N
Ural Mountains
Volga River
Dnieper
Don R.
OPE
Dniester R.
rpathian Mts.
Danube R.
Balkans
Black Sea
Caucasus Mts.
aspian Sea
ASIA
Tigris River
Euphrates R.
Zagros Mts.
Sea
ARABIAN DESERT

SPECIAL PRICE
NO RETURN

~~I I 59~~

I 2 65

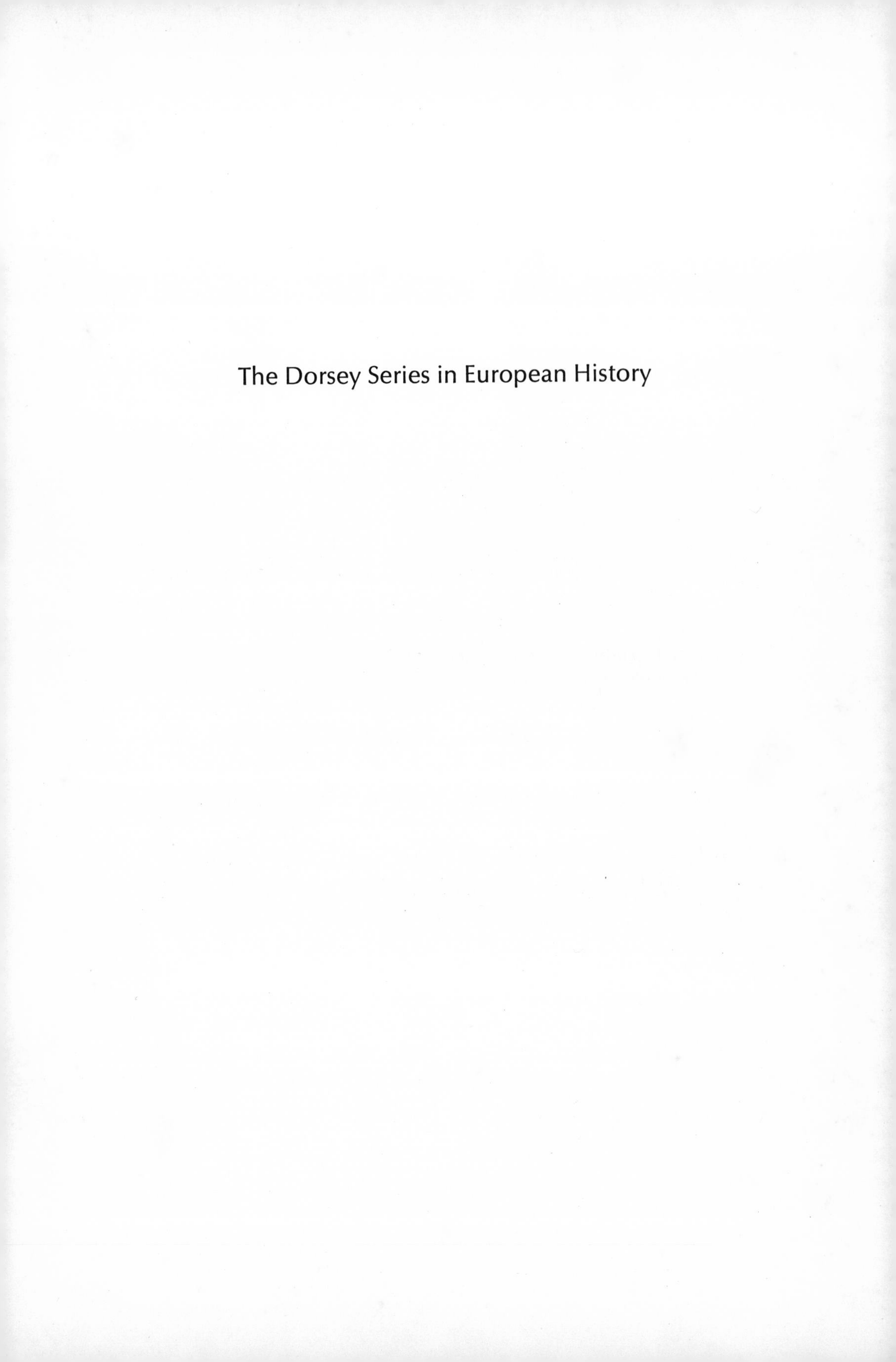

The Dorsey Series in European History

THE DORSEY SERIES IN EUROPEAN HISTORY

EDITOR THEODORE S. HAMEROW *University of Wisconsin*

Black (ed.) *Posture of Europe, 1815–1940: Readings in European Intellectual History*

Funk (ed.) *Europe in the Twentieth Century: Source Studies on Contemporary Issues and Problems*

Gooch (ed.) *Interpreting European History* Volumes I and II

Jones *From the Tigris to the Tiber: An Introduction to Ancient History*

Senn *Readings in Russian Political and Diplomatic History* Volumes I and II

Stromberg *A History of Western Civilization* rev. ed.

White *Medieval History: A Source Book*

A History of Western Civilization

A History of Western Civilization

ROLAND N. STROMBERG
Professor of History
University of Wisconsin–Milwaukee

Revised edition • 1969

The Dorsey Press, Homewood, Illinois
Irwin-Dorsey Limited, Georgetown, Ontario

Revised Edition

First Printing, April, 1969

Library of Congress Catalog Card No. 68–56868

Printed in the United States of America

Table of contents

INTRODUCTION: The study of history

The past is one of the dimensions of human existence. Its reminders lie about us everywhere—visibly, in the form of buildings, monuments, pictures, and many other objects. We may gaze on Stonehenge, the Sphinx, or something much nearer such as family heirlooms in the attic; they all remind us that people were here before us, and they normally stimulate a curiosity concerning what such people did, what they were like. Invisibly, but just as clearly, the past is present in our institutions of society and government, our laws, our language—our life itself. A distinguished modern philosopher has written that "History is the systematic science of that radical reality, my life." He meant that what we are is largely a product of the cultural inheritance into which we are born, and which shapes our experiences. Even if we decide to rebel against aspects of that inheritance, we are indicating its decisive importance in determining our lives.

Few societies have been without a sense of the past or have failed to write about it. For our Western civilization, which began in the eastern Mediterranean some 5,000 years ago, history has been especially important. The Bible, both Old Testament and New, abounds in vivid narrative of actual happenings pictured as a great drama in which God's plan or Providence is unfolded. The ancient Greeks, who began so many of our sciences with so much genius, produced Herodotus and Thucydides, the fathers of historical inquiry. They turned the searchlight of critical scrutiny on the tragic data of human events, on wars and revolutions and class strife, in order to find what caused these things. Medieval monks, when they could do little else for knowledge, recorded the events of their times in chronicles. And so to the Renaissance and Machiavelli; the Enlightenment and Voltaire; and the modern flood of detailed historical studies based on archival documents. No age has lacked a keen interest in the study of the past.

The reasons for such study have been various. There is a natural interest that flows from the excitement of memorable events. History is the story of human life; it includes all the manifold and varied expressions of man's thought and action. There are gripping adventures, heroic deeds, strange customs, notable achievements. The canvas of history is painted with great men, whether they are the Platos and Galileos and Einsteins, giants of the intellect; or the Caesars, Napoleons, and Bismarcks, leaders of state. It is filled with the clash of arms, the rise and fall of empires, much cruelty and suffering but also much triumphant achievement. In brief, it is a good story, the better because it happens to be true. We may well agree with Walt Whitman that, compared with "facts properly told, how mean appear all romances." Narrative history, well told, will always find a place in the world of literature as long as there are people to read.

At a higher level, historical writing has served the purposes of social solidarity. Most modern nations owe their very existence to the awareness of their common past, that "memory of great deeds done together" which Renan named as the definition of nationalism. Such great historic peoples as the Jews and the Romans felt a deep piety toward the "goodly inheritance" of their ancestors; and this was the social cement holding them together. They remembered and enshrined the actions of the past in order to ensure present unity. So do modern nations; Americans have always been taught about the *Mayflower* and George Washington, as the French have about Joan of Arc and the Revolution. Any group, large or small, that wishes to achieve a social identity finds itself using the past in this way. It is quite natural, for example, that American Negroes, anxious to find themselves as a cultural people, have turned eagerly to their history in recent years. The great resurgence of history in the 19th century owed much to the fact that this was a time of nationalism. The patriotic uses of history may inspire a certain cynicism in some quarters; but *any* human grouping or cause finds itself using the past in this way.

More ambitiously yet, serious students of history since its birth have hoped that the critical examination of past situations could provide the wisdom with which to avoid future troubles and thus aid mankind in its constant struggle against the evils that afflict it. Thucydides believed that an understanding of the causes of the war between Sparta and Athens could help avert future wars; it was this that impelled him to write his masterpiece. We learn from history and profit by the lessons of the past: such has been the faith of historians from the great Athenian down to the present. It is not, alas, easy to apply the lessons of history. Some of the apparent "lessons" are dubious; we can know that much apparent evil issued from a course of action but we cannot guarantee that as much or more would not have arisen from an alternative course, and sometimes it looks as if trouble lies in either direction. James II, as we will see, refused to govern with Parliament, tried to dismiss it and rule absolutely—he was overthrown by a revolution. A century later (exactly) the French king Louis XVI, pondering on the fate of his English predecessor, decided he would *not* rule absolutely and summoned a great national parliament—with the result that he was overthrown by a revolution and had his head cut off. At Paris in 1919 a distinguished historian studied the Congress of Vienna as a guide to present decisions and decided that it had erred in treating the defeated power too leniently; the Treaty of Versailles was to be reproached by the next generation of historians for having dealt with the defeated power too severely, thus sowing the seeds of new war. So it goes.

Montaigne, that delightful sceptic, told of the general who decided to attack, was beaten, and heard the lesson of history pronounced against him: rashness is fatal. But the next general remained on the defensive and lost; he, of course, was told that timidity invites defeat. (Something like this happened between World War I and World War II, the French having spent the intervening years preparing for the last war.)

Historians above all others should know that the world changes, and thus what worked yesterday may not work today. If a simple faith in the "lessons of history" tends to evaporate under the light of careful study, past experience remains a depository from which we should be able to derive wisdom to be applied to contemporary problems. If we cannot find that wisdom here, where else can we find it? The past is the experience of the human race, and surely we learn, if at all, from experience. Mankind cut off from its history is like an individual who never remembered anything of his previous life, and who therefore would always remain an infant. The possibility of accumulating knowledge and preserving a body of culture to be passed on to the next generation is what distinguishes man from the other animals. It is what "civilizes" him: men without history are barbarians. It is what makes him a creature of reason, insofar as he is that: rational knowledge must gradually develop through long experience and the cumulative contributions of many minds.

It can fairly be claimed for the study of history that it leads to some qualities of mind which equip one much better to evaluate contemporary problems. The historian learns to weigh all the evidence judiciously; he learns that situations are invariably complex and that no one cause ever explains everything. History is the enemy of fanaticism and monomania. It accustoms us to search widely and deeply for all the factors, and to subject these to critical scrutiny. No person well trained in historical methods is likely to rush into "simplistic" conclusions or to be credulous of the claims of cranks and ideologists. The historian knows how difficult it is to be sure about any human situation, even the smallest one; he is wary of facile generalizations and sceptical of sweeping claims. His is, in the broadest and best sense, the scientific spirit applied to human affairs, and this spirit or method can usefully be applied to present situations as well as past ones. Having learned how hard it was to find out the truth about the massacre of Saint Bartholomew's Day, or the origins of the World Wars, he is not likely to believe that it will be easy to find out the truth about any current puzzle. But he knows that patient inquiry can unravel the truth.

It is perhaps more obvious that we should be interested in the history of our own country, the United States of America, than in "Western civilization." What is Western civilization? We read, sometimes, about "American civilization" or "French civilization"; then, again, the phrase "World civilization" has been used. It is apparent upon a moment's reflection that if there is such a thing as American civilization, it is very closely related to that of Europe—related linguistically, culturally, intellectually. It is in fact a part of the larger unit of Western civilization. We share our language with the English, but that language has in it many words derived from the French, akin to the German, and based on Greek or Latin roots. (As a sample, check the derivation of the following words: physics, democracy, republic, journalism, engine, senate, kindergarten, university, president, sheriff.) All European "countries" such as France, Italy, Germany, and Great Britain, though their languages may differ somewhat, have in common a large stock of ideas and institutions, reaching back to their roots in an ancient Mediterranean civilization which once was unified under the Roman Empire and which has always known a large measure of cultural unity even when political units assumed an independent existence. Such common denominators include the Christian, or Jewish, religion; legal systems based on the Roman law; scientific and philosophical ideas derived from the Greek thinkers; modes of literature and art; and, beyond that, all kinds of customs which one might assume were simply human, and not specifically Western, until one visits a wholly different culture, such as that of India or China, and finds that people do things quite differently. We are all Greeks, Jews, Romans, and Germans every day without realizing it; for Western civilization is an amalgamation of elements from these cultures, shaped through many centuries. The United States was, of course, originally settled by people from Europe and this imprint has remained on the nation. We cannot cease to be members of Western civilization, though we may evolve some special version of it.

Should we study "world history" rather than just European or Western? We need not deny the great importance of civilizations other than Western to deny that such a thing as "world civilization" (and, by extension, world history) exists. That we are today less Europe-centered in our view of the world than we used to be is one of the more obvious of modern trends. A distinguished Indian historian, S. K. M. Panikkar, has recently put it well, and irrefutably: We can no longer, he asserts, hold to "the faith which was so firmly held in the past that everything of value developed on the shores of the Mediterranean. . . . The past of the Great Asian peoples has gradually come to be considered as part of the general heritage of civilized man, and this may in time lead to a breakdown of the narrow Europeanism, which considered everything outside the experience of the West to be of secondary importance." He could have added "the African peoples." Everyone should be encouraged to learn more about the other civilizations of the world. But the fact is that they are quite different from our own. One can perhaps compare them with ours (there are a number; no one "Asian civilization," but many Asian civilizations, from the Arabs and Iranians in western Asia through Indians and Chinese and Japanese in east Asia.) One cannot say that we are all part of the same global civilization. Perhaps in the future all these civilizations will fuse to form one. Some think this process is going on now. But in the past they grew up separately. If we study them, we should do so without mixing them in with Western civilization; study them in their own right, as unique and different entities, just as valuable as our civilization, but not at all the same as ours.

Our chief reason for absorbing the history of Western civilization is to understand and thus to liberate ourselves. We are in fundamental ways the product of this history. Our institutions of government, our laws, our learning, and our customs grew from this soil. When we understand how they grew, we understand better our own nature; and when we see our place in the entire pattern we are freer to choose and to act. Viewed in this light, history is a preparation for life. It is a means of achieving the Socratic maxim, "Know thyself."

Our Western civilization has always been a dynamic one. It has had a time dimension, it has moved, whereas some cultures seem not to move at all, or to move with glacial slowness. European visitors to Africa used to comment that "Time seems to stand still." It gallops on in the West. About a century ago, Western man had the idea that this movement is a progress, that the development of man is onward and upward, better and better—a long story of steady gain, starting from primeval ignorance and backwardness and culminating in utopia, perhaps not too far off. The 20th century has unfortunately all but shattered this fond illusion. No doubt there are areas of progress, measured by gains in efficiency or power; but in other ways we seem to regress, to stand still, perhaps to go around in circles. Of one thing most historians are now sure: we cannot predict the future in any large sense, we do not know the fate of man. It is exciting, nevertheless, to seek clues to such a fate in the patterns of the past. Such clues as are vouchsafed to us are found here, in the record of human experience.

When all is said, perhaps the greatest appeal of the study of the past is that stated by the 18th-century philosopher and historian David Hume: "To see the human race, from the beginning of time, pass, as it were, in review before us . . . what spectacle can be imagined so magnificent, so various, so interesting?" No historian can possibly tell all of that story, or anything like all, but he can try to present something of the drama and the magnificence of this great spectacle. It begins in the dimmest mists of prehistory, and proceeds down to the latest age of man. For all we know, it may be nearing its end; more likely, it is still in its merest infancy. All we know is that it is an amazing story, and it is us.

Australopithecus, earliest man-like creature, lived in Africa a million years ago. Remains have been found in South Africa and Tanzania.

1

The emergence of man and the first civilizations in the Near East

chronology

c. 1,000,000 B.C.
Beginning of Pleistocene age; first man-like creatures.
c. 500,000 B.C.
Middle Pleistocene; *pithecanthropus erectus*, forerunners of man.
c. 100,000 B.C.
Neanderthal man; cave dwellers. Late Pleistocene.
c. 35,000 B.C. to 8000 B.C.
Homo sapiens; Stone Age hunting culture.
c. 8000 B.C.
Last glaciation. Mesolithic age.
Beginnings of agriculture. "Neolithic revolution"; pottery and settled communities.
c. 4000 B.C.
Beginnings of copper metallurgy in southwest Asia.
c. 3200–2800 B.C.
Early Sumerian, Egyptian, and Minoan civilizations.
c. 2340–25 B.C.
Sumerian imperial state; capitals at Accad and Ur.
c. 2130–1775 B.C.
Middle Kingdom in Egypt.
c. 2000–1580 B.C.
Middle Minoan period in Crete.
c. 1800–1760 B.C.
Reign of Hammurabi; Babylonian dynasty.
Conquest of Egypt by barbarian Hyksos.
c. 1600 B.C.
Hittite invasion of Babylon; Kassite dynasty, to 1171.
c. 1580–1400 B.C.
Late Minoan period; conquest by Mycenaean Greeks, 1400.
c. 1570 B.C.
Beginning of New Kingdom in Egypt; eviction of Hyksos.
c. 1275 B.C.
Moses leads flight of Hebrews from Egypt.
c. 1100 B.C.
Dècline of Egypt begins. Hebrew conquest of Palestine.
Invention of alphabet by Phoenicians.
Rise of Assyria, conquering Babylonian Empire.
950 B.C.
King Solomon. Division of Jewish kingdom, 933.
800–730 B.C.
Prophets Amos, Hosea, Isaiah I.
Indian Upanishads.
Zoroaster.
722 B.C.
Destruction of northern Jewish kingdom of Israel by Assyrians.
586 B.C.
Fall of Jerusalem; Babylonian captivity of Jews; period of great prophets of Exile (to 539 B.C.).
539 B.C.
Conquest of Babylon by Persians under Cyrus II; end of Jewish exile.
Persian rule over all of southwestern Asia, to 330 B.C.
Buddhism in India.
444 B.C.
Nehemiah; Jewish autonomy within Persian Empire.
Reorganization of Jewish religion; priestly code.
Book of Job (? fifth century B.C.)
334–30 B.C.
Conquest of Persian Empire by Alexander the Great of Macedon.
323 B.C.
Death of Alexander. Rule of Ptolemies in Egypt, Seleucids in western Asia.

The origin of civilization

Emergence of man

The ability to walk upright, on two feet instead of four, seems to have been the critical step on the road to man's evolution as a creature capable of intelligent thought and rational action. The skillful hand was decisive; not merely because with it man could make tools, but because he could protect his head and procure his food, thereby releasing the skull from a weight which limited brain capacity. Early types of man, such as the *pithecanthropus*, were still "bone-heads" compared to us, with massive jaws and jutting visors to protect the eyes. The development of forearms and hands specialized for purposes more cunning and creative than walking made possible the development of a cranium better fitted for high-quality gray matter. The brain owes almost everything to the hand, and the hand owes its dexterity to the feat of balancing on two legs rather than four. Many names have been suggested for man—*homo faber*, man the toolmaker, is better than *homo sapiens*, someone has said. Perhaps even better is *homo erectus*. The two-legged performance, which we take for granted, was probably an essential feature of man's surprising development into a speaking and thinking animal.

Man evidently attained something close to his present physical makeup as long ago as 100,000 years. Hominid types like Neanderthal man, the cave dwellers, appear about this time, though *homo sapiens* probably did not emerge clearly until later. The whole process of evolution has taken an enormously long time. Life began roughly a billion years ago. Monkeys and apes reach back millions of years, and man-like creatures appeared more than a million years ago. (The diminutive *australopithecus*, who lived in Africa, certainly goes back that far.) As early as 300,000 years ago we can see men using primitive tools and weapons, devising traps, working together to kill large animals. Much of the story remains shrouded in mystery. For example, it is still a matter of dispute whether Neanderthal man, who lived in Europe as late as 40,000 years ago, was conquered and destroyed by *homo sapiens*—modern man, our direct ancestors—or whether modern man evolved from him; whether Neanderthal man, that is, was a separate species or one of our ancestors.

Modern archaeology is now engaged in unearthing much new information about prehistory. The apparently invincible obstacle imposed by the absence of written records has in some small measure yielded to techniques such as the radio-carbon method of dating ancient remains, and to the accumulation of data from all over the globe. If we shall never know as much about prehistoric man as we know about historic, we know much more than we used to.

Clearly one of the most potent stimuli shoving the human species along the path of evolution was the cycle of climatic changes connected with the ebb and flow of glaciers in the Ice Age. A million years ago or so there began an age marked by the advance and retreat of glaciers—altogether some 15 of them. Alterations in vegetation speeded up evolution. When the forests thinned, apes adapted to them were forced to change or perish, and these

Prehistoric man crawled deep into the recesses of caves to paint marvelous colored pictures of animals as found in the Lascaux caves in southwestern France.

types that could manage to go upright were better fitted to survive. Later, changes in rainfall and climate forced men to stop hunting and take up the cultivation of grains. To be periodically confronted with an abrupt alteration of environment meant the sacrifice of thousands to the stern law of life, the survival of the fittest, but it also meant biological progress.

Life in the open on two feet only must have been dangerous, and we may surmise it put a premium on the wits. Only the ingenious survived. Teamwork, too, was probably encouraged. It has sometimes been said that sociability is one of man's unique traits, but this is doubtful, for upon close examination many lower animals reveal remarkable examples of group cooperation. However, it is clear that from the first, men worked together in food-finding. We may conjecture that *language* grew up largely as a result of the intense cooperation forced upon this two-legged hunter who lived by his wits. And, once this priceless gift of language was obtained, men could use it to create new forms of collaboration.

In the region between Europe and Asia, we can clearly make out the existence of men much like ourselves in physical characteristics about 35,000 years ago, possessing an advanced Stone Age culture, based on hunting, which went on until some 10,000 years ago. Much of the intervening eon was spent in the often pleasant occupation of hunting, pursuing the reindeer and the mammoth across grassy Ice Age plains. As a roving food-gatherer the human animal could not create what we call civilization. We have no reason for doubting that he felt the same creative impulses as modern man—the desire to know, the desire to make, the desire to worship and to sing. Stone Age man has in fact left behind artifacts which testify not only to his toolmaking ingenuity but to religious and artistic instincts. He carved statuettes, and he crawled deep into the recesses of caves to paint marvelous colored pictures of animals by lamplight. He tried, touchingly, to restore life to the dead by painting them the color of life, and he certainly practiced communal religious rites. We must imagine him, too, telling stories around the campfire, as did the red Indians of early America, which explained in mythological terms how things began and why things happened. Man is a natural storyteller, and a listener to stories. He is a mythmaker.[1]

The millenium prior to the emergence of civilization was the time of a lively "industrial revolution"—aided by inventors whose names must forever be unrecorded—in which men first learned how to make wheeled vehicles, sailing vessels, and above all metal tools, with the arrival of a copper metallurgy. The human species had started at last on the road that led to Parnassus—and to Pittsburgh.

But without a permanent abode and without written language, countless generations of hunters and storytellers were condemned to be like those of whom it was written "some there be which have no memorial, who are perished as though they had never been born." Another climatic revolution intruded to force man out of this sterile pattern. The ice cap retreated, and with it the animals man had hunted and the environment he had hunted them in. Evidently this was what turned him toward other occupations, economically more rewarding. The domestication of animals and the tilling of the soil preceded the coming of civilization, for they made possible both permanent settlement and a surplus of production which permitted economic diversification and specialization. This agricultural revolution probably began about 9000 B.C. and slowly spread. In western Asia aridity replaced plentiful rainfall and pushed men toward the cultivation of certain wild grasses found on the upland plateaus. Perhaps the greatest of all human revolutions was this agricultural revolution, for it made possible permanent settlements, a food surplus, and thus civilization.

Civilization means literally living in cities; a soil fertile enough to sustain a population not concerned with agriculture is its essential prerequisite. When the rich alluvial soil of the Tigris-Euphrates and Nile river valleys was harnessed to great productivity, with the aid of dikes, canals, and irrigation, cities appeared. A complex type of society could develop. Specialists of all sorts came forth—administrators, tradesmen, metal workers, soldiers, and many others. The arts of civilization, the hallmark of a civilized society, included monumental architecture, large-scale government with tax collectors and law codes, large-scale business marked by the use of money; they also included, above all, the arts that came from the greatest art, that of writing: literature, and knowledge set down in writing, embracing astronomy, medicine, mathematics, and the literature of proverbs and epics. A revolution in human knowledge could occur with the discovery of writing. This revolution in turn meant a new power over nature, derived from development of a

[1] In the aboriginal "bushmen" of Australia we have an exceptionally interesting survival of something approximating Stone Age man; one notable characteristic of this appealing people is their elaborate, involved, and lively mythology, as well as an extremely complicated system of familial relationships.

vast array of skills from metallurgy to accurate calendars, from building plans to government records. Thus did humanity enter its stage of civilized society, rather suddenly, after tens of thousands of years of slow preparation. It happened in Mesopotamia and in Egypt.

The first civilizations

The first civilizations arose in the river valleys of the Nile, Tigris and Euphrates, and Indus. The Indus civilization much farther to the east does not come into our story; but in area it exceeded, and in time was almost as early as, the Fertile Crescent and Egyptian civilizations.

Whether these several early civilizations were separate and largely independent developments, or whether one came first and the others derived from it, is an old controversy and one not yet settled, if indeed it ever can be. It seems likeliest that priority should be given to the Fertile Crescent, i.e., the Tigris-Euphrates area in Mesopotamia, now modern Iraq. But if Egypt, India, and China borrowed from this seedbed of civilization, they very quickly fashioned their own unique societies. It is possible that all were branches of a common parent stem. All this took place within the decisive millenium 4000–3000 B.C. And so "history," the record of human civilization, is a very recent development on the enormous clock of geological time—something that has happened just in the last minute of the year, if we place it in reference to the history of the earth.

The Near East nurtured the first civilization for a number of plausible reasons. It was a natural crossroads, where tribes of men met and exchanged ideas. Farming was first developed in the upland regions of western Asia; then it moved to the fertile river valleys where high levels of food production were possible. But irrigation was necessary, and the need for artificial irrigation encouraged social and political organization. In this area, too, copper was first mined and smelted. On the great rivers goods could be carried to far places to be exchanged for other goods.

The kingdoms of Sumer on the Euphrates and Egypt on the Nile introduce us to human civilization. Civilization includes many things. It implies economic specialization and social stratification: some men are not growing their own food but are performing other functions and trading these for food. They have become craftsmen, merchants, perhaps priests, scholars, and governors. The growing specialization and complexity in society enhanced the need for some sort of organized political authority, thus giving rise to the state. Most societies on the road from barbarism to civilization evidently passed through a "heroic age" when "there was no king in Israel, and every man did what was right in his own eyes." But for every man to do so becomes intolerable when society has become interdependent. In these first civilizations political authority took the form of despotic monarchy, backed by religious sanctions.

In order to govern a state and to run a fairly complex economy, writing and figuring are necessary; there is evidence that the first writing was indeed used for such very practical purposes. Once invented, however, the momentous ability to write down could lead to whole new mental horizons for man. Education, literature, science, philosophy could emerge. Human knowledge could be pooled, and preserved for posterity to build upon. In brief, man could begin to make himself something other than an aimless wanderer condemned to repeat each generation what had been done before. His history could begin.

The ancient Near East gave us the first writing—developed in a series of steps over a millenium, from crude pictures of objects to ideography (conventionalized symbols standing for objects and ideas) and finally to the phonetic principle and the alphabet, a step even the gifted Chinese far away to the east never took. The cuneiform writing on clay of the Sumerians, and the hieroglyphs or picture-writing of the Egyptians, began the greatest of all human discoveries, and the Phoenicians finished it by inventing the phonetic alphabet. In these river valleys of western Asia, where archaeologists dig up cities while scholars labor to decipher ancient scripts, we are learning what was done with this ability to write things down. Not only verses and proverbs, but also legal codes, were written down. The famous Babylonian legal code of Hammurabi (c. 1800 B.C.) no longer appears as a sole example, but as the descendant of a whole series of earlier codes. In modern Turkey, a whole records office of the Hittites has been found, with documents written in eight languages and indicative of an extensive diplomatic service. The creation of the state meant a new epoch in human affairs. Courts of law, enforcing elaborate laws relating to such matters as divorce, alimony, banking, and military service give us a rather good picture of the complexity of these societies.

The ancient empires

The first of the great ancient civilizations were the Sumerian (c. 3000–2000 B.C.), Egyptian (c. 3000–1100 B.C.), Cretan (Minoan, c. 2800–1400 B.C.). In the Euphrates valley of Mesopotamia, Babylonians replaced Sumer; then came Assyrians, Chaldeans, and finally Persians, to establish great empires. There were Phoenicians and Lydians, Hittites, who made a major state in Asia Minor and were the first to make iron, and of course the Hebrews, through whose writings most Europeans formerly acquired what familiarity they had with these peoples of the ancient world. We have learned much more about them in very recent times through the labors of archaeologists, philologists, and historians. Under their hands whole civilizations, previously most obscure, have sprung to life. In Egypt, impressive monuments of stone had been preserved; the world had long marveled at Sphinx and Pyramids. (Europe only began to know and study ancient Egypt in Napoleon's time, however.) But in Mesopotamia immense amounts of work had to be done in mounds of crumbling brick to reveal the contours of cities and civilizations. On the island of Crete, the brilliant Minoan civilization emerged from complete obscurity in this century, as men found fabulous palaces buried beneath the ground. In Egypt, archaeological investigation discovered additional rich

Phoenecian ship carved on a rock sarcophagus at Sidon

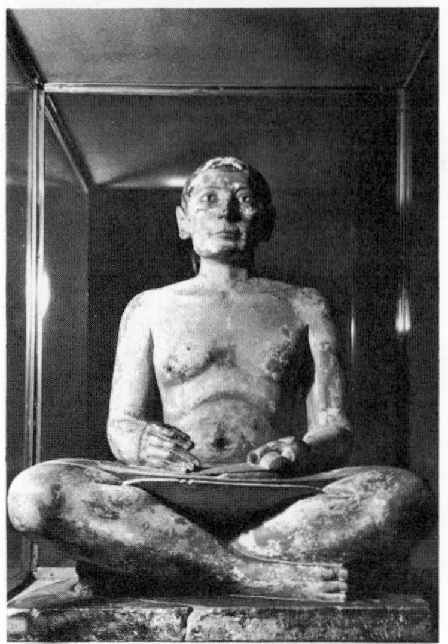

Egyptian scribe (c. 2700 B.C.) now in the Louvre, Paris

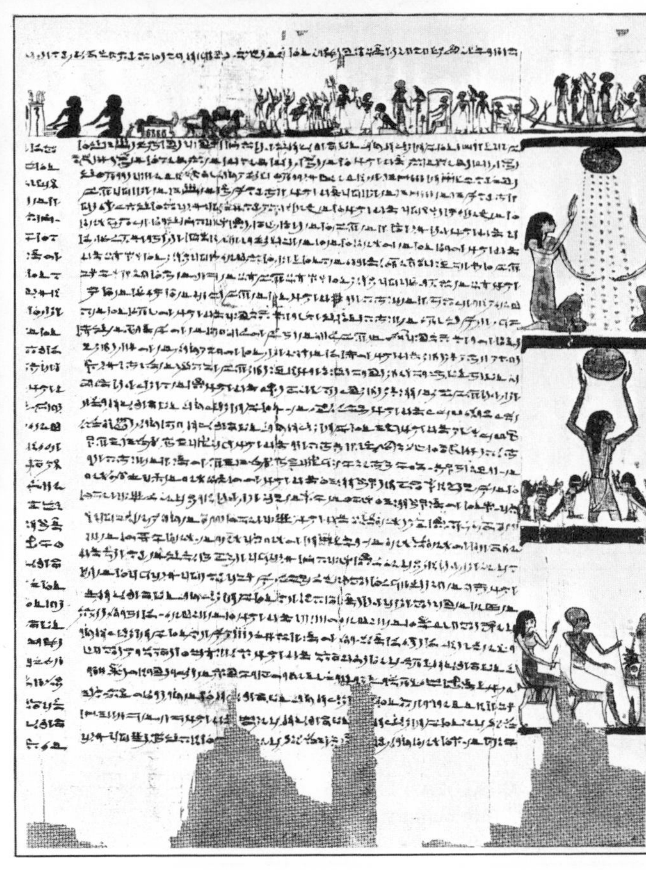

Egyptian papyrus. The art of writing, developed in the ancient world, made government possible and advanced civilization.

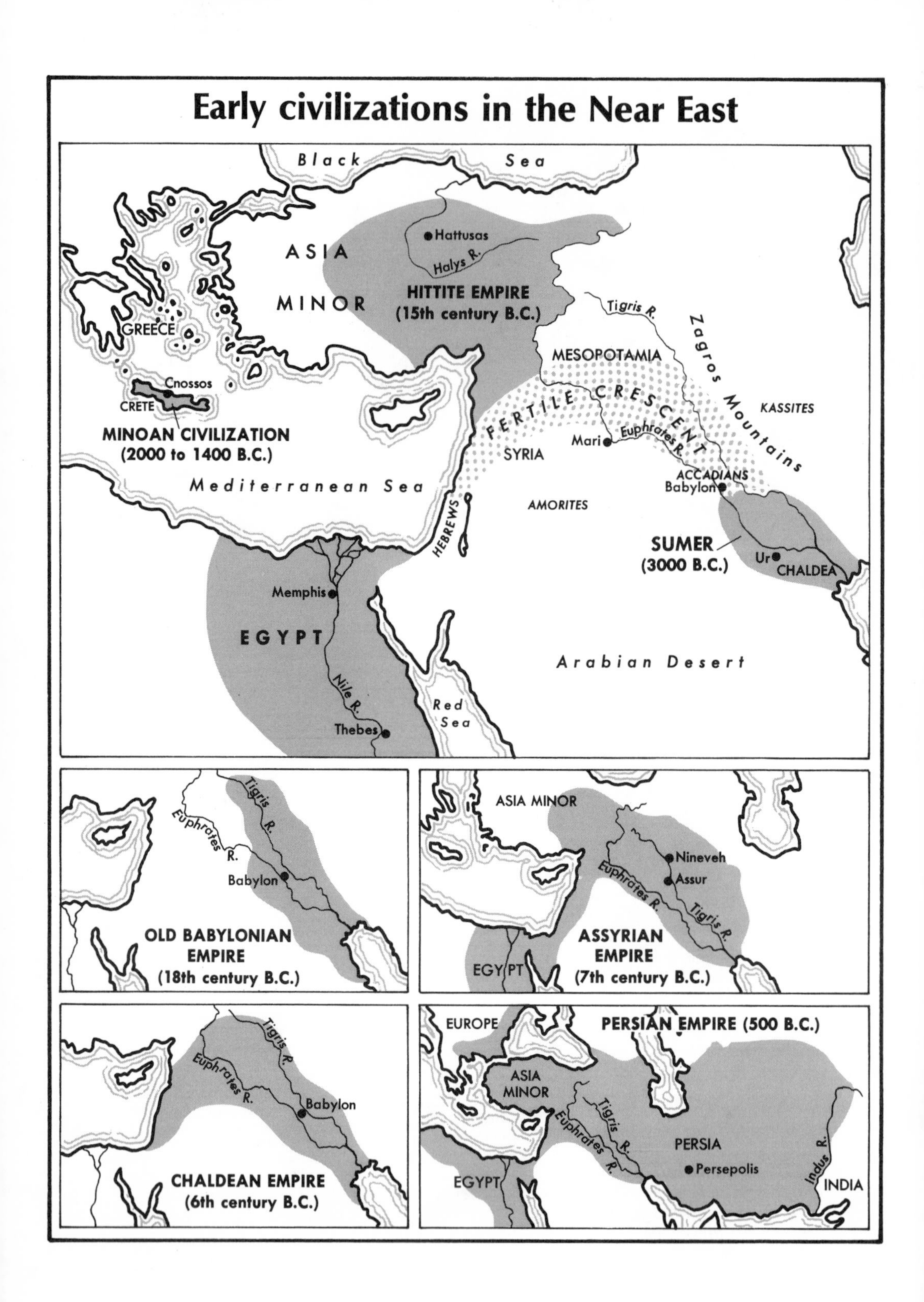
Early civilizations in the Near East
Black Sea
Hattusas
ASIA
MINOR
Halys R.
HITTITE EMPIRE
(15th century B.C.)
Tigris R.
Zagros Mountains
GREECE
MESOPOTAMIA
Cnossos
CRETE
FERTILE CRESCENT
KASSITES
MINOAN CIVILIZATION
(2000 to 1400 B.C.)
Mari
Euphrates R.
SYRIA
Mediterranean Sea
ACCADIANS
Babylon
AMORITES
HEBREWS
SUMER
(3000 B.C.)
Ur
CHALDEA
Memphis
EGYPT
Arabian Desert
Nile R.
Red Sea
Thebes
Tigris R.
Euphrates R.
Babylon
OLD BABYLONIAN
EMPIRE
(18th century B.C.)
ASIA MINOR
Nineveh
Assur
Euphrates R.
Tigris R.
EGYPT
ASSYRIAN
EMPIRE
(7th century B.C.)
Tigris R.
Euphrates R.
Babylon
CHALDEAN EMPIRE
(6th century B.C.)
EUROPE
PERSIAN EMPIRE (500 B.C.)
ASIA
MINOR
Tigris R.
Euphrates R.
PERSIA
Persepolis
Indus R.
INDIA
EGYPT

treasures in the tombs. Throughout the Middle East region today this work continues and discloses material which enables us to know something of how these peoples lived and thought. Along with this spade work, linguists have labored to decipher a dozen lost languages, with increasing success.

Achievements of ancient civilizations

With gains in knowledge has come greater respect for achievement: achievements political, administrative, economic, and cultural by these ancient peoples who made the first civilizations and developed them through a cycle of more than 2,000 years. Roman government and Greek philosophy and science, as well as all the higher religions, undoubtedly owed a more fundamental debt to these pioneers in all the arts and sciences than used to be supposed. In this history of European civilization, no account of the ancient Orient will be attempted. But some summary of its achievements forms a logical and necessary introduction to Europe. For these were passed on to Europe via Greece and Rome. Despite the ways in which Greek thought broke sharply with that of the Orient, the indebtedness of Greece to it was much greater than we used to think. Similarly, too, Hebraic religion, which broke away from the dominant oriental pattern, no longer appears quite so original, but obviously owed much to Babylonian mythology and other eastern strains.

Geometry made its first appearance in Egypt as a practical art; arithmetic and astronomy in Babylonia. It is difficult to name a field in which our fundamental habits of thought and practice do not stem from these most ancient sources. For example, the habit of dividing the week into seven days, and hours and minutes into units of 60, goes back to Babylon. A "remarkable literature of epics, and legends, of history, of law, and of astronomy" included most of the stories, myths, and parables which later appeared in the Bible or in Greek and Roman mythology, thus forming the basic literary material of Europe. This establishment of basic patterns extends to such areas as medicine, engineering, and architecture. Egypt worked the copper mines of Sinai, built canals and dams on the Nile, altered the course of that mighty river, reclaimed land for cultivation.

Long famous have been the pyramids and temples of Egypt. In modern times we have learned of such buildings as the temple to the goddess Inanna in Ur of the Chaldees, almost as impressive in its dimensions and structure. Americans have not ceased to wonder at the "modern" plumbing found in the great palace at Cnossus in northern Crete, nor Frenchmen at the chic styles of the bare-breasted Cretan ladies; while Englishmen might well be impressed by the wealth this island empire drew from maritime commerce developed and protected by naval power.

Babylon was the mighty city whose streets were of marble and whose walls were wide enough for two chariots abreast. It was the city whose wickedness shocked the simple Hebrew shepherds brought there in captivity; whose famous "hanging gardens" were one of the seven wonders of the world. Today all its glories are only a pile of debris, but archaeological genius and patience have been able to reconstruct them on paper.

Hammurabi (c. 1765 B.C.) the Amorite king whose name is attached to the most famous, though by no means the only, ancient code of laws.

Highlights of ancient history

Here we will briefly outline the history of the early civilizations. In the Mesopotamian area, the "classic" age of Sumerian civilization began about 3000 B.C., with its capital at Ur where were found the Royal Tombs and the clay tablets, oldest existing writings. About 2350 the Semitic Accadians took over the kingdom and brought it to its zenith of power and civilized progress, ruling over all of Mesopotamia and a good part of Syria c. 2200 B.C. The last of the Ur dynasties ended about 1950 B.C. after invasions from the West by the Semitic "Amorites." There followed a period of breakup into smaller states, along with infiltration by another barbarian people, the Hurrians from the northeast. But much wealth based on an extensive commerce continued to exist. The 18th century B.C. is richly documented, the correspondence of the king of Mari exhibiting a high degree of administrative efficiency and state activity, such as the taking of censuses, provisions for military defense, fire protection, and of course irrigation. To this century belongs the famous code of Hammurabi, who having defeated Mari and other states established a large Amorite empire with its capital at Babylon. Not heretofore an important town, Babylon at this time began to display its "wonders of the world," among them the temple-tower known as the "tower of [King] Babel."

But Babylon was destroyed by the Hittites about 1550 B.C. and did not rise again for two centuries. The Hittite state in Asia Minor (present-day Turkey) rose to power in the 17th century, conquered much of that region, destroyed the Babylonian dynasty in a raid, but soon broke up in internal

Ebih II, Governor of Mari, at left.

Imhotep—scientist, engineer, and sage.

dissension, to rise again later. Meanwhile the mountain people called the Kassites assumed power in Babylonia, became assimilated, and ruled for some 400 years until 1171. The Hittites, and for a time the Hurrians, erected strong states to the north and northeast, developing an art and literature of considerable interest. It is at this time, too, that the Assyrian state, with its capital at Assur, begins its rise, though the Assyrians do not come into their own until several hundred years later: they have conquered the entire region by the eighth century B.C.

Egypt

Civilization in Egypt and on the island of Crete showed a similar chronological pattern. Egyptian civilization emerged with the unification of the land of the Nile about 3200 B.C. (the earlier dates cannot be calculated with any precision). The Old Kingdom, as it is called, corresponds roughly to classical Sumer, getting into its stride about 2600 B.C. when the celebrated Imhotep, scientist, engineer, and sage, appears as "the first known genius of historic times." Temple and pyramid building, along with a brilliant painting and sculpture, revealed the distinctive Egyptian style. Around 2180 the Old Kingdom broke up, not from external invasion but from the breakdown of internal authority. The problem of the local or "feudal" nobility existed for these kingdoms as it did for Europe later. But within a century the Middle Kingdom began its 400 years of splendor, with its architectural and engineering feats, its pyramids and Labyrinth and canals equally the wonders of the world. Amonemhet III, who built dams 20 miles long, was approximately the contemporary of Hammurabi—a great age, obviously.

By 1700 the decline of the Middle Kingdom coincided with invasion by Semitic mountain peoples whom the Egyptians called the Hyksos (they were perhaps the same Amorites who had taken over Mesopotamia) and regarded as barbarians. The Hyksos captured the North, with the capital at Memphis, around 1700; but from Thebes, in the South, the Egyptians redeemed the country and went on to reach another peak of power and prosperity in the New Kingdom, whose zenith was about 1400–1350. It was at this time that the Hebrews, who had enjoyed favor from the Hyksos kings, suffered enslavement. The temple building of the 17th to 20th dynasties exceeded all previous examples; literature and the arts flourished; Egyptian power extended into the Palestine-Syria region. The splendid temples near Thebes, such as those at Karnak and Deir el-Bahri, amaze the modern tourist as much as they amazed Herodotus, the Greek historian. But about 1200 B.C. Egypt began to crumble and, after struggling with the Hittites, succumbed to the Assyrians, the warlike people who also conquered Mesopotamia. Then came the Persians to conquer all.

Crete

Similarly, we have Minoan civilization, on Crete, rising about 2800 B.C., reaching a high point in the Middle Minoan period c. 2000–1580 and another in the Late period 1580–1400, falling thereafter to the Mycenaean Greeks. The digging up of the enormous stone palace at Cnossus, and with it the revelation of a highly developed civilization preceding the Greeks in Europe (if we may so place this island, which lies in the Mediterranean off the southern shore of Greece) has been a work of this century, to a large extent due to the genius of one man, Sir Arthur Evans. Not even the Egyptians have anything to match the palace for elegance and architectural perfection as well as size. The Cretan "palaces" were much more than royal residences, being almost cities in themselves. Possibly early migrants from Egypt founded this civilization. It developed a thriving commerce, being a crossroads for communication with both Egypt and Asia. These people built excellent roads, kept elaborate written records, constructed a powerful fleet to safeguard their maritime interests. But it is above all their graceful art that delights us, with its revelation of a way of life that seems joyous and spontaneous.

Wars and gods

Thus the magnificence of the ancient empires. They reached their zenith, in general, about 1500 B.C. At that time the Egyptians, under the New Kingdom, were at their peak, as was Crete. Hammurabi ruled in Babylon two centuries earlier than that. But one may roughly think in terms of a cycle that began about 3000, reached its ripe glory in the half millenium from 1900 to 1400, then began to decline, arriving at its low point by 300 B.C. Our own cycle of modern European civilization may be put on a comparable time scale: rise from 500 to 1500 A.D., great power and glory for a few hundred years—then symptoms of decline? Some great historians have seriously proposed a cyclical theory. Meditating on the ruins of ancient empires has always been a cure for complacency.

War

One reason the empires did not last was that much of the ancient world was almost constantly at war. Victorious armies razed cities, slaughtered men and enslaved the rest, deported whole peoples. Passages of the Old Testament, and also from the wars of the Greeks as reported in Thucydides and Herodotus, are a sufficient reminder of the melancholy face of war in the ancient world. It was war endemic, and some scholars argue cogently that it did quite as much damage as our modern wars, all things considered. There is a mighty tribute here to the vitality of the human race. Cities are destroyed, but new ones arise. Kings lead their peoples on mighty enterprises. "I cut through steep mountains, I split rocks, I opened passages," Nebuchadnezzar boasts. But the Persians come and smite down the Babylonians. Well might the Jewish prophet muse on the theme of "How art the mighty fallen!" Ancient history seems like a sequence of mighty rises and mighty falls, punctuated by merciless battles.

This at least is true of the Fertile Crescent area, open to invasion from several directions. The same geographic reasons which had caused it to conceive the first civilization out of its lively social intercourse also forced it to endure waves of invasion from the surrounding uplands. This did not prevent the region from breeding cities and cultures in profusion, continuing to

Fresco of the bull-leapers from the palace at Cnossus, Crete.

be in general the zone of greatest civilized activity. But the impression is one of turmoil and instability, a steady rise and fall with much destruction and much syncretism or blending of cultures. There was more stability in Egypt, for geographic reasons. Egyptian pharaohs had to contend with African tribesmen to the south as well as occasional invaders from Asia, but they had natural defenses in both directions. During the Middle Kingdom the upper Nile was cleared and a canal built around the Cataract so that military forces

Assur-nasir-pal, King of Assyria (883–859 B.C.) from Nimrud.

could more easily be shipped to subdue the southern tribesmen. Nevertheless, Egyptian rulers loved to boast their military prowess. "Splendid in valor, in might, and in triumph," they had inscribed on their tombs. "Almost every Egyptian king . . . had to make a display of force on his frontiers to ensure a peaceful reign." It was a warlike society, if less turbulent than the Asiatic lands.

In brief, ancient history seems filled with

> The noise of the whip, and the noise of the rattling wheels; and prancing horses and jumping chariots; the horseman mounting, and the flashing sword, and the glittering spear; and a multitude of the slain and a great heap of carcasses. . . .

which is a Biblical comment on the Assyrians. The ancient empires, which introduced government and highly organized society with all the advantages thereby entailed, brought also the curse of war. We may suspect that these mighty monarchs exaggerated the frightfulness of their bloodshed and did not really raze as many cities or cut through as many mountains as their scribes recorded. But there is enough violence left after making allowance for such exaggeration.

Ancient gods

Religion, too, filled the ancient Orient. These vigorous peoples worshiped as wholeheartedly as they fought and built. The god of Assyria, Ashur, was quite as warlike as the people of that nation. There were demons, which afflicted people with everything from bad luck to headaches, and which had to be driven out by ritual and magic. The Babylonians studied the stars diligently, and became the first astronomers of the world, but to them astrology was the chief interest: "If the planet [Jupiter] emerges from behind the moon, there will be strife in the land," and so on. Marduk, chief divinity of Babylon, created the stars as abodes for the lesser gods. With childlike eyes in this infancy of human thought and expression, the ancient peoples looked at nature and projected personality into it, a thing natural enough to do. It was a first effort at understanding and control of their cosmic environment. Religion entered into the foundations of the earliest human cultures. The ancient city was literally a temple, a sacred place. Religion suffused every phase of life.

Almost all these religions were polytheistic. And the many gods were nature gods, representing the earth, the sky, and so on. Egypt worshiped the pharaohs as gods, representing the natural order of society and the state. Most peoples worshiped a fertility goddess, who brought forth the crops in the spring in the annual miracle of rebirth. The Canaanite fertility deities were particularly full-blooded, sexual, and warlike. Anath, "progenitress of the peoples," represented naked, astride a horse and armed, was given to ferocious massacres; she killed her brother, cut up his body, and sowed the fragments over the country, according to the myth. She resembles the Assyrian goddess Astarte. The themes of battle and fertility are mixed together in the archetypal images of ancient religion.

The people of Israel broke drastically with the rest of their Semitic neighbors, and others of the ancient world, in conceiving of a single God above and beyond nature, a "transcendent" deity of whose hands the heavens are the work. About 1300 the Egyptian king Ikhnaton tried to consolidate the numerous Egyptian deities and to elevate the sun-disc above all others, on the basis of which a claim for him as the first monotheist was formerly made, but few experts now think that this is a fair claim. In any case it did not last. The Egyptians had sun gods and earth gods, creator gods and regional gods; their kings were gods too; they evidently felt no need to choose just one deity but were prepared to pay tribute to a rich abundance of them. The priesthood, of course, profiting from this lively trade in religion, had no desire to destroy any of its branches. Plain people perhaps felt that in a world filled with so many risks and terrors it was well to have as many gods on your side as you could get. Later, in the Hellenistic and Roman Empire period, the Near East exported most of the religions that were popular with the urban masses; these included Isis, the Egyptian goddess whose white-clad priests sang hymns and sprinkled Nile water in the rite of baptism; Cybele, the Great Mother, an offspring of Astarte, also appearing in Greece as the cult of Demeter; and Mithras, the Persian soldier-god, popular in the army, whose disciples believed in a heaven and a hell.

The last-named descended from the great Persian religious tradition, which as early as the sixth century B.C. produced the nearly monotheistic creed taught by the famous Zoroaster or Zarathustra. Deficient though most of the ancient peoples were in religious vision when compared to the later Hebrews, they produced in their literature many of the themes found in the Old Testament. They possessed a "wisdom literature" which produced the prototype of Job (why must a righteous man suffer?) or Ecclesiastes (how futile are human pleasures and glories). It is a literature by no means lacking in mercy, humanity, and love. If a poor man owes you money, forgive him two thirds of it, an Egyptian maxim advises, and you will sleep better. "Do not laugh at a blind man or tease a dwarf." The proverbs of the Biblical books of Proverbs draw on a common stock which the Hebrews acquired at least in part from their neighbors among the peoples of the ancient Orient. The position of women was high in Egyptian and Cretan civilization, higher than among the Greeks or in medieval Europe probably, as is revealed in many paintings and statues depicting men together with their wives or mothers, and revealed also in the proud bearing of the women and in the Egyptian laws of inheritance. Isis, wife and mother, was an outstanding Egyptian deity; later, her devotees made her one of the leading religions of the Roman Empire for a time.

In Persia (Iran), the religion founded by Zoroaster was followed after the sixth century B.C. by a reversion to dualism and polytheism. Zoroaster had taught that there was a supreme being. Ahura Mazda, who struggled against the embodiment of all evil, Angra Mainyu, each supported by a battery of spirits, angels and demons. Ahura Mazda would ultimately prevail over the forces of evil. Persian dualism issued later in Mithraism and then in Manichaeism, exerting some influence on both Judaism and Christianity. It was probably the most important single religion distilled by the ancient ferment

Ikhnaton, King of Egypt

Religious worshiper of ancient Sumer (c. 2700 B.C.) from Tel Asmar, Iraq (above left); and Minoan snake goddess of the 16th century B.C.

Egyptian musician. The position of women was high among the Egyptians.

of religious belief except for that which was produced by the Hebrews. The latter people, meanwhile, were creating out of war, captivity, and suffering, the most notable spiritual achievement of the ancient world.

The Hebrews

Of all these oriental peoples, one of the most obscure was to leave by far the greatest mark on Western and world civilization. The story of the Hebrews (more often called Jews from the fifth century B.C., after their state Judah or Judea) has seemed to Christians as well as Jews to represent a unique divine revelation, granted by God to this people alone. Critical history, applied in modern times, has found the Bible to be far from "infallible" in a literal sense; indeed, historical criticism has shown it to be in some respects a confused document, requiring much clarification. Nor is it entirely unique, for many of the Old Testament stories, such as the Creation, the Fall, the Deluge, are myths found in other places and may well have been borrowed by the Hebrews. Yet when all is said, the Bible of the Jews is still unique as a spiritual biography of a people in search of God, the story of religious evolution by a nation with a special genius for religion, and perhaps the greatest of all historical dramas.

The story of Israel as recorded there is filled not with abstract ideas or scientific discoveries but with events of profound and dramatic import, with "mighty acts of God" and thundering words of the prophets. In a series of remarkable happenings, the people of Israel escaped from Egyptian slavery about 1300 B.C., saved by their God and their prophet-leader Moses. If historians cannot quite credit the tale of the Red Sea drying up for the escaping Israelites and reappearing to drown the pursuing Egyptians, they can wonder at the vitality of a people who so firmly believed in the miracle of this deliverance that they celebrate it to this day, in the feast of the Passover. This desert nomad people clothed every historical experience with vivid poetic imagery.

The Bible

The problem of the actual historicity of the events narrated in the Bible, as seen in the light of modern historical knowledge and other critical study of the Bible, is too large and too complicated a subject to go into. But in general it may be said that historians do not doubt the basic authenticity of most of it, though it is history occasionally overdramatized, oversimplified, and embellished with legend in a manner common to all "folk" history. Consider the legends that have grown up about such a figure as Abraham Lincoln in quite modern times. The popular and the critical accounts of Lincoln will differ, but the fact of his existence and his general position in history would not be in doubt. The earlier books of the Bible were not written until many centuries after the events they described, and had to rely on oral tradition. The real work of collecting and editing the various Hebrew writings was not done until after the sixth century B.C., and was then done by scholar-priests whose point of view was not that of the modern critical scholar.

Thus the Bible is a great series of dramatic scenes and memorable events—a "story-telling masterpiece." But it is more than that, of course. Most primitive peoples have strong imaginations, desert peoples perhaps most of all. What was singular about the Hebrews was their monotheism—their One God, a jealous god whose unity and soleness was attested by all the prophets. Yahweh, as described by Moses, was more than a tribal god to be summoned up on military occasions. In Hebraic history he was a powerful living presence who dominated the historical process and controlled all of nature. At length he became a universal God, who had picked Israel as his special agent but who reigned over all men. With them he made a Covenant, a solemn pact binding the people to honor and worship him alone, and keep his laws. By means of history and by poetry, the Jews discovered a philosophical idea of profound import.

Hebraic monotheism

Monotheism is not natural to man. Some sort of religion is found everywhere, but the strict monotheistic faiths are just about confined to Israel and her offspring, including Christianity and Islam as well as Judaism. Polytheism has been the more normal tendency. Agricultural peoples were especially prone to fertility cults in which the origin of things was explained by the mating of male and female powers. In one of the dramatic encounters with which the Old Testament abounds, the prophet Elijah (ninth century B.C.) denounced and finally defeated the cult of Baalism, just such a fertility religion, which was threatening to dethrone Yahweh. Monotheism may be arrived at by the philosophers as an abstract idea; but religions are born of the concrete experiences of unlettered folk. It is certainly remarkable how the Jews clung persistently to their one God, not as logical doctrine but as life experience, resisting every tendency to syncretize him with other deities or deprive him of absolute power. His chief significance lay in being not a nature god but a god who transcended nature, creator and controller of it but standing above it; at the same time, he guided the destinies of men and peoples, rewarding good and punishing evil.

A universe peopled by miscellaneous gods and demons, or even a "dualism" where a good and evil principle contended as in Iranian religion, is a universe of chance and caprice. The omnipotent God of the Hebrews was a guarantee of order and law in the world, as well as of its ultimately beneficent purpose.

The prophets

The men who expressed this impulse were not academic philosophers, but the prophets, who came from the people and spoke to them in powerful and often strange language. These men who claimed to speak with divine inspiration might be a simple shepherd like Amos, a village priest like Jeremiah, or more rarely a "proud citizen of Jerusalem" like Isaiah. All of them heard the call to prophesy in connection with some particular attribute of Yahweh they felt impelled to preach about—Amos his righteousness, Jeremiah his wrath, Isaiah his holiness, and so on. The prophets did not hesitate to attack kings and bitterly assail their own people for their sins. All nonconformists, all critics of their own society, owe a fundamental debt to the prophets of Israel. While Socrates was put to death in enlightened Athens, the Hebraic prophets seem more often than not to have triumphed in unpopular causes.

Growth of Hebraic religious thought

Hebrew history

The evolution of the "ethical monotheism" of the Hebrews was a gradual development. In the early, patriarchal age it was there, but in extremely crude form. Its development proceeded through the experiences described in the Old Testament, familiar to most of us. The Hebrews appear first in history about 1400 B.C. as an obscure, apparently rather barbarous nomadic people who were enslaved by the Egyptians. To the world at that time, it must have been utterly without significance that a certain Moses both helped the Hebrews to escape from slavery and persuaded them to give up polytheism—if indeed the latter is true. (The problem of the Biblical text is an epic one, hardly yet solved if it ever will be; but all scholars would agree today that the early books of the Bible contain a good deal of material written much later than the events they describe—many centuries later.) The books of the Old Testament about kings and "judges" are remarkable for their historic and narrative sense; Samson, David, Solomon are vividly realized people at the center of a stirring saga. The world still took little note of what this small kingdom did, however, and politically the Hebrews were destined to failure. They waged long war with the Canaanite inhabitants of Palestine, partly blending with this people in the process; then they encountered an invasion by the sea-going Philistines. After surmounting these obstacles, for a time the Kingdom of Israel almost became a power in the world. King Solomon (about 950 B.C.), as all Bible readers know, lived in what seemed splendid luxury. The archaeological recovery of his palace has confirmed this magnificence. Egypt had declined and Assyria had not yet entered as the new conqueror. But the state made by David and Solomon soon divided into two parts, and the Assyrians destroyed the northern one with its capital at Samaria (722 B.C.). Judah, the southern and poorer state, was then reduced to desperate straits by the powerful Chaldeans of Babylonia who took over the Assyrian empire. In 586 B.C. King Nebuchadnezzar of Babylon destroyed Jerusalem and took numerous captives to Babylonia.

The captivity

Conquered and carried into exile into Babylon, the Jews had their faith put to its severest test. Out of this disaster to the political fortunes of the tiny kingdom came a theology deepened and enlarged by suffering. This was the time of the greatest prophets, Jeremiah, Ezekiel, and the Second Isaiah. A truly universal ideal emerged in which Israel became the "suffering servant" destined to carry the message of salvation to all men even at the cost of its own national defeat. The unknown prophet called simply Deutero-Isaiah was one of the greatest teachers of all history. The general idea that emerged from the prophets of this period was that whatever happens may be part of a divine plan not evident to man. That plan may require the suffering and sacrifice of some toward a larger good. Adversity is therefore no reason for doubting a moral order in the universe. It is the lesson that appears in its fully developed form in the Book of Job, perhaps the greatest Hebraic philosophical writing. Shaken by unmerited suffering, Job clings to his faith and finally sees that God's ultimate purposes must be beyond his merely human perspective. The position is one quite similar to that adopted by the philosophically trained Stoics of Athens a century or more after the writing of the Book of Job.

The great historian-sociologist Max Weber argued that Western civilization derived the basis of its distinctive technological-economic order—its "economic rationality"—from ancient Judaism. We are probably more likely to think of the Greeks in this connection, but the fact is that Judaism reached the conception of an orderly, planned universe too. Albert Einstein and other great modern Jewish scientists and scholars have testified to the foundations of their science in the Jewish faith.[2]

Later Jewish history

Upon their return from exile, and especially after 444 B.C., the Jewish people entered a period which was perhaps less creative but nonetheless remarkable. The stress was on the law, not the prophets. The elaboration of a fixed custom and ritual governing almost all conduct assured the nation of survival, acting as cement to hold this amazing people together through all history in the face of national dismemberment and persecution. Coming once again under foreign sway, this time that of the Seleucid monarchs of Antioch (a product of the decentralization of Alexander the Great's empire), the Jews organized a great uprising, the Maccabean revolt, and won their independence anew (168 B.C.). But by 64 B.C. they fell like everyone else under the sway of invincible Rome. Twice they tried courageously but vainly to rebel. The intense nationalism developed by the Jews in this period tended to negate Isaiah's lofty vision, and an excessive legalism produced a certain feeling of dissatisfaction among some Jews. The prophetic movement was not dead, despite a heavy predominance of ritual and law. This popular messianic tradition continued to expect the coming of a Savior and the achievement of Israel's great mission, in one stupendous climax to all history.

The messianic idea

Messianism—the idea of a messiah—is one of the most striking contributions of Hebraic thought; precedents for it may be found in the earlier religions of Egypt and Babylonia, but the Jewish development of it was uniquely powerful. Its chief significance lies in its suggestion of an ethical goal in history. The messiah or redeemer would come as a climax to all history, ushering in a final kingdom of God, in some sense. The notion of an individual messiah, either a political or a purely spiritual leader, was deeply planted; Deutero-Isaiah, however, conceived of the whole Israelite people being collectively the "servant of the Lord," the redeeming elect of mankind.

John the Baptist and Jesus of Nazareth were products of this spiritual ferment within Judaism. So also were the sectarians at Qumran whose manuscripts were found in one of the most sensational archaelogical discoveries of recent times, the so-called "Dead Sea Scrolls." These were presumably Essenes, a sect which emerged in the second century B.C., following a Teacher of Righteousness and practicing baptism. They may have influenced Christianity.

Jesus of Nazareth

The teachings of Jesus were the objections of a passionate reformer to the legalism of the dominant Pharisee group who, though pious, stressed a body of customary regulations in a manner that obstructed the spiritual element in religion. In so objecting he faithfully followed the prophetic tradition. In his

---

[2] Some historians (see particularly the books of Cyrus H. Gordon) have argued that the traditional view of Greek and Hebrew separateness needs to be modified; they were in fact parts of a single cultural complex which embraced all the ancient Near East.

sympathy for the poor and socially outcast, whom the Pharisees were inclined to dismiss as the undeserving in a way that reminds us of some of the later Puritans, Jesus also was following in the footsteps of Amos and Ezekiel. The ethical teachings of Christ were not, however, very different from orthodox Jewish rabbinical precepts of his day—or indeed from those of some other religions. The much earlier Babylonian wisdom literature contains a close parallel to the Golden Rule, for example. But Jesus summed up and beautifully expressed the unparalleled religious experience of the Hebrew nation from Moses to the Pharisees. He did more than that. Christianity will be discussed in a subsequent chapter. Here we may note that some have found in Jesus elements coming from beyond Israel, perhaps from the genius of Greece which by then had formed and been spread over the oriental world. Turned inward on their own rich national consciousness as they were, the Jews could not escape a Hellenistic influence from the third century B.C. on. Jesus came from the most cosmopolitan part of the Jewish land, where Iranian and other eastern currents of religion, as well as Greek, mingled with native strains. The most distinctive difference between Christianity and orthodox Judaism was the universalism of the former; it may be related to the period in which Jesus lived. That period belongs to the next phase of world history, but into it went the wisdom of the whole ancient cycle.

The Jews proved unable to follow the universalism of Jesus. But Christians concede that their Savior is inconceivable save as a Jew against the background of Jewish history, and regard the Hebraic books as part of their faith. The Hebraic contribution was the exalted idea of a single God, who looked after his human children. It was the striving after righteousness as the way of pleasing Yahweh. It was the conception of an orderly and purposeful universe, and of purpose in history, of a final goal toward which all human happenings pointed.

Oriental religions

It may be noted that Judaism and Christianity, with their qualities of monotheism and teleology, contrast with the dominant types of Far Eastern higher religions, represented by Buddhism. These religions, which were developing at about the same time, had no sense of an ethical goal in history, or of a God who watches over the daily affairs of men. They sought, rather, the extinction of all sensual experience by an escape into a realm of pure being unbounded by time and space, uncontaminated by matter. Something of this spirit came into western civilization through Gnosticism and later Neo-Platonism, but the historical concreteness and sense of human destiny bequeathed by the Hebraic tradition was always dominant in the West.

Karl Jaspers has suggested that the period from about 800 to 200 B.C. was the "axial age" of world history, in which all major religions and philosophical systems came into being. That would include Confucius and Lao-Tse in China, Gautama the Buddha and the Upanishads in India, Zoroaster in Persia, as well as the Hebrew prophets and the Greek philosophers. In a book devoted to Western civilization, we cannot describe the Oriental creeds and civilizations. But we may be permitted a few lines simply to point out some comparisons and contrasts. Between 800 and 500 B.C. the Indic writings known as the Upanishads became the basic texts of all subsequent Indic religion. They contain its most characteristic doctrines, including the goal of escaping from the illusion of self and sense experience by merging into the cosmic spirit, the Brahman. This was not a theistic religion, nor a priestly one. The object is not to worship God but to achieve unity with the ultimate reality by a rigid and prolonged self-discipline. This reality is not a God who transcends the world, i.e., is beyond it and who created it; it is just the world itself in its spiritual aspects. In the sixth century B.C., Buddhism (and also Jainism) grew out of this Brahmanism, eventually to become one of the greatest and largest of the world's higher religions as it migrated to China and elsewhere. The Buddha taught that one must learn to extinguish the self and reach Nirvana, which is release from the sorrow and pain of the ever-changing realm of temporal existence. This is to be accomplished by one's own efforts, not reliance on God, who does not exist. In time various versions of Buddhism introduced notions of deity, but these were always regarded as vulgarizations by the high Buddhist tradition. The Orient in general believed in no messiah-savior who offered mankind salvation; it regarded this world as meaningless, or painful, or illusory, and saw no "salvation" except in the extinction of individual consciousness. (Later, to be sure, the religion of Islam penetrated parts of the Far East.) Oriental religion has been much more tolerant than Western, not insisting on any single faith which must be followed at the expense of all others. It has been less optimistic, and less humanistic in the sense of affirming value, hope, and purpose in the life of this world.

The source of the West's distinctive ethical outlook is Judaism. The impact of their unique historical religion on the Jews made them a people apart. They were "the *one* people of the [Roman] Empire who remained obstinately faithful to their national traditions in spite of the attractions of Hellenistic culture." This strong conviction of their own uniqueness not only gave the Jews a separate identity all through history, but also passed into Christianity and contributed to its success in the Roman era.

The decay of the ancient empires

Assyria

"One generation goeth, and another generation cometh; and the earth abideth forever." The ancient Orient watched the decline and fall of many a splendid empire. The great city of Ur, center of the Sumerian state whose ruler boasted that he was "king of the four quarters of the earth," went down before invaders from the Arabian desert. Amorites, Hittites, and Kassites had their day and fell. Later it was the Assyrians' turn to "come down like a wolf on the fold." This warlike people at the peak of its power in the seventh century B.C. conquered and occupied Egypt, the other great river-valley region of civilization, before being themselves overcome by Medes and Chaldeans. It is perhaps not surprising that the religious and literary themes of the

Sphinx and pyramid at Gizeh in Egypt

later Mesopotamian civilizations are fundamentally pessimistic, seeing no escape from the evils of life and no answer to the question about its meaning. Then even the age-old Kingdom of Egypt succumbed to a malady that was apparently as much internal as external, and was never again a great power. Assyria and then Persia conquered her before Alexander of Macedon made her a part of the Hellenistic world in 332 B.C.

Persia

"When Cyrus entered Babylon in 539 B.C., the world was old. More significant, it knew its antiquity." So writes the historian of the Persian Empire, A.T. Olmstead. Another modern historian, Arnold J. Toynbee, has theorized that civilizations in their old age go into a "universal state," when out of smaller units a world empire is created. For the world of the ancient Orient, Persia supplied such a state at the end of its cycle. It is typical of this phase (if we concede that a cyclical trend does exist in history) that "the periphery triumphs over the center." Macedon and Rome provide subsequent examples of the same thing. In this case, Persia, which lay well to the east of the classic Nile-Euphrates twin axis of ancient civilization and had not previously been noted for its civilization, played the part of barbarian-conquerer of an old and rather tired civilization. Like the Romans later, the Persians both respected and adopted the higher culture they conquered and organized. Cyrus, Darius, Xerxes—these names of the great Persian monarchs are familiar to us both from the Hebrew Bible and the Greek historians. For after

Persian cylinder seal inscribed to Darius the King shows him lion hunting.

conquering and organizing vast reaches of Asia and Africa, the Persians pressed into Europe but were thrown back by the Greeks on the field of Marathon and later at Salamis. The Persian Empire had broken down when Alexander the Great swept through Asia near the end of the fourth century B.C. But it prepared the way for him as he in turn prepared the way for the Romans.

To go with their abortive "universal state" the Persians produced a notable universal and higher religion, that founded by Zarathustra and developed in the cult of the sun-god Mithra, as already mentioned. Twice, it has been said, Persia almost conquered the West: the first time at Salamis, the second some centuries later when Mithraism competed with Christianity for the soul of the Roman Empire. But the Persians failed. Their civilization had many very attractive features. Its poetry and art as well as its religion are among the noblest ever produced. But geography favored powers more centrally located in the great Mediterranean basin.

Ancient society

Politically, the ancient peoples hardly attained much of that personal liberty of free citizens which the Greeks made the foundation of their states. Originating in control of the great river valleys, these "oriental despotisms" seem to most historians to have failed to escape from the somewhat dreary pattern of all-powerful monarchs and passively obedient subjects. Whether Hittite, Babylonian, Egyptian, or Persian, a common denominator of the ancient empires is this cult of the state personified in the king who is sometimes made into a god. With all their impressive achievements, they fail to present us with a picture of progressive development; instead we see one mighty potentate succeed another without much change in the essential pattern of society. Conceivably the most important cause of their final collapse lay here. The social structure almost universally was marred by slavery. This was probably the result mainly of war and conquest, but it was sanctioned by the gods and recognized in the laws, even those of relatively equalitarian peoples such as the Hebrews, Hittites, and Greeks. Not all slaves were completely without rights; a careful study of ancient society reveals many degrees of enslavement and suggests that the concept must be evaluated differently from more recent forms of slavery. However, a society based on rather rigid classes and castes was typical.

This was the end of the road for the world of the ancient Orient, a whole cycle of human history—the first cycle. Nine centuries later it would produce another great empire, that of Islam, then subside again. It had created some imperishable monuments in stone and metal, and some which perished until they were rediscovered and dug up in our own time. It had laid the scientific, mathematical, political, and literary foundations for all later civilizations. Out of its many religious mythologies, it had distilled some degree of rational thought and two higher religions, the Persian and the Hebraic. The moral and religious foundations of the West were laid up in Israel, right in the middle of the ancient civilizations; and the Greeks were influenced more than we used to think by these peoples whom they encountered in trade and in war. It is now time to turn to Greece and to the West.

Bibliography

Introduction

A note on the end-of-chapter-bibliographies: (a) The name of the publisher is given. If no date is given, the book is in a paperback edition. (*b*) For full information about paperbacks, see the annual *Paperbound Books in Print* published by R.R. Bowker, New York. For all books, *The Publishers' Trade List Annual* and, for Great Britain, *The Bookseller* contain the publishers' lists; check here if you know the publisher and want to find out if a book is in print and how much it costs. Or, consult *Books in Print*, an annual index of the *Publishers' Trade List*. (c) These bibliographies are necessarily highly selective. In general, the books selected are the most scholarly recent publications. Probably the best way to learn about additional historical writing is to look at the bibliographies which most of these books contain; see especially period textbooks such as Starr, below, Stephenson-Lyon in Chapter 4, Chabod in Chapter 9, the volumes of the Harper Rise of Modern Europe series, *The Oxford History of England*, etc. Especially valuable for everything since 1450 is *A Bibliography of Modern Europe*, edited by John Roach as an accompaniment to the *New Cambridge Modern History* (New York and London: Cambridge University Press, 1968). Generally useful, though now a few years out of date, is *The American Historical Association's Guide to Historical Literature* (New York: Macmillan, 1961). Finally, needless to say, the student should become acquainted with the card catalog of his college or university library; if this is not extensive, see the bound volumes of the catalog of the Library of Congress, arranged both alphabetically by author and, more usefully, by subjects.

Chapter 1

Competent and attractive introductions to the earliest men include Grahame Clark, *World Prehistory* (Cambridge University Press); Herbert Kahn, *On the Track of Prehistoric Man* (Modern Library, College Editions); R. Colbourn, *The Origins of Civilized Societies* (Princeton, N.J.: Princeton University Press, 1959); and the lavishly illustrated cooperative book, Stuart Piggot (ed.), *The Dawn of Civilization* (London: Thames & Hudson, 1961). Clark and Piggott have collaborated on *Prehistoric Societies* in the History of Human Society series (New York: Alfred A. Knopf, 1965). Also see David Diringer, *Writing*, in the excellent Ancient Peoples and Places series, published in this country by Frederick A. Praeger (New York, 1962). The romance and the reality of archaeology are suggested in V.G. Childe, *New Light on the Most Ancient East* (Grove Press, Evergreen); Kathleen M. Kenyon, *Digging Up Jericho* (Frederick A. Praeger, 1957), as well as *Archaeology in the Holy Land* (2d ed.; London: E. Benn, 1965); and James B. Pritchard, *Archaeology and the Old Testament* (Princeton University Press, 1958).

Specifically on the civilizations of the ancient Near East, Sabatino Moscati has provided summaries in *The Face of the Ancient Orient* (Doubleday, Anchor) and *Ancient Semitic Civilizations* (G.P. Putnam's Sons, Capricorn). See also Henri Frankfort, *The Birth of Civilization in the Near East* (Doubleday, Anchor), and *Before Philosophy* (Penguin). More specific yet, S.N. Kramer, *History Begins at Sumer* (Doubleday, Anchor); Sir Alan Gardiner, *Egypt of the Pharaohs* (Oxford: Clarendon Press, 1961); John A. Wilson, *The Culture of Ancient Egypt* (University of Chicago, Phoenix); O.R. Gurney, *The Hittites* (Penguin); and A.T. Olmstead, *History of the Persian Empire* (University of Chicago, Phoenix). H.W. Saggs, *The Greatness that was Babylon* (New York: Hawthorne Books, 1962), and the same author's *Everyday Life in Babylonia and Assyria* (London: Batsford, 1965), are attractive introductions to one of the two main centers of ancient civilization. A vast project of international scholarly collaboration, the UNESCO History of Mankind series, begins with a volume by Jaquetta Hawkes and Sir Leonard Woolley, *Prehistory and the Beginnings of Civilization* (London: George Allen & Unwin, 1963).

B.L. Van der Waerden, *Science Awakening* (New York: Oxford University Press, 1961), assesses the contribution of Egyptian and Babylonian science. On religion, E.O. James, *The Ancient Gods* (G.P. Putnam's Sons, Capricorn), provides a general background; while Martin Noth, *The History of Israel* (London: A. & C. Black, 1960), H.H. Rowley, *The Faith of Israel* (Philadelphia: Westminster Press, 1957), and S.R. Driver, *An Introduction to the Literature of the Old Testament* (World Publishing, Meridian), are good guides to the enormous literature on Judaism and the Bible. Also outstanding are the paperbacks by T.J. Meek, *Hebrew Origins* (Harper Torchbook); E.W. Heaton, *The Old Testament Prophets* (Penguin); Isidore Epstein, *Judaism* (Penguin); Norman H. Snaith, *The Distinctive Ideas of the Old Testament* (Schocken Books). See also W.O.E. Osterley and T.H. Robinson, *Hebrew Religion: Its Origin and Development* (Macmillan, 1937), and C.F. Whitley, *The Exilic Age* (Westminster Press, 1957). Among many other excellent works of scholarship in this area, Y. Kaufmann, *The Religion of Israel*, translated and abridged by M. Greenberg (Chicago: University of Chicago Press, 1960), is a recent outstanding one; a more specialized work than Cecil Roth, *The Jews*, in the History of Human Society Series (London: Hutchinson, 1967). Salo W. Baron, *A Social and Religious History of the Jews* (11 vols.; New York: Columbia University Press, 1952–67), is a monumental achievement. On Persian religion, see R.C. Zaehner, *The Dawn and Twilight of Zoroastrianism* (London: Weidenfeld & Nicolson, 1961). Reliable guides to the much-discussed subject of the Dead Sea Scrolls are Matthew Black, *The Scrolls and Christian Origins* (London: Thomas Nelson & Sons, 1961), and Jean Danielou, *The Dead Sea Scrolls and Primitive Christianity* (New American Library, Mentor). A famous, very readable synthesis is H. Daniel-Rops, *Jesus in His Times* (Doubleday, Image).

In addition to the Bible (see *New English Bible*, or an annotated edition such as *The Dartmouth Bible* [Boston: Houghton Mifflin, 1950]) and Kramer's *Sumer*, above, which contains texts, there are some fascinating sources, including W.G. Lambert (ed.), *Babylonian Wisdom Literature* (Oxford University Press, 1961), and T.G. Allen, *The Egyptian Book of the Dead* (University of Chicago Press, 1960). A good general textbook is Chester G. Starr, *A History of the Ancient World* (Oxford University Press, 1965).

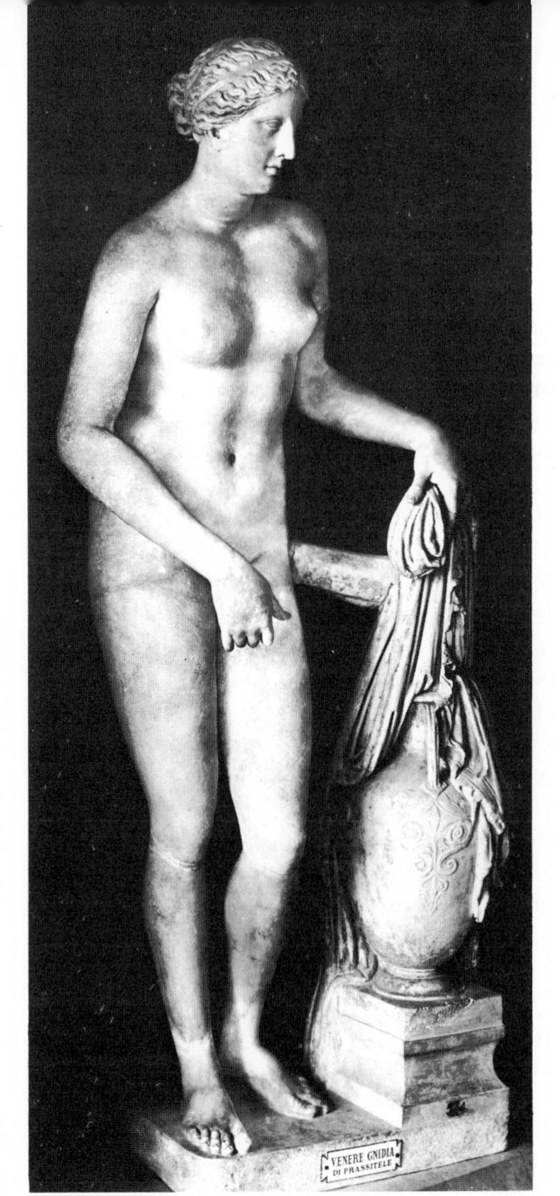

Copy of Praxiteles' "Venus" (Venus of Cnidus), considered perhaps the most beautiful Grecian statue.

2

The Greeks

chronology

c. 1200 B.C.
Mycenaean civilization; King Agamemnon; Trojan War.

c. 1100 B.C.
Dorian migration into Greece.

c. 900 B.C.
Homer. Formation of city-states begins.

c. 590–500 B.C.
Thales and Anaximander, Ionian science.
Pythagoras and Heraclitus, successors of Thales, to 500.

490–79 B.C.
Persian Wars.

461 B.C.
Pericles elected leader of Athens. Expansion of Athenian empire. Aeschylus.

438 B.C.
Completion of Parthenon. Sophocles.

431–404 B.C.
Peloponnesian War. Defeat of Athens.
Euripides, Socrates, Thucydides.

399 B.C.
Death of Socrates.

390–60 B.C.
Peak of Plato's thought.

371 B.C.
Theban victory over Sparta. Recovery of Athens.

359–36 B.C.
Philip of Macedon; conquest of Greece by Macedonians.

336–23 B.C.
Alexander the Great; conquest of Asia. Founding of Alexandria.

323– B.C.
Successor-states of Alexander: Ptolemy, Seleucid monarchies.
Rebellion in Athens put down (322); end of age of city-states.
Hellenistic age.

270–63 B.C.
Death of Zeno, Epicurus, leading Hellenistic philosophers.
Euclid, Aristarchus, Hellenistic science flourishes.

The development of Greek civilization

That other supremely gifted people of antiquity, the Greeks, were developing at the same time as the Hebrews, but in a different direction. Here too was a people, small in numbers and in power, making their contribution in the realm of the mind and affording evidence for the thesis that the most creative states are small ones.

In the case of ancient Greece, geography seems to have had something to do with it. The mainland harbors and island-dotted seas produced a race of seafarers. The salient fact of the economy became sea-going commerce and Greeks journeyed to Asia Minor, Syria, Egypt, Crete, and the other civilizations of the Mediterranean world, developing trade not only in goods, but in ideas. It is possible to explain the Greek genius for intellectual synthesis and generalization as the result of their wide contacts. They assimilated the knowledge of all antiquity: the Phoenician alphabet, Egyptian geometry, Babylonian astronomy, and others. The first important Greek scientist-philosophers came from the shores of Asia Minor. There was a strong Minoan influence on the Greeks quite early. Some scholars hold Plato's philosophy derived in part from a tradition which led back through Pythagoras to the Orient. All this considered, however, there can never be any question about the ascendancy of the Greek mind in the realms of science, philosophy, and rational thought in general.

Early Greek history

Like the Hebrews, the Greeks emerged dimly from prehistory during the second millenium and had an "heroic age" in roughly the 13th century, at the end of which the Achaean-Mycenaen king, Agamemnon, attacked and destroyed Troy, as related most memorably by the poet Homer, an Ionian probably of the ninth century, who remained for Greeks a veritable Bible. ("Homer" may well have been more than one person—this is a famous literary-historical puzzle.)[1] The Bronze Age Mycenaean Greek civilization, heavily indebted to the Cretan Minoans, and so called from having its most imposing center at the city of Mycenae in southeastern Greece, began about 1600 B.C. and reached its climax about the time of the destruction of Troy as related in the *Iliad*. Between 1400 and 1200 the Mycenaean Greeks inherited much of Crete's commercial wealth and power, and built impressive cities. Thereafter they declined, and for several centuries there was a "dark age." Barbarian intrusions from the north (Dorians, Thessalians) considerably disturbed the peninsula. As Thucydides says, "A long time elapsed before Hellas with difficulty achieved stability and was no longer subject to shifts of population." By the eighth century, however, a varied Greek world, from the Ionian islands to powerful Athens and over to "Dorian" Sparta, and including many other local traditions, formed a reasonably stable society. The Greeks were a mixed people, racially as well as politically. They never succeeded in mak-

[1] Scholars are inclined to date Homer's *Iliad* in the ninth century, but assign the *Odyssey* to a later date, eighth or even seventh century.

ing a nation politically. The constant wars between their cities are well known, as is the fact of the differences between their great cities Sparta and Athens, representing different facets of Hellenism. They did however make a culture, a manner of living, with a general sort of unity which set them off from the others and caused all Greeks to look upon non-Greeks as "barbarians"—even when they were fighting bitterly among themselves.

The Persian wars

They achieved from the sixth century on a unique civilization marked by conquests of the mind to which the entire world has been forever indebted. It is interesting that the Exilic Age of the Hebrews is the period of the Ionian scientists. The same Persians who, conquering Babylon, delivered the Jews from captivity, attacked the Greek cities but were hurled back in the famous battles of 490–79 B.C., Marathon, Salamis, Thermopylae, Plataea. The Greek cities led by Athens were thus able to hold their independence long enough to produce the great age. The period from the birth of Socrates in 470 B.C. to the death of Aristotle in 322 (by which time the era of the independent city-states was reaching its end) has often been called "the most memorable in the history of the world." It was memorable not for religious vision—though there was some of that—but for rational, speculative thought, the "love of wisdom" which the Greeks named philosophy. They did not distinguish sharply between philosophy and science: both were a part of that desire to know, and to know rationally, which represented the genius of Hellas.

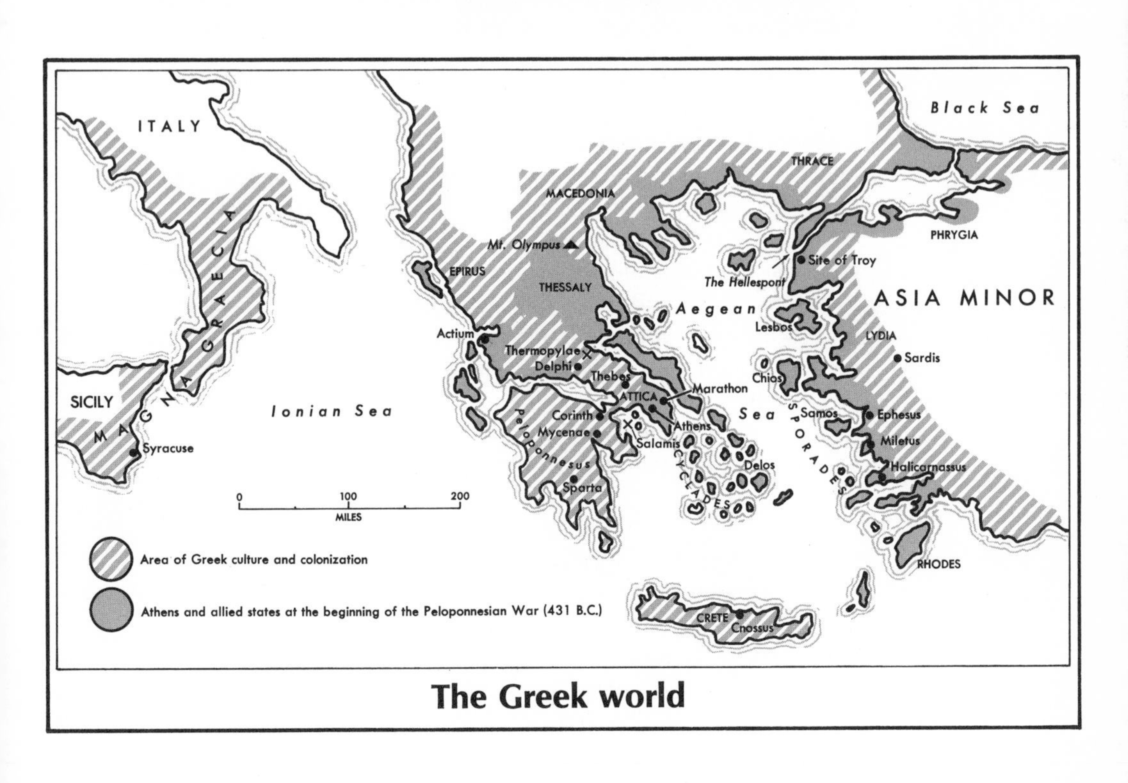

The Greek world

Socrates

Plato

The "polis"

The flowering of Greek thought, art, literature occurred within the framework of the *polis* or city-state. The mountains and the many ocean inlets form a geographical environment in Greece peculiarly favorable to small political units. Moreover, the economic foundations of classical Greece lay in the urban occupations of commerce and industry. Athens especially became a great center of international trade, as her mines and workshops, manned in good part by the labor of slaves, supplied commodities for export in return for the foodstuffs and other goods not produced by the rocky soil of Greece. And so the city—with a fairly restricted area of territory around it—became the focus of political as well as social and economic life in ancient Greece.

The cities were self-governing, independent, and proud of their independence. The smallness of these political units made possible—at least in Athens—the development of a "pure" democracy. Each citizen (but by no means all residents were citizens, some being slaves and others aliens) participated directly in the making of laws, and also in the hearing of important jury trials. Executive officials were selected by drawing lots; generals could be fired summarily by the assembly, which any citizen of Athens could attend and at which he was entitled to vote. Scholars are inclined to believe that this Greek *polis* was a unique institution, created by the Greeks, its free political institutions contrasting with the despotic states of the Near Eastern peoples. Quite possibly it was the supreme contribution of the Greeks to civilization. The slave basis of Athenian democracy marred it, though evidence indicates Athenian slavery was mostly mild and not extensive; while in other Greek cities—notably Sparta—a frankly oligarchic type of government developed. Nevertheless, the remarkable civic consciousness of all the Greek cities, together with the cultural advantages that can come from small cohesive groups, contributed to their great achievements. "Man is a political animal," Aristotle wrote. Man then is destined to live together in cities, and act together in self-government. All the Greeks in their mature stage of civilization felt the same way. In the realm of ideas where they excelled everyone before or since, the classic figure of the Greeks was Socrates, who went abroad into the streets and *agora* and talked to all Athenians.

The Greek philosophers

The birth of philosophy

Greek philosophy was a persistent search for first principles, for the reality that underlies the uncertainty of sense impressions and of temporal sequences. More recently, some of our philosophers have told us that we should not make such inquiries, for they are vain. Many in our positivist age have not much liked "metaphysics." The ancient and medieval worlds were immersed in it. We must at least recognize the legitimacy of their motives. The intelligence of the Greeks led them to see that the world as perceived in our senses lacks clarity and certainty. Behind this flux of experience must lie something else if the world is to be intelligible.

The Ionian scientist-philosophers of the seventh and sixth centuries B.C. dedicated themselves to a search for the one basic, unchanging substance out of which everything else was made. Thales, Anaximander, and Anaximenes failed to find it, but their intellectual curiosity set off an age-long inquiry. Pythagoras, influenced by these Ionians, suggested that the ultimate nature of the world is to be like mathematics. The world of mathematical relations is a world of logic, clarity, apparent certainty. Two and two do not just roughly equal four most of the time if nothing else interferes, as events in the sensory world so often do; the equation stands exactly and forever. And mathematics is a vast as well as an orderly system. Pythagoras was a brilliant geometrician. Certain relations between numbers and music (between rates of vibration and concordant notes) led Pythagoras to suggest that the real world is built on mathematical principles. Pythagoras and after him Plato believed the world to be intelligible only if approached through pure mathematics.

Plato

Plato, meditating on such problems raised by earlier Greek thinkers, produced his famous doctrine of Ideas, or Forms: a realm of rational essences which the reason can grasp through mathematics or pure logic. By the time of Plato, disciple of the immortal Socrates as well as of the earlier genius, Pythagoras, Greek philosophic thought had attained an amazing subtlety and skill. While other peoples were still thinking in mythological terms, the Greeks had carried abstract, conceptual thought almost to its limits. They dealt in terms such as form, essence, nature, reality, mind, matter. With a Socratic zest, a Platonic acuteness, and a Aristotelian thoroughness they raised all possible questions, and answered them by "reason." Plato uses myths, but usually only as illustrations of some point he wishes to make in logical analysis. The Socratic dialogue became one classic method of presentation—the form of an argument, with the dramatic interest of personality involved in it. But, apart from the fact that the dialogues were only a popular form of presenting philosophy, they are considerably more intellectual than, say, the Book of Job, which is also an argument and a masterpiece of serious literature. The reasoning is closer, the thought keener, above all the terminology is less mythical and metaphorical.

Greek rationalism

The "conceptual" or "intellectualist" bias of the highest Greek thought as represented by Aristotle and Plato has come under some attack in modern times, but throughout most of European history it has been a mighty force. "All men have an instinctive desire for knowledge," Aristotle begins his *Metaphysics*. It is not for its practical value but for its own sake that knowledge is prized. Man is marked by the power of reason: he is *homo sapiens*. Knowledge that is merely sensory is imperfect; real knowledge is of the essences of things, qualities which are accessible to the pure reason alone. Aristotle thought that one had to begin with sensory particulars, not with Plato's pure ideas, but he agreed that the goal is the same: it is to define essential qualities, which are not tangible but abstract. There had been materialists, vitalists earlier in Greek philosophy. There had been Heraclitus of Ephesus, for example, (c. 540–475) who believed that reality was change, and thought the servant of will. The Sophists had doubted all knowledge, and the atomists, led by Democritus, believed the universe was blind chance, without God or purpose. But Plato and Aristotle taught men to believe that these were crude and imperfect theories. This "autonomy of reason" was obviously an optimistic, energizing idea. Man is not determined by life, he rises above it. His divine gift of reason makes him half a god, marked off from the rest of nature. He is proud and free and may know Truth, not just opinion.

It is true, however, that much Greek thought in its later epochs—even Plato's Academy—came back to skepticism. In the last analysis, reality remained unknowable. The metaphysical quest ended in failure. But Platonic rationalism found its way into Christianity and bequeathed to medieval Europe its confident certainties. The profound skepticism of Pyrrho of Elis and Sextus Empiricus, teaching that nothing can be known, was set aside and remained unknown until the 16th century A.D.

Whatever truths Plato and his fellows may have found or not found, their way of inquiry was always the same as that of the sciences, from which they were indeed not separated: the way of free inquiry, discussion, critical analysis, patient and open-minded search for truth. This legacy was summed up for the West in Plato's account of the trial of his master, Socrates, who told the Athenians:

> If you were therefore to say to me, "Socrates, we will let you go, but on this condition, that you cease from carrying on this search of yours, and from philosophy; if you are found following these pursuits again, you shall die"—I say, if you offered to let me go on those terms, I would reply, "Athenians, I hold you in the highest regard and love, but I will obey God rather than you; and as long as I have breath and strength I will not cease from philosophy, and from exhorting you, and declaring the truth to everyone of you whom I meet."

Socrates

With utter candor and absolute integrity, the easy-going Socrates, who talked to everyone and charged no fees for his teaching, came to believe that most of what passed for knowledge was ignorance, and with "Socratic irony" affected a naive ignorance himself, the better to bait the pretentious ones and lead them to admit their confusion. This critical method of Socrates ruthlessly demolished all sorts of conventional beliefs and prejudices; but though Socrates was a gadfly, and unflinchingly honest, he was no mere debunker (though some of his disciples apparently were). He was a staunch foe of sophists and skeptics, basically a conservative rather than a radical. He believed that man had a soul, or that there was something of this sort in which men share: a higher reality, spiritual in nature, existing somehow behind or beyond the apparent world of body and senses. It was this which guaranteed that Truth and Justice really existed, to be traced down amid the welter of shifting opinion and the amoral clash of political factions. To all future generations Socrates bequeathed this tremendous idea. Christianity would silently absorb much of the Socratic soul into its system; a Christian humanist of the Renaissance like Erasmus of Rotterdam would virtually canonize "Saint Socrates." Socrates left a myth for the West to build on; it was described in immortal language by his most renowned pupil, Plato.

The Hellenic genius

Practically all this intellectual development was finally concentrated in the city of Athens, the "school of Hellas" and of all mankind, "the envy of nations" as Aeschylus called her, where free civic institutions flourished along with philosophy and the great drama and architecture of this golden age. Athens, where Socrates taught (and was executed for allegedly subversive activities) and where his disciple Plato wrote—city of the Parthenon, the Winged Victory, of Sophocles and Euripides—was also the city of the first effective democracy, a pure democracy. A city also of slavery, and of an imperialistic foreign policy which ended by ruining her. With her faults as well as her glories, Athens became a symbol for the West, for here more than any other one place Western civilization began.

Greek science

Many have tried to express the meaning of Athens and of the Greek spirit. Enthusiastic Hellenists have possibly overidealized it. But the establishment of the foundations of all western thought is a solid, a staggering achievement that cannot be denied to Greece. That the names of almost all our sciences are of Greek origin is enough evidence. The popular view of

The Parthenon on the Acropolis of Athens

Greek science underestimates rather than overestimates it. Most people would probably say that the Greeks did start it all, but were imperfect scientists, largely through an excess of speculation and deficiency of observation, and their mistakes had later to be corrected. Partly true, but fuller knowledge reveals often that the Greeks were surprisingly modern. Anaximander and Empedocles anticipated Darwin in suggesting evolution. The atomic theory was developed. Aristarchus of Samos found that the earth went around the sun. In these areas, different viewpoints won the field and the lines of development mentioned were not carried forward until much later. But in all cases this was because the experimental evidence then available seemed to support another position. The Greeks explored all hypotheses and always followed where scientific inquiry, untrammeled by prejudice or authority, led. They thus established western science on a secure foundation, whatever mistakes they necessarily made in the infancy of human knowledge. Their spirit was that of Hippocrates (460–400 B.C.), who founded the science of medicine not by being right about all the diseases—we have not yet gotten that far—but by setting forth the rules of scientific diagnosis: careful observation, thorough analysis, painstaking collection of evidence and comparison of it. This is not to deny that Greek science showed by modern standards a tendency to let its speculative interests outrun its observational data. This was natural in the early stages of science, and must not be construed as meaning that the Greeks showed no interest in or aptitude for exact and careful observation—they did. In Hellenistic times science became more experimental.

Earlier peoples cannot be said to have lacked "science," if we agree to

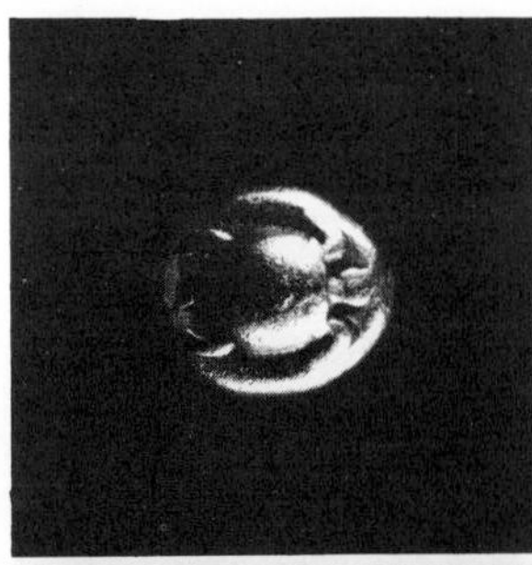

The stater of Aegina, issued about 700 B.C., was the first silver coin.

The decadrachm of Syracuse, issued to commemorate the end of the Peloponnesian War.

apply the term to rather unsystematic discoveries. The Greeks themselves granted credit to the Egyptians in medicine and mathematics. Metallurgy and other practical techniques; practical geometry; Babylonian astronomy, clocks, calendars—the ancient peoples had bequeathed a great miscellany of lore to the Greeks. The genius of the latter lay in building a coherent body of theory, generalizing these data into systems and laws, reducing them to order. Together with mathematics, the Greeks excelled in its sister study, logic. They tried to find the rules of reasoning, the methods of systematic inquiry. If logic was a Greek discovery, and Euclid perhaps the greatest Greek thinker, it is wrong to say they neglected experiment—a thing which has often been said since Francis Bacon said it 350 years ago. Numerous sophisticated experiments are recorded in Aristotle, in the Hippocratic medical treatises, and elsewhere. Two thousand years later, Greek science was found to have contained some errors and perhaps even to have been wrong in its basic premises. What is amazing is that it should have lasted so long, and that it provided the sources of all the sciences. Greek science reached maturity in Hellenistic times, i.e., the period from about 300 to 100 B.C., when Galen, Archimedes, Eratosthenes, Ptolemy the astronomer, Hero of Alexander, and many others flourished.

Greek art

To this scientific achievement, the Greeks added many other unique gifts. Unlike the Hebrews, who left little in the arts except their Biblical writing, the Greeks excelled in architecture, the plastic arts, and the drama. The difference between the Grecian style in the visual arts and practically all that went before is as startling as their leap forward in philosophy and science. This style com-

Carved marble chairs for dignitaries at theater of Dionysus, Athens (c. 330 B.C.)

Late Hellenic bronze boxer

Temple of Athena on the Acropolis of Athens (427–24 B.C.)

Pericles, political leader of Athens in the Golden Age

bines perfect proportion, and a touch of the ideal, with a naturalism that gives us the feeling of reality. In the mature Hellenic style, which gradually evolved over the centuries from an earlier formalism somewhat resembling the Egyptian or Etruscan, we see real people, alive and natural, in the many magnificent sculptures which have been preserved. The same is true of the marvelous tragedies of Aeschylus and Sophocles and Euripides, wherein great men, possessing dignity and free will, pit themselves against the implacable laws that rule the universe. These are among the noblest works of mankind, and today we are astonished that every Athenian was able to follow the performances of these plays with sustained interest. Greek tragedy was an organic union of drama, music, and the dance. In their glorious temples and theaters, too, the Greeks put into esthetic form, with naturalness and spontaneity, something of their vision of life and their careful observation of it. We have lost their music, their painting, and indeed a good part of their literature. How little we have is sometimes forgotten. It is a further tribute to Greece, for these fragments were rich enough to nourish civilization for ages. Greek art, drama, and poetry are basic in Western civilization.

The Dionysian element

It must not be thought—lest we exaggerate—that all Greeks were free-thinking rationalists or philosophers. Far from it. Before each of the countless battles in those interminable wars on which the Greeks often seem to have spent most of their time, they sacrificed animals and read the entrails for omens, refusing to fight if these were unfavorable. This was the custom among Socrates' contemporaries. Socrates himself was put to death for stirring up the Athenian youth to doubt the ancient gods. (This at least was the nominal charge. Under the impact of war and plague the Athenian democracy almost broke up in disorder in the years just prior to Socrates' trial. Bitter internal strife had broken out in this atmosphere, and corrosive factionalism existed; Socrates was really a victim of this.) Out of Greece came orgiastic cults and mystery religions as wild as anything the Orient knew. Indeed, a part of the soul of Hellas was an enthusiasm which led it into extremes in all directions; the passion for perfection in thought was matched by other passions, in politics and religion, which were far from scientific. The famous Hellenic maxim "nothing in excess" is misleading. It was not typical of the Greeks, which is probably why they adopted it. They had to rein in a tremendous vitality.

Greek religion was a varied and miscellaneous thing; there was no one religion common to all Greeks, no church, no central body of doctrine. The Olympian festival began as a religious ceremony and became an athletic event; the oracle at Delphi turned into a kind of "Dear Abby" where Greeks sought advice on personal problems. The "mystery" religions, such as the cult of Demeter practiced at Eleusis, produced marvelous myths and hymns; in the wild Dionysisan frenzies associated with Orphism, music and the dance were heavily involved. The Greeks told rather scabrous stories about their gods, who were a quarrelsome, immoral lot, constantly stealing, seducing, and warring on each other. All these popular cults seem to testify to the basic humanism of the Greek people, to whom the gods were less an object of solemn worship than a source of very worldly satisfactions. But on a higher level the lofty speculations of Plato and other Greek philosophers about the nature of God, who shaped the universe according to reason (see especially Plato's *Timaeus*), and about the soul, the immortal and immaterial element in man, were destined to exercise a deep influence on Christianity.

The Peloponnesian War and the decline of the Greeks

Athens and Sparta

Athens and Sparta were the two "great powers" of the little world of Greek politics. Rivals for more than a century after the Persian War, they were totally unlike: trade and industry formed the economic basis of one, self-sufficient agriculture of the other; cosmopolitan Athens, "isolationist" Sparta; the art, learning, literature and free spirit of the city of the Acropolis contrasting with the antiintellectualism and austerity of the hardy farmers. And above all, democracy versus oligarchy. Somewhat like contemporary South Africa, Sparta controlled a large helot (serf) population by force and by rigid hostility to all change. Yet the amazing discipline and self-control of the Spartan army

Portions of the shrine of Athena at Delphi

testified to a society with deep civic spirit, and in fact to Sparta rather than Athens belonged the creation of the first constitution and the first *polis*.

Among Sparta's allies in the fifth century B.C. was the strong naval and commercial city of Corinth. This Spartan alliance confronted the might and pride of Athens at the onset of the Peloponnesian War. Athens, in her pride, became imperialistic. The outstanding city both in strength and in culture, Athens aspired to dominate all Greece but found that the formidable troops of Sparta stood in her way; and even more, the fierce love of independence felt by even the smallest Greek city. The Athenian empire was an outgrowth of the Delian League, originally a free association of many small Greek states; but the wealth and power of Athens so much exceeded that of the others that she gradually assumed power over them, finally treating as rebels the citizens of a small state that attempted to withdraw from the League.

The Peloponnesian War

Not long after the Persians were defeated, the Peloponnesian War began (431) and went on for a quarter of a century except for a truce between 421 and 416. It produced not only ferocious fighting in which the customary respect for the rules of war, which Greeks had shown in the past when

fighting with each other, was no longer evident, but also bitter civil conflict within the cities, leading often to mass proscription by one side or the other —democrats and oligarchs. It was an experience which morally even more than physically destroyed the Greeks. The comparatively small numbers of men lost in battle might be replaced, but no one could restore the atmosphere of civic unity or Greek national spirit after this. Perhaps the one good thing that came out of the war was Thucydides' classic work of history which described and attempted to account for it. ("The real cause of the war," Thucydides concluded, "was Athens' power and Sparta's fear, which compelled them to go to war.") Thucydides was fully aware that his subject was a tragic one; he tried to write "for all time" in order to learn from history and help prevent men in the future from making the same sad mistakes. It was a typical Greek achievement.

Sparta was the nominal victor in this long war. There was no real victor for the Greeks; they never recovered their balance. Bigger states from outside—Macedon and then Rome—were to press upon them before they were able to heal their wounds and establish some sort of federal unity. The fourth century B.C. was nevertheless the golden age of Athenian thought. The execution of Socrates, 399, was a part of the bitter political conflict of the period; the political theory of Plato and Aristotle was stimulated by the task of finding some answer to *stasis* (civil strife). Aristophanes' comedies are full of satire and a bitter wit which deals with the political conflicts of his Athens. In philosophy and literature, this age was the boldest and finest. One might conceivably compare this period to 20th-century Europe. The awful failure represented by the two destructive world wars has cracked the old structure of sovereign states in our time and indicates a crisis which may presage the end of Europe as previously known. Yet it has been a brilliant century for the arts, sciences, philosophy. In such times of social breakdown and political upheaval there seems to be an additional stimulus to thought. It is a fact, at any rate, that the Athens of Plato and Aristotle, who would dominate European thought for centuries, was an Athens already in steep political decline.

Alexander the Great

The Macedonians, from the land just north of Greece, were in contact with the Greeks and their rulers spoke Greek, but they were not considered to be Greeks; the Macedonian dialect was not comprehensible to the latter. Their elective kingship and tribal social organization marked them as a people just emerging from the stage of barbarism. As peoples in this phase often did—it was their "heroic age"—they excelled in war. Philip, the father of Alexander the Great, was a skillful diplomatist as well as military leader. He led a great army while the Greek cities were now typically employing mercenaries, no longer producing virile citizen-armies. The orator Demosthenes urged the Athenians to strike Philip before it was too late; but to little avail. The Athenian democracy, once overbold in its policies, now was too slow and cautious. Some Greeks, perceiving the bankruptcy of the city-

Alexander the Great

Demosthenes, orator and statesman

states and believing Philip to be a true Greek, secretly hoped he would prevail and unite the states at last.

The Macedonian conquest

Philip did indeed worship Zeus and Apollo, the Greek gods, and claimed to have descended from Heracles. Though half barbarians, the Macedonian kings shared the spirit of Hellenic culture. Philip, had employed the famous philosopher Aristotle to instruct his son, Alexander. Thus the brilliant youth acquired a deep respect for the ideals of Greek culture. Philip defeated Athens and her allies in 338, but did not proceed to destroy her. Instead, he organized a League of the Greek states and imposed peace upon them. He was assassinated in 336 at the age of only 46; he had laid the foundations for his son Alexander to spread Greek culture far and wide over the world.

Conquest of the East

There was a mixture in Alexander of the philosopher-king and the barbarian conqueror that has always fascinated posterity. His amazing career as world conqueror began immediately on his assumption of the throne at the age of 20, and continued through a meteoric career of 13 years; he died in 323 at the age of 33. He established Macedonian authority as far north as the Danube in Europe, as far east as Persia. He conquered the Persian empire and even pushed briefly into India. In Greece, of course, all resistance was crushed. In one day Alexander (335) captured Thebes, a powerful city as the Greek cities had been accustomed to measure power, and utterly destroyed it—save, typically, for the house of Pindar the poet. It was enough to intimidate the rest. As news of the victories of the mighty Macedonian phalanxes in Asia returned in the years following, some Greeks forgot their old local pride in a surge of admiration for a man who was, after all, a Greek by cultural adoption. However, Greeks were less enthusiastic than some of the orientals. For many of them, as for Demosthenes, the Macedonians remained something less than barbarians. Alexander's empire was to belong not to Greece but to the world.

It has seemed to most historians that this world of the eastern Mediterranean was ripe for unity, and that Alexander was an instrument, a splendid one, of historical destiny. Most of the people seemed to welcome a unification, whereas formerly they would have fought to the death for their independence. Some of them still did; but the Egyptians welcomed Alexander as a liberator (from Persia), as did numerous other peoples and cities of Asia Minor. He founded the city of Alexandria there in Egypt, and was accepted as the pharaoh—god.

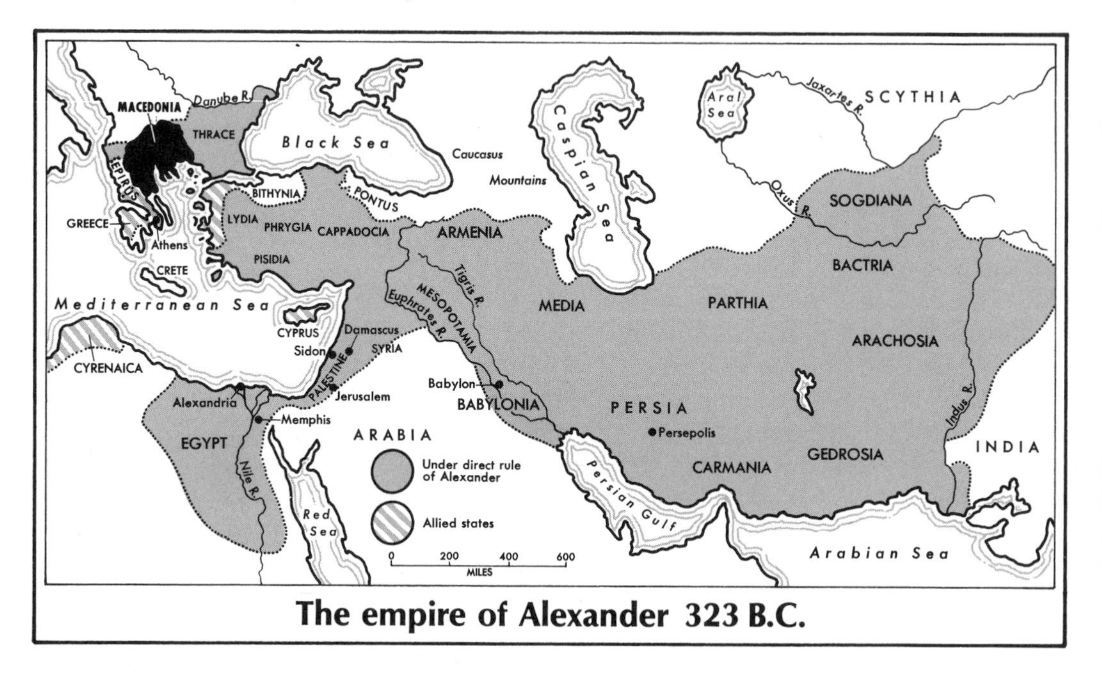

The empire of Alexander 323 B.C.

Spread of Greek culture

It must be recalled that Persia had earlier rehearsed this world state. Alexander usually was tolerant and enlightened in his rule. Commerce flourished under a single coinage and general pacification. The Greek influence was spread far and wide. The Greeks always had been energetic colonizers, having earlier settled as far west as Sicily, Italy, and southern France, as well as on the shores of Asia Minor. Indeed, the great colonizing epoch of the Greeks dates back to the seventh and eighth centuries B.C. But now there tended to be a single great area of culture in which the Greek civilization made a profound impact but received back influences, since Alexander tolerated local religions and traditions. Thus was created virtually a "world state." Alexander himself, as he pursued his conquests, had some sense of almost a religious mission to achieve a united world in which civilizations were blended. It was a preparation for Christianity and for the Roman Empire. "Particularism was replaced by the idea of the 'inhabited world,' the common possession of civilized men. . . . Men began to feel after the unity which must lie beneath the various religions."

Successor states

Alexander's dream did not, however, fully survive his own premature death. The immense size of this empire so quickly conquered presented staggering difficulties, which the equally immense energy and vision of Alexander could barely keep up with. Had he lived longer, this incomparable genius of both war and administration might well have done what it remained for Rome to do: conquer and effectively organize the entire Mediterranean world. He possessed the same combination of military efficiency (with occasional ruthlessness against incorrigible foes or rebels) and political wisdom, which led him to tolerate a variety of cultures, provide enlightened government, and encourage peaceful commerce. But the Empire split soon after Alexander's death. Egypt became a separate kingdom under Ptolemy, one of Alexander's generals. Athens and other Greek cities rebelled, were crushed by Antipater, and lost their freedom to a Macedonian governor. Antioch became the capital of another successor state under the Seleucid kings. Conflict between these various successor states of Alexander's Empire, along with a destructive eruption of the Celts (Gauls) into Greece and Asia Minor, disturbed the Mediterranean world until about 270 B.C.; by that time it reached an uneasy equilibrium based on the empires of the Ptolemies, the Seleucids, and in Europe the Antigonids (line of Antigonus Gonatas, descended from one of Alexander's greatest generals).

This splitting up of the Alexandrian empire did not mean an end to the process of making the civilized world both more cosmopolitan and more Hellenistic. Those who ruled it were men who had served under the great leader, and they continued his methods. The mingling of cultures and ideas continued. This cosmopolitan world, in which every people of the antique age found some place, awaited almost inevitably a new unification.

Hellenistic thought

During Alexander's empire, Greek thought and culture penetrated Asia and received some influence in return. Other cities of the eastern Mediterranean became important centers of "Hellenistic" thought: Greek, but Greek with a difference, influenced by various oriental strains and now no longer tied to the Greek city-states. Alexandria in Egypt was outstanding among these cities. Its Museum assumed leadership from the Lyceum and Academy of Athens, which, the creations of Aristotle and Plato, had once been without peer. (The latter, however, continued to be important for a long time after Athens lost her independence.) The philosophical schools of Stoicism and Epicureanism were the most significant, with the influence of Aristotle also continuing; Aristotle, the scientific-minded disciple of Plato, had brought the latter's high idealism down to earth, as it were, and made it practical. Along with science, universal religions appeared, such as the cult of Isis, and, before long, Christ. Emerging from the East and blending with elements of Greek philosophical thought, they appealed to larger multitudes than did the purely intellectual systems. As Greek culture spread to fuse with many other popular cultures and to play the role of world-culture, it lost something in purity and creativity, to become "mass" culture. These movements will be discussed in the context of the Roman Empire, in the next chapter.

Hellenistic science and culture

Science did not die: on the contrary, Euclid, Archimedes, and Aristarchus, all of the century following the fall of Athens, brought ancient science to its pinnacle. It would seem defensible to argue that this interlude between the end of localism and the rise of the Roman Empire, roughly the third and second centuries B.C., constituted the richest period of ancient civilization. At least, the process by which Greek thought was taken to a wider world and came into contact with oriental strains was one of the most fruitful in all history. Alexandria itself—intellectual capital of the Hellenistic world—was a cosmopolitan city where Greek, Jew, Syrian, Egyptian, and Hindu mingled.

The vast literature produced during the Hellenistic period was perhaps as a whole less original and creative than Athenian thought of the classical age. Much of it was vulgar, much of it routine. There was an exquisite but rather "decadent" Hellenistic literature, represented by Theocritus and Meleager; there was also a great deal of pedantry and imitation of former styles. Historical writing declined from the austere heights of Thucydides to become mere rhetoric. All in all, the Hellenistic age can remind us strongly of 19th- and 20th-century Europe. Empirical science flourished; Eratosthenes could measure the circumference of the earth quite accurately, and the theory of Aristarchus that the earth went around the sun was tested by a variety of experiments, though ultimately rejected. Stoicism and Epicureanism, however, were somewhat less elevated and penetrating philosophies than Platonism and Aristotelianism. Their interest was ethical rather than metaphysical; they had somewhat less of that sublime curiosity and far-ranging criticism of the Athenian schools. The Hellenistic world was rather like our modern age in its cosmopolitanism, its worship of practical efficiency, its rather bewildered search for values, its mass-ism. Yet its sciences and thought were far above anything the western world was to know for many, many centuries. The great library at Alexandria with its 400,000 books was not in fact equaled in any part of the world until the Arab cities of Córdoba (Cordova) and Baghdad in the 10th century A.D. This library was totally lost between the second and seventh centuries A.D.

Universalism

The critical leap made was, above all, to abandon localism for an international, cosmopolitan outlook. About this leap opinions may differ. A society is not better because it is bigger; a leading historian of our time has written a book persuasively arguing that only small states are really creative, and the examples of Athens and Judah go far to prove it. But there comes a time when the larger unit must prevail, and it has its own kind of grandeur. Bursting the bonds of the small community and experiencing membership in the entire human race was a tremendous revolution, perhaps the most staggering the human mind has ever experienced.

The date of 322 B.C., when Athens was utterly subdued after rebelling against the Macedonians, may be taken as ending the age of the city-states. If it was the final landmark in the history of the ancient Greeks, it is also considered the terminal date by historians of the ancient Orient. Up to that time the oriental empires had dominated the Near East and sometimes threatened Europe. Now, they passed under the political domination of a European power, and were subjected to its cultural influence. There would not be another great empire rising from the Near East for nine centuries.

The power of the rising giant of the future, Rome, was felt in Greece by the third century B.C., and by 146 both Macedonia and the Greek Leagues were under Roman sway. The empires of Asia Minor and Egypt were soon to fall. The power and the glory of all the Mediterranean world passed to the military genius of the Italian city. The universal empire foreshadowed by Darius and Alexander was achieved by Pompey, Caesar, and Augustus.

The legacy of Greece

The Greek genius belonged to the world and not just to Europe. Indeed, it remained in the East after "the fall of Rome" in the fifth century A.D. cut it off from the West. The ancient Greek philosophers were inclined to think of Greece as a bridge, mediating between East and West. During the Roman Empire, Greek thought made its way into Europe, but few of the peoples there were yet ready to receive it. The Byzantine and Arab states preserved it for future transmission to Europe. During the Middle Ages, Greek learning, thought and literature lay largely unused, except by a very small number, because European civilization as a whole was not ready for it; but it was preserved, and provided the basis for the renewal of intellectual culture beginning with the Renaissance of the 14th and 15th centuries.

Later revivals of Hellenism

That story lies ahead. But one understands the massive achievement of the ancient Greeks best if one knows that their culture reigned supreme for nearly 1,500 years. Both the Near East and Europe returned to it as soon as they became organized and civilized, and for centuries did not dream that anything more could possibly be said than had been said by Aristotle, Plato, and the Hellenistic scientists. So we shall meet the Greeks again and again in Western history. Briefly, these will be the principal occasions of that influence: first, Christianity absorbed much Stoic and Neo-Platonic material, largely through St. Augustine at the end of the Roman Empire; then in the "medieval renaissance" of the 12th and 13th centuries Aristotle became king, while a good deal of Greek science made its way into the European mind, and the university philosophers attempted a synthesis of Christian theology and Greek philosophy; finally in the Italian Renaissance of the 15th century a revival of Plato as well as other Greek poets, dramatists, and philosophers broadened and matured the mind of Europe. We could add the important neoclassical movement of the 17th and 18th centuries.

Classicism

No summary of what all this meant can hope to convey much meaning, for the subject is too vast. But a general reminder may be in order. The Greek "style" in art, sculpture, architecture, going under the rubric of "classicism," has been revived again and again: an American monument or public building is still likely to be some sort of an imitation of the Greeks (cf. Washington D.C.'s Capitol, White House, Lincoln Memorial, and National Gallery of Art). Classicism is something more than just a certain plan of architecture; it is an enduring mode of expression, based on the acceptance of limits and the setting up of orderly rules. Classicism is nothing less than the rule of reason in the arts, and as such has never died as one main stream in the western tradition. The baroque challenged it in the 16th century and romanticism in the 19th, but their tendency to throw off all restraints led them into extremisms that caused many to return again to the wisdom of classicism. A modern philosopher has written that no true civilization in the West has ever existed except on a classical foundation.

Greek speculative philosophy has never gone out of date: we have the opinion of one of this century's leading scientist-philosophers, A.N. Whitehead, that Plato's thought is thoroughly relevant to our own day, indeed has gained in relevance in recent decades. On a humbler level, our theater derives ultimately from Greek drama, even if a modern "chorus" girl is unaware of her traditional roots. The list might be extended almost indefinitely.

That we no longer expose girl babies or hold slaves may be a matter of gratification, and we should not make the mistake of saying that all our civilization came from Greece. Christianity, fusing with the Hellenic in some degree, was nevertheless in some respects a radically different thing; nor were the Germanic tribesmen of northern Europe, from whom we more directly derive, living in anything like the environment of a Mediterranean city. Despite the importance of Greek terminology in our political ideas (democracy, aristocracy, republic, constitution, and many others), these ideas do not have a lot in common with theirs, as the reader of Plato's *Republic* may learn.

The fact yet remains that, in the striking words of a distinguished modern scholar, "there is less intellectual difference between the modern thinking man and his Hellenic precursor, some 2300 years ago, than there was between the educated Greek of the fourth century B.C. and the learned Near-Eastern scribe of the same period." In other words, the Greeks made the decisive break with the previous mode of thought; they invented rationalism.

It was within the matrix of this powerful intellectual achievement that Europe was to grow up. As we shall see, the Romans who conquered the Greeks in a military sense were conquered by them culturally, and made the legacy of Greece a part of the legacy of all the civilized world for all times to come. Long after the Roman conquest and the creation of the Roman Empire, Greek thought in the sciences and philosophy continued to dominate. In some sense, it never ceased to do so. So long as intellectual culture lives, it will owe its basic debt to Athens.

Bibliography

To the earliest ages of Hellas, Leonard R. Palmer, *Myceneans and Minoans* (London: Faber, 1961), and T.B.L. Webster, *From Mycenae to Homer* and *Greek Art and Literature 700–530 B.C.* (New York: Frederick A. Praeger, 1959 and 1961), provide excellent introductions; to which can be added M.I. Finley, *The World of Odysseus* and *The Ancient Greeks* (London: Chatto & Windus, 1956 and 1963), and A.R. Burns, *The World of Hesiod: A Study of the Greek Middle Age 900–700 B.C.* (London: Kegan Paul, 1936). George E. Mylonas, *Mycenae and the Mycenaean Age* (Princeton, N.J.: Princeton University Press, 1966), deals with recent excavations at Mycenae. A more popular introduction to archaeology in the Greek lands is Paul L. MacKendrick, *The Greek Stones Speak* (New American Library, Mentor). Anthony Andrewes, *The Greeks* (London: Hutchinson, 1967), is in the History of Human Society series. Other attractive general surveys are C.E. Robinson's *Hellas, A Short History of Ancient Greece* (Beacon Press), and Maurice Bowra's *The Greek Experience*, one of the History of Civilization series (New American Library, Mentor). A more detailed history, recent and authoritative, is N.G.L. Hammond, *A History of Greece to 322 B.C.* (New York: Oxford University Press, 1959).

A.E. Zimmern, *The Greek Commonwealth* (Oxford University Press), and A.H.M. Jones, *Athenian Democracy* (Oxford: Blackwell, 1957), takes us into the Greek city-states; see also Fustel de Coulanges' older classic, *The Ancient City* (Doubleday, Anchor), and Walter A. Agard, *What Democracy Meant to the Greeks* (University of Wisconsin Press). Jill N. Claster (ed.), *Athenian Democracy*, is in the European Problems series, published in paperback by Holt, Rinehart & Winston, supplying readings and a carefully selected bibliography. *Sparta* is the subject of a book by H. Michell (New York: Cambridge University Press, 1964) and another by A.H.M. Jones (Blackwell, 1968). A work of impeccable scholarship is J.A.O. Larsen, *Representative Government in Greek and Roman History* (Berkeley: University of California Press, 1955); a modern classic is Werner Jaeger, *Paideia: The Ideals of Greek Culture* (3 vols.; Oxford University Press, 1939–44).

In the all-important sphere of Greek thought, among many see A.E. Taylor, *Socrates* (Doubleday, Anchor); G.M.A. Grube, *Plato's Thought* (Beacon Press); Ernest Barker, *Greek Political Theory* (Barnes & Noble); Eduard Zeller, *Outlines of the History of Greek Philosophy* (World Publishing, Meridian); R.G. Collingwood, *The Idea of Nature* (Oxford University Press); and Bruno Snell, *The Discovery of the Mind: Greek Origins of European Thought* (Harper Torchbook). More specialized are John Burnet, *Early Greek Philosophy* (World Publishing, Meridian); Marshall Clagett, *Greek Science in Antiquity* (Macmillan, Collier); and E.R. Dodds, *The Greeks and the Irrational* (Beacon Press). W.K. Guthrie, *The Greeks and Their Gods* (Beacon Press), is a lively introduction to its subject. A special topic of great interest was dealt with by a distinguished French historian, Henri Marrou, *A History of Education in Antiquity* (New American Library, Mentor).

W.W. Tarn, *Alexander the Great* (abridged version, Beacon Press), is by the greatest modern authority on that great subject. Tarn and G.T. Griffith, *Hellenistic Civilization* (3d ed.; Cleveland: World Publishing, 1961), is more succinct than the masterly *Social and Economic History of the Hellenistic World* in three volumes by M.I. Rostovtzeff (Oxford: Clarendon Press, 1941). In the realm of original sources, C.A. Robinson, Jr. (ed.), *Spring of Civilization: Periclean Athens* (Grove Press, Everyman), gives us a selection of the great writings and speeches, which are available in fuller form in many editions: see the Penguin editions of Thucydides, Herodotus, and Xenophon; and T.V. Smith (ed.), *From Thales to Plato* and *From Aristotle to Plotinus* (University of Chicago, Phoenix). The glories of Greek art and architecture are revealed in many superb books of photography, for example *The Birth of Western Civilization: Greece to Rome*, edited by Michael Grant for McGraw-Hill (New York, 1964), which manages to get 727 illustrations into its 360 large-sized pages.

3

The Roman Empire

chronology

c. 700 B.C.
Etruscan civilization in Italy.
509 B.C.
Traditional date of founding of Roman Republic (more likely c. 475).
c. 400–350 B.C.
Celtic invasions.
295 B.C.
Rome becomes dominant power in Italy.
264–41 B.C.
First Punic War.
218–201 B.C.
Second Punic War; Hannibal invades Italy.
168–48 B.C.
Defeat and absorption of Macedonian empire by Rome.
146 B.C.
Destruction of Carthage.
133–21 B.C.
Gracchi; period of social revolution.
125 B.C.
Beginning of conquest of Gaul.
88–82 B.C.
Civil war in Rome; rivalry of Marius and Sulla.
65–62 B.C.
Pompey's campaign in Asia.
58–51 B.C.
Conquest of Gaul by Julius Caesar.
49 B.C.
Caesar defies Senate and marches on Rome.
45 B.C.
Caesar defeats Pompey, becomes dictator.
44 B.C.
Assassination of Caesar.
43–42 B.C.
Triumvirate of Antony, Lepidus, and Octavian; execution of Cicero; defeat of Cassius-Brutus republican forces at Philippi.
36 B.C.
Marriage of Antony and Cleopatra; conflict between Antony and Octavian.
31 B.C.
Naval battle of Actium; defeat of Antony. Suicide of Antony and Cleopatra, 30 B.C.
27 B.C.
Octavian, as Emperor Caesar Augustus, "restores the republic" with special powers for himself.
4 B.C.
Probable date of birth of Christ.
9 A.D.
Defeat of Romans by Germans at Osnabrück, checking Empire at Rhine.
14
Death of Augustus; Tiberius Emperor.
43
Subjugation of British isles begins, under Emperor Claudius.
64
Nero's persecution of the Christians. Arrest of Paul, 65.
66–69
Revolt in Judea.
Vespasian begins Flavian dynasty of emperors.
70
Destruction of Jerusalem.
84
Conquest of Britain completed.
117–38
Emperor Hadrian; Empire at peak.
135
Dispersion of Jews.
161–80
Marcus Aurelius, philosopher-emperor, last ruler of golden era.
212
Roman citizenship conferred on subjects of the Empire.
235–84
Period of anarchy; emperors made and murdered by army.
Plotinus, Neo-Platonic philosophy.
285–337
Diocletian and Constantine; administrative reforms.
301
Edict of Diocletian: state regulation of economic life.

Etruscan art, dancing maenad and sileni. "Life, ardent and spontaneous," D.H. Lawrence describes it. The Etruscans were known for their delight in sensual pleasure and their utterly amoral attitude toward sex

The rise of Rome

The Etruscans

The inhabitants of Rome, and surrounding Latium (hence "Latin"), were originally one among many other peoples of the peninsula known as Italy, and were by no means the most civilized or important. Italy, and all of western Europe, lagged well behind the eastern Mediterranean in civilization. The first important cultures in Italy came from the Greek colonists in Sicily and southern Italy, and from the Etruscans in the north, a non–Indo-European people of mysterious origin, probably themselves migrants from the Near East (Anatolia). The Greeks were active colonists, Syracuse in Sicily especially being one of their great cities; and thus very early a Hellenizing wind blew over the Italian landscape. As for the Etruscans, they were an amazingly creative people, who not only absorbed and transmitted Hellenism but also possessed deeply original traits. It is certain that both these cultures contributed much to the inferior native cultures. It is enough to point out that the Etruscans invented not only the arch and the vault in architecture, but also the "Roman" numerals as well as gladiatorial contests. The Etruscans ruled over Rome along with much of Italy in the sixth century B.C. Another source important for Italy was the Phoenician (Punic) influence, which emanated from Carthage and its colonies in Sicily—destined to be the classic foe of Rome.

It was to be neither Greek nor Tuscan nor Carthaginian who finally ruled Italy, the western Mediterranean, and then the classical world, but rather a people initially much smaller, poorer, and backward. As nearly everyone knows from the poet Vergil's epic account, the Romans came to believe that they were descended from Aeneas who escaped from the fall of Troy, to settle at the mouth of the Tiber under divine auspices after years of arduous wandering. One of his descendants later married the god Mars and from this relationship sprang the twins Romulus and Remus. Historical criticism can find little basis for the legends, though such tales usually embroider on some factual cloth. But they testify to the important Roman characteristics, piety and a deep historical sense. Rome preserved and honored her symbols of ancestral origins: the she-wolf who suckled the exposed twins was from earliest times a Roman emblem. About the end of the sixth century B.C. (509 according to the traditional account), Rome was liberated from the Etruscan kings, the last of whom had been a hated tyrant; and from this the city derived a powerful republican tradition. So this little people fancied that they were descended from gods, nourished by wild animals, and defenders of their liberty against foreign tyrants. It seems an invigorating heritage, and Romans became famous for their spirit. Like the Hebrews, though to a different end, they made use of a strong historical sense to fortify themselves.

Geographic factors

But other factors worked for Rome to lead her on her amazing course. Of these a notable one was geographic position. Geography is always pregnant with historical destiny, though sometimes we tend to take it for granted. "All roads lead to Rome": the adage was an important historical fact. The city on the Tiber stood at one of nature's intersections. From early times seven roads radiated from Rome to all the other parts of the spiny, much-divided peninsula. Rome had easy communication with both the Greek south and the Tuscan north, while the Tiber, a navigable river, gave access both to the sea and to the interior. Rome was the natural hub of Italy, and it is not surprising that a vigorous and warlike people who controlled it would go on to control the whole country.

The symbol of the city of Rome, Romulus and Remus suckled by a wolf.

This result was not obtained without bitter and almost ceaseless fighting. Perhaps the greatest of military historians, Hans Delbrück, found the secret of Roman success in war not in superior bravery, much less in brilliance of strategy, but in discipline. In later days conservative Romans like Cato were to recall the austerity of former times and try to summon their fellow citizens back to this spirit. Austere the early Republic certainly was, for there was no choice. Here was no Athens or Alexandria, but a poor city which had to be an armed camp. The patrician (upper class) influence dominated, but the plebs, or lower class, gained a share in the state because they too had to fight. The armed peasants filled the legions of Rome from early times. The image which the Romans had of themselves was that of a hardy, simple folk who worked and fought hard and had no time for nonsense: a sort of ancient Puritanism. Later, when Rome had risen to the leadership of the world, she held the same austere view of her function. "Let others be artists," wrote Vergil. "Your job, O Romans, is to rule nations, impose peace, spare the fallen, strike down the insolent."

Expansion of Rome

The Romans carried out this job with enthusiasm. They gained Italy in a long series of wars and alliances which we need not detail here. From 264 to 241 B.C. they contended for possession of the western Mediterranean with the brilliant city of Carthage, in the first of the three Punic Wars. The Phoenician city of Carthage had built a large empire in Africa, Spain, and Sicily. It was in the Second Punic War that her great general Hannibal invaded Italy from Spain, crossing the Pyrenees and the Alps to do so, and winning a tremendous victory at Cannae before he finally had to leave without achieving a permanent defeat of the tenacious Romans. In 146 B.C. the Romans completely destroyed the city of Carthage and took her empire.

To the civilized Orient this must have seemed like a barbarian conquest. But there was no vigor to withstand the Roman legions, and soon Greece and the states of Asia Minor were in the fold. It may again be recalled that there had been ample preparations for this "world state." It was a cosmopolitan age, and had been ever since the Macedonian Empire. The Near East was already ruled by the successor states of Alexander, and all Rome had to do was take them over. Sometimes, as in the case of the monarch of Pergamum in Asia Minor, these smaller empires actually surrendered themselves voluntarily.

In addition to the three wars with Carthage, Rome fought three wars with the powerful Macedonian state, which had produced the conqueror Alexander the Great earlier and had continued as a major empire. The total defeat of that Greek and Balkan power was accomplished in 168 B.C., though there was another revolt before Macedonia became a Roman province in 148 B.C. The conquest of Gaul (France) began in 125 B.C. The popular general Marius, who reformed the military system, not only put down revolts in Africa and Gaul but went far toward militarizing and imperializing the Roman state—a development described in the next section. Another great general, Cornelius Sulla, successfully countered a threat from the East in the person of monarch

Mithridates and began an extension of the Roman Empire in Asia Minor and the Near East. Pompey completed that job in 65–62 B.C.

All this hectic expansion went along with numerous revolts and with a severe crisis in the affairs of the Roman state which soon led from republic through military dictatorship to an imperial monarchy. That the expansion nevertheless went on suggests not only that the Roman legions were invincible—which they sometimes were not—and that the Roman will to power was irresistible—in which there is much truth—but also that conditions were ripe for a world state. There was not much life left in the ancient city-states, and except in a few places there was not much of what we call nationalism. Someone almost certainly would have had to organize the Mediterranean world. That Rome filled the role, rather than Carthage or some other state, is a tribute to the vitality of her people.

Secrets of Roman success

The recipe for success the Romans used in building an empire appears to have been one that combined ruthlessness with mildness. The utter destruction of rival Carthage, notorious in history as an example of the harshest of treatments of a vanquished foe, was by no means an isolated case. Corinth was another city wiped off the face of the earth, an unpleasant habit the Romans formed in dealing with a troublesome enemy or rebel. Equally well known is the crushing of the slave revolt led by Spartacus, on which occasion 6,000 crucified rebels lined the Appian Way; and later, the dispersion of the Jews in A.D. 135. With these and other examples before him no historian is likely to accuse the Romans of gentleness. On the other hand, no such empire could have lasted as long as it did without other features. The greatest of all Roman discoveries was that a noncitizen could become a citizen of Rome as well as of his native city; and throughout their rule the Romans freely tolerated local autonomy and local customs, becoming intolerant only when political rebellion seemed involved. Rome never attempted to Romanize her subjects, or impose a doctrinal uniformity on them. Perhaps that was because she had practically no culture of her own. She was "the mother that took all peoples unto her bosom."

From Republic to Empire

Roman government

The Roman government during the time of the Republic was that of an aristocracy somewhat tempered by democracy. The class distinction between patricians and plebeians goes well back into Roman history. The Senate, to which the patricians alone could belong, holding office for life, became the dominant organ of government, along with the two annually elected consuls, who disposed of military and police powers—executives who though elected by a supposedly popular assembly were also almost invariably taken from the patrician class and nominated by the Senate. (Holding of the treasured consulship automatically ennobled a family forever, and ex-consuls sat in the Senate.) The plebeians, who had developed their own organization, gained some share in government in the fourth and third

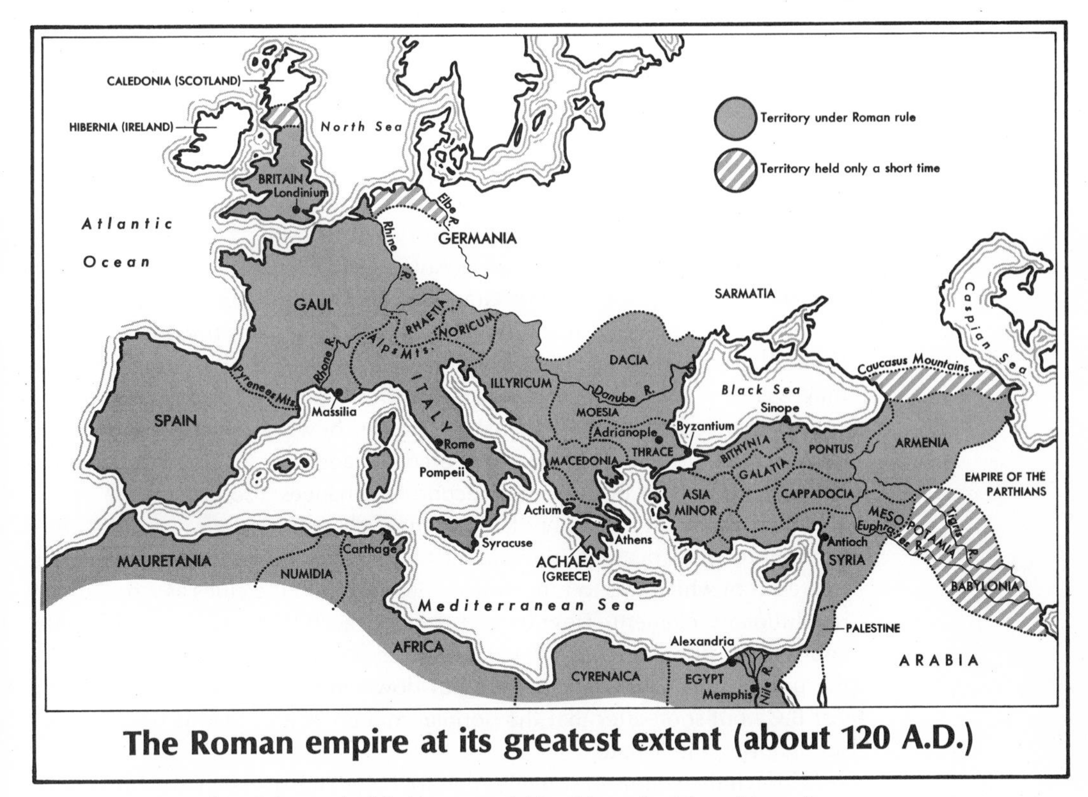

The Roman empire at its greatest extent (about 120 A.D.)

centuries B.C.: the right to hold the consulship (though this seldom happened), legal equality with the patricians, and a right of intercession for their own officers, the tribunes. Nevertheless both political and economic power tended to remain in the hands of the upper class, and the growth of the Empire added to it, one reason being that the Senate appointed the magistrates who went out to govern the provinces and who returned to sit in the Senate themselves.

Political theorists like the historian Polybius thought that the Roman constitution was a judicious blending of democracy, aristocracy, and monarchy—tribunes, senators, and consuls nicely checking each other. But the reality was that a small group of aristocratic families—sometimes, it is true, fiercely competitive with each other—had a tight grip on the state. The Romans also had a tradition of emergency dictatorship which stood them in good stead at moments of national crisis. Despite their intermittent protests the plebeians came to count for rather less than they once had; in the period of imperial expansion from about 300 to 135 B.C., the office of tribune fell into decay. Another class, the knights or *equites*, came into the picture—a middle class or *bourgeoisie*, they would be called in modern Europe. These wealthy merchants, government contractors, and tax collectors might buy or marry their way into the nobility, but on the other hand pride of ancient birth counted for much and the "new men" had a reasonably hard time breaking into the political elite. Thus did the Roman state stand on the eve of a series of explosions that were finally to blow it apart and reconstitute it in the century from 132 to 31 B.C.

Decline of the Republic

The Republic, under which Rome had first risen, became in time incredibly corrupt. Violent civil strife accompanied its collapse, ending in dictatorship and then emperorship. This dramatic story involved the great names of Pompey, Caesar, and Augustus, as well as Antony and Cleopatra, and before them the tribunes Tiberius and Gaius Gracchus. During the period of war and expansion in the third and second centuries B.C., Rome was ruled by the senatorial oligarchy, a group of 300 old landed families holding office for life; they were proud and often arrogant, but their spirit had kept Rome on the course that led to world leadership. Finally, however, forces of rebellion against this aristocratic control gathered. In addition to creating a middle class of traders and businessmen, economic changes also caused the rise of a restive "proletariat." Most notable of these changes was a transformation of agriculture from peasant freeholding to vast plantations using slave labor, the result of which was to force former peasants into the cities as a potentially revolutionary element. Tiberius and Gaius Gracchus, reviving the tribunate, appeared as popular leaders demanding "land reform" and cheaper food for the urban poor. The Gracchi were put down in violent civil strife (132 and 121 B.C.) but soon after that the popular military leader Marius became consul, ignoring the Senate.

Through the confused struggles that followed, it became evident that senatorial rule no longer sufficed for a vast empire with large military problems and equally imposing social ones. The partisans of the generals Marius and Sulla took turns slaughtering each other while the Senate looked on helplessly. The old aristocratic families counted for less and less as popular demagogues gained power. As it had in the Greek cities, class struggle made its appearance and resulted in revolutions or dictatorships. In 81 B.C. Sulla became dictator, though he did not wish to destroy the senatorial class, to which he was attached. Marius championed the plebs. Pompey, a great military commander who extended Roman power to the east, was the next strong man. In a triumvirate with Caesar and Crassus he swept aside the objections of the Senate, even though the latter possessed the eloquence of Cicero. The Republic was going fast. As it turned out, the man to watch was not Pompey but Julius Caesar. It was Caesar's brilliant military successes against the Gauls to the north (58–51 B.C.) which caused Pompey to fear him and to seek a showdown with him. The issues related to a conflict between the aristocracy and the plebs, with Pompey representing the upper class and Caesar the common people. But neither strong man was prepared to respect the traditional forms of government.

At the showdown, it was Caesar who won. He "crossed the Rubicon" in 49 B.C. and pursued Pompey to defeat in Spain, Africa, and Egypt (where he met Queen Cleopatra). Caesar's glamour and genius brought him the dictatorship for life and ended the Republic. The last blow in its defense was Brutus' in the famous assassination of Caesar in 44 B.C. It did not succeed in saving the Republic, but only delivered it, after a further series of struggles, familiar to all readers of Shakespeare's plays, to Caesar's grandnephew and adopted son, Octavian.

Antony and Octavian

Mark Antony (Marcus Antonius), a relative and protegé of Caesar, sought to assume Caesar's position as dictator but was opposed by the Senate, which Cicero's oratory encouraged. Antony and the young Octavian joined forces to crush the republican cause, executing 300 senators, while Brutus and Cassius committed suicide following the battle of Philippi, 42 B.C. Then the two ambitious tyrants fought each other for the prize. A triumvirate of Antony, Octavian, and Lepidus undertook to rule, a geographic division being made in which Antony got the East and Octavian the West (Lepidus, who soon was squeezed out, being assigned Africa). Antony's marriage to the sister of Octavian was supposed to cement the alliance, but it eventually became an added irritant. Antony went out to attend to affairs in the troubled East, where the Parthians were making mischief and where after finally defeating them he presided over a general reorganization of the Empire, quite brilliantly. But his absence left Octavian virtually a free hand to build his following at the capital.

The Emperor Augustus, a frail youth when he assumed the imperial office, was destined to a long and successful reign.

Mark Antony
and Cleopatra

Antony's attachment to the glamorous Egyptian queen Cleopatra cost him favor in the eyes of Rome. It is unfortunately only a romantic myth that Antony lost his head over Cleopatra. The Egyptian Queen was no longer young or very beautiful, although a woman of strong intellect and personality; her alliance with Antony was at least as much a diplomatic as a love match. But the Romans feared and suspected her; Octavian's propaganda made the most of this. Octavian and Antony's struggle for power still creates rows among historians. The fact is that both were men of great ability, imperious will, and restless ambition, and, as Hobbes has said, two men cannot both ride in front on the same horse. A struggle to the death between them was all but ordained, and both men probably sensed this early. They jockeyed for position against each other from the beginning. Octavian had the great name of Caesar, and showed himself no unworthy heir, being courageous, bold, eloquent—and unscrupulous. Antony was the older, and had won the field at Philippi; he probably had on his side more of the propertied, conservative, and republican families, who mistrusted any Caesar. Perhaps more of a gentleman, Antony let himself be outmaneuvered by the tireless young Octavian, who had the advantage of being in Italy while Antony's duties kept him in the East. It was at any rate the young Caesar who had the luck to win the final round; had Antony won, the future might not have been much different, for the old Republic was dead and a new kind of imperium would be installed by either man. Octavian became the unquestioned commander of the state after defeating Antony and Cleopatra in 31 B.C. at the great battle of Actium. Within a few years he received the imperial title of "Augustus," under which name Octavian was known henceforth.

Beginning of a new order

Historians agree that the Republic could not have survived as it was. "A government designed for a modest city-state had failed to prevent violence and corruption, or to control the commanders who could not be dispensed with in so enormous an empire." A handful of old Roman families was too narrow a social base for the vast polyglot Empire, while the old machinery of government was inadequate. There was a need for symbols of government that could appeal to all the varied peoples of the world Empire; also for wholesale reform of the corrupt and chaotic methods of imperial government. There was need for a hand firm enough to control the army and its popular commanders who from time to time threatened the state and caused intolerable civil war. It may be that wiser leadership and better luck could have somehow altered the Republic into an instrument at once more effective and more democratic. But the internal constitutional crisis took place at the same time as foreign wars on all the numerous frontiers of the Empire, and violent social transformations: the threat of slave revolts constantly entered the picture, and the urban proletariat was almost equally violent. There was not much time to think calmly or devise a better solution.

The aristocratic republic had been agrarian and traditionalist; its senatorial families had looked down upon the capitalists who, being only of the class of *equites* or knights, belonged to a lower rank and though often of great wealth were largely excluded from the highest political offices. The new order of the Caesars was more democratic in a social sense: there was more mobility between classes, less patrician pride of birth. Looked at in this light the Roman revolution of Caesar and Augustus was not wholly unlike the French Revolution (see Chapters 18–19) which overthrew an aristocratic "ancient regime" to introduce social equality along with a Napoleonic dictatorship. The Romans, however, never did accept full equalitarianism in theory; the three classes remained, though it was less difficult to move up the ladder in imperial times. The new order was more frankly "plutocratic": commercial wealth was the key to position and power. An aristocracy of new men replaced the old patrician families, without acquiring their antique dignity.

Continuation of constitutionalism

And so, as it happened, the legacy of the Roman Empire was monarchy, emperorship—not, however, without the rule of law. The Senate continued in existence, though it conferred large powers on the Emperor. Not until the third century did he become an oriental despot with absolute authority. Augustus avoided pomp and placated the Senate, a spirit in which most of his successors acted in the next two centuries. Officially he announced in 27 B.C. that he "restored the Republic." The success of the Empire did cause widespread adulation for the abler emperors, to the point of virtual deification; but the idea of the government in its best years was that of a constitutional monarchy, ruled by law, with the old "mixed" constitution of tribunes, patricians, and consuls kept, at least in theory. Until Rome began to crack up in the third century, her old republican spirit with its doughty civic pride and cooperative political order survived in part despite the establishment of a strong power in the person of the emperor, and the ruin of the old republican nobility during the civil wars. Augustus sought to restore the old morality, revive the ancestral religion, and inculcate patriotism—a task which enlisted the genius of Rome's greatest poet, Vergil. The *Aeneid* belongs to the first decade of Augustus's reign. So does Livy's *History*, which, deploring the moral collapse, hoped to revive morale by recalling "the heroic past."

The Empire

Despite some shocking emperors like Caligula and Nero, the period from Augustus (31 B.C.) to Marcus Aurelius (180 A.D.) possessed at least a measure of those qualities so glowingly described by Gibbon in his tribute to these years as the happiest in the history of the world. The Empire was ruled by a single benevolent law, and peace and prosperity prevailed. Even Christians of this era—for example, Tertullian—admitted the material if not the moral achievements of the Roman state. The impressive physical monuments of Roman genius, which still delight the tourist, were built: the excellent roads, the marvelous aqueducts, the luxurious public baths. In this era also Vergil, Tacitus, Seneca, and other great Roman writers contributed to the harvest season of a rich literature.

The Roman Colosseum, ancestor of all sporting arenas, where gladitorial contests and chariot races amused the urban populace.

The Roman Empire rimmed the Mediterranean (*mare nostrum*) and straddled three continents. It included the Hellenistic East, north Africa, and portions of Europe. But most of central and northern Europe lay beyond the Roman frontier, and if Gaul (France), southern Germany, and Britain were eventually made significant parts of the Empire, the Mediterranean was certainly its center. The Romans were led into Europe in large part as a result of a pattern familiar to empire-builders, by which you are compelled to control the neighboring region to defend what you have. The best way of coping with wild tribesmen who raided the frontier was to seize their lands. This led the Romans all the way to Britain by 43 A.D. However, the Rhine and the Danube marked the limits of the Empire in Europe. Caesar had subdued the Gauls in France and Belgium; but in 9 A.D. a Roman army was shattered by Germanic tribesmen under Hermann (Arminius) in a battle near Osnabrück which led the Emperor Augustus to decide against extending the boundary to the Elbe. Spain, southern France, and southeastern Europe (Illyricum, in present-day Yugoslavia, as well as Greece) were integral parts of the Empire. Eastward, it stretched through the rich Near East and Asia Minor to the Black

Aqueduct, built in the time of Emperor Trajan (53–117), still in use at Segovia, Spain.

Sea, the mountains of Armenia, and the deserts of Palestine and Arabia. North Africa above the Sahara was a valued heartland of the Roman realm.

Law

By A.D. 212, citizenship and a single law prevailed over this wide area. Roman citizenship was at first jealously withheld by the Romans, but in 91 B.C., following a rebellion by Italians who demanded the privilege of Roman citizenship, Rome took the step of extending it beyond the bounds of the city. Rome's pride was her law—prime source of all enlightened legal codes in the West. It was binding on rulers as well as ruled. There developed the concept of a law of nations which was ideally above man-made law and constituted a moral check on tyranny and injustice. Whatever imperfections there were in practice, we find much evidence of high standards of justice. Law was a subject the Romans excelled in; it was the most distinguished of careers, to be prepared for by long training in the art of rhetoric as well as study of records of legal enactments and cases. Citizens or noncitizens throughout the Empire had a higher degree of protection against wrong and assurance of justice than at any time before in history.

Peace

Next to justice, the greatest blessing Roman rule brought was peace. Probably enough has already been said to make it clear that war had been endemic in the ancient world. Now, for the two centuries between Augustus and Marcus Aurelius, there was scarcely any of it. Ample contemporary testimony confirms the fact that war had vanished from the experience of men. Even piracy and brigandage were greatly reduced. It appears that the corruption in government characteristic of the late republican period sharply declined if it did not completely disappear. Under these conditions trade expanded. Throughout the Empire, from England and Spain to Egypt and Syria, a far-flung commerce flourished, stimulated by the common currency (kept up to par in these centuries, later to deteriorate badly) and by easy and cheap customs. Tribute to the material success of Rome may be found in many places: in the facts that the tin mines of England supplied an international market not to be equaled until modern times, that cities flourished in north Africa where even today there are only villages, that most of the major cities of Spain, France, and the Rhine were originally founded by the Romans—who filled even these provincial outposts with fine public buildings, monuments, and amphitheaters. It hardly needs repeating that the Romans were great builders of such eminently practical structures as roads, bridges, and aqueducts. Some of the latter, in Spain, southern France, and northern Africa, are still in use today. And modern highways still run along the routes the Romans so efficiently selected.

Roman flaws

Having said the good things—and no historian could say less than the above—it is fair to mention some of the less lovely features of Roman society even in the "golden age." While the Romans excelled at such things as highways and sewers, they had little artistic taste, and were always dependent on Greek or oriental craftsmen and artists in their design and ornamentation. They remained a people without much intellectual culture or social refinement. The immorality and vulgarity of urban life in Roman cities became notorious. The disgusting spectacles in the amphitheaters, in which slaves or prisoners were torn by wild beasts, provide a famous example. We hear of public houses of prostitution. Slavery disfigured the Empire; and torture, applied chiefly to slaves, marred the Roman law. Roman satirists from Horace to Petronius show us a picture of crass materialism among the vulgar rich, and callous contempt for the poor, along with a brutalized populace bought by bread and circuses, amused by the sufferings of slaves. The greatest Roman historian, Tacitus, left us a horrifying picture of cruelty, corruption, and selfish greed at the imperial court. A study of the life of such a city as Pompeii, where many rich Romans lived, reveals the almost exclusive predominance of materialism and hedonism. One is reminded of Matthew Arnold's lines:

On that harsh Roman world
Disgust and secret loathing fell
And bitterness and sated lust
Made human life a hell.

Such was the price of power and the curse of bigness.

Economic stagnation

Science, from Euclid to Galen, was not Roman but Greek-oriental, though it profited from the services Roman rule provided. The backwardness of Rome in this respect seems to have been paralleled in the general area of industrial technology. One would expect the Romans to excel here, if not in the higher realms of pure research. But most historians find a pattern of economic stagnation in the West which ultimately contributed to Rome's downfall. Slave labor and tribute from the industrious East evidently brought Rome so much wealth that she felt no need to develop machinery on a large scale. The economic center of the Empire remained in Asia Minor. And never did the ancient world proceed toward the kind of advanced technology we know today. The ideas were there: Alexandrian scientists certainly knew, as pure theory, many of the principles upon which modern technology is based. But no one applied them. A complex set of economic conditions no doubt explains this absence of "growth." But the fact that it was absent may go far to account for the eventual "decline and fall."

Roman thought and literature

Latin style

As has been noted, and as might be expected from a people so exclusively dedicated to war, conquest, and politics, the Romans had little intellectual culture of their own. It may be going too far to assert, as did Walter Bagehot, that "they have not left a single discovery in any abstract science; not a single or well formed work of high imagination." They produced a charming poetry which included one great epic work, Vergil's *Aeneid*. Historical writing appealed to the Romans, and if Tacitus is not quite the equal of Thucydides, he stands at the head of an imposing school. Under Greek influence, it is true,

Silver bowl, found at Hildesheim, Germany, probably part of the table service of a Roman nobleman of the Augustan period.

but capable of standing on its own feet was this Roman literature, which included the dramas of Seneca and Terence. The Renaissance of the 15th century in Europe returned to the fountains of Roman classical literature with delight, finding there a rich humanistic tradition. The Romans were enchanted by rhetoric, and learned to write as well as speak well. The rolling periods of classical Roman style came echoing down the centuries, preserved in the writings of the late church fathers such as Augustine and Jerome as well as in Cicero, Vergil, Tacitus, and other secular Roman authors. It molded the speech and prose of the West for all time. It appears (as Gilbert Highet reminds us in his book *The Classical Tradition*) in such familiar pieces as Abraham Lincoln's "Gettysburg Address," with its use of tricolons. Lincoln, as Highet remarks, had not read Cicero, but he had read writers like Gibbon the historian who were "steeped in the cadences of Ciceronian Latin."

Latin literature grew into a rich storehouse of quotations on almost every facet of man and his ways; it was deeply "humanist" in the sense of being intensely interested in man, and it was "classical" in the sense of being marked by the Grecian virtues of economy and elegance. Latin was a language of extraordinary conciseness, saying in a few words what others required many to express. One example among innumerable possible ones: Seneca's remark that

> *Lectio certa prodest, varia delectat.*

is translated as:

> Desultory reading is delightful, but, to be beneficial, our reading must be carefully directed.

Fourteen words in English—five in Latin.

Cicero—orator, philosopher, defender of the Republic

Roman intellectual contributions

Relatively uncreative themselves, Romans assimilated well the culture of others. They took over a great deal of Greek thought, using Greek ideas almost entirely in building what came to be a fine educational system. There was initial resistance to this by rugged old Romans who thought any such civilized refinement inappropriate for warriors, but Rome finally succumbed completely to the charms of Greek literature and philosophy. "Captive Greece took captive her capturer," as Horace wrote. Though they did not ever fully understand it, the Romans transmitted, and in a measure transmuted, the heritage of Greek philosophical thought. They built a rich literature of their own on this foundation. Had it not been for Roman writers, that priceless interitance would have been lost to the West; for during the dark centuries after about A.D. 500 the Greek language was virtually lost to Europe. As it was, much science and philosophy never got out of the Greek tongue. The Roman society was bilingual, and Greek remained the chief vehicle in areas other than business, law, and government. Expert at engineering and building, the Romans did little with medicine and could not even construct a calendar without Greek help. Their matchless law had to be systematized by a Greek. Pliny's Natural History is a repertory of facts without organization or generalization. But Vitruvius on Architecture, Horace on the Art of Poetry, Ovid on the Art of Love, Cicero on almost any question of conduct and life—these and other great writers immortalized a precious freight of lore and learning.

Stoicism

The Romans were most attracted by the later Greek philosophical schools of Epicurus and the Stoa, especially the latter. Most people probably think of Stoicism as Roman. It was in fact initially a product of Athens in the post-Aristotelian era, its founder the Phoenician Zeno from Cyprus. The practical Romans were interested in its moral and ethical aspects. In some degree, Stoicism played the role of a religion for the cultivated minority, as Christianity and other cults did for the masses, in the period of the Empire. It provided a sense of purpose in the world, gave men a code of conduct to live by, offered them the consolations of philosophy.

Zeno had stated that the good life can better be lived in a world society than in a local one. Stoicism believed in a providential world order, of which man was a part, and stressed the concept of natural law, a single set of moral precepts which were essentially the same for all men. The universe is a great unity, and man is in harmony with it. God (by which the Stoics conveyed something much more impersonal than the Christians) decreed that each has his part in this larger harmony; he must play it and should be happy to do so.

> God has assigned you a post; you must not leave it without his orders.

Man-centered rather than god-centered, Stoics proudly declared that the philosopher can face his lot without aid from anyone. They did not believe in survival after death in the Christian sense of a personal immortality. The spirit of Stoicism was inner fortitude, imperturbability, via the strength that one can find within when one faces the worst that life has to offer—and accepts it as inevitable. Stoics (and Epicureans too) taught that the wise man can defy fate and show himself stronger than any adversity. Their writings, such as those of the blind slave Epictetus, or the great Emperor Marcus Aurelius, tended to be maxims or aphorisms on this theme, the courage to endure. A notable and somewhat curious doctrine was the injunction to curb all passions, including even the most natural, such as grief for the loss of a loved one. For the wise man will not so yield to weakness, knowing as he does that all is as it must be, and cherishing as he does his own imperturbable soul.

Stoicism bequeathed much to later European thought, though as such it passed from view with the fall of Rome and the triumph of Christianity, not to reappear until the Italian Renaissance of the 15th century. A great deal of it passed silently into Christianity. Some of the Stoics, like the poet and playwright Seneca, could come quite close to Christianity, so close that medieval Christians erroneously claimed they had been secret converts to Christianity. Others were more notable for the stress on the absolute rationality of a pantheistic world order, and the proud independence of the man who lived according to reason. The brotherhood of man, and the Natural Law which, rooted in divine reason, stood above all man-made law—these Stoic concepts above all others entered deeply into the European inheritance. And Stoics believed in a soul which survived the destruction of the body and returned to join the World Soul of which it was a part—a doctrine which influenced and blended with the Christian doctrine of life after death.

Neo-Platonism

Later in the imperial period Stoicism tended to be replaced by Alexandrian Neo-Platonism as the most fashionable philosophy for intellectuals. The saintly Plotinus (204–70 A.D.), mystic and metaphysician, was the celebrated founder of this school, which was carried on by Porphyry and Proclus. The Platonic element in this philosophy was the concept of a realm of eternal ideas with which the mind can make contact by pure thought or contemplation. Neo-Platonism arranged these ideas in an ascending scale of existence rising from the crudest matter to the Absolute (not a personalized God as with the Christians but a metaphysical Pure Being). To be liberated from matter, regarded as negative and evil, and to ascend the ladder of being, to live in the higher realm of the supersensual, was the goal. The Egyptian-born Plotinus had traveled in the East and made contact with Persian and Indian strains, which may have found their way into his mystic philosophy. He lived long in Rome and served as the tutor of imperial families. His semioriental thought was too esoteric for Rome, undiluted; but it was to have a powerful influence on medieval Christianity after St. Augustine merged it into his Christian philosophy at the end of the Roman age. Boethius was another who passed it along to medieval Europe.

Clearly neither Stoicism nor Neo-Platonism were faiths for the masses. They were somewhat alien even for educated Romans, despite their vogue in such circles. Marcus Aurelius wrote his *Meditations* in Greek; Augustine, like Plotinus, was from north Africa, a flourishing part of the Empire but culturally somewhat alien. The Roman public schools, which were not for everybody, provided an education heavily oriented toward the practical subjects of law, rhetoric, and applied mathematics, along with much reading of the Roman poets and historians. They were chary about Greek philosophy, of which smatterings only were taught. For the masses, and even for some of the elite, the spiritual element was provided by another oriental product, but one of a different kind—the so-called "mystery religions."

Religious cults of the Empire

The old Roman religion, which included such deities as Jupiter, Juno, and the household gods, was a cult of patriotism which all good Romans felt called upon to uphold, much as Americans salute the flag, sing the *Star Spangled Banner*, or celebrate Washington's birthday. It offered very little of either spiritual or intellectual content. The religion of emperor-worship did take on some vitality. This was an Asiatic custom, imported into Rome. The earlier emperors modestly postponed their deification until after their death ("Dear me! I think I am becoming a god!" Vespasian jested on his death-bed). But in the eastern provinces people worshiped the living emperor. Encouraged because it furthered the unity of the polyglot Empire, emperor-worship developed an elaborate organization and at times was genuinely popular. But it is not always exciting to treat as a god a man of flesh and blood, especially if he seems less than perfect and is installed and then murdered by the palace guard—the fate of all too many emperors in the third century.

Mystery religions

For humbler or less intellectual people than those who studied Stoicism or Epicureanism, this spiritual vacuum came to be filled by a picturesque variety of "mystery religions." Any number of them existed, coming from Asia Minor, Egypt, Greece. They tended to be wild and weird. The orgiastic cult of Dionysus-Bacchus, which featured sexual debauchery, was scarcely less startling than that of Cybele, the oriental mother-goddess, whose devotees practiced self-mutilation, or of Mithra, the Persian sun god. Even Isis, the Egyptian goddess who was more tender than Cybele and may even have influenced the Christian conception of the Virgin Mother, had frenzied followers. All of these cults promised salvation of the soul for a future life and included elaborate initiation ceremonies marked by various ordeals, which have lived on in college fraternities.

These cults offer material for the abnormal psychologists, yet they were extremely popular, appealing even to some upper-class and well-educated Romans as well as the sodden proletariat. It is possible upon reflection to understand why. In the first place, there was nothing else, and assuredly human beings require some sort of spiritual sustenance. No society has ever existed without religion, construing the word broadly as a faith to live by. The "consolations of philosophy" were not for the many, and until Christianity arrived there was little in the way of popular religion except these gods which came from the Orient. In the second place, the Roman world was a cosmopolitan society in which individuals had been uprooted from their local attachments to lose their identity in a huge and frightening mass. Through salvation religions one could gain some sense of purpose, of identity, and of solidarity with others. It is most significant that all these cults

The Pantheon, temple to all gods. Rebuilt with its great concrete dome at the time of Hadrian.

offered promises of personal immortality, and that they also featured the rites of initiation into a secret and solemn fellowship. No longer members of a secure group, human beings sought such membership in these societies. The yearning for immortality may be traced to fear of loss of identity in a mass society, and to a confusion and despair about the meaning of life in this world which certainly afflicted many in the Empire.

Rise of Christianity

None of these religions was exclusive, and none very well organized. They were regarded tolerantly by Roman authorities, for they did not seem inconsistent with the state religion. Mithraism, popular in the army, received the favor of several emperors. It had no professional priesthood, and sometimes blended with the other cults. The rest were perhaps too primitive, superstitious, and depraved to have more than a temporary success. When Christianity appeared, its higher moral and philosophical tone was evident, even though Tacitus tells us that the early Christians were "notoriously depraved," indicating they may sometimes have fallen into the habits of the cultists, though more probably indicating the great historian's ignorance and prejudice in this case. And Christianity stood apart as the one popular religion which would not be assimilated or syncretized. Christians would not even join in the worship of the Roman state. For this they were regarded as "antisocial" and subjected to persecution. The stubborn differentness of this religion was eventually to win it success. That quality was rooted in the long national tradition of Jewish monotheism. And yet, too, this religion had added to itself some other features, making it more appealing to Greco-Roman culture.

Christianity was evidently extremely obscure during its first century and a half. There are very few references to it in Roman sources. We know from Tacitus that Nero made the Christians in Rome a scapegoat for the great fire of A.D. 64, subjecting them to cruel torments. This is evidence of a remarkably rapid expansion; but as late as the later second century A.D., Christianity is confused with other mystery cults and regarded as an ignorant superstition. The first educated Roman who took it seriously enough to argue with was apparently Celsus, who wrote a book against it in 178. It was in the troubled third century that Christianity made its bid. In that century it had to survive ferocious persecution, but came through the ordeal with triumphant courage and went on to conquer the Empire in the fourth century.

The Christian faith

Sources of Christianity

Christ emerged from the messianic consciousness of the Jewish people. The messiah-king, and the related Son of Man image, which he invoked, were familiar to the Jews; so also was the apocalyptic vision of a last day and a new age coming. But the idea of a savior-god who dies and then returns to life is also to be found in the mystery religions, sometimes including the idea of the Redeemer who is raised to heaven where he prepares the way for the entrance of the faithful. Sacraments such as the baptismal immersion and the holy meal were likewise shared by Christianity with many of the religions of the Near East. The careful historical investigation of Christianity may seem to leave little that is unique. The fact remains that from these familiar ingredients Christianity shaped a uniquely powerful religion, one which, it seems fair to say, conquered because it was far superior in spiritual qualities to any other of the religions of the Empire. It may well be that its recipe for success lay in the blending of a Judaic element—released from the exclusive possession of the Jews and universalized—with influences from other currents of faith abroad in the Hellenistic age. At the same time Christianity preserved its separate organization, avoiding the fate of being "syncretized" or swallowed up in the cosmopolitan Roman world with its many cults and philosophies.

Teacher, prophet, worker of miracles, Jesus to his early Jewish followers was above all the one who after being crowned with thorns and crucified had been raised from the dead and made Messiah, soon to return as Son of Man to judge and to save. The early Christian communities regarded themselves as part of Israel. But, rejected by the dominant elements in Judaism, the sect universalized its message, cut loose from Israel after earnest discussion, and offered its message of salvation to all. The first apostles and evangelists hastened to bear the "good news" everywhere, and to the energy and enthusiasm of these early missionaries Christianity owed its success.

Paul

It seems clear that Paul, the great evangelist who may be regarded as the chief creator of historic Christianity, brought to Christianity more than was there when he found it. Paul was a Jew of the Dispersion, born and raised in the Hellenistic city of Tarsus where Greek science and Stoic philosophy would have been familiar. He knew the Greek language and many of the concepts of Greek culture, while at the same time he was steeped in the traditions of Judaism. He knew also the oriental cults and mythologies. In brief, he was very much a citizen of the world. He had not known Jesus directly and was independent of the first disciples; indeed, as everyone knows, Paul at first was a foe of the Christians. As convert and apostle, Paul labored to expand the faith and preserve its identity, against both Judaizers and syncretizers—that is, the tendency to keep Christianity as a branch of Israel or, on the other hand, to merge it into Hellenistic philosophy. Paul was not the only missionary of the apostolic age—far from it—nor was he even the first, but he was the greatest. These missionaries who were inspired to "carry the gospel to the ends of the earth" were the founders of historic Christianity.

Paul's significance, it has been said, lay in creating not a religion but a church. At the same time, his magnificent writings, in the form of letters to various congregations, exhorting, encouraging, and sometimes rebuking them for aberrations, contain important additions to Christian doctrine. Paul systematized Christianity, gave it a "doctrine." But he was no mere organizer of church and doctrine, as New Testament readers know, but also one of the most moving writers of religious literature who ever lived—one who knew better than to bury the "existential" impact of Christianity with *too much* theology. Christian ideas of the meaning of Christ, sent as the Son of God to atone for sin and bring redemption, stem largely from the Pauline theology. While the accounts of Christ's life and martyrdom in the synoptic Gospels chiefly present the appealing story itself, Paul shaped these events into a coherent body of doctrine.

No adequate account of Christian doctrine can be offered here. But a few of its outstanding traits may be mentioned, with special reference to answering the historic question why Christianity proved the most successful of all religions.

Aspects of Christian belief

First, Christianity dared to ask of its followers total faith and complete commitment. "If Christ be not risen, then is our preaching vain": the cardinal tenet was the actual historic happening, the resurrection and ascension of Christ. Not an abstract or metaphysical idea, mankind's salvation was on the contrary the result of a concrete event to which the first disciples bore eyewitness and in which all Christians passionately believed. As a modern Christian historian, Herbert Butterfield, has written, "We are not left with a religion of nebulous love and a mere sentimental good fellowship; and we are not asked to grope hazily for an unidentifiable God." To this day, the acceptance or rejection of an event that transcends rational understanding is the crucial Christian hurdle. "Unto the Jews a stumbling block and unto the Greeks foolishness," as Paul wrote, it may be rejected by the skeptical but if believed it is bound to alter one's entire life. It demands complete commitment. It is hard to enter the kingdom of God (Mark 10:25–25), it means the abandonment of worldly ways. One cannot serve two masters, God and Mammon (Matthew 6:24). One must even be prepared to break family ties to follow Christ (Luke 14:26). One could hardly be just half a Christian, or a part-time Christian. Again, one might decline such a formidable challenge but if one accepted it, one's whole life would be involved. The converted person became a "new man," "born again."

The joyous news brought by Christ was the promise of life eternal. All the mystery religions yearned for immortality, but Christianity gave the greatest assurance of it, it would seem. If our hope is in this life only, we are of all men the most miserable (I Corinthians 15:19). Death is swallowed up in victory and has lost its sting; "whoever lives and believes in me shall never die." Whatever exactly the Christian doctrine of eternal life means, the depth of its conviction and its ability to offer consolation are well known. This promise of salvation is held out to everyone who has faith. Early Christians did not doubt the imminence of the last reckoning when "the Lord himself shall descend from heaven with a shout" to condemn the wicked to hell and raise the saved to heaven. Conviction that the end of this world was at hand enabled Christians to exhibit contempt for it, and to show an extraordinary disdain for death. They confidently awaited the wrathful judgment of God on all sinful earthly institutions, including the Roman state itself.

This revolutionary quality in Christianity may be suggested as another reason for its success. Though not as such a political movement, it stood apart from all other cults in refusing to worship the emperor, and Christians predicted the final downfall of Rome ("Babylon") which would be overcome by the Kingdom of God. The symbolic sense in which this was meant was not so clear to people at that time, and we find Roman officials assuming that these bothersome followers of "Chrestus" were disloyal or subversive, wishing to pull down the existing state and install their own king. This brought down intermittent persecution on the Christians, but the blood of martyrs is good seed for any church and by their courage in meeting death they won many converts. In such places as Egypt it is clear that Christianity fused with a nationalistic feeling of resentment against Rome. The view that Christianity was exclusively a movement of the lowest classes of society is no longer held, but it did appeal notably to the poor and dispossessed. To them it offered a democratic creed, in that all are equal in Christ, the poorest may find a place among God's elect if only he truly believes. God cares for the least of His children, and may care more for them than for the rich, who cannot easily enter the kingdom of heaven. Jesus himself was a humble carpenter. The mighty would be cast down and the lowly exalted at the last judgment. This element in Christianity could lead to Christian Socialism in modern times; it could cause Friedrich Nietzsche to claim that Christianity was the revenge of the weak on the strong.

Christian ethics

Meanwhile, while awaiting final justice and eternal life, Christianity taught its followers to live not in revelry and debauchery but in sobriety and unselfish love, in chastity and humility of soul. The higher ethic of Christianity as opposed to the rival cults seems beyond question. It possessed a moral superiority that told in the long run. And this spirit of sobriety and self-help made the Christian communities prosper in a material sense, though this was not their aim. Throughout the long history of Christianity this theme has manifested itself: beginning in holy poverty, Christian groups have accumulated wealth in virtue of their very contempt for it. It happened to the Knights Templar in the Middle Ages and the Quakers in the 18th century, and apparently it happened to the early Christians: within a comparatively short time these communities of hard-working, honest, frugal people grew wealthy.

It was a distinctive quality of Christians that while despising the "things of this world" relative to the glorious everlasting life that lay ahead, they did not absolutely despise them; they did not ordinarily become hermits, fakirs, or profligates out of a complete rejection of this world, as happened to a number of other faiths. Some branches of early Christianity were Gnostic, teaching a dualism in which this world is absolutely corrupt and mystic knowledge is necessary to escape from it; but these sects were rejected. The dualistic Gnostics and Manichees, who appeared in the Middle Ages as the Cathars of Languedoc, tended in this direction along with some of the oriental, Hindu creeds. Christ had lived on earth as a man, God cared for men as such, therefore no Christian could hold human life worthless: the Incarnation barred the way. In loving one's fellow men as well as in living a righteous life, one pleased God. The ecstatic expectation of life after death was not inconsistent with a useful life here on earth for the Christian.

Organizing the church

Equipped with these sterling qualities, Christians were afflicted with severe growing pains as their movement spread. It ran the danger of falling apart in disunity, or else being annexed by or dissolved into one or another of the many cults and philosophies that filled the huge Empire. Its leaders struggled to preserve a coherent body of doctrine, in the face of many deviant versions of the creed that appeared here and there, often influenced by local traditions. And Christianity had to shape an organization. All this it had to do in the teeth of a persecution extremely severe at times, driving the Christian movement quite literally underground, or into the wilderness. Some of the numerous "heresies" or deviations of doctrine are discussed in the next chapter. Organizationally, the church began to create that great centralized administration which eventually became Roman Catholic in the West with its hierarchy of bishops, archbishops, and pope. The Eastern Church centered at Constantinople became similarly centralized.

The mood of the later Empire fell into grooves quite congenial to such a religion as Christianity. Late classical writers, watching the decay of a great worldly power structure, brooded on the fragility of all such enterprises; living amid a civilization ruined by greed and sensuality they rejected the worth of these goals. With Juvenal they meditated on the vanity of human wishes: "the only path that surely leads to a life of peace lies through virtue." The close connection between Christianity and classical culture cannot be too strongly stressed. The view that the two were radically different, and that Christianity was something alien to Roman ideals, must be rejected. In the sad centuries of Rome's decline the two came very close together.

Beginning of the end

The Roman Empire reached its maximum territorial expansion in A.D. 117, after which it stood on the defensive over its far-flung frontiers. The climax of its career as governor and law-giver to the civilized world came at about this time. But the great Antonine Emperor, the philosopher Marcus Aurelius, faced the outbreak of war in his reign (161–80). Beyond the Euphrates lay the Parthian state, which embraced Persia and aspired to regain Mesopotamia. Within a few years it was to be reorganized as the Sassanid monarchy of Persia, a powerful and ambitious state; thus once again the Persians confronted the West. More menacing to Rome itself were the barbarian Germans, especially the Goths who were held at bay across the Danube. Military expenses increased while the imperial economy seemed to stagnate.

Political troubles

From 235 to 285, the empire was afflicted with a severe case of succession trouble. The army began to choose the emperors—and to murder them with

Hadrian, in whose reign Rome attained her peak of power and glory.

Marcus Aurelius, "My city and country, so far as I am Antonius, is Rome; but so far as I am a man, it is the world."

monotonous regularity. There were 26 emperors in this period, of whom only one escaped violent death. "This criminal gains the gallows, that a crown," Juvenal had written in disgust, even in better days of the Empire (c. 100 A.D.); the great satirist put his finger on a problem endemic in hereditary monarchies and never solved at all satisfactorily by Rome, except in the second century when the principle of adoption was regularly adhered to. Now there was a breakdown in orderly government and imperial authority from which in many ways Rome never really recovered. Her foes took advantage of it to breach the defenses, and local warlordism appeared in the absence of any firm or respected central authority.

The Illyrian emperors

There was a rally. From 285 to 337 the vigorous emperors Diocletian and then Constantine enjoyed long reigns and introduced basic reforms. The reforms of Diocletian were at the expense of personal liberty and brought in the evils of statism, bureaucratic centralization, and heavy taxation. Only by creating such a structure of government, this able man thought, could predatory warlordism be curbed. Diocletian's edicts even sought to freeze people in hereditary professions and fix prices and wages by state decree. An interesting experiment in state socialism, it checked the debasement of the coinage (inflation) and some other economic maladies. But it has been observed that "The state which Diocletian saved lived under such conditions that it is questionable whether it was worth saving." "A political organism which requires the permanent, forcible subjection of large groups of its population is likely to end by totally brutalizing and stultifying itself." Roman imperial history shows the steady enlargement of the unfree classes, the steady growth of despotism and concomitant decline of individual initiative. Under Diocletian the price extracted for imperial efficiency became intolerably heavy. The emperorship in the hands of Diocletian and his successors became autocratic and despotic in a way that the Augustan "principate" never was. The Roman constitutional state was transformed into a despotism or continuing dictatorship.

Decay of the Empire

Much earlier, Livy had written that Rome could bear neither her ills nor their remedies. The remedies of Diocletian—a centralized, bureaucratic, regulatory system—cured some abuses but created others. They did not stop the dry rot in the Roman Empire.

The malady, historians have held, was in part internal. The pressure from without was heavy, but it might not have prevailed but for the decay within. At least there are many signs of such decay; the deterioration of the emperorship, the decline in civic spirit, the growing weight of taxation, and the loss of personal liberty. Serfdom, the attachment of the farmers to the land, came into existence in the fourth century. In this century the influx of "barbarians," even into the armies and government, reached such proportions that one could hardly any longer speak of a "Roman" empire. And the Roman Empire as such was to withdraw to the East, setting up its capital at Constantinople, abandoning the West to the barbarians.

Nevertheless the structure built by Rome showed a remarkable tenacity. It won the allegiance of the barbarians and continued to exist for some time. Perhaps it never fell at all. The question is one which we will attempt to answer in the next chapter. It seems clear, however, that the fourth century brought at least the change from one sort of society and empire to another, with the "triumph of Christianity and of barbarism." The old Roman Empire no longer existed in the West.

Bibliography

Raymond Bloch, *The Origins of Rome* (New York: Frederick A. Praeger, 1960), explores its fascinating topic with both learning and style. Bloch has also, in this same series (Ancient Peoples and Places), done justice to the fascinating people who preceded and influenced the Romans, *The Etruscans*. Michael Grant's *The World of Rome* (Cleveland: World Publishing, 1960; also New American Library Mentor paperback) is a good, well-illustrated survey of Roman civilization at its zenith. The older classic *History of Rome* by Theodore Mommsen is in paperback (World Publishing, Meridian) in abridged form, as is M. Rostovtzeff, *Rome* (Oxford University Press). A brilliant account of *The Roman Revolution of the Caesars* is provided by Sir Ronald Syme (Oxford University Press), while A.H.M. Jones, *Studies in Roman Law and Government* (Oxford: Blackwell, 1960), supplements the previously cited work of J.A.O. Larsen (see Chapter 2). See also Wilhelmina M. Jashemski, *Origins and History of the Proconsular and Pro-praetorian Imperium to 27 B.C.* (Chicago: University of Chicago Press, 1950). For a rather underworked subject, see B.H. Warmington, *Carthage* (Penguin). On culture, literature, and society, each of the following is outstanding: M.L. Clarke, *The Roman Mind* (London: Cohen & West, 1956); S. Dill, *Roman Society* (2 vols.; World Publishing, Meridian); J. Carcopino, *Daily Life in Ancient Rome* (Yale University Press); Arthur Koestler, *The Gladiators* (New York: Macmillan, 1939); Michael Grant, *Roman Literature* (Penguin); William H. Stahl, *Roman Science* (Madison: University of Wisconsin Press, 1962); Thomas Africa, *Rome of the Caesars* (New York: John Wiley & Sons, 1965).

Tenney Frank's *Economic History of Rome* (Baltimore: Johns Hopkins, 1927) is still standard; the same historian edited, with others, a six-volume *Economic Survey of Ancient Rome* (Paterson, N.J.: Pageant Books, 1959). H. Mattingly, *Roman Imperial Civilization* is a Doubleday Anchor book; on the question of the decline and fall, Gibbon's famed work, available in many editions (a condensed version is published by Viking paperbacks), may be compared with Richard A. Haywood, *The Myth of Rome's Fall* (New York: Crowell, 1958), a book which attempts to sum up modern scholarship on the subject; and, more weighty, A.M.T. Jones, *The Later Roman Empire 284–602* (Blackwell, 1964). Anthony Birley, *Marcus Aurelius* (Boston: Little, Brown & Co., 1966), provides a good picture of the Empire in the mid-third century. H.J. Rose, *Religion in Greece and Rome* (Harper Torchbook), and E.V. Arnold, *Roman Stoicism* (New York: Cambridge University Press, 1911, reprinted 1960), each sheds light on the spiritual dilemma of ancient Rome. See also Ludwig Edelstein, *The Meaning of Stoicism* (Cambridge, Mass.: Harvard University Press, 1967), and A.J. Festugière, *Epicurus and His Gods* (Blackwell, 1956), the latter on the other Greek-originated creed popular among the Romans. For early Christianity, Sherman E. Johnson, *Jesus in His Own Times* (London: A. & C. Black, 1958), is a useful survey; Michael Gough, *The Early Christians*, in the Ancient Peoples and Places series (Frederick A. Praeger), stresses the physical remains; R. Bultmann, *Primitive Christianity in Its Contemporary Setting* (World Publishing, Meridian), is by one of the masters of modern Biblical interpretation; J.N.D. Kelley, *Early Christian Doctrines* (2d ed.; A. & C. Black, 1960), is authoritative on its subject. The first 2 volumes of H. Daniel-Rops' multivolume *History of the Christian Church* (World Publishing, Meridian), by one of the outstanding Roman Catholic scholars, are evocative of the spirit of the early church. In *Pagan and Christian in an Age of Anxiety* (Cambridge University Press, 1965), E.R. Dodds evokes the mood of the later Empire.

As source reading, the works of Caesar, Cicero, Tacitus, Livy and Plutarch are available in numerous editions (Penguin has a fine series), while useful anthologies include N. Lewis (ed.), *Roman Civilization: Selected Readings* (Columbia University Press, Records of Civilization series); Ernest Barker (ed.), *From Alexander to Constantine: Social and Political Ideas* (Oxford: Clarendon Press, 1956); Moses Hadas (ed.), *The Stoic Philosophy of Seneca* (Doubleday Anchor); and B. Davenport (ed.), *Portable Roman Reader* (Viking Press). Under the editorship of Moses Hadas, Time-Life offers *Imperial Rome*, a picture book.

Seventh century East Christian manuscript of New Testament with painted wood cover

4

The barbarian kingdoms and the Christian church

chronology

313
Edict of Milan, recognition of Christianity.
325
Council of Nicaea.
330
Founding of Constantinople by Emperor Constantine.
361–63
Emperor Julian reverses policy toward Christianity.
370
Huns appear in Europe.
378
Barbarian invasions; battle of Adrianople, defeat of Romans by Visigoths.
395
Separate emperors in East and West.
410
Capture of Rome by Visigoths.
430
Death of St. Augustine.
476
Last Roman emperor in West deposed.
481–511
Frankish kingdom of Clovis; civil war among his sons after his death.
489–526
Theodoric, Ostrogoth Emperor of Rome.
527–65
Reign of Justinian the Great, Emperor at Constantinople; reconquest of Italy from Ostrogoths.
Codification of Roman law.
543
Death of Benedict of Nursia; age of monasticism.
568
Lombard conquest of Italy begins.
570–90
Slavic movement into Balkans; military threat from Avars; decline of Eastern Empire, also at war with Persians and soon with Muslims.
590–604
Pope Gregory the Great establishes prestige of papacy at Rome.
597–664
Conversion of England to Roman Christianity; compromise (664, Synod of Whitby) with Celtic Christianity.
613–38
Frankish kingdom reunited under Merovingian house.
622–32
Expansion of Islam begins.
638
Frankish Merovingian kingdom starts to disintegrate; beginnings of feudalism.
As mayors of the palace, Carolingian line emerges.
673–718
Constantinople attacked and besieged by Arabs.
711–15
Muslim conquest of Spain.
726
Iconoclastic controversy between Constantinople and Rome.
732
Charles Martel's victory at Tours checks advance of Muslims into Europe.
Boniface begins work of organizing monasteries on the Continent.
752
Pepin, Charlemagne's father, elected King of Franks
756
Donation of Pepin, alliance between papacy and rising Carolingian monarchy.
757–96
Kingdom of Mercia, fairly strong English state; broken up after latter date.
771
Charlemagne begins his reign.
774
Charlemagne conquers, absorbs Lombard kingdom.
778
Battle of Roncesvalles (*Song of Roland*); Charlemagne's invasion of Spain checked.
785
Charlemagne completes subjection and Christianization of Saxons.
787–95
First Norse attacks on England and Ireland.
795
Charlemagne defeats Avars; sets up numerous marches to hold conquests.
800
Coronation of Charlemagne as Emperor by Pope at Rome, reestablishing Western Empire.

Decline in the West

Causes of Rome's fall

The "fall of Rome" is the classic historical problem, alluring yet elusive. Men of every age have felt that if only they knew the answer to it they might hold in their hands the key to human success. The distinguished author of a recent study of economic growth, W. Arthur Lewis, remarked that "All the problems dealt with in this book would be settled if we understood the rise and decline of Greece and Rome." Was the chief cause of decline economic? Or political? Or moral? We know the symptoms. They included crushing taxation, loss of liberty under a bureaucratic despotism, loss of the old Roman civic spirit, loss of control over the military, declining population, increase of the servile classes, the pursuit of strange gods. Can we be sure which, if any of these, was the "fundamental" factor? Did the economy decline because men lost their probity and industry, or vice versa? Was the imperial anarchy and its sequel, the despotism, purely a political question? Was crushing taxation the cause of economic stagnation, or the result of it?

Even the ripest students of the Roman Empire hesitate to speak dogmatically about such questions. They do point out that with rare tenacity Rome staved off disaster for several centuries and tried almost every conceivable remedy. It was no sudden collapse. Perhaps the real miracle was not that the Empire broke down but that it ever existed. Clearly the wondrous period between Augustus and Aurelius—not much more than a century—had been quite exceptional in the affairs of men, for war and strife was the rule rather than the exception, both before and afterward. Quite possibly so unusual an accomplishment, the rule and pacification of so large a realm, was too much for anyone to sustain in the world as it then was. Possibly it is true, as philosophers long believed, that every society is subject to decay as the price of its success. At any rate, the leaders of the Empire for several centuries tried everything they could think of in an effort to solve the problems of the overgrown state. The rally which began near the end of the third century, led by the Illyrian emperors (Aurelian, Diocletian, Constantine) supplied, as we have seen, an energetic program of military action against the barbarians, and internal reform with heavy admixtures of state regulation.

Division of the Empire

In so doing they took one momentous step: recognizing that the Empire was too vast to be governed by a single authority, they split it in two. As early as 285 A.D. there was a division for administrative purposes, and Diocletian resided in the East. Constantine then moved the capital to the city on the Bosporus, at the entrance to the Black Sea where Europe meets Asia, which long bore his name (330 A.D.). By 395 there were separate emperors of East and West, widening the breach. This change had ominous potentialities for the western half, little though this was intended in the beginning. For both the wealth and the civilization of the ancient world which Rome had conquered remained preponderantly in the East. The fact that Constantinople was a more natural center of the Empire than Rome was what caused the settling of the capital there when it became desperately necessary to cut losses and defend what could be defended. It was the East that had the deeper civilization, and more advanced social and economic development; the West was still barbarous, or civilized only skin deep. To make a separation was to raise the possibility that Europe would be prematurely cut off from its source of civilization. And this was what happened. A partition which was at first only administrative and provisional at length became permanent and complete.

Acceptance of Christianity

Constantine, the great emperor who transferred the capital to his city in Asia Minor, is known even more in history for another memorable decision: it was he who took the decisive steps toward making Christianity the religion of the Empire. In 312 Constantine defeated the rival claimant to the imperial throne, Maxentius, in a battle outside Rome before which, according to legend, he saw a sign of the cross in the sky and embraced the Christian emblem as his standard. In 313 the Edict of Milan granted full legal rights to the Christians, who had in fact been free from persecution in the West since 306, in the East since the death of Galerius in 311. Constantine grew more and more sympathetic to Christianity, but he did not receive baptism until just before his death in 337. He extended it many privileges, though he never made it the official state religion or banned other cults. There was an increasingly Christian tone to his policies, including a greater humanitarianism; but it seems likely that Constantine remained, as would be natural, still half a pagan. In 325 he presided over the great Council of Nicaea which ruled against Arianism and established criteria of Christian orthodoxy. At his death Christianity had clearly triumphed in the Empire, though not until the reign of Theodosius (378–95) did it become the sole and official creed of the Empire, Julian (361–63) having tried meanwhile to restore a pagan faith. Intermittent persecutions, the last of them under Constantine's predecessor, Diocletian, had not destroyed the Christians but only made them stronger and more united.

Constantine's conversion has sometimes been construed as a political move, a desperate maneuver to save the dying Empire: join the Christians since you can't beat them. The fact is that his belief was quite sincere. Christianity had been growing in the esteem of the educated classes for some time, being no longer a despised sect but one with an increasing appeal to the philosophical. Blending with Greco-Roman thought, it had already attracted or was about to attract minds of the caliber of St. Jerome and St. Augustine. But to Gibbon, and other historians, the adoption of Christianity has seemed a confession of failure and a further cause of decline. For Christianity, which had proved its vitality as a personal religion, was hostile to many features of Roman patriotism and civic spirit. It subordinated the kingdoms of this world to other and higher interests. But it had become a force almost too strong to fight, and rulers hoped that some of its success would rub off on them. Certainly Christianity, once adopted by Rome, threw itself behind the empire and supported it fully.

When adversity continued, the Emperor Julian, who came to the throne in 360, in desperation reversed the former policies. He tried to decentralize and debureaucratize, reversing Diocletian's methods; and he turned against Christianity, undoing Constantine's work for a time. A crusading reactionary, Julian was a man of considerable intellect and force, but he could not stop the dry rot either. The Delphic oracle, it is said, told him that

> . . . *the carven hall is fallen with decay*
> . . . .
> *The stream is dry that had so much to say.*

Barbarian threat

The date of the conquest of Rome by the Goths, as the marauding Germanic barbarians were called, was 410. Since the battle of Adrianople in 378, it had been evident that the western Empire could no longer contain these peoples. One should not think of Rome being deluged under hordes of barbarians; they do not seem to have been very numerous, and if Rome could no longer keep them out the fault lay in her weakness as much as in their strength. For quite a while the imperial armies had used auxiliary troops from among the barbarians; in good part, the process was one of gradual infiltration rather than frontal assault. But the barbarians were engaged in an exceptional amount of migrating at this time, the result of the fierce Asiatic Huns pushing the Ostrogoths out of their homeland in the Russian steppes about 370, which set in motion a whole train of tribal movements. These Germanic tribesmen were in any case seminomadic, engaging in some agriculture but moving about a good deal with herds as their chief source of sustenance. War to them was the normal course of existence. They had been controlled in the past not merely by applying superior force but by hiring their services or making treaties with them, on behalf of a power they respected. As this power melted away, they tended to take over the Empire.

The more important of these Germanic peoples spoke a similar language and tended to the tall, blond "Nordic" type but were divided into various nations often warring against each other. The Lombards, the Burgundians, the Vandals, the Goths, the Saxons, the Franks, the Alemans (Alamanni), the Bavarians—their names were to leave a stamp on Europe. Not until 476 did the western Empire formally cease to exist; in that year the last of the western emperors was deposed by a barbarian general named Odoacer, who sent word to the emperor in Constantinople that he did not wish to be named emperor himself. By this time, western Europe was almost altogether in German hands; a few isolated Roman magistrates held out for a time, and Celtic "provincials" in Brittany, Wales, Scotland, half-Romanized, cherished the memory of Rome but soon reverted to a tribal condition. The Visigoths in Spain, the Vandals in north Africa, Burgundians, Franks, Saxons in western Europe dominated former imperial regions.

The barbarians and the Roman heritage

All this involved much suffering and death, and profoundly shocked those of the Roman world who had to watch it. It is hardly surprising that it seemed

Basilica of St. Antimo, Siena province, Italy—example of Lombard architecture

like the end of the world. "My voice sticks in my throat; and, as I dictate, sobs impair my speech. The city which had taken the whole world was itself taken." So wrote St. Jerome, the Christian scholar, when the news of 410 reached him. Christian though he was, and as such believing in the higher worth of another and eternal City, Jerome wrote in despair, "if Rome be lost, where shall we look for help?" During the fifth century Rome had to endure another barbarian sacking, this time by the fierce Vandals. The horrors which these tribesmen could visit on peoples long accustomed to peace should not be underestimated. The Vandals reportedly followed the pleasant custom of reducing walled cities by piling the bodies of the dead around the walls until the stench forced capitulation. We learn from the surviving writings of a Romanized Celt, Gildas, in Britain, c. 540 A.D., what terror the invading Saxons brought as they slaughtered, enslaved, destroyed cities and villas of which they had no understanding nor could make any use. So it went, in many places, for a long time.

Continuity

It is nevertheless common today to emphasize the continuity of civilization that managed to prevail. Hardly less startling, if we accept the picture of marauding savages, is the fact that a Gothic king, Theodoric, strove to restore Roman government and culture at the end of the fifth century. The Goths were susceptible to Christianization and Romanization—some of them, at any rate. While Vandals and Saxons came as fierce enemies, the Goths were allies of Rome early, and had already been Christianized. They responded to the Roman world with the same mixture of admiration and suspicion with which modern "colonial" peoples often look upon the European. However, there was probably much less rejection, for Rome never was nationalistic or racially discriminatory in her outlook, and her truly international ideas of law and government could readily be adopted by others.

The answer, then, to the ancient historical question, "Why did Rome fall?" may be that she didn't, at least not in 476. The Empire was taken over by the Germans of various sorts, who adopted its religion and its law, its social and economic institutions, as best they could. The disturbed conditions of the time, resulting from profound population dislocations, as well as their own level of culture, prevented them from making much progress; yet in many ways this "fall of the Roman Empire" did not change the basic situation in Europe very much.

What did matter most of all was the fact that the western world of Europe, including even the civilized Mediterranean shore, gradually lost contact with the eastern half of the Empire which had always been its source of higher civilization as well as wealth. The period between about 400 and 750 has often been looked upon as a single epoch—this was the traditional view—but many historians today have found that it may better be understood as two; or, rather, that the crucial date for the relapse of Europe into darkness should be put in the sixth–seventh century. From about 410 to 565 the Ostrogoths, Visigoths, and Franks still greatly respected the Empire, tried to be Romanized, and though they did not succeed at least they made every effort to preserve as much of the Roman heritage as they could grasp. Moreover the

The Byzantium influence on architecture is shown in the sixth century basilica of San Vitale, Ravenna. A mosaic in the church (p. 85) depicts Emperor Justinian I.

eastern Roman Empire remained fairly close to them, and they usually acknowledged its sovereignty. Only later, as a result of the decline of Byzantium and the rise of the Arabs, did this fructifying source of influence get cut off.

The eastern Roman Empire and the role of Islam

"To a Roman citizen of even moderate culture in the fifth century, it would probably have seemed that the future of Europe and civilization depended on Constantinople and its fate." It was now the capital, and a great city, where resided the emperor together with all the symbols of imperial power and classical culture. And despite increasing schism between the eastern and western Christians (of which a furious controversy about the nature of Christ, discussed at the Council of Chalcedon in 451, was a sign), most Christians even in the West still saw Constantinople as the center of the church.

So this Byzantine civilization, as it came to be called (Byzantium being the old name of Constantinople) exercised a stronger influence on Europe at this time than it did later. In theory there still was only one Empire, and its chief seat was undeniably at Constantinople, whatever decentralization there might be in practice. The barbarian kings scarcely questioned the theoretical supremacy of the emperor, who at Constantinople took on the awe-inspiring trappings of an oriental potentate. And the Mediterranean was the center of civilization still. Byzantine influence on the arts may be seen throughout the civilized western world at this time.

"I think that in early Byzantium, maybe never before or since in recorded history, religious, esthetic, and practical life were one." William Butler Yeats

Justinian's attempted reconquest

Constantinople held on to the Balkans (Illyricum, Greece, Thrace) against barbarian pressure, though the Goths raided them freely. With her great navy controlling the sea, Byzantium in the sixth century made an effort to recover Italy. The great Emperor Justinian I, known to posterity for the work of ordering and digesting the Roman law, led an offensive which succeeded in regaining north Africa from the Vandals, who alone of the Germans had refused to acknowledge the imperial supremacy, and marched to Rome where the thoroughly Romanized Ostrogoth king accepted Justinian's overlordship. But most of the Goths construed this as cowardice and treason and waged war on Justinian. After a considerable struggle he subdued them (540–54) and, turning his attention to Spain, succeeded for a fleeting moment in restoring something very near the old Roman Empire in the West: "the Mediterranean was once more a Roman lake."

It was a crucial moment for Europe. The successors of Justinian could not hold onto this reconstructed Empire; exhausted by the effort, the Byzantine state all but collapsed, and the Lombards came into Italy bringing an even worse barbarism. It was at this time, if ever, that "Rome fell": the wars of Justinian followed by the Lombard invasion ruined and depopulated most of Italy, caused Rome to lose most of her population, brought to an end the imperial epoch.

To its east, Byzantium was beset by Persians and Arabs, in the Balkans by Avars, an oriental people akin to the Huns who moved into that region. Plagued also by internal dissension, the eastern Empire experienced bad times for the next century after the death of Justinian in 565. It staved off disaster and finally rallied, but constant warfare brutalized and impoverished it during most of the seventh century. Constantinople saw the Arabs at the very gates of the city in 717. It held, counterattacked, and finally regained Asia Minor. But from that time on it tended to face East, while the Bulgars and Slavs, settling in southeastern Europe up to the borders of Greece, formed a barrier between it and the West. The Arabs conquered and long held most of the Mediterranean. Only in southern Italy did Byzantine rule touch the West, feebly, in the 10th and 11th centuries (875–1068).

Constantinople was to go on to build a brilliant civilization in the 9th and 10th centuries, and to exert a deep cultural influence on the Bulgars and Slavs, who received their Christianity from the Orthodox eastern church (the Bulgars fought ferocious wars for possession of the Greek throne); but by that time the gulf between Byzantium and Europe had widened appreciably, the former having become orientalized while the latter had begun to go its own way. The overt sign of this cleavage was the break between the two churches, the popes at Rome claiming independence. At any rate in the crucial period from about 565 to 800 the eastern Empire was itself so hard pressed and impoverished that it had little to offer Europe, which found itself abandoned to another wave of barbarism. And meanwhile the great Arab surge brought virtually the entire Mediterranean basin into the hands of an alien power.

Of all the events which conspired to isolate and impoverish Europe, the most important was the Arab conquest of a good part of the Mediterranean

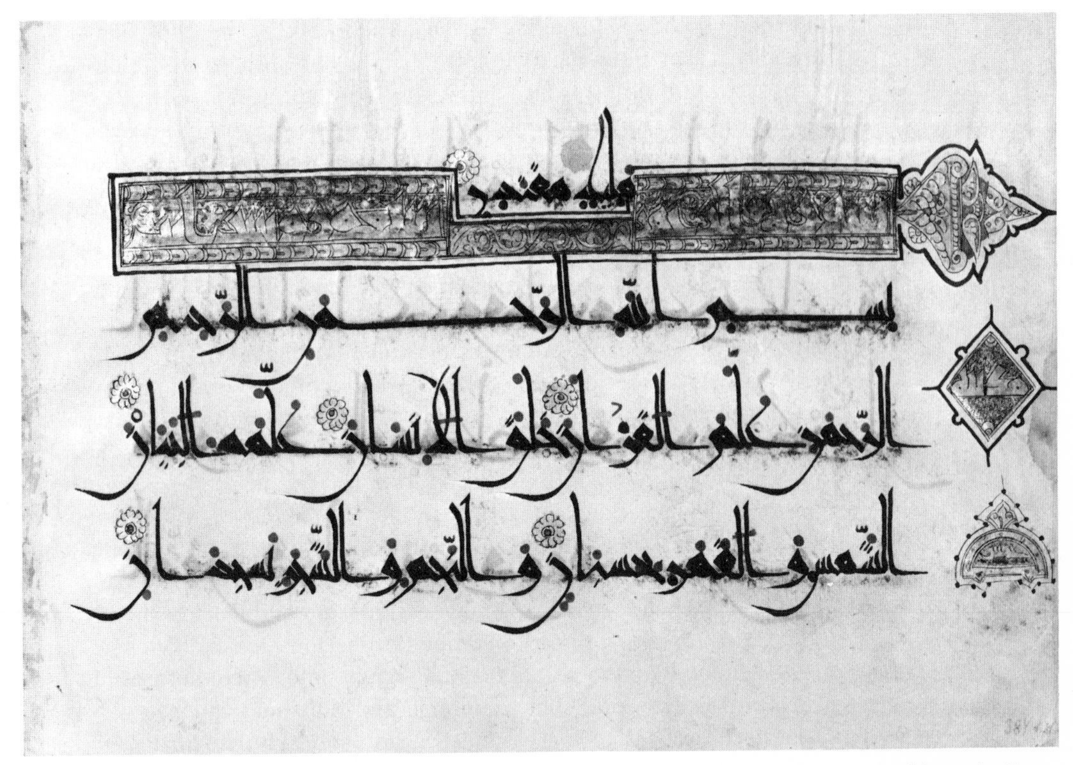

Leaf from the Koran or Qur'ān, the sacred book of Islam, 10th century Persian

in the seventh century. The eruption of Islam is a famous story. Within a century after the death of the prophet Muhammad, in 632, the militant religion he founded—strongly influenced by Judaism and Christianity, and sharing some fundamental traits with them[1]—had conquered Persia, the eastern Mediterranean, north Africa, the important islands of the Mediterranean, and Spain. It spread more rapidly than any religion in history, gaining great numbers of converts within a century after its birth, not only in Africa, the Middle East, and Europe, but also in India, the Indies, and China.

The Islamic conquests

Being without a priesthood in any organized sense, Islamic government was more "theocratic" than the dual church–secular state situation of medieval Europe. At its zenith Islam besieged Constantinople and pushed on from Spain

[1] Muslims share with Christians and Jews a belief in the unity of God (Allah), if anything placing an even stronger stress on the absolute power, wisdom, and transcendence of God. Muhammad, the founder of the Muslim faith, is considered to be an apostle or prophet, through whom God sent his message to the Arabs, as he sent Moses to the Jews, and Jesus to the Christians to bring a further message to the world. Muslims respect the Bible of the Christians and Jews and regret their separation. Islam has no ordained priesthood, only lay teachers. Fasting, almsgiving, and pilgrimage have always played a large part in this religion. Its Koran, or holy book, is much simpler and briefer than the Bible. "Islam" means submission to the will of God; a "Muslim," derived from the same root word, is one who has thus submitted to God and worships him according to the Koran. "Mohammedanism" is incorrect, for Muhammad is not regarded in the same way as Christians regard Christ. A simpler and more straightforward monotheism, along with a universalism, marks the religion of Islam, which is of course worth far more study than we can allow it here.

into southern France, being, however, turned back by the Christians at each extremity. Islam subsequently went much further into Asia and Africa. For Europe, it was both a negative and a positive factor. It was negative in that it barred access to the East and to the sea, took over the Hellenic heritage, preempted a whole place in the world that previously had been Roman or Christian. That place was of course the very heartland of ancient civilization, as well as the center of trade and the key to riches. Moreover, the Arab conquest took Spain, the part of Europe that except for Italy itself had been most strongly Romanized. It captured Sicily and southern Italy, too, at its peak.

Positively, Christian Europe was eventually to make fruitful contact with the Arab world. But this did not come for a long time. Arabic[2] numerals, so superior to the clumsy Roman system, did not even get widely adopted in Europe for centuries. Arab scholars, who made use of paper as a cheap yet durable writing material, soon began to translate and preserve great quantities of Greek and oriental learning. In the 12th century Europe would draw heavily on this source. Meanwhile, the Muslim world, or Islam, appeared as strange and devilish, full of heretics and black magic. After the battle near Tours in 732 when the Franks turned back an Arab probe across the Pyrenees, Islam posed no strong threat to Europe beyond the Alps and Pyrenees, being fully occupied with the task of maintaining the integrity of her existing holdings. The Islamic world split up into several different "caliphates" and lost some territory back to the eastern Roman Empire. But in Spain a rich and highly civilized Islamic society existed, far superior to anything found in Europe in the Dark Ages. That Europe was not much affected by it until the 12th century was in good part the result of her own backwardness; and yet a friendlier and less alien culture might have penetrated her shell of barbarism.

The Germanic peoples and kingdoms

Thus the period between 450 and 750 was—to sum up—a period of confusion in which the gradual infiltration of the barbarians into the western Empire was followed by the temporary eclipse of even the eastern Empire, the loss of contact with the Mediterranean, and the threat that something like total barbarism would extinguish the heritage Roman civilization had left behind.

Germans

One thing at least was clear: Europe was largely in the hands of the Germans. These were the barbarians who, as Vandals, Visigoths, Ostrogoths, Franks, Burgundians, Bavarians, Saxons, and other tribes, had first overflowed the western Empire (including north Africa) and threatened the eastern. After much migration the Vandals ended in north Africa, the Visigoths in Spain, the

[2] They were originally Hindu. The Arabs adopted them in the eighth century, along with algebra, which they also later transmitted to Europe. Paper was another invention they obtained from China.

Franks in France, the Saxons and Bavarians in Germany. Goths, Vandals and Visigoths were later borne under by other invaders. But the Germanic peoples in general were to dominate Europe and form the basis of its modern nations west of the Elbe. They were quite uncivilized to begin with. They had no written language, their organization was tribal, they knew no science or philosophy, their law was crude and primitive, based on such practices as the *wergeld*, by which a murderer simply paid a sum of money, varying in amount according to the rank of importance of the slain person, or judicial combat and ordeal by fire. But they were capable of agriculture and metal-working, and possessed a high degree of skill in some arts. The Romans encountered them as wandering warriors, but this was partly the result of their being pushed out of their homelands by the impact of the nomads from Asia, the Huns. They showed a tendency to settle down after a time, and occasionally to imitate the higher civilization of Rome with surprising alacrity. In any case Romanized populations remained, particularly in Italy and southern France, where the Germanic rulers formed no more than a thin layer on top.

Celts

The Germans replaced the Celts, partly pushing them out, partly killing them, and partly keeping them as a lower class. Today the Celts are found in Wales, Ireland, the Scottish Highlands, and Brittany, where they were driven at this time. Once they had been widely spread over Europe, having captured Rome itself in 390 B.C. (the last time the city was taken until Alaric and his Visigoths in 410 A.D.). They were the Gauls of France, the Iberians of Spain, the Britons of the British Isles. Rome had subdued and partly Romanized some of them. They too were tribal but were gifted in art, literature, and religion and apparently capable of a rich civilization. They developed a remarkable culture in Ireland between the fifth and ninth centuries. But elsewhere they were submerged under a Germanic tide, though mingling in many cases with their conquerors. In one of his poems A. E. Housman writes of his ancestry:

The Saxon got me on the slave.

So it was, no doubt, from the Rhine to Wales. But the blond conquerors set the tone of civilization, or the lack of it, through the early "Middle Ages."

Germanic qualities

The folk tales of the Germanic peoples were rather grim and lurid. Theirs was a violent world, filled with slaughter, rapine, constant burnings and battles; it was also a world of heroism and loyalty. There are some ghosts and other supernatural elements, too, in these stories. There is not much humor and not much joy, but men are brave and sometimes magnanimous; if they are crafty and cruel they usually get their come-uppance. Thor and the other gods remind us of the gods of pagan Greece. These barbarians resembled in many respects the American Indians or African tribesmen of more recent times; or the Greeks of the Homeric age. They were in the tribal stage of human social development, which seems to exhibit comparable characteristics wherever it is found.

The Germanic peoples had some attractive qualities. They were a hardy, courageous folk, who made good farmers as well as good soldiers and who lived without unfree classes initially, though they had a military aristocracy. Nineteenth-century historians held the view, now somewhat discredited, that the source of modern democracy was in the original institutions of these Germanic tribesmen. Tacitus, the Roman historian, admired them for virtues the Romans had when they were conquerors but no longer possessed—a view perhaps guilty of romanticizing. It would seem that they had decided gifts in the practical arts. For several centuries Europe had to live with the melancholy fact that they were not yet capable either of much culture and education or mature political institutions. They had a basic cultural kinship—common institutions and similar language—but no awareness of themselves as forming a single people. Their loyalty was to the tribe, or more specifically to the chief or king who headed the tribe. They gradually built up larger states, but these were based on the tribal spirit.

Romanization of barbarians

The period of the Barbarian Kingdoms from about 400 to 700 is a difficult one to understand. We see on the one hand the tribal barbarism of these peoples and their rulers, with themes of cruelty, savagery, constant war, and an appallingly low standard of morality and social behavior. On the other hand these kingdoms were much more Romanized, politically at least, than later, for there was a conscious attempt to keep alive the Empire, which even the barbarians accepted, and they dropped their Germanic institutions in their admiration for the Roman ones in many places. Our knowledge of the secular kingdoms is somewhat meager, but such remnants of Roman literacy as Gregory of Tours, a Gallo-Roman aristocrat and a bishop of the church who wrote a history of the Franks near the end of the sixth century, supply us with accounts. Isidore of Seville, who wrote an encyclopedia which served early medieval Europe, tells us something about the Visigoths in his native Spain, and a bit later Paul the Deacon, himself a Lombard, wrote his people's history at the famous Benedictine abbey of Monte Cassino. If the mixture of barbarism and Romanism is bewildering, we can perhaps find some parallels in our own day among peoples who, as in parts of Africa and Asia, have emerged from tribalism to modern civilization almost overnight, so that one can find mud huts and skyscrapers side by side, figuratively and sometimes literally speaking. The barbarians, we may feel, were at first *too* susceptible to the lures of a superficial Romanization, and were demoralized by it. Their effort to make the leap across a huge cultural gulf brought forth some strange social phenomena.

Franks

At any rate their political affairs showed little of a constructive nature. In Spain, where Roman civilization had been strongly established, the Visigoths might have achieved a strong state but soon fell easily to the invading Muslims, 711–13. The Franks, Visigoths, Burgundians, and other German tribes and nations fought constantly with each other, as well as with any other peoples who might be about (such as the indigenous Basques in Spain). The Franks, who settled in Roman Gaul, early showed signs of being capable state makers. Clovis, greatest of the line of Merovingian kings (named after Clovis' father Merovech), was an able barbarian, though thoroughly brutal and amoral, who carved out a substantial kingdom in France early in the sixth century which his successors sought to maintain. By the eighth century the Franks believed they were "a most glorious nation" for whom God had a most special love. They were to live up to this proud boast when they produced Charlemagne. But in the main their story for much of the period was one of unstable political units, personal in nature, marked by the violence of the blood feud, falling far below the dignity of a state despite superficial trappings of Romanism. Their custom of dividing the territory of a king among all his sons made for constantly shifting areas of rule and bloody family battles for power. The Franks preserved a good deal of the Roman heritage, including towns, something of the Roman law, and the Latin language. But, as Clovis' kingdom fell apart and loss of contact with eastern trade and culture increasingly impoverished the land, this heritage seemed to grow weaker and not stronger in the seventh and eighth centuries.

In Italy, the Lombards, who became dominant after 568, were more primitive than the Visigoths and Ostrogoths who preceded them, and subjected Italy to a century or more of anarchy before they achieved anything like stability. The Saxons who invaded Britain were yet more primitive, being from those portions of Europe which had not felt Roman rule at all. Their homelands in northern Germany were not brought within the Christian framework until the eighth century; in England, they received Christian influences both from Celtic Ireland and from Rome earlier than that. All in all, the numerous tribal kingdoms of Germanic Europe showed only a little promise of rising above barbarism in the seventh and eighth centuries. It seemed to the few contemporary men of culture that the Roman heritage might gradually drown in a sea of barbarism.

The church

But "above the confused contrasts of nations and kingdoms" was raised the Christian faith. Christianity was the common denominator of medieval Europe. Its missionary activities eventually brought all Europe within its fold.

The church which preserved and represented this faith had been shaped initially in the days of persecution. During its early days, when it spread by word of mouth throughout the Roman Empire, Christianity had confronted not only the hostility of the Roman state but severe problems of internal unity. It was apparently a very simple faith—fervent belief in the historical fact of the crucified Christ, his Resurrection and Ascension as the Son of God who had died to redeem mankind from their sins, and in whom it was necessary to believe to be saved. But it was beset with disputes about many matters as it went forth in the Hellenistic world to convert all kinds and sorts of people. Deeply rooted in Hebraic national consciousness, Christianity clung to

Christ predicts Peter will deny him thrice before the cock crows in this fourth century sculpture from Roman Gaul.

its identity and exclusiveness; it demanded and kept unity. "Is Christ divided?" the apostle Paul asked the contentious Christians. "To be perfectly joined together in the same mind and the same judgment" was essential. But in order to preserve its unity—and then to survive the fearsome assaults on it—the early church was forced into a definition of dogma and the creation of an organized and disciplined structure. When it became a recognized religion under Constantine, the emperor himself assumed the authority of defining and enforcing orthodoxy.

Christian controversies

Numerous were the Christian controversies of the early centuries. They appear again and again in the history of the church; we will encounter them notably at the time of the Reformation. Noteworthy were those about the person of Christ, a Christian paradox: whether human or divine, or in what sense both; whether created by God or coeval with him. The great Council of Nicaea in 325 A.D. strenuously debated and finally defined this point, at the cost of alienating the followers of Arius about whom we have already heard. The Arians refused to concede that Christ was of an equal nature with God the Father, regarding him as divine but as a being created by and thus subordinate to God; against them the famous Nicene trinitarian creed was accepted by a majority of the Council, and those who would not accede to it were then treated as heretics. A long struggle with Arianism, which was planted early among the Germans, lay ahead before it was finally rooted out.

Efforts to make Christianity into an ascetic dualism, which went under the name of Gnosticism, were previously mentioned. In the second century followers of the Phrygian, Montanus, indulged in excessive emotionalism and prophesying—a kind of "chiliastic" enthusiasm which threatened authority and discipline in the church. (The early Christians believed quite generally in the reality and imminence of Christ's second coming on the final day of judgment.) Many regional centers of Christianity simply asserted a local autonomy—they were the Congregationalists or perhaps the national churches of their day. St. Augustine, greatest of the church fathers of the later Empire, concerned himself with the heresy of Pelagianism and nearly fell into the opposite heresy, some thought, thus setting up a long medieval debate. The question here was the degree to which human nature of its own free will could choose Christ and achieve redemption, as against the view that man as a fallen sinner could obtain redemption only through the gift of God's grace.

These controversies—there were others—will give an idea of the difficulties encountered. The result was the evolving of a rather elaborate theology and the imposing of a good deal of authoritarian discipline. Christianity had the natural intolerance of a creed which did not doubt that truth was one and that departure from it entailed ruin and damnation. Discipline in the church, as reflected in the power and prestige granted to the bishops (episcopoi), already existed before the church was called from the catacombs to rule the Roman Empire, beginning with its legalization in 313. The church was already regarded as one, holy (being in effect the body of Christ), catholic (that is, universal, coextensive with the entire Christian community), and apostolic (handed down from the original disciples of Jesus through a succession of bishops). The sees of Antioch, Alexandria, and Rome held special distinction because Peter, Paul, or Mark had taught at these places.

The popes at Rome

When Constantine, who raised the Christian faith to primacy within the Empire by embracing it, moved the capital to his city on the Bosporus in 330, he left behind in "Old Rome" bishops who never accepted the supremacy of this "New Rome." The basis was thus laid for a quarrel which split Christendom, though in fact it was probably the barbarian and then the Arab invasions which made this split effective. In the middle of the fifth century Pope Leo the Great (Leo I) of Rome, who had to deal with the Vandals, refused to accept Constantinople's claims to supremacy. At the end of this century Pope Gelasius asserted that the pope shared with the emperor "the rule of the world." Thus was born a famous doctrine, that of the two swords, temporal and spiritual, which shared the governance of man—the popes urging that, naturally, the spiritual is higher than the temporal.

St. Augustine

Augustine had already sketched it out. This greatest of Christian philosophers, who brought to the faith a classical education and a philosophical background, defined many questions in a way that would serve as a standard of authority for many centuries. He is thus the chief source for the intellectual culture of the Middle Ages down to the 12th century. Living 354–430, he watched the first great barbarian wave break over Rome. His *City of God*, preeminent among his many writings, almost exultantly proclaimed that the Empire of Rome had fallen because no earthly city can do otherwise, being absolutely corrupt. The City of God would endure. It was, in this world, represented by the church, though imperfectly. The spiritual authority of the church ought to take precedence over the authority of whatever worldly kingdom there might be. The only worthwhile function for government was

Fifth century fresco of St. Augustine

to provide for the security of the church and further its work. Thus at least he was construed in early medieval times. Actually one can find in Augustine something of the view that the state has more positive functions, aiding man in a social life which has value in itself, though a lesser value—the position later developed by St. Thomas Aquinas.

Revealing was the intellectual odyssey of this educated Roman citizen (a Berber from north Africa) who was to do so much to shape the mind of medieval Europe. He had known the sensual pleasures of Rome, but turned away from these in disgust in search of a higher ideal. Dissatisfied with the skepticism in which later Greek philosophical thought ended, he became first a Manichee (Persian dualistic religion), then a Neo-Platonist. His full conversion to Christianity in the garden at Milan became famous through the *Confessions*, and was a classic example of the conversion experience so often met with among Christians; but Augustine's philosophical background remained with him, and he argued that philosophy is valuable as preparing the way for faith, in turn being illuminated by faith. Despite his "I believe in order to understand" (*credo ut intelligam*), Augustine made a place for classical literature and learning in his thought, and this place it maintained all through the Middle Ages.

Because of his attacks on the Pelagians, and the radically dualistic mood of *City of God*, in which this world sometimes appears as almost utterly worthless, Augustine became known as the theologian of original sin, denying all value to natural man and to this life as such. And doubtless this suited the mood of much of the Middle Ages as well as of his own generation, which saw the glory of Rome vanish. But the fact is that the Bishop of Hippo lived a busy and active life (though at first he had sought to withdraw into seclusion), administering a city as bishops generally had to do in those times and writing voluminously in his spare moments. The Christian, as Augustine taught, must live in this world though he looks forward to the next. The life and doctrine of St. Augustine expressed the situation of the whole Christian church, which took charge of much of Europe's affairs even as it taught the relatively low value of any such activity.

The role of the church in the Dark Ages

The church in government

Amid the confusion and instability of the barbarian kingdoms, the church supplied much of what there was of government and law. In the days of the invasions bishops appeared as military leaders, and they supervised the administration of cities. We see Augustine, for example, in between his hours of writing, devoting himself to the busy life of a political leader—doing everything from sitting on the judicial bench to taking care of a sick child. With the withdrawal of Roman civil government there was no one else to perform these functions. Pope Leo I goes forth to plead with the Vandals not to sack the city, and succeeds in getting them to rob it in an orderly manner. Something over a century later, Pope Gregory the Great (Gregory I) must direct the defense of Italy against the Lombards, and supervise the care of all the plague-stricken refugees the Lombard war had created. In Merovingian France (sixth-seventh century), bishops shared in political and judicial affairs. This was virtually of necessity, for the clergy alone possessed the knowledge. This involvement of the church in the affairs of this world continued, and the higher clergy came to own great estates, have special privileges under the law, and later serve as ministers to counts and kings. It was a tribute to the strength of the church and the weakness of secular government. Also it was a perpetual menace to the purity of religious leadership.

Conversion of pagans

Chief among the tasks of the church was the conversion of peoples to a single Christian faith. This work went forward all during the Middle Ages. Some, like the Saxons, had to be converted from paganism; the Goths had to be dissuaded from their Arian version of Christianity and brought within the pale of orthodoxy as the Roman church conceived it. More important, all the barbarians had to be Christianized in a real sense. Nominally Christian, the peoples of Europe were still close to being pagans under the skin in this period. They might continue to worship the gods of Rome if they lived in areas such as Spain or southern France where that influence had been strong. Martin of Braga, a Spanish bishop of the later sixth century whose works survive, chides his flock for continuing to believe in divinations, auguries, Minerva, and Venus. The Germans, of course, had their own pagan deities. In order to adapt Christianity to their understanding the church sometimes recognized these barbarian nature gods as saints or angels. For example, Halloween, the vigil of the Christian All Saints' Day, contains relics of Celtic paganism. It took a long struggle to Christianize the peoples of Europe, and in the process the church itself underwent change. But missionary work went on.

Unquestionably the church was dragged down from the lofty height of an Augustine during the Dark Ages. Even Gregory the Great, a man renowned for his learning as well as his courageous leadership, chided a bishop for reading literature other than the Scriptures. The average cleric became almost as illiterate as the rest of society. In the eighth century the church fell into considerable disorder, and this was often an excuse for the seizure of its lands. It was in the monasteries, chiefly, that something of civilization survived.

Monasticism

Monasticism was imported from the East, having originated in Egypt. The recent discovery of the Dead Sea Scrolls in a monastery of the Essenes, founded in the second century B.C., reminds us that monasticism existed among the Jews in Hellenistic times. It became significant in Greece in the third century, and spread to Italy in the troubled times accompanying the decline of the Empire. There were many individual examples of monasticism before the renowned Benedict of Nursia organized it into a set pattern for the Christian West in the sixth century. Cassiodorus, about the last learned Roman, who served under the Ostrogoth King Theodoric, established a monastery at Squillace on the Adriatic when he retired, and his monks rendered

Chapter house of the abby of Notre-Dame-de-Pontaut (Cloisters collection, Metropolitan Museum of Art, New York).

worthy service there translating and copying. Earlier, as early as the later fourth century, monasteries had been formed in southern France, Ligugé about 360 and Saint Victor of Marseilles around 415. The institution spread widely all over Europe: in far-off Ireland, there developed a vigorous Celtic monasticism rather different from that of continental Europe. Encouraged by popes and patronized by kings, monasticism was the movement of the day in sixth–seventh-century Europe. The reasons for its popularity may readily be guessed: like the church itself, but more obviously so, the monastery or convent was a refuge from the barbarism which now filled the world, attracting the more sensitive souls and enabling some art and learning to survive. Many devout Christians prized the quiet seclusion of monastic life. At the same time the monks could usefully serve the church by propagating the faith and developing its liturgy and doctrine. Even barbarian secular rulers showed respect for these communities of the learned and pious. In most places, too, the monasteries provided about all there was of such services as education, hospitalization, care of the handicapped.

Benedictine rule

From Ireland came Columba, from Devonshire in England the great Boniface, to set up monasteries in northern Europe. But it was Benedict, working

Monastery of Montserrat in northeastern Spain

in Italy, whose "rule" prevailed. Benedict's rule did not fully triumph until Charlemagne's time, and there were some hermit monks even much later, for example, the Carthusians. But his system received the backing of the popes, Gregory the Great especially being its ardent proponent. Carefully regulating each hour, almost each moment of the monks' lives, Benedict set up a rigid routine of prayer, holy services, labor in the fields, and study. This was a highly social type of existence, as compared with the lonely, hermit-like monasticism often found earlier. Shut up in the same community for his lifetime, following the same changeless discipline, the monk lived a life based on contempt for this world. At the same time, the fellowship of literate people—all monks were supposed to know how to read and write—created conditions far more favorable to the survival of culture than the chaotic world outside the monastery walls.

Through the monasteries flowed most of the creative impulses of the Dark Ages. They nourished scholarship as well as piety. Monastic life often degenerated from the high ideals set by its founders, but from time to time one monastery or another produced something truly creative. Few historians have failed to conclude that European civilization owed its greatest debt during its dim and squalid infancy to the monasteries—pinpoints of light here and there amid the darkness. This was as true in the ninth and tenth centuries as it was in the sixth and seventh. It is in part a tribute to the savagery of the times, no doubt, that many of the early monasteries were situated in wild and inaccessible spots: the island of Lerins, at the mouth of the Rhone; Monte Cassino, Benedict's greatest establishment, on a spur of the Apennines; Lindisfarne, an island off the northeastern coast of England; Montserrat, on a mountain crag in Spain. But the shaven men, kindly, humble, and perhaps holy, gained the respect of the peoples around them in this period. It should be added that at a time when serfdom was becoming the rule, monasteries were places where no class distinctions among the brethren existed. But in time many monasteries came to hold serfs.

Quarrel with the eastern church

Thus the church, "all that remained of the Roman Empire," held together, provided leadership in dealing with the barbarians and in keeping government and society going, and brought forth a new institution, monasticism, to shelter some minimum of learning against the storm. In the fifth to seventh centuries it laid the foundations for that immense power it possessed in the later Middle Ages. A distinctive European civilization began to grow first around the church, and an emerging sense of identification as a "Christian republic" of the West, with Rome, not Constantinople, as the capital. In 726 there began a controversy with the eastern church which resulted in widening the breach between the two branches of Christendom and indicated an increasing independence on the part of the West. The eastern church began a crusade against icons or representations of the human image, especially of Christ. The Roman church strenuously opposed this "iconoclasm" and it was a burning issue for a century. The dispute was related to the old controversy about the nature of Christ. Islamic religious art was also iconoclastic, purely abstract. By contrast the churches and monasteries of Europe were filled with carvings and paintings of holy people. It was a symbol of the difference between East and West, perhaps indicative of a greater humanism, if also less intellectual sophistication, in Europe. For the church at Rome, it was a chance to assert its own authority and virtually to declare independence from the eastern emperor in the name of the Roman pope.

It is nevertheless true that in the eighth century the church showed signs of slipping into the general morass of barbarism which was threatening Europe in the aftermath of its loss of contact with the Mediterranean and the Roman Empire in Constantinople. Politically, socially, economically, and culturally, all of Europe just about touched bottom. In France, the decay of the Merovingian state was complete, and the possessions of the church were often seized by needy or greedy warrior chieftains. Almost miraculously for Europe, she was to be rescued by a great Frankish king in alliance with the church.

Charlemagne

Battle of Tours

The greatest event of the eighth century—one which stirred the imagination of Europe—was the turning back of the Muslim tide by Charles Martel in 732 at Tours in north central France. After the Frankish warrior-king beat back the Saracens in that battle, the Franks went on to produce the first significant political state since the emperors departed from Rome. Since Clovis (c. 500) their record as state makers had hardly been much better than the other Germans, including the "foul and leprous Lombards" as Pope Gregory the Great called them. Their history was largely a mournful if not entirely uninteresting record of wars and tortures and murders, the blood-feuds of tribal chieftains, the making and then the dividing of personal kingdoms. There was really no state; the "kingdoms" of Austrasia and Neustria, names which appear on the map, were temporary conglomerations of political power in the incessant and ferocious feuds of individuals.[3] Between 613 and 628 there was a temporary revival of the Merovingian kingship but the ensuing reversion to anarchy ended that line; the Carolingians emerged from among the "mayors of the palace," into whose hands power devolved in a manner that foreshadowed the feudal age.

But the Franks had been allowed to stay from the fifth century on in one region, and that a region in some of which Roman institutions had been well planted. While Spain fell to the Muslims and Italy passed from Visigoth to Ostrogoth to Byzantine to Lombard amid constant fighting, the Franks settled down in Gaul and stayed there. It can hardly be said that they lived

[3] After the death of Clovis in 511 his lands were divided, as customary, among his four sons, who established capitals at Paris, Orléans, Soissons, and Metz respectively. Conflict among the sons ended with only one of them surviving; but Lothair again left four sons and four kingdoms, and another feud resulted in three hostile domains, Neustria, Austrasia, and Burgundy. The three were temporarily reunited in 613. This is the story of the Frankish kingdom at all times, the kingdom dividing or coalescing according to the accidents of battle and inheritance.

peacefully. Charles Martel himself ("the hammer") fought the Saxons, the Bavarians, the Duke of Aquitaine, and other enemies of his rule in France, as well as the Saracens, and in so doing almost ruined the land, exploiting its wealth mercilessly in his search for the sinews of war. But his vigor and prestige laid the foundations for a firm monarchy. His son Pepin the Short (king 751–68) made himself the master of all France and extended his power beyond France. He foreshadowed Charlemagne's policy by allying himself with the pope at Rome; the Donation of Pepin in 756 was the basis for papal temporal power over the region known as the papal states.

The unfortunate Frankish custom of dividing a kingdom among all the sons had not ceased, but as it happened both Charles Martel and Pepin were able to avoid the worst problems of the succession and keep their possessions intact. Pepin's brother Carloman ruled jointly with him before retiring to become a monk. Pepin divided his kingdom between two sons but Charlemagne's brother, who promised to be troublesome, soon died (771).

Rise of Charlemagne

This exceptional family culminated in the figure of Charlemagne—Charles the Great, or Karl the Great. Thrust up like a torch right in the middle of the Dark Ages was the great Emperor who revived the conception of Roman civilization. Charlemagne was a man of unusual intelligence and energy. He was kept busy fighting throughout his reign, spending virtually his whole life in the saddle, yet he found time to make himself literate—a rare feat at that time for Germanic rulers—and conceive large educational and administrative reforms. Conqueror of the Lombards, the Saxons, and the Avars, Charles was a great military commander and strategist. Converter of Saxons, Slavs, and Avars, he stood forth as the champion of Christianity; he too defended the Spanish frontier against the Saracens, carrying on his grandfather's work. It was from a campaign here that medieval Europe derived its greatest epic, the story of Roland's heroic stand in the mountain pass.

Charlemagne found himself, together with his lieutenants, in possession of much of Europe by the year 800, by virtue of a military career unparalleled since the days of Caesar. Its capital was at Aix-la-Chapelle, or Aachen, in the middle Rhineland. His empire stretched from the Spanish March to the Elbe, from the Muslim frontier to the Slavic. He entered into close relations with the papacy, appearing at Rome in 799 to defend Pope Leo III against violent attack. Charles drew about him learned men from all parts of Europe, the leading one being the Englishman Alcuin. These scholars knew much about the former Roman Empire; they also were devout Christians, of course.

Coronation of December 25, 800

It happened that at this moment the title to the eastern Empire at Constantinople was regarded as vacant, being in the possession of a murderess, the Empress Irene, a Messalina of innumerable horrid crimes. Charles found himself at Rome on Christmas day, 800, where the Pope crowned him at St. Peter's and the crowd hailed him as emperor. That Roman title he bore thereafter. Never before had there been a separate emperor in the West, ignoring or rejecting the one in Constantinople. There had been a separate western emperor 395–476, but by agreement with Constantinople; this time, the eastern emperor did not recognize Charlemagne's title, and indeed the latter seemed to be claiming sole power as emperor. Some of the details of this event have been endlessly debated by historians; but whoever had taken the initiative, or whatever was in their minds, the event was of enormous significance for Europe. It was nothing less than the revival of the Roman Empire in the West, but this time a Christian empire in which the independent role of the church was evident. Rather than a "caesaro-papism" as in the East, here emperor and pope appeared as equal partners. Charles had allowed himself to receive the crown from the Pope.

From the fifth century on, as we noted, the Roman popes tended to claim supremacy within the church, energetically quarreling with the religious decrees of Constantinople and sometimes ignoring them. An open break had occurred in 728 over iconoclasm. There was to be no formal divorce until 1054, but the real separation certainly should be dated from the eighth century. About 750 the papacy conveniently created for itself the famous "Donation of Constantine," much later shown to have been a forgery, which supported the papal claim to have received from the Emperor Constantine acknowledgment not only of the primacy of the Roman see among all other Christian sees but of the pope's right to temporal rule in Rome.

The papacy crowned these actions by its alliance with Charlemagne in 800. Thereafter the Roman Empire in the West was conceived as having two heads, the one temporal, the other spiritual, the two swords ruling together, corresponding to men's bodies and souls. This conception gave rise to many disputes in the future, but it forestalled a caesaro-papism on the eastern pattern and thus served the cause of liberty. It also strengthened the papacy.

This alliance between the Roman church and a Frankish king was the logical culmination of the period between 400 and 800. For a long time both bodies had been feeling their way through a fog of barbarism, yet it had been evident that they were the important, creative elements in society. In 800 they came together in an act which symbolized the unity of Europe under their twin banners. This act guaranteed the preservation of the Roman past and the Christian European future. At least it set up an ideal toward which western Europe would strive for many centuries to come, and has perhaps not yet quit striving for.

Carolingian Renaissance

The "Carolingian Renaissance" included a strong effort to regain literacy and to write purer Latin, and especially to perform the services of the church with proper dignity and correct form. It scarcely reached the laity at all but led to the establishment of cathedral schools, some of which played a crucial role in the later emergence of higher learning. A new handwriting script, the "minuscule," appeared, and Carolingian books are of a high artistic quality. Much of this reform came from Anglo-Saxon sources, which in turn owed much to the Irish. Alcuin, the English-born educational adviser of Charle-

Contemporary statuette of Charlemagne

Ninth century carved ivory book cover from Lorsch on the Rhine shows Carolingian craftsmanship.

The Ardagh Chalice—Celtic work in silver and gold of the eighth century

magne, worked in Europe through the monasteries of Tours, Fulda, St. Gall, Reichenau, Lorsch. At the latter village on the Rhine, not far from Heidelberg, there still stands a fine example of Carolingian architecture. It is striking that this renaissance, slight though it may have been, came from the north, not the south. Europe was beginning to create its own civilization, rather than taking it altogether from the ancient classical culture of the Mediterranean. The heart of Charlemagne's world lay along the Rhine; its culture was intrinsically Germanic though it borrowed from Rome.

Erigena

To the Carolingian Renaissance belongs the first medieval philosopher, another transplanted Irishman, known as John Scotus Erigena, who appears at the court of Charles the Bald around 850 near the end of the epoch. In western Europe only the Irish could then read Greek. Irish Christian culture was distinctive, differing in a number of respects from European, but making the monastery the basic form of social organization. The most famous mother-abbey was that of Iona. Featuring itinerant rather than resident bishops, the Celtic church was strongly missionary; and in the Dark Ages it was, quite amazingly, far ahead of Europe in knowledge of Greek and Roman literature. Erigena had read the Neo-Platonic work of the Pseudo-Dionysius, itself derived from the philosopher Proclus. Because it was believed that this work was by the convert of St. Paul (see Acts 17:34), it received Christian acceptance, and a copy came to Louis the Pious, Charlemagne's successor, from the Byzantine emperor. By such accidents did the thought of the ancient world seep into the early medieval mind. Erigena attempted a synthesis of Greek philosophical thought and Christian theology that is prophetic, in general, of later Scholasticism. Without intending it, he strayed close to heresy.

He entered into the debate about predestination, again anticipating later things, but his thought was almost lost in the long period of darkness that lay ahead.

For unfortunately at the very moment when Charlemagne led a political renaissance, and presided also over this distinctive if short-lived renaissance in the arts and learning, economic conditions were turning worse, not better. Despite the valor of Charles Martel and Charlemagne in turning back the Saracens at the borders of Spain, the latter held the Mediterranean, including Spain and Sicily, and closed off the avenues of commerce, forcing the still backward, agrarian economy of Europe into an isolation which condemned it to poverty. So the Carolingian renaissance was to prove abortive, and the great Emperor's work was largely if not entirely wiped out in the unhappy century that followed his death.

Bibliography

A.H.M. Jones, *Constantine and the Conversion of Europe* (in the Teach Yourself History series; New York: Macmillan, 1948), Norman H. Baynes, *Constantine the Great and the Christian Church* (London: H. Milford, 1931), and Jacob Burckhardt's older classic *The Age of Constantine the Great* (Doubleday Anchor), deal with the beginning of the Christian Empire. Martin Werner, *The Formation of Christian Dogma* (London: A. & C. Black, 1957), and C.N. Cochrane, *Christianity and Classical Culture* (Oxford University Press) are two good works on the further development of Christianity (see also under Chapter 3); H. Marrou, *Augustine and His Influence*, in the Men of Wisdom series (Harper Torchbook) presents the reader to the greatest founder of medieval Christian thought. John W. Barker, *Justinian and the Later Roman Empire* (Madison: University of Wisconsin Press, 1966) is a well-written survey which offers some challenging interpretations. The entrance of Europe into the Dark Ages is the theme of many books; among them, A. Dopsch, *The Economic and Social Foundations of European Civilization*, a famous appraisal (London: Routledge & Kegan Paul, 1937); Margaret Deansley, *History of Early Medieval Europe 476–911* (London: Methuen History of Europe Series, 1956); H. St. L.B. Moss, *Birth of the Middle Ages* (Oxford University Press); William C. Bark, *Origins of the Medieval World* (Stanford, Calif.: Stanford University Press, 1957); F. Lot, *The End of the Ancient and the Beginnings of the Middle Ages* (Harper Torchbook); R.S. Lopez, *The Birth of Europe* (New York: J.B. Lippincott, 1967). On the theme of monasticism and the church, John Chapman, *St. Benedict and the Sixth Century* (London: Longmans, Green & Co., 1929); Eleanor S. Duckett, *Gateway to the Middle Ages: Monasticism* (University of Michigan, Ann Arbor); H. Daniel-Rops, *The Church and the Dark Ages* (World Publishing, Meridian).

M.L.W. Laistner, *Thought and Letters in Western Europe 500–900* (Ithaca, N.Y.: Cornell University Press, 1957) is a brilliant and scholarly survey of Europe's intellectual life in the so-called "Dark Ages." Henri Pirenne's *Mohammed and Charlemagne* (World Publishing, Meridian) is a classic; cf. *The Pirenne Thesis* in Raytheon's Heath "Problems" series. Recent treatments of the greatest of Dark Age figures include Richard Winston's serviceable biography, *Charlemagne* (Random House, Vintage), H. Fichtenau, *The Carolingian Empire* (New York: Oxford University Press, 1957), and Eleanor Duckett, *Alcuin, Friend of Charlemagne* (Macmillan, 1951). Further on the Byzantine Empire, after Justinian's time, see, among many works, Steven Runciman, *Byzantine Civilization* (World Publishing, Meridian), A.A. Vasiliev, *History of the Byzantine Empire* (2 vols., University of Wisconsin) and Norman Baynes and H. St. L.B. Moss, *Byzan-*

tium (Oxford University Press). For the Franks, see J.M. Wallace-Hadrill, *The Long-Haired Kings and Other Studies in Frankish History* (New York: Barnes & Noble, 1962), by one of the leading authorities on this era of European history.

Worthwhile source readings include Augustine's works, especially *City of God* (Doubleday Image Book); Einhard's *Life of Charlemagne* (University of Michigan, Ann Arbor); *The Rule of Benedict*, Paul the Deacon's *History of the Lombards*, and Bede's *Ecclesiastical History of the English People*, all available in the Thomas Nelson & Sons Medieval Texts. E. Emerton's edition of the *Letters of St. Boniface* (New York: Columbia University Press, 1940) takes one close to the monastic age. A good overall collection of readings is Donald A. White (ed.), *Medieval History: A Source Book* (Homewood, Ill.: Dorsey Press, 1965).

Readable textbooks on medieval history include Carl Stephenson, revised by Bryce Lyon, *Medieval History* (4th ed.; New York: Harper & Row, 1962); Robert S. Hoyt, *Europe in the Middle Ages* (2d ed.; New York: Harcourt, Brace, & World, 1966); Friedrich Herr, *The Medieval World*, in History of Civilization series (New American Library, Mentor). Much more detailed, and useful primarily for reference, are the volumes of the Cambridge Medieval History. Norman F. Cantor's *Medieval History* (Macmillan, 1963) is more than a textbook, with sustained and forceful interpretations, especially good on intellectual history.

5

Feudal Europe: 9th to 11th centuries

Eleventh century medallion of Christ from monastery at Jumati in Russia

chronology

814
Death of Charlemagne; weakening of Empire under his successor, Louis the Pious.
813–33
Zenith of Muslim caliphate at Baghdad.
827
Muslims begin conquest of Sicily.
843
Treaty of Verdun, dividing Charlemagne's Empire into three parts.
Norse attacks.
850
Beginning of great period of East Roman Empire; schism with Rome.
John Scotus Erigena.
863–85
Slavic conversion to Orthodox Christianity (mission of Cyril and Methodius).
871–99
Alfred the Great checks Danes in England.
877
Breakdown of Frankish Empire; strife for crown.
885
Count Odo defends Paris against Norsemen. Peak of Norse invasions.
887
End of Carolingian dynasty with deposition of Charles the Fat.
900
Magyar invasions become serious menace to eastern Europe.
910
Abbey of Cluny founded.
911
End of East Frankish line of Carolingian monarchs.
Normans settled in Normandy by treaty.
919
Beginning of Saxon line of kings (Henry the Fowler).
Development of feudalism.
955
King Otto of Saxons defeats Magyars at Battle of Lechfeld.
962
Otto the Great crowned Emperor at Aachen.
972
Gerbert, at Reims, begins advanced studies.
987
Election of Hugh Capet as King of France.
991
Renewal of Danish invasions in England during reign of Ethelred the Unready.
999
Gerbert becomes Pope Sylvester II.
St. Stephen King of Hungary; westernization and Christianization of Magyars.
1002–22
Henry II, German Emperor. Great fiefs become hereditary.
Decline of Omayyad Muslim dynasty in Spain.
King Canute, England (1017–35).
Conquest of Bulgaria by Basil II of East Roman Empire.
Byzantine forces also hold domination in southern Italy against Lombards and Normans.

The renewal of anarchy

Of Charlemagne's Empire it has been well said that "it did not endure, but its effects were enduring." It left an ineffaceable memory of a great state, rising above the personal kingdoms of the Franks, in the image, if only the image, of ancient Rome. It had brought also a brief renaissance of education, art, and culture in general. The cathedral schools established by Charlemagne's order never quite flickered out in the ensuing three centuries and finally flamed up in the grandeur of the medieval universities.

But the Empire did prove to have been built on foundations too insecure to last, and a discouraging reversion to anarchy lay ahead. The interlude, lasting for more than a century, has been called "Europe's second dark age." With the death of Charlemagne in 814 the largely personal nature of his achievement became evident. Despite valiant efforts, no permanent structure of government could be built in so short a time. The economic and technological conditions of life in ninth-century Europe were inadequate for such a state. Unfortunately for Europe the emergence of the Frankish state coincided with the Arab conquest of the Mediterranean, making economic conditions worse as political conditions were improving. Barred from access to Mediterranean commerce, Charlemagne's Empire confronted a large-scale economic recession, the symptoms of which were a decline of trade and of currency, with an agricultural economy built around the large estate or manor becoming virtually the sole foundation of life.

Division of Charlemagne's Empire

Renewal of barbarian invasions—Norsemen, Bulgars, Hungarians—must be accounted a prominent cause of the confusion that ensued. But before that there was political breakdown. Divided into three parts in 843 after Louis the Pious, Charles' son, had ruled without success, the Holy Roman Empire then went all to pieces among Charlemagne's successors in the unhappy later ninth century. In 843, when the Treaty of Verdun made the three-way division of the empire, the future outline was set for three great states—France, Germany, and Italy. However, in the short run the divisions set up by the Treaty of Verdun were not permanent. The middle kingdom of Lothair, running all the way from the North Sea to Rome, had so little unity that it fell apart completely; and the crown disappeared altogether. The treaty ended the Roman Empire in the West, never again to be restored fully. It is an age whose futility seems reflected in the names of the Frankish kings—Louis the Stammerer, Charles the Bald, and Charles the Fat. In 887 the deposition of the latter ended the Carolingian dynasty altogether. The Empire was revived permanently only in 962 and by another line of European kings, Saxons, while France became a separate kingdom. The late Carolingian period was a time of dreadful anarchy. Sorrowfully did those who had known the mighty Charles watch the dissolution of his Empire into ever smaller pieces in the years after his death.

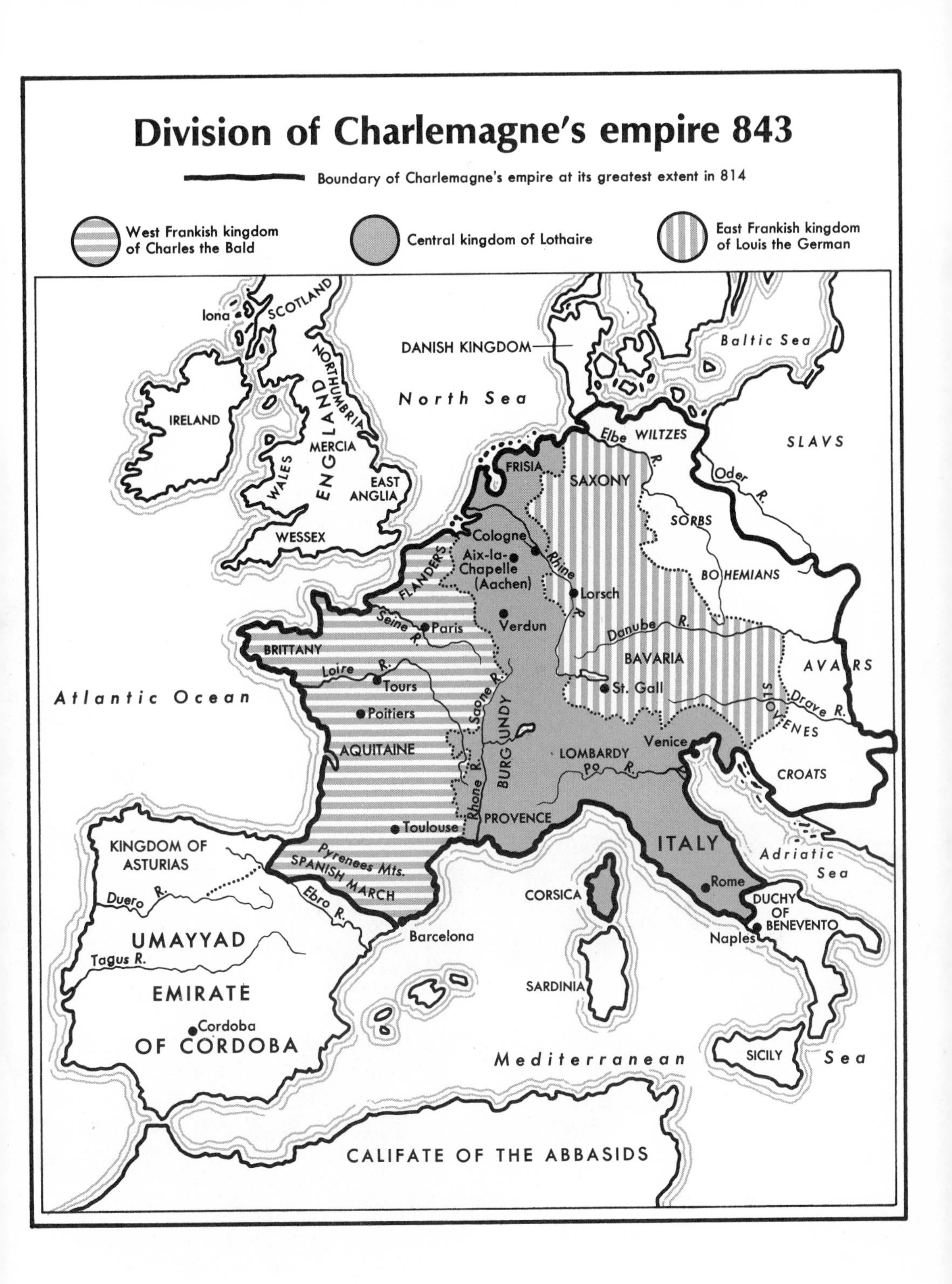
Division of Charlemagne's empire 843
Boundary of Charlemagne's empire at its greatest extent in 814
West Frankish kingdom of Charles the Bald
Central kingdom of Lothaire
East Frankish kingdom of Louis the German
Iona
SCOTLAND
NORTHUMBRIA
DANISH KINGDOM
Baltic Sea
North Sea
IRELAND
ENGLAND
MERCIA
WALES
EAST ANGLIA
WESSEX
Elbe R.
WILTZES
SLAVS
FRISIA
SAXONY
Oder R.
SORBS
Cologne
Aix-la-Chapelle (Aachen)
Rhine R.
FLANDERS
BOHEMIANS
Lorsch
Seine R.
Paris
Verdun
Danube R.
BRITTANY
BAVARIA
AVARS
Loire R.
Tours
St. Gall
Atlantic Ocean
Poitiers
Saone R.
BURGUNDY
SLOVENES
Drave R.
AQUITAINE
Venice
LOMBARDY
Po R.
CROATS
Rhone R.
PROVENCE
Toulouse
ITALY
KINGDOM OF ASTURIAS
Pyrenees Mts.
SPANISH MARCH
Adriatic Sea
Duero R.
Ebro R.
CORSICA
Rome
DUCHY OF BENEVENTO
UMAYYAD
Barcelona
Naples
Tagus R.
EMIRATE
SARDINIA
Cordoba
OF CORDOBA
Mediterranean
SICILY
Sea
CALIFATE OF THE ABBASIDS

Viking attacks

Had the Frankish kingdom remained united and sound, it might perhaps have coped with the twin threat that appeared from east and west in the last half of the century, when the Hungarians from one direction and the Vikings from another attacked Europe. The latter terrorized Britain and France especially, but eventually raided far beyond. At the end of the eighth century the "Viking age" of Scandinavia began, the age of sea voyages, which meant raids on neighboring countries by these still barbarian peoples to whom war was a way of life. Norwegians and Danes attacked western Europe while the Swedes mainly adventured in Russia. They sacked and burned all over northern Europe in the 9th and 10th centuries. Paris itself was not spared, nor Aachen, Charlemagne's capital, during the raid on which in 881, symbolically enough, the very tomb of the great Emperor was destroyed. While Arabs choked off the Mediterranean trade, from the other end Viking attacks paralyzed the once flourishing ports of the Low Countries. In England the Danes conquered the area of the North where, in Northumberland, the finest of Celtic-Saxon monastic life had flowered. They were largely responsible for the collapse of effective government in England and France at this time. In

In vessels such as this, in the ninth century, Norse warriors raided and terrorized the north and west coasts of Europe and sailed as far as North America.

England the barbaric Saxons had made progress between 600 and 800, gradually consolidating small kingdoms into larger ones and producing outstanding men of letters, including Bede of Jarrow, and Alcuin, the adviser of Charlemagne. The Viking raids and invasions of the ninth century caused extensive destruction and disruption.

Finding the lands they raided pleasant, the "northmen" settled there, areas being given to them sometimes in the hope of bribing them into more peaceful habits. They proved fairly assimilable because they too were Germanic peoples, utterly untouched by the Roman-Christian culture but sharing with the other Germans basically similar traits of language, folklore, customs. Eventually they did adopt Christianity, settle down, and make a contribution to the common culture.

Persuaded to settle down in the province of western France known thereafter as Normandy, home of the Normans or Norsemen (a region larger than the present-day province), these sailors and warriors soon adopted Frankish ways, and showed themselves the ablest political organizers in France. They were to conquer and organize England in the next century; they played a powerful part in the restoration of some degree of order in France, which they had initially disorganized. In England the Danes made a not insignificant contribution to the development of civilization in the 10th and 11th centuries, historians now recognize.

Magyar invasion

From the east, Magyar horsemen (later called Hungarians) from the steppes pushed up the Danube valley about 900. This was the latest of a series of invasions from Asia which had started with the Huns in late Roman times and had included the Avars and Bulgars with whom Charlemagne contended. Nomads unused to settled agricultural life, these people lived by plundering and were fierce warriors. They raided central Europe as far as Bavaria, burning villages and forcing men to seek refuge in well-defended castles or burgs. Not until 955 were they defeated near Augsburg by the Saxons and turned back, after which they began to settle down in their present homeland. During these years each region had to look to its own defense and central government broke down. It is the time in Germany of the emergence of the territorial duchies—Saxony, Franconia, Swabia, Bavaria, and Lorraine.

It is also the time of castle-building—at first of wood, only by the year 1000 beginning to be stone (the age of the great stone fortified castles is the 11th–12th centuries). In time they became vast fortresses, imposing still as we view them today, situated at strategic high points not easily to be assailed; at first they were crude wooden stockades and blockhouses, yet still a protection. They were the bastions of the feudal nobility, but also the protection of the people in time of invasion.

Under such circumstances, it is not surprising to learn from chroniclers that "robbery and burglary became the custom, and everybody was a brigand." The lords who were supposed to defend poor people sometimes were as bad as the foreign marauders. In the general demoralization of society, law and order can break down completely. It is not surprising that the peasant would forfeit his freedom in exchange for protection. He was fortunate to survive at all. It was essential that he become the servant or vassal of a lord who had a castle, to which in time of trouble he might withdraw.

Feudalism: Origin and nature

Under such conditions did feudalism arise, as the central conception in society and government. Feudalism represented an effort to *secure order* during a period of economic stagnation and weak central government. It gave to society and government a definite organization, in which duties and obligations were carefully defined in order to establish a military force, protect individuals, maintain law. Existing in a rough age, it nonetheless represented the reaction of the forces of law and order to a severe challenge.

Vassalage

Feudalism ought to be distinguished from some other institutions with which it was indeed associated, but which are not the same thing. "Vassalage" was older than feudalism. A strong feature of the Germanic people was a keen sense of personal loyalty to one's chief or lord; probably all peoples in the tribal stage (and others as well) have it. Vassalage had earlier been associated with the Germanic institution known as *comitatus*, the service which members of a warrior-band swore to their chief, pledging him their loyalty to death, and in return being accepted, as it were, as one of the "gang," entitled to a share of the loot. Any reader of *Beowulf* or *The Song of Roland* knows that to die in defense of one's chieftain or kinfolk was regarded as the chief virtue, to fail in such duty the chief infamy. The oath of loyalty was a sacred thing. The Frankish kings bound all their servants to them by oaths of allegiance. (Governments still do.)

The fief

From the Roman side, similar practices existed in the late Empire, in the private armies which we would call freebooters. The vassals in these cases were poor, though free, men, and the conditions were the crude ones of barbarian warfare and pillaging. But the idea of vassalage became familiar and was even occasionally formalized in documents—certainly in ceremonies. It would be incorporated in government when the primitive political society of the tribe gave way to more advanced and generalized relationships.

The other ingredient which went into feudalism was the benefice, or fief, granting land not in outright ownership but for an indefinite period on condition of performing certain services. It appears that for various reasons this had become a familiar practice earlier, as a means of land distribution during the barbarian intrusions. Feudalism was, then, the marriage of vassalage and fief—in other words, *the granting of land on condition of service to the king.* This practice began with the early Carolingians, Charles Martel and Pepin the Short, who did it, seizing lands from the church, in a desperate quest for soldiers. It originated with the Carolingian kings as a result of economic and political weakness; and even Charlemagne found it extremely difficult to govern his vast realms without it. He had neither a large trained bureaucracy nor much money. It was natural to turn to the granting of power to individuals in the form of landed estates, in return for their promise to help him govern and fight. In Charlemagne's time, this granting of land to vassals (now a class of persons of considerable power and importance) who would carry out the work of government and also provide military support, became common. This association of vassalage with the holding of a fief in return for administrative and especially military service is what we properly term "feudalism."

Thus there was feudalism in Charlemagne's time, and even earlier; but it is more usual to stress it in the period that followed, when there was an even heavier dependence on it as central government grew weaker. It should be stressed that where a money economy scarcely existed, and land was almost the only source of wealth, this was about the only kind of a military or political system possible. A modern government collects taxes, and with that money trains and employs huge numbers of soldiers and bureaucrats. A medieval government had no such fiscal resources, yet had the same needs, especially for soldiers. Feudalism existed when money had all but disappeared, and one had to gain soldiers and officials of government by offering them rights to land and labor instead.

Feudalism implies a weakness on the part of central government, which cannot itself *directly* operate the services of government. However, *some* central government is logically the focus of the whole system. This government was compelled to hire its servants in a different way than a modern state would do, or any state in an advanced economy. Yet it did hire them, and the whole rationale of the feudal order was toward erecting a form of stable and effective government. Moreover the superiority of the kings had to be accepted if only theoretically. Students of feudalism have pointed out that it may actually have saved the monarchy from being extinguished altogether in the 10th and 11th centuries; "slight as was this recognition," F.L. Ganshof writes of the acknowledgment by the territorial princes that the king was in theory their superior, "it was its survival in these centuries that prevented the complete fragmentation of France."

King versus nobles

At the same time, it must be conceded that any central government which has to rely on the promise of a wealthy local potentate is not much of a government. The key men were those potentates, the great territorial vassals rather than the king. In principle, the king only gave the land "in fief" to the nobles in return for their commitment to provide him with military service on call. But the great nobles, who controlled the manors and commanded a monopoly of military might, might well be more effectively powerful than the king for obvious reasons. If the President of the United States commanded no armies directly but had to call on the governors of the states for troops, it is easy to see who would have the power even if in theory the governors were obliged to the President. The fact is that feudalism did signify the inability of political society to exist in units as large as the kingdom; it had to function in smaller units from grim necessity. During the ninth century the royal power was steadily eroded until almost none remained.

It may be said, however, that for much of Europe real government had never existed on a larger scale, and indeed the duchy or county unit represented a considerable advance over the tribalism which had existed previously. One must beware of assuming that such a "kingdom" as that of Clovis, or even Charlemagne, was something like a modern state, from which there was a huge regression in the ninth century. These kingdoms actually rested on an underlying basis of tribalism. Feudalism was in many ways, if not all, a step beyond this.

The mounted warrior

Feudalism doubtless conjures up in many minds a picture of mounted knights. Mounted knights too might exist without feudalism, and feudalism might perhaps use other kinds of vassals. But of course the change in the mode of warfare to a specialized and expensive cavalry army had much to do with the development of medieval feudalism. The old Germanic custom was that every freeman owed military service: the origins of the colonial American militia are in ancient Saxon life. But after the eighth century only a few relatively wealthy men could afford to equip themselves with horse, armor, lance—all the expensive accouterment of the medieval warrior. A technological revolution in warfare had occurred, silently, between about 700 and 850; it involved the discovery of an improved stirrup, along with the breeding of better horses, and it brought to military power the mounted and armored knight. He was costly, much more so than the old infantry or light cavalry. The equipment was expensive: horses, and armor, swords, and lances of scarce, high-quality metal.

So it became the more necessary to give substantial rewards to those who would serve as knights. Warfare became aristocratic, and helped make society so. An aristocracy existed in the ancient world, and was rapidly developed among the Germans who succeeded the Roman Empire; a landed aristocracy increased its power from the eighth century on. It now became associated with a virtual monopoly of warfare—something new—and with the feudal and manorial systems. Land and serfs were given to nobles in return for their periodic donning of the knightly panoply in order to venture forth to war, and for the protection their donjons gave to the people against rapine and pillage.

The feudal nobility

One may well stress, then, the fact that there was in feudalism some conception of central government rather than the fact that it was weaker than the modern state. But after Charlemagne kings were weak. Territorial nobles called dukes or counts (the highest vassals in the feudal hierarchy) tended to become the focus of the system, ruling over smaller territories, called duchies or counties.

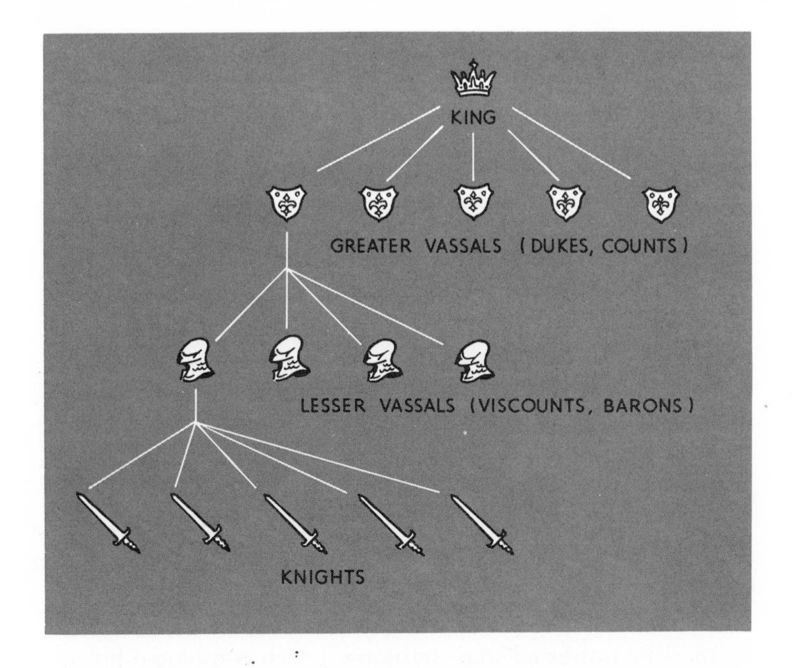

Subinfeudation

Feudalism typically involved the practice of "subinfeudation" by which each rank in the feudal hierarchy contracted with those both above and below. That is, the king gave large amounts of land to a few dukes or counts in return for their providing a number of warriors; then these high nobles turned to lesser nobles, who in turn might bargain with still lesser ones, and so on down the ladder until one got to the landless knight. So the higher nobles were dependent on lesser ones in much the same way that kings were dependent on them. The baron or chatelain or viscount, the vassals of the great vassals, just below the duke or count in the feudal scale (in France the word "vavassal," a vassal holding of a vassal, appeared), might well possess a castle of his own, command many knights; and be strong enough to defy his superior. We know of many occasions when such a breach occurred, the vassal alleging some violation of the feudal contract and solemnly renouncing allegiance. Often there was little enough the lord could do about this. Later in the Middle Ages, the great dukes might be bound closer to the king because they needed support against their own unruly barons.

Feudalism was a long chain of personal allegiances—more accurately, not one chain but an intricately interlocked series of chains. In addition to an elaborate hierarchy from the poorest knight to the proudest duke, there developed some extremely complex plural allegiances: a vassal might hold land of a half dozen different lords and in turn be himself a lord to scores of vassals. To illustrate the point only at the highest level, the Plantagenet kings of England were in one of their aspects vassals of the King of France, by virtue of being also possessors of several French dukedoms, and it would have been quite possible for the French King to have been reciprocally their vassal at the same time. Feudal relationships become incredibly complicated, and to add to the difficulty customs varied from place to place—so that a thorough understanding of the system is a matter for the experts and involves almost a lifetime's labor. Plurality of allegiances worked to weaken further the monarchy, for the king became only one liege lord among many, not *the* sovereign one: a vassal, that is to say, might owe fealty to a couple of counts as well as the king and feel them of about the same significance.

Whatever the theory, effective power concentrated in the hands of those who had castles and manors, which meant the higher levels of vassals. In feudalism each step in the hierarchy depended on the services of the vassals beneath; but the simple knight at the bottom of the ruling class did not possess any castle or have any retainers. These knights might be little more than rank-and-file soldiers, landless and in effect the dependent servants of their overlord. But they were still marked off by a large gulf from the tillers of the soil; as possessors of horse and armor, and swearers of oaths of allegiance, they belonged to the ruling aristocracy. The peasant, on the contrary, was wholly outside this circle.

Power of greater vassals

The king possessed some territories which constituted his own royal domain. But Hugh Capet, for example, the founder of the French monarchy, held only a tiny percentage of France: a scattering of lands in the Ile de France, the region around Paris. Gradually, by persistence and luck, more by alliance and marriage than conquest and war, the French state would grow from this tiny nucleus. Meanwhile the overwhelming bulk of France, or what then was known as France, consisted of the great fiefs, some of which were considerably more important than the monarchy in feudal times. Normandy, Flanders, Burgundy, Champagne, Aquitaine, and Anjou represented dynastic duchies and counties, some of them at one time kingdoms themselves, whose courts were grander than the king's, though technically they were his vassals. A similar role was played in Germany by the five great duchies of Franconia, Saxony, Swabia, Bavaria, and Lorraine. In Italy, the Iron Crown of Lombardy had no real significance; the various duchies and marquisates—for example, Tuscany, Spoleto, Benevento, and Naples—shared the field with the free cities, which represented the chief survival of urban life in Europe during the feudal centuries and which were the first cities to revive beginning in the 11th century—Venice, Genoa, Pisa, Milan, Florence, as well as Rome. In the northern part of the former middle kingdom, the county of Burgundy (that portion detached from the dukedom of Burgundy, which remained within the French zone) developed into a kingdom, but usually a weak one. If monarchy was altogether lacking from some regions, it was not much of a factor, for a long time, even where it theoretically existed.

Thus it was the dukes and counts rather than the kings who became the ganglia of power in the feudal world. They commanded the troops, issued the orders, administered such government and dispensed such justice as there was within their realms. They made their titles hereditary—which the strict theory of feudalism could hardly have admitted—while keeping the kingship elective, they being the electors. The bargain between themselves and the king they increasingly looked upon as one in which the king owed them as much as or more than they owed him; and for centuries, in France and even in England (where, as we shall see, after 1066 the monarchy was stronger than any other in Europe) a king who attempted to exercise too much power would feel the weight of their opposition. They were the effective rulers of Europe for centuries.

Life of the feudal nobility

What sort of life did the average noble lead? One thing at least is clear, that it revolved around the profession for which he existed, war. Ensconced inside their castles where there was little to do, the nobles were liable to boredom except in time of war. Hunting, as everyone knows, was one of their favorite distractions, and became a jealously guarded monopoly of the noble class; others were the various jousting and fencing encounters. Though capable of tender feelings for family and chateau, these seigneurs obviously had little taste for the quiet life, and dreamed of doing battle against man or beast when not actually so engaged. The Crusades of the 12th century represented a natural organization of their impulses. The tournament became their principal sporting event. And much medieval literature exalts war—war conceived as heroic hand-to-hand encounters between brave knights. That it might involve the desolation of peasants did not usually disturb them. Living, often, by what was in effect brigandage, becoming "robber barons" or kidnapping barons, they were often in peacetime a menace to society—to churches, monasteries, and cities, as well as peasants. The 10th-century knight was undoubtedly a rough fellow. The church attempted to soften his brutalism by such devices as the Truce of God and the Peace of God, which gradually established a custom that certain days and certain precincts were off limits for the sort of brawling that was a way of life with the feudal nobility.

Seigneurial functions of government

Still, the feudal nobility must be thought of as performing a few actions other than waging war, jousting, hunting, and brawling. They were, after all, the source of what law and government there was; the justice they dispensed might be rough, but they did serve that function. Collecting taxes and exacting other duties from his peasants, the lord in return acted as the policeman and heard disputes at a feudal court. His "seigneurial rights" included powers of keeping the peace, taxing, administering justice, and others, so that the lord was in effect mayor, tax-collector, sheriff, register of deeds, and many other functionaries all in one. His power was not in theory unlimited, for he was bound by oath to his superior and by *noblesse oblige* to honor contractual or customary agreements with his inferiors. In practice, though, it must have been difficult for a mere peasant to question or appeal from the seigneurial justice. That is one reason why the king, whose dispensation of justice served as a court of appeal later became popular with many plain people.

To his lord (the king, in the case of the higher nobles), the vassal owed both aid and counsel. The king was his "suzerain" (a very different thing from "sovereign," the later concept) to whom as such he had given an oath of loyalty; a loyal friend gives support when necessary but also advice. The remote origins of later parliamentary democracies are to be found in the feudal court where vassals assembled to confer with their suzerain. There may not have been much majesty in this arrangement in the dark period of which we write; more, perhaps, like a gangster talking with his "mob," or a tribal chief with his elders, than an orderly representative government. But in time it took on the features of majesty and dignity. In the later Middle Ages, orderly representative assemblies, along with the concepts of government by consent and the rights of subjects, such as are set forth in Magna Carta, developed out of the feudal council. It is one of the great contributions to civilization of these so-called "Dark Ages."

Peasants, serfs, and manors

The economic base that supported the feudal fighters was the manorial system. When a vassal pledged his loyalty to his lord, he was given one or more large estates with a number of unfree or semifree serfs that went with the land. It was the manor which served as the vassal's wage in return for his services to the king or other noble. Such plantations had been in existence, however, since Roman times, and only later became associated with feudalism. An effort to solve pressing agricultural problems had led the late Roman Empire to bind peasants to estates as serfs. The Roman villa often directly became the medieval one, and was a typical institution. The Germans also contributed to the institution of slavery and serfdom, for they made slaves of conquered peoples. Free farmers existed in Carolingian times, but so did the manor or villa, with its central estate-house of the noble or royal landowners, receiving rents in services and in commodities from peasants who were bound for life to their task. In the bad times of the 9th and 10th centuries, free farmers tended to disappear as all were driven to the

Scene of hunting, and pasturing swine, from an 11th century English manuscript.

protection of the guarded estate and as the need for vassals caused demand for more serf-manned estates.

The concentration of both political and economic power in essentially military hands was not a good thing. The barons were a turbulent class who lived by fighting and had little respect for the peasants who worked their lands; they frequently made bad estate managers. The tiller of the soil they typically despised as another and lesser breed because he did not fight or swear fealty; a mere beast of burden. Of course such had usually been the lot of the poor; the medieval serf was not worse off than the Roman *colonus*. But he had little chance to improve his position under this system. He was what held up the entire structure, and since his labor was so indispensable it was necessary to keep him at it. It was a static order, geared to the production of knights and not economic wealth.

The manor lord (or his bailiff) who ran the estate was seldom selected for his knowledge of agriculture or his skill in dealing with human beings. He belonged to a fighting caste, and if there was no fighting to do for king or duke he might well organize some of his own. This class became a serious problem to society in the 10th and 11th centuries. But so long as there was no safety for men outside the moated manor, and so long as the knights held a monopoly of military power, there was not much to do about them. The villeins or serfs worked their estates for them, supplied them with labor for other products made in the simple, largely self-sufficient manorial economy, and paid them rents in kind for their own land.

Status of peasants

Certainly not all medieval tillers of the soil were slaves or serfs. The villein or peasant was a free man, though in practice this might not mean much in the grimmest days of feudalism. The manor usually contained a gradation of workers ranging from household slaves or landless manual workers up to the free peasants holding land of their own on terms of service. The unfree were probably descendants of those enslaved in war, and many free peasants were part of the contractual world of feudalism, having initially made a bargain with the lord as his vassals, and being at least theoretically free to renounce it and leave. Probably in practice there was not much distinction between the free and the unfree in the earlier Middle Ages, for they were all in much the same boat. Information about the lower class of medieval times is scarce. But we know that in the course of time slavery and serfdom diminished and finally all but disappeared.

During the Crusades, the church declared that serfs had the right to take the cross and if they did so were thereby freed. In any case we should be careful to distinguish serfdom from slavery. Slaves were not very numerous in medieval society, and grew less so as the church waged determined war on slavery. Serfdom was a recognized institution, and there were at one time a great many serfs; but a serf was not a chattel; he could hold property and have his own family. His lack of freedom consisted in being bound to the soil and in having to pay services to the lord. On the other hand he was immune from military service and received the protection of having his piece of land and his niche in society, in return for the duties he owed to his lord.

The manor

On the manor, with its typically attached peasant village, a form of agriculture was practiced which we know from many familiar accounts. It was a cooperative arrangement, wherein labor and goods were pooled and the produce was shared out equally. The "open field" and "strip" system scattered the holdings of each peasant, presumably in order to equalize the good and bad land, though the plowing pattern also determined the division into strips. The heavy plow, pulled by up to eight oxen, was needed in northern Europe to break the heavy soil; the invention of this plow had much to do with making this agricultural system what it was. Working together in this cooperative system (not communist, since each took what was raised on his own acres after jointly sowing, cultivating, and harvesting the crops), the peasants could work for themselves part of the time but had to supply labor for the lord's demesne (his property) the rest of the time—a period that varied from region to region and according to the status of the individual. The worker might be completely at the mercy of the lord; he might be a free man who owed very little; or more typically he would owe a specified number of days a week, perhaps three—a heavy but at least limited burden.

Seigneurial taxes

The various taxes, fees, and exactions which the lord demanded weighed heavily on the serfs; some of them, on free peasants as well. In addition to the *corvee*, or work duty, taking a certain number of days of labor for work on the demesne, they included the banalities or fees for the use of mill, winepress, bakery, and so on—a monopoly system on the manor for which the proprietor exacted his price. And there were other taxes. A serf could pass on property to his children only if he paid a fee (*heriot*), representing the waiver of a lord's right to all his property; and there was always a marriage tax. Now all these rather arbitrary exactions may seem harsh, as indeed they were, but it must be remembered that they were the equivalent of taxes which local and national governments would collect today—the lord was the government then. We have the modern version of the *banalité* in the sales tax, and it still costs money to buy a marriage license or pay an inheritance tax; while military service, at least, is still subject to a *corvée*. It should not be forgotten that times were hard for everyone in the early Middle Ages. We must not think of the nobles as living in luxury in the 10th and 11th century. They too suffered from the lack of trade, the crudeness of the economy, the inefficiency of labor. "Fine stone castles, silken raiment, and spices had to await the reappearance of merchants and the money to hire skilled labor."

Ways of escaping serfdom

Of the serf system in general it may be said, as is said of slavery in the old South of the United States, that while it was productive of much cruelty and injustice, at least a lord or bailiff's interest had to lie in keeping his

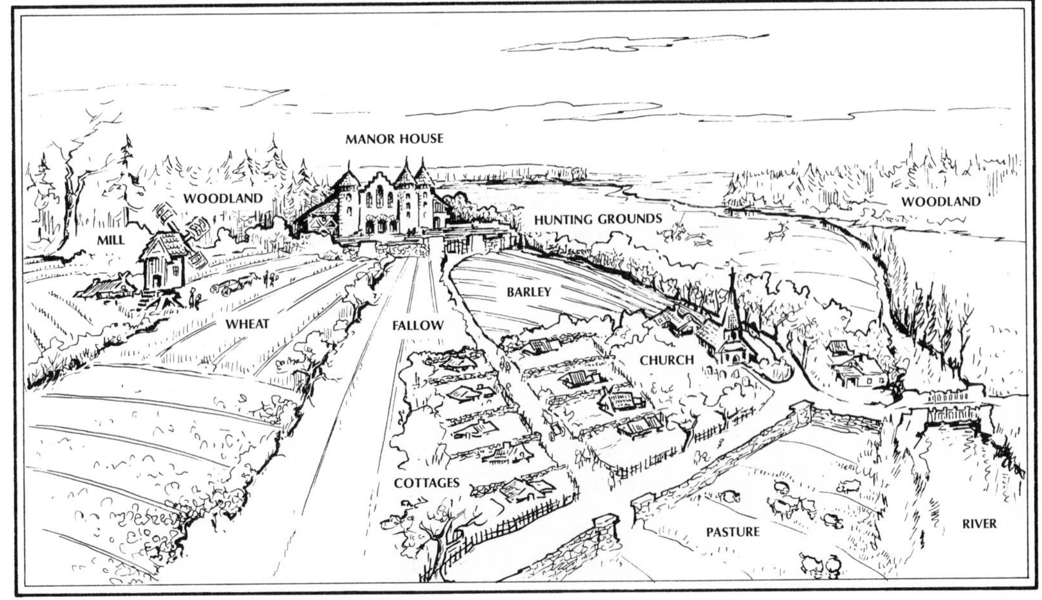

A medieval manor

workers reasonably content, certainly not in killing them off through excessive exactions. Labor was scarce and valuable at this time, population being quite small by later standards. Custom, the efforts of the church, and the economic self-interest of the lords combined to mollify the ill-treatment of serfs. In the 12th century seigneurs encouraged the planting of new villages by holding out release from serfdom to those who would settle them.

Peasants could not ordinarily dream of leaping the gulf that existed between the toiling and the fighting castes. They might enter the church with the permission of the lord, and conceivably rise high. The serf might shake off his servitude by marrying a free peasant (the rule was that children took their mother's status), by living in a town for a year and a day, or later by commuting his work services to a cash payment. Later, when towns and cities appeared in significant numbers with the revival of trade, he might get to the city; but opportunities to escape from the dismal trap of manorialism were hardly plentiful until the later Middle Ages. However, serfdom undeniably diminished rather steadily through the Middle Ages. Whether theoretically free or bond, the laboring class had in practice little choice but to continue toiling on the manor and paying the lord's price for his protection. Nevertheless what information we have about the life of the medieval peasant does not suggest that it was entirely joyless. There were holidays, on which the folk danced and sang; there were fairs, which brought strange sights and sounds; and from earliest medieval times there were wandering minstrels.

As for the lord's uncertain justice, there had been an appeal from it in Charlemagne's time to the *missi dominici*, the traveling emissaries of royal justice, who occasionally checked in to see if things were going properly;

Otto the Great who founded the Holy Roman Empire.

The crown imperial made for Otto the Great, about 960. Gold plaques surrounded with emeralds and sapphires depict the secular and sacred roles of the emperor.

and later, when the kings recovered some power, they would do the same. The age of feudalism proper, however, lies in the centuries between the 9th and 12th when the royal power was at its nadir.

The beginnings of recovery

In the 10th century Europe began to dig herself out of the blizzard that hit her about 850 to 900, a dreadful half-century which included the final disintegration of the Frankish Empire, the destructive attacks of Norsemen and Hungarians, the reduction of society to its lowest common denominator, the self-sufficient manor, and the fragmentation of political rule down almost to the level of the robber baron. It is significant that the 10th century brought church reform as one of its few bright spots. For the church, degraded though it was in this era, was to be very much involved in the process of recovery. The great events and institutions of the era that lay ahead included crusades, cathedrals, universities, papal supremacy.

Otto the Great and the Saxon emperors

But the recovery of civil order was the basic process. Only when life was once again reasonably secure could trade and industry revive, or intellectual culture appear. Progress in this direction came slowly. In Germany, the Saxon leader Otto the Great defeated the Hungarians at Augsburg in 955 and reconstituted the Empire in 962. By his prestige won as savior of Europe from the Hungarians, Otto deserved the imperial title in the opinion of his vassals. After struggling awhile with the duchies, Otto perceived that a single powerful state was out of the question. The strength of localism is indicated by the fact that while Otto was able to defeat and remove the rebellious dukes and appoint new ones from his own family, these allies turned against him after living for a time in their territories. Local patriotism in the duchies was a very real force. It should be realized that even today such units as Bavaria, Saxony, and Swabia preserve their regional characteristics and sense of identity.

But the monarchy in Germany was at this time stronger than elswhere: out of the wreckage of the Carolingian Empire, France (or what was then called the West Frankish kingdom) emerged the most fragmented, in part because of the Viking attacks. The classic pattern of feudalism developed first in France. The old eastern kingdom in Germany held together somewhat better at this time; its turn to dissolve came later.

Otto allied himself to the church on terms which made the church as useful to his Empire as he was to the church. Virtually controlling the papacy, having deposed the unworthy John XII and put one of his own subordinates in the chair, Otto went far toward making the territorial church an arm of his state. He built a magnificent Empire by conquest and statesmanship, though he had to accept the local dominance of the dukes (Lorraine, Franconia, Swabia, Bavaria) who would recognize him as Emperor only with limited powers. Otto's Empire extended into Italy and even into part of France, while on the Slavic frontier he pushed eastward. Some historians have criticized him for setting his sights too high and bequeathing to his successors an impossibly large domain. But at the time it was a great achievement and raised the hopes of men for restoring a true state. Otto I was in many ways no unworthy successor of Charlemagne. His descendants preserved the Ottonian Empire for two centuries. Thus was the idea of the Roman Empire kept alive. It was in the process of evolving toward the Holy Roman Empire. But Otto was also the German king. This confusion of roles was in the future to prove costly to Germany.

Capetian kings of France

In France, 987 is the date from which the great French monarchy began a long career destined to last until 1792. Hugh Capet, elected by the magnates to the kingship in 987, was the offspring of a family that had been important for a century, ever since Eudes or Odo, Count of Paris, distinguished himself in warfare against the Norsemen and was elected King of the West Franks in 888. Hugh Capet gained the throne after Otto II attacked the Franks in a quarrel over Lorraine; allying himself with the German Emperor, he sacrificed his claim to this province—not a very glorious way for a French ruler to begin. Hugh Capet demanded and secured the succession of his own son, and the Capetian line successfully carried on this practice; but for long they were still in theory elected by the feudal magnates.

Thus Hugh Capet, the first of what turned out to be a long dynasty, was actually neither much more nor much less impotent than the kings immediately preceding and following him. The great nobles—Burgundy, Flanders, Aquitaine, Champagne, Poitou, Gascony, Brittany, Anjou—elected the king; it now happened that the royal power stayed in one family. But for a long time the king was still much at the mercy of his powerful vassals, the dukes and counts. France was the classic land of feudalism, and its provincial tendencies took strong root. Nevertheless, the Normans having ceased to be disturbers of the peace, reconstruction began. Though organized at first around the duchy rather than the kingdom, stable government based on law began to develop.

Wessex kings of England

In England, the Danish troubles brought forth a great King, the Wessex leader Alfred, whom England named "the Great" and who lived in legend ever after. The Wessex kings beat back the Danes, reconquered the "Danelaw" and became rulers of a united England with its capital at Winchester, a remarkable achievement for this stage of European history. It was the first time all England had been united in one kingdom. In 973 King Edgar, who received the submission of Welsh and Scottish kings, had, so we are told, 3,600 ships, doubtless an exaggeration but indicative of considerable power. The Danes, like the Normans in France, settled down to become Christians and good citizens. Numerous place names in East Anglia and the north of England betray a Danish origin. Unfortunately more Viking raids came, and the Wessex line deteriorated, the last king bearing the revealing name of Ethelred the Unready. In 1016 there came to the throne a Danish king, the famous Canute, a well-liked and capable ruler. Whether the English state was in good or bad shape when the Normans came remains a matter of some controversy. It seems to have been at least as united as anything on the Continent. But in 1066 the Norman conquest brought in a new era, from which time dates the emergence of a really strong monarchy.

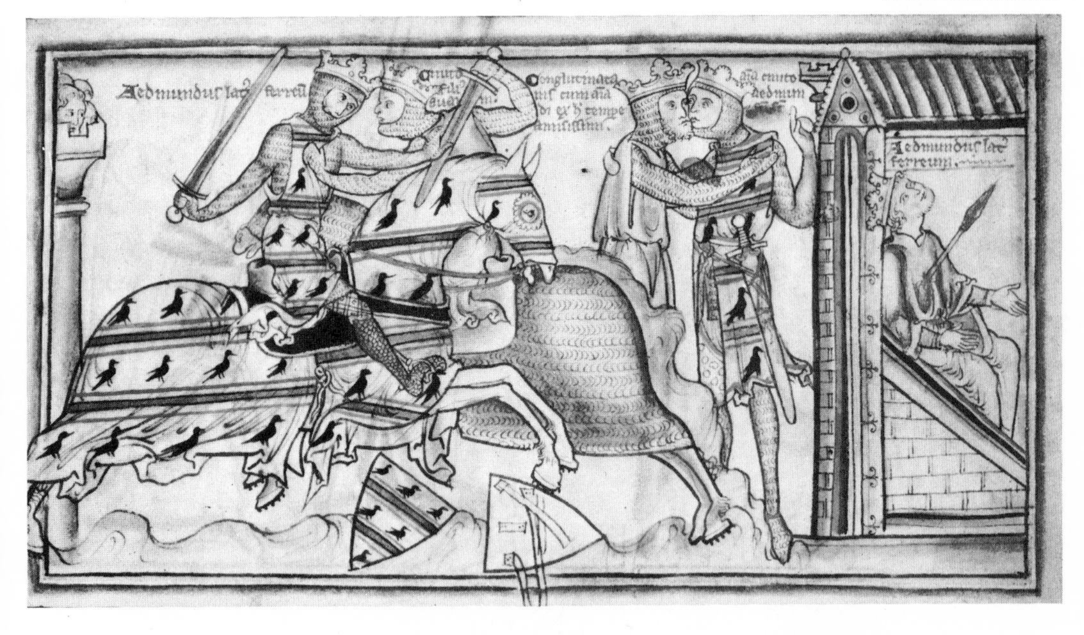

Canute defeated Edmund Ironside and was made king at Edmund's death.

The papacy

Italy suffered from Saracen as well as the Magyar raids and from internal dissension. During this period of degradation everywhere in Europe, the papacy shared in it to the fullest. It became the plaything of political intrigue, and was the cause of dozens of petty wars. Ambitious nobles from across the Alps, from France or Burgundy or southern Germany, came there to seek power and wealth. The domination of the Saxon emperors after 962 did not please the Italian nobles, and also set up a conflict with the papacy. But the 11th century saw a noble revival in the prestige and the power of the pope; Gregory VII came to lead the medieval papacy toward its place at the pinnacle of all Europe. Of this more later.

Thus in general the period between about 950 and 1000 brought some advance, if slow and uneven, toward more orderly society and competent government. The emergence of towns or cities accompanied this advance. While fortified places never ceased to exist during the worst times of disorder and poverty in the ninth century, often on the site of what had been and would again be important cities, these places were not at that time engaged in any commercial or industrial activities of any consequence, nor did they have an independent organization. In other words, there were virtually no cities as we think of them through much of the 8th, 9th, and 10th centuries. Ahead there lay a most significant place for them, as they became occupied

leofode. 7 on þisum gere ec swac Harðacnut Eadulf eorl
under his griðe. 7 he wæs þa wedloga.
M.xlii. Her geforð Harðacnut swa þ he æt his drince stod 7 he
færinga feoll to þære eorðan mid egeslicum anginne
7 hine gelæhton ðe þær neh wæron 7 he syððan nan word
ne gecwæð. 7 he forðferde on vi. id. iun. 7 eall folc
underfengan Eadward to cinge swa him gecynde wæs.
M.xliii. Her wæs Eadward gehalgod to cinge on Wincestre on for-
man Easterdæg mid mycclum wyrðscype. 7 ða wæron
Eastron .iii. non. apl. Eadsige arcebiscop hine halgade
7 toforan eallum þam folce hine wel lærde. 7 to his agenre
neode 7 ealles folces wel manude. 7 Stigant preost
wæs gebletsad to biscop to East englum. 7 raðe þæs se cing
let geridan ealle þa land þe his modor ahte him to handa.
7 nam of hire eall þ heo ahte on golde 7 on seolfre.
7 on unasecgendlicum þingum. forðam heo hit heold ær
to fæste wið hine. 7 raðe þæs man sette Stigant of his
biscoprice. 7 nam eall þ he ahte þam cinge to handa.
forðam he wæs nehst his modor ræde. 7 heo for swa
swa he hire rædde. þæs ðe men wendon.
M.xliiii. Her Eadsige arceb forlet þ biscoprice for his untrum-
nysse. 7 bletsade þærto Siward abb of abbandune to bi-
scope be ðæs cinges leafe 7 ræde. 7 Godwines eorles.
Hit wæs elles feawum mannum cuð ær hit gedon wæs.
forðam se arceb wende þ hit sum oðer man abiddan
wolde oððe gebicgan þe he wyrs truwode 7 uðe gif hit
ma manna wiste. 7 on ðisum gere wæs swyðe mycel hungr

Page from the Anglo-Saxon Chronicle. Compilation of this early history begun under Alfred the Great extended from 892 to 1154.

by a new class, the bourgeoisie, and developed their own distinctive form of communal organization. They will be the means by which the stagnant and static class system of the manor breaks up, and by means of which kings will regain their lost powers. In the later or high Middle Ages urban life will be the crowning glory of Europe, a vast transformation indeed from the days of castles, manors, and serfs in unrelieved monotony. When exactly did these cities begin? It is a question which is much the same as asking when Europe began to recover and advance toward medieval civilization. The answer is, pretty clearly, at the end of the 10th and during the 11th centuries, for most of Europe. Venice was always the great exception, and the Italian cities stirred earlier than those on the other side of the Alps.

For Europe generally the year 900 marked about the low point, and the 10th century was an improvement on the 9th, suggestive of a man who has been felled by a knockout blow slowly getting to his feet and clearing his head. In the 11th century he will be ready to resume his battle to build a civilization, with the signs of his success appearing markedly in the 12th century.

Monastic culture and reform

Learning in the early Middle Ages

Meanwhile, the monasteries continued to serve as the chief foci of culture. Within their walls learning was at least preserved, books sometimes written. Nevertheless the great classical heritage wore pretty thin. Between Augustine and Anselm (c. 400 to 1100) there is almost nothing in Europe that can be called really original or monumental in thought. There are interesting lesser figures. The notion of complete darkness is a myth, but compared to both earlier and later epochs thought was definitely inferior. There was some good local history; there was Scriptural commentary, which tended to repeat the patristic writers (Ambrose, Jerome, Augustine, Gregory) with little change, while a passion for allegory and symbolism led the theological imagination into bizarre paths. The isolation of men from each other due to difficulties of communication was responsible for this stagnation. Advanced thought demands the possession of a great many tools which are present only when society is secure, with many libraries, institutions of learning, places where men of letters may mingle together. These conditions were not met in the Dark Ages. It is significant that an approach to intellectual renaissance came when Charlemagne established his state, and wilted away when that ephemeral Empire dissolved; similarly, a kind of renaissance is associated with the Ottonian emperors. The Ottonian Renaissance was fairly slight but did produce some interesting minor art and some new schools—all centered on the monasteries.

The monasteries were invaluable, yet they tended to isolation, so that what might be done in one was with extreme difficulty transmitted elsewhere to become part of a social accumulation of knowledge. We read of monks who set out to search for others who were working in their field of interest, but not knowing where to find them they could only wander for years until

INCP LIBER
MACHABAEOR
T FACTUM E
postquam percus
sit alexander phi
lippo macedo qui
primus regnauit
in grecia.
Egressus de terra
cetthim darium
regem persarum et
medorum constituit
prelia multa et om
nium obtinuit muniti
ones et interfecit re
ges terrae et pertransiit usq; ad fines terrae et ac

Book of Maccabees in the Alcuin Bible, with minuscule script and ornamented initial, produced in ninth-century monasteries.

they found, or perhaps did not find, some kindred spirits. It is the story of early medieval life.

But some excellent art existed, as monks in their daily work illuminated manuscripts and wrote music for the church services—or sometimes for their own delight made verses. The origin of the later medieval music, drama, and poetry is to be found in the ninth century. The glories of the 13th century lie well ahead, but it is possible to see a great epoch of civilization germinating much earlier.

Outstanding abbeys

Thus the monasteries—some of them at least—were capable of producing a rich if cloistered and narrowly clerical culture. One must not suppose that all of them were centers of light. Most were not, but there were many, and at one place or another something creative was going on. It has been suggested that the diversity of European society saved it, for unlike a single-headed Byzantine state, it had many small ganglia and even the savagery of the Dark Ages could not kill them all. At one time Cassino and the Irish centers, at another Fulda and St. Gall, Northumberland, Bec, or Cluny—all these places played crucial roles, and there were others. Fulda, in Franconia, and other monasteries founded by Boniface of England in the eighth century were prominent among those which placed stress on scholarship. So also the Irish-founded St. Gall in Switzerland.

In 910, a movement began in the abbey at Cluny, in Burgundy, the initial goal of which was simply the restoration of religious discipline, piety, adherence to Benedict's rule. It received the active support of the dukes of Aquitaine. By a system of daughter abbeys which maintained a close relationship to the original foundation, the spirit of Cluny spread all over Christendom. It was responsible for the reformed papacy of the next century, but it flowered into learning as well as piety. The Cluniac monastery at Fleury on the Loire played a significant part in the recovery of knowledge early in the 11th century. It is worth noting that Cluny had the unusual status of exemption from the feudal order and thus was in a position to combat the pernicious effects of this system on the church and religious life, effects which often turned bishops and abbots into feudal warriors.

Gerbert, a man who studied in Spain and learned Arabian science, and who then became head of the cathedral school at Reims, was a product of the Cluniac movement. He became Pope Sylvester II in the year 999. Earlier, we see him playing some part in getting Hugh Capet established on his throne. It is from Gerbert's appearance at Reims in 972 that we can date the dim beginnings of the new era in Europe that succeeded the Dark Ages and led on to the impressive civilization of the 12th and 13th centuries. The schools at Reims and at Chartres, founded by a pupil of Gerbert's, led the way toward the medieval universities.

St. Anselm

Thus certain monasteries invariably produced the movements of intellectual and cultural significance. The Norman abbey of Bec was another such: there in the 11th century taught Anselm, the first original philosopher since Augustine, save for John Scotus Erigena in Carolingian times. The Italian-born St. Anselm, prior of Bec and also Archbishop of Canterbury, illustrates the cosmopolitan character of medieval thought; he may also be said to have been the initiator of Scholasticism, the typical medieval system of ideas which flowered in the 13th century. Scholasticism was concerned to reconcile faith (Christian dogma) with reason (Greek philosophy) through the method of formal logic. Anselm's "entire position rests upon the primacy of faith" to a much greater degree than does St. Thomas Aquinas' later; but he believed with St. Augustine that faith unlocks the doors of reason and that the rational proofs of Christianity are of value. He was most famous for his "ontological" proof of the existence of God, an argument from the existence of the idea of God in our minds to the reality of God, involving the ingenious proposition that if we can form the notion of an absolutely perfect being then that being must exist, for existence is an attribute of perfection!

It need not be pointed out that Anselm was hardly a typical monk. The monks, as well as the higher secular clergy, were drawn into feudalism. As landowners the monasteries managed their estates much as any other lords of manors in the feudal era. Indeed, because the monks kept better records, we know more about life on a medieval manor from them than from other sources. They were probably somewhat more efficient and humane than other landlords, but their serfs and peasants performed their duties in much the same way as elsewhere. Abbeys often were to become very wealthy later in the Middle Ages. They might supply knights like other manors, though they sometimes paid an army tax in money or in supplies. The originally secluded monks were drawn into the world of affairs as time went on; seldom could they maintain their aloofness from life. It is the reason why Cluny had to arise in order to purge the church of laxness and worldliness, and recall it to the service of God which it was inclined to forget.

Bibliography

The complex question of feudalism is handled from varying prespectives by Carl Stephenson, *Medieval Feudalism* (Cornell University Press); R. Coulborn, *Feudalism in History* (Princeton, N.J.: Princeton University Press, 1956); F.L. Ganshof, *Feudalism* (Harper Torchbook); and Marc Bloch, *Feudal Society* (Chicago: University of Chicago Press, 1961). See also I.J. Sanders, *Feudal Military Service in England* (New York: Oxford University Press, 1956). The social and economic pattern of the manorial age can be studied in such works as G.G. Coulton, *Medieval Village, Manor, and Monastery* (Harper Torchbook); H.S. Bennett, *Life on the English Manor* (though descriptive of a somewhat later period) (Cambridge University Press); and Robert Latouche, *The Birth of Western Economy* (rev. ed.; London: Methuen Publications, 1967), a valuable book. The distinguished French medievalist Marc Bloch also has had his *Land and Work in Medieval Europe* translated into English (London: Routledge & Kegan Paul,

1967). Lynn White, Jr., *Medieval Technology and Social Change* (Oxford University Press), is a rich and revealing work of synthesis on an extraordinarily interesting subject. Additionally for those interested in medieval agriculture, C.S. Orwin, *The Open Fields* (3d ed.; Oxford: Clarendon Press, 1967), and Vol. I of the Cambridge Economic History of Europe, edited by M.M. Postan, *Agrarian Life of the Middle Ages*.

The political history of this period of the dim beginnings of national states is covered in Robert Fawtier, *The Capetian Kings of France* (New York: St. Martin's Press, 1959); Geoffrey Barraclough, *The Origins of Modern Germany* (G.P. Putnam's Sons, Capricorn); Peter Hunter Blair, *An Introduction to Anglo-Saxon England* (New York: Cambridge University Press, 1956); and Doris M. Stenton, *English Society in the Early Middle Ages* (Pelican History of England, Penguin Books). H. Arbman, *The Vikings* (London: Edward Arnold, 1962), further documents the singular story of the Norse eruption. The other people whose expansion so affected the destiny of Europe is the subject of books by X. de Planhol, *The World of Islam* (Ithaca, N.Y.: Cornell University Press, 1959); G.E. von Grunebaum, *Medieval Islam* (University of Chicago Press, Phoenix); H.A.L. Gibb, *Studies in the Civilization of Islam* (Boston: Beacon Press, 1962), and the same distinguished orientalist's *Mohammedanism: An Historical Survey* (Oxford University Press, Galaxy).

C.W. Oman, *The Art of War in the Middle Ages*, covering an important topic, has been reprinted by the Cornell University Press in paperback. Leon Gautier's *Chivalry* has been translated from French and issued by Barnes & Noble (New York, 1959). The striking portrait of this age of European thought and culture by R.W. Southern, *The Making of the Middle Ages*, is now in a Yale University Press paperback. David Knowles and R.N. Hancock, *The Religious Orders in England*, Vol. I (Cambridge University Press, 1948), continues the always fascinating story of monastic life. Knowles' *Saints and Scholars* (Cambridge University Press) is selected from his larger works. Southern has also written of *St. Anselm and His Biographer* (Cambridge University Press, 1963).

For some source readings, see Norton Downs (ed.), *Basic Documents in Medieval History* (D. Van Nostrand); in the Thomas Nelson & Sons Medieval Texts, Asser's *Life of Alfred*; and in the Columbia University Records of Civilization series, *The Peterborough Chronicle*. A recent edition of the *Anglo-Saxon Chronicle*, Whitelock, Douglas, and Tucker (eds.), has been issued by Eyre and Spottiswoode. Jacqueline Simpson, *The Northmen Talk* (Madison: University of Wisconsin Press, 1965) is an important collection of Icelandic tales. Southern has edited *The Life of Anselm by Ealmer* for the Nelson Texts (London: Thomas Nelson & Sons, 1962).

Christopher N.L. Brooke, *Europe in the Central Middle Ages 962–1154* (New York: Holt, Rinehart & Winston, 1964), and Zachary N. Brooke, *A History of Europe 911–1158* (Methuen Publications, 1951), are standard accounts for this general period. In the series on Social and Economic History published by Longmans and edited by Asa Briggs, Vol. I is H.R. Loyn, *Anglo-Saxon England and the Norman Conquest* (London: Longmans, Green & Co., 1962).

6

Europe advances toward civilization: 1000-1200

chronology

1050
Beginning of Byzantine decline.
1054
Final schism between Roman and Eastern (Greek Orthodox) churches.
1066
William, Duke of Normandy, invades England and takes throne; reorganization of English political order.
1073–85
Gregory VII, Pope.
1077
German Emperor does penance before Gregory VII at Canossa.
1079–1142
Peter Abelard, pioneer teacher and philosopher.
1080–1100
Romanesque architecture. Rise of towns.
Construction of St. Mark's, Venice.
Recovery of Toledo and Valencia from Islam.
1090–1153
Bernard of Clairvaux.
1095
Pope Urban II proclaims First Crusade.

The 12th century walled city of Carcassonne in France.

1099
Death of the Cid, Spanish national hero.
Capture of Jerusalem by crusaders.
1108–37
Louis VI, beginnings of effective monarchy in France.
1109
Death of Anselm, first medieval philosopher.
1122
Concordat of Worms, compromising investiture controversy.
1125
Guelf-Ghibelline feud, new papal-imperial conflict.
1137
Union of Catalonia and Aragon in Spain.
1143
Arnold of Brescia, Roman revolt against papacy.
1147–49
Second Crusade; influenced by Bernard of Clairvaux.
1152–90
Frederick I (Barbarossa), Hohenstaufen emperor.
1154–89
Reign of Henry II in England.
1159
Peter Lombard's *Sentences*. Period of translations from the Arabic.
Barbarossa invades Italy.
Henry the Lion, Prince beyond the Elbe, develops that region of Germany.
1162
Clash between Henry II of England and Thomas Becket, Archbishop of Canterbury.
1170
Becket's murder at Canterbury.
Beginnings of University of Paris; rise of universities.
1176
Defeat of Barbarossa by Italian burghers at Legnano.
1180
Death of John of Salisbury, medieval humanist.
1180–1223
Philip II (Augustus), King of France.
1189–92
Third Crusade (Philip Augustus, Frederick Barbarossa, Richard Coeur de Lion).
1194–99
War between Philip II and Richard of England over latter's holdings in France.
1197–1212
War between the Guelfs and the Ghibellines.
1202–4
Fourth Crusade; Venetian conquests in the Near East.
1208–13
Albigensian crusade.
1212
Alfonso VIII's decisive victory over the Muslims in Spain.

The advance of Europe

Europe in 1000

Let us sum up the condition of Europe about the year 1000. Apart from a few monks, there was little real civilization, even among the ruling class. "Inheritance and environment had combined to give the nobles of eleventh-century France the personal characteristics of fierce, undisciplined warrior chieftains," begins a distinguished book by Sidney Painter on the subject of chivalry. Warlike and arrogant, the nobles gained their living from the serfs or villeins who tilled the soil, but they did not themselves live in anything like luxury, for Europe was still economically primitive. Not much that could be called architecture yet existed, nor painting nor sculpture. Population was small by later standards; much of the land was still covered with forests. Clothing, food, and housing were crude. In relations among men, force—naked and brutal—was likely to be the determining factor. True it was that the feudal system provided for certain clearly recognized, even legally enforceable rules: chiefly the duties of a vassal to his lord, defined rather exactly and subject to sanctions if not fulfilled. This was the beginning of a legal order in Europe, but it was only a beginning. Kings were thoroughly intimidated, and the barons held a monopoly of military power. A mercantile class was as yet confined to a few peddlers, except for fairs held from time to time. Only a few cathedral schools kept learning alive at an elementary level; nor had the revival of cities begun save in a few exceptional instances. Wherever you look, in whatever phase of society, the story is much the same.

In the next three centuries all this was to change enormously. By the time we reach the end of the 13th century—the France of Philip the Fair, say—we have entered another world, which ought not to be placed in the category of the earlier Middle Ages, though old custom decrees the use of the same term to cover both. It is a world of breathtaking architecture, costly raiment, fine towns and cities. Kings have again become great and have impressive courts. The nobility itself has lost its crudeness and has taken up the soft ways of courtly chivalry, making verses or love where they formerly made war. Forests have been cleared, and population has increased. There is a money economy. Universities teach advanced studies, while the most energetic of the religious orders are no longer monks living in seclusion but friars who live in and serve the cities. The Roman law has been revived and parliaments are meeting.

Thus these three centuries, between about 1000 to 1300, mark probably the most exciting advance in the history of Europe. They include a "renaissance"—the Twelfth-Century Renaissance—which some historians have held to be more important than the more renowned Italian Renaissance of the 15th century. They include the making of the state, the revival of economic life, and the emergence of cities.

Causes of European recovery

How did this change come about? First, after the Hungarians and Norsemen settled down, western Europe was not disturbed by any more wholesale incursions of barbarian peoples. Later, Mongols and Turks came, but the

11th century Benedictine abbey, Jumiéges, France

The 12th century church of the Magdalen at Vézelay is a splendid example of the assurance and mastery of Romanesque style.

Nave of the Romanesque Durham cathedral with probably the earliest rib-vaults in Europe.

The cathedral of St. Martin at Lucca, Italy.

blows were absorbed by the unfortunate peoples of eastern and southeastern Europe. Settled political and economic life had a chance to take root. There was at the same time a recession of the Arab tide, which gave Europe an opportunity to renew contact with far more advanced places in the Mediterranean, from which both knowledge and wealth were to flow. Christian access to Spain and Sicily was the prime cause of an intellectual awakening in the 12th century. The first four Crusades, 1095–1204, furthered this contact with older and richer civilizations. An important revival of trade came, and with it towns and cities, breaking up the stagnation of the manorial economy, making many political and social changes possible.

One such was the significant matter of central government. Feudalism and the manorial economy deprived the king of power because he had no funds. By collecting taxes, kings could create their own military forces and governments, breaking their dependence on the nobility.

Standing out above the rest in the realm of politics were two significant events of the 11th century: the Norman conquest of England and the struggle of the papacy with the imperial power. The Battle of Hastings, 1066, and the Emperor's penance at Canossa, 1077, find their way into every list of great dates.

The Norman conquest

In regard to the former, historical opinion today generally agrees that the Norman conquest was for England a major step forward. The conquest of Anglo-Saxon England by foreigners was a bitter thing, and there have always been Englishmen who remember it as a wrong. There have also been those who identified the Anglo-Saxon society of preconquest times with freedom, and wrote of "Norman tyranny." In reaction, another opinion has insisted that England was on the verge of disintegration until the Normans brought over some organization.

The best recent scholarship emphasizes some continuity. The English had already made much progress in government; the Normans who came over in 1066 led by the claimant to the throne of England, Duke William (William I of England), were hardly any more civilized. They had been settled in Normandy but a century and a half, and were notable chiefly for a considerable enthusiasm for monastic Christianity. (The importance of the abbey at Bec has already been noted.) But the erstwhile Vikings were still none too gentle, and William, after gaining the victory over Harold Godwin in 1066, proceeded to scourge the country ruthlessly of all resistance. In the North he left no village standing between York and Durham, an enterprise which for sheer destructive barbarity hardly has an equal even in the bloody annals of the Dark Ages.

Nevertheless the new order the Normans imposed upon England proved in the long run much stronger and more stable than the old. They made strong and able kings. A well-organized feudalism was established, with all lands held either by the crown directly or by the great nobles. Norman feudalism already had a strong central power before the invasion of England; it was a less decentralized feudalism than elsewhere in northern Europe. Subtenants, the lesser vassals subinfeudated by the tenants-in-chief, owed a loyalty directly to the king, not just to their immediate feudal superior. This was a novelty in feudal agreements. If a tenant-in-chief died without an heir his lands reverted to the crown. Having made it clear at the beginning by terrible tactics that they intended to rule in England, William and his successors held the upper hand over the feudal nobility to a greater extent than most other places in Europe. As everywhere under feudalism, the nobles held great power, but they came closer to being controlled in England. The Normans, as newcomers making a clean sweep, were able to establish a uniquely strong kingdom in England. And except for a brief period of anarchy, 1135–54, there was over a century of continuously energetic rule, culminating in the enlightened genius of medieval England's greatest King, Henry II, 1154–89. This was perhaps "tyranny," but in fact what Europe needed for growth at this time was stronger government, for purposes of order, protection of life and property, and economic units large enough for trade. Norman England led the way in this direction.

Canossa

Elsewhere in Europe, the battle between the German emperors and the papacy held the center of attention. While the King of France was still of no great account, the German Emperor was a personage of considerable dignity and importance. In the middle of the 11th century he received the homage of peoples all the way from French-speaking Lotharians to Poles and Bohemians of the Slavic frontier; as "Holy Roman Emperor of the Germanic nation" he dominated the church and was suzerain in northern Italy. It is true that he no more directly controlled these vast fiefs than did the King of France; he merely received an oath of allegiance from the nobles as they continued to rule their own local domains. He spent a great deal of his time going about to suppress or cow rebels, and indeed had no fixed residence or capital. But his role as Emperor and the nominal allegiance of so many vassals gave him a standing much beyond any other prince in Europe at this time.

Cluny and church reform

In the 11th century he faced a papacy reviving from a period of abysmal disorder in the previous centuries. In feudal Europe the church had become feudalized, and was the plaything of the nobility. Popes had been elected through disgraceful violence and intrigue; bishops and archbishops were hardly distinguishable from barons and counts. The Cluniac movement brought in a spirit of reform. The reform party struggled to purge the church of such laxities as simony (selling church offices) and the marriage of priests, which had become common. They also worked to free the church from the grip of the secular rulers—especially the Emperor, who controlled the papacy and used it to strengthen his state. Reform and papalism were here closely associated: to free themselves from feudal nobles, bishops would look to a strong leader at Rome. The church required such leadership to win inde-

The Battle of Hastings, 1066. Harold is struck down and killed by a Norman.

pendence, to shake itself free from a worldly order. But the spirit of Cluny was slow to capture the papacy, permeated as it was by politics.

Emperors and kings, accustomed to use churchmen in the tasks of civil administration, tended to think of these as their servants. The church had become so involved in the feudal system that bishops received fiefs in the same manner as lay lords and it was natural to think of them as of the same order. Monasteries and churches being protected by the monarch or noble, the latter thought it reasonable that he should make the appointments. In any case no one thought of a separation between civil and ecclesiastical authority, *regnum* and *sacerdotium*—they were two aspects of the same order. And Roman precedent, from Constantine to Charlemagne, supported the idea that the apex of the pyramid was after all the emperor, source of all power. The effort of the papacy to wrench itself free, declare its independence of secular domination, also inevitably involved a counterassertion that it was the pope rather than the emperor who occupied the top spot, and could if necessary overrule secular authority. But initially the goal of reform seems to have been the more immediate one of simply shaking off what was felt to be degrading and corrupting lay control. The emperors had grown accustomed to dictating the choice of the pope himself; but in 1059 control of papal elections was invested in the College of Cardinals. The papacy turned for support against the emperor to the Norman rulers of Naples and Sicily, playing them off against the emperor as well as threatening to release his feudal vassals from their obligations. In connection with this great revival of the papacy, which is so important a process in the 11th century, the final break with Constantinople (1054) should be mentioned; it expressed the full independence of the western church, which had determined to assert its own authority and make pretensions to universal power.

Investiture controversy

Although several reforming popes preceded the great Gregory VII (Pope from 1073–85), none asserted more energetically his power against the emperor. Gregory VII was a monk named Hildebrand, of humble birth, who had been at Cluny, that focus of all religious reform. The great conflict in which he became involved with Emperor Henry IV was about the right of a lay ruler to *invest* a bishop or abbot, that is, formally give him the insignia of his office. It had become the custom of the monarch to do so and in return receive an act of feudal homage. The issue clearly concerned the independence of the church or its control by the secular state. After the Emperor replied to Gregory's prohibition of lay investiture by declaring him deposed, Gregory did not hesitate to excommunicate the recalcitrant German Emperor and declare his subjects released from their oaths of obedience. Henry's vassals in Germany seemed only too happy to oblige the Pope. For three days at Canossa in 1077, the temporarily checkmated Emperor had to do penance in the snow outside the castle where Gregory was staying. The singular nobility of Hildebrand's character and the loftiness of his ideal—a purified church freed from worldliness, acting as the spiritual leader of all Europe, correcting even kings if they strayed from the path of righteousness—sank deeply into the consciousness of Europe. Eventually Henry overcame his recalcitrant vassals and marched on Rome to depose Gregory and elect another pope (1084). Gregory in defeat and death was the maker of the medieval papacy. Despite his tragic end, he had done much to free the papacy from its humiliating subjection to the secular authority.

Urban II, French Pope who wore the tiara soon after Gregory, vigorously carried on the policy of a papacy independent of control by the emperors. He was the Pope who proclaimed the First Crusade in 1095 (see below). The

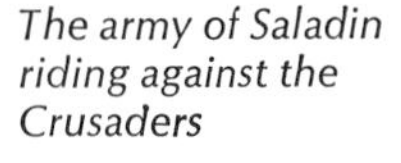

The army of Saladin riding against the Crusaders

relative success of this enterprise added luster to the papal crown, and subsequent popes were emboldened to continue their struggles with kings. Battles over investiture went on. In 1122 at the Concordat of Worms, a compromise formula was agreed upon, which actually followed closely the terms of an earlier agreement between the Pope and the English King: the formal installation of bishops and abbots would be performed by a clergyman, and they would be chosen by the cathedral or monastic chapter; however, the chosen prelate had to be acceptable to the King and had to pay homage to the King. This compromise scarcely settled all the issues in the smoldering feud between the two swords.

Bernard of Clairvaux

When, in the 12th century, the higher clergy again showed signs of weakness and corruption, new reformers arose to renew the spirit of Cluny. Of these the greatest was Bernard of Clairvaux (1090–1153). Saint and mystic as well as vigorous reform leader, the leading spirit of the Cistercian abbeys was a remarkable figure. In his attitude to the new learning then beginning to enter Europe he appears as a reactionary, but his spirituality was deep and real. Almost four centuries later Martin Luther would find in him an important basis for the Protestant theology that shook the unity of Christian Europe. But St. Bernard chose to remain within the church, purifying it rather than destroying it; his spirit insured that the church would remain united and strong through the Middle Ages, able always to struggle against secular control and worldliness if not always able to achieve the high ideals of a Gregory or a Bernard.

The Crusades and the expansion of Europe

So with the leadership of the church once again vested in the papacy, the church raised the banner of the Crusades to rescue the Holy Land from the "infidel," as the Muslims were called. The spirit of the Crusades goes back to the first missionaries of the church; it was but an extension of the missionary spirit which had never stopped because it was of the essence of Christianity. Some minor episodes preceded the First Crusade; and one may well regard the long Christian struggle in Spain as a continuous crusade, as also the Norman conquest of Sicily and southern Italy earlier in the 11th century, or the war against Slav and Balt by the Teutonic Knights. But the Crusades with a capital "C" were a series of European invasions of the Near East that occurred over two centuries.

The first four Crusades

At the end of the 11th century, the Emperor of Constantinople, threatened by the Seljuk Turks, requested help from the Christian princes of Europe. The specific object was to preserve Jerusalem as a Christian holy city and place of pilgrimage. Pope Urban II responded and preached the "Crusade," a word taken from the symbol of the Cross, in 1095. The papacy was continuing its struggles with the kings, and Urban had quarreled with the King of France; his appeal went to the nobles and knights. The success of the First Crusade

The crusading Knights Hospitallers held Le Krak des Chevaliers in Lebanon from 1142 to 1271.

represented a victory for the reformed papacy. The crusaders came chiefly from France, and from the region of Cluny's greatest influence. Despite their own jealousies and some friction with the Emperor they had come to help, the crusading barons threw back the Seljuk Turks and captured Jerusalem. An army of perhaps 30,000 was transported to the Near East with the aid of the Italian cities. Under Godfrey of Bouillon a feudal kingdom was established in Jerusalem. But most of the crusaders came back home, and the French who remained could not sustain their position in the long run. A less successful aspect of the First Crusade involved poor people who left home inspired by Peter the Hermit and filled with vague expectations of millenial justice; but this People's Crusade, ill-equipped and poorly led, met with speedy disaster.

The Second Crusade, 1147–49, represented the initiative of the famous Bernard of Clairvaux, a religious leader of unparalleled influence in Christian Europe, as well as that of the pious, unstable French King Louis VII. The German Emperor Conrad III also joined it, but the Second Crusade achieved little. Forty years later, the great Muslim leader Saladin recaptured Jerusalem from the Christians and thus precipitated the Third Crusade (1189–92). This one featured the rising monarchs of Europe, including the brilliant Frederick Barbarossa of Germany, Richard I of England, Philip II (Augustus) of France; papal domination had now yielded to the kings. After some initial successes, the jealous monarchs quarreled with each other and gained no more than the promise of temporary Christian access to the holy city.

The Fourth Crusade, 1202–4, was a fiasco in which the Pope was forced to excommunicate the crusaders who, under the commercial instigation of

Walls and donjon of the 12th century castle of the royal Anjou family at Loches, France—residence of the kings of France from the 13th to 16th centuries.

The 12th century Castle of the Counts of Flanders at Ghent, Belgium controlled the countryside.

the Venetians, attacked Constantinople and sacked it. So far from rescuing the eastern Christians, the crusaders from Europe had waged war on them!

Though it is customary to speak of the four Crusades as completing a cycle, there were others. St. Louis, the French King, embarked upon two in the course of his long 13th-century reign, both highly unsuccessful (he died during the second one, 1270). The brilliant German Emperor Frederick II also crusaded, was excommunicated by the Pope, and returned with some understanding of the Muslim world. There were many other minor crusades or attempted crusades.

Meaning of the Crusades

The Crusades have always been among the most storied events in European history. From the religious point of view, they testify to the extent of Christian zeal in medieval Europe; also, they point to the ambition and power of the popes, who planned and inspired the first one, as well as to the rising cult of chivalry among the knights and barons of Europe. They had a variety of other meanings. It has been suggested that they were a means of draining off from Europe the arrogant nobles and knights whose combativeness was a menace more than a protection after the Dark Ages. Indeed, Pope Urban openly referred to this motive. The wilder ones went off to vent their energies on the Saracens, to be killed or perhaps to carve themselves out domains in the Near East, as many did.

The Holy Land was the medieval equivalent of the American "Wild West" or British "Outposts of Empire" in more recent times, places of romance and adventure where the bolder or less civilized spirits went and about which others read or heard with interest. And where, also, the younger sons and other landless knights might find economic rewards. We know that these allegedly religious enterprises were usually more noted for the rivalry of knightly arms as well as for the jealousy of proud nobles and monarchs. The Crusades also included some disgraceful exhibitions of cruelty and greed. But they were exciting, and they satisfied the human lust for martial adventure.

The Crusades meant in a broader sense that Europe was breaking out of her isolation and making contact with an area where civilization had always been higher. The economic implications of this renewal of contact with the Near East were very considerable. Old trade routes were restored and new ones opened up. Here was the wealth of Asia, which since time immemorial had been a revelation to Europe. When Alexander the Great saw the tent of Darius the Persian after the battle of Issus, he knew what it was to be a king; and so it was with Richard and Philip and Frederick now, as well as a host of lesser men. A taste for oriental luxuries, and the means of satisfying that taste through trade, awakened in Europe. It was the commercial spirit of the Venetians which corrupted the Fourth Crusade and turned it against Christian Constantinople rather than the Muslims. As large-scale enterprises involving the equipping, supplying, and transporting of thousands of soldiers, the Crusades directly stimulated the European economy.

Christianity ultimately lost its battle for the soul of Asia. The Crusader states in Syria lasted only a few decades, the Muslim reconquest of this area being completed by 1291. Tiny Christian communities in Syria, Egypt, Iraq, and Persia remained, but became less and less important. While Islam retained its hold on western Asia, Buddhism remained the most powerful faith through most of East Asia. The barbarian Mongols, whose spectacular career of conquest disturbed both Asia and Europe in the 13th century, were courted by Christianity as well as by Islam and Buddhism (King Louis IX of France sent emissaries to the Great Khan in Karakorum), but in the end the Mongols divided their religious allegiance between Islam and Buddhism. Medieval Europe's most magnificent offensive, the crusade to carry Christianity to Asia, thus ended in failure. But it had many fruitful by-products and its impetus carried on into the later Age of Exploration. Portuguese and Spanish explorers who made their way to India and the New World were still motivated by a zeal to carry the message of Christ to the far corners of the earth, to convert the heathen and confound the infidels. If it had not been for this missionary impulse, the result of a deep religious faith, Europe in all likelihood would not have reached out to Asia and to the discovery of America nearly so soon.

Failure of the Crusades

Economic Recovery and urban development

Especially in Italy, with the great city of Venice in the lead, did revival of trade renew urban life and bring wealth. But cities arose also on the trade routes which led up from Italy, over the mountains and along the Rhine and Loire rivers. The Low Countries rivaled Italy, Antwerp and Bruges being among the greatest centers of the new commercial wealth at this time. Europe found a variety of products it could export in return for eastern spices, silks, perfumes—and slave girls. There were metals, furs, lumber, horses, wool, wine. Soon many people, in addition to the enterprising shippers of Genoa and Venice, were getting rich from this trade, and cities were growing.

Alliance of cities and king

Cities obtained from kings charters of self-government, purchasing their privileges with money which kings badly needed. The city bourgeoisie and the monarchs were natural allies. Kings could build up their governments and get free of the curb of the nobility if they could obtain money, while merchants needed the protection of the royal power so that they might trade. The brigands were numerous and included those "robber barons" who regarded any passing merchant as fair game. Toll stations every few miles were only a milder form of brigandage to the harassed merchant. Cities formed leagues for protection, but an effective royal government was the best answer. Thus rising princes and rising merchants often worked together to break up the sterile pattern of feudalism.

Some little trade there had always been in some parts of Europe, even in the darkest times. Venice, especially—a part, however, of Byzantium more than the West in early medieval times, protected from Germanic warriors on her island fastness—had continued to be a great city. Regional fairs had provided a means of exchanging goods. But the revival of commerce and cities which took place in the 12th century made the urban pattern a significant one rather than the rare exception, and trade a constant rather than an occasional happening.

Cities and feudal society

The city, as a place outside the feudal order, brought in a new kind of society, which worked as a dissolvent on the older pattern. In the city men were free, that is, no longer serfs. "The city air makes men free," an old German proverb ran. They were by no means "free" from the often very stringent city laws, but they were free from the restraints of the manor and the lord. By custom, a serf who had lived in a city for a year and a day was no longer a serf. And of course the cities proved magnets drawing the more ambitious peasantry away from the country. The citizens of the cities won their privileges to be free and self-governing—not without a struggle in the beginning, but in time they were recognized as a part, and a valuable part, of the country. Many of the cities, particularly the ecclesiastical ones, i.e., those under the jurisdiction of bishops or archbishops, became free "communes" only after violent insurrection; other cities evolved in a much less revolutionary manner.

Civic life of medieval cities

Civic life evolved new forms of government and law, as well as economy. Medieval cities seem to have been marked by a high degree of mutual cooperation, which made them in all respects "communes," as their government came to be known. Politically, the burghers needed and demanded their own government, parting company with the feudal system; city government featured officials elected annually, being considerably more democratic than the feudal type, though usually dominated by a mercantile elite rather than the whole populace. Civic spirit was very high, and citizens showed much enterprise and ingenuity in solving the problems of urban life and government. Proud of their hard-won liberties, and distinguished by the walls with which they surrounded themselves (for security, but later also from custom and pride), the medieval cities were to stand forth as independent social and political organisms, playing a role such as they had not played since antiquity and would not play again after the rise of the modern state, which has swallowed them up.

Economically, it was still necessary for merchants to stick together, for individual capitalists were not yet powerful enough to go it alone. The master institution of the cities was the guilds. Initially this was the merchant guild, a union of the burghers for self-protection which also served as the basis of town government. In any medieval city the guild hall was likely to be the grandest building, except for the cathedral. Later the craft guilds developed, as the workers in each occupation organized to set standards and control production. These guilds constituted a form of social regulation of industry which some modern reformers have admired: they supervised the quality of workmanship, looked out for the welfare of artisans, and sought to bring supply and demand into balance. The craft guilds provided one means of practical education in an age which lacked our sort of public school system: the familiar custom by which a young boy would be taken as an apprentice to live in the household of a master craftsman and learn his skills.

Capitalism

In late medieval times (earlier in exceptional cities like Venice), capitalism developed. One sign of the times was the entry into banking of Christians. The expulsion of the Jews—a brutal business, which took place in most west European countries in the 13th century—ended the monopoly of finance which Jews had enjoyed in the earlier Middle Ages because it was regarded as an unclean business, forbidden to Christians. Medieval restrictions on usury and on other business practices regarded as unethical were eased. If, however, we include in "capitalism"—as is usual—economic individualism, and a class division between owners of tools and wage workers, then the typical medieval town was not yet capitalistic. It was still cooperative and communal, though engaged in the production and sale of goods for profit, often for a wide market.

The existence of the cities undermined the manorial economy. Based on a nonmonetary exchange of services, that economic order was upset by the introduction of money. Peasants went to the city, or managed to get hold of enough money to purchase their freedom or commute it to rent. Nobles were attracted by the lure of money, with which they could buy luxurious goods, and were tempted to exchange the old system for the new. There is a special sense in which capitalism meant freedom: the economy of money and profit destroyed the manorial economy and the feudal system with its binding of the serf to the land.

Settlement of new land gave another boost to the burgeoning economy of this era of economic growth. Forests were being cleared and new land brought into production; it was a frontier age in which the rising population of Europe was expanding primary production. New towns were growing up where no previous settlement had existed at all. Frontiers are usually free from old customs and restrictions; such was the case here. The fact has already been mentioned that serfs who went to the new lands became free men. The most important new monastic order, the Cistercians, dedicated themselves to this frontier movement by pledging to settle virgin land and also not to keep serfs. New farming areas were less bound to the old order and more commercially minded. (Even the Cistercians, going in for wool production, in time became disgracefully rich!) Trade and the development of cities profited from this avenue of economic growth.

The development of the monarchies

Henry II of England

The long reign of Henry II of England (1154–89) created the basic machinery of state for England and raised the monarchy to a new dignity as well as power. Between 1135 and 1154 a period of anarchy accompanying a dispute over the throne caused much suffering as, according to the *Anglo-*

Saxon Chronicle, a contemporary account, the nobles ran wild and tortured people for their money. It was with especial relief, then, that England accepted the rule of a strong King. Henry II, first in the Plantagenet line, was Duke of Normandy, Count of Anjou and Maine, and by marriage Duke of Aquitaine, as well as King of England—an impressive empire which was unfortunately to involve his descendants in many quarrels with the kings of France. Despite the distractions of his French domains, he stamped out the lawless habits of the recent interregnum in England and, giving ceaseless attention to all the details of administration through a reign of 35 years, laid

A 13th century miniature of the killing of Thomas Becket. Contemporary representations of Becket were ordered destroyed by Henry II.

down foundations for effective royal government. In those times the King moved about, just as Charlemagne had done long ago; the government was himself and his "household"; his chief task was to hear cases and take appeals from baronial justice. Henry, a born lawyer, never wearied of this, and won fame for the fairness of his decisions. Like his contemporary Philip Augustus of France he tried to get away from reliance on the knights as a military force by setting up a small national army. He also warred against the nobility by requiring them to have licenses for castles and tearing down any unlicensed ones. In general, the "king's peace" reached out under Henry II to undermine the independent power of the nobles and begin the journey that led to a genuinely sovereign national government. There would be a long journey to travel before this goal was attained, but Henry saw that it was begun.

Martyrdom of Becket

Like all strong monarchs he clashed not only with the magnates but with the papacy. Henry's ambitions to create real royal government ran afoul of the reformed papacy's energetic defense of the church's autonomy; it is a story which contains much of the tragic conflict of the high Middle Ages. The particular issue here was the immunity of churchmen from the lay courts, even in case of criminal actions; the church had its own law courts, and a "criminous clerk" had to be released and handed back to them. In this case, the overzealous actions of Henry's henchmen who murdered Thomas Becket, the Archbishop of Canterbury, thus creating a martyr, forced the English king to yield most of the points in dispute. Canterbury became the most famous of medieval shrines, to which pilgrims came from all over Europe and to which were attributed many miraculous cures. There were those even within the church who had thought Becket's uncompromising position an error; but his martyrdom changed all that, and won a great victory for the church.

Philip II of France

Henry's counterpart in France was Philip II, called Philip Augustus (1180–1223), another commanding figure. In France, as in England, a trend toward stronger royal government had been noticeable since about the beginning of the 12th century: at that time Louis VI (1108–37) was the first Capetian to be much more than the slave of his vassals as King of France. It was in the footsteps of this fat but energetic and popular King, who allied himself with urban bourgeois elements and sought to reduce his neighboring vassals to obedience, that Philip Augustus trod. Philip, like Henry, may be taken as an example of what able and constructive monarchs were doing. He contributed much to the advancement of Paris, his capital, by building, paving, and walling it. He was diplomatically astute, making an alliance with Henry II of England when he needed support against rebellious barons, but later intriguing against Henry. He engaged in a duel with the English kings for possession of the lands they claimed in northern France. He appointed new royal officials who formed the basis for a regular, professional administrative system responsible to the king. He played off the nobles against each other, and turned for support to the town bourgeoisie. Attending to the question of taxes, Philip Augustus increased the royal revenues, with which he paid not only his civil servants but his own soldiers. Something like a small regular royal army came into existence in his time, a fact of the highest significance.

The Albigensian crusade

Philip was also the king in whose reign occurred one of the least savory of medieval episodes, the destruction of the culture of Provence. Pope Innocent III proclaimed a crusade against the Albigensian heresy which had taken root in southern France, where in the 12th century a most attractive civilization had developed in the land of the troubadours. Albigensianism, named after the town of Albi in Languedoc, or Catharism, had affinities with the old heresies of Gnosticism and Manichaeism, whose basis was the duality of the good and evil principles in the universe. Between flesh and spirit, the dualists insisted, there could be no reconciliation; it followed from this that Jesus had not really lived in the flesh, but had only seemed to. The Cathars of southern France may have come by way of a Greek Orthodox sect in Bulgaria called the Bogomiles, who held similar views in the 10th century, and whose churches still may be found in Yugoslavia. It is not altogether clear where the heresy came from, but it flourished in Languedoc from the beginning of the 12th century on. The church had already been alarmed by the followers of Peter Waldo, "the poor men of Lyons," who claimed to be true Christians but denied the Real Presence in the mass and, worse, assailed the right of the church to own property, were absolute pacifists, and refused to accept the jurisdiction of the criminal courts of law. Such deviations were as old as Christianity. But when the yet more extreme Cathars appeared it seemed to clerical conservatives that the whole of southern France might be lost to Christendom unless the heresy was stamped out. The Cathars, while preserving a few Christian terms, were really quite outside Christianity. Rejecting most of the sacraments and condemning the Christian clergy, some of them practiced an extreme form of asceticism, akin to that of the Hindu fakirs. These were the pure, the Perfect ones (the name "Cathar" coming from the Greek word for this). Catharism was a fascinating but exotic spiritual growth; it is easy to see why it shocked the Christian orthodox.

Eager to eliminate this aberration in the church, Innocent III in 1209 called the Albigensian crusade. Philip II permitted the northern nobles to take part in the crusade. Rich portions of the South were devastated and heresy stamped out with much cruelty. The movement involved the independence of southern feudal lords, and Philip undoubtedly saw in it separatist tendencies which conflicted with his monarchical ambitions. The kings of this epoch had in them qualities of realism, of unscrupulous sagacity, which subsequently were called "Machiavellian." Such qualities were doubtless necessary for the large task of building the modern state.

Growth of royal power

These monarchs brought better law and justice to wider areas, chipping into the arbitrary personal power of local tyrants. Feudalism was by no means dead. These kings still were far from absolute. A weak or unpopular monarch could expect setbacks at the hands of his vassals such as King John encountered in 1215 (see next chapter). But there were large gains in order and organization. Previously stressed was the important point that feudalism could mean a monarchy of some dignity, the center of the system, though with power considerably decentralized. While feudalism might mean the tyranny of the local lords, or it might mean something akin to anarchy, it could also mean a hierarchy of which the king was the natural and glorious pinnacle. The "feudal monarchs" of the 12th century had barely begun to create a machinery of government adequate to make them able to rule by their own power. They still had to consult with the higher nobility; they might be able to coerce notoriously bad ones but there was no question of ruling without the cooperation of most. There was a great difference between a king of the 10th and of the 12th century, nevertheless. The latter had raised both the prestige and the power of his office over the years. And it would continue to grow.

The kings who achieved this were not the crusaders who went off to seek excitement in the remote East. Louis VII of France and Henry II's son Richard the Lion-Hearted of England have been accused by historians of neglecting the vital if somewhat drab tasks of administration in order to embark upon pointless and expensive adventures. Philip Augustus was drawn into the Fourth Crusade by pressure of public opinion but was not happy there and soon returned. The sound instinct of the really great kings was to do the spade work at home, not seek empty glory abroad.

Germany: continued conflict with papacy

The German Empire, sprawling over much of central Europe and involved in constant wars with Poles, Bohemians, and Hungarians, as well as in Italy, did not develop so satisfactorily as a political community. It was too big and too heterogeneous. There were strong kings there, too, but they wasted their achievements on the vastness of their realm, while the bitter feud with the papacy was a constant and debilitating factor. Henry V, son of the emperor who had dueled with Hildebrand, waged war against Poland, Hungary, Bohemia, and in Italy; he succeeded in thoroughly humiliating Pope Paschal II, gaining ample revenge for Canossa. The investiture controversy, you will recall, was settled by compromise in the Concordat of Worms, 1122, but this hardly stilled the ill-feeling. The papacy played some part in a feud over the succession to the imperial throne which broke out in 1125, and which long divided much of Germany and northern Italy into Guelfs and Ghibellines—supporters of different candidates for the throne, with an overtone of clericalism versus anticlericalism. The Ghibellines were anticlerical supporters of the claims of the Swabian Hohenstaufen family, who by 1152, after a destructive civil war, had mastered their rivals and went on to be one of the great medieval dynasties. They were too prone to go crusading or empire building in far places, however. The presence of Conrad III and then Frederick Barbarossa at the Crusades may be recalled.

Frederick Barbarossa

Frederick Barbarossa (1152–90) reigned as the contemporary, roughly, of Henry II and Philip Augustus; in a great era of kings, he outdid both of them in personality and perhaps even in ability. The red-bearded Emperor long lived in German national legend for his fabulous feats. When not going on crusades or conducting displays of feudal pageantry, Barbarossa did much to tame the territorial nobles and organize the Empire, which he was the first to call the Holy Roman Empire. But he was involved in constant wars in Italy, where the cities of the north, led by Milan, defeated him in 1176 in a battle (Legnano) which ranks as the first defeat of feudal cavalry by commoners and infantrymen.

The feud with the papacy, and the ambition to control Italy as well as Germany, along with the unusual frontier problems of a region lacking in essential unity, were to plague the German emperors, and prevent them from succeeding in the way that French and English kings would do. There was another bout of civil war between Guelfs and Ghidellines between 1197 and 1212, during which the nobles profited by the disorders of the crown. The Hohenstaufen dynasty could not get the hereditary principle accepted though they struggled to do so, Barbarossa getting his son Henry VI onto the throne before he himself died. The last of the dynasty, Frederick II, would meet defeat in the next century and Germany as well as Italy would remain a land of small states, failing in the search for a larger unity on imperial foundations. But the Empire with its many cities had its glories in medieval times.

Eastern Europe

In lands farther east, the most important racial group was the Slavic. While today the Slavs are the most numerous, and conceivably the most important, of the peoples of Europe, they were not of much significance in Europe until the sixth century A.D. and after that played a subordinate role for many centuries. They lived in Russia and Poland and gradually penetrated eastern Europe—Bohemia, the Balkans—much where they are today. Even where they lived, the first states were often the work of non-Slavic invaders: in the case of Russia, Swedish Vikings. A good portion of them were to be Christianized from Constantinople and come under the cultural influence of Byzantium. The Black Sea and the Russian rivers formed a natural route from Constantinople to the Baltic. Russia lay almost beyond the purview of western history in the Middle Ages, but a Byzantine-inspired civilization flourished there, especially in the city of Kiev. The Kievan civilization was at its peak in the 11th century, when that city on the Dnieper headed a considerable kingdom, built great cathedrals, and participated in an extensive commerce. The destructive sweeps of Asiatic barbarians across Russia constantly blighted her efforts at civilization, however.

The Serbs also created their own state in the 11th century. The Bulgars, originally an oriental people, finally succumbed to Byzantine rule in the 11th century after ferocious wars, their independence being restored in the 13th when the Byzantine state began to collapse. For western Europe, the Poles and Bohemians were more important, along with the Hungarians. A Polish

A medieval town—Rothenburg ob der Tauber, Germany

state emerged in the 11th century. But it had trouble surviving its own dynastic rivalries and the pressure of Germans, as well as Hungarians, and subsequently the Mongols. Poland was a crossroads, its great plain being open in almost every direction. The Poles accepted Latin Christianity in the 10th and 11th centuries and thus were to be tied culturally to the West. The same was true of the Bohemians, who had even greater trouble maintaining independence and were made a part of the German Empire in the course of time.

These Slavic peoples were culturally more backward than western Europe, having received Christian and Roman (or Greek) influences late, and long maintaining tribal customs which had the familiar effect seen earlier among the Germanic peoples, of unstable kingdoms. But they developed institutions similar to those of western Europe: Christianity, monasticism, feudalism, monarchy, Roman law. Some of them joined in the Crusades which made up so prominent a part of the century.

A summary, then, of political developments in this formative period of the 12th century shows that kings were trying to increase their power and create a centralized, consolidated government reaching over all their kingdom. But feudalism was still very much alive, and the kings could go but a little way down the road leading to the modern state. Yet a discerning observer might have foreseen the future. The efforts of energetic kings to expand their powers often led them into conflict with the greater nobles, who naturally resented the encroachment on their power. It also led to clashes with the church, which was undergoing a parallel consolidation under the popes and which jealously guarded its independent power and administration. But in France and England the trend was in favor of the throne. In the Holy Roman Empire, however, the reverse was true, because the emperors tried to do too much and failed to consolidate their overly large realm, which stretched from Germany into Italy, while engaging in bitter conflict with the papacy. In the lands farther to the east, the Slavs generally had not yet developed the beginnings of national states or of independent kings.

The intellectual renaissance of the 12th century

A medieval library prior to about 1100 did not contain many books. The Bible, the four western Fathers of the Church (especially Augustine and Gregory), a bare smattering of philosophy in Boethius' *Consolations of Philosophy*, and a rather debased version of Hellenistic scientific knowledge in Isidore of Seville's *Etymologies*—this, apart from local history, was likely to be about all. The sparseness of literature was not the result of any dislike of knowledge, for the most part, but of conditions which made the writing and publishing of books by able scholars extremely difficult.

In the towns, grammar schools were so-called because the most important subject was Latin grammar, the "trivium" of grammar, rhetoric, and logic being more important than the "quadrivium" of arithmetic, geometry, music, and astronomy—a time-honored classification which went back to Roman times. Cathedral and abbey schools varied in quality, but the best of them (and these were the seeds of the universities) could not teach much. A movement of recovery began in the 11th century in small ways. The most significant place for the 11th-century preliminary advance, in addition to the Norman abbey of Bec where Anselm worked, was the cathedral school of Chartres. But by the end of the 12th century books were plentiful; the great universities at Paris, Bologna, and Salerno were underway; really advanced work was being done in the arts and sciences. Whole realms of philosophy, science, and mathematics had been opened up. This century also produced the Provençal lyrics and the greater epic poetry of France. Another major achievement was the revival of systematic and careful study of Roman law, both civil and canon.

Sources of the new learning

While manuscripts copied and preserved in the monasteries were important sources for the revival of learning, translations from the Arabic were probably the chief medium by which new blood was pumped into European thought. In Spain, especially at Toledo, and in Sicily—places where the Arab and European worlds met—translators worked; but they also traveled as far as Asia Minor in their eagerness to tap this rich vein of knowledge. A general spirit of inquiry was abroad; the atmosphere of an intellectual renaissance existed. Men boldly declared with Peter Abelard that nothing should any longer be accepted merely on authority.

Fortunately for Europe, at this moment when conditions had stimulated a thirst for knowledge, the nearby Arab world supplied oceans of it. The Arabs had preserved and added to ancient philosophy and science. Aristotle, the leading source of the medieval philosophical and scientific renaissance, was interpreted for Europe by such great Arab commentators as Averroës and Avicenna. But much else was recovered from the ancient Greeks through the Arabs: the medical texts of Galen, the geometry of Euclid, the astronomy of Ptolemy. Some, too, came from the Greeks of the Byzantine Empire, where classical Greek thought had been cherished.

Byzantine culture reached the peak of its revival in the early 11th century. From 867 on there had been an amazing renaissance of power, prosperity, and culture in the old imperial state, marked by a considerable reconquest from the Arabs in Syria and the eastern Mediterranean. It was during this period that Byzantine controlled the Balkans and converted far-off Russia to the Orthodox faith. This increase in power and influence was paralleled by a "golden age" in the arts. The dazzling Byzantine style in art and architecture exerted an influence on western Europe, especially by way of Venice. Constantinople was a fabulous center of wealth and world trade. After about 1050 Byzantium began a period of rather abrupt decline.

The final separation of the eastern and western Christian churches in 1054 involved a dispute about possession of southern Italy. Norman forces, supported by the papacy, expelled the eastern Empire from this area. Norman adventurers had appeared in the south of Italy beginning in 1016 and begun to conquer that area, held rather feebly by Byzantium. Thus hostility existed, but also contact, and western Europe came in touch with a higher civilization than its own, at the time when it was beginning its own economic and political recovery. This contact became closer during the Crusades.

But the more important source for the revival of learning was Muslim Spain. Islamic Arabs and Berbers had occupied almost all the Iberian peninsula after their victories of 711–13. They built there a rich culture with its center at Cordova. The beautiful decorative arts of Islam worked a spell even over those Christians who returned as the bitter foes of its faith. Moorish industry and agriculture enriched the country. In the North some Basque and Visigoth Christians held out. Gradually, aided by quarrels among the Moors and the general decline of the vast Arab empire, the small Christian states of the North began to expand. The mark of the Moors would always be on Spain, but the Spanish character would also be molded by the centuries-long Christian crusade to drive them out. In the 10th and 11th centuries this work of redemption succeeded to the point where the northern half of the peninsula was Christian, under the king of Leon and Castile. Already Spain had her national hero, the warrior known as the Cid.

Warfare between Christian and Moor went on intermittently until the final victory of the former in 1492. But by 1085 the Christians were in possession of such centers of Muslim culture as Cordova and Toledo, a principal source of the recovery of learning in Europe. In 1212 Castilian King Alfonso

Court of the Lions at the Alhambra in Granada, Spain shows the delicate traceries of Muslim architecture.

VIII won a decisive victory over the Muslims, after which they never really rallied. Christian Spain had a relatively backward economy and society, the result largely of protracted warfare and of isolation from the main currents of Europe. However, contact with the intellectual riches discovered in Arabic Spain was of the highest importance for all Europe as scholars flocked there from England, France, Germany, and Italy, to read and to translate the dazzling books of Aristotle, Galen, Euclid, and others.

Intellectual revival

This new knowledge gradually flowed in during the 12th and 13th centuries. It was apparent that Europe welcomed it eagerly. The long night had ended, and the 12th century's enthusiasm for learning and thought has seldom been matched in all history. Whatever lay to hand was taken up and eagerly examined, but what most excited Europe in the 12th century was the Logic of Aristotle. It opened up new horizons of ordered thought to people yearning for some way of synthesizing the chaotic world into a unity. Peter Abelard (1079–1142), bold thinker and great teacher who virtually began the University of Paris, undertook to examine conflicting or troublesome passages of Scripture with the aid of logic. This exciting intellectual game could lead to highly unorthodox conclusions. It prepared the way for the reception of Aristotle's main body of writings, including the *Metaphysics*, which came a little later and supplied the great controversies of the 13th century. Abelard also reopened the philosophical question of the reality of universals, a topic Europe had never quite lost sight of since Boethius presented it in one of the few philosophical texts known all through the Dark Ages.

Realism and nominalism

Plato's effort to establish the objective existence of pure ideas or forms as the object of knowledge, and Aristotle's concern with this problem, made up the background of the famous medieval controversy between "realists" and "nominalists." One may get close to the issue by reflecting whether an individual object, say a table, does not require membership in the class of objects, tables in general, to be understood; and, if so, what is the status of this general class. Do class-names, such as "mankind" as distinct from an individual man, exist only as words, or are they in some sense realities, as the realists claimed? If they are real, do they inhere in the individuals or apart from them? In attacking the extreme realism of William of Champeaux, Abelard advanced philosophical thought to a more sophisticated level and stirred up interest in critical analysis in general. It has also been suggested that the realist-nominalist controversy was not without its practical implications. The rising interest in Aristotelian and seminominalist modes of thought reflected intellectual tastes which were more scientific and naturalistic, less theological and metaphysical. Aristotle's philosophy led one to begin by observing the particular, sensible object; it was, at least by comparison with the sort of Platonism earlier held, empirical. Thus as men grew more confident and successful in their affairs they moved cautiously toward a more naturalistic outlook, toward a scientific empiricism.

12th-century humanism

The 12th century also produced a humanism—in the sense of an interest in the "humanities"—which reminds us of the Italian Renaissance of several centuries later. Bernard of Chartres and John of Salisbury, minds typical of the 12th century, "modelled their style on Ovid and Cicero, and exchanged scholary epigrams and epistles like the humanists of a later age." They prided themselves on their style and on their breadth of knowledge. John of Salisbury wrote an outstanding treatise on politics, the *Policraticus*, which is a storehouse of classical allusions, with a particular debt to Cicero. It was Bernard, master of the celebrated cathedral school of Chartres, who made the famous remark that the moderns were like dwarfs standing on the shoulders of giants. Though he could not do without the ancients, the 12th-century scholar was ready to believe that he might yet see a little further than they did. The remark was typical of the 12th-century humanists with their deep respect for the past combined with a wise and independent outlook. The rigorously logical Schoolmen of the next century often dismissed them as dilettantes, as the Italian humanists in turn considered the Schoolmen to be crabbed logic-choppers.

St. Bernard of Clairvaux, that fabulous figure of the medieval church, threw his influence against the speculative philosophy of Abelard in a mighty encounter between giants: the sharp, skeptical intellect of the pioneer Schoolman against the thundering eloquence of the greatest of medieval preachers. But Hugh of St. Victor sought to mediate between these two protagonists in order to reduce the tension between philosophy and faith.

Roman law

The most popular subject in the universities was neither philosophy nor classics but law. Recovery of the *Corpus Juris Civilis*, the compilation which included Justinian's Digest and Code, led to systematic study of Roman law, which had never been entirely lost during the Middle Ages.

The study of Roman law had never quite died out in Italy, and customary law in southern France bore its faint stamp. But the stream had thinned to a trickle; about 1100 it suddenly began to flow and was soon almost a flood. The university at Bologna in northern Italy, where the celebrated Irnerius taught, became its leading fount. More basically, society seemed ready to receive it. It suited the age's intellectual urge for logic and order, a reaction from so many centuries of confusion. Kings and nobles welcomed it for practical reasons: it helped them organize, consolidate, and govern their realms. The forces of civilization saw in it a weapon against the blood feuds, ordeals, and other barbarous practices of Germanic law. The Roman law in both church and secular state goes along with the general intellectual and cultural revival of the 12th century. The renaissance of the papacy encouraged this subject, too, for from Rome came volumes of the church decretals, which are pronouncements by the pope on canon law. The first of these was Gratian's famous edition, which formed the basis for the study of canon, or church, law.

The 12th-century scholars laid the foundations for the brilliant thinkers of the next century. They translated the books, began the universities, and developed the methods which were to be typical of Scholastic philosophy. This "Twelfth-Century Renaissance" provided the foundations for later intellectual development and may be regarded as the basic civilizing process in western history. Thus the 12th century, which for excitement had the Crusades, reveals on closer examination a pattern of growth and development in all fields that is more truly exciting. This growth was economic, political, and intellectual. It was also artistic and architectural, a theme reserved for the next chapter: this is the time of Europe's first great churches, abbeys, and castles. Europe had arrived on the threshold of a brilliant civilization.

Bibliography

The crowded 12th-century historical scene is surveyed in a cooperative work, M. Clagett (ed.), *Twelfth Century Europe and the Foundations of Modern Society* (Madison: University of Wisconsin Press, 1961). Charles H. Haskins' classic study, *The Renaissance of the Twelfth Century*, has been reprinted (World Publishing, Meridian), as has his *The Rise of Universities* (Cornell University Press), the witty and urbane essay of a great scholar. A.C. Crombie, *Medieval and Early Modern Science*, Vol. I (Doubleday Anchor), and Gordon Leff, *Medieval Thought* (Penguin), are both outstanding.

R.W. Southern, cited for Chapter 5, is also useful here. The rise of urban culture can be approached via a well-known study, Henri Pirenne, *Medieval Cities* (Doubleday Anchor); more recently John H. Mundy and P. Riesenberg, *The Medieval Town* (Princeton, N.J.: D. Van Nostrand, 1958); Maurice Beresford, *New Towns of the Middle Ages* (New York: Frederick A. Praeger, 1967); or for a specific community, Mundy's *Liberty and Political Power in Toulouse 1050–1250* (New York: Columbia University Press, 1955). E.M. Carus-Wilson, *Medieval Merchant-Venturers* (London: Methuen Publications, 1954) is by a master of medieval economic history; see also Vols. II and III of the *Cambridge Economic History*.

Steven Runciman, *A History of the Crusades*, by the leading modern authority, is in three volumes (New York: Cambridge University Press, 1951–54); a photographic record of these storied events is Regine Pernoud, *In the Steps of the Crusaders* (New York: Hastings House, 1959). Watkin Williams has written a great life of *St. Bernard of Clairvaux* (Westminster, Md.: Newman Press, 1952), while H. Daniel-Rops continues his history of the church with a volume for this epoch entitled *Cathedral and Crusade* (World Publishing, Meridian). Additionally on the most dramatic events of this period, Kenneth M. Setton and Marshall W. Baldwin (eds.), *A History of the Crusades*, Vol. I (Philadelphia: University of Pennsylvania Press, 1956), and James Brundage, *The Crusades: A Documentary Survey* (Milwaukee: Marquette University Press, 1962). Richard A. Newhall has written an attractive short paperback, *The Crusades*, in the Berkshire Series in European History (Holt, Rinehart & Winston). The anniversary year 1966 brought forth a spate of books about 1066, including Henry R. Loyn, *The Norman Conquest* (London: Hutchinson, 1965). G.O. Sayles, *Medieval Foundations of England*, first published in 1948 and now available in paperback (A.S. Barnes, Perpetua), is a useful survey, which may be supplemented by A.L. Poole's distinguished volume of the Oxford History of England for this period, *From Domesday Book to Magna Carta* (1955), or Sir Frank Stenton's *The First Century of English Feudalism 1066–1166* (New York: Oxford University Press, 1961).

Still worth reading, though needing to be checked against more recent scholarship (see again Barraclough, *Origins of Modern Germany*, cited for Chapter 5), is James Bryce's old *The Holy Roman Empire*, now available in a Schocken paperback. For other areas, each of the following is renowned: A. Castro, *The Structure of Spanish History* (Princeton, N.J.: Princeton University Press, 1954), and George Vernadsky, *Ancient Russian and Kievan Russia*, Vols. I and II of his History of Russia (Yale University Press). J.J. Bagley has an interesting volume, *Life in Medieval England* (London: Batsford, 1960). Compare U.T. Holmes, Jr., *Daily Living in the Twelfth Century* (University of Wisconsin Press); Eileen Power, *Medieval People* (Doubleday Anchor); and Joan Evans, *Life in Medieval France* (London: Phaidon Press, 1957). Norman Cohn has supplied an absorbing account of one striking phase of medieval life in his *The Pursuit of the Millennium* (Harper Torchbook). For a wide variety of topics, Sylvia L. Thrupp (ed.), *Change in Medieval Society* (Appleton-Century-Crofts) provides up-to-date essays.

Among many sources, De Joinville and Villehardouin, *Memoirs of the Crusades* (Penguin); John of Salisbury, *Historia Pontificalis* and *Letters* (Thomas Nelson & Sons, Medieval Texts); Otto of Freising and Rahewein, *The Deeds of Frederick Barbarossa* (Columbia University Records of Civilization). Byran Tierney (ed.), *The Crisis of Church and State 1050–1300* (Prentice-Hall, Spectrum) is a judicious selection of documents. See also the bibliography for the next chapter.

7

The climax of the Middle Ages: 1200-1300

chronology

1194–1250
Life of Frederick II, *stupor mundi*, King of Sicily and Holy Roman Emperor.
1198–1216
Pontificate of Innocent III, zenith of medieval papacy.
Papal victory over John of England, 1213.
1199–1216
Reign of John in England.
1212
Battle of Las Navas de Tolosa, decisive victory of Christians over Moors in Spain.
1214
Battle of Bouvines, victory of French King over King John of England and over the French feudal nobility.
1215
Magna Carta.
Fourth Lateran Council sets church creed and ritual.
1220–23
Franciscan and Dominican Orders organized and accepted.
Official foundation of Paris University.
1226
Teutonic Knights undertake conversion of Prussia.
1226–70
Reign of St. Louis (Louis IX) of France.
1227–29
Crusade of Frederick II, great German Emperor; excommunicated by the Pope, violent feud between emperor and popes.
1236
Recapture of Cordova from Moors.
1237–41
Great Mongol invasion of eastern Europe, gaining suzerainty over Russia and devastating Poland, Hungary, Bohemia and the Danube valley.
1244
Final loss of Jerusalem by Christians.
1250
Death of Frederick II during war with papacy.
1254–73
Great Interregnum in Holy Roman Empire; end of Hohenstaufen dynasty and power of medieval Empire.
1260
Mongols stopped in the Near East.
1265
Simon de Montfort's Parliament in England, landmark in emergence of representative government.
Birth of Dante.
Charles of Anjou takes crown of Sicily.
1271–95
Second voyage of the Polos to the Orient.
1272–1307
Edward I, King of England; advance of English government.
Model Parliament, 1295.
1273
Rudolf I, first Hapsburg Holy Roman Emperor.
1274
Death of Thomas Aquinas, greatest medieval philosopher, author of *Summa Theologica*.
1282
Sicilian Vespers (anti-French revolt in Sicily).
1285–1314
Reign of Philip the Fair (Philip IV) of France; advance of power of French monarchy.
1294
Death of Roger Bacon, medieval scientist.
1294–1303
Pontificate of Boniface VIII.
1302
Bull *Unam Sanctam* issued by Pope Boniface. Seizure and humiliation of Pope by Philip IV of France.

Reims cathedral

The political background

The 13th century has been called "the greatest of centuries," and it certainly was without much question the greatest since the second century A.D. Building on foundations laid down in the 12th century, the 13th produced a more sophisticated, a more intellectualized, a more urbanized civilization. The 13th century's claims to glory are many and various. They include an extraordinary architectural renaissance with highly developed decorative arts to go with it, universities where scholars tried to synthesize Greek philosophy and Christianity, kings with increased power, growing cities, an international unity under the popes, and a century of relative peace.

King John and Magna Carta

Western Europe had brilliant monarchs in this century, and a significant political evolution. England began with the unfortunate rule of John, brother of the equally unfortunate knight errant, Richard Coeur de Lion. A serious king, John tried to carry on the system of his great father, Henry II, but ran into ill luck. Richard left him an empty treasury with which to defend a realm that included possessions in France. It will be recalled that the Plantagenet kings of England were also dukes of Aquitaine and Normandy and counts of Anjou. John was no great warrior, and met defeat in France. To get money he pressed hard upon the barons, and they revolted against him. The baronial revolt produced that familiar document, the Magna Carta, which the lords forced him to accept in 1215. The Great Charter included among its significant provisions the prohibition of any new taxes without the consent of the Great Council, later Parliament; and no "freeman" to be arrested or otherwise molested by the monarch without "the lawful judgment of his peers and by the law of the land." That the Great Charter was a vindication of liberty against tyranny, the traditional view, has been strenuously challenged by historians who point out that it was "a reactionary feudal document . . . imposed on the king by a rebellious baronage . . . its purpose to limit the rights of the crown not as against the people but as against the tenants-in-chief." The fact remains, however, that Englishmen later did look back to the Magna Carta as their great precedent for freedom from arbitrary rule.[1] And out of the council of barons grew Parliament and representative government.

Growth of Parliament

The English Parliament was by no means the only one in the 13th century, although it survived better than the others. The practice of summoning representatives, armed with full legal powers to speak for their communities or corporations, seems to have begun in the papal dominions about 1200; it spread through much of Europe, including Spain and France as well as England. Broadening of the feudal council to include townsfolk and other important groups went on nearly everywhere, too. The evolution of government from the time of Henry II and Frederick Barbarossa to Edward I and Frederick II is from the personal and largely unorganized to the more impersonal and institutionalized form of consultation with the king's subjects.

More effective royal government

It is customary to date the English Parliament from the middle of the 13th century, and its emergence was associated with the long reign of a weak king, Henry III (1216–72). In 1265 met a Council which included knights and burgesses as well as the greater nobles. Then came Edward I, "the English Justinian" (reigned 1272–1307), who strengthened the monarchy at the same time that Parliament began to meet regularly. Law and government became systematized. When Edward died after a reign of 35 years, it was possible to

[1] It is interesting that 1222 is the date of an extraction of feudal privileges similar to the Magna Carta from the monarch in Hungary, at the other end of medieval Europe. Andrew II of Hungary, like Richard of England, had bankrupted himself by going on a Crusade to the Holy Land.

say that England had become a mature political community, a nation in the real sense of the word.

The same transition from the personal to the institutionalized that we see in Parliament may be seen in the executive power of the crown; it becomes less the king's person and more something impersonal that will finally be known as "the State." Kings cease to be wanderers and develop permanent capitals; whole departments of government emerge from what was previously just the king's household. In England and France there are new local officials representing the king—sheriffs, bailiffs, seneschals—while the king is no longer completely dependent on the feudal nobles to carry out his decrees. At the king's court there are important developments in his council, in law courts, in administrative departments. The complex governmental machinery of the modern nation was slowly emerging, with its laws that are binding on all its subjects, its methods of enforcing these laws, its courts for interpreting them, its machinery for collecting taxes, its armies, and its numerous other services. All this was beginning to happen in the 13th century. The modern state grew out of the medieval kingship.

The development of regular parliaments, Roman law, permanent departments of the government, and more effective royal administration is a story repeated in 13th-century France and elsewhere in Europe. St. Louis (Louis IX, 1226–70) issued ordinances which had effect over the whole realm on his authority, and he used them to ban private warfare. By the end of his reign, too, France had a royal currency circulating over the whole kingdom. Philip the Fair (Philip IV, reigned 1285–1314), Edward I's contemporary and sometimes enemy in war, followed the famous St. Louis on the throne and proved to be the strongest monarch France had seen since Charlemagne. Assemblies of the feudal nobility met in France, too, but they did not develop into a national parliament as in England, chiefly because France was much less a single community. But the royal courts were expanded and improved, and by means of the right of appeal from the feudal law, as well as by gaining direct control over some matters, there grew up a national law alongside the feudal. A theme common to France and England was a running fight with church and papacy, marking the effort of a real national state to escape from the bonds of clerical domination. It will be referred to again.

Throughout the Continent the evolution toward an order both more dignified and more complex expressed itself not only through the development of representative institutions but also through the Roman law. Taught at the universities, the Roman law had become more rigorous and more carefully defined. Because of its tendency to deposit "sovereignty" in a single place, monarchs used it to justify their increased power.

Frederick and Germany

To Germany the 13th century brought Frederick II (1194–1250), called *stupor mundi* because of his amazing talents as a philosopher and scientist as well as jurist and soldier. But the fantastic disunity of this realm may be judged by the fact that Frederick was born in Sicily and spent much of his time fighting for that Mediterranean island, as well as for northern Italy. He was forced to recognize and even extend the dominion of the territorial princes in Germany. It was a trend contrary to what was happening in France and England, where the kings were beginning to chip away the privileges of the local nobility. It continued the fateful course of German history in which the national state did not develop as in France and England. Barbarossa, Henry VI, and Frederick II, great as they were, could never break the powerful German territorial nobility nor the Lombard cities.

Significantly, however, Frederick erected in Sicily a centralized, absolutist state of a sort new to Europe. He was the first "enlightened despot," a man far in advance of his time in many respects. The University at Salerno, Arab-influenced, became the first medical school of Europe; Frederick founded the University of Naples, also. This Hohenstaufen monarch, who fought in northern Italy with the Lombard cities, as had his grandfather Barbarossa, entered into a ferocious struggle with Pope Gregory IX. This renewal of the papal-imperial conflict resulted in warfare which laid waste much of Italy. The Hohenstaufen dynasty died with the great Frederick (1250), whose tomb is appropriately in Palermo.

His successors were unable to cope with the popes, who summoned aid from Charles of Anjou, the brother of the King of France. Frederick had been unable to consolidate domains too vast and disparate. His long struggle with the papacy left a mark on both Italy and Germany that would long remain. The papacy had ruined the German emperor, though at terrific cost to itself. The failure of the Empire should not obscure the prosperity and relative stability of Germany in the 13th century, an era of rising cities, flourishing trade, and more orderly law and government locally. That Germany became a collection of little states was a fact of more moment for the future than the present.

Eastern Europe: The Mongol invasion

In the 13th century eastern Europe experienced the shattering force of the Mongol invasions. This was the latest surge from out of Asia, which in the past had so often proved disastrous to Europe. The Mongolian-speaking tribes of the steppes of central Asia embarked upon breathtaking conquests toward the end of the 12th century. United under Chingiz Khan ("universal ruler"), these fierce horsemen subjugated most of central Asia, began the conquest of China, and swept like grass fire through western Asia and eastern Europe before their leader's death in 1227. They were more attracted by the wealth of Persia and the Near East, to which they did enormous damage, visiting fire and sword on what were then the world's greatest cities, including Baghdad with its palaces, mosques, and libraries. This branch of the Mongols was finally checked by the Egyptian Mamluks in 1260, after their unity of leadership had begun to falter.

One wing of their armies pushed into Russia, crossing the Volga in 1237 and putting Moscow to the torch. But the Golden Horde, as this wing of the Mongol nation called itself, continued to rule Russia for some time from their headquarters on the Volga. They became content to receive tribute and acknowledgement of their suzerainty. But their influence tended to cut Russia off from Europe. The Kiev and Novgorod cultures declined, to be replaced by Moscow, much farther to the east, as the leading Russian center. Beginning with the great Alexander Nevsky, the Muscovite Russians cooperated with the Tatars, as they called the Mongols, while waging war against Swedes and Germans to the west. Thus did the Mongol invasion, one of history's great forces, affect the destinies of a part of Europe.

Even where the Mongol invasion did not endure it left the way open for local lords to increase their power at the expense of the central monarchy. After burning Moscow the Golden Horde swept on into Poland, Bohemia, Hungary, and the Danube Valley. They turned back in 1241 owing to the death of the Great Kahn (Ogadai) and never returned to this part of Europe. After the Mongols left, the nobility gained the upper hand in Hungary. Poland was also devastated, and one result was an increase in the German influence as the Polish state weakened. The glories of the 13th century chiefly lay in western Europe.

Cities and friars

The free towns and cities, which had appeared during the 11th and 12th centuries, blossomed in the 13th. The institutions and environment described briefly in the previous chapter developed into maturity. Commerce and the new city economy now exerted a corrosive influence on the manorial economy. In the more advanced areas of this urban economy—Flanders, for example—attachment to the soil in the old manner virtually ceased to exist by the middle of the 13th century. A money economy enabled thrifty peasants to buy their freedom and encouraged lords to welcome money rents in place of personal services. The new commodities tempted the nobility, but they required money to buy them. The cities, in turn, paid cash for food. In short, agriculture could not resist being drawn into the money economy.

Free cities

The bourgeoisie of the cities played an increasing role in affairs. In 1176 the Italian burghers defeated the German cavalry, as noted; in 1214 at Bouvines, when the French King Philip Augustus beat King John of England and his allies among the French nobility, thus vindicating the strength of the monarchy, he relied heavily on soldiers from the cities. Typically, kings allied with burghers, though this pattern did not prevail always and everywhere. In the 13th century there arose great and proud "free cities." Such were the *Reichsstädte* or imperial cities of the German Empire. The first of the German cities to receive "privileges" from the emperor was Worms, in 1074. But the golden age of the German free cities came in the 13th century, when they developed vigorous civic institutions. Following the death of Frederick II and the collapse of the Hohenstaufen dynasty, the cities of the Rhine formed a league: Strasbourg, Basel, Mainz, and Cologne are some of these famous old places In some of them an anticlerical tradition stemmed from the fact that they had won their independence from the control of a bishop or archbishop. In any case they prized their freedom, and the strength of their local traditions may readily be seen to this day.

In Italy, the breakdown of feudal and royal government during the struggle of pope and emperor aided the evolution of cities as the basic form of government; here they grew into states, controlling the country around them and often waging war with each other. They also were the most direct gainers from the revival of trade with the Orient; and so the Italian cities, already producing Dantes, soon Giottos and Petrarchs, prepared for the brilliant Renaissance of the arts which was to revolve around their unique civic institutions in the 14th and 15th centuries.

Some cities of southern France, too, especially Marseilles, were virutally independent. But in the more feudalized areas of Europe, such as central and northern France, or in the strong monarchy of England, the cities were not so independent. There the feudal nobility normally resented them and gave them trouble; the kings, and sometimes the greater vassals, increasingly saw in them a valuable ally but wished to exercise some surveillance. The French cities eventually were absorbed by the territorial state. St. Louis subjected them to financial supervision in 1262; and yet so strong was the pride in being a "commune" that Paris revived this tradition and attempted to secede from the rest of France as late as 1871. (A "commune" was a city which had won its independence by rebellion.)

The merging of Christian and urban culture

Though sometimes nobles came to the cities (especially was this true in Italy) and ex-serfs became artisan-workers, the cities were, almost by definition, dominated by the bourgeoisie, often in an oligarchic manner. The 13th-century city seems unique in the blending of this secular, commercial element with the church to create an urban Christian culture. The universities, described in the next section, are one example: staffed by men of the church (there was no other learned class), they nevertheless taught and thought in ways that were not exactly clerical, and their outstanding philosophers undertook to vindicate the natural reason of man. So it was with that chief glory of the times, the vast and splendid cathedrals. The masons and craftsmen who built the great churches were mostly laymen. So also the painters and sculptors who decorated them. These great buildings were in the cities, clearly expressions of urban wealth and skills. Though places of Christian worship, they were also products of the creative talents of urban craftsmen, and of course they testified to the wealth of the cities. We may suggest without intending any irreverence that they were monuments to civic pride as much as to Christian piety. This does not mean that the latter was absent. There was little if any real anti-Christian sentiment; there was simply a blending of secular culture with the church.

The new orders of clergy were also a sign both of the urban trend and of the blending of clerical culture with the cities. The persistent tendency of the cloisters to fall into worldliness or decay had been countered by the great

Cluniac movement of the 10th century and by the Cistercian movement of the 12th. The Cistercians did not reach the cities, however. Indeed, they made their greatest contribution as frontiersmen, helping in that process of pushing into the forests which expanded the arable lands of Europe in this era.

Dominican and Franciscan friars

The friars who came in the 13th century were religious men who did not live in secluded monasteries but went into the cities to preach, teach, and serve. Dominicans and Franciscans aimed their activities in this direction. Followers of among the greatest of medieval saints, they were at first wandering beggars, practicers of holy poverty. Francis of Assisi was an Italian, Dominic a Spaniard; the two mendicant orders emerged separately at almost the same time (1220, 1223) with different backgrounds. The Dominicans were a response to the Albigensian (Catharistic) heresy in neighboring Provence, and militant preaching against heresy was their hallmark. They were prominent in the Inquisition, established in 1231 for the purpose of checking the spread of heresies. The Inquisition operated under the authority of the Holy Office. Men were arrested on suspicion and tried in secret; torture was used to get confessions; and there was no appeal from decisions. With such tactics, the Inquisition became a dread instrument of repressing nonconformity in religion.

The Franciscans followed the gentler ways of their saintly founder, St. Francis of Assisi, seeking to imitate the life of Christ, conceived as joyous, spontaneous, meek, and loving. But they made the bolder missionaries, being among the earliest to adventure into the Far East from Europe.

These orders became prominent in the universities, and in the running of urban charitable institutions and hospitals. Benedictine or Cistercian abbeys

Gothic sculpture of the Virgin in Reims cathedral

Contemporary fresco of St. Francis in Sacro Speco di S. Benedetto, Subiaco, Italy

were once the highest expression of Christian life. That was no longer so. The vital forces in the church flowed into urban channels, into activities within society and not withdrawn from it.

Perhaps it was owing to the devoted energies of these "mendicant orders" that urban life remained within the clerical fold. Except in Italy, and somewhat later, there was not much distinctly bourgeois culture in the higher sense. Schools for the bourgeois laity did appear in the cities, but mostly on a primary level and a practical one. In medieval cities the great cathedrals, in the Gothic style, were the most imposing architectural monuments; their decorations were the leading art. Medieval civilization in its splendid development remained Christian and church-centered as it moved into an urban era.

The medieval universities and Scholasticism

The founding of the universities, and the establishment there of advanced studies, crowned the intellectual life of the Middle Ages. Nearly all the important thought of the 13th century took place within the universities. It was a situation unlike the modern world, where much of what is original and creative in philosophy and literature has been done outside the universities. They almost had a monopoly in the Middle Ages. The universities were in the towns and cities; above all Paris, Bologna, and Salerno, later Oxford, Naples, Montpellier, Padua, and subsequently others. These unique institutions—the ancient world had not known anything quite comparable—stemmed from the cathedral schools in most cases. But earlier there was not enough knowledge, nor enough students, to sustain advanced educational establishments. Now there were both. In the beginning the students took the initiative, flocking to hear some popular lecturer such as the celebrated Abelard. Only gradually did the universities become well organized. They were self-governing bodies. Though licensed by the church and staffed with clerics, chiefly of the two renowned mendicant orders, their clericalism should not be exaggerated, for theology was not the only item on the curriculum by any means. Especially important at all times was the teaching of the Roman law. Several times in the 13th century the papacy tried to prevent the study of Aristotelian philosophy at Paris, without much success. The verdict of an outstanding student of the medieval universities (Charles H. Haskins) is that there was very little restriction on the teaching freedom of professors.

The students were by all the numerous accounts a frolicsome breed, leaving behind as their chief gift to posterity the jolly drinking songs of the so-called "Goliardi poets." But we also know of those whom Chaucer immortalized:

For he would rather have at his bed's head
Some twenty books, all bound in black and red,
Of Aristotle and his philosophy
Than rich robes, fiddle, or gay psaltery.

Influence of Aristotle

Dominating the realm of knowledge was indeed Aristotle, "master of those who know," *the* Philosopher. But Aristotle and his Arabic commentators (Averroës and Avicenna became familiar names to intellectual Europe in the 13th century) did not by any means monopolize learning. Chaucer's physician was well read in Esculapius,

And Deiscorides, and in Rufus,
Hippocrates, and Hali, and Galen,
Serapion, Rhazes, and Avicen,
Averrhoës, Gilbert, and Constantine,
Bernard, and Gatisden, and John Damascene

—an imposing list of authorities both ancient and modern, western and oriental. Intoxicated with new learning, Europe's appetite for books was voracious. The main charge against the medieval "Schoolmen," or Scholastics, is that they were too bookish. They had had for so long so few books that now they feasted on those volumes "all bound in black and red."

Scholasticism

Paris and her daughters (practically all universities north of the Alps were offspring of the French university) stressed the method of the disputation: conflicting sources cited, solutions stated and challenged, and mastery of formal logic assumed with all the terminology of classical metaphysics. Scholasticism is usually defined in terms of its method, that of Aristotelian logic and the formal disputation, but the word may also mean the general goal which the scholars adopted: that of reconciling Christian faith and ancient philosophy. The 13th-century philosophers became the most renowned examples of high medieval thought. Their rigorous logic, careful distinctions, and long chains of argument represented an intellectual exercise which in its complexity and discipline was far in advance of anything since the age of Plato and Aristotle. Nor is it correct to say that they merely revived the Greek philosophy. They were heavily indebted to Aristotle, but their adaptations of his philosophy to Christianity showed originality.

St. Thomas Aquinas

The greatest of these 13th-century Schoolmen was Thomas Aquinas, an Italian who, beginning his education at Frederick II's University of Naples, joined the Dominican order, studied at Cologne under the famous Albertus Magnus, and then taught at Paris. He dedicated his powerful mind to the task of making Aristotelianism compatible with Christianity. In 1228 Pope Gregory IX had tried to remove Aristotle from the universities, reproaching the Paris faculty of theology with teaching the text of the Philosopher above the word of God. Yet papal fiat could not stop the advance, and to preserve the unity of Christian thought Aquinas labored to show that reason and revelation, philosophy and faith, Aristotle and Christ do not contradict each other, but take separate roads to the same goal. Aquinas has been called the greatest of all apologists, and his masterpiece, the *Summa Theologica*, remains a classic of philosophical writing. He can be seen as more than an apologist, for he allowed reason autonomy and regarded man as by nature a reasoning animal, his intellect not radically impaired by original sin as some Augustinians had taught. The often repeated assertion that medieval Scholastics relied on authority rather than reason has little truth in it. Aquinas explicitly declares that the appeal to authority is the weakest of all arguments, and endeavors to defend every proposition by the most rigorous use of reason. In the last analysis reason will not contradict faith, so he believed; but it is not to be directly guided by faith. Faith supplements rather than controls reason. Grace, as Aquinas puts it, perfects nature but does not abolish it. His own works came under papal suspicion, and he was not canonized as the Angelic Doctor until the 14th century—by which time other doctors, using his own methods, had gone beyond St. Thomas in proclaiming the independence of reason from faith.

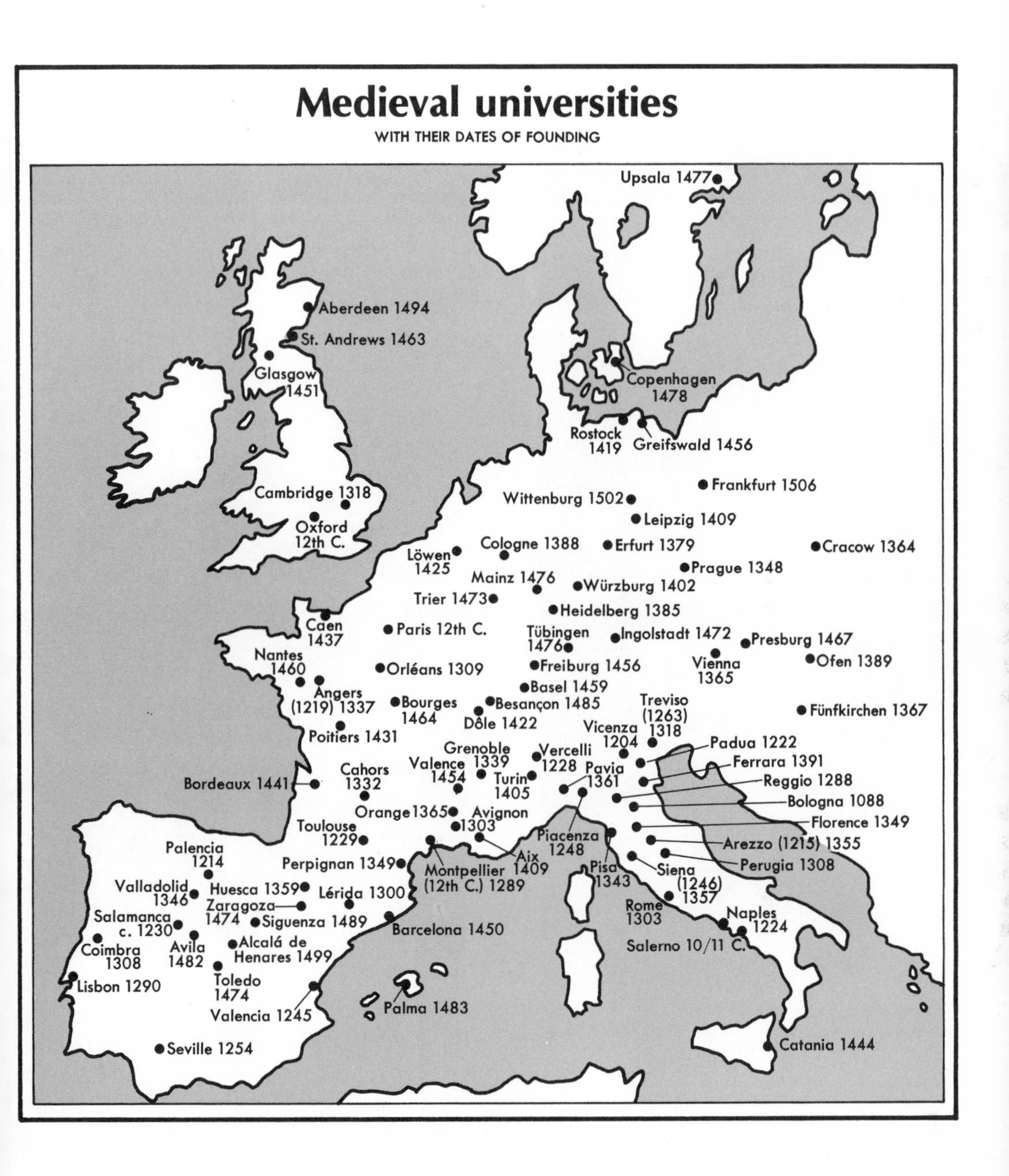

Medieval universities
WITH THEIR DATES OF FOUNDING
Upsala 1477
Aberdeen 1494
St. Andrews 1463
Glasgow 1451
Copenhagen 1478
Rostock 1419
Greifswald 1456
Frankfurt 1506
Cambridge 1318
Wittenburg 1502
Leipzig 1409
Oxford 12th C.
Löwen 1425
Cologne 1388
Erfurt 1379
Cracow 1364
Prague 1348
Mainz 1476
Würzburg 1402
Trier 1473
Heidelberg 1385
Caen 1437
Paris 12th C.
Tübingen 1476
Ingolstadt 1472
Presburg 1467
Nantes 1460
Orléans 1309
Freiburg 1456
Vienna 1365
Ofen 1389
Basel 1459
Angers (1219) 1337
Bourges 1464
Besançon 1485
Treviso (1263) 1318
Fünfkirchen 1367
Dôle 1422
Poitiers 1431
Vicenza 1204
Padua 1222
Grenoble 1339
Vercelli 1228
Ferrara 1391
Cahors 1332
Valence 1454
Pavia 1361
Reggio 1288
Bordeaux 1441
Turin 1405
Bologna 1088
Orange 1365
Avignon 1303
Florence 1349
Toulouse 1229
Piacenza 1248
Arezzo (1215) 1355
Palencia 1214
Aix 1409
Perugia 1308
Perpignan 1349
Montpellier (12th C.) 1289
Pisa 1343
Siena (1246) 1357
Valladolid 1346
Huesca 1359
Lérida 1300
Zaragoza 1474
Rome 1303
Naples 1224
Salamanca c. 1230
Siguenza 1489
Barcelona 1450
Coimbra 1308
Avila 1482
Alcalá de Henares 1499
Salerno 10/11 C.
Lisbon 1290
Toledo 1474
Valencia 1245
Palma 1483
Seville 1254
Catania 1444

Thomas Aquinas, "the angelic doctor."

Globes like this revealed medieval man's interest in the heavens—late medieval globe by J. Stoffler of Tübingen University.

The vast, imposing synthesis of Aquinas marks an epoch in European thought. It is typical of the 13th century in the harmony which it finds everywhere, in its avoidance of extremes, and its blending of secular and clerical ideas.

Medieval science

Contrary to an impression once prevalent, the high Middle Ages did not completely neglect science, despite a preoccupation with metaphysics. Leonard of Pisa led an advance in the realm of mathematics that was most fruitful, not only recovering Euclid but making some original contributions. Saturation with the spirit of ancient Greek philosophy was bound to arouse something of the scientific spirit, meaning an interest in experimental inquiry with careful analysis to attain truth of a general character. It is by no means true that the medieval scholars disparaged experiment. Especially at Oxford, under Robert Grosseteste and Roger Bacon, was there a significant advocacy of experimental science. Modern science is now believed to have been an outgrowth of late medieval work, in which the Aristotelian University of Padua and the 14th-century Ockhamists at Paris as well as Oxford played important parts. (For Ockham, see the chapter following.)

It is true that Aristotle's framework of ideas eventually proved unsatisfactory for physical science. It is also true that the Schoolmen by their nature were not professional scientists and tended to theorize more than they practiced in this area. Laboratory science was largely missing from the medieval universities; the approach was bookish. Still, we must always be on our guard against condemning past science because it was not as good as ours. It could not be, since science is cumulative. Our own science will doubtless some day be obsolete and appear laughable in many particulars. The test is whether an age made its due contribution to the advance of scientific discovery. The verdict of recent historians of science has been that the Middle Ages passes this test comfortably. Serious historical scholarship no longer assumes that the Schoolmen discussed only such apparently frivolous issues as whether angels were corporeal or immaterial. They did discuss such issues, which then seemed important, but the range of medieval thought was much wider, and came close to the universality of Aristotle himself, whose works on scientific method (*Analytics*), physics, and biology were among the most important of his writings.

More obviously, the medieval universities neglected the humanities, the classics of literature, which in revenge the Renaissance was to turn to so enthusiastically. Logic ruled, not literature. There were humanists in the Middle Ages, but they scarcely made their way into the universities. Troubadours sang, and so did students; but professors did not teach literature.

Medieval art and architecture

Medieval art as communication

Philosophy, science, law, and theology were not for the great majority in the Middle Ages. For them, within the spacious walls of the cathedrals unrolled the sumptuous pageantry of the church services. Visual imagery was its key: in an age before books were plentiful or many people could read, this was natural. "The Church educated people to understand painting as a language and to look at it for the expression of their sincerest feeling," wrote Bernard Berenson, the famous student of Italian Renaissance painting. Popularly, ideas were then conveyed chiefly not by the printed word but by painting and sculpture filled with symbols, and also by direct speech or the performance of dramatic ceremonies. Within the cathedral, sculpture and the glorious splendor of stained glass—an art we cannot duplicate today—offered riches for the eye, while music heightened the impressive ceremonies of the colorfully dressed clerics. The mass lives on, and anyone who has watched it performed in a great European Gothic cathedral can get an idea of its imaginative power, even in a rationalist age. In a medieval city, the effect would have been enhanced by the costumes of the worshipers and penitents themselves, for it was a time of color and individuality in dress, far more so than in the relatively standardized modern world.

Architecture

The cathedral itself was a triumph over space on behalf of beauty, and the culmination of a long journey in the building arts since the end of the ancient world. One can make out distinctive styles in the Dark Ages (4th–8th centuries), in the Carolingian "renaissance," and the Ottonian (11th century, imperial)—and perhaps others. Not much survives, and building was never very advanced in these centuries; there was not enough wealth or pooled skills, and art styles expressed themselves in much smaller things, sometimes exquisitely done: ivory reliefs, metalwork, crucifixes, manuscript illustrating. Byzantine influence was strong, though the Germanic peoples had their own decorative styles.

But in the 11th and 12th centuries we get a significant change, corresponding to that major renaissance described in the previous chapter. This was the age of the Romanesque. "Romanesque art is essentially architectural"; some splendid cathedrals were built, though at this time it was still the monasteries more than the urban churches which claimed the center of the architectural stage. Abbey churches and chapter houses provide most of the gems of the Romanesque, but the solid massiveness of such a cathedral as Durham in England is a tribute to the strength of Europe in its first great renaissance. Compared to the Gothic, Romanesque is unsophisticated, but it is powerful. In the early examples of it the roofs were not yet vaulted, but were built flat. The blunt strength of the Norman architecture in England is well expressed in the enormous castles they built, as for example at Dover, startling still in the sheer ability to handle huge masses of stone with perfect competence. Romanesque decoration tends to the stereotyped and abstract, without much originality. We feel with this style that we are in the presence of a society still young and crude, yet possessed of tremendous vitality—as was indeed the case.

Gothic began in the middle of the 12th century and lasted, in some places, until the 16th; in England it still flourished gloriously if a bit over-ripely in

Triumph of soaring Got[h]
space—Laon cathedral [in]
France, begun in 1170.

Tudor times, but in Italy the Florentine Renaissance pushed it out of all but the North by 1450. Without much question its zenith fell in the 13th century. French in origin, it spread widely throughout Europe to become a truly European style. France was at this time the cultural and intellectual capital of Europe; the court of Saint Louis and the University made Paris and its environs a unique center of all the arts and sciences. St. Denis abbey church, near Paris, is usually accounted the first Gothic structure. French architects and sculptors worked on cathedrals as far afield as Canterbury in England and Bamberg in Franconia.

Gothic architecture with its pointed arches (differing from the ordinarily round Romanesque) and its soaring vertical effects, culminating in the spires, seems quivering with aspirations toward heaven; but the conquest of space in the almost miraculous interiors is a triumph of reason for human purposes; outside, the flying buttresses intricately arranged, which make the interior effect possible, boast openly of the technical achievement. To many, these huge harmonious edifices, made up of reason balanced with faith, have

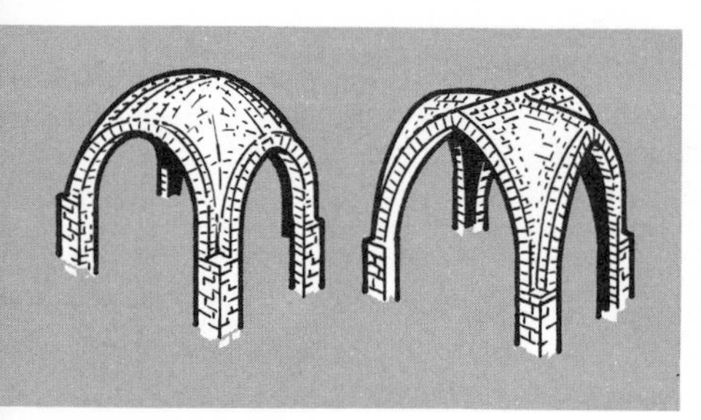

Romanesque and Gothic arches

Gothic light and lightness—13th century Lorenzkirche, Nürnberg, Germany

seemed comparable to the *Summae* of the Scholastic doctors, "encyclopediae carved in stone." The sculpture which filled the interiors and adorned the exteriors of the Gothic cathedrals is more naturalistic, more human, more personal than earlier. It is a myth that this feeling for the natural and the real had to await the Italian Renaissance.

The abundance of artistic treasure surviving from the 13th century leaves no doubt about the immensity of the achievement. And much was lost, especially during the anticlerical vandalism of the Reformation and from the normal attrition of time and war, to which such things as stained glass windows have been more than normally vulnerable. While pride of place belongs to architecture, sculpture and painting underwent tremendous development and music had its own glories. There was an interesting medieval theater, too. The greatest drama was the mass itself. The visual and dramatic arts excelled because of the relative paucity of a popular written literature. In all the art forms of the century there is evident a balance, though with tension, between reason and faith, nature and transcendence.

Naturalism in German Gothic sculpture—the Bamberger Reiter, left, and Ekkehart and Uta, by the celebrated Naumberg Meister, done about 1250–1260.

Dante

The search for a gigantic synthesis of life in all its phases, found in the Gothic cathedrals and in the *Summae* of the Schoolmen, may also be glimpsed magnificently in Dante, greatest of medieval poets. The great Florentine's life reaches into the 14th century and he is sometimes treated as a pioneer of the Renaissance, as indeed he was; but Dante also summed up the Middle Ages in his *Divine Comedy*. This vast poem is a sort of *Summa* itself, almost an encyclopedia of medieval knowledge; at the same time it is a work of art, filled with as much intricate craftsmanship and beauty as a cathedral. The fervent Christian faith that inspired it is evident even as Dante sharply criticizes some popes. But there is also science and philosophy. No reader of the *Commedia* can fail to feel its force, or rise from reading it without recognizing that the age that produced it was, however different from our own, a great one.

"The title Dark Ages, given to the medieval centuries, is, respecting art, wholly inapplicable. They were, on the contrary, the bright ages; ours are the dark ones." So wrote John Ruskin, in the 19th century.

Chivalry and song

While the cities, where most of the great universities settled and where the cathedrals grew toward the sky, held a good part of the 13th century's culture, the courts of the feudal lords made some progress, too. The nobility showed a tendency to become more civilized. In their cruder days the barbarian warriors, who became feudal knights, attached worth to sheer physical prowess and bravery. To be able to beat up the next man was their childish idea of achievement. Highly prized too was that quality of loyalty which contributed so much to the spirit of feudalism; and also *largesse*, generosity. In time the knights grew less fierce. The knightly class developed a sense of proper behavior, at least between themselves: the word was "courtesy." This was the first of several varieties of "chivalry."

Varieties of chivalry

Courtesy came to include, in addition to loyalty and bravery, the qualities of mercy and kindness, fair play and generous treatment of prisoners of war, even gentleness. This went so far that knights turned war into a series of sporting encounters between individuals, and eventually spent most of their time fighting in the jousts or tourneys which were simply games. These great games were, of course, a high point of medieval color, pageantry, and sport. Modern sports events still borrow the name of "tournament." Armored warriors jousting at each other on horseback represented some improvement over the Roman habit of allowing wild animals to maul slaves, and clearly foreshadowed the modern sporting event.

The church attempted unceasingly to propagate a higher ideal of life than that of constant brawling, and eventually succeeded in suffusing chivalry with a Christian content. In the 11th century the "Peace of God" idea spread with the vigorous backing of the clergy to become the "Truce of God," which restricted war to certain days. The Crusades, obviously, involved a diversion

Knight of the 13th century

of the nobility toward religious goals. St. Bernard of Clairvaux helped found the Order of the Temple, white-clad soldiers of Christ, spiritual knights pledged to service and self-sacrifice. (The Knights Templar failed sadly to live up to Bernard's high ideals, unfortunately.) By the later 12th century we get elaborate discussions of the qualities of a Christian knight. He should serve the church, help the poor, spare the weak, and live a chaste life. Such classic medieval romances as the *Song of Roland* and the Quest for the Holy Grail include a strong religious element: the service of God as well as emperor, the holy pilgrimage. It should not be supposed that all knights became models of saintly virtue; their habits of living by war and ransom were too deeply ingrained. But it can be agreed that Christian chivalry was an important idea with many practical consequences.

A medieval tournament

Courtly love

A third version of chivalry—as inconsistent with the other two as they were with each other, it has seemed to some students of the subject—was that connected with fair ladies, damsels in distress, and "courtly love." "The ideas of courtly love first appeared in the lyric poetry composed by the troubadours of southern France." This love poetry probably came from neighboring Muslim Spain, thus being another import from that source of the medieval renaissance. Troubadour love lyrics were passionate and often sensual: the chemical reaction known to occur between members of opposite sexes seldom have received franker or more joyous recognition. This poetry was a part of that Provençal culture so brutally crushed in the Albigensian crusade early in the 13th century. But the exalted opinion of sexual love which it propagated had already spread to other parts of Christendom. Courtly love fused with the cult of chivalry. A knight would be braver because of a beautiful lady. Indeed, it was "doubtful whether a man who did not adore a lady could be a true knight." The court of the counts of flourishing Champagne, where Chrétien de Troyes wrote in the 12th century, became its leading center. Credited with bringing the troubadour tradition into northern France from her native province was the celebrated Eleanor of Aquitaine, the wife successively of King Louis VII of France, who divorced her, and King Henry II of England, who finally imprisoned her after she sided with her sons in a rebellion against Henry (1173–74). Eleanor's own life was material for a romance; it was fitting that she and her daughter, the Countess of Champagne, tirelessly supported the literature of courtly love.

John of Salisbury, writing in this century, was not at all sure it was seemly for renowned nobles to sing and play love songs, as they seemed to be doing. One of Chrétien's tales is of a knight, Eric, who fell so madly in love that he neglected his knightly duties for his marital ones. Nor was courtly love always confined within the bounds of monogamous marriage. A favorite medieval story, that of Tristan and Iseult (Tristram and Isolde), posed the dilemma of courtly love at odds with Christian morals: what if there was true love between a man and another man's wife? The 7th and 10th commandments clearly indicated the answer if one wished to avoid mortal sin by Christian standards, but the medieval romancers were by no means sure. Love, too, had its claims, to deny which was more of a sin than adultery to these writers. Their Bible was Ovid, whose *Art of Love* constituted one of the chief sources of this cult.

Anthropologists and sociologists declare that romantic love in the form it has been found in Western civilization is not a universal human instinct, but is a peculiarity of our culture, which we owe largely to the Middle Ages. Obviously sex, and in some sense love, are found everywhere, but the whole complex of girl and boy "falling in love," and endowing this with qualities of tenderness and sentiment, etc., is uniquely Western and may be traced back to the troubadours. It should be added that the medieval form of romantic love was more daring than later, since it was so often associated with a married woman who was permitted to have lovers. The custom, which a later Puritanism found so shocking, by which in European aristocratic circles both wives and husbands were permitted and even expected to have extramarital love affairs, goes back to medieval romance.

Thus it appears that knightly, churchly, and courtly chivalry were uneasy and perhaps flagrantly inconsistent companions. If the first abjured a knight to go forth and fight, albeit fairly and "courteously," the second encouraged him to champion worthy causes and live a chaste life, while the third suggested that he please and woo beautiful women. One might fuse these strains. The familiar story of the knight who overthrows an oppressive tyrant to rescue a beautiful imprisoned maiden, and is rewarded with her hand, manages to combine all three. In real life there probably was a shortage of such ideal circumstances. But the modern love story has not got much further. Modern life still appears to bear the stamp of the age of chivalry and romance.

As for the knights, they were obviously being softened and tamed by this process, as well as becoming just a bit ridiculous. Rough and crude though it had been, given to murder and rapine, the earliest knighthood of Europe was unquestionably brave and had played a part in saving society from utter anarchy. When its usefulness declined with the rise of more orderly government, of cities and civilization, the feudal nobility tended to become superfluous and decadent. By the time of Cervantes and his *Don Quixote*, it had become pathetic or absurd, though even then it upheld generous ideals.

St. Louis, from a French Bible of the 13th century

Saint Louis, the ideal king of chivalry

That time lay well ahead of the 13th century, however, and during this summertime of the Middle Ages knighthood was still in flower. The ideal of the Christian knight appeared in the famous Saint Louis, king of France (Louis IX, 1226–70). Zealous for religion to the point of suppressing heresy via the Inquisition, Louis went on two Crusades against the infidels, but courteously yielded a province to England to avoid war with a Christian monarch. As king, he strengthened the throne and improved royal justice. He waged war on private warfare, and made his own court a center of chivalry. During Louis' reign, French medieval civilization in all its glory broke forth: Gothic cathedrals were built, the University of Paris became the center of the philosophical renaissance. A vital part of this rich civilization was the literature and the practice of chivalry.

The role of the papacy

Recurring through the Middle Ages are the fights between the kings and the popes for the ultimate power. The church claimed to be the mentor and guide of kings and kingdoms in all their activities, but the secular rulers seldom gave way easily. The issues generally concerned appointment of the clergy, immunity of the clergy from secular law, and collection of taxes. On paper and in battle the "two swords"—the temporal and the spiritual—quibbled and struggled for mastery, until finally men came to believe that there was not room for two masters in a sovereign state.

Innocent III

The 13th century began with the tremendous pontificate of Innocent III (Pope from 1198–1216) who gave classic expression to the theory of a universal Christian society under papal leadership. In Innocent's Lateran Council of 1215 the creed and ritual of the church received their classic medieval formulation, the Sacraments being declared the means of grace, and specifically defined, while the administration of the church was more systematically organized. At the same time papal authority over the secular powers was insisted upon with a new clarity and firmness. Innocent did not hesitate to rebuke all the powerful monarchs of Europe—John of England, Philip II of France, and the Holy Roman Emperor. Ever since the 11th century, the papacy had retained its Hildebrandine conception of the spiritual power effectively disciplining the temporal. It did not usually have much luck carrying out this program, but there were auspicious occasions when it succeeded. A century after Canossa, Henry II of England was forced to yield most of the points in dispute with the pope after his men had murdered, and made a martyr of, Thomas Becket, the Archbishop of Canterbury. Forty years later King John, the same unfortunate monarch who lost to the barons of Magna Carta, had to accept defeat in his quarrel with Innocent, swearing to become the Pope's vassal (1213). (In return the Pope condemned Magna Carta and rebuked the barons who drew it up, 1215). And, as related, the papacy secured the downfall of Frederick II and the Hohenstaufens after a fierce struggle.

The unity of Europe in the 13th century still found its symbol in the unity of Christendom under a single church. Both the monarchs and the papacy had grown in power and pride, and at times they clashed. But they also were able to cooperate, and in their dual reign over the souls and bodies of men, medieval people beheld that essential unity. While at times much of Europe seemed divided into "Guelfs" and "Ghibellines," papalists and imperialists, there was still no doubt of there being but one great society in which spiritual and temporal rulers must somehow divide power.

The church and its powers

The theory by which the papacy was "the father of kings," whose task it was to keep peace among them and correct them when they erred, had in it majestic and noble elements. It was not always persuasive in practice. The papacy became wealthy and worldly. It did not scruple to command its own military force, though mostly it called upon other kings or princes to join in disciplining a recalcitrant ruler. For reasons of their own these rival powers might oblige. Thus the papacy was drawn into the political arena and appeared to be only another interested power. In the 13th century the pope often seemed like the leading monarch of Europe: indeed, Innocent III received the homage of half the states of Europe as their feudal superior. Owning huge quantities of land, controlling education, and collecting great revenues, the pope excited the natural envy of kings, and when he claimed a power to veto their actions as rulers they were unlikely to acquiesce. The papacy was able at times to dominate the kings because its spiritual authority was great, and excommunication was a dread weapon; because, also, the clergy monopolized learning and kings could scarcely yet do without them in government.

Because students have a tendency to exaggerate the powers of the medieval church, often thinking of it as a sort of counterpart of modern totalitarianisms, it ought to be stressed that even at its zenith the church remained heavily dependent on the other "sword," too. The papacy exercised direct power over an area around Rome, but elsewhere it had to rely primarily on moral force or the willingness of the secular ruler to cooperate. At most times and places those rulers had a keen sense of their own interests and were not particularly religious. In any case all government was so weak in the medieval age that it can hardly be compared to modern government.

But the papacy, a worldly institution, always ran in danger of losing its spiritual purity and abusing its powers. Criticisms of obviously ungodly popes, complaints about corruption in the clergy and scandalous lapses in the monasteries, were not heard for the first time in the Reformation era; they were common enough in the Middle Ages. The vitality of Christianity had revealed itself in the series of reforms and renewals which came from below: from Cluny and Citeaux, from St. Francis and St. Dominic. But the upper reaches of the church constantly tended to lose their spiritual character. The last of the great medieval popes, Boniface VIII, at the end of the 13th century, seems more worldly than spiritual. It was this Pope who produced in 1302 the most famous and extreme statement of the direct supremacy of the church through the papacy over all temporal rulers—the bull *Unam Sanctam*.

Extreme papalist claims

Unam Sanctam argued that the two swords, the temporal and spiritual, are both in the keeping of the church, though the former is not exercised directly *by* the church; she has the power but chooses to delegate this power to others. "There is no power but from God" and this power the holy, Catholic and apostolic church holds by virtue of Christ's commitment to Peter. The spiritual power is superior to the temporal in dignity and nobility, and therefore may judge the temporal one, just as man's soul is the director of his body. Therefore, "Every human creature is subject to the Roman Pontiff." The bold claims of *Unam Sanctam* were soon hotly disputed by "imperialist" writers, who employed a variety of arguments but relied mostly, perhaps, on "My Kingdom is not of this world": Christ, and therefore his church, is not properly concerned with the governance of temporal matters, but only with the purely spiritual. The church should stay out of politics, as we might put it. Diagramatically, the difference between papalists and imperialists might be given as follows.

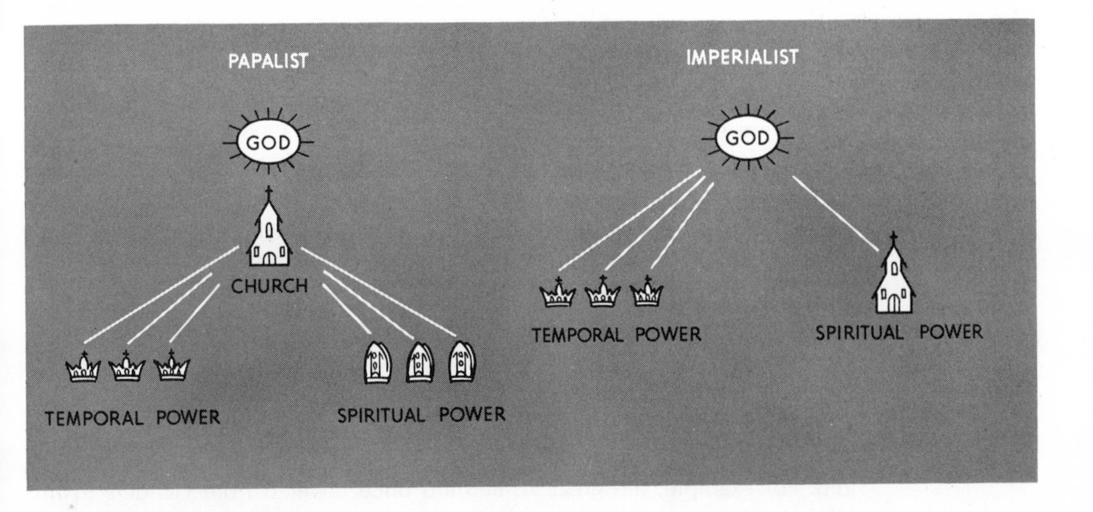

The imperialists did not think the monarchs got their power from the church, but directly from God.

Defeat of the papacy

Boniface was not afraid to clash head on with the powerful rulers of Europe—Edward I of England, Philip IV (the Fair) of France. He lost, as these powerful and popular monarchs showed that they could master the clergy within their domains. Boniface ended in defeat and humiliation. It was the last gasp of the medieval papacy, which soon fell into sad decline. It is possible to be sympathetic to the claims of an international institution, possessing terrific spiritual resources, against the upsurge of the national monarchies; and yet it is difficult not to feel that the ambitious Boniface had become just another politician and forfeited his spiritual authority. The fact is that, right or wrong, the monarchies of western Europe, backed by public opinion, were announcing a new era, which marked the passing of the zenith of medieval civilization. In the 13th century, however, a rough equilibrium existed between nationalism and internationalism, monarchs and papacy.

Intolerance and inequality

Repression of heresy

While granting the grandeur of the Gothic, the technical proficiency of Scholastic philosophers within their field, and all the interesting features of medieval life—chivalry, guilds, parliaments, and so on—most moderns resent and reject such undeniable facets of medieval life as heresy hunting, the Inquisition, anti-Semitism, and in general the monolithic conception of society and culture: one faith, one church, one point of view. These cannot be assigned to the darker past, for they flourished in the 13th century and were matters of pride. The *beau ideal* of a Christian king, St. Louis, considered it glorious to repress heretics; the Dominicans devoted their talents to it. The medieval Inquisition had nothing like the power associated later with the Spanish one, and in general the 13th century was not as aggressively intolerant as the 16th, when Protestant and Romanist waged war on each other. Nevertheless there was no room for other than Christians; baptism was necessary for citizenship, excommunication meant loss of all civil and political rights. Jews were despoiled and expelled from France in 1306, England in 1290—treated with contempt virtually everywhere at all times.

Of these deplorable features all one can say is that their roots lay deep in both human nature and tradition. St. Thomas taught that the perfection of the Christian life lay "primarily in the love of God, derivatively in the love of our neighbor." "Where there is hatred let me sow love," St. Francis prayed. But few medieval people apparently thought of this love as extending beyond the circle of Christendom. The doctrine of the "just war" included sanction for any war waged by Christians on infidels, and the obligations of knightly courtesy did not extend to non-Christians. We should be careful to discriminate between what the church taught and what the mob sometimes did. For example, the great St. Bernard once traveled from Flanders to the Rhineland to stop a vicious anti-Jewish outburst which had broken out in several of the cities of the Rhine. The greater spiritual leaders of the church never appproved of such pogroms, or the massacres and looting which a brutalized feudal army might inflict, as during the crusade against the Albigensians. But they did approve of the extirpation of heresy, and instigated it. St. Bernard was quite willing to deliver the persistent heretic to the stake.

Medieval anti-Semitism was caused in part by the identification of the Jews with money-lending and other forms of "capitalism," long forbidden to Christians. There are numerous examples of high churchmen seeking to protect the Jews from popular hostility. On the other hand, the spirit of religious intolerance, thoroughly approved by the medieval church, was bound to excrete anti-Semitism as a by-product.

Sources of intolerance

Christianity was, of course, a religion that assumed one revelation, one Christ, no other pathway to salvation save utter faith in him. That this might be a matter of indifference seemed to medieval man a most shocking idea. And the classical tradition of political thought in certain ways reenforced this intolerance. Aristotle's *Politics* held that the state is natural to man, a part of his very being: in and through it men derive all their rights. There was no political individualism here; that was an invention of the postmedieval centuries. The state existed to promote the "good life" in positive ways, according to Greek political theory. This point is worth stressing in view of the common belief that only Christianity was responsible for medieval intolerance while the Greeks were more enlightened. Plato's advocacy of religious intolerance, in the *Laws*, is specific and extreme: religious disbelief is to be punished with imprisonment or in incorrigible cases, death. (This was to be done by the state: the Greeks knew no church.) The later liberal idea, of a state which confined itself to keeping peace, allowing each individual to go his own way with as little interference as possible—this conception of the state emerged after the Reformation and was unknown in the Middle Ages.

Medieval governments were in practice weak; but in theory they claimed full powers to supervise men's souls as well as their bodies. The former, of course, were the concern of the church, considered one of the two arms or "swords" of government. But the secular authorities were usually eager to punish heretics, too. Men could not conceive of a society that lacked basic ideological unity.

Also somewhat foreign to the modern mind is another medieval political axiom, that of natural inequality. Society was viewed as an organism, of which the parts were necessarily unequal. The feeling was for hierarchy, not equality. Men, like the parts of the body, had unequal functions. It would be absurd to talk about the equality of the feet with the head, and medieval thought found it equally absurd to speak of an equality of serf with noble. No doubt they both had rights, but the rights were appropriate to their differing stations in society. This point of view reflected the realities of feudal society, but also came naturally to the medieval mind which saw the universe as a hierarchy of being.

Constitutionalism

Intolerance and inequality mar the Middle Ages from the viewpoint of most moderns but they seemed proper then. We should realize that they went right along with many conceptions which the modern mind regards as eminently reasonable. The Middle Ages were saturated with the idea of law, conceived of as not made by men but found and declared—its foundations being the eternal natural laws decreed by God. Completely foreign was the notion of absolute or despotic power. Rulers got their power from God and the people: there is constant reference to "the consent of the people" as the source of law and government even though in practice popular institutions might be crude or lacking. Parliaments grew up in the 13th century, and so did the Roman law with its high standards of equity for all men. Feudalism, in theory at least, was a ladder of consent and contract, resting on agreement not compulsion. The political legacy of the Middle Ages included constitutionalism, law, and representative government—a valuable heritage indeed. Though obviously true, this fact is still probably not popularly appreciated. Perhaps people have difficulty in understanding how an age that produced the Inquisition could also produce parliaments, or that feudalism included both inequality and liberty. But so it was.

Medieval civilization in summary

The 13th century indeed stands in European history as a great one, the climax of medieval civilization, which had been in creation since the fall of Rome and which was, in the 14th century, to show signs of disintegration. For a moment it blossomed in glory. The visible signs of that glory, still standing, are majestic Gothic cathedrals with craftsmanship of matchless skill and beauty. The medieval philosophers provided a happy synthesis of reason and faith and a summation of all knowledge. Chivalry tamed the unruly fighting barons into "courteous" knights. Town life grew, and was stabilized by craft guilds, which gave economic stability while guaranteeing craftsmanship. (In our time, some "Guild Socialists" have proposed this medieval system of production as a model of social justice which we could well imitate.) The forces of society were in equilibrium: the papacy, at its peak of influence, checked kings, kings restrained nobles, town and country were in harmony. Relatively at least, there was peace: the wars of nationalism had not yet begun, while the anarchy of the Dark Ages was at an end. The thriving cities and the rich churches of Europe gave evidence of prosperity. It was an age of intellectual development in which thought broke through the bonds of a strict religious confinement without losing its essential unity. Science and philosophy made progress. This century brought to birth our modern parliamentary political institutions and modern law. It is the century of St. Francis, Thomas Aquinas, the scientist Roger Bacon, Dante, Saint Louis, Edward the "English Justinian," Frederick *stupor mundi.*

Such at least is the more favorable judgment. The 13th century was certainly not wanting in either conflict, ignorance, or evil. It was marred by intolerance, it was unable to resolve fundamental problems which caused a breakdown in the next era. It was far from perfect, though entitled to a distinguished place in history on anybody's reckoning. In retrospect, we can see that the equilibrium it attained could not last. The most apparent political conflict bound to occur was that just described: the monarchs were certain to challenge the claims of the papacy, with great wealth and power as the stakes. Two sovereigns there could not be. In fact, this conflict, as we have noted, was persistent all through the Middle Ages. The 13th century itself was racked by it: it ended with the ruin of the papacy which itself had brought down the Empire.

Medieval philosophy was also unstable in its alleged reconciliation of the claims of reason and faith. Fourteenth-century philosophers rejected the Thomistic synthesis as untenable. The range of medieval thought was relatively narrow, its bases thin. Unity was possible only because thought was in its infancy. Its explanations ceased to satisfy as knowledge accumulated and the critical intellect continued to probe. The forces set in motion by the Schoolmen proved stronger than the bonds of faith in which they wished to confine them. Once unleashed, the spirit of Socrates was bound to carry on beyond any dogmatic limitations.

To this we might add that the economic and social balance of medieval economy, represented by the guilds, also proved unstable. In time the commercial spirit would produce individual capitalists and destroy the cooperative features of medieval town life; class conflict would arise with great extremes of wealth and poverty. A more complex economy would develop. The high Middle Ages was a fruitful period for technological improvement. Technological change—the development of new machines, tools, techniques —undermined the social foundations of medieval life. (The old view that the Middle Ages were technologically backward will no longer hold up; leading students who have carefully investigated this subject in recent years think that this was a time of decisive discovery in technology as well as in some of the sciences.) Modern capitalism broke through the restraints of the guilds just as the modern state repudiated the shackles of the papacy and modern thought refused to stop at the boundaries of Christian belief.

Diversity of medieval life and thought

Those who know the Middle Ages best—students of medieval art, literature, philosophy, music—emphatically do not accept the old bromide about the changeless rigidity of medieval culture, any more than they accept the verdict of sterility and stagnation. On the contrary, medieval modes of art and expression reveal innumerable variations to the trained eye. The variations are within a different range than the modern and thus can be missed at first sight. The range of the medieval *was* in a sense narrower than that of the modern, but infinite variations can be played on just a few notes, and this happened in the Middle Ages. Scholastic philosophers are *not* all alike, nor are Romanesque cathedrals. Within the limits of certain basic similarities they exhibit considerable difference in detail.

The medieval world was one of a diversity that may seem disorderly but can impress one as delightful. Society was chiefly organized on a local basis; the all-embracing and omnipotent state had not yet made its appearance. While monarchs were strong enough to provide some unity, the many towns, cities, universities, guilds, church units and other "corporations" led their own vigorous life with more autonomy than is true today. In theory they were all supposed to be parts of a single, organic society. Each corporation and each class had its special functions, duties, and rights within the hierarchical framework.

In leaving the Middle Ages it is perhaps worth remarking that a good many undesirable traits associated with this period are the result of false history, or rather propaganda. In later times the Renaissance, the Reformation (in Protestant countries), and the Enlightenment each had its special reasons for being unfair to the Middle Ages. They picked out certain features and condemned them because their own cause profited thereby. To Protestants it was the age of popes, and most popes were villainous; to *philosophes*, it was the age of religion, and all religions were odious. There is little in the way of cruelty, intolerance, or any other depravity that one cannot find somewhere in the long period between 500 and 1400. But the same could be said of any such period of time, and hardly constitutes a fair judgment. It would be as easy to blacken the modern age, or any other, by similar selective use of evidence. It should be repeated, first, that there was a vast difference between the 8th or the 10th century and the 13th; second, that Europe started from barbarism and one must judge by the amount of progress made, which was immense on any just reckoning; third, that in many particulars the civilization of the 13th century was probably superior to what came later: industrial organization, arts and crafts, ability to synthesize knowledge, absence of arrogant nationalism, and perhaps others. And finally that most of the stereotypes or labels placed on the "medieval" are quite false.

Medieval gloom?

One such stereotype is the view that these were gloomy times, when nobody had any fun, everybody wore hair shirts, and human nature was despised. That myth is a part of the propaganda of the Renaissance. One does not have to look far in the Middle Ages to find such things as a frank sexuality, boisterous and bawdy songs and stories, erotic poetry, fun poked at the clergy, drinking songs, music to which the people danced. Indeed, this is all part of a picture which some 19th-century romantics saw as the "merrie England" of olden times. One may find it in the Goliardi poets, the romances of chivalry, the love lyrics of Provence, the *fabliaux* and farces of the people. A choice selection of medieval song and story can be delightful. And there are a number of other medieval people and institutions we have not mentioned, but which came near the lives of the humble: jugglers and tumblers and minstrels, fairs and festivals and dances. Sunday, in these times, was a merry day for the common folk, as also were the numerous saints' days. Memories of pagan festivities mingled with these Christian holidays. Visitors to Europe today know of the many colorful festivals and holidays, some of which are purely local, others like May Day or the *Fasching* fairly general. Contrary to a widespread opinion, one of the chief legacies from medieval times is fun.

Bibliography

Walter Ullman, *Principles of Government and Politics in the Middle Ages* (London: Methuen Publications, 1962), and the same author's *The Growth of Papal Government in the Middle Ages* (New York: Barnes & Noble, 1955) are excellent works of synthesis. The papacy, key institution of the Middle Ages, was the subject of one of historical writing's most monumental achievements, Ludwig von Pastor's old *History of the Popes* which runs to 40 volumes in the English translations (St. Louis; Concordia Publishing House, 1891–1953). Daniel Waley has written more recently and more succinctly on *The Papal States in the Thirteenth Century* (New York: Macmillan, 1961). As for the secular monarchies, a large literature includes E. Kantorowicz's very distinguished *Frederick II* (London: Constable, 1958) and the same scholar's *The King's Two Bodies: A Study in Medieval Political Theology* (Prrinceton, N.J.: Princeton University Press, 1957). The best biography of *King John* is probably that of J.C. Holt (London: Eyre & Spottiswoode, 1961). *Magna Carta* received more than its usual attention in 1965, its 750th birthday; among the books of that year were one by J.C. Holt (Cambridge University Press), and a very usable little New American Library Mentor paperback, *The Great Charter*, a collection of essays by S.E. Thone and others. Norman Cantor, *Church, Kingship, and Lay Investiture in England* (Princeton University Press, 1958), is among those who have recently considered the famous medieval dualism of royal and ecclesiastical authority. John B. Morrall, *Political Thought in Medieval Times* (London: Hutchinson, 1958), is a useful survey, the older and longer classic being R.W. and A.J. Carlyle, *A History of Medieval Political Theory in the West* (2d ed. 6 vols., New York: Barnes and Noble, 1927–36). A distinguished American medievalist, Gaines Post, has written *Studies in Medieval Legal Thought: Public Law and the State* (Princeton University Press, 1964).

Turning to medieval culture, David Knowles provides a broad view of *The Evolution of Medieval Thought* (Random House, Vintage). F. Copleston, *Medieval Philosophy* (Harper Torchbook), is by an acknowledged master of the history of philosophy; so is

Etienne Gilson, *A History of Christian Philosophy in the Middle Ages* (New York: Random House, 1955). Grace Frank, *The Medieval French Drama* (Oxford: Clarendon Press, 1954), is one of the best books in its area; on the famous cathedrals, Otto G. von Simson, *The Gothic Cathedral* (Harper), Emil Mâle, *The Gothic Image* (Harper), and E. Panofsky, *Gothic Architecture and Scholasticism* (Macmillan), provide diverse approaches to the Gothic genius. Jessie Crosland, *Medieval French Literature* (Oxford: Blackwell, 1956), is a serviceable introduction. A less savory side of medieval life may be glimpsed in A.S. Turberville, *Medieval Heresy and the Inquisition* (Hamden, Conn.: Shoe String Press, reprinted 1964); and on the same subject, Henry Charles Lea's three-volume classic has been condensed and reprinted by Eyre and Spottiswoode, 1963.

Sources are rich; Thomas Gilby has a splendid edition of *St. Thomas Aquinas* in Oxford University Press paperback; J.B. Ross and Mary M. McLaughlin have selected widely and well from medieval thought and literature in *The Portable Medieval Reader* (Viking); and there are such special collections as Lynn Thorndike's *University Records and Life in the Medieval Ages* (Columbia University Press) and Jacob R. Marcus, *The Jew in the Medieval World: A Sourcebook* (World Publishing, Meridian). Andreas Capellanus, *The Art of Courtly Love* (Columbia University Press), or the E.P. Dutton Everyman paperback edition of *Aucassin and Nicolette and Other Medieval Romances*, represent one pleasant aspect of medieval life. See also Ralph Lerner and Muhsin Mahdi (eds.), *Medieval Political Philosophy: A Sourcebook* (New York: Free Press, 1963).

8

Transition from medieval to modern: 1300-1450

By the 15th century illuminated manuscripts were rich with vivid color and incredibly detailed decoration. New printing processes were soon to render them obsolete.

chronology

1271
Marco Polo sets out on his voyage to the Orient.
1305–77
Babylonian captivity: Avignon papacy.
1306
Expulsion of Jews from France.
1314–47
Louis the Bavarian, Wittelsbach claimant, disputes imperial title with Hapsburgs.
1321
Death of Dante, greatest medieval poet.
1328
End of the Capetian kings of France; beginning of Valois line.
Rival claim of Edward III to French throne.
1337–1453
Hundred Years War between England and France.
1341
Reaffirmation of Magna Carta, victory of feudal magnates in Parliament over Edward III in England.
1346
Battle of Crécy, English victory.
1348
University of Prague founded.
1349
Death of William of Ockham.
1348–50
Black Death epidemic in northern Europe.
Ottoman Turks enter Europe.
1356
Golden Bull (Holy Roman Empire)—electoral system established.
1358
Jacquerie of French peasants, resulting from misery caused by Hundred Years War.
1360
Peace of Bretigny, truce in war. Weakening of French monarchy.
Wycliffe's doctrines in England, c. 1360–85.
Petrarch, Boccaccio, beginnings of Italian humanism.
1369
Resumption of war in France.
1371
Voyage of Sir John Mandeville.
1377
Nicole Oresme postulates diurnal rotation of earth.
1378–1417
Great Schism in church.
1381
Peasant revolt in England.
Economic distress, uprisings in France. Paralysis of French monarchy under Charles VI.
Founding of Brethren of Common Life, Netherlands.
1384
Death of Wycliffe.
1389
Battle of Kossovo; Turkish conquest of Balkans.
1399
Murder of Richard II, England; end of Plantagenet dynasty.
1400
Death of Chaucer, author of the *Canterbury Tales.*
1402
Beginning of Hussite movement in Bohemia.
Thomas à Kempis, religious mysticism of Lowlands.
1414–17
Council of Constance. Execution of Hus. End of the Great Schism.
1415
Battle of Agincourt, victory of Henry V over French.
1418
Explorations of Prince Henry of Portugal begin.
1420–33
Hussite wars in Bohemia.
1429
Joan of Arc leads army to relief of Orléans.
1431
Council of Basel (schism, Hussites, church reform dealt with).
Execution of Joan of Arc by English at Rouen.
1438
Pragmatic sanction of Bourges (conciliarism, French national church).
Hapsburgs return to the throne of Germany.
1450
Jack Cade rebellion, England.
Invention of the printing press.
1453
End of Hundred Years War. Reform of French royal finances by Jacques Coeur, merchant prince.
Capture of Constantinople by Turks.
1455
Beginning of War of Roses, English civil war.

Troubles of the papacy

The 13th century had given the impression of a balance of forces, a happy equilibrium between extremes, in all areas—political, social, economic, intellectual. It was to break up in the stormy 14th century. This was an age of "profound upheavals and ferocious conflicts," an age of rapid, almost cataclysmic change. It saw the almost complete breakdown of some typical achievements of the high Middle Ages. In general, the "unities" of the 13th century, whether in political, social, economic, religious, or intellectual life, fell apart and were replaced by conflicts and divisions. There was schism in philosophy as there was in the church; both Aquinas' synthesis of reason and faith and Innocent's combination of monarchy and papacy proved inadequate. Among the disturbances and catastrophes of the century were the Babylonian Captivity and the Schism of the papacy, the Hundred Years War between France and England, the advance of the Turks into southeast Europe, the Black Death, peasant insurrections, class war in the cities, and, among the thinkers, a radical break with the Thomistic tradition of rational theology. The general impression is of a disturbed era, though certainly not one in danger of reverting to anything like Dark Age barbarism. There are gains which once made are not unmade, though they may go astray. Cities, universities, national governments, technology, complex systems of ideas—these persisted, in many respects they grew. But almost all historians agree that the period from about 1300 to 1450 has many of the attributes of an age when "one world was dying, another struggling to be born."

The Babylonian captivity

The decline of the papacy, that central institution of the Middle Ages, was one of the most important of such signs. In the aftermath of Boniface VIII's disastrous attempt to coerce the strong kings of both England and France, King Philip of France proposed Clement V (reigned 1305–14) for Pope. His election marks the beginning of French control of the papacy; and residence in Avignon, instead of Rome, which was torn by the Guelf-Ghibelline battles, indicated the temporary end of papal independence. The popes stayed in that lovely city on the Rhone, subject to the pressure of the French, for more than 70 years. That this was a period of exile, of "Babylonian captivity" (1307–77), most Christians instinctively felt, for the true home of the church was at Rome. The German emperors and people particularly resented the Avignon papacy, the more so since most of the popes opposed them and favored France politically. A similar reaction could be found in England. There was a long struggle for southern Italy between the French house of Anjou, supported by the popes, and the Spanish house of Aragon. In Italy, dislike of the French as ambitious imperialists combined with a natural desire to have the papacy returned to Rome. The Avignon popes were bitterly criticized (by Petrarch, among others) for luxurious living and personal immorality, though this criticism was perhaps somewhat prejudiced. The papacy was,

Schism in the papacy. The German emperor Sigismund sends envoys to two popes urging they resign.

in spite of itself, a plaything of the potent monarchs who struggled for greater power in Europe and were beginning to engage in the great game of international politics.

The scandal culminated in 1378 when "the Great Schism" divided the church in two, as separate sets of cardinals each elected a pope, one at Rome and one at Avignon. In 1409 a general council of the church deposed both popes and elected a third, but the other two refused to recognize the act, and thus there were three popes. The great Council of Constance, 1414–17, which also had to deal with the schism caused by John Hus and his followers in Bohemia, succeeded in restoring papal unity, with the Avignon line ending. But this body also affirmed the doctrine that a general council of the church is superior to the pope. Conciliarists hoped to make the "papal monarchy" into a parliamentary, constitutional one. The Pope just elected at Constance refused this doctrine and dissolved the body. The conciliar movement, supported by the European monarchs, who saw in it a method of gaining control of the church in their lands, remained strong. From a church thus bitterly rent into factions, kings availed themselves of the opportunity to extract generous privileges, such as those obtained by the French King in the Pragmatic Sanction of Bourges (1438), when went far toward nationalizing the church in France. The Sanction diverted church revenue from Rome to Paris and struck at the pope's power in matters of church administration and doctrine. Similar privileges passed to the German princes.

John Wycliffe

In the past, movements of reform had sooner or later arisen to rescue a church in trouble. They were not altogether lacking this time. But it appeared that the age of the medieval papacy had passed. Internationalism and spiritual unity no longer existed. Certainly it is true that some of the stronger religious expressions of this age either sailed close to the brink of "heresy" or actually passed right into it. Religious mysticism and late Scholastic skepticism are described later on in this chapter, in connection with the intellectual temper of the age: a temper which departed almost violently from the serene assurance of St. Thomas Aquinas that reason guarantees God and Christianity. Here we may note one figure of the church in the later 14th century: John Wycliffe (or Wyclif;[1] 1320?–84), frequently called a forerunner of the Protestant Reformation. This Yorkshireman studied theology at Oxford where the somewhat unorthodox philosophies of Duns Scotus and William of Ockham were already rampant. In arguing against the pope's power over the king or even over the church, Wycliffe was not going farther than imperialists or conciliarists, prominent at this time. But, as he went on with his project to translate the Bible into English, he came (c. 1370) to reject the sacramental powers of the church and preach a doctrine somewhat similar to that which Martin Luther later announced as salvation by individual faith alone. When the Pope tried to discipline him, Wycliffe received support from both people and rulers, being defended by the London commoners and by the powerful John of Gaunt, of the house of Lancaster, a claimant to the throne. The Great Schism then arrived to remove all threat of papal punishment, and Wycliffe never was troubled.

But monarchs no more than popes wished to overturn all authority in the church. The followers of Wycliffe, called Lollards, were persecuted in the 15th century, after being associated with the revolution of 1381. It is certain that Hus, the Czech rebel, read Wycliffe among others, and it seems that Lollardy never quite died out as an underground movement in England. If the hour was not yet quite ripe for the Protestant revolt, it definitely was foreshadowed here, 150 years before Luther. The trend was toward national control of religion, at the expense of the international, pope-controlled church. The latter proved unable to reform itself and rally, even after the healing of the "great schism" of 1378–1415.

---

[1] The uncertainty about the spelling of the names of medieval people reflects their own, in an age when orthography had not been invented and the written word counted less than the spoken. As most students know, even Shakespeare two centuries later had difficulty in deciding how he would spell his name.

Troubles of the monarchies: England and France

Thus the affairs of the church were about as confused as they could be, and the consequences for a Europe accustomed to the church's intellectual and spiritual supremacy were serious. One cause of this confusion was the rise of nationalism and national states. This period of European history stands as one in which national unity was being shaped, and kings would emerge with greater power on the ruins of the old feudal nobility. Nevertheless, if this was the ultimate result, it was not discernible through most of the 14th and early 15th centuries. On the contrary, kings were in as much trouble as popes; the feudal nobility experienced a resurgence, a last flare-up before being extinguished forever. Kings were on the whole weaker than in the 13th century, nobles stronger. And the common people suffered far more.

In England, the century after the death of the masterful Edward I saw a breakdown in the royal power and a rise of the barons. This baronial opposition was not always reactionary or benighted, for some of the magnates had constructive ideas; but they did demand a share in the governance of the realm. In so doing they unwittingly served the cause of a later parliamentarianism, but they caused considerable disorder at the time. They beat down Edward II who lost prestige through his shattering defeat by the Scots in 1314 (Bannockburn) and was murdered in 1327. They went on to increase their power under the able Edward III, who had to engage in foreign war in France. In 1341 they forced the King to concede parliamentary powers in a renewal of Magna Carta, and England entered upon an era of aristocratic government. An outstanding event was the deposition and murder of Richard II (1399), a King who had aspired to greater powers than he could wrest from the high nobility. With him the Plantagenet or Angevin kings of England came to an end; the power of Parliament, dominated by the baronage, continued over most of the next century, which was marked by a struggle between the dukes of York and Lancaster for the throne.

In France, the Valois kings, a collateral line, took over from the Capetians in 1328, sustained defeat at the hands of the English in war, and were forced to make concessions to the Estates-General, the French equivalent of England's national Parliament, while the great duchies tended to pursue independent courses. At the end of the century civil strife between Burgundy and Orléans in France was the counterpart of the English Yorkists and Lancastrians. In Spain, this was the great age of the Córtes, an institution corresponding to Parliament and Estates-General; the feudal nobility were also in the ascendancy there. Everywhere, including the German Empire, the central authority seemed to be torn by conflict between the great ducal houses, or weakened by their resistance to the royal power.

Causes of the Hundred Years War

England and France struggled in the throes of the Hundred Years War. This epochal struggle (on and off for more than a century, actually, 1337–1453) seems, like most wars in retrospect, a foolish one. Though the Hundred Years War was an agent which precipitated nationalism and, by ruining the old

English besieging a French castle in the Hundred Years War.

nobility, helped prepare for the modern state, its causes lay deep in the feudal age. By long tradition the English kings had interests in France; even Henry II, it is said, was more interested in his continental possessions than in England. Henry, Richard, John, virtually all the kings of England from 1154 on, squabbled or fought intermittently with the king of France over that substantial area of western and southern Franch which the English monarch's held as their feudal domain. In the long run, their possessions lacked sufficient community of interest to cohere in a single state.

Nothing was more natural than that the French kings would try to draw into their exclusive orbit such important adjoining regions as Aquitaine and Poitou. Philip Augustus had taken Normandy away from the luckless John; Philip the Fair tried to convert his feudal vassaldoms into something like direct possessions. It must be remembered that neither the French or English king was sovereign except in limited areas; for the most part the territory in dispute was feudal. At the beginning of the Hundred Years War, the issues in dispute were certainly not "national," but rather feudal: they involved, for example, the fact that the King of England, being also Duke of Aquitaine, was obliged in his latter capacity to do homage to the King of France. The background of the war included conflicts of this sort over the English fiefs in western France. Edward III laid claim to the throne of France through his mother at the beginning of the war, though this was much more a pretext than a cause of the war. It would be an error, so it appears, to ascribe to either side any conscious effort to establish a national territorial state in the modern sense: such a view would be anachronistic, that is, it would ascribe later motives and ideas to a period when these scarcely existed.

This sort of combination of feudal claims was inflamed by popular beliefs about a warrior's honor. This feeling is apparent in Shakespeare's play, *Henry V*. "Your brother kings and monarchs of the earth," Exeter tells Henry V, "Do all expect that you should rouse yourself, As did the former lions of your blood." The Archbishop of Canterbury had just delivered a long and learned exposition concerning why the Salic law did not apply in France and therefore Henry could lay claim to "certain dukedoms, and generally to the crown and seat of France."

There were economic interests at stake, too. The cloth industry of Flanders, the most advanced in Europe, used English wool and was a bone of contention; the French certainly resented close economic ties such as existed also between Brittany and England. French kings had strong ambitions to incorporate the duchies of Flanders and Brittany more closely into the French state.

The war and its results

To speak of the war lasting 100 years is misleading; this was not yet war in the modern sense, waged by well-organized national armies; it was closer to "a series of raids," though this war brought some significant growth in the direction of national organization. The early English victories came about because of superiority in archery: the crossbowmen and the longbowmen beat the French knights in a way that long lived in English song and story. Gun-

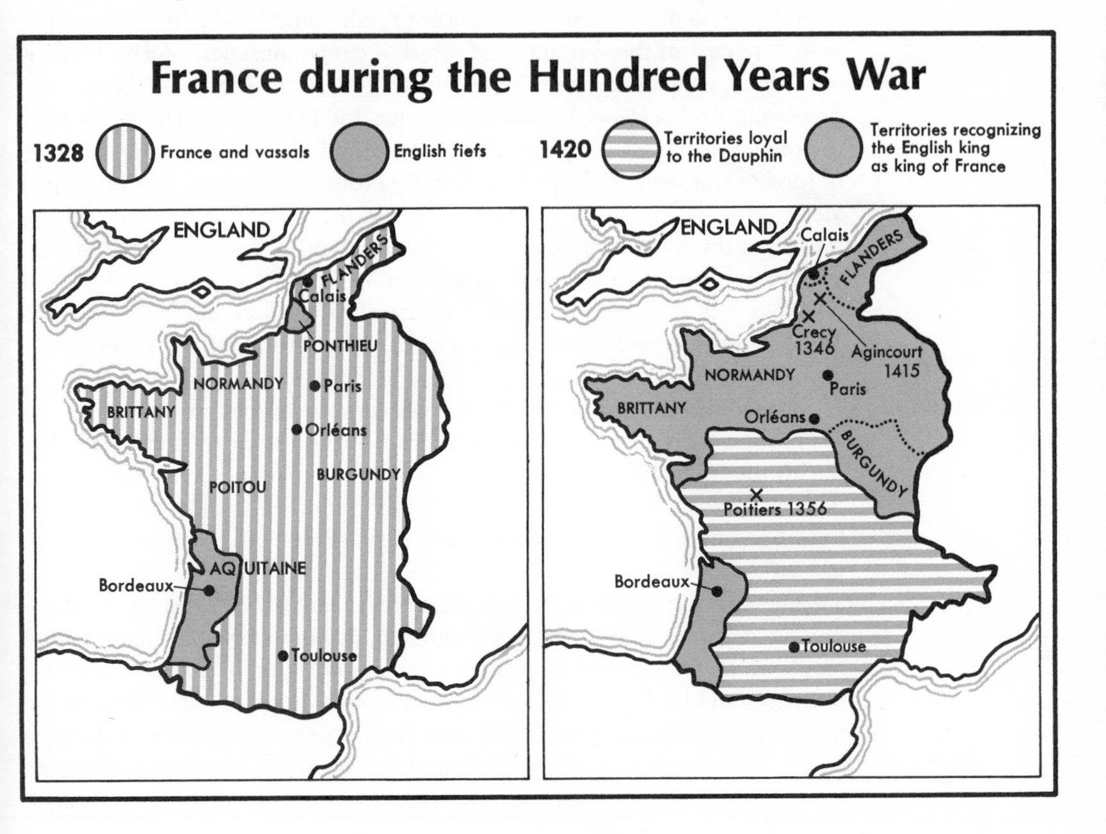

powder had made its appearance in Europe, but was not yet of much importance. The English wasted brilliant victories and arduous compagns in France, during which Edward the Black Prince and Henry V covered themselves with glory. For in the long run they could not maintain their position on the mainland against a rising French nation. In the course of time the terrain was bound to tell; really large and well-organized armies could not be sustained on foreign soil.

Whatever its causes, the results of the long war were momentous. Besides creating the first national symbol of modern Europe, Joan of Arc, it brought about a substantial extinction of the feudal warriors. The longbow vanquished the armored knight at Crécy, Poitiers, and Agincourt. The English nobles continued their own mutual extermination in the War of Roses which followed the Hundred Years War in England. The English, in being thrown out of France (they maintained only a tiny foothold at Calais for some time) received a blessing in disguise, for involvement in continental wars could now be avoided and naval power concentrated upon. The French monarchy emerged greatly strengthened. The English did not, in the immediate sequel; but after the civil war just mentioned they were to develop strength, under Yorkist and especially Tudor kings. As an agent precipitating nationalism and a stronger state, the Hundred Years War undoubtedly has its chief significance.

At the time this somewhat beneficent result could hardly have been foreseen. The cost of the war appalled sensible contemporaries. Much of northern France, which had been the fairest land of late medieval civilization, lay desolated. (In his *Henry V*, Shakespeare has the Duke of Burgundy describe the ruin in matchless eloquence.) England fared little better, for the expenses of foreign war weighed heavily on her. Onerous taxation was a cause of two major popular rebellions, in 1381 and again in 1450, though some scholars insist that the major depression of these years did not spring from the war. There was a *jacquerie*, or peasant rebellion, in France, too, in 1358, the result of intolerable financial exactions. A peace of exhaustion, between 1360 and 1369, allowed some recovery, but renewal of war brought fresh disorders.

Plague and revolt

Meanwhile, the Black Death stalked Europe, taking an awful toll. Its worst years were 1348–50. The Black Death has seemed to some historians the symptom of a long-term weakening process in Europe rather than a sudden, inexplicable catastrophe. Population had increased while the supply of food had not kept up, and thus dietary deficiencies weakened resistance to disease

The 14th-century economy was less sound than that of the 13th. Momentous socioeconomic changes were going on, most notably the waning of the medieval land economy as peasants commuted their feudal dues to cash payments and landlords became oriented toward a cash market. In the cities, the guild as an efficient regulatory agency of supply and demand also broke down; there were now fierce class struggles in many of the towns between a propertyless (and voteless) working class and a capitalist plutocracy. Through all the confusions of this age of transition, a notable theme is revolution, indicative of the profound social dislocations going on.

The 1381 rebellion in England was a great one, sweeping over many parts of the country. Among its apparent causes was the Black Death epidemic, which had caused wages to rise and speeded up the freeing of the peasants from serfdom by making men scarce, but which had been followed by an attempt to force wages back down. Furthermore, a less stable class of free but impoverished hired farm workers arose, partly replacing the old peasant-serf class. The Wycliffe-Lollard religious disturbances caused some of the poorer clergy to preach a kind of Christian communism to the lower classes, much as the Anabaptists later did in Germany; and of course, the war brought high taxes. The murder of tax collectors marked the beginning of the rebellion. This great rebellion lacked effective leadership and direction, and was crushed. The aristocracy triumphed; the feudal magnates often dominated the affairs of the whole nation, making this a period of what some have called "bastard feudalism."

The poor suffered under whatever rule there was. To this era belongs Langland's *Piers Plowman*, a voice from the lower classes written in the vernacular and expressing with simple eloquence the plight of the poor, "too sad to speak of or to say in rhyme"—the plight of those "charged with children and overcharged by landlords" who "suffer much from hunger" and must live on "bread and penny ale" when "the mouths are many and the money scarce." Langland thought, significantly, but perhaps wrongly, that the "olden times" had been far better for the poor peasant. All in all, this epoch appears as far from a happy time for any of the protagonists in this "first war of modern times." At the same time there were certainly many who drew a profit from the war, as always happens; in this case not only financiers and contractors but nobles who could seize and hold for ransom another noble according to the time-honored custom of knightly warfare. Breakdown in political affairs to the point of civil war occurred in both countries. Charles VI (1380–1422) of France, weak and unstable, was king in name only while the powerful dukes of Burgundy and Orléans fought each other when not fighting the English.

Central and eastern Europe

While this prolonged bloodletting was going on between France and England, central and eastern Europe was not at peace. While the Holy Roman Empire in Germany showed signs of severe crisis, with warfare both civil and religious breaking out there, the most startling development was the incursion of the Ottoman Turks into southeastern Europe.

Turkish invasion of Europe

These Ottoman Turks first appear as a power in the distressed Near East about 1326. The Eastern Christian Empire at Constantinople had been showing signs of decay for some time. To the Greeks and other civilized peoples the Turks seemed savage nomads, but they possessed a talent for government as well as fighting. By the end of the 14th century they were besieging Constantinople and had penetrated deeply into southeastern Europe, defeating the Serbs and Bulgars at the long-remembered battle of Kossovo in 1389. In 1396, another crusade against the Turks, which attracted a goodly number of European knights, revealed the incompetence of those brave warriors, who seldom were able to conceive of battle as more than a series of individual charges. Though subject to their own internal feuds, the fierce Turkish warriors were irrepressible; before long they were attacking in Hungary. In 1453 fell Constantinople, an event of profound psychological significance, though in fact the great imperial capital had long since ceased to be more than a shell of its former self. It seemed scandalous that Christian Europe could not combine against the "infidel" Turks (they had early adopted Islam) who were enslaving the peoples of southeastern Europe. But western Europe had its own troubles.

Hungarians and Venetians, with aid from the Persians on the other flank of the Ottoman Empire, did something to stem the tide, but could not prevent Turkish conquest of the eastern Mediterranean and southeastern Europe to the borders of Hungary and Croatia (see map p. 384). Turkish control of the trade routes diminished their profitability for the Italian cities and others dependent upon them. The Venetians, after a costly war with the Turks, lost some of their bases and had to pay an annual tribute for permission to trade in the Black Sea.

German affairs

In central Europe, occupied largely by the shadowy Holy Roman Empire, the 14th century was also confused and turbulent. After the catastrophe that befell the Hohenstaufen Empire with the defeat and death of Frederick II, there was no emperor at all 1254–73 (the Great Interregnum), after which the rather obscure Swiss nobleman Rudolf of Hapsburg was elected Emperor. The Hapsburgs from the beginning paid less attention to the imperial ambition than to building up their own holdings. The great nobles invariably exerted their authority over any overly ambitious emperor, deposing him or deliberately electing the weaker of the family. In the years 1314–47 there was a struggle between two emperors, one a Hapsburg and the other Louis the Bavarian, of the Wittelsbach family. The papacy backed the Hapsburg while most Germans backed Louis. This struggle brought forth famous political treatises by Marsiglio of Padua and the poet Dante on the side of Louis, boldly arguing for the supremacy of the secular state in all matters of government. Under the Luxembourg emperors, 1347–1438, the deterioration of the imperial office continued. The Golden Bull of 1356 signified the triumph of federalism, establishing the election of the emperor by seven electoral princes of the Empire. Finally in 1438 the Hapsburgs resumed what was to be an unbroken succession for many centuries. But they, too, failed to fulfill expectations of a genuine German national state.

The most notable war affecting the Empire was that which broke out in Bohemia. This land of Slavic peoples had been gradually brought into the

John Hus, leader of the Czech religious revolt.

Empire from the 10th century on and infiltrated by Germans. The Germans constituted the upper class and the native Czechs the lower class of workers and peasants. In the 14th century Bohemia grew in wealth and importance, its capital city, Prague, becoming one of the great cities of Europe. The University at Prague, founded 1348, was the first university in central Europe. Though linked to the Empire, Bohemia had an independent king and a tendency toward separatism.

The Hussite wars were a revolt of Bohemia against the Holy Roman Emperor, and to a large extent of the Czechs against the Germans. John Hus, a Prague university professor, was something of an early Luther. Drawing on native sources as well as the ideas of the English theologian Wycliffe, he not only assailed abuses in the church and demanded reform but also went on to challenge the authority of the pope and then assert the authority of Scripture, presumably as interpreted by the individual. In taking the first three steps he was not doing any more than many others in this era of the conciliar reformers; it was the last one which got him branded a heretic. But Hus' heresy quickly became involved with a *national* movement, as did Luther's later. There is a parallel with Luther also (see pp. 249–53) in the divisions that occurred among the rebels. However, they united against the crusade against Bohemia proclaimed by the Pope, after the Council of Constance treacherously seized and executed Hus who had appeared there under a safe-conduct (1415). The Bohemians defeated the invaders; war went on for some years, occasionally including civil war between the right-wing and left-wing factions of the Hussites. A compromise was eventually reached between the church and the more conservative wing of the Hussites (1436), but the heresy was never really suppressed in Bohemia, and constitutes an important preliminary for the Protestant Reformation a century later.

The rise of national states

Out of all this confusion and crisis emerged important new institutions. It is a time of significant changes politically, economically, and culturally. Of these changes the most important of all was perhaps that of nationalism.

The new political climate of Europe was one in which strong national states were shaping up. This evolution seems to us natural, and no doubt in some degree it was. The roots of nationalism lie deep in the past, and it is possible to see the various nations dimly shadowed in the Middle Ages. But a later patriotism probably exaggerated these roots. French nationalist historians have written as if ninth century feudal counts were really dreaming of *la patrie* to come, which is surely false. Europe got sorted out into reasonably stable political units only gradually and by accidents of power and personality more than "nationality." None of the major states, of course, was or is racially pure, whatever that may mean. Geography sometimes suggested demarcations but seldom compelled them. In general, it was the state which made the nation more than the nation which made the state. That is, royal dynasties built up territorial states and then, subsequently, a sentimental attachment to these states arose. A common language definitely followed, not preceded, the establishment of the state. The dialect of Paris became the French national tongue because Paris was the capital and its speech was imposed on the various local dialects.

In medieval times it was not to France but to the person of the king that loyalty was felt—a loyalty which extended only to the greater vassals. The humble serf can have felt little attachment to anything, except his hearth and his rare holiday. The cities produced a local or civic patriotism, but not a national one. In sum, neither feudalism nor the church nor the cities, those chief medieval institutions, had anything to do with nationality, nor did the political philosophies of the time recognize it.

National unity and sentiment arose, however, for a number of reasons. There was the romance of kingship: a popular attachment to a great ruler, who was conceived as doing wondrous things for his people—in which, of course, there often was much truth. The "King *in* England," as that officer was first known, might then easily become the King *of* England, and being English would take on brave qualities. Important in nation making was the decline of the feudal nobility, and the rise of a free peasantry. Feudalism was inherently antinational. It was built on the proud independence of great lords who were themselves little centers of sovereignty, and its nexus was the personal one of man to man.

Decline of feudal nobility

This is not to deny that by the 14th and 15th centuries the nobility itself had become more national than at an earlier time; though they checked the king and demanded a share in the government, they were now more bound to the realm. In England this is especially true. Feudal warlords were turning into a national aristocracy. The extinction of these nobles, at least in their old capacity, was the result of forces that were economic, political, and military, which went on over a long period. With their passing, and the rise of commoner men to places of importance, the way opened toward a more national state. When the peasant was not only a free man but a person who wielded the longbow or the pike in the king's army for defense of his country, rather than a serf who crouched behind the wall of the mounted knight, he was far more likely to feel an attachment to king and country. The arch-symbol of modern nationalism was a peasant girl who fought in the war of France against England.

St. Joan

The person of Joan of Arc, peasant maid of Domrémy, is shrouded in the mists of the past. There is surprisingly little agreement about whether she was blond or dark, short or tall, beautiful or plain, feminine or masculine in nature. What we know is that she heard voices calling her to courage for her country's sake. The awe-inspiring effect her personality had on all who came within her orbit is well documented. She became a symbol of will and bravery for her countrymen. The woman who led an army to raise the siege of Orléans (1429), turning point of the long war, was bound to become legendary. Captured and delivered over to the English, she was charged with witchcraft and burned at the stake at Rouen in 1431 after a trial which has always seemed among the most dramatic in all history. (See George Bernard Shaw's modern treatment, *Saint Joan*.) Her words at the trial give an impression of considerable intellectual power, above all else a directness and decisiveness remarkable in so young a girl. Presumably born in 1412, Joan was 17 when she rescued France and 19 at her death. She was in large part, it would seem, still a medieval figure: her visions put her in the tradition of the saints, she was pious, she also obviously shared in the ideals of chivalry. She is the knight in shining armor, suffused with an exalted purpose and with the aura of ideal femininity.

The whole story of Joan has come in for some modern debunking, some claiming that the famous act was staged. We do suffer from too little real knowledge about Joan, and the story may be criticized. It is probable, however, that like other such stories it is essentially true though encrusted with myth. Certainly Joan had her greatest meaning as a myth—a symbol of nationalism. To some at the time it seemed most inappropriate that one who pretended to be a saint should go forth to war, and serve one side only in a national war. Joan herself cannot readily be made to fit a pattern of "nationalism": her patriotism seems to have been personal as much as national. That is, she thought in terms of liege loyalty to the king, not devotion to an abstract state or an image of "the French people." But eventually she became to all Frenchmen a legend and a symbol, whose meaning was devotion to *la patrie*, hatred of the foreign invader, willingness to fight and die for national

Joan of Arc is led to the Dauphin to urge him to assume the throne as Charles VII and unite France.

liberty—by all classes, not just a few. It should be said, however, that Saint Joan was not really canonized as the French national heroine until the 19th century, when modern nationalism came fully into its own.

Hus played something of a similar role for the Czechs, Luther subsequently for the Germans. Loyalties which had once flowed in the direction of the church, with its saints and patriarchs, hereafter would go increasingly toward national heroes or heroines. It was a stage in the evolution of modern times out of medieval.

Economic changes

Agrarian revolution

The end of the Middle Ages occurred in conjunction with an agrarian revolution which in western Europe broke up the medieval manor and resulted in new forms of commercial agriculture, marked by a cash rather than a service basis. That is, tenants no longer paid their landlord in labor obligations, but gave him money. Many peasants "commuted" their obligations into money rent. In England "villeinage" was diminishing in the 14th century and was virtually gone by the reign of Elizabeth in the 16th. The Black Death which visited northern Europe in the middle of the 14th century allegedly hastened this process by making labor scarce and improving the bargaining position of those who survived its terrible assault.

The peasant became free, but not necessarily better off. The old system had security if not opportunity. Men had been guaranteed some minimum of land and shelter. They now took their chances in a commercial world. They might be forced into a new form of wage slavery, becoming an ill-paid agricultural proletariat. But they might rise to become proprietors, and "gentle" their condition. In England, it is a familiar story how the profitability of wool caused the eviction of tenants in order to make way for sheep ranches. The number of beggars, hoboes, petty criminals, and other specimens of derelict humanity multiplied in the later Middle Ages. One of the prime reasons for England's interest in New World colonization was the desire to get rid of this troublesome element by packing them off. On the other hand, some were able to rise in society. England, particularly, was full of new men entering the upper classes from below, making English society unusually fluid and mobile, without hard and fast class lines. A vigorous, acquisitive economic society was the result.

Capitalism

A more individualistic and aggressive capitalism was on the way. A few commodities, in particular, came under the sway of this form of economic life marked by large-scale operations carried on by great individual capitalists. One such commodity was wool. In 1421, 74 percent of the customs revenue of England came from raw wool. (Preeminent in growing it were still the Cistercian monasteries.) The Woolsack on which the Lord Chancellor still sits was a symbol of the chief commercial interest of England. A 15th-century English pamphlet says that no country can do without it, hence "we might rule and govern all kings" by it. It was indeed a mighty force in Europe. The

Hundred Years War was fought in part because of it. In the Tudor era of the 16th century, England, which had previously lagged behind foreign competitors in weaving, became proficient in the manufacture of cloth as well as the production of its raw material, and grew fabulously wealthy. In the 14th and 15th centuries English wool was still being exported to the manufacturing cities of Flanders and Italy, where the most skilled weavers flourished.

The clothiers were among the first great capitalists of Europe. In the time of Henry VIII, the famous Jack of Newbury employed several hundred weavers, if contemporary accounts may be believed. An incipient factory system existed, but more common was the "domestic system," by which merchant capitalists farmed out production to the looms of individual "cottagers" in their homes. The 15th century saw the rise of great capitalists like the celebrated Jacques Coeur of Bourges, who built a vast commercial empire based on trade with the East and then financial services to the crown, and the equally celebrated Fugger family of Augsburg, bankers to the royalty of Europe. Mining and metallurgy were other important areas of capitalist development.

Great inventions

Medieval technology, contrary to an older opinion, was progressive and fruitful. Modern science owes much to medieval artisans who developed, for example, the art of lens grinding from which would come the telescope, and who made the marvelous clocks which adorned medieval cathedrals. The great inventions which in the 15th century signaled the birth of a new age were the results of a long tradition of craftsmanship and experiment. "Printing, gunpowder, and magnet have changed the world," Francis Bacon wrote. The greatest of them was printing, that is, the use of movable metal type to produce printed material in large quantities cheaply. Though Johannes Gutenberg of Mainz is accorded priority, the process was actually developed almost simultaneously at Avignon, Bruges, Haarlem, and Mainz (c. 1450). Though the growth of literacy was slow, in the long run this epochal discovery had too many results to be named. The further growth of the state could take place when documents could be printed and widely distributed. What bureaucracy could do without them? The growth of nationalism owed more, probably, to the popular press and the resulting development of uniform languages over wide areas than to anything else. Reading of books about far places, such as the popular Marco Polo adventures, stimulated the voyages of discovery. Above all, of course, science and knowledge began to expand with the possibility of easy communication between men all over Europe. It became possible for experts to write or edit books on a professional basis when a large market was assured and publishing houses came into existence. The higher standards of scholarship in textual matters, attributed to the humanists of the Italian Renaissance (see next chapter), were actually made possible by the economics of the new publishing industry.

Jacob Fugger of Augsberg—banker the royalty of Euro Painted by the gre artist Albrecht Dür

Jacques Coeur, famed merchant and adviser of kings, built this grand Gothic house in Bourges, France.

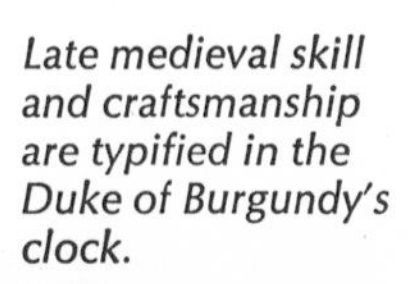

Late medieval skill and craftsmanship are typified in the Duke of Burgundy's clock.

Philosophy and religion

The turbulence of Europe's political and social affairs had some counterparts in the world of thought in this period. In the 14th century the unity of Scholastic philosophy was lost, as the post-Thomist philosophers, among whom the outstanding figure was the Englishman William of Ockham, abandoned the Thomistic harmonizing of reason and religion. It will be recalled that St. Thomas Aquinas had attempted to show the harmony of reason and Christian revelation, nothing in either being contrary to the other; he had offered rationalistic proofs of God's existence and had explained away certain disagreements between Aristotelian philosophy and Christian doctrine, such as those on the origin of the world, God's providence, and the nature of the soul. The successors of Aquinas, using his tools of logical analysis, doubted his conclusions. Perhaps in some measure the jealousy of rival religious orders was a factor, for Duns Scotus and William of Ockham were Franciscans whereas Aquinas had been a Dominican. But the potency of their intellects cannot be denied. Ockham taught that religious truths cannot be proved; theology is not science but faith. The realm of nature is of a different order than the realm of grace. Reviving the old controversy between realism and nominalism, Ockham gave to his nominalism a new meaning. The acute English Franciscan sensed the radical subjectivity of all conceptual thought: that is, the ideas we have in our heads are different from the things that are outside us. The latter may be known intuitively but only "thought about" by using an arbitrary set of symbols dependent upon our mental structure.

These views bring Ockham and some of his followers surprisingly close to much later philosophers such as Hume and Kant. Here we need only note that Ockham sundered what Aquinas had joined together, reason and religion. Ockham rejected all of St. Thomas's proofs of the existence of God, along with much else. Belief in God and the Christian revelation must be an act of faith, not of reason. The followers of Ockham and Scotus were not the less pious for rejecting the rational approach to religion, but they tended in the direction of mysticism or nonrational religious experience. On the other hand, they showed an interest in purely naturalistic science, too. Divorced from theology, it was the better able to proceed its own way unimpeded. So we have in the 14th century a tendency for dualism to replace the harmonious unity of Thomism, and for this dualism to express itself on the one hand in a more empirical science and on the other in a less rational religion.

Religious mysticism

The religious mystics played a large part in popular culture and looked ahead to the Reformation. One of them, Meister Eckhart, wrote some of his books in the German vernacular. The Brethren of the Common Life, founded in the Low Countries, became a significant *lay* religious order. St. Catherine of Siena, who helped bring the popes back from Avignon, was a popular figure who combined mysticism with humanitarian activities. Richard Rolle has been claimed as the father of English prose, the first to use the English vernacular successfully in literature. Thomas à Kempis wrote a tract, *The Imitation of Christ,* which has maintained its popularity with a religious reading public steadily down through the centuries. All these were important figures in the revival of mysticism in the 14th and 15th centuries. Mystics sought contact with God through some sort of inner illumination that came about not through learning and logic but quite otherwise—by an experience that transcended or bypassed the reasoning intellect. They often strained the limits of orthodoxy, since to them neither church nor formal creed was the most important thing. Few of them sought to be deliberately antichurch, yet unquestionably they helped prepare the way for the Reformation. Martin Luther was deeply influenced by various writings of the German mystics, collected in the book *German Theology.* The lack of a firm authority at the helm of the church during the era of the Great Schism did not, of course, encourage rigid doctrinal orthodoxy.

Imperialist theories

There was some political significance in the religious mystics, who were sometimes laymen writing in the vernacular to a popular audience and ignoring clerical authority. William of Ockham, the giant of thought referred to above, belonged in politics to the "imperialists" who challenged the papal theory of sovereignty and supported the claims of the temporal authority. The church should give up all connection with politics and become a purely spiritual force, they believed. In all that concerned government, the state ought to rule. The "two swords" idea had led to constant strife, and the only practical solution was to give the sword altogether to one, which must be the temporal. Ockham supported the Holy Roman Emperor against the Pope. A supporter of his "imperialism," meaning the supremacy of the temporal power over the church, was Marsiglio of Padua, most famous political writer of his time (*Defensor Pacis,* 1324). It is easy to see the trend toward the sovereign secular state in this political theory. Ockham and Marsiglio showed themselves here as in theology to be sharp separators of the two domains, religion and reason, church and civil society. Each had its place, but they should not mix. It was an idea Luther would take up.

Decadence of Scholasticism

After the great Ockham, in the early 14th century, there is a certain degeneration in northern Scholasticism, which corresponds to the widespread devastation of France in the Hundred Years War. Paris was no longer the university it had been. The Great Schism hurt the university by forcing it to choose between loyalties to France or Rome. It was at this time that the major dispersal of Paris scholars took place, some going off to found universities in Germany. Though Germany was prosperous in these years, and many of her finer universities were created as offshoots of Paris (for example, Heidelberg, 1389), much of northwest Europe was sterile. It is a time of widespread belief in witchcraft, more a phenomenon of the 15th century than of the earlier medieval. Papal bulls against witchcraft were issued in 1484 and 1487. Scholasticism seemed to many to be played out. Its "obscure glosses and frivolous ques-

14th century students at the college of the Ave Maria in Paris

tions," to quote a slightly later indictment, were hallmarks of a method which no longer yielded results compatible with its elaborate skills; it had become too much of an esoteric verbal game. At least to many people, the doctors became figures of fun, and the verdict—just or unjust—was found in the alleged derivation of the word "dunce" from Duns Scotus. The greatest of the Franciscan doctors actually had one of the most powerful metaphysical minds the world has ever known. But its subtleties, too abstruse for the average mind and apparently without relevance to experience, caused his system to become a byword for learned foolishness.

More significant perhaps than this somewhat unlearned reaction was the fact that these Scholastics had in a sense slain their own system. Scotus and Ockham themselves led in the direction of metaphysical skepticism, as previously remarked. They encouraged an abandonment of metaphysics and rational theology in favor of other modes of speculation, including empirical science.

Late medieval science

Late medieval science was promising, but failed to fulfill its promises. The most important names are Jean Buridan, Nicole Oresme, and Albert of Saxony, to which might be added the speculations of the remarkable religious mystic *and* scientist, Nicholas of Cusa. They challenged Aristotelian theories of matter and motion. On the premise of Ockham's famous "razor" (the simplest possible explanation of the phenomena should be preferred), Oresme suggested that the earth might be in motion around its own axis. He also challenged the accepted Aristotelian theory of motion. These 14th- and 15th-century Schoolmen came near to reaching the breakthrough Copernicus and Galileo were to achieve two centuries later. But their promising beginnings were not immediately followed up. As for the Bishop of Cusa, he shows us a curious if fascinating mixture of scientific and metaphysical speculations tinged with the mysticism of the age. He theorized that the earth moves, the universe is infinite, and the earth is not the center of it; nor is there any distinction between terrestrial and celestial matter. All of these propositions were quite at variance with the cosmology taught in the schools. But the arguments of this mystical theologian were often of a sort we would not regard as scientific. Nowhere does it appear more evident than in its scientific and cosmological aspects that this age was one of transition between medieval and modern.

Also promising was late medieval literature. This was the time of Chaucer, and of Froissart who chronicled the Hundred Years War. Important writers were beginning to express themselves in the vernacular, or popular language, as distinct from the traditional Latin; Chaucer is an outstanding example. This reflected the development of nationalism away from medieval universalism and could be most exciting and creative, but as a departure from tradition it seemed to some a symptom of disorder at this time.

By this time (c. 1350–1400), influences from the humanist revival of arts and letters in Italy were being felt. Chaucer, the great poet who came close to creating the modern English language in the *Canterbury Tales*, knew Petrarch, the pioneer Italian humanist. There were many signs that the North was unsure of its direction in the 14th century, despite sporadic examples of individual genius. Evidence for this can be found in many places: in the somewhat decadent overornateness of the late Gothic style in architecture, which was still magnificent but had lost the purity and unity of the early Gothic; or in the equally decadent forms of late chivalry, such as the Order of the Golden Fleece in the Netherlands. These new orders featured much pomp and ceremony, much rhetoric and rhodomontade.

Geoffrey Chaucer

Europe begins to look outward

Marco Polo

From Venice, "the proudest city in all the Western World," through whose famous harbor passed the goods of the Orient on their way to the markets of Europe, Nicolo and Maffeo Polo set forth in 1260 on a journey that took them to the court of the great Kublai Khan, who headed the vast Mongol Empire in China. These wealthy merchants returned nine years later and soon went out again, this time with the young Marco Polo, on a still more fabulous voyage. Though the Polos were scarcely the first to make contact with the Far East, such journeys as they made were still so rare and so dangerous that this one became justly famous. The Polos visited lands some of which were not again reached by Europeans until the 19th century. This most fabulous of voyages found immortality when Marco, with the aid of a Pisan romancer, wrote it into a book in 1298. Many, including at length Christopher Columbus of Genoa, would read that book. Modern investigation has vindicated the essential accuracy of most of what Polo set down about the Orient, especially the teeming, wealthy country of China with all its wonders. His fellow Italians apparently could not believe all of it, and small wonder; yet they listened and were enchanted.

Other Venetian traders went to China during the next century; so also did fearless Franciscan friars. We must, in this respect as well as others, revise upward the old estimate of the Middle Ages: there was an "age of discovery" in the 13th and 14th centuries, too. But about 1350 the Mongol dynasty fell, and was replaced by rulers unfriendly to men from the West. The Turks at the same time threw up another barrier across the old routes to China. But men continued to read about the voyages, and the new printing methods produced popular books of this sort. One of the most famous of all literary hoaxes or plagiarisms, the *Voyage of Sir John Mandeville*, was first published in 1371 and went through many later editions and translations. "Mandeville," who was probably a Flemish writer, actually cribbed from authentic travel books in making up his own entirely imaginary journeys. The book's popularity testifies to a widespread interest in real travel adventures, a type of literature which was competing with the feudal romance.

Prince Henry the Navigator

Thus Europe began, albeit cautiously and on a small scale, to look outward, farther than the traditional interest in the Holy Land of the Near East. During the first half of the 15th century, the place of most importance for this fateful process was not proud Venice or her maritime rival Genoa, but the land of Portugal in the far southwest corner of Europe. Prince Henry the Navigator is one of history's most celebrated people, and he takes rank with his contemporaries Joan of Arc and John Hus as an embodiment of his nation's soul as well as its greatest personality. It was in 1416 that this feudal magnate founded a naval station at Sagres which became a center for study and research in geography and navigation. Henry's navigators explored the west coast of Africa and penetrated the interior of that continent. One of their

Prince Henry the Navigator

achievements, unfortunately, was the establishment of the Negro slave trade. In addition to profit, glory, and knowledge, Henry's principal motive appears to have been a crusading religious zeal, born of long warfare against the Muslims, and in particular a desire to rescue Europe from the Turkish menace. He hoped to cross Africa and strike the infidels from the rear, perhaps making contact with the legendary Christian state which folklore placed in Abyssinia. He showed amazing persistence in exploring and sailing along the African coast. That persistence was later rewarded when the Portuguese rounded the Cape (1488) and made their way to India, some years after Henry's death in 1460. He more than anyone else provided the tools which both Da Gama and Columbus were to use with such good effect—the knowledge of ship design, maps, charts, and instruments of navigation. In 1477 Columbus settled in Portugal and there he absorbed this spirit of exploration.

The end of an age

Pessimism of later Middle Ages

These revolutionary changes opened up all kinds of possibilities for the future. The latter half of the 15th century will experience the refreshing breezes of the Italian Renaissance, with perspectives on art and life which break through the dry formalism of the Scholastics; it will feel the impact of the printing press, the first voyages of discovery, and the "new monarchy," together with the new capitalism. For the north of Europe at least, all this came to relieve a profound pessimism which seemed to settle over things in the first half of that century. The historian J. Huizinga, who has studied the mood of these times as carefully as any one, speaks of "a sombre melancholy," "immense sadness," in the sermons, chronicles, poems, and documents of the period. Ridden by wars and plagues for a century, with some tendency for the old anarchy to return with its violence and insecurity, much of Europe seemed tired and dispirited. We might review the sad situation as of 1450, over Europe as a whole. The church struggled in the throes of the conciliar controversy, with the papacy about to carry off victory at the price of reform. The Hussite troubles in Bohemia still dragged on. The Turks were about to complete the conquest of Constantinople, Serbia, Bosnia. In the aftermath of the Hundred Years War, civil strife began in England, the war of Lancaster and York. France, completing the expulsion of the English, was looking up, but famine, pestilence, and anarchy had just recently been the plight of much of the country. It could be added, among other things, that Castile was subject to a bout of feudal anarchy at this time. In northeastern Europe, too, there was a pattern of strife. The German Teutonic Knights struggled in fierce warfare with Poles, Lithuanians, and Estonians throughout most of the period from 1326 to 1466. Russia was painfully extricating herself from the Tatar yoke and trying build a state; Ivan the Great, first important national figure of modern Russia, came to the throne in 1462 after a long preceding period of anarchy.

Toward the Renaissance

The later years of the 15th century, by contrast, rather clearly mark a change of such proportions as to permit the judgment that the modern era of history then began. It was not merely that the Italian Renaissance introduced new themes of thought and expression at this time. Important though these were, their novelty and importance has probably been exaggerated. They did not constitute so decisive a break with the medieval as has sometimes been claimed. For such a break in the realm of basic ideas, one must wait for the scientific revolution of the 17th century. But the Italian city-states did develop a new kind of political order, and the nation-states of northern Europe, with some aid from this Italian example, also emerged into a new political era, marked by a more powerful centralized monarchy. Medieval social and economic institutions gave way to modern ones. Basic technological breakthrough occurred. Nationalism developed. And Portugal pioneered in a momentous seaward thrust to the Indian Ocean and beyond. Sad as they seemed at the time, these were the most fabulously creative years of European history in many ways.

At the same time the Italian culture of the Renaissance came as an infusion to a Europe much in need of fresh blood. We should turn next to a consideration of this Renaissance.

Bibliography

The best account in English of the Hundred Years War has been written by Alfred H. Burne in two volumes, *The Crécy War* and *The Agincourt War* (London: Eyre and Spottiswoode, 1955, 1956); E. Perroy's *The Hundred Years' War* has been translated (Bloomington: Indiana University Press, 1960). For political developments, V.H.H. Green, *The Later Plantagenets: England 1307–1485* (London: Edward Arnold, 1955), is an excellent survey; so is the older book by a master of prose, G.M. Trevelyan's *England in the Age of Wycliffe 1368–1520* (Harper Torchbook); also Paul M. Kendall, *The Yorkist Age* (London: George Allen & Unwin, 1961); and, more narrowly focused, Harold F. Hutchinson, *The Hollow Crown: A Life of Richard II* (Eyre & Spottiswoode, 1961). J.R. Landers, *The War of the Roses* (London: Secker & Warburg, 1965), is intended for the general reader. Covering continental affairs, two generally satisfactory texts are Daniel P. Waley, *Later Medieval Europe* (New York: Barnes & Noble, 1964), and William T. Waugh, *A History of Europe from 1378 to 1494* (London: Methuen Publications, 1949). John R. Hale (ed.), *Europe in the Late Middle Ages* (Evanston, Ill.: Northwestern University Press) brings together some recent scholarly articles. Varying views of the alluring but elusive female founder of French nationality are given in Lucien Fabre, *Joan of Arc* (New York: McGraw-Hill, 1954); Sven Stolpe, *The Maid of Orleans* (New York: Random House Pantheon Books, 1956); A. Guerin and J.P. White, *Operation Shepherdess* (London: William Heinemann, 1961); and Regine Pernoud, *Joan of Arc* (Grove Press, Evergreen); among others.

On the church, T.S.R. Boase's biography of *Boniface VIII* presents the Pope who began the troubles of the papacy (London: Constable, 1933); G. Mollat, *The Popes at Avignon 1305–1378* (London: Thomas Nelson & Sons, 1962), is the translation of the authoritative work on the subject, one which dispels some legends. E.F. Jacob, *Essays in the Conciliar Epoch* (Manchester: Manchester University Press, 1953), is by a master of this period, author also of the Oxford History of England volume covering the 15th century. Paul E. Sigmund has made a worthy contribution to the understanding of the conciliar movement with *Nicholas of Cusa and Medieval Political Thought* (Cambridge, Mass.: Harvard University Press, 1965). K.B. McFarlane, *John Wycliffe and the Rise of English Nonconformity* (New York: Macmillan, 1953), is a brief introduction to the subject. The Hussite revolt has been treated by M. Spinka, *John Hus and the Czech Reform* (Chicago: University of Chicago Press, 1941), as well as by F.G. Heymann, *John Zizka and the Hussite Revolution* (Princeton, N.J.: Princeton University Press, 1955), dealing with Hus' successor in a work of splendid scholarship. J. Ancelet-Hustache, *Master Eckhart and the Rhineland Mystics* (Harper), presents in popular format another leading religious theme of the late Middle Ages.

For the whole period, J. Huizinga has provided an evocative portrait in his *Waning of the Middle Ages* (Penguin). More specialized studies in intellectual and literary currents appear in H.S. Bennett (ed.), *Chaucer and the Fifteenth Century Revolution* (New York: Oxford University Press, 1954). Pierce Butler has dealt with *The Origin of Printing in Europe* (University of Chicago Press, 1940). Late medieval science, a fruitful development, is treated in Vol. II of A.C. Crombie, *Medieval and Early Modern Science* (Doubleday Anchor); see also G.W. Coopland, *Nicole Oresme and the Astrologers* (Harvard University Press, 1954). In philosophy, Vol. III of Frederick Copleston's admirable *History of Philosophy* covers Ockham to Suarez (London: Burns & Oates, 1953). Gordon Leff, *Medieval Philosophy* (Penguin) is particularly good on the late medieval philosophers. J.H. Parry gives an excellent general survey of exploration and discovery in *The Age of Reconnaissance* (New American Library, Mentor). A.P. Newton, *Travels and Travellers of the Middle Ages* (New York: Alfred A. Knopf, 1930), is good background for the Age of Exploration. Edgar Prestage, *The Portuguese Pioneers* (London: A. & C. Black, 1934), and E. Bradford, *Southward the*

Caravels (London: Hutchinson, 1961), are equally good on the era of Prince Henry. Henry H. Hart has the best biography of Marco Polo in his *Venetian Adventurer: Marco Polo* (Stanford, Calif.: Stanford University Press, 1942). Also see Albert B. Kerr, *Jacques Coeur, Merchant Prince of the Middle Ages* (New York: Charles Scribner's Sons, 1927). A. Mahn-Lot, *Columbus* (Grove Press, Evergreen), is an excellent brief treatment; a longer and probably definitive account is Samuel Eliot Morison, *The Admiral of the Ocean Sea* (Boston: Little, Brown, 1942).

Sources of interest include W.S. Scott (ed.), *The Trial of Joan of Arc* (London: Folio Society, 1956); John Froissart, *Chronicles* (E.P. Dutton, Everyman); the Library of Christian Classics, Vol. XIV, *Advocates of Reform from Wycliffe to Erasmus* (1953); A. Gewirth (ed.), *Marsilio of Padua's Defensor Pacis* (2 vols.; Columbia University Records of Civilization); S.B. Chrimes and A.L. Brown (eds.), *Select Documents of English Constitutional History 1307–1485* (A. & C. Black, 1961). *The Travels of Marco Polo* is Volume No. 306 of Everyman's Library (London: J.B. Dent).

9

The Renaissance

Bellini's "Portrait of a Condottiere" conveys the individuality with which Renaissance painters portrayed their subjects.

chronology

1434–94
Medici rule in Florence; height of the Renaissance.
Portuguese navigational experiments.
1454–80
Development of printing processes. (Gutenberg Bible, 1454; Caxton press, England, 1476.)
War of Roses in England.
Maturity of Italian city-states; age of humanism.
End of schism within church; restoration of papal authority.
1461–83
Louis XI of France. Defeat of Burgundy (battle of Nancy), 1477.
1469
Marriage of Castile and Aragon, Spain.
French Estates-General requests king to rule without them.
1471
Lorenzo and Giuliano de' Medici rule Florence.
Victory of York (Edward IV) in War of Roses, England.
1475
Sistine Chapel begun. Birth of Michelangelo.
1478
Establishment of Spanish Inquisition.
1484
Papal Bull against witchcraft.
Ficino's translation of Plato, at Florentine Academy.
1485
Battle of Bosworth Field, beginnings of Tudor dynasty, Henry VII, in England.
1486
Mirandola, "Essay on the Dignity of Man."
1488
Bartholomeu Diaz rounds Cape of Good Hope.
1492–1504
Voyages of Columbus.
Papacy of Alexander VI, Borgia Pope.
Conquest of Granada, expulsion of Jews from Spain, 1492.
1493–1519
Maximilian I, Hapsburg Emperor, fails to create strong central state.
1494
French invasion of Italy.
Savonarola in Florence.
1497
John Cabot's voyage to North America.
1498
Da Gama reaches India.
Fall of Savonarola.
Turkish attacks on Hungary.
1502
Leonardo's "Mona Lisa."
1508–10
Michelangelo's ceiling frescoes for Sistine Chapel.
1509
Henry VIII assumes throne of England.
1510
John Colet founds St. Paul's humanist academy, in London.
1511
Erasmus, *In Praise of Folly*.
Entrance of humanism into Germany, northern Europe.
1515
Invasion of Italy by Francis I of France; end of political power of Italian city-states.
Thomas More, *Utopia*.
Letters of Obscure Men.
Titian, "Sacred and Profane Love."
1516
Erasmus' New Testament translation.
Machiavelli, *The Prince* and *Discourses*.
1519–22
Magellan's voyage around world. Spanish conquest of Mexico begins.
1528
Castiglione's *The Courtier*.

Renaissance in Italy

"Renaissance" is a term hallowed by long usage and inextinguishable from our historical vocabulary. Like "feudalism," "capitalism," and other large concepts, it suffers sometimes from vagueness; different or even contradictory meanings have led some historians to doubt its utility. It once was applied sweepingly to the entire early modern period from about 1400 to 1700, but this usage is no longer common, and is clearly confusing. On the other hand, historians have discovered previous "rebirths," as we have seen, most notably in the 12th century. However, the Italian Renaissance of the period from about 1380 to 1520 remains a valid, real, historical phenomenon, which spread to other parts of Europe and is of great importance, though we must be careful not to attribute to it too much. It was not, as is still sometimes wrongly suggested, a total recovery of European civilization from darkness.

In all sorts of ways, life was quickened and made more interesting in the 15th and 16th centuries by what came from Italy. Once again the land of classical culture seemed to bloom with all the flowers of learning and art; the grandeur of antiquity was revived, and all Europe absorbed it. The land which had been the seat of ancient civilization in Europe had since 400 A.D. gone through a long series of ordeals and misadventures which had prevented its playing a leading role. While Muslims and then Byzantines controlled the southern part of the peninsula, Lombards and then Hungarians ravaged the north; after which Italy had been a battleground of the often titanic struggle between popes and German emperors. Not until the 14th century did Italy find it possible to come into her own. Then she blossomed with a late splendor. Especially was this true in the arts.

In many ways the taste of the Italian Renaissance was different from the medieval, and it produced exciting new ideas in the arts. The Renaissance style has more detail, more movement, more sophistication in its craftsmanship, more feeling for the concrete and particular. It is by no means without an ideal element. By contrast much medieval art tends to be "Byzantine" in its elimination of unnecessary detail, its portrayal of ideal forms. Medieval painting uses color brilliantly and can have a strong emotional impact, but the Italian painters introduced dramatic technical advances. While the Italians went too far in asserting that nothing before Giotto was worth consideration, one cannot deny the creative originality of Italian Renaissance art. It also created a new style in architecture, less grand but more symmetrical than the Gothic, and even more exquisitely adorned.

Expansion of classical sources

It is also clear that the Renaissance had a wider range and quantity of ideas. Since the 12th century Europe had known a great deal of classical literature, but it now recovered a great deal more. Some Italian scholars learned Greek, threw themselves passionately into the game of rediscovering old manuscripts, and made highly significant findings. All of Plato became available, compared with a smattering before. Important ancients such as Lucretius the Epicurean, Pythagoras, and the Stoics became known. It is necessary to be judicious here: on the one hand, the medieval scholars knew many of the ancient writers and treasured them—a few, like Vergil, being admitted to the company of Christian saints; on the other hand, the Renaissance did make important and numerous additions. There were also better editions. Textual scholarship advanced, aided by the economics of the newly invented printing presses.

Humanism

More important was the different spirit in which literature was approached. The Italians of the Renaissance had a sense of style and elegance that made them essentially "humanists." This word originally meant a stress on that course of studies we still call the "humanities" that is, literature, the fine arts, languages, history. Renaissance humanists rebelled against the Scholastic scientific spirit, which cared nothing for style, was impersonal and abstract-logical. They loved Cicero the essayist, Demosthenes the orator, Polybius the historian—and Plato, the *poet* of ideas. They aspired to the cultivation of the personality by means of a literary education. They certainly seemed more refined, sophisticated, and esthetically mature. They made the Scholastics look like crabbed pedants and the poets of the North seem primitive. There were a few such humanists in the Middle Ages: John of Salisbury is a notable example. But they were then very much a minority movement.

Florentine Platonism

At the same time, medieval philosophy continued in the universities without much change, still preoccupied with older issues, especially the nominalist-realist controversy as revived by William of Ockham. The humanists were not usually much interested in philosophy, certainly not the sort associated with Scholastic methods. But they approved of Aristotle and Plato, seeking to interpret them in rather new ways. There was a notable Platonic revival. The Florentine Academy, created in the high noon of the Renaissance and sheltering the most notable of humanist philosophers, Marsilio Ficino and Pico della Mirandola, proudly revived the name of the great Athenian's school. This was Platonism with a difference. There was considerable stress on the unique position, dignity, and power of man, the being who stands as the center term of the entire hierarchy of existence, sharing mind with the angels and body with the lower beings. Still, the eclectic Platonic philosophy of the Florentines may be seen as essentially traditional, new only in its wider knowledge of Plato's writings and of other ancient Neoplatonist philosophers. Ficino was not seeking to revolt against anything, but rather to show—in a way not too remote from the Scholastic purpose—that Christianity and Platonism could merge in a single theology. If this was an intellectual revolution, it was a mild one.

Classicism

One must be on guard against an excessively "romantic" interpretation of the Renaissance. There is some rather exuberant wickedness in the Italian Renaissance, as there was also in the Middle Ages; but most Renaissance humanists were too close to the classical age of ancient Greece to wish for immoderation. While a quest for new experience was present, there was also a sense of human limitations. These men were, after all, classicists, with all that implies as the very opposite of romanticism: restraint, balance, limits. The anti-Christian and antiphilosophical features of the Renaissance have been much exaggerated. "Christian humanism" was a typical product of the Renaissance: it applied a different spirit to religion, but was nonetheless deeply religious. And the leading philosophical school of Florence was a Platonism or Neoplatonism which delighted in the idea of a hierarchical and ordered universe.

When the word "humanism" is used today it generally implies such beliefs as rejection of all supernaturalism, refusal to accept traditional Christianity, the basing of values on human nature alone. It may almost be said that nothing was farther from the spirit of the Renaissance "humanists." Typically, like their famous pioneer Petrarch, they embraced Christian piety and Platonic transcendence, adding to these a Ciceronian eloquence. Theirs was a gentler humanism by far than the raucous atheism of a later time.

Humanism may be defined in another sense: as an impulse to embrace all of human experience, something expressed in Seneca's famous cry, "Nothing human is alien to me." The men of the Renaissance seldom honored this in any wildly romantic way, but a desire to embrace as many creeds as possible is clearly evident in leading humanists like the famous and precocious Pico of Mirandola, whose "Oration on the Dignity of Man" is so often reprinted as a Renaissance set piece. Discovering so many other ancient philosophies and religions, humanists tried to fuse them all in a single synthesis. But they believed, with Pico, that they all pointed to the same God and were not just so many fragments of experience. Philosophical relativism or skepticism is not very strong in the humanist period proper, though a century later we meet it in Montaigne. The discovery of the ancient skeptics, such as Pyrrho, who denied the possibility of any certain knowledge, can be attributed to Renaissance scholarship but came somewhat later.

Literature as humanism

Two other products of the Italian Renaissance must be mentioned: literary humanism and civic humanism. In literature, Petrarch and Boccaccio introduced fresh themes into Europe. What seems most significant about this literary humanism is its insistence on the high value of literature as such, especially its moral value. A gifted writer in both Latin and the vernacular Italian, Petrarch communicated a joy in good writing for its own sake, as he assailed the gloomy monks and graceless Aristotelian philosophers who wrote in bad Latin. Petrarch firmly believed, as did all the literary humanists of the Renaissance, that literature has a moral value. The Petrarchians came close to preaching good writing as an ethic and religion. (Plato had thought music necessary to morality.) They insisted upon the high value of literary style. "Literature was the means of self-improvement, of improvement in society; literature, in a word, was life." This message has not since been ignored in the West. It can just about be said that we owe the serious study and practice of literature to the Renaissance.

Civic humanism suggests a passionate local patriotism, a civic pride, which conveyed memories of antique republicanism, memories of Athens and of ancient Rome. Without this intense pride in their city the Florentines would not have adorned it with all the beauties of architecture and sculpture as, to the delight of the tourist, they did. At the same time, this spirit in the Italian cities entailed jealous rivalries and wars between them, to their ultimate sorrow, as they invited foreign intervention by the more powerful states beyond the Alps. Civic humanism, however, was a gift to all Europe in its insistence upon the value of participation in the affairs of the community—the dignity of citizenship and of politics.

Civic humanism

When all is said and done, there came out of the Italian cities something very new and very attractive. It has exercised its charm down through the centuries ever since. We must not do what some of the Italians themselves were too prone to do, assert in their pride that they were the first to paint, to sculpt, and to enjoy the delights of literature, or to be citizens. Yet this was an artistic and literary renaissance of the highest magnitude. It also brought solid advances in scholarship: the mastery of new languages (Greek and Hebrew), the editing of texts, the learning of ancient history. Humanists were welcomed at the courts of the northern European states not alone

Lorenzo de'Medici, humanist and patron of art and literature. Sculpture by Andrea del Verrocchio.

Renaissance cathedral in Florence—a style wholly different from Gothic. The dome by Brunellsechi, the bell tower by Giotto.

because they were charming and could quote poetry and write elegant Latin; they made good diplomats and counselors because they knew languages and knew history.

Realism in Renaissance urban culture

The Italian cities were the birthplace of this movement. Since the 12th-century revival of trade they had won its chief prizes, and had developed an urban life beyond anything else in Europe. Venice was a gorgeous city of 100,000, the head of a great maritime empire, with bases and colonies all over the eastern Mediterranean. Genoa, the city of Columbus, was for a time a worthy rival of the great city of lagoons, whose Doges annually cast a ring into the Adriatic to symbolize the marriage of Venice with the sea. Milan, Naples, and Florence, along with papal Rome, were the other major cities. They played a role unlike any cities in the North, for feudalism had not developed far in Italy, and there was no king of Italy. Therefore the cities were preeminent, and built up states themselves. Culture was more exclusively urban than it was beyond the Alps. Especially was this true in northern Italy.

Sources of the Renaissance

Why did the humanist passion sweep Italy? Of course, the memory of classical antiquity was closer there; the ruins of Rome inspired Brunelleschi to a new architecture which was based on their spirit. In good part, as Renaissance students have always recognized, the Renaissance was a manifestation of Italian nationalism or patriotism, which included pride in the ancient glories of the peninsula. On the other hand, a *civic* pride and patriotism was much in evidence, too, as we have seen. Like the Greek cities of old, the Italian cities engaged in wars with each other, cultivated their differences. They proved unable to unite in defense of Italian independence against foreign invasion beginning at the end of the 15th-century.

Why it was that Florence proved the most creative may only be conjectured. Venice was half Byzantine and looked overseas; Rome was tied to the papacy. Florence was in Tuscany, where a highly artistic people lived. But it is almost impossible to explain such bursts of creativity. Athens had had it, Rome had it in politics, Paris had it in the 12th century. The era of the Medici, rulers of Florence, lavish patrons of the arts and themselves sometimes poets and artists, began in 1434 and lasted until 1494—the high noon or perhaps afternoon of the Renaissance, the age of Leonardo da Vinci, Michelangelo, and Machiavelli. The Medici themselves, especially Lorenzo, were humanists, manuscript collectors, enthusiasts for art and literature. Patrons are always important to the artist and scholar. The patronage of the Renaissance popes, and of Ludovico Sforza in Milan, provide other examples.

But the Florentine renaissance in the arts preceded the coming of the Medici to power. At the beginning of the *quattrocento*, as the Italians call the 15th century (the 1400's), the paintings of Masaccio, the famous Donatello statues which still stand in Florence (David, St. George), and Ghiberti's fabulous golden doors for the cathedral's baptistry marked the glorious dawn of a century that was to culminate in Raphael, Leonardo de Vinci, and Michelangelo. Brunelleschi began to create the architecture of the city, in the Duomo, many other churches, and the Pitti Palace. These artists set the tone for all that followed; the real miracle of Florence therefore seems to have happened around the years 1400–1420.

Art in northern Europe

As in Italy, wealth and enlightened patronage stimulated the northern renaissance. Notably was this true in the Burgundian state (including the Low Countries), where the painting of Jan and Hubert van Eyck (Flemish, that is, present Belgium) and the sculpture of Claus Sluter are good examples. Philip Commines of Charles the Bold's court markedly resembles Machiavelli. That the cities of the Low Countries and the Rhine were able to produce something resembling the Italians, independently, suggests that a "renaissance" was likely to occur wherever there was wealth, an urban environment, a lay bourgeoisie, a sympathetic government.

Characteristics of Italian art

It may be suggested that art of a greater naturalism or realism is likely to appear when men feel themselves comfortably at home in their environment.

Abstract, formalistic art seems typical of less well-adjusted eras (which can help explain the 20th century's return to the latter type). A feeling for nature was plainly present in the art of Italy. The human figure was depicted with realism. Men were not estranged from life, but wished to enter into it fully. The same was almost true of the 13th century, and much Gothic sculpture is realistic; while the great cathedrals themselves, meant to hold seemingly all the world, spacious and soaring, obviously had a humanist element. But medieval painting lacked the technical advances which enabled Italian painters to give an impression of realism, and also had a somewhat less secular spirit. Through the centuries men have marveled at the technical skill of the great Italian painters combined with their feeling for life.

Machiavelli

The realism of the Renaissance also emerges vividly in the political writings of Machiavelli. Medieval political tracts often took the same form as Niccolo Machiavelli's *The Prince*, that is, advice to the ruler of the kingdom on how to manage his affairs. But the earlier tracts are simply moral homilies exhorting the prince to become virtuous and govern in a Christian manner. They do not betray much feeling for the actualities of politics. Machiavelli's works are different. *The Prince*, in particular, earned its place of immortality among political writings by exactly this quality of realism.

Machiavelli's famous book was both a tract for the times and a treatise for all times. As the former, it noted with indignation that "Italy has been overrun by Charles, plundered by Louis, violated by Ferdinand, and insulted by the Swiss"; she was the prey of all those people north of the Alps whom Machiavelli regarded as "barbarians." For this Machiavelli blamed much in Italy, particularly the military system and the absence of Italian patriotism, and he called for reform and unity in order to liberate his country. Here he was anything but the dispassionate scientist; in the last chapter he called for something like a miracle of national resurgence to save Italy. Throughout much of the book, however, Machiavelli was drawn to a consideration of power as such. He approached it as a practical rather than a moral question. "He who neglects what *is* done to follow what ought to be done will sooner learn how to ruin than to preserve himself. For a tender man and one that desires to be honest in everything must needs run a great hazard among so many of contrary principle." It is a rough world, and omelets are not made without broken eggs, Machiavelli implies. He was ready to license his prince to do some evil that good may come of it. Do the ends justify the means? Machiavelli dared to say yes. He went on to make a study of the ways to get and keep power.

Machiavelli was conscious of having broken drastically with tradition and introduced a new teaching which could be dangerous as well as useful. For many people for many years, Machiavellianism was an evil word, a synonym for satanism. In some pious circles possession of the Florentine's works was enough to ruin a person's reputation. Kings and princes did nevertheless secretly make use of *The Prince*, and other manuals of practical wisdom for

Niccolo Machiavelli: portrait by Santi di Tito in Palazzo Vecchio, Florence.

princes appeared. Beyond the various maxims of practical statecraft which Machiavelli scattered through his writings—and which may or may not be useful, always depending on the circumstances—there was his basic proposal that politics be treated as a science or discipline of its own, apart from religion or ethics. It became an autonomous study. Machiavelli did for politics what Adam Smith later did for economics. In his daring, his originality, his realism, and even in his touch of wickedness, he represents for many the spirit of the Italian Renaissance.

Statesman and political scientist, Machiavelli was also historian, as was his distinguished contemporary Guicciardini. The revival of history reflected the interest in concrete human affairs, not abstract generalities.

In this sense, "humanism," the word used to describe the new thought and culture of the Renaissance—meant something more than its narrower connotation at that time—that is, the study of the humanities. As applied chiefly by later scholars, it has meant the greater sense of realism that one finds both in art and literature, whether in Donatello's sculpture, Titian's vo-

luptuous nudes, or Machiavelli's writings on politics and history. It should not be used indiscriminately to imply the absurd theory that no one before the Italian humanists was ever "interested in man" or "aware of human nature." But a more vivid awareness of psychological realities and a sharper eye for the nuances of natural things may fairly be claimed for them. One is safe in saying that no such political treatise as Machiavelli's had appeared during the Middle Ages, even though medieval kings and nobles frequently *acted* like the Florentine's prince. It is also fairly safe to say that no medieval painter or sculptor could have matched Titian's "Venus" or Michelangelo's "Dawn."

The art, literature and thought of the Renaissance thus appears to be closely related to a greater awareness of human and social reality, and this in turn to urban life. It is not really surprising that in these cities there should be this greater awareness of the subtleties of life as it actually is. There is more human contact, more society and politics, more humanity concentrated in cities. Life was both freer and more varied than in the country. There was more wealth, more leisure, more sophistication. There was also more conflict; the city-states of the Italian Renaissance were no freer from both internal and external strife than were their counterparts in the Greece of old.

"The naked form is the central core of the humanist art of the Renaissance"—as it had been for ancient Greeks. Michelangelo's "Dawn" and Titian's "Venus."

Spread of the Renaissance

Machiavelli's classic had been called forth by the depredations of foreigners; it did not suffice to save Italy. The city-states of Italy developed the arts of diplomacy, of statecraft, of international relations to a high degree in the 15th century. They introduced, in fact, the first permanent foreign service; they formed the concept of the sovereign state, drew treaties, made alliances and leagues with a new precision. That some of their leagues were based on an idea of stabilizing the status quo by means of "collective security" did not save them from continually getting into wars. These wars invited the renewal of an old plague, the intervention of outside powers. Beginning with the French invasion of 1494, Italy became a battleground and lost her place in the sun. Slipping behind in power and wealth, converted into possessions or satellites of the larger kingdoms (Spain, France, or Hapsburg Austria), the Renaissance cities sank in political importance and gradually lost even their cultural ascendancy. Venice indeed maintained independence, but settled into apathy after the 16th century, while Milan lost her independence altogether to Spain, and Florence, as the Duchy of Tuscany, ceased to have importance. In 1527 Rome itself was sacked by the Emperor's troops in an orgy that stunned all Europe. Naples became a possession of Spain in 1504.

Decline of Italy

Thereafter Italy was again in decay. Not that she failed to contribute great minds to movements of European thought after that. The names of Galileo, Vesalius, and Torricelli during the scientific revolution (see Chapter 12) are a sufficient reminder; the University of Padua has been accorded pride of place in that international movement. Yet with the emergence of the strong national kingdoms of the north and west, especially England, France, and Spain, and with the revolution in trade routes that followed the Atlantic voyages, Italy became of secondary importance in the affairs of the world. What she had created in the great age of the Renaissance, however, spread to all Europe. It was carried back across the Alps by invading soldiers and scholars alike.

Humanism in the North

No part of Europe was untouched by it, except those unfortunate regions of the southeast which were being overrun by the Turkish tide. There was a Spanish renaissance, later submerged by the Counter-Reformation but vigorous for a while. There, reformers of the church like Cardinal Ximines used the "new learning." France, the home of medieval culture, of the Gothic and the Scholastic, showed some resistance to the "new learning" but succumbed, and produced humanist scholars and writers in the 16th century. Germany and the Low Countries shared fully in the Renaissance. Indeed, humanism flourished in the small states of Germany almost as much as in the Italian cities. The painter Albrecht Dürer of Nürnberg ranks on a par with the great Italians. Erasmus of Rotterdam—scholar, stylist, humanitarian, educational reformer—has seemed the perfect embodiment of the humanist spirit, and became the most celebrated single figure of the entire literary renaissance. John Colet

Sir Thomas More, humanist and Lord Chancellor of England, was executed for defying the religious claims of Henry VIII. Painting by Hans Holbein the Younger.

and Thomas More brought the new learning to England. More's *Utopia* (1516) took rank with *The Prince* as the other political classic of the age. Most of these humanists were close to the governments, for royal courts sought their services both for practical and ornamental purposes.

Humanism in the North was only one ingredient among several in the intellectual history of this age. "Scholasticism" was by no means dead; the debate between nominalists and realists which William of Ockham had revived went on heatedly during the last portion of the 15th century. Ockhamism, Scotism, and late medieval schools of mysticism flourished. Erasmus himself owed much to the pietistic religious movement known as *devotio moderna,* strong in the Low Countries, which produced schools of a new sort and stressed a direct and human approach to Scripture. The *via moderna* of Ockham fought its battles with the *via antiqiua* of the conservative realists, while the followers of Duns Scotus were a third force. Scholasticism was divided into a right and a left wing, and might be Thomist or Ockhamite, Scotist, or even Averroist, the most nonreligious form of Aristotelianism. Humanists entered this scene as another vigorous party, generally though not always hostile to Scholasticism of all sorts. They did not, certainly, push it out. And yet the most glamorous and celebrated men of learning remembered from this epoch were humanists: Erasmus, More, Reuchlin, Lefèvre d'Etaples.

Humanist education

In 1520 the Reformation intruded and altered the situation so that, especially in the north of Europe, humanism as a distinct movement gradually became indiscernible, almost lost in the mightier flood of religious revolt. Whether one preferred rhetoric to logic or Italian Renaissance to Gothic architecture became rather less important than whether one stood with the Church of Rome or against it; and the humanists were divided on this question. Yet the thrust of the Renaissance left imprints too deep to be wiped out. Education, learning, art, politics—none of these could ever be the same. Educationally, the humanist movement produced a flock of new schools and penetrated the older ones. Thus many of the great preuniversity "public schools" of England go back to a humanist origin, St. Paul's of London, founded by Colet, being the best known example. The nature of this education, with its heavy stress on classical literature and also physical culture has endured down to our own time. Humanists got into the universities, where they often competed fiercely with the entrenched Scholasticism for honors and preferment. The introduction of a humanities or arts curriculum, modify-

IMAGO · ERASMI · ROTERODA
MI · AB · ALBERTO · DVRERO · AD
VIVAM · EFFIGIEM · DELINIATA ·
ΤΗΝ · ΚΡΕΙΤΤΩ · ΤΑ · ΣΥΓΓΡΑΜ
ΜΑΤΑ · ΔΕΙΞΕΙ
· MDXXVI ·
AD

Erasmus of Rotterdam, noted leader of the "revival of learning" in Europe at the end of the 15th century. Engraving by Albrecht Dürer.

ing the medieval preference for logic, metaphysics, and mathematics, originated with the humanists. For example, a lectureship on "works of the poets and orators" at newly founded Christ's College, Cambridge, about 1500, reflected the influence of the humanist chancellor, John Fisher, who soon brought Erasmus to Cambridge to teach Greek.

The ideals and the accomplishments of the northern Renaissance were most notably reflected in its outstanding representative, Erasmus of Rotterdam, who also taught in Switzerland and England. Like his friend Thomas More, he dreamed of a human nature refined by proper education; of enlightened princes who devoted themselves, with the aid of Renaissance scholars, to uplifting the morals and minds of their subjects; of a purified Christianity which would make men free. He admired the great "pagan" philosophers, such as Socrates and Cicero, almost as much as Christ, and lived long enough to deplore Martin Luther's fanaticism; but he was a devout Christian yearning to make Christ's ideals a living reality. A sharp critic of existing society, deeply concerned about the plight of the poor, Erasmus expressed his classical moderation in rejecting violent revolution and in seeing that human society will never escape some amount of imperfection. His scathing assaults on monks, warmongers, unequal taxation, and many other evils stamp him as a reformer, a liberal, one of the greatest social critics who ever wrote; yet his dream was of the Christian prince and not the proletarian revolutionary. Classical humanism, to which Erasmus was true, warned against the sin of pride and saw man as a limited creature.

Christian humanism

Thus the Renaissance brought forth many and various ideas; and it is difficult to say that any one of them predominated. But there was a persistent religious theme. The religious ideas of Renaissance humanism were highly important not merely for their own sake but in the light of what was to happen in the 16th century, when Europe entered into the struggle of the Reformation. The humanists, both Italian and northern, did have strong religious interests and a powerful impact on the church. Between 1447 and 1521 the Renaissance "captured the papacy." Popes were patrons of the Renaissance, a fact which Michelangelo's Sistine ceiling has immortalized. They were themselves scholars, manuscript collectors, and art enthusiasts, as well as rather unscrupulous politicians—that typical Renaissance combination. They were not necessarily bad men for being bookish and artistic, but their "worldly" interests and Renaissance politics made them rather unspiritual. However, this was nothing new in the papacy. Deeply spiritual popes there had been, mystics and even hermits; but the nature of the office had always tended to the election of political types, and to a luxurious, monarchical way of living which had periodically shocked pious commoners. This was as true in the time of St. Francis or of St. Catherine as of Savonarola and Luther. Dante wished as strongly in the 14th as Erasmus in the 16th century to exclude certain popes from heaven.

Humanists and the Bible

But humanism did not usually mean a complete transfer of interests from religious to secular. Most humanists were earnest Christians. They wanted to rescue Christianity from the grip of Scholastic theology, to "humanize" it. To some this meant an infusion of Neoplatonic mysticism. To others it meant just the reading of the Bible and church Fathers as literature, and the use also of pagan literature for inspirational purposes. Erasmus devoted himself to the translation of the New Testament into good literature (Latin), so that, as he hoped, every plowboy might be able to read it; and More told Oxford that knowledge of God should come from Scripture and the early Fathers, not from Scholastic riddles. Assailing the allegorical interpretation of Scripture, humanists stressed the historical, biographical approach. John Colet lectured on St. Paul the man rather than the Pauline theology as such. "Christian humanism" was an effort to put personal, emotional meaing into the dry abstractions of theology. As such, it was a prominent concern of the Renaissance.

Humanists put the powerful armory of their scholarship at the service of textual reform of Scripture. The truth is that the Christian holy writings were in a most uncomfortable position textually. There was no one unquestioned text, far from it, but a large number of imperfect copies from which it was terribly difficult to puzzle out the original. The official "Vulgate" version of the Bible in Latin, St. Jerome's old translation, was full of errors. Erasmus and company corrected some of them, but only started the long road of Biblical scholarship. This interest of the humanists reflected a growing interest in the Bible on the part of a literate laity. It is not true that the church refused to permit vernacular translations and new editions, but it did tend to view them warily, feeling that the difficulties and dangers were too great.

In 1511 appeared Erasmus' *In Praise of Folly,* in which the sharpest pen of the age turned his weapon of satire on monks, Schoolmen, and ignorance in general. It was the high tide of humanism in the North. The years just before Luther witnessed a stirring "battle of books" in Germany in which the humanists, led by the great scholar Johann Reuchlin, contended with the Scholastic doctors of Cologne, who attacked them for encouraging the use of Hebrew and the reading of allegedly profane material in that language. The humanists in reply charged their foes with ignorance and obscurantism, and defended the scholarly approach to Scripture. The scholastics accused Reuchlin of knowing no more theology than a babe; the humanists used satire with searing effect in the very bold *Letters of Obscure Men.*

Humanism and religious reform

Within a few years (1511–16) Erasmus gave to the world his New Testament translation and *Encomium Moriae*, Machiavelli his *Prince*, Thomas More the *Utopia*. Reuchlin had published his Christian-Hebrew grammar in 1506 and the ensuing controversy brought forward the *Letters of Obscure Men*. The implied stress in all these works on religious reform, at a moment when the Protestant revolt was breeding, seems too significant to miss. With their interest in reform of religious habits, in Bible reading by the laity, with their sharp attacks on popes, monks, and medieval theology, the humanists might seem to have prepared the way for the Reformation. The view is a common one. People said at the time that Luther hatched the egg Erasmus had laid. However, Erasmus was to break with Luther and remain loyal to Rome. A majority of humanists did so, in the long run, though at first attracted to Luther. Few of the humanists were rebels. They wished a gentle reform from above, with a spirit of piety based on education and culture. They were frightened by the violence of the upsurge that seemed to accompany the Lutheran theology, much as they may have welcomed it initially.

Humanism and science

The story of the Reformation is found in the next chapter. The Reformers took the center of the stage and held it for a century, turning the issues in a direction that humanism had hardly intended. With all its importance for the West, and its perennial fascination for students of the human spirit, Renaissance humanism did not point entirely in the direction Europe was to go. It was aristocratic, it was international, it was esthetic. It did not contribute much to science and technology, despite the private interests of Leonardo da Vinci. The association of "Renaissance" with "scientific revolution" is a strong one in the popular mind, but the scientific movement of Kepler and Galileo not only came later but owed less to the humanists than it did to the late Scholastics (see earlier, pp. 212–13, on Oresme and Buridan). Humanism was so strongly literary and moral in its interests that it threw its influence largely against the scientists, along with the logicians and pedants. In the perennial opposition of the "two cultures" about which C.P. Snow has written recently, humanism was firmly on the side of "the humanities," from which its very name derived, and against the scientists. The Renaissance produced an impulse toward getting power over nature, but in the 15th century this issued in magic, astrology, alchemy, and other forms of occultism, more typically than in what we would call science. Historians of science have alleged that the humanists marked a regression in scientific methodology from the late Scholastics. On the other hand, their interest in nature was strong though largely misdirected, and may well have contributed indirectly to the scientific revolution in the age of Copernicus and Galileo.

The Renaissance was not exactly like anything that came after it, heavily though later developments may have borrowed from it. It was *sui generis*—at its purest, the culture of an urban civic life which was even then disappearing before the great national states of the West. Its most enduring legacies were educational, scholarly, and literary. Never again would logic dominate the universities without challenge; never again would there be wanting men deeply learned in philology and related subjects. Never again, above all, would cultivated men in Europe be without a knowledge of "the classics."

Revival in the North

The new monarchies

The kingdoms of Europe—most of them, at any rate—emerged in the later 15th century stronger than ever. The word is of the "new monarchy," which means a state entirely released from feudal restraints, tending toward absolute despotism, disposing of resources previously unknown. In France, it comes in the reign of the wily Louis XI, who consolidated the monarchy after the exhausting wars, secured the defeat of the powerful Duke of Burgundy by shrewd diplomacy as well as arms, and, while bringing feudal anarchy to an end through organizing an effective financial and military system, pursued economic policies favorable to commerce and industry. It was a typical pattern. The new kings favored the bourgeoisie, from which class they tended to take their ministers. They were shrewd, realistic, often unscrupulous in their diplomacy, but aimed at the good of the state; they were "Machiavellian" even before Machiavelli. These northern states certainly learned much from Italy, applying the lessons of the city-states to broader areas; but historians are inclined to think that this was not simply a matter of Italian influence. There were indigenous forces at work here as in Italy, pushing aside the old political order and structuring the new.

Louis XI

Louis XI, the "spider king," outmaneuvered Charles the Bold of Burgundy, bought off his allies, took advantage of his mistakes, and ended by having the Swiss pikemen administer the *coup de grace* at the great Battle of Nancy (1477), where Charles was killed and much of Burgundy added to France. The powerful house of Anjou also fell to the French Valois king. The powerful French territorial nobility were subdued by this King of feeble body but strong mind and will. In marked contrast to England, the French Estates-General abdicated completely and asked the King to govern without them.

Tudor kings of England

In England, the Battle of Tewkesbury in 1471 brought the civil War of the Roses to an end, with full victory for the white rose of York. Edward IV proved a strong and able ruler, and actually began the new monarchy. After his death Henry Tudor seized the throne from the tyrannical Richard III. Some historians now believe Shakespeare's pro-Tudor version of the famous intrigue and murder story is considerably biased, but Richard was widely believed to have murdered his nephew, the young King Edward V. The red rose won the last triumph in the person of the somewhat obscure Tudor, victorious over Richard at the battle of Bosworth Field in 1485, who as Henry VII began a line of monarchs destined to lead England to greatness.

The Tudor monarchs showed in classic form the traits of the new monarchy: realism, a commercial orientation, an instinct for power, dedication to the military and economic reform of the state, tough and able diplomacy. The Tudors presided over those economic and naval gains which brought England to a leading position in Europe under Queen Elizabeth and laid the foundations for her future greatness. Remarkable in England was the virtual extinction of the old nobility. By 1509, it was reported that only one duke and one marquis were left of the old families. War, crusade, and civil strife had done this, along with the generous use of attainder (using judicial powers without the procedures of the common law) by Henry VII, no man to tolerate

Richard III, last king of the House of York

Henry VII, first king of the House of Tudor

opposition. The Tudors created new nobles, who were not likely to be enemies of the state. It became a common saying in England that nobility was only ancient riches: any man who had money could buy a title.

Despite the often ruthlessly despotic behavior of the monarchs, Parliament did not disappear in England. Edward IV bypassed its tax powers in a manner the Stuarts later took up, to their ultimate sorrow; Richard III browbeat it into ratifying his inheritance of the throne but did not attack it; Henry VII and all the Tudors were to flatter it, use it, perhaps pack it, but never rule without it. Its roots were already too deeply put down in English political soil. In this period Sir John Fortescue (1394–1476) contrasted the constitutional English monarchy with the absolutist French, the English common law with the Roman—already drawing a distinction later centuries were to make familiar. A strong monarchy, but also a strong Parliament—this was the miracle England accomplished.

Unification of Spain

The same strengthening of the monarchy went on in Spain. The marriage of Isabella, heiress to the throne of Castile, and Ferdinand, heir to Aragon, in 1469, was a landmark in the affairs of Spain. With the aid of the cities this royal combination tamed the great feudal magnates. Aragon and Castile remained separate kingdoms administratively for some time, the union being only dynastic and the Inquisition the only common political institution; but the union led to an attack on the last remaining Moorish territory (Granada in the extreme South) which succeeded, 1482–92, in completing that centuries-old crusade. On the Iberian peninsula Portugal remained separate and so did the kingdom of Navarre in the north, bordering France; but the rest, a considerable majority of the peninsula, had drawn closer together and would before long emerge as the most powerful state in Europe.

Germany

But the German Emperor did not succeed in unifying his country. In Germany the role played by kings in France and England fell chiefly to the territorial duchies. The reason, according to an explanation we have already encountered, was that the German king had long been the Holy Roman emperor, an office with vague claims to universal authority, and definite relationships to Italy and the papacy. There was also a matter of geographic disunity. The German north, fronting on the Baltic and dominated for long by the Hanseatic League of cities, was not related to the south, which looked in the direction of Austria and Bohemia. The frontiers of Germany, racially and physically, were not well defined. The west of Germany was interested in France and Burgundy, while far to the east the Teutonic Knights struggled with Poles on the Slavic frontier. It seems likely that this political geography played as much part as the nature of the imperial office in disuniting "Germany."

Germany prospered in the later Middle Ages and early modern period, boasting rich cities and a highly developed economic life, welcoming humanist culture, as we have seen, but loyalties remained focused on city or territory, not on a national state. The duchies of Bavaria, Saxony, Swabia, and so on, and the various free cities of the Empire, along with some of the domains of the church (for example, the Archdiocese of Mainz), often became great places, but the fact remains that Germany settled down into a situation of many small political units with no central state or centripetal force such as France and England possessed. A sense of frustration at this failure inspired a sentiment of German patriotism which flared up in Luther's era. The emperor made his headquarters at Vienna after 1438 when the Hapsburg family began a long era of unbroken succession in the imperial office.[1] The office was traditionally elective, with the seven "electoral" states of the Empire doing the honors after 1386. It became customary, however, to choose the eligible Hapsburg. The line produced some hard-working and capable rulers, but they did not dare aspire to the destruction of the powerful territorial states. The Hapsburgs strove to build up their own domains, extending the area under their direct control mostly in the direction of Bohemia and Hungary, while playing the role of a strictly feudal, that is, limited or even figurehead monarch through most of the unwieldy Empire. As such they constituted one of the great dynasties of Europe; and some accessions by marriage were to make them even greater in the 16th century.

In brief, throughout northern and western Europe large national or territorial states were emerging. This was not inevitable; it did not happen in Germany, and we also see centrifugal forces at work in Scandinavia. Territorial contiguity need not necessarily mean community of interest. A seaport city, such as Venice or Hamburg, might feel more of a pull to regions far across the ocean than to its own neighboring hinterland. In northern Europe, the league of Hanseatic cities, a group of ports on the Baltic including the widely separated places of Hamburg, Bremen, Lübeck, and Danzig, at one time in the later Middle Ages developed common political institutions based on similar economic interests. But by the 15th century this urban league and others like it were waning. Territorial states based on national consciousness seemed to be the pattern of the future.

New World discoveries

Medieval ideas of geography

Contrary to a popular myth that still exists, medieval men of education knew that the world was round, a fact established by the ancients; they did not imagine, either, that people would fall off the earth on the other side. They did entertain extremely fanciful notions of geography, telling tales of mythical kingdoms, mythical animals, and mythical peoples, much as present-day science fiction does of "creatures from outer space." Thus Joinville, the well-educated 13th-century biographer of St. Louis, tells us that spices flow out of the river Nile in Egypt, which emerges from an earthly paradise bearing all kinds of treasure, fished out of the river with nets by the natives. Men

[1] The "capital" of the Empire was not at Vienna, a distinction to be noted. While Vienna became the seat of the Hapsburgs' personal domains, destined to grow mightily, the Reichstag or Imperial Diet moved around from city to city. After 1663 it met at Regensburg (Ratisbon).

Early map of the New World from Cosmographica by Peter Apianus, 1524. Not much was then known of North America.

Christopher Columbus

thought that it was quite impossible to reach the southern "antipodes" because of a torrid zone that could not be crossed. What held back voyages to the west, where a mythical "Atlantis" was supposed to lie, was primarily the lack of sufficiently seaworthy ships to brave the terrifying Atlantic, so different from the placid Mediterranean, and also lack of other navigational knowledge. That is why the Portuguese hugged the coast of Africa for so long. This had not prevented the Vikings of Scandinavia from reaching Greenland and Newfoundland in North America in the 10th and 11th centuries; but these remarkable feats of a barbarian folk led to no permanent settlements in America and were not well known in the rest of Europe.

Renaissance learning and the age of discovery

In a variety of ways, the great process of exploration was related to the Renaissance. The recovery of Ptolemy's *Geography* in 1410 was part of a resurrection of ancient knowledge which was a central task of Renaissance scholarship. Needless to say Ptolemy's picture of the world was inaccurate, and yet it stimulated curiosity and inspired experimentation. In addition to the design of ships and sails, where the Portuguese learned much from the Arabs, the other vital area of advance was in navigational instruments, whereby the navigator might locate his position when out of sight of land, by means of observations of the stars. Astronomers consulted by the Portuguese also learned from the Arabs, who in turn had built on Ptolemy's *Almagest*, which summed up the ancient world's knowledge. Though science was not a major interest of the typical Renaissance humanist, the renewed interest in and translation of ancient books was bound to affect the sciences. The whole of history is bound up together, and one cannot separate the seamless web that binds Petrarch, Columbus, and Copernicus together. So Renaissance learning had something to do with the age of exploration. Nevertheless the most important contribution came from the practical experiments of practical men—sailors, shipbuilders, chart-makers. Perhaps it is best to say, with a leading historian of this subject, that "All this achievement was due to an unprecedented combination of sea experience and academic knowledge."

The knowledge that led to the Atlantic expeditions grew up mainly in Portugal, as we know, but Prince Henry's school drew on many Italians and indeed gathered together an institute of cartographers, astrologers, mathematicians, travelers, and seamen from all over Europe.[2] Columbus settled in Portugal, and there absorbed this spirit of exploration.

Columbus

Our conception of the Renaissance would not be complete without Columbus and the vision of a new world. It is true that this great vista was a little remote from the humanists of Italy or the politics of Europe as yet.

[2] Most Europeans and Americans probably are still unaware that in the 15th century the Europeans were well behind other peoples of the world in maritime knowledge and achievement. Arabs had long sailed the African coast and across the Indian Ocean. In 1405 and 1433 the Chinese sent out great expeditions to India, Arabia, and East Africa which were far more impressive than Prince Henry's relatively small and cautious ventures. But they failed to follow up these expeditions with colonization and further explorations.

Columbus made use, or rather misuse, of the Florentine geographer, Toscanelli, who was a product of the golden Medici age of the Tuscan city, and other geographers. Columbus persuaded himself that the distance between Europe and Asia was far less than it was. That another continent lay almost exactly where he erroneously put Asia was his good fortune. The immortal admiral himself, of course, was a native of Genoa with its fine maritime traditions. In the courage with which he ventured on what seemed a foolhardy expedition he no doubt reflected the adventurous spirit of his age and culture. He came from a land which had already given the world Marco Polo and was drawn toward that Orient with which it long had carried on trade. Columbus, as everyone knows, thought he had sailed to the isles of the East and stubbornly refused to believe otherwise. Bartholomeu Diaz rounded the Cape of Good Hope in 1488, and by 1509 the Portuguese had secured for Europe the mastery of the eastern seas, while the Spanish were yet uncertain about what they had blundered upon through having backed Columbus.

Spanish and Portuguese discoveries

All Americans learn about the voyages of exploration when they study the history of their own country; here, then, we may be forgiven for making but brief mention of these. The Portuguese hour of glory, which made Lisbon the chief focus of trade with the Orient in the 16th century, ensconced them in Macao near China and Goa in India; later little Portugal had to relinquish most of these staggering commitments to the Dutch and the English, but she was the true pioneer of modern world trade. Spices were the chief source of wealth. Meanwhile the Spanish *conquistadores* were writing a chapter without equal in world history as they conquered, organized, and exploited—often with extreme cruelty, but with amazing energy—an empire as large as Rome's had been, and probably more profitable, in the Americas. The Portuguese took possession of Brazil (1500), and in 1501 the Italian navigator Amerigo Vespucci, destined to give his name to the whole of the New World, explored the South American coast under the Portuguese flag. But Spain sent Balboa across the Isthmus of Panama to glimpse the Pacific (1513) and Ferdinand Magellan on his great voyage around the globe (1519–22), finding his way around the southern tip of South America. A papal bull of 1493, and a treaty of 1494, divided the newly discovered outer world entirely between Spain and Portugal! Francis I of France soon asked to see the clause in Adam's will that excluded him from his share; but the two Iberian countries deserved their preeminence at this time. Soon the Spaniards conquered the rich Aztec empire of Mexico (1518–21), central America (1522–35), and the fabulous Inca domains in Peru (1531–36). They soon derived enormous wealth in gold and silver from the mines of Mexico and Peru. Exploring to the north (Florida and Carolina coast, Ponce de Leon and De Soto, 1521–43; Texas and the Colorado country, Coronado, 1540–42), the Spanish largely left North America, save for Mexico, to concentrate on the more profitable southern half of the New World.

Stirred to its depths by the Reformation, Europe as a whole was not very

Sailing close hauled, in mid-16th century.

conscious of the significance of all this until the latter half of the 16th century. Though sending out the Italian, John Cabot, early (1497) to discover the mainland coast of North America, England proved languid in response to the challenge until later; there was an almost total lack of interest in works of geography or overseas exploration for a half century after Columbus. She was engaged then in building a state and undergoing the Reformation. John Cabot's son Sebastian tried to find the storied Northwest Passage through Labrador and Hudson Bay, but failed; trying for the Northeast Passage, he found Russia instead. Jacques Cartier sailed in the service of France in 1534 but nothing came of it for 70 years. France was fighting wars in central Europe against the Holy Roman Emperor, and then being torn by internal strife stemming from the religious revolt.

Influences of the discoveries

In the long run, the implications for Europe of the New World and overseas trade included the relative decline of Italy, southern Germany, and the old trade routes in favor of the Atlantic states; vast wealth to be made by large-scale commercial enterprise; new horizons of thought and imagination which accompanied the widening of the physical world and the discovery of new peoples, customs, products; the building of colonial societies in the Americas, Africa, and Asia, which extended the range of Western civilization while creating civilizations which were not entirely European; and too many other effects, in a widening circle, to be enumerated.

It is natural for use to include under "Renaissance" a process which did so much to break up old patterns of thought and action and create new ones, even though most of these results would show up later. And there is at least the example of Thomas More to support the connection. His famous *Utopia* was a criticism of certain policies of European governments: especially, irrational wars (the French in Italy) and bad social policy (enclosure of the commons land in England). But More, the classic humanist, went on to depict an ideal society in the New World. He had no intention of migrating, being far too busy attempting to reform the English educational system and correctly advise King Henry VIII. It was a literary device. But the thought that in the "brave new world" some better society might be created was one that stuck. Sir Humphrey Gilbert carried More's book with him on his ship to America.

Concept of the Renaissance

We may close this chapter by critically reviewing the concept of this age as "Renaissance," that is, rebirth. There are indeed many reasons for deciding to begin "modern history" about 1450 or 1500. The ending of feudal domination, the rise of the new state and of nationalist sentiment, the rise of capitalism, discovery of the New World and of new trade routes to the Orient—these are the chief ones. In the realm of thought and expression, men as diverse as Machiavelli and Da Vinci strike a note of realism which is substantially original. All these developments, however, had their roots in the Middle Ages, and one should not make the error of thinking of them as a miraculous awakening from a long sleep. There should be no real difficulty in thinking of change *and* continuity, for they are really aspects of the same thing. A child grows and changes, until one day we decide he has become a man. A river flows on over rocks and through narrows, and may come to a waterfall, but it is the same water. Revolutions happen in history, but they are prepared in the past. There was little interruption to the continuity of history in the 15th century, and new things evolved out of old over a long period of time.

There is some tendency to extend the word "Renaissance" to cover an even wider stretch of time, including under it some things, like Shakespeare's plays or Galileo's science, which appeared a century later. Unless we are to think of all European history as a perpetual renaissance—in which of course there is much truth—we ought not stretch the term to cover so much. It has established itself ineffaceably as the term descriptive of what happened in Italy in the period from about 1380 to 1520; it may be extended to include other developments in the later 15th century which had little to do with humanists and scholars but mingled with them in the pattern of the age.

Like all creative epochs it left enduring legacies—so that the Renaissance, but also the Middle Ages, are in a sense still going on. But after 1520 the Reformation—to which we now turn—seems to mark a new historical epoch.

Bibliography

The Renaissance has brought forth whole libraries. A good start might be Wallace Ferguson's *The Renaissance in Historical Thought: Five Centuries of Interpretation* (Boston: Houghton Mifflin Co., 1948). Another thoughtful summation is F. Chabod, *Machiavelli and the Renaissance* (London: Bowes & Bowes, 1957), which contains a valuable bibliographical essay; while the volume by M.P. Gilmore in the Rise of

Modern Europe series, *The Rise of Humanism* (Harper Torchbook), and the first volume of the *New Cambridge Modern History* (1957) are both outstanding. A splendid essay by the eminent Renaissance scholar Paul O. Kristeller has been printed in paperback (Harper) as *Renaissance Thought: The Classic, Scholastic, and Humanist Strains.* One cannot go far without mentioning the 19th-century classic by the great Swiss historian Jacob Burckhardt, *The Civilization of the Renaissance in Italy,* in paperback as two volumes of the Harper Torchbooks. F. Schevill, *The Medici,* is a fine account reprinted also by Harper Torchbooks, as is his *Medieval and Renaissance Florence* (2 vols.). See also Denis Hay, *The Italian Renaissance* (New York: Cambridge University Press, 1961), and more recently Peter Laven, *Renaissance Italy 1464–1534* (London: Batsford, 1966), a succinct introduction. Hans W. Baron, *The Crisis of the Early Italian Renaissance* (2 vols.; Princeton, N.J.: Princeton University Press, 1955), is an outstanding work of scholarship. Directed at the intellectual movement are Frederick B. Artz, *Renaissance Humanism 1300–1500* (Kent, Ohio: Kent State University Press, 1966), and Lauro Martines, *The Social World of the Florentine Humanists 1390–1460* (Princeton University Press, 1963). Tinsley Helton (ed.), *The Renaissance: A Reconsideration of the Theories and Interpretations of the Age* (University of Wisconsin Press) is an up-to-date summary of interpretation. Further light on the Italian Renaissance comes from Roberto Ridolfi, *The Life of Niccolo Machiavelli* (Chicago: University of Chicago Press, 1963). Also see J.R. Hale, *Machiavelli and Renaissance Italy* (London: English Universities Press, 1961).

The Renaissance north of the Alps suggests above all Erasmus; the prince of humanists can be approached via J. Huizinga's *Erasmus and the Age of the Reformation* (Harper Torchbook). Albert Hyma, *The Christian Renaissance* (New York: Century, 1925), pioneered in calling attention to the role of the Low Country piety in the thought of Erasmus and his age. H. Holborn, *Ulrich von Hutten* (New Haven, Conn.: Yale University Press, 1937), is another good biography. R. Weiss has written on *Humanism in England during the Fifteenth Century* (2d ed.; New York: Oxford University Press, 1957), while of great interest for the English Renaissance is R.W. Chambers, *Thomas More* (University of Michigan, Ann Arbor), as well as Leland Miles, *John Colet and the Platonic Tradition* (Open Court Publishing). Kenneth Charlton, *Education in Renaisance England* (London: Routledge & Kegan Paul, 1965) is a recent study of a theme near to the heart of humanism.

Some books about Columbus and the Age of Discovery were cited in the preceding chapter's bibliography, but here we may add Boies Penrose, *Travel and Discovery in the Renaissance 1420–1620* (Cambridge, Mass.: Harvard University Press, 1952).

Art, sculpture, architecture books are plentiful. Bernard Berenson's influential *Italian Painters of the Renaissance* is available in Meridian (World Publishing) paperback. Two Harvard University Press publications, S.J. Freedburg, *The High Renaissance in Rome and Florence* (2 vols., 1961), and Erwin Panofsky, *Early Netherlandish Painting* (2 vols., 1961), may be singled out. *The Horizon Book of the Renaissance* (New York: American Heritage Publishing) contains a wealth of color illustrations.

From the singular riches of original sources, a selection has been made by Ross and McLaughlin, *The Portable Renaissance Reader* (Viking Press); but all should read *in toto* such works as Machiavelli's *The Prince* and *Discourses* (several editions); Castigilione's *The Courtier* (Doubleday Anchor); and Erasmus, *In Praise of Folly* (University of Michigan, Ann Arbor). There are also Vasari's *Lives of the Artists* (New York: Simon and Schuster); Sebastian Brandt, *Ship of Fools* (Columbia Records of Civilization); Allan H. Gilbert (ed.), *The Letters of Machiavelli* (G.P. Putnam's Sons, Capricorn), the editor being also the author of *Machiavelli's Prince and Its Forerunners* (reprinted, New York: Barnes & Noble, 1968). A selection from Erasmus under the title of *Christian Humanism and the Reformation* has been made by John C. Olin for Harper's paperback Sourcebooks in European History series, which also contains the *Letters of Obscure Men* and other Renaissance documents.

Protest of 1517 against John Tetzel and the selling of indulgences.

JOHANNES TECELIUS PIRNENSIS
Dominicanus, Nundinator Romani Pontificis, anno
1517. à μεγαλανδρῳ LUTHERO territus & in fugam versus,
uti talis ejus effigies visitur in templo Pirnensi.
O ihr Deutschen mercket mich recht/
Des heiligen Vaters Bapstes Knecht
Bin ich/ und bring euch jtzt allein
Zehn tausent und neun hundert carein/
Gnad und Ablaß von einer Sünd/
Vor euch/ ewr Eltern/ Weib und Kind/
Sol ein jeder gewehret sein/
Soviel ihr legt ins Kästelein/
So bald der Gülden im Becken klingt/
Im hun die Seel in Himmel springt.

10

The Reformation

chronology

1513–21
Pontificate of Pope Leo X.
1517
Luther's 95 Theses.
1518
Heidelberg Disputation; Luther accused of heresy; hearings at Augsburg.
Luther appeals to general council of church.
1519
Zwingli begins preaching in Zürich, moves toward Protestantism.
1520
Charles V Holy Roman Emperor, as well as King of Spain.
Luther burns papal bull, writes pamphlets against papacy.
Suleiman the Magnificant, zenith of Ottoman Empire.
1521
Luther refuses to recant at Diet of Worms. Edict of Worms against him.
War between French King Francis I and Charles V.
1522
Lutheran controversy spreads. Luther begins translation of Bible into German.
Loyola at Manresa.
1525
Battle of Pavia, imperial victory over French.
Peasant revolt in Germany, denounced by Luther.
Marriage of Luther.
1527
Henry VIII appears to Pope for annulment of his marriage to Catherine of Aragon.
Sack of Rome by imperial troops. Advance of Turks into Hungary.
1529–30
Augsburg Confession: Luther-Zwingli split. Reformation Parliament in England.
1531
Schmalkaldic League of German Protestant princes and cities.
1534–35
English break with Rome; Act of Supremacy.
Anabaptist movement in Germany; seizure of Münster.
Foundation of Jesuit order.
1536
Calvin in Geneva; first edition of *Institutes of Christian Religion.*
Suppression of English monasteries.
1540
Society of Jesus approved by Pope.
Six Articles, England.
1542–44
Fourth Valois-Hapsburg war.
1545–63
Council of Trent.
1546
Death of Luther.
1546–47
Schmalkaldic War.
1551
Articles of the Anglican Church drawn up by Cranmer.
1553
Trial and execution of Michael Servetus in Geneva.
Reign of Mary of England, 1553–58; restoration of Catholicism.
1555
Peace of Augsburg.
Pontificate of Paul IV, 1555–59; spirit of Counter-Reformation.
1559
End of Hapsburg-Valois wars.
1563
Huguenot Wars in France.

Background of the religious revolt

The existence of a single church had been axiomatic for Christian medieval Europe. Accustomed to pluralism and diversity in the modern world, the student may well wonder why; but there is no difficulty in understanding it when the historical situation is grasped. The indivisible church rested on imposing grounds both psychological (it was the binding force for peoples at a time when nationalism and other modern political ideologies scarcely existed) and philosophical. Historically, the church represented, as few if any yet doubted, the continuation of Christ's own disciples by an unbroken apostolic succession: it could hardly be false unless Christ himself was a deceiver. It seemed hardly possible to doubt the unity of all Christians in the same faith, Christ having taught one way to salvation and not many; and the need of a visible, earthly church to serve as the vehicle for Christ's message, the means of salvation, was hardly less obvious. In addition, the conditions of life in earlier medieval times had solidified the power of the church. Amid general ignorance it alone held together as the source of religious truth.

Forerunners of Protestantism

The medieval church did not always escape criticism and difficulty. There were many preliminaries and partial precedents for the revolt Martin Luther launched in 1517–21. Among those already mentioned, we may here recall the following from the preceding two centuries: John Wycliffe, the unorthodox English theologian; John Hus, the Bohemian rebel; the conciliarists, who challenged the supremacy of the pope; the imperialists, who asserted a power of state over church in all that concerned organization; the mystics, whose path to God bypassed both sacraments and formal doctrines; the humanists, whose zeal for religious reform accompanied an attack on Scholastic theology and a keen interest in lay reading of Scripture. There were also monarchs who had long wished to dominate the church within their domains, striking down any interference from Rome. None of these, it must be understood, was Protestant, though Wycliffe and Hus came close. Most did not dream of breaking with the official church, yet each contributed something to a formula that added up to revolt when Luther put it together.

Luther drew on all of these and on older traditions as well. Appealing to the writings of Paul, Augustine, and Bernard, Luther would express, in reality, a perennial impulse within Christianity (and Judaism before it) for a personal, emotional religion as against an overly formalized and externalized one. This was in some sense a conflict as old as the prophets versus the law in ancient Israel, and had been repeated in the early years of the Christian church. During the Middle Ages such voices as St. Bernard and St. Francis expressed it though they did not create a schism within the church. For that matter, the Waldensian and Albigensian movements remind us that there were some who did rebel completely from the church even in the Middle Ages. Christianity constantly strained between the opposing tensions of a fervent personal faith and an effective ecclesiastical organization, both representing deeply rooted needs and traditions.

The immediate background of the Reformation included abuses and corruption in the church during the era of the Renaissance popes, more interested in art and politics than religion and morality. The undeniable need to cleanse the Augean stables of the church does not, however, explain why the Protestant reformers were to *leave* the old church altogether. Possibly of greater importance was the political situation within Germany, where the great movement began. Here there was widespread disappointment at failure to achieve national unification. The most recent disappointment was the Emperor Maximilian, who had been expected to pump fresh blood into the imperial office but had ended in frustration. All the restlessness of an age of revolutionary change was to be injected into the Protestant Revolt once it began. There was nationalism, social discontent, the rise of capitalism, ambitious kings, and greedy nobles. A recent historian has tried to sum up the causes under three great crises: a crisis of authority (whom should men obey? to what should they pay their loyalty?); a crisis of unity (the old medieval Christian republic breaking up, the nation-states merging); a spiritual crisis. It was an age of unease, a deeply religious age, one which had witnessed wars, revolutions, tragedy. Many men were deeply troubled about the conditions of their souls. One such was an obscure German monk.

Crises in Germany

In considering Luther and the Protestant revolt it will be necessary to ask not only why Luther thought as he did but why his thought, in many respects not new, led this time to a major break with the historic church. First let us look at the man himself, a rather humble individual who became to his surprise the leader of perhaps the most significant revolution in European history.

Luther's road to the Reformation

Luther's early years

Martin Luther was born in the village of Eisleben, in Thuringia, probably in 1483, of a family which was apparently reasonably well off (contrary to a long-established belief that the hero of the Protestant revolt had a "peasant" background). His father became associated with the mining industry in Mansfield, and provided his son with a good education. He attended the University of Erfurt, one of the largest and most famous in Germany. It would appear that young Martin was influenced there by Ockhamism, but not much by the humanists. Why he decided, against his father's wishes, to abandon his law studies for theology is something about which there is really very little knowledge. Luther himself later told the story about making a vow to become a monk when frightened by lightning in 1505. At any rate he entered a monastery of the Augustinian friars, and remained in that capacity thereafter until his final break with the church. This did not mean a life of withdrawal from the world; the order was known for scholarship and Luther soon was lecturing at the University of Wittenberg, where he was promoted to a professorship in 1511. His subject was the Bible.

A sensitive young man of high ideals, Luther was perhaps born to be a rebel. Familiar is the story of how he vainly sought relief from torment of soul in fastidious performance of monastic duties, in vigils, prayer, and fasting.

The worldliness of the church, with its gaudy externals and its absence of sincere inner religion, repelled a personality who would probably have been a Rousseau in the 18th century or a Nietzsche in the 19th. Of Luther's high seriousness and intense inner life there can be no doubt. Unquestionably he exaggerated the "horrible corruption" of the papacy and the sins of the "scholastic doctors" who in their pride talked of man *by his own power* gaining God. Such men as Luther always exaggerate. Most angry young men grow up after a time to be complacent middle-aged ones. Luther alone was destined to realize a dream of tearing down the world. But when he began to attack various abuses of the church in 1517 he can hardly have realized what would be the consequences.

Luther's war with the church

Most people are familiar with the story of how John Tetzel came selling indulgences, preaching—as it seemed to plain people, at least—that it was possible to purchase the remission of one's sins by gifts of money to the church, and how Luther, the young divinity professor, reacted by a public statement (95 theses) challenging this practice. It was the beginning of the road that led Luther within three years to defy ecclesiastical authority and

The church at Wittenberg where Luther posted his 95 theses. Woodcut by Lucas Cranach.

break with the Roman church. Luther was given a chance to defend his views, and engaged in a memorable debate with the learned John Eck, which was referred to the universities of Europe for a decision. Appealing at first to the Pope, then to the Council, Luther finally came to rest on Scripture and defied all the authorities. When a papal bull condemned his opinions, Luther publicly burnt it (December, 1520) and followed with pamphlets in which he set forth the revolutionary doctrines of justification by faith alone, the "priesthood of all believers," and reliance on the Bible alone as foundation for church discipline and organization as well as doctrine. There turned out to be grave difficulties in these affirmations, and Luther was to retreat from some of them later. But meanwhile he had made himself a symbol of rebellion, and had found that Germany welcomed him as such. Old dislike of the papalists, a heritage of the medieval conflicts between emperor and pope, mingled with new nationalism in Germany to make Luther an easy victor in any popularity contest with the hierarchy of the Roman church.

Excommunicated, Luther was invited to Worms by the Emperor, who was charged with carrying out sentence on him but hesitated because of German opinion. Luther refused again to recant.

Martin Luther burning the papal bull in 1520

Luther before the Imperial Diet at Worms, 1521

The courage of Luther, as he raised the standard of revolt against Rome between 1517 and 1521, is not in doubt. But the ground was well prepared for his action. In fact, Luther grew bolder because he was encouraged by a roar of approval from all classes of Germans. The 95 theses which he had posted on the Wittenberg church door on October 31, 1517, relating to the sale of indulgences, were not intended as a defiance of church authority. By 1520, Luther had come to regret the theses as being too mild; he had now moved further along. He was denouncing "the tyranny of Rome" completely and was ready to defy its authority. Sometimes overlooked is the fact that Tetzel, the "indulgence monger" who first aroused Luther's ire, was repudiated by the Pope and died in disgrace. There were many others *in* the Roman church who wished to reform it of various undeniable abuses, and therefore these abuses do not explain why Luther *left* the church. The road he traveled led him by degrees toward the final step of rejecting any central authority in the church and proclaiming "the priesthood of all believers." On that memorable journey to Worms in 1521 where he was to defy both Pope and Emperor —a lone professor against the powers that be—Luther was cheered every step of the way by crowds of people who lined the roads to pay him their tribute; his pamphlets sold by the thousands. The Lutheran Revolution was in large part made possible by a movement of popular German nationalism.

Popular support for Luther

When Luther refused to repudiate his writings before the great Diet at Worms, he was saved by his popularity throughout Germany. Charles V, the Emperor, was ready to seize and execute him, but, protected by Frederick of Saxony, Luther withdrew to Wartburg Castle and safety. There he busied himself with a great translation of the Bible into German. It is not true that this was the first such translation; there had been for some decades a growing interest in the Bible on the part of the laity, and the demand had been met by a number of translations into the vernacular. One of the strongest influences on Luther was the movement known as the Brethren of the Common Life, originally founded in the Low Countries but popular in Germany, which catered to such lay religious interest. Luther's translation, however, was much the most popular. It came to be known as the German Bible.

Thus the Lutheran revolt was the product not only of a sensitive soul's torment and of the seeming inadequacy of institutionalized and rationalized religion; it was also the product of political change, in which nationalism and the secular state were heavily involved. Many other emotions and impulses—social, economic, psychological—were to become intermixed with this titanic movement. But the one most evident was that of nationalism. Luther has remained a German national hero, a sort of combination of George Washington and Joan of Arc, sometimes admired even by that part of Germany which remained Catholic.

Luther's creed

The theology of faith alone

Luther built his theology out of traditional materials. Regarding the originality and power of his thought there are no two opinions, but it is equally clear that he drew generously on past doctrines. He himself acknowledged a debt to St. Paul and to Augustine. From Paul he learned that faith alone saves (Luther interpolated the "alone," but argued stoutly that Paul meant this), that works without faith are hollow. This was the passage that rescued Luther from his distress of soul and struck him with the force of a revelation: the just shall be saved by *faith*. Augustine, "doctor of grace," had long ago held that man in his natural condition, his intellect as well as his will radically impaired by the Fall, is helpless to choose the good until God bestows divine grace upon him. The theology of grace had never been lost during the Middle Ages, despite the prevalence of Scholastic theology in the 13th century. Among numerous medieval Augustinians was Bernard of Clairvaux, the great 12th-century figure in whose words Luther found one of his first answers to the spiritual torment that beset him. Luther also received some influence from the theology of William of Ockham, which urged that philosophy had nothing to do with faith, rejected the alleged proofs of God's existence, and asserted that God's will was entirely arbitrary. Luther's rather startling pronouncements on the arbitrariness of God's will—He chooses to bestow His grace on some of His disobedient children, entirely unmerited, for no reason that can be understood—thus had a background in 14th-century theology.

Luther and humanism

Luther reacted somewhat negatively to humanism. He knew, admired, and used the Biblical translations of Erasmus, and believed in studying the classical languages as an aid to Bible understanding. He also reflected humanist views in his insistence on the *literal* meaning of Scripture. But he disagreed profoundly with much of the humanist position on religion. The measure of the difference emerged later in a famous debate between Erasmus and Luther on the issue of free will. The Christian humanist believed that men by education could train their will to the good, but Luther insisted that this form of "good works" was as futile as the sacraments of the church. There must be a good will—a state of grace—otherwise all practice is vain, and will only lead the corrupted soul deeper into sin. To the pure all things are pure, but to the impure all things are impure. Doing good deeds from a selfish heart is no good. Luther insisted on the absolute impotence of "natural" man to achieve love of God and spiritual salvation. Man without the gift of divine grace is capable of reason, which is sufficient for his worldly needs; but he cannot attain grace by any power of his own—it is an act of God toward man.

Luther was reacting, with typical energy, to the laxities into which Roman Catholic worship and theology had fallen. Thomas Aquinas and most Scholastics had held to a mild, compromising theology which allowed good works to prepare the way for faith and man to collaborate with God in the task of salvation. On the other hand, the Roman church satisfied human nature's craving for the emotional by the rich liturgy of the services, held in the majestic surroundings of a Gothic cathedral and featuring a music, art, and drama developed over many centuries. It was an impressive combination of intellectualism and ceremonialism. But it tended to split the Christian world into two parts, the priests and the laity, and to split off an intellectualized theology from an emotionalized liturgy. There is an important sense in which Luther wished to restore the unity of Christianity. His "priesthood of all believers" slogan, of course, along with his attacks on monasticism and his approval of a married clergy, represented his belief that there should be no special priestly caste with extraordinary powers.

His theology, in all its severity, was also an effort to rescue religion from the sterility into which he thought it had fallen. Scholastic theology was both pallid and conceptual. It was an exercise for the few and not the many. It was close to being a humanism which looked tolerantly on human nature and spoke little of its sinful side. It did not satisfy Luther's cravings for spirituality. In the last analysis perhaps all one can say is that the formula which had long satisfied men no longer worked. All through religious history men like Luther had arisen. The prophets of Israel were of the same stamp: protesters against an overly institutionalized religion, demanding, often with a grim note, the return to inner righteousness. In the Christian Middle Ages men

Fredrick of Saxony flanked by Luther, left, with Zwingli and Melanchthon on right. Painted by Lucas Cranach.

like Bernard of Clairvaux, powerful and turbulent personalities with a deep inwardness, had remained *within* the church while greatly transforming it. The appearance, as recently as 1490, of a Savonarola (the Florentine prophet), suggests how frequently this theme repeated itself in Christian history. These prophets were seldom mild, often fanatical.

Men like Luther, then, were not altogether unknown. But the Saxon professor created a potent mixture out of elements drawn from Paul (the importance of faith in Christ as means of salvation); Augustine (the necessity of divine grace, the corruption of human nature without it); Bernard (the need for an inner religion, true for *me*); perhaps Ockham (the irrelevance of philosophy and dialectic to faith); and others, including indirectly Erasmus and the Brethren of Common Life (a Bible-reading laity, every man his own priest). Of course, the Scriptures themselves, of which he was a profound student, in their entirety weighed most heavily in Luther's Bible-centered Christianity.

Luther was in revolt against Scholastic methods, and is a writer of paradoxes and some apparent contradictions. His inconsistencies can seem dismaying, but he was a creative thinker with a superb prose style and a mighty sincerity. The numerous Germans who responded to his electrifying message were responding less to a theological creed than to a call to revolt, and were perhaps more nationalist than Christian.

Reformation motives and factions

Nationalism

There were to be other places besides Germany where opposition to the papacy, though not necessarily to existing religious forms, was associated with nationalism. Almost everywhere, indeed, the national state asserted itself in one way or another against the position of the medieval church, which had privileges no longer regarded as tolerable by kings and not popular among the people. These, it may be recalled, had included the levying of taxes, exemption from ordinary laws, responsibility to Rome and not the king on matters of policy, and possession of huge amounts of property. In some countries, such as France and Spain, the national monarchy remained orthodox while managing to secure a large measure of control over the church in its domains. Power was transferred while doctrine and ritual remained the same. Many historians have found it significant that the "Reformation" usually erupted most strongly in countries where a strong monarchy was lacking. Examples are Germany, Switzerland, and Scotland. The fiscal exactions of the papacy, and other privileges, had not been dealt with, so that violent popular reaction took place. Nationalism gathered around the symbol of a national church in the absence of a national monarchy.

It is also true that countries of the North tended to secede from the Roman church while those of the South by and large did not. This is not to say that the division was that simple: everywhere there was a struggle, everywhere there were Protestants and Roman Catholics. But when the smoke finally cleared from the big explosion, Protestantism had prevailed in England and Scotland (though not in Ireland!), in the Scandinavian countries and in Holland, in northern Germany but not southern; while France, Spain, Italy, but also what is now known as Belgium remained loyal. England, however, where there was a strong monarchy, went Protestant only slowly and cautiously. France was torn by civil strife for 40 years before reaching a decision. Far-off Poland held to Rome, though not until after a severe struggle, while in nearby Switzerland Protestantism found its strongest leader in a Frenchman from Picardy, John Calvin. Thus the association of Protestantism with distance from Rome, or northernness, is only roughly true. But unquestionably the northern countries felt less attachment to the papacy because they had less representation in it. The papacy and the College of Cardinals were almost monopolized by Italians, Spaniards, and Frenchmen. Such essentially political motives were everywhere prominent. The examples of Ireland and Poland make it evident that if a powerful and disliked neighbor was Protestant, the other faith would receive support by reaction.

The range of motives

All kinds of motives, good and bad, entered into the pattern of revolt once it had begun. All revolutions bring out this range of motives: everyone with a grievance or an interest seizes the opportunity. Macaulay, the popular 19th-century historian, caught this feature in colorful prose: "Sovereigns impatient to appropriate for themselves the prerogatives of the popes, nobles desirous to share the plunder of abbeys, suitors exasperated by the extortions of the

Roman camera, patriots impatient of a foreign rule, good men scandalized by the corruptions of the Church, bad men desirous of the license inseparable from great moral revolutions, wise men eager in the pursuit of truth, weak men allured by the glitter of novelty, all were found on one side. . . . Within fifty years from the day on which Luther publicly renounced communion with the papacy, and burned the bull of Leo before the gates of Wittenberg [December, 1520], Protestantism attained its highest ascendancy." But it suffered from lack of unity.

Protestant disunity

Disunity among the rebels was evident from the beginning, marring the Lutheran movement within a year of the drama at Worms. Luther was soon disturbed by news about "the violent conduct" of some of his followers, and wrote an *Exhortation* against "insurrection and rebellion." Returning to Wittenberg in 1522, he plunged into a series of bitter quarrels with his erstwhile disciples and with other aspiring reformers. From this time on the rapid spread of "Protestantism" was hardly more remarkable than its internal divisions. Luther was soon appalled at the wildfire he had started, and began to try to put it out.

The more extreme Protestants destroyed statues, paintings, organs, and altars (this vandalism wrought grievous damage to European art) and drastically altered church services. This "left wing" of the Reformation came to be lumped together under the name of Anabaptists. Luther engaged in lively polemics with the radicals, but he also differed with other relatively conservative reformers, such as the Swiss, Ulrich Zwingli, a contemporary of Luther's who exerted great influence in Switzerland from his city of Zurich.

Luther's conservatism

Luther clung to much of the old in his religion. Historians have spoken of "the innate conservatism" of Luther: strange, indeed, in the man who was the greatest of all revolutionaries between 1517 and 1521. He was more conservative on the Holy Eucharist than other Protestants, holding stubbornly to a doctrine of the real presence of Christ in debates with Zwingli and other Protestants. His was not the same as the Roman doctrine of transubstantiation, as defined in 1215 and based upon the Aristotelian distinction between accident and substance. This Luther rejected, along with the conception of the mass as a sacrifice of Christ renewed upon the altar to impart saving grace to the communicant. But Luther would not agree, either, with Zwingli and other Protestants who wished to make the ceremony merely symbolic or commemorative.

Above all, Luther could not watch without dismay the dissolution of the church into contending factions. He turned against the anarchy of sectarianism as fiercely as he had denounced the tyranny of Rome. He wished to enforce unity on a reformed church. Luther was impaled on the horns of the most ancient of human dilemmas, liberty versus authority. His mighty blasts had caused the authority of Rome to crumble. But, released from authority, much of Europe seemed prone to dissolve into a chaos of private beliefs.

This Luther had not wanted. He was shocked by it, and, along with his great Protestant successor John Calvin, made an effort to stabilize the Protestant movement by giving it unity of creed and a disciplined organization. "This power the Church certainly has, that she can distinguish the Word of God from the words of men," Luther had written even in 1520. He had intended no mandate to every man to believe as he liked. It is a point still sometimes sadly misunderstood. Luther must not be regarded as something in the nature of a modern liberal. Turning to the state as a substitute for Rome, he came close to underwriting a new kind of tyranny, some have thought.

Spiritualists and Brethren: Protestant sectarians

The peasant revolt

Most dramatic was the peasant uprising which broke out in Germany (especially in the Black Forest region) in 1525. It was a social revolution mixed with religious fantasies. The Black Forest peasants preached a form of Christian millenarianism in which the ungodly were identified with the rich, while the saints or "elect" were the poor; and the Day of the Lord was at hand. This movement had been touched off by Luther, yet he could not approve it, and at length denounced its excesses and called in immoderate terms for its suppression. The tragic episode had a good deal to do with splitting the forces of German religious reform into two hostile parts. It illustrated the entry of social-economic motives into the Reformation. The poor peasantry, naturally enough, wished to turn the revolt into channels which would benefit them as against the rich. The same sort of impulse appeared a few years later (1534–35) among the lower class revolutionaries who seized the city of Münster in Westphalia, under the leadership of one John of Leyden, and began exterminating the rich on religious grounds. They were captured and cruelly punished by a union of Lutheran and Catholic princes and prince-bishops.

Anabaptists and other sects

The term "Anabaptist" was loosely applied to all these lower class movements, which were put down with considerable severity. Some of these sectarians, particularly the first generation, were often extreme and violent, preaching the imminence of the Second Coming and occasionally sanctioning violence by the "saints"; the second generation was almost invariably nonviolent. The Protestant sects proliferated into hundreds, and contributed enormously to the civilization of the western world. Though almost exterminated by cruel methods on the Continent, they appeared in England in the next century and found their fairest haven in the New World colonies of England. Their origin was really in the Germany of Luther's day, but the spirit of sectarianism spread to other places in Europe.

Fundamental to many of them was the doctrine of the inner light. Like George Fox, the 17th-century founder of the Quakers, they "heard a voice" and set off to preach. The holy spirit, they held, might manifest itself in all men. Sometimes this idea issued in strange behavior, and it was a defiance of authority intolerable to the conservative forces in society. The Protestant sectarians, one might say, only carried the doctrine of Luther to its logical and extreme conclusion. They would have no official church, and sometimes no church at all. The church was invisible, it was in its earthly form "wherever two or three are gathered together," or even where any one felt the spirit of God. Typically extremist, usually rising from the poorer classes where strong emotions and small education went together, these private religions were sometimes pathetic or ridiculous. At the same time they testify to the wonderful vitality of the human spirit, and its capacity to suffer and die for what it believes in.

Antinomianism

One of Luther's own disciples, Carlstadt, argued that the spirit of God is not subject even to Scripture. Left-wing disciples of Calvin were subsequently to adopt the "antinomian" position that the regenerate or elect, those who have experienced the saving grace of God, are not bound by the law. Thus bolder Protestants quickly took the doctrines of the Reformers to an extreme that the founders could not sanction, and caused a breach in the ranks of the Reformation. They caused Luther and Calvin to react in the direction of discipline, law, objective standards, and an organized church. The sectarian outburst, which appeared as sheer anarchy to many people at that time, helps explain why Luther and Calvin eventually adopted, or tried to adopt, a conservative position after an initial radicalism.

Spiritual brethren

Another enduring wing of the early Reformation began with the reforms of Zwingli in Switzerland, then broke away from his Reformed Church in 1525, and continued as several doctrinally united but severely persecuted small sects. These related sects almost always chose the simple title of Brethren, but their critics ridiculed them by uniting them and many other more radical and more spiritualistic sects under the common and derisive label of Anabaptist. The reformers of the Swiss Brethren quickly spread into Austria, Moravia, Germany, and down the Rhine to the Low Countries. In the Netherlands the movement was led by a converted priest, Menno Simons, who lent the name "Mennonite" to the largest single body of the Brethren. Though politically impotent, and numerically small during the two early centuries of intense persecution, the Brethren contributed a distinct and enduringly influential theology to Protestantism. In purest form, this doctrine is still present in the various Mennonite, Amish, Brethren, and Freewill Baptist sects. Along with several versions of Calvinist theology, it is the main doctrinal source of the major Baptist Churches of today. The Brethren also first anticipated the radically free-will and perfectionist strains of early Methodism.

The early Brethren broke with the moderate Zwingli over two compelling issues—his advocacy of a state church and his acceptance of infant baptism. The early movement was typically sectarian, with a small, voluntary membership, high moral standards, baptism at conversion, lay ministers, and a congregational church government. The Brethren were usually simple folk, artisans in the main, who developed a simple theology notable more for its

Ulrich Zwingli, and at right, Emperor Charles V, painted by Titian.

straightforward consistency and its courageous rejection of compromise than for logical subtlety. Unlike the spiritualistic sects, they were narrowly Biblical and were determined churchmen. Adhering to what they believed the most obvious intent of the New Testament, they viewed the church as the perfect, holy body of Christ, or as the now persecuted but ultimately triumphant Kingdom of God. Salvation was thus impossible outside the church. They accepted the primacy of faith in securing salvation, but tended to define faith more in terms of rigid obedience to the law than of correct belief or inward experience. Though without sacraments or priests, they practised excommunication of sinful members. Unlike the Calvinists, the Brethren rejected the orthodox doctrine of original sin, thus eliminating any reason for infant baptism. Thus baptism marked the conscious and free profession of faith by an adult, his entrance into the church, and the accompanying gift and continuing succor of the Holy Spirit.

The Brethren were most distinctive in their determination to follow the advice of St. Paul literally and be completely separated from the world. Their closed communities, with varying degrees of communal cooperation, resembled Protestant monasteries. The pure church could not be implicated in worldly concerns; neither could the Christian be a captive of pride and the secular lures of the encircling domain of sin. Whereas the Lutherans allied themselves with the state, and the Calvinists even tried to dominate it, the Brethren endeavored to ignore it. To them, forced membership in an established church and persecution for religious belief were abhorrent. Conversely, the good Christian rendered unto Caesar only the required services consistent with a good conscience. Thus, the more orthodox Brethren refused to vote, to hold public office, and to contribute to or participate in war. In persecution, the Brethren meekly submitted. In war, they fled. When left in peace they invariably prospered, but remained aloof from their neighbors. Driven from country to country, many welcomed a haven in America when such a boon was proffered by William Penn in 1681. In many ways they resembled the Quakers who invited them to share Pennsylvania with them.

The spread of Protestantism

Faced with the "swarming" of the sects and bitter quarrels among the Protestants, Luther had grown pessimistic by 1527: "Up to now I have been cherishing the vain hope that men can be directed by the Gospel. But the fact is that they destroy the Gospel and wish to be constrained by law and sword." But revolt against Rome was just beginning to spread. Luther's disillusionment and his reaction toward conservatism aided its spread among the princes of Germany. They adopted Lutheranism in the knowledge that by so doing they might seize church lands, free themselves from papal exactions, and yet keep a relatively conservative church order which staunchly supported their authority. Perhaps reluctantly but almost inevitably, Lutheranism was driven to rely on the state to maintain the Lutheran church.

Troubles of Charles V

The German princes were encouraged by the inability of the Emperor to enforce the Edict of Worms against Luther. Charles V, by virtue of his role as King of Spain and of Burgundy as well as Emperor, found himself engaged in a long war with France, and unable to devote his energies to the suppression of Lutheranism in Germany. The Turks also pressed him from the southeast. No religious zealot, Charles preferred peace within Germany and a successful issue to his foreign wars, and was not averse to temporizing tactics. There were hopes for compromise and reconciliation. Of course, Germany was a land of local autonomy. It became evident that the territorial princes, not the Emperor, would decide the religious question. The word "Protestantism" comes from the manifesto sent to Charles in 1529 by a large number of Lutheran princes and cities, the "protesting estates," which included Saxony, Brunswick, Brandenburg, Hesse, and numerous free cities. The Lutheran territories were the northern ones, probably because they felt safer from the imperial power; but such southern cities as Nürnberg, Strasbourg, and Ulm were Protestant, though tending toward Zwinglianism after 1529.

In Switzerland, the city of Zürich under Zwingli's leadership mounted a militant Protestant drive which led to war with the "forest cantons" in which the Swiss prophet was eventually killed. But while rural Switzerland remained Catholic, Berne and Geneva were to join Zürich as strongholds of the reforming theology. Martin Bucer of Strasbourg and before long John Calvin of Geneva emerged as leaders.

Protestant league

Weakened by their own failures to achieve agreement between Zwinglians and Lutherans, the Protestants of the Empire nevertheless profited by Charles' distractions to entrench their position. The Schmalkaldic League (1531) was an alliance of Protestant estates which grew in power under the energetic political leadership of Philip of Hesse, until the latter's bigamy, which Luther reluctantly approved, caused a reaction against him. It looked for a time as if all Germany might go Lutheran. Meanwhile Lutheranism spread to Scandinavia. Whereas in Germany it was a tool of the territorial princes against the Emperor, in Denmark it entered into a struggle between the King, backed by the bourgeoisie, and the nobles. Seizure of the church lands strengthened the kings in an area where politics were rough and brutal.

The English break with Rome

So it was also in England. The desire of King Henry VIII to get an annulment of his marriage to Catherine of Aragon was only the occasion and not the cause of the English Reformation, it has been said frequently; but we cannot be sure that the break with Rome would have come had it not been for this famous matrimonial dispute. The Roman Catholic writer Hilaire Belloc vigorously presented the view that England's departure from Rome was sheer accident, and an accident that proved decisive, since without England the Protestant cause would have failed. The English monarch wished to put aside his Spanish spouse and marry a lady of the court, Anne Boleyn. Applying to the Pope (Clement VII) for a special dispensation to annul the marriage, Henry met refusal. These negotiations leave little doubt that the Pope would have liked to accede. Such requests had been granted in the past. But Clement was a prisoner of Charles V, nephew of Catherine.

The English people, on the divorce, were not altogether with their King; they cheered Catherine and insulted Anne out of natural sympathy for a wronged and blameless wife. However, Henry could count on a great deal of animosity toward the papacy and the clergy. As in Germany, so in England: the foreign control of the church, its taxes, and its laxities aroused a resentment which combined nationalism, moralism, and economic interest. Henry's break with Rome was approved every step of the way by a Parliament which was roughly representative of the people of England who counted. It was not of course democratic, but represented wealth, yet wealth which was now as much bourgeois as noble. It was subject to some pressures from the throne, yet it appears likely that it did agree with the King on this issue. The various acts which marked this revolution included the Act of Restraint of Appeals; the Act of Supremacy, which made the King head of the English church; an act diverting papal revenues to the English treasury; and two acts dissolving the monasteries (all between 1533 and 1539). The church, in brief, became national, its head was now the King, its ties to Rome were broken. But it was not otherwise much changed.

Henry VIII of England, painted by Hans Holbein the Younger.

More's martyrdom

The only resistance to this came out of the North, where a popular protest known as the Pilgrimage of Grace, led by one Robert Aske, was suppressed and brutally punished. The most distinguished of the King's counselors, and perhaps the most distinguished man in England, the famous humanist Thomas More, died on the scaffold for refusing to subscribe to the Act of Supremacy, in which he, like Aske, sensed a new and awful tyranny. So also did the humanist educator John Fisher, while a number of humble monks were cruelly put to death. Thomas Wolsey, long Henry's chief minister, a proud and powerful man with a genius for foreign policy, fell afoul of the divorce proceedings and was also destroyed. The ruthlessness of Henry's seizure of the monastic properties impressed many as tyrannical. Undoubtedly the "new

Glastonbury abbey, suppressed in 1539, its abbot executed, fell into decay.

monarchy" was throwing its weight around in a way that dismayed thoughtful men. But on the issue of the church there was nothing to stop it; the cause of Rome was not popular.

Dissolution of the monasteries

The monasteries, which possessed much land and owned great wealth, were unpopular in some areas but apparently not greatly resented in most. Few, however, cared to defend them, and the monks themselves acquiesced in their extinction with surprising resignation, most of them receiving pensions or posts in the secular church. Roman Catholics themselves recognized the need for reform or abolition of some orders, which occurred in Catholic as well as Protestant countries. Historians have frequently concluded that monasticism was an obsolete institution at this time. But few have found much that was edifying in the seizure of monastic wealth. Most of this wealth ended in the hands of a new class of powerful gentry-capitalists.

Anglo-Catholicism

In leaving creed and ceremony of the church unaltered, Henry was probably acting in accordance with popular instincts as well as his own. The King was soon beheading doctrinal Protestants as a warning to those who wanted to go too far. Wolsey's successor, Thomas Cromwell, suffered the same fate as his predecessor for the opposite reason, being too much of a Protestant (1540). This also, though, was mixed up with the King's marital problems. The much-married monarch executed Anne Boleyn for adultery in 1536, the future Queen Elizabeth, Anne's daughter, being then declared illegitimate; he next married Jane Seymour, who died after giving birth to the future king Edward VI; then he married Anne of Cleves on Cromwell's advice, for political reasons, without having seen her. The King was disillusioned both with Anne and the Protestant cause. The Six Articles of 1540 affirmed transubstantiation, the celibacy of the priesthood, auricular confession, private masses. In 1543 Parliament passed an act forbidding reading of the Bible by the uneducated. The monarchy appeared to prefer a situation in which it got the power and wealth of the church but otherwise made as few changes as possible. In the next 15 years, England was to experience a violent swing from extreme Protestantism, under Henry's young son Edward VI (1547–53); to extreme Catholicism, under his daughter Mary (1553–58), who attempted to return to Rome; and then back to something like center under Henry's daughter Elizabeth (1558–1603), who steered a calculating Machiavellian course between the two churches and under whom the Church of England's ambiguous position became somewhat defined.

On the Continent, this sort of calculated Machiavellianism also prevailed. The Emperor, Charles V, was willing to compromise with the Lutherans when it suited his interests; and his rival in war, the King of France, Francis I, sought the aid of the Pope but also of the Protestant states and the Turks. If he stayed with Rome, it was from considerations of practical policy more than sentiment. Sovereigns had, of course, to consult such practical considerations. In this period they were typically strong, ruthless, clear-sighted, determined to build a powerful, efficient state. It is an essential part of the drama of this era that the religious revolution and the political-national one coincided and interacted.

Swashbuckling French King Francis I, painted by Titian.

Calvinism

Crisis in Protestantism

"No sooner did religious Protestantism attempt to formulate its positive beliefs than disintegration began." Luther began by announcing the "priesthood of all believers" and the personal nature of salvation, as an interior experience, the result of God's saving grace. He did not really mean for each man to arrive at his own faith, however, and as we have seen was shocked by the sectarian anarchy that broke out. He had no intention of going back to Rome, but he was prepared to use force on the Anabaptists and he groped for a principle of authority.

Sacramentalism, or the doctrine that saving grace comes through the church and its ceremonies, had to be rejected by Protestants. Luther kept two of the seven Sacraments (Baptism and Eucharist) but they could not assume the role they played in the Roman church. Luther's authority for the two Sacraments was the Bible, which Protestants tended to erect into the basis of their creed, as against the authority of popes or councils. But the Bible is too large and varied a collection of ideas to make for Christian unity if left to the vagaries of individual interpretation. Luther, on the whole, simply assumed that right reason would construe the Bible as he did, and all other versions must be the devil's work. But he differed with other learned and responsible Protestants even on the nature of the Eucharist, and on other matters as well. Who was to interpret the Bible for Protestants? Where would their church—assuming the need for one—get its strength?

The question became a pressing one as the initial strength of the Protestant movement, based on widespread discontent with existing conditions in the Roman church and drawing on all the other motives we have mentioned, seemed in danger of losing itself in disunity. The cry of Luther for personal experience against clerical ceremony as the grounds of religion could never be forgotten; without it there was no Protestantism. On the other hand, there was also the church, there was Christian fellowship, there was the simple fact that Christianity could not be whatever some silly person said it was. In fact, as God's revealed truth, it was *one* thing, presumably, not many. So John Calvin was to argue forcefully.

Calvin comes to Geneva

Calvin became the leader—some called him "the Protestant pope"—who made a powerful effort to restore doctrinal unity and church discipline. He had a more logical mind than the unsystematic Luther. Many regard Calvin as the less attractive figure: a narrower mind, a less creative soul. But Protestantism seemed to stand in need of his powerful intellect in its second phase. John Calvin had an excellent education, at the University of Paris as well as other schools (Orléans, Bourges), learning from Scholastics as well as humanists. Converted to Protestantism, and disappointed in France's progress toward the new creed, he made his way to the city of Geneva, with which he was long to be associated. Protestantism had spread rapidly in the free cities of Switzerland. The "man of a book and a city," Calvin was to dominate Geneva and organize its church, while writing his *Institutes of the Christian*

John Calvin

Religion, over a period of years between 1536 and 1564. To Geneva and to Calvin came Protestants from all over Europe seeking the consolidating force they needed. By 1555, when he had become unquestioned master of Geneva and the most internationally famous Reformer, he was indeed what his assistant Theodore Beza called him, "the oracle of the Christian world"—the Protestant part of it, at any rate.

Role of Calvin in Protestantism

Lutheran churches were largely confined to the German states and Scandinavia; Calvinist churches became international, including the Dutch Reformed, Scotch Presbyterians, the Puritans in England and New England, the French Huguenots, as well as branches in Germany, Hungary, and indeed almost everywhere. Calvinism gave the impression of a lucidly explained and clearly defined Protestantism. Calvin was the foremost Biblical theologian of his time, and to this he added the gifts of a systematizing mind and a practical talent for government. In addition to his Biblical commentary, elaborated in the long and thorough *Institutes*, Calvin devoted himself to the complete reform and reorganization of the church. A system based on presbyters, elders, teachers, and deacons replaced the old hierarchy; the old ceremonies and rituals became drastically simpler; the stress was on the preaching of the Word, not the Sacraments. All this was based on practical experience, and Geneva stood forth as a great model of the reformed and reorganized Christian society.

With Calvin's *Institutes* as a guide, Protestant church organization and beliefs seemed clear. To those who said that Calvinism was the same as Romanism except with Calvin in place of the pope, the answer given was that Calvin's was the correct doctrine because more Scriptural. But this was not the Bible alone; it was the Bible as construed by Calvin. It was backed by iron authority. Geneva was a place where the civil government enforced the decrees of the elders of the church, suppressing both heresy and loose behavior with an iron rod. The grimmer side of Calvinism was seen in Geneva in the inquisitorial supervision of conduct, the death sentence for crimes such as adultery and disobedience to parents, and in the burning of the heretic Michael Servetus at the stake in 1553. The political foes of Calvin were dealt with in summary fashion, too. Contrary to a common belief, he was not the "theocratic" ruler combining church and state in a single office; but he was able to exert strong influence on the state.

Predestination

The Calvinist theology struck many as a grim one, stressing as it did the omnipotence of God and the helplessness of man; and to this Lutheran theme was added a particular emphasis on the predestination of both saved and damned. Certainty that the elect were unalterably bound for heaven gave Calvinists a strong sense of assurance. It they had had an experience of grace, they felt certain they were among the saints and could never relapse. Thus the doctrine of predestination tended, somewhat paradoxically, to release men for vigorous action.

It was ironic that the original revolt of Luther in the name of freedom had come to this. But Luther had believed in reform, and this was thorough reform. Calvinism insisted upon an educated clergy, a church purified in every way, a citizenry practicing as well as understanding the Christian virtues. To Calvinism probably belongs the chief credit for the idea of compulsory education for all, which has now prevailed throughout Western civilization. More so than the Lutherans, Calvinists stressed the Bible as the only source of salvation; its every line must be read, pondered over, understood, preached about. Every Christian must be equipped to read and understand the Word of God, which is all he has in a corrupt world. Self-righteous and narrow, Calvinism was also for many individuals a source of great spiritual strength. Calvinism made good citizens and hard workers; the English Puritans are our most familiar witnesses to that. It has been suggested that it helped form modern capitalism, by which is meant economic individualism together with practices of thrift and hard work; and the influence may be conceded, though Calvin exercised in Geneva a medieval control over usury and other unethical economic practices. Calvinism has been credited with making labor dignified and worthy for the first time since its fall at the hands of the Greeks.

Calvinism and capitalism

The well-known thesis (associated with R.H. Tawney and Max Weber) that Calvinism and capitalism were intimately related must not be stated too crudely. Both Luther and Calvin showed strong anticapitalist feelings, natural enough in men who were in many respects returning to an earlier Christian orthodoxy. They were both as doubtful as Christ himself about the chances of a rich man getting to heaven. If their movements did in a sense help "capitalism," this was owing to the fact that the virtues they encouraged —self-discipline, thrift, hard work, simple living—happened also to create wealth. So it had been with the earliest Christians. Calvin put a special stress on a conception of the Christian "calling" as consisting of faithful performance of one's duties in whatever occupation one might be in. To him the Christian vocation was not confined to the church, but was in the world; you serve God in your occupation, whatever this may be. The shoemaker as well as the clergyman does God's work and must do it well. By a slight but significant extension of this idea, more typical of later Calvinists, success was equated with godliness, and to make money became a sign of election to the ranks of the saints. The religion of gain was a perversion of Calvin's original thought yet a rather natural outgrowth of it. Max Weber thought that this Protestant ethic of work and success helped significantly to fortify and advance the "capitalist spirit." This spirit was certainly not born in the 16th century, but according to the "Weber thesis" it was critically magnified and played a prominent role—not the only one—in the creation of the kind of economic society typical of the modern Western world.

The Counter-Reformation and Catholic reform

Delay of Catholic reform

For a number of years the Roman church seemed helpless to stop the ebb of its fortunes. It was paralyzed by the lack of machinery for dealing with such an unprecedented crisis, by the low state of its morale and education, and especially by the war between the Emperor and the French king—a war which found the papacy, not strongly led in these years, ground between. The scandal of Charles' war on Rome in 1527, during which the Holy City was pillaged and sacked, appeared to many people as a sign of God's judgment against the corrupt papal city, now being freely denounced by Protestants as the "whore of Babylon."

Charles V, the Hapsburg leader, found himself, by a singular number of the right deaths, the reigning monarch not only in the Holy Roman Empire but in Spain, and, via the Burgundian inheritance, in the Low Countries. (This is treated more fully in the next chapter.) The French, for their part, were ambitious, fearful of Charles' great power, and a rival claimant to the lands of Burgundy, a large part of which they had taken after the victory of 1477. Francis I was a thoroughly "Machiavellian" king; and Charles, too, was solely concerned with the preservation of his estates. Each would deal with the Lutheran powers if the alliance was advantageous. It seemed impossible to call a general church council and begin the work of reform and counterattack against Protestantism until the two great Catholic princes were at peace. But they fought off and on all through the years from 1521 to 1559, in a series of Hapsburg-Valois wars.

Council of Trent

The great Council of Trent was finally convened in 1545 but, subject to interruptions and breaking up in discord on two occasions, it did not complete its work until 1562–63. Pope Paul III (1534–49) made a start at reform, but could not get very far. A reforming faction existed within the church. In 1537 they submitted a report omitting none of the abuses, finding them at every level from papacy on down. The meetings of the Trent council produced heated arguments between reformers and conservatives, both on reform of abuses and statement of doctrine. The issues were numerous and complex. Broadly speaking, a liberal faction urged both reform and some concessions to the Protestants on doctrine, while also reviving the conciliarist position, that is, the authority of general councils over the pope. The final outcome, however, was reform of abuses *without* doctrinal concessions or limitation of papal power. The vigorous Popes Paul IV (1555–59), Pius IV (1559–65), and Pius V (1566–72) brought about a revival of the high office and used it as a potent instrument of reform.

Reform of abuses and definition of doctrine: the Council of Trent proceeded to tackle both. In regard to the latter, the definitions produced after long debate seemed to exhibit both how thin was the line that separated Protestant from Romanism, and how wide a gulf it could become. The Bible was declared to be the basis of the Christian faith; *but* traditions in the keeping of the church were made indispensable in the interpretation of the Bible. To the Lutheran theology of justification by faith alone, the Catholics at Trent replied that faith is necessary, and comes through God's grace; *but* men may resist grace or cooperate with it, thus maintaining a measure of free will. On the matter of the seven Sacraments, purgatory, indulgences, and so on, there was no compromise on doctrine with the Protestants, but there was an effort to clean up many of the practical abuses that had crept in. In general, on dogmatic questions the spirit of Trent was one of defiance to the Protestants rather than compromise with them, under Jesuit influence; but today many of the careful statements in the long and closely reasoned decrees of Trent would be acceptable to many non-Catholic Christians.

In regard to reform, great progress was achieved despite many obstacles. With no inclination to deny or hush up the abuses, the spirit of Trent was to reaffirm doctrine, though with a new precision and thoroughness of statement; but, having refused change there, to proceed with all the more vigor toward the reformation of practical abuses. It is true that here also conservatism manifested itself in the rejection of any fundamental changes in organization. Thus, the clergy were not to marry, the hierarchy of the church remained the same, papal power was strengthened. The major attack was on the corruptions of the system, not the system itself. Pluralities and nonresidence of bishops were forbidden. Seminaries were to be established in every diocese for better training of young men for the clergy. To these decrees of the Council must be added the work of the reforming popes in cleaning up Roman morals, suppressing simony, and removing other corruptions.

Loyola and the Jesuits

More important than reforms in the ecclesiastical machinery was the renewal of morale and spirit in the slumbering church. In addition to the papacy, new religious orders supplied this. The Society of Jesus was easily the

The Council of Trent in session

most important of these. The Jesuits were to become "the most powerful missionary organization the world has even seen." Hatred of this redoubtable elite of trained "soldiers" of the Counter-Reformation by Protestants was in direct proportion to their effectiveness. Constituted in 1540 by Paul III, they were already, at the Council of Trent, the intellectual leaders of the clergy. St. Ignatius Loyola, a Basque soldier who, after receiving a crippling wound, vowed himself to Christ and became the founder of the Society, was almost a contemporary of Luther (Loyola 1491–1556). The year that Luther went to Worms was Loyola's year of decision. In 1522 he lived as a hermit in a cave near Manresa, close to the monastery of Montserrat in northeast Spain; like Luther, seeking relief from his acute anxiety of spirit. In 1523, after a pilgrimage, he began to write his manual called *Spiritual Exercises*, a course in self-training and self-mastery. Loyola's path owed nothing to Luther; it was the independent struggle of another great religious soul. The strange, intense cripple was himself suspected of heresy by the Spanish Inquisition. His message was slow to ripen. Loyola attended school in Spain and then at Paris, where he encountered the Lutheran doctrines and was a classmate of John Calvin. A small circle of disciples clustered around him and took a vow to joint together in 1534 at Montmartre, near Paris (today, in it). These were mostly laymen; Ignatius was no priest at this time. Ordained in 1537, he won the support of the Pope for his new order by 1540, overcoming some opposition.

The message of Loyola was discipline, organization, intellectual clarity, and action. Theologically, the Jesuits stood at the opposite pole from the Calvinists, affirming within Christianity an extreme version of free will, as against Calvinist predestination. There was nothing here of the Protestant introspection. Jesuits overcame inward feelings of doubt by training of the will. But the results were not dissimilar, for in militance, dedication, commitment, the Calvinist and the Jesuit seemed well matched. One could almost say that they struggled for the soul of Europe between them in the following half century. Both were activists, who fought their battles in the world, not away from it. The Jesuits took their famous vow of obedience and complete service to the church; then the candidates underwent the most rigorous training for 15 to 17 years, with only the elite being selected. Thoroughly educated and schooled in self-mastery, the Jesuits then went forth into the world prepared to serve in any capacity. Education, statesmanship, and missionary work proved to be their special fields of superb accomplishment.

Other new orders

Numerous other new orders also arose, including the Oratorians, whose scholarship became renowned, Capuchins, Theatines, and the Ursuline sisters. In its revival the church drew also upon a mystic tradition, the Spanish Theresa and John of the Cross being especially notable. There was a tendency for the Catholic revival to center in Spain, where crusading zeal was outstanding in the ensuing age of Philip II. But it spread all through Catholic Europe. In contrast to Protestantism, where Puritan elements tended to drive art out of the church, if not out of life altogether, the so-called "Counter-Reformation" produced a rich and distinctive art. It is true that there was an ascetic, puritanical element, expressed in the austerity of a Paul IV or Pius V, whose efforts at moral reform resemble Calvin's. But later in the century the rebeautification of Rome established a style, the baroque, which is sometimes regarded as the art form of the Counter-Reformation. The church drew on the humanist traditions of Scholasticism and also the Renaissance.

Religious intolerance

Catholic intolerance was quite as pronounced as Calvinist. Two outstanding achievements of the Council of Trent and the reforming papacy were the reestablishment of the Holy Office, or Inquisition, and the creation of machinery for censorship, as represented by the index of prohibited books. Zeal, austerity, and discipline went along with a persecuting spirit. Virtually no one was yet prepared to accept the possibility of various versions of Christianity coexisting. The voice of Sébastien Castellion (Châtillon) of Basel was raised against Calvin's execution of Servetus. It was a brave and a precocious voice, but most people probably thought Calvin's answer crushing. How can we be indifferent on matters of such importance, and how can there be more than one Christian truth, which is God's revelation? Would God have deceived us by making His word unclear? No, there must be a single orthodoxy and all else is horrible heresy. Sad though later generations might find this logic, it was persuasive in the heated atmosphere of the Reformation.

Results

How may we sum up the results of this vast convulsion, the Protestant Reformation? It is another process that is still going on, for however much religious faith may have waned in the modern world, there are still millions for whom it is urgently important. And the millions of Christians in Europe and her offshoots are still divided into Roman Catholic and Protestant, with the Protestants further subdivided innumerable times. The modern age has seen the development of a significant "ecumenical" movement in world Christendom, aimed at healing the old wounds. It has made some progress, especially in reuniting Protestant sects. It has also found some of the old arguments still too tough to wash away. Protestantism continues to be fissiparous, as a glance at the records of new sects will indicate. The Roman church still stands outwardly with the monolithic unity constructed at Trent, though it has moved far from some of the positions then adopted. Hostility between the two religious worlds can still strongly influence modern society and politics.

Catholic and Protestant still hurl reproaches at each other and betray lack of understanding of the other's position, though there has been much recent improvement on this score. Catholics have said that Protestantism breeds a deficiency in both the philosophical and esthetic senses, has yielded too readily to secular forces, has fostered civilizations that are mere assemblages of individual atoms. Protestants think that Catholic civilizations betray ignorance, "superstition," and too much passive herd spirit. Ecumenical writers often urge that the two groups represent different but complementary qualities which ought to be united in a mature civilization. It seems easier to do this on paper than in reality.

Our text cannot resolve such debates, but can only point to their enduring relevance. The conflict of Catholic and Protestant which produced a "schism in the soul" of Western civilization was productive of much evil, obviously: ferocious persecution, bigotry, and hatred. But it led also to some things which may be accounted progressive. Competition can be a good thing, even in holy matters; and the competition of religious dogmas did lead to improvements in scholarship, education, literacy, thought. Each side labored to produce better works of scholarship and of theology to buttress its claims.[1] The gains made were not confined to the purely religious sphere, but influenced other realms of knowledge. And in the domain of social life, the reform movement in both camps tended to reduce ignorance, laxity, and corruption, producing a clergy and a laity better informed, soberer, living a more Christian life. Another area where religious competition proved a stimulus was overseas exploration and colonization: one motive, among others, was the desire to Christianize the natives according to "the true faith."

[1] Modern historical scholarship is frequently said to have originated as a result of the Reformation. Monumental collections of documents from church history were published by both sides; fabulously learned scholars tackled the complicated question of Biblical and other texts, continuing the work begun by Erasmus; and though initially each side was wholly biased, in time historians arose who saw the need to adopt a moderate position.

Skepticism

Ending the virtual monopoly of one faith meant an opportunity for thought to diversify. Little though the first Protestants intended it, they had introduced an inevitable skepticism or relativism into Europe. They had assailed the single orthodoxy and set up another. Amid the welter of contending theologies which soon arose, the average man was likely to gain the gradual impression that none of them was true. "Free thinking" appears by the end of the 16th century. Greatest of all skeptics was the urbane essayist Montaigne, possibly the foremost literary figure, next to Shakespeare, of the century. Religious strife helped make Montaigne doubt the possibility of finding truth, as he took refuge with ancient Epicureans and skeptics. One may believe in religious dogma, but largely as a matter of convenience; the civilized man turns his interests elsewhere. Montaigne's interest in personality for its own sake, in human nature and psychology as such, opened new perspectives. From another direction came the great scientific movement, which is to be discussed in a later chapter. These important new interests were an indirect result of the Protestant revolt.

In time this tendency toward skepticism exerted its profound influence on civil society, leading in the direction of tolerance and a new conception of the state. For the time being, however, religious zeal entered into close collaboration with nationalist sentiment in this age of emerging national states. It has been observed how intimate the connection was at all times between Reformation religious forces and nationalist political ones. The age of Luther and Calvin happened also to be the age of Henry VIII and Charles V. To this temporal struggle of "principalities and powers," which accompanied the religious one, we should now turn.

Bibliography

Oustanding books which cover the whole of the Reformation era, or which seek to appraise it broadly, include the following: Harold J. Grimm, *The Reformation Era* (New York: Macmillan, 1954); G.R. Elton, *Reformation Europe 1517–1559* (Harper Torchbook); Owen Chadwick, *The Reformation* (Penguin, History of the Church); Hajo Holborn, *A History of Modern Germany: I, The Reformation* (New York: Alfred A. Knopf, 1959); Wilhelm Pauck, *The Heritage of the Reformation* (Chicago: University of Chicago Press, 1961) Lewis Spitz (ed.), *The Reformation: Material or Spiritual?* (Raytheon, D.C. Heath, Problems in European Civilization series); K. Holl, *Cultural Significance of the Reformation* (World Publishing, Meridian); and J.S. Whale, *The Protestant Tradition* (Cambridge University Press). The Protestant bias of the last two may be counteracted by turning to Philip Hughes, *A Popular History of the Reformation* (Doubleday, Anchor); H. Daniel-Rops, *The Protestant Reformation* (World Publishing, Meridian); or the delightfully acute Hilaire Belloc, *Characters of the Reformation* (Doubleday, Anchor). On individual countries, see M. Powicke, *The Reformation in England* (Oxford University Press); A.G. Dickens, *The English Reformation* (London: Batsford, 1964), the most thorough inquiry; Gordon Donaldson, *The Scottish Reformation* (New York: Cambridge University Press, 1960). For light on the Reformation as a whole, see J.W. Allen, *A History of Political Thought in the Sixteenth Century* (Barnes & Noble). C. Parmiter, *The King's Great Matter* (New York: Barnes & Noble, 1967), is a close study of Henry VIII's famous and fateful effort to annul his marriage.

The prime figure of the Reformation may be studied in R.H. Bainton, *Here I Stand* (New American Library), a deservedly popular biography; H. Boehmer, *Martin Luther* (World Publishing, Meridian); R.H. Fife, *The Revolt of Martin Luther* (New York: Columbia University Press, 1957); Gordon Rupp, *Luther's Progress to the Diet of Worms* (Harper); Albert Hyma's provocative *New Light on Martin Luther* (Grand Rapids, Mich.: Wm. B. Eerdmans Publishing, 1958). Also, Ernest Schwiebert, *Luther and His Times* (St. Louis, Mo.: Concordia Publishing House, 1958). C.L. Manschreck, *Melanchthon: The Quiet Reformer* (New York: Abingdon Press, 1958), is a good study of one of Luther's colleagues. George H. Williams, *The Radical Reformation* (Philadelphia: Westminster Press, 1962), introduces the world of the sectarians; good also is the older work, reprinted, of Rufus M. Jones, *Spiritual Reformers of the Sixteenth and Seventeenth Centuries* (Beacon Press), and Ernst Troeltsch, *Social Teaching of the Christian Churches* (2 vols., Harper Torchbook), a generally valuable study.

History and Character of Calvinism, by John T. McNeill (New York: Oxford University Press, 1954), and *John Calvin*, by Georgia Harkness (Abingdon Press, Apex), are useful introductions to the great Genevan reformer; see also J. Forstman, *Word and Spirit in Calvin* (Stanford, Calif.: Stanford University Press, 1962). The late R.H. Tawney's famous *Religion and the Rise of Capitalism* (New American Library) is a cardinal document in the celebrated "Weber thesis" on Calvinism's relationship to capitalism; cf. Kurt Samuelsson, *Religion and Economic Action: A Critique of Max Weber's "The Protestant Ethic and the Spirit of Capitalism"* (Harper Torchbook).

On the Catholic Reformation, P. Janelle, *The Catholic Reformation* (Milwaukee: Bruce Publishing, 1949); H. Boehmer, *The Jesuits* (Philadelphia: Castle Press, 1928); J. Broderick, *St. Ignatius Loyola: The Pilgrim Years* (New York: Farrar, Straus & Cudahy, 1956); and Herbert Jedin, *A History of the Council of Trent* (London: Thomas Nelson & Sons, 1957). Broderick has also written a life of Robert Bellarmine, the famous Jesuit leader (Westminister, Md.: Newman Press, 1961).

E.M. Plass (ed.), *What Luther Says: An Anthology* (Concordia Publishing House, 1959), is among the many collections of Luther's works. A shorter selection, edited by John Dillenberger, is a Doubleday Anchor paperback; *The Reformation Writings of Martin Luther*, edited and translated by B.K. Woolf (New York: Philosophical Library, 1953), are more extensive. See also Calvin, *Commentaries*, edited by Joseph Haroutunian (Library of Christian Classics, Vol. XXIII), and *John Calvin*, edited by Albert-Marie Schmidt (Harper); Castellion, *Concerning Heretics* (Columbia Records of Civilization); G.A. Williamson (ed.), an abridgement of *Foxe's Book of Martyrs* (London: Secker & Warburg, 1965); G.H. Williams (ed.), *Spiritual and Anabaptist Writers* (Library of Christian Classics, XXV). Lewis H. Spitz has edited a useful short collection in paperback, *The Protestant Reformation* (Prentice-Hall).

11

Religious and national conflict in the 16th century

chronology

1556
Abdication of Charles V; division of holdings between Spanish and Austrian thrones.
Philip II, King of Spain.
1558
Elizabeth, Queen of England. Acts of Supremacy and Uniformity.
1559
End of Hapsburg-Valois wars (Peace of Cateau-Cambrésis).
Death of Henry II of France.
1561
Mary, Queen of Scots, begins reign. Opposed by Scottish Protestants.
1562
Beginning of Huguenot religious wars in France.
1563
Thirty-Nine Articles; establish Anglican church
Council of Trent completes work. *Profession of Tridentine Faith*, 1564.
1567
Murder of Mary's husband Darnley in Scotland; abdication and (1568) flight to England of Mary.
1568
Revolt of Netherlands begins. Execution of Egmont and other Netherlands leaders.
English seizure of Spanish treasure.
1570
Excommunication of Elizabeth by the Pope.
1571
Lepanto, great naval victory of Spanish over Turks.
1572
Massacre of St. Bartholomew. Fourth Huguenot war in France.
Progress of Counter-Reformation, especially in southern Germany.
Spread of revolt in Netherlands; recall of Duke of Alva, 1573.
1576
Sack of Antwerp. Union of Dutch provinces against Spain (Pacification of Ghent, 1576; Union of Utrecht, 1579).
Catholic League in France backs Duke of Guise for throne. Fifth Huguenot War.
1580
Philip of Spain assumes throne of Portugal.
1584
Assassination of William of Orange.
Death of Ivan the Terrible, first Tsar of Russia.
1585
English aid sent to Dutch.
1587
Execution of Mary, Queen of Scots.
Drake's raid on Spanish at Cadiz.
Beautification of Rome; emergence of baroque style.
1588
War between Spain and England; defeat of Glorious Armada.
War of Three Henrys, France; murder of Henry of Guise and Henry III.
Intervention of Spain in French wars.
Montaigne, *Essays*.
1590
Victory of Henry of Navarre, Huguenot leader, in French religious war.
1593
Henry of Navarre renounces Protestant religion, crowned King of France (1594).
Plays of Shakespeare, 1590–1613.
1598
Edict of Nantes.
Death of Philip II of Spain.
1600
East India Company chartered.
1601
Elizabethan poor law.
Execution of Lord Essex after an unsuccessful rebellion.
1603
Death of Elizabeth.
1604
Beginning of "Time of Troubles" in Russia.

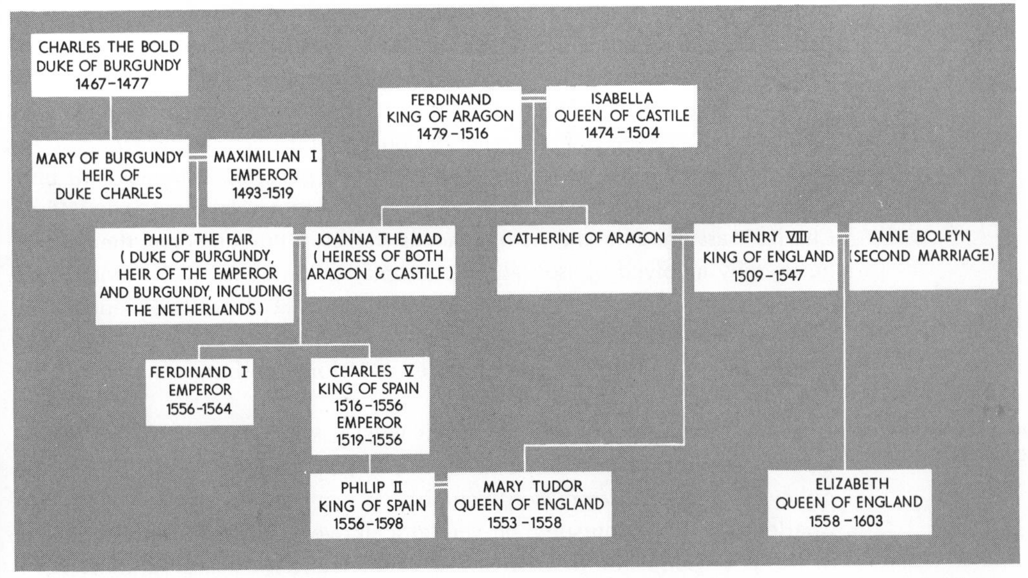

Lineage of the Emperor Charles V

Political factors in the Reformation era

Martin Luther's arrival on the scene to usher in the Protestant movement coincided with the coming of a new era in European politics. The intimate connection between the two has already been noted. Charles V, the emperor who presided at the famous Diet of Worms in 1521, had just inherited a truly majestic domain. By marriage to the house of Burgundy his grandfather, the Emperor Maximilian, added greatly to the family glory; but in 1477, it will be recalled, Burgundy had been defeated by France. Remaining to the Burgundians, however, were valuable Low Country and Rhineland possessions. Charles was a grandson of the German emperor, a son of the Duke of Burgundy, and on his mother's side of the Spanish royal house, his mother being Joanna, daughter of Ferdinand of Aragon and Isabella of Castile (see chart). This somewhat complex regal lineage became of high importance to Europe when, by a singular series of deaths, Charles became the possessor of all: Burgundy, Empire, Spain. Mightiest emperor since Charlemagne, Europe called him, and many expected him to restore the medieval unity of Europe. Charles was a hard-working if somewhat pedestrian monarch who strove manfully to live up to this high ideal and solidify his magnificent but overly vast and scattered patrimony. In the long run he could not succeed.

Rise of France

Unfortunately, among his other inheritances was a bitter feud with France. At this time France was the rising power of Europe. It is true that her kings were too prone to go marching off to Italy, as far as Naples, where there were traditional French claims. In his famous *Utopia* the humanist statesman-writer Thomas More had criticized this failure to pursue national policies that were realistic rather than romantic. Nevertheless, the French throne steadily drew within its orbit of effective control the various once-independent duchies of what is today France. Thus Brittany lost its autonomy in 1491 despite efforts of Spain, England, and Empire to preserve it; much of Burgundy had been taken after 1477. The brilliant reign of Louis XI, 1461–83, set the French state on solid foundations. France and Spain became persistent enemies, not only because of frontier quarrels but because of clashing claims in Italy. When Charles V assumed the throne of Spain as well as of Burgundy and the Empire, he thereby involved himself almost automatically in wars with France. Two great powers seemed fighting for the control of all Europe. The French king, Francis I, young and dashing, came to the throne at about the same time as Charles and fought him in a long series of Valois-Hapsburg wars.

Duel of Hapsburg and Valois

In this drama the equally glamorous English King, Henry VIII, also played a part sometimes, but mostly had the wit to stay out. The Tudors followed a policy of shying off from continental wars whenever possible. Francis and Charles were left to pursue their vendetta all over Europe: in Italy, in France, in the Low Countries, in Germany. In 1525 Francis lost the Battle of Pavia (northern Italy) and renounced his claims to Italy and Burgundy; but he found this vow easy to repudiate as soon as he recovered his balance, and war was renewed 1527–29. When Francis allied with the pope, Charles' troops took and sacked Rome in the shocking event to which reference has already been made. The French again had to sue for peace. Charles at this time was able to turn his attention to the affairs of Germany, and attempted to stamp out the Lutheran heresy. The Protestant princes and cities leagued against him (Schmalkaldic League), and the French conspired with them. The third war of Charles and Francis came in 1536–38, the fourth in 1542–44. Francis even made a treaty with the Turks (1536), which scandalized European moralists. The Schmalkaldic War within Germany, 1546–47, and then a final war between Charles and France, 1552–56, rounded out an epoch of violent political instability in Europe.

Part of the instability was of course due to religious factors; for the Lutheran league fought Charles partly over ecclesiastical questions, while in the background of the age's violence lay the Peasant Rebellion, the Commune of Münster, the rise of Calvin and of the Jesuits. But the issues between the monarchs were those of naked power. Time and again Charles, Francis, and Henry of England showed how ruthlessly they could sacrifice religious or moral principles to the successes of their reign. The alliance between France and the infidel Turks was only an unusual example of this.

The outcome of the Charles V era showed that no one power could dominate Europe; for the French sustained themselves with the aid of diplomacy and stalemated the Emperor despite his nominally vast holdings. There was no unity or solidity to the various Hapsburg domains. The Emperor could not even dominate Germany, for the Protestant territories, maneuvering between the larger quarrel of the Emperor with France and the Turks, kept their independence and their religion. Meanwhile the Turks advanced into Hungary, besieging Vienna itself in 1529, and continual warfare against the sultan's forces did not succeed in recovering much of Hungary. Charles V also engaged in a Mediterranean naval war with the Turks.

The later 16th century

Peace of Augsburg

About 1555 or 1560 Europe seemed to enter a new era, marked by a different set of actors, who were to hold the stage for a half century. The old players departed. Luther died in 1546, Loyola in 1556, Calvin in 1564. The retirement of Charles V in 1555 (he died in 1558) was a major landmark. The Emperor confessed defeat in an important peace with the Lutherans in the Empire, the Peace of Augsburg (1555), which recognized the right of each prince to choose Lutheranism or Catholicism for his domain. His subjects were supposed to follow his decision, or else migrate. Lutheran states might keep the church lands taken prior to 1552, but thereafter any bishop, archbishop, or abbot who turned Protestant was supposed to forfeit his lands. It was a victory not only for Lutheranism but even more for territorial particularism over the central government of the Empire. It did indeed, like most treaties, only recognize what was already an accomplished fact. But the Peace of Augsburg and the passing of Charles, accompanied by separation of the imperial and the Spanish thrones, ended an epoch.

At about the same time (1559) the death of Henry II of France began a long period of internal disorder and strife which knocked her from the ranks of the major powers for almost half a century. In place of France and the Empire, the two rising states were Spain and England, under Philip II and Elizabeth respectively. The Turkish Empire too began to decay after the death of Suleiman in 1566.

A new era

The completion of the Council of Trent's work in 1563 was another landmark. The era of theological preoccupation had ended, with the dogmatic consolidation of each side's position. Hereafter a united and at least partially reformed Roman church, armed for action with militant new organizations like the Jesuits, confronted a Protestantism at least partly consolidated behind the banner of Calvin. The powerful states associated with these causes were to be Spain in her golden age, and, ranged aganist her in a "Protestant" camp, Elizabeth's England with help from the rebelling Low Country possessions of Spain.

It was an age extremely rich in "history": incident and development both. The flowering of England in the age of Elizabeth is of the greatest interest to all English-speaking peoples. The revolt of the Netherlands was by any reckoning one of the most dramatic events in modern history. The French civil war, which pitted Calvinist Huguenots against Catholics, was both a religious and a constitutional crisis of the highest significance, out of which emerged finally the great French monarchy of the 17th century. These events were bound together by threads of diplomacy and intrigue.

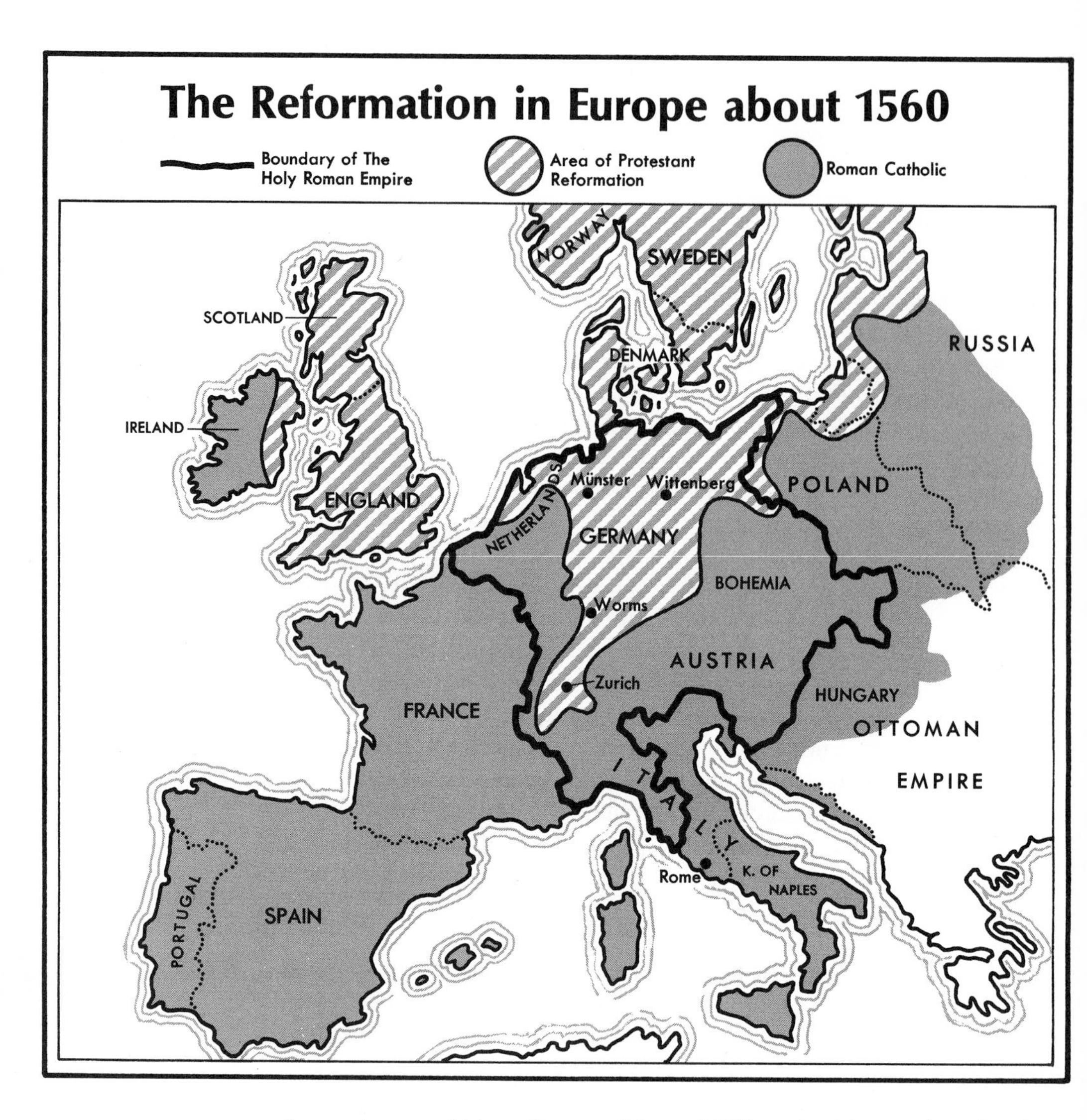

It was the age of Mary, Queen of Scots, William the Silent, Admiral Coligny and Henry of Navarre, Francis Drake, Walter Ralegh, and John Knox. Individual episodes, such as the Massacre of St. Bartholomew, the massacre at Antwerp, the execution of Mary, the defeat of the Spanish Armada, are among the classic tales of history. Over the age hangs the rising importance of New World exploration and exploitation, of colonial riches beyond telling, of a new economic order. For northern Europe it was still in some regards the Renaissance age: an age, that is, of exciting frontiers in knowledge and art. And of course the cruelty and courage of religious warfare and religious martyrdom are there.

With all of this, though, it must be known preeminently as the age of Spain. When Charles V wearily laid down his burden, confessing defeat in what has been called the last real effort to restore the medieval Christian empire of Europe, he split his cumbersome realm in two. Spain, with her possessions in Italy and Burgundy and the Netherlands, passed to Charles' son Philip; the imperial crown and the Hapsburg lands to his brother Ferdinand. With the wealth of the New World and the moral force of the Counter-Reformation both in possession of Spain, Philip's part of the inheritance became easily the more important. Spain was about to have her golden age.

The predominance of Spain

Marriage of Aragon and Castile

The earlier history of Spain had been violent and dramatic. The Moorish conquest and the centuries-long Christian reconquest dominated the history of this land of dramatic and contrasting landscapes. Expulsion of the last of the Islamic "Moors" was not completed until 1492. The Spain which sent out Columbus was filled with the zeal of crusaders and redeemers of the holy faith against all the heathen. The marriage of Aragon and Castile completed a unity which the psychology of solidarity against the Moor had aided, and which was expressed in that powerful compulsion to national conformity, the Spanish Inquisition. From its establishment in 1480, the Inquisition remorselessly hunted out heresy. The prominence of Spain in both the Christian Renaissance and the Counter-Reformation was rooted in her history, and prepared the way for the crusading era of Philip II.

Conquistadors

The conquistadors who followed up Columbus' voyages conquered a great empire for Spain in the next 50 years. There streamed out of Spain a throng of high-born adventurers ready for this challenge to adventure and wealth, a tribute to the peculiar vitality of the Spanish temperament when thus challenged. Tales of incredible courage and energy, and on the other hand of unbelievable cruelty and treachery, come from this movement. A fierce lot, consumed with the lust for gold, the Spanish were responsible for the death or enslavement of millions of the native Indians. They wrought enormous damage before the Spanish government was able to exert some control over their actions. But the world will always marvel at the fact that a few hundred of them were able to conquer the great Inca and Aztec empires; the sagas of Cortes in Mexico and Pizarro in Peru are among the most familiar of all historical episodes. The Spanish explored both continents, discovered the Pacific Ocean (Balboa, 1513), ranged far into the interior of North America (Coronado, De Soto). They let North America alone because the rewards were much greater to the south, in the highly developed Indian empires of Mexico and Peru. Soon, however, Magellan and his crew sailed around the Horn, to the Philippines, and all around the world. Though Portugal was already entrenched in the East Indies, Spain annexed the Philippines.

In the long run, Spanish and Indian cultures fused in the New World to form an interesting society. Unlike the English subsequently in North America, the Spanish did not come in large numbers as homesteaders, but in small numbers as conquerors and rulers. They did not eject the Indians, as the

English did, but governed them, and eventually fused with them. The Spanish formed the upper class, and the Indians the lower, being at first only serfs; but in time a single society tended to emerge. Jesuit missionary work, exceptionally dedicated and selfless, aided in this process.

Such New World themes are a bit outside a history of Europe. So far as concerned Europe, the wealth and prestige derived from this colonizing naturally made Spain much more powerful. Precious treasure from the mines of Peru paid for a Spanish army which was far better than any other in Europe. It have been on the whole the judgment of historians that all this treasure was a curse to Spain in the long run. It raised prices wildly, encouraged reckless foreign policies, discouraged industry, made the Spanish upper classes lazy and unproductive, and incited other peoples to prey on their treasure ships. In good part, though, the evident failure of Spain to use all this wealth productively, spending it on wars and not investing it in a productive way, may have been caused by basic economic and social conditions in Spain. Be that as it may, Spain's "golden age" was impressive while it lasted, though it faded rapidly in the next century, leaving a poor country and a second-rate power to dream of her hour of glory.

Extent of Spanish empire

The Spanish empire at its zenith included much more than the New World possessions. Half of Europe was under Spain's sway. She controlled both the Low Countries and another remainder of the Burgundian state known as the Franche-Comté (Free County), on the eastern border of France. She held extensive lands in Italy, including Sicily and Naples in the south and Milan in the north. And in 1580 Spain took over Portugal with all that enterprising little country's colonial possessions in the Far East and Africa. In Vienna, the ruler of the Holy Roman Empire was tied by close family relationship to Spain. No wonder the rest of Europe feared this power, when to it was added the wealth of the New World—and the zeal of the Counter-Reformation.

Philip II

Philip II of Spain was devout, ascetic, learned, able, hard-working. He dedicated these talents almost wholly to repressing Protestantism and restoring the true church. But he also restored order to the turbulent overseas empire, curbed the nobility, and worked hard to make an effective administrative system, though probably his gifts here were not the highest. It is generally conceded that his economic policies were not sound, though he followed the prevailing mercantilist philosophy of trade regulation. Under him the notorious zeal of the Inquisition did not flag, the Moriscos (converted Muslims) being treated with especial severity after they rebelled in 1569 (eventually they were expelled); and the Spanish were led on a crusade all over Europe. It fitted the national character but eventually led to disaster.

The Dutch revolt

Philip's foreign policy was based on a firm agreement with the papacy as well as the imperial Hapsburgs. He intervened in the civil wars in France on

Philip II of Spain. Painting by Rubens.

The battle of Lepanto, 1571. Detail of painting by Vincentino.

the side of the Catholic League. He fought with the Pope and the Venetians against the Turks and defeated them in the famous naval battle of Lepanto, 1571, the fleet being commanded by Don John of Austria. After the death of his wife, Mary of England, he wooed the evasive Elizabeth in order to draw her toward the Roman church, and when this hope was abandoned he intrigued to secure her overthrow and the enthronement of Mary of Scotland. He saw himself as the champion of Christian Europe, the restorer of Christian unity, the enemy of heretics. But his plans were destined to miscarry. His troubles began in the Netherlands.

The revolt of the Netherlands followed close on Spanish efforts to root out heresy, using the dreaded Inquisition, in an area where Protestant currents had long existed and where Calvinism was now spreading rapidly; there were also efforts to centralize the government in an area of strong local interests. There was resentment on the part of prosperous Dutch burghers at having to pay heavy taxes to the Spanish; and there was simple dislike of foreign rule. All virtue was not necessarily on the side of the patriot rebels. Their behavior was at least not exemplary. Mobs incited by Anabaptists as well as Calvinists sacked churches, smashed statues and windows, destroyed books and manuscripts. The Spanish replied with fierce repression. The name of the Duke of Alva became synonomous in the Netherlands with a reign of terror in which thousands were executed and thousands more fled. But resistance from the bays and inlets of the northern Netherlands, carried on with a kind of sea guerilla warfare technique developed by the Dutch, could not be put down.

Alva was recalled, and the Spanish tried more conciliatory tactics. But hope of compromise ended in 1576 at Antwerp, when a massacre occurred. This "Spanish fury" was in fact not an act of the Spanish authorities, though the Dutch believed so. It was the result of a mutiny of soldiers who had not received their pay; they escaped control and burnt buildings, murdered, raped. Whatever the cause, it had the same effect as the massacre of Huguenots in France four years before in further embittering and prolonging the struggle.

Eventually, the statesmanship of the Duke of Parma pacified the southern part of the Low Countries, that area which is today Belgium, then called the Spanish Netherlands. There was a sorting-out process in which the less tractable spirits migrated to the North. The South did receive substantial liberties, while the seven provinces of the North (of which "Holland" was but one though the largest) formed the Union of Utrecht and proclaimed independence (1581). Their greatest leader and first *Statthalter* of the United Provinces, William of Orange, called William the Silent, was assassinated in 1584. Despite internal squabbles after that, the Dutch won their fight to hold on to the independence of the northern provinces, which were staunchly Calvinist in their religion, while the South became a center of the Catholic Counter-Reformation. The defeat of the Spanish Armada in 1588 helped them do it. Queen Elizabeth was actually not very generous in her aid to the Dutch, but by getting into war with Spain she contributed much to their salvation.

The restoration of France also helped them, for the new King of France, Henry IV, had little reason to like the Spanish and soon allied himself with the United Provinces. Since 1559 the great French nation, which had been strong enough to repulse the world power of Charles V, had been in serious trouble, involved in civil strife which often goes by the name of the Huguenot wars.

The French civil war

The Huguenots

"Huguenot" is a word of mysterious origin. But the principles of the French Huguenots were not mysterious; they were Calvinist. The practical strength of John Calvin's ideas was never shown more vividly than in their use to knit together the previously disunited and insignificant French Protestants into a powerful movement, all in the short period of a few years, around 1550 to 1560. Their Calvinism had strong political overtones. Huguenot theorists developed the idea of a right of rebellion against kings, an idea which had an influence on the English Puritans later. This Protestant revolutionary movement attracted support from nobles who still felt a feudal resentment toward the monarchy, and from bourgeois elements in certain areas. It was also strong in outlying regions of France which had never quite accepted the dominance of Paris. In brief, around it clustered all the centrifugal forces in a land still not quite knit together in a single nation. In France as a whole, the Protestants were a small minority at all times, but they were strong in some regions—mostly the extreme south and southwest—and they produced notable leaders. Above all, they profited by the weakness of the French monarchy in this era of strong religious passions.

Massacre of St. Bartholomew

Rebellion and civil disorder broke out during the reign of the boy king Charles IX, under the regency of the Queen Mother, Catherine de' Medici, of the famous Italian family. The first period of strife seemed healed with a truce in 1570 followed by a reconciliation of the Huguenots through the marriage of their leader, King Henry of Navarre (tiny, independent state in the Pyrenees) to the sister of Charles IX. Huguenots flocked to Paris for the marriage at Notre Dame cathedral. What followed became notorious as the Massacre of St. Bartholomew's Day. The belief long held by Protestants, that this was a deliberate plot from the beginning to lure the Huguenots into a trap and slaughter them, does not appear to be true. Much subsequent investigation by historians into the tangled story disclosed that Catherine, along with the powerful Guise family (the Duke of Guise, Catholic leader, had previously been assassinated) originally intended to assassinate only the Huguenot leader Coligny, who was exerting an influence on the young king. When the plot misfired, Catherine panicked and organized a coup to kill all the leading Huguenots. The Paris mobs did the rest. August 24, 1572, was the black day when throughout France some 20,000 Protestants or alleged Protestants were killed.

Massacre in Paris of the Huguenots on St. Bartholomew's Day, August 24, 1572.

The result was not to destroy Protestantism but to return France to civil war, as outraged relatives and friends of the victims took up arms all over the country. Charles IX soon died and was succeeded by Henry III, a weak though well-meaning king. Henry wished to compromise with the Huguenots, but could not hold the Catholics, who formed a Catholic League under Henry of Guise and rejected the monarchy. Distracted France was treated to the spectacle of the War of the Three Henrys: the King, the Catholic League, and the Huguenots under Henry of Navarre, who had managed to escape the carnage of Bartholomew and finally joined the Protestant army. Duke Henry of Guise seemed to have the support of most Frenchmen, but he was murdered, and Henry the rightful king joined forces with Henry of Navarre, only to be assassinated in turn. Before his death, he commanded his followers to recognize Navarre as King of France. Throughout all this the Pope and the Spanish gave support to the Catholic League; under Alessandro Farnese the Spanish helped bar Henry IV from Paris though he won notable victories elsewhere in France in 1589 and 1590.

Henry IV and the Edict of Nantes

Henry of Navarre, now Henry IV of France, gradually won recognition of his title by courage and ability. He profited from a reaction against intervention by Spain. In 1593 he made his famous decision to become a nominal Catholic. Never a very religious person, Henry did not really represent the

Henry of Navarre rescued France from civil war and established the Bourbon dynasty in 1589.

stricter Calvinists. By becoming a Catholic he was able to unite much of war-weary France behind him. He was to be one of the ablest French kings in history, this founder of the Bourbon line, though dissolute in his personal life; he found a great minister in the Duke of Sully. Spain, meanwhile, had been blasted by blows from England as well as from the rebelling Dutch. In 1598 Henry issued the Edict of Nantes, declaring Catholicism to be the official church but granting liberties to the Huguenots, who were granted certain areas in which they might worship and given access to public office. It was a momentous step toward toleration, incomplete though it was. Though he had to make abject obeisance to the Pope before he was recognized by most Frenchmen, Henry's victory had been made possible by the party known as the *politiques*, who wished to elevate expediency above religion, as Elizabeth did in England. The toleration of the Edict of Nantes was almost as imperfect as that of the Peace of Augsburg, or Elizabeth's broad state church. But it did bring peace to France. In the same year Henry made peace with Spain, as Philip II ended his life and reign.

Twelve years later, Henry himself fell victim to a final act of fanaticism in this bitter struggle. But he used the intervening period to good effect in restoring the government of France to order and dignity. He seemed about to embark on a war against the Hapsburgs at the time of his assassination. That would have been a popular policy, and was in fact to be pursued some years

Henry of Navarre, Henry IV of France, assassinated by François Ravaillac, May 14, 1610.

later by the brilliant Richelieu, who took up the work of strengthening the state. After Henry's untimely death, there followed 14 years of uncertain rule, with one renewal of outright civil war, before the firm hand of the great Cardinal took hold, as chief minister of Louis XIII.

French political thought

Huguenot political thought contributed to modern liberalism in its development of ideas of popular sovereignty, social contract, and right of rebellion. On the other side, the French political crisis also brought forth the divine-right theory of kingship, with the argument that a single absolute sovereign is necessary for civil peace. The *politiques*, for their part, developed a new conception of the state as ethically neutral, properly concerned only with civil peace, not religious opinion. One of the greatest of all writers, the essayist Montaigne, lived during these years and derived his astringent skepticism from the unhappy conditions around him. Thus these were creative if troubled times. France as a whole, though, learned chiefly the lesson of authority. Too much civil war, wasting the land and murdering citizens, caused the French to seek recourse in a powerful central authority all through the 17th century. It makes an interesting study in reaction: the English, who had a strong state under the Tudors, sought liberty through revolution in the next period, while France reversed this pattern.

England in the age of Elizabeth

The death of Henry VIII in 1547, after a long reign which had been in many ways enlightened but which had left England disturbed about the religious question, brought to the throne a nine-year-old boy, Edward VI, only son (by Jane Seymour) of Henry's numerous marriages. It was a reign marked by the apparently unwise decision of Edward's protectors, Lords Somerset and Northumberland, to push more rapidly toward Protestantism than the English people wished to go. In any case they were not strong or popular rulers. After six years the death of the young king brought to the throne his half-sister Mary, daughter of Catherine of Aragon, now nearly 40 years old.

Marian reaction

Mary attempted to turn back to the papacy. Her husband was the fiercely Catholic King of Spain, Philip II, just entering upon his long reign. Mary was not a popular ruler. Her Spanish husband was so unpopular he did not dare appear in public in England, where he seldom came. Mary's efforts to suppress Protestantism by persecution proved one of the most spectacular failures in history. Some 300 martyrs suffered death, and thousands more went into exile. The blood of the martyrs proved the seed of the Protestant church in England, and the Marian Exiles went to Geneva, Strasbourg, and Zürich, where they studied under the great continental Protestant theologians, John Calvin, Martin Bucer, Theodore Beza. When Mary died after four years they were able to return.

Long before Mary's death eyes were on "my lady Elizabeth," Anne Boleyn's daughter, next in line for the crown; she was in fact imprisoned for a time, suspected of involvement in a rebellion. In 1558 she entered upon what few then could have known would be the longest and most successful reign in all the previous annals of England. While Elizabeth was a shrewd, extremely intelligent, on occasion quite unscrupulous ruler who had sense enough to surround herself with able advisers, the glory that was to adorn her reign was hardly due mainly to her own qualities. Indeed, in some ways she was a weak ruler, given to indecision and also to bouts of shrewish temper. She gradually won the love of her subjects because of the great success of her reign. This success sprang from forces in English society which had been preparing the way for a national renaissance. England leaped to the forefront of Europe in wealth, power, influence, and in literature and the arts.

Reign of Queen Elizabeth

The queen who put her name on the age was in many ways worthy of it, despite her failings. Not exactly beautiful, Elizabeth had a good deal of feminine glamour, and carried on a love affair with her subjects as she played the role of the grand lady up to the hilt. She was obviously dedicated to England and her job as queen, and had such commanding qualities of intel-

The young Queen Elizabeth

lect and personality that there was no doubt about her position as real ruler. Elizabeth once boasted in her picturesque speech that if she were turned out in nothing but her petticoat, she could make her way without help. In truth the Tudors all had something of the common touch to go with their strong royal leadership, for the family had come up from obscurity only a few generations back. No one doubted that Elizabeth would have been capable of holding her own in a man's world anywhere or any time. Francis Bacon said of her after her death, when he presumably had no reason to flatter, that "Elizabeth . . . was a wonderful person among women, a memorable person among princes." He marveled that the warlike English should have been governed by a woman. Elizabeth was capable of it. As she told her army at Tilbury on the eve of the Spanish invasion in 1588, "I know I have the body of a weak and feeble woman, but I have the heart and stomach of a king."

The south front and the Marble Hall of Hatfield House, built by William Cecil, Elizabeth's chief minister, reflect the affluence of her reign.

Elizabethan policies

Elizabeth continued the wise policies of her father and perhaps improved upon them in some areas. These included a jealous watch over the royal finances, a concern to build up the navy and overseas commerce, a habit of choosing advisers from among commoners not great nobles, and a shrewd attention to the balance of power in diplomacy. She had all the Tudor calculating realism, and something of the harshness and cruelty. Admirers of Elizabeth must deal with the charge that she introduced the use of torture into England, along with lesser unpleasantries such as *agents provocateurs*, informers, spies. "Reason of state" justified almost anything. Elizabeth's famous religious policy was a case in point. It has been admired because it sought to "comprehend" as many as possible, was deliberately vague and flexible, never sought to impose religious uniformity for its own sake. But it cynically made religion an engine of state, and it dealt ferociously with both Catholic and Puritan whenever these seemed to threaten the state. The Acts of Supremacy and of Uniformity, 1559, included ambiguities designed to conciliate Protestants and Catholics alike. But the Elizabethan church was as intolerant and authoritative, though less dogmatic than Calvin's or the Pope's. Queen Elizabeth was in the place of the Pope, and anyone who challenged that authority—whether Jesuit or Puritan—felt her heavy hand. It is true that most of the executions in England were Catholics between 1588 and 1603 when the war with Spain was on and all Romanists were suspected of disloyalty. Most of them were, however, unjustified on the grounds of danger to the state. Elizabeth also harried those Protestants who ventured to criticize her church, with its bishops and archbishops, as too Romish.

The Elizabethan church

However, England avoided the religious wars which plagued France at this time, and remained reasonably united. Elizabeth's illogical Anglo-Catholic church with a Protestant creed—Romish in liturgy and Calvinist in doctrine, it was said—managed to preserve a large degree of national unity. After the capricious tyranny of Henry, followed by the rash haste to protestantize of Edward and then the bloody Marian reaction, most of England was ready for a compromise, on the basis of a church that would "comprehend" as many as possible. Illogical though it might be, the Anglican church had roots in English history. Few could yet visualize a state without a single public form of religion; but Elizabeth's church was as broad as the times permitted. In the mood of patriotic national unity that settled over England in the Elizabethan age as she battled the Spaniard and rose in strength, neither Romanism nor the wilder forms of Protestant sectarianism were at all popular. The Church of England actually had drawn eclectically on a good deal of continental Protestant theology, including influences from Bucer and Zwingli as well as Calvin and the medieval church.

Elizabeth's realistic diplomacy, handled with the sage advice of ministers like William Cecil and Francis Walsingham, kept England at peace for 30 years while extracting the maximum of advantage from the complications abroad. It would be wrong to see in Elizabeth anything like the "Protestant champion" in her intentions, though circumstances eventually made her something like that. She sought England's practical interests and nothing else. Thus, she gave little aid (and that little vitiated by the incompetence of her favorite, Leicester) to the struggling Dutch, for fear of antagonizing Philip and because of commercial rivalry with the enterprising Hollanders. She was, herself, profoundly mistrustful of Calvinists, with their habit of attacking royalty. One such, John Knox, had appeared already in the British Isles.

Elizabeth, Mary, and Philip

Mary, Queen of Scots

In 1568, Mary of Scotland fled to England and sought refuge with her cousin Elizabeth. Mary, whose mother was a French Guise and who had married Francis II of France, came back to Scotland in 1561 to confront a land already in revolt against Catholicism, in a movement stirred up by the intrepid Calvinist Knox and supported by both nobles and common people in much of Scotland. To the Scotch, like the Germans, Protestantism became a symbol of nationalism. Elizabeth cautiously aided this revolt, though disliking both Knox and revolutions, because the English interest required the elimination of French influence from Scotland, where it had long been troublesome. The lovely young queen, now a widow, ignored Elizabeth's advice, married a Catholic, Lord Darnley, and sought to suppress Scottish Protestantism. Mary's policies unfortunately got mixed up with her personal love life. She fell in love with a Protestant noble, Lord Bothwell, who was strongly suspected of the subsequent murder of Darnley. Soon after this murder Mary and Bothwell were married. This scandal caused Mary's downfall in Scotland, her complete loss of popularity leading to her abdication and flight. Mary's implication in the Darnley murder, long a controversial matter, does not seem to have been established, but her indiscretion in marrying Bothwell is obvious.

Mary Stuart, Queen of Scots, prisoner of her cousin Elizabeth from 1568 until executed in 1587.

Catholic opposition

As a "guest" of Elizabeth for 19 years, Mary became a natural focus for plots against the Queen. She was next in line for the throne if Elizabeth died childless. In 1570, Pope Pius V had excommunicated Elizabeth and declared her deposed, a rash act which much weakened English Catholicism. It is somewhat uncertain how many of the numerous Catholic "plots" against Elizabeth were real and how many manufactured by Elizabeth's own efficient secret service to add to her popularity. However, beyond doubt was the hostility of the papacy, the activity of courageous Jesuit agents trying to reconvert England, and the growing danger of war with Philip II. The "bloody question" put to English Catholics forced the cruel choice between queen and pope, religion and country. Hundreds paid the penalty for the wrong answer.

Mary was finally put to death in 1587 with the use of a good deal of trumped-up evidence. But Parliament demanded it; the English people as a whole were now passionately convinced that the danger from Catholicism and Spain was too great if Mary lived.

War with Spain

The execution touched off Philip's war against England. For many years hostility had been growing. Outstanding among the causes were English raids on Spanish ships and ports in the New World, a form of piracy which the English justified by refusing to recognize the Spanish monopoly of the New World, papal-granted. In 1568, while still on presumably friendly terms with

The Spanish Armada under attack of the English fleet and its fireships at the battle near Calais in 1588.

Spain, England seized a large shipment of Spanish bullion which had put into English ports to escape pirates. Drake marauded the Spanish Main periodically thereafter, Elizabeth being careful to draw the line just short of war. This activity was immensely helpful to Elizabeth's usually empty treasury, but hardly very neighborly. After 1570 one may well speak of a state of limited and undeclared war between the two great powers. They only awaited the right occasion. Philip's hands were tied by the revolt in the Netherlands. Elizabeth's aid to the Dutch in 1585 and the execution of Mary he considered the last straws, and he determined to make the insolent pirate-Protestant island feel the awesome weight of Spanish military might. And so he mounted a great naval expedition against England.

The Great Armada

The Great Armada returned from England a shattered wreck. It was a blow from which Philip never really recovered—or Spain. The battle in the channel has been often related. Drake had just returned from a raid on Cadiz and the Azores which demonstrated the superiority of English gunnery and seamanship. In the battle of 1588, the Spanish were no match for the English on the sea—for several centuries, few others were to be. The Spanish ships were destroyed by the superior gunnery of the smaller English vessels, and the storms finished the work. In England, the fear of invasion caused a rallying around the Queen, who responded with manly courage and great speeches; the victory brought wild rejoicing: "Such night in England ne'er had been, nor e'er again shall be." The victory of 1588 saved not only England, but also quite possibly the Netherlands and France, from the power of Spain. The last years of Elizabeth's reign were in many ways an anticlimax; her work seemed to have been finished when she led an aroused nation to victory in 1588. The war with Spain dragged on for some years, but England had no fears about its outcome after the destruction of the Armada.

The first North American colonies

In the context of the duel to the death with Spain may be put the first English colonizing expeditions to North America. The ill-fated Ralegh-Gilbert attempt to plant a colony on Roanoke Island, 1584–91, had as its most prominent motive the desire to "singe the King of Spain's beard" by creating a naval base on the flank of his Caribbean lifeline. Already, intrepid Spanish Jesuits had penetrated the Chesapeake Bay area. A few years later, the English Jamestown settlement vindicated Ralegh's vision, but it had a future even he could scarcely have foreseen. Ralegh's cousin, the greatest publicist of New World colonization, Richard Hakluyt, found a variety of reasons other than this one, but did not neglect to point out that "this enterprise may stay the Spanish king from flowing over all the face of that waste firmament of America" and that "if you strike Philip in the Indies, you strike him in the apple of his eye." In addition, Hakluyt made much of New World colonies as a place to send unemployed ex-soldiers, young wastrels, "the fry of the wandering beggars of England," and other expendable elements who, a nuisance at home, might "people the waste countries to the home and foreign benefit, and to their own more happy state." Further, the colonies might grow commodities for England's use, and accept in return English goods, to the furtherance of prosperity; and "we shall in planting there enlarge the glory of the gospel, and from England plant sincere religion." The mixture of strategic, social, economic, and religious motives was typical of the many-sided Elizabethan age, so fruitful of developments in all these spheres.

Political, social, and economic changes

The death of Elizabeth, of Philip, of Henry, the ending of the Dutch revolution, of the wars of England and Spain, and of the civil war in France, all took place within a few years of the turn of the century, and marked the definite passing of an age, as measured by the leading political issues and conflicts as well as the leading personalities. What had been the themes of this era? One, certainly, was the explosive association of religion and politics. Whether we look at the Scottish kirk, the Dutch rebels, at the tragic fate of Mary or the sanguine strife in France, or at Elizabeth and Philip's duel, we find it hard to disentangle the lines of the two, but see them clearly intertwined. Most historians, without doubting the intensity of religious faith shown by many individuals, and in no wise discounting the importance of religious ideology, would say that these wars were primarily social and political, not religious. Power, profit, and pride were more fundamental than

Sir Walter Ralegh—soldier, explorer, adventurer—a favorite of Elizabeth, executed by James I.

church and creed. Chief if not sole cause of the cruel persecutions "for conscience sake" was the demand of the state for loyalty, the fear that Catholic in Protestant state or Protestant in Catholic state would be disloyal. In certain areas not dominated by the power rivalry of great states, as for example Switzerland, Catholic and Protestant quickly learned to live side by side peacefully. There is a famous church in Switzerland always shared by Catholics and Protestants–hardly a typical case, unhappily, but indicative of the possibilities of coexistence where conditions otherwise were favorable.

Nationalism

Nationalism, then, was the leading force. It can be seen in Elizabethan England, which witnessed the birth of a real national consciousness—much of it built on the themes of hatred of the papist and Spaniard, admiration for the fighting sea dogs, love for the dazzling queen, and gratitude for the economic prosperity that accompanied naval power and national strength. It can be glimpsed in the loving care Shakespeare bestowed on his great cycle of history plays, based on the kings from Richard II through Henry VIII:

> *A kingdom for a stage, princes to act*
> *And monarchs to behold the swelling scene!*

The common Englishman's dislike of foreigners was frequently commented upon in this era. So also in Spain: the crusade for the faith cloaked an exuberant Spanish pride in country. Dutch nationalism was forged in their rebellion, and in France patriotism finally vanquished clerical partisanship. In Ireland, enthusiasm for the Roman religion obviously fed on hatred of the Protestant English at this time, and is closely associated with a process by which an Irish nation was being made out of Celtic tribesmen. Catholicism in Ireland played a similar role to Presbyterianism in Scotland as a national symbol. That patriotic nationalism might be associated with religious symbols, indeed usually was, did not necessarily mean that it was primarily religious in the strict sense. The church or creed was for the majority a symbol of solidarity, of nationhood.

Capitalism

At the same time, these years witnessed striking economic and social changes, quietly going on behind the sensational political events. Basic changes that had begun earlier continued: the freeing of the "villeins," emergence of a money economy, beginnings of modern capitalism. In England, the "gentry" became dominant: a class of commercial gentlemen who farmed for profit and invested their profits in a variety of enterprises. Wealth seized from the church and placed in private hands served as a fillip to capitalism. The Elizabethan age was a time of tremendous accumulation of wealth in England; the evidences of it are still to be seen in the fabulous country houses of gentry and nobles, which are among the most splendid examples of private architecture the world has ever known. And even strife-torn France shows us something similar. With the wealth from the New World flowing into Europe and creating a "price revolution" (inflation), "never in the annals of the modern world has there existed so prolonged and rich an opportunity for the businessman, the speculator, and the profiteer . . ." (John Maynard Keynes). In the latter days of Elizabeth's reign, enriched by booty from the Spanish Main, English capitalists created the great overseas joint-stock trading companies, the Levant, Muscovy, and East India companies. Henry IV sent out the advance agents of the French commercial empire in Canada.

The plight of the poor

On the other hand, revolution in agriculture and extinction of the monasteries, along with the inflation, caused an apparent worsening of the condition of the poor.

They burnt the homes of the shaven men, that had been quaint and kind
Till there was no bed in a monk's house, nor food that man could find.
The inns of God where no man paid, that were the wall of the weak
The King's Servants ate them all. And still we did not speak.

(G.K. Chesterton)

As charity waned, so did the old manorial society where the peasant at least had a place. The medieval land system had been one of separated strips plus commons and wasteland—a communal system, not an individualistic one, and based on a sustenance, not a monetary, economy. The trend since the Middle Ages, now accelerated in Tudor England, was to consolidate these into compact farms. The pursuit of this end by aggressive capitalistic farmers often involved the squeezing out of tenants or villeins. Widespread poverty and vagabondage were symptoms of a social crisis which the state tried, though inadequately, to meet: Elizabethan poor laws and economic regulations—as, for example, the Statute of Apprentices—show us the modern welfare state in its first dim outlines. The state, indeed, began to interest itself in economic policy in a mature way. The system known as mercantilism emerged.

Beginnings of mercantilism

"Mercantilism was the economic counterpart of nationality in politics." Some details of the well-developed mercantilistic systems of the 17th and 18th centuries will be given later. Here we may note that the state stepped forward to perform functions formerly done by the church, or the guilds, or the manorial village, as these medieval institutions waned. Whether it was the administering of charity or the regulating of wages and prices, the state now had to do it. There was still a general belief in the need for such regulation. The medieval legacy was a regulative, communal one, assuming that in the interest of order and morality there should be rules for economic life. Tudor legislation even tried, though somewhat vainly, to stem the "enclosures" with their eviction of honest plowmen to make way for sheep. At the same time charters were granted to the great trading companies, a practice which gave rise to the charge of monopoly.

Social mobility

Society was becoming more mobile. In England, at least, titled lords did not disdain to take a hand in trade or even manufacturing. A callous attitude toward the sufferings of the poor went along with an admiration for success, and a cheerful willingness to recognize the gentility of any man who had become rich. Politically, land was the key to influence; but wealth could buy land, and with it a secure place in society. There was a tendency for "new men" from the urban capitalists to invade the countryside, buying up land from the old gentility. This mobility was a strong reason for the economic progress of England. Elsewhere, in Spain especially but also in France, one found a nobility of blood which disdained trade. The feudal nobility might be losing its monopoly of military, economic, and political power, but it continued to exist on the Continent as a social caste. Not so in England.

Survival of Parliament

Very significant, also, was the survival in England of Parliament and its transformation into an effective national legislative assembly, whereas this medieval institution was falling into disuse elsewhere. The powerful Spanish monarchy dispensed with this reminder of the weak kings of the past, and in France, too, where a national meeting of the "Estates-General" met in 1614 for the last time until 1789, these institutions were becoming associated with feudal weakness. The Imperial Diet of the German world met, but was not associated with a sovereign state, being rather a congress of almost independent states. In England, perhaps because, unlike France, Spain, or Germany, this land had constituted a *single* feudal community, the king's council evolved into a national parliament. Under Queen Elizabeth, singularly enough, this body not only survived but flourished. This led England on a path that was very different from the other major states of Europe.

Central and eastern Europe

Germany

This chapter has been a description largely of the Atlantic states. Without any doubt this period of the later 16th century made their fortunes and more or less marred those of the other parts of Europe. Italy, after having seized the intellectual, artistic, and economic leadership of Europe from about 1400 to 1500, sank into political dependence and commercial decline. Germany also suffered. Charles V, the greatest emperor since Frederick II in many ways, had sacrificed German interests to those of his other far-flung possessions, and was in fact not a German at all by birth and outlook. After his passing, with the Reformation having divided the small German states even more sharply against each other, there was no hope for a central German monarchy. The Counter-Reformation succeeded brilliantly in restoring the prestige of the Roman church in the south of Germany, Bavaria and Austria being its strongholds, while the north remained Protestant. The Hapsburg emperors resumed their inclination to extend their own personal possessions on the eastern frontier, leaving Germany alone. The Turks, who were powerful foes through most of the century, ran into difficulties for a time after 1580, and the Hapsburgs pushed their influence in Bohemia and Hungary. It was this whole situation which prepared the way for the catastrophic Thirty Years War, dealt with in the next chapter.

Poland

The Reformation had spread into Poland and the Baltic lands too, as usual associated with nationalism: demands for a national church with a more Slavonic liturgy accompanied complaints about the corruption of the clergy and an interest in novel theological doctrines. Socinus, leading European reviver of the antitrinitarian heterodoxy, taught in Poland. But the monarchy stayed Catholic, and the Counter-Reformation recovered Poland for the Roman faith. There remained some Greek Orthodox influence.

Ivan the Terrible

Poland was subject increasingly to the pressure of a reviving Muscovite Russia. The years 1547 to 1584 were the dates of the effective rule of Ivan IV, Ivan the Terrible, the first of the grand dukes of Moscow to assume the title of tsar (caesar, that is, emperor). Like so many Russians a fantastic blend of cruelty and selfless dedication, he began to lead this strange and wild land, which had been for centuries a great highway for invasions from the Asiatic plains and deserts, toward an effective government. A kind of feudalism, including an estate system of unfree peasants and a powerful nobility, naturally took root in a country where life was so precarious. It was hard to prevent peasants running off in that vast region, and on the southeastern frontiers wild Cossack communities grew up. Central government had to contend with almost insuperable difficulties; but from time to time a tsar of tremendous energy sought to tame the *boyars* (the feudal nobility) and establish a strong central administration. It was a sporadic process subject to all kinds of interruptions. Contending against various nomadic orientals in one direction, the Muscovite state faced Swedes, Poles, and Balts in another. Ivan's reign was followed by a difficult period, climaxed during the 1604–13 "Time of Troubles," when the throne had no occupant and there was the utmost confusion, including Cossack revolt, foreign invasion, *boyar* particularism.

These lands of the East suffered from the absence of well-defined or defensible frontiers. Where Poland stopped and Russia began might be a matter of yearly alteration, and the boundaries between Poles and Germans, represented chiefly by the Teutonic Knights, were about as turbulent and transitory. Not for a good many years would this straighten itself out and stable political entities develop. A series of wars revolving about the valuable trading area of the Baltic Sea lay ahead in the 17th century. Many other decisions about the political contours of Europe in an age of national states would be made in that century.

Bibliography

Karl Brandi (English translation, 1939), and Royall Tyler (1956), join G. von Schwarzenfeld, *Charles V, Father of Europe* (London: Hollis & Carter, 1957) as eminent students of the great adversary of Martin Luther and Francis I. His colorful contemporary, Henry VIII of England, has found many biographers, among them A.F. Pollard (London: Longmans, Green & Co., 1951) and (an accessible Bantam paperback) Francis Hackett; more recently, and more sympathetically, John Bowle, *Henry VIII* (London: G. Allen & Unwin, 1964). Other regal personalities in this great age of kings have been handled with notable skill by G. Mattingly, *Catherine of Aragon* (Random House, Vintage); Marguerite E. Wilbur, *The Unquenchable Flame: Life of Philip II* (New York: Hastings House Publications, 1952); H.F.M. Prescott, *Mary Tudor* (London: Eyre & Spottiswoode, 1953), the wife of Philip and predecessor of Queen Elizabeth. Of the latter perhaps the leading modern biography is J.E. Neale, *Queen Elizabeth I* (Doubleday, Anchor); Neale has also written on *The Age of Catherine de Medici* (London: Jonathan Cape, 1943); while another distinguished British historian, C.V. Wedgwood, is the biographer of *William the Silent*, the Dutch Washington (W.W. Norton). Henry D. Sedgwick's *Henry of Navarre* (Indianapolis: Bobbs-Merrill, 1930) is one of the few works in English on the pioneer of French absolutism. Jean Heritier, *Catherine de Medici* (G. Allen & Unwin, 1953), is the only full-scale biography in English.

Further on the rise of Spain: R. T. Davies, *The Golden Century of Spain* (Harper Torchbook); F.A. Kirkpatrick, *The Spanish Conquistadores* (London: A. & C. Black, 1946); R.B. Merriman, a massive four-volume work on *The Rise of the Spanish Empire* (New York: Macmillan, 1918–34), on which see also J.H. Elliott, *Imperial Spain 1469–1716* (New American Library, Mentor), readable and scholarly if fairly general. John Lynch, *Spain Under the Hapsburgs: I, 1516–1598* (New York: Oxford University Press, 1964), is more detailed. So is Elliott's *The Revolt of the Catalans: A Study in the Decline of Spain 1598–1640* (New York: Cambridge University Press, 1963). On the Dutch rebellion there is an outstanding treatment by P. Geyl, *The Revolt of the Netherlands* (London: Williams & Norgate, 1932, reprinted E. Benn, 1959). James W. Thompson covers *The Wars of Religion in France 1559–1576* (New York: Frederick Ungar Publishing Co. Inc., 1957).

On the Elizabethan era a whole library exists; Neale has written on *Elizabeth I and Her Parliaments* (Jonathan Cape, 1957), A.L. Rowse vividly on *The England of Elizabeth* (Macmillan), G.R. Elton on *The Tudor Revolution in Government* (Cambridge University Press); A.H. Dodd on *Life in Elizabethan England* (London: Batsford, 1961), featuring illustrations. J.A. Williamson, *The Age of Drake* (A. & C. Black, 1961), is outstanding, as are the works of the American scholar Conyers Read, including *Lord*

Burghley and Queen Elizabeth (Jonathan Cape, 1960). Garrett Mattingly has contributed an excellent account of *The Defeat of the Spanish Armada* (Jonathan Cape, 1959), on which see also Michael Lewis, *The Spanish Armada* (Batsford, 1960). Mattingly has also written a brilliant study of *Renaissance Diplomacy* (Penguin Books), which sheds light on much of the statecraft of this period. The Elizabethan religious settlement is appraised by Carl S. Meyer, *Elizabeth I and the Religious Settlement of 1559* (St. Louis, Mo.: Concordia Publishing House, 1960).

Sources: R.H. Tawney and Eileen Power, *Tudor Economic Documents* (Longmans, Green & Co., 1924); G.R. Elton (ed.), *Tudor Constitution: Documents and Commentary* (Cambridge University Press); A.F. Steuart (ed.), *The Trial of Mary Queen of Scots* (London: W. Hodge, 1951); Philip Carman (ed.), *The Other Face: Catholic Life under Elizabeth I* (Longmans, Green & Co., 1960). Hakluyt's *Voyages* are in eight volumes in the Everyman's Library (London: J.M. Dent).

12

The intellectual and scientific revolution

Demonstration of use of the sextant, 1583

chronology

1543
Copernicus, *Revolution of the Heavenly Bodies.*
Vesalius, *Anatomy of the Human Body.*
1554
Castellion, *Concerning Heretics.*
1556
Agricola, *On Metals.*
1576
Jean Bodin, *The Republic.*
1577
Tycho Brahe's observations on comet.
1579
Vindiciae contra Tyrannos, Huguenot writings against royal absolutism.
1589
Galileo begins his scientific career.
1600
Gilbert, *The Magnet.*
Execution of Giordano Bruno.
1605
Francis Bacon, *Advancement of Learning.*
1610
Robert Bellarmine, *Power of the Pope.*
Galileo's discovery of Jupiter's satellites.
Kepler's laws of planetary motion, 1610–19.
1614
Napier's discovery of logarithms.
1616
Papal rejection of Copernician theory (except as "hypothesis").
William Harvey, lectures on circulation of the blood. (Published, 1628).
1619
Descartes' dream.
1620
Bacon, *Novum Organum.*
1627
Bacon, *New Atlantis.*
1632
Galileo, *Dialogue concerning the Two Principal Systems of the World.*
1633
Condemnation of Galileo.
1636
Corneille, *The Cid.*
1637
Descartes, *Discourse of Method; Geometry.*
1640
Cornelius Jansen, *Augustinus.*
1643
Torricelli's experiment with atmospheric pressure.
Thomas Browne, *Religio Medici.*
1644
Descartes, *Principles of Philosophy.*
Roger Williams, plea for religious toleration.
1649
Gassendi's revival of Epicurean atomic theory.
Pascal's work on conic sections.
1651
Hobbes, *Leviathan.*
1654
Pascal's conversion.
1660–1673
Plays of Molière, Racine; Restoration drama, England.
1661
Malpighi's observations of capillary action.
1662
Royal Society, England. Work of Robert Boyle.
1666
Academy of Sciences, Paris.
1670
Spinoza, *Theological-Political Treatise.*
1677
Leeuwenhoek's microscope observations of germ life.
1684
Leibniz's discovery of differential calculus published (discovered independently by Newton).
1687
Newton's *Principia Mathematica.*
1689
Locke, *Two Treatises of Government.*
1690
Locke, *Essay Concerning Human Understanding.*
Huygens, *Treatise on Light.*

Toleration and the limited state; Political thought

"Agreement in religion is the only social basis of the state; there can be no real unity without it." So everyone had felt for many centuries. Moral disunity would be so profound, they thought, that political life in common would be impossible. So long as religion was the major interest of man this proposition was hard to confute. Not only did Christianity teach a single church in a single state, but classical philosophy—Plato and Aristotle—held that the state exists as a moral institution, to "promote the good life." To regard the state as something ideologically neutral, which exists only to preserve order, leaving each man free to believe as he pleases provided only that he does not disturb the public peace—this modern conception of the state, which emerged in the 17th century, would have been alien to the city-state philosophers of antiquity, as it was to medieval popes or to Calvinists and Lutherans during the Reformation. One is tempted to say it is not the natural thing to believe.

Calvin versus Castellion on toleration

Looked at from the point of view of religion itself, rather than politics, toleration of diverse creeds was equally repugnant. The debate between Castellion and Calvin has already been mentioned. Castellion's *Concerning Heretics* (*De Haereticus*), 1554, was the most notable plea for toleration in the 16th century. Castellion argued that no one can be sure about the answer to such vexed theological questions as free will and predestination, the nature of the Trinity, and so on. There have been numerous opinions about them, men of good will have differed, there can be no clear standard of orthodoxy. Quite sincere people may differ with Calvin, and it cannot be right to kill good men for matters of opinion of this sort. No doubt there are essentials of the Christian faith which must be maintained, but these are few, simple, and clear—that God exists, that His commands must be followed. Even Castellion conceded that one who totally denied God, or Christ, or the immortality of the human soul, might be punished, though not with death.

The reply delivered by Calvin and Beza included arguments that God cannot have deceived us about the faith, there *is* truth in all these matters, and there is a duty to maintain it. We punish thieves and murderers; is not spiritual sin even more abominable and dangerous to society? Perhaps the heart of the matter was this belief that wrong belief is quite as reprehensible as wrong conduct, that heresy is a kind of murder of the soul. In the 16th century, there seems little doubt that the great majority of thinking men agreed with Calvin, his reasoning of course being essentially the same as the Roman church and most other Protestant denominations. They disagreed only on what authority they accepted to uphold faith. It probably cannot even be said that most of the smaller Protestant sects were really tolerant, though they were in a natural position of pleading for an extent of the range of toleration to include themselves. Most of them were exclusivists in their conception of the church, regarding it as only for the elect or saving remnant. Toleration owes a debt to the simple existence of so many courageous dissenters, but their beliefs were fanatically held.

Progress of toleration

Castellion's seedling grew, and circumstances aided it. The important Dutch anti-Calvinist Arminius, of the University of Leyden, should be mentioned among his disciples; much of the softer Protestant theology of the 17th and 18th centuries in England as well as on the Continent went under the name of Arminianism. By 1630 the Calvinist theocrats in Holland were no longer dominant, and the Dutch Republic became famous as a land which flourished impressively while harboring more than one theology. Meanwhile, with the Edict of Nantes, France had embarked upon an experiment in toleration; then the Thirty Years War convinced men of the folly of religious conflict. In England the debate about toleration went forward during and after the Puritan revolt. The Presbyterians, as we noted, were far from tolerant, while the Independents, who became dominant with Cromwell, believed in substantial toleration for all Protestants but not for Catholics or Anglican Episcopalians. The debate went on with a barrage of pamphlets.

Most Americans are familiar with the contribution made by Roger Williams, who migrated to Massachusetts and quarreled with the Puritan theocrats of that colony. Williams was distinguished, but only one of a number of 17th-century English writers on the limits of public control of religion. The atmosphere after 1660, when the Restoration brought in a strong reaction against theology itself, encourage toleration, despite some Anglican vindictiveness against Puritans expressed in legislation against them. Not until 1689 did England enact something like full religious toleration, but the battle in the minds of men was well on the way to being won before then. The Puritan Revolution in England and the Thirty Years War on the Continent marked a point beyond which men turned away from contending religious factions in disgust and proceeded in new directions.

In reading the history of these debates (the American historian W.K. Jordan) has done a magnificent job of surveying them for 17th-century England), one is impressed by the negative character of the arguments. That is, the best argument for toleration was the stark fact that society could not live with a variety of religious opinions—which now existed—if it persisted in demanding religious unity. Whatever the theory of the thing, the *fact* was that society would tear itself to pieces unless it learned to tolerate. Strife and war forced the mind into new patterns. The actual historical situation was the strongest argument for toleration.

New conception of state

Men began to think of the state in a new way. Its purpose is not to enforce any particular doctrine, but to see that men do not cut each other's throats. It it can do that, it will have done enough. Williams urged that government is like the command of a ship on which many different creeds have embarked: its job is simply to see that the ship does not sink, that all are kept safe to reach whatever destination it is that they have. No doubt previous ages would have regarded this as an ignoble view of the state, abdicating all its grand moral functions. But under conditions of the larger national states of Europe after the Reformation it became quite necessary.

And, one might well argue, truth is after all individual; it cannot be enforced by a state. The philosophy of toleration was strengthened by John Milton's magnificent expression of faith, in *Areopagitica*, of truth's ability to conquer alone, without force, if given a fair field. "Though all the winds of doctrine were let loose to play upon the earth, so Truth be in the field, we do injuriously by licensing and prohibiting to misdoubt her strength. Let her and Falsehood grapple; who ever knew Truth put to the worse, in a free and open encounter." And the reverse is true: force cannot compel sincere belief, it can only make hypocrites.

This revolution in men's conceptions of civil society and the state, the result of pluralism in beliefs and a degree of skepticism about final truths, is possibly the most significant and distinctive element in modern Western civilization. It has blended with the medieval heritage of constitutionalism to create the liberal society of the West.

Sovereignty and royal power

Spurred by religious conflict and by the rapid growth of the secularized state, 17th-century writing produced a wealth of new political ideas. Some of them looked in the direction of absolutism. Jean Bodin, the brilliant French writer on political and economic affairs of the later 16th century, isolated the "sovereign power" that in every state must inhere in one place only. Others, such as the Franco-Scot, Barclay, argued that any right of resistance to the sovereign must entail anarchy, and supported the absolute power of the monarch with arguments both old and new, Biblical and scientific. These men were seeking refuge from civil war, and were concerned to refute Huguenot arguments for a right of resistance to the crown.

Thomas Hobbes

In the 17th century, the Grand Monarchy of Louis XIV found a buttress in the works of the learned mentor of the Sun King, Bishop Bossuet; and the English Royalists had spokesmen such as Robert Filmer, at whom John Locke tilted. Thomas Hobbes, the eccentric and radical genius of English thought, included among his chief works the famous tract entitled *The Leviathan*, which sought to explain political society in a "scientific" way as the result of fear and self-interest. These led men to establish government by means of a "social contract" which handed over absolute powers to a sovereign (not necessarily one man, but Hobbes thought a monarchy the best). Hobbes witnessed the Puritan Revolution and the civil war, which persuaded him that liberty leads to anarchy and men must have omnipotent government if they are not to cut each other's throats. "Hereby it is manifest, that during the time men live without a common Power to keep them all in awe, they are in that condition which is called Warre: and such a Warre, as is of every man, against every man." It was not an uncommon conclusion in this age of internal strife: the British Tories as well as the continental despots made it an article of their faith.

The period of the Puritan revolution (discussed in the next chapter) gave rise in England to a diversity of political ideas, some of them looking toward

English political philosophers Thomas Hobbes and John Locke

democracy. In general, the wiser tended to agree on a "classical republicanism" of the sort propounded by James Harrington and John Milton: a system of checks and balances, in which the crown and the aristocracy checked the popular representative body, and all power was considered limited by a fundamental law corresponding to natural law. Debates in the Puritan army raised the question of whether all men should have the right to participate in governmental processes, or only those who owned property; and the verdict went, in practice at least, to the latter position. At the end of the century came the Glorious Revolution and the political treatises of John Locke. Locke carefully summed up the moderate political position seemingly vindicated by the events of 1688, when England fired one king and hired another without undue disturbance.

John Locke

Against Hobbes, who denied the existence of natural rights based on natural law, Locke affirmed them: men are by nature free and equal, with rights to life, liberty, and property, which rights they cannot ordinarily alienate except by their own consent. In framing a social compact for the better protection of these things, they did assign powers to government, but only within specified limits. Even the elected legislative body cannot exceed its limits. A tyrannical government may be resisted. Such assertions were not made for the first time by Locke; indeed, he can seem strongly reminiscent of the medieval Schoolmen when speaking of natural law and constitutionalism.

But Locke managed to give these ancient ideas both greater precision and an air of being up-to-date. Locke was a believing Christian, but his political theory appeared to rest on a natural, not a supernatural, basis. Like Hobbes he offered a purely rational, naturalistic analysis of government, yet unlike that scandalous atheist he provided men with basic liberties and did not turn them over to a leviathan-state.

Thus, a new kind of constitutional, limited state was one outgrowth of the post-Reformation debate about the nature of political society. It must be admitted that for most of Europe it was royal absolutism that replaced the old Christian republic. Only England among the major powers went the way of liberal constitutionalism, as our next chapter explains.

The scientific revolution

Meanwhile there were even more momentous vistas of thought. At the beginning of the 17th century exciting new developments turned great European minds in the direction of astronomy and the physical sciences. Perhaps this movement itself developed because the better minds wearied of theology and looked in new directions. It is certainly true that the end of the Reforma-

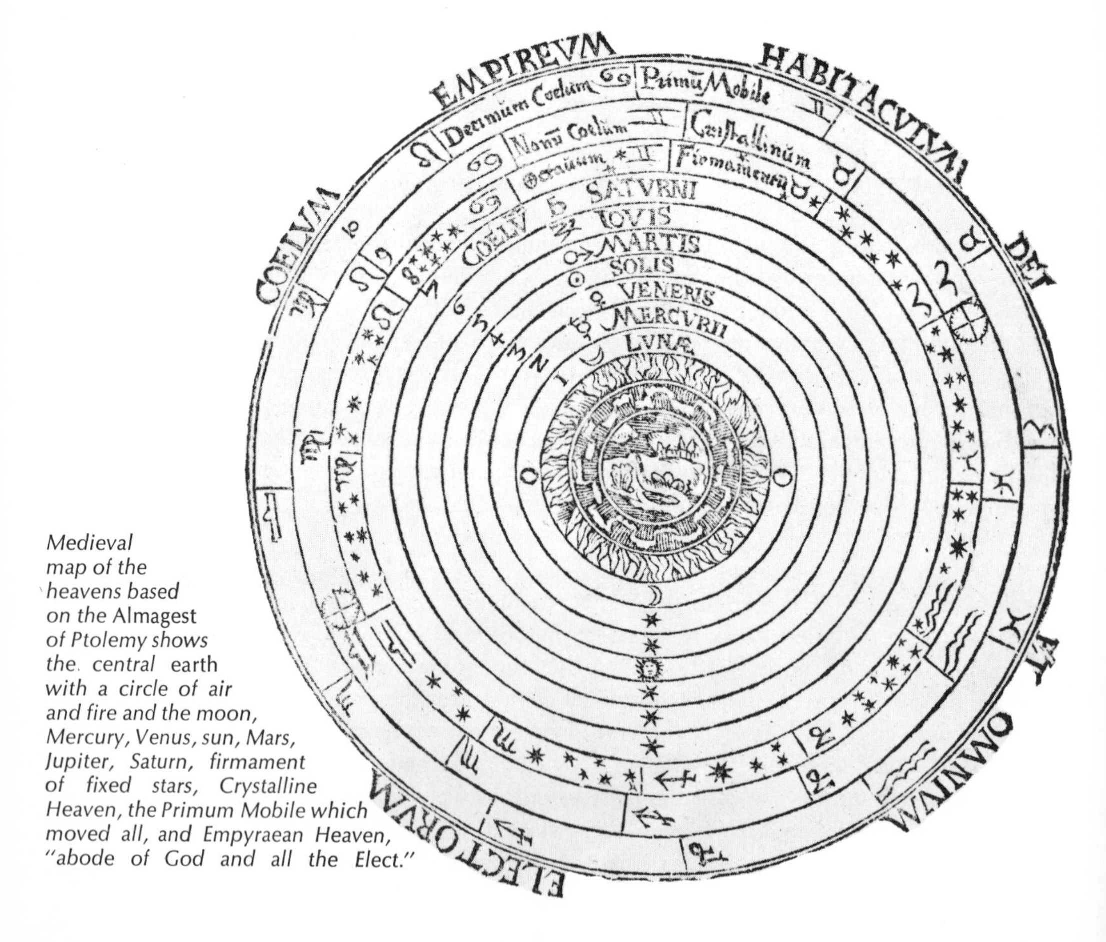

Medieval map of the heavens based on the Almagest of Ptolemy shows the central earth with a circle of air and fire and the moon, Mercury, Venus, sun, Mars, Jupiter, Saturn, firmament of fixed stars, Crystalline Heaven, the Primum Mobile which moved all, and Empyraean Heaven, "abode of God and all the Elect."

tion, with its passionate concern for theological problems and religious experience, and the end of Renaissance humanism, with its typical interest in literature and the arts, coincided with the coming of a new and fascinating zone of mental experience. Involved was nothing less than a cataclysmic revolution in man's conception of nature, his view of the universe in which he lived and his picture of how it operated.

Medieval view of universe

The cosmogony or model of the universe which medieval man knew had come from Ptolemy and Aristotle, with some insertions to shore up Christian faith. Most of us probably know its general contours. This world stood motionless in the center of the universe, while all the celestial bodies revolved around it in a series of spheres. They were weightless, being made of an entirely different kind of substance than earth—which explained why they could move. They were borne on glass spheres, like balloons on an invisible ferris wheel. The key to this older system was the law of motion. For until Galileo and others were able to demonstrate the startling law of inertia, men could not believe that motion could take place in a heavy body without a mover. The earth, being heavy, must be motionless, and the stars and planets, since they moved, must be very light and moved *by* something. This view was not based on ignorance; though wrong, it corresponded to what observation indicated, until a sensational breakthrough in the 17th century opened up new horizons. Medieval thought believed with less evidence that there were ascending levels of matter in the universe, with earth at the bottom, then water, air, fire, and the celestial ether in that order. The whole made a parallel to the Neo-Platonic chain of being in which everything ascended from lowest to highest—which was God—in an orderly manner.

It should not be supposed that no one before Copernicus had ever questioned all this. In the ancient world, Aristarchus of Samos was one who had argued for a heliocentric system; indeed, there was lively controversy among various schools before the Aristotelians carried off the triumph. In the 14th century, Nicole Oresme and Jean Buridan postulated the diurnal movement of the earth and suggested problems connected with the movement of bodies. When Platonism was revived during the Renaissance, it brought with it a tradition of disagreement with the Aristotelian school on various scientific questions. Kepler and Galileo, the pioneers of modern physical and astronomical science, were, interestingly enough, adherents of one of the most ancient of schools. They were Platonists. Less empirical than the Aristotelians, the Platonists were both more mathematically oriented and in some important ways less dogmatic about the natural universe and its laws. The mathematical mysticism of Pythagoras, too, became known and was an important influence on Copernicus.

Copernicus

To demonstrate the movement of the earth and perform the most drastic intellectual revolution in Western history, more was necessary than mere hypothesis. Copernicus, the Polish-German astronomer who published an epochal book in 1543, did little more than propose the hypothesis. We still read in popular encyclopedias that this book (*De Revolutionibus Orbium Coelestium*) "proved that the planets, including the earth, revolve around the sun." Alas for the writers of encyclopedias, it was not so simple. Copernicus did not prove it. It took more than a century of collective effort by the best minds in Europe to do that. His claim to fame was in starting a movement destined to lead on, through Kepler, Galileo, and Newton (and innumerable others) to a completely different conception of the universe. The canon of Frauenberg cathedral was well aware that he had made no more than a suggestion which others must work out. It was enough to assure him immortality.

Kepler

Largely ignored for some time, the Pole's hypothesis gradually made its way. Tycho Brahe, Danish astronomer who observed also in Prague, and the great Johannes Kepler of Stuttgart (1571–1630), sought to place it on firm foundations. Kepler, by dint of incredible labors, managed to discover the true motions of the planets: elliptical rather than circular, but revealing an essential harmony. This truly great man was the contemporary of Galileo,

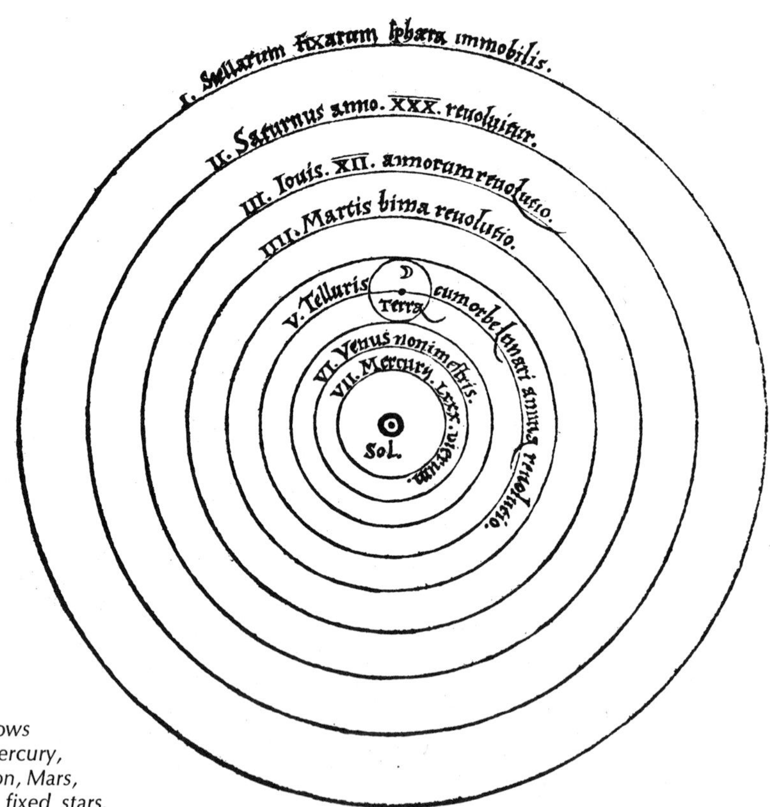

A drawing of the solar system by Copernicus shows a central sun with Mercury, Venus, the Earth and moon, Mars, Jupiter, Saturn, and the fixed stars.

and is now accorded equal rank with the great Italian as founder of modern physical science.

By detecting new stars and comets, Brahe helped overturn the old Ptolemaic system, but he did not decide in favor of Copernicus' heliocentric pattern. Instead he proposed another alternative, in which the planets circled the sun but all of these went around a static earth. Kepler, a Pythagorean mystic seeking the harmony of the universe in numbers, broke through "the tyranny of the circle," and also arrived at an impressive example of the mathematical universe he believed in: his law of the proportion between the periods of the planetary orbits and their distance from the sun. Concomitant developments in mathematics and technology aided these advances. The formula for scientific progress is always a complex one involving many factors. Kepler's age saw the invention of the slide rule, of logarithms by John Napier, and important work on conic sections. It also brought forth the tools with which finer observations could be made: telescopes, quadrants, and so on. Technological developments in such humble areas as mining, metallurgy, navigation, gunnery, suggested new mechanical models to scientists.

Galileo

William Gilbert, court physician to Queen Elizabeth, contributed another fruitful idea with his treatise on magnetism (1600). Galileo thus arrived in a world excited by the apparent destruction of old cosmologies yet unable to make out the shape of the new. The great Italian was by no means always on the right track, yet his stimulating prose as well as his powerful scientific imagination led him to establish the Copernican "hypothesis" beyond reasonable doubt in the minds of educated men. His observations through the telescope, and vivid descriptions of these, startled all Europe in 1610. He succeeded in refuting many of the stock arguments against the earth's movement, for example, that centrifugal force would whirl it to pieces, or that a body thrown into the air would come down in a different spot. Then he found the law of acceleration of falling bodies, working with superb genius on a problem that had been discussed for a long time. Most crucial of all was his virtual discovery of the law of inertia—that objects, contrary to the old (and apparently commonsense) view, need not have a constant mover to be in motion, but will continue in motion by their own momentum once started. Galileo, however, did not arrive at Newton's law of universal gravitation.

Galileo and the church

Well known is the story of Galileo's clash with clerical authority. His trial, forced recantation, and subsequent confinement to his farm (which did not, however, entirely end his scientific labors) occurred in 1633. The position of the Roman church is sometimes misunderstood: it was prepared to tolerate the Copernican theory if presented as a mere "hypothesis," not a fact, and indeed did so. Galileo, a genuinely pious man by every account, had no desire to flout religious authority or discredit the faith. He argued powerfully—and prophetically—that the Bible was not intended to be a textbook of physics and that religion would be discredited if this view prevailed. But the church, dominated by the spirit of the Council of Trent, would not accept the facticity of Copernicus' and Galileo's universe in the teeth of certain clear Biblical passages to the contrary. Protestants sometimes reacted similarly: Luther declared Copernicus to be a "fool," and Kepler was harassed by Protestant rulers. However deplorable, this ecclesiastical obscurantism was not effective, for in Catholic countries as well as Protestant the scientific revolution went ahead. Borelli and Torricelli in Italy, Descartes and Pascal in France, are outstanding proofs of this. These men did often accept the convention of presenting some of their scientific work as "hypothesis" rather than fact. Descartes held up some of his writings until after his death.

Galileo had dedicated his career to disposing of the numerous classical objections to a theory of the earth's movement. Frequently called the greatest of experimental scientists, the Italian actually excelled in scientific imagination: in the conception of hypotheses, in knowing *what* experiments should be performed. He thought of his method as mathematical rather than (primarily) experimental. A leading historian of the scientific revolution has observed that "the modern law of inertia was hardly a thing which the human mind would ever reach by experiment." Yet the experiments which Galileo's genius conceived struck Europe's imagination. His forceful prose and his clash with the papacy in 1633 contributed to establishing his reputation as the pioneer of a new era in man's conception of his world. Few men have ever so combined power of intellect with a daring imagination.

The new world-view

Martyrdom of Bruno

Conservative reaction to the startling change in a whole world-view was doubtless to be expected, since the proofs were not as yet overwhelmingly convincing and men naturally clung to the old. The leading victim of the new form of intolerance was Giordano Bruno, a philosopher-scientist who stressed the plurality of worlds and preached a mystical pantheism. Bruno, a combative personality, met death at the stake in 1600 for a number of heresies. Plurality of worlds was the most disturbing aspect of the new universe to theologians, since it destroyed the uniqueness of the earth and hence of Christ's role. It was also probably the most disturbing to the mind on other grounds. The universe now appeared as infinitely large, full of vast empty spaces—"these infinite spaces frighten me," said Pascal.

But it was to take on the attributes of a machine over which the human mind could by understanding gain power. Galileo and, especially, the remarkable French scientist and philosopher René Descartes took the important step of regarding the physical world as subject to mechanical principles. To the modern mind it may seem an obvious step, but the whole ancient and medieval tradition was against it. The famous Cartesian *dualism* established a divorce between mind and matter, the latter being conceived as a deterministic system, a machine governed by the laws of motion. Physical nature could be isolated and dealt with as an order outside the realm of the spiritual, an order subject to "laws" mathematically stated.

Galileo Galilei, 1564–1642

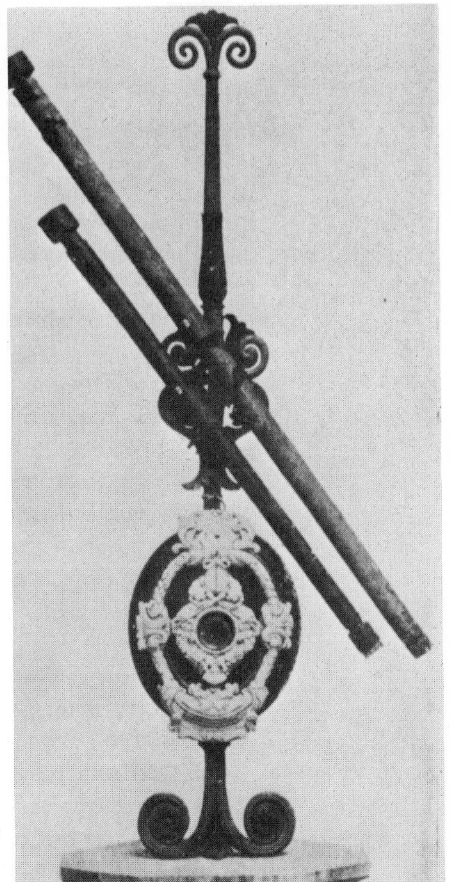

The telescope with which Galileo studied the planets

René Descartes

Francis Bacon

Descartes and Bacon

Descartes, a great mathematician, was fascinated by the geometrical method. Start with a firm axiom and one may proceed step by step to deduce everything else. His celebrated *cogito ergo sum* gave him the starting place, he thought, and from the intuitive certainty of his own existence the great philosopher passed to the existence of God then quickly to his physics. His *Discourse on Method* shared honors with Francis Bacon's *Novum Organum* as a primer of the new scientific method in the 17th century.

Both the French mathematician and the English jurist believed that the time had come for a wholly new method of knowledge. They disagreed in their attempts to describe this method, Bacon being on the whole an advocate of empiricism and Descartes of geometrical deduction. But they combined to unleash a potent attack on the old Aristotelian-Scholastic metaphysics with its essences, its explanations in terms of purpose, its "occult qualities." They helped persuade men that an intellectual revolution was in process. They proposed the goal of power over nature rather than an abstract understanding of it. Their interest was directed toward a nature conceived as wholly different from and external to man, but a nature with regularities which men could find out by the proper methods and then exploit.

This intellectual revolution is usually considered the greatest that western man ever experienced; one that wiped out the fundamental outlook on nature which had existed for a thousand years. Nothing like this had really occurred since the Greek philosophers of the fourth century B.C. Certainly both the humanism of the Renaissance and the Protestantism of the Reformation were still pretty thoroughly ancient and medieval in their conception of nature.

Nature as a machine

"Each age has a dominant world view" (Alfred North Whitehead) and that of the modern age has been the scientific outlook shaped in the 17th century. Until quite recent times (the revolution in physics associated with Einstein and Planck) this view has prevailed. Prior to the 17th century the mental map or frame of reference was different in basic respects. The most significant change was probably that from an organic to a mechanistic model. The representative medieval world-view saw nature, and also human society, as a great body, in effect; a hierarchical chain of being with no breaks, an order of which the principle was not mechanical—a dynamic system of bodies in motion—but like that which exists between parts of the body. The new model was the machine.

In connection with this change came the sharp dualism between living and dead matter, not previously found. Aristotelianism considered all things to be a combination of form and matter, potency and act, a potential form struggling to actualize itself through matter. The idea that there was a continuous unbroken "chain of being" from the crudest object to the most perfect had been incorporated into medieval thought, too. It followed that differences between things were of degree, not kind. Nonliving as well as living things had forces within them pushing them toward their fulfillment. This psychophysical unity of all things taught by Aristotle and Aquinas gave way to Galileo's doctrine of primary and secondary qualities and Descartes' dualism. In brief, matter became something with only the qualities objectively measurable—mass, shape, movement. Nature was a machine! Today we are not so sure that it is, but the "error" was the most fruitful one in history.

Rejection of teleology

Also, the medieval-ancient search for essences and substances was abandoned. One now measured and classified the observable properties, and no longer bothered with those ultimate purposes that concerned Aristotle. The doctrine of Aristotelian science most sharply attacked was that of teleology, the theory of final causes or purposes in nature. This was an answer to the ultimate question "why," which modern science does not give. Teleology, said Francis Bacon, is like a virgin consecrated to God: it is noble but produces no offspring. The Aristotelian answer that a thing's cause is, ultimately, its essential inward nature, its striving-principle or purpose, came to seem meaningless. There is a famous satirical passage in a play of Molière's in which the Scholastic pupil repeats by rote the profound thought that opium makes one sleep because it is possessed of a dormitive virtue. The wisdom of Aristotle had grown stale; modern science wished knowledge which aimed lower but got somewhere. If one forgot about ultimate explanations, which could never be verifiable, and gave full attention to the effective causes only, one gained power over nature.

Progress of science

The "century of genius" was now in full swing. Galileo and Kepler were joined by Torricelli, Boyle, and Harvey. The latter spectacularly broke free from classical anatomy to describe the action of the heart and the circulation of the blood as a *mechanical* system. And there came others too numerous to mention. Science was in the air, and men turned to it as they turned to metaphysics or theology in an earlier age. Philosophical speculation based on or related to the new science became exciting too, and such unorthodox philosophies as pantheism and ancient Epicurean atomism were revived.

Mathematics dominated the era. The development of higher mathematics made possible discoveries by Kepler and Galileo; Descartes, a mathematician, was philosopher of a mathematical universe. Thomas Hobbes and Benedict Spinoza, enthralled by geometric reasoning, sought to apply it to ethics and politics; ladies in their Paris salons studied Euclid.

Yet experimental science was not completely neglected. In England, particularly, where the Baconian influence was strong, Robert Boyle and the Royal Society were dedicated "empiricks" and made the laboratory respectable; it was identified with medieval alchemists and rather shunned by the continental Cartesians as insufficiently rational. The Dutch stood high among the scientists of this age; Huygens, who ranked second only to Newton at the end of the century, attempted to mediate between the Newtonian and Cartesian systems, while the Dutchman Leeuwenhoek won fame for his use of the microscope to discover the tiny organisms invisible to the naked eye.

Newton

From England, significantly, came the final triumphant synthesis of the scientific century: Isaac Newton's exact formulation of the laws of motion and of universal gravitation. The victory of the Newtonian over the Cartesian system was a victory for empiricism. Not that Newton neglected mathematics; on the contrary, he shared with Leibniz the discovery of the differential calculus, without which his formulas could not have been precisely verified. But whereas Descartes was dogmatically committed to a deductive system experimental almost only in its initial premises, Newton held that hypothesis must be checked at every step by experiment and must never go beyond the empirically verifiable. Mathematics he considered only a tool of research, not the language of nature. It should express in exact terms what experimental data indicated, and no more.

With the god-like Newton's masterful summation of the laws which seemed majestically to "govern" all physical matter, the scientific revolution appeared to have found its ideal method as well as its most important conclusion. The Lincolnshire genius seemed to have cleared up all the mysteries and fitted together all the pieces. He explained the movement of the heavenly bodies, terrestrial objects, and the tides, indeed every kind of motion, according to a few simple laws; he revealed the cosmic order, expressing it in exact mathematical formulae. For 200 years physical science would do little more than expand the footnotes to his masterful outline, *The Mathematical Principles of Natural Philosophy*.

William Harvey, English physician, discovered the manner of circulation of the blood.

Sir Isaac Newton, founder of modern physical science.

Baroque architecture of the 17th century, an outgrowth of late Renaissance forms, broke up the severe classical facades and made the symmetry a more complex one of dynamism rather than repose. Bernini's piazza at St. Peter's in Rome, above, and the facade of the Neumünster at Würzburg, Germany, show the flowing curves and adornment.

Baroque

The upheaval in the sciences was both a profoundly disturbing influence and, eventually, one leading to order and reason. In the time of Galileo the removal of old landmarks caused quite a few sensitive and thoughtful souls to feel as did the English poet John Donne when he wrote of "all coherence gone." Descartes brought in a strong sense of a universe more completely rational than the old one, but the Cartesian philosophy was not altogether convincing, and not until Newton did there come the removal of virtually all doubts about the orderliness of nature. The titanic figure of Blaise Pascal suggests some of the tensions of mid-century: Pascal, the mathematical prodigy, whose conversion to mystical religion pulled him somewhat away from a science the implications of which he feared.

The baroque style

Perhaps this helps explain why the artistic style typical of the earlier part of the century is the baroque, a violent and disturbed style. This style has also been associated with the Rome or Spain of the Counter-Reformation. Bernini, the Neapolitan architect and sculptor who did much of the extensive rebeautification of Rome in the 17th century, was its primary genius in his field. In painting, the Flemish master Rubens and the Spaniard, Velásquez, among others, would unhesitatingly be put down as "baroque." Between about 1580 and 1650 there were outstanding examples of a style marked by "a grandeur without restraint, a wild extravagance, and a luxury of detail that would have been distasteful to Michelangelo." "Mannerism" is a term often used to describe the more extravagant post-Renaissance style, highly decorative and overly ornate. Baroque and mannerism disregarded conventions and experimented in startling effects. Some of this was very exciting art indeed, and it is foolish to declare dogmatically that it is "worse" than the Renaissance style or the neoclassical. The baroque mood, somewhat like romanticism later, was a reaction against the sedate classicism of the preceding period. Classicism, with its rules and boundaries, can sometimes seem too tame. The baroque-romantic rejection of such limitations is exciting, but is prone to eccentricity, becoming grotesque and aimless without the classical discipline. Then men again turn back to classicism. At its best, however, the baroque was richly voluptuous without losing its balance.

Baroque architecture spread to France and to southern Germany, where a little later it produced masterpieces of exquisite beauty and delicacy. Many students of art history see baroque as essentially Spanish (Naples belonged to Spain, which would bring in Bernini), but, while it admittedly had less impact on England and France than on Italy and Spain, it was hardly confined to any one place. In England, there has been some objection to applying the term to the "metaphysical" poetry of such as John Donne and Richard Crashaw, with its tightly packed layers of meaning, its conceits and extravagances, its effort to keep different worlds in balance; but Jacobean drama was wild and violent, using themes of murder, rape, and incest. In France, the same taste for "flamboyant fancy" was present, with some importing of

Spanish tragicomedy, before, after mid-century, the neoclassical age ushered in clarity, order, and discipline.

The triumph of neoclassicism late in the 17th century, extending into the 18th, coincides with Newton's triumphant vindication of harmony in the universe, and sets the scene for the 18th-century Enlightenment. Contributing also to this movement were ideas stemming from the 17th-century ferment in philosophy.

The new philosophy

The 17th century, "century of genius," contributed more great minds to the world than any other, in all probability. To the titantic scientists, from Kepler and Galileo to Boyle and Newton, and the penetrating political thinkers Hobbes and Locke, it added the philosophers Descartes, Spinoza, Leibniz, and —again—John Locke, in whose shadow most of modern philosophy has lain ever since.

Descartes

We have already referred to Descartes as scientist; his philosophy was closely related to his science and especially his scientific methodology. But the Frenchman had the rare distinction of being great in both science and philosophy. In order to put his science on firm foundations, he resolved to find the basis of certainty in the cosmos by subjecting all knowledge to systematic doubt pushed as far as it could be carried. Ancient skepticism, from the school of Pyrrho of Elis and the late Platonic Academy, was again brought to light in the 16th century; Montaigne is one who exhibits the profound influence of this "pyrrhonism," which held that nothing could be known for sure. Descartes thought he was able to establish the existence of certain truth after all the reasons for doubt had been examined. I have at least a certainty of my own existence; and from this Descartes reasoned to the existence of God and thus to a guarantee of the truth of any clear and simple idea which I know intuitively. As already suggested, he proceeded to develop his method of reasoning in the geometric mode which he felt could disclose full and clear and certain truth about nature, and then to create a system of physics. That this last turned out to be more fiction than truth, overthrown by Newton's superior physics, impaired the prestige of the great Frenchman but could not remove his vision of a rational universe, knowable by the rational mind, subject to exact laws expressible in mathematical terms.

Spinoza, Leibniz

Other great philosophers who, influenced deeply by Descartes though differing from him in some matters, affirmed reason in nature and man were the Spanish Jew, Baruch Spinoza, who lived in Holland, and from the German world the Leipzig-born genius, Wilhelm Leibniz. The latter was a mathematician, scientist, philosopher, and inventor whose career can stand comparison with those of Descartes and Newton. With the latter he disputed the primacy of the discovery of the calculus, and in fact published the first and best system; while with John Locke he argued concerning the validity of pure empiricism,

Benedict Spinoza and, right, Gottfried Wilhelm Leibniz

remaining true to the continental tradition of rationalism though offering some revisions of Descartes. From his fertile brain flowed plans alike for technological inventions and political solutions. One of these many ideas was reunion of the churches under a scientifically based theology. He was chiefly responsible for establishing in Berlin an academy of sciences on the model of the French academy. Harmony was the keynote of the Leibnizian philosophy, and in fact he had stronger roots in the medieval Scholastics than most other 17th-century philosophers.

The 18th-century Enlightenment was to be much affected by this idea of the harmony of reason and religion, in a manner different in detail but agreeing in its fundamental spirit with that of the 13th century: a sense of the orderliness of the universe, and of nature with human reason. Spinoza, too, radiated such a faith in order: nature and God were in fact to him but different aspects of the same substance. The 18th-century Enlightenment under the influence of Locke was to react against the abstract rationalism of these 17th-century metaphysicians, but would keep their vision of law and order in an almost deified nature.

Locke

Newton's friend, the philosopher John Locke, was the man who taught England and Europe to forego metaphysics and follow the method of science. This method was conceived to be little more than glorified common sense. Careful observation, clear analysis—a combination of Descartes' "clear and distinct ideas" with Newton's "experimental method"—this was the conception of science which percolated down from the great scientists to the average cultivated mind. Locke conceived it to be his mission—and for more than a century he was assumed to have accomplished it—to remove "the rubbish that lies in the way to knowledge" and disclose a new and more simple way to philosophy, "which is nothing but the true knowledge of things." If "God said, Let Newton be! and all was was Light," the Deity had sent John Locke to remove the bushel from Newton's light. This pair had more to do than any others with the Enlightenment which followed.

Challenge to religious orthodoxy

Whether Cartesian, Spinozist, or Lockean, the new philosophy posed some problems for traditional religious belief. Descartes' world machine, pious critics complained, left nothing for God to do after giving the first push to the first atom. Spinoza's pantheism, which made God and nature the same, was considered to be in effect atheism and got the lens-grinder of Amsterdam thrown out of his Jewish synagogue as well as scandalizing Christians. Locke was alleged to lead to deism, i.e., belief in God on the grounds of reason alone without need for the Christian revelation. The 17th century was filled with clandestine atheism, deism, and "libertinism," though little of it could be published or openly acknowledged. It remained for the 18th-century Enlightenment, treated in a later chapter, to bring these unorthodoxies into the open. The new science, the new philosophy, and new political ideas thrown into the crucible of thought in the 17th century fused in the 18th to make that movement of the Western mind and culture we call the Enlightenment.

Bibliography

The theme of toleration is dealt with by Joseph Lecler, *Toleration and the Reformation* (2 vols.; New York: Association Press, 1960), and W.K. Jordan, *The Development of Religious Toleration* (4 vols.; Cambridge, Mass.: Harvard University Press, 1932–40). W.J. Stankiewicz, *Politics and Religion in Seventeenth Century France: A Study of Political Ideas* (Berkeley: University of California Press, 1960), and P. Zagorin, *A History of Political Thought in the Puritan Revolution* (London: Routledge & Kegan Paul, 1954), are useful for political ideas. The large subject of *The Origins of Modern Science* is introduced beautifully to the general reader by Herbert Butterfield (Macmillan, Collier); equally good is A.C. Crombie, Vol. II of *Medieval and Early Modern Science* (Doubleday, Anchor). One of the several multivolumed histories of science is the Rise of Modern Science series published by Harper & Row, in which the second volume is by Marie Boas, dealing with the Renaissance period, and the third by A.R. Hall, *From Galileo to Newton* (New York, 1963). Other books on a fascinating theme include T.S. Kuhn, *The Copernican Revolution* (Random House, Modern Library); Max Caspar's fine biography of *Kepler* (London: Abelard-Schuman, 1960); Arthur Koestler's stimulating *The Sleepwalkers* (London: Hutchinson, 1959); G. de Santillana, *The Crime of Galileo* (University of Chicago, Phoenix), a scintillating study of the famous case. For the biological sciences, C. Dobell, *Anthony von Leeuwenhoek and His Little Animals* (New York: Dover Publications, 1960); K.D. Keele, *William Harvey* (London: Thomas Nelson & Sons, 1965). Overall, the brilliant essay by C.S. Lewis, *The Discarded Image* (New York: Cambridge University Press, 1964), makes clear the nature of the transition from premodern to modern modes of thinking about the universe, on which see also A. Koyré, *From the Closed World to the Infinite Universe* (Harper Torchbook), and R.G. Collingwood, *The Idea of Nature* (Oxford University Press).

The Age of Grandeur: Baroque Art and Architecture, by V.L. Tapié (Frederick A. Praeger), is pictorial. There are other picture books. On the 17th-century philosophers, F.H. Anderson, *The Philosophy of Francis Bacon* (Chicago: University of Chicago Press, 1948); Jacques Maritain, *The Dream of Descartes* (New York: Philosophical Library, 1944); L. Roth, *Descartes' Discourse on Method* (Oxford: Clarendon Press, 1937); R.W. Meyer, *Leibnitz and the Seventeenth Century Revolution* (Chicago: Henry Regnery, 1952); Ernest Mortimer, *Blaise Pascal* (London: Methuen Publications, 1959); Maurice Cranston, *John Locke, A Biography* (London: Longmans, Green & Co., 1957); Richard Peters, *Hobbes* (Penguin); F. Copleston, *History of Philosophy,* Vol. 4, *Descartes to Leibniz* (Doubleday, Image). Again on Hobbes, see Howard Warrender, *The Political Philosophy of Hobbes* (Clarendon Press, 1957), and Leo Strauss, *The Political Philosophy of Hobbes* (University of Chicago, Phoenix).

Sources. The Rationalists (Doubleday, Dolphin) and *The Age of Reason* (New American Library) are paperback selections of the writings of the 17th-century philosophers. Bacon's *New Organon,* F.H. Anderson (ed.), is a Bobbs-Merrill Liberal Arts paperback. Thomas Hobbes, *Leviathan* (Bobbs-Merrill, Liberal Arts), edited by H.S. Schneider; *Newton's Philosophy of Nature* (Hafner), H.S. Thayer (ed.); and John Locke's *Two Treatises on Government,* preferably in the New American Library Mentor edition, Peter Laslett (ed.), are other basic documents of intellectual history.

*A 17th century Dutch warship
and East India Trading Company
vessel approaching Amsterdam harbor*

13

Revolution and war: 1600-1660

chronology

1603
Beginning of reign of James I in England.
1604
"Apology" of Parliament.
1605
Gunpowder Plot, England.
1608–9
Catholic League v. Protestant Union in Germany.
1609
Truce in Dutch-Spanish war; independence of northern provinces.
1610
Assassination of Henry IV of France.
1610–17
Regency of Marie de' Medici, France. Louis XIII, 1617–43.
1611
Completion of great English translation of Bible (King James version).
1614
"Addled" Parliament.
1616
Coke's decision against forced loans in England, dismissal from office.
1618
Ferdinand II, Holy Roman Emperor. Revolt in Prague; beginning of Thirty Years War.
1620
Battle of White Mountain.
1621
Renewal of Dutch-Spanish war.
Protest of English Parliament; arrest of its leading members.
1625
Charles I to throne of England.
Richelieu becomes first minister of King Louis XIII, until death in 1642.
Grotius, *De Jure Belli et Pacis.*
1626
Defeat of Danes by imperial forces, Lutter.
1628
Petition of Right.
Siege of La Rochelle.
1629
Arrest of Sir John Eliot, dissolution of Parliament by King Charles.
Edict of Restitution, Holy Roman Empire.
1630
Entrance of Sweden into Thirty Years War. Victories of Swedes under King Gustavus Adolphus, 1630–32.
1637
Ship Money case.
Revolt in Scotland against Anglican religious services.
1638–39
Solemn League and Covenant; Bishops' War with Scotland.
1640
Short Parliament, England.
1641
Long Parliament; Grand Remonstrance; impeachment and execution of Strafford.
Abolition of royal courts by Parliament.
1642
Beginning of English Civil War.
1643
Battle of Rocroi, French victory over Spanish.
Death of Louis XIII; minority of Louis XIV.
Cardinal Mazarin, chief minister.
1644
Execution of Archbishop Laud by Parliament act of attainder.
1645
Battle of Naseby, parliamentary victory over the Royalists.
Surrender of King Charles.
Swedish-French victories in Thirty Years War.
1648
Renewal of English Civil War. Battle of Preston Pans.
Pride's Purge.
Peace of Westphalia.
The Fronde, rebellion of the nobility in France, 1648–53.
1649
Execution of King Charles.
1653
Oliver Cromwell, Lord Protector of England.
1658
Death of Cromwell.
1659
Treaty of the Pyrenees between France and Spain. Negotiations to restore Charles II to throne of England.

Parliament and king in Stuart England

Parliament was a medieval institution. It grew out of the king's feudal council, the haughty barons who had the right and the duty of advising the king in earlier times. This was typical of feudalism and found almost everywhere in Europe. With the rise of strong monarchies and centralized states it tended to disappear elsewhere, but in England it survived and was gradually transformed, a prominent reason being, as we have mentioned, its status as the only such body of the realm. Since the 13th century there had been precedents in England for the occasional summoning of a body that included the lesser knights and burgesses (bourgeoisie) as well as the great nobles. It became established that a law which "touches all" would have to receive the consent of a "Commons." Under the great King Edward I in the late 13th century, Parliament had developed into a regular lawmaking institution. During the troubled times that followed, it sometimes came to seem like a synonym for misrule by the barons, but it did not die; on the contrary it extended its influence. A significant development was its becoming a two-house body rather than three. In other places the traditional arrangement was clergy, nobility, and commons sitting separately; we will meet this arrangement in France on the eve of the great 1789 revolution. In England the House of Lords embraced the clergy while the House of Commons came to include some of the lesser aristocracy—a significant strengthening of the lower house.

James I

The Tudors, perhaps because they were commoners who could scarcely claim much hereditary glory, chose to flatter and use Parliament rather than try to destroy it, and were able to do so. It is striking that Parliament—and Commons especially, as distinct from Lords—actually increased its stature under Queen Elizabeth, mightiest of English monarchs. It did not quite dare challenge that imperious lady on a major issue, but it gave obvious signs of feeling that it had a large share in the governing of the realm, that it was a body of great dignity and many privileges—which it did not derive from the king's will but from "ancient custom."

Elizabeth's successor lacked both her charm, prestige, and will. The offspring of that fateful marriage between Mary of Scotland and Darnley, he impressed people as learned and mentally quick, but weak of body, unprepossessing in appearance, rather unstable of character, and lacking in manners or tact. His court was to become a byword for immorality and corruption. If James I had numerous drawbacks as a king, he had also been left in an awkward situation. After years of living with Elizabeth, all kinds of pent-up grievances were ready to burst forth. Elizabeth's unsatisfactory religious settlement, in particular, had been generating a large amount of suppressed steam. Many protests which had been suspended due to her age and the awe in which she was held were sure to come forward after Elizabeth's death. In addition James had to face the problem of royal revenues at a time when the price revolution was diminishing the income and raising the expense of governments.

Contemporary impression of the Gunpowder Plotters, alleged to have tried to blow up Parliament

Early in James' reign (1605) the Gunpowder Plot convinced most Englishmen, if they needed further convincing, that the Catholics were enemies of the state. One Guy Fawkes was arrested on November 4, 1605, and confessed (under torture) to a conspiracy aimed at blowing up King and Parliament on the opening day of Parliament immediately following. Some historians have been skeptical of the plot's authenticity, suggesting a government stratagem to discredit the Catholics. If so, it worked well. There was no further danger from this quarter; but by the same token, the Puritan wing of Protestantism was strengthened. Calvinists who demanded the further reform or "purification" of the ambiguous Anglican church had been heard from under Elizabeth, but she had sternly repressed them. They now loudly reaffirmed their program. James was no friend to these people, but rebuked them when they came to him at the beginning of his reign. "A Scottish Presbytery," he said, "agreeth as well with monarchy as God with the Devil." He was to hear more from them, for Puritanism was on the rise. Though the Puritans and other Protestant dissenters (among whom were those to be called Congregationalists, Separatists, and Independents, men who held to a substantially sectarian view of the church as purely voluntary, a gathering of the elect) were not yet strong enough to shake any throne, they were one of the stubborn forces the Stuart kings were to break against.

Parliament asserts its rights

Parliament was assuredly the greatest of these. In its "Apology" of 1604 that body told James in no uncertain terms that its rights and privileges came to it from "ancient custom," not the will of the king. James for his part,

James I of England

much given to theorizing about government, seemingly adopted the new view of an absolute "divine right" monarch. That this was substantially a new view must be emphasized: we need hardly repeat that medieval kings were both in theory and practice subject to many limitations. The idea of a purely secular absolutism arose amid the contending religious factions of the Reformation era. When both Calvinists like John Knox and Jesuit-advised popes claimed a power to depose the king, theorists arose to assert that kings might rule regardless of the church. We have seen also how the Protestant revolt, by placing the pope's power in the hands of the monarch, strengthened royal despotism in England. But the Tudors, though they might exercise absolute power, were careful not to boast of it. The theory of monarchical absolutism, formulated by theorists such as the Franco-Scot Barclay, 1599, emerges more clearly in England with Sir Robert Filmer a little later, but King James seems to have held something like it. He certainly was more outspoken than Queen Elizabeth in declaring that Parliament could only act at his will and sufferance.

In contradition to his imprudent theoretical claims to power, James was in practice too passive to lead, and allowed Parliament to get out of control. Elizabeth had dedicated herself unceasingly to tactics of domination over

Parliament, by cajolery as well as by intimidation, and most of all perhaps by always telling them what she wanted. James neglected these tasks; Parliament was left much more to its own devices and had to find its own leadership; it is not surprising that this leadership tended to oppose rather than follow the royal wishes. On this analysis James' troubles stemmed from not following the old maxim "speak softly and carry a big stick." He spoke loudly, but he did not really exert a masterful hand over England—quite the reverse.

Stuart finances

The parliamentary opposition criticized waste and money squandered on the royal favorites, especially the Duke of Buckingham, perennial favorite of both father and son; after persistent efforts to impeach him, Buckingham was finally assassinated, to the satisfaction of much of England but the royal displeasure. Men asked what had become of the "grave and wise council" of Queen Elizabeth's day. They especially assailed the Stuart foreign policies, perhaps somewhat unjustly. From first to last, money was a sore problem. Financially the Stuarts barely scraped along, starved for taxes by the absence of parliamentary cooperation. It was this which drove them to some desperate expedients that further alienated Parliament. It appears that Parliament was to blame for refusing to grant additional funds to the government in a time of inflation which rendered previous incomes inadequate; but on the other hand it is difficult not to agree that Stuart despotism inspired far less confidence than the Tudors had.

Quarrels of King and Parliament

Whatever the reasons, the fact is that James could not get along with Parliament, nor could his son and successor, Charles. James quarreled with the first one in 1604, dismissed it and did without until 1614, when the "Addled Parliament" never passed a measure and had four of its members sent to the Tower for strong criticism of the king's policies. The Thirty Years War caused James to assemble Parliament again, but again he found its members readier to express grievances than grant money, with the result that England played very little part in that war. (Yet the successes of the Catholic side in the 1620's led to criticism of the Stuarts for not aiding the Protestant cause.) If the King could not live with Parliament, neither could he live without it, for war and other emergencies created a demand for funds and the English people were stubbornly convinced that no tax was legal unless Parliament approved it. So the stalemate continued.

Illegal taxes

In an effort to find a source of revenue beyond Parliament the Stuarts resorted to various dues, resurrecting old customs like "ship money," selling monopolies, and forcing gentlemen to be knighted and pay a fee. These proved irritating and, as might be expected, were challenged as illegal. The King was able to have his money-raising devices declared legal because he controlled the royal courts of Chancery, Exchequer, and Star Chamber, which had been created only in Tudor times. Reaching back far beyond these relatively upstart tools of absolutism were the common law courts, with roots in medieval times: a peculiarly English[1] custom of determining private law not by reference to a code (like Justinian's) or any one collection (like the canon law Decretals) but by interpreting a great mass of precedent cases. In Yorkist and Tudor times the royal courts had been superimposed on the common law Courts of Common Pleas, and claimed supremacy over them in case of a clash of jurisdictions. But in 1616 the doughty veteran, Edward Coke, climaxed a long career of being a thorn in King James' side by refusing to accept this superiority of the "prerogative" law over the common law.

The common law

Coke asserted, on the contrary, the supremacy of the common law courts, with a right to overrule either king or Parliament. Coke's claim for this doctrine of "judicial review" did not prevail, but it helped to stir up discontent. The courageous judge was removed from office for defying the royal will, and the lesson was not lost on the other judges, who tended to ratify the king's wishes thereafter; but for thousands of Englishmen the conflict between royal fiat and realm of law had been dramatized in this clash. Those who objected to paying taxes to the king resorted to the courts on several notable occasions thereafter.

Charles I

Charles, who came to the throne in 1625, was a handsomer and more impressive man than his father, but he had no better luck with Parliament, lawyers, and Puritans—indeed, considerably worse. The 1628–29 Parliament produced the Petition of Right ("the second Magna Carta") and broke up in a brawl with the King. So desperate was Charles' need for funds that he was forced to accept the petition, which declared against forced loans, imprisonment without legal process, and so on—a definite precursor of the Bill of Rights. In so declaring Parliament had in mind chiefly the famous case of the five knights, gentlemen who had refused to pay forced loans to the crown, and had been imprisoned. The knights were released and the petition accepted. But a year later, angered by the continued demands of Parliament, Charles dissolved it and arrested opposition leader Sir John Eliot, who subsequently died in the Tower. On this dramatic occasion men of Parliament held the speaker in the chair while they finished their business, refusing to concede that the King could dissolve their body.

Period of personal government

Charles then resolved to have no more to do with Parliaments, and managed to get along without them for 11 years. A widely publicized test case against ship money, the latest form of royal financial exaction, occurred during these years. Ship money was a levy traditionally imposed on port towns in emergencies; now it was extended all over the country and made a regular levy. The tax was upheld in 1637, yet it was significant that 5 of the 12 judges in the Exchequer Chamber dared to vote against the King.

[1] Peculiar to England in the importance it assumed as compared to the civil law; but customary law was widely in use in the earlier Middle Ages and had roots in Roman practice.

King Charles I, overthrown by the Puritan Revolution of 1642.

But it was the church question that eventually got Charles into real hot water. Charles I's religious policy, administered by Archbishop Laud, whose name became odious to the Puritans, aimed at purging these troublesome malcontents from the English church.

Religious feelings still ran high; in England, many murmured at the alleged influence of "papists" at the King's court. King Charles was not in fact a Roman Catholic, but his French wife was, and papal delegates enjoyed favor at court, while the Elizabethan laws against Catholics were not enforced. Puritans continued to insist on the thoroughgoing "purification" of the English church from all remnants of Romanism. Get rid of the bishops, Puritans cried; also the elaborate ceremonies. They were content with "four bare walls and a sermon." As for the clergy, let them be chosen by the church-going laity. These Puritans were fortified by their faith, usually Calvinistic but sometimes including an inner-light mysticism. Puritans might denounce games and maypole dancing as immoral—an extremism which was a reaction against the sort of Anglicanism that turned Sundays into days of feasting and athletics; also they inveighed against the flagrant immorality of the theater, in an age when actress and prostitute were practically synonymous terms. They were ridiculed as joyless hypocrites by many writers of the day, including Shakespeare and Ben Jonson; but they *were* moral, in a dissolute age; and this strength of character increasingly appealed to the better sort of person, especially among the middle class but not excluding the landed gentlemen. Puritanism had become somewhat fashionable.

Persecution of the Puritans

The Puritans were definitely a minority; but the inquisitorial methods and harsh persecution of Laud (no heads were cut off, but some ears) did not sit well. It was during the Laudian 1630's that the more intransigent of the Puritans migrated to Massachusetts, obtaining a rather generous charter. England might have submitted to their being purged, but Charles and Laud made a fatal mistake when they sought to do the same in Scotland. In 1637, when the Book of Common Prayer was read in St. Giles', Edinburgh, in place of Knox's book, an enraged Scotswoman hurled a stool at the offending bishop. It was really the first blow in the great Puritan Revolution. For in order to handle the Scottish war that ensued, Charles had to recall Parliament, which had been last seen in the stormy proceedings of 1629 and now came back fighting. The final break, and civil war, soon followed.

Causes of the revolution

The above summary of this famous quarrel suggests that obviously money played a great part in it, complicated by a breakdown of trust between King and parliamentary leaders, and by the religious question. The Stuarts could not carry on the government without funds, and Parliament may well be criticized for its refusal to grant them; but Parliament did not trust the kings and asked a share in government, which the absolutist Stuarts would not concede. Then their efforts to raise money without the consent of Parliament ran into the common law and into the instincts of Englishmen who believed no tax was legal unless authorized by Parliament. Under such conditions Charles' unwise decision to force religious conformity on Scotland proved his undoing.

If Puritans objected to religious policy, others complained of the King's neglect of the liberties of his subjects, his cavalier disregard of Parliament, and his unsuccessful foreign policies. Charles I was not a great king though he was a gracious one. But he was quite sure that he *was* the king—king by grace of God and responsible only to God. His rather simple mind clung stubbornly to the simple logic of royal sovereignty: the king determined law and determined policy for his realm. Who else? He might and should *consult* his loyal subjects gathered in Parliament (at his summons, and to be sent away when he chose), but then he made up his mind, and it was not theirs to question this decision. If a king was not this, then he was not a king, Charles felt, though he might be "a Doge of Venice." Charles did not propose to be a Doge or a figurehead. Unhappily, he saw in criticism only treason, in opposition rebellion.

The English civil war

After hastily dismissing one Parliament in 1639 (the "Short"), Charles soon was forced by need of funds to issue the call for another, which became the

Long Parliament, destined to sit until 1653 and preside over war with the King, his execution on the block, and finally the emergence of a leader from its own ranks who would dismiss it and rule alone. Charles found himself deserted by much of England in his war with the Scots and had to give in to Parliament, which imposed upon him a sweeping program of parliamentary supremacy. Summed up in the Grand Remonstrance of 1641, it was expressed in the passage of bills abolishing all irregular taxation and the royal courts, impeaching Laud and Lord Strafford, Charles' able minister, and soon executing the latter by act of attainder (Laud met the same fate in 1644), establishing triennial Parliaments and denying the right of the king to dismiss a Parliament. There was a threat to abolish the bishops. Changing his mind again, Charles sought to arrest five leading members of Commons, but he encountered the hostility of London and fled to the North with a portion of Parliament and the great seal, setting up his standard at Nottingham on August 22, 1642. The civil war had begun. "Roundhead" and "Cavalier" would fight for the possession of England.

Issues of the war

It was not a large or a bloody war, and its issues at times seemed unclear. It was not exactly royal tyranny versus free parliamentary government (though this view is still widely prevalent), for Charles did not wish to rule without Parliament, and Parliament was capable of acting tyrannically enough, as in the acts of attainder (declaring a person guilty without judicial process). Still less was it tyranny versus *democracy:* for Parliament did not at all represent the majority, the vote being confined to that small minority which held real property. After the revolution began some democratic viewpoints emerged, but these never dominated the revolution. Parliament was dominated by the wealthiest squires in England, a small oligarchy that held the land and lorded it over tenant farmers and laborers on their estates. Nor was the struggle entirely one of Puritan versus Anglican, for many of the more conservative Parliamentarians did not want a presbyterianized church and soon broke with the more radical Puritans.

The gentry

Did some more basic economic or social cleavage lie behind the quarrel? Not very clearly. Most historians now reject the explanation of the Puritan Revolution as a class conflict in which the "bourgeoisie" overthrew the "landed aristocracy." For one thing, in Stuart England the landed gentry and the men of trade and industry were almost the same class. Typically, a man of means was both, as were leading revolutionaries like Hampden, Pym, and Cromwell. There was, indeed, only one class which counted for anything, and that was the "gentry." The civil war began and was largely fought out as an internal quarrel of this class, some for the King and more against him. The amorphous lower classes stayed out of it or followed their superiors.

Rising or falling gentry?

A question that has greatly exercised some historians in recent years—perhaps unduly so—is whether this all-important gentry class was "rising" or "falling"—getting better off or worse off. One school has sought to explain the revolution as a result of the vastly increased wealth and power of this landed aristocracy, grown strong enough to challenge the king. Another insists that the gentry class was losing wealth and reacted in a revolutionary manner because hard-pressed. The latter hypothesis seems less convincing, though naturally some landowners might prosper less or not at all. What is important is that the gentry, or nontitled aristocracy, occupied a strong place in English society; sturdy and accustomed to local authority, these squires still had something of the common touch, being in the main not titled peers. Practically no English aristocrat boasted of having blue blood or an ancient lineage.

It may be said that the wealthier gentry made this revolution against a king who taxed them without their consent. It was a defense of property; but it also was a defense of basic liberties against arbitrary government. It is difficult to avoid the judgment that in some ways it was a defense of privilege: the oligarchy which largely ruled England, and ruled it corruptly, was being challenged by a bid for a royal absolutism which might well have been more honest and efficient. Study of the workings of government in Charles' reign shows that administration was largely a monopoly of an upper class who used it to enrich themselves.

Sovereignty

A clear cause of the conflict was the effort to locate the seat of sovereign power. It was an age of rationalism, and the concept of "sovereignty" had come to the fore—that power which, as Bodin had said, must ultimately rest in one place in the body politic. Heretofore Englishmen had vaguely agreed that somehow king and parliament shared power, each with its rights and together governing the realm. Now it seemed to be necessary to decide which one ruled. If two men ride a horse, observed Thomas Hobbes, one must ride in front. In most European countries which were becoming organized as modern states at this time, the king succeeded in identifying sovereignty and unity with his undivided will, while the "estates" or parliaments passed into oblivion as a relic of the medieval past. So it was in France and Spain. But in England Parliament was unusually strong and unusually national. In the course of the long debate with the king it began to claim sovereignty for itself alone, arguing that Commons spoke for the people, the king being but a servant of this will.

Cromwell and his army

If the civil war between Roundheads and Cavaliers (Puritans and Royalists) was not to be as vast and bloody as that waged between Americans 200 years later, this was primarily because the resources of the state were not as great, and because the great bulk of the people were scarcely involved at all. Armies contained a few thousand men, and while passions sometimes ran high, it was on the whole a quarrel among gentlemen. On the one side were about half the country squires plus some of the commoner sort, especially in London; on the other, most of the higher nobles and the rest of the country squires, with their retainers. In the long run, the power of the purse told. For the Parliament side held London, with its money, its customs house, its access to foreign trade, its industrial skills. The fleet went over to Parliament, and money enabled Parliament to raise and equip something like a small professional army, while the King had to rely on volunteers. Many brave men followed him loyally, and he won some victories, but they were indecisive, for he was never able to capture the City. And in a captain of horse named Oliver Cromwell the Puritans turned up the leading military genius and outstanding political personality of the war—a man destined to go down in history with the very greatest leaders of men. Brave Oliver led the New Model Army, an army inspired with religious zeal—a fighting force perhaps unique in modern history.

As revolutions are prone to do, the English revolution changed its character as it went along, having a momentum of its own. No one at the start could have foreseen the execution of the King and the rise of a military dictatorship, preceded by a drastic purge of the Long Parliament itself. Or that the Scots, who had begun it by fighting against Charles, would join him to fight against Parliament. Such was the case. While the war went on indecisively the first couple of years, Cromwell distinguishing himself at the important battle of Marston Moor in the north but the Royalists having the better of it in the south, Parliament discovered that it had as much trouble agreeing among itself as it had had agreeing with the King. Presbyterians and Independents parted company on church policy and other matters: a breach roughly between the more conservative and the more radical.

In 1645 the battle of Naseby marked a decisive victory for the New Model Army under Cromwell. Though Montrose fought gallantly for the King in Scotland, where the Highlands were royalist, Charles gave up the cause as hopeless in 1646. But subsequently, though captured, he made a secret agreement with the Scottish Presbyterians, who now disliked Cromwell's faction more than they did the King's. By this treaty Charles agreed to abolish the bishops and install a Presbyterian system! But Cromwell beat the Scots also, at Preston Pans, 1648. The next move was to bring the King to trial.

Execution of King Charles I

Before he could be convicted, it was necessary to purge Parliament. With Colonel Pride doing the honors, the army forcibly threw the Presbyterian members out of Commons, leaving only the "rump," while suppressing Lords altogether. Only after Pride's Purge had taken place did the rump legalize the trial of Charles, who denied the legality of the proceedings, as well he might. A majority of Commons and all of Lords had been purged. The army council essentially dictated the death sentence to Charles, who died with dignity and courage. Soon, the royal martyr's last words were being hawked about England and the regicide revolutionaries began losing in popular esteem. But the left-wing Puritans justified the killing of the King with many a Biblical quotation. They had indeed bound their King in chains and their nobles (some) with links of iron.

The Protectorate

The revolutionary dilemma

The death of the King brought to a head the revolutionary dilemma. The makers of the revolution, though triumphant, could not reconstruct the kind of government they desired because they could not agree on what that was. With magnificent simplicity, Oliver Cromwell once summed it up when he remarked that he could say what he would *not* have better than what he *would* have. This is a common, almost inescapable dilemma of revolutionaries: having overthrown the old authority, a negative achievement, they face the formidable problem of erecting a new one, and that quickly. They are less likely to agree on this than they did in opposition. The chaos of opinions that a revolution is likely to unloose makes their task the more difficult. In this case, England broke out in a rash of sectarian religions. "A Bohemist, a Bidellian, a Digger, a Traskite, a Philadelphian, a Christadelphian, a Seventh Day Baptist. . . ."—so historians call the roll. There were Fifth Monarchy Men, Muggletonians, Seekers, Quakers, Shakers, several kinds of Baptists. The flock of small and sometimes strange sects were all jeered at as "ranters" by the respectable, but tremendously inspired by their fervent faith. There were those among them who believed in the world's coming to an end, preceded by the kingdom of Christ on earth, when all wealth would be shared equally. Gerrard Winstanley the Digger demanded agrarian communism. Others, in

The execution of Charles I at Whitehall on January 30, 1649

an intense state of ecstatic and millennial excitement, went in for all sorts of extravagances of behavior. This "swarming" of the sects closely resembles the Anabaptist phase of the German Reformation, and indeed many of them were the same or related ideas. There was no unity of thought on church or state.

Varieties of revolutionary opinion

Debates in the army produced an encounter between the democratic view that every man should have a vote, and the more conservative opinion that "no person hath a right to an interest or a share in the disposing of the affairs of this kingdom . . . that hath not a permanent fixed interest in this kingdom," that is, the vote should go with property ownership. The Leveller pamphleteers, Richard Overton and William Walwyn along with John Lilburne, supported not only a large measure of political democracy, but social legislation to aid the poorer classes, such as abolition of imprisonment for debt, free education, medical care, an end to land monopoly. The Fifth Monarchy men, significant for a time during the revolution, represented an English counterpart of the left-wing Anabaptists of the previous century in Germany: at the millennium, all brethren would be equal and private property would be abolished. Winstanley, whom modern Communists hail as a forerunner, asked why economic democracy, by which he meant confiscation and redistribution of land, should not implement political democracy. The Puritan Revolution produced many other theories of government, including those of John Milton, Thomas Hobbes, and James Harrington. These are all deeply significant, but they pointed in no one direction. While Milton justified the execution of King Charles the tyrant, and Harrington supported a balance of forces within society, Hobbes, the greatest of them all, believed that only by turning over complete power to a single sovereign could men curb their naturally antisocial instincts and live in peace. Hobbes called the right tune, in the short run, for the final upshot of the revolution was dictatorship.

The left never controlled this revolution, unlike the later French and Russian revolutions. Cromwell's center group struck down the Leveller and Millenarian left at the same time that it struck down the royalist right, and kept the revolution firmly in the hands of men of property.

Cromwell as dictator

Oliver Cromwell was a reluctant dictator, perhaps strictly speaking not a dictator at all. On December 16, 1653, he took an oath as Lord Protector of the Commonwealth of England, Scotland, and Ireland. The title did not formally imply a dictatorship. Cromwell and his advisers, among whom John Lambert was notable, had twice tried to erect a workable government on the basis of an elected Parliament, but felt that it was not then possible. The last Parliament had been dissolved, but Cromwell declared that it had resigned authority into his hands. Whatever it might be called, this was in effect one-man rule backed by the army. The truth is that the disturbed and divided state of England made this unpalatable solution almost necessary, unless the revolution were to be abandoned altogether and the royal authority

Oliver Cromwell, Lord Protector

restored. It is instructive to compare this revolutionary dilemma with rather similar situations in the French Revolution of 1789 and the Russian Revolution of 1917. (See the discussion of these events later in this book.) Nevertheless it was supreme irony to see Cromwell lecturing and dissolving Parliaments as the Stuart "despots" had once done. He also scolded judges and demanded that they follow his will, more crudely than Charles had ever done.

Cromwell's reign

The Protectorate of Cromwell proved a vigorous government during which English trade and naval power expanded; a naval war with sinking Spain yielded important possessions in the West Indies. Seeking perhaps to "busy giddy minds with foreign quarrels," Cromwell also took on the Dutch. He continued to summon Parliaments and as regularly dissolve them. The Anglican church was suppressed along with the Catholics, and there was an effort forcibly to impose Puritan morals on the country. Banning of the theater, censorship of the press, and rigorous enforcement of the Sabbath soon made Puritan rule unpopular. Cromwell ruled ably until his death in 1658, but after that the only feasible solution was a restoration of the monarchy.

The Restoration

Oliver named his son, Richard, to succeed him, but Richard was not of his father's stamp and soon resigned when faced with widespread opposition.

General Monk, a veteran lieutenant of Cromwell, assumed control, restored the Long Parliament, and entered into negotiations with Charles II, son of the executed king. And so it happened that early in 1660, to the acclaim of great crowds, another Charles came back to reclaim the throne of England, while Cromwell's bones were dug up and scattered to the winds.

Cromwell's reputation

Despite his failure, no English ruler did more to shape the future of his people than Oliver Cromwell. Poets praised him while he lived (see the odes of Milton, Marvell, Dryden) but when he died he had few friends, and in later times he was reviled as a tyrant. Today his reputation perhaps stands higher. As ruler of England, he showed moderation and moved toward religious toleration. Earlier, he had sown the seeds of long Irish hatred for the English when he slaughtered captured soldiers and Roman Catholic clergy in an orgy of bloody destruction, exterminating or dispossessing the local gentry and replacing them with new owners drawn from his army or other pro-Puritan capitalists. But ironically the same man who scourged Ireland in the name of the true church stands as the beginner of religious toleration in England. He treated the defeated royalists with some clemency, and honestly tried to find a political solution consistent with Parliamentary government. A deeply religious man, he helped put the Puritan stamp on the English common people, especially the middle classes—a stress on hard work, good conduct, discipline, piety—much though the immediate reaction was against it. He seems a tragic figure, caught in the toils of revolution. But when he died England was heartily sick of one-man rule and Puritan grimness.

When King Charles II came back he promised toleration to the Puritans and confirmation of estates seized during the revolution, along with amnesty to all. Though no formal Bill of Rights was signed as in 1688, he gave tacit agreement to respect the rights of Parliament and common law. The Restoration brought no reversion to the prerevolutionary state of things, despite Charles' inability to carry out all his promises. Regular Parliaments, an end to illegal taxation, abolition of the royal courts—such reins on absolutism proved permanent. It remained for the 1688 Glorious Revolution to make them certain.

France under Richelieu

France and England exhibit in this period a reversal of roles. While the Tudor strength gave way in England to the Stuart weakness, in France the era of Huguenot wars and uncertain kings was replaced in the 17th century by a powerful monarchy—the strongest state Europe had yet seen. Chief architect of this power, classic state-maker of the modern age, was one Armand Jean du Plessis, better known as Richelieu. He became a cardinal as well as a duke. He was in fact placed in the church because he was of noble blood, not because of any particular spiritual qualities, and he made politics his passion from the beginning. Weak physically, Richelieu possessed extraordinary energy and powers of concentration. His genius arrived on the scene at a crucial time. Henry IV, it will be recalled, had done much to restore the battered French monarchy, but had died the victim of an assassin's dagger in 1610 after not many years on the throne. His death threatened to throw France back into the melancholy civil strife of the previous period. The regency of Marie de' Medici, 1610–17, saw the nobles regain power and the central government diminish. Louis XIII, when he came of age (he was only 16), was not of commanding personality or brilliant mind.

Rise of Richelieu

Between 1617 and 1625, Richelieu, then bishop of Luçon, got himself established at the court and strove ambitiously for a position of power. He obtained it, not without the use of a talent for intrigue. But though Richelieu could always use the slipperiest of ways, he was commanded by a vision, an ideal. It was to serve France by strengthening the state, which meant the monarchy. To this simple goal he dedicated himself quite selflessly; it was a religion for which he would make any sacrifice and use almost any means. His obvious ability as much as his shrewd maneuvering gained him the coveted place as Louis XIII's first minister. This position he had attained by 1625; but he was not secure in it until 1630, having to fight against jealous enemies in an atmosphere of intrigue. He governed France until his death in 1642, having the unquestionable support of the King the last 10 years. This was not a long period, for a sickly man in a troubled world, and one must be amazed at the energy and ability of Richelieu in achieving what he did.

Methods of government

His goals were marked out with that clarity of intellect which the philosopher René Descartes, his contemporary, was also displaying. To make France the first power in Europe, the monarchy must be strengthened, the prestige of the state raised. The very concept of a "state"—one supreme, impersonal power binding on all its subjects—was a new one; Richelieu, it has seemed, invented it. The king exercised power in its name. Great nobles must be humbled, Huguenot separatists made to acknowledge the royal authority. In his *Political Testament* Richelieu expressed the belief that absolute monarchy was the only alternative to anarchy; it alone could represent the nation and serve the general interest. The methods by which the cardinal accomplished this goal followed Machiavelli's advice to make the king both feared and loved. Richelieu seemed to be Machiavelli's prince in action: calculating, ruthless, cruel, though clear-headed, wise, selfless. He struck off the heads of a few high nobles, executing a Montmorency on one famous occasion, and another noble simply for dueling, "in order to encourage the others." He smashed the independence of the Huguenots. By the Edict of Nantes they had been left in full possession of some fortified cities, of which La Rochelle was the chief, as well as of some seigneurial jurisdictions, but now they were made to acknowledge the royal authority, then extended religious toleration on condition that they not disturb the public peace. Better a few suffer, even unjustly, than that the safety of the state be endangered—this was Richelieu's motto.

Cardinal Richelieu

In his zeal to bolster central government Richelieu ran roughshod over legal obstacles, ignored the protests of the Parliaments (there were several in France), and greatly expanded the powers of the royal *intendants*, who served as agents of the king throughout France, at the expense of local liberties. The iron hand in the velvet glove—Richelieu combined force with diplomacy, dispensing favors as well as penalties to draw men to support of the king.

Richelieu's diplomacy

Richelieu's was the era of the Thirty Years War, further described in the next section. It was necessary for him to restore the military strength of France before he could take advantage of its opportunities. In the interim the cardinal developed an amazing diplomacy. There was no question about his goals: Richelieu continued the anti-Hapsburg policies of the Valois and Henry IV. France might be a Catholic state and Richelieu a cardinal of the church, but the interest of France dictated an alliance with the Protestant states against the dangerous power of Spain and Austria. He financed the Dutch, the Danes, and the Swedes, and by a diplomatic and spy network strove to neutralize other areas or win them as allies. He was a master of stratagem and finesse. At the same time, Richelieu with furious energy threw himself into war, supervising the famous siege of the Huguenot port of La Rochelle (when a wall built in the sea around the harbor forestalled an English fleet sent to relieve the city), rebuilding the French army and fleet. In the later stages of the Thirty Years War he intervened with maximum success for France, which came out of that long struggle as the top power.

Though he usually appears in history books wearing a grim if efficient guise, Richelieu did not confine his activities for the glory of king and France to the administrative and military. One of his outstanding creations was the French Academy, designed to raise the standard of French art, scholarship, and literature by granting prizes, honors, and subsidies. The system of official academies, extended by Louis XIV, imposed a considerable degree of state control over the arts and, incidentally, harnessed them to its service in a kind of "cultural diplomacy," whereby French art and letters worked for the greater glory of the monarchy. But it also furthered the arts and sciences.

One defect of all this was financial. Richelieu poured out money recklessly in these enterprises, which did not come cheap. New taxes falling on the peasantry sometimes caused violent uprisings which were suppressed with ruthless efficiency. The fact is that Richelieu had gotten the nobility largely on his side, by a combination of bribery and terrorization. They became the officers of the new national army, the diplomats and administrators of the new state machine. He could afford to ignore the peasants. But the result was a financial system in which may be seen the seeds of the ruin of the French monarchy at a later date.

The Fronde

After the death of Richelieu his policies were carried on ably by his disciple Mazarin, who however inspired less fear and became cordially hated. The minority of Louis XIV coincided with a last outburst of noble-led revolt against the royal authority in 1648–53, an episode known as the Fronde. But Louis XIV restored order and continued to build a mighty structure on the foundations so well laid by the cardinal who was always "for the King."

The Thirty Years War

Causes of the war

The Thirty Years War of 1618–48 began as a German war, between Catholic and Protestant states of the Empire, but spread to become a general European war in which virtually everybody became involved. Its issues in the wider sense were the familiar ones of balance of power and conflicting national ambitions between the greatest states. The Hapsburg coalition, the Madrid–Vienna axis, if one likes, was the strongest power in Europe in 1618, and other powers, fearing its victory in the German struggle, then intervened to keep the Hapsburgs in check. Like the previous wars, it is not quite correct to speak of it as "religious." The issues were nominally such, but actually were matters of power. The alliance against the Hapsburgs included Catholic France as well as Protestant Denmark, Sweden, United Provinces, and German Lutherans. The balance of power pushed Lutheran Saxony into the Hapsburg camp and devoutly Catholic Bavaria at one time into the other side.

In the Empire the uneasy truce between Lutheran and Catholic states had long threatened periodically to produce war. While Protestants were divided between Lutherans (themselves subject to many angry controversies following the death of Luther, though gradually they settled these) and Calvinists (the Reformed, who spread into Germany from 1559 on), they continued to make gains; while on the other hand the Counter-Reformation revived the Catholic morale and began to recover ground for Rome. The Peace of Augsburg had expected to freeze the *status quo*, but the dynamic forces of religion would not yet submit to this process. Consequently the terms of the peace were freely violated. Both sides had an incentive to gain control of the Electoral College and the Imperial Diet. Complex questions arose over the terms of the Augsburg agreement, and the two sides quarreled bitterly over them. The old machinery of the Empire broke down. Under such circumstances it seems vain to ask who was the aggressor; while the Protestants clearly violated Augsburg in many instances, the fact is that Catholicism was showing the most strength toward the end of the century, for the Protestants as usual squabbled among themselves while the Jesuit-led Counter-Reformation grew in power and regained area after area. A Protestant Union of most of the Lutheran and Reformed princes and cities took shape in 1608, to rally the Protestant forces; the reply was a Catholic League, led by Bavaria. Thus it seemed that civil war was almost inevitable sooner or later.

The Bohemian revolt

It finally came when Ferdinand II succeeded to the emperorship, a strongly Catholic prince whose arrival coincided with a revolt in Prague, Bohemia, against policies aimed at the Bohemian Protestants. The Hapsburgs had been pursuing bold policies in both Hungary and Bohemia. The Bohemians offered the throne of their kingdom to the Calvinist Elector of the Palatinate (southwest Germany), who accepted but was soon badly defeated by the imperial forces, the Lutheran Protestant princes giving him little help. Not only was Bohemia severely punished after the defeat of Frederick the Count Palatine at the Battle of White Mountain (1620), but his own lands were taken from him. This upset the balance of power in the Imperial Diet and everybody tended to break loose from that body, with anarchy breaking out in the Empire. The Emperor, with the aid of Spain, then undertook to exterminate Protestantism in the Empire.

At the same time, Spain renewed her efforts, after a long truce, to subdue and regain the Dutch provinces. With France suffering from the difficulties of 1610–24 and England from the feud of King and Parliament, there was

Count Wallenstein and at right King Gustavus Adolphus of Sweden, military heroes of the Thirty Years War. Paintings by Van Dyck.

little to stop the powerful Hapsburgs, it appeared. Their goal was regarded as nothing less than the conquest and re-Catholicization of all Europe, and perhaps they did entertain such dreams. They did in any case win numerous victories in the first part of the war, under the Spanish general, Tilly, a native of the Spanish Netherlands, and the imperial commander Wallenstein, a Bohemian.

Hapsburg successes

Denmark and then Sweden were drawn into the war by the threat to the north German-Baltic area. But Christian of Denmark was smashed by the redoutable Tilly and Wallenstein (at Lutter, near Brunswick). The Edict of Restitution, 1629, came at the height of Hapsburg success and decreed a general restoration of all property taken from the church since 1552, as per the often violated "ecclesiastical reservation" of the Peace of Augsburg. It involved large quantities of property and was an evident effort to begin the destruction of Protestantism throughout the Empire.

Swedish intervention

The hard-pressed Protestants found a champion at last in Gustavus Adolphus of Sweden, the greatest soldier the war produced, and a great king of his country. Sweden had been rising fast under its able line of Vasa kings, and aspired to control the Baltic, an ambition which placed it squarely in opposition to Hapsburg plans for northern Germany. The Swedes entered the war in 1630 and racked up a series of victories in the next three years before Gustavus was killed, in the battle in which he defeated Wallenstein, at Lützen near Leipzig in 1632. The fast-firing Swedish musketeers and artillery revolutionized military tactics. Without Gustavus the Swedes eventually met defeat, but with the aid of France continued to exert a decisive influence on

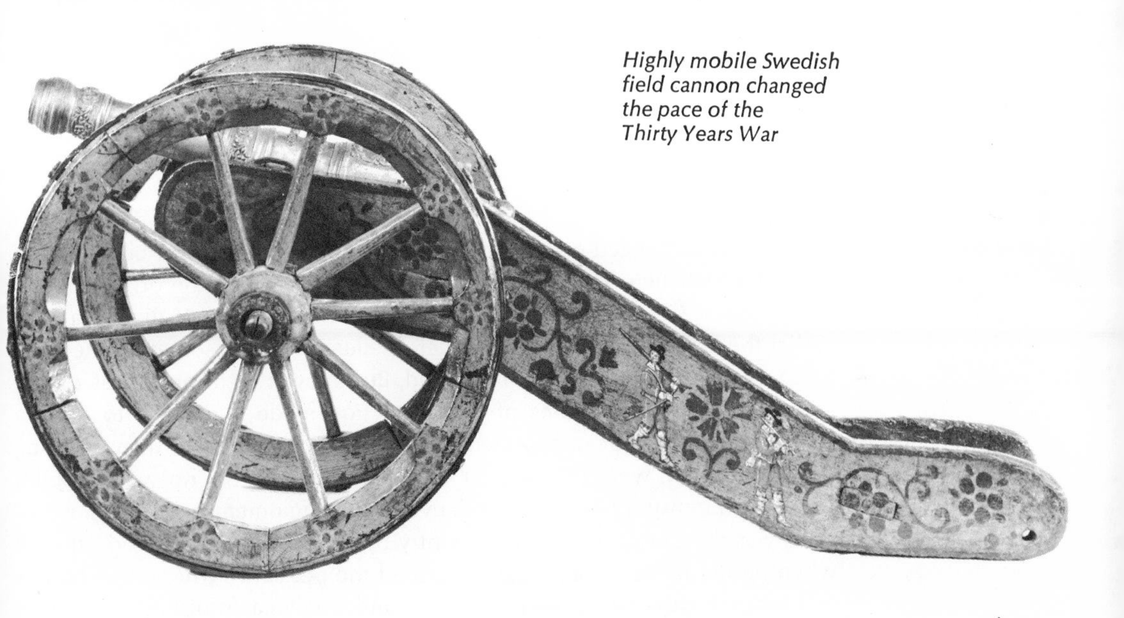

Highly mobile Swedish field cannon changed the pace of the Thirty Years War

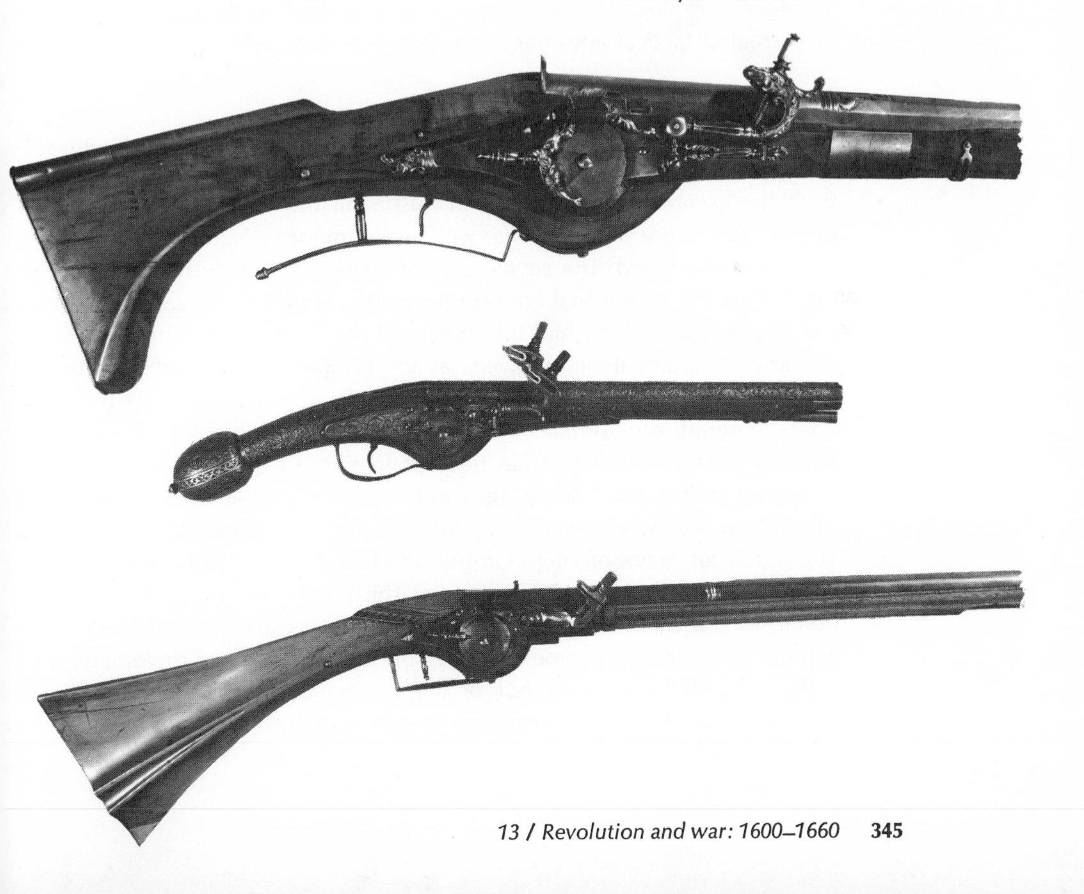

Wheel lock small arms of the Thirty Years War period from the armory of Louis XIII

the course of events. In the last years of the war they were again winning victories under their commander, Torstensson, while the French under Marshal Turenne and the Prince of Condé invaded southern Germany, and the Hungarians under their leader Rakoczi assailed the Hapsburgs from the other side.

Ravages of the war

As the war dragged on, it became more and more a contest between the masterful Richelieu and the Spanish-Austrian power, with the original issues of the war in Germany rather forgotten. Ferdinand died in 1636, and a little earlier the fabulous professional soldier, Wallenstein, who sometimes seemed to be a power in himself, was murdered. But the war went on. It was a slow war because the conditions of military action made it difficult to force a battle, and the major engagements, while on a bigger scale than anything heretofore seen, were few and far between. Armies were not very mobile; supply and transport were weak relative to the equipment being used. Notorious was the devastation of the country by the soldiers, who lived off of it when on the move. Cruel tragedy pursued the peasantry when these hordes of human locusts descended. Germany and Bohemia furnished the battleground for almost the entire war. In the last stages of the war particularly, the ravages were frightful, especially in southern Germany and Moravia; Italy also suffered. This is sometimes blamed on the habit of using professional soldiers, under hireling *condottieri* like Wallenstein; but the worst damages were done by the national armies of the Swedes and the French as they created tactical advantage out of pillage and sack.

The Peace of Westphalia, 1648

Organization of the state system

The protracted peace conferences which brought the war to an end brought about the first international organization of Europe's state system. With the exception of England and Russia, all the major European powers present and future were there, as well as the minor ones. Procedure, "protocol," was developed. The sovereignty of states was clearly recognized. This meant that the impersonal conception of "the state" as a legal entity above and beyond individuals had fully replaced the feudal and dynastic concept of *individuals* and their followers, as the fundamental fact of government and politics. It meant that these states, considered to have definite territorial limits, entered into formal relations with each other on the basis of legal equality. It is a system that has become familiar to the modern world, but it did not exist in the Middle Ages and had only gradually been shaping up since then. It now received clear-cut recognition and careful organization. The significant work of Hugo Grotius, the Dutch philosopher and jurist (*De Jure Belli et Pacis*), appeared during the Thirty Years War: a form of international law based on state sovereignty but seeking avenues to cooperation among these units. In some measure, the development of diplomatic procedures could bring order out of the international chaos which afflicted Europe in the Thirty Years War, though wars did not cease.

Results of the war

In separate proceedings at Osnabrück and Münster (both in the province of Westphalia) which finally resulted in three treaties, the various tangled issues of the war got sorted out. The results, briefly stated, were to confirm the sovereignty of the individual German states, and the impotence of the Emperor *qua* Emperor, which meant of course the disunity of Germany, the triumph of localism or "particularism"; to confirm and recognize the independence of the Dutch Republic from Spain; and to reward the real victors of the war, Sweden and France. The Swedes gained valuable Baltic territory in north Germany (Pomerania, Bremen), while France received strategically valuable areas on her eastern borders (Metz, Verdun, Toul, Alsace). Sweden, after a meteoric career as king of the North, was to prove unable to hold her great-power position in the century after Westphalia, but France mounted to the top of the European ladder and stayed there. The Dutch came out very well, seizing the Spice Islands and other colonial areas from Spain and Portugal, and blossomed for a time as the leading maritime and commercial power of Europe. Spain could now be seen in decline. Her war with France went on another decade before the Treaty of the Pyrenees (1659) gave France control of strategic points on the frontier.

Hugo Grotius, author of the first important textbook of modern international law.

Effects of the war on Germany

The Hapsburgs fell back in both Spain and the Empire, while their foes, from petty German princes up to France and the Netherlands, gained their objectives. Never again would either Madrid or Vienna, or the combination, threaten to be "overmighty" in Europe. The fear now would be of France. Classically, the Thirty Years War is known for its disastrous effects on Germany. While the Protestants, including now Calvinists as well as Lutherans, maintained their right to exist, the accompanying victory of territorialism insured the division of Germany into petty states for two centuries. And the terrible devastation of the war fell on Germany.

The tendency of Germany to succumb to forces of local rather than central government had been established long before this: we should recall this from medieval history, when the emperors had failed to make the beginnings of a national state that were being made in France and England as early as the 12th century. The Reformation and the Thirty Years War did not, then, cause this trend; they may indeed be seen as results of it. The causes were as much geographic as traditional. But at this time the trend became disastrous. Previously, *Kleinstaaterei* (the little-state system) had not been inconsistent with wealth, culture, and at least some power. Now, with Richelieu and Louis XIV shaping a mighty French state on their borders, the Germans would find it fatal to be divided.

Whether the Thirty Years War caused the economic decay of Germany or whether it only hastened deeper-laid causes has been the subject of a long debate; recent careful inquiries based on considerable data seem to support the view that for much of Germany, subject to local exceptions, the war itself was indeed the prime destructive agent. Before 1618 most of Germany was prosperous. Had she kept pace with developments in the other major areas, there seems no reason why this should not have continued. The shocking destructiveness of the war in numerous regions led on to the miserable rule of petty despotism that afflicted the German world after 1648. Something more than a hundred small units each had to have its court and army and bureaucracy, its customs and regulations of trade. Moreover the French and Swedes reserved a treaty right to intervene in German affairs, and quickly reduced many of the small states to the status of their clients and servants. Within another generation, the wars of Louis XIV again brought grief to western Germany. Not for two centuries could Germany get back on the road to unity, and then she was forced to do it in the wrong way. The whole experience constituted a disaster almost without parallel in the modern world, creating the "German problem" for which our own time has paid dearly.

Aftermath

From this appalling cycle of war and revolution some of Europe seemed to recover rapidly after 1648. The Dutch, their independence secure, launched upon a veritable golden age, and France embarked upon its most glorious era, that of the "Sun King" Louis XIV. England quickly rebounded from a civil war that had done relatively little physical damage. If most of Germany sank into despair, there were islands of progress even there; the phenomenal rise of Brandenburg-Prussia, the future kingdom of Prussia, began at this time. (See map on facing page.)

Holland's golden age

For the Dutch, it was not merely the age of their maritime glory, in which they acquired the prize of the East Indies, discovered Australia and New Zealand, became the only European traders in Japan, and settled New Amsterdam in North America—but also the age of Rembrandt and the other masters of painting, of Grotius, the famous philosopher Spinoza, and the scholars of Leyden University. Amsterdam not only became the financial capital of Europe—which it clearly was in the middle of the 17th century—but had strong claims to be considered the intellectual capital. The Dutch were able at this time to hold their own in several naval wars with England; indeed, on one glorious occasion they took on France and England together (1672–78) and gained a draw. In the long run the small republic could not quite stand up to the competition of its two powerful rivals and neighbors.

The Dutch were attached to their provincial rights and suspicious of a strong central government. The House of Orange customarily held the position of statthalter but often ran into stout opposition from the States-General. That the Dutch succeeded so well with a large measure of political liberty, decentralized government, and religious toleration impressed itself deeply upon Europe in the years after mid-century. According to the English champion of religious toleration, Henry Robinson, when men were asked in what country they would prefer to live, they answered "in their own or in Holland." From Spinoza's pen came a powerful argument for the liberty of the rational mind. William of Orange, who became William III of England in 1688, was the European leader who rallied opposition to the French threat to Europe (see Chapter 14).

The Swiss Confederation

Another of Europe's "sturdy midgets" was Switzerland. The Treaty of Westphalia recognized the formal independence of the Swiss Confederation from the Empire. Between Italy, France, and Germany lay this unique political entity, which had expanded slowly since its origins in 1291, until by 1513 it included, counting subject and allied districts, substantially what is present-day Switzerland. Switzerland, which had contributed so much to the Reformation, also played a significant part in the Thirty Years War, when the mountain passes connecting north Italy with Austria became an important strategic area. The Swiss Confederation as such was officially neutral, but Swiss groups backed by Spanish and French contended for control of the passes. The Swiss had long been the best soldiers of Europe, their services at a premium in the hiring of mercenary troops. (Many a wealthy burgher of Berne today can trace the family fortune back to such *condottieri*.) If Switzerland became the classic European neutral, it was largely because of internal disunity. While the Catholic–Protestant division was outstanding, there also was a French-speaking versus German-speaking cleavage, and a diversity of environment between alpine, rural, and urban communities. Always, the mountainous character of their beautiful land made the Swiss locally independent. This absence of a national spirit and a national government (the Confederation was only a loose league of provinces or cantons) took its toll during the 18th century: the Swiss do not seem to have been as prosperous or happy as they later became in their neutrality. But here in the cantons of Switzerland, protected by fate and the mountains from becoming a "great power" afflicted with statism and war, people practiced real grass-roots democracy, and kept alive its values while most of Europe went the other way.

End of an era

The changes which came over much of Europe in basic ways of thinking in the 17th century were so important that they must be dealt with in a separate chapter. The year 1648 conventionally marks the end of an entire epoch and the beginning of another. It is the end of the Reformation era, in the sense that new interests became predominant over religion, religious toleration was accepted, and a different conception of the state developed. It is the beginning of the modern scientific era, in which respect it breaks with some traditions of thought that went far back into the earliest times.

The state

The 17th century's weightiest political contribution was the territorial state. Richelieu may well have been the man of the century. While England kept her ancient Parliament and constitution, this came to be a rarity: a century later a prominent English statesman made the remark that there was only one other such constitution remaining in Europe, that of the small German state Württemberg. Though this was not quite true, on the Continent absolutism's triumph was well nigh complete, and so was its identification with the strong state. This state now disposed of power which, though slight by comparison with modern ones, was infinitely greater than anything known in medieval times. It commanded its own force and no longer leaned on the services of feudal warriors: this is the pattern of the mature states, led by France, and is the model which other aspiring ones copy. One of the sometimes overlooked "revolution" of the century was a military one: it may be seen emerging during the Thirty Years War, and included the development of permanent standing armies. The first regular national navies also date from this century.

The powerful state may sometimes have been the enemy of liberty, but it made possible a large number of substantial achievements: among them overseas expansion, economic growth, large-scale scientific research, and technological improvements. At a time when private capital was still scarce and private enterprise small in size of operations, only the state could promote such projects as planting colonies, building roads, and draining swamps, to name but a few examples. Thus once more we may say that a terrible war proved constructive as well as destructive. At any rate there is no doubt but that Europe entered a new era after it was over.

France's predominance

In terms of national influence, it was to be the age of France. Spain, invincible during the 16th century, faded rapidly during the 17th; the victory of French troops over Spanish at the battle of Rocroi in 1643 symbolized a transfer of supremacy which the Peace of Westphalia and the Treaty of the Pyrenees ratified, and by the end of the century vultures were fighting over the Spanish Empire in Europe. With England still weakened by internal strife, and the Austrian Hapsburgs by the victory of particularism in Germany as well as by a resurgence of the Ottoman Turks (see Chapter 15), the way was clear for France. The most populous of the countries of Europe, France now had a strong government, a powerful and ably led army, and a cultural supremacy which the decay of the Italian cities and of the Roman papacy assisted in bringing about. Under Louis XIV she was to advance rapidly to the first position in Europe and then threaten to overwhelm the entire continent.

Bibliography

Generally valuable for the first half of the 17th century are *New Cambridge Modern History*, Vol. VI; Carl J. Friedrich's volume, *The Age of the Baroque*, in the Rise of Modern Europe series (Harper Torchbook); *Oxford History of England*, Vol. IX, by Godfrey Davies; David Ogg, *Europe in the Seventeenth Century* (Macmillan, Collier); Sir George N. Clark, *The Seventeenth Century* (Oxford University Press), and also his *War and Society in the Seventeenth Century* (New York: Cambridge University Press, 1958). G.P.V. Akrigg, *Jacobean Pageant* (London: Hamish Hamilton, 1962), is a vivid portrait. Another good recent publication is Christopher Hill, *A Century of Revolution, 1603–1714* (W.W. Norton).

The English—and some Americans too—have naturally written much about their great revolution and civil war. Biographically, there is David H. Wilson, *King James VI and I* (New York: Holt, Rinehart & Winston, 1956); E.C. Wingfield-Stratford, *Charles, King of England*, *King Charles and King Pym*, and *King Charles the Martyr* (London: Hollis & Carter, 1949–50); Catherine D. Bowen, *The Lion and the Throne: Life and Times of Sir Edward Coke* (Hamish Hamilton, 1957); C.V. Wedgewood, *Strafford* (rev. ed.; London: Jonathan Cape, 1961); J.H. Hexter, *The Reign of King Pym* (Cambridge, Mass.: Harvard University Press, 1941); and H.R. Trevor-Roper, *Archbishop Laud* (2d ed.; New York: Macmillan, 1962). Further light is shed on the coming of the revolution by William Haller, *The Rise of Puritanism* (Harper Torchbook), and Valerie Pearl, *London and the Outbreak of the Puritan Revolution* (New York: Oxford University Press, 1961), as well as David Mathew, *Social Structure in Caroline England* (Oxford: Clarendon Press, 1948), and G.E. Aylmer, *The King's Servants: The Civil Service of Charles I* (New York: Columbia University Press, 1961). Lawrence Stone has apparently said almost the last word on the famous gentry controversy in his impressive *The Crisis of the Aristocracy 1558–1641* (Oxford University Press). John H.F. New, *Anglican and Puritan: The Basis of Their Opposition 1558–1640* (Stanford, Calif.: Stanford University Press, 1965), stresses the importance of theological views in the civil quarrel. Miss Wedgwood has handled the immediate background as well as the civil war in two masterful volumes, *The King's Peace 1637–1641* (1955) and *The King's War 1641–1647* (1958), both published in London by Collins. She has continued her series on the civil war period in *A Coffin for King Charles* (Macmillan, 1964). Cromwell has of course found innumerable biographers, among them, John Buchan's very readable *Oliver Cromwell* (Boston: Houghton Mifflin, 1934), Maurice Ashley, *The Greatness of Oliver Cromwell* (London: Hodder & Stoughton, 1957), and C.H. Firth, *Oliver Cromwell and the Rule of the Puritans*, an older classic reprinted in 1953 (Oxford University Press). Another illuminating study of the Puritans is Leo Solt, *Saints in Arms: Politics and Puritans in Cromwell's Army* (Stanford University Press, 1959). Perhaps the most illuminating discussion of the Levellers is in C.B. Macpherson, *The Political Theory of Possessive Individualism* (Oxford University Press, 1962). Austin Woolrych has examined the *Battles of the English Civil War* (London: Batsford, 1961). An excellent and inexpensive summary of the whole process is provided by G.E. Aylmer in a New American Library Mentor paperback, *Short History of Seventeenth Century England.*

Equally important continental events are less well covered in English. The versatile C.V. Wedgwood has also written the best study of *The Thirty Years War*, available in Doubleday Anchor paperback; *Gustavus Adolphus* has found a keen student in Michael Roberts (2 vols.; London: Longmans, Green & Co., 1953–58), a work which considers the whole of the great Swede's surroundings. P. Geyl continues the Netherlands story with his scholarly *The Netherlands in the Seventeenth Century 1609–1648* (New York: Barnes & Noble, 1961).

Sources. J. R Tanner (ed.), *British Constitutional Documents 1603–1625* (Cambridge University Press); S.R. Gardiner (ed.), *Constitutional Documents of the Puritan Revolution 1625–1660* (rev. ed.; Oxford University Press, 1951); J.P. Kenyon (ed.), *The Stuart Constitution 1603–1688; Documents and Commentary* (Cambridge University Press, 1966); William Haller (ed.), *Tracts on Liberty in the Puritan Revolution* (3d ed.; Columbia University Press, 1934); and *The Leveller Tracts* (New York: Peter Smith, 1964).

Louis XIV of France, "The Sun King." Sculpture by Bernini.

14

The age of Louis XIV

chronology

1660
Beginning of Louis XIV's personal reign.
Restoration of Charles II, England.
1662
Colbert, finance minister of Louis XIV.
Act of Uniformity, exclusion of English Nonconformists from the churches, schools, and government.
1665
Death of Philip IV of Spain.
Great Plague in London. Great London fire, 1666.
English-Dutch naval war, 1665–67.
1665–1700
Reign of Charles II in Spain.
1667–68
War of Devolution, France and Spanish Netherlands.
1670
Treaty of Dover between England and France.
1672–78
Dutch War; Netherlands, Spain, and Empire versus France and (until 1674) England.
1673
Test Act excludes Catholics from office.
1678
"Popish plot" hysteria, England.
1680
Chambers of Reunion, instrument of French aggrandizement.
1682
"Gallican Liberties" of French church proclaimed by Louis XIV. Papal protest.
1683
Rye House Plot, England. Whigs back Exclusion Act.
1685
Revocation of Edict of Nantes by Louis XIV.
Accession of James II. Monmouth Rebellion.
1688
Glorious Revolution; William and Mary replace James II.
1689
Bill of Rights, Toleration Act.
1689–97
War of League of Augsburg; Grand Alliance against France.
1690
Battle of the Boyne, in Ireland.
1694
Censorship of press ended in England; Triennial Act.
Charter of Bank of England.
Death of Mary; William III sole ruler of England.
1697
Treaty of Ryswick, ending War of League of Augsburg.
1700
Death of Charles II of Spain.
1701
Act of Settlement passed by Parliament.
1702–14
Reign of Queen Anne.
1702–13
War of the Spanish Succession.
1704
Battle of Blenheim.
Suppression of Port-Royal, center of Jansenism, by Louis XIV.
1706
Battle of Ramillies.
1707
Act of Union between Scotland and England.
1709
Battle of Malplaquet.
1713
End of War of Spanish Succession, Treaty of Utrecht.
1714
George I, first Hanoverian on England's throne.
1715
Death of Louis XIV.
Failure of Jacobite rebellion in Britain.

An age of power; The Grand Monarchy of Louis XIV

The last years of the 17th century were crucial ones for western Europe. England moved through the reign of the restored Charles II (1660–85) to James II and another revolution, the "Glorious" one of 1688, following which she developed a political system unique in Europe, one destined to have a profound effect throughout the Continent. France, having attained the pinnacle of power and glory, had to engage in a series of fierce wars with practically all the other states—a new struggle for the balance of power, with France now as the principle threat and "aggressor." The shifting fortunes of nations, which sent Spain tumbling down from the top, raised up others; the chief of them in this period, perhaps, was the north German state of Prussia. But it is also a time in which Russia emerges from the dim condition of virtual nonnationhood to become a great power and one with a European orientation. There were enough other changes to make this an exciting period for the study of European politics both internal and international.

It has been described as an "age of power." Better organized and fully "sovereign," the states especially of western Europe became more formidable. Battles were fought on a grander scale than anything hitherto seen. If the ability to kill some 30,000 men in one day, as was accomplished at Malplaquet in 1709, might be considered a questionable victory for civilization, it at least indicated that states possessed substantial powers of organization, finance, as well as national morale, hitherto unknown. The states and the national cultures of Europe were beginning to mature.

Power was not always oriented solely toward destruction. It is evident in the energy with which Louis XIV built a whole new city at Versailles, and Peter the Great at St. Petersburg; in the draining of swamps and the building of canals, so typical of this age, from England to Russia. It is evident also in the outburst of colonial and mercantile activity, for this is the era of the great overseas empires of France and Britain in the New World. Others who could not quite carry out this task, such as the Great Elector of Brandenburg-Prussia, dreamed of it; little Holland and Sweden made the effort but ultimately failed in the New World, the Dutch however performing fabulous feats in the East Indies. The administration of government became regularized in a trained permanent bureaucracy of civil servants.

The two leaders were France and England, and they form a dramatic contrast. For France, the age of the Grand Monarch, Louis XIV, the Sun King, brought great power and glory, magnificent cultural achievements and immense prestige, under the shield and symbol of royal absolutism. For England, the Glorious Revolution of 1688 turned out to be the foundation on which was built a structure of ordered liberty under the supremacy of Parliament, a source of enormous strength to the island kingdom, which checked and defeated Louis XIV at the end of his reign to usher in an era of British ascendancy. England laid up her treasure for the future in a series of events which thrust her away from absolutism forever; but the years 1660 to 1700 belonged indisputably to France.

France without rivals

The dominant position of France resulted in part from the weakness of others. Early in his reign (1661) Louis wrote himself a memorandum in which he noted with complacency the comforting fact that every other power of Europe seemed to be in serious trouble. In particular both Spain and the Empire, erstwhile greats, were in decline. The fall of the former from world power to an impoverished second-rate nation in a few decades has few parallels in history for sudden eclipse; while the Vienna Hapsburgs, shattered by the Thirty Years War and facing a revived Turkish power in the ensuing years, presented no threat for some time, though they eventually made a comeback. It will be recalled that the French army came out of the Thirty Years War the best in Europe, matched only by the Swedes, whose role as a world power was to prove ephemeral because of their small population and limited resources. The Swedes in any event were kept busy in struggles for the Baltic with Poland, Denmark, and especially Russia until their defeat at the hands of Peter the Great, 1709–21. With England still weak during the reign of Charles II, Louis hardly had to fear any check on France's power except from the small Dutch state—with which he waged almost constant war.

If the misfortune of others has to be accounted a prime reason for the mightiness of France, there were other, positive causes in her own internal development. The French state led the others in centralization, organization, and hence power. Her population was then the greatest in Europe, for the fertile French soil supported more people than any other European nation; to this large and homogeneous population had been added a military and administrative system which concentrated more money, men, and power in the hands of the central government than was true of any other large unit in Europe. Richelieu had laid the foundations; Louis XIV, an able, hard-working, and power-conscious king, built up the structure of strength during what was the longest reign in the history of Europe until Queen Victoria and Emperor Franz Joseph surpassed it in the 19th century.

The elaborate ceremony which surrounded the monarch, the "cult of majesty," would seem foolish to a later generation. But it was a part of the system by which men were turning to the national state and its symbols. It helped, too, in the task Louis carried out so successfully: the converting of a formerly unruly nobility into courtiers who fawned on the king. As such, they were at least not a danger to the peace. They became servants of the crown. It was a prime factor in the new equation of state power.

"L'Etat c'est moi." The alleged remark of Louis XIV was symbolically true, but by no means actually. The state was now much bigger than an individual. It included a large bureaucracy of professional soldiers, administrators, diplomats. A ministerial system was necessary to supervise it. The King was by no means an unchecked despot. "Absolutism" might be mentioned, and the King now said to be a regent of God ruling by "divine right." But there was a strong spirit of law abroad. In France no less than in England there existed the concept of a "natural law," which limited the actions of the sovereign to what was reasonable; and even apologists for absolutism declared the King

Marriage of Louis XIV. Tapestry by Gobelins, designed by Charles LeBrun.

to be no capricious despot. The classical ideal so potent in this era found symmetry, harmony, and law pleasing, not caprice and tyranny, and Louis posed as the natural apex of the national pyramid, not a remote and awesome tyrant.

And there remained within France, especially in the outlying provinces, many ancient local rights which the King hardly dared interfere with. He had no great system of police, but relied on his prestige and a relatively small number of his agents, the *intendants*. Nevertheless, the power of the state was increasingly felt.

Colbert's mercantilism

Three things may be taken as representative of that power in the reign of the Sun King. One was the system of mercantilist economic administration developed by Colbert, Louis' great minister, which covered a good part of France with a rational system designed to regulate and develop France's economy. This was also the time of the expansion of the great French mercantile empire of the St. Lawrence and the Mississippi in North America. "Mercantilism" is a term we have met before; the 17th and early 18th centuries marked its zenith in Europe, with Colbert's model the prize one. Mercantilism meant state regulation and supervision in a variety of ways, from the inspection of goods to the granting of concessions to work the mines; it also meant direct state activity in the economic arena, as for instance by building roads, bridges, and canals. The goal was the enlightened one of aiding industrial development, though the economists of a century later criticized the means. Mercantilism also, unhappily, meant protectionism, as statesmen pursued the fetish of a favorable balance of trade, especially in manufactured goods, and tried to keep from trading with rival nations, instead building up self-sufficient empires. Mercantilism was related to the ideal of unity and symmetry: society was conceived as a single organism of which the state formed the head. Not yet could society be thought of as a collection of atoms; the age of laissez-faire had not quite come. But mercantilism did not, of course, destroy private enterprise; regulatory and paternalistic, it was far from "socialist." (On mercantilism, see further pp. 403–4).

Gallicanism

Another sign of the monarchy's power was the Gallican church, i.e., French national control of the church at the expense of the papacy. Gallicanism was related to the old conciliarist position, always a favorite of the French monarchs: a general council of the church was said to be above the pope. The argument was then extended to declare that a council of the French bishops should have power over the French church. Bishop Bossuet, Louis' apologist, raised such extreme claims for French control of the church that all elements of papal power would have been eliminated: not only appointment of the clergy and control of the church, but even determination of doctrinal questions should reside within France, its king and its bishops. The Gallican church resembled the Anglican in freedom from Rome. A compromise with the pope was finally worked out which saved the appearance of attachment to Rome; but in practice the pope was allowed very little right of interference. "Ultramontanism"—"beyond the mountains," referring to the pope beyond the Alps in Rome as the ultimate authority in the church—became suspect.

Louis was not interested in theological subtleties; he did wish to preserve the unity of his French society. He showed himself hostile to the Jansenists, a formidable faction within the church, who adopted an almost Protestant (Augustinian) view of the role of divine grace and entered into bitter controversy with the Jesuits. But he showed an equal disinclination to let Rome decide these matters. Louis was genuinely pious, and his court respected the forms and rituals of religion; except in the most clandestine manner, no attacks on religious orthodoxy, such as appeared in the next century, were permitted. It was, however, more a nationalist than a purely Christian orthodoxy.

Revocation of Edict of Nantes

Finally, there was the revoking of the Edict of Nantes in 1685. The Edict of Nantes had allowed the French Protestants, called Huguenots, to practice their own religion and to live in peace as citizens of France. When Louis XIV demanded their conversion to Catholicism and revoked the Edict of Nantes, he faced the emigration of a valuable group of artisans and tradesmen. The act considerably shocked Europe, especially Protestant Europe, and went contrary to the age's trend toward religious tolerance. Thousands of useful citizens left the country, to France's loss, and the action did not escape criticism by leading French writers. (See Moliére's *Tartuffe*.) Yet it seems to have been generally supported by public opinion. Its motivation was by no means religious, but primarily national. The Pope did not initiate the action, nor privately approve of it; one of Louis' motives seems to have been to be more Catholic than the Pope, to make a display of orthodoxy that would shame the Pope and redound to his own glory. The unity of France, a perfection in which the classical idea of perfect symmetry and order was involved, required the elimination of alien elements such as the Huguenots were alleged to be. Similarly motivated was the eventual suppression of the Port-Royal convent where Jansenism had flourished. Few cared much about the theological issues, but the unseemly quarrel marred the perfect unity of Frenchmen, so highly treasured. It must be added, however, that neither Protestantism nor Jansenism was fully destroyed in France by this repression.

Cultural glories

The chief glories of the Age of Louis XIV were cultural. French art and letters blossomed in a grand Gallic renaissance and all Europe did France the honor of imitating a dazzling civilization that seemed to center on the Sun King's court. The chief motif of this art was a "neoclassical" one. Harmony, order, and unity were its watchwords. The dynamic stresses and violent disequilibriums of the earlier baroque became abhorrent. Drama and poetry were purged of all that was wild, boisterous, disorderly, and required to obey the rules. This stress on decorum, strict discipline, and the removal of all loose or rough ends was the unique hallmark of this movement, which permeated not only literature and the arts, but all of life. Buildings, gardens, furniture, music, each revealed it in their balanced proportions, their stately symmetry. The court musician of Louis XIV was Lulli, a low-born Italian, whose music is heavily, even theatrically classical in exactly the spirit of the age. The blending of baroque and neoclassical achieves its full triumph in the music of the Saxon immortal, J.S. Bach, in the earlier 18th century. Elegance and good manners, with heavy stress on ceremony and dignity, were introduced to much of Europe through the court of Louis XIV. It is possible to see remnants of the baroque in a tendency toward the massive and big. Those gentlemen in powdered wigs and knee pants, dancing the minuet with sophisticated, lovely, and completely artificial ladies; the delicately tinted, fragile, exquisite scenes of Watteau, Boucher and Fragonard—these were signs of the spirit which only began to assume command of Europe at the end of the 17th century. The authentic Louis XIV style is heavier, tending toward the grandiose while determinedly symmetrical; the 18th century brought a more delicate touch. Yet to Voltaire, greatest of 18th-century writers, the age of Louis XIV was the great age, perhaps never again to be equaled.

The elegance as well as the magnificence of Louis' establishment at Versailles bowled over Europe. It was the quality which has made Paris the world's fashion center ever since—good taste, refinement, chic-ness. French

"Ceres" by Antoine Watteau, the fashionable French painter.

Versailles in 1668, the vast palace and famous gardens created by Louis XIV to house his court in appropriate pomp and splendor.

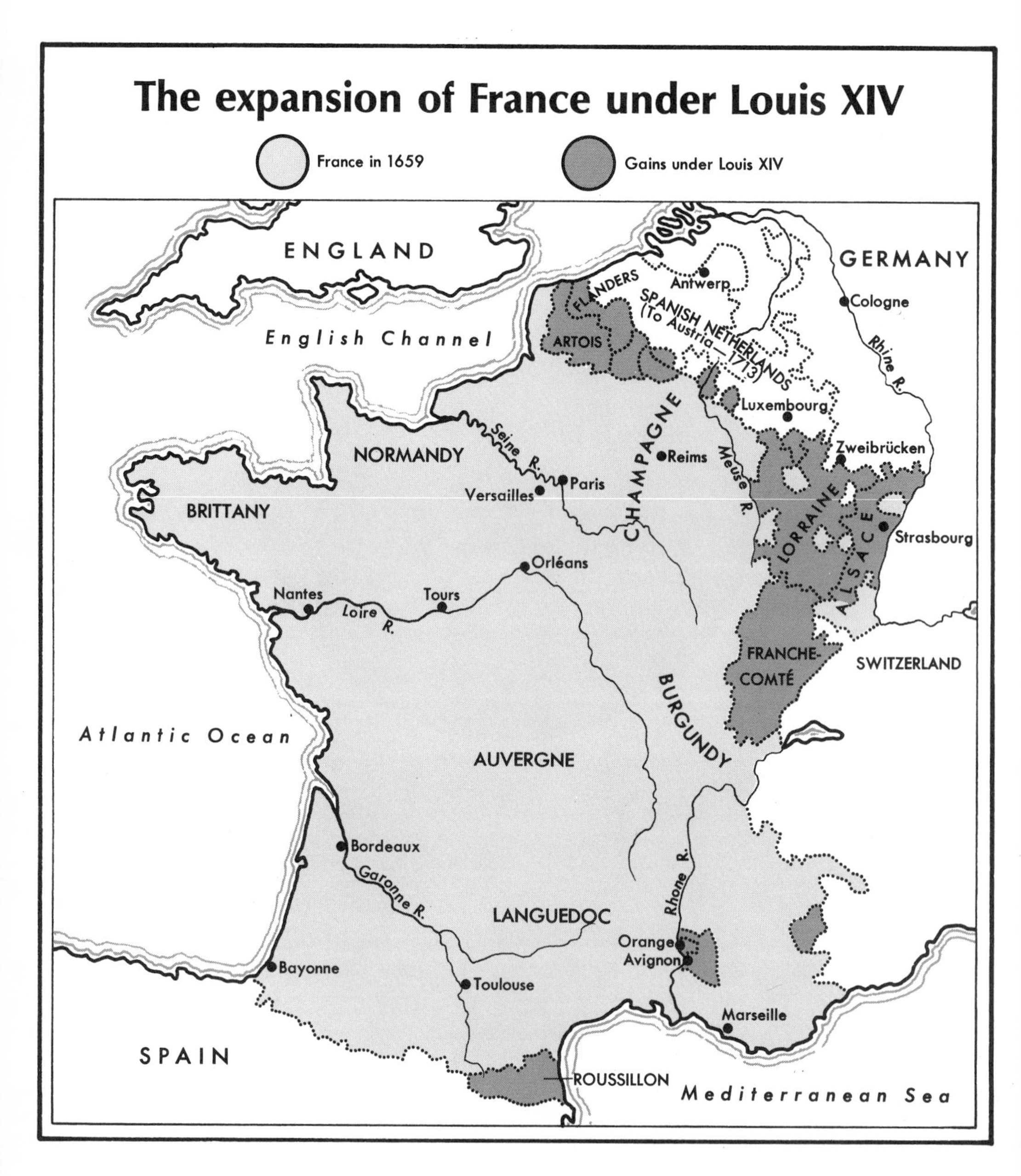

literature, manners, and taste attained undisputed ascendancy. From England to the German world, from St. Petersburg to Lisbon, imitations of the gardens and buildings at Versailles spread, along with acceptance of French guidance in matters ranging from dress to poetry. We hear of the very pious Lutheran prince of Brandenburg having an official mistress, little though he was personally disposed to her, because this was customary at Versailles!

The Classical Age produced its imposing giants of thought and literature.

Descartes and Pascal, whose clarity of thought emerged in limpid crystal-clear prose, set the general philosophical tone for the age. The dramatists Racine and Molière excelled in purity of language and flawless perfection of the technical side of drama. In the keen wit of Molière some of the growing scientific interest is revealed: unforgettable was his satire on the medical doctors who were slaves to the book authority of Galen and the ancients. In Paris and Versailles the French contributed a unique institution, the *salon*, presided over usually by charming ladies, which was a meeting place for the *literati* and indeed all of cultivated society. Here, at the rich and scintillating capital of the powerful French state, European thought and letters undeniably had their center.

French ambitions

The wars in which the Grand Monarch embroiled France and most of Europe were a serious drain on his treasury and perhaps a blot on the enlightened character of his reign. They certainly were largely futile in the long run. The years between 1688 and 1713 were to be filled with the sound of what has been called the first world war of modern times. The tendency among historians has been to blame the pride and arrogance of France and her King for these wars. About half of his long reign (28 years out of 54), Louis was at war. Dignified, far from tyrannical, a bit stuffy, very proud, Louis was not by nature particularly warlike; French national pride was aroused, however, indeed intoxicated—as well it might be—by the power and especially the prestige of France. Europe did France the honor of learning her language and imitating her manners. Was not "civilization" itself French? There was talk of a world monarchy. There was also talk about the "manifest destiny" of France to reach her "natural frontiers"—the Rhine, ocean, mountains.

Intoxicated by pride and seeking ever more "gloire" for the glorious monarchy, France demanded that all other nations recognize her supremacy, conducting a "prestige diplomacy" which insisted upon the lowering of flags and the seating of diplomats to the honor of France. She also showed aggressive intentions toward, particularly, the Spanish Netherlands on her northeastern border, which alarmed the Dutch and involved them in wars with France; also toward the small territories and free cities of the German Empire on the east. Louis also seized the Avignon enclave from the papacy. Expansion at the expense of the Dutch, the Spanish, the German princes, and the pope seemed carried out by brutal and cynical methods, as French "courts of reunion" exploited the legal complexities of feudalism to annex cities and provinces. The taking of the free city of Strasbourg made the worst impression. Finally, the claim of France to the throne of Spain appeared to be a real bid for the dominion of all Europe.

However, like most nations accused by their foes of "aggression," the French thought they were acting reasonably, in self-defense. They still feared their old foes, the Hapsburgs. Acquisition of Strasbourg and other frontier regions they looked upon as necessary to forestall the Emperor. As for Spain, which became the key to European policy, its situation was an unusual one. Philip IV, who died in 1665, had two daughters, one married to Louis of France and the other to the Hapsburg Emperor. He also had a feeble-minded invalid son. The situation set up a competition for the Spanish dominions, now in decline but still vast—Belgium, Naples, Milan, the Franche-Comté in Europe, as well as the overseas possessions. The French feared Austrian possession of all this as much as the Emperor feared its acquisition by France. Either way, it would upset the balance of Europe. What was to be done? Before his death Philip decided to let the weakly Charles, his son, rule; it was certain he would have no offspring, and it was believed he would soon die. Philip also said that after Charles' death the throne should go to Austria, that is, to the children of his daughter who was then espoused by the Emperor. It was this which angered and frightened France.

War of the League of Augsburg

But even sympathetic historians concede that Louis went too far in his countermeasures. Both sides, to be sure, intrigued incessantly over Spain. Charles II, Philip IV's son, surprisingly lived until 1700, prolonging the issue for years. Between 1689 and 1697 occurred the War of the League of Augsburg, the name of the first alliance organized against Louis XIV by William of Orange, who then became William III of England. When William of Orange came over from Holland to be King of England as William III in 1688, he brought with him a war. The Alliance included Sweden, Spain, the Emperor, and the German princes of Bavaria, Saxony, the Palatinate. To them

were added England, the Netherlands, and Savoy. France fought alone, and this "Grand Alliance" was rather too much for her, though she won her share of victories. The British did not send any troops to Europe, but contented themselves with smashing the strong French navy at the great sea battle of La Hogue in the English channel. It was a crushing blow to Louis' ambitions to make France a naval and colonial power as well as the mistress of Europe. The power of France, great as it was, did not prove great enough to sustain this dual demand, and after La Hogue France was to fall back steadily on the overseas front, in India as well as the New World, finally to be thrown out of both by Great Britain in the 18th century. But at this time the weakness inherent in coalitions enabled the French to make the short-lived peace of 1697, the Treaty of Ryswick. This treaty forced France to give back some of the areas she had "reunited" by allegedly illegal means, and Louis never regained the peak of expansion reached about 1685. But he kept Strasbourg, the Franche-Comté, and Alsace, while giving back Lorraine, Luxembourg, and Zweibrücken, and renouncing far-ranging claims along the Rhine.

War of the Spanish Succession

In 1700 the childless Charles of Spain finally died at the worst possible moment for the peace of Europe, having just made a will. He had designated as his successor the grandson of Louis XIV, the Duke of Anjou. When the latter mounted the Spanish throne as Philip V, it was the signal for a renewal of the war, the War of the Spanish Succession, 1702–13. While many were ready to blame France for trying to assume the supremacy of Europe, it should be

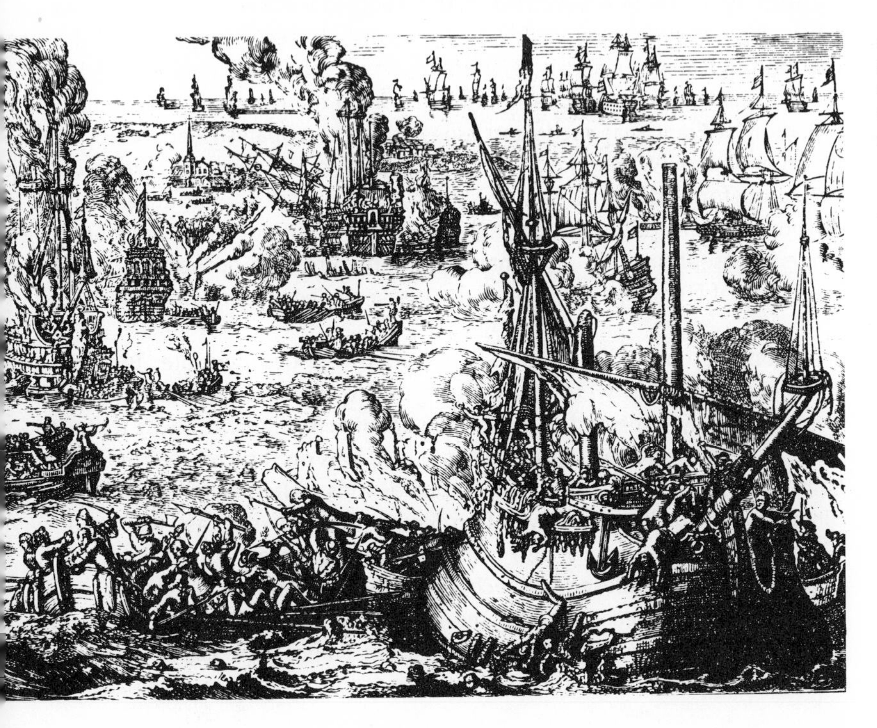

Battle of LaHogue, a contemporary engraving showing the final destruction of the French fleet at the close of the six day battle, May 19, 1692.

pointed out that Louis did not force the decision on Charles II and did not even much welcome it, since he knew it would threaten war. He was prepared to compromise with William III and the Emperor on the sharing of the Spanish spoils. It was Spain that refused to contemplate any partition of the "seamless garment" of her Empire, and thrust it on France because she thought the latter best able to defend it. It is far from clear that France was the greedy aggressor in this war, but probably most of her foes sincerely thought so. "The Pyrenees have ceased to exist!" someone said, and everyone repeated it. The union of Spain and France would be fatal to the other states of Europe, they thought.

Again the Grand Alliance confronted France, though this time Louis found a couple of allies (Bavaria, in addition to Spain). The Alliance added Portugal and the rising state of Prussia. The war featured the military exploits of the famous English general John Churchill, Duke of Marlborough, and Eugene, Prince of Savoy, the military leader of the imperial forces. The powerful French military machine was well led as usual, but again the numbers of her foes proved too much. She faced Marlborough and the Dutch in the Low Countries and Prince Eugene of Italy. The two united to repel the French drive for Vienna at the battle of Blenheim near Ulm. The great battle of Ramillies secured the Low Countries for Marlborough, one of those rare generals who never lost a battle. The English captured Gibraltar, and Prince Eugene decisively defeated the French at Turin. But for the disunity of their numerous foes, the French again might have come off worse than they did.

After the battle of Malplaquet (1709), England wearied of the war. It was a particularly bloody battle with heavy English losses, though the Duke of Marlborough might claim it as another victory. The Tory faction in England did not think it sensible to continue the war to the complete defeat and humiliation of France, at such cost, especially as the Spanish people appeared to favor Philip. When the Whigs continued to demand the exclusion of Bourbons forever from the Spanish throne, the Tories, who accused Marlborough of corruption, gained power in England. The death of the Hapsburg Emperor Joseph in 1711 also changed the picture. The upshot was peace—the Peace of Utrecht, 1713, one of the major settlements in European history.

The Peace of Utrecht

Among its numerous provisions, the following deserve note: the crowns of France and Spain were never to be united in the same person, but the Bourbon family remained in Spain. The Spanish Netherlands went to Austria but the Dutch were to control strategic garrisons on the French frontier. The Emperor also took over the Spanish possessions in Italy (Naples, Milan, Sardinia), except Sicily, which went to Savoy. A separate treaty was made in 1714 between the Emperor and France at Rastadt, largely confirming Utrecht, but the Emperor refused to recognize the Bourbon monarchy in Spain. Prussia and Savoy became kingdoms. Great Britain kept Gibraltar and got the Maritime Provinces in the New World from France. The island of Minorca and the *asiento* or slave-trading contract for the Spanish colonies also were

The first Duke of Marlborough

thought to enhance the power of Britain, who came out a major winner.

France lost virtually nothing in Europe, in fact made a few small gains, but she did not recover what the Peace of Ryswick had taken from her. Much of what she had sought, the Spanish inheritance in Europe, passed to the Emperor. However, the "family compact" of Bourbons gave her a relationship to Spain which often resulted in close cooperation between the two states during the 18th century. She was shorn of some colonial possessions by rising England, and came out of the war thoroughly exhausted, with an empty treasury. A sullen people cheered the death of Louis XIV in 1715.

France had been able to fight all of Europe and gain virtually a draw, even though her ambitions had been checked and her power contained, and she emerged from the wars of Louis XIV enlarged and strengthened. Her proud motto "Not unequal to many" had been fully sustained. But the cost was great; and there seems something significant in the fact that among the great buildings erected in and around Paris by Louis, including the Louvre and the palace at Versailles, one of the greatest was the Invalides (still standing), the military hospital. Heavy debts and a tax problem, which never was solved until the great Revolution, were included in the legacy.

Effects of the wars on lesser powers

What were the effects of Louis XIV's wars on the less powerful nations of Europe? Both Spain and the Dutch Republic were in relative decline. These two erstwhile mortal foes found themselves fighting on the same side in the War of the League of Augsburg against the now common and giant enemy, France. The long struggle against France exhausted the Dutch; they kept their colonial empire in the East Indies and maintained their independence and indeed their prosperity, but they were overshadowed in power by the English on the seas and the French on the land, as well as by the other powers of the European state system as it shaped up in the 18th century: Prussia, Russia, and Austria. They had won themselves a place in Europe as a sturdy midget, like the valiant Swiss, and as a progressive land from which much could always be learned in government and economics. Whenever they ventured to go to war with the big powers, though, they came off badly (1780–84, and during the French Revolution).

Spain remained at the level of a secondary power. After being shorn of the last of her European possessions at Utrecht, Spain made some efforts to regain the Italian ones in the years following, taking advantage of quarrels among the major powers. Intrigue of this sort paid off in the recovery of Naples and Sicily (Kingdom of the Two Sicilies) and establishment of Spanish princes in several small duchies. The Bourbons were not bad rulers: inheriting a Spain somewhere near total economic collapse, they struggled manfully to bring about a revival by typical mercantilist policies. It was a difficult task. The trouble with Spain, so it appears, lay deep in the social structure and even more in the national psychology of a land where men of birth and ability held trade in contempt—and where everyone claimed to be a noble, so it seemed. A particular factor was the enormous power of the church and the high percentage of ecclesiastics in the population. Philip V, Ferdinand VI, and especially Charles III, decidedly a member of the society of "enlightened despots," did tackle the task of reform. It was a question of making the administration of government more efficient, of regularizing taxes, removing obstacles to trade, encouraging commercial and naval pursuits. These measures bore some fruit: if Spain never again became as mighty as in 1580, by the latter part of the 18th century she was hardly so impoverished and demoralized as she had been in 1680.

Italy, like Spain, suffered from economic sickness, and politically she stagnated like Germany in the reign of petty states, while the powerful monarchies to the north passed her by. The papacy was in severe decline. In the northern corner of Italy the state of Savoy, which contributed the great Eugene to the service of Austria in the War of the Spanish Succession, won new lands and the title of kingdom as a result of that war, but was far from being a major power. For the failure of Italy to achieve unity, the reasons given by Machiavelli earlier and repeated by Napoleon Bonaparte later held true: the long, narrow peninsula had no community of interest, and the popes constituted a special obstacle to a national state; and weakness feeds on itself by inviting foreign intervention.

The balance of power

The statesmen of Europe had begun to talk about the "balance of power." It had been exemplified in the wars of Louis XIV; it was supposedly embodied in the Peace of Utrecht. The leaders of Europe had once fought for moral and religious ends; they now fought for the power of the state, and in a famous phrase of the day, they employed the concept of *raison d'état*, reason of state—the rational analysis of national interest as a tool of statecraft. But peace, rather than incessant war, was in the interest of all; and peace, it was thought, could be best assured by the balance of power.

It is certainly true that one of the reasons for this cycle of wars in the latter part of the 17th century was the disequilibrium of power. The rapid decline of Spain and the Empire, together with the enhanced strength of France, had created a situation favorable to French aggression. There were, in brief, too many areas of weakness on the borders of France and they constituted an irresistible temptation. Few great powers can resist such opportunities to expand. Moral rationalizations, such as the need for "natural frontiers" or the "manifest destiny" of the nation to spread its beneficent civilization, are readily available. Only power can check power. At Utrecht, a conscious attempt was made to arrange matters so that French power would be contained. The elevation of Prussia and Savoy to kingdoms, as well as the Dutch-Austrian garrisoning of Belgium, should be seen in this light. To judge by the relatively long period of peace that now began, the plan worked with some success.

The Glorious Revolution in England

The Restoration of Charles II

The English state and nation advanced in rather different ways. The Restoration, it will be recalled, had brought back the hereditary monarchy, in the person of Charles II, son of the beheaded Charles I, but with his tacit acceptance of much of what had been accomplished during the Puritan Revolution. Charles made no explicit promises, but he was recalled by Parliament, which proclaimed in so doing that the government of England was "in King, Lords, and Commons." The Church of England did come back, and in spite of Charles' promise he could not altogether prevent some vengeance being visited on the "Nonconformists." For a time, Presbyterians, Quakers, all except Anglicans were rather severely dealt with. However, a more tolerant spirit developed within the Church of England itself. The spirit of the age was now against religious persecution. Charles himself, a dissolute and rather lazy king, was not a religious bigot. He proved a good friend to William Penn the Quaker, and to American colonization in general (it offered an easy way of rewarding impoverished followers with a claim on his gratitude, as well as getting rid of troublesome religious dissenters). The King's marriage to the Portuguese princess, Catherine of Braganza, also, brought Bombay as a dowry—the seed from which the great British Empire in India was in time to grow. He also was a good friend to the Royal Society of scientists. He was shrewd and tolerant enough to avoid extreme conflicts with Parliament such as had brought his father low.

The reaction against the Puritans was a strong one, and the Restoration period in England is indeed known for its naughtiness. Charles came back from French exile with a French wife and not a few French habits; his court

Charles II of England, the Restoration king.

John Dryden, who refined the English language to a new purity.

popularized French dress and, as some critics complained, French morals. The "merry monarch" himself kept numerous mistresses. Reigning literary fashions cheerfully followed his lead, and the restored theater (it had been banned under the Commonwealth) grew a crop of comedies which dwelt on the theme of sexual passion with a sophisticated wit. In Restoration plays, like modern novels, most husbands betray their wives and all wives are unfaithful to their husbands. The more serious side of the literary movement, which produced such large figures as Dryden and Congreve, featured as in France a move to purify the language, gain in technique, and avoid the extravagances of earlier writers. Dryden, who wrote in metrically flawless couplets, confessed that

> *Our age was cultivated thus at length,*
> *But what we gain'd in skill we lost in strength.*

However, the period did see the emergence in England of a prose style that was admirably clear, a vehicle of exposition far superior to the exuberance of earlier prose writers. It was an elegant, civilized age, often but not always frivolous. After all, it produced Boyle, Newton, and Locke. It also produced Christopher Wren and the architectural renewal of London in neoclassical taste after the great fire of 1665.

Charles II and Parliament

Relations between king and Parliament were not yet sound. The period was not a satisfactory one for either foreign or domestic policy, though disaster was averted. In foreign policy, Charles' lack of funds, for which Parliament was partly responsible, together with his previous relationship with the French during his refugee days, led him into a scandalous acceptance of money from Louis XIV. French gold bribed other English politicians, including the leader of the opposition to Charles in Parliament. This helps account for what many English felt was a deplorable weakness in England's reaction to the aggressive power of France. An alliance between England, Holland, and Sweden was negotiated by Charles' foreign minister in 1668, but Charles made a secret treaty in which he promised to support Louis in his wars. It has often been regarded as the most disgraceful treaty in England's history. These were the secret portions of the Treaty of Dover, 1670. Two years later England joined France in attacking the Dutch.

Anti-French feeling, mingled with suspicions about the government's policies, lay behind the furor over the "popish plot" which swept England in 1678. One Titus Oates threw the country into a panic by alleging to have proof of a new "gunpowder plot," and the ensuing witch-hunt sent several leading Catholics to the gallows before it was discovered that Oates was a liar and the whole plot a hoax. It was the leading example of England's uneasy state during Charles' reign. England found no stable basis of government during these years. "Whigs" and "Tories" made their initial appearance in English history—the source of later political parties. But effective government through political parties had not yet been learned. A series of violent national oscillations threatened renewal of civil war.

King
D.r Oates discouereth y.e Plot
to y.e King and Councell.

Playing card design on the "popish plot"

Parliament, on the whole, maintained its ascendancy. Charles never really tried to dispute it, and in 1673 Parliament won a resounding victory when it forced the fall of Charles' whole cabinet, called off the unpopular war against the Dutch, and passed a bill to exclude Catholics from office (the Test Act). The Catholicism of Charles' brother James, apparently next in line for the throne, became a crucial issue. Charles himself was secretly Catholic; James was avowedly so. Parliament's Whig leaders did not trust Charles, nor he them, both with good enough reason. Cooperation between the two, necessary to stable English government, did not exist. Charles was able to ride out the storm and die in bed—where, indeed, some of his most celebrated triumphs had taken place. But the merry monarch had the ill luck to leave no legitimate heir, though numerous bastards, and so the Catholic James II ascended to the throne in 1685.

The Glorious Revolution

He was to be the last of the Stuarts, and his fall to be the triumphant beginning of the modern English constitution. In his short three-year reign before ignominious flight in 1688, James showed himself courageous but wholly wanting in judgment. His Catholicism, and suspected commitment to Louis XIV (whose revocation of the Edict of Nantes just then aroused Englishmen afresh against him, and whose claims to the throne of Spain were making him the more feared) put James in a bad position. There was a rebellion led by the Duke of Monmouth, an illegitimate son of Charles II, at the time of James' accession, but it was ill-timed and ill-led. The execution of Monmouth and many of his followers left Protestant hopes firmly fastened on William of Orange, the leader of the Dutch, whose wife Mary was James' daughter. William had the merits of being staunchly Protestant, a great foe of Louis XIV, and in possession of substantial armed forces.

James meanwhile proceeded in headlong haste to act on his theory that the king must override Parliament and assert his mastery. It can be said in his defense that the existing situation was almost intolerable, and that Louis XIV was teaching Europe that the absolute monarchy was the way to wealth and power. But James' insistence on Catholicizing England was a gross blunder if he hoped to succeed in his plans. He made an effort to ally himself with the Dissenters (Presbyterians and Independents, former Puritans) against the Anglicans but they refused the bait and stood shoulder to shoulder with their foes of yesterday against the greater threat, as they saw it, of Romanism. James drove ahead energetically with a program designed to install Roman Catholics in the universities, the army, and the government as well as in the church; he attempted to pack Parliament and raised a standing army made up largely of foreign mercenaries. He succeeded in alienating almost all possible elements in the country. At this point, James II had a son, and the prospect of a succession of Catholic rulers galvanized the Whig and Tory leaders into action.

The significant fact in what followed was that *both* Whig and Tory chiefs in Parliament joined in issuing an invitation to William and Mary to assume the throne forfeited, in their opinion, by the unlawful acts of James. This was not the first time, needless to say, that an English monarch had faced revolution. Medieval kings had been insecure enough (witness poor Richard II), and we may recall the fate of Henry VI and Richard III, before James' father lost his royal head in 1649. The importance of 1688 was not, then, altogether in the act of successful revolution as such. It was important because the entire nation, in effect—both of the quarreling political factions, men of all shades of opinion—joined in the revolution, which then went through without violence or divisions among them. It was that rare thing, a moderate revolution. It is true that Whigs and Tories developed disagreements concerning exactly what happened in 1688. The fact remains that the entire nation was then at one against James.

In 1688 Whigs and Tories agreed that James II could no longer be king, but they did not altogether agree on their reasons. Whigs adopted the social compact theory, agreeing with John Locke that government derives from a solemn compact between ruler and people, the latter represented by Parliament. Tories repudiated this as subversive of the necessary authority and alleged that the principle of hereditary monarchy had not been destroyed by James' abdication. Further developments in the next 25 years, down to 1714, helped cement the victory of the Whigs.

Bill of Rights

After William sailed into Torbay with the aid of a "Protestant wind," James' forces melted away and he fled to France.[1] Parliament solemnized the proceedings by issuing the great Bill of Rights, which specified, for all to read, the rights of Parliament and people against king—rights of free speech, judicial fair play, parliamentary control of taxation. Many of them found their way a century later into the American Bill of Rights. It constituted a concrete example of the "social compact" between the ruler and an entire people. Thereafter all English constitutional development rested on this basic act, which made a solemn bond of political unity among all Englishmen. Factions might thereafter bicker, but their common acceptance of the "revolutionary settlement" of 1688 allowed them to agree on fundamentals and thus prevented further revolution and armed strife. Moreover, the years that ensued brought England prosperity and progress as an accompaniment of civil peace under a competent government.

The two daughters of James II, Mary, who ruled jointly with her husband until her death, after which he ruled alone, and then Queen Anne, who reigned 1702–14, were Protestant Stuarts, and next in line for the throne on hereditary principles except for the son of James II, who had been an infant in 1688. Either James II or his son was the legitimate king on strict principles of heredity; and William III had no hereditary claim of his own at all. But Mary and Anne did. Neither of them left any children, and in 1701 Parliament attempted to resolve the question of the succession by the Act of Settlement, which settled the crown on the nearest Protestant branch of the royal family. This was the German house of Hanover, into which Sophia Stuart, a cousin of the royal family, had married. When Anne died in 1714 this Hanoverian dynasty was duly enthroned, after an attempted revolt by the followers of James III failed badly. It has been there ever since. England was determined to exclude any Stuart pretenders of the Catholic faith, and seemed quite content with the dubiously regal George I of Hanover.

Victory of Parliament

It was not quite clear what principle of the monarchy had been adopted; yet plainly Parliament had made the rules, whatever they were, and was in possession of the field against any brand of absolutism. The events of 1714–15 constituted a victory for the Whigs against the Tories, part of whom had tied their cause to the coattails of James III and now were wholly in disarray. For the next half century the Whig chieftains dominated both Parliament and the crown, the first two Hanoverians, George I and George II, being without much interest in the proceedings. Gradually what remained of the Tory faction accepted 1714 as well as 1688 and reconstructed the party on a basis other than Jacobitism (loyalty to James III). An uprising in Scotland in 1745 in favor of the Young Pretender, Bonnie Prince Charlie, received virtually no support in England and was crushed.

---

[1] James came back to Ireland in 1690, where he was sure of a friendly welcome, but lost a major battle—the battle of the Boyne—to English forces and gave up the effort. The Stuart pretenders were allowed to live in France until the death of Louis XIV in 1715; thereafter they lived in Rome.

Allegorical painting of King William III

The House of Commons in the 18th century

England, which became Great Britain in 1707 through the union with Scotland, prospered and rejoiced in freedom in the 18th century. It seemed to have achieved the miracle of liberty *with* authority, a strong state, yet one that did not oppress its subjects. European experience since the age of feudalism had suggested a rather grim choice between one or the other. Liberty had meant anarchy, to which tyranny seemed the only antidote. "Despotism, it had been thought, was the secret of efficiency," writes George M. Trevelyan. "Freedom was a luxury to be enjoyed by small communities like the Cantons of Switzerland, the Seven Provinces of Holland—and Holland's power after a short period of glory was waning fast before the rising might of the French King." The success of 18th-century England surprised and impressed Europe, and was a potent factor in the new political outlook of the Enlightenment.

Bibliography

Vols. V and VI of the *New Cambridge Modern History*, and the volumes by F.L. Nussbaum and J.B. Wolf in *Rise of Modern Europe* Series (Harper Torchbooks), are basic. The background for the age of Louis XIV in the age of Richelieu may be found in C.V. Wedgwood's summary, *Richelieu and the French Monarchy* (Macmillan, Collier), and in *Richelieu*, the recent study of the great cardinal by D.P. O'Connell (London: Weidenfeld & Nicolson, 1966), which dispels some legends. Henry Bertram Hill has edited *The Political Testament of Cardinal Richelieu* (Madison: University of Wisconsin Press, 1961). J. Boulenger, *The Seventeenth Century in France* (G.P. Putnam's Sons, Capricorn), is the reprint of an old work by a French scholar; cf. Geoffrey Treasure, *Seventeenth Century France* (Doubleday, Anchor). In *The Splendid Century* (Doubleday, Anchor) and *Louis XIV: An Informal Portrait* (London: Andre Deutsch, 1959), W.H. Lewis has ticked off the grand monarchy as enjoyably as anyone. Another graciously written study is that of Albert Guérard, *Life and Death of an Ideal: France in the Classical Age* (Harper & Row). Soberer but important are J.E. King, *Science and Rationalism in the Government of Louis XIV* (Baltimore: Johns Hopkins Studies in History and Political Science, 1949); C.W. Cole, *Colbert and a Century of French Mercantilism* (New York: Columbia University Press, 1939); and *French Mercantilism 1683–1700* (Columbia University Press, 1943). The Sun King himself is given sympathetic treatment by Vincent Cronin, *Louis XIV* (London: Collins, 1964); Vincent Buranelli, *Louis XIV* (New York: Twayne Publishers, 1966); and especially John B. Wolf, *Louis XIV* (W.W. Norton), which may be contrasted with the treatment in Maurice Ashley, *Louis XIV and the Greatness of France* (Free Press). Louis O'Brien has told the story of *Innocent XI and the Revocation of the Edict of Nantes* (Berkeley: University of California Press, 1930).

R.T. Davies, *Spain in Decline, 1621–1700* (New York: Macmillan, 1957), is an account of the country whose rapid decay caused a profound disturbance in the European balance of power. More appealing to the general reader, perhaps, would be the engaging book by John Nada, *Carlos the Bewitched*, i.e., the ill-fated last Spanish Hapsburg, Charles II (London: Jonathan Cape, 1963). On England in the Restoration period, there is Arthur Bryant, *Charles II* (Collins, 1955), a biography which overlooks most of the merry monarch's faults and sees his virtues. John H. Wilson, *Nell Gwyn* (New York: Pellegrini & Cudahy, 1952), is quite content to find little virtue in the most celebrated and colorful of the royal mistresses. David Ogg has made a brilliant contribution to our knowledge of the period in his two-volume work *England in the Reign of Charles II* (Oxford University Press), and continues his study with

England in the Reign of James II and William III (Oxford: Clarendon Press, 1955). On the Glorious Revolution, George M. Trevelyan, *The English Revolution 1688–1689* (Oxford University Press), is distinctly "Whiggish," and may be compared with the account in Keith Feiling, *History of the Tory Party 1640–1710* (Clarendon Press, 1954). Sir Winston Churchill wrote of his distinguished ancestor, *Marlborough: His Life and Times* (reprinted, 2 vols.; London: George C. Harrap, 1947); cf. Malcolm Hay, *Winston Churchill and James II of England* (London: Harding & Moore, 1934), a reply to certain features of Churchill's book. Stephen Baxter, *William III and the Defense of European Liberty* (New York: Brace & World, 1966), is the outstanding recent study of the Dutch-English king. Nicholas Henderson, *Prince Eugene of Savoy* (London: Weidenfeld & Nicolson, 1964), is the best recent book in English on the subject of the great Hapsburg minister. Michael Foot, in *The Pen and the Sword* (London: MacGibbon & Kee, 1957), has told the story of how the great writer Jonathan Swift fought the battle for a peace settlement short of total victory over the French. George Trevelyan's *England Under Queen Anne* (3 vols.; New York: Longmans, Green & Co., 1930) is in the best style of this master of the vigorous narrative.

Sources. Lucy Norton (ed.), *Saint-Simon at Versailles* (London: Hamish Hamilton, 1958), a selection from the famous court memoirs of the Duke of Saint-Simon; Voltaire, *The Age of Louis XIV* (E.P. Dutton, Everyman's Library); James H. Hanford (ed.), *The Restoration Reader* (Grove Press, Evergreen).

15

Central and eastern Europe

chronology

1462–1505
Ivan the Great, Grand Prince of Moscow, begins consolidation of Russian state.
Throwing off of Tatar yoke, 1480.
1466
Defeat of Teutonic Knights in Poland. Decline of Hanseatic League.
1533–84
Ivan the Terrible, first Tsar of Russia. Struggles with nobility and with Tatars; first contacts made with West.
1613
Beginning of Romanov dynasty in Russia. Gradual consolidation of Russian state after "Time of Troubles." Expulsion of Poles from Moscow.
1621
Revolt of janissaries, Ottoman Empire.
1640–88
Great Elector, Brandenburg-Prussia.
1645–64
Turkish-Venetian war. Rise of Kiuprili rulers of Ottoman Empire.
1654–67
Russo-Polish war for Ukraine, Russian victory.
1660
Brandenburg given full sovereignty over Prussia.
1661–64
Hapsburg war with Turks.
1670
Peasant revolt in Russia (Stephen Razin).
1677–81
Russo-Turkish war.
1682–99
Renewal of Austro-Turkish war. Siege of Vienna by Turks, 1683. Polish King, Sobieski, leads army to relief of city. Defeat of Turks by Austria allied with Venice. Treaty of Karlowitz, 1699, liberating Hungary from Turks.
1688–1713
Frederick I of Prussia. Prussia becomes kingdom.
1689–1725
Peter the Great of Russia. Internal reforms, westernization, territorial expansion, access to Europe secured.
1697–98
Peter's journey to Europe.
1700
Great Northern War begins (Sweden, Denmark, Poland, Russia).
1709
Battle of Poltava, Russian victory over Swedes.
1711
Hungarian revolt against Hapsburgs. Charles VI to Hapsburg throne.
1718
Death of Charles XII of Sweden.
1721
Treaty of Nystadt, ends Great Northern War; Russia acquires Baltic ports, becomes European power.
1733
War of Polish Succession; weakness of Polish state.
1739
Treaty of Belgrade, stabilizing southeastern Europe between Austrian and Turkish Empires.

The handsome baroque city of Warsaw in the 18th century as painted by Bernardo Belloto Canaletto

The Holy Roman Empire

The Empire whose roots went back to Charlemagne, and which had once included part of Italy as well as something of what is now France, Switzerland, and the Netherlands, had diminished in size and power. The Peace of Westphalia recognized the official departure of the latter two regions, also giving some of Alsace to France and control of the ports on the Baltic Sea to Sweden. It turned the Empire itself into little more than an empty name: a "ghost," Thomas Hobbes called it; "an irregular body resembling a monster," the German jurist Pufendorf wrote. The Thirty Years War represented the victory of state sovereignty over the union, as one would say in the United States; it was as if the South had won the Civil War. The ambitions of the Hapsburg emperors to convert the Empire into a united state were ended forever, and after this they concentrated entirely on their own hereditary domains, which led them to look to the southeast more than to Germany. The machinery of the Empire indeed remained. While the imperial crown still remained with the Hapsburgs, the Imperial Diet, in which some 160 of the 360 "estates" of the realm were represented, continued to meet; nor can it be rightly said that this Diet, along with the Empire's judicial machinery, performed no useful services. It was a kind of United Nations and World Court for the world of petty states within the Empire, and often helped resolve disputes between them. But there was no executive authority, military force, or power of taxation; the Diet resembled the Articles of Confederation under which the United States lived between 1781 and 1789, a mere confederation of sovereign powers.

Decline of Germany

Of the numerous small principalities and free cities, only two or three had the resources to become strong states. Germany was in economic distress and therefore social decline in this period. The frightful ravages of the marauding armies of the Thirty Years War left a legacy of misery for some time after the close of the war, as brigandage and freebooting were carried on by discharged soldiers from force of habit. In Germany as elsewhere, the passions of the Reformation had now largely spent themselves and the religious question gave little further trouble, people tending to settle down in the faith they held. So civil war within the Empire was comparatively a minor problem. But Louis XIV's troops did serious damage particularly to the Palatinate (southwest Germany), and economic stagnation accompanied political fragmentation.

The chief difficulty stemmed from a permanent pattern of economic stagnation. The causes of this included the shifting of trade routes, the control of the river mouths by foreign powers, and especially the failure of Germany, for want of a central government, to keep up with the large mercantilist economic units being shaped by France and England.

Petty despotisms

So the picture was in the main depressing. The misery of the peasants accompanied the decay of the free cities and the degradation of the nobility, far less cultured than in France and less industrious than in England. This decline took place in an area once as prosperous and civilized as any part of Europe. The small princes along the Rhine became paid clients of France; the Palatinate was ruined; Bavaria had the misfortune to choose the wrong side in the War of the Spanish Succession, when the battle of Blenheim forced the Wittelsbach ruler to flee the country. As best they could, the German princes tried to imitate Louis XIV's grand monarchy and make their governments more powerful and efficient, though few of them had anything like the resources with which to do so. They almost slavishly imitated the architecture and manners of the Versailles court, and visited it frequently. The palace of Nymphenberg at Munich is a lesser Versailles, and there were other examples of this. Later in the 18th century the French classical influence mingled with baroque strains to produce a beautiful architectural and especially decorative art in Germany.

But these petty despotisms with their mock-heroic effort to rival the Sun King were a drain on the people. Each tiny area had to have its own royal court and bureaucracy, its own army and customs. The result was crushing taxation, economic backwardness, and a self-perpetuating pattern of stagnation. No healthy political or economic life could grow.

Saxony

Of the German states, Brandenburg-Prussia and Saxony stood out as relative successes. The latter, with its great city of Leipzig and its famous porcelain industry at the capital, Dresden—a land which could well claim to represent the cultural heart of Germany, and which somewhat escaped the pattern of economic decay—was for a time the chief German state. In Bavaria and Saxony, and indeed in some other places, the 18th century in Germany was artistically and intellectually distinguished. The name of Johann Sebastian Bach, of Leipzig, should be a sufficient reminder of this. The celebrated philosopher Leibniz also came from the distinguished University of Leipzig. Some of the smaller states kept alive a vigorous constitutionalism. Thus, for example, the parliament or Estates of Württemberg waged a vigorous battle against the dukes' efforts to install absolutism, and in good part succeeded—a story hardly unique in Germany. The absolutist state of Prussia was to emerge and eventually impose its dominance on Germany, but the world of the smaller states was one where, by and large, ancient constitutional practices maintained themselves and a tradition of representative government did not die—a point sometimes overlooked. Not all Germans are Prussians.

Yet it is to the Prussian story that one must look for something vigorous and vital in this period of German history. Fortunately or not, with immense consequences both for Germany and for the entire world, the previously somewhat obscure principality of Brandenburg-Prussia had the human resources to make a strong state out of very little on this northeastern frontier of the empire.

The German rococo porcelain cabinet in the palace of the margraves at Ansbach

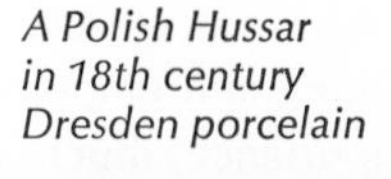

A Polish Hussar in 18th century Dresden porcelain

The rise of Prussia

The Elector of Brandenburg had been a personage of some importance in the little world of the Holy Roman Empire for several centuries, but this was far from making him a world power. However, he came out of the War of the Spanish Succession the King of Prussia, and thereafter the progress of this state was almost sensational.

Earlier history of Prussia

Prussia, in medieval times, had been conquered from the Slavs and Lithuanians and governed by the Teutonic Knights, an order of crusading feudal warriors. It was a frontier society, in which the planting of missions and towns went along with warfare against the "natives." The knights penetrated heathen Lithuanian and Christian Poland alike, and carved out a large Baltic empire at one time, its peak being in the 14th century. A union of Poland and Lithuania at length defeated them, and they decayed badly in the later 15th century. Prussia became Polish, but it also had a feudal connection with Brandenburg. In 1605 the guardianship of the duchy of Prussia was transferred to Brandenburg; the Great Elector, Frederick William, of Brandenburg gained full sovereignty over it in 1655–60 after a war with Poland.

In earlier times this northeast sector, nominally a part of the German world of the Holy Roman Empire, actually belonged more to the Baltic-Scandinavian orbit and hardly seemed civilized to south Germans; "it would not have occurred to anyone to choose a north or northeast German prince as king and emperor," as Veit Valentin observes. Brandenburg had no great importance, much less Prussia. Quite early one may detect a difference between the south German and the north German; on the northeast frontier particularly, the stamp of a military frontier was on the people in the form of a stern authoritarian sense of discipline.

In the 15th century the house of Hohenzollern, originally from Franconia, gained control of Brandenburg and proved to be energetic and ambitious from the start. In the time of Martin Luther, Protestantism found a congenial environment in north Germany, where its ethic merged readily with the existing spirit of dedication to hard work and duty. The Elector of Brandenburg, at first Lutheran, went over to the Reformed (that is, Calvinist) Church out of sympathy with, and desire for the support of, the Dutch, around the beginning of the Thirty Years War. Then came the acquisition of Prussia (separated from Brandenburg by the "Polish corridor") and, gradually, other miscellaneous pieces of land in northern Germany, including especially the Rhenish territory of Cleves-Jülich.

The Great Elector

Thus enlarged, and beginning to assume the leadership of the somewhat bedraggled Protestant states of Germany, Brandenburg-Prussia under its Hohenzollern kings blossomed as a modern state. The able and unscrupulous Frederick William, the Great Elector, who reigned 1640–88, had evidently taken some leaves from the book of Richelieu. But his education was Calvinist and he brought to Prussia the Calvinist spirit of hard work and dedicated effort. He showed himself a master of the strategy and tactics of state making, which involved as elsewhere breaking the power of the feudal estates, getting money, building an apparatus of government. He adopted "Colbertism" or French mercantilism in state economic policy, and in general learned assiduously from the French monarchy as well as from the Dutch government. It was he who made Berlin a great city by building a canal linking the Elbe and Oder rivers. The Great Elector even wished to create a navy and organize colonies, to which the German emigrants then flocking to Pennsylvania might go. He could not carry out these far-ranging plans, but they indicate his foresight and ambition. He was a superb statesman.

Hohenzollern foreign policy

He profited by granting asylum to the French Huguenots, not so much because he believed in toleration as because they were fellow Calvinists and would make useful citizens. This state was not a rich one. Poor lands and absence of natural resources made it necessary to husband every resource and strain every nerve. This fact stamped itself upon the Prussian state. The Hohenzollern foreign policy was a devious and slippery one. For example, the Great Elector made a secret treaty in 1679 binding himself to Louis XIV in return for an annual subsidy, which he used to develop his navy; but in 1685 he deserted France for William of Orange's alliance against France. It was at this time that the Elector replied to the revoking of the Edict of Nantes by an edict granting asylum to the Huguenots, some 20,000 of whom came to greatly enrich the German state with their skills. Prussia played very little part in the subsequent war against France, yet managed to come out of it with the recognition of her status as a kingdom and the gain of some territory.

Tactics of shrewd realism in foreign policy on the part of a small power were only a necessity of life, and not necessarily to be condemned unless the whole state system is to be condemned. Prussia certainly was not the only state to practice them. In many ways the Prussian state was an enlightened one, though increasingly despotic, rather grimly Calvinist, and very ambitious to climb in its fluid part of Europe. Prussia was also involved in the fortunes of the Baltic, where Sweden rose and fell, with Denmark, Poland, and the emergent state of Russia as other rivals. At the close of the Second Northern War in 1721 Prussia received the Pomeranian coast which the Swedes had long controlled—an important acquisition. Thereafter she did not worry about the fading Swedes but acquired an even larger cause for concern in the expanding Russians.

The great philosopher Leibniz and the scholars Thomasius and Pufendorf —the latter a political theorist admired by John Locke—came to Berlin, where a scientific society on Leibniz's plans was founded in 1701. The University of Halle formed the religious movement of Pietism, in which some of the free spirit of the old German mysticism replaced theological dogmatism. An academy of the arts on Richelieu's model also grew in Berlin—all this under Frederick I, 1688–1713. Prussia is so often described as a kind of garrison state, a modern Sparta where all was duty, discipline, and work, that it seems

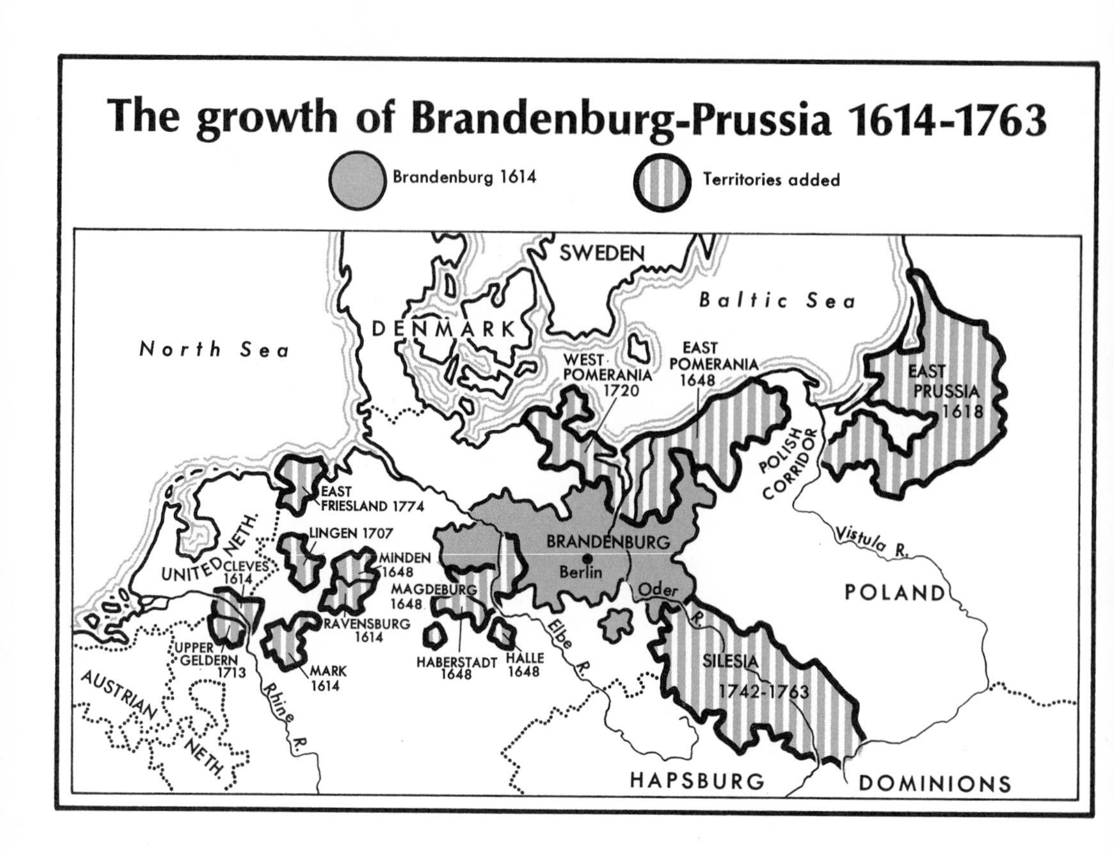

well to mention these other features. The harsher features were indeed there, reflecting the traditions of a frontier state—a "march"—without great natural wealth, where competition for survival was extremely keen. And reflecting also, perhaps, the impact of a Protestant ethic in which the spirit of Calvin, coming chiefly by way of the Netherlands, was as strong as Luther's.

Role of the army

A salient factor at all times in this somewhat miraculous rise of the Prussian state from most unpromising circumstances to become one of Europe's major powers was, in addition to the energy and Machiavellian shrewdness of its rulers, the army. "Other states have had armies; Prussia was an army which had a state." The epigram is close to being the truth, for the Prussian army was an extraordinarily large one for such a small and poor population. Built on the staggering taxes extorted from a groaning peasantry, it developed as the key institution in a manner almost unique. Numbering 30,000 in the time of the Great Elector, it grew steadily to reach 200,000 by the end of Frederick the Great's reign, a more than six-fold increase in a century. Its reputation as the best in Europe was won at the battles of Rossbach and Leuthen in the Seven Years War, when it defeated French armies that were much larger numerically. The nobles who officered it grew to identify their interests with the state's through the army, and in almost any Prussian town the military installations became the center of life. A proud tradition grew around it; about all one can say is that what art was to Florence in the Renaissance, or the kirk was to Scotland during the Reformation, the army, the military life, was to Prussia. Around it clustered the virtues, manners, and morals which became associated with "the Prussian style": duty, fortitude, loyalty, steadfastness, discipline.

Frederick William I

Armies of this caliber command respect, and before long the Prussian state counted for a good deal in Europe. It was its good fortune to have four able rulers in a row. The Great Elector (1640–88); after him the humane and civilized Frederick I, under whom Prussia became a kingdom; then the coarse, narrow-minded, but fanatically hard-working Frederick William I (1713–40) preceded the brilliant Frederick the Great (II). Stories about the old "Potsdam Fuehrer" who so tried the patience of his gifted son, and vice versa, are legion; he devoted his life to the state and army, had no feeling for the arts, husbanded his country's resources with a miser's instinct, pursued a timid foreign policy and evaded war, and died with his uniform on. He was a philistine drill-sergeant of the worst sort, yet the people loved him for his honesty and dedication to the state. His son, whose fabulous career in the middle and later 18th century brought Prussia into great-power status, had the good fortune to come after the foundations had been well put down by his three capable ancestors. The royalty of Europe with its habits of inbreeding could produce degenerate stock, as the Spanish Hapsburgs were just then engaged in proving. It could also do very well. Among the ancestors of Frederick the Great, a result of the intermarriage of royal houses, were William the Silent of the Netherlands and George I of Great Britain.

The Hapsburg domains and Poland

Austrian domains

As titular head of "The Empire," doubtless it will be remembered, the reigning Hapsburg had little power at any time and none whatsoever after 1648. But as ruler of his own domains he was a true monarch, and these domains increased steadily. The crowns of Hungary and of Bohemia were now hereditary in the Hapsburg family. Having resigned themselves to the futility of their role in the Empire, the Hapsburgs concentrated on their own lands and on redeeming Hungary from the Turks. After 1713, these lands were widely scattered, including as they did the former Spanish possessions in Italy and the Low Countries, as well as Hungary, Bohemia, and other southeastern areas acquired from the Turks. They yielded Naples to the Spanish within a few years. The rest constituted a mixture of races, religions, and cultures. Rebellion in Bohemia had set off the Thirty Years War; rebellion in Hungary was endemic throughout the 17th century, though it lapsed in the 18th. Apart from their native Austria, a land of hardy peasant and mountain folk who became devoted to them, the Hapsburgs did not rule over homogeneous or contented people. But the house was tenacious, proud of its position as one of the oldest dynasties in Europe, and of its role in holding the Turk out of Europe. Nearly ruined in the Thirty Years War, it did much to centralize administration, encouraged trade and banking, and by the end of the century was again a major power in Europe.

The Pragmatic Sanction

In 1711 a revolt in Hungary subsided with promises of some local autonomy. Charles VI, who reigned from 1711 to 1740, devoted himself to getting all the various Hapsburg lands to follow the same principle of succession. The Hungarian Diet had accepted the male Hapsburg line as its king; so, earlier, had the Bohemian. Charles VI's "Pragmatic Sanction" was an effort to secure European acceptance of the passing of the crowns to his eldest daughter, in the absence of a son, as well as of the indivisibility of the lands belonging to his state. In the Austrian and Bohemian lands no law or custom prevented the female succession, but in Hungary this was not the case; and also the imperial crown could not be worn by a woman. Charles got Hungarian acceptance of the sanction by promising to preserve the Hungarian Diet and rule Hungary according to her own laws. The object of this was to prevent any possible dismemberment of his variegated domains, as well as to solve the problem presented by the absence of a male heir, and Charles felt it necessary to get the consent of all the European powers to these changes in the rules of his kingdom. In so doing he threw them a political football which was thereafter kicked around for 15 years, and finally became the pretext for a major war. Charles had obviously feared that *not* asking the other states for their consent would give them an excuse for intervening after his death; he seems naive in thinking that he could forestall it in this way. The fact is that the "new Hapsburg Empire" was something of an invitation to robbery, and there were states on the prowl around Europe.

Poland

Poland was even more a temptation to the greedy. In 1733, France and Spain fought a short war with Austria and Russia over the succession to the Polish throne. To this degree of scandal had the election of a Polish king come: it was an invitation to a wholesale descent of everybody with candidates, money, and men—somewhat like an American political party convention. The War of the Polish Succession, just referred to, occurred when the French got one set of Polish nobles to elect the father-in-law of Louis XV, while the Russians and Austrians induced another set to choose the Elector of Saxony, and each side sent in troops to back up its choice. (The Russians, not the French, won). This state of affairs boded ill for Poland.

At one time, from about the end of the 14th to the middle of the 15th centuries, Poland had been an important state. Victory over the Teutonic Knights and the subsequent absorption of Lithuania gave it command of the northeast sector of Europe. It was an enlightened state, too, largely avoiding the religious wars of the Reformation, producing intellectual leaders of the stamp of Copernicus (half Polish, born in Cracow). Initially attracted to Protestantism, Poland was later drawn to the baroque culture of the Counter-Reformation.

Jan Sobieski, great soldier-king of Poland

Jan Sobieski

In the 17th century the Poles had to do battle with Turks to the south, to the east Tatars, Muscovite Russians, and Cossacks of the Ukraine. The Polish hero of this century was Jan Sobieski, who saved Vienna in 1683. Let us pause for a moment on his life, bringing history down to concrete cases for once in a chapter that is mostly devoted, of necessity, to general trends. Surrounded by Turks and Tatars as his land was, Sobieski was born in an atmosphere dominated by the crusading spirit and by concepts of fighting patriotism. He visited France for two years in his youth, indicative of the pull of that region for young easterners anxious to make contact with polite society. A wealthy man, Sobieski became hetman or commander-in-chief of the army at a time when the commander might find it necessary to pay the troops out of his own pocket. He studied soldiering by serving for a while with Charles Augustus of Sweden, the Swedes still being known as the masters of the art of warfare. Later he fought against the Tatars, the Ukrainian Cossacks, the Swedes, and the Muscovites. And, of course, also against the Turks. In 1674 he was elected King of Poland, as John III: the Polish kingship had remained elective, a source of grave weakness. Sobieski had trouble with the proud independent nobility and gentry of his land; nor did he, as a mere elected monarch, command much respect from the other kings of Europe, powerful hereditary rulers such as the King of France, the Holy Roman Emperor, the Tsar of Russia, or even the Elector of Brandenburg. The Romanovs had already conquered many of Poland's former holdings and the pressure would grow.

Sobieski took French gold, schemed to make the monarchy hereditary, played the game of high politics. But the high point came when he, in cooperation with the Pope, Innocent XI, forged an alliance with the Emperor and then led the allied army which defeated the Turks before the gates of Vienna. A Christian Holy League directed against the Turk soon included the Pope, the Emperor, Poland, and Venice, with Russia subsequently coming in. But the lion's share of the territory redeemed from the receding Ottoman Empire was to go to Russia and the Hapsburgs, in spite of Sobieski's hour of glory. For Poland was not able to keep up with these stronger states, a fact evident by the time of Sobieski's death in 1696 at his beautiful baroque palace of Wilanow near Warsaw.

Weakness of Polish government

Sobieski had led Poland for a moment to a height of power she would not attain again for 230 years, if ever. Lack of adequate central authority was the apparent reason for Poland's fall—in the 18th century she became the classic and awful example of this defect. With her elective king, jealously independent nobles, and parliamentary system in which unanimity was required on important issues, "Poland remained the extreme case in which elements of the medieval assembly of states acquired political power beyond that of the king." A figurehead king without adequate powers of government was a fatal handicap when taken together with the rise of powerful neighbors around Poland and her open frontiers. Poland was destined to become the prey of these neighbors who achieved greater success in power if not in liberty: Prussia, Russia, Austria. The partition of Poland, accomplished in 1772, was impending for almost a century. Such were the hazards of life in a Europe rapidly changing and growing in the 17th century. Poland failed to keep up.

The Baltic and the rise of Russia

Charles XII

Sweden was a northern country that fell from glory. It is rather amazing that the Swedes, with their sparse population, made it at all. But at one time, under the able rule of the Vasa kings, including the great Gustavus Adolphus of Thirty Years War fame, they dominated almost all the Baltic. The climax of Swedish power came under the brilliant Charles XII, who died in 1718 after defeats in Russia. Charles XII of Sweden, "the last Viking," ranks in his country's history as the greatest of heroes and was widely so regarded throughout Europe in the 18th century. Voltaire's judgment that Charles was the greatest of all historic men received the endorsement of the Swede's foe

King Charles XII of Sweden. "The last gasp of chivalry."

and conqueror, Peter the Great of Russia; it appears, however, that Charles' abilities took a military direction almost exclusively. A simple, democratic person, Charles had no airs, was a fighting man to the core, and thus won the devoted love of the common soldiers in his army. Certainly he was a great natural leader of men. At the zenith of his career he had beaten Denmark, Russia, and Poland, while all Europe marveled and even trembled before this "lion of the North." Unfortunately Charles could not beat all the odds when he invaded Russia in 1707, and he ended, like most romantic warriors, by leaving an almost ruined country. What struck the imagination of Europe was exactly this heroic mold: Charles was a throwback to the medieval warrior; he was no calculating politician or practicer of "statecraft" at all; his simple nature could only conceive the soldier's life. He was the last gasp of chivalry.

These wars for the Baltic reflected the existence of a "northern system" of power in this area, with the Baltic Sea and its rich trade as a focus. All the powers which rimmed that sea, including Denmark, Sweden, Poland, Russia, and some of the north German states, took some part in it. The Swedes dominated it for a while in the 17th century, but the Battle of Poltava, 1709, signaled the arrival of a new master.

Emergence of Russia

The emergence of Russia to become an important part of Europe's affairs was of course a development of the highest significance. In the 15th century, the principality of Moscow was a state of only 15,000 square miles, utterly remote from and without significance for Europe. There had been an earlier civilization around Kiev in the Middle Ages, Byzantine Christian, sharing in the commercial routes that emanated from Constantinople. But conquest by the oriental Tatars blighted this civilization and largely cut Russia off from the West. In 1240–52 Alexander Nevsky defeated the Swedes and the Teutonic Knights, preventing a European domination of Russia; while at the same time he cooperated with the khans, who were willing to leave government to the local princes in return for tribute and suzerainty—a pattern to be followed for two centuries. The backwardness of Russia in all respects must be explained by geographic factors as well as oriental influence. Opening eastward on Central Asia, the Slavs were subject to the continual invasions of the nomadic warriors of that great plain. Distances were immense and communications poor, except along the long north-south rivers. It was difficult for so huge and amorphous a mass to find its center and its goal. At length, after incredible difficulties and sufferings, Russia found its center in the city of Moscow, its goal in liberation from the Tatar yoke and contact with the West, together with a sense of its own mission to continue its unique culture.

Role of Moscow

Moscow first won its position as a center which served the khans of Mongolia as collector of tribute. But in the course of time it came to expand and to become the nucleus for a Russian state. It produced a series of remarkable princes, including Ivan III (1462–1505) under whom the Mongol yoke was thrown off and other principalities, particularly Novgorod, absorbed. With the fall of Constantinople to the Turks, the Muscovites came gradually to believe that the mantle of the Christian empire had fallen on them. For Christianity had reached Russia (in the 10th century) from Byzantium and became a vital force in Russian life after 1453. Moscow seemed the only remaining fastness of the Orthodox faith, the "third Rome." The princes of Russia tried to trace their descent back to the Emperor Augustus. This myth did a good deal to give Russian nationality its sense of destiny and goal, so important for a movement of consolidation. Thus Russia was to be a part of the Christian world, in a sense a part of the West. But "the Byzantine inheritance and the Tatar threat had combined to make the course of Russian history, in spite of superficial resemblances, incommensurable with that of the states of Latin Christian Europe." Russia, in brief, was never the same as the West.

Ivan IV

Yet she was drawn to it. In that direction lay commerce, wealth, techniques, and technology from which backward Russia could learn. Fighting intermittently with her western neighbors the Poles, Russia sought nevertheless to attach herself to this world. Expansion, so much a theme of the Muscovy state which started from almost nothing and increased with snowball-like proportions, meant expansion toward the seas, and commerce with wealthier regions: the Baltic, and to the south the Black Sea. The reign of Ivan the Terrible (Ivan IV, 1533–84) was a time of state building by a "tsar" (Ivan was the first to use this imperial title) who smote the power of the local landlords, conquered the Volga from the Tatars, and established contact with western traders. He even aspired to wed a lady of Queen Elizabeth's court, and received English merchants. But after Ivan there came a "time of troubles" marked by struggles for the throne and civil strife. In 1613 a national movement drove out the Poles, who had taken advantage of Russian weakness, and established the Romanov dynasty on the throne. It was to last until 1917. Not until about 1675, however, was the state firmly established. Wars with the Poles on the one side, Tatars and Turks on the other, were perennial; and in 1670 came a great peasant revolt, led by Stephen Razin. For this was a land where serfdom was a part of the social order, for reasons similar to those which had established it in Europe in the 10th century: it was one way of getting some degree of order and security out of an anarchic and lawless situation.

From the middle of the 17th century, Russia gained the Ukraine and came in contact with the Turks. As mentioned, she entered into diplomatic relations with European states at the time of the Christian League against the

Ivan IV combined political foresight with incredible brutality.

Turks. She also drew close to the Baltic, that inland ocean which had long been a route to commercial prosperity, whether for the cities of northern Germany, the Danes, or the Swedes. Russia was drawn into this system of power by the increase of western influences, and by her desire to shake off her backwardness through access to the West. But until the reign of Peter the Great, Russia remained amost unknown in Europe, vaguely dismissed even by educated Europeans as somewhere far to the east, with Persia and Abyssinia.

Peter the Great

The Byzantine inheritance made the Russian Tsar absolute beyond anything known in the West, while the numerous invasions, and geographic problems, encouraged a more brutal social order than had been seen in

Peter the Great, energetic westernizer of Russia

Peter cuts the beards of the boyars

Europe since the Dark Ages. Russia, indeed, was advancing quickly out of the Dark Ages, endeavoring to catch up with Europe. The cost was often great in human suffering, as it has continued to be in that land's history down to the present epoch. Having lost valuable centuries through being removed from the orbit of Greco-Roman civilization by the Mongol conquest, Russia was always struggling to catch up. Her history has been marked by titanic outbursts of effort to catch up, along with interludes of doubt about this course and an effort to mark out for Russia a separate mission.

Peter's visit to Europe

Russian expansion brought them into wars, with the Turks in the region of the Crimea and the Black Sea, and in the Balkans as well. The Turks were for long a pretty tough nut for the Russians to crack; progress in that direction was slow but remorseless. At first the European armies were also too much for the Russians. It was this, primarily, which determined Peter the Great to intensify the westernizing of his country. The giant Tsar, possessed of boundless energy and a flair for engineering, visited Europe in 1697–98, inspecting shipyards and even working, incognito, in European establishments in order to satisfy his curiosity about western technological ways—one of the most famous visits of all history. Later he brought hundreds of workers from Europe to build his city of Petersburg on the Baltic.

Defeat of Sweden

In the first part of the Great Northern War with Sweden, Charles XII defeated the Russians. But between 1700 and 1709 Peter made a vigorous effort to westernize his armies and build a fleet. At Poltava, Peter shattered Charles in 1709. The dynamic Russian ruler moved his capital to St. Petersburg to be nearer Europe, demanded the removal of beards and Russian costumes along with other symbols of a nonwestern orientation, and conducted in general a fierce war on the "reactionaries" who resented being pushed into imitation of Europe. Headstrong and violent, but intelligent and enlightened, Peter represents in Russian history the classic example of the forced pace toward catching up with Europe. He faced revolt from the nobles, the church, and other outraged conservatives, but crushed them and went on to centralize the state administration, introduce western education, and also encourage the adoption of western technology.

This colorful autocrat impatiently drove backward Mother Russia to adopt modern ways, laying on the lash when she faltered. He probably went too far too fast. His death was welcomed in Russia, and the pace of change slackened for a while. It should be noted that Peter had been raised to power with the aid of foreign officers, and the westernizers then and later were actually Europeans, not Russians—Germans, English, Swiss, Swedes—in the employment of a country which still largely lacked a native intelligentsia.

The link to Europe

Out of the Great Northern War Peter had gained (Treaty of Nystadt, 1721) territory on the Baltic, an area including Estonia and present-day Latvia. Russia now became a part of the European system of power. Her intervention in the Polish succession in 1733 has been mentioned. She was a party to the Treaty of Belgrade with Turkey and the Austrian Empire in 1739, having joined in that war against the Turks. The Russian state created by Ivan and Peter was still backward relative to most of Europe, but it became powerful enough to exert an influence on Europe, as well as receive one. It soon began to play a major part in European political affairs, and to be knit to the European economy. From the time when Peter gained access to the Baltic, and built canals (as for example between the Volga and the Neva) to link Russian communications with that sea, Russian trade increased mightily. Her lumber, iron, foodstuffs, and furs passed to Europe in return for a variety of manufactures much needed in Russia. It was a decisive step forward. Peter the Great had moved with a sure instinct when he saw in his "window on Europe," the Baltic ports, the road to westernization.

Byzantine and Ottoman

If eastern Europe was a different world, related yet estranged from the West, one reason was the sundering of East and West when the late Roman Empire moved one capital to Constantinople, or Byzantium.

Responsible for bringing civilization to much of eastern Europe was this Byzantine Empire which was Christian and Greco-Roman yet also subject to oriental influences. Byzantium had been very hard pressed by Islam in the mighty eruption of the Arabs in the seventh century, but it had held out, and went on to greater glories before it finally fell in 1453 to the Ottoman Turks. The Slavs of the Balkans and Russia, and the Bulgars, learned their Christian faith and classical culture from Constantinople. We now recognize also that the art of medieval western Europe owed a considerable debt—its exact dimensions are a matter of dispute among the experts—to Byzantium. Far richer than the West in medieval times, the Byzantine Empire had a powerful and orderly government and an advanced economy when Europe was suffering from the feuds of Frankish tribesmen or the spoliations of robber barons. Its Emperor was absolute, without limitation, his power considered to come from God; he was head of the church also, Pope and Emperor in one (though subject to some censorship by the patriarch of Constantinople). Its culture proudly preserved the great Greek learning and art of antiquity.

Between the eastern and western Christians there were differences which led to the final schism of 1054 after long theological quarrels. The schism, which was an accomplished fact by the time of Charlemagne, reflected basic differences in the culture and orientation of the two civilizations. Byzantium was a part of the East, part of a different economic as well as cultural world. Yet the Greek church was proud of its missionary activities among the Bulgars and Slavs. In the course of time these areas came to possess brilliant civilizations based on Byzantine models. The church art of medieval (12th- to 14th-century) Serbia is of surprising magnificence. These areas were to pass under the barbarous yoke of the Ottoman Turks and deteriorate sadly, but before that they had shared in the medieval glories of Byzantium.

SVLTAN SOLIMA
Imperador de Tur:
chi Entro al gouer:
no L'anno 1519 et
mori L'anno 1566

Sultan Suleiman I, through conquests, alliances, and tributes, made his Empire rich.

Ottoman Turks

All this fell to the Ottoman Turks in the 14th and 15th centuries. The Turks originally represented a barbarian conquest; they were hard, primitive tribesmen conquering an old, rich civilization. Formidable warriors, these lean Asiatic nomads had a mountain fierceness and a close tribal organization. They adopted Islam and, becoming rulers of the caliphate, won the position of guardian of the Moslem world. When Constantinople fell to them, the Turkish Sultan added the title of Emperor. Sweeping into Europe and across the Arab world as well, the Turks had for a time the greatest of empires. The revenues of Suleiman the Magnificent (1520–66) were twice those of his contemporary, Charles V. This was the potentate who took Budapest and besieged Vienna itself; had it not been for this Turkish threat, Charles V and the Hapsburgs would surely have beaten France and perhaps erected their monarchy over all Europe. The "scandalous" alliance of France and the Turks will be recalled.

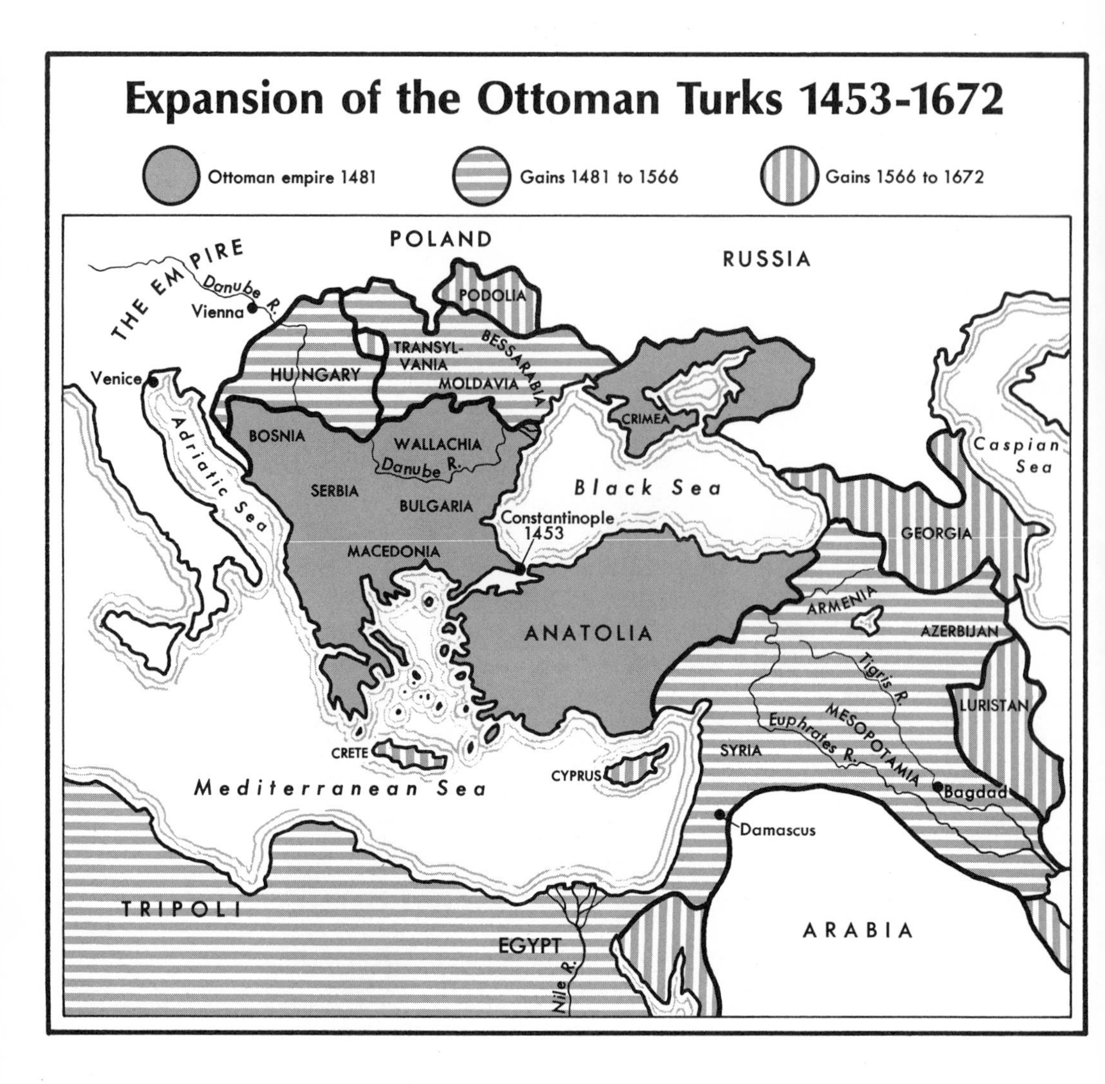

They seemed men of destiny, these yellowish leaders from the interior of Asia. But in the course of time they too were softened by the pleasures and wealth of old Asia. They had a remarkable system of governing by the use of specially trained slaves, called janissaries, who, selected and taken from their subjects at an early age, were kept apart as a ruling caste. Many even of the sultans came to be half Russian, or Greek, or Albanian. The high officers of state and the army were drawn from this janissary class, which reflected its rigidly supervised education in being absolutely loyal and honest—for a long time, at least.

The Turks governed, but they had little interest in technological and scientific development; in fact, for Christian Europe their long rule was an almost unmitigated disaster. The Ottoman Empire declined not only because of technological backwardness but because of the corruption of the sultanate. Polygamy, the harem, and intrigue over the succession finally made the Sublime Porte a fearful example of monarchical decadence and debauchery. The janissaries revolted and murdered a sultan in 1621, which was an ominous sign of the machine turning on its master. Before their last decline the Turks had a revival in the 17th century under the Kiuprili grand viziers (Albanians), and in 1683 they were again at the gates of Vienna, playing a part in the wars of Europe. For the Hapsburgs were again having trouble with France, and were weakened in war with Louis XIV by this back-door intrusion. We have seen how Sobieski and the Poles helped turn back the Turks.

But after being checked before Vienna by Sobieski's international Christian army, the Turks again ebbed. The Emperor defeated them severely and chased them down the Danube a good way, reclaiming Hungary, Transylvania, and Serbia, but losing Serbia back. The fighting went on intermittently until 1739, when the Treaty of Belgrade stabilized the frontier. The Turks were also under pressure from Peter the Great of Russia around the Black Sea, pressure which continued under Catherine the Great later in the 18th century. However, they remained in southeastern Europe, holding much of Serbia and Rumania (the provinces of Wallachia and Moldavia) as well as Greece, until the 19th century. They owed this survival chiefly to the rivalries of the European powers, who could not agree on a partition of this zone and watched each other more warily than they did the sultan. In 1772, after having started out on a plan to divide up the Turkish Empire in Europe, Russia and Austria, following the suggestion of Frederick the Great, turned instead to the more convenient partition of Poland.

That the Turk remained in Europe and subjected this area to a rule which was retrograde in the extreme meant much for the future of Europe: southeastern Europe became in the 19th and early 20th centuries the powder keg of Europe, racked by explosive hatreds and innumerable racial antagonisms. This was a legacy of imperialism in a part of Europe where imperialism was the usual thing.

Eastern Europe as a whole

How eastern Europe differed from the West

Taking eastern Europe as a whole, there were some general features which marked it off from the West. Its peoples were different: this was a world largely of Slavs, with a mixture of others such as Balts, Magyars, Albanians, Bulgars, Turks, but not many of the Germanic races who dominated in the West. (But the German Hapsburgs governed a portion of it, and advisers and officials from western Europe made up a part of the Russian government. The eastern part of the Prussian state, too, might in many ways be counted as part of this zone.) Its religion was different: Orthodox Christian or even Moslem, though Roman Catholic and Protestant were represented. (Poland was Roman Catholic, the Hapsburgs Romanized their domains as best they could.) Its cultural, social, political, and economic affairs were all more "backward," though we must be careful to state what we mean by so pejorative an adjective. The peasants were generally more degraded, since serfdom still existed and often amounted to something like slavery. Cities were fewer, trade less brisk, agriculture overwhelmingly predominant. Landlords, of a sort somewhat reminiscent of medieval Europe's feudal barons, played a large role in society. Politically, the rule of the Turk was benighted by European standards, while the inadequacies of Polish kingship contrasted with the semioriental despotism of Russia. The Hapsburg realms, too, involved methods of goverment inconsistent with any ordered constitutional state.

By and large, cultural backwardness accompanied social and economic backwardness. There were old and rich cultural traditions in this part of Europe, for example those of the Magyars, the Serbs, the Poles, the Bohemians, the Ukrainians, the Lithuanians, not to speak of the Greeks, or those Rumanians who traced their descent to Rome. Western Europe often did not appreciate these traditions because barriers of language and custom interfered, and because of lack of contact and knowledge at this time. Russia was extremely remote from most Europeans; the Turk was a hateful legend. Many of these cultures had been submerged by foreign conquest. For this was an area of imperialism, meaning rule by aliens. The hard hand of the Russian tsar and the Turkish sultan oppressed people who deserved better.

This was also the European frontier with Asia. It was exposed to the assaults of a continent, and bore the brunt of many a ferocious attack. Behind it western Europe led a sheltered existence, and owed the frontier peoples a large debt for that reason. If Turk and Mongol did not sweep into Europe it was because the great Slav body existed and absorbed the blows.

State building in eastern Europe

However, by the 18th century there were signs of improvement. If Poland, the leading Latin Christian society, a land of rich churches and universities in later medieval times,[1] was in decay, Russia was becoming more civilized and the Hapsburgs were rationalizing their ramshackle empire. The kingdom of Prussia had emerged to stabilize a portion of the area. Most people thought the ejection of the Turk only a matter of time. It must be conceded that as a general rule the price of a stronger state and an educated upper class was the subjection of the mass of peasants to serfdom. Much noted was the fact that in the East, builders of states—Romanovs, Hapsburgs, or Hohenzollerns—worked differently than monarchs had done in the West. In the latter zone they typically allied with the middle classes, or a commercial gentry essentially bourgeois in outlook, to bear down the proud territorial nobility, extinguish serfdom, and set up a law which touched all, though all might not yet be equal under it. In the East, the power of the landlord nobility was too great, under the economic circumstances, to be removed. States were built on the basis largely of deals between kings and landlords. The latter retained local political autonomy, governing their serfs entirely on their own vast holdings. *Boyars*, *schlachta*, *junkers*, the holders of great *latifundia*—eastern Europe was full of such local potentates, and would be down until very recent times, whereas they were declining in the west of Europe, the last of their privileges going with the French Revolution. They granted powers to the monarch, sent their younger sons into his bureaucracy or army, and paid

[1] An example of this is the magnificent wood-carved altarpiece of St. Mary's Church in Cracow (1477–89), perhaps the most extraordinary specimen of this sort of art in Europe.

some taxes into his till, but in return they expected a free hand locally, where they unlimitedly exploited the serfs—often, as in Hungary or east Prussia, people of another race, or if not actually so regarded at such in practice (Russia). The result was that each advance in the power of the state tended to drive the country's masses deeper into slavery. Peter the Great's reforms had this result, as did Catherine II's later. The story was similar in Prussia and in the Austrian Empire. It was not a happy situation.

Bibliography

General surveys of the eastern part of Europe include Oscar Halecki, *Borderlands of Western Civilization: A History of East Central Europe* (New York: Ronald Press, 1952) and F. Dvornik, *The Making of Central and Eastern Europe* (London: Polish Research Centre, 1949), also *The Slavs in European History and Civilization* (1962). On the various countries, there are *The Cambridge History of Poland* (2 vols.; New York: Cambridge University Press, 1941), the first volume going to 1691; S. Clissold (ed.), *A Short History of Yugoslavia* (Cambridge University Press, 1967); D. Sinor, *History of Hungary* (New York: Frederick A. Praeger, 1959), with stress on the earlier centuries; and S.H. Thompson, *The Czechs in European History* (2d ed.; Princeton, N.J.: Princeton University Press, 1953). D.M. Vaughan, *Europe and the Turks* (Liverpool: Liverpool University Press, 1959), along with R.B. Merriman's biography of *Suleiman the Magnificent* (Cambridge, Mass.: Harvard University Press, 1944), and A.D. Alderson, *The Structure of the Ottoman Dynasty* (New York: Oxford University Press, 1956), will provide insights into the role of the Ottoman Empire. F. Bengtsson has written a recent *Life of Charles XII*, the great Swedish leader (New York: Macmillan, 1960); F. Schevill, *The Great Elector* (Chicago: University of Chicago Press, 1954), and F.L. Carsten, *Origins of Prussia* (Oxford: Clarendon Press, 1954), concern the emergence of Brandenburg-Prussia. See also the brief paperback by Sidney B. Fay and Klaus Epstein, *The Rise of Brandenburg-Prussia to 1786* (Holt, Rinehart & Winston). Hajo Holborn's second volume of his *History of Modern Germany* (New York: Alfred A. Knopf, 1964) covers 1648 to 1840.

An interesting biography is J.B. Morton, *Sobieski, King of Poland* (London, 1932). John Stoye, *The Siege of Vienna* (London: Collins, 1964) is excellent on 17th-century military affairs. Russia of course bulks largest; George Vernadsky's *History of Russia* continues with Vol. III, dealing with *The Mongols in Russia*, and Vol. IV, *Russia at the Dawn of the Modern Age*. J.L.I. Fennell has a good study of the 15th-century ruler *Ivan the Great of Moscow* (Macmillan, 1961). An interestingly written biography of *Ivan the Terrible* is by Jules Koslow (London: W.H. Allen, 1961). A brief general history is J.D. Clarkson, *A History of Russia From the Ninth Century* (Longmans, Green & Co.); while a good specialized work is Jerome Blum, *Lord and Peasant in Russia from the Ninth to the Nineteenth Century* (Atheneum). James H. Billington, *The Icon and the Axe* (Alfred A. Knopf, 1966), is a thoughtful interpretation of Russian culture. Stephen Graham has made himself the biographer of both *Ivan the Terrible* (New Haven, Conn.: Yale University Press, 1933) and *Peter the Great* (New York: Simon & Schuster, 1929), the latter having attracted many students including B.H. Sumner, *Peter the Great and the Emergence of Russia* (Macmillan, Collier). The greatest of Russian historians was V.O. Klyuchevsky, whose *History of Russia* in five volumes has been translated into English and published by Russell & Russell, Publishers (New York, 1960); his *Peter the Great* is in a paperback edition (Random House, Vintage).

An interesting collection of source material is Marthe Blinoff (ed.), *Life and Thought in Old Russia, 1466–1881* (University Park: Pennsylvania State University Press, 1961). The first volume of Thomas Riha's *Readings in Russian Civilization* (University of Chicago) covers 900–1700; Vol. II, 1700–1917.

16

Europe in the Age of Enlightenment

chronology

1715
Accession of Louis XV (regency until 1721). Failure of Jacobite revolt in Britain.
Whig supremacy in England 1715–60 (George I, George II).
1720
Robert Walpole chief minister, England.
1733
War of Polish Succession, defeat for French influence in East.
Family Compact between France and Spain.
1735–59
Charles IV, "enlightened" ruler of Naples and Sicily.
1738
Treaty of Vienna, Polish and Italian settlement.
1739
War of Jenkins' Ear between Spain and Britain.
1740
Death of Emperor Charles VI, accession of Maria Theresa, beginning of War of Austrian Succession. Frederick the Great to Prussian throne.
1748
Treaty of Aix-la-Chapelle, ending War of Austrian Succession.
1755
Great earthquake at Lisbon.
1756
Reversal of alliances; beginning of the Seven Years War.
William Pitt, British Prime Minister.
1757
Battles of Rossbach and Leuthen, brilliant victories of Frederick the Great over French and Austrians.
1759
British capture of Quebec.
Charles III, "enlightened" ruler of Spain, 1759–88.
1760
George III becomes King of England.
1762
Death of Elizabeth of Russia, withdrawal of Russia from war.
Catherine the Great assumes throne of Russia.
1763
Treaties of Paris, Hubertusburg, ending Seven Years War.
1765
Joseph II Emperor of Austria.
1767
Catherine the Great's "Instructions" to assembly of deputies.
Expulsion of Jesuits from France and Spain.
1768
Wilkes affair in Great Britain.
1772
First partition of Poland.
1773
Pugachev's revolt, Russia.
Dissolution of Jesuit order by the Pope.
1774
Death of Louis XV, coming of Louis XVI to French throne.
Russian acquisitions from Turkey.
1775
American Revolution begins.
Turgot dismissed by Louis XVI.
1778
Franco-American alliance.
1780
Gordon Riots in London.
1781
Edict of Tolerance and other reforms of Joseph II.
Constitutional struggle in Holland.
1782
Fall of North Ministry in Britain.
1783
Treaty of Versailles, ending war of American independence.
1786
Death of Frederick the Great.
1787
Assembly of Notables summoned in France.
American Constitution.
1789
Gustav III of Sweden proclaims legal equality.
French Revolution begins.

The dawn of the 18th century

An age of repose

As the 18th century began, most of the main countries of Europe settled down into a more placid mold than that of the churning, turbulent 17th century with its wars and revolutions. Louis XIV's reign came to an end, and with the advent of Louis XV, at first under a regent, France entered tamer waters under far less adventurous leadership. In any case war had exhausted her, and the rest of Europe, which now entered upon a long period of peace. The 1713 Peace of Utrecht signaled the restoration of the balance of power. England, too, saw her last political crisis upon the death of Queen Anne and the installation of George I in 1714, which ushered in an era of repose. Prussia between 1713 and 1740 was ruled by Frederick William I, who avoided war and husbanded his country's resources. Russia, following Peter the Great's brilliant, stormy, and revolutionary reign, was more than ready to call a temporary halt to such moves. The Dutch and Spanish were as ready as the French to exchange war for peace; Austria busied herself with her southeastern

Frederick the Great playing the flute at Sans Souci, his palace at Potsdam.

frontier, where she was building an empire in this area redeemed from Turkish rule. In their internal government, the states of Europe were consolidating the gains made during the previous century.

Intellectual progress

This period of retrenchment, peace, and repose, well expressed in the motto of England's "prime minister" Robert Walpole that it was best to let sleeping dogs lie, coincided with the culmination of the intellectual and scientific revolution in the work of Isaac Newton, John Locke, and others at the end of the 17th century. With these achievements went the intoxicating sense of a new method of knowledge which might be applied everywhere with unlimited potentialities; a feeling of release from centuries of stagnation, a feeling of "breakthrough" or—as the term was—Enlightenment, illumination, *Aufklärung.*

So the 18th century dawned bright and clear, and through much of it, developments continued to be encouraging. Not since the high point of the Roman Empire had men felt the sense of security and well-being they felt in the 18th century. In England, this was dubbed the "Augustan age," and in France, too, people stressed the classical motif, as if conscious of this comparison between their age and that of Augustus. True, there was no world state. But the great states of France and England with their imperial possessions seemed a reasonable approximation. War between them, so incessant in earlier times, was much less frequent and also much less destructive in this century. Between the close of the War of the Spanish Succession in 1713 and the War of the Austrian Succession in 1740 there were only a few minor skirmishes. Between 1740 and 1763 lay two major wars, but these wars mainly concerned Prussia and Austria. France and Britain contended chiefly in their overseas empires, where much was at stake, indeed, but where the fighting was remote from the homeland.

The civilization of war

The manner in which the 18th century waged its wars should be noted: it went far to achieve the goal of civilized war, war as a game with rules, in which calculating statesmen used armies as tools of state policy but were at the same time aware of their place in the European community. There was nothing like the fearful ravages of the Thirty Years War or even of the wars of Louis XIV. Well-disciplined professional armies, commanded by aristocrats with a high sense of *noblesse oblige,* sparred warily in the field, in a game of maneuver wherein the object was as much to avoid battle as to seek it. War might scarcely disturb the normal tenor of life: it was in fact this ideal at which statesmen avowedly aimed.

18th-century cosmopolitanism

There was a notable cosmopolitanism about the thought of the Enlightenment; it ignored or disparaged the sentiment of nationalism and talked in terms of the human race, or of men as united by the common denominator of natural reason. In practice as well as in theory, internationalist phenomena of a surprising sort existed. Frederick the Great, who advanced the Prussian state to a position of world leadership, chose to speak, write, and read French, because it was much more the language of learned Europe than his own German. So also did the courtiers of Imperial Russia, preferring French to their own supposedly more barbarous tongue. Englishmen of the upper class, in order to qualify for a career and complete their education, embarked upon the "grand tour," a leisurely journey through France and Italy which was felt necessary to make one a civilized European. In return, Voltaire and Montesquieu, the leaders of French thought, inordinately admired the English system of government and ridiculed their own inept despotism. Men of letters tried to write in accordance with classical precepts which were the same everywhere, giving to literature an international flavor.

Classicism, or neoclassicism, now replaced the 17th-century baroque almost everywhere, reflecting the calmer and more confident spirit. To be elegant, exact, symmetrical, and unified was the acme of perfection in a work of art; men were asked to purify their language, their conversation and literary style. But at the same time a bolder and more critical spirit was abroad. In France this was true from the very start of the reign of Louis XV, who could not overawe men as had his illustrious predecessor; Montesquieu and Voltaire were the young men of the hour. And England, after the Glorious Revolution, developed an amazing freedom of thought and expression. This freedom to criticize became a hallmark of the Enlightenment, and in it some sensed the possibility of a subversion of the established order of government and society such as did occur near the end of the century. But such a result was as yet far off; the established order was safe enough in the earlier 18th century.

Economic prosperity

Mercantilism

It must be admitted that there was not, as in Hellenistic and Roman times, a single international economy with common coinage and no tariff barriers. Until rather late in the century the precept as well as the practice favored "mercantilism," though a few voices had been raised against it. The word "mercantilism" has become attached to the economic policies pursued by states from the 16th to the 18th centuries, though like all such general terms it is easy to point out its inadequacies. It has been previously mentioned: Queen Elizabeth in the 16th and Louis XIV in the 17th centuries were said to have practiced mercantilism. By this is meant that they used the powers of the state vigorously to advance trade, commerce, and sometimes manufacturing, thus regulating a good deal of economic life. "The one common feature was the exercise of state power over every side of economic life." (Herbert Heaton)

Now this use of state power was undeniably constructive in its time, or at least had some constructive features. It was the counterpart in economics of the victory of the national state over feudal localism. It took the nation as the unit, and one of its goals was the destruction of all local barriers to trade, creating a national market. Such barriers, the relics of medievalism, were formidable indeed, especially on the Continent. And state aid in the establishment of various industries and of transportation was often vital. All Englishmen took for granted that the Navigation Acts constituted the indispensable basis of England's naval power and thus of her whole economic position. These laws gave a virtual monopoly of the carrying trade of England and her colonies to British ships. Even in the 19th century, long after much mercantilist economic thought had been rejected, subsidies helped build canals and railroads, as students of American history know. They might otherwise not have been built.

Jealousy of trade

However, the obvious corollary of a nationalist economic system was that it was not internationalist; it was exclusive and jealous against a foreign state. Planning and regulation within the confines of the nation always implies keeping out any foreign competition which would be outside the planning or regulatory area. Subsidies of the sort just mentioned took the form of monopolies granted to English shippers only, who were protected from foreign competition. To build up a domestic industry by means of a tariff which penalizes foreign goods is a familiar phenomenon even down to the present day. The so-called "mercantilist system" was sometimes, too, less a rational system than a tendency for each special economic interest to get favors from the government. In any case tariffs, monopolies, prohibitions on imports or exports, attempts to lure skilled workers away from other countries and prevent the migration of one's own skilled workers, and treatment of colonial empires as an adjunct to the national economy—all these were familiar features of mercantilism which were sometimes productive of wars between the rival economic units. International trade war, not international trade, was the rule in the 18th century.

Economic growth

Nevertheless, there was some tendency throughout the 18th century for men to deplore the worst features of international beggar-my-neighbor policies and to realize what Adam Smith authoritatively demonstrated in 1776, that if each country specialized in its own most efficient products and all traded freely with each other everyone would be richer. Meanwhile the rapid progress of the national economies, with their overseas possessions, made for unexampled prosperity, especially in England and France. Great Britain waxed fat on the proceeds of unity at home, colonies abroad, and a government favorable to trade and industry. The Atlantic ports profited at the expense of the older Mediterranean trade routes; Venice declined as London, Bordeaux, and Amsterdam continued to climb. It was the English city on the Thames that now became the most populous of all cities in the Western world. Paris was second.

Role of colonies

Up until the last quarter of the century, this was still the age of the merchant prince, not the "industrialist." Industries such as textiles and iron made much progress, but it is too early to speak of the "industrial revolution."

The great fortunes were likely to be made in India, or in the slave trade, or in "factoring" for the American mainland colonists, or in the sugar plantations of Jamaica. It is significant that colonies were valued as producers of certain raw materials rather than as markets for the products of home industries. The latter view began to prevail only in the latter part of the century. England long valued the Sugar Islands more than the North American colonies, and in 1763 debated earnestly whether to take Guadaloupe or Canada from France. Profits from such mercantile enterprises were huge. West Indian sugar barons and "nabobs" home from India were the glamorous rich of the hour in England. The slave trade still brought fortunes. Most of the gold and silver from the Spanish and Portuguese New World colonies found its way into the hands of French and English merchants.

End of medieval economy

By the 18th century the economic world was beginning to show the cumulative effect of a series of changes going on since the end of the Middle Ages. In western Europe the medieval land economy had all but disappeared, and had been replaced by commercial farming. The peasant village, with its villeins bound to the soil, its "commons" and manor, had given way to large farms worked by wage laborers; or in other places, the peasants had gained land as small renters or freeholders. In the cities, the dominant medieval institution had been the guilds. By the 18th century these too had greatly declined, and with them declined the medieval craftsman—at once workman, foreman, employer, and merchant. The strict regulation of production, wages, and trade which the guilds had once exercised was taken over by the state; but by the 18th century every form of regulation was gradually retreating in favor of the free play of enterprise. Workingmen were becoming wage laborers dependent upon capitalists who owned the tools and the materials. Cities were growing, markets were expanding, transportation had greatly improved. There was more wealth. Merchants, shippers, manufacturers, and financiers made up a more numerous, wealthy, and powerful bourgeois class than ever before. Peasants and workers, however, got little of the new wealth.

Prelude to the Industrial Revolution

The "Industrial Revolution" was approaching. That is swooped down upon the world suddenly is a view no longer held. Several centuries of gradual change prepared the way for it. By the end of the 18th century, the proper conditions were present, and the pace began to quicken. Throughout the 18th century the basic groundwork was being laid. In summary, these were the significant developments: foreign trade expanded, and greatly augmented wealth; there was technological progress in a wide variety of areas, the most important of which included steam power, coal and iron smelting, textile machinery; and a "transportation revolution" began to knit nations by canals and improved roads into effective economic units. It is interesting that the roots of the great 19th- and even 20th-century inventions—railroads, telephones, telegraphs, and even automobiles and airplanes—can be detected in the 18th century; they are as yet not commercially feasible but they are being approached as engineering ideas. Thus, for example, in 1770, Joseph Cugnot demonstrated a steam-driven vehicle designed to pull heavy artillery; it did so, but used too much water and jerked too violently to be practicable. The aerial feats of the brothers Montgolfier are rather well known. In 1804 Sir George Cayley made the first successful glider. There was tinkering also with telegraph and telephone, but progress in electricity was not yet sufficient to make them feasible. Two Italians, Volta and Galvani, whose names are preserved in its parlance, gave electrical science its real start at the end of the century, after the fascinating games played with Leyden jars and lightning rods earlier in the century.

Domestic system

The day of the factory, using power machinery and employing hundreds of laborers, was not yet. More typical was the "domestic system" in which rural families worked on products in their homes, to be picked up and assembled by merchant capitalists; or, in the cities, still the small workshop. There were a few exceptions but not many. England and Scotland were the farthest advanced; even here, by 1780 one could just glimpse the dawn of the Industrial Revolution. The rural gentry still dominated English social and political life as the aristocracy did in France and elsewhere in Europe.

The political and social order: Great Britain

By the Act of Union of 1707 England was united with Scotland and thus became Great Britain. In 1714 the British emerged as a first-class power, perhaps the leading one in Europe, as the long struggle with France ended in a qualified victory: Britain picked up naval bases and gains in the colonial world. In the same year as the Peace of Utrecht, the constitution received its definitive settlement with the Hanoverian George I assumed the throne under the direction and control of the Whig leaders of Parliament. Thus fortified by political success, England went on in the 18th century to thrive as never before. Her population and trade increased, especially after mid-century; and in textiles, iron, and coal, the incubation period for the 19th-century birth of a technological age took place.

English liberty

Europe was deeply impressed by the English government because it was both free *and* successful, and accompanied by economic success. With a limited monarchy, a strong Parliament, and large freedoms of speech and press, the British presented a model not of turbulence but of stability, and led the other states in wealth as well as personal liberty. After 1689, when the Toleration Act was passed, there was in practice no barrier to the free exercise of religion, and though that act disqualified Nonconformists as well as Catholics from political office, ways were found of evading this in practice. Catholics and unitarians, as well as non-Christians, were not placed within the bounds of toleration in 1689. But, by 1700, they were not in practice subject to persecution. (Not until 1828–29, with the repeal of the Test and Corporation Acts and passage of the Catholic Emancipation Act, were Dissenters

1783 balloon ascension from Versailles witnessed by the King and family

William Hogarth's pen depicts voting by the blind, the crippled, and the deranged in 18th century England.

and Catholics granted full, formal political equality. Jews and atheists did not gain admission to Parliament until 1858 and 1888 respectively.) When the Licensing Act was allowed to lapse in 1693, an era of substantial freedom of the press began. Deists and unitarians, who boldly criticized Christian doctrines, wrote insistently and virtually without restriction beginning in the 1690's; hardly half a century before, such "blasphemy" was punishable with imprisonment or even death.

In the Whig political philosophers, of whom John Locke was foremost, Englishmen read nothing about an organic state with a divine-right monarch, but about a social compact between individuals, which created a government of limited powers, against which there might be under certain circumstances a right of rebellion. A few Tories might grumble at this. But after 1715 there were few old-fashioned Tories left, and the long period of Whig ascendancy began which lasted until 1760.

Continental writers made much of English liberty in their propaganda for change in their own countries, and the mood of the Enlightenment with its faith in reason and its hopes for progress owed a good deal to this English achievement. However, historians have been constrained to point out that the realities of English political life differed not a little from the ideals of the publicists.

Realities of the English constitution

They tended to see it as a system of checks and balances, separation of powers, all solemnly devised according to the classical model. In some ways this was true. The independence of the judiciary from the royal power, cherished since the assaults of the Stuart kings on the common law, was regarded as settled. The common law developed majestically, finding its great commentator in Blackstone during the 18th century. Neither king nor Parliament could lay hands on the courts. On the other hand, the secret of English stability lay in no separation of powers between executive and legislative, but in the virtual resignation of Kings George I and George II and their permitting the leaders of Parliament to run executive affairs. And the surprising unity between Parliament and throne was also the result of a secret system of "influence" which Montesquieu never discussed. The House of Commons was controlled through a variety of corrupt practices, of which the crown's disposal of offices, honors, and gifts was the most important. It was not a democratically elected body, save in a very few counties or boroughs. It really came closer to being the preserve of a wealthy oligarchy, which at this time controlled both Parliament and the crown. Thus behind the formal facade of the political system, the realities were quite different, and much less inspiring.

English social structure

This England was by no means equalitarian or democratic. The social structure of England was inequalitarian, consisting of four main layers. There were the peers, the hereditary nobility, entitled to a seat in the House of Lords—a group small in number in England, unlike France. These dukes and marquesses, the "great oaks that shade the country" in Edmund Burke's admiring phrase, had great prestige and often functioned as the nucleus of the leading political factions, but they shared power with the other branch of the aristocracy, the gentry. These were nontitled, but often very wealthy. The line between the wealthier gentry and the peers was not always very distinct; the former were not servile toward the latter, and indeed prized their independence. They had made a revolution once and were proud of their social status, which in England was based on land ownership. The squire's house and estate was the focus of English society, for here there was no Versailles, nor indeed any Paris—London despite its size and commercial importance was no such center of all the arts and civilization as was the French capital.

The squires

At its bottom end the gentry class slid into the smaller freeholders, who might be yeoman peasants possessed of only an acre or two. (Consider the difference in tone between Squire Allworthy and Squire Western in Fielding's *Tom Jones*, that matchless picture of 18th-century English life.) Toward their tenants and laborers the squires displayed a paternal benevolence; it was the Frenchman, Montesquieu, who said that in case of war the French peasants would cut the *seigneurs'* throats while the English would defend the lives of theirs. The squire was the local government, and he usually determined the election of the member of Parliament for his district. An important feature of the English system of land and title was primogeniture, which made the younger sons seek a trade or profession since they inherited nothing—an invigorating factor which also strengthened the House of Commons, as distinct from the House of Lords, for many younger sons, well educated and of aristocratic family, went into Commons rather than Lords. In Dr. Samuel Johnson's pungent phrase, primogeniture made but one fool a family. But if a man made money in trade, he bought land, for it alone conferred prestige and political power. The 18th-century electoral system notoriously discriminated against the cities, and included many "pocket boroughs" or "rotten boroughs" which were small or even nonexistent, and completely at the disposal of the local squire or lord.

"He is naturally a very dull animal," a French observer said of the English squire at this time; the picture of the beef-gorging, beer-guzzling, fox-hunting roughneck is familiar enough. But certainly there were the Allworthys as well as the Westerns, the gentry of some education and good taste as well as those who ate with their hounds and slept with their pigs. Less cultivated than his counterpart in France, the English aristocrat was closer to the people and politically more independent. He did not scorn trade and industry. Below him, the lines were somewhat blurred between his class and the "middling sort." Anyone who made money could become a member of the English aristocracy, and no questions asked, if he bought land and learned to ride to the hounds. There was no aristocracy of privilege as in France, for whatever the social inequalities, all were equal before the law in England.

The Dissenters

The middle classes, consisting of a miscellaneous group of tradesmen, better-off tenant farmers, the lower ranks of the professions, and the men of manufacturing, found little snobbishness of birth to overcome in England. In the burgeoning industrial economy of the later part of the century this class produced most of the great industrialists. They were more likely to be of the Dissenting or Nonconformist Protestant religion—Presbyterians, Independents, Baptists, or Quakers. This marked them off from the squires, who were Anglican (nominally so, in actuality far from a deeply religious group), and caused them to be subjected to some mild forms of discrimination. Dissenters could in theory not hold office; but in fact they were permitted to evade the disqualification by attending the Church of England once a year, and by special acts of Parliament which suspended even this requirement on an annual basis. More serious was their disbarment from the universities, Oxford and Cambridge; but the Dissenters developed their own academies, offering an education less classical and more practical. (The Scottish universities, Glasgow and Edinburgh, helped England's industrial growth much more than the traditional English universities.)

The poor

The poor might be rural workers with some claim on the squire's charity, or skilled artisans with a chance of working their way up in the social scale; or they might be the gin-sodden wretches whom Hogarth depicted in his famous paintings. The London underworld, the public hangings on Tyburn hill, the "press gang," the beggars, pimps, and prostitutes, were all an unhappy part of the 18th-century scene. Public education and the welfare state had not yet taken up the task of doing anything about the unlucky and ill-

Despite general prosperity, life remained sordid for many in the 18th century. Gin was cheaper than tea.

equipped. There was some private charity, but the drift of the century was away from rather than toward public responsibility for poverty. Most writers on the subject, from Defoe to Fielding, said that the best medicine for the poor was to force them out of their idleness by refusing to grant them easy sustenance either from the state or from private charity.

The Methodists

It was, relative to all previous examples, a free society, with little limit on freedom of press and pulpit after 1700. The debates in Parliament, though not yet legally published, actually were made known to the public. While the upper classes fattened on the increasing wealth of a prosperous century, the lower class quite frequently rioted, but never cared or knew enough to make a revolution. The chief agency reaching the poor in mid-18th-century England was the rising Wesleyan or Methodist religious movement, product of the remarkable evangelist John Wesley. Scandalizing much of British respectability, Wesley preached to the poorest people, gained their attention, taught them not revolution but the reform of their own character, manners, and morals. It has been said that this evangelicalism was "the true nursing mother of the spirit and character values that have created and sustained free insti-

John Wesley preaching at Bolton Cross

tutions throughtout the English-speaking world." But the Methodists were widely despised as fanatics in the complacent atmosphere of the mid–18th century. It was a time when many Church of England parsons thought more of fox-hunting with the squire than of discharging their religious duties.

British pragmatism

English government by contrast with the French was less expensive and less centralized, indeed less extensive. Whereas France and Prussia kept large standing armies, all honest Englishmen hated the army and refused to support anything more than a tiny one. The British army numbered less than 20,000 when France and Prussia boasted 200,000. The navy, it is true, ranked high in English eyes, as the proper means of defending the country and securing its interests, but it absorbed no very large amount of government money. By long tradition and perhaps by "national character" (something that does seem to exist, even if often difficult to define with exactitude), the English desired to be governed less, planned-for less, than the French. They trusted more to individual enterprise, to local option, and to muddling through without any comprehensive central scheme of organization. The English also relied less on a centralized bureaucracy and more on the amateur efforts of the local squires, who administered justice and government in an informal way. They believed the French to be slavish and dogmatic; even British neoclassicism as a literary and artistic style was more experimental, less subservient to the rules, than French.

Their colonial empires exhibited this pattern too, and here the British came out much better. Overregulated from Paris, the great French empire in the New World had a brilliant start but never succeeded in attracting large numbers of settlers. The British, by contrast, let their colonists alone and they flourished. Unhappily for the government at Westminster, they also gained the feeling that they were perfectly self-sufficient and could get along without any connection to the home government.

France: The Ancien Régime

French troubles

France in the 18th century did not find as much political success, hence the readiness of her intellectual classes to criticize and point to England. While continuing to lead the world of letters and thought brilliantly—never more so than in the age of Voltaire, Buffon, Rousseau, Montesquieu, D'Alembert, and others—France lost ground in many ways. The Grand Monarchy ceased to be grand. Louis XV and Louis XVI were no weaker than George I and George II, but what was a blessing in England, with her strong parliamentary tradition, was dangerous in France, where the monarchy was the keystone of the whole system and a national parliament did not even exist. With the largest population of Europe and natural wealth, augmented until 1763 by a large colonial empire, France remained a great power, with a rising standard of life. But she was to lose international prestige, coming out of the wars of mid-century with stinging losses, and being excluded from the New World by Great Britain, from eastern Europe by Prussia and Russia. Worse still, her internal situation grew alarming. While the monarchy lost authority through the ineptitude of the kings, there were urgent basic reforms crying for attention. The royal finances grew ever more desperate.

The trouble lay in an unequal tax structure which granted exemptions freely to the nobility while bearing too heavily on the poor; a system which was unwieldy and inefficient in its feudal foundations and corrupt in its collection. A vigorous, courageous king with able ministers was needed to push through tax reform against the opposition of powerful entrenched interests. Few in France thought much of parliaments as a solution. There were several regional *parlements* in France,[1] with the status of courts of registry for royal decrees, but while they had some power and sometimes courage, they did not have the stature of national representative bodies. Moreover, they had become a refuge of the privileged orders, who used them to oppose any basic reforms.

The coming of the French Revolution is treated in the chapter on that great event (Chapter 18). Here something should be said briefly about the social order of the Old Regime, as it became known after the Revolution—

---

[1] There were twelve *parlements* altogether by 1685, some of them very ancient; Paris was the most important, but regional *parlement* cities included such places as Rouen, Rennes, Bordeaux, Aix, Dijon, Toulouse, Grenoble, Metz.

an order based on aristocratic privilege. Aristocracy in the 18th-century manner must be distinguished from the old baronial class. It had now become courtly and elegant. It was by no means impossible for the crown to create nobles out of commoners, a practice, however, less rare in England than in most continental countries. The aristocracy still had a strong relationship to the land: protected by laws preventing the breakup of an hereditary estate, landed domains still marked the noble, though he no longer fortified himself against the king in a moated castle. In France the erstwhile serfs had become free peasants, but they were sharply marked off from the *seigneur* whose tenants they typically were. However, the greater nobles now lived at court if they could and seldom visited their uncomfortable rural residences. This absenteeism caused the French landed aristocrats to have a less healthy relationship with the peasantry than in England, where they stayed on the land; though, to be sure, only a small percentage of the nobles lived at Versailles.

Privileges of the nobility

The nobility held a monopoly of high offices in army, church, and state, and they were exempt from many taxes. During the fiscal crisis which mounted in France from about 1760 and which eventually set the French Revolution in motion, the "privileged orders" were able to defeat all efforts to subject them to equal, proportional taxation—a fact of the highest importance. The French nobility, and also the German, unlike the English, tended to scorn trade and industry as occupations. This nobility was divided into the "nobility of the sword"—ancient in origin, military in its orientation—and the more numerous "nobility of the robe," raised up from bourgeois rank chiefly in the 17th century, a class which monopolized the civil offices of the government. In practice the two kinds of nobles held pretty closely together; and there was also a *haute bourgeoisie* of rich bankers and businessmen who often intermarried with the nobility and were accepted in high society. The nobility thus was not a completely closed caste; it *was* a privileged one. There seemed no rational reason why it should not at least have borne its fair share of taxes.

Irregularities of the Old Regime

Rational considerations did not prevail under the Old Regime. That is to say, the state and society showed little regularity or uniformity in their laws and practices: everything varied from place to place and even from individual to individual. France was still an amalgamation of formerly independent provinces, and the feudal principle of local custom still largely prevailed. A significant distinction existed between the old body of the kingdom, in central France, and others which either had traditional separate status as "états" (states)—Brittany, Burgundy, Languedoc—or had been added later than the rest—Alsace, Lorraine, Provence, Flanders. The latter paid, on the whole, less taxes, and retained more provincial privileges, including tariff rights: there were customs borders between these provinces and the rest of France. The making of a single nation with uniform laws had been started by Richelieu and Louis XIV, but had a long way to go. Louis XV's and Louis XVI's reigns marked a halting along the road. But it was inevitable that the task be completed. Inequality and irregularity in the basic rules of society, the basic duties of a citizen, could not long be tolerated. Against both the injustice and the inefficiency of the Old Regime, voices were raised in increasing volume all through the century.

Such an order had obvious flaws. On the other hand, it must be recognized that the arts of gracious living flourished here as seldom before or since. The elegance that appears in the furniture, tapestry, costume, music, *decor*, painting, and literature of the French 18th century is a familiar witness to this fact; the salons of the Paris nobility nourished the brilliant writings and science of the Enlightenment. Charm, subtlety, and sophistication became dominant in society as never before in Europe. Paris society lionized Voltaire and Rousseau, sent Lafayette to fight for American independence, bought the delicate paintings of Watteau, Boucher, Fragonard. Without question aristocratic society was immoral and frivolous, but these were not its only traits.

The clergy

Within the clergy, a division between upper and lower classes also existed. The high clergy was a preserve of the nobility who often (though certainly not always) lived like lords, neglected their duties, and accordingly earned the dislike of the humbler priests. The church held much property (in certain parts of France it was the chief landowner, though this situation must not be thought of as typical), and defeated efforts to tax it; thus in some eyes it ranked

The exquisite rococo interior of the Amalienburg lodge at Munich.

as a part of the order of privilege and aristocracy—a fact which goes far to explain the animosity toward it felt by *philosophes* and later displayed during the Revolution. But the clergy was not unduly numerous and did perform many useful social functions.

Peasants

The classes in France below these privileged orders ranged from the bourgeoisie down to the most unfortunate pauper, in a series of steps. By and large the peasant landholder did well in France during the 18th century, up until the later part. France was (and long remained) a nation of peasants, unlike other countries in Europe, including England, where big estates were squeezing out the smallholders in the 18th century. Fairly good times, with rising prices for foodstuffs, helped many peasants to become quite well-off, and many tenants or sharecroppers became independent proprietors in the years from about 1730 to 1775. The system of *métayage* or sharecropping remained common, while a landless or nearly landless rural proletariat always existed. Again, conditions varied widely; but taking France as a whole it appears that peasant proprietors (whose ownership was seldom in fee simple, but in practice amounted to it) held between a third and a half of the land. But a fall in prices after 1777, and heavier taxes falling on his shoulders, made the plight of the French peasant unenviable. It has been estimated that taxes took 50 percent of his income; while the additional land he needed too often rested in the idle hands of the privileged classes. "Seigneurial rights," which were relics of feudalism, closed certain lands and forests to him, and caused him to pay taxes (*"banalités"*) to the local lord in a number of ways. These were irritating, and they became worse than that in the difficult times of the 1780's.

The wars of 1740–63

Frederick the Great

The rising state of Prussia reached its zenith in the reign of Frederick the Great, a brilliant and versatile figure who came close to being the man of the century. Frederick's father, the dour, penny-pinching disciplinarian Frederick William I, led the northern state from 1713 to 1740. He watched over the treasury and built an army famous for its discipline, while staying at peace. When Frederick the Great came to the throne in 1740, he immediately launched Prussia on a new and more aggressive course. At that moment died the Emperor Charles, whose concern about leaving the Hapsburg domains to a woman, his daughter Maria Theresa, will be remembered. The war which Frederick unleashed in 1740 broke a long period of peace and was destined to transform the affairs of Europe after a quarter century of struggle.

Outbreak of war in 1740

Frederick desired to possess the rich province of Silesia, adjacent to Prussia, to part of which his house had a shadowy claim, and took advantage of the confusion attendant upon the succession of Maria Theresa to the Austrian throne (there were several other claimants) to grab it. It was a seizure which the bright young monarch, an enthusiast for the fashionable

Maria Theresa, empress of Austria

Enlightenment doctrines, scarcely bothered to justify otherwise than on the grounds that Prussian interests required it. In that, at least, he appears to have been correct. If Prussia was to hold her place as a great power, which the careful husbandry of the earlier Hohenzollerns had made it, she needed more population and natural resources. Frederick argued that *Realpolitik* must prevail; state leaders must know the interest of their state and act accordingly, without too much regard for conventional morality. In a famous book written by this author statesman, he boldly defended the Machiavellian doctrine that private and public morality cannot be the same. (In later editions, however, he pointed out that on realistic grounds it is not good for a state to be known as a violator of treaties.) It should be added that in grabbing Silesia he was seeking a limited gain, for which he was prepared to offer Austria some compensation, and he did not wish to begin a major war.

Frederick found that he had started one nonetheless. Traditionally anti-Hapsburg France backed him, and brought along her junior partner Spain, while Bavaria, whose prince was the chief rival claimant to Maria Theresa's throne, also helped him. The young Queen's cause appeared bleak at first as Frederick won victory in Silesia, but she did not lose courage and her army fought back stoutly. Her plight aroused the sympathy of her people, and she was to become Austria's most popular ruler. She gained an important ally in England. England's hostility to France combined with King George II's interest in German politics through his native Hanover, a small state of the

Frederick the Great at battle in Silesia, June, 1745.

Madame Pompadour, mistress of Louis XV, epitome of 18th century style.

north fearful of Prussia, to lead her into war. Events in England, involving the fall of long-time Whig "boss" Robert Walpole as Prime Minister, suggested that that country was weary of quietude after 30 years of peace and prosperity and was spoiling for action. In fact England began war with Spain in 1739 over the momentous issue of "Jenkins' ear," an atrocity charged against the Spanish in Caribbean waters, where Anglo-Spanish commercial disputes were an old story. The war between Prussia and Austria went on from 1740 to 1742, then was renewed in 1744.

Results of the war of 1740–48

Frederick found his French allies languid in their military support of his fighting with the Austrians, which took place to a large extent in Bohemia and Saxony. Indeed, France and England turned out to be more interested in fighting each other for quite other purposes. Hard-pressed for a time, Frederick recovered to win victories, and Maria Theresa was forced to agree to a peace in 1745 which conceded Silesia to Prussia. Frederick thus kept the province he called "my Peru." England and France continued a war in which the latter with her Spanish ally sought to win back Gibraltar and Minorca and abolish the English *asiento* privilege won in 1713, while skirmishing in North America. It was rather a desultory war, and fitted the pattern of 18th-century warfare not only in that respect but in the diplomatic maneuvering which accompanied it, and in the tendency to settle for limited gains. France and England made peace in 1748 with no important changes. Maria Theresa had lost, in addition to Silesia, a few districts in Italy to Sardinia and Spain; she gained recognition of the Pragmatic Sanction.

Diplomatic revolution

Neither Austria nor Prussia had found its allies very satisfactory in this war, a fact which helps explain why they traded them for the next one. The famous "diplomatic revolution" by which France joined Austria and England joined Prussia, an exact reversal of roles, seems startling. It may be taken as typical of 18th-century international politics, which involved no deep-seated ideological affiliations or national sentiments. It was a game of power dedicated to the interests of states, and switches of this sort were made as easily as, say, a delegate at an American political convention might desert one candidate for another. However, the several years between the end of War of the Austrian Succession (1745, 1748) and the beginning of the Seven Years War (1755–56) saw some classic maneuvering. The Austrians actively wooed France, which was much more feasible now that the pro-Austrian Marquise de la Pompadour reigned as mistress of the weak Louis XV. The real surprise was this reconciliation between those ancient enemies France and Austria, one cause of which was the rise of Prussia and a general shift in the balance of power. Austria entertained ideas of offering to France the Austrian Netherlands, in return for backing against the nearer menace of Prussia.

Renewal of war in 1756

Russia came into the picture, too. The court at St. Petersburg had begun to enter into the spirit of European politics; and a conspiracy began to shape up between Vienna, St. Petersburg, and Dresden (Saxony), the details of which have given generations of subsequent historians employment. Recent historians have not attached much weight as a Russian motive to the old story that the Tsarina Elizabeth had been insulted by Frederick and bore him a grudge; it appears that the main councillors of state at her court agreed on such a war being in the Russian interest. In 1756 Frederick again suddenly began the war with an assault on Saxony, but this time he claimed to have knowledge of a conspiracy to crush him which he had been forced to anticipate. Historians who have carefully studied the episode generally agree that there was such a plot. They have come to the conclusion, which even Frederick did not seem to suspect (he blamed the plot chiefly on Austria and Saxony), that the most active conspirator was Russia. In any case something was afoot, and Frederick did find himself at war with three powerful states on every side of him—the three most powerful in Europe against one. He found an ally in England, and England found an immortal war leader in William Pitt, but the English gave only money, not troops; their war was again—and this time on a far larger scale—with France in America, and in India. Frederick became a tremendously popular figure in England after his defeat of the French at the battle of Rossbach, but the Prussians were less impressed, for understandable reasons, with British victories in Canada.

Frederick's military feats

It was in this war that Frederick made his military reputation. He fought off a host of foes, rushing from frontier to frontier with incredible energy, brilliantly exploiting his interior lines and the lack of coordination among his enemies. By 1762, however, he was on the ropes. Prussia was saved at the last possible moment by England's victory over France and by the death of the Empress Elizabeth of Russia in 1762. The new Tsar completely reversed her policies and took Russia out of the war. It was a surprising conclusion to these wars of mid-century which were full of surprises. Prussia managed to hold on to her domains, including Silesia. Frederick became a legend, and devoted the rest of his life and his great gifts to the work of peaceful reconstruction. Prussia had made the grade. The consequences of this for later history were enormous. Prussia went on to become eventually the power which united all Germany, a task the Hapsburg monarchy could never achieve. Had Prussia been defeated and partitioned in 1763, as all but happened and was prevented only by an accident, what would have been the fate of Germany—and Europe?

Enlightened despots

Decisive results of Seven Years War

The Seven Years War (or the Third Silesian War, or in America the French and Indian War) decided many things. It decided the continued existence and success of Prussia. In the colonial world it was decisive as between France and Britain, for the French lost their whole North American empire, and lost out in India too. Perhaps it decided the coming of the American Revolution, for the quarrel between Britain and her American colonists

Catherine the Great, empress of Russia

was the immediate outgrowth of this war. It also made clear that Russia would be a power in Europe hereafter. It inflicted an additional humiliation on France and thus helped prepare the way for the great Revolution that was to come in 1789. It also disillusioned some of the 18th-century "philosophers" (see next chapter).

Frederick and Catherine

One of its results was apparently to convince Frederick to leave off making war. He had escaped by the skin of his teeth and had no further taste for such adventures. In regard to the Russians, he laid it down as a maxim that "we must make friends with those barbarians": it was dangerous for Prussia to alienate this vast state on its flank. Fortunately for Frederick the Russian ruler was the fabulous Catherine the Great. She took over after a brief interlude of her husband Peter, the admirer of Frederick who had taken Russia out of the war. Peter was probably murdered by cohorts of his wife, who preferred the masterful Catherine to her weak-willed husband. Catherine was a German princess (of Anhalt-Zerbst), and according to unverified rumor was actually an illegitimate daughter of Frederick. She was as astute, intelligent, realistic (or unscrupulous), and "enlightened" as he, and together they constituted the classic examples of "enlightened despotism." The intellectual bond between them was cemented by a common friendship with Voltaire, Diderot, and other French high priests of the Enlightenment. A more practical bond, subsequently, was to be Poland, which they partitioned.

Enlightened despotism

The next chapter deals with the Enlightenment as an intellectual movement, a new philosophy or outlook which permeated European thought in the 18th century. It may be mentioned here that this was far from a merely literary or "intellectual" movement. Through the mediation of that remarkable group of *philosophes* of whom Voltaire was first and foremost, ideas became practical, statesmen became philosophers, and philosophers became statesmen. Frederick was himself a writer, musician, conversationalist, patron of the sciences, and friend of the French writers. Voltaire lived for some time at Sans Souci, Frederick's palace at Potsdam. The two finally became incompatible as housemates, but their mutual respect continued, and many other Frenchmen were invited to Prussia, among them the brilliant scientist Maupertuis. As for Catherine, Voltaire hailed her as the wonder of the world, and she engaged in correspondence with him, Diderot, Grimm, and a wide circle of the French writers, contributing generous financial aid to many a cause of the *philosophes*. They found her their intellectual equal. Frederick, Catherine, and Voltaire made this amalgamation of monarchy and modern thought fashionable, and lesser princes all over Europe imitated it. They all strove to be "enlightened" rulers.

What did it mean to be "enlightened," besides corresponding with Voltaire? Religious toleration and freedom from religious "superstition" was one hallmark. To be enlightened was to be emancipated from the narrower forms of Christian orthodoxy, though it was fashionable to believe in a God of nature demonstrable by "reason." An enlightened monarch patronized the sciences, setting up royal institutions for their encouragement. He regarded himself as an instrument of popular welfare: Frederick declared that he was a servant of the state, not vice versa. Though a despot, Frederick in his writings went a long way in paying tribute to the principle of popular sovereignty. So did Catherine: her famous instructions for the composition of a new code of laws, based on the ideas of Montesquieu and Beccaria, declared that citizens are all equal under the law and though the sovereign must be absolute her aim is the welfare of all. There were stories about how Frederick yielded to the law when it affected him: a poor miller whose land he wanted to add to his estate refused to sell, and the king after first threatening the man repented and saw that the laws of property should bind even the king. Frederick showed an interest, too, in popular education: he is credited with being the first head of a state to propose compulsory primary schooling.

Achievements of enlightened despots

The enlightened despot centralized the government and built an efficient and honest bureaucracy. He adopted the latest economic policies, which meant mercantilism until the 1770's, when laissez-faire became more popular. He drew up new legal codes, more humane as well as equitable. Catherine, whose achievements in Russia were alleged to be far more on paper than in actuality, did succeed in abolishing torture and sought to draw up a code of law for Russia, a far-reaching enterprise for which she assembled a national legislative commission in 1767. Of course an enlightened monarch kept his finances in order and taxes reasonable and equitable, while spending money on industry, seaports, the draining of swamps, and so on, as well as on the army. He preferred peaceful diplomacy to war. He was energetic, hard-working, just, efficient.

In brief, this model despot provided good government, pretty much as it has always been understood. There can be no doubt but that "Old Fritz" in his later years went far toward meeting these exacting requirements. Catherine undoubtedly did her best—she was a woman of enormous energy and great ability, though vain—but was handicapped by the vast dimensions of reform in her exceedingly backward country. Joseph II of Austria, son and successor of Maria Theresa, also plunged enthusiastically into reform and attempted what Frederick and Catherine never did: to abolish serfdom. However, he did not entirely succeed. "You write only on paper and I must write on the skins of men," Catherine once wrote to Diderot. To describe the enlightened ruler was not the same thing as carrying reforms into actual practice, for harsh realities intruded. One of them, which affected Frederick, Catherine, and Joseph, was the old factor of dependence upon the landlords in these eastern lands. You could not abolish serfdom without alienating a class you needed to administer the state. Some of Catherine's high Enlightenment ideals were pathetically or laughably out of touch with Russian reality.

A further weakness of enlightened despotism was, of course, the need for an enlightened despot. Prussia flourished under Frederick, but he left a system highly dependent on the person of the king, and his successors were not nearly so competent. Nevertheless, enlightened despotism appealed to Voltaire and other *philosophes* as the ideal form of government. Why this was so may be clearer after a consideration of the state of affairs in the privilege-ridden Old Regime, discussed a little further on. It would have been hard to make the sweeping reform and rationalization of the whole system, evidently so necessary, without a power strong enough to beat down the innumerable special interests which blocked the way. Frederick advised by Voltaire came near to Plato's philosopher king. The great writer Goethe counseled Duke Karl August of Weimar; all over Europe, kings and princes felt it incumbent upon them to consult men of learning. Even in France, where the weakness of Kings Louis XV and Louis XVI caused essential reforms to be postponed and so prepared for the great Revolution of 1789, there was throughout the century a tendency to raise the standards and improve the efficiency of government. In Spain, Charles III shook up that somnolent land of privilege and almost succeeded in making it a modern state.

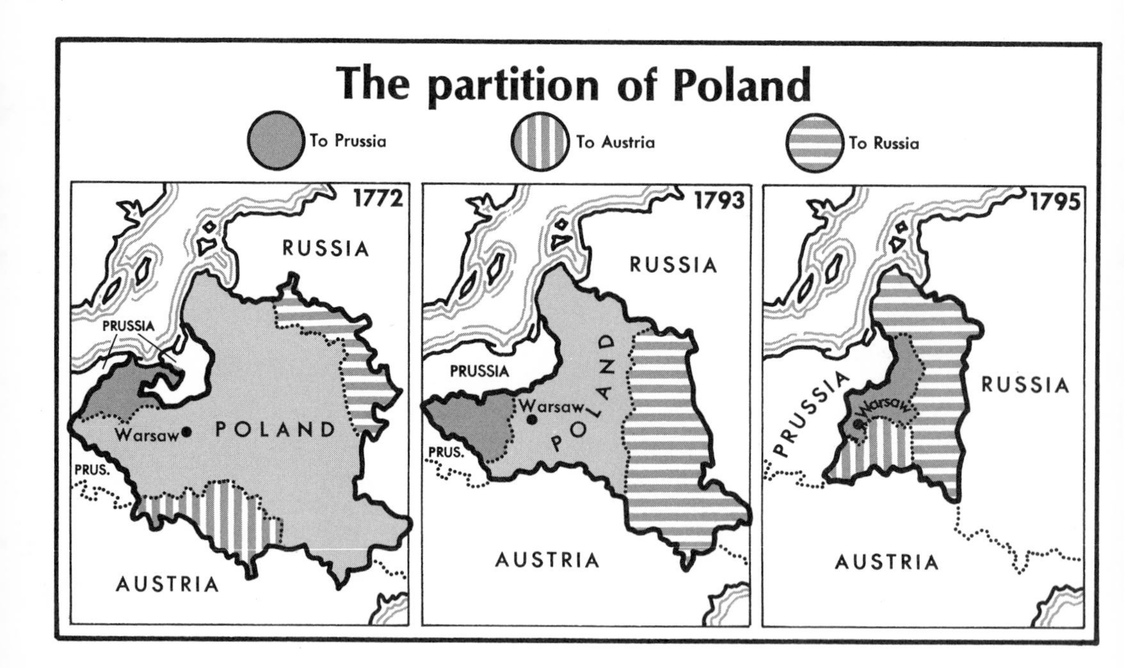

Crucial role of royal leadership

In Sweden, in the same year that France slid into revolution because the King could not wrest necessary reforms from the nobility, King Gustav III proclaimed the equality of rights of all citizens, and followed it up with a substantial land redistribution to improve the lot of the peasants. He paid for this act by being assassinated in 1792, but the Swedish nobility did not recover its special privileges, and Sweden avoided revolution. This example reveals the crucial role that royal leadership could play. One might suggest the generalization that the French Revolution found support in those countries where there had been no enlightened despotism, and failed in those where it had vigorously existed. Portugal, Denmark and Tuscany provide other examples of countries which benefited from enlightened despotism. Even though it usually did not accomplish sweeping social changes, it often prepared the way for them by creating the machinery of government necessary to carry them out in later times.

Partition of Poland

Some enlightened despots, as can hardly be overlooked, pursued a cynically realistic statecraft which was partly—if paradoxically—a result of their "enlightenment"; for it was enlightened not to be fanatical, that is, ideological, but rather to be guided by rational self-interest. Frederick would never have fought a war for some high-flown moral or religious ideal; this would have seemed to him and the *philosophes* like returning to the Dark Ages. He *would* grab Silesia, as Catherine grabbed provinces from Turkey, to advance the interests and welfare of his subjects. The outstanding example of this rather dubious sort of enlightenment was the partition of Poland, an event which considerably shocked the moral sense of some old-fashioned Europeans. The weakness of Poland has previously been referred to. It is possible to argue that this weakness invited and even justified the partition, since it was a standing source of trouble. However, the cynicism of the monarchs was abundantly in evidence. In the background of the initial partition, 1772, lay a complex diplomatic situation. One essential was Frederick's desire to be on good terms with Russia, from fear of her and of an Austrian bid to recover Silesia as well. But neither did the canny Prussian want an overly strong Russia; nor an Austro-Russian war in which Prussia might get involved. In brief, the gobbling up of Poland was a device for maintaining a balance of power and amicable relations between Russia and Prussia, with Austria as a possibly reluctant addition to the dinner party. The second and third partitions of Poland (1793–95), during the French revolutionary period, resulted principally from the greed and skill of Catherine, and the ineptitude of her rivals. Russia got the lion's share of Poland, and Catherine the Great became a hateful figure to every Pole.

Though Edmund Burke indignantly remarked that "chivalry is dead," Europe took the partition of Poland in stride, that unhappy country having long been politically a scandal. Voltaire praised the partition as enlightened statesmanship: it had at least avoided war. Perhaps the great publicist was pleased because the government of Louis XV, as usual, was made to look ridiculous. French diplomacy had been outwitted and completely excluded from an area traditionally of deep interest to France. It was another blow to French prestige.

Toward revolution: Unrest in Britain

The serenity of the British government under its Whig leadership was considerably disturbed after 1760 by a series of new developments. These disturbances foreshadowed revolutionary change and undoubtedly helped stimulate both the American and the French Revolutions. At the end of the war of 1756–63, the British reached a zenith of power and prestige: victory over France, complete ascendancy in the New World and in India, unchallenged commercial leadership, a political and social system apparently as solid as the oak of which, in English patriotic song, the hearts of her sailors and soldiers were said to be made. Yet within a few years the English experienced a serious internal crisis and the rebellion of her American colonists.

George III and the Whigs

Considerably disturbing the political scene, first, was the revival of the monarchy. King George III determined to exert the powers of royalty himself instead of delegating it to others as George I and George II had done. He threw out the Whigs, an act which was popular because of the corrupt and oligarchic character of Whiggish government which had so long (since 1714) exercised power. George was not, however, able to make himself and his "personal government" successful in the long run. The Whigs, chagrined, went into opposition in Parliament and showed that they possessed more ability than the "King's friends."[2] The onus of corruption now fell on the King, for he controlled Parliament by the same questionable means as had made the Whigs unpopular. Meanwhile arising in British life were democratic forces threatening to break through the old aristocratic forms of government.

Pitt

William Pitt, the "Great Commoner," brilliant war leader during the struggle with France 1755–63, was the first popular Prime Minister in British history. "You have taught me to look for the sense of my subjects in another place than the House of Commons," George II told Pitt. "A minister given by the people to the King," this mercurial genius sometimes, though not always, inclined toward bringing the people themselves closer to government. He was but a cautious supporter of parliamentary reform, being himself a product of the rotten-borough system; nor did he join altogether with those Whigs who began to oppose George III's resurrection of the royal powers. His intense and high-minded patriotism, however, included a feeling for the worth of all Englishmen, not just an aristocratic few.

The Wilkes affair

Then in 1768 a wayward playboy, John Wilkes, found himself the leader and symbol of a popular uprising from below. Wilkes had incurred the displeasure of the law by publishing in his newspaper, *The North Briton*, what was held to be a seditious libel on the King. He was under arrest for this offense when the voters of Middlesex County (near London, and one of the few reasonably democratic English electorates) returned him to the House of Commons. Commons refused to accept him and finally declared his opponent duly elected. The result was an outcry for "Wilkes and Liberty" which seemed to affect Englishmen of all classes: Parliament had shocked a national instinct for political fair play. There were extensive riots in London. In the end Wilkes won a victory for his principle.

Demands for annual Parliaments, electoral reform, and the elimination of the spoils system were heard along with the cry that the people who elected a member should not be defied by an unrepresentative Parliament. Pamphlets such as the *Letters of Junius* gained fame, and newspapers which purveyed political news to a growing body of readers won the right to report on parliamentary debates. Reformers thereafter labored for the goal of political reform in the sense of a more representative and popularly responsible Parliament.

The American Revolution

Causes of the Revolution

The American Revolution was the first of the two great revolutions which transformed the western world in the last quarter of the 18th century. The

[2] It should be pointed out that political parties *in the modern sense* did not exist in the 18th century; "Whig" and "Tory" were terms that stood for no well-organized or coherent units. In actuality politics was governed by the influence of factions which were based chiefly on family connections. The small electorate and the highly aristocratic society made this possible. Nevertheless, the various combinations through which Walpole, Newcastle, and Pelham "managed" Parliament all passed roughly as "Whig."

The "Wilkes and Liberty" excitement

English Revolution of 1688 had been a victory also for the British colonists of North America, since it rescued their own elective assemblies from the despotic plans of James II. They shared fully during the 18th century in the pride all Englishmen took in their liberties. But they grew to feel that these rights were embodied and expressed in their own colonial assemblies. This view was encouraged by the laxness of rule from Westminster prior to 1763. However, no British lawyer could accept the theory that colonial assemblies were coequal with Parliament.

The influence of practical events forced this difference to a showdown after 1763. After the war in which Britain and her American colonists joined in expelling the French from the continent, an argument about taxation arose. Confident in their strength and fully prepared to defend their liberties under the law, Americans rejected the direct tax placed on them in 1765 as unconstitutional (Stamp Act). To the British this opposition did not seem reasonable, for the revenue was to pay for the war and expenses of administering and defending the territory gained by the war, which was for the colonists' advantage as much as the home country's. Americans replied by denying that they owed any debt of gratitude and by pointing out that they paid abundant taxes to Britain via her monopoly of colonial trade.

Benjamin Franklin at the Court of France, 1778.

The Americans were certainly aware that they could now get French aid against Britain at a pinch. French policy made this clear very soon after the Seven Years War. As a means not so much of "getting even"—18th-century statesmen were not that emotional—as of redressing the balance of power and restoring French supremacy, Vergennes, the French foreign minister for many years, pursued a policy of striking at Britain through her American colonies. The French helped bring on the American Revolution, and aided it generously after it began.

French aid to the Americans

Quite contrary to Vergennes' calculations, it in turn helped produce the French Revolution, through effects both direct and indirect. For one thing, this policy of aid to America cost a great deal of money, and the already tottering French financial structure could not bear up under the load. The "enlightened" Turgot, who served the new King Louis XVI for a short time 1774–76, argued against the pro-American policy on financial grounds, but to no avail. Directly, the war of independence in America attracted volunteers from France—of whom, of course, the enthusiastic young noble Lafayette was the most famous. Some of these men came back with an enthusiasm for liberty and an experience in successful revolution. They had gone over mainly seeking simply adventure; they returned partisans of political change.

The American Revolution, though viewed at a distance and not very well understood, had an enormous effect on Europe, especially France. It seemed to sum up the age of Enlightenment. The Americans were seen as "natural" men who exhibited the reasonableness of man when released from ancient encumbrances and superstitions. They pointed the way to progress. Their Revolution showed that popular movements in the direction of liberty and even democracy need not always end in violent anarchy and a new sort of despotism, as had happened in Europe's revolutions. The American Revolution was that rare thing, a successful revolution which produced a moderate regime. The reasons for this we need not enter upon here, in a book whose center is European history. It is enough to note that "the image of America" for the European mind was an image of the Enlightenment in action.

Lower-class unrest

British troubles with subject peoples were not confined to North America; in 1782–83, partly as an outgrowth of the American problem, the Irish demanded autonomy and despite concessions from London began some clandestine violence. In 1780, an outburst of prolonged rioting known as the Gordon Riots shook London; ostensibly aimed at Catholics, its bigotry concealed a restiveness among the lower classes that was perhaps potentially revolutionary. The Industrial Revolution was barely beginning to exert an influence in Britain. Probably of more importance was the rising demand, led by respectable people, for parliamentary reform. Redistricting, annual elections, and even universal manhood suffrage were forcefully advocated by the Yorkshire Movement and other reform groups.

Removal of the King's ministry

Moreover, as a result of defeat in the American war for independence, George III was forced to bow to the Whig opposition and remove his minister, Lord North. In 1780 the House of Commons passed a motion that "the influence of the Crown has increased, is increasing and ought to be diminished." But the North ministry survived until the British surrender at Yorktown in 1781. Its fall was a landmark in the evolution of British parliamentary government. The Whig leaders—of whom the talented orators Edmund Burke and Charles James Fox were foremost—did not believe in much direct popular influence on legislation. The outbreak of revolution in France was to cause Fox to move in that direction but Burke and the majority to react against it. The fact remains that England, though she escaped revolution and even hardened against it after the French Revolution, had pointed a finger in the direction of drastic political change.

Other premonitions of revolt

Other miscellaneous disturbances around Europe have given rise to the view that this was a revolutionary era not only for France but for all of the western world. In the Netherlands (United Provinces) between 1781 and 1784 a struggle arose over the efforts of the Statthalter to increase his power at the expense of the Estates, a contest in which a radical faction appeared among the commoners. All over Europe there was either enlightened despotism, bringing about reforms from the top, or restlessness, leading to occasional revolutionary violence. In most places, old aristocracy was vigorously defending its privileges against a rising bourgeois–lower class force.

Nevertheless, it remained for France to make this truly the age climaxed by a great revolution. The troubles in Ireland were remote, Holland was a small place now, and Great Britain, for all the occasional riots (which were far from a new phenomenon), gave absolutely no evidence of being about to have a major revolution. Few people anywhere in the 18th century thought in revolutionary terms—a concept much too romantic for this neoclassical century. Men were sure that reason now exercised such sway over the minds of men that steady peaceful progress would be possible. The explosion in Paris in 1789 caught the world unaware.

Bibliography

Vol. VII of the New Cambridge Modern History is *The Old Regime 1713–1763;* somewhat less voluminous are David Ogg, *Europe of the Ancien Regime 1715–1783* (Harper Torchbook) and the reissue in translation of the work of an older master, Albert Sorel, *Europe under the Old Regime* (Harper Torchbook). Among several other recent short 18th-century histories, C.B.A. Behrens, *The Ancien Regime,* is in the well-illustrated History of European Civilization Library series, published in paperback by Harcourt, Brace & World.

General accounts of the separate nations include, for England, Basil Williams, *The Whig Supremacy 1714–1760,* which is Vol. VI of the Oxford History of England (2d ed., 1962). Among many specialized studies of 18th-century English politics and statesmen, J.H. Plumb's biography of *Sir Robert Walpole* (2 vols.; Boston: Houghton Mifflin, 1956–60), and *The Four Georges* (London: Batsford, 1956); Sir Lewis Namier's celebrated study *The Structure of Politics at the Accession of George III* (St. Martin's Press); and George Rudé, *Wilkes and Liberty* (Oxford University Press), are worth singling out. Also Richard Pares, *Geoge III and the Politicans* (New York: Oxford University Press, 1953); Namier's *England in the Age of the American Revolution* (New York: Macmillan, 1962); I.R. Christie, *Wilkes, Wyvill and Reform* (Macmillan, 1962). (For books dealing with culture and thought see the next chapter's bibliography; for the age of the French Revolution, Chapter 18.)

Enlightened despotism is the dominant theme on the Continent in this period. The leading figures are the subjects of biographies by G.P. Gooch, *Frederick the Great* (London: Longmans, Green & Co., 1947) and *Catherine the Great and Other Studies* (Longmans, Green & Co., 1954). Another recent account of the fascinating empress of Russia is Ian Grey, *Catherine the Great* (London: Hodder & Stoughton, 1961). Edith Simon, *The Making of Frederick the Great* (London: Cassell, 1963) is a recent fairly popular treatment; a more scholarly study is Herman Weill, *Frederick the Great and Samuel von Cocceji* (Madison: University of Wisconsin Press, 1961), stressing the judicial reforms of the Prussian King; cf. Hans Rosenberg, *Bureaucracy, Aristocracy, Autocracy: The Prussian Experience 1660–1815* (Harvard University Press, 1958). D.B. Horn, *Frederick the Great and the Rise of Prussia* (English Universities Press) is in a popular series, brief, but by a master of the period. Saul Padover wrote a life of *The Revolu-*

tionary Emperor: Joseph II, 1741–1790 (New York: Columbia University Press, 1954) while Edith M. Link, *The Emancipation of the Austrian Peasant 1740–1798* (Columbia University Press, 1949) has dealt with an important part of the Josephist reforms. Richard Herr, *The Eighteenth Century Revolution in Spain* (Princeton, N.J.: Princeton University Press, 1958) is a valuable and important book.

Franklin L. Ford, *Robe and Sword: The Regrouping of the French Nobility after Louis XIV* (Harper Torchbook) is a piece of careful research on a question basic to the Old Regime in France. Among countless writings on the Ancien Régime, Alexis de Tocqueville's *The Old Regime and the French Revolution* (Doubleday, Anchor) stands out as a classic; F. Funck-Brentano, *The Old Regime in France* (New York: Henry Holt, 1935), is another older work by a distinguished historian, containing much information; on the lighter side is Nancy Mitford's biography of *Madame Pompadour* (Hamish Hamilton, 1954), while Elinor G. Barber, *The Bourgeoisie in Eighteenth Century France* (Princeton University Press, 1955), is a rigorous sociological analysis. G.P. Gooch provides a lively discussion of *Louis XV: The Monarchy in Decline* (Longmans, Green & Co., 1956). Albert Goodwin examines the aristocracy in a series of essays on *The European Nobility in the Eighteenth Century* (Harper Torchbook).

Eighteenth-century diplomacy and war are handled in the following monographs: D.B. Horn, *Sir Charles Hanbury and European Diplomacy 1747–1758* (London: George C. Harrap, 1930); Lawrence J. Oliva, *Misalliance: French Policy toward Russia during the Seven Years War* (New York: New York University Press, 1963); Herbert H. Kaplan, *The First Partition of Poland* (Columbia University Press, 1962), somewhat revisionist in seeing Austria as the leading instigator. The penetrating essay by the great German historian Friedrich Meinecke, translated as *Machiavellianism* (German title *The Idea of Reason-of-State*) is worth consulting for basic changes in attitudes toward state-craft (Frederick A. Praeger). Herbert Butterfield has an absorbing essay on the origins of the Seven Years War in his *Man on His Past* (Beacon Press). Kaplan has also written on *Russia and the Outbreak of the Seven Years War* (Berkeley: University of California Press, 1968).

The *Memoirs of Catherine the Great* and of Frederick the Great are sources of prime interest; the former has been printed in translation by Macmillan, 1955. For France on the eve of the Revolution, Arthur Young, *Travels in France 1787–1789*, ed. C. Maxwell (Cambridge University Press, 1929) is a famous document. E.N. Williams (ed.), *The Eighteenth Century: Documents and Commentary* (Cambridge University Press, 1960) deals with the significant political evolution of the British constitution.

17

The Enlightenment

chronology

1693
Locke, *Some Thoughts concerning Education.*
1697
Bayle, *Dictionnaire historique et critique.*
1702
John Toland, *Christianity Not Mysterious.*
1704
Death of Locke.
Beginning of deist controversy in England.
1713
Berkeley, *Dialogues.* Abbé de St. Pierre, *Project for Perpetual Peace.*
1714
Leibniz, *Monadology.*
1721
Montesquieu, *Persian Letters.*
Berkeley, *On Motion.*
1726
Swift, *Gulliver's Travels.*
1727
Death of Newton.
Vico, *The New Science.*
1734
Voltaire, *Philosophical Letters.*
Alexander Pope, *Essay on Man.*
Johann Sebastian Bach, oratorios.
1735
Linnaeus, system of classification of plant and animal life.
Measurement of earth, verifying Newtonian theory.
1738
John Wesley founds Methodist Association.
1747
Franklin's experiments with electricity.
La Mettrie, *L'homme machine.*
1748
Montesquieu's *Spirit of Laws.*
Hume, *Enquiry concerning Human Understanding.*
1749
Diderot, *Letter on the Blind.*
Buffon, *Discourse on Nature.*
1750
Voltaire visits Potsdam.
Rousseau's prize essay.
Turgot, *Tableau philosophique.*
1751
First volume of *Encyclopédie.* Maupertuis, *System of Nature.*
1754
Rousseau, *Discourse on Origin of Inequality.*
Condillac, *Treatise on Sensations.*
1758
Quesnay, *Tableau économique.*
Helvétius, *De l'esprit.*
1759
Voltaire, *Candide.*
1760
Rousseau, *Nouvelle Héloïse.*
1762
Calas case.
Rousseau's *Social Contract* and *Émile.*
1764
Voltaire, *Dictionnaire philosophique.*
Beccaria, *Treatise on Crimes and Punishments.*
1770
D'Holbach, *Le système de la nature.*
1772
Lavoisier's first experiment on combustion.
1774
Goethe, *Sorrows of Werther.*
1776
Adam Smith, *Wealth of Nations.*
1778
Buffon, *Epochs of Nature.*
1780
Lessing, *Education of the Human Race.*
1781
Kant, *Critique of Pure Reason.* Herschel's observation of Uranus.
Rousseau, *Confessions.*
Schiller, *The Robbers.*
1783–84
Montgolfier, Robert brothers, balloon ascents.
1785
James Hutton, *Theory of the Earth.*
1787
Mozart, *Don Giovanni.*
1794
Condorcet, *Progress of the Human Mind.*

An 18th century salon. Conversation, witty and worldly, was an art.

The idea of progress

Something of what "Enlightenment" meant has already been suggested. There were certain key words which the "enlightened" employed to indicate what they opposed. "From half Europe superstition, bigotry, ignorance, mental slavery were abolished at thy command," Mirabeau wrote to Frederick the Great. Now everyone, it is safe to say, is always against such things as superstition, bigotry, and ignorance. But different ages attach different meanings to them. Exactly what this 18th-century movement of the mind was, remains to be explained. But first of all, there is great significance in the simple fact that numerous men—the dominant men of the day, both intellectually and politically—*felt* their age to be one of a unique "Enlightenment." The word appears in every language with the same connotation of an illumination, a clearing up, a rising of the sun after ages of darkness (in German, *Aufklärung*). These men may all have been deluded or biased, their claim of enlightenment an arrogant one. But it remains a profound historical fact that Europe felt a surge of confidence, the birth of a new day, a fresh and exhilarating breeze. It seems likely that at no other time in European history was this feeling so strong.

The causes of this feeling were not one but many, as is usual in such historical phenomena. The events and trends mentioned in the last chapter played their part: relative peace, political stability, economic growth, the English revolution, overseas expansion, able monarchs. Perhaps the most significant single idea that emerged during the Enlightenment was the idea of progress. To the modern mind it may seem strange that this idea was scarcely even known to the thought of Europe prior to the 18th century. But this is because of our modern bias; there is nothing so strange in *not* accepting the idea of progress, really. One might readily admit the possibility of advance in certain areas of human activity, for example, technology, but by the idea of progress we mean the belief that the *whole* of human society is *constantly* moving forward, showing a record of steady advance from earliest times. To the ancient Greeks, it had seemed more likely that, since human nature remains about the same, and fate is capricious, the affairs of man show a cyclical up-and-down pattern. Machiavelli, the Renaissance sage, held that there must always be about the same total of vice and virtue in the world, and that decay is at least as normal a social process as advance. This seems plausible enough, when one reflects upon it. More pertinent, perhaps, was the simple historical fact that through all his vicissitudes man had not revealed any steady ascent. He had built great empires, and then lost them. The decline and fall of the ancient empires, especially the Roman, was the greatest event that stared the historian in the face.

Quarrel of ancients and moderns

Near the end of the 17th century, both in France and then England a "quarrel of the ancients and moderns" broke out, a "battle of the books" initially brought on by the brash assertion of a French critic that the modern writers were superior to the ancient. Neoclassicism ridiculed this claim that Homer and Vergil could have superiors, though the "moderns" succeeded in winning acceptance of the obvious point that science and technology might show a cumulative growth. In general, the victory went to the ancients. But during the 18th century the belief grew that all of history shows a forward advance, and even that mankind was now on the last lap, or last but one, of its march toward perfection.

Sources of the idea of progress

Where did they get this belief? Obviously the triumphs of 17th-century science encouraged it. Not merely the achievements of Newton, Harvey, and others were in question, but the scientific *method* which it was thought could be applied to *all* areas of human experience and yield similar results. Historians of thought have also pointed out that the idea of progress was nothing other than a secular version of the Christian doctrine of the millennium. That it now was transferred to the secular arena, with heaven placed on earth as it were, was a striking change, yet the basic contours of thought were an inheritance from Christianity. Christianity involved a keen time-sense, and the concept of a progression through history toward a final glorious consummation. All one had to do to get the idea of progress was to substitute an earthly utopia for the saints' everlasting rest. Denis Diderot remarked that "posterity is for the philosopher what the other world is for the religious man." An historian has written of "the heavenly city of the eighteenth century philosophers."

Events in the 18th century were encouraging enough to foster this faith in posterity. A number of historian-philosophers from the Abbé Saint-Pierre to the Marquis Condorcet supported it with their pens. Writing near the end of the century and in fact while in hiding from the Reign of Terror during the French Revolution, Condorcet displayed the whole of human history as a continuous progress, through 10 ages, of which Europe was then (1793) living in the 9th. The 10th and last age would be attended by equality, by the "perfectability" of knowledge, virtue, and bodily condition.

By no means all significant thinkers in the 18th century shared so naive a view, and in fact there was a good deal of "historical pessimism." The king of all the 18th-century "philosophers," Voltaire, paused amid his optimistic reflections in 1755 to question (anent the Lisbon earthquake) whether there was any evidence for benevolent purpose in the world, and his satirical masterpiece, *Candide*, is an attack on facile optimism. Its parallel in England was Samuel Johnson's equally pessimistic *Rasselas*, or Swift's mordant disgust at the human race. However, there was enough of the idea of progress to be most significant. The German sage, Lessing, wrote of God's revelation as continuous through history, rather than having happened just once (*The Education of the Human Race*), and both Herder and Kant, greatest of 18th-century German philosophers, suggested a progress toward moral perfection. Voltaire himself, most of the time, conveyed an impression that reason was gradually purging the world of error, virtue replacing vice. Rousseau, who of all the great writers of the century most ferociously assailed the existing social order, seemingly held out the prospect of a vast improvement if this corrupt and decadent society were swept away to make place for a new one, more natural, more democratic, purer. The temper of the age was against what Condorcet called "that discouraging philosophy which regards error and corruption as the habitual state of societies."

Philosophy and science

It was through "philosophy" that the world was to be purged of error. "Philosophy" was the word used to mean enlightenment as against ignorance, reason as against superstition. Playwrights, novelists, and journalists, in which categories men like Voltaire, Diderot, and Rousseau would appear to fit more nearly than in that of philosophers, called themselves *philosophes;* society ladies in their boudoirs and salons were "philosophical." The fact is that the 18th century believed philosophy had been brought down from the clouds to earth, and made comprehensible to all. Previously there had been difficult philosophers, but these "metaphysicians" now stood exposed as dunces if not mountebanks, parading their ignorance in turgid phrases. When properly understood, philosophy turned out to be simple enough for all to grasp. It really was only common sense.

Locke's philosophy

The men who had made this wonderful discovery included Descartes and John Locke. The latter especially dominated the century after his death in 1704 as few men of thought have ever done. Locke stood for empiricism, with just enough rationalism to round out a sturdy, optimistic, "common-sense" system. "Rationalism" is here to be defined as a belief in man's ability to understand the nature of reality by pure reason, using, particularly, geometric modes of reasoning; one started with an unassailable fact, but deduced the rest, as Descartes did. Empiricism connotes observation, experimentation, and as the guarantee of truth, sense experience rather than abstract reason.

The same method which stood Newton in such good stead should, Locke

Voltaire

felt, be applied to the very principles of human knowledge. Our mental processes, he thought, our "ideas," are all we can know. Let us examine them carefully but not go beyond them; this will tell us what our minds are fitted for; and when we do that, we find that certain types of questions are futile because we cannot possibly know anything about them. There are no "innate ideas" in the mind, only a "blank tablet" into which are fed sensations, "simple ideas" which are then combined in the mind to produce more complex ideas. And thus our most elaborate thoughts are buildings made from the bricks of simple sense experience. All knowledge is based on experience. With surpassing clarity, so it seemed, Locke declared the human "understanding" capable of attaining real and certain knowledge, not fantastical and visionary, if it followed the right rules and stuck to the "plain historical method" of observation.

Returning in 1730 from a period of exile in England, made necessary by his amorous escapades as well as his literary ones, the brilliant young dramatist Voltaire (as he called himself) brought back an admiration for Newton, Locke, and the English political order. In the ensuing years he and his mistress, the Marquise du Châtelet, steadily propagandized for Newtonianism as against the Cartesian and Leibnizian rationalism which prevailed on the Continent. Montesquieu, too, whose *Persian Letters* with their cleverly implied criticism of government and the church had been a sensational literary success in the 1720's, was an ardent admirer of Locke; his famed *Spirit of Laws* sought to apply a more empirical, yet scientific law-seeking method to the study of politics. To the French *philosophe* movement which flourished around mid-century, the method of Locke and Newton was virtually synonymous with philosophy and enlightenment.

Spirit of the Enlightenment

Permeated by the spirit of Locke and Newton, the 18th century felt itself solidly based on a scientific method which, while empirical and therefore solid, could be counted upon to discover the laws of an orderly universe. This method could be applied everywhere—to government, wealth, education, even literature, morals, and religion. Later generations were in a position to see how much all this was *not* proven, but rested on a number of uncertain assumptions and analogies. The 18th-century philosophers ushered in "an age of reason based on faith," in Alfred N. Whitehead's striking phrase. In other words, their belief in a natural order of things everywhere, which investigation would surely disclose, was itself an act of faith, an assumption and not a fact.

But it was a most exhilarating error, and a fruitful one. Convinced that nature was an open book, not a mysterious terror, men turned eagerly to its study. And in many fields they made exciting discoveries. The natural sciences continued to arouse great interest, and produced in this century a catalog of important figures, though perhaps nothing to match the 17th century's pioneering titans. Educated men in the 18th century all had scientific interests if they wished to be up-to-date. Most Americans are probably familiar with the scientific dabbling of Benjamin Franklin and Thomas Jefferson, those splendid specimens of Enlightenment culture.

Scientific progress

A succession of interesting developments in the sciences kept alive an enthusiasm for science throughout the century—an age in which gentlemen, ladies, clergymen, indeed almost everyone had a passion for experimental science that occasionally approached the rhapsodic. Measurements to see if the earth was flattened at the poles, which sent scientists as far as Peru, resulted in a dramatic vindication of Newton, whose gravitational principles implied such a phenomenon. Astronomers found new planets, stars, comets, and even galaxies; they measured distances to the heavenly bodies accurately and thus disclosed the awesome immensity of the cosmos. Herschel and Laplace formulated hypotheses, near the end of the century, concerning the origin of all celestial bodies. The latter in 1796 summed up the new "system of the world" in a treatise of great potency which offered evidence for the orderliness of nature and the success of science in finding out her secrets. It was a Newtonian century: the bases of it all were Newton's laws and Newton's methods, but the confirmation and extension of these proved exciting indeed. They disclosed to western man the vision of the universe as he saw it until quite recently.

Astronomers, professional and amateur, had to share the limelight with others. There was the work in electricity; the emergence of chemistry as a science, finding its Galileo at the end of the century in the Frenchman Lavoisier after a great deal of lively controversy earlier; the birth also of geology, a science destined to come into its own in the next century but already in the 18th stirring up great interest and evoking pious resistance as it gained insight into the enormous age of the earth. It became a passion in England, especially, toward the end of the century.

The biological sciences possibly interested the 18th century even more than the physical. The name of Buffon led all the rest; he was a veritable god to the 18th century, and his ponderous *Histoire naturelle* in some 30 volumes became a best seller. The age's most popular naturalist expressed in his writings a spirit of scientific naturalism applied to the realm of life. He had the ubiquitous faith that such a method would reveal a system of "laws." Here, too, the fruits were to be reaped in the 19th century, especially by Charles Darwin, but the 18th began the examination of biological phenomena which eventuated in modern theories of life and its evolution. A number of 18th-century scientists and philosophers considered the evolutionary hypothesis. (Also suggested was the idea of vitalism, that physical and mechanical factors cannot explain life.)

All in all, the quickening popular interest in science and the faith in its methods was the leading intellectual feature of the Enlightenment. At the same time, we ought not exaggerate the progress made. On the wrong track in chemistry until 1790, the age of Enlightenment could also get derailed badly in other areas: one of the century's most honored experiments (1748)

Thomas Jefferson

allegedly proved the fact of spontaneous generation, and Voltaire ridiculed the claims of geologists to have found fossils embedded in stone. Like the 13th-century philosophers, the 18th-century ones were frequently better at speculation than experiment. Mistakes in science are normal; the only point here is that the Enlightenment was not anything miraculous, but seems simply to have contributed about its due measure of scientific discovery—no less, but probably no more than other centuries.

It was, perhaps, in the *social* sciences that the Enlightenment displayed its most significant and characteristic interest. "The proper study of mankind is man," Alexander Pope announced. "Philosophy" became psychology, sociology, political science. The search was, indeed, for a single "science of man" to parallel Newton's science of all physical objects. If this quest was destined to fail, it found many interesting things on its route. This century produced the first systematic study of economics as a separate science, with the Scotsmen David Hume and Adam Smith sharing paternal pride along with the French "Physiocrats."

Environmentalism

An important key to the many hopes for progressive social reform in this era was Locke's doctrine of the *tabula rasa*, the mind which was blank at birth and shaped by external experience into whatever it became. Locke did not fully believe this but many of his disciples in the 18th century did, asserting that human nature is not fixed but completely malleable. It followed that if you could somehow break through the vicious circle of depraved humanity leading to depraved government, and by a season of enlightenment refashion political and social institutions for the better, you could make men better. Man is only what his environment makes him; he can be made "good" or "evil," or specifically what you want him to be, by control of that environment. "The character of men originates in their external circumstances," Helvétius wrote. Turn to Diderot's article on "Vice" in the *Encyclopédie* and you find a lecture on the determination of ethics by the social environment. Helvétius in France and David Hartley in England sought to work out the principles of a deterministic psychology on the basis of *association*, the laws which decide how we put our ideas together. Helvétius' *De l'esprit*, 1758, pushed Locke's idea of the waxy-tablet mind far in the direction of a materialism which denied the existence of mind as such (as Hobbes had done earlier).

The "philosophes"

While Locke and Newton were undoubtedly the seminal thinkers for the Enlightenment, not England but the Continent, and above all France, took the lead in popularizing, glamorizing, and applying Enlightenment ideas.

Pierre Bayle

There were important continental inspirers of the Enlightenment too. One was the Protestant refugee from Louis XIV's intolerance, Pierre Bayle, who became a freethinker and stimulated the young *philosophes* with the skeptical inquiries in his *Historical and Critical Dictionary*, published in Holland. Others were Spinoza and Leibniz, already mentioned. Newtonians might assail Cartesian rationalists but the latter had laid a potent foundation for scientific and critical studies.

If France took the lead in 18th-century thought, it was because her superior population and wealth made her the natural leader of Europe; because her great capital city Paris belonged to all the world, a uniquely endowed center of European civilization; and because her social institutions encouraged cultivated discourse and the arts. Richelieu and Louis XIV had devoted money and effort to improving the arts. The *salons*, run by fashionable hostesses who vied with each other in putting on exhibit the most brilliant conversation, provided a uniquely favorable setting. Thus there emerged in France the most famous generation of literary and intellectual leaders in modern history. According to some they helped bring on the French Revolution; it is certain that in their own lifetimes they were the confidants and counselors of kings and ministers. And their works were more widely read than any such categories of literature had ever been in all history. They wrote to influence people to action in the direction of "enlightened" reform. The pen of Voltaire, it has been said, was the mightiest destructive force history has known. Rousseau's lagged very little behind; the *Encyclopédie* entered almost every fashionable home and it was widely read and discussed.

The French Encyclopedia

This famous *Encyclopédie*, edited by Diderot and D'Alembert, included contributions from practically all the leading French luminaries in its 17 volumes which appeared over a number of years at mid-century. Preceded by the *Historical and Critical Dictionary* of Pierre Bayle and by the *Chambers Encyclopedia* in Scotland, it was much more ambitious than either; it endeavored to reassess human knowledge *in toto*. It was eagerly awaited and bought by nearly everyone of importance in France until at length it fell afoul of troubles with the censorship. The *Encyclopédie* sought to encourage knowledge of the sciences and technology. It obliquely criticized orthodox religion; alarmed conservatives believed it to be a vehicle for "deism, materialism, and irreligion," and in 1759, when the *philosophes* had been discredited by Helvétius's *De l'esprit*, they had it condemned and suppressed, the eighth volume being then in press. The enterprise was ultimately renewed and completed. Few works did more to disseminate the outlook of the Enlightenment.

Montesquieu

By this time, the 1750's, Voltaire, now immensely rich and growing old but still with many years of his fabulous career left, had been joined in the circle of accredited *philosophes* by many others: Diderot, D'Alembert, Helvétius, Holbach, Rousseau, Condillac. In 1748 Montesquieu made his last and greatest contribution. In his book *The Spirit of Laws* (1748), he sought to establish the science of politics on an empirical basis. Like Newton, he would find general laws not in abstraction, as had Hobbes and Spinoza, but on the basis of concrete facts. It is certain that Montesquieu did not achieve this audacious goal, but equally certain that *The Spirit of Laws* represents a large advance on any previous treatise in its field. It is in part a classification of the forms of government, in part a series of essays on the relation of political institutions to such environmental factors as climate and geography, and in part a scheme of historical development. For Montesquieu was deeply versed in ancient history, one of his other works being as essay on the decline of the Roman Empire, which anticipated Edward Gibbon's much larger 18th-century work on this subject. The *Spirit of Laws* as a work has never ceased to interest the student of politics, whatever its faults as a coherent presentation of "the science of politics." Montesquieu did not succeed in excluding his own views and prejudices from this supposedly scientific study; ideologically, it presented the case for the "feudal monarchy"—monarchy checked by the aristocracy—which the baron, himself a magistrate of the Bordeaux *parlement*, clearly thought the best form of government for his time. Democracies or republics, he thought, worked only in the small community and belonged historically to the city-states of antiquity. He expounded the idea of checks and balances, separation of power, and the division of government into three branches. To live in liberty, men must arrange matters so that "power should be a check to power," for "experience shows that every man invested with power is apt to abuse it."

Voltaire criticized Montesquieu for seeing in the feudal estates a valuable

Montesquieu

check against tyranny. Still, all the *philosophes* respected the Bordeaux noble, and in spirit he was one of them; in particular, his search for a science of politics, his anticlericalism, and his trenchant style endeared him to them.

Voltaire

The acknowledged king of French literature, Voltaire was preeminently a playwright but also wrote tales, essays, and history, during a literary career that lasted more than half a century (1715–78). It is not easy to extract a wholly consistent doctrine from his works. He assailed all manner of stupidities, abuses, and injustices. His pen was indeed a mighty destructive force, probably less of a constructive one. He believed on the whole in "enlightened despotism" to redeem the world, and had as his friends Catherine of Russia and Frederick of Prussia. He did not believe in democracy, at this stage at any rate, and spoke contemptuously of the "mob." He was shocked by both Rousseau's tendencies toward socialism and his apparent hostility to organized society. But his own savage attacks on organized religion helped weaken the foundations of civil authority. Optimistic in his youth, the older Voltaire found himself severely disillusioned by the march of events, including not only the Lisbon earthquake of 1755 which gave rise

Voltaire and Frederick the Great at Sans Souci

to a celebrated controversy about the meaning of evil in human affairs, but even more the wars, and the failure of basic reforms in his beloved France. Of this pessimism, or rather somewhat chastened optimism, the immortal *Candide* is a souvenir. Voltaire, one of the wittiest, wisest, and most quotable commentators who ever surveyed human affairs, was probably the most influential writer of the century, maybe of all times.

Other "philosophes"

The dashing Denis Diderot, chief editor of the *Encyclopédie*, was a versatile, original and unorthodox thinker, less respectful of religion even than Voltaire, a man who could write novels (one of them quite indecent) as well as scientific articles. Condillac built a mechanistic psychology on Lockean foundations. Helvétius's book *On the Mind*, which caused such a stir in 1759, supported a hedonistic ethic, pleasure being defined as good and pain as evil. This was indeed subversive of moral principles, and from Helvétius the road of the Enlightenment, in one direction, may be interpreted as leading toward the Marquis de Sade and his completely depraved glorying in vice. At the fashionable salon of the rich atheist Baron d'Holbach, Jean Jacques Rousseau heard things which shocked him and caused him to reject these

Denis Diderot

Jean Jacques Rousseau

philosophes. Rousseau broke personally with Diderot and Voltaire and left Paris to preach a cult of rustic simplicity with a fervent religion of nature. Rousseau, who had leaped into prominence in 1749 with his prize essay arguing that the arts and sciences had corrupted rather than purified morals, was from the beginning of another type than the rationalistic *philosophes*, though his unorthodox views and brilliant style marked him for a time as one of them. He might be regarded as the *philosophe* who became an *anti-philosophe*.

Though Voltaire remained active and a popular idol until his death in 1778, just prior to which he received a mighty acclamation in Paris, by that time the *philosophes* as such were somewhat passé. But this remarkable group of writers had proved themselves perhaps the most influential as well as most colorful generation of literary men and men of ideas in European history. Closely associated with them were such kindred spirits from other countries as the Scotsman David Hume, the German Lessing, and the Italian Beccaria. To most people the *philosophe* movement means almost the same thing as the Enlightenment.

Political ideas

These writers mightily influenced the mind of a century. What were their leading ideas and, in particular, their political ones? Some have already been suggested. While Montesquieu indicated a preference for a balanced monarchy based on the feudal constitution, most of the others wished a total reform of the ramshackle Ancien Régime to make it more orderly and rational. Total reform in the name of reason would have to come from the top, from an enlightened despot. Few of the *philosophes* had any enthusiasm for democracy in the sense of turning political power over to the people. The people were too ignorant. A dictatorship of the Enlightened would have to come first.

Rousseau is something of an exception to this generalization, his *Social Contract* expressing a more democratic impulse. Among the magic words in the 18th century, recurring in the titles of books and chapters of political thought, were "nature," "natural law," and "social compact." The idea of natural law was as old as the Stoics, and had been emphasized by medieval philosophers; it now received a new twist. The idea of a social compact as the basis of government was also old, but had never had such popularity as it had in the century between Hobbes and Rousseau (1653–1762). David Hume, the skeptical prince of 18th-century philosophers, had already rejected it as historically false and logically redundant by the latter date. So did Montesquieu. But the image long persisted of nations being founded in a solemn ceremony when men "gathered in a crowd around the sacred altars of the country which is being born," and gave up a part of their liberty in order to form society, but on condition that the government do its duties properly. Whether or not this was an actual historical event did not worry the 18th century much. It did not have a strong historical sense. The social compact, as interpreted by Locke, seemed an admirable example of ordered liberty under law, with rational men forming a government for rational ends. And this suited the spirit of the Enlightenment very well.

Religion

Deism

The *philosophes* and the Enlightenment will always be associated with their assault on Christianity. Religious "free thought," born in France early in the 17th century, came into its own in England in the tolerant and free atmosphere of the postrevolutionary era, from 1690 on through the 18th century. Unitarians, skeptics, and "deists" proceeded to criticize the very foundations of Christian orthodoxy. After 1695 there was practically no effort to silence them by persecution. Eighteenth-century England valued its freedom too much and its religious orthodoxy too little to do that. The English deists, a group that included John Toland, Matthew Tindal, and others, were the proponents of a "natural religion" with which they proposed to replace Christianity. No revelation was needed to give man enlightened religion, they held. The Bible was only an old book full of superstitions. Jesus had been an excellent teacher, but he only taught what all religions the world over taught. The deists attacked Christianity while they claimed to believe in God, whose existence, they thought, could be proved by natural reason, and in a code of morality available to all men by the light of reason.

The Calas case

The English deists were not intellectual giants, but their viewpoint was presented persuasively and they made much of the differences that existed among orthodox Christians. In 18th-century England, the Puritans had lost their zeal and had become quietly respectable, while the Anglicans were dominated by the "latitudinarian" or "low church" wing which wished to impose a minimum of doctrinal orthodoxy. Voltaire and the French *philosophes* adopted deism and used it against the more intolerant French church. "The enemy is clericalism," cried the patriarch of Ferney. The church was a privileged order, attached closely to the nobility in France, and there were instances of cruel intolerance such as the Calas case for Voltaire to attack. Jean Calas of Toulouse was an elderly Protestant charged with the crime of killing his son in order to keep him from becoming a Catholic, and was subjected to the most inhuman torture in an effort (unsuccessful) to make him confess this crime, of which he was undoubtedly innocent. Voltaire's pen made the case internationally notorious as an example both of injustice and religious fanaticism, and he eventually succeeded in getting the decision reversed and the judges rebuked.

It should be noted that deism, the typical religious system of the Enlightenment philosophers, agreed with the faith in a natural order of things, running without divine intervention, self-contained and deterministic. Religious principles must be the same everywhere, said the deists, and must be discoverable by the natural reason of men without recourse to divine revelation. The God of the deists was much like the Cartesian Great Watchmaker who wound up the world-machine and thereafter let it run itself. Their interests were really not religious at all, but secular; what they wanted was a God who guaranteed that the universe was orderly and benevolent.

Deists insisted that a natural religion, a "religion of nature," was possible *without any need for the Christian revelation.* It *alone* was enough. Natural reason by itself could lead the ordinary man to a correct understanding of God and of proper morals. The corollary of this was the often-repeated deist claim that all religions were really the same, and Christianity itself was just "a gospel as old as the creation," the "republication of the religion of nature." Even the untutored savage had inklings of this universal religion of nature. One could read it in the stars, and perhaps men had an innate moral sense which taught them the same truths of ethics.

A little factual knowledge about primitive religious beliefs proved fatal to the deist case, and deism as such was discredited by mid-century. But the orthodox Christians, who were of course far more numerous, were infected by the spirit of the age to the point of lacking inner emotional content in their religion, and making it a matter of external evidences. In the guise of "Arminianism" and "Arianism" or "Socinianism" (unitarianism), both Anglicans and Dissenters in England grew extremely liberal in their theology, denying original sin and stressing the benevolent side of human nature.

Suppression of the Jesuits

There were similar trends on the Continent. The Jesuits had always been mild in their theology and worldly in their interests; these trends seemed intensified in the 18th century. Among the charges which enabled the enemies of the society to secure its expulsion from France (1762) and finally its dissolution by the papacy (1773) were its confessional laxities, its identification with politics and commerce more than religion, and the flexible nature of its theology. The militant arm of the Counter-Reformation was thus severed from the church. Catholicism itself seemed weak and decadent again in the 18th century. So also did the official Lutheranism of the German and Scandinavian states.

It will not surprise us to learn that there was little religious piety among the elite of the Ancien Régime. It must not be thought that Voltaire, Helvétius, Diderot, and company escaped challenge; the orthodox devout remained well entrenched in the established church (though some abbés and bishops even turned *philosophe*), and some wrote well against the new infidelity: Fréron is a good example. Even Rousseau reacted against the cold rationalism of the *philosophes,* though his own religion was highly unorthodox. Nevertheless the tide of taste ran strongly against anything that smacked of Christian piety. It was fashionable for educated men to make fun of Christianity, and the courts of Louis XV and Louis XVI felt less faith than that of Louis XIV. The public forms were respected, but behind this outward conformity lay no real religious sentiment.

Religious revivals

Against this decline of Christianity there were certain countertrends. The Wesleyan movement in England was an important one, John Wesley being by all odds one of the century's greatest spiritual leaders; he reached the lower classes with an enthusiastic "evangelical" Christianity. In faraway New England the colonial theologian Jonathan Edwards reinvigorated Calvinism, or neo-Calvinism, against the weakening influence of Arminian theology which he thought destructive of Christianity. The condemnation of Jansenism in France (1713) partly cut the Catholic church off from a vital religious movement, but this pietistic form of Catholicism actually survived there. German pietism continued to be an influential popular force. The "Great Awakening" in America was probably the most significant intellectual and social event in American colonial history. Not all was deism and skepticism in the age of Enlightenment; yet these undeniably stood out as generallv the most significant.

Neoclassicism

Qualities of neoclassicism

It has already been suggested that neoclassicism became the dominant style of Europe in the later 17th century, its chief prophets being French, but with Restoration England falling into substantially the same camp. The 18th century was to remain rather determinedly neoclassical in its tastes. The style fitted well into the mood of the "age of reason"; it both subtly influenced and was influenced by the scientific, rationalistic outlook. Eighteenth-century classicism might well be called the rule of reason in the arts. It abhorred the rough, the extravagant, the unduly subjective, the "enthusiastic." It required symmetry and perfect form, with every word falling into its proper place. Its watchwords were clarity, good sense, and the elegance of precision. In support of these canons of good taste neoclassicists appealed to reason and to the *consensus gentium*, or the best taste of all men throughout history. They also appealed to "nature," that ambiguous term so much in vogue during the Enlightenment. "Nature" to them as to all the enlightened meant order, harmony, simplicity, and they often cited the marvelous symmetry of natural forms such as flowers and petals, beehives and crystals.

18th-century art and literature

Neoclassicism produced its masterpieces. The romantics may have reacted violently against it, but Alexander Pope's poetry shares with Fragonard's paintings and 18th-century architecture a marvelous and pleasing skill. Voltaire's heroic couplets have perhaps gone stale, but the literature and music of the age can still delight us: Bach and Mozart, Pope and Dr. Johnson. In England, the novelists and satirists, from Defoe and Swift to Richardson and Sterne, including the splendid *Tom Jones* of Henry Fielding and the *Humphrey Clinker* of Tobias Smollett, produced landmarks of English literature familiar to every student. An age that gave birth to such works, and to the inimitable conversation of Dr. Johnson, cannot be called sterile. In Germany, the 18th century brought a rebirth of German literature under the guidance of the great critic Lessing. In France, the *philosophes* lamented a decline from the great age of Racine and Molière in literature, but their own satires, plays and novels made it at least a lively era.

Subsequent generations came to feel nevertheless that this was a literature *manqué*. It lacked passion, sincerity, and individuality, the romantics were to charge. Neoclassicism disparaged originality and real feeling; it refined away emotions and concealed the individual under its pat formulae. This charge is only partly true, for there is variety, sentiment, and wit in 18th-century literature at its best. But it is true that between 18th-century literature and the romantic 19th-century writers a considerable gulf extends. The former did not think primarily in terms of individual self-expression, but was a social art concerned to find and communicate the common sentiments and ideas of mankind, rather than the unique, personal ones. It shied off from the abysmal depths of the human psyche and deliberately sought to express "what oft was thought, but ne'er so well expressed"—to communicate, in perfect form, the ideas and experience *shared* by all men. Nothing further from the modern mode of "alienated" souls celebrating the visions of their private worlds can be imagined. In this respect the 18th-century writers for the most part lacked range and depth, on a modern view; and yet there were certain things they did much better than Romantic individualists. There seems no reason to deny this era the title to a really great literature and art, adding only that it was different from what came after.

Johann Sebastian Bach

In any case not all 18th-century literature can be classified as strict neoclassic. The latter half of the century explored, cautiously, some new esthetic dimensions. Richardson and Rousseau popularized a cult of sentimentalism. And the more solemn sort of neoclassicism turned into the rococo style. "Plays, books, pictures, statues, homes, everything is subject to the taste for ornamentation and coquetry, to the graces of a delightful decadence," wrote the Goncourts. This is the spirit that breathes from the court of Louis XV, in the delicately lascivious pictures of Fragonard and Boucher and Greuze, in the Petit Trianon, in the exquisite costumes. Artificial, modish, and delightful, it too was in its way classical. It was also decadent—the style of the aristocracy in its last stage of uselessness, a style for the most part merely pretty. Yet, lest we dismiss it airily thus, we should remember that it gave us the music of Mozart.

Economic thought

The Physiocrats

The belief in a "natural order" subject to self-operating "laws" analogous to Newton's "laws of motion" had significant results in at least one domain of social science, that of economics or "political economy." The Physiocrats, a French group, have been granted recognition as the "founders of modern political economy." They began their school about 1758. Economics they conceived as a distinct and separate science. Before them, the economic outlook known as mercantilism had existed for some time, as we have seen. There is doubt that it was systematic or general enough to take rank as economic science. The mercantilists did indeed discuss phases of economics in a thoroughly analytical manner, being particularly concerned with phenomena of money and prices. What the French and Scottish pioneers of modern economics did after about 1750 was to weld these isolated fragments into a coherent system, in which the world of economic behavior was conceived as a single order with its own methods and laws. They also attacked specific mercantilist policies, especially its protectionist and jealousy-of-trade features. Hume and Montesquieu (and others) had already asked whether it was not true that a nation profited when the commerce and industry of its neighbors flourished. The French Physiocrats, among them Quesnay and Turgot, and Adam Smith went far in the direction of hostility to all forms of state subvention or direction of the economic order. The best rule, they thought—with some few exceptions—was *laisser-passer, laisser-faire:* let goods pass freely, let them alone.

Adam Smith

Let commerce be free—free from tariffs, taxes, other artificial restrictions; and let competition prevail—no monopolies—and the result would be maximum wealth and maximum justice. The Physiocrats, who strongly influenced Adam Smith, the famous Scottish author of *The Wealth of Nations* (1776), saw the economic world as a single whole which should be treated as a deterministic system, studied as an autonomous area. Their views began to exert a strong influence after mid-century. The "enlightened despots" had

The Petit Trianon at Versailles, built in graceful neoclassic style with a rococo element by Louis XV for Madame Pompadour.

followed mercantilist policies, that is, state intervention, but the doctrine of free trade and laissez-faire tended to replace mercantilism in advanced thought later in the century. Turgot, who held power under Louis XVI for two years before being dismissed (1774–76), declared free commerce in grain throughout France and sought to abolish the guilds, among his other attempted reforms.

Laissez-faire

It should be noted that laissez-faire was then a radical idea. Some people in our century have associated it with highly conservative businessmen, but in the late 18th century we find Tom Paine, apostle of revolution and radical of radicals, holding to the opinion that government is an evil which will vanish altogether when enlightenment has spread. Adam Smith's famous textbook has often been presented as a kind of capitalist manifesto, but it was in fact most sympathetic to the "laboring poor" and hardly so to large capitalists. In any case the idea of a natural economic order which would run itself according to regular laws was congenial to the 18th-century mind. The assumption of Smith that men may be counted on to see and follow their own interests agreed with Enlightenment thought; so did his claim that there is a natural harmony of interests, which makes the combination of all selfish actions add up to the public good. It was like each particle of matter obeying Newton's laws of motion and together making up an orderly, harmonious universe!

Right or wrong, the economists succeeded in founding a science which has flourished ever since. Adam Smith's book was very nearly the book of the century, and its basic assumptions guided Western economic thought or "political economy" for a good part of the next century. In the course of time many of those assumptions came to be questioned, but on the whole this was the Enlightenment's most successful venture into the social sciences, in which it so fondly believed and of which it expected so great an improvement in the condition of man.

Other social sciences

The Enlightenment's search for a science of man and society gave birth to the modern disciplines of sociology and psychology, as well as economics, and likewise to modern methods in history. To this may be added anthropology, wherein the indefatigable Buffon excelled. It did not really develop any of these areas save economics very far by later standards, but it conceived the idea of them.

It may well be doubted whether the search found its goal. Perhaps no science of man ever will quite succeed. But certain persistent if conceivably illusory modern quests had their origin here. For example, the Italian historian Vico, the Toynbee of his day, tried to find the "laws of history," and thought he had discovered the natural cycle of civilization. Montesquieu, the giant to whom reference has already been made, sought the general laws or principles behind social and historical phenomena: he wrote on the causes of the fall of Rome as well as on "the spirit of laws." Condillac, Hartley, Priestley, and La Mettrie explored the possibilities of a deterministic, mechanistic psychology. Rousseau and also Diderot began to explore the mysteries of the subconscious mind in a more modern manner.

The application of "scientific" method to human affairs, in the sense of a careful, patient, and thorough collection of facts, was clearly rewarding, resulting in the acquisition of much new data about societies and the workings of human institutions. Europeans began to study primitive societies in other lands, obtaining the first real body of knowledge about such peoples. In their treatment of history, writers such as Hume, Voltaire, and the incomparable Edward Gibbon brought historical writing to a plateau it had not previously attained. Voltaire demanded history's extension beyond the narrow domain of court politics to include social, economic, and intellectual history, and also the history of other civilizations, such as the Muslim world, China, and India. Nevertheless, it has been denied, probably correctly, that they had a genuinely historical outlook; they were too much the prisoners of the Enlightenment's preconceptions about the past, and notably falsified the medieval record. Their outlook was rather alien to the 19th-century vision of history as a plan of continuous growth in which every epoch has its necessary place. To them the past was simply a record of inexplicable error, from which it had suddenly been released in the 17th century: a patently unhistorical view. They did, however, often exhibit high standards of accuracy in their search for the true facts of the past.

In this methodological sense, few could deny the usefulness of Enlightenment social science. The effort to discover sweeping "laws," to see man as a machine, society as rigidly determined by "laws" and men as rigidly determined by society, is another matter. The greatest of the *philosophes*, such as

Montesquieu, rose above this dogmatic limitation. The merits of this sort of sociology must remain under serious doubt. Nevertheless it was an exciting idea and stimulated a whole new arena of thought and action.

Breakup of Enlightenment rationalism

Rousseau

Despite its permanent achievements, its enduring impact on the western mind, from mid-century on, even as the Enlightenment hit high noon, there were signs of a certain crisis in its characteristic affirmations. Even the Enlightenment's belief in reason faltered somewhat. "Reason" was assailed or undermined from two different directions: We may call them romanticism and empiricism. The former found its chief prophet in the famous Genevan, Jean Jacques Rousseau, a poor wanderer and second-rate musician whose writings were filled with a magic the brittle, sophisticated *philosophes* lacked—the magic of sincerity, individuality, and sensitivity. After he had made a brilliant leap to fame, Rousseau rejected Paris and its salons, quarreled with Voltaire (and almost everyone else in his life), lived in rural seclusion where he practiced as well as preached the simple life. Voltaire ridiculed this man who wished to return the human race to savagery; Rousseau denounced the *philosophes* for despiritualizing man with a materialistic determinism that was shallow and degrading. There was enough truth in his indictment, and enough genius in his writings, to insure Jean Jacques a fame as great and enduring as that of his foe Voltaire.

In assailing the *philosophes* along with the court aristocracy which lionized them, Rousseau expressed a democratic sentiment in 18th-century France which was of considerable political importance. He himself, an extreme individualist, was seldom interested in politics, but became after his death the hero of a good many in the French Revolution. His short tract on *The Social Contract,* often reprinted, expressed a more democratic version of the famous myth of a general agreement establishing the first government among men. Rousseau's major interest was in the human mind, as a psychologist and educationalist. Readers of his semiphilosophical novels, who were legion in the 1760's, learned that human nature had been corrupted by a false civilization and false ideas, but is capable of marvelous development when properly treated. "All is well when it leaves the hand of the Creator; all degenerates in the hands of man." Rousseau has many affinities with modern criticism of an overly rationalized or intellectual culture. In his own day, he was eagerly read by many of the lesser bourgeoisie in France who found in him a weapon against the proud upper classes. Here was a great writer who taught that the uninstructed hearts of simple people were worth more than all the chatter of court and salons! But everyone wept over the fate of Julie in Rousseau's sensationally successful novel, *La Nouvelle Héloïse.* It introduced a new spiritual dimension to Europe.

Rousseau would hardly have approved of all that was subsequently done and said in his name, but this is the usual fate of genius. There can be little doubt about his authentic genius, though his strange life and odd personality

The spell of Rousseau. This 1778 engraving shows "Émile learning through play with village children." His novel Émile taught Jean Jacques' innumerable disciples the virtues of simple life and the return to "nature."

caused him to be ridiculed, and his influence has been thought pernicious for various reasons. Rousseau has on occasion been blamed for almost everything in the modern world, including democracy, socialism, fascism, and progressive education. He might well be praised for discovering some of the wonders and mysteries of the human mind within, and affirming its uniqueness and its value against a tendency in the Enlightenment to reduce man to a mechanical object. A society in which Rousseau's influence was strong could hardly treat men as cogs in a machine. However, Rousseau's concept of the "general will" and his political theory in general has been accused of opening the doors to a "totalitarian" system by sanctioning a sort of mystic unanimity of the people. He was to be quoted incessantly by the more extreme factions of the French Revolution. After denouncing existing society as unjust, Rousseau held up a new, equalitarian, but also anti-individualist social contract. For in Rousseau's society men would seemingly have no rights except through society, and would be bound to the community very closely, much as in the Republic of Plato.

Hume

The other force undermining Enlightenment rationalism came, as we observed, from within "reason" itself. The principal individual concerned in this process was the Scottish philosopher David Hume. Hume was a thoroughgoing rationalist, in the sense of possessing a keen analytical intellect and a skeptical, hard-headed outlook. He carried on the tradition of British empiricism as represented in John Locke. It will be recalled that Locke proposed to base all knowledge on sensory experience, by which he hoped to make knowledge both real and certain, abolishing all the obfuscations and mistiness which he thought he detected in previous "metaphysical" systems. The trouble was, as Locke himself partly realized at times, that real and certain knowledge of the outer world cannot be had if all we know is our sense perceptions. If we confine ourselves to these perceptions we can know *them*, no doubt, but they contain no guarantee that they represent what is out there in the world. Something is, but it is transmitted through the screen of our senses, hence known only indirectly, and may be quite unlike what common sense thinks it is. (Discoveries of modern science in the era of Einstein and Planck have made Hume's analysis something more than a bit of verbal ingenuity.) We have certain knowledge only of our sense impressions, not of what set them in motion.

The analyses of Hume, and of Bishop William Berkeley, also showed Enlightenment empiricism leading disconcertingly in the direction of complete skepticism or of subjectivism. We make no attempt here, of course, to set forth these complex works. Most educated people in mid–18th century did not allow themselves to be unduly disturbed by what they regarded as probably only the rather far-fetched paradoxes of an overly subtle brain. However, the acid of Hume's skepticism proved gradually corrosive. The uncomfortable feeling grew that Enlightenment optimism rested on the smuggling in of a good many entirely unproven assumptions. It was indeed an "age of reason based on faith." Hume, today, is recognized as a greater philosopher than Locke—one of the greatest of all time.

Kant

It remained for Immanuel Kant, aroused from his "dogmatical slumbers" by Hume, to make the grandest of examinations of the nature of human knowledge. The Königsberg philosopher was to present the powerfully argued thesis that our knowledge really depends on the kind of minds we have: that what we see, in brief, is determined by the mental glasses we wear. Gone was Locke's *tabula rasa*, his simple ideas combining themselves in some mechanical way into complex ones, his innocent belief that we can abolish all except something called sense impressions and with these bricks construct an impregnable fortress of certainty. Kant, who was influenced by Rousseau as well as Hume, and his German successors, Fichte and Schlegel, opened a new era in philosophy. It is a strain of thought we will refer to later. In other ways Kant was a magnificent summarizer of the Enlightenment, as in many ways Hume, too, was a specimen of his times. But he points clearly to a significant change in the basic "climate of opinion." It is a change on the whole from a naive optimism to a warier, if not wearier, skepticism.

Thus by about 1780 the magic of the Enlightenment had worn off a bit, the more advanced were seeing its flaws and looking for something new. The peak of it had come from about 1730 to 1760; few in this generation with any brains at all remained unaffected by Voltaire or Rousseau, the *Encyclopédie*, deism, environmentalism, the vision of mankind perfecting itself by means of some social science corresponding to Newton's law. Few doubted that Europe was on the verge of a new golden age. This habit of mind spread widely through a new reading class, the lesser bourgeoisie, and certainly had a great deal to do with the French Revolution, to which we now turn.

Bibliography

George R. Havens, *The Age of Ideas* (Free Press), and Kingsley Martin, *French Liberal Thought in the Eighteenth Century* (Harper), are both rather uncritically sympathetic toward the 18th-century philosophers, but can serve as readable introductions, as can Paul Hazard, *European Thought in the Eighteenth Century* (World Publishing, Meridian). The best recent general survey of Enlightenment thought and culture is Peter Gay, *The Enlightenment: An Interpretation* (New York: Alfred A. Knopf, 1966). Older classics that are not likely to lose their place are Ernst Cassirer, *The Philosophy of the Enlightenment* (Beacon Press), and Carl L. Becker, *The Heavenly City of the Eighteenth Century Philosophers* (Yale University Press). Lester G. Crocker, *An Age of Crisis: Man and World in Eighteenth Century French Thought* (Baltimore: Johns Hopkins University Press, 1959), and its sequel, *Nature and Culture: Ethical Thought in the French Enlightenment* (*ibid.*, 1963), probe deeply into the thought of the era.

On the individual *philosophes*, there is an excellent biography of *Montesquieu* by Robert Shackleton (New York: Oxford University Press, 1961). *Diderot: The Testing Years 1713–1759*, by Arthur M. Wilson, and Crocker's *The Embattled Philosopher: Denis Diderot* (Lansing: Michigan State University Press, 1954), are both good. Voltaire and Rousseau have elicited innumerable writings. Recently translated and reprinted with a critical commentary, Gustav Lanson's *Voltaire* (John Wiley & Sons) is still a sound introduction, though new information has come to light since then. The best place to search for it is probably in the numerous volumes of the series *Studies on Voltaire and the Eighteenth Century*, edited by Theodore Besterman and published since 1958 at the Voltaire Institute and Museum in Geneva, Switzerland. Peter Gay, *Voltaire's Politics* (Random House, Vintage) is useful; Nancy Mitford, *Voltaire in Love* (New York: Harper & Bros., 1957), is an intimate portrait. David D. Bien, *The Calas Affair* (Princeton University Press, 1960), carefully examines the most famous case in which Voltaire became involved. On Rousseau, there is a sound brief study by F.C. Green, *Jean-Jacques Rousseau* (New York: Cambridge University Press, 1955); Jean Guehenno's 2-vol. *Jean-Jacques Rousseau* (New York: Columbia University Press, 1966) is more detailed. John W. Chapman, *Rousseau: Totalitarian or Liberal* (Columbia University Press, 1956), and Alfred Cobban, *Rousseau and the Modern State* (Hamden, Conn.: Shoe String Press, 1965) may be compared as interpretations of Rousseau. Cf. also J.L. Talmon, *The Origins of Totalitarian Democracy* (Frederick A. Praeger).

On the English Enlightenment, see R.N. Stromberg, *Religious Liberalism in Eighteenth Century England* (Oxford: Clarendon Press, 1954); A.R. Humphreys, *The Augustan World: Society, Thought and Letters in Eighteenth Century England* (Harper); Ernest Mossner, *Life of David Hume* (London: Thomas Nelson & Sons, 1954). Further on 18th-century religion, Frank E. Manuel, *The Eighteenth Century Confronts the Gods* (Cambridge, Mass.: Harvard University Press, 1960). J.B. Bury, *The Idea of Progress* (Dover Publications), an older classic, deals with an Enlightenment theme further pursued by Charles Frankel, *The Faith of Reason: The Idea of Progress in the French Enlightenment* (Cambridge University Press, 1948), and Henry Vyverberg, *Historical Pessimism in the French Enlightenment* (Harvard University Press, 1958), which points out exceptions to the belief in progress. Elizabeth Souleyman, *The Vision of World Peace in Seventeenth and Eighteenth Century France* (New York: G.P. Putnam's Sons, 1941), and Shelby T. McCloy, *The Humanitarian Movement in Eighteenth Century France* (Lexington: University of Kentucky Press, 1957), relate to the humanitarian impulse, on which see also Alfred Cobban, *In Search of Humanity: The Role of the Enlightenment in Modern History* (London: Jonathan Cape, 1960). William Letwin, *The Origin of Scientific Economics* (London: Methuen Publications, 1963), is an excellent recent treatment of an important topic, stressing British economic thought from the mercantilists to Adam Smith. W.H. Bruford, *Germany in the Eighteenth Century* (Cambridge University Press, 1935), is an introduction to the German Enlightenment.

Source readings: N.L. Torrey (ed.), *Les Philosophes* (G.P. Putnam's Sons, Capricorn book), a convenient little anthology with useful notes; J. Lough (ed.), *Selections from the Encyclopedie of Diderot and D'Alembert* (Cambridge University Press, 1954); Isaiah Berlin (ed.), *The Age of Enlightenment* (New American Library, Mentor Books), a good philosophical introduction; Ben Ray Redman (ed.), *The Portable Voltaire* (Viking Press). Rousseau's *First and Second Discourses* (St. Martin's Press) as well as his *Social Contract* (numerous editions) are readily available; his *Confessions* have been printed in paperback by Penguin Books. Peter Gay has edited a splendid edition of Voltaire's *Philosophical Dictionary* (2 vols.; New York: Basic Books, 1962).

18

The French Revolution

chronology

1788
Announcement of convoking of Estates-General.
1789
Opening of Estates-General, May 5; Tennis Court Oath, June 20; first session of National Assembly, July 9; storming of the Bastille, July 14; Great Fear; Night of August 4; Rights of Man and Citizen, August 26; March of the Parisians to Versailles, October 5.
1790
Civil Constitution of the Clergy, July 12.
Burke, *Reflections on the Revolution*.
1791
Death of Mirabeau; conflict with the Pope; attempted flight of Louis XVI, June 20; Declaration of Pillnitz, August 27; convening of Legislative Assembly, October 1, under new Constitution.
1792
War between France and Austria, Prussia; storming of the Tuileries by Parisians, August 10; massacres of prisoners and aristocrats, September 6–9; French victory of Valmy, September 10; first session of Convention, proclamation of French Republic, September; victory of Jemappes, invasion of Belgium, November; beginning of trial of Louis XVI, December 4.
1793
Execution of Louis XVI, January 21; war between France and England; revolt in the Vendée; Committee of Public Safety established April 5; defeat of the Girondists; assassination of Marat, July 13; *levée en masse* adopted.
1794
Execution of Hébert and Danton; Reign of Terror at peak, March–July; suspension of judicial protections, Law of 22 Prairial; Festival of the Supreme Being, June 8; fall and execution of Robespierre, July 28–29; end of Terror, dissolution of Commune of Paris, suppression of Jacobin club.
1795
Government by "Directory."
Suppression of Royalist uprising by Captain Bonaparte.
"Conspiracy of Equals" suppressed.

The sans-culottes, armed Parisian workers, controlled the narrow streets of the city during the years of the Revolution.

The "Old Regime" of aristocracy and monarchy

Monarchy in Europe

Inasmuch as the French Revolution which began in 1789 changed European society in some of the most significant ways it has ever been changed, a brief repetition of what that society was like on the eve of the Revolution will be useful. Perhaps the two most important generalizations that can be made are that the Old Regime was marked by the rule of monarchy and aristocracy. In regard to the former, except for the now declining Italian city-states of Venice and Genoa and the small, rather isolated country of Switzerland, every European state of any consequence was headed by a king or emperor, and usually one whose powers were spoken of as "absolute." The British monarchy, "limited" since 1688, was an exception to absolutism, but the kings of Britain had not yet become mere figureheads. The Russian tsar was a complete despot in a sense not known in western Europe, where the sense of unwritten restraints on the power of the monarch—those of custom and moral obligation—were strong. There were many things the "absolute" kings of France and Spain could not and would not do. But they reigned without parliaments and were the fountainheads of all policy and law.

Privileges of the nobility

The proud and ancient aristocracy of Europe had once constituted a check on the royal power and in the eyes of some political theorists it still did so. But the tendency from 1500 to 1789 had been for the aristocrats gradually to become servants of the king. Powerful all over Europe in the aristocratic 18th century, they did not normally oppose the throne. In some places a kind of bargain had been struck—this was notably true in Russia and in Prussia—whereby in return for their supporting the king and serving as his high officials in army and government, the nobles gained even greater power locally, to rule over the peasants on their great estates. Even in England, the nobility or gentry presided over local government as a matter of course. In France, though the upper crust of the aristocracy now preferred to live at the glittering royal residence of Versailles, the local nobility retained many of their "seigneurial rights"; these privileges were to be a prominent cause of the French Revolution.

These privileges of the aristocracy should be noted. Except in England, they were a separate legal caste with special rights and exemptions setting them apart from other citizens. (In Britain, they dominated society and government but the great bulk of them held no special legal status; their supremacy was a matter of wealth and custom.) These privileges included rights of local government; certain monopolies such as hunting, ownership of winepress and bakery oven, etc.; exclusive right to high offices of state; and above all, exemption from taxation. The extent of these special privileges varied in Europe, being the greatest in the East, where Russian and Polish nobles lorded it over serfs who were little better than slaves; where Hungarian nobles paid no taxes at all; and where East Prussian barons ruthlessly exploited the peasantry. The Revolution was to occur in a country where the peasant was relatively well off. Yet the French nobles were scandalously exempt from the major taxes and resisted all attempts to make them pay their fair share. And they jealously hung on to what remained of their "seigneurial rights," to the great annoyance of the peasants, who, though no longer serfs, were still obliged to pay taxes and sometimes give work service to a now useless aristocracy.

Aristocracy in the 18th century

The rights of the nobility had made some sense in former times when it actually had provided protection and local government. But when feudalism ended and the nation began to shape itself around the centralized state, these special privileges became an anachronism. During the 18th century, commerce was bringing wealth to a growing number of commoners; at the same time the French nobility became increasingly parasitic. It also, blindly enough, became increasingly restrictive. An aristocracy can perpetuate itself readily if it is willing to welcome into its ranks the rising and ambitious people from below. This was notably true in England, where almost any person of humble birth who acquired wealth could buy land and soon be accepted as one of the "gentry." In France, Louis XIV had encouraged the bourgeoisie and even created a special branch of the nobility, the *noblesse de robe*, to provide them with aristocratic status. In the 18th century, under the weaker Kings Louis XV and Louis XVI, this avenue of social mobility was cut off. The old aristocracy jealousy guarded its impressive array of privileges.

The hierarchical society

The institutions of monarchy and aristocracy prevailed, then, all over Europe, from Moscow to London, though practices varied, the West displaying more liberal features than the East. The great Revolution that began in France but was in some important respects less a French than a European revolution was to sweep aside the social order of the Old Regime, which was hierarchical, corporate, and class-divided. That is to say, it was an order with a class system from lower to higher, frankly recognized as such, and one where membership in a class determined every person's status. The basic meaning of the Revolution was its destruction of this social order, throughout most of Europe, and the substitution of an order based on the legal equality of all citizens in the nation-state. The French Revolution also destroyed the monarchy, though in its beginning no one wanted this and many felt that a limited, constitutional monarchy modeled after Great Britain's would be desirable.

Reasons for the Revolution

It was a generally prosperous France that headed toward revolution. The 18th century witnessed a huge increase in trade, chiefly from the colonial areas of the New World and from India, in which France participated. While she lagged somewhat behind Great Britain in this respect, and had not developed her domestic industry and agriculture so far as the latter country, where the Industrial Revolution was getting under way, she was economically more advanced than any other country and many commoners had gained wealth. They were denied an appropriate share of political power and social recognition. The French Revolution, one of its leading historians has said, came to "restore the harmony between fact and law." This analysis is worth pondering.

"The middle classes have become rich," Voltaire observed; "industry has opened up a thousand roads unknown formerly." Growing in population as well as wealth, France still dominated Europe culturally, socially, intellectually—never more so than in the era of Louis XV and Louis XVI, when French writers were read all over Europe, French art and architecture exported everywhere, French manners and dress imitated by everyone. It is true that after 1763 economic progress seemed to have slowed down or become much more uneven. A serious "depression" formed the immediate background of 1789. But by and large, the century had brought encouraging progress for the first time in many centuries. Famine had decreased, the peasantry was relatively better off. But it was the bourgeoisie, especially the upper bourgeoisie, who waxed prosperous; and the bid of this class for political power may well have been the primary force behind the Revolution. An English visitor (the writer Smollett) commented in 1765, "Many of the commoners, enriched by commerce and manufacturing, grow impatient of these odious distinctions, which exclude them from the honors and privileges due to their importance in the commonwealth." In other words, the upper middle classes had gained in wealth, but were largely excluded from political power and forced to watch the haughty nobility monopolize social prestige.

Bourgeois ideas

A good share of the leadership of the first phase of the Revolution came from ambitious and successful bourgeoisie who found the road to social recognition and high office blocked because they could not show the proper quarterings of blood. Bourgeois indignation against a system that rewarded birth rather than merit broke out in many places before it became a regular storm of protest in 1789. It fed on the writings of Voltaire and Rousseau, and was expressed in popular plays, such as Beaumarchais' *Marriage of Figaro*. ("Figaro killed the nobility," said Danton.) It was ventilated in the clubs and lodges, of which the Freemasons were the most celebrated, organized prior to the Revolution: places where the middle classes met and exchanged ideas. We may be sure they talked much of aristocratic snobbery, the injustice of inequality, and why commoners ought to enjoy as many rights as nobles.

The weakness of the monarchy

Louis XV

Revolutions are as likely to be the result of weak government as of oppressive government, of prosperity as of misery. If a weak government is also oppressive, and if prosperity falls to the lot of some, leaving the rest in misery, one has the best soil for revolt. A powerful and ruthless tyranny (such as modern totalitarian regimes in Germany under Hitler or in Russia under Stalin) may not allow any opportunity for rebellion. A part of the picture of France before 1789 was the weakness of the monarchy. It was not very oppressive, though some unsavory practices existed. Louis XV, whose long reign stretched from 1721 to 1774, was a lazy and unintelligent king who certainly disabused the average Frenchman of any great respect for the monarchy. Unlike his magnificent predecessor he totally lacked the grand manner. "The word failure is written in big letters across the whole record of his reign," writes G.P. Gooch. Modern historians, so far from reproaching Louis with tyranny, speak of the "aristocratic reaction" which was the result of royal weakness: the King let power slip from his hands and it fell into the hands of the upper classes of France. He should have been stronger—strong enough to impose reforms and break the power of a privileged aristocracy.

Louis XVI

After Louis XV's unlamented passing, much was hoped for from his successor; but the next Louis, destined to meet his death on the scaffold 19 years after he mounted the throne in 1774, while conscientious and more intelligent than his grandfather (also more moral), lacked presence and self-confidence, and therefore failed to oppose powerful interests and insist on the sweeping reform demanded if France was to avoid a crisis. By no means ill-intentioned, Louis XVI seemed to do the wrong things. He poured millions into the American Revolution, but only intensified his financial problems while building up French sympathy for republicanism, brought back by returning French soldiers who had fought in the New World. This was not his intention, needless to say; his ministers told Louis that by helping the Americans, France would weaken Great Britain and thus elevate herself. It did not turn out that way. Without this French help, the Americans could probably not have gained victory over the British and won their independence at this time. Ironically, without it Louis XVI might have saved his treasury from bankruptcy and his throne from revolution.

The financial dilemma

Louis XVI sought reform only to have it backfire against him. He proclaimed religious freedom and abolished the use of torture; he reestablished the *parlements* which partially limited the royal will (they had to register an edict before it became law); and reformed the army. But the *parlements*, controlled by the aristocracy, blocked his reform of taxation. This was the most pressing problem. Plunging toward bankruptcy because it consistently spent far more than it collected in revenues, the King's government had to be able to tax the rich if it hoped to balance its budget. But the "privileged orders" were able to defeat efforts to tax them. Thus economic reform led back to fundamental social change. It was the impossible financial situation that led finally to the summoning of the Estates-General in 1789—signal for the Revolution.

Louis began in 1774 by appointing the philosophical Turgot as his chief minister, but after two years dismissed him because of complaints from the privileged orders. Subsequently, the able Swiss minister of finance, Necker, strove manfully with the sorry financial situation, 1777–81, before giving up. A fundamentally bad situation existed in which the court and government were cut off from the people, with no effective instruments of popular representation existing. The *parlements* were never able to fill the part of popular bodies, and in fact were more often the citadels of reaction.

Queen Marie Antoinette

The court at Versailles, set apart from the rest of France, a center of aristocratic influence and regal gayety, was a natural target for criticism by an increasingly self-conscious bourgeoisie. The Austrian Queen, Marie Antoinette, was far from being the Messalina she often was said to be, but had the misfortune to be unpopular. The affair of the Diamond Necklace, 1785, is a case in point. Counts and countesses were involved in a sordid escapade of theft and fraud in which the Queen was an innocent victim but received much of the blame.

By comparison with other regimes there really was not much "oppression" emanating from the crown in France. The Enlightenment writers had little difficulty evading an inefficient censorship, which in any case did not seek to prevent all freedom of expression. When the mob stormed the Bastille on July 14, 1789, they found in that alleged citadel of tyranny exactly seven prisoners, the prison being guarded by a few score of old men. This is not to say that arbitrary practices did not exist under the Old Regime. The *lettres de cachet*, letters of arrest directly from the king, were a notorious abuse. Never widely used, they were extremely rare under Louis XVI. The sins of the Old Regime government were more of omission than of commission. Much had to be done in France that was not being done. In addition to the need to curb the privileged classes, the Old Regime badly needed regularizing to conform to the structure of a modern state. It had no unity; its taxes, laws, administration varied widely from place to place. To a significant number of historians, the French Revolution seemed to have begun nation making and state making, rather more than just accomplishing social justice or reform of abuses. It was destined to make a centralized state out of feudal remnants, thus completing the task Richelieu had begun. If Louis XV and Louis XVI had continued the strengthening and ordering of the government in the manner of Richelieu and Louis XIV, the chances are good that the Revolution would not have come to put an end to the dynasty of the Bourbons.

The coming of the Revolution

We have just seen that two of the most basic causes of the Revolution were (*a*) the rise of commoners or "bourgeoisie" in wealth together with the refusal of the aristocracy to grant them social status and political power; (*b*) the failure of the 18th-century French kings to carry out reforms of government designed to strengthen and rationalize the administration of a nation. There was, then, a *political* crisis and a *social* crisis. Relevant also is an *intellectual* crisis, indicated in the last chapter: the whole spirit of the Enlightenment, critical and secular, questioning and reformist, was implicitly asking for change while an authoritarian regime refused to allow it. Finally there was, more immediately, an economic crisis. Much of the century had been

Queen Marie Antoinette

relatively prosperous, but for some years prior to 1789 a downward turn in the economic cycle gave rise to great suffering.

Summoning of the Estates-General

Few, however, really expected revolution. The summoning of the Estates-General in 1789, to deal with the mounting fiscal crisis of the government, was not thought to portend revolution but rather the opposite, the harmonious solution of prolems by a solemn national conclave. Persistent deficits led Calonne, the latest finance minister, to write a memoir in 1786 stating that basic tax reform could no longer be put off. The last budget of the Old Regime showed deficits running at about 20 percent, with service to the debt absorbing more than half the total. Louis XVI preferred to turn the difficult question over to a national assembly, surely not an ignoble solution, but one that was to lead to trouble. There was no existing national assembly

The French Revolution opened sedately with the assembling of the Estates-General, May 6, 1789.

The storming of the Bastille on July 14, 1789.

of France with a regular habit of meeting. A special "assembly of notables" met in 1787, but seemed not to have the legal power to authorize basic changes. Efforts to secure fiscal reform by royal edict encountered opposition from the *parlements*.

"Qu'est-ce que le Tiers-État?"

Amid the sense of a developing crisis, the call went out at length for a meeting of the Estates-General of France. This body harked back to feudal times; it had not met since 1614, had never met often, and was of uncertain procedures. It met in three orders or "estates," Clergy, Nobility, and—the rest, the "Third Estate." The three houses were to vote separately, and the consent of all three would be required to approve a law. Such a procedure, though traditional, now infuriated much of the nation, and the "Third Estate" showed its confidence and boldness. "What is the Third Estate?" the Abbé Siéyès asked in a famous pamphlet. It was nothing; it should be everything, he replied to his own rhetorical question. It was the nation; it was being treated as less than the privileged orders. A cold contempt for the nobility shone in the Siéyès tract and others that appeared while the nation awaited the assembling of the Estates, which finally took place in May, 1789. Why should 3 percent of the nation outvote 97 percent? Could a *nation* exist except on the basis of the legal equality of its citizens? This mood and these questions announced a psychological revolution.

Tennis court oath

Once in session, the Third showed itself determined to have a single assembly with voting by head, rather than the voting by order which gave the privileged classes a veto on the nation. It found able and eloquent leaders in such men as Siéyès, Mirabeau and Lafayette, leaders who refused compromise and finally defied a threat of force from the king. "A nation assembled cannot be dismissed," they announced, and they received support from some members of the other two orders. Indeed, the nobility appeared ready to yield up at least some of its privileges on the altar of national welfare. Under these circumstances Louis yielded and the assembly became a single body. A bloodless revolution seemed accomplished, and the tennis court in Versailles where the Third had pledged not to leave without a new French constitution assumed the status of a sacred place. This was the "great step" of June 10–17.

Storming of the Bastille

But meanwhile, amid the excitement and tension of more than a month, mob violence broke out in Paris. The events of July 14, coming right after the constitutional crisis seemed to have been resolved, announced a power that would subsequently dominate the course of the revolution: the armed populace of Paris. They suspected that the King was gathering troops to dismiss the assembly. They were hungry, restive, and harangued by colorful orators and unemployed journalists. Seizing guns from the Invalides, they attacked the Bastille, captured it, and lynched its governor; then they took over the government of the city of Paris.

The great fear

The King, shrinking from the use of force against the people, withdrew his troops from Paris and accepted the revolutionary regime there. There was a similar pattern in other French cities; and in the countryside at many places, peasants marched about (in fear, they said, of brigands) and burned manors. Historians have debated whether this revolutionary upsurge was planned or spontaneous. Whatever may have been the case later, the evidence is that this first surge was spontaneous, largely unplanned, just an emotional reaction by a people tense with excitement. Pent-up forces seemed suddenly released. Thus do great revolutions begin.

Night of August 4

At Versailles, the new assembly observed these events and joined in the enthusiasm. On the night of August 4, all privileges of a feudal and aristocratic nature were declared to be at an end; nobles joined in the ceremonies and renounced their feudal rights. "The National Assembly destroys entirely the feudal regime." This exciting session was subsequently (August 5–11) substantially embodied in a series of decrees, but the King delayed approving these measures, and some of the nobles, even some of the upper bourgeoisie, began to wonder if events were not moving too fast and too far. In any case, the question of just what the new government of France was to be like, now that there was an assembly and a new social order, early began to cause dissension. Men knew what they would *not* have better than what they *would* have; it is easier to overthrow an authority than to reestablish a new one. The most notable specific issues at this time were what veto power the king should be given—absolute or suspensive—and whether there should be one legislative house or two.

March on Versailles

As uncertainty at Versailles continued, agitation in Paris went on. Inflammatory newspapers sprang up, such as Marat's *Ami du Peuple*. The mob which had shown its power on Bastille day was not disposed to relinquish it. The flight from Paris of nobles and rich people left the city more firmly in the hands of the *sans-culottes*, as the people were being called (though at this stage middle-class leadership tended to assert itself). On October 5 one of the most colorful events of the Revolution took place, the march on Versailles. Led by women, and demanding the King's acceptance of the August decrees, food for the city, and removal of troops from the city (the presence of a royal regiment had touched off the demonstration), a long procession wound its way the few miles out to Versailles, broke in on the King, and compelled the royal family to come to Paris. The crowd was on the whole a happy one, and did not mistreat the King but cheered his frightened acceptance of their demands. It had been engineered by middle-class leaders like Barnave. However, the landmark was an unmistakable one. In Paris, the King and the assembly, which also migrated, were under the threat of the armed multitude. The more conservative classes now began to break away and the King himself, whatever his feelings before, searched for ways and means of breaking with the Revolution—and breaking it.

Declaration of the Rights of Man

Meanwhile on August 27 the assemby had sent forth into the world the Declaration of the Rights of Man. In general terms the declaration announced all men to be equal in rights, and declared the state to exist for the maintenance of those rights. It was a memorable piece of propaganda for the Revolution, but subject to the objection, within the context of events in 1789, that different groups might construe differently the "rights" to which they were entitled, and thus intensify the dissensions within the nation. These rights were not very precisely defined. They included "the unrestrained communication of thought and opinions," as well as a "sacred and inviolable right to property"—but in both cases it appeared that there might be exceptions, "in cases of evident public necessity." (See Articles XI, XVII). It was asserted that "the law ought to prohibit only actions hurtful to society" (V) and "ought to impose no other penalties but such as are absolutely and evidently necessary" (VIII). These are examples of what critics of the "natural rights of man" school would call a tendency for such "rights" to be equivocations or tautologies. If taken as goals to be striven for, a set of hortatory slogans, they could perhaps do no harm; but if excited people construed their ambiguous language as an immediate assurance of some hoped-for remedy, they might lead to grave confusion. Their authors probably did not anticipate—any more than had Martin Luther 270 years before—how eagerly men would adopt and how ardently act upon the "Rights of Man and of the Citizen" published August 27, 1789.

In October the Parisian populace marched to Versailles and compelled the King and assembly to come to Paris.

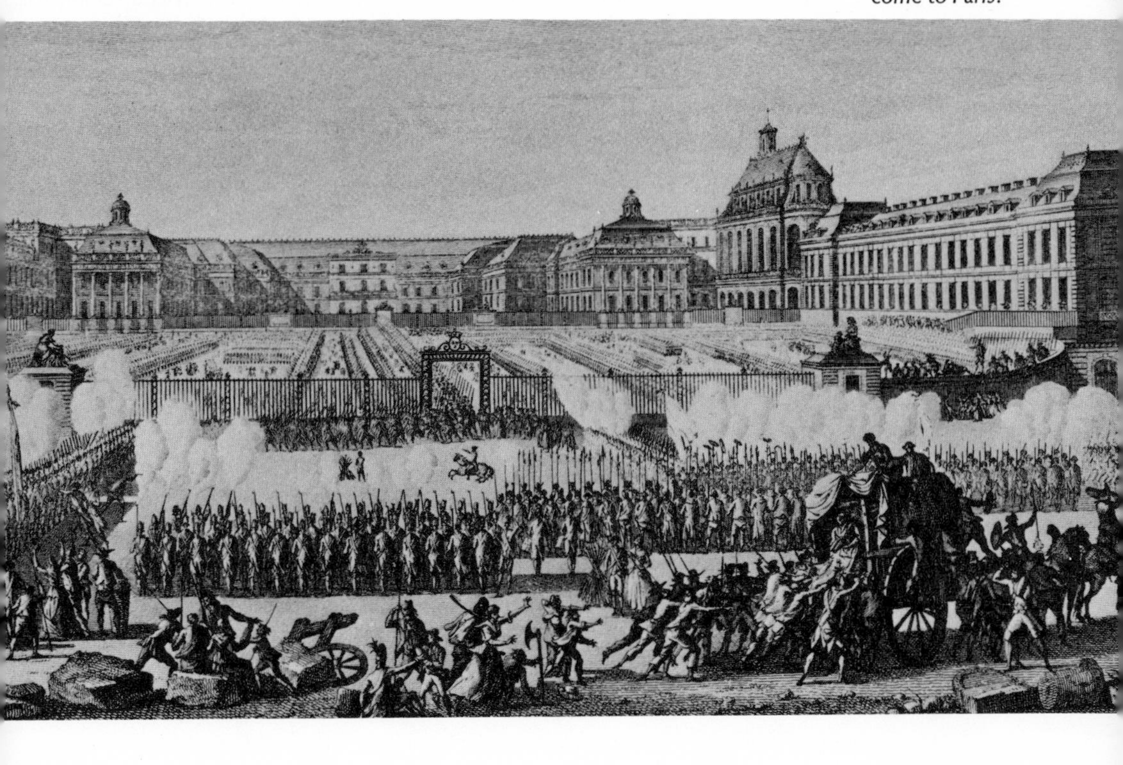

Honeymoon phase of the Revolution

With what acclaim the people hailed the Revolution in these first months! Wordsworth, the famous English poet of later years, found the French people mad with joy when he visited France in 1790 on the first anniversary of Bastille Day, July 14, 1790: dancing in the streets all night, gayety and friendship everywhere. Others described the air filled with waving flags, the burning of incense upon altars of liberty, parades in which a hundred thousand men marched. France for a time was delirious with joy, and the rest of Europe seemed to catch the contagion too. Always well filled with foreigners, Paris attracted Englishmen, Germans, Italians, Belgians, Dutchmen, Spaniards, even Poles and Russians, who sometimes decided to become French citizens, or went home to spread the word about the great events. In this early period of excitement, many people had the impression that the whole world was destined to become a kind of international republic of human brotherhood. "War will cease, conquest is abjured!" Wordsworth exclaimed. "Rejoice, all nations and all lands!" Such were the extravagant hopes of a time which seemed like the Apocalypse, a predestined hour of glory for all men. Unhappily the imperfection that mars human affairs soon made its appearance.

Reconstruction and disorder

Burke's indictment

Edmund Burke, the British statesman, in the most renowned book written against the French Revolution (1790), claimed that it went wrong because the revolutionaries tried to scrap an entire political system and put a new one in its place overnight. Burke thought, needless to say, that this was a recipe for disaster, and reproached the French for not building on the existing structure. Though it is hard to see how the mistake could have been avoided, there is something in Burke's criticism. The abolition of the feudal order had swept away the old, and everywhere the new had to be put in its place. The army, for example, had been run by the nobility. Now that army offices were open to all, with some of the high officers fleeing, the army tended to decompose; and it was some time before a new officer class could be trained and discipline reestablished. The seigneurial authority in the villages had ended, so that there must be another system of local government. Sweeping changes in the judicial system were decreed (elected judges, a jury system). Reform of the clergy also seemed urgent. In brief, area after area of the national life came under drastic alteration; and however desirable the changes, confusion resulted during the transformation.

Dissension among the revolutionaries

In any case, revolutions are hardly conducive to respect for authority. People tended to do what they chose, the hour being one of an exhilarating freedom. The assembly was respected only so far as it was in accord with popular opinion. Real power clearly lay in the hands of the people of Paris, and the National Guard which they controlled. Under these circumstances, more and more conservatives and moderates drew back from the Revolution. For a moment at the start all France, as "patriots," seemed united, but a division soon appeared between those who wished to stop the Revolution quickly and those who wished to see it go on. Some of the former, frightened by the violence, before long turned against the Revolution completely and wished to restore the Old Regime. The same thing, we recall, had happened in the English Puritan Revolution.

The assembly, an unwieldy body at best, lacked leadership. Among the men who were prominent, the Marquis de Lafayette, the "hero of two worlds," had great prestige, but was no orator and stayed out of the affairs of the assembly; while Count Mirabeau, a dynamic and able man with oratorical ability, failed to inspire confidence in his personal integrity. The king liked and trusted neither of these men. Louis was a sore problem, for, influenced by the Queen, he was not disposed to cooperate at all if he could help it, and thus he weakened the position of the moderates who counted upon a constitutional monarchy.

The new Constitution

Violence subsided for a time. Attention was focused on the new Constitution, brought forth in 1791, proclaiming the extinction of the old order and the birth of a new one based on equal rights. The King became "King of the French," not "King of France," and was expected somehow to share the powers of government with the national assembly. Louis was not happy in his new role. His wife, the unpopular Marie Antoinette, hoped that her brother, the Emperor of Austria, would send troops to break the Revolution and restore the King to his old rights. The assembly lacked effective leadership, the more so after the death of Mirabeau, strongest figure of the early part of the Revolution.

Reforms and reorganization

The assembly nevertheless went forward during the next year to pass measure after measure to create a new order and deal with old problems. The old provinces were abolished and a new system of territorial units erected, France being divided into "departments." There were provisions for the election of local administrators and national legislators, on the basis of a tax-paying requirement for the vote. (This despite the Declaration of the Rights of Man, which implied a democratic electorate in several places, though not quite making it explicit.) A new judicial system; dissolution of most of the monastic orders; the Civil Constitution of the Clergy, a basic reform which made the clergy elective; the issuing of a new money, the *assignats*, government notes backed by confiiscated church lands—these were among the most important of the acts. On paper, an entirely new France existed. In actuality, the flesh and blood covering these paper skeletons had yet to appear. And many of these actions left deep scars on the nation. In regard to the church, particularly, the rather drastic anticlerical program caused a portion of the clergy to feel deeply aggrieved. The lower clergy at least had originally supported the Revolution; now nearly half of them became "refractories" by refusing the oath to the Civil Constitution.

Stopped in his flight, the King is forced to return to Paris, June 20, 1791.

Increasing opposition to the Revolution and dissension among its followers heartened the reactionaries. The King, whose basic lack of sympathy with a constitutional regime made his position hopeless, finally made his move on the night of June 20, 1791, when the royal family tried to escape from France. Halting at Varennes, the coach was discovered, and peasants summoned by the tocsin grimly forced the royal family to return to Paris. It was a dramatic moment in the history of this Revolution which seemed to unfold like a great play. The "flight to Varennes" closed the second act and led into a new phase of the Revolution. From then on, France was in effect a republic, for the King, though technically still that for a time, was in fact a ruined figure and a prisoner of the people of Paris. The plight of Louis also threatened to bring a declaration of war against France by his fellow monarchs of Europe, particularly the brother of Queen Marie Antoinette, Leopold of Austria. Perhaps, as Napoleon later remarked, it would have been better had the postmaster of Saint-Menehold been less observant, and the King's carriage allowed to leave France. For as it was, his position now became a source of embarrassment and difficulty.

The second Revolution

Declaration of Pillnitz

Disgruntled nobles and the Queen had from the beginning shown a desire to appeal for help abroad. Indeed, Marie was indignant with her brother for not rushing to her aid with an army long before this. But Leopold had his problems elsewhere. He did recognize an obligation. On August 27, 1791, the second anniversary of the Declaration of the Rights of Man, the sovereigns of Prussia and Austria issued the Declaration of Pillnitz, which suggested that the other monarchs of Europe might join in intervention to reestablish order in France. But these monarchs were reluctant to respond; and in France, moderates were for the time being able to control those who called for the royal scalp. Already, on the 17th of June, a large meeting of the Left had been dispersed by armed force on the Champ-de-Mars with numerous casualties, the National Guard remaining loyal to Lafayette. While the moderate "Feuillants" held an uncertain majority in the assembly, the situation remained tense, with Varennes and Champ-de-Mars and Pillnitz far from forgotten. Emigration continued, and the finances of the nation were in wild disorder.

Girondins

Leadership soon slipped a few more degrees leftward with the dominance in the new legislature, convening in October, 1791 (under terms of the Constitution as drawn up by the National Assembly, which had had the status of a constituent body), of the "Girondins," a group headed by Brissot and Vergniaud. The Girondins were ready to lead France into war, a "crusade for universal liberty." They were inclined to the doctrinaire opinions of the *philosophes*, and historians have reproached them with a penchant for oratorical slogans accompanied by an absence of practical ability.[1] However that may be, Austria, now under Francis II, seemed willing enough also to fight. Soon the war began. It seems fair to distribute the blame for it about equally. It had perhaps been inevitable since Varennes. Few could have known that the struggle begun on April 20, 1792, would not really end until 1815 and would change the face as well as the soul of all Europe.

Uprising of August 10

The French army, torn asunder by the Revolution, had not yet been wholly reconstructed. It met defeats at first, and France seemed about to be invaded. Under these conditions, and with economic affairs also going badly, a patriotic outcry against the "traitorous" aristocrats arose, encouraged especially by the left-wing Jacobins.[2] On the 10th of August, 1792, the tocsin sounded in Paris and the *sans-culottes* seized the local government, engaging in a massacre of the king's guard. The conquest of Paris boded ill for the assembly. Whoever ruled the Paris Commune would eventually rule the national body. Power in France had passed by direct action to the people, or whomever they chose to bestow their favor upon. Lafayette, after failing to lead a counterrevolution against Paris, fled to the Austrians. The man who had symbolized the first French Revolution thus became an enemy of the second—as this new phase of the Revolution, beginning in 1792, was often to be called.

---

[1] Recent historians have been inclined to doubt that the Girondins were ever really a cohesive or well-defined party in terms of positive principles.

[2] The Jacobins took their name from a political club (originally the Society of the Friends of the Constitution) which met in the convent of the Jacobin order in the Rue Saint-Honoré. The Girondins have been so-called because Brissot, Vergniaud, and others of their leaders came from the province of Gironde.

September Massacres

The victorious revolutionaries of August soon mounted a campaign of ferocious terror against their foes, and "the rights of man" seemed not to exist for those who were suspected of being aristocrats. The mob took the law into its own hands. The September Massacres were encouraged by Marat, the popular journalist, "the friend of the people," who demanded a slaughter of the aristocrats as the only means of saving the Revolution. These gruesome events, which went far to disillusion the world with the French Revolution, took place under the influence of foreign invasion, it must be recalled. While the second Revolution proclaimed a democratic republic with universal suffrage, unfortunately for French democracy it was dominated by a spirit of fear and hatred. About 1,200 people were murdered in Paris in the bloody September days.

Valmy

On September 20, the French army won what seemed a miraculous victory against the invading Prussians at Valmy. The truth is that France's monarchical foes were weakened by their own divisions. While Prussian and Austrian troops were in the west, Catherine of Russia was availing herself of the opportunity to take Poland, and the second partition of that unhappy country had to be arranged. But naturally enough, revolutionaries attributed the victory to the democratic principle of the new French nation and army. The French enthusiastically pushed on into Germany and the Low Countries. Had France showed some restraint, she could perhaps have had a favorable peace and broken up the shaky coalition against her. But the intoxication of victory and the dynamism of the popular revolution carried her on to an ideological war abroad—to bear the principles of the Revolution all over Europe—and toward further revolutionary activities within France. Of these the trial and execution of the King soon took the most prominent place—a grand climax to Act Two of the Revolutionary drama.

The Convention

The Legislature having given way to a new elected body based on nearly universal suffrage according to the demands of the August revolutionaries, this new body—the National Convention—met September 20, 1792. It was declared to be year I of the Republic: a new epoch would have a new calendar, and the monarchy was officially at an end. The new assembly was in fact representative of a minority; most Frenchmen had not voted in the elections, which were frequently held under the shadow of the Terror. The convention held all power, as representative of the national sovereignty. There was no restriction legally on the power of the single legislature, and this legislature was dominated in fact by the will of a fairly small minority. That Jacobin democracy could become totalitarian dictatorship was the sobering lesson of this phase of the Revolution. The Gironde faction was soon overcome in a struggle with the left Jacobins—the "Mountain" (Montagnards), in the parlance of the assembly. The Girondins, supported by the main body of the bourgeoisie, wished to protect property, establish freedom of commerce, and preserve essential liberties against the omnipotent state.

The Montagnards spoke for the *sans-culottes* of Paris—the violent mob, or the august people, depending on one's viewpoint.

"Sans-culottes"

These *sans-culottes* or *bras nus* (those without breeches, the bare-armed ones) who made the second French Revolution were not exactly like the 19th-century industrial working class. They were not, in the main, socialists. They were moved by a fierce hatred of the richer classes, by a strong feeling that in various ways they were the victims of social injustice. But what knowledge we have about them suggests that they wanted just more property for themselves, not communal property: in Marxist terms, their psychology was "petit bourgeois" rather than socialist. Their most passionate ideal was social equality; their prophet was Rousseau. Remarkable was the degree of organization they achieved and the militant courage with which they came forth to do battle whenever the tocsin sounded. They developed their own *mystique*, their symbols—the famous songs, costumes, and emblems of the Revolution. Of all revolutions, the French was the most dramatic, inspiring, and terrible. For several years the people of Paris by the vigor of their action dominated the affairs of France and shaped the destinies of the world.

Execution of the King

Louis XVI went to the scaffold on January 21, 1793. The death sentence passed the Assembly by the close margin of 387 to 334 on the final count, most Girondins voting against it. As in the case of Charles I of England in 1649, the act profoundly disturbed some and drove a deeper wedge between Frenchmen. Martyred, the King was a more effective symbol against the

January 21, 1793, King Louis XVI, now called merely Louis Capet, is executed.

Revolution than he had been alive. A ruler more weak than wicked, he was an almost inevitable sacrifice to this phase of the Revolution. His consolation, had he been able to know it, was that many of those who voted for his death were to follow him to the guillotine before many months. For the habit of solving problems in this grim way proved hard to stop.

Holy war and Reign of Terror

Spread of the Revolution

In many places outside France, the French Revolution raised an echo. The Old Regime, after all, was somewhat the same all over Europe, and burghers in Rhenish, Swiss, or Italian cities faced much the same problems as their fellows in France. There were many who turned away after an initial enthusiasm, or who, like a celebrated German, wished to be warmed by the fire of the Revolution but not burnt up by it. But it was hardly possible to prevent the Revolution from leaping the borders of France. And the revolutionaries, swept away by enthusiasm, conceived a mission to spread the sacred fire all over Europe. Moreover, they argued that the monarchs would have to be crushed or they would crush the Republic. Along with this went much talk about the familiar "natural frontiers" of France or perhaps her mission to restore the ancient unity of Europe. The Revolution unleashed forces of patriotism and nationalism as well as political and social ideologies. No sentiment seems less resistible than that which equates national expansion with human progress.

Thus the war went on, and the French turned into the invaders and aggressors, sometimes with and sometimes against the will of the populations concerned. They proclaimed the abolition of feudalism wherever they went and often received much support; on the other hand, assaults on the church or simply arrogant behavior, affronting national instincts, sometimes caused a reaction against these soldiers who came bearing revolution on their bayonets—or was it just French imperialism in a new guise?

British reactions

In Britain, Tom Paine, William Godwin, and the London Correspondence Society voiced a threat of radical change. Paine, self-appointed American apostle of world revolution, returned to the England in which he had been born to publish *The Rights of Man*, a ringing reply to Burke's indictment of the Revolution, which for a time sold like hot cakes in England. But the September Massacres turned British opinion against the Revolution, and turned Burke's *Reflections on the Revolution* into a remarkable prophecy. While Charles James Fox embraced the cause of the Revolution, Burke led some of the Whigs away from it. In Scotland, Robert Burns celebrated the cause of revolution, but English political practice and national instinct was hostile to the violence, dogmatism, and melodrama of the events in Paris. (It remained for a Scot, Thomas Carlyle, to write an appreciative history of these events for Englishmen many years later.) Above all, the execution of the King shocked an England which had once done this herself but had come to regret it.

But the Prime Minister of Britain, the younger William Pitt, declared that factors not of ideology and sentiment but of national security were paramount. It was the French conquest of the Low Countries which caused him to take steps in 1793 leading to war with France. For most Englishmen, the war combined self-defense and a crusade against the French Terror.

Purge of the Girondins

Before long the Terror was a reality. In 1793 the French Republic faced war abroad and insurrection at home. Disaffection with the developments in Paris caused a major uprising in the Vendée, in southwest France, while in the north Dumouriez, the general of the French forces on the Belgian front, followed Lafayette's course and fled to the enemy after trying and failing to lead an army against Paris to dethrone the revolutionary government. It was under these conditions of war abroad, civil war at home, and "treason" evidently everywhere, that the Reign of Terror began its grisly course. The Gironde faction fell to the left-wing Montagnards at the beginning of June when the Convention was purged by action of the Parisians. This event was extremely reminiscent of "Pride's purge" in the Puritan Revolution; it marked a stage at which power had definitely passed to an extralegal revolutionary force and foreboded a dictatorship. The Cromwell of the French Revolution as for a time it seemed, soon appeared. His name was Maximilien Robespierre.

Robespierre

Leadership of the government was likely to fall to the person most effective in haranguing the Paris *sans-culottes*. For a time the dominant figure in the political clubs and in the Convention was Danton, a truly able man who, like Mirabeau before him, was compromised by his corruptness. Robespierre rose on a reputation for probity as well as eloquence and a constant thundering against aristocrats, traitors, and rebels, who ought all, he said, to be put to the sword. "The enemies within, are they not in collusion with the enemy without?" cried Robespierre. Faced with the problems of war under revolutionary conditions, the Convention granted emergency powers over the state to a Committee of Public Safety, made up of 12 men. Robespierre for some time played the leading role in this body though he never completely dominated it. He was not a soldier, like Cromwell, but an orator, an idealist and ideologist, a phrase-maker. He was never "dictator" in name, but only one of the committee of 12 with vast emergency powers delegated by the assembly. He owed his power to his hold over the Parisians gained from his flamboyant speeches in the Jacobin club. Armed with this power, he freely denounced all who opposed his faction as traitors and secured their proscription. Posterity has not agreed in its estimate of this remarkable man. He has been variously seen as a sickening tyrant, a weakling disguising his impotence with force, or a great revolutionary, a splendid leader betrayed by the abnormal conditions of the time.

The Reign of Terror

The Committee of Public Safety showed energy in organizing France for war, and many of its actions in providing the sinews for the first modern war were notable. Recruitment, requisitioning, economic mobilization for a war, a huge army raised by wholesale enlistments and also by conscription, came under its far-ranging eye. Unfortunately the Committee, which did so much to organize France against her enemies, is chiefly remembered for its equal vigor in sending to the guillotine all those suspected of treason. This soon got out of hand. Had the Terror been used judiciously to check the genuine counter-revolutionaries in an emergency situation, it would have been difficult to condemn it, for no state tolerates treason in time of war. But the fearful scope of the executions soon caused a reaction. With normal judicial safeguards entirely suspended at the peak of the "Grand Terror" (law of 22 Prairial, June 10, 1794), the Revolutionary Tribunal secretly condemned men to death on the slightest evidence. These were not merely "aristocrats"; it has been estimated that 85 percent of those executed were commoners. To have signed a petition several years ago was enough to send one to the guillotine. Robespierre was terrible in his demands that the dread blade invented by Dr. Guillotin be used to remove the heads not just of a few examples but of everyone in France who *might* be a traitor. The "Grand Terror" at its zenith was claiming dozens of victims each day at the public executions in the Place de la Révolution (now Place de la Concorde). The extent of the Terror can be exaggerated: the Grand Terror lasted less than two months, whereupon Robespierre fell a victim to his own machinery of death and to the hatred and fear he had aroused. There were 1,376 executions in Paris in this period. Altogether, throughout France in the entire period of 1792–94, the number of victims of the Revolution (counting those who died in prison) was perhaps 35,000. It was enough to shock the nation and the world. The first popular republic seemed more bloodthirsty than any tyrant of former times.

In addition to punishing all foes or alleged foes of the Revolution and organizing the nation into something like total war, the Terror stood for certain vague ideological goals summed up in the phrase "Republic of Virtue." Robespierre, whom for a time no one dared contradict, was an enthusiastic follower of Rousseau, a fanatical crusader for moral right. As a disciple of the great Genevan, he stood for equality, the simple life, the moral regeneration of the people. An enemy to the "atheism" of the rationalist *philosophes*, he organized a great "festival of the Supreme Being" which was intended to inaugurate a sort of state religion *a la* Jean Jacques Rousseau. A pitiless policy toward the rich found its justification in the strictures of the Robespierrists against luxury and opulence, viewed as corrupting the nation. Thus the ideal of a kind of Spartan democracy permeated the leaders of France under the Terror. Blood shed by the guillotine was to result supposedly in a nation purified into the Republic of Virtue.

The reaction; results of the Revolution

Fall of Robespierre

On July 28, 1794, Robespierre fell, and with him collapsed the dynamic, frenzied thrust of the Revolution, which thereafter searched for some plateau of rest on which the gains could be consolidated. There had been a truly

Robespierre—the small town lawyer whose revolutionary oratory carried him to near dictatorial powers in 1793 and to the guillotine in 1794.

awesome exhibition of "the revolution devouring its own children," in a famous phrase of the day. *Sans-culottism* finally became too much for the Jacobin leaders themselves. The Committee of Public Safety began to mistrust the mob, and tried to repress it. When Robespierre struck down Danton and the "Indulgents," who wished to moderate the Terror, he at the same time struck down the extreme left-wing followers of Hébert, called the *enragés*. At the last, when Robespierre and his colleague Saint-Just were outmaneuvered and brought to the scaffold, the armed Parisians did not rise in their defense: a breach had appeared even between Robespierre and the *sans-culottes*.

Robespierre, his jaw fractured in the arrest, on the day of his execution. A pencil sketch by his friend Jacques Louis David.

One by one, the men who had started the Revolution and led successive stages of it had become its victims. Factions had risen to power only to be discarded and destroyed by new leaders—who met the same fate in turn. Popular heroes like Camille Desmoulins, Danton, Hébert, and Robespierre—all guillotined—or Marat—murdered—had paid the penalty. Others like Lafayette and Dumouriez had fled. Tom Paine, the American apostle of revolution, arrived in Paris as a hero and soon found himself imprisoned as a traitor. So it went. Small wonder that people grew weary of this grim farce, and yearned for a little peace and quiet.

Evaluation of the Terror

"Thus perished the fiercest of the savage beasts, the most monstrous criminal that nature ever conceived"; "the most horrible plot ever devised against human liberty was discovered, foiled, and punished." With such words Frenchmen of '94 expressed their abhorrence of the Terror and their relief at the death of Robespierre. "I could never believe that men were so cruel and unjust"—these last words of Camille Desmoulins, hero of the early Revolution who was guillotined along with so many other revolutionaries during the Reign of Terror, express what many felt about the course of events between 1792 and 1794. From these events the great French historian Taine drew the gloomy conclusion that "man is a wild beast, carnivorous by nature, delighting in blood." Examples of the Revolution "devouring its own children" abound: of the 12 jurors who condemned Queen Marie Antoinette to death, 9 (along with a number of the witnesses) soon suffered the same fate; few of those who started the Revolution were alive at its end. A melancholy tale, indeed. But the revolutionary regime of the Reign of Terror has not gone undefended. In extenuation, it can be said that war was going on, with all the danger of foreign invasion, and with the aristocratic emigrants a part of the invading force. A pitiless policy toward the "enemy within" was part of the revolutionary government's mobilization of the nation for total war, which was, overall, successful: France was saved, the Revolution was defended.

Thermidor

After the execution of the Robespierrists on the Tenth Thermidor (July 28 by the old calendar) the Terror subsided. Thermidor came to mean Reaction. Hereafter, the Jacobins were to sink, though they made a few more efforts to rally their old forces. Such political persecution as there was took the form of a "white terror" in which revenge was taken on the Jacobins. On the whole, the reaction was against all things Jacobin, including grimness, death—and democracy. A gay and frivolous spirit returned, as aristocrats again dared to frolic and ladies specialized in the extremely daring "Directory" dresses. There was a sharp reaction against popular democracy: the Constitution of the Year III severely restricted the suffrage, while the Directory itself, an executive of five men with extensive powers delegated to it by the new legislature, was a new version of the Committee of Public Safety, but without its revolutionary fanaticism. A young army officer named Napoleon Bonaparte showed how the army, using artillery, could sweep rioters from the streets. (Royalist rioters, however, in this case; a part of Napoleon's appeal lay later in the pose of defender of the Revolution against reactionaries as well as extreme revolutionaries.)

Period of the Directory

Revolutions are immensely exciting, but society cannot stand revolutionary excitement and violence for long. The atmosphere of France after Robespierre's fall and the end of the Terror was one of glorious release from tension, rather like Restoration England in the swing back to pleasure seeking. Meanwhile (1795–99) France searched uneasily for its political moorings. In Paris, the young Corsican army officer watched the spectacle. "Ease, luxury, and good form have all returned," he wrote to his brother. "The memory of the Terror is just a nightmare. Dances, theatres and the women, who are the most beautiful in the world, have become the great business of life." Not averse to beautiful women, the young Corsican dreamed mainly of military glory. France was still at war, and the opportunity would arise. A young officer could rise fast in those times if he was capable and not politically tarnished either by royalism or Jacobinism. As for the Directory, it was not satisfactory, becoming corrupt and seemingly incapable of energetic action. And it, too, soon was forced to use arms against the people. Napoleon Bonaparte's hour would come.

Results of the Revolution

Since the Revolution had come to a halting place, it may be a good time to survey its achievements. The results of the Revolution may be summed up as follows: first and foremost, the old corporative and hierachical society, founded upon birth and privilege, conceived of frankly as a hierarchy of classes, was replaced by a legal equality of individuals. The old nobility and clergy lost their special privileges, feudal rights, titles. Men were proclaimed to be equal under the law. Not until Napoleon supervised the new legal code did this become definitely embodied in positive law, but it was the obvious goal of the Revolution all the way. It was, indeed, accepted by almost everyone the first few months of the Revolution.

Before long, lower-class spokesmen argued that equality under the law meant little except plutocracy, but socialist or semisocialist ideas did not get far during the Revolution, though they appeared. In 1795 the "Conspiracy of the Equals," led by one "Gracchus" Babeuf, failed badly and would earn little more than a mention in a history of the Revolution except that, in retrospect, Babeuf appears as about the first modern socialist revolutionary. He had been inspired by Rousseau and the socialistic writers deriving from Rousseau, Mably and Morelly. "Bourgeois individualism" was the triumphant principle; the French Revolution nevertheless left behind a tremendous myth for later revolutionaries of all varieties. Men returned to it for inspiration in 1848, 1871, and 1917. Jacobins such as Robespierre, though not socialists, were powerful symbols of equality and "social justice."

The state greatly increased its power, and a uniform centralized administration came into being (again, largely on paper only until Napoleon, but the intention was clear). The power of the state was shown in the emergency dictatorship of the Committee of Public Safety; it was far greater than the Bourbons had ever wielded. That this power was more popular, backed often by the will of an aroused people, might make it more benevolent, but it certainly *was* more powerful. It might be seized by a popular demagogue of a military leader and used in various ways. It had been used in 1793–94 to requisition wealth as well as manpower in the public interest. It had created a new kind of army, too—a mass, patriotic one.

The course of the Revolution through mob violence and the ruthless fanaticism of a Robespierre ended by thoroughly frightening the bourgeoisie into a desire for a strong state to keep law and order. These men wished to keep the fruits of the Revolution in the form of legal equality and the new property relations; they had grown heartily sick of the tocsin and the Faubourg St. Antoine. The Revolution was looking for an organizer and stabilizer from 1794 on, and finally found one in Napoleon Bonaparte.

Nationalism

During the Revolution nationalism and national unity were enormously strengthened. This was partly a natural result of equality, and the end of a class system. Men were equal—equal as what? Classes no longer existed as legal orders—what was the basis of society? The nation, the state, Frenchmen, France. All became *enfants de la patrie*, as the revolutionary and French national anthem said. The administrative unification assisted, by imposing the same laws, tariffs, standards, all over France, where before there had been a welter of local differences. And the defense of the Revolution by a "people in arms" against outside attack completed the identification of the Revolution with patriotism. It is possible to speak of nationalism existing before the Revolution, of course; but the sentiment now reached far more people, became more intense, and had fewer rivals in its claims on men's minds and spirits.

Thus the Revolution helped bring to birth nearly all the social and political features of the modern world: democracy, liberalism, nationalism, the strong state, total war, and standardization, to name a few. In the years that followed, these results were to be consolidated under the rule of Napoleon and spread all over Europe in a mighty war. It would be wrong to say that the Revolution *caused* these things, though. One can see them gathering strength all through the 18th century, perhaps for some time before that. Had the old monarchy had the courage to introduce the legal equality and national order for which France obviously yearned, the Revolution itself might have been avoided. Revolution came because (it seems) forces of change got dammed up, rather than flowing normally, and finally burst through the dam in a mighty torrent.

Bibliography

Two of the leading present historians of this epoch, Robert R. Palmer, *The Age of the Democratic Revolutions* (2 vols.; Princeton, N.J.: Princeton University Press, 1959–64), and Jacques Godechot, *France and the Atlantic Revolution*, tr. by H.H. Rowen (New York: Free Press, 1965), put the Revolution in broad prespective. Good general accounts include M.J. Sydenham, *The French Revolution* (G.P. Putnam's Sons, Capricorn), stressing political developments; A. Goodwin, *The French Revolution* (Harper Torchbook); N. Hampson, *A Social History of the French Revolution* (London: Routledge & Kegan Paul, 1963, now in a University of Toronto Press paperback). The respected French scholar, Georges Lefebvre, whose works lack something in dramatic quality but contribute much new knowledge, is represented in English by *The Coming of the French Revolution, The Thermidorians*, and *The Directory* (all Random House, Vintage). *The French Revolution*, by the socialist historian, Albert Mathiez, has been published in a paperback by Grosset & Dunlap.

C.B. Rogers, *The Spirit of Revolution in 1789* (Princeton University Press, 1949), gets at the popular literature of the day, while George Rudé, *The Crowd in the French Revolution* (Oxford: Clarendon University Press, 1959), gets even closer to the sources of revolutionary emotion. Equally valuable on this aspect is Albert Soboul, *The Parisian Sans-Culottes and the French Revolution* (Clarendon Press, 1964). Studies of the personalities and factions involved in the Revolution are numerous. A leading British scholar, James M. Thompson, has a two-volume biography of *Robespierre* (Oxford: Blackwell, 1935), or see his shorter *Robespierre and the French Revolution* (Macmillan, Collier Book). M.J. Sydenham has recently reappraised *The Girondins* (London: Athlone Press, 1961); Crane Brinton, *The Jacobins* (New York: Russell & Russell, Publishers, 1961), is a standard authority; R.R. Palmer's study of the Committee of Public Safety, *Twelve Who Ruled*, was reissued in paperback (Atheneum). Louis Gottschalk, *Jean-Paul Marat, A Study in Radicalism* (reprinted; New York: Benjamin Blom, 1966), is by another well-known American scholar. Brinton's popular *Anatomy of Revolution* (Random House, Vintage) provocatively compares the French Revolution to other major revolutions of modern times. Alfred Cobban, *The Social Interpretation of the French Revolution* (New York: Cambridge University Press, 1964), offers some rather unorthodox opinions. Two examples of recent approaches: Joan McDonald, *Rousseau and the French Revolution* (Athlone Press, 1965), shows how much the revolutionaries distorted the ideas of Jean-Jacques Rousseau; while J. Kaplow, *Elbeuf during the Revolutionary Period* (Baltimore, Md.: Johns Hopkins University, 1964), shows how little difference the Revolution made in the life of one French town.

In addition to the first two books cited, the following deal with the era of the French Revolution in other countries: G.P. Gooch, *Germany and the French Revolution* (London: Longmans, Green & Co., 1920); W.T. Laprade, *England and the French Revolution* (Johns Hopkins University, 1909); Paul H. Beik, *The French Revolution Seen from the Right* (Philadelphia: American Philosophical Society, 1956), which includes the influence of Edmund Burke's indictment of the Revolution; Edith M. Johnson, *Great Britain and Ireland 1760–1800* (Edinburgh: Oliver & Boyd, 1963); Maurice R. O'Connell, *Irish Politics and Social Conflict in the Age of the American Revolution* (New York: Oxford University Press, 1966); G.S. Thomson, *Catherine the Great and the Expansion of Russia* (Macmillan, Collier Book). The whole revolutionary decade is covered in Crane Brinton, *A Decade of Revolution 1789–1799* (Harper), one of the Rise of Modern Europe series.

E.L. Higgins (ed.), *The French Revolution As Told by Contemporaries* (Boston: Houghton Mifflin, 1938), is an exciting presentation through the actual sources. More recently, Georges Pernoud and Sabine Flaissier, *The French Revolution* (Fawcett, Premier Book), have done something similar. J.M. Thompson has edited *French Revolutionary Documents 1789–1794* (Blackwell, 1966). Edmund Burke's *Reflections on the Revolution in France* is required reading; it has been presented along with Tom Paine's reply in a Doubleday Dolphin Book. A. Cobban (ed.), *The Debate on the French Revolution 1789–1800,* in the British Political Tradition series (Barnes & Noble), conveys the excitement of controversy over the principles raised by the Revolution.

19
Napoleonic Europe

Napoleon in 1799

chronology

1795
Third partition of Poland.
Rule of Directory in France.
1796
Napoleon Bonaparte's victories in Italy.
Death of Catherine the Great.
1798
Napoleon's expedition to Egypt. Second Coalition against France formed.
1799
Napoleon's *coup d'état*, establishing consulate.
1800
Reorganization of French administration by Napoleon.
1801
French Concordat with Pope; peace with Austria, Russia.
1802
Peace of Amiens with Great Britain; Napoleon consul for life; revolt in Santo Domingo.
1803
Sale of Louisiana by France to United States; breakdown of Peace of Amiens.
1804
Promulgation of Code Napoleon; Napoleon proclaimed Emperor; execution of Duke of Enghien.
William Pitt resumes British premiership.
1805
Napoleon crowned King of Italy; Third Coalition against France; capture of Austrian army at Ulm; British naval victory of Trafalgar; battle of Austerlitz, Napoleon's greatest victory.
1806
Death of Pitt.
Napoleon's brothers on thrones of Naples, Holland; dissolution of Holy Roman Empire, creation of Confederation of Rhine.
Fourth Coalition; Napoleon defeats Prussians at Jena, enters Berlin.
Berlin Decree proclaiming Continental System, blockade of England.
1807
French victories of Eylau and Friedland; Russian Tsar forced to make peace at Tilsit; creation of Grand Duchy of Warsaw; Jerome Bonaparte made King of Wesphalia; reforms in Prussia, including abolition of serfdom; Milan Decree.
1808
Insurrection in Spain against Joseph Bonaparte.
1809
Wellington and British Army in Spain; victory of French over Austrians at Wagram; Napoleon excommunicated, arrests Pope, seizes Papal States.
1810
Marriage of Napoleon to Marie Louise of Austria; Holland annexed to France; Alexander of Russia breaks with Continental System.
1812
Sixth Coalition; War between the U.S. and Britain; Napoleon's invasion of Russia with Grand Army; entrance into Moscow; retreat from Moscow.
1813
Battles of Dresden, Leipzig; Congress of Prague, Napoleon refuses terms; revolt in Holland against French.
1814
Invasion of France by Allies; Treaty of Chaumont between Allies; abdication of Napoleon; first Treaty of Paris; opening of Congress of Vienna.
1815
Napoleon's return from Elba; the Hundred Days; Battle of Waterloo; completion of Congress of Vienna; exile of Napoleon to St. Helena; Holy Alliance and Quadruple Alliance.

Napoleon's mission

Reaction against revolutionary idealism

Between 1795 and 1800, France hovered between republic and dictatorship, much as England had done in the period of the Commonwealth. The Directory, a five-man body wielding powers granted to it by an unrepresentative legislature, was tolerated only because of the absence of any better alternative. Few wanted to return to the Old Regime. But no one wanted any more Jacobin mob rule, either. "Everybody was disgusted with the Revolution," it was said. The great majority of the French people were not street-fighters, any more than they were Royalists; and these, the "indifferent ones," overawed by the energetic crusading minority earlier in the Revolution, now made their presence felt. A writer remarked that Robespierre was really overthrown by "Joseph Prudhomme"—in English we would say John Smith or John Doe, the Average Man. The intense revolutionary idealism of a Robespierre could not long be sustained. It became evident that the Jacobins had lost their hold on the Parisians and could no longer summon insurrections at the sound of the tocsin.

Most Frenchmen wanted stable government, even at the sacrifice of democracy, if this government preserved the solid fruits of the Revolution: land for the peasants, property rights for the bourgeoisie, an end of feudalism, equal civil rights for all. Meanwhile the war went on, and France began to succeed in it. Successful wars produce popular generals; and it was not difficult to predict that a France in search of leadership would support such a man against the Directory. The latter body became increasingly corrupt, and was widely regarded as a most unsatisfactory system of government. It steadily grew more dictatorial and less representative.

Bonaparte

On September 4, 1797, the Directory was forced to call on the army to preserve it against the legislature, and from this time on it really existed at the tolerance of the military, and was moreover virtually a dictatorship. There were several candidates for the role of Pompey or Caesar in this situation, but Napoleon Bonaparte soon eclipsed his rivals and became the man of the hour. He had risen from a lieutenant to a general in six years, was only 27 when he became France's foremost military idol, and was master of France at the age of 30. Within eight more years he had laid all Europe at his feet. One had to go back to Alexander the Great for anything comparable. This glamorous prodigy was destined to take charge of revolutionary France and lead it to the near conquest of the continent.

Napoleon Bonaparte was born in Corsica, an island which had passed from Italy to France just a year before his birth in 1769. The Corsican-Italian youth felt himself an alien during his education in France, and was moody and sensitive. Fortune was to treat him kindly enough, however. The Revolution made it possible for junior officers to advance with extreme rapidity. Bonaparte was lucky enough to escape incrimination in the various factional fights, though as a follower of Robespierre he narrowly avoided difficulty at the time of Thermidor. His chief stroke of good fortune was being on hand

England, as this 1798 cartoon indicates, saw the struggle as one between civilization and barbarism posing as liberty.

when a royalist uprising occurred on October 5, 1795—he quelled it with his artillery. He got the reputation of being *both* a child of the Revolution and a man who could keep order. He obtained the command of the Army of Italy in 1796 at a time when the tide of battle was beginning to turn in favor of France everywhere. Its national army, now thoroughly reorganized, was both larger and more enthusiastic than the old professional armies of Europe.

Though he lived under a lucky star and owed his success partly to social forces, Napoleon's own genius cannot be denied. He was an electrifying leader who knew how to inspire his men; more than that, he had studied the art of war and applied to it new ideas with surpassing genius. Better roads and better guns had created a silent revolution in the conditions of warfare. The great development of French artillery actually began under the Old Regime, its most recent advances having been made largely by the officer Gribeauval in the 1760's and 1770's. This was a matter of improvements in materiel and technology, making guns both more mobile and more accurate. Napoleon was not only aware of these changes, he was able to apply them brilliantly to warfare.

Italian campaign

The hour, the circumstances, and the man seemed to collaborate magnificently in Bonaparte's case. His genius and his luck brought him to the front at

Admiral Nelson

just the moment when, to quote his own remark, "France needs a master." It also gave him command of a nation charged with forces strong enough to overturn the balance of power and sweep through Europe. After the sensational Italian campaign of 1796–97, during which he defeated the Austrians and forced them to yield northern Italy to France, Napoleon secured command of an expedition to Egypt, in which he came out badly. Victorious against the Turks, he was cut off by England's Admiral Nelson, who destroyed the French fleet.

Seizure of power

This somewhat untoward outcome did not appear to hurt Napoleon's popularity when he returned to France in 1799 to find the moment propitious for an overthrow of the unpopular Directory.[1] On November 9–10, 1799, the 18th and 19th Brumaire of the Year VIII, Napoleon did this with the aid of one director—Siéyès, curiously, the same man who had virtually started the Revolution with his famous pamphlet in 1789, and who now ended it, 10 eventful years later. At first Bonaparte was theoretically only one of three consuls, but there can have been few people fooled. Soon he was the only one; in 1802 he became consul for life, in 1804 he was proclaimed Emperor. He was un-

[1] While Bonaparte was in Egypt, Marshal Masséna brilliantly defeated the Austro-Russian army in two battles near Zurich, giving the Republic a lease on life.

questioned master of France, and soon he was the master of almost all Europe. Perhaps he was a tyrant—a valiant band of Frenchmen of high ideals thought so from the beginning—but the French people voted for him overwhelmingly in the plebiscite which was held.

The Napoleonic regime

Napoleon did not immediately turn to conquest. He inherited a country much in need of reconstruction after years of civil and foreign war. In his seizure of power Napoleon had promised peace. In a couple of years he got it, on very favorable terms. A smashing though somewhat lucky victory at Marengo in northern Italy persuaded the Austrians to make peace again and England soon came to terms also. Apart from the expedition to Santo Domingo, apparently meant as preliminary to the reestablishment of a great French colonial empire (Spain having secretly returned Louisiana Territory to France), Napoleon remained at peace between 1802 and 1805. Great Britain declared war on France in 1803 after only a year of peace, following quarrels over Malta. But there were no military results until 1805, save for a naval blockade by Britain and some preparations at Boulogne by the French for an invasion of England across the Channel, which never materialized. The Santo Domingo expedition foundered on the bitter resistance of the native Negroes, and Napoleon sold Louisiana to the United States in 1803, preferring to deposit it there than allow Britain to seize it.

Organizing the Revolution

His superhuman energies were seldom satiated by just one task, but in these years Bonaparte turned them toward the reconstruction of France, the pacification of its internal quarrels, the consolidation of his government. These were the years of the drawing up of new legal codes (the "Code Napoleon"); the framing of another constitution (the fifth since 1789); a concordat with the Pope, settling for the time being a long quarrel harking back to the law of 1790; and a substantial number of other "enlightened despot" projects. "We have finished with the romance of the Revolution, let us make it practical," Napoleon announced. It was his job to "organize the Revolution."

Napoleon undeniably did carry out many of the practical goals of the Revolution. The legal codes, a vast and much-admired project, were based on the principle of equality of all under the law. Peasants secured legal title to the lands they had acquired from the nobles during the Revolution. Napoleon's motto was "the career open to talents": let everyone go as far as his merits could take him. The centralized administrative system aspired to by many of the revolutionary leaders, but not then achieved, was now accomplished. It was an orderly system made up of departments, *arrondissements*, and municipalities, headed by prefects, subprefects, and mayors—officers nominated by the central government and tied to it by the chain of command. The departments (prefectures) can roughly be compared to the states in the United States. If we were under the French system, our state governors would be in effect appointed by the President—one can readily see the greater administrative centralization of the Napoleonic system, which has survived in France substantially to this day. What it lacked in democracy this system could make up for in efficiency, provided one had at the top a man as able as Bonaparte. It could also lead to bureaucratic inefficiency. But the logical clarity of this system gave it strong appeal. It could be extended to other lands coming under French sway during the wars of Napoleon.

The Code Napoleon

The same application of common principles to all of France is seen in the famous Civil Code, which went into effect in 1804 after Bonaparte and a commission of jurists had worked it into shape. The code combined revolutionary principles with conservative ones. Citizens were equal under the law, feudal practices were outlawed, rights to property acquired during the Revolution were made secure—a practical keystone of Napoleon's power was this confirmation of everything gained during the Revolution. Property, in general, was protected, while authority—the authority of the husband in the family, for example—was affirmed.

Under Napoleon French troops were to continue to appear in Europe as the destroyers of feudalism, the bearers of equalitarianism. In all these ways he consolidated the Revolution and was its loyal son. In pacifying France, too, even in suspending government by the legislature, he was perhaps not betraying the Revolution. For it had been evident quite a while that the strife of factions was not what France wanted. However, *liberté* as well as *egalité* and *fraternité* had been the slogans of the Revolution, and Bonaparte gave France little or no liberty. The press was muzzled, the opposition thrown out of the Tribunate, critics of the regime were subject to arbitrary arrest and banishment.

Napoleon developed an enormous cynicism. Having experienced everything at the age of 30, he had no more illusions. Men, be believed, are selfish. They are led by their stomachs; they can also be led by "baubles"—for which reason he created a "new nobility" as well as awards such as the Legion of Honor. He did not think men were often led by ideals, or valued liberty in the abstract.

Agreement with the papacy

Napoleon, who privately sneered at sexual morality and religion, publicly believed that society required a strong family and a strong church. His other great internal achievement was the concordat with the Roman church, ending a long quarrel begun early in the Revolution. Napoleon had observed that the great majority of the French people were equally attached to the Republic and to the religion of their fathers. After long and difficult negotiations with Rome, the agreement was reached in 1801, with the Pope conceding at least as much as Bonaparte. The church accepted the loss of her properties and promised never to try to regain them. The Catholic religion was recognized not as the "religion of the state" but as that of "the great majority of French citizens." The bishops who had held office under the Old Regime were compelled to resign their offices, new ones suitable to Napoleon being named—a most unprecedented violation of episcopal tenure. At this price the Catholic religion was again established in France under the protection of the state. Bonaparte, himself a thoroughgoing skeptic in religious matters, felt that this step pacified France and solidified his government. He was right.

Napoleon's new nobility

This combination of realism and conservatism with devotion to the basic ideals of the Revolution was Napoleon's keynote throughout. He wished to abolish all distinctions of birth, and reward men according to their abilities alone—"careers open to talents." The Revolution having abolished the old nobility, Napoleon set up a new one, an act sometimes taken to mean that the Emperor had fully broken with the equalitarian spirit of the Revolution. But in fact this new "Imperial Nobility" had to be earned, and could not easily be handed on to descendants. Cabinet ministers, senators, judges, mayors, decorated soldiers would be made counts, barons, or chevaliers, but only after they had proved themselves by winning these honors. The title could be inherited only if the family possessed enough money to support it (the idea being not to have the state support any idle aristocracy). So this new nobility, while it may have displayed the conservative Napoleon anxious to create a new ruling class, also revealed his dislike for an aristocracy of birth and unearned privilege.

The career open to talent

Under Napoleon's Empire a new class of upper bourgeoisie gained great power. He interpreted "all equal under the law" to mean that the rewards should go to those who had the energy and initiative to earn them. This was not far from 19th-century British middle-class liberalism, with its motto of "a fair field and no favors." It released great energies. It was not economic equality, in the Jacobin sense, but was equality of economic *opportunity.* There was little freedom to oppose the government under Napoleon, but much encouragement to new men of ability to make their way forward. There was security for property against the threat of more political upheavals. In some ways a cynical tyrant, Napoleon in other ways was the bearer of enlightenment to Europe. That is perhaps why neither posterity not his contemporaries could quite make up their minds about him.

So the question whether Napoleon "betrayed the Revolution" or fulfilled it is open to argument; in some ways he did both. But whatever he was doing, he did it with extraordinary ability and success. A marvelous intelligence and a fantastic energy united in him, along with a terrific ego. Such a man could not stop at the mere reorganization of France, especially since the principles of the Revolution were widely considered to be articles for export. And the armies of revolutionary France led by the greatest military genius of modern times threatened to be invincible.

The Emperor Napoleon

In 1804 Napoleon showed signs of becoming increasingly ambitious. His suppression of all opposition in France intensified, with the arrest of the popular general Moreau and others on conspiracy charges. The young Duc d'Enghien, a prominent Bourbon, allegedly involved in conspiracies to kill Napoleon, was kidnapped from neutral territory in Baden not far from the French frontier and shot without trial. The episode did much to alarm Europe at the arbitrary violence of Bonaparte. Two months later, Napoleon crowned himself Emperor at Notre Dame in the presence of the Pope: another Charlemagne. It is true that this was only as Emperor of the French. But the title itself, and in addition the pomp and circumstance with which the new Emperor proceeded to surround himself, made it apparent that he aspired to include more than France in his domains. He soon began to intrigue toward the seizure of additional territory. And in 1805 when assuming the Iron Crown at Milan he wrote "I am not the successor of Louis XIV but Charlemagne."

The revolutionary Republic had turned into an imperial monarchy with all the trappings. But behind it remained the power of the popular forces unleashed by the Revolution. Lord Castlereagh, the British statesman, had earlier remarked that "It is the first time that all the population and all the wealth of a great kingdom have been concentrated in the field; what may be the result is beyond my perception." Place at the head of this force a military genius with insatiable ambitions, and the result would astound even Castlereagh.

Napoleon at the battle of Jena, October 14, 1806.

Napoleonic wars

England succeeded in welding Austria, Russia, and Sweden into a coalition to contain France. This was the Third Coalition. The First Coalition, which came into existence at the beginning of the wars with France in 1792, had consisted of Austria, Prussia, Spain, and Britain; it broke up in 1795 when the Prussians made a separate peace. Austria fought on, with British help, until 1797, when Napoleon forced her to sign the peace of Campo Formio. The Second Coalition lasted from 1798 to 1801, Austria and Britain being joined by Russia at this time. Austria was knocked out by 1801, and after 1802 there was a pause in the war for two years. The chief trouble with all the coalitions, obviously, was that Napoleon was always knocking them to pieces. But they also suffered from a lack of close cooperation among the members. The same difficulties afflicted the Third Coalition. Moving large armies with a speed astonishing to his foes, Napoleon proceeded to devastate this coalition and bowl over Europe in brilliant campaigns which saw him at his military zenith. He captured an Austrian army at Ulm, took Vienna, then smashed the Russians and Austrians together in the great battle of Austerlitz (December, 1805), perhaps the most scintillating of all his victories. A panic-stricken Prussia took the field in time to be crushed at the battle of Jena. In 1807 the defeat of Russia at Friedland completed the breathtaking conquest

The battle of Trafalgar, October 21, 1805.

of virtually all Europe. The Tsar, Alexander I, made peace at Tilsit and allowed France to have her way even in Poland, creating the satellite Grand Duchy of Warsaw. Both Austria and Prussia had been forced to make humiliating peace. The Holy Roman Empire was formally dissolved, ending its thousand-year existence, and in its place Napoleon completely reorganized the German world, abolishing dozens of tiny estates and regrouping the others, chiefly in a Confederation of the Rhine subordinate to him.

Napoleon's relatives rule Europe

It was difficult to keep up with all the changes. Napoleon himself became king of an Italian state, and when the Pope objected to the Napoleonic rule and system he was seized and held prisoner. In the south of Italy the throne of Naples passed from the Bourbons to Napoleon's brother Joseph, later to his brother-in-law Murat. Napoleon sought to organize his accumulating conquests in a curious family system, reminiscent of the Corsican clan. Brother Louis became King of Holland; Jerome, of Westphalia; while Joseph was soon promoted from Naples to Spain. A particularly high-handed act against the Spanish royal family (the "ambush" of Bayonne, a virtual kidnaping) preceded the installation of Joseph in their place and perhaps capped Napoleon's arrogance. He had only to speak and ancient dynasties fell, to be replaced by his own upstart Corsican kinsmen. Truly it was an astonishing spectacle. But, again, Napoleon appeared in the guise of enlightened reformer and liberator to at least some of these peoples. He brought with him the Code Napoleon and a new social order. He was pulling down political structures which the Revolution had rendered obsolete.

Resistance to Napoleonic rule: Spain

Would Napoleon succeed in uniting all Europe under a single rule? He soon ran up against strong forces of resistance. He had already tasted defeat, though not personally or by an army. The British fleet had shattered the combined French and Spanish fleet at the great naval battle of Trafalgar off the Spanish coast in 1805. For the English it was the greatest victory since 1588 and exploded Napoleon's plans for an invasion across the English Channel. Britain was in a position to follow Francis Bacon's maxim that the power that commanded the seas "might take as much or as little of the war as it chose." She would exploit every weakness in Napoleon's somewhat ill-digested continental empire. The best chance was in Spain. There, the Spanish people were outraged at Napoleon's cavalier treatment of their king and his foisting on them of a French regime. A nationalistic uprising against the French began and received the aid of a small, crack British army under Arthur Wellesley, who became the Duke of Wellington, a tough and able Irishman whose military genius was not far behind Napoleon's. While Spanish guerrillas fought with ferocious courage against the French, Wellesley's Peninsular Army, using hit-and-run tactics, helped make Spain a "running sore" for Bonaparte. It cost him thousands of his best troops, tied down 300,000 men, and never was brought under control. Spanish courage and national spirit—or, as Napoleon fulminated, their superstitious reverence for their kings and priests—opened the first breach in his European empire. The British army, under the ablest opposition general the war produced, moved into that breach and made it a gaping hole. The extreme difficulties of Spanish geography and communications helped. A Portuguese army restored by the English also contributed.

The Continental System

Napoleon was far from through. When the Austrians once again renewed the war Napoleon beat them at Wagram (July 5, 1809). The Continental System, Napoleon's economic plan for the integration of Europe, and a reply to the British blockade, was tightened up. This system, embodied in the two Decrees of Berlin (1806) and Milan (1807), theoretically closed all European ports to the goods and the ships of England or her colonies, and authorized seizure not only of English ships but of any neutral vessels that cooperated with the British blockade. Europe, even France herself, found it difficult to do without British goods, and some parts of the Continent, particularly the eastern countries, were hard hit. The embargo could not be fully enforced, and both as a war measure and as a propaganda measure the Continental System largely failed. There was a good deal of resentment against it in Europe on the grounds that it really represented French economic imperialism, not a true "continental system." But Bonaparte would tolerate no criticism of it.

Metternich

Repression became more severe, both in France, where censorship was tightened and critics exiled, and in the occupied countries, where resistance was likely to be punished by the firing squad. Napoleon's enemies increased apace. One of them was Prince Metternich, the Austrian genius of diplomacy, who along with British foreign minister Castlereagh began the job of molding a firm coalition among all the other states of Europe—something that had heretofore proved impossible. Others were the French exiles, among them her greatest writers—Mme. de Staël, Chateaubriand, Benjamin Constant—who denounced Bonapartism as execrable tyranny. Another was the Tsar of Russia. And in 1810 the Bonaparte clan itself cracked: Louis, the King of Holland, abdicated and fled, refusing to enforce the Continental System to the detriment of the country he ruled.

War of 1812

One of Napoleon's few later triumphs occurred when French diplomacy succeeded in embroiling Great Britain in a war with the young United States, in a row stemming chiefly from British interference with American shipping in enforcement of the blockade against trade with the Continent. But the Americans were not able seriously to impair the British war effort against Napoleon. Meanwhile, though gaining this one distant and minor ally—for the American Republic had yet to become powerful—Napoleon made a powerful enemy in Europe. He was about to go to war with Russia.

Napoleon's downfall

Sources of war with Russia

The break with Russia came about as a result of inevitable jealousy and friction between the powerful French Emperor and the only other major land power not subject to his will. Napoleon demanded that the Russians end their trade with England and cooperate with the Continental System, and was enraged by their refusal. In addition there was a direct territorial clash of ambitions. When Napoleon beat Austria in 1809, he took from her large territories in eastern Europe, some of which he added to his Grand Duchy of Warsaw and others of which he organized in an Illyrian province under a French duke. Napoleon's evident ambitions to the east also included grandiose dreams about Constantinople and the Orient. Alexander could hardly ignore such challenges on his very doorstep, and Napoleon, rashly enough in view of his growing troubles in Europe, was determined to push them. Many historians think that Napoleon's judgment foundered on power and that he became a megalomaniac in the later years. He seemed to show that trait here, as he prepared for a mighty invasion of Russia. On the other hand, this crusade was a means of uniting many Europeans against the Russian menace, and if he won, his prestige would surely have been sufficient to overawe all opposition. It was a gigantic gamble worthy of Napoleon at his most romantic.

The Grand Army invades Russia

The Grand Army which Napoleon assembled in the summer of 1812, the greatest military force the world had yet seen, was made up of Italians, Poles,

Prince Metternich

Viscount Castlereagh

Napoleon in 1812

Swiss, Dutch, Germans, and Austrians as well as Frenchmen. Prussia and Austria contributed only a few troops reluctantly, but the Poles undoubtedly fought with their hearts in it, against their traditional foe and oppressor Russia; while Napoleon always had friends in the Italian, Swiss, and Rhenish cities. The Russians for their part were joined by the Swedes, who deserted France though under the rule of the former French Marshal, Count Bernadotte. England was their ally, Prussia and Austria secretly so, but these allies could do little to help Russia. The Russian generals no doubt intended to fight at the border, as Napoleon expected, but were too weak to face the 600,000 man Grand Army. Their successful strategy of retreat was thus partly unintentional. However, from Wellington's tactics in Spain they had learned how to destroy supplies as they retreated, thus making life difficult for the invader. They burned Smolensk as Napoleon followed them on toward Moscow. At Borodino a fierce battle occurred, immortalized by Tolstoy's description in *War and Peace*. It was a costly victory for the Grand Army. The Russian army remained in existence and continued to retreat. Napoleon found Moscow deserted, barren, and soon in flames. Alexander would not surrender or make a treaty, and Napoleon could only sit in the Kremlin as winter rapidly approached—the fierce Russian winter.

The retreat from Moscow was a terrible one, as the Grand Army froze, starved, and was harassed by Russian regular and irregular fighters. When it reached the Niemen 500,000 of the 600,000 had died. This was a military disaster hard to equal in all the annals of war, and it just about doomed Napoleon. It is true that he raised a new army and managed to stave off

The Grand Army in retreat from Moscow—winter 1812.

defeat for two years, but the odds were increasingly against him. National wars of liberation sprang up everywhere—first in Prussia, then in other parts of Germany, while Austria once more (for the fifth time) renewed the war, after Metternich had exhausted all the diplomatic resources of peace. Thanks to his and Castlereagh's labors, a solid coalition of Russia, Prussia, Austria, and Britain shaped up. In August, 1813, Napoleon defeated an Allied army at Dresden, but it was his last real victory. He had several chances after that to make a favorable peace, but with characteristic pride spurned them. In October the great "battle of the nations" at Leipzig went disastrously for the French and their remaining allies.

From here on, the pattern was one of a triumphal Allied advance toward French soil, while Napoleon's satellites fled the ship like drowning rats. Wellington also advanced into France from Spain. Still, late in 1813, Napoleon refused a peace offer that would have left France intact, with the boundaries

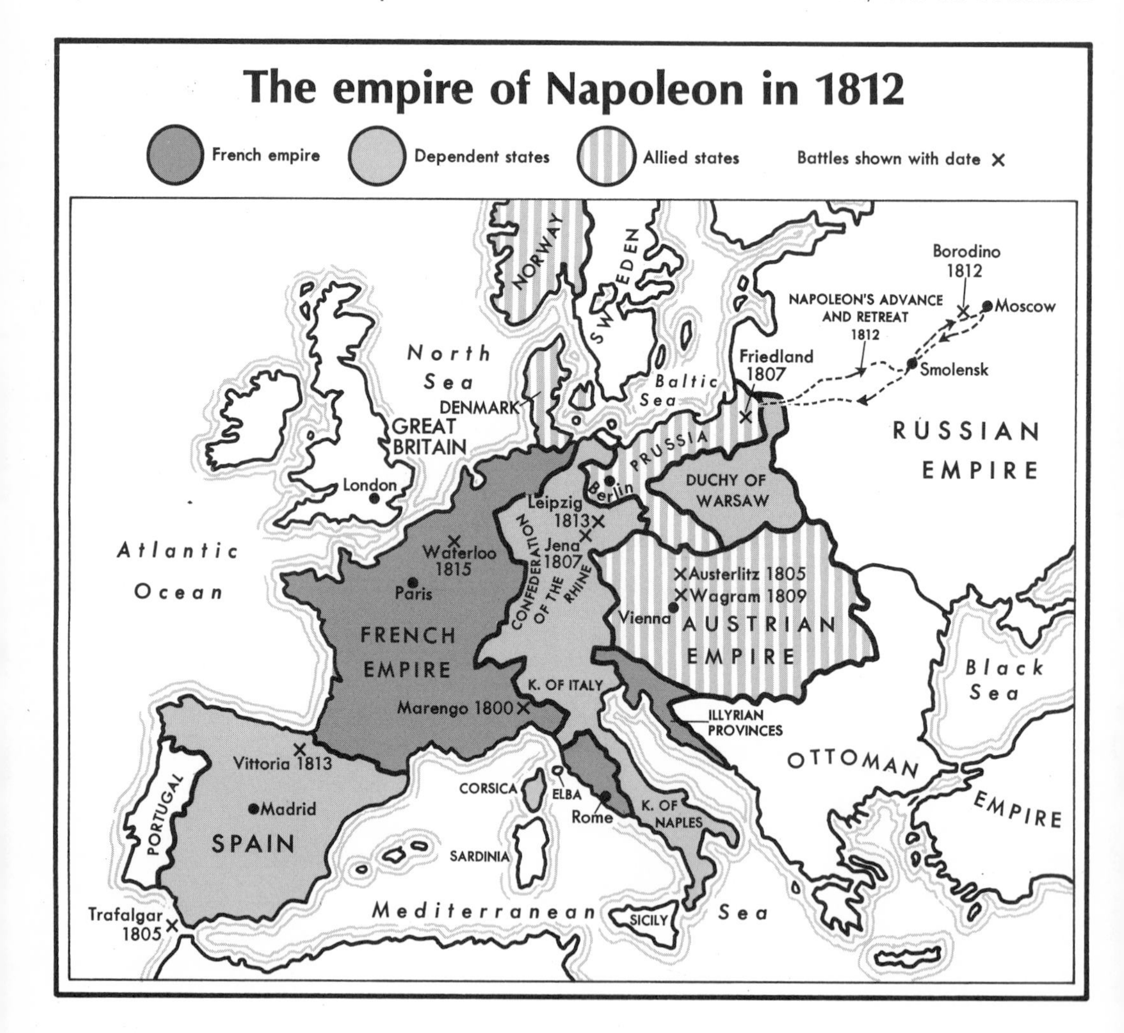

Duke of Wellington

of Alps and Rhine. Driven within France, he turned savagely and defeated Blücher, the famous Alsatian general, but could not long stay his fate. The Allies pounded their way toward Paris, and took it on March 30, 1814. Napoleon abdicated, and the Allies graciously granted him the island of Elba as his principality, with a generous pension. His last stand in 1813–14 was both gallant and able, against great odds; at the same time it was wildly unrealistic, and uselessly sacrificed many more lives.

The meaning of Napoleon

The Hundred Days

The saga of the little Corsican lieutenant who rose to the dizziest heights of any European in modern times, and fell about as rapidly, was not completed, for there remained the Hundred Days. After a year of Louis XVIII, the Bourbon king restored by the Allies, signs of discontent in France, and also discord among the victorious allies at Vienna, caused Napoleon to return to France. Landing almost alone in the South, the magic of his appearance made all France rally behind him once more. Troops sent to oppose him by the government in Paris rushed to his standard. He declared that he now intended peace not war, but the Allies, understandably enough, were taking no chances. They raised a great European army which, headed by the Duke of Wellington and Blücher, defeated Napoleon in the dramatic battle of Waterloo, a fierce engagement which the French came close to winning.

Napoleon was then taken far away to the island of St. Helena where he was treated as a prisoner, to his great chagrin and that of Bonapartists ever since. He died within a few years, and his body was subsequently (1840) brought back to Paris. Thirty years after his death his nephew was to show that the Bonapartist appeal was far from dead.

Judgment of Napoleon

Around the Corsican, controversy has swirled ever since. Was he "the greatest of historic men"? Or an international gangster unaccountably allowed to run amuck? Was he liberator or enslaver, organizer of the Revolution or greedy tyrant? Did he aspire to the lofty goal of uniting Europe or the ignoble one of subjecting it to foreign domination? Was his defeat a victory for blind reaction, or national freedom? Many other questions have been raised, and they submit to no easy answer. That Napoleon was a military and administrative genius no one has doubted. His critics have said he was also a barbarian with no ideals and no manners, an egoist whose insatiable ambitions cost millions of lives in vain, a tyrant who snuffed out liberty. His admirers saw in him a bearer of enlightenment along with the dream of a united Europe.

It is difficult not to agree partly with both sides. Beyond doubt Napoleon *was* an intolerable egoist with some of the instincts of a gangster, practically no real culture, a basic contempt for human nature. He also, however, faithfully represented the progressive social creed of the French Revolution and did strive for an association of Europe which must seem to us today better than the nationalism which caused World War I. To Goethe and Nietzsche, he was the "good European." To Schopenhauer, he was "the finest embodiment of human will power"—for good and evil both. To Mme. de Staël and Chateaubriand he was the classic tyrant described long ago by Aristotle. The reader of his collected writings and sayings today cannot but be impressed by a razor-sharp mind, a keen and restless intellect capable of discerning many profound truths, if with a heavy indebtedness to others—a man who read voraciously and assimilated an astonishing amount. Though his own career was romantic enough for any poet, Napoleon in his literary and intellectual tastes remained true to the 18th-century Enlightenment, showing no liking for the romantic movement then growing in Germany and England. Chateaubriand, the great French representative of the romantic movement, was his determined foe. Thus Napoleon has been regarded as a reactionary in this respect, and certainly his close supervision of the arts and letters blighted them. He was capable of saying that the only reading he enjoyed was the statistics of his armies! In the last analysis we are left groping for the real Bonaparte, uncertain whether he was a barbarian or a man of considerable intellect as well as a great statesman. He remains a paradoxical figure.

Permanent significance of the Napoleonic era

More objectively, the Napoleonic years left Europe permanently altered. The Old Regime had been destroyed and could not be replaced. Directly, Napoleon had given many people a taste of the revolutionary principles of legal equality. Indirectly, he had aroused a sense of national patriotism. He had scrapped old political entities, such as the Holy Roman Empire. In France, the system of administration and of law established under him remained (and still does). Abroad, his foes themselves did France the honor of imitating his system: Prussian reformers came to the conclusion that a military power as strong as the French could only be had by scrapping the class system and adopting the "career open to talents" idea. These reforms, associated with the name of Baron von Stein, did not all last; but many did, including the end of serfdom. They illustrate Napoleon's impact on Europe. "France did more than conquer Europe, she converted her," wrote the historian Albert Sorel. Historically Napoleon was the man destined to destroy the old order of Europe. But the new order did not follow the contour of his vision, or his ambition, in important respects. He had inadvertently opened up the force of nationalism, and Europe, though modernized socially, was not to be united politically. One may feel that the most constructive part of Bonaparte's schemes was thus frustrated to the detriment of Europe.

He never understood the sentiment of nationalism; why should not all peoples accept the same enlightened social order? Why should they cling to ancient superstitions like hereditary monarchy and priestcraft? But nationalist sentiment existed, and was stimulated, ironically, by Napoleon's conquests. Nationalism thus represents a key both to the success and the failure of Napoleon's mission. The principles of the French Revolution spread throughout Europe—or much of Europe—because these peoples were ready for its message of equality, democracy, an end to the old order of privilege. To them this meant a new nation, which would be made up of Italians or Germans and not just princes, nobles, and subjects. Nationalism thus took on a new meaning wherever the Revolution spread its ideas. The similarity of ideas and movements gave a cosmopolitan character to the Revolution and created the concept of a single great nation of Europe, formed on the new foundation of liberty and equality. *But* it also produced nationalism which resented being dominated by the French and soon saw in Napoleon's armies only a fresh form of enslavement to the will of others and a threat to the newly born ideas.

The peace settlement

The Great Powers which had won the war pledged themselves to solidarity forever. The situation was somewhat similar to that which prevailed in 1945 after World War II, when a coalition forged in the fires of a frightful war believed that it could hang together always and thus provide the basis for permanent peace. As on the later occasion, such hopes proved illusory. However, the powers did gather at Vienna for a congress of all Europe, a meeting comparable to that in Westphalia after the Thirty Years War and at Paris after World War I. There in 1815 they quarreled, patched up their quarrels, settled the fate of Europe for a generation, and created an international organization for peace.

Peace terms with France

The leniency of the terms of peace with France surprises those who have compared this peace settlement with later ones. The cry for vengeance did arise, but it was firmly resisted. "It can safely be said," writes the British historian Wingfield-Stratford, "that with a popular press capable of whipping up patriotic propaganda on 20th-century lines, no government would have dared incur the odium of losing the peace by . . . allowing an enemy . . . to get off with a far easier settlement than he had either the power to exact or the right to expect." The Allies had the power over France as of 1814 and again in 1815, but on the other hand they were wise enough to want a lasting settlement and realistic enough not to want to keep troops in France to uphold an unpopular one. The truth is that they were still a bit in awe of France, and also there was enough *noblesse oblige* left among European gentlemen to suggest gallantry toward an honorable foe. No modern "popular press" backed by an irresistible King Public then existed, even in Britain, though Castlereagh was cruelly attacked.

More concrete motives included the decision to reinstall the Bourbons, which made it desirable not to make their position difficult—it would be difficult enough already—by saddling them with a humiliating peace. And balance-of-power thinking, axiomatic with these statesmen, led them to think in terms of preserving a reasonably strong, though not overstrong French nation. The Prussians wanted annexations from France; Britain and Russia opposed them. They wanted Prussia to be strong enough to hold down France, and gave her territory along the Rhine, but they did not want her to be too strong. Therefore even after Napoleon's return from Elba made it necessary to renew the war against France, the terms were mild enough. France renounced all those other countries she had controlled, but the boundaries of France remained as they had been in 1792, while an indemnity (imposed only after the Hundred Days) was paid off in three years. No bitter humiliation was left to rankle in French hearts. In fact France was soon to resume her place as a member of the inner circle of great powers. For this, however, the quarrel among the victors was chiefly responsible.

Congress of Vienna

Having made the two Treaties of Paris, the powers convened for the Congress of Vienna. (The Hundred Days and the second Treaty of Paris interrupted their sessions there.) While all Europe was there, as usual the decisions were made by the great. "The Congress never met," it was said; more than 200 delegates, and thousands of people with grievances, assembled at Vienna, a mob of such confusion that it was never formally organized; the Big Four simply went ahead and made their treaties, claiming to speak for all of Europe. Their job was big enough. They had to provide a general European settlement after the wholesale upheaval wrought by Napoleon, and their discussion became acrimonious at times. The balance of power had to be weighed against national aspirations; one nation's pride and demands for security against another's. It is not surprising that there were serious clashes. These centered on two areas: Poland and Saxony.

Statesmen of Europe at the Congress of Vienna, 1815.

Russia wished to control Poland, a familiar theme which has made trouble more than once. It was not surprising that she wished to do so, but the other powers feared an upsetting of the balance. Prussia for her part aspired to Saxony, her neighbor on the south, a state which had shown notable sympathies for France until very late in the war and was thus vulnerable. Prussia and Russia joined forces in backing each other's claims, while Great Britain and Austria resisted this strengthening of the eastern powers. It was this division which allowed Talleyrand, the veteran French minister (who had served Napoleon but secretly treated with the Allies in the last days of his reign), to become an important member of the inner circle of the great powers at Vienna.

It was difficult (as after World War II) to argue with Russia about Poland when her troops were in occupation. Alexander, whose prestige was high, insisted that Russia wanted an independent Poland, though under his protection. In the end, after much diplomacy and a severe test of strength, Alexander got a large part but not all of Poland, as a kingdom under his protection, and Prussia got a slice of Saxony plus other territories in the west of Germany, not contiguous with her home territory. Austria and Prussia retained parts of Poland, with Cracow being made a free city; Austria was compensated in Italy. It was a somewhat awkward arrangement, but it served the purpose of preventing a breach and possibly war between the powers.

Balance of power

The Peace of Vienna was to be accused of "bartering peoples about" without attention to their wishes or to the principle of nationality. The charge

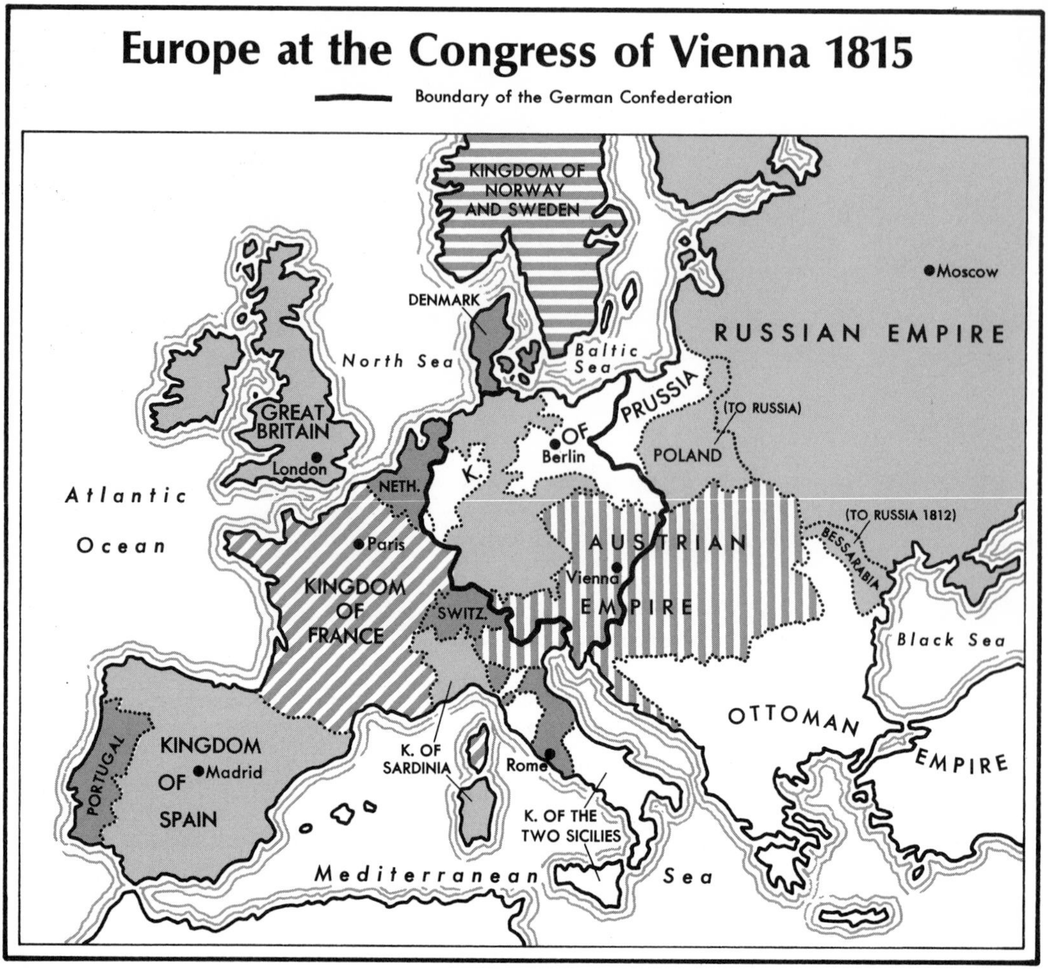

Europe at the Congress of Vienna 1815

Boundary of the German Confederation

is true. The statesmen of 1815 were not impressed with the wisdom of nationality as the basis of a settlement; they *were* concerned both with composing their own quarrels—which often dictated territorial "compensations"—and with securing a stable balance of power. They put Belgium under the Netherlands, in order to strengthen that area, an arrangement which did not work out. They returned much of north Italy to Austria, because the Austrians had made concessions elsewhere.

Legitimacy

For nationality or popular consent the peacemakers of Vienna attempted to substitute the principle of "legitimacy," or government by the hereditary ruling house. The Bourbons returned to France, Spain, and Naples. Many of the princes were restored where they had been deposed in Germany and north Italy; the pope returned to his papal domains. Germany remained a preserve of small principalities, though the Holy Roman Empire was not revived and the number of states was substantially reduced from 1789. It was not possible there to put back the old system, and something of Napoleon's Confederation of the Rhine could be seen in the confederation created in 1815. However, Austria and Prussia returned to it, with the emperor as presiding officer.

"Legitimacy" was a phrase which no doubt reflected the feelings of the peacemakers of 1815, conservative opponents of popular sovereignty and nationalism as they were. But in practice they seem to have ignored or violated the principle more than they honored it. Bernadotte, no "legitimate" or pre-1789 monarch, was permitted to keep Sweden, and Norway was added to his kingdom; the Dutch had no "legitimate" right to Belgium, nor of course Tsar Alexander to Poland; in northern Italy, some old ruling houses were replaced by members of the Hapsburg family since expediency dictated the compensation of Austria in this region. It is possible to find numerous such instances of lapse from the principle acclaimed as the basis of the peace. In Germany, many former sovereigns were not restored. The peacemakers of 1815 were not doctrinaires but realists, on the whole, and really did not attempt any blanket imposition of their doctrines. The victorious Allies were often to be accused of wishing to put back the clock to 1789. In fact they were neither able to do so, nor did they wish to. Metternich and Castlereagh, the leading architects of this peace, were conservatives, not reactionaries; realists who paid attention to existing forces but did not want to thrust beyond them. They certainly did feel that the French Revolution had overthrown the peace of Europe and ought to be reined in as sharply as possible.

International organization

This conservative and balance-of-power peace also produced the first real effort at European international organization, by the cooperation of states associated together for a common purpose, that of keeping the peace. The great powers decided to meet regularly and act together on European problems, and they did so for the next seven years. Alexander of Russia, an extraordinary personality who had passed from Enlightenment ideas to a kind of social Christianity, was keenly interested in an idealistic way in world peace. It was he who proposed solemnizing the international cooperation of the powers into a "Holy Alliance," a league based on Christian principles of brotherly love. Metternich and Castlereagh were more hardheaded, and made fun of Alexander's mysticism, but they were not averse to the experiment of cooperation; Britain refused to associate herself with the Holy Alliance, urging constitutional obstacles. After the three continental despots Alexander, Francis, and Frederick William signed the Holy Alliance, Britain joined them in signing the more prosaic Quadruple Alliance late in 1815, pledging the Big Four to keep together, help each other, and preserve the peace of Europe against any troublemakers.

This system of regular conferences included only the Big Five, France sometimes being added, save for rare occasions (1856, 1878) when a full congress of all European states might be summoned. It was not a formal organization like the present-day United Nations but included many of the same ideas. Like the United Nations, it was supposed to provide an international police force, with the great powers stomping out any breach of the peace. Like the United Nations also, it failed to consider what happened when the great powers themselves clashed, as was bound to happen. In 1822, Great Britain withdrew to "go it alone" because she could not agree with the policy of intervention to suppress rebellion in Spain. (See further next chapter.) Fundamentally, it was a matter of her interests diverging from those of the continental powers. For the British, who had acquired Malta, the Cape of Good Hope, Ceylon, and some other overseas bases through the war, were more than ever slanted toward overseas commerce. They hoped to forget European wars—and they wanted the trade of the Spanish colonies.

Nevertheless the "Concert of Europe," vague as it was, perhaps marked an achievement for Europe and meant something, if not much, throughout the century. For the time being Europe relaxed and rested from the long siege of revolution and war. The times between 1815 and 1830 favored conservatism. Men were weary of ideological strife and needed time to assimilate the lessons of the Revolution and Napoleon. The Congress of Vienna made a peace which though pedestrian and not very stable—practically all of it was overturned in 1830, 1848, 1861, and 1870—turned out to be surprisingly successful. Though the next 50 years brought some important revisions in Europe's boundaries, there was not to be another major war for exactly 100 years. It seems likely that the main reason for this was the satisfaction of all the great powers, none of which had a gnawing grievance.

The great powers satisfied

For the victors had rewarded themselves well enough: Russia with the lion's share of Poland; Prussia with large gains all over northern Germany even if she had not gotten all Saxony; Austria with control of northern Italy including the commercial wealth of Venice; Great Britain with—only a few remote overseas territories. But the British well knew that in overseas trade and a stable balance of power in Europe lay the basis for greater wealth than the world had yet known. The future for the next half century would favor no continental empire but the industrial capitalism of the British, backed by their global naval power.

The fact that it was a great-power peace, in which all the victors rewarded themselves generously while even the defeated one, France, suffered little, helps explain the relative success of the settlement of 1815. Judged by its particular provisions, it was singularly short-sighted, except in the clement treatment of France. Belgium, Italy, Germany, and Poland are examples of what seem both unjust and unsound assignments of peoples to a rule they did not want and would rebel against at the first opportunity. Belgium rebelled against Dutch rule in 1830, Poland against Russia in 1830 and again in 1863, though unsuccessfully; Italy and Germany were in ferment until finally, in the 1860's, they organized themselves in a wholly different way. Despite this, the treaties of 1815 led to a century of substantial peace. For this it would be rash to credit altogether the decisions made by statesmen in 1815; more basic social forces obviously were at work, too. But they would seem to deserve at least some credit. To see that the great powers are contented is a good way to keep the peace, if not to do justice to all, for large wars stem from the grievances of large states, not small ones. Throughout most of the 19th century the five major powers remained in reasonably stable equilibrium, more interested in maintaining what they had than in aggressively seeking more territory.

Bibliography

George Rudé, *Revolutionary Europe 1783–1815* (Harper Torchbook), is especially good on Napoleon. Felix Markham, *Napoleon and the Awakening of Europe* (Macmillan, Collier Book) is aimed at the general reader. E.E.Y. Hales, *Napoleon and the Pope* (London: Eyre & Spottiswoode, 1962), deals with a special subject of considerable importance. H. Rose's older *Life of Napoleon* (2d ed.; New York: Macmillan, 1934) is still valuable. Monica Sterling, in *A Pride of Lions* (London: Collins, 1961), cast light on the great man by studying his remarkable mother. Later interpretation by historians and others can be found in P. Geyl's excellent work, *Napoleon For and Against* (Yale University Press). On the military career, R.S. Quimby, *Background of Napoleonic Warfare* (New York: Columbia University Press, 1957), a careful analysis, deals chiefly with military thinking in the French army just before Napoleon, theoretical studies on which Bonaparte drew. Sir Charles Oman, *Studies in the Napoleonic Wars* (New York: Charles Scribner's Sons, 1930), is among the standard works in a large and distinguished field which includes John Fortescue's *Wellington* (3d ed.; London: E. Benn, 1960) and, on the Russian campaign, Eugene Tarlé, *Napoleon's Invasion of Russia* (New York: Oxford University Press, 1942), as well as the famous Karl von Clausewitz, *The Campaign of 1812 in Russia* (London: G. Bell & Sons Ltd., 1843). Recently, David G. Chandler, *The Campaigns of Napoleon* (Macmillan, 1966), is encyclopedic. *The War in the Mediterranean 1803–1810* has been well covered by the historian Piers Mackesy (London: Longmans, Green & Co., 1957). See also J. Christopher Herold, *Bonaparte in Egypt* (New York: Harper & Row, 1962) and Owen Connelly, *Napoleon's Satellite Kingdoms* (New York: Free Press, 1966).

Arthur Byrant, in *The Years of Endurance* and *Years of Victory* (Harper & Bros., 1942, 1945), captured the excitement of the war in Great Britain, 1793–1814. Its impact on other parts of Europe may be glimpsed in E.E.Y. Hales, *Revolution and Papacy 1769–1846* (Eyre & Spottiswoode, 1960), A.A. Lobanov-Rostovsky, *Russia and Europe 1789–1825* (Durham, N.C.: Duke University Press, 1947), and Walter M. Simon, *The Failure of the Prussian Reform Movement, 1807–1819* (Ithaca, N.Y.: Cornell University Press, 1955). C.S.B. Buckland traced the diplomacy of Napoleon's downfall in *Metternich and the British Government 1809–1813* (London: G. Bell & Sons Ltd., 1932). On the peace conference, Harold Nicolson, *The Congress of Vienna* (Viking Press), and Sir Charles Webster, *The Foreign Policy of Castlereagh 1812–1815* (London: G. Bell & Sons Ltd., 1931, 1950) and *The Congress of Vienna 1814–1815* (Barnes & Noble University paperback). Crane Brinton, *The Lives of Talleyrand* is a W.W. Norton paperback. A serviceable new biography of *Castlereagh* has come from C.J. Bartlett (Charles Scribner's Sons, 1966).

Sources. J.C. Herold (ed.), *The Mind of Napoleon* (Columbia University Press), and John E. Howard (ed.), *Letters and Documents of Napoleon* (2 vols.; London: Cresset Press, 1961); A. Brett-James (ed.), *Wellington at War 1794–1815* (Macmillan, 1961); Count Phillipe-Paul de Ségur, *Napoleon's Russian Campaign* (Boston: Houghton Mifflin Co., 1958). *The Horizon Book of the Age of Napoleon* (New York: American Heritage, 1963) is richly illustrated.

Cattle and goods carriages on Liverpool and Manchester Railway, 1833

chronology

1815
Passage of Engish Corn Laws.
Restoration of Louis XVIII in France.
Burschenschaften, students' societies for liberal nationalism, appear in Germany.

1819
Peterloo massacre, Manchester; Six Acts, repressing free speech and assembly.
Carlsbad Decrees, directed against revolutionary activity in Germany.

1820
Revolution in Naples; in Piedmont, 1821. Intervention of Austria under auspices of Alliance (Troppau Protocol).
Carbonari movement.

1822
Death of Castlereagh: George Canning, foreign secretary.
English withdrawal from Continenal alliance, 1823.
Greek war of independence against Turkey; declaration of Greek independence.

1823
French troops put down Spanish revolution in name of European Concert, Great Britain dissenting and withdrawing from conference system.

1824
Charles X to French throne; program of reaction, clericalism. Liberal opposition.
Spread of Prussian *Zollverein*, started in 1819.

1825
Failure of Decembrist revolt in Russia. Nicolas I, Tsar.

1827
Intervention of powers (France, Great Britain, Russia) in Greek-Turkish war. Battle of Novarino.

1828
Repeal of discriminations against Catholics and Nonconformists, Great Britain.

1829
Treaty of Adrianople, settling issues in Near East with independence for Greece.
"Ultraist" cabinet appointed by Charles X in defiance of Chamber of Deputies.

1830
Revolutions in France, Belgium, Germany, Poland. Abdication of Charles X, constitutional monarchy under Louis-Philippe of Orléans.
Separation of Belgium from Netherlands. Absorption of Poland into Russia.

1831
Uprisings in Italy (Parma, Modena, Papal States), repressed.
Young Italy society founded.

1832
Reform Bill enacted, Great Britain.
Further repression by Metternich of liberal movements in Germany.

1834
Civil war in Spain (Carlist war, followers of claimant to throne Don Carlos) 1834–39.
English Poor Law.
Mazzini flees to London after failure of a revolutionary movement in Savoy.

1837
Queen Victoria becomes ruler of Britain.
Rise of Chartism.

20

Beginning the century of progress: Europe 1815-40

Industrial Revolution

1738
Kay's flying shuttle.

1765
Hargreave's spinning jenny.

1771
Arkwright's water frame.

1775
Watt's steam engine.

1779
Crompton's "mule."

1785
Cartwright's mechanical loom.

1793
Whitney's cotton gin.

1800
Volta's battery.

1805
Jaquard's silk-weaving machine.

1807
Fulton's steamboat in regular operation.

1811
Luddite riots in England (machine breaking).

1814
Stephenson's first locomotive.

1831
Insurrection of silk weavers in Lyon.

1833
First Factory Act, England, Following investigations of child labor in textile mills.

1834
Effort to form general union of all workers in England.

Romanticism, Science, Social Thought

1796
Goethe, *Wilhelm Meister.*
Laplace, *System of the World.*

1798
Malthus, *Essay on Population.*
Coleridge, Wordsworth, *Lyrical Ballads.*

1799
Schleiermacher, *Discourse on Religion.*
Beethoven, *Pathétique* sonata.

1801
Chateaubriand, *Atala;* Schiller, *Maid of Orléans.*
Lamarck's theory of origin of species.

1803
Say's treatise on political economy.

1804
Beethoven's *Eroica* Symphony.

1805
Chateaubriand, *René.*

1808
Fichte, *Addresses to the German Nation.*

1812
Byron's *Childe Harold.*

1814
Ingres, Goya paintings.

1817
Ricardo, *Principles of Economics.*
Poetry of Shelley.

1819
De Maistre, *On the Pope.*

1821
Saint-Simon, *Système industriel.*

1832
Hegel, *Philosophy of History.*

1835
Tocqueville, *Democracy in America.*

Perspective on the century

The advance of Europe in power

The teeming, dynamic 19th century had begun. It would be well to outline in advance something of the stature of this century, for which the dates 1815–1914 are standard: between two world wars. To begin with, Europe attained her maximum of power and glory in this century, measured not merely by material standards but by cultural influence. We are all aware of the terrific impact western civilization has had on the entire world—for better or worse. In the 20th century we have lived and are living under the shadow of that influence and the disturbances it has caused. In the 19th century, Europe by sheer weight of technology, wealth, population, and vigor burst out on the rest of the world, conquered or simply permeated it, battered down the walls of its native civilizations and forced it willy-nilly to adopt European ways. Though this process occurred chiefly after mid-century, the British began it earlier and Europe was preparing for it earlier. It was chiefly the result of Europe's stupendous technological development, behind which lay the mighty "Industrial Revolution"—a phrase covering an entire complex of which machinery, science, and economic organization are only the most evident parts.

The Industrial Revolution made Europe wealthier, more populous, and in possession of tools of commerce, navigation, and war such as enabled her to thrust herself on the outer world of Asia and Africa. It brought her also a whole range of new problems and new ideas. While economic progress went forward at the cost of huge dislocations in the traditional habits of men, the century rang with arguments about capitalism, socialism, economic policy, the welfare of the working class. No less than in the arena of science and technology, the 19th century is mighty in the realm of ideas. With a far more literate population and a far larger range of knowledge, Europe produced social and political ideologies in profusion. These ideologies—of liberalism, socialism, nationalism, democracy—made their way around the world, too. The 19th century produced most of the ideas on which the world has since been living. No historian can ignore them: Bentham, Hegel, Carlyle, Comte, Mill, Marx, Mazzini, Darwin, Nietzsche, Tolstoy, and all of the other great names of the century's thought shine with a splendor which is not exceeded by the politicians and the industrialists.

Ideologies

Some reasons for this being "an age of ideologies" may be suggested. Formal Christian religion was waning in its general influence, and every field of thought grew rapidly secularized. In some measure the new "isms" filled the part of substitute religions. Then, too, the French Revolution had swept away so many moorings of security that men needed to redefine all sorts of fundamental political and social relationships. The Industrial Revolution, likewise, arrived with all the drastic changes and urgent issues it presented, creating an impulse both to analyze its workings and protest against its results. Popular interest in political, economic, and social doctrines reflected the existence of a larger literate population, with reading and serious thinking no longer confined to a small upper-class elite.

Writers were being read in the millions of copies and making their living by writing, often a very good living as they became famous beyond most other leading citizens. It is true that Voltaire and Rousseau had accomplished something similar in the 18th century, but most earlier writers had lived off the patronage of king or nobles and had written for a small audience. The 19th century made household words of Dickens, Eliot, Thackeray, Balzac, Hugo, Goethe, and how many others. These, it is true, were chiefly novelists. But their novels had high intellectual content. It was a serious age, deeply interested especially in social and political ideas—an age which valued education, built primary schools, and taught millions to read.

The sciences

At the same time, the sciences wrote chapters in human progress which will not yield to any other field in their importance. It was an age of revolutions in hygiene and medicine, as well as in industrial power and machinery. Wherever one looks, the century shows these dynamic aspects, along with grave disturbances—more revolutions, political changes, class conflict, cultural crisis. As the legacy of the French Revolution worked itself out, Europe turned in the direction of political liberalism and democracy. Despite the turmoils which accompanied so large a shift in political power, most Europeans after about mid-century believed that they were on the high road of general progress. They believed—it is difficult to blame them—that science, technology, and popular enlightenment were combining to produce a new era of the human race. But there were thoughtful men who were deeply concerned about the loss of values and of cultural stability in a mad race for wealth and power and in the rise of mass democracy. These doubts increased at the end of the century. Only a minority entertained them seriously until the debacle of 1914. It was a century of progress.

Nationalism

This economic, social, and political progress took place within the confines largely of the national state. One of the leading paradoxes of the century was the development of an international economic and intellectual society side by side with the growth of the religion of nationalism. While goods were exchanged as never before—mercantilism had bowed to free trade—and industrialism built a society which had common features in all countries, and while ideas like liberalism, socialism, or the sciences were international, one also found the various national communities becoming more and more the focus of life, so that to be French, British, or German was the crowning mark of identification and source of satisfaction. There was a surprising parochialism in a world more and more interdependent and international. The citizen in London every day consumed goods from all over the world, held ideas to which Frenchmen and Germans had contributed, read in his newspaper information from the four corners of the globe—but sang "Hail Britannia" and considered England to be uniquely wonderful, Frenchmen and Germans to be queer kinds of aliens. The same, of course, was true *mutatis mutandis* of his counterpart in Berlin or Paris.

No doubt it is because we are closer to the 19th century that all its splendors and failures, its triumphs and paradoxes, its ideas and conflicts seem important to us. It is the immediate parent of our own age, and we are naturally more interested in our parents than in our remoter ancestors. There is justification for spending as much time on the last century and a half as we spent on the previous millenium. One of the chief functions of history is to elucidate the present age, the one in which we live. And the 19th century is the parent of the 20th.

An interlude of reaction: Political developments 1815–32

The Holy Alliance

Those who fought the French Revolution and Napoleon for a generation were naturally conservatives, and their triumph was a triumph in some degree of that conservatism. For about 15 years, between 1815 and 1830 or 1832, this mood was dominant; then it yielded to liberalism. The Concert of Europe, otherwise known as the Quadruple Alliance or the Holy Alliance (unholy to some), bestrode Europe under the guidance of Prince Metternich, who became for many people the arch-symbol of conservatism, busying itself with the maintenance of "legitimacy" and the suppression of revolutions, which it construed as a threat to the peace and hence within its jurisdiction. In 1820 and 1821 such a police power in the cause of reaction was exercised in Naples and in Genoa, to sustain respectively the unpopular Bourbons and Hapsburgs. And though Great Britain conspicuously withdrew from this action, troops were sent into Spain in 1822 on the occasion of a rebellion against the restored Bourbon monarch there. The spirit of revolution was still abroad in some parts of Europe. In northern Italy, placed under the control of Austria, there was the Carbonari movement (which Metternich blamed on Russian agents, but which actually had a strong native base); insurrectionists in Greece fought Turkish dominion revolution in Spain against the restored Bourbons, and in the South American colonies, created another zone of trouble. Metternich, the fabulously skillful diplomatist, who secured passage of the Carlsbad Decrees in the German Confederation in 1819 following the assassination of the writer Kotzebue, and who kept a keen eye on the Carbonari, appeared as the great watchdog of conservatism, "the *status quo* incarnate"—for Austria of all states was the most vulnerable. In Germany, a movement of futile protest, chiefly among students and university teachers, was directed against the discouraging Vienna settlement which had continued disunity and particularism, and also against the failure of King Frederick William, in Prussia, to carry through the social reforms initiated by Baron Stein during the Napoleonic wars. Here, too, the hour seemed to be one of stark reaction.

British withdrawal from the Quadruple Alliance

Great Britain balked at intervention in Spain. George Canning, who succeeded Lord Castlereagh as British foreign secretary after the latter's suicide, announced bluntly that Britain would not cooperate with the continental powers, and most Englishmen heartily agreed. It was on this occasion that the United States, fortified by the British support, sent forth the famous Monroe Doctrine warning against interference by the continental monarchists in the New World (1823). British opposition effectively put a stop to whatever plans there may have been for restoration of the Spanish colonies in Central and South America, which had rebelled and proclaimed their independence during the Napoleonic years when Spain had been so gravely weakened and preoccupied at home. British withdrawal dealt a severe blow to the dreams of the internationalists for permanent cooperation among the great powers; its cause was in good part the reactionary policies of the Holy Alliance. British withdrawal did not prevent the Alliance from putting down the liberal revolt in Spain, as well as in Naples, or from upholding the unpopular Hapsburgs in Genoa.

France: Bourbon restoration

Europe watched with interest the experiment of putting back a Bourbon king in revolutionary France. Louis XVIII was not, fortunately, an "Ultraist" who wanted to go back to 1789. He had accepted a charter in 1814 when he assumed the throne, a document which affirmed that Frenchmen were equal before the law and provided for religious liberty and some freedom of the press. It also set up a two-house legislature, including an upper house of Peers, not elected, and a lower house elected by a very restricted electorate. It was closer to the British system than any other. There were, however, many "Ultras" among the returning emigrés—those of whom it was said that they had learned nothing and forgotten nothing. They caused some difficulties. They did not get back the lands they had lost, but were granted monetary indemnification in a controversial piece of legislation, and they tended to be given the high political posts, to the indignation of many. The years of the revolution and Napoleon had established a class of wealthy bourgeoisie who were not to be removed from positions of great influence and power in society. The returning aristocrats had to contend with a new ruling class.

Charles X attempts to restore absolutism

In 1824, Louis died and was succeeded by Charles X, much more sympathetic to the Ultraists. These extreme conservatives were those to whom the Revolution and all its works smelled of heresy, who wished to restore a full-fledged aristocracy, give education altogether to the clergy, and in general get back to the Old Regime. Charles had himself crowned at Reims in ceremonies reminiscent of the old monarchy, and indicated some intention to carry out an Ultraist program. Opposition to this arose, much of it being based on anticlericalism; i.e., fear of the return of the church to political and social power. Rising criticism of the government caused it to react by attempting to muzzle the press; and at length Charles and his chief minister, Prince Polignac, decided to get rid of the Chamber, which after the 1827 elections had a "Liberal" majority, largely agreed on the need for constitutional government and a moderate parliamentary regime. (But the term "liberal" as used in France at this time covered a number of different factions, including Bonapartists.)

Charles forced the issue on a point not made clear by the charter, the critical question of whether an adverse vote of the Chambers required the resignation of the king's ministers. In 1830 the King sought to dissolve the Chamber and amend the constitution by his own decree. The question was whether king or parliament was master, and Charles found out. The Parisians went to the barricades again, the army refused to attack them, Charles had no choice but to abdicate, and France had made another revolution.

Tory rule and popular discontent in Britain

England followed somewhat the same course from conservatism to a moderate liberal victory. There, the long war had left in power Tories of the deepest hue, "pig-tailed Tories" to the younger generation. Since, as Pitt had said, "You cannot repair your roof during a thunderstorm," all reform had been put off for the duration of the war. Even after the war, the Tories showed no disposition to move. They had suspended *habeas corpus* in 1794 and they did it again in 1819, confronted with a postwar movement of social protest which they identified with sedition. The Six Acts of 1819 restricted public meetings, forebade the right to bear arms, and taxed out of existence the cheap press, which men like William Cobbett had been using to denounce the government. The impulse to this assault on traditional British liberties had been provided by a very considerable stir among the working classes and the lower middle classes, a result in good part of a severe economic depression which struck postwar Britain. During the long Napoleonic Wars British agriculture and industry had both prospered, European competition being withdrawn. The end of the war found them over-expanded, agriculture in particular. In response to the golden lure of high profits, the squires had enclosed land, increased their yield, and brought marginal land under cultivation.

In addition, the "natural British impulse to resist authority" (Walter Bagehot) had been reined in for a generation, while need for political reform continued and the effects of the Industrial Revolution were beginning to be felt. Opposition to the government appeared among such working-class demagogues as Thomas Spence and "Orator" Hunt but also in the intellectually imposing middle-class movement of Utilitarianism.

Followers of "King Ludd" smashed machines in their anger at the ruin visited upon artisans by the new textile manufacturing processes, while such popular writers as the incomparable Cobbett cursed the new factory owners as well as the new gentry for their callous indifference to all but their own profits.

The Six Acts intimidated the opposition but caused great bitterness. The "Peterloo" massacre (named ironically after Waterloo) of 1819, when a crowd was fired upon in Manchester, long rankled in English memory. This phase of repression did not really last long, but while it lasted it was the ugliest estrangement between British government and people since 1688. In February, 1820, the police discovered, just in time, a plot to blow up the entire Cabinet—the famous Cato Street Conspiracy. It was led by a workingman who had watched the "Peterloo massacre." Strikes, demands for political reform, unrest again in Ireland, the scandal of the royal divorce case, the Six Acts—all this hit Britain in the early 1820's.

The Corn Laws

Faced with a return of European imports and falling prices, the landed interest demanded and received tariff protection in the form of the Corn Laws of 1815, which prohibited imports of foreign grain if the market price was below a certain level. But the workers complained of costly bread, the manufacturers of high wage costs because of high food costs, making it difficult for them to compete with foreign goods. The Corn Laws, difficult to defend yet demanded by the politically powerful landed interest, remained a source of political agitation until repealed in 1846 after a tremendous debate.

The monarchy in eclipse

There was restiveness and agitation, which the incumbent Tories, haunted by memories of the French Revolution, thought foreshadowed a similar revolution in Britain and handled with severe repression. The country suffered from the absence of a strong leader. The monarchy had fallen into sad state. An "old, mad, blind, despised and dying king," as Shelley called George III, had given way in fact to his son, George IV, who became regent in 1810 and then reigning monarch on the death of his father in 1820. George IV became one of the least liked of all British kings, and in the 1820's could not appear in public without exciting hostile hoots and jeers. His desertion of his wife and subsequent attempts to obtain a divorce, along with his riotous immorality and unstable character, brought him an unpopularity which a few have felt was not wholly deserved; but on any showing the fourth George was the worst of the lot. It has been said that "George IV was the king who came nearest to persuading the British people that monarchy was a useless institution."

These years seem in retrospect a crucial turning point. They might have forced Great Britain to abandon constitutional government and drown her great parliamentary experiment in the blood of class war. But she rallied her usual good sense and overcame the crisis by enacting a series of reforms.

Between 1822 and 1827 the more moderate Tories, George Canning, William Huskisson, and Robert Peel came to the front. Canning's foreign policy of breaking loose from the Holy Alliance, that is, from continental despots and the danger of war, was popular. At the Home Office, Peel made many reforms in penal and legal codes—all the world identifies him with the establishment of an orderly police system. Huskisson at the Board of Trade began to move toward free trade by dismantling some of the mercantilist regulations. Soon a liberal move toward political reform, spearheaded by the Utilitarians, picked up steam. It came to a head in 1832.

The emergence of liberalism

The French revolution of 1830

The year 1830 was a year of revolutions, but in the main these revolts followed a surprisingly moderate pattern, and reflected a victory for what was then called "liberalism." The French uprising of that year which brought to an abrupt and inglorious end Charles X's effort to restore royal absolutism set the example. The revolutionaries of 1830 were a mixed group of workers, students, and bourgeoisie, opposed by very little armed force. This revolution, hearteningly, did not lead to protracted strife and violence. Liberals offered the crown to the Duke of Orléans, son of the king's younger brother who had been a radical in the French Revolution. Louis Philippe was known as a liberal. Lafayette, the old hero of 1789, persuaded Paris to accept this choice. Without further trouble the charter was amended and a constitutional monarchy existed. The revolution was so reminiscent of what happened in England in 1688 that men spoke of "historical plagiarism"—and expected to duplicate England's success. The new charter was far from democratic; the vote was still confined to a few. But it was clear that the Chambers came before the king and that safeguards against absolutism existed.

"Grande bourgeoisie" to power

The revolution of 1830 expressed in political terms the social and economic dominance of an upper bourgeoisie of rich bankers and manufacturers, a class called by a recent French historian the *grande bourgeoisie*. This group carefully distinguished itself as much from the old nobility as from the lesser folk beneath it. Politically the old nobility was legitimist, the *grande bourgeoisie* Orléanist. The latter had arisen largely since the Revolution and wanted no part of the Old Order based on blue-blood aristocracy; they were new, self-made men. But they also wanted no part of democracy, and were quite snobbish toward the nonwealthy. They came into their own under the Orléanist regime of 1830 to 1848, whose conservatism was expressed in extremely restricted suffrage based on wealth and in an upper chamber resting on money rather than titled nobility, but which was in a certain sense "liberal"—constitutional, parliamentary, and with guarantees of property rights and considerable freedom of expression. Men referred to Louis Philippe as "the bourgeois monarch," or the "king in a business suit."

Liberalism

Liberals preferred liberty without democracy, parliamentary but not popular government, freedom of speech but protection for property, constitutional and legal safeguards against both monarchical tyranny and popular attacks on wealth. In economic policy the word was laissez-faire, and in foreign policy liberals tended to be peaceful, preferring lucrative commerce to glory and conquest. It was very much a political movement suitable to the upper ranks of the bourgeoisie. It might, however, be supported at least for strategic reasons by others who were potentially more radical. For the common denominator of liberalism was a stress on freedom, civil equality, rational persuasion, "a fair field and no favors" in the realm of ideas as well as economic activity. Using these liberal methods, one might arrive at other goals which were not the same as the policies usually associated with middle-class Liberals. Liberalism was to become especially strong in Great Britain, and there too its decisive triumphs came between 1828 and 1832.

Reform bill of 1832

The great reforms carried through in England, above all the Parliamentary Reform Act of 1832, were backed by a coalition of various groups who could agree on the framework of political liberalism. Catholic Emancipation in 1829 and repeal of the Test Acts at the same time removed discriminations against those Christians who were not of the Church of England (Jewish emancipation still had a few years to wait). Many who favored these reforms could not bring themselves to approve the sweeping overhaul of the ancient system of voting and districting which became the main target of reform. But the need for it seemed overwhelming. "Rotten boroughs" and corrupt elections, the domination of England by a small oligarchy using this system, the underrepresentation of populous new cities in the industrial Midlands—such were the abuses. Die-hard conservatives—some, indeed, who were enlightened ones, like the great poet-philosopher Coleridge—believed that a whole new theory of government was being introduced, which would have unforeseen consequences. It was nothing less than the theory of democracy. However, few suggested giving the vote to everyone; the reformers proposed only a relatively small extension of the vote. It was a middle-class program.

After 15 months of unparalleled public discussion and agitation, during which England seemed at times on the brink of civil war, the Reform Bill was carried, not before a threat by the king, now William IV, to "swamp" the House of Lords by creating new peers. Britain, led by many of her outstanding statesmen, had decided for liberal reform. The 1832 act scrapped the old, disorderly and unfair system of voting and representation in the House of Commons by regularizing the suffrage, redistricting, and admitting new groups to the electorate. It fell far short of either democracy or equality, for most Englishmen remained without the vote and irregularities in the districts while diminished were not erased. Some corruption and "pocket boroughs" remained. But a substantial change came about for the first time in centuries and paved the way for further reforms later. The most notable classes admitted to the vote in 1832 were the urban middle class ("10-pound householders," i.e., anyone who owned or rented property to that annual amount) and rural leaseholders and copyholders of substance—those, that is, who did not own land but rented or held it in significant amounts. The squirearchy lost its near monopoly of political power. The electorate almost was doubled. The new industrial cities, such as Manchester, Leeds, Liverpool, Birmingham, received representation, to the extent of 78 seats taken from small boroughs. (Sixty-five others passed from the boroughs to the shires, which was a small step in the direction of fair play.) The new electoral law did not really cause much change in the nature of the House of Commons for the next few years, but the passing of the act considerably eased and cheered the popular mind. Reform was not impossible! The Municipal Corporation Act soon followed (1835), giving the vote in municipal elections to all taxpayers.

A victory for Liberalism

The victory of parliamentary reform thus may be construed as a victory for the urban middle classes in Britain, though it led to no startling changes in politics for some time and in fact included concessions to the rural interest. Its chief significance lay in once more settling the constitution of the realm by peaceful compromise, and in symbolizing the new outlook and philosophy of Liberalism. That word was not used in any creditable sense in England until the 1840's, and then it became the name of one political party, the successor of the erstwhile Whigs. But in a broader sense all England had become "liberal."

Other 1830 revolutions

Elsewhere than in France and Britain, the years around 1830 brought some disturbances, but suggested that liberalism was weaker in the east and south of Europe, where the middle classes were weaker and the economic order less advanced. Germany stirred in 1830 against the Metternich system but little came of it. Italy showed renewed restiveness but revolts there were put down. Also in 1830, stimulated by the French Revolution, Belgium rose up and threw off the Dutch rule imposed on her unwisely by the peacemakers of 1815; at the same time the Poles attempted a revolt against Russia with less luck. By rebelling the Poles may have prevented Russia from sending troops to put down the French and Belgian movements. Thus the Poles rendered crucial aid to the cause of liberalism in the West in 1830, but at much cost to themselves; their revolt was suppressed, its leaders were subjected to cruel punishment, and all vestiges of Polish autonomy now disappeared as Poland was incorporated directly into Russia. In southeastern Europe, the Greeks struggled for their independence from the Turks between 1821 and 1831 finally winning it after a bloody and confused struggle into which the great powers were sometimes drawn. The 1829 Treaty of Adrianople, which ratified the independence of much of Greece under a German king, also guaranteed the autonomy of Serbia and game Russia a protectorate over the Rumanian provinces of Moldavia and Wallachia. In Bulgaria the Turk remained.

As for Russia, the giant of the East continued to be thoroughly reactionary. Alexander I had had a liberal phase, but was succeeded by the autocratic Nicholas I who shared with the Austrian Emperor a firm belief that western liberal ideas could only poison the eastern countries. In 1825 a feeble uprising led by a handful of liberal intellectuals failed pitifully (the so-called Decembrist movement), and after that for a long time it was not possible to speak out for liberal causes in Russia. (On Russia and Austria, see further in the next chapter.)

Political and social thought

Tocqueville and American democracy

France and Great Britain set the pace for politics, as they had done in the previous century. There was some influence also from the new republic of the New World, the United States, where independence led to a successful example of popular government. British liberals and radicals tended to admire America, Tories to disparage it. In 1835 a brilliant young Frenchman, Alexis de Tocqueville, published the first of two volumes on *Democracy in America*, one of the major political classics of the century. Innumerable other travel books described life in the United States, with horror or with admiration or a mixture of both; none was as penetrating and philosophical as the Frenchman's. Tocqueville was a liberal. By birth an aristocrat, his feeling for liberty was aristocratic in origin, but he was wise enough to see the path humanity was taking. "Today all men are impelled by a force which we may hope to regulate or check, but cannot hope to vanquish—a force pushing them . . . towards the destruction of aristocracy." Like Metternich, Tocqueville watched this new force in some amazement, not unmixed with fear; but unlike the German he accepted it and sought to live with it. Despite his generous praise of much in the United States, observed in a careful and objective spirit, Tocqueville was not really a democrat. He feared especially a leveling-down of culture, and suspected democracy of destroying all independence of mind. Tocqueville affrmed the value of liberty and individualism against "the tyranny of the majority" no less than the tyranny of kings. He lived to denounce another Bonaparte in France. His book exerted a strong influence on the classic British liberal philosopher, John Stuart Mill.

Romanticism

Romanticism, the reigning spirit in literature, also affirmed an element of personal integrity and uniqueness against any sort of external authority. What romanticism meant exactly was and is a matter of dispute, but its existence was a fact. Romanticism began as a reaction from the Enlightenment, or at least that part of the Enlightenment which tended to eliminate

Romanticism in art. Eugene Delacroix, the most celebrated painter of the romantic school, showed typical romantic traits in the choice of exotic themes and turbulent scenes. Romanticism had a special fondness for the medieval. This painting is "The Entry of the Crusaders into Constantinople."

Percy Bysshe Shelley in 1819. Lord Byron in Albanian dress, 1813.

the personal and subjective, the poetic and the intuitive. Some of the more superficial *philosophes*—like Helvétius and Holbach, whom the young Goethe found so dull—insisted that man was only a part of physical nature, wholly determined by his environment, soulless and mechanical like the universe itself, which they held to be a machine. Literature and religion had sagged; it was "an age of prose," an age of deism, an age of science. In time men wearied of this, as they usually weary after a while of any dogma or intellectual fashion. Undoubtedly the romantic mood was helped along by a reaction against French rationalism on the part of peoples who were fighting the French in the era of the Revolution and Napoleon. It had been on the way earlier. It did not become widely accepted for a generation, the pioneers of the 1790's long being almost as suspect by the conventionally minded as modern painting was for many years after 1908. In England, romanticism is usually dated from the *Lyrical Ballads* of Coleridge and Wordsworth, 1798; but these remained obscure, and held up to ridicule so far as they were noticed at all, for a number of years. In France, where classicism was strongly entrenched, romanticism did not prevail until 1820–30, the time of Victor Hugo. Germany was its principal homeland; there it was associated not only with poetry and drama but with the music of Beethoven, the idealist philosophy, and the new theology of Schleiermacher. A return to Christianity, if perhaps to a slightly unorthodox kind, marked romanticism, which was reacting against the weary skepticism and the dull mechanism of the Enlightenment.

Any complete account of romanticism would have to include the philosophical writings of Immanuel Kant, greatest philosopher of the later 18th century, and his followers. No such account is possible, but it may be suggested that Kant, by severely criticizing the naive empiricism of Locke, and by showing an a priori element in our knowledge (relationships which we do not get from experience, but which are there in the mind before we can rationally experience), brought down the house of the Enlightenment. He went on to hint that we may know ultimate reality not by analysis but by intuition, and his followers in Germany—Fichte, Schelling, Schlegel—developed this further in the direction of romantic idealism. Romanticism tended to be German in its origins. Pioneers of romanticism in other countries—Madame de Staël in France, Coleridge and Wordsworth in England—were usually Germanophiles, and it became fashionable to contrast the profound German soul with the glib and superficial French. Most of the cardinal tenets of romanticism may be traced to its roots in post-Kantian philosophy. Here was the doctrine that truth comes not to the analytic intellect but to the poetic insight; the conception of the universe as spiritual, not mechanical; the feeling for a personal religion involving mystic communion with God; the sense of history.

Romanticism in politics

Romanticism restored poetry to a place in the universe of knowledge; the poet became, in Shelley's phrase, "the unacknowledged legislator of the world." It revitalized music and created a new school of painting. It brought excitement to a generation reared on the melodrama of revolution and war, which now found the previous century's style too tame. Its implications for a large number of fields—even science—were great. Politically, the romantic spirit was ambiguous. Quite often in the period around 1815 romanticism went with conservatism, for the two were both fashionable at about the same time and they shared a dislike of the Enlightenment. However, for obvious reasons romantics made good rebels. Shelley wrote some fiercely revolutionary verse, Byron romantically went off to fight and die for Greek independence ("I dreamed that Greece might still be free.") A good deal of the socialism and other radicalism of the 19th century is tinged with romanticism. It was difficult for a romantic to be a bourgeois liberal; he might go to either of the extremes, right or left.

An age of ideologies: Conservatism

The early 19th century was a seedbed of new ideas. Historians have written of "the proliferation of '-isms,' " of "the age of ideology." We have mentioned liberalism and romanticism. Conservatism also appeared as a formal creed, its major prophets being Edmund Burke and a brilliant French Restoration group including Charles Bonald and Joseph de Maistre. The political theory of conservatism, a reaction against the utopianism and rationalism of the 18th century, stressed the limitations of abstract reason, the need to be specific and concrete, the necessity also of foregoing large dreams and utopias. It had a strong feeling for the wisdom embodied in tradition, and the value of piety for political purposes: traditional monarchies, traditional churches, institutions rooted in the past. It glorified authority at the expense of liberty, though maintaining that true liberty does not consist in an anarchic individualism but rather in acceptance of limitations: thus, no creature in nature is "free" to do anything, but rather to do what nature fits him for. Man as a political animal must accept society and the state. From Hegel and the Germans, particularly, came a good deal of stress on the state as the highest embodiment of human purpose.

Maistre, a writer with mordant insights, abhorred nationalism while accepting the need for state power, and looked to the papacy as a higher power mediating between states and between peoples and rulers. Protestant Germans and Englishmen would scarcely approve such a program, but Burke, Coleridge, Adam Müller, and Novalis could agree with Bonald and Maistre on much, and this conservative group represented imposing intellectual powers—the most impressive in Europe, perhaps, in the realm of political thought, during the generation from about 1800 to 1830. Their stress on the corporate features of life, their piety, their sense of the past, constituted ties with the older Europe; but at the same time this was a new ideology in many ways—new at any rate in *being* an "ideology," a self-conscious philosophy of politics intended to meet the needs of a Europe recovering from the ravages of the French Revolution (which to most of the above was simply a black and inexplicable interlude, perhaps, as Maistre thought, something sent by God to punish Europe for her sins).

The situation that faced Europe after the French Revolution and Napoleon was in many ways a unique and uniquely critical one. The post-1815 generation had seen the roots of the past torn up, the traditional foundations of political life destroyed, and it felt the need to re-create the bases of order. If Europe was not to lurch forward blindly into anarchy, there must be a redefinition of social purposes and ideals. Socialists like Saint-Simon felt this as strongly as conservatives like Bonald, or liberals like young John Stuart Mill. "After Napoleon, what?"—the question Chateaubriand asked himself—was one that posed itself to all thinking men. So it is not strange that this generation produced just about all the social theory, in embryo, that the modern world has been chewing on since. It was its mission to call into existence a new world. Some of these ideologies are discussed further in the next chapter. The more radical of them became entangled in the revolutions of 1848. Though we may associate socialism with Karl Marx, who was just beginning his stormy career in the 1840's, actually the true pioneers of socialist theory belong to the 1820's and 1830's: especially the Frenchmen, Henri Saint-Simon and Charles Fourier. As background for these ideas, it would be well to discuss the tremendous transformation of economic and social life that was coming over much of Europe during these years.

Industrial epoch

Little of what happened between about 1810 and 1840—whether Peterloo massacres, reform bills, revolutions in France, or the growth of social doctrine—was unrelated to the massive alterations in economic life then going on. Politics was affected by it: the leading issues included relief to the poor, factory legislation, tariffs. Literature was affected by it: whether one's choice was a novel by Dickens or an essay by Carlyle, the theme was there. Everything was affected by it, and not surprisingly, for these changes associated with the Industrial Revolution were obviously among the greatest that had come over Europe in all her long history.

Historians have taken issue with the phrase "Industrial Revolution" insofar as it conveys the idea of something happening without warning or preparation, for clearly this vast movement had been ripening for centuries. Behind it lay almost innumerable changes which finally meshed into one big change.

Sources of the Industrial Revolution

It has been questioned whether *the* Industrial Revolution took place between about 1780 and 1830. First of all, a number of other industrial revolutions have been identified, or more accurately, a continuous revolution. Once upon a time the Middle Ages were written off as sterile, not least in the mechanical arts; but, as we know, this is not true. That era brought into use an improved plow and other implements making possible a "medieval agricultural revolution" which formed the foundation for urban life. It also "is the period of decisive development in the history of the effort to use the forces of nature mechanically for human purposes," according to a distinguished historian.[1] Historians have also discovered an "industrial revolution" in Elizabethan times. European inventiveness, in a word, had existed ever since the Dark Ages. In the light of full knowledge the progress of technology appears as a long, gradual process, not an innovation of the 18th century. There were times when social and political conditions were unfavorable, when life was insecure and property hard to keep. But there was never a century when technological advances were not being made.

Invention continued in the 18th century at a quickening pace. Probably what accounts most for this was the *political* success achieved by the modern state, in suppressing disorder, making life and property secure, organizing large areas under a single jurisdiction. This process had advanced furthest in Great Britain in the 18th century. Neither external attack nor internal strife marred the British way of life, as a mild but sufficient government kept order with a minimum of expense and coercion. After the union with Scotland in 1707, the extent of the land over which this single government held sway was unusually large. France in the 18th century, before the Revolution, was not a single economic unit, but became so after the Revolution. Add to this the British overseas empire, and a large market for goods was available to British manufacturers.

---

[1] See Lynn White, Jr., *Medieval Technology and Social Change.*

Accumulation of capital

Capital was available. Capital is surplus money looking for profitable investment. It had been accumulating for a long time, mostly through trade. The great East India Company, and the other trading companies, had brought together great amounts of money and had led to large profits. West Indian sugar plantations, too, made the fortunes of merchant princes. Merchant capital preceded industrial capital; the profits that flowed in from overseas trade would then be invested in productive enterprise. With this kind of big business came the machinery of banking and finance that is so important to a capitalistic economy. The Bank of England received its charter in 1694; in 1721, the so-called South Sea Bubble revealed how extensive and important investment in speculative "joint-stock" companies could be. Was it to her naval supremacy, her many colonies, her great merchant marine that England owed the lead in the Industrial Revolution that she secured in the 19th century? Very likely, in good part, along with her stable government and avoidance of costly wars. And this, too, one might argue, the fortunate islanders owed to their geographic situation. However, it has been pointed out there was plenty of capital in the 16th and 17th centuries, as indicated by the fabulous country homes of the aristocracy. These homes testify to the expenditure of that capital in "conspicuous consumption," whereas the 19th-century bourgeoisie preferred to live frugally and plow the profits back into industry. Evidently a psychological or intellectual revolution was the basic factor here.

An Agricultural Revolution

Preceding the Industrial Revolution was what is often called an Agricultural Revolution. During the 18th century, and especially in the latter part of it, significant changes were underway in the countryside. A more commercial spirit, and the lure of profits, caused squires to seek to enclose the common lands and end the old system of strips and open fields, developed during the Middle Ages, a system based on group cooperation rather than individual ownership. Under the open-field arrangement individual farmers had worked strips of land separated from each other, rather than all in one piece, and there were also "common" lands used by everybody, belonging to the village collectively. In 1700, half the arable land of England still conformed to this medieval pattern. During the next century much of it was to be "enclosed," i.e., fenced or hedged around, and added to the large estates of the landowners. Those rural people who, squatting on the commons or holding land as "copyholders" and not outright owners, lacked title to their land were squeezed out, bitterly and sometimes violently protesting. Whatever its hardships and injustices, this made it possible to increase production, for commercial farmers could now engage in more scientific agriculture, aggressively seeking to increase yields in order to secure greater profits. Meanwhile the displaced agriculturalists went to the cities to supply cheap labor, so it used to be alleged.

The above picture, a traditional account, has been much modified in the light of recent research, we should hasten to say. The extent of enclosure was not nearly so great as once alleged. We find that rural population increased, not diminished, through the 18th and earlier 19th centuries, though not so rapidly as urban population. Yet the fact remains unaltered that there *was* a significant "agricultural revolution" in that men learned how to produce a great deal more for each acre and each unit of human labor. Again, this increase in productivity did not come suddenly; it is spread over the decades and has gone on into modern times. But there were dramatic breakthroughs in the 18th century. Rotation of crops, scientific livestock breeding, and soil fertilization were increasingly practiced.

This jump in agricultural production was one reason for the coming of the Industrial Revolution. A substantial urban population could be supported with the aid of such an increase in food supply. The poor wretches driven from the land by enclosures were forced into the cities to labor in the new factories for miserable wages, according to one familiar account of the process. It was not quite that simple. There was a substantial *increase* in population, beginning in the last half of the 18th century. During this period the population of Great Britain grew from about 5 or 5½ millions to 9 millions. This was basically because improved sanitation and medicine were keeping more people alive. This population rise, taking place mostly in towns and cities, was itself a cause of the farmer's desire to improve his methods of production; the market was there, demanding to be supplied. During the Napoleonic Wars of the 1790's and 1800's, agricultural demand in England further increased, owing to the absence of foreign competition.

Transportation

There was also a Transportation Revolution. Or at least it is undeniable that the later 18th century saw a renaissance of road and bridge building, soon to be followed by a rage for canals, before the steam-driven railroads took over. Macadam, a Scot, left his name on a paving process. A fellow countryman, Telford, goes down in history as one of the master bridge builders. Neither roads, bridges, or canals were new to the human race, needless to say, but the quantity and quality of them built in England between 1760 and 1830 is impressive. This took money, and once again the presence of capital willing to invest in such projects is perhaps the most impressive thing. And the *need* for more and better roads and river transport testifies to an increased volume of trade. In the Industrial Revolution, factors worked together. When manufactured goods could be shipped cheaply, they could find profitable sales beyond the local market, and thus manufacturing enterprises could become quite large. Trade would grow, and the principle of the division of labor would make everyone better off. Obviously cheap and effective means of transport are a prerequisite to economic growth. But the money to build the roads, canals and bridges, and to dredge harbors, is not likely to come forth *until* the likelihood of profitable trade exists.

A takeoff stage

So the factors worked together. But once a certain level is reached, there seems to be a "takeoff" stage when each boosts the other and the whole economy excitedly rushes forward. Factories beget transportation, and transportation in turn begets more and bigger factories. Capital is invested and earns more capital to be reinvested. Surplus agricultural yield, the result of applying capital as well as skill to farming, is traded to the city people in return for their products. Banking and credit facilitate the exchange of goods. An economy may stand relatively stagnant for centuries, gradually gathering strength for the explosion. Great Britain reached this pay-off stage at the end of the 18th century, and western Europe was not far behind.

Role of invention

The sudden outburst of invention was a response to this improving economic climate. The Watts and the Kays and the Hargreaves, who now arose, and whose names are familiar to all, were ingenious men, but we have no reason to suppose this period of the 18th century produced any larger number of ingenious men than formerly. "Inventors invent things when the community wants them," it has been said. The community issues its call when the capital and the market are both present, and the lure of profit beckons. It is going too far to say that inventions automatically spring forth when the right economic conditions are present; but these conditions can provide a powerful incentive. Hero of Alexander, in ancient times, made a toy steam turbine, but no one built a real one until modern times. James Watt was certainly not the first to notice (as the old legend would have it) that steam pushes up the kettle's cover; men had known this ever since they first boiled water. But suddenly, in Watt's day, the use of steam power became practicable. Many men, in actuality, collaborated to invent the steam engine, to which Watt added only the final element, a separate condensing chamber. Hundreds and thousands of men collaborated in building the industrial order. Watt required the skills of iron makers, he required capital to back him, he required various sorts of theoretical knowledge, and so on.

Watt's engine, the new processes in iron and steel, and the inventions of Arkwright and Crompton in the textile industry came at about the same time (about 1760 to 1790), to cause the impression of an "industrial revolution." Economic historian T.S. Ashton cites the schoolboy who wrote on his examination that "about 1760 a wave of gadgets swept over England." Remembering again that gadgets had been creeping, if not sweeping, over Europe ever since the early Middle Ages, they certainly now quickened their pace, as the record of patents applied for indicates. Especially was this true in Great Britain, the classic land of the Industrial Revolution, which was to steal a considerable lead over all her rivals early in the 19th century, and not be caught until near the end of the century.

Population increase

Population growth worked with the other factors. A certain concentration of people is needed for an industrial economy. Obviously masses of people alone, without the capital, the skills, the transportation, mean nothing. But when capital and skills have developed to a certain point, a large enough agglomeration of people becomes a boosting factor. Industrialization

James Watt, great pioneer of industrial power

in the United States of America was slow until late in the 19th century, not because capital and skills, enterprise and inventiveness, did not exist, for they existed there perhaps more than anywhere else. But a vast continent beckoned, good virgin soil was plentiful, population sparse, and the economics of transportation were therefore discouraging. The steady population growth that began in England in the 18th century and continued at an accelerating pace in the 19th stimulated the economic growth of the country.

Raw materials

Raw materials were a necessity. Coal and iron, the prime materials of the new industrial age, existed in plentiful supply and close proximity in England, as elsewhere in Europe. A dirty story, and a grim one, was the coal-mining story, but coal fed the industrial machine. It not only supplied winter warmth to the urban masses, but stoked the iron-processing furnaces and supplied the steam power that soon ran factories and railroads. The age of steam began with the Newcomen apparatus that pumped water out of the mines; soon, the steam engine was creating an enormous new demand for coal. Iron had been mined in Europe for centuries, but now leaped forward in quantity and quality. Formerly it was processed with the aid of wood (charcoal), the iron industry therefore growing up near forests. In England, the

Early 19th century iron foundry

exhaustion of the forests caused a search for new fuels, and then for good quality iron smelted with coke. Throughout the 18th century gradual improvement took place, until by the end of the century ironmasters had learned to produce relatively abundant high-quality iron and steel using coal as the fuel. Henry Cort's puddling and rolling techniques, first used 1783–84, are a milestone in the Industrial Revolution. And it was from this industrial complex of the Birmingham area that James Watt emerged with the improvement that began the age of steam. Watt had learned the theoretical principles of the steam engine from professors at the University of Glasgow; he then found help from the skilled ironmasters of northern England who could make the valves and other fittings he needed.

Britain's secret of success

Why it was that the British led the way toward industrialism does not seem mysterious. Chiefly, it was because war and revolution did not interrupt the growth of society as they did on the Continent. In studying the development of business enterprise based on new technologies one is impressed by the value of a long nurturing period, for it was necessarily a slow process. A company is formed in someone's back room, slowly accumulates skills, customers, and capital, and gradually grows, to be carried on in another lifetime or two by the family before it finally emerges as some great industrial enterprise in the 19th century. This is the story told time and time again. This sort of growth obviously depended upon social and economic stability. Capital accumulation and investment, so essential a part of the process (and what heroes of self-denial those early capitalists were, living on little and "plowing back" everything into the business) clearly requires a long period of time in which men can be reasonably sure that no economic or political disruption will deprive them of their property; in which they are not distracted by abrupt change or made to feel that progress for their children is unsure.

The Protestant ethic

The English common law gave property unusual protection. In addition, one is struck by the Puritan or "Nonconformist" influence on British capitalism. Independents, Quakers, Presbyterians, and Unitarians seem to have made the best capitalists, if not the only ones: their habits of hard work, frugality, and almost incredible perseverance were rooted in the ethical precepts of their faiths, along with the natural drive of a once despised and persecuted minority to assert its worth. In the last analysis, what this perhaps comes down to—since these were the beliefs of the lower middle class—is that in England the sturdy middle class was strong, stronger than anywhere else in Europe. France had a yeoman peasantry, which Britain altogether lacked, the English land being largely in the hands of wealthy farmers while the poor were driven to the cities. For this very reason the *industrial* middle class, or urban bourgeoisie, became uniquely strong in England, able successfully to challenge the landed interests for political power in the 19th century.

England possessed coal and steel in proximity, and, as is often pointed out, a climate which however unpleasant for many purposes was eminently suitable for the spinning of yarn. But in these respects the British were not unique: they had no monopoly on minerals or a damp atmosphere. They did have a unique political heritage and class structure at this time, and these seem the more important factors.

The Industrial Revolution as a European phenomenon

But in fact this revolution was a European phenomenon and would come to all countries in time. It rested on that European scientific heritage which was not the monopoly of any one people: the heritage of Kepler, Galileo, Descartes, Newton. It rested also on the basic technology of Europe which had always possessed a fundamental unity: windmills, plows, and clocks had not existed just in one part of medieval Europe. In regard to the social structure, one sees the middle classes rising all over western Europe at this time. The French Revolution brought them up in France and other places in Europe (Rhenish cities, Italian cities, Flemish cities). And before long the other peoples joined in the "wave of gadgets." Jacquard invented silk-weaving machinery in France, the counterpart of spinning jenny and mechanical loom for cotton goods in England. An American, Robert Fulton, pioneered in the steamboat. Subsequently the most dramatic improvement in iron and steel processing came from the Germans, Siemens and Bessemer, who took up where the British left off.

Chemistry

Such a list is endless. At the end of the 18th century chemistry also made its great breakthrough. Stagnant almost since Aristotle, with medieval alchemists unable to achieve any orderly scientific development, it made itself a modern science roughly between the time of the German Stahl (1717) and the Frenchman Lavoisier (1783), who died on the guillotine during the French Revolution. Chemistry participated in the Industrial Revolution, of course, in all sorts of ways, from bleaching processes for textiles to removal of impurities from iron ore.

Electricity

The other great scientific advance of the 18th century was in the field of electricity. In 1746 a Dutchman, Van Musschenbroek, invented the Leyden jar, and in 1752 Benjamin Franklin came over from America to conduct his famous experiments showing that lightning is electricity. In 1800 an Italian, Alessandro Volta, found a way to store electrical energy in a primitive battery. The names of Ohm, Galvani, and (later) Hertz suggest the continental, especially German and Italian, contributions to the science of electrical energy, but it remained for an Englishman, Michael Faraday, to formulate the basis of the age of electricity through huge mechanical generators. This came in the mid–19th century.

The Industrial Revolution did not stop in 1830, but was really only just getting under way. This is another objection to the concept of a "revolution"

John Kay's 18th century flying shuttle, which increased weaving speed and stimulated the invention of spinning machine to keep pace

in the 1780–1830 period. The second generation of the industrial age created the Bessemer process and the electrical generator; it vastly improved the primitive railroad engines and equipment developed first in the 1820's; brought in the telegraph, oceanic cable, the typewriter, and many another basic process of modern technology. The average consumer scarcely felt the impact of industrialism until after 1850. The Crystal Palace Exhibition of 1851 was its ceremonial initiation. So the 19th century—and the 20th—have been a continuous industrial revolution, ceaseless in their discoveries, a "wave of gadgets" without end.

And, lest we forget, this gadgetry is always closely linked with theoretical science. James Watt studied under theorists at the University of Glasgow; the age of electricity grew out of the theoretical discoveries of Faraday and his colleagues; at every stage, theory and practice must be closely associated. And this requires a sophisticated society. There must be great universities equipped with expensive laboratories, as well as great factories with expensive machinery. The basis of economic progress is research, as we know. Research takes money, skill, organization. These things must grow, and they grow slowly at first, but then with ever-accelerating speed.

Social results of industrialism

A revolution is not less a revolution for having been long in preparation, and the mixture of all these ingredients did rather suddenly explode about the beginning of the 19th century. "Explosion" is the right word: the overt signs of this "revolution" were violent ones. From 1806 on, the ruin of the handloom weavers by factory machine methods caused violence: frame

1856 typewriter by Sir Charles Wheatstone, developer also of musical and electrical instruments

breaking, machine wrecking. The relative suddenness of change in the cloth industry, giving little time for readjustment, may be judged by figures which indicate that in Manchester the number of "mills" grew from 2 in 1782 to 52 in 1802, and the number of power looms for weaving from 2,400 in 1813 to no less than 100,000 by 1833. A good part of the violence was associated with this industry, so long the proud preserve of skilled workmen who now faced and fought complete ruin at the hands of the machine. In France, the insurrection in Lyon in 1831, perhaps the most celebrated single example of protest against the coming of industrialism in that country, involved this same industry, though silk was the textile. Readers of the German literary classic, Hauptmann's *The Weavers*, know that the same thing happened in Silesia. Much of the discontent among the "working class" at this time, taking the form of Chartism in England, with the emergence of socialist ideas, agitation, and occasional violence, occurred not among the "operatives" of the new mills—a sodden and oppressed lot not yet capable of protest, mainly women and children—but among the handcraftsmen and artisans who had been well off and were able to put up some resistance.

Condition of the working class

This same industry produced the chief scandal of the early industrial epoch, the condition of these women and children operatives. Well known is the story which emerged from parliamentary committees of investigation, from 1816 to 1840: the story of people working 76 hours a week in the textile mills; the unbelievable and uncontrolled (for long) exploitation of women and children to the detriment of the race but the profit of cotton capitalists. It was the scandal and shame of Europe. One should not forget that the evil touched off a storm of tracts, novels, investigations, and efforts at legal control which eventually did something to cure the abuse. It is necessary to see this question in perspective: long working hours were the custom, on farm and in household, and were not invented by cruel factory owners. It does not appear that most of the poor who came from rural areas to the mills were any worse off than they had been. But the other part of the scandal was the crowded and unsanitary conditions in the rapidly swelling factory cities. Terrible epidemics of cholera in Britain and France resulted. It is true that few European cities had ever been very sanitary, and Paris was no more immune from the cholera than Leeds. But the squalor, ugliness, and misery in these industrial cities made a sad commentary on the machine age.

Capitalism as villain

The first stage of mechanization and urbanization through the Industrial Revolution involved severe suffering wherever it appeared. Even in the wealthy United States, its effects were demoralizing in the 1870's and 1880's; in Soviet Russia under Communism since 1929 the suffering has been even more severe, despite the alleged control by working class leaders rather than "the bourgeoisie." Some have been inclined to blame "capitalism" for an immense amount of suffering, caused by an "exploitation" of the "working class." It is a familiar interpretation, subscribed to by Karl Marx and indeed by

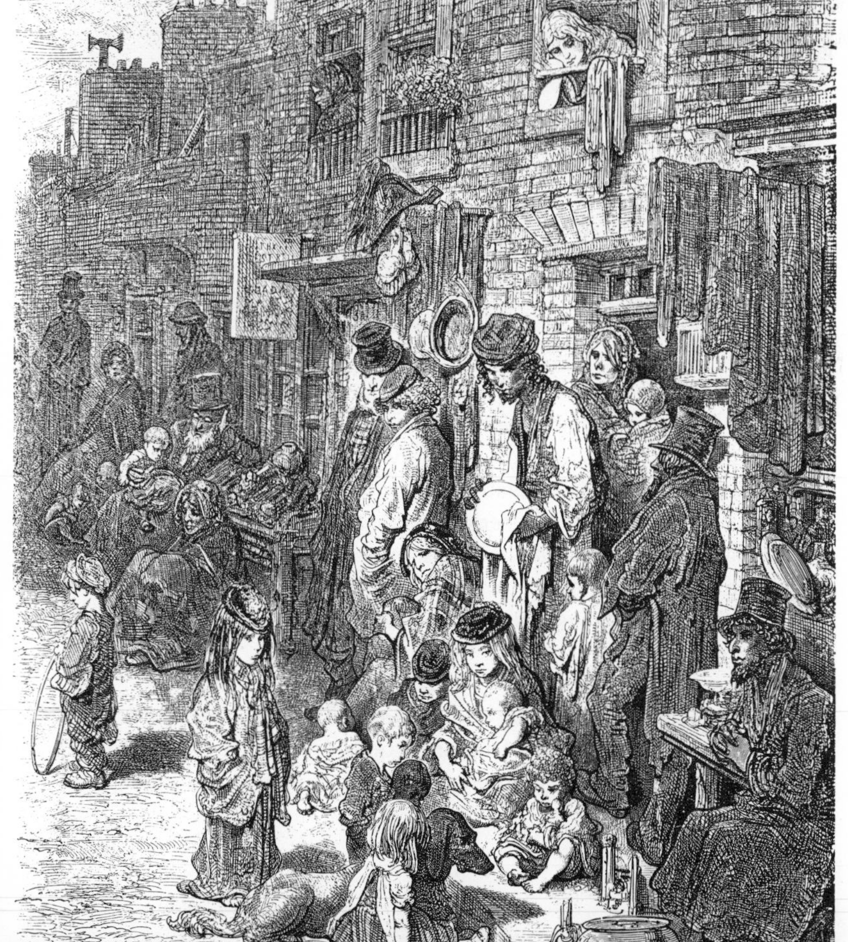

Worker revolts in Lyon in 1831, 1834, and 1839 were severely repressed. Contemporary drawing of the 1834 siege.

"Wentworth Street," by Gustav Doré, shows 19th century London slums.

Thomas Carlyle, 1795–1881, critic of laissez-faire capitalism. Painting by James MacNeil Whistler.

socialists of all persuasions, and quite frequently accepted uncritically by historians. But much recent research has corrected this picture, noting for example that poor housing and unsanitary conditions in the cities owed more to obsolete government regulations than to "capitalism." As for "exploitation," it is a purely subjective term until one defines it with care, as enemies of "capitalism" seldom did. It seems more accurate to say that industrial capitalism was a progressive force bringing greater wealth for all, though with severe early growing pains. Statistics reveal a rising standard of life for the working classes throughout the industrial epoch, as measured by real wages.

It is nevertheless a fact that the masters of the new wealth, the owners of factories and employers of labor, acquired a reputation in this era for both unexampled greed, indifference to the sufferings of their hirelings, and for a lack of culture. Wealthy men had usually been gentlemen before this; there was nothing gentlemanly about Plugson of Undershot, as Thomas Carlyle named a mythical but all too recognizable industrialist. Romantic writers as well as socialist agitators believed that the new industrialism as run by Plugsons spawned ugliness and social evil. Their picture was probably one-sided, but it exerted a tremendous influence on Europe.

The phrase "Industrial Revolution" was apparently first used in the 1830's. One of the first to use it was the French revolutionary socialist, Blanqui. Another who called attention dramatically to the primacy of "the mechanical age" and "the social question" was this Thomas Carlyle (*Chartism*, 1839, and *Past and Present*, 1843). Carlyle was influenced by the French nobleman, Henri Saint-Simon, who has perhaps the best claim to the title of father of modern socialism. Saint-Simon had declared that those who count in modern society are the industrialists, not the politicians. If all the politicians were to die, France could get along; but take away a hundred of the leading engineers and the nation could scarcely survive. It followed that the most urgent task of modern times was to create the best sort of industrial society. The industrial epoch was really only beginning in the 1830's, but this was the period which felt its first impact.

"Were we required to characterize this age of ours by any single epithet," Carlyle wrote in 1829, "we should be tempted to call it, not an Heroical, Philosophical, or Moral Age, but, above all others, the Mechanical Age. It is the Age of Machinery. . . ." But Carlyle went on to point out that the machine was seemingly a curse more than a blessing. "We have more riches than any Nation ever had before; we have less good of them than any Nation ever had before." It was the paradox of modern times.

Bibliography

European diplomacy in the years after 1815: Sir Charles Webster, *The Foreign Policy of Castlereagh 1815–1822* (G. Bell, reprinted, 1947); Henry A. Kissinger, *A World Restored* (Grosset & Dunlap, Universal): Paul W. Schroeder, *Metternich's Diplomacy at Its Zenith 1820–1823* (Austin: University of Texas Press, 1962); E.E. Kraehe, *Metternich's German Policy* (Princeton, N.J.: Princeton University Press, 1963). On France: Frederick B. Artz, *France Under the Bourbon Restoration* (Cambridge, Mass.: Harvard University Press, 1931); M.D.R. Leys, *France between Two Empires, 1818–1848* (London: Longmans, Green & Co., 1955), a general survey; André Maurois, *Chateaubriand* (New York: Harper & Bros., 1958), an attractive biography of the outstanding all-around figure. Recent general accounts of this era include the left-oriented E.J. Hobsbawm, *The Age of Revolution, 1789–1848* (New American Library, Mentor), and the contrasting J.L. Talmon, *Romanticism and Revolt: Europe 1815–1848* (New York: Harcourt, Brace, & World); see also Talmon's *Political Messianism: The Romantic Phase* (New York: Frederick A. Praeger, 1960), an examination of the visionary social and political ideas of the Romantic generation. Covering Great Britain, E. Halévy's *The Liberal Awakening 1815–1830* is Vol. II of his classic *History of the English People in the Nineteenth Century* (Barnes & Noble, University paperback); E.L. Woodward, *The Age of Reform 1815–1870*, in the Oxford History of England (1938); E. Lipson, *The*

Growth of English Society (4th ed.; London: A. & C. Black, 1959); more recently, Asa Briggs, *The Age of Improvement, 1783–1867* (Harper Torchbook). For a biography, Roger Fulford, *George the Fourth* (G.P. Putnam's Sons, Capricorn). K.S. Pinson, *Modern Germany: Its History and Civilization* (New York: Macmillan, 1964), and Veit Valentin, *The German People, Their History and Civilization* (New York: Alfred A. Knopf, 1946), are distinguished books, valuable for most phases of modern German history.

A.G. Mazour, *The First Russian Revolution, 1825* (Stanford University Press), may be compared with Marc Raeff, *The Decembrist Movement* (Prentice-Hall). Raeff has also studied the Russian statesman *Michael Speransky*, adviser to Tsar Nicholas (The Hague: M. Nijhoff, 1957). R.F. Leslie, *Polish Politics and the Revolution of 1830* (London: Athlone Press, 1956), deals with another of the revolutions. The French 1830 may be viewed through T.E.B. Howarth's biography of *The Citizen King* (London: Eyre & Spottiswoode, 1961). An older but still standard monograph, J.R.M. Butler, *The Passing of the Great Reform Bill* (Longmans, Green & Co., 1914), handles Britain's near-revolution of 1832. In his *Social Romanticism in France 1830–1848*, David O. Evans succinctly and elegantly discusses the ideologies of this age of ideologies (Oxford: Clarendon Press, 1951). For the beginner, D.C. Somervell's *English Thought in the Nineteenth Century* (David Mackay, Tartan) is also useful. Vol I. of G.D.H. Cole's mammoth *History of Socialist Thought* (New York: St. Martin's Press, 1953) covers the early socialists; the most important of them has been given a distinguished treatment by Frank E. Manuel, *The New World of Henri Saint-Simon* (New York: Harvard University Press, 1956). Asa Briggs (ed.), *Chartist Studies* (Macmillan, 1959) reflects recent research into this movement of the British working class.

The Industrial Revolution is a part of this endlessly creative era; it has given rise to an endless number of books and articles. T.S. Ashton provides a good introduction in an Oxford paperback, *The Industrial Revolution*, and has also done essential research on *Iron and Steel in the Industrial Revolution* (Manchester: Manchester University Press, 1951); his *Economic History of England in the Eighteenth Century* is part of a five-volume Methuen series under his editorship. To the older classics of economic history written by such stalwarts as Sir John Clapham, L.C.A. Knowles, and Mr. & Mrs. John L. Hammond have been added some recent syntheses: J.D. Chambers, *The Workshop of the World: British Economic History 1820–1880* (New York: Oxford University Press, 1961), and H.L. Beales, *The Industrial Revolution 1750–1850* (Macmillan, 1958). Chambers and G.E. Mingay have an admirable survey of *The Agricultural Revolution* (New York: Schocken Books, 1967). Vol. VI, parts I and II of the Cambridge Economic History, *The Industrial Revolution and After*, edited by H.J. Habbakuk and M. Postan (New York: Cambridge University Press, 1965), is exhaustive and authoritative. Two recent works of social history have received high praise: F.M.L. Thompson, *English Landed Society in the Nineteenth Century* (London: Routledge & Kegan Paul, 1963), and E.P. Thompson, *The Making of the English Working Class* (London: Gollancz, 1963), the latter rich in content though with certain ideological peculiarities. As an antidote to the latter's enthusiastic hatreds for the "bourgeoisie" one might read the essays in F.A. Hayek (ed.), *Capitalism and the Historian* (University of Chicago, Phoenix). John T. Ward, *The Factory Movement 1830–1855* (St. Martin's Press, 1962), treats the effort, led by aristocratic landowners, to secure legislation protecting the industrial workers. S.G. Checkland, *The Rise of Industrial Society in England 1815–1885* (St. Martin's Press, 1965), is a broad summation. A.L. Dunham has surveyed *The Industrial Revolution in France 1815–1848* (New York: Exposition Press, 1955); and Rondo Cameron's *France and the Economic Development of Europe 1800–1914* (Chicago: Rand McNally, 1967) provides a broader perspective. A. and N. Clow, *The Chemical Revolution 1749–1828* (London: Batchworth, 1952), excellently handles one aspect of the Industrial Revolution.

Primary material for this chapter can be found in the following samplings: H. Temperley and L. Penson, *Foundations of British Foreign Policy* (Cambridge University Press, 1938), a selection of documents useful throughout the century; G.M. Young and W.D. Hancock (eds)., *English Historical Documents 1783–1832* (Oxford series); Robert Baldick (ed.), *Memoirs of Chateaubriand* (Hamish Hamilton, 1961); H.E. Hugo (ed.), *The Portable Romantic Reader* (Viking Press); John Bowditch and Clement Rashland (eds.), *Voices of the Industrial Revolution* (University of Michigan, Ann Arbor), a selection from the classical economists and socialists. Robert Owen's *New View of Society* is in Everyman's Library.

21

The revolutions of 1848

"Third Class Carriage." Daumier's painting caught the image of the lower classes in mid-19th century France. Farm women and workers mingle with some of the petit bourgeois.

chronology

1840–48

Anti-Corn Law agitation, England; repeal of the Corn Laws, 1846; famine in Ireland, 1846.

Economic depression generally throughout Europe 1846–47; working-class discontent.

Growth of middle class in France, Germany, Italy. Demands for constitutional and representative government, enlargement of suffrage.

In France, socialist ideas of Proudhon, Louis Blanc.

Movements of liberal nationalism in Italy and Germany.

1848

Great Britain: Chartist demonstration, presenting petition to Parliament; brief insurrection in Ireland, July 29 (Tipperary); no other revolutionary activity.

France: Campaign for electoral reform led by liberal-democratic elements in the Chamber; great banquet of February 22 prohibited by government; insurrection in Paris, abdication of Louis Philippe, February 24; republic proclaimed; "right to work" recognized and work-relief to unemployed given; alarm of bourgeois republicans at socialist–working–class demands; after April elections, termination of the "national workshops," which led to bloody "June Days," socialist insurrection crushed with heavy loss of life. New constitution provided for a strong president, universal suffrage. Louis Napoleon, nephew of the great Emperor, overwhelmingly elected President December 10.

Hapsburg Possessions: Revolutions in Vienna and Budapest Marcch; resignation of Metternich, March 13; Five Days in Milan, March 18–23; revolutions among Czechs, Poles; flight of Emperor from Vienna, May 17; Pan-Slav Congress at Prague, June; defeat of Czechs by army under General Windischgrätz, of Italians by General Radetsky; capture of Vienna by Windischgrätz, October 31; abdication of Emperor Ferdinand, replaced by grandson Francis Joseph; war against Hungary.

Germany: March Days in Berlin; King Frederick William promises liberal reforms and dons tricolor; Heidelberg committee arranges for Frankfurt assembly, May 18, to frame an all-German constitution; difficulties over Schleswig and Holstein, war with Denmark; quarrel with Prussian King, who regained control of Berlin, dissolved the Prussian constitutional assembly, dictated a conservative constitution. Divisions within Frankfurt assembly between Left and Right, *Kleindeutsch* and *Grossdeutsch* parties.

Elsewhere: Revolution in Naples, which collapsed in May; in Rome, November, flight of Pope; new constitutions granted in the Netherlands, Tuscany, Piedmont.

1849

Dissolution of National Assembly by President Louis Napoleon; French intervention to suppress Roman Republic; repression of liberals and radicals in France.

Continuing conquest of revolutions in Austran Empire; seige and starvation of Venice, defeat of Hungarians with Russian aid.

Frankfurt Constitution completed, March 27, rejected by King of Prussia; dispersal of rump assembly at Stuttgart; King Frederick William plans his own north German union, vetoed by Austria (humiliation of Olmütz, 1850).

Great Britain and liberalism

The hungry forties

Europe passed through a period of crisis in the 1840's—the "hungry forties," as they were called. Hunger stalked Ireland during the potato famine which drove so many Irishmen to migrate to the New World. It also stalked Europe, with crop failures and hunger in the cities contributing no small amount to the revolutions of the year 1848. The cholera continued its ravages. The pains of early industrialization still afflicted certain parts of society. Europe emerged into something like the sunlight of 19th-century high noon during the next decade; but the 1840's, and to some extent the whole of the period since 1815, found its climax in the excitement, violence, and eventual disillusionment of the revolutions which rumbled from one end of the Continent to the other in 1848.

1848 was a turning point in the history of almost every country, so that we may conveniently survey developments in all the major countries using this as the key date. Among the countries which managed to *avoid* revolution in 1848, two were notable: Russia and Great Britain. The reasons were diametrically opposite. Russia suffered under an iron despotism and had a society too backward to produce the social classes that everywhere made revolution in 1848, the urban bourgeois and the industrial working class; Britain, on the other hand, was the pioneer of the Industrial Revolution and the leader in free political institutions. It is true that there were disturbances in the British Isles: industrialism had caused sporadic machine breaking earlier, and in the late 1830's a working-class movement of considerable proportions, known as Chartism, put in its appearance. The British middle class, however, had largely gained its objectives, and did not associate itself with this lower class protest.

British liberalism

Great Britain took rank as the classic land of "liberalism." The word came widely into use in the 1840's. Liberalism generally meant an economic, political, and social individualism which treated each man as an independent unit, and was suspicious not only of the state but of any other form of association (business corporations, trade unions, religious groupings) which claimed him as member of a group. It also meant, at this time, the specific economic doctrines of the "Manchester school"—rather dogmatically holding to a faith in pure competition and no state regulation as the wisest policy. This was a popularized version of the "political economy" of such penetrating minds as David Ricardo, Nassau Senior, and John Stuart Mill, who had built on the foundations put down earlier by Adam Smith and the French Physiocrats. It is now clear that the popular versions oversimplified, if they did not distort, the highly complex teachings of the theoreticians.

Political economy

The popular version of economics assumed free competition among free men as its starting point, and spent much of its intellectual energy in explaining why the "natural" economic order would result in maximum production of wealth and maximum social justice. Attempts to legislate on such matters as wages and profits, or to impose "artificial" pressures such as trade union organization and bargaining, would do no good and perhaps much mischief. Sentimentalists who looked at poverty and misery and demanded that "government do something" were only demonstrating their ignorance of economic science. Let all men be free to pursue their own interests, let freedom of contract and freedom of the market be maintained, let government protect property rights and a sound currency, giving no man special favors, and all would come out for the best.

Economic fatalism

It is not difficult to see why Thomas Carlyle and others spoke of "the dismal science" and of a "gospel of Mammon." Radical in its origins, political economy came to rest in the patronage of industrial capitalists, who found it as comforting to be told that wages must remain low as to be assured that in seeking their own maximum gain they were serving civilization. "Through the wise and beneficent arrangement of Providence," a popular tract of 1850 stated, men serve the public when thinking of their own gain. This was a *carte blanche* to selfishness, as well as "a gospel of economic fatalism."

But the dominant industrial middle classes nodded their approval, and, as a great modern socialist, Harold Laski, has written, "from Waterloo until the outbreak of the Great War no other doctrine spoke with the same authority or exercised the same widespread influence" as this liberal creed which rested at bottom on the classical economists. Freedom, in the negative sense of freedom from restraint, appeared to be not only enjoyable but a duty enjoined by science, the way to wealth and prosperity.

The medicine for poverty

Not all reform was denied to the lower classes. In 1834, it is true, a new Poor Law gave brutal expression to the middle-class view of poverty as something to be cured by making it as unpleasant as possible. No longer able to receive "outdoor relief," the unfortunate pauper would have to go to a workhouse, and these places, by deliberate design, were made highly unpleasant. Degradation and humiliation awaited the man or woman, perhaps crippled or aged, unfortunate enough to be thrown into one of these "bastilles." The ideology of laissez-faire and self-help filled the mind of educated England at this time. It was wrong to hand out charity, for then the poor would not work. It was right to fortify their character by making them labor. So odious was the workhouse system that it was not actually carried out in full, but it expressed quite well the dogmatic convictions of those who followed political economy and Utilitarianism, the new schools of social thought.

Factory legislation

A few noble voices were raised against this inhumanity. A significant number of these were among the Tory landowners, a group not always notable for reform but more likely than factory owners to defend the factory workers. It was in part because they often intensely disliked the new industrialists; and at any rate it did not cost the squire anything to demand better conditions of work in the factories. A genuine spirit of charity did exist in such notable Tory reformers as the deeply religious Lord Shaftesbury, who crusaded many years for factory legislation. But some liberals who had supported religious liberty and parliamentary reform balked at attempts to regulate conditions and hours of work, because they opposed any government interference with individual freedom of contract. Only gradually, in a series of acts between 1833 and 1847, was progress made against the evils of child labor, inhumanly long hours, unsafe and unhealthy working conditions. These evils were exposed in investigations undertaken by parliamentary committees. To this crusade such great writers as Charles Dickens and Thomas Carlyle lent their powerful pens. Factory and Mining Acts were pushed through in 1844 and 1847. Far from perfect, these measures eliminated child and female labor in the mines, set a 10-hour limit per day in the factories, required dangerous machinery to be fenced off. They also set a precedent for subsequent welfare legislation.

Chartism

To the seemingly rather bleak creed of bourgeois liberalism, which advocated votes for the propertied only and frowned on any helping hand stretched out to the poor, many workers objected. They demanded political democracy and economic socialism. Not adequately led for some time, these inchoate and inarticulate elements in society grew better organized in the 1830's and 1840's. "Chartism" was their first major rallying cry, reaching into every working-class district in Great Britain. It took its name from the Charter of reform which was the basic national platform of the party. The reforms asked for were political ones: universal male suffrage; no property qualification for holding public office; annual Parliaments; pay for members of

Kennington Common, 1848. Chartist orator demanding political reform.

Parliament, to enable workers to sit in Parliament. These were demands for full political democracy which hardly seem extreme, though daring at that time. Some Chartists were socialists, and sought the vote in order to bring about a completely new economic order. The manner of some of the more notorious Chartist leaders, like the Irish socialist Feargus O'Connor, alienated respectable people. Detailed studies of this working-class movement reveal innumerable local leaders developing in a pattern of groping for self-identification by an industrial "proletariat" that felt itself to be apart from the rest of the nation.

Repeal of the Corn Laws

Chartism, therefore, left behind a large deposit in the working-class consciousness, but as such it passed out of existence. Its only major national political offensive crumbled in 1839. It revived but feebly in the revolutionary years (for Europe) of 1847–48. During the 1840's other political issues came to the fore and gave rise to an exciting national debate in which all classes joined. The leading one was the tariff on grains—the "Corn Laws," in the parlance of the day. Protection, the landed interest claimed, was essential to the survival of British agriculture, and agriculture was a prime national interest. The manufacturers disagreed, urging that if the tariffs were repealed, some inefficient farmers would doubtless go under, but the English workingman would get his food cheaper, English industries would thrive on the resulting lower wages, and export markets would contribute to the national welfare. The essential argument of Richard Cobden and the Anti–Corn Law League, which covered the isles with an unprecedented publicity campaign, was that agriculture might well be sacrificed to industry since Britain was better suited to specialize in the latter.

Protection also violated the sacred canons of free competition. Political economists threw their weight against the landlord and for the industrialist. To the disciples of the great David Ricardo, especially, the landlord was the enemy of economic progress, crippling industry by keeping wages high. Advisers of statesmen, editors of influential newspapers and journals—these political economists exerted great influence from the 1820's on. They converted the Liberal party—which now took that name—to free trade. A faction of the Conservatives joined the Liberals, too, in the final vote which secured the repeal of the Corn Laws in 1846.

In the Corn Law agitation both sides attempted to appeal to the British workingman—a fact which illustrates the growing maturity of elements in the population heretofore largely ignored politically. The whole campaign was indeed a milestone in the public debate of an urgent political issue before a mass audience. If the result was hardly any great victory for the workingman, he had reason to believe he might make his voice heard before long. At this time the 10-hour act was passed after sensational hearings on conditions in the factories.

Britain escapes revolution

Chartism faded away. Britain escaped revolution in 1848 almost alone among the major nations. Helping her solve her problems was a free political system, which allowed major groups in the nation a fair chance of achieving their legitimate aspirations by the ballot. Helping also, to be sure, was the extensive migration of surplus population to the United States and the British colonies; and, in general, that wealth which came with leadership in the Industrial Revolution. Throughout most of the 19th century, Great Britain held the lead in this area, as measured by the indexes of manufacturing, iron and steel, coal. She was to be exceeded in the last quarter of the century by Germany and the United States. At mid-century, her leadership was firm enough to arouse the awe of foreigners, who sought to decipher the British secret of success. "The creation of wealth in England in the last ninety years is the main fact in modern history," Ralph Waldo Emerson wrote in his book *English Traits*.

France and socialism

The era of the July Monarchy in France, 1830–48, was intellectually a brilliant one. This was the romantic generation, for, with the triumph of Victor Hugo's *Hernani* in 1830, Romanticism prevailed, and not only the great Hugo but George Sand, Alexander Dumas, the poets Lamartine and Musset, and perhaps Balzac and Stendhal, may be placed within its ranks. The pedestrian quality of the Bourgeois Monarchy contrasted sharply with the brilliance of the writers. In other areas Frenchmen also excelled: while Daguerre invented photography, Corot, Courbet, and Delacroix set the fashions in painting for Europe. Tocqueville, the socialist writers, and Auguste Comte, founder of "positivism," would be included in any list of the century's major political and social thinkers.

The birth of socialism

Socialism was preeminently a French creation, as political economy of the Adam Smith–Ricardo sort was typically British. Modern socialism had its origin in the French Revolution, and might be regarded as the reaction of frustrated *sans-culottes* to the discovery that formal, legal equality did not make them any better off. Early socialism owed a good deal to certain utterances of Rousseau, and appeared in the "Conspiracy of Equals" led by Babeuf in the late stages of the French Revolution (1795). Crude at first, it was developed in rather different directions between 1800 and 1830, chiefly by Charles Fourier and especially by the colorful, eccentric aristocrat, Henri Saint-Simon, a scion of the bluest blood in France who spawned social ideas in profusion and left behind a religious cult dedicated to the creation of a planned industrial society. Fourier, along with the famous Scottish manufacturer Robert Owen, encouraged the founding of model communities; but the Saint-Simonists looked toward a national or even international economy, managed by a trained scientific elite of engineers and social scientists, where order and planning would take the place of chaotic individualism. Students of national character have often asserted that the French, as compared with the English, prefer logic, order, and general ideas. For their part the empirical Anglo-Saxons mistrusted broad theories, liked to "muddle through," and were incurably individualistic.

Varieties of socialist theory

At any rate Paris was undeniably the headquarters for revolutionary or reformist social ideas. Karl Marx learned his socialism there. Saint-Simon was the true prophet of socialism, the author of most of its slogans such as "the exploitation of man by man," "to each according to his need," the struggle of the "proletariat," the need to plan, etc. He had numerous successors. Whereas Saint-Simon frankly spoke of a managerial and scientific elite, some brands of socialism appealed to the nascent working class. The idea that somehow the employers cheated the workers out of their proper wages, unfairly appropriating value created by labor, was deeply if not very precisely implanted in working-class circles long before Karl Marx elaborated it into a complex economic theory. One prominent source, ironically, was the "capitalist" economic theory of David Ricardo.

In explaining the appeal of socialism to the working class, one can stress too much the role of certain thinkers and too little the effect of simple tradition; for socialism was not really a novelty, if one means by this the social control of industry and trade. In most parts of Europe the old guilds were not dead; the artisan working class, threatened by the new factory system with its unregulated competition, was accustomed to regulation and now looked to the state to protect the workers.

Social romanticism

In the aftermath of the half-way revolution of 1830, and stimulated by the first impact of the Industrial Revolution, a *mélange* of socialistic ideas filled the 1830's and 1840's. Lamennais, a Catholic priest and formerly a follower of the conservatives Bonald and Maistre, became an enthusiastic social demo-

Louis J. M. Daguerre, 1844, as recorded by his own invention, the daguerreotype

Henri de St. Simon, pioneer socialist, who dedicated his life and fortune to the idea of a new social order, planned and cooperative

Victor Hugo, the greatest figure of French romanticism, inspired much of the political idealism that erupted in 1848.

Louis Philippe and his sons. The bourgeois monarch ruled from one revolution (1830) to another (1848).

crat with his popular *Words of a Believer* (1835) which gave lyrical expression to the "tremendous revolution going on at the heart of human society," a revolution of "the peoples" destined to produce a "new world." In accents comparable to those of Thomas Carlyle in Britain, this Breton denounced "wage slavery" and castigated the rulers of society for neglecting their responsibilities. Hugo, Sand, and Lamartine evoked a similar mood in many of their novels and poems. The French Revolution was restored to favor and seen as a splendid if terrible upsurge of the people. Under the influence of this "social romanticism" men felt a new social order advancing, with "the people" on the march and tyrants trembling. It was a messianic or apocalyptic mood, vehement though rather vague. The revolution that came in 1848 owed a great deal to it. Both socialists and republicans participated in it, without any very sharp distinction. 1848 was to reveal a split between the two groups, but prior to that the two strains mingled in a chorus of slogans about social justice, popular rights, and the march of the masses. In some ways these slogans harked back to the Jacobinism of the French Revolution of 1792.

Discontent with the bourgeois monarchy

New socialist voices of the 1840's included Louis Blanc, *The Organization of Labor* (1839), as well as Pierre Proudhon, *What is Property?* (1841). Proudhon's was a more radical voice than that of the gentle Fourier or the theoretical Saint-Simon. He declared roundly that "property is theft" and talked of class war, revolution. Such ideas were in vogue on the Paris boulevards. A young German, Karl Marx, came there in 1843 to share the excitement of socialist debate in the cafes. Amid this excitement, the monarchy of Louis Philippe went its unexciting way. The Orléanist king who owed his authority to the liberals and had accepted the superiority of constitution and charter, symbolically kissing the tricolor flag, was a solid, unemotional man who for a time won popularity in the role of "citizen king." He offered France peace, free enterprise, equality under the law. Under this "bourgeois monarchy" there was considerable economic progress, along with the sufferings produced by the dislocations of early industrialism. The businessman king lacked glamour, and in time "France grew bored," as Lamartine said. More substantial as an explanation of the decline of the Orléanist government was its thoroughly unrepresentative character in an era of rising popular democracy. The suffrage remained restricted to a few, though the press was largely free. Therefore one had agitation without the possibility of its political expression —a good formula for explosion. In Paris, dozens of newspapers were read, some quite violent in their expression. Bad factory conditions and epidemics of the cholera provided a somber background for these radical attacks on the *status quo*. The years 1846–47, just preceding the revolution of 1848, were years of economic crisis, of unemployment as well as poor harvests. The laissez-faire government provided virtually no relief for such sufferings, though, as in Great Britain, an antichild-labor law was passed in 1841.

As an example of how the years between about 1820 and 1848 increased the wealth of some, but augmented economic inequality, the following statistics relating to Paris and comparing the years 1820 and 1847[1] were meticulously compiled by the French historian Daumard, studying the records of inheritances:

	1820	*1847*
Those who left no inheritance at all (presumably dire poverty)	69.1%	72.6%
Those who left an inheritance of less than 2,000 frances (extreme to moderate poverty)	14.1	12.1
Those who left an inheritance of between 2,000 and 20,000 francs (petit bourgeois wealth)	8.4	6.9
Those who left an inheritance of 20,000 to 500,000 francs (middle to upper bourgeoisie)	7.5	6.9
Inheritance of more than 500,000 francs (great wealth)	0.3	0.8
(Remainder unevaluated)		

Broken down another way, the percentage of fortunes over 100,000 francs increased from 2.4 percent to 3.6 percent. France was not industrializing as fast as Britain, nor was Paris a startlingly industrialized area. The figures are nonetheless revealing both for the amount of sheer poverty that existed, its tendency to increase, and the tendency for great fortunes to grow the most. The *size* of growth of the less than 1 percent at the top was also remarkable. The number of those leaving wealth of more than 2 million francs increased from 2 to 10. In all of France, total wealth increased about a third between 1820 and 1847. "Enrich yourself," the motto of the Orléanist monarchy, was surely an apt slogan for the upper classes, the figures reveal, but hardly for the masses. These figures also suggest that, at least for the great city of Paris, the "bourgeoisie" *decreased* from around 30 percent to around 25 percent, in numbers, while increasing the total wealth held by members of this "class." The revolution of 1848 becomes more explicable in the light of such figures.

Origins of the 1848 revolution in France

The scholar-statesman Guizot, a formidable person, dominated affairs under Louis Philippe. Guizot was a classic "conservative liberal" who wished to keep the powers of government out of the hands of the ignorant multitude, while presiding over an economic policy based on the reigning theory of full economic freedom. He was a great 19th-century figure, and one of his contributions was in the area of public education. He certainly meant his country well, but his policy of withholding all political power from the masses was destined to prove disastrous. On this he would not budge. In 1848 a combination of liberals and socialists assailed the government, protesting against the narrow suffrage and alleging corruption in government. They drew on the example of the Anti–Corn Law League of recent British origin in organizing meetings, speeches, and dinners under respectable middle-class leadership. They planned a huge protest dinner in Paris on February 22, 1848, which the government sought to prohibit. The ban touched

[1] The price level declined slightly between 1821 and 1847.

Barricades were a regular feature of city uprisings in France and elsewhere in the 18th and early 19th centuries.

off huge demonstrations, and on February 23 the barricades went up again in Paris. The old king had no desire to fire on the people. He had gained the throne from their hands and would lose it to them. Louis Philippe's abdication led to the proclamation of a republic—the Second French Republic—on February 24.

It was not certain in which direction the new Republic would go, if it went at all. The makers of the revolution, somewhat surprised, did not really know what to do with their victory. They decided that the people should decide; let universal suffrage be proclaimed, and elections be held. So, quite suddenly, France prepared for an election in which more than 8 million men, rather than 250,000, were to cast ballots. So came universal manhood suffrage to modern Europe.[2] It was a solemn moment.

The June Days

But perhaps it came too suddenly; at any rate the results of this first European democracy were not encouraging. The Second Republic, born of the

[2] Universal suffrage with *indirect* elections had chosen the National Convention in 1792, during the French Revolution; the 1793 constitution provided for direct election by universal suffrage but was never put into effect.

1848 Revolution, never was able to get started. In the Constitutional Assembly elected in April of 1848 there was a conservative and moderate majority—rather surprising to the liberals and radicals, but not so surprising in view of the rural-peasant character of most of France outside the city of Paris. In sharp contrast, socialist influence in Paris was so strong that a somewhat intimidated provisional government made concessions to it by setting up large-scale work relief under the name of the national workshops, and by bringing Blanc into the government. But the bourgeois republicans became more and more frightened of this whole scheme, and a break between the two revolutionary factions neared. It came in June with a bloody struggle between Parisian workers and government troops. These were the "June Days," long of dreadful memory in France. On them the revolution foundered.

Louis Napoleon elected president

The new Constitution provided for a strong president elected by universal suffrage, as well as an Assembly; when the elections were held in December, the easy winner of the presidency was Louis-Napoleon Bonaparte, nephew of the great Emperor (son of his sister Hortense). France had again chosen a Bonaparte to bring it peace; and this one, like his famous uncle before him, was not long in doing away with the Republic. The *coup d'état* did not take place until 1851, but the Second Republic's doom was sealed before that. A democratically elected Assembly had again produced upheaval and failed to secure the respect of France.

Germany and nationalism

German nationalism

In Germany the unsatisfactory settlement of 1815 left behind seeds of protest. Already noted was the fact that demonstrations among university students and professors encountered the reprisals of the "Metternich system" in the 1820's and proved too weak to resist. Petty absolutisms afflicted Germany. Not all but many of the small states were illiberal in their policies. Writers, both popular and philosophical, gave expression to the need for union—and liberty, but especially union. Those writers who led the German liberal-nationalist movement included Ernst Arndt and "Father" Jahn, founder of the singular "Turnverein" gymnastic movement, designed to strengthen German youth in body and mind; and, at the less popular end of the intellectual spectrum, the great philosophers Herder, Fichte, Hegel. The latter reveal significantly the preoccupation of even the loftiest minds of German philosophy with this problem of national unity. From them came much of the more serious mental underpinning of 19th-century European nationalism. Hegel's imposing edifice of thought, the leading philosophical synthesis of the century, assigned to the state the highest expression of man's ethical goals and made the nation the instrument through which the spirit of the world expresses and realizes itself.

Doubtless the political weakness of Germany was the more glaring because at this time, coming out of a long slump, Germans assumed leadership of European thought and letters. That at least was a common opinion in the period from roughly 1780 to 1830, during which could be encompassed Kant, Hegel, Fichte, Herder, Goethe, Schiller, the historians Ranke and Niebuhr, the political theorists Humboldt and Müller, and a good many other assorted philosophers, poets, scientists, and scholars, not to speak of incomparable musicians. (The English, sighed Heinrich Heine, are lords of the sea, the French of the land, the Germans of—the air.) In developing romanticism and philosophical idealism, the German savants usually brought in an element of nationalism or statism. No German of education and culture in this age could do other than turn away from anarchic individualism and toward the desired unity of a splendid state like other historic peoples possessed. They did not, however, despise liberty. They assumed it would be possible within the boundaries of an ordered state. Hegel's historical dialectic found the ancient Orient to have been dominated by despotism, the Greek city-states by individual freedom; the modern European nations combined these into a synthesis whereby liberty was possible within the framework of the larger state.

The 1815 Bund

Philosophers and historians, however great their authority in Germany, could not make this dream come true. Thirty-eight states meeting together in the loose German Confederation (Deutscher Bund) did not make a nation. Two of these were great powers: Austria and Prussia. This fact prevented either one or the other of these two rival monarchies from undertaking the unification of the Reich—even if other powers such as France or Russia would not have objected, as they surely would have. Of the two, Austria assumed priority between 1815 and 1848, with Prussia largely content to play the part of her junior partner. And Austria would have no part of German nationalism.

The "Zollverein"

The helplessness of the parliament (Bundestag) at Frankfurt, a meeting of the diplomatic representatives of sovereign states dominated by the interests of Prussia and Austria, persuaded the last optimist that this was no road to national unification. Economic distress in the 1840's lent urgency to the cause of a more effective political organization. But how could the circle of frustration be broken through? A glimmer of hope lay in the *Zollverein* or customs union which slowly grew between 1819 and 1834 until it embraced most of the German lands; but this was a matter of treaties between sovereign states who jealously guarded their sovereignty. Many liberals were ready for some sort of revolution which would break the power of the petty princes and their entrenched bureaucracies, in order to clear the way for a national German government.

1848 revolutions in Germany

The signal from Paris in 1848 seemed to provide the answer. Heinrich Heine, perhaps their greatest poet in this generation, had chided the Germans with being too mild and orderly to make a revolution. But the February Days in Paris were followed by the March Days in Berlin. King Frederick William

IV of Prussia proved himself easily intimidated by the barricades and showed an admirable disinclination to shed the blood of his people. He gave in and promised (March 18) not only a constitution and liberal reforms, but to merge Prussia in a united Germany.

Metternich, keeper of the citadel of conservatism in Vienna, meanwhile had been overthrown by the Viennese barricades, and there was no conservative leadership in the German world. Similar movements sprang up all over Germany, where restiveness had been stirring against the petty despotisms. The demands of all Germans centered on a national parliament. Already, early in March, a congress had assembled at Heidelberg, and issued the call to a general constitutional convention to meet at Frankfurt. It hoped to accomplish the job of uniting Germany under a liberal regime, as the Americans had done in 1787–89. The national assembly at Frankfurt, as well as the new Prussian parliament, were elected by universal suffrage: democracy was the word of the hour all over Europe.

The Austrian Empire

Censorship of ideas

In the Hapsburg monarchy, the "revolutionary absolutism" of that energetic enlightened despot, Joseph II, had given way during the French Revolution and after to a very different system. The "Francisist" system of Emperor Francis II (1792–1835) was, broadly speaking, based on the view that the mad ideas of the French Revolution were like a dangerous virus to which the body of Austria was peculiarly susceptible; and that therefore the proper remedy was to keep them out if possible and wage war on them if they got in. "It became necessary to introduce a sort of spiritual customs duties," as Oscar Jaszi writes, "more complete and ramified than perhaps the world had ever seen." Under this blanket condemnation lay practically every idea that came out of the intellectual ferment of Europe we have been discussing, whether silly and dangerous or deeply important and significant. Kant, Fichte, Bentham, and Ricardo were as suspect as socialist or antireligious propagandists. Spies filled the state. The Carlsbad Decrees, previously mentioned, put all the universities under police supervision and extended the Austrian system, under Metternich's influence, to much of Germany for a time. Ruling over various peoples, the Hapsburgs were especially sensitive to the venom of nationalism.

The fall of Metternich; Revolution in Vienna

Vienna, where the great Hapsburg Empire had its center and where Metternich held sway (though, as he said, he "sometimes ruled Europe but never Austria") was the key to much of eastern and central Europe. The Viennese rose up in the chain reaction of urban revolutions early in 1848, and aided by his enemies within the imperial council, they forced the resignation of the "crown prince of reaction" (March 13). The "last of the aristocrats" made a typically graceful and sardonic exit. He was heard playing the Marseillaise all night on his violin while stopping off at a Rhenish castle en route to exile in London. The news of Metternich's fall hastened revolution throughout the Hapsburg realms as well as in the German states of the confederation.

Two places particularly were eager to get the signal: Italy and Hungary. The former had been discontented ever since its return to Austrian domination in 1815. Milan and Venice, great and proud cities of the North, had been annexed directly by Austria, while the rest of Italy was divided into small states mostly ruled over by dukes subordinate to Austrian influence. Only the Kingdom of Sardinia (Piedmont) seemed strong enough and independent enough to lead Italy, but under King Charles Albert it had not been aggressive in that direction. Italy spawned revolutionaries; the picturesque "Carbonari" became famous all over Europe. In 1830, uprisings had been crushed by Austrian troops. Shortly after that the eloquent pamphleteer, Giuseppe Mazzini, attempted to march on Italy from Switzerland, confident that the people would rise up. They did not do so; a quarter of a century later, the Mazzini prophecy would come true, but not in 1834.

Italy in revolt

But in 1848 revolution broke out in Milan and Venice; the *cinque giornate* in Milan (March 18–22) were tremendous, the Italians forcing the retreat of an Austrian army under Radetsky. Prodded by his minister Cavour, the King of Sardinia declared war on Austria. The revolution spread to Rome, where the Pope, who had turned against the cause of Italian independence, was driven from the city and a republic proclaimed under the famous revolutionary exile, Mazzini. There was also revolution in Naples. For a few moments in 1848–49 it looked like Italy might achieve the miracle Mazzini dreamed of and the Red Shirts of Giuseppe Garibaldi fought for. But these hopes were destined to cruel disappointment.

Hungary and the Austrian Empire

In Hungary, there never was much incentive needed to rebel against Austrian rule. A firebrand leader of the caliber of Mazzini and Garibaldi put together emerged in the person of Louis Kossuth, one of the leading personalities of 1848. At the time of the revolt in Vienna and the subsequent control of the capital city for several months by a revolutionary committee (the Emperor himself fled to Innsbruck in May), national minorities all over the Austrian Empire began to secede and set up governments—Czechs and Croats as well as Hungarians. A great Pan-Slav Congress met at Prague, but proved to be mostly Czech in its attendance. It looked as if the whole Empire would be dissolved into a number of parts. But it turned out differently. The Austrian armies, under vigorous leadership, remained loyal to the Emperor and determined to crush the rebels. One by one the Czechs, the Viennese, the Italians, and the Hungarians were to be picked off. They failed to cooperate effectively.

Russia and reaction

The system of repression

Liberalism had little chance to flourish in countries where the middle class was weak, serfdom and slavery existed, industrialism lagged, and the great landowners held economic power. After the failure in 1825 of the

"Decembrist" revolt, the Russian Pestel, a leader of this revolt, said in his last speech that conditions were not ripe for liberalism; "we tried to gather the harvest before the seed had been planted." Perhaps a few seeds of liberalism had been planted in Russia by Catherine the Great and her son Alexander I; but if so they were ripped up by Nicholas I, the next tsar (1825–55). A hard-working public servant thoroughly dedicated to his country, Nicholas can be regarded as continuing one phase of enlightened despotism; he sponsored a new code of law, encouraged railroad building and did much to improve technical education in Russia. He also pursued a vigorous and, until his last years, successful foreign policy which secured the expansion of Russia at the expense of Turkey and Persia. On the other hand, there was suppression, censorship, the secret police, the Siberian prison camps for political offenders—all that made Russia a byword for the blackest sort of government. The development of this repressive system, notorious throughout the 19th century (and the 20th), must be charged to Nicholas. It was responsible for some of the chief scandals of the century: as, for example, sending writers of the stature of Dostoyevsky to the dreadful Siberian prison camps and driving into exile many of Russia's major men of letters.

In 1830, following the rebellion in Poland, Russia incorporated Poland directly into Russia and began a policy of "Russification." Polish exiles thereafter formed significant circles in the western cities, especially Paris. But the Russians themselves produced great figures of revolt who left their native country to plot revolution from abroad. The dimensions of reactionary oppression in Russia seemed matched by the stature and extremism of the revolutionary exiles. A giant of international revolution was Michael Bakunin; an intellectual giant was the emigré writer Alexander Herzen. Throughout the century a small minority in Russia suffered severely under the cruel backwardness of political and social life, and their spasmodic efforts to rescue their motherland from this fate made up some of the more dramatic chapters of European history. But they could not succeed.

Russian backwardness

A degraded serf-peasant class ruled over by landlords formed the basic social structure of Russia, and urban industry developed with painful slowness. The middle class was small, literacy low, government without any roots in "the people"—for 80 percent of these "people" would have to be liberated, civilized, and educated first. No national legislature existed, or even any institutions of local government beyond the feudalistic rule of the gentry.

Not until after defeat in the Crimean War and the death of Nicholas was there to be any break in the grim pattern in Russia; the exiles, while sometimes potent in foreign countries, had power only to stir up a good deal of secret discussion in Russia among the "intelligentsia"—young officers, perhaps a few liberal nobles, some journalists, and teachers. The Tsar's dreaded "third section" kept a sharp eye out and shipped any suspected subversives off to Siberia. But behind closed doors men talked in Russia, and perhaps read the paper edited by Herzen and smuggled into Russia, picking up there socialist ideas fresh from Paris or London; they would soon begin to conspire. (It is said that the Tsar himself read Herzen's journal because it was so interestingly written.) This dismal pattern of official repression by an unmitigated autocracy, and revolutionary conspiracy by frustrated liberals, continued largely on down through the century until it finally culminated in the revolutions of 1905 and 1917.

Russian aid to counterrevolution

In the revolutions of 1848, the role of Russia was therefore a reactionary one. Nicholas offered to help his brother monarchs in distress. Francis (Franz) Joseph of Austria, who replaced his father on the throne in December, accepted the offer and Russian troops marched into Hungary to help put down the revolution in that country. Thus began the undistinguished Russian tradition of suppressing Hungarian revolutions. But reaction had already triumphed in Vienna, in order for the invitation to be issued; Nicholas I did not come without the consent of the Austrian government.

Collapse of the revolutions of 1848

Causes of failure of revolutions

The help so generously given by the Tsar of Russia to the cause of reaction did not do the revolutionaries of 1848 any good, but even without it they would have failed. The chief causes of this failure related to their internal divisions, their lack of experience, and their lack of clear objectives. The first of these—internal divisions among the revolutionaries—included socialists versus liberals, and members of one nationality against another. In Paris, the "June Days" brought a ferocious civil war fought between the socialist-led workers of Paris and the bourgeois-dominated Republic which had been installed in February. It shattered the morale of the Republic almost as much as it broke the power of the Parisian socialists, and prepared the way for Louis Napoleon's emergence as all-powerful President and then Emperor of France.

Similar quarrels existed in Germany. The middle-class constitutionalists were frightened enough to retreat back into the arms of the princes, as various radicals and socialists sought to exploit the revolution to very unbourgeois ends. One of them was Karl Marx, who edited a newspaper in Cologne for a time; he did not however play any great part in the events of 1848. It cannot be said that socialists were very strong outside a few major cities. But then neither were the bourgeois revolutionaries. Unity was indispensable if the revolution wished to consolidate its triumph.

In France, in the elections based on universal suffrage, the surprise was the strength of conservative monarchists reflecting the views of French peasants. Louis Napoleon's victory in the presidential election by an overwhelming vote was the result of disenchantment with the Republic. "The more I see of the representatives of the people the more I love my dogs," said Lamartine, the poet-orator who had been one of the leading bourgeois revolutionaries of 1848. The reaction against representative government and toward a new authoritarian dictatorship was the result of confusion and conflict in the legislative body. The leap to full universal suffrage, without preparation, seemed to have landed France in another 1790 situation where too much happened too fast and the result was confusion. The Paris mob had put on its customary performance, invading and intimidating the Chambers. And in the last analysis, most of France turned out not to be liberal, socialist, or revolutionary at all. The gulf between city and country, Paris and the provinces, was a startling dualism in French life. Elsewhere in Europe during the revolutions of 1848 a similar pattern occurred: by and large only the cities rebelled. Bismarck dreamed of the King's "loyal peasants" restoring him to this throne; the army, not the peasants did so, but the fact that the rural areas were either actively or passively hostile to the urban reformers and radicals goes far to explain the failure.

Revolutionary disunity

In the Austrian Empire, the people of Vienna who held the city for a while did not know what to do with it, and failed to make contact with Kossuth's Hungarians. Notable also was an outbreak of conflict between the Hungarians and the Slavs, who were both against Austrian rule but violently opposed to each other. Here, in the state which in some respects held the key to central Europe, the chances seem to have been the best and the failure the greatest. At one time or another, revolutionary movements controlled just about every part of the empire, from Vienna to Venice and Prague to Budapest. But they failed conspicuously to coordinate. General Radetsky, who smashed the Piedmontese and then plucked the Italian cities one by one, was the leading spirit of the counterrevolution.

It should be mentioned that not only did the Russians send him help, but help also came from another, rather surprising, quarter. In order to gain favor with the Roman Catholic peasants whom he represented, the new President of France, Louis Napoleon Bonaparte, helped restore Rome to the Pope, defeating Garibaldi's gallant little army and forcing that romantic revolutionary hero into desperate flight through the swamps of Ravenna. Napoleon turned down an appeal from Charles Albert of Piedmont to help him in the war against Austria. Thus ended the short-lived Roman Republic.

Frankfurt assembly

Thus did the various revolutionary regimes fail to cooperate. In Germany, a talented congregation of lawyers and professors met at Frankfurt and deliberated solemnly over Germany's new constitution. First they set up a provisional all-German government. But events, particularly a war which broke out in Schleswig-Holstein, made it all too clear that this government had no real power. The 600 members of the assembly included Germany's most brilliant men, but they were deeply divided; the Frankfurt gathering epitomized the many divisions of Germany, not only into democrats, liberals, and conservatives, but Protestants and Catholics, and also *Grossdeutscher* and *Kleindeutscher*, that is, those who wanted to include Austria and those who would exclude it. If Austria were to be included the question arose of the status of her non-German lands, such as Hungary and Czechoslovakia. "The question of German unity was itself full of disunity," as Karl Marx wrote. By autumn, the assembly got around to writing the constitution, a long and admirably liberal one, including a bill of rights specifying all manner of civic rights based on equality before the law, freedom of expression, the removal of class distinctions and special privileges. Election to the popular branch of the legislature was to be by manhood suffrage while in the upper house, representing the states, Prussia's representation was not to be great enough to secure her domination.

Failure of the assembly

It was, in brief, an ideally liberal constitution, on paper, though according to some unduly long, its 197 paragraphs not exactly complying with Napoleon's advice to make constitutions as short as possible. But its worst defect was the absence of any power to turn the statements of the constitution into a living reality. When the delegates finished the constitution, they found that there was no one to put it into effect. Offered the crown by the Frankfurt assembly if he would head the constitutional German state, Frederick William of Prussia refused it. Austria, too, made it clear that she would not accept such a constitution. The monarchs had regained control of the situation with the aid of the army by this time (April, 1849) and were of no mind to surrender their power to another government, least of all a liberal one. While some of the constitution makers gave up and went home, a radical group stayed in Frankfurt and tried somehow to put the constitution in effect, only to be turned out by the Prussian army; further sporadic uprisings were then easily suppressed.

Collapse of the revolutions

Here in Germany as elsewhere, a year of remarkable happenings and great courage, of stirring events and generous hopes, ended apparently in—nothing. Whether from ill-luck or their own ineptitude, or the absence of popular

Hero of two worlds, Giuseppe Garibaldi began his revolutionary career in 1848 and carried it on for two decades.

Emperor Napoleon III

support, the revolutionaries were in confusion and defeat, the old regimes were back in power, and severe reprisals were being taken against unfortunate patriots and rebels. While Garibaldi managed to get back to Staten Island, New York (though his beautiful wife Anita died in the flight), and Mazzini back to the literary salons of London, more than a hundred leading Hungarians were not so lucky, being shot by the Austrians; and the several thousand Parisian victims of the June Days might sympathize from beyond the grave with those Venetians who died from cholera and starvation during the siege of their city. The results everywhere were profoundly disillusioning to liberals and radicals, after so much suffering and sacrifice.

Results of 1848

Second Empire in France

A storm as violent as that of 1848 could not blow over without making some changes, even though the general impression was that all the noise and blood had ended with things much the same. Of overt changes, there were indeed not too many. France had traded King Log for King Stork, Louis Philippe for Louis Napoleon, and after 1851 had less freedom and self-government than before. True, universal suffrage had been established once and for all; even Bonaparte had himself confirmed by it. But the experience of 1848–51 led most of France to embrace an authoritarian rather than a parliamentary government. The greater powers in the constitution of the Second Empire were lodged in Bonaparte himself and in a Council and Senate appointed by him; the lower house had little power. The new government, which lasted nearly 20 years and achieved many good things (it is discussed further in the next chapter), was not noted for its toleration of political opposition or freedom of the press. It was much less free in this respect, for some time at any rate, than the pre-1848 government. And France had developed a pronounced and long-standing distaste for republics. Writing amid the civil war of 1871, the writer Edmond Goncourt expressed this sentiment: "The Republic . . . is a fine, foolish dream of thoughtful, generous, and disinterested minds; it is not practicable with the evil, petty passions of the French populace. To them, Liberty, Equality and Fraternity mean nothing but the enslavement and destruction of the upper classes." On the other hand, a minority cherished in bitterness memories of the barricades of June and the severe repression, while others such as Victor Hugo and Alexis de Tocqueville never forgave Napoleon for the crime against liberty committed in 1851. Political feuds, dividing the country bitterly, deepened as a result.

German disillusion

For Germany the outcome was no less disillusioning. Hundreds of thousands of Germans migrated to the United States in the next few years, some for political reasons, from a feeling that Germany had missed another chance. (This politically conscious element made a signal contribution to American life; the statesman Carl Schurz is a good example of the "forty-eighter" who, despairing of liberalism in Germany, came to find it in the United States.) After he refused the crown from the Frankfurt assembly, the Prussian king made an effort to unify Germany on a more conservative basis, but found the road blocked by Austria, backed by her friend Russia. One meeting of the parliament of this German union actually took place, at Erfurt, in 1850; but as soon as she finished putting down the Italian and Hungarian revolutions, Austria, backed by Russia, challenged it, restoring the old confederation. Prussia shrank from such a war and accepted the "humiliation of Olmütz," as this ultimatum was known.

Prussian constitution

Prussia, along with many of the smaller states, did get a new constitution, but like the French one it did not allow for much liberty or democracy. This Prussian constitution of 1850, which remained in effect until 1918, also included universal suffrage but like Louis Napoleon's gave the real power to an upper house which was not elected. Even the lower house, in this case, was elected by the famous three-class system, which while giving everybody a vote gave the wealthier people in effect more than one vote. Voters were divided into three groups according to the amount of taxes paid, each group electing a third of the Landstag, the result being that the upper income class chose a considerable majority of the deputies (17 percent chose about two thirds). The election was also indirect. Virtually all the other German states adopted similarly conservative constitutions.

In regard to unification, the experience of 1848, with its fine constitution that never went into effect, gave the Germans an unfortunate conviction that mere talk got you nowhere, that power was the only necessity. German liberalism, so strong a force in this generation, withered during the next one and all but died. However, the impulse toward unity continued to be strong and had eventually to be recognized. And Olmütz rankled even in conservative Prussian hearts.

Italian hopes

From the stirring events of 1848–49, Italy derived somewhat less disillusionment, even though the end had been terrible defeat. Garibaldi and Mazzini left behind a legend to inspire Italians in the next decade. North Italy grew ever more hostile to the Austrian rule, and the whole peninsula began to be swept by something like the lofty patriotism of Mazzini's ideal. Piedmont got a constitution, and King Charles Albert abdicated in favor of Victor Emmanuel, a more vigorous Italian leader. The great diplomat Cavour became prime minister, and from Turin spun webs of intrigue to get the powers of Europe behind Italian unification. These forces were to sweep Italy to liberation and unification within a dozen years. But for the time being reaction was in the saddle, not only in the Austrian-held north but in the Papal States, where Pius IX was in profound retreat from Mazzinian liberalism and indeed all liberalism; and in the south, where the Neapolitan kingdom became a fair approximation of what the British statesman Gladstone once called it—"the negation of God erected into a system of government." Moreover, even the achievement of unification in 1861 owed more to moderate realism than to revolutionary idealism.

Austria

In Austria came reversion to the static and repressive system of Metternich, under an even tougher conservative, Schwarzenberg. During the revolutions the old Emperor had been replaced by young Franz Joseph, who sat on the throne of the Hapsburgs until 1917. In time, he became loved as no Austrian ruler had been since Maria Theresa, but the political problems of the highly mixed empire grew worse until they exploded in 1914, blowing up Europe along with the Dual Monarchy (as it became in 1867). The remains of feudalism had ended during the revolution, a solid accomplishment if one overdue by western standards. Only in Russia, now, did there exist a genuinely servile population, class-ridden though much of eastern Europe might still be. The process of emancipating the Austrian peasant, undertaken by the enlightened despot Joseph II, was completed by the revolution of 1848.

The smaller states

The smaller states of Europe—which so often get neglected in our preoccupation with the big ones—felt the liberal and revolutionary current of the day. Thus in 1849 Denmark got a new constitution and became a limited monarchy. Norway and Sweden did not follow this example until 1864, but there was a liberal movement all through this period which gained concessions to free press and religious freedom. (Norway and Sweden were at this time united under a single monarchy, a union which was peaceably dissolved in 1905.) Switzerland in 1847 experienced a brief civil war between Catholics and liberals, and in 1848 established a new government under a new constitution—one marked by somewhat larger powers for the central government, reflecting nationalist and "liberal" trends among a people traditionally conservative and extremely jealous of local (canton) liberties. In the Netherlands, 1848 caused an increase in the powers of the parliament and a decrease in those of the monarchy, along with the emergence of a vigorous party of liberal reform. To Belgium, which had rebelled and won independence from the Dutch in 1830, 1847–48 brought reforms in the direction of increased suffrage and parliamentary government. The small countries fared better than the big ones in 1848: they usually escaped violent revolution but managed to secure liberal reforms, not startling ones but steps on a road of progress. The countries mentioned flourished under the influence of these reforms in the following period.

Eastern Europe

Eastern Europe in general was scarcely touched by the storm. The Poles, crushed in their revolutionary uprising of 1830, did not stir again until 1863, when another rebellion was put down; in this area the power of reactionary Russia was simply too great.

The Ottoman Empire had lost some territory since 1815. Greece had gained her independence; Serbia was now for all practical purposes independent. While Russia maintained a protectorate over the Rumanian provinces of Moldavia and Wallachia, Turkish rule continued to blight Bulgaria and Albania. The Treaty of Adrianople of 1829 had established a sort of joint supervision of this troubled region by the great powers, but threats to the peace of Europe continued to emanate from southeastern Europe all through the century until the great explosion of 1914. The Balkan countries proved violently unstable whether ruled by Turks, foreign kings, or their own monarchs. To the factors of poverty and a highly mixed population was added the unhappy legacy of centuries spent without self-government under the Ottoman yoke. In general these peoples were not yet ready to respond to the call of the liberal-democratic-socialist slogans of 1848, so much a product of the urban intellectuals.

A reaction against idealism

Karl Marx and Friedrich Engels published *The Communist Manifesto* in 1848, and spent the rest of their lives preparing for another revolution which, they were convinced, would complete the work of 1848. (They regarded the latter as a "bourgeois" revolution, not the final proletarian one.) An era of revolutionary romanticism and political idealism closed out with 1848. A "toughness of mind," a greater realism and sophistication, was typical of the European mind in the next period. The *Realpolitik* of Bismarck and Cavour was to be the chief political phenomenon. Democrats or socialists, the revolutionaries of 1848 appeared to have been naive ideologists dreaming dreams without much relevance to reality, living in a world made up of slogans; the rights of man, or the right to work, or the sovereignty of the people, were mere words. Clearly there is something to the diagnosis that the revolutions of 1848 were to an unusual degree inspired by general theories and led by political romanticists; Lamartine, Blanc, Kossuth, Garibaldi and Mazzini, or the Frankfurt liberals (heavily sprinkled with college professors) speak for themselves. In the aftermath of the terrible disillusionment of 1848 such people often gave up politics completely, and turned to art and literature; or they became complete reactionaries; or if they remained politically active and hopeful, they adopted a practical, short-range outlook and spoke of giving up misty dreams and utopian expectations. "I did not die, but I have aged," Alexander Herzen wrote in a famous commentary on 1848. "I am recovering from those June days as if after a grave illness." It was a cataclysmic experience for the liberal European mind.

Meaning of 1848

The larger meaning of 1848 was that democracy and nationalism had arrived in Europe and could not be denied, though they could prove troublesome. Despite apparent retreat from democracy, future regimes were not really able to ignore it. Universal suffrage has never ceased to exist in France since 1848. Louis Napoleon proclaimed himself the Emperor Napoleon III, but he was careful to get the people's approval in plebescites held from time to time. In Germany, not even the conservatives could ignore the pressure for unification—soon, one who had bitterly opposed the 1848 movement was making masterful moves in that direction. Italy too returned to the goal of national independence, this time under more moderate and realistic leadership, not as flamboyantly radical as that of Mazzini and Garibaldi but much more effective. Within 20 years Hungary, also, won by quieter means what she had fought for in vain at the barricades in 1848. Not all European peoples were so fortunate, but 1848 announced the presence of popular sovereignty as a power that would have to be reckoned with in the contemporary world. The halt that took place in most countries between 1848 and about 1870 was only a short delay in the march of this power.

Bibliography

On the events of 1848, outstanding books are Raymond Postgate, *Story of a Year: 1848* (New York: Oxford University Press, 1956); Veit Valentin, *1848, Chapters of German History* (London: G. Allen & Unwin, 1940); Lewis Namier, *1848: The Revolution of the Intellectuals* (Doubleday, Anchor); Arnold Whitridge, *Men in Crisis: The Revolutions of 1848* (New York: Charles Scribner's Sons, 1949); Priscilla Robertson, *The Revolution of 1848: A Social History* (Harper Torchbook). M. Kranzberg has edited *1848* in the useful Problems in European Civilization series published in paperback by Raytheon Education's D.C. Heath. R.J. Rath has studied *The Viennese Revolution of 1848* (Austin: University of Texas Press, 1957). P.H. Noyes, in *Organization and Revolution: Working-Class Associations in the German Revolutions of 1848–1849* (Princeton, N.J.: Princeton University Press, 1966), provides materials on an often neglected aspect of the revolutions. Among other studies which put the revolution in a somewhat wider context are E.L. Woodward, *Three Studies in European Conservatism* (reprinted;

Hamden, Conn.: Shoe String Press, 1963), including Guizot and Metternich, essential for an understanding of the forces against which the revolutionaries rebelled; Richard H. Thomas, *Liberalism, Nationalism, and the German Intellectuals, 1822–1847* (London: W. Heffer, 1951); Kent R. Greenfield, *Economics and Liberalism in the Risorgimento . . . 1814–1848* (Baltimore: Johns Hopkins University Press, 1934), the work of a distinguished American historian; and Theodore Hamerow, *Restoration, Revolution, Reaction: Economics and Politics in Germany 1815–1871* (Princeton University Press, 1958). G.H.F. and J. Berkeley, *Italy in the Making* (3 vols.; Oxford University Press, 1932–40), is a generally useful study of the emergence of Italian nationality, while A.J.P. Taylor, *The Italian Problem in European Diplomacy 1847–1849* is a closer analysis (Manchester: Manchester University Press, 1934). Harold Acton, *The Last Bourbons of Naples* (London: Methuen Publications, 1961), is a vivid portrait of the ancient dynasty which collapsed a few years after facing revolution in 1848. See also some of the books cited for Chapter 20.

The revolution of the romantics was rich in personality; among excellent biographies of the important actors are G. Salvemini, *Mazzini* (Stanford, Calif.: Stanford University Press, 1957); Leo A. Loubère, *Louis Blanc* (Evanston, Ill.: Northwestern University Press, 1961); Peter De Polnay, *Garibaldi: The Man and the Legend* (London: Thomas Nelson & Sons, 1961); and D. Mack Smith, *Garibaldi* (London: Hutchinson, 1957). George Woodcock, *Pierre-Joseph Proudhon* (London: Routledge & Kegan Paul, 1956), is about the leading socialist writer of the time; cf. Henri Lubac, *The UnMarxian Socialist* (New York: Sheed & Ward, 1949), and J. Hampden Jackson, *Marx, Proudhon, and European Socialism* (Macmillan, Collier Books). One of the best books on the classical economists, which dispels some popular misconceptions, is Mark Blaug, *Ricardian Economics* (New Haven, Conn.: Yale University Press, 1958). E.E.Y. Hales has written on *Mazzini and the Secret Societies* (London: Eyre & Spottiswoode, 1956). E.H. Carr, *Studies in Revolution* (Grosset & Dunlap), and Eugene Lampert, *Studies in Rebellion* (Routledge & Kegan Paul, 1957), include the Russians Bakunin, Herzen, Belinsky, and other international revolutionary leaders. Alan B. Spitzer, *The Revolutionary Theories of Blanqui* (New York: Columbia University Press, 1957), is devoted to the Parisian left-wing socialist; Donald Read, *Feargus O'Connor* (London: Edward Arnold, 1961), to the radical Chartist who failed to persuade the English workers to make a revolution. Hales has written a biography of *Pio Nono* (Doubleday, Image), the Pope who was involved in the Italian drama of 1848–61.

Alexis de Tocqueville, *Recollections,* ed. J.P. Mayer (World Publishing, Meridian), includes a commentary on the 1848 revolution and afterward by the great French political writer, who held office for a time in the short-lived Second Republic. *The Living Thoughts of Mazzini,* Ignazio Silone (ed.), presents the foremost ideologist and political pamphleteer of this epoch (London: Longmans, Green & Co., 1939). R. Postgate has edited *Revolution from 1789 to 1906: Selected Documents* (Harper).

Queen Victoria at the beginning of her reign

22

Realism, science, and nationalism: 1850-71

chronology

1848
Marx and Engels, *The Communist Manifesto*.
1851
Herbert Spencer, *Social Statics*.
Great Crystal Palace Exhibition, London.
Coup d'état of Louis Napoleon; plebiscite; Second Empire proclaimed.
1853
Extension of *Zollverein* in Germany to include all states except Austria.
1854
Outbreak of Crimean War. Battles of Balaclava, Inkerman.
1855
Siege of Sebastopol. Austrian threat to enter war against Russia. Russians seek peace.
1856
Peace Congress at Paris, ending Crimean War.
Prestige of Napoleon. Beautification of Paris, promotion of economic development by state.
1858
William I, Prussian King. Clash with legislature over military policy.
1859
Darwin's *Origin of Species*.
Mill, *On Liberty*.
French-Piedmont war against Austria; battle of Solferino. Withdrawal of France from the war.
1860
Garibaldi and March of the Thousand. Unification of most of Italy, via plebiscites.
1861
American Civil War, 1861–65.
Emancipation of Russian serfs.
Kingdom of Italy proclaimed.
1862
Bismarck becomes Prussian chief minister. Continues fight with *Landtag*.
1863
Unsuccessful rebellion in Poland. Prussia assists Russia in defeating it. Schleswig-Holstein question.
1864
Invasion of Schleswig by Austria and Prussia.
First International Workingmen's Association, organized by Karl Marx.
Syllabus of Errors, Pope Pius IX.
1865
Lister's antiseptic surgery.
French withdraw support from Emperor Maximilian in Mexico under U.S. pressure.
1866
Seven Weeks War, defeat of Austria by Prussia. Battle of Königgratz (Sadowa).
German Confederation ends; Austria excluded from German affairs.
Venetia added to Italy, during Austro-Prussian war which Italy joined.
Napoleon vainly demands compensation from Bismarck.
1867
Unsuccessful effort by Garibaldi to capture Rome, defended by French.
Second Reform Bill, England.
Reorganization of Austrian state into Dual Monarchy.
North German Confederation.
First volume of Marx's *Capital*.
1868
Overthrow of Queen Isabella of Spain. Hohenzollern candidacy for Spanish throne.
1869
Completion of Suez canal by French.
1870
French demands for withdrawal of Hohenzollern candidacy. Franco-Prussian War.
Battle of Sedan; defeat and abdication of Napoleon. Siege and surrender of Paris.
Withdrawal of French troops from Rome, seizure of Rome by Italians; completion of Italian unification.
1871
Proclamation of German Empire at Versailles. Treaty of peace signed at Frankfurt; annexation of Alsace and Lorraine by Germany.
Paris Commune.

Victorian stability and progress

The years around 1848–50 mark a dramatic and startling change in the mood of Europe. The revolutions of 1848 had a sobering, if not chilling, effect on the romantic idealism of the previous years. In politics, and in literature, art, and philosophy as well, the word is "realism." This means a retreat from romanticism in literature, from idealism in philosophy, from utopianism in politics. The "in" things, as we might put it, were science and a scientific philosophy called positivism; writing and art that avoided exotic or misty subjects for prosaic, even sordid, ones; hard-boiled and hard-headed political methods. This is the age of Comte, of Darwin, of Flaubert, and of Bismarck: names that suggest, in their various fields, a common denominator of scientific realism. At the same time, it is an era of stability and prosperity, following the hungry and revolutionary forties. Europe settled down for a generation to enjoy the fruits of industrialism after having gotten through its early growing pains.

The age took its name from England's queen. Queen Victoria arrived on the throne of England in 1837, after a period during which the British crown had commanded anything but respect. She was herself a not terribly handsome German girl whose popularity at first was very slight, she being a niece of the unlamented George IV. She soon began to set an example of virtue, of domestic felicity and respectability—her marriage to Prince Albert being among the happiest on record—which affected her entire court. No breath of scandal or indecorum was permitted to touch it. There were no more divorces, royal mistresses, or lovers as formerly. Victoria created a monarchy in the image of the respectable middle class. In so doing she did much to stabilize society and politics. As her long reign wore on, she took on the attributes not only of a national symbol but even an international one. For in this era of British ascendancy, when Lombard Street was the world's economical capital, and English liberalism the most widely shared article of political faith, "Victorian" became an adjective used to describe civilization over much of Europe and the United States.

It is an adjective which carries overtones of stability and of respectability, of the great middle class in its heyday, and of a complacent belief in the certainty of progress. It almost goes without saying that not all the phenomena fit this general description. There were rebels and radicals in Victorian times, and indeed few of its major writers, of whom there were many, were complacent. Some of them even dared treat of sex, allegedly taboo under Victoria.

Beginnings of trade unions

Still, the major trends were as described. Almost miraculously, the hungry forties gave way to the prosperous fifties. Between 1850 and 1874, real wages rose, modestly but steadily. While a 60-hour week generally prevailed, inordinately long by modern standards, the worst abuses of woman and child labor had been removed by the factory acts; and trade unions began, in a modest way, to help factory workers further improve their condition. The laws had been hostile to the growth of workers' organizations: in France even during the Revolution they had been forbidden (1791), and in England the act of 1799 did so; after a brief interlude of liberalization in 1824 they were subjected in 1825 to severe restrictions, though permitted to exist. Few respectable perons then doubted that they were "a fearful engine of mischief, ready to riot or assassinate," as a prominent Englishman wrote; and laissez-faire liberalism opposed them on principle. The political economists had impressed deeply upon the mind of middle-class England the idea that trade unions are a violation of the fundamental principle of free society: liberty of contract. Each individual worker must be free to make a bargain with his employer, they argued. But the unfairness of this principle became more and more evident, for the individual worker was so powerless compared to the great business concern that there was no equality at all.

Between 1850 and 1870 there was a significant tendency for unions to become respectable. They became, not large and general associations attempting to embrace all the working class with vaguely revolutionary goals, but *trade* unions representing a single craft: engineers, carpenters, tailors, bricklayers, and so on, each with their own craft union. Displaying a sense of responsibility as well as greater bargaining strength, the unions got their magna carta of legal recognition in 1871 in Great Britain (not until 1884 in France), though many disputes about the exact boundaries of their power lay ahead. They became an all-important instrument both for improving the material lot of at least some of the workers, and for raising them to the level of responsible and respectable members of society. The skilled workingmen were learning to organize and bargain for higher wages; their leaders were at pains to stress that this was not a revolutionary movement, but an effort to improve the condition of the workers within the boundaries of the existing capitalist system. Appearing before parliamentary committees, union leaders impressed that gentlemanly club with their intelligence and moderation: members of Commons discovered to their surprise that working-class leaders were not all shouting rabble-rousers.

An improving age

But it was the era of the bourgeoisie, not the workers, and testifying to the success of bourgeois capitalism was the steady advance of technology. A landmark in British history was the so-called Crystal Palace exhibition of 1851. With Queen Victoria and Prince Albert glowingly presiding, the exhibition was a monument to national pride and to the age of progress. The vast "palace" of glass and steel erected in suburban London to house the fair impressed people as an architectural wonder; within its spacious walls the products of British industry testified to the rising standard of living, at least for the middle classes. Nineteenth-century inventiveness had begun its long parade of useful gadgets: the telegraph, the telephone, the oceanic cable, the locomotive, electricity with all its consequences. The 1851 exhibition appeared on the threshold of this age of invention.

It was an "age of improvement." The history of improvements in human comfort is one too often unwritten. Most 17th-century cities had displayed

The Crystal Palace exhibition which Queen Victoria opened in 1851 exemplified Britain's industrial prosperity and self-confidence.

sanitary conditions comparable to those of Madrid, where every night at 11, on a signal, the sewage was thrown into the streets. The more advanced countries were beginning to do better than that by the age of Louis XIV, but even the Sun King's Versailles was both uncomfortable and unsanitary to a degree appalling to present taste. Historians of London give credit to a certain Myddleton for making perhaps the greatest contribution to the welfare of that city ever achieved by one man, when in the later 17th century he gave her a fresh water supply. It remained for the 19th century to bring a sewerage system. Napoleon I, who made vast improvements in the city of Paris, provided the city with adequate fresh water for the first time, and also, among other things, organized an effective fire-fighting system which still survives. His nephew's thorough modernization of the city with sewers and water systems was one of his greatest achievements. And in Britain "Victorian comfort" meant running water and modern plumbing, paved streets and improved public health. The growing size of cities posed formidable problems of providing for human needs; in meeting these an heroic generation of engineer-reformers did much to better the condition of the appallingly dirty and dreary urban masses. Of these men, the most famous in Great Britain was Edwin Chadwick, author of the Sanitary Report of 1842 and thereafter for many years crusader for public health through effective public sanitation.

Liberal government

Free trade helped distribute prosperity in this period. Between the repeal of the Corn Laws in England in 1846 and the revival of protectionism in Germany and the United States in the 1870's lay the classic "free-trade" era, in which the gospel according to Manchester was seldom questioned. The growing economy of the United States of America went free trade in 1846, though during the Civil War this began to be modified. A crowning event was the free trade treaty between Britain and France in 1860. Dozens of other such treaties were exchanged. The German *Zollverein* (customs union) prepared the way for the political unification of Germany under Bismarck, and until 1879 the new German state pursued liberal economic policies.

Depressions, "panics," periods of severe economic crisis, which were an unnerving feature of the capitalist economy, did not strike severely during this interval. There was no major depression until the mid-1870's, the short ones of 1857 and 1867 not being prolonged or disastrous. Perhaps the Crimean War (1854–55), the American Civil War (1861–65), and the Franco-Prussian War (1870–71), along with several other minor wars, helped feed the economies at crucial times. But the welfare state had not yet arrived, and the watchword in government expenditures was economy. Gladstone made his reputation in England by reducing taxes while balancing the budget. The great Liberal statesman regarded an income tax as simply dishonest, a view shared by most of his contemporaries. The prosperity of England in this, her most prosperous era, was based on free enterprise, competition, full protection for property rights, low taxes, cheap government—policies which received the endorsement of the economic theorists of the time.

Victorian stability rested on a firm economic foundation, it appeared, while it manifested itself in a successful social and political order. England gave the world a prime example of orderly government on a popular basis, a balance of limited monarchy, Parliament, and people, with political parties providing the threads that bound them all together. In politics too this was an "age of equilibrium," as one historian has named it. Mass democracy had not yet arrived. Writing in the 1860's, the erudite and elegant Walter Bagehot, in the best book ever written on the English constitution, attributed its success precisely to the fact that the lower classes still exhibited a proper deference to their betters: they elected gentlemen to Parliament.[1] In any case only about 1 in 5 adult male Englishmen had the vote. Victorian society showed sharp class divisions. But somehow, with the aid of political parties and able

[1] The landed gentry of England continued to prosper in this era; fears that agriculture would be ruined by the repeal of the grain tariffs did not materialize until about 1880, for the growing cities provided an abundant market and foreign competition did not become formidable until later. Some thought this era the crowning one for the squires, and it was still true that successful industrialists and merchants tended to buy land in order to acquire the prestige of being a country gentleman.

leaders of these parties, the system worked. The most important innovation appeared to be the political parties. Successful operation of the party system presupposed a fundamental unity—in Bagehot's words, "a people so safely at one that they can afford to bicker." Liberal and Conservative could engage in mock warfare because they now knew it would never pass beyond the stage of words. With one party to take the ball and carry it as far as it could, and the "loyal opposition" trying to bring it down, the game was played within the confines of public opinion.

By 1864, after an era dominated by the personalities of Lords Palmerston and Russell, came the age of Gladstone and Disraeli. The Liberal and Conservative parties each presented an imposing figure, national in his appeal, to win the attention of the increasing British electorate as none had done before. They engaged in a mighty clash of phrases and, in some measure, principles. The party system enabled reform to take place peacefully.

Extension of the vote, 1867

In 1867 another electoral reform bill increased the percentage of voters among the adult males from about 20 percent to 35 percent—doubling the electorate, a step criticized by some as "shooting Niagara," in Carlyle's phrase, but inevitable and supported by both major parties. The outcome of the Civil War in the United States had something to do with this trend. Believing now that democracy was inevitable sooner or later, each of the rival political parties wished to gain credit for bestowing the vote on the working class. When the Liberals brought forth a moderate reform bill, Disraeli trumped their ace with a stronger one! The wily Conservative leader had a supple, sophisticated mind, along with a sense of humor more than a little aroused by the thought of beating the Whigs or Liberals at their own game. He would "steal their clothes while they were in swimming." A few Tories broke away, but he held together enough to carry the bill, aided by Liberal votes, after a series of amendments had made it even stronger. Accompanied by cries of anguish from those who declared this "leap in the dark" to be fraught with danger, the Second Reform Act of 1867 gave the vote to practically everybody living in cities who could claim a permanent residence, whether property owner or not. In brief, it enfranchised the urban working class. The rural wage workers were not let in until 1884. But the critical step toward universal adult suffrage had been taken.

Gladstone and reform

Galvanized by this action, Great Britain moved immediately into a great reform period, the greatest perhaps of the century, during Gladstone's first ministry, from 1868 to 1874. The people as well as Parliament followed a man they had come to worship as few statesmen ever have been worshipped. One politician confided that when he was asked a puzzling question at a political rally, his strategy was to mention the name of Gladstone; this was sure to set off five minutes of cheering, and he had time to think of his answer! Gladstone was to head the government four times, for a total of some 15 years, before his death in 1898 (1868–74; 1880–85; 1886; 1892–94). He

Gladstone

Disraeli

was to lose some of his popularity, with some people, in the course of the many political wars he fought. But he remained the greatest political figure of the time; this was the Age of Gladstone. His popularity rested on a combination of great ability with tremendous moral earnestness—and on his faith in the people.

The Elementary Education Act of 1870 began the momentous job of setting up a public school system for all children; attendance was made compulsory in 1880. Robert Lowe, a notable opponent of the suffrage extension of 1867, allegedly was the author of the remark, after its passage, that, "We must educate our masters." Edward Cardwell's reforming years in the War Office under Gladstone resulted, among other things, in ending the old aristocratic system of purchasing commissions. In 1870, too, as noted, the trade unions received their "magna carta," though picketing had yet to be granted legal approval.

The "people" came closer to government. Gladstone, who did so much to make politics popular, once generously praised the English public for having been, on major issues, righter than their leaders, and he saw the masses improving themselves steadily. It is a fact that crime, poverty, and drunkenness decreased steadily after 1842, when they had been at a peak. The middle classes and lower classes both shared an evangelical Christian piety, the result of the Methodist movement perhaps more than anything else, which expressed itself in an impulse to reform morals and vanquish such social evils as drunkenness, crime, prostitution. Anyone who has ever read a "temperance tract" of the times (in England or the United States) knows what this spirit was.

Belief in progress

The improvement should not be exaggerated. Much misery and degradation remained at the bottom of the Victorian social scale. In England class lines were still sharp, and there was as yet no "welfare state." But with the export trade increasing by leaps and bounds, some workers dressing and acting like gentlemen, social evils overcome, and the constitution in successful and increasingly democratic operation, it is no wonder that Victorian England believed in progress, and was optimistic to the point of complacency. Its chief intellectual figures were John Stuart Mill, the classic spokesman of liberalism, and Charles Darwin, whose clinching arguments for biological evolution constituted this generation's most sensational discovery, and was perhaps even the discovery of the century. The chief prophet was Herbert Spencer, who combined the doctrine of natural selection (survival of the fittest) with economic liberalism, and told the Victorian middle classes, to their great satisfaction, that they were right to compete as fiercely as they could and let those who could not keep up in the race perish. This was, he assured them, the rule of nature and the path of progress. Thus was the great prestige of science thrown over the reign of the Victorian middle classes. But it would be unfair to present Spencer as fully representative: a more generous spirit of reform could be found in Evangelical religion, in Mill's liberalism, in the famous novels of Charles Dickens and George Eliot, and in the social criticism of Matthew Arnold and John Ruskin.

The Second Empire: Stability and statism

France under the rule of Napoleon III differed somewhat from England in the age of Liberals and Conservatives. The Emperor permitted a "fig-leaf for autocracy" in the form of a popularly elected parliament, but no real power was allowed it, and no opposition permitted—"loyal" or otherwise—for many years. The *coup d'état* of December 1–2, 1851 had dissolved the legislature, and Louis Napoleon arrested and deported all who resisted. He submitted both the suspension of the old constitution and the erection of a new empire, headed by himself, to a popular plebiscite. The vote overwhelmingly favored both. The plebiscite was not entirely fair, but there is not much doubt about the fact that a great majority of Frenchmen did favor this move. "If the *coup d'état* was a crime France was less its victim than its accomplice," it has been said. Many great Frenchmen, however, never forgave Bonaparte his calculated blow against liberty.

Napoleon III

Napoleon III as a personality was hardly a good imitation of his famous uncle. Personally he was so unprepossessing that many had thought it impossible even with his name for him to get anywhere in politics. He came to power more as a myth than as a man, his name appearing as a refuge against the disorders of the revolution and evoking fond memories of past glory. He was hailed by those who could claim to have frozen a nose at Moscow, but also by those who remembered that Bonapartes restored order and protected property. Once in power, he proved by no means a cipher. History has not made up its mind about the nephew any more than about the uncle. That the former was the less brilliant man would be agreed, but in some of Louis Napoleon's achievements during his 20-year domination of France, one can see considerable value. The image of him as the tyrant pure and simple—a view held by some—appears much too simple. His intents were to pacify France, to secure a consensus, and to lead the way back to responsible self-government.

Napoleonic policies

Napoleon's wish to serve his people by solid social achievements was unquestionably sincere. He had written and thought much about what "the Napoleonic ideas" meant. His book on "the extinction of pauperism" indicated a Saint-Simonian bent to his thought, and in fact the emperor called himself, half humorously, a socialist. Some of his ideas for bringing the state into fruitful cooperation with private industry were truly constructive. And he sought to relax the dictatorship when France was ready for liberty, introducing some measure of representative government in the latter years of his reign. "Order precedes liberty" was Napoleon's maxim. But liberty would come in its season, he promised, and proceeded to carry out this promise in the later years of his reign. In the 1860's he proclaimed a new phase, the "Liberal empire," marked by increasing liberties and parliamentary government. There was less laissez-faire and more government in the French economy than the British. There were great public works programs, among them the wholesale face-lifting job done on the city of Paris: the boulevard system, the Opera, a good part of Paris as tourists have known it ever since, came into being. There was also the construction of the fabulous Suez Canal by a French company with state backing. As Prince Albert had done in 1851, Napoleon III did in 1855 and again in 1867—he promoted a huge industrial exhibition, designed to display the wonders of modern science and technology, and incidentally bring tourists to see the new capital. These international shows were a fad of the times. The United States had one in 1876 on its hundredth birthday. They were a tribute to the idea of progress, under the banner of science.

Use of the state to stimulate a basically private enterprise economy reminds one somewhat of the later American "New Deal," and was as controversial: critics pointed to jobbery and corruption and said France would have flourished at least as much without Bonaparte's state banks and resettlement projects. But his conception of the state as "not a necessary evil but the beneficent engine of the whole social organism" was original and challenging.

Socialism and trade unionism got short shrift, however. It was a crime until 1864 to go on strike; unions were only legalized in 1868. But Bonaparte made a free-trade treaty with Britain against the protests of the manufacturers, and listened to advice from Saint-Simonian planners. He entered into war in 1859, with Austria, largely if not completely out of zeal for the cause of national unity for Italy; then he became Bismarck's dupe perhaps chiefly because he was too much a man of peace. Though the man who overthrew the Second Republic appeared as a cruel tyrant to some great Frenchmen such as Victor Hugo and Alexis de Tocqueville, he can be regarded as having prepared France for the Third Republic that followed. At any rate France did proceed toward liberal democracy in the next era.

The liberal decade

This decade of the 1860's could well be described as the high point of 19th-century liberalism. It began with Garibaldi, and the Russian emancipation of the serfs; it included the victory over slavery in the American Civil War, and the 1867 Reform Act and Gladstone's ensuing reform administration in Great Britain. The free-trade treaty was a part of its liberalism. By the 1860's Louis Napoleon had moved away from dictatorship and toward the "Liberal Empire" and was sharing power with an elected legislature while permitting free speech. The greatest writings of the decade addressed themselves to the theme: John Stuart Mill's *On Liberty* and *Representative Government*, for example. And the unifications of Germany and Italy were widely regarded as triumphs for the liberal principle of national self-determination, however illiberal the methods used to secure this goal.

Nationalism and realistic statecraft: The "Risorgimento"

These unification movements were the most sensational achievements of these years. Accustomed to playing star roles, France and Great Britain had to yield the stage to Italy and Germany from 1860 to 1870. These formerly weak, divided nations found their way to national unity at last, and this achievement dominated the decade. The means by which this was done were those of the consummately skillful realists, Otto von Bismarck of Germany and Count Camilli di Cavour of Piedmont, men who raised the realistic spirit in statecraft to its highest point. Because they accomplished the seemingly impossible with the aid of a bag of diplomatic tricks, legends grew around both men. Actually they only made skillful use of the opportunities presented them by the rivalries and feuds of the other powers of Europe.

The Crimean War

Probably the best place to begin this chapter of diplomatic history is with the first major outbreak of hostilities in 40 years, which took place in 1854. In that year Europe had had a war, seemingly a rather meaningless one—the Crimean War. Famous for the Charge of the Light Brigade and Florence Nightingale, it has sometimes been dubbed the most futile of wars. Its origins chiefly concerned the plans of Nicholas I of Russia for disposing of the remains of "the sick man of Europe," as he called the Ottoman Empire. Though it was hard to deny that the Turk was indeed sick, France and Great Britain did not intend that his possessions should fall into the hands of Russia. The British, including Queen Victoria and the Prime Minister, Lord Palmerston, were quite anti-Russian. A concern about Russian encroachments in the direction of India was probably the chief reason for this hostility, along with the unpopularity in a progressive country of the power which represented reaction and despotism. The war was bitterly opposed by some British liberals, but was tremendously popular when it began. Perhaps people simply were weary of peace after 40 years of it.

The Emperor Napoleon, who had announced that "the Empire means peace," was nevertheless expected as a Bonaparte to possess a little martial glory. He made himself the champion of Roman Catholics in the holy city of Jerusalem, and sought to revive the traditional Napoleonic interest in the Near East. Nicholas of Russia, grown old and irritable, took peremptory action in sending troops into the Turkish provinces of Rumania, which were under Russian protection. The Turks defied Russia, were backed by Britain, and the western powers sent an equally peremptory ultimatum to Russia to stay out of Turkey. The opinion of most historians has been that a reasonable compromise should have been possible, had there not been a good deal of war fever in the air. It was not the last time, though, that the "eastern question," caused chiefly by the weakness and misrule of Turkey in Europe, and the rivalry of all the great powers over this strategically important area of southeastern Europe, would cause severe trouble.

After a spell of quite bloody fighting on the Crimean peninsula, the Allies got a victory and ended the war forcing the Russians to promise to keep

their warships off the Black Sea. From the Crimean War France and Louis Napoleon emerged with some prestige, the British with little except memories of the hapless but gallant Charge of the Light Brigade and of Florence Nightingale's heroic nursing, the Russians with a sobering lesson in their technical backwardness. The chief gainers were the two master diplomats, Cavour and Bismarck, who took little part in the war but turned it to their advantage by astute diplomacy. Cavour brought Piedmont (Sardinia) into the war, not because he cared anything about the war as such but because he wished to gain support for Italian unification. Bismarck observed the estrangement of Russia from the western powers, and from Austria, which Russia blamed for her "ingratitude" in not lending aid. It would provide him with opportunities for maneuver. The Crimean War marked a change in the whole pattern of European diplomacy since 1815 in that the "Holy Alliance" was ruptured, Russia emerging with a real bitterness against Austria for not standing by her, while Britain joined her old foe France.

"Realpolitik"

In the aftermath of the failures of 1848, both Italy and Germany turned to *Realpolitik* as a means of achieving their goals. *Realpolitik* as practiced by these master poker players might be defined as diplomacy which was

The siege of Sebastopol in the Crimean War, October 23, 1854, a high point in the Anglo-French war against Russia

shrewd and devoid of all scruples. More particularly, it meant forming alliances without regard for sentiment or ideology. There was nothing new in this, doubtless, and yet since 1815 there had been strong traditional alignments based on sentiments and ideologies, especially between the monarchical states of the East. Bismarck thoroughly shocked the Prussian king by suggesting an alliance with France. Soon men were to realize that probably never before in European history had a diplomatic craftsman of Bismarck's skill existed. He was a combination of Richelieu, Frederick the Great, and Metternich—or so, at least, an astounded Europe soon came to feel.

Franco-Austro-Italian War

The dramatic unifications of Italy and of Germany began to unfold in the late 1850's. Louis Napoleon, who had fought with the Carbonari in his youth, had the Italian sympathies of his family and was in addition enthusiastic for the cause of nationalism in general. Early in 1858 the Italian patriot Orsini tried to assassinate the Emperor with a bomb, and while executing the would-be regicide Napoleon was moved by Orsini's plea that he "do something for Italy." In 1858 Cavour got Napoleon to agree secretly to join Piedmont in a war on Austria if it could be so arranged as to make it look like Austria was to blame. For a man of Cavour's talents this was a mere trifle.

France was to get Savoy and Nice, while Piedmont was to absorb Lombardy, Venetia, and the rest of Italy north of the Papal States (see map). Austria fell into Cavour's trap and was made to appear the aggressor. France entered the war and fought two engagements with the Austrians at Magenta and Solferino, the latter an extremely bloody battle. Revolutions took place in the duchies of northern Italy (Tuscany, Modena, Parma), and a nationalist feeling began to sweep over the whole peninsula. But Napoleon lost his taste for the war and withdrew, causing Cavour immense anguish. The French Emperor doubtless wondered why he was fighting for Italy when he needed to stand guard against rising Prussia. However, it was too late to stop the national uprising of Italy. Garibaldi returned with an army of Red Shirts and, after coming to Genoa to fight the French for Nice, decided to go to Sicily and help a rebellion which had broken out in the Kingdom of Naples.

Garibaldi: and the "Risorgimento"

The "March of the 1,000" quickly became one of the most sensational exploits of the century. This national hero, acclaimed by the people, overthrew the Neapolitans in Sicily, crossed the straits and marched on triumphantly to Naples, the King fleeing. Revolution broke out next in the Papal States. Garibaldi advanced from the south and Sardinian troops from the north, defeating papal forces and Neapolitans. The eventual result of all this was the proclamation of the Kingdom of Italy in 1861. French troops defended the city of Rome, and Venetia remained in the hands of Austria, but the rest of the peninsula voted by plebiscite to join the new kingdom, under the King of Sardinia and with the 1848 constitution of that state. Garibaldi continued to organize efforts to seize Rome. French defense of that city poisoned relations between France and the new Italy.

Venetia was to be gained in 1866 and Rome in 1870, completing the unification of Italy. It had been a stirring process, but one in which the guile of Cavour was as important as the courage of Garibaldi. Indeed, the intrepid guerrilla chieftain became something of a nuisance to the Italian government in his later years, since he was always gathering an expedition to march on something, usually Rome, the result of which was to further irritate the French and invite intervention.

Contrary to what was widely believed, the *Risorgimento* had not owed its all to a vast and spontaneous movement of nationalism which united all classes. When Cavour succeeded in persuading Garibaldi to halt his march on Rome and accept orders from Piedmont, his maneuvers reflected the fear of moderates lest the flamboyant radical hero get out of hand. The moderates desired national unity for practical purposes but—rather like the American Federalists of 1787–89—sought to dissociate it from a too democratic movement. Under Cavour's skillful leadership they largely succeeded; he was the Hamilton of the *Risorgimento*. Both Mazzini and Garibaldi subsequently denounced the new Italy as a betrayal of all they had been fighting for. Other Italians were to complain that they had been annexed to Piedmont and that there was too little local liberty.

Unification of Italy 1859-1871

Independent states joined Kingdom of Italy in years shown on map.

Northern Boundary of Italy, 1871

Kingdom of Sardinia, 1815–1859

Joined to Sardinia and Kingdom of Italy, 1860–1861

Joined to Kingdom of Italy 1866–1870

The American Civil War

But for much of liberal Europe Garibaldi was a romantic symbol; he was the spirit of a people, the soldier of freedom, the liberator of humanity. In 1861 Europe watched the Italian drama with greater interest than it did that other drama being played out in the far-away United States: the American Civil War. As the British public cheered the name of Garibaldi, the British Navy had tacitly helped him to invade Italy.

The Civil War did excite Europe to some extent. The cause of the South generally appealed to conservatives, that of the North to liberals and radicals. Popular opinion in Britain probably helped prevent a policy of recognition of the Confederacy and aid to it which might have changed the complexion of the war. The Northern victory and the figure of Lincoln advanced the cause of democracy in Europe. Upon the outbreak of the American Civil War, a tense drama began, familiar to students of American history, upon the outcome of which the result of the American war may have hinged: would Great Britain recognize, and aid, the Confederate secessionists? Counting on the power of "King Cotton," the South was sure they would. Union diplomacy exerted itself to the utmost to prevent this. British public opinion strenuously debated the pros and cons of the American strife, wondering whether South or North was morally right. Though the North represented antislavery, it threw away this advantage at first by stating that the aim of the war was not to overthrow slavery but to prevent secession. Some English liberals sympa-

Prince Otto von Bismarck

thized with the Southern cause on grounds of freedom, self-determination, and the right to independence. But the working class rallied strongly to the North, and after much hesitation, and after allowing two powerful warships to be built for the Confederacy, the British government withheld recognition, refused to break the Union blockade, built no more warships for the South.

Blunders of Louis Napoleon

Louis Napoleon, who usually looked bad in foreign affairs in his later years, made no exception in the Italian matter. He had gained Savoy and Nice, but while helping to create a strong new state he had not gained its friendship, for his abrupt withdrawal from the war and his garrisoning of Rome convinced most Italians of his hostility to them. British opinion had been favorably stirred by the Italian cause, and Palmerston had helped Garibaldi cross the straits from Sicily; the greed of the French in acquiring Nice and Savoy aroused old British suspicions of France, and so the French Emperor lost much of the friendship he had gained when France allied with Britain in the Crimean War. He also went astray when he tried to take advantage of the American Civil War to put a puppet emperor on the throne of Mexico.

Bismarck and German unification

Bismarck watched this episode with an eye to exploiting the jealousies, ambitions, and ill-feeling it had produced. Otto von Bismarck was a conservative, and as such not initially a German nationalist. He was temperamentally hostile to the vague abstractions and misty ideals of literary leftists; his strength lay in his realistic power to understand and mold concrete, immediate situations. He had opposed the revolutions of 1848 and was a Prussian patriot, not a German one. Independent, headstrong, and impulsive, Bismarck in his youth was an extreme reactionary and hailed the defeat both of the 1848 revolution and of a unified Germany, which he feared would submerge the Prussian aristocracy under a tide of south German liberalism. It is one of the chief ironies of history that he himself was to lead such a movement later. Sent down to be Prussia's delegate to the Confederation precisely because he was thought to be pro-Austrian and antinationalist, his combative instincts, always extremely strong, led him soon to oppose Austrian domination of the Confederation. He found the Austrians arrogant and was too proud a Prussian to accept the part of second-fiddle to the Hapsburgs. Thus he was to become the instrument of Prussian aggrandizement which turned into German unification.

Bismarck and the liberals

Bismarck first came to the notice of Europe, rather unfavorably, when he fought the liberals in Prussia in a quarrel over the army. As chief minister of the new King, William (Wilhelm) I (1861–88), Bismarck defied the *Landtag* (parliament) which had refused to vote money for an expansion of the regular army. (The liberal-dominated parliament preferred to base the military system in good part on the more democratic *Landwehr* or local militia, which the professional soldiers scorned and wished to abolish.) He went ahead with the army plans anyway, an apparently unconstitutional act which aroused a storm of protest and convinced many that Bismarck was a madman. But the army that Prussian generals Moltke and Roon were building was no ordinary army.

Schleswig-Holstein affair

Bismarck moved rapidly to make his gamble pay off. In 1863, a complex dispute arose with Denmark over the duchies of Schleswig and Holstein (which had caused trouble inopportunely before, in 1848). The duchies had long been in a personal union with the King of Denmark, who now died leaving no male heir. They were largely German-speaking (especially Holstein) but some of the inhabitants wanted autonomy under the Duke of Augustenberg. Bismarck succeeded in persuading France and Britain of the merit of the Prussian case based on nationality. Austria claimed a right to share in this decision. Bismarck picked a quarrel with Austria as an outgrowth of this action, turned quickly on her, and almost before Europe could catch its breath, crushed the Austrians at the great battle of Sadowa in 1866.

The Seven Weeks War

Austria had been well isolated. Bismarck noted that she had alienated Russia in the Crimean War, while Italy was ready to join Prussia against her in order to redeem Venice. France and Austria, who had fought against each other in 1859 upon the occasion of Napoleon's pro-Italian intervention, had drawn a bit closer together again, but Bismarck correctly calculated that France would not fight for Austria (as Austria was to refuse to fight for France in 1870). Bismarck played upon Napoleon's pro-Italian and pro-nationalist sympathies. His evidently reckless course was in reality carefully prepared. The army showed its technical and organizational superiority, moving troops via the railroads with great speed and carefully planning its strategy with the aid of the famous general staff system. Moltke, probably the greatest of all students of war, had learned much about the uses of railroad and telegraph. The new and more easily loaded "needle gun" was another Prussian innovation. At one great battle (Sadowa, or Königgrätz) not far from the border, the Austrians were smashed and the war ended almost as soon as it started. The Prussian defeat of Austria in the Seven Weeks War of 1866 amazed and shocked Europe, which had regarded Austria as stronger than Prussia. Europe woke up to the fact that it had a double genius on its hands: the diplomacy of Bismarck and the military leadership of Moltke.

What Bismarck intended was not yet clear. He persuaded the Kaiser (with difficulty) to treat Austria with great leniency, only dissolving the Frankfurt Confederation and excluding Austria from German affairs. It was an amazing example of clemency toward the foe, and the realism of Bismarck may be seen in his remark that, "We will need the Austrians later." With Austria excluded, Prussia was the undisputed master, and the small states were helpless; she now annexed several of them and organized others in a new North German Confederation. South of the Main, Bavaria, Württemberg, and Baden remained independent but had to ally with Prussia.

Meanwhile Napoleon, for whom this Prussian success, as he belatedly realized, represented a staggering defeat, moved toward conflict with Prussia. The blundering Emperor first asked for compensation in the form of Luxembourg and Belgium. Bismarck refused; later he used this French demand, which had been unwarily put in writing, to increase British suspicions of France and neutralize Britain during Germany's war with France. From 1867 on Napoleon prepared himself for inevitable conflict with Prussia, while Bismarck too assumed that war with France would have to come. He now had adopted definitely the goal of a greater Germany under Prussian leadership, and probably wished to attach the south German states to a German Reich, too. They would have to go some place, and Bismarck had gone too far to stop short of complete success. He had become a convert to nationalism because as a practical statesman he recognized that it was a force too strong to resist. In his memoirs, written years later, the great realist wrote that, "Only through a common national war against the traditionally aggressive neighbor," i.e., France, could the north-south breach in Germany be healed. However, there is some evidence that this was an afterthought, and that Bismarck, who cared little for the Catholic South Germans, really had this next step largely forced on him by the flow of events and the anger of France. Some historians have warned against the "Bismarck legend," which he attempted to establish in his famous memoirs—the legend that he had a master plan and foresaw all contingencies far in advance. It only looked that way later.

Defeat of German liberals

Cultural and religious differences between south and north Germans existed; so also did opposition between German liberals and conservatives. The idea of being unified by Bismarck's "blood and iron" methods was not pleasing to numerous Germans. They feared Prussianism, militarism, autocracy. The Prussian defeat of Austria weakened them, but there remained much opposition in these southern states to their absorption by Prussia. In Prussia, however, Bismarck's success melted opposition. The Liberals in the Prussian parliament yielded in their fight, and a portion of them as National Liberals came over to his side. Conservative Prussians were not so sure they liked this man whose methods were so unconservative, but there was no serious opposition to Bismarck, rapidly assuming the stature of the century's greatest statesman.

Significance of Seven Weeks War

The Seven Weeks War of 1866 thus was of great significance. It broke up a connection of many centuries between Austria and Germany and by doing so cast the die for a new Europe, with a nationalistic Germany emerging under Prussian leadership while Austria was condemned to be an uneasy ruler over non-Germanic peoples in southeastern Europe. The rise of Prussia at Austria's expense consummated a process begun long before, no doubt, and yet the statesmen of 1815 had realized how important it was for the balance of power that Prussia be kept in check by means of a strong Austria.

The events of 1866 went far to increase the force of nationalism in Europe. Italy picked up Venetia at this time and thus virtually completed her unification. Last but not least, the triumph of Bismarck over the forces of constitutional liberalism in Germany—which were very much in existence heretofore—meant that the new Prusso-German national state would tend to be a militaristic and authoritarian one.

The Franco-Prussian War and its results

Origins of the war

Helping to kindle Franco-German enmity was the candidacy of a Hohenzollern (of the southern German, Catholic branch of the family, not the Prussian royal family) to the vacant throne of Spain. A revolution in that country in 1868 drove out the immoral and incompetent Queen Isabella. Bismarck did not initiate the Hohenzollern candidacy, but was suspected of having used it to provoke the French. It is not clear that this was so, but the hostile reaction of an already alarmed France was understandable. Napoleon, whose prestige had by now been badly shaken, demanded the withdrawal of the Hohenzollern. At Ems, the French ambassador imperiously asked William of Prussia not only to disavow the candidacy but to apologize and promise never to renew such claims. He went considerably beyond what was necessary, and gave Bismarck an opportunity, which he did not miss, to publish to the world evidence that the French were being intolerably aggressive.

Some later historians accused Bismarck of deliberately bringing on war by his editing of the "Ems dispatch." The fact is that the French were already well along on the road to war; Bismarck for his part did not refuse the challenge. Since 1867, the French had known they could not let Bismarck wrest control of Europe from them without a war, while the latter knew that he would have to beat France if he wanted to erect a powerful German state on her borders. While the French Emperor himself wavered—not wanting war but not wanting peace either, as he once said—important members of his cabinet definitely pushed for war, with the apparent approval of a considerable majority of Frenchmen. So the showdown took place, but once more Bismarck was the master.

Again, diplomacy had isolated the foe in advance. Russia was brought off with Prussian support for her denunciation of the Crimean War Black Sea clauses, while Britain heard about France's desire for Belgium. Italy saw a chance to drive the French out of Rome and add that city to the Italian kingdom. Austria, too, stayed quiet. In the last analysis, it was probably the blunders of Louis Napoleon which caused him to be isolated. No one in Europe in 1870 trusted the French monarch. On the other hand, the French were supremely confident of their ability to crush the upstart Prussians and march quickly to Berlin, without any need for allies. Most of Europe was betting the same way, for in past times, France had normally been much the stronger. ("The first serious encounter between the Prussian army and the French," wrote British Prime Minister Palmerston, "would be little less disastrous to Prussia than the battle of Jena.") So the rest of Europe stood aside and held the ring, content to watch the war between the luck and skill of Prussia and the apparently greater strength of an aroused France, led again by a Bonaparte.

This Bonaparte was not like the last one. Never warlike, Louis Napoleon was now old and ill. Prussian strategy was again based on knowledge and use of the railroads, and this strategy again went like clockwork while the French seemed inadequately prepared. Overconfidence certainly played its part in the French defeat—an overconfidence completely unjustified in view of Prussian progress in war while the French had largely stood still since the time of Napoleon I. The French capital soon reeled under the news of defeats.

The French debacle

This war was decided within six weeks. On perhaps the darkest day in French history—for even Waterloo had been more glorious—an army commanded by the Emperor himself surrendered at Sedan on September 2, following which Napoleon abdicated. After this a republic was proclaimed and a new government rallied something of the national spirit to fight on for several months, but the task was hopeless, the citizen army being more zealous than skilled. Émile Zola called his novel on the war "La Debacle," and it was nothing less than a debacle for France. It was a triumph of science and organization over the mere enthusiasm, the patriotic *élan,* on which the French had counted. Neither numbers nor spirit seemed any longer to count against scientific knowledge and thoroughness. The defeat has often been construed as an adverse judgment on the whole reign of Napoleon III, too sweeping a judgment; but he did make a sad exit.

Civil war in France; Paris Commune of 1871

The aftermath of the Franco-Prussian war was civil war in Paris. More casualties resulted from this struggle than from any one battle against the Germans. Frenchmen fought each other while Germans outside the city looked on in amazement and contempt. Seeking a stable French government with which to negotiate peace, Bismarck had granted an armistice during which elections were held to a new national assembly. It is difficult to think of another war in which the defeated people voted, under the auspices of the victors, to decide whether to fight on or make peace. The result was overwhelmingly in favor of peace, almost everywhere except in the city of Paris. The city of Paris proudly refused to accept the government of the *"capitulards"* or the humiliating peace it was prepared to make. The Parisians rebelled against the Germans, proclaiming their autonomy as a "commune," i.e., free city. Parisian radical thought was then much influenced by the "federalist" idea of such socialists as Proudhon, to whom the ideal state was a loose federation of locally self-governing communities. As the Germans stood by and watched, the regular French government's troops first beseiged and then stormed Paris, in an attack that France was not soon to forget. A good deal of historic Paris, including the Tuileries palace, was destroyed and 20,000 people lost their lives in this grim civil war; thousands more fled or were deported in the punishment that followed. It was worse than 1848 or 1792. Both sides seemed to have been equally bloodthirsty and averse to

Communards of the 1871 Paris Commune destroy the Napoleon Column in Place Vendôme.

compromise. France, it must be remembered, was suffering from the trauma of military defeat and from the political confusion attending the shamefaced abdication of Napoleon III. The "bloody week" of Paris in May, 1871, climaxed probably the worst year France had ever had.

Terms of peace

France made peace at the price of ceding Alsace and part of Lorraine to the Germans, paying an indemnity of five billion francs, and, more humiliating yet, watching the official creation of the German Empire in ceremonies (January 18, 1871) at the palace of Versailles. It has seemed to historians that Bismarck would have served Germany better by a more magnanimous treatment of the vanquished foe. However, in the intoxicating hour of triumph after centuries of being humiliated by France, it was perhaps too much to expect of human nature to be less jubilant. German military leaders insisted upon the retention of the strategically vital Metz-Strasbourg area in order to prevent French renewal of the war at a later date, and Bismarck was inclined to believe that France would always be a mortal foe in any case.

France became a republic, but only because the monarchists could not agree, as between Orléanists and Legitimists. The veteran statesman Adolphe Thiers presided over an interim government and soon began to feel that "a republic divides us least"—a conservative republic. But for several years the life of the Third Republic was precarious. France paid off the indemnity within a few years and resumed her usual economic life; this short war had

Unification of Germany 1815-1871

Prussia, 1815

Added to Prussia, 1866

North German Confederation (with Prussia), 1866

Added to NGC to make German Empire, 1871

Boundary of North German Confederation, 1866–1871

Boundary of the German Empire, 1871–1918

not devastated or crippled her. It had severely injured her pride, and deprived her of territory the memory of which was continually kept alive by refugee leaders from the "lost provinces," but as decades went by without further war Europe's confidence in an era of peace and prosperity grew. Not until 1914 was there to be another major European war. There was a serious war scare in 1875, when Germany apparently contemplated a preventive war against a France that seemed to be recovering with alarming rapidity. But Bismarck thought better of it and thereafter successfully pursued a policy of both keeping France diplomatically isolated and plying her with small favors.

The Second Reich

Germany became the German Empire, in conscious imitation of the old medieval Reich. The German states of the south—Bavaria, Württemberg, Baden, Hesse—joined the northern confederation to create a new, unified state, with the King of Prussia as the Emperor of Germany and a national Reichstag or assembly. There was also an upper house in which the representation was by states; and the states retained a good many rights and powers. They executed the laws and ran the courts. Only certain specified powers were given to the national government. But Prussia was the giant among these states; in the Bundesrat or upper house she held about 30 percent of the seats, and controlled others among the tiny states of the north. Since a change in the constitution required a two-thirds vote of the Bundesrat this gave her a veto over constitutional change. The Reichstag was elected by universal suffrage on the basis of population, but it did not have power to control the ministers appointed by the Emperor. The great Bismarck received a post created expressly for him, that of Chancellor, responsible only to the throne and holding large powers. It should be remembered that the Emperor of Germany was also King of Prussia, and Prussia, much the largest and most powerful of the German states (of which there were some 25 now[2]), had its own rather undemocratic constitution, dominated by the aristocracy.

It was a joyful moment for many, if not all, Germans, despite the limitations and possible weaknesses of the Reich. Amid national rejoicing "the centuries-old hopes of our forefathers, the dreams of German poets," as the Crown Prince's pronouncement put it, were fulfilled. Like Italy, Germany was not quite united in spirit, and there remained severe tests ahead, especially between Catholic South and Protestant North; also between the old liberalism of the smaller states and Prussian authoritarianism. But the ensuing years brought such prosperity and strength that nationalism flourished.

"An immense revolution has been accomplished in Europe"; "Europe has lost a mistress and gained a master." So men said all over Europe. For 200 years France's role as the strongest continental power had scarcely been questioned; now it was the turn of Germany. While France fumed in frus-

---

[2] Among the *Mittelstaaten* or states of medium size were Bavaria, Saxony, Würrtemberg, Baden, Hesse, and Hanover, in approximate order of size. Among the rest, Brunswick (Braunschweig), Weimar, and Mecklenburg had historic significance, as did free cities such as Hamburg. The names of Reuss, Coburg, Meiningen, Oldenberg, Nassau, and Altenburg are likely to be remembered by few outside Germany.

The Houses of Parliament on the Thames are a good example of 19th century Gothic architecture in Victorian England.

tration, the British were rather inclined to welcome the new situation. They saw in Germany a balance-of-power check not only on their old rivals, the French, but also on their new ones, the Russians. It could be argued that a strong Germany would provide Europe with stability, especially as she seemed in Bismarck's later years to be a "satisfied" power, ready to settle down and digest gains made in the decade from 1861 to 1870. However, a change of profound import had been made, and only the future could tell what it portended.

Intellectual and cultural trends

These middle decades of the 19th century, though marred by some short wars, were in the main optimistic and successful years. Europe was being transformed by the railroads, by telegraph and transatlantic cable, by a variety of practical inventions. Popular education expanded the circle of literacy, and popular magazines and newspapers supplied the reading market. Middle-class culture was at its zenith. In architecture and the arts generally this meant something not very inspiring. "Victorian" architecture and decor were in the first place heavily eclectic. All previous styles were imitated—there was a Gothic revival, a Renaissance revival, a neobaroque. Modern taste has sometimes rejected the Victorian; it seems heavy, staid, comfortable, and a bit stupid, like the Victorian middle classes with their money and their prudery. The 19th-century bourgeoisie earnestly patronized the arts, building great museums and, if they were rich, filling their houses with past masterpieces. The impressiveness of some of the Victorian public building cannot be denied; and in the field of painting, the French impressionist school evolved under the leadership of Monet and Pissarro, destined to revolutionize painting in the 1870's.

Realism

If, as not all would agree, the visual and plastic arts were not very creative, in literature it was an impressive generation. Romanticism was replaced by, or at least blended with, realism. Flaubert, Gautier, and Baudelaire led one of the most brilliant generations in French literature, one which reacted against romantic effusiveness by a painstaking craftsmanship and against romantic social idealism by a tough-minded interest in the details of life as it is. In Britain this was the time of the Victorian novelists George Eliot and William Thackeray, and the post-romantic poets Tennyson and Browning. In the German world of music, Richard Wagner arose to revolutionize the opera. The novel, in particular, a form especially suited to assiduous, detailed observation of the external world, flourished as never before. In England Charles Dickens had made the novel the favorite of the Victorian reading public, who were edified as well as amused by it; Thackeray, Eliot, the Brontes, and any number of lesser talents turned this stream into a literary flood. The French novel was more daring and less respectable, but even more exciting—here the master Flaubert, along with the Goncourts, passed their uncompromising realism along to a younger generation that included Zola and Maupassant. Also living in Paris at this time was the Russian novelist, Turgenev. "Realism" was the theme of this generation of writers and artists; they too were post-1848 reactors against romanticism, they too shared the admiration for science. In painting, the impressionists, by contrast to the later expressionists, explored the outer world of phenomenal experience, not the inner world of private visions and dreams. "Realism" meant cool, detached, thorough, careful observation, set down with technical skill; objective in tone, avoiding enthusiasm or moral preaching. It could be, by implication, mordantly critical of man and society, as in Flaubert's famous *Madame Bovary*, a sad story of culturally impoverished lives. But it was not a crusading literature. In some degree the artist began to draw away from society, though with rare exceptions he was not yet as "alienated" as he would be a generation later. The first of those who would later be called the *poètes maudits*, the accursed poets, alienated from a society they despised, was Charles Baudelaire, whose spare, symbolical, and daringly introspective verse was to exercise a deep and lasting influence on later generations of poets in all countries. But more typical of the 1860's was the school of Parnassus, which demanded a return to classical purity and the expulsion from verse of all rhetoric, preaching, and teaching—a pure work of art.

In these years also the great Russian novelist Dostoyevsky began his career. For such writers can be claimed an almost unique literary glory. The man of letters became the member of a distinct profession. Mostly in the past he had written on the side, literature being the avocation of clergymen, educators, or perhaps even businessmen. If the independent writer began in the previous century with Voltaire and Rousseau, in the 19th century the *literati* became almost a distinct class, living in "bohemia" as the writers' and artists' section of big cities was known.

Positivism

The theme of realism or, as the word soon was, naturalism in literature corresponded to the vast prestige of science in this generation from 1848 through the 1870's. Science had never lost much prestige since the time of Newton, but romantics had tended to disparage it, urging that the deeper truths were not obtained by this method, but rather by intuition and poetic expression. The renewed prestige of science owed something to such philosophical movements as Utilitarianism in England and the Positivism of Auguste Comte in France.

The age of the Second Empire in France was intellectually speaking the age of Positivism. Comte, an amateur philosopher and social theorist who exerted an influence comparable to that of Herbert Spencer or Karl Marx, announced the arrival of the positive or scientific age, succeeding the earlier ages of religion and of metaphlysics. Positivism was the supposed method of the sciences—the collection of sense data alone, the experimentally verifiable and nothing else—applied to everything. Comte included in his blueprint for the new society a Positivist Church, based on a "religion of humanity" which worshiped great men of the past. Between 1852 and 1870, most leading Frenchmen sought to apply the spirit of positive science in all fields, and searched for a "religion of science." Literature, too, was to be made scientific. The inheritance of Descartes and Voltaire reemerged in France; men sought the hard fact, the clear statement, eschewing all mysticism and moonshine. Never since has "scientism"—the effort to base all values on the scientific method—had such a vogue. It was in this period that Karl Marx and Friedrich Engels elaborated their system of supposedly scientific socialism.

Science

The prestige of science owed most to new and startling developments within science itself. Active areas included chemistry, where a revolution comparable to the Newtonian in physics had occurred; and electricity and electromagnetic phenomena, associated with the names of Michael Faraday, James Clerk Maxwell, and others. No field of science was unexciting, and there was a particular vitality in the world of medicine. But the chief honors were certainly taken by the biological sciences, and in particular by Charles Darwin's enunciation of the theory of the evolution of species in 1859, in his famous book *The Origin of Species*.

Theory of evolution

Like the road that culminated in Newton's laws of motion and gravitation, the road to Darwin was a long one leading past many previous contributors. The story is quite as fascinating as that other scientific revolution. One may trace speculations about evolution all the way back to the Greeks, as usual; and one can point out that a thread of evolutionary theory remained alive all through the Middle Ages. However, down through the 18th century the evidence against transmutation of species was taken to be conclusive. Maupertuis in the 18th century has been given credit for genuine pioneer work, but the large authority of Buffon was thrown on the whole in favor of the fixity of species. Buffon, however, was part of a major growth of interest in biological science in the 18th century. Rapidly developing also, especially in England—where it became something like the favorite ourdoor sport of the landed upper classes—was the science of geology. Most people know how much geology contributed to the evolutionary hypothesis, by focusing attention on the appearance and disappearance of species over very long periods of time. A revolution in men's conception of the age of the earth sprang from the findings of the geologists.

Embryology also contributed data. The exciting thought that all life might have evolved through eons of time from the simplest forms to the highest was being entertained by many people some years before Darwin's *Origin of Species*. The Scottish publicist Robert Chambers created a sensation by proposing this theory in 1844. He did not, however, offer convincing proof,

Charles Darwin

and until Darwin's book professional opinion remained quite skeptical.

One of the most fascinating things about the Darwinian theory is the extent to which it drew on other ideas of the age, outside the realm of science proper. Darwin, and also Alfred Wallace, the man whom he barely beat to the wire with the theory of evolution, got the idea for an explanation of how evolution could take place from reading Thomas Malthus. The well-known Malthusian theory of population suggested a struggle for existence in which some were always dying off because reproduction outran food supply. If so, would not those survive who were biologically most fit, and might not this account for gradual changes in organisms? Lamarck, the French paleontologist, had already raised the question whether changes induced by environment are not inherited. Darwin, who was not aware of the mechanism of inheritance since this was not generally known until 1900 (Mendel, the Austrian monk, learned about this earlier but his work remained unknown for some time), supposed that somehow "natural selection" could take place over sufficiently long periods of time: the giraffe's neck, presumably, got stretched inch by inch because longer necked giraffes had a survival advantage. It has been necessary to modify Darwin's views in some respects, but most biologists have accepted the importance of natural selection—the survival of the fittest—as a part of the picture of evolving life.

Indirectly important for the rise of evolutionary thinking, too, was the whole climate of opinion of the century, with its bent toward the historical. Especially was historicism prominent in the German philosophers, from Herder to Hegel. Evolution is a cosmic process, these thinkers taught. Hegel, the most famous philosopher of the century, who died in 1831 but whose striking *Philosophy of History* appeared in the years after his death, fathered a vision of human history as a dialectical process, thought in motion, working itself out to a predestined conclusion like a growing thing. Comte joined Hegel in seeking to place his sociology on historical foundations, while the careful study and writing of history, stimulated by these philosophical currents (in which there is also a place for Maistre, Bonald, and the historical conservatives), flourished in the 19th century. Mommsen, Ranke, and Niebuhr took their place as the founders of the modern profession of history. Thus, it seems, everything conspired in Darwin's age to direct his attention to the evolutionary hypothesis.

What Darwin offered was a patient and thorough summation of all the evidence available for evolution, plus a persuasive hypothesis by which to account for it. In many ways Darwin's was a less brilliant work of scientific revolution than Newton's, and some have even denied him the title of genius. But all great scientific discoveries are composite products, and Darwin's genius was not the less for being that of thoroughness. Doubtless the popularization of science in the later 19th century owed much to this fact. Darwin had done nothing anyone could not do by hard work. The grandeur of science lay in its method, and this was accessible to all—an idea that fitted the democratic trends of the times.

The Darwinian controversy

However, the implications of Darwin's theory of natural selection soon caused a storm of controversy. Contrary to a popular opinion, Biblical literalism does not seem to have been the chief obstacle. And while theologians objected, theirs was perhaps not the most significant reaction. Many men of good will who were not necessarily orthodox Christians became deeply disturbed by the implications of Darwinism, because it evidently reduced man to the denominator of the animal world. The unbridgeable gulf between man, a creature of reason and of moral freedom, and the world of animal instinct, was wiped out. Moreover, the purpose of life seemed abolished in favor of accident, blind will, irrational life-force. So it seemed to some. It is enough to recall that Herbert Spencer quickly drew from evolution the social idea of a devil-take-the-hindmost race in which no one ought to pause to assist the suffering, for they are the weak who must perish to improve the species. The crude form of social Darwinism saw life as a cruel war for survival. An ethic of this sort seemed intolerable; but was it not what one inferred from Darwinian evolutionism?

Whatever the objections to his theory accounting for it, and whatever emendations future research would necessitate, Darwin had established the fact of evolution beyond reasonable doubt, and mankind had to readjust to this fact. The general public got from Darwin further evidence for its optimistic belief in progress. By struggling and striving things do go forward, they interpreted him as saying. Some doubtless fall by the wayside, but posterity benefits. Nothing is fixed, all things are possible. Scholars, for their part, learned to look at everything from a genetic point of view: to explain something, you traced its history. Historical studies continued to flourish as never before; and it was said that history could become an exact science. To be scientific and to be evolutionary was of the essence.

Agnosticism

In matters of religious faith the "agnosticism" professed by Darwin himself, more emphatically by Herbert Spencer and by the influential Darwinian Thomas Huxley, became most fashionable. Agnostics might simply say, with Comte, that the human mind is not equipped to understand anything of ultimate purposes and essences; or they might aggressively assert that God is an unnecessary hypothesis. Darwin himself came to feel that the realm of life contains so much blind chance and accident, as well as cruelty and suffering, that it affords no evidence for a purposeful creation and beneficent deity. There were many Victorian "rationalists" and "freethinkers" who claimed that science had outmoded religion, and saw the latter as an enemy of progress. The outspoken atheist Charles Bradlaugh created a scandal when he was elected to Parliament and refused to swear the required oath because it referred to God. Thus did the Victorian age, so respectable and devout, bring on itself through its most prized possession, scientific knowledge, an enormous scandal, soon described by Friedrich Nietzsche as "the death of God." What might follow from the removal of the bulwarks of religion and conventional morality could well prove the undoing of Victorian stability.

Foes of the Cambridge scientist's famous theory were shocked at the idea of man's descent from the lower animals.

Further than this, faith in progress on Darwinian terms presented difficulties. True, the species might "progress," that is, become more efficient; but what of the individual? Tennyson's famous poem "In Memoriam" was only one expression of an agony of doubt that afflicted sensitive souls in the very middle of the Victorian age of optimism:

> *Are God and Nature then at strife,*
> *That Nature lends such evil dreams?*
> *So careful of the type she seems,*
> *So careless of the single life. . . .*

Countless individuals suffered and died for the benefit of—posterity, perhaps the human race, perhaps some inscrutable design of providence, but clearly not for the individual as an end in himself. The proposition that individuals are ends, not means, proclaimed by Immanual Kant and upheld by John Stuart Mill, had been the cornerstone of liberalism. It was now seemingly overthrown by the authority of science itself. The intellectual and moral crisis that this caused was a profound one.

Bibliography

The following are splendid introductions to the Victorian age, on which an enormous amount has been written and continues to be written: G. Kitson Clark, *The Making of Victorian England* (Cambridge, Mass.: Harvard University Press, 1962); G.M. Young, *Victorian England: Portrait of an Age* (Oxford University Press); W.E. Houghton, *The Victorian Frame of Mind, 1830–1870* (Yale University Press); Asa Briggs, *Victorian People* (Harper & Row). W.L. Burn, *The Age of Equipoise* (W.W. Norton) is a good general account of the years around mid-century. G. Kitson Clark, *Peel and the Conservative Party* (Hamden, Conn.: Shoe String Press, 1964); Norman Gash, *Politics in the Age of Peel* (London: Longmans, Green & Co., 1953); and Donald Southgate, *The Passing of the Whigs 1832–1886* (New York: St. Martin's Press, 1962) provide a glimpse of politics; a recent biography by Herman Ausubel of *John Bright: Victorian Reformer* (John Wiley & Sons), and probably the definitive biography of *Disraeli* by Robert Blake (St. Martin's Press, 1967) can fill in some details. A recent monograph of much interest is F.B. Smith, *The Making of the Second Reform Bill* (New York: Cambridge University Press, 1966).

Louis Napoleon's regime has stimulated numerous notable works of scholarship, including J.M. Thompson, *Louis Napoleon and the Second Empire* (W.W. Norton), Theodore Zeldin, *The Political System of Napoleon III* (New York: Macmillan, 1958), and T.A.B. Corley, *Democratic Despot* (London: Barrie & Rockliff, 1961). Interesting is David H. Pinkney, *Napoleon III and the Rebuilding of Paris* (Princeton, N.J.: Princeton University Press, 1958). In paperback, Roger Williams, *The World of Napoleon III* (Free Press). Zeldin has also written *Emile Ollivier and the Liberal Empire* (Oxford: Clarendon Press, 1963). Less sympathetic to the Emperor's political system are G.P. Gooch, *The Second Empire* (Longmans, Green & Co., 1960), and H.C. Payne, *The Police State of Louis Napoleon Bonaparte 1851–1860* (Seattle: University of Washington Press, 1966). On the Crimean War, C.M. Woodham-Smith, *The Reason Why* (E.P. Dutton, Everyman), is concerned with the famous charge of the Light Brigade; Olive Andrews, *A Liberal State at War* (Macmillan, 1967), a study of the war and its critics in England; W.E. Mosse, *The Rise and Fall of the Crimean System, 1855–1871* (St. Martin's Press, 1963), the peace settlement and its aftermath in European diplomacy.

Mosse has also authored *The European Powers and the German Question, 1848–1871* (Cambridge University Press, 1958). The great political events of this era, the unifications of Italy and Germany, have produced a large literature. On Italian unification, probably the two best recent books are D. Mack Smith's *Cavour and Garibaldi 1860* (Cambridge University Press, 1954), and Raymond Grew, *A Sterner Plan for Italian Unity: A History of the Italian National Society* (Princeton University Press, 1963). But George M. Trevelyan's old *Garibaldi* (Longmans, Green & Co., 1933) may still provide more pleasure. A useful collection is Charles F. Delzell (ed.), *The Unification of Italy 1859–1861: Cavour, Mazzini, or Garibaldi?* (Holt, Rinehart & Winston, European Problem Series). See also Derek Beales, *England and Italy 1859–1860* (London: Thomas Nelson & Sons, 1961). The most impressive examination of Bismarck in English recently has been undertaken by Otto Pflanze in his *Bismarck and the Development of Germany 1815–1871*, of which the first volume was published in 1963 (Princeton University Press). Briefer is F. Darmstaedter, *Bismarck and the Creation of the Second Reich* (London: Methuen Publications, 1948). Theodore Hamerow's *Bismarck* (Raytheon Education, D.C. Heath, Problems in European Civilization series) provides a splendid overview. A.J.P. Taylor, *Bismarck* (Norton), is the most interesting short life of the great Chancellor; Erich Eyck, *Bismarck and the German Empire* (W.W. Norton), is critical; Eugene N. Anderson, *Social and Political Conflict in Prussia 1858–1864* (Lincoln: University of Nebraska Press, 1954), a learned monograph on the constitutional crisis. Richard Milman, *British Policy and the Coming of the Franco-*

Prussian War (New York: Oxford University Press, 1965), and Lawrence D. Steefel, *Bismarck, the Hohenzollern Candidacy, and the Origins of the Franco-Prussian War of 1870* (Harvard University Press, 1962) join Mosse in making real contributions to the background of the war; on the French side, see Lynn M. Case, *French Opinion on War and Diplomacy during the Second Empire* (Philadelphia: University of Pennsylvania Press, 1954). A fine account of *The Franco-Prussian War* comes from Michael Howard (Macmillan, 1962); Melvin Kranzberg, *The Siege of Paris 1870–1871* (Ithaca, N.Y.: Cornell University Press, 1959) and Frank Jellinek, *The Paris Commune of 1871* (Grosset & Dunlap), complete this dramatic story.

On the intellectual currents of the age, D.G. Charlton, *Positivist Thought in France 1852–1870* (Oxford University Press, 1959); Gertrude Himmelfarb, *Darwin and the Darwinian Revolution* (Macmillan); Loren Eiseley, *Darwin's Century* (Doubleday, Anchor); W. Irvine, *Apes, Angels, and Victorians* (World Publishing, Meridian); Walter Houghton, as cited in the first paragraph above.

Darwin's *Origin of Species* (Doubleday, Dolphin) and Bert J. Loewenberg (ed.), *Evolution and Natural Selection* (Beacon Press), are convenient sources; B. Wishy (ed.), *Prefaces to Liberty: John Stuart Mill's Political Writings* (Boston: Beacon Press, 1959), is one recent presentation of the era's outstanding liberal. George Bonnin (ed.), *Bismarck and the Hohenzollern Candidature for the Spanish Throne: Documents in the German Diplomatic Archives* (London: Chatto & Windus, 1957), provides a glimpse of high diplomacy. See also Queen Victoria, *Leaves from a Journal*, ed. R. Mortimer (New York: Farrar, Straus & Cudahy, 1961); *English Historical Documents 1833–1874* (Oxford University Press, 1956). Robert Baldick's edition of *The Goncourt Journals* (Oxford University Press, 1961) contains Edmond Goncourt's dazzling observations on the events of 1870–71 in Paris.

chronology

1841–42
Opium War; European penetration of China.
1849
Livingstone begins his exploration of Africa.
Subjugation of Algeria by France in process.
1850–64
T'ai-P'ing rebellion in China. European intervention in China, Japan.
1857
Great Mutiny in India, leading to end of East India Company, direct rule by British Crown.
1862–85
French occupation and annexation of Indo-China.
1867
Creation of Dominion of Canada, with substantial autonomy in internal affairs.
1869
Opening of Suez Canal.
1871
Stanley's search for Livingstone. Further exploration of Africa by Europeans.
1873–74
Ashanti war.
1875
British purchase of Suez Canal shares. Imperialism of Disraeli.
1876
Opening of Korea to Europeans.
King Leopold of Belgium organizes association for African exploration and development.
1877
Queen Victoria proclaimed Empress of India.
1878
Afghan War; Zulu War.
Franco-Italian rivalry for Tunis.
1882
Occupation of Egypt by British troops following bombardment of Alexandria.
1883
Establishment of German Southwest Africa; Germans enter race for colonies.
1885
"Congo Conference" at Berlin; treaties dividing up Africa.
British defeat in Sudan. King Leopold assumes personal rule of Belgian Congo.
Anglo-German partition of New Guinea.
Germans annex Solomon and Marshall Islands.
Burmese War, followed by British annexation of Upper Burma.
1886
Birth of Indian Nationalist movement.
1890
French penetration of African interior.
Cecil Rhodes prime minister of Cape Colony.

Model of Zimbabwe (chiefs' graves) and walled village rebuilt from stone ruins in Southern Rhodesia. Of native origin, the main structures are thought to be of the 17th and 18th century with traces of habitation from the 9th century.

1891
Beginning of Trans-Siberian railway.
1894
Sino-Japanese war. Scramble for concessions in China by all European powers ensues.
Sun Yat-sen founds Chinese revolutionary societies.
1895
Jamestown Raid on Transvaal; tension in South Africa between British and Dutch settlers.
1896
Battle of Adua, defeat of Italians by Ethiopians.
1898
Recapture of Sudan by British. Fashoda crisis between Britain and France.

23

Imperialism: The West conquers the world

Spanish-American War; United States annexes Philippine Islands, Hawaii.

1899–1902
Boer War.

1900–1901
Boxer Rebellion in China; international punitive expedition sent to China.

1901
Commonwealth of Australia, union and self-government provided.

1903–5
Protest and investigation of conditions in Belgian and French Congo; enslavement of natives to work rubber plantations. Eventual reform.

1904
Russo-Japanese war. Stimulation of Asiatic nationalism as a result.
Anglo-French entente.

1905–11
Moroccan crises—see Chapter 26.

1908–10
Self-government for Union of South Africa within British Commonwealth.

1909
Minto-Morley reforms in India, expanding Indian participation in government.

1911
Chinese Revolution.

Earlier imperialism

The Jesuits in China

Between Europeans and peoples outside Europe there had of course been some contact for many centuries. Thus, European relations with the Orient go far back, as our old friend Marco Polo well testifies. The modern history of such contacts may well be said to begin with the names of St. Francis Xavier and his Jesuit brethren, who were active in Japan from 1549 to 1633 and in China from 1578 to about 1700. They labored to convert these peoples to Christ, though they experienced great difficulty in doing so, for the Chinese had their own long philosophical traditions, the Christian faith seemed odd to them, and a gulf of language and culture existed which all the energy and zeal of the Jesuit fathers could not bridge. They were expelled from both Japan and China, the latter blow coming after a long fight in Rome about whether the missionaries could make concessions to Chinese customs (the Jesuits' "Chinese rites" incorporated ancestor-worship practices)—a fight which finally went against the missionaries' practices of accommodation. And, as we recall, the Jesuits were dissolved altogether in the 18th century.

Thereafter European influence in the Far East diminished until the 19th century, though in the 18th a small trade with China existed through two ports, handled by Chinese merchants. Efforts to establish diplomatic relations with the government at Peking failed. The Chinese at first suffered from an absolute inability to comprehend that everyone outside of the Celestial Empire was not some kind of "barbarian" whose quaint ways might be ignored. To them China was the world; the oldest of civilized states it was, indeed, one which the Europeans hardly understood any better than the Chinese understood them. The proud Chinese emperors demanded the *kowtow*, symbol of submission, from the foreigners and were reluctant to enter into diplomatic relations with European states on a basis of equality. This haughty isolationism eventually exposed China to reprisals.

But not until well into the 19th century could European merchants, backed by the armed force of their governments, force their way through the barriers China imposed to contact with the West.

The British in India

In India, the British extended their influence in the 18th century, while the Dutch remained established in the East Indies. Having ejected their rivals the French from India in 1763, the British extracted vast wealth from that fabulous land, but in the 18th century there scarcely existed any imperialist sentiment as it later developed. It was a business proposition, with the East India Company representing the authority of Britain in India. In fact it was the scandals that developed during the 18th century, when agents of the company amassed vast fortunes by illicit means, that led to the British government's assuming greater powers in India. This did not grow into full sovereignty until 1858, but during the 1770's and 1780's the company was brought under closer control of the government at Westminster; the scandals of the nabobs received a thorough airing during the famous trial of Warren Hastings (governor and governor-general 1772–85), a case which dragged

"The Horn Blower," an example of the highly prized art of Benin (present Nigeria)

on for seven years and enlisted the energies of the great Edmund Burke. From this time on, the British government gradually extended both the scope and the extent of its power over the great subcontinent of India—a process which bore some resemblance to the famous description of it as done "absentmindedly," in that there was no master plan but rather a series of responses to particular conditions. The British found that their rule was the sole alternative to lawlessness, anarchy, and civil war among various petty states and banditti in India. By 1819, at the close of the Maratha war, the British were in effective control of India, absentmindedly or not; yet few people in England had yet any full sense of what this implied.

Early contacts with Africa

Of Europeans to venture into the adjacent continent of Africa in modern times, the Portuguese were the first, followed by Dutch, French, and English in the 16th and 17th centuries. The coastal regions could readily be reached by the seafaring whites, but formidable geographic barriers stood between them and the interior of the "dark" continent. In this interior there flourished, largely unknown to Europe, some rather highly developed civilizations, only today being studied carefully.[1] But fundamentally, Africans were "primitive":

[1] Only a few of these can be mentioned. The Meroë civilization flourished in the Sudan in the Roman Empire period. In medieval times the kingdom of Ghana in western Africa possessed great trading cities and could put 200,000 warriors into the field, according to the testimony of an 11th-century Muslim scholar. The legendary city of Timbuktu was the capital of a great state, Mali, which began in the 13th century and still existed in decadent form in Algeria and the Sudan when the Europeans came in the 19th century. Benin, in interior Nigeria, prospered on the slave trade; its impressive art is particularly well known today. There were other African civilizations, about which the student may learn in the courses on African history which are now increasingly offered.

Early 19th century African slave market

that is, though often gifted artistically, their religions were animistic, they lacked written thought and literature, their political organization was usually based on the tribe. Influences penetrated Africa from outside, coming from the Muslim East as well as the Christian West; but these influences were often not of a very edifying sort. For the trader seeking ivory, gold, and slaves early dominated outside relations with Africa.

The slave trade

The slave trade, a prime source of riches in early modern Europe, was clearly responsible for cultural regression on a major scale among the peoples of Africa, unleashing as it did forces of warfare and social disorganization. This trade went on on a vast scale in the 18th century, taking literally millions of slaves from Africa, mostly to the New World. A modern Negro historian has estimated that the slave trade may have cost the lives of as many as 100 million people, counting indirect as well as direct losses—an estimate which may be too extreme but suggests the immensity as well as the inhumanity of this vast business in human flesh. But the international slave trade was gradually suppressed from 1807 on and the British abolished slavery in the Empire in 1833—important preliminaries for the great antislavery movement in the United States, which owed a good deal to its British predecessor. The government of the French Revolution had abolished slavery in the French Empire, and Napoleon failed in his effort to reimpose it in Haiti. The 1815

Congress of Vienna issued a declaration against the slave trade, which had little immediate effect but reflected the increasing weight of opinion against the nefarious business. Over the next decades the British, responding to organized antislavery groups and perhaps also to the economic obsolescence of slavery in the machine age, waged war on the slave trader. By midcentury some European settlements in Africa were actually diminishing or being abandoned because of this decline of what had always been the main industry.

Midcentury decline of imperialism

In other ways too, imperialism, which had always been an affair of economics and of individual merchants more than of governments and of politics, received a setback in the earlier 19th century. At the end of the 18th century, the successful revolt of the United States, an example followed subsequently by the South American colonies of Spain, led to the pessimistic view that colonies would inevitably break away as soon as they reached maturity, dropping off like "ripe fruit." And liberalism in its Adam Smith–Jeremy Bentham phase disapproved of any interference with the natural course of trade, thus undermining the mercantilist foundations of the "old colonial empire." In the leading imperialist nation, England, the Liberal era from 1850 to 1870 brought forth strains of antiimperialism; the granting of autonomy to Canada in 1867 and withdrawal of troops from Australia and New Zealand in 1870 being significant expressions of this feeling. Why waste money defending colonies which would sooner or later be free and whose trade would not in any case follow the flag? Richard Cobden, the famous Liberal, poured his scorn on those "gorgeous and ponderous appendages to swell our ostensible grandeur, but, in reality, to complicate and magnify our government expenditure, without improving our balance of trade."

The great mutiny

However, the expansion of Europe did not stop in this period but only slowed down. France acquired Algeria by slow stages between 1830 and 1870, beginning from an initial expedition which intended only to punish an insult to the French consul at Algiers. It was a good example of acquiring colonies "absentmindedly," as the British did in India, where events continued to pull them on from trading post to imperial rule over the whole subcontinent. Lord Dalhousie, governor-general 1848–56, was perhaps the first ardent imperialist in India. His enthusiasm helped bring on the Great Mutiny of 1857, a dramatic uprising against the British which led to the end of the East India Company's rule, with the British crown taking over direct power in India. India struck the British imagination, and Disraeli successfully climaxed his campaign against Liberal antiimperialism in the 1870's by getting Queen Victoria—to her immense pleasure—proclaimed Empress of India. Their stake in India led the British to penetrate Persia and Afghanistan from the 1850's on.

The Opium War

Meanwhile the British waged war on the emperor of China to force that vast oriental nation to trade with Europeans. It was at this time (1842) that

David Livingstone, famous missionary and explorer of Africa

the British obtained Hong Kong, and in the aftermath of the so-called "Opium War" China opened a number of ports to Europeans and Americans. In 1853–54 Japan received visits from the American admiral, M.C. Perry, under whose more or less friendly persuasion she likewise decided to establish commercial intercourse with the outside world.

Among many other examples of European interest in imperialism might be mentioned the ill-planned attempt of the Emperor Napoleon III to put Maximilian of Austria on the throne of Mexico and establish a French protectorate. The unpopularity of Maximilian in Mexico, the ending of the Civil War in the United States and strong American reactions against this move, and Napoleon's own troubles in Europe, caused the collapse of this enterprise in 1867. All in all, despite the opposite trend in some places, men at about this time felt that colonial empires were diminishing, not growing.

The age of imperialism

Revival of imperialism

But there came about a mighty upsurge of imperialism between 1870 and 1900. It is sometimes dated in England from Disraeli's victory over Gladstone in the election of 1874. It was in 1871 that the veteran missionary-explorer David Livingstone, who had been tramping over Africa for many years (important expeditions in 1849, 1853–56, and 1858–61), seemed to be lost in the region of Lake Tanganyika and became the object of a much-publicized search, which ended in the famous discovery of the doctor by an enterprising journalist named Henry Stanley. This thriller, eaten up by the newspaper-reading public, was a symbolic launching of the era of imperialism.

Ship carrying the Empress Eugenie at opening of the Suez Canal on November 17, 1869

"Within the limits of two feverish decades, 135,000,000 inhabitants of the nonwhite world accepted under the stimulus of gold, gimcracks and gunpowder the doubtful blessings of white domination." The eruption of Europe into all corners of the globe in a "new imperialism" which brought westerners into direct control of African and Asian countries was a gigantic process. Few of the nonwhite peoples escaped. The exceptions simply proved the rule. Brought under the European sway was all of Africa, except Liberia and Ethiopia—the one virtually an American protectorate, the other able to defend itself in an unusual example of a military victory over Europeans (against Italy, battle of Adua, 1896); and all of Asia, in one way or another—by "protectorate," if not outright annexation, or by economic "spheres of interest." Those countries which maintained a nominal indepedence had to accept European advisers and European capital, and grant favored status to Europeans. The exception, Japan, was a power which so successfully imitated Europe that she herself earned a sort of status as a westernizing and imperialist state. Such was the pattern in this generation of imperialism.

Occupation of Egypt

The many episodes in this vast drama are too numerous to be related. One or two must serve. In 1875 the ruler or "khedive" of Egypt, which technically still belonged to the Ottoman Empire but had actually been independent since about 1840, had run himself into enormous debt by incredible extravagances. He had borrowed money from Europeans, who were clamoring for their funds. He had also invested heavily in the Suez Canal, which had just been built by French engineers. When he decided to sell his shares in

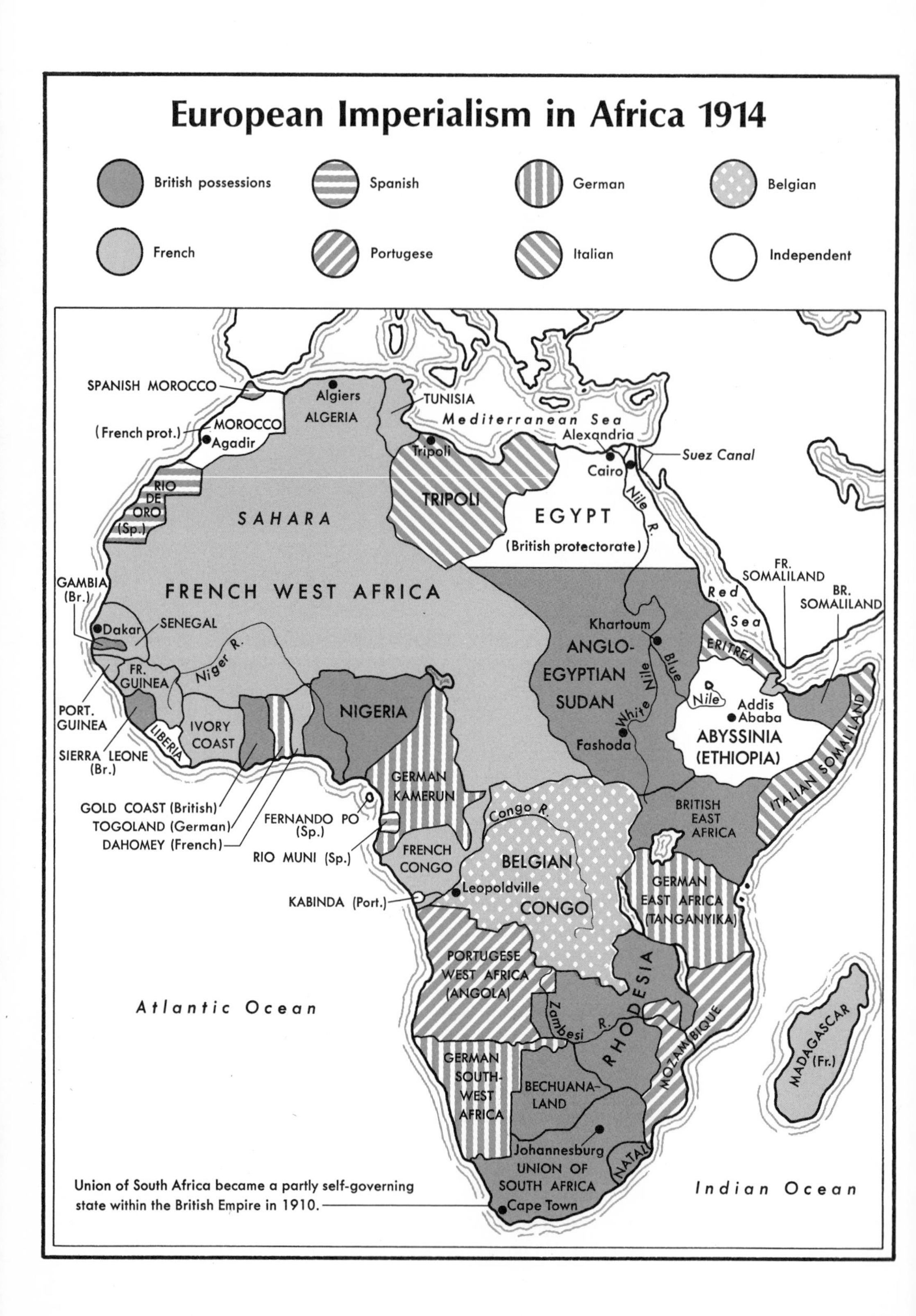
European Imperialism in Africa 1914
British possessions
Spanish
German
Belgian
French
Portugese
Italian
Independent
SPANISH MOROCCO
(French prot.)
MOROCCO
Agadir
Algiers
ALGERIA
TUNISIA
Mediterranean Sea
Alexandria
Suez Canal
Tripoli
TRIPOLI
Cairo
Nile R.
EGYPT
(British protectorate)
RIO DE ORO (Sp.)
SAHARA
FRENCH WEST AFRICA
GAMBIA (Br.)
Dakar
SENEGAL
Niger R.
FR. GUINEA
PORT. GUINEA
SIERRA LEONE (Br.)
LIBERIA
IVORY COAST
NIGERIA
GOLD COAST (British)
TOGOLAND (German)
DAHOMEY (French)
FERNANDO PO (Sp.)
RIO MUNI (Sp.)
GERMAN KAMERUN
FR. SOMALILAND
BR. SOMALILAND
Red Sea
Khartoum
ANGLO-EGYPTIAN SUDAN
Blue Nile
White Nile
Fashoda
ERITREA
Nile
Addis Ababa
ABYSSINIA (ETHIOPIA)
ITALIAN SOMALILAND
BRITISH EAST AFRICA
Congo R.
FRENCH CONGO
BELGIAN CONGO
Leopoldville
KABINDA (Port.)
GERMAN EAST AFRICA (TANGANYIKA)
PORTUGESE WEST AFRICA (ANGOLA)
Zambesi R.
RHODESIA
MOZAMBIQUE
Atlantic Ocean
MADAGASCAR (Fr.)
GERMAN SOUTH-WEST AFRICA
BECHUANA-LAND
Johannesburg
UNION OF SOUTH AFRICA
NATAL
Cape Town
Indian Ocean
Union of South Africa became a partly self-governing state within the British Empire in 1910.

the canal, British prime minister Disraeli beat the French to the draw and bought them up, giving Great Britain a dominant share in the canal, to the great delight of those imperialists who saw it as a lifeline of empire connecting India and the Mediterranean. Before long, in order to safeguard both the solvency of Egypt and the security of the canal, the French and British found themselves establishing a joint fiscal control over the country, as the spendthrift khedive agreed to quit in return for an annual expense account. Riots broke out against this intervention, in response to which the British bombarded Alexandria in 1882. The French withdrew; the British remained for 70 years, in what was supposed to be a temporary intervention. Not Disraeli but the liberal, antiimperialist Gladstone ordered the bombardment of Alexandria, indicative of the fact that "imperialism" quickly crossed party lines. The British ably straightened out Egypt's finances and provided efficient government. From Egypt they were led into the Sudan, which borders Egypt on the south, for this region was a source of trouble to Egypt. There in 1885 they lost an expeditionary force led by General George Gordon. This they had to avenge by an invasion and conquest of the Sudan.

Partition of Africa

Meanwhile the French, pushed out of Egypt, found consolation in extending their sway over northern and western Africa. The King of the Belgians, who financed Stanley, was promoting his own Congo schemes. Germany, at first uninterested in African colonies, asked for her share because of the demands of public opinion. In 1885, Bismarck presided over a "Congo Congress" at Berlin in order to share Africa among the powers so that hostile incidents might be avoided. This did not entirely end the competition, for Italy, elbowed aside in north Africa by France, continued to seek colonies until she succeeded in wresting Tripoli (renamed Libya) from Turkey in 1911–12. And within a few years France and Britain seemed on the verge of a war for the control of central Africa.

Imperialism in China

Something similar happened in Asia in the aftermath of the Opium War and the Indian Mutiny, both of which revealed the weakness of Oriental states when faced with the power of the West. Ever since 1842 the Chinese had been subject to some coercion by Europeans. In the 1850's a vast peasant rebellion, aimed largely at foreign intrusions, swept China and caused the European powers to send troops into China. The ancient and proud Celestial Kingdom gave up her satellite states of Indo-China to the French between 1862 and 1885. Here as elsewhere the missionaries were among the first to come; Vietnamese monarchs provided an excuse for intervention when they tried forcibly to eradicate Christianity. The British established themselves at Hong Kong and Russia nibbled away at the north of China. Then in 1894 Japan attacked and defeated China; this proved to be the signal for a full descent of European imperialism on the unfortunate country, a giant with feet of clay; she was rapidly carved up into "spheres of interest" or "influence." In these zones the European powers obtained for themselves sweeping economic concessions, amounting to virtually complete economic domination. While China kept a nominally independent government, it was forced to hand over much of its power to Europeans, who set its tariffs, built its railways, developed its industries. This too was "imperialism."

All the powers participated in this acquisition of overseas possessions and spheres of influence, except Austria-Hungary. The lion's share went to the British lion, with France a strong second; Germany belatedly entered the race, securing some areas in Africa and the Pacific, as well as a leasehold in China. Italy, though defeated in Ethiopia, took Eritrea, Tripoli, and part of the Somaliland in Africa. Russia expanded by land into Manchuria, Korea, and Mongolia, where she clashed with Japan; she split Persia with Great Britain in 1907. The United States, previously unconcerned with such matters, reached out as far as the Philippine Islands. The King of Belgium, a pioneer in African explorations, acquired a huge Congo empire. To name all the acquisitions would take much space; a glance at the map of the world in 1914 can give us the picture. Some of these possessions were older ones: thus the Dutch, the Portuguese, and the British kept older possessions, while the United States took over from Spain in several places. However, additions to empire after 1874 were enormous.

Causes of imperialism

It is difficult to generalize about the causes of so vast a process. Clearly it was in the broadest sense a tribute to the enormous vitality of western civilization—which simply overflowed. The technological superiority of Europe was obvious. Armed with modern weapons a handful of Europeans could cow hordes of "natives." Indo-China, which required 500,000 American troops to hold it in 1967, was taken in this period by a mere handful of Frenchmen. But it was not altogether a matter of force, though force was unfortunately much in evidence. The economic system of the Europeans was much more advanced; politically, Europe often was able to govern where there had been anarchy or weakness; culturally, European civilization was at a peak of confidence. "We assert," a prominent American said in 1898, "the proposition that the Anglo-Saxon stock are by their industry and their indomitable perseverance the chosen ones to sway the affairs of men." This was an intolerable arrogance, perhaps, yet a source of strength.

Imperialism was in general the work of individuals, not governments. If governments annexed, it was usually because individuals had gone out and created some sort of situation which impelled government action. Lord Salisbury, who annexed much of the British Empire in the feverish 1890's, had no enthusiasm for it; he said Africa had been invented to plague the foreign office. The individuals who went out and stirred up the natives were of all sorts. There is a tendency still to follow the analysis of the Marxists and talk of an exclusively economic process. But among the first to go, actually, were a very different sort, the missionaries—who were often among the most ardent annexationists, too. There also came adventurers, scientists, journalists,

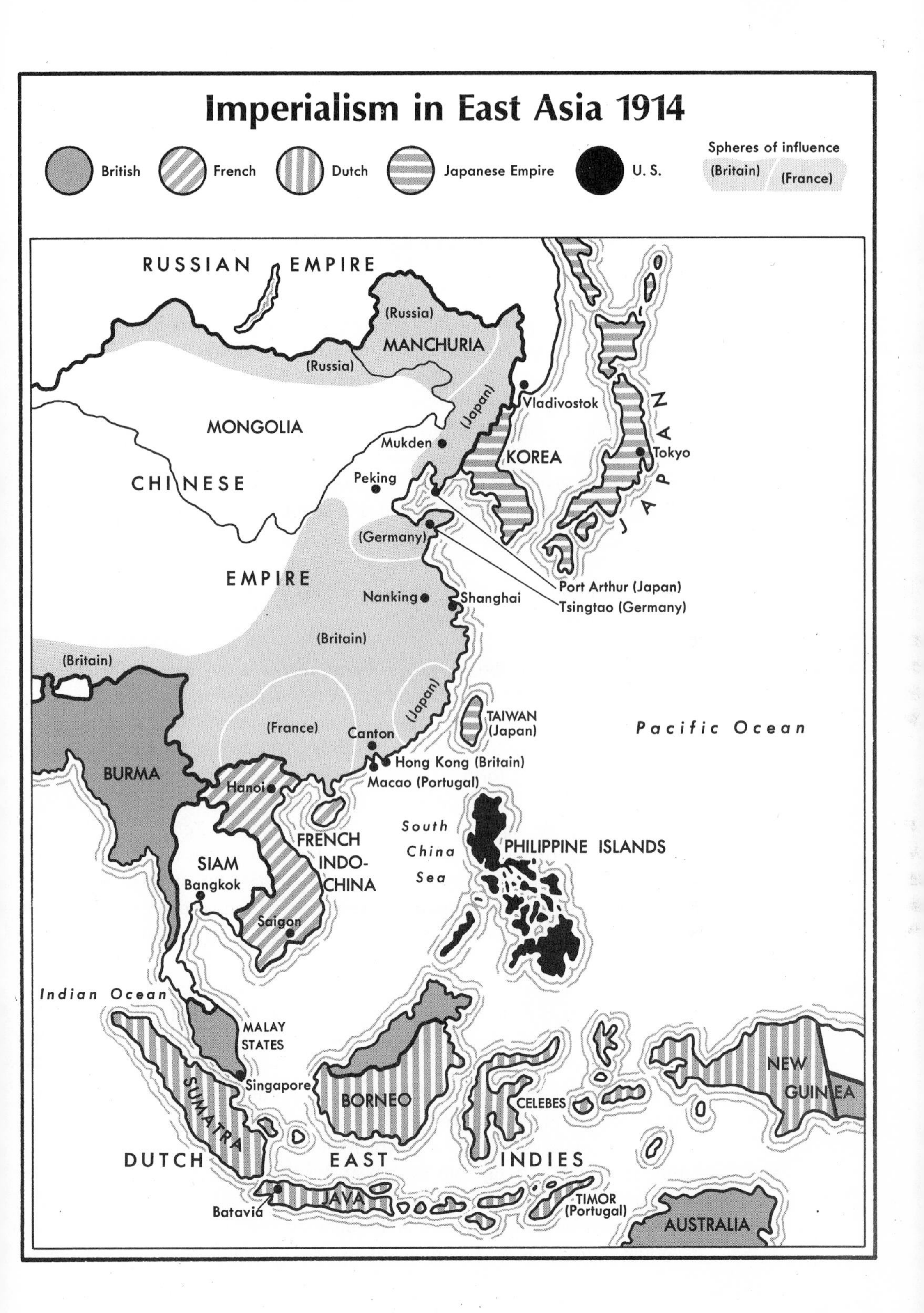
Imperialism in East Asia 1914
British
French
Dutch
Japanese Empire
U. S.
Spheres of influence
(Britain)
(France)
RUSSIAN EMPIRE
(Russia)
MANCHURIA
(Russia)
(Japan)
Vladivostok
MONGOLIA
Mukden
KOREA
Tokyo
JAPAN
CHINESE
EMPIRE
Peking
(Germany)
Port Arthur (Japan)
Tsingtao (Germany)
Nanking
Shanghai
(Britain)
(Britain)
(Japan)
TAIWAN
(Japan)
Pacific Ocean
(France)
Canton
Hong Kong (Britain)
Macao (Portugal)
BURMA
Hanoi
FRENCH
INDO-
CHINA
South
China
Sea
PHILIPPINE ISLANDS
SIAM
Bangkok
Saigon
Indian Ocean
MALAY
STATES
Singapore
SUMATRA
BORNEO
CELEBES
NEW
GUINEA
DUTCH
EAST
INDIES
Batavia
JAVA
TIMOR
(Portugal)
AUSTRALIA

freebooters. Big capital, being prudent, did not ordinarily come until the ground had been well prepared. In the symbolic episode which first caught the imagination of Europe, the search of Stanley for Livingstone in "darkest Africa," one of the key figures was a missionary and scientist, the other a journalist looking for a good story.

Adventure

Much of imperialism may be explained in terms of its glamour; it was the great adventure of a Europe somewhat bored by peace and prosperity in this era. Strange names and far places, brave men doing great deeds, fighting Zulu warriors seven feet high, scaling mighty peaks, finding diamonds, playing games of deep intrigue with inscrutable natives or foreign agents—all this became the favorite reading of the late Victorian public. "In place of our T-V.I.P.'s, pop-singers, film stars and racing drivers, fans of the later 19th century had the African explorer," writes Elspeth Huxley. "Hirsute, virile, brave, tough as old boots, quarrelsome, as handy with the pen as the chronometer, these manly figures bestrode the jungle world like a whole group of colossi, vanishing for years on end and reappearing with tales of freakish cannibals, savage kingdoms, lakes bigger than whole civilized countries, hair-breadth escapes and tragic disasters, all on the heroic scale." The names of Rudyard Kipling and Rider Haggard in England may be enough to suggest the imaginative side of imperialism.

Social Darwinism

An application of the pervasive theme of evolution lent intellectual respectability to the movement. Nothing in this generation escaped the influence of that idea, and "social Darwinists" borrowed the idea of life as struggle and exertion to apply to the realm of politics. The white races were proving their vigor by going forth to conquer and to rule. The onward march of things demanded such competitions of peoples, with the stronger rightly surviving even at the expense of the weaker. So ran the *Zeitgeist* of this era. Respectable historians and sociologists added their voices to those of popular newspaper publishers in praising Europe's outward thrust, in all its exuberance and brutality, almost without reservation. Those who opposed it were accused of ignoring the call of destiny and failing to heed the law of existence.

Economic motives

Business soon entered the field. There were enormous profits to be made, developing virgin countries where cheap native labor and rich natural resources might make a veritable paradise for the enterprising capitalist. The economic potentialities were sometimes overestimated. There was much talk about the 40 million naked African backs waiting for Manchester shirts, and the United States annexed the Philippines in 1898 as an entrance to the "illimitable markets of China"—which never developed. Still, there were fabulous windfalls. A notable feature of this economic imperialism was the stress on investment, rather than merely trade as formerly. Oil, rubber plantations, mining, railroad building brought European engineers, capitalists, technicians to areas as a permanent fixture. The railroad was the greatest single key to the new imperialism; everywhere that the white man came, he soon set about building one. Ownership or long-term leasing of valuable properties and the importing of expensive machinery meant that westerners had a direct stake in these societies, one that had to be protected.

The religion of imperialism

The motives to imperialism were as many as the motives to human action of any kind—greed, idealism, adventure, curiosity, itch for power, instinct to build, desire to dominate. Among typical "empire-builders" the fabulous Cecil Rhodes might be taken as a sample. Rhodes luckily made a fortune in diamonds in South Africa early in his career; but what drove him thereafter to be an ardent imperialist was not so much a search for riches as a soaring dream of development, of a Cape-to-Cairo railroad, and parliamentary governments all over Africa. Imperialism became a religion and a mission with such as Rhodes.

"The Rhodes Colossus"—Cecil Rhodes and the completion of the Cape Town to Cairo telegraph. Punch, *December, 1892.*

Marxist explanation

The Marxist analysis of imperialism, elaborated by J.A. Hobson and by Lenin, is thus much too simple and of dubious validity at many points. It claimed that capitalist countries were able to postpone economic collapse and proletarian revolution at home only by finding large new profits in the exploitation of colonial economies. Thus the prime motive for imperialism was alleged to be industrial-economic; governments are regarded by Marxists as only tools in the hands of the great industrialists whose constant concern is an ever-diminishing stream of profit. Foreign policy becomes little more than a reflection of capitalist economics. Very little research is needed to dispel most of these fantasies. The economic factor in "imperialism" should not be overlooked, but can be exaggerated.

Politicians or military men sometimes pushed for annexations on grounds not directly related to economics. For example, we find France taking Tunisia because the military men wanted it, not the businessmen, while the exploration and annexation of central Africa involved such key figures as Count de Brazza, aristocratic adventurer sent by the Foreign Office. Jules Ferry, as Prime Minister of France in the 1880's, turned his attention to overseas acquisitions because he wished to present the image of vigorous national leadership, and because he wished to divert French attention from the quarrel with Germany over Alsace and Lorraine. No great amount of French capital was ever invested in the colonial empire, nor was trade with it nearly so important as trade with European countries. It began and remained a somewhat expensive political hobby, kept up because national prestige demanded it. A few French firms made large profits, especially in Indo-China, but this group did not bulk large by comparison with the whole business community.

To Great Britain, of course, the colonies were rather more important; still, Britain's chief markets and outlets for investment capital were in the increasingly self-governing white dominions (Canada, Australia, New Zealand) and in the United States, not in her African acquisitions.

Sometimes there was a strategic motive for annexation; thus, the British felt stability in Egypt to be essential to the Suez Canal. Sometimes it was a desire to protect an existing colony, sometimes a simple matter of prestige and "keeping up with the neighbors." There was a natural impetus to the scramble once it started. Africa was divided up in 10 years because once the grabbing started, everybody had to grab before the others did, or risk being left out, which would have caused an adverse popular reaction. Annexation often seemed forced on statesmen. A familiar situation was the necessity of annexing an outlying region to control what you had—as, for example, possession of Algeria brought France into the neighboring areas of Tunis and Morocco. And entrance of European business into non-European countries frequently brought on a situation in which these interests wished to have their rights safeguarded. They might get into conflict with the natives, or it might simply be that local law was unable to cope with the situation. Native governments were unaccustomed to such complex property arrangements and commercial rules as Europeans brought. A recent student of imperialism has coined the phrase "the imperialism of free trade" to express this factor: even if wishing only to trade, the Europeans drew the other peoples into their network of law and then found that they had to supply the law.

European privileges

Europeans in "colonial" areas demanded special legal privileges, exemplified in the famous Turkish "capitulations" or Chinese "extraterritoriality": exemption from Turkish or Chinese law and the right to have their own courts, even when a case involved the claims of a native against a European. They lived and carried on their affairs as a privileged elite. This imperialist movement was not usually mass migration, though there were a few places where this occurred. Though quite a few Frenchmen went to Algeria, Italians to Libya, and British to Canada, Australia, New Zealand, and Cape Colony, more Europeans went to the United States in the period 1870–1914 than went to all their colonies put together. Imperialism typically brought a comparatively small European elite to colonial or quasi-colonial areas—active, aggressive, and usually backed by the force of their home governments, but not numerically large.

Neomercantilism

Governments found other motives to annexation of empire, in addition to a sometimes reluctant protection of their citizens who had ventured afar. A prominent motive in Great Britain, one finds, was a fear that the age of free trade was over and a protected market would be needed. The free traders had argued that colonies were a burden, since their trade would always flow in the direction dictated by economic forces, not political sovereignty. But after 1870 this came to seem doubtful. It would surely be wise to prepare for the worst by building fences around an economic empire, many felt. "Neomercantilism" in economics went along with imperialism, as in the 17th century.

When all is said and done the motives of sentiment or even humanitarianism bulk as large as economic self-interest. In England the missionary societies exerted a steady and strong influence; to them the ideal of Christianizing and uplifting the benighted savage was real, and they frequently looked to the home government to take the natives under its protecting wing, saving them from the exploitation European capitalist penetration was likely to bring.

Imperialist conflict

Anglo-French rivalry

Such large-scale seizure of territory was not accomplished without armed conflict. On the whole, non-European peoples lacked powers of resistance and the European states were able to divide up other people's territory amicably enough among themselves, so that there was surprisingly little conflict in view of the magnitude of the process. But clashes did occur. For 20 years after they parted company in Egypt in 1882, France and Britain were unfriendly rivals in Africa. This rivalry culminated in the Fashoda incident 16 years later, when France and Britain seemed on the brink of war in 1898 as their paths crossed in Africa, deep in the continent's heart, near the head-

British armored reconnaissance train, Boer War

waters of the White Nile. The incident passed off without violence, but caused a severe diplomatic crisis.

African wars

Meanwhile, in Africa, a Sudanese army had defeated the British, for which the British later took ample revenge, and an Ethiopian one defeated the Italians in 1896; and in South Africa events were leading toward the Boer War of 1899–1902. African resistance to European control was more considerable than is usually indicated. Little wars of native tribesmen, like the Zulus, Matabele, Ashanti, were as persistent as those of the American Indians against the white settlers, though about as futile. A formidable list of such "wars" can be made up: two in the Sudan, one ın Ethiopia, several uprisings in Algeria, attacks of Riff tribes of Morocco, four Ashanti wars in British West Africa, two Dahomey wars, uprisings in the Congo and Angola, the great Herrero revolt in German Southwest Africa, Arab uprisings in East Africa, Zulu wars, the Matabele war, the Wahehe war, troubles in Uganda and Nyasaland—and so on.

The Boer War

The largest war, however, was that between the Dutch settlers and the pushing British imperialists for possession of South Africa. The Dutch had been there since 1652; but the Cape Colony passed from the rule of the United Provinces to Great Britain during the Napoleonic Wars. A long and bitter feud between British and Dutch for supremacy in South Africa went on during the 19th century. The Dutch migrated to the frontier. Then Disraeli annexed the region of the Transvaal, settled by the Boers, as the Dutch farmers were called, but Gladstone allowed it to resume self-government after an armed clash (1881). Dreams of a great African empire linked by a Cape-to-Cairo railway drew the ambitions of British imperialists again toward control of the Dutch-inhabited frontier regions; missionary desire to protect the natives against Boer intolerance also played a part, and the presence of diamonds and gold added motives. Cecil Rhodes as governor of the Cape Colony, and the popular imperialist Joseph Chamberlain as colonial secretary, formed a combination conducive to British aggressiveness, which other men in the Conservative government then in power did not altogether approve. For the bitter fighting that broke out in 1899, most of the world was inclined to blame the British. However, the proud and uncooperative Dutch farmers had been a difficult group to deal with.

In the Boer War they put up a surprisingly sturdy resistance before finally succumbing to the much greater strength of Britain. In the first months of the war the Dutch farmers shook the British, administering defeats to them. It was a profound blow to British pride and a shock which caused a wholesale reevaluation of British policies, even though in the end the Boers had to yield.

The Boxer Rebellion

This was a case where European imperialism came up against Europeans who were already there. In most instances, European imperialism faced native governments which were too weak to put up much resistance. But the Boxer Rebellion of 1900 in China illustrated the kind of reaction that could take place. Reacting to the humiliation of the 1890's, a Chinese national uprising in 1900 threatened to throw out the Europeans. The "Boxers," a league of antiforeign youth, attacked Europeans and Americans and destroyed their property all over China, though mostly in the north, especially at Peking. In response, the whites mobilized an international expeditionary force and visited ferocious punishment on China, engaging in quite disgraceful looting and killing.

Slowly the sleeping giant that was China started to gather her forces again. A revolution began in 1911, but bore little fruit until 1927. China remained subject to the economic domination of Europeans, who lived in a special status as a privileged class in certain sections of the coastal cities. They brought to China European capital, technology, and political and social ideas. But they also brought humiliation to a proud, ancient culture.

Like Africans, Asiatics usually put up what resistance they could but were unable to fight off the Europeans. In French Indo-China, revolts in the interior were chronic, in a region remote and difficult to control. Burma was brought under British rule from India only after a series of wars in the 19th century, and after the annexation of Upper Burma in 1886 some guerrilla resistance went on for a long time. Throughout the 19th century the Dutch extended their control over the islands of the East Indies at the cost of much military action; in Sumatra and Bali, the process was not completed until into the

20th century. After Japan and Russia fought for the possession of Korea, the victorious Japanese faced a desperate revolt by the Koreans, who wanted independence but were finally suppressed. So it went everywhere.

The Russo-Japanese War

Most of the time, the European powers were able to compose their own quarrels over the spoils of empire. Colonial rivalry seldom seriously interfered with accords between the powers when other motives dictated such accord. In 1904 France and Britain patched up their African differences at the expense of Morocco, which passed largely under French "protection." (The aggrieved power here was Germany, but the Germans were appeased in 1911 with territory in the Congo.) In 1907 Great Britain and Russia, often bitterly competitive in the Far East, arranged a division of Persia (Iran) into spheres of influence; which considerably eased their tensions, though the arrangement did not work out altogether satisfactorily. This was the typical pattern, illustrated in China, where the Europeans made treaties defining each other's "spheres" and joined forces when the Chinese rebelled. In 1904–5 occurred the great exception to this rule. Two imperialist states—though not both European ones—clashed in a bloody war brought on by an apparently irreconcilable conflict for colonial empire. This was the Russo-Japanese War.

Both Russia and Japan felt a vital attachment to the region of Korea-Manchuria. To Japan, it was much more than a matter of prestige or the interests of a few capitalists and missionaries; Manchuria was felt by that island kingdom to contain nothing less than the resources needed for survival: food to feed the growing population of Japan and mineral resources to supply her industries. Russia, for her part, had been the most aggressive of the European powers in China because of a strong feeling of "manifest destiny" to expand to the Pacific and carry western civilization there. One of the most heralded enterprises of its time was the great Trans-Siberian Railway, begun in 1891 and reaching completion in 1904, linking Asia to Russia. To complete this link, Siberia badly needed the ice-free Manchurian ports. It was over the ports of Dairen and Port Arthur, together with the railways of which they were the termini, that the rival interests of the two powers most sharply clashed.

Russia also considerably underestimated Japan, as did most of the world. Here was another Asiatic people, and none had yet stood up before Europeans. However, Japan was allied with Great Britain (1902) and supported diplomatically by the United States. The most westernized and nationalistic of the oriental peoples surprised everybody by winning some smashing victories over the Russians, who were handicapped by a revolution at home in 1905 and forced to make peace on rather humiliating terms. The war was a rehearsal for 1914 in its bloodiness. It was a premonition of 1917, too, in the inefficiency of the Russian army and the low morale of the men. The Japanese, by contrast, fought with fanatical dedication.

The Japanese fleet bombards the Russians in Port Arthur, 1904.

It was a distant sign, too, of the ending of the imperialist epoch. The Japanese victory had an immense effect on Asia. The myth of European invincibility had been overthrown. "Asia was moved from one end to the other," writes an Indian historian, asserting that the most ignorant peasants in his region knew of the event and responded. It is certainly true that as far west as Turkey there was a response, and all the important nationalist movements of Asia sprang to life after 1905. Japan had not only destroyed the white man's aura of godlike unconquerability, but had pointed the way to Asiatic success: one must adopt European ways in order to beat Europeans. By 1914, the revolt of Asia was only just beginning; it profited greatly from World War I and went on to augment its strength after that.

Relation to 1914 war

The European powers were able to discharge their restless ambitions on the colonial world and thus perhaps avoid conflict at home. One rather facile interpretation of imperialism sees it as a source of conflict between the major European powers which led on into the great world war of 1914–18. But, as we shall see in a later chapter, that clash bore no direct relationship to anything outside Europe. Nor did colonialism usually lead to wars between the European states. It may be a better interpretation to say that the *frustrating* of overseas ambitions led to war in Europe, as disappointed states sought prestige in other and more dangerous areas. This would hold true of Russia, at least. After her humiliating defeat by Japan, Russia turned in the other direction, to southeastern Europe, with sharpened ambitions to recoup her lost prestige. She began to pose as the big brother and liberator of the Slavic peoples there, some of whom were ruled over by the Austro-Hungarian

Empire. This involved her in a quarrel with Austria and, indeed, may be said to have tossed a match into the explosive "powder keg of Europe." Those inclined to speculate on the "ifs" of history have sometimes wondered if it would not have been better had Russia beaten Japan and continued her activities in the Far East. Occupied in that direction, she would not have troubled the peace of Europe.

On the other hand, imperialism aggravated the tendency of most European peoples to be intolerably chauvinistic in this period. "Jingoism," an arrant form of nationalism which was boastful and militaristic, prevailed in every major country. It fed on news of conquest and superiority in all corners of the globe, and contributed to the mood of national arrogance which had a good deal to do with the flare-up of war in Europe in 1914. But this arrogance was as much cause as consequence of the imperialist movement itself. It was, in the last analysis, the *hubris* or pride of a Europe which had grown too strong for the rest of the world. "All power tends to corrupt."

Evaluation

Thus continued a great movement involving the destinies of hundreds of millions of people—peoples black, white, brown, and yellow. It is difficult to moralize about this vast process. The impact of peoples was productive of so much, directly and indirectly, that the good and the bad would appear to be inextricably mixed. Few Europeans at the time doubted the worth of what they were doing. Arrogantly they assumed that all these "lesser breeds," whether Africans, Chinese, or whatever, were far behind Europe in the arts of government, administration, technology, and even culture. To them the white man brought superior justice, superior sanitation, and a chance to break out of the cycle of misery in which he thought they all lived. He knew little about these alien peoples, and assumed they were all hopelessly backward, whereas some of them had old and rich civilizations. He talked piously of the "white man's burden," as if Europeans were doing a big favor out of their generosity to these peoples.

In compensation, later generations adopted an exaggerated idea of the evils of "imperialism." The word became a synonym for the worst in man. It was widely assumed, especially in the United States, that wicked European capitalists went out to exploit, rob, and murder the poor natives. Both these views are certainly wrong, in part. The Europeans were unjustifiably arrogant, but they did have much to offer to Asia and Africa. They did some of them seek to give to the nonwhite peoples, as well as to exploit them. They went as missionaries, teachers, devoted public servants as well as carpetbagging profiteers and adventurers. It was in any event not possible to halt this process. The spilling out of Western civilization took place like an act of nature, and for good or evil it had to happen. Much was done that was cruel, much that was kind, as always in human affairs, whether at home or abroad. Perhaps we should remember that there was infinite tragedy and heartbreak also in the Paris streets, the American prairies, the Australian bush, the Russian ghettoes in this era. Man's inhumanity to man was not confined to relations between peoples of different cultures. It is true that misunderstandings come more readily when alien peoples are thrown together. But it is fairly safe to bet that the man who mistreated his native workers in the Congo would have mistreated his employees in his own country if he had remained there.

British Commonwealth

It is unsafe to generalize, because the situations lumped under the name "imperialism" differed widely from place to place. At one extreme were the self-governing British dominions of the evolving Commonwealth system. The word "imperialism" was a good one in Britain, carrying connotations there of this mighty union of free peoples, voluntarily associated; and in theory all of Britain's possessions, the dependent colonies included, were expected at some future date to proceed along the road that led to self-government. The Commonwealth idea did not at this time mean complete voluntarism, but it was substantially that, and a series of landmarks from the Durham Report on Canada (1839) to the Ottawa Declaration of 1926 ("the Dominions are autonomous communities within the British Empire, equal in status, in no way subordinate one to another in any aspect of their domestic or external affairs") carried the white dominions steadily toward self-government. It is remarkable that a few years after the bloody Boer War, Britain granted (1908–10) powers of substantial self-government to a Union of South Africa which included the Dutch provinces. Those who doubted that the nonwhite colonies would ever be granted such rights were eventually confounded, after World War II, when India became the first nonwhite dominion and others followed.

Good effects of imperialism

Thus "imperialism" at its best might stand for an almost holy concept of the helping hand extended to less fortunate peoples, giving them support until they were able to stand on their own feet. One can hardly deny that Europe had much to offer in the fields of science, economics, and political administration. Indeed, very few Asiatics and Africans would deny it today. For example, Egypt under the firm but benevolent despotism of Lord Cromer was better governed than under the khedive who had bankrupted it. In India, the advantages of British rule included effective and honest government, a common language, railroad building which helped prevent famines. At the same time cheap factory-made English textiles, though providing clothing for the Indian masses, ruined native handcraft industries. In the long run perhaps the most significant process involved in British rule was a typical mixture of good and bad: educated Indians, products of the British universities in some cases, found themselves excluded from the government of their country and, acquiring European ideas of liberalism and nationalism, began to lead the movement for independence.

At its best imperialism was a religion of service, a kind of Peace Corps for the British upper classes, who believed they were discharging a solemn duty

The first locomotive in Indore, central India, 1875

to humanity. Kipling warned them that those who nobly bore the "white man's burden" could expect no reward except

> *The blame of those ye better,*
> *The hate of those ye guard.*

Lifting up the benighted, redeeming them from sloth, ignorance, and superstition, was a thankless task, but it would be performed in a spirit of selfless dedication. Told by left-wing publicists that they were a greedy and unprincipled lot of robbers, the imperialists stood honestly aghast. They meant well; the real reproach is their naive inability to comprehend that spreading the civilization of 19th-century Europe was not a vast boon to all humanity.

The most valid criticism of European rule is that it failed to recognize the need to use native institutions, but instead sought to impose European institutions as they were. Two colonial administrators with enough imagination to attempt a preservation of native institutions within the framework of western tutelage were Sir Frederick Lugard in British East Africa and General Louis Lyautey in French North Africa. Most colonial empires eventually made progress in this direction as they learned through painful experience.

But native leaders complained of foot-dragging on the path to autonomy. By 1910 India, disappointed at the pace (a degree of Indian participation in

the government of India was extended in 1909) and aroused by the Russo-Japanese War, had produced a nationalist movement given over to violence. Not until 1916 did the Dutch East Indies have a legislative council at all. This sort of body, partly elected and partly appointed, with advisory powers only, was the usual beginning. Its powers and its representative character would then gradually be increased. The honest belief of white administrators was that the native peoples were not yet ready for full self-government. The latter naturally disagreed. There was probably about as much error on one side as the other.

Evils of imperialism

The seamier side of imperialism must not be glossed over. Economic exploitation could be found at its worst, perhaps, in the Belgian Congo, where forced native labor amounting to slavery became an international scandal. It was investigated and reformed, 1905–10, and the French also reformed their administration in the Congo. Similar conditions were to be found in Portuguese Angola and elsewhere. White settlers typically developed harsh attitudes toward the native blacks, somewhat comparable to those of the American settlers toward the red Indians. Living among much larger numbers of natives, who at times burst forth in violence, they were inclined to favor the harshest measures of security. And since their economic interests required native labor, they did not scruple to secure this labor by compulsion if necessary. In other more advanced countries where the white man penetrated, such as China or India, he often was guilty of snobbery and greed. The French were better than the English at mixing with the native peoples, but worse in maintaining honest government and ethical economic practices.

The behavior of the Europeans in China in 1860–64 after the T'ai-P'ing rebellion, and in 1901 after the Boxer uprising, seems completely indefensible, since authorized troops engaged in orgies of looting which despoiled the oldest civilized nation in the world of priceless treasures. Even the United States of America, which rested her national traditions on the right to independence of a colonial people, found herself led into singular actions during the war against the Filipino rebels in 1900. Having fought a war with Spain supposedly to liberate Cuba, the United States succumbed to the temptation to take over much of the Spanish Empire herself. The motives were by no means all unworthy. But they led to deeds which many Americans found odd in an antiimperialist republic. The United States also took part in the international expedition to punish China for the Boxers. She seized Hawaii after an American clique overthrew the native government, and intervened numerous times in the smaller states of the Caribbean area. Such were the forces and the dilemmas of the outward movement of the western world at this time.

But the student should not be left with the impression that imperialism was a sort of conspiracy of evil, any more than it was a brightly charitable enterprise. It was a tremendous meeting of peoples, with incalculable potentialities, in which evil and good mingled as they do in human nature at all times. The dynamic agent was Western civilization, for such were its qual-

"Moonlight revelry at the Dozo Sagami." Painting by Utamaro of Japan, 18th-19th century.

ities that it could not help exerting the driving force of power. The recipients were civilizations sometimes older and richer but less dynamic. They were roughly prodded out of ancestral patterns by the pushful Europeans, and today we live in an epoch marked by the readjustment of these civilizations to the impact of the West, an impact they could not ignore.

Self-sufficient, primitive economies were drawn into the web of modern commerce; tribal cultures were destroyed. The Europeans brought not only a new law and government, but new ideas, often excitingly attractive to some of the natives. They worked as a dissolvent and as a ferment in the lives of these peoples. It has been a painful process, like all great social changes, but may give rise in the future to extraordinary things. For its part, the white world received some influences from the East—quieter, perhaps, and slower, but maybe just as potent in the long run.[2] Historians in the 20th century came to speak of a possible "world civilization" that would fuse East and West in some new synthesis.

Differing reactions to Western influence

On the vast spectrum of this mighty mingling of peoples and meeting of cultures, there were many different colors. Consider Japan, at one end—able with astonishing ease and rapidity to assimilate western ways; already, a generation after her first modern contact with the West in the 1860's, in many important ways half westernized. The Japanese adopted Europe's political and administrative practices as well as her machinery, read European literature, took over European architecture. Japan was never a victim of European imperialism because she so thoroughly adopted European ways as to become, herself, almost an "imperialist" nation in relation to other Asiatic countries. Japan was the great exception to almost all the rules about imperialism. On the other end, the highly civilized Chinese were much more resistant to Western civilization—capable of rising up in fury as in the great T'ai-Ping or, later, Boxer rebellions; absorbing the West's injections of alien culture with the slow metabolism of a sick giant.

With their old and rich civilizations, Chinese and Indians obviously differed vastly from African tribal cultures, as did Persians (Iranians) and other ancient peoples of Asia. But all had to deal with the same great problem—how to react to the powerful influences radiating from Europe, brought there by energetic white men whose dynamism could not be repelled; how to borrow without losing their own identity, how to fend off the rapacity of the Europeans while accepting the valuable things they had to offer.

Whatever resentments African and Asian peoples might understandably harbor against the white man who so often treated them with cruel disdain,

---

[2] Indian philosophical and religious thought, fully available to Europe through the labors of translators and scholars since about the beginning of the century, influenced European thought through Schopenhauer, Emerson, and many others. Japanese painting played some part in the impressionist revolution in painting in the 1870s. Chinese and Japanese poetry interested the important Imagist school just prior to 1914. These are examples of an Oriental influence that was especially notable in the fields of philosophy, art, literature. The influence has increased in the 20th century.

it could hardly be denied that they had been awakened by the touch of the white man's civilization, and would later use that civilization themselves in their march to a new era in their history.

Bibliography

General surveys of modern imperialism include Parker T. Moon, *Imperialism and World Politics*, an older standard (New York: Macmillan, 1926); and a recent Frederick A. Praeger paperback, quite useful, Stewart C. Easton, *The Rise and Fall of Western Colonialism*. Works which seek to analyze and explain imperialism are numerous and interesting. J.A. Hobson's *Imperialism*, a work which influenced Lenin, has been reprinted in paperback (University of Michigan, Ann Arbor). Lenin's *Imperialism: The Highest Stage of Capitalism* has been supplied to us by International Publishers, in paperback. Criticism of the Leninist theory may be found among other places in R. Strauz-Hupé and H.W. Hazard (eds.), *The Idea of Colonialism* (New York: Frederick A. Praeger, 1960). In *The Imperial Idea and Its Enemies* (New York: St. Martin's Press, 1959), A.P. Thornton offers a brilliant discussion of the concept; see also C.A. Bodelsen, *Studies in Mid-Victorian Imperialism* (reprinted; London: William Heinemann, 1960); and Klause E. Knorr, *British Colonial Theories 1570–1850* (Ontario: University of Toronto Press, 1944), for the background of thinking about imperialism. An important analysis is Bernard Semmel, *Imperialism and Social Reform* (Cambridge, Mass.: Harvard University Press, 1960). See also Joseph A. Schumpeter, *Imperialism and Social Classes* (Harvard University Press, 1951).

Some of the earlier European penetrations of Asia are treated in I.C.Y. Hsü, *China's Entrance into the Family of Nations* (Harvard University Press, 1960); R.P. Masani, *Britain in India* (New York: Oxford University Press, 1961), a good brief account; and John F. Cady, *The Roots of French Imperialism in Eastern Asia* (Ithaca, N.Y.: Cornell University Press, 1954). In *Asia and Western Domination*, a distinguished Indian scholar, K.M. Panikkar, has told the story from an Asiatic point of view (London: George Allen & Unwin, 1953). Also on China's imperial experience Peter Fleming, *The Siege at Peking: The Boxer Rebellion* (London: R. Hart-Davis, 1959), and Victor Purcell, *The Boxer Uprising* (New York: Cambridge University Press, 1962). Donald C. Gordon offers an excellent study in British actions in southeast Asia in his *The Australian Frontier in New Guinea 1870–1885* (New York: Columbia University Press, 1951).

On African imperialism: R.E. Robinson and J. Gallagher, *Africa and the Victorians* (Macmillan, 1962); Alan Moorehead's brilliant *The White Nile* (Dell), and *The Blue Nile* (Dell); Henry Rudin, *The Germans in the Cameroons: A Case Study in Modern Imperialism* (New Haven, Conn.: Yale University Press, 1938); Ruth Slade, *King Leopold's Congo* (Oxford University Press, 1962), a study of one of the least creditable episodes of Western imperialism. E. Holt, *The Boer War* (New York: G.P. Putnam's Sons, 1958) examines this important British imperial experience. Philip D. Curtin, *The Image of Africa* (Madison: University of Wisconsin Press, 1964) is a study in stereotypes.

From the viewpoint of the European countries, the following works cover the emergence of imperialism and imperial policies. France: H.I. Priestley, *France Overseas: A Study of Modern Imperialism* (New York: Appleton-Century-Crofts, 1938); Thomas F. Power, *Jules Ferry and the Renaissance of French Imperialism* (New York: Columbia University, King's Crown Press, 1944); and Henri Braunschwig, *French Colonialism 1871–1914* (London: Pall Mall Press, 1966). Germany: William H. Dawson, *The German Empire 1867–1914* (2 vols.; Hamden, Conn.: Shoe String Press, Archon, 1967); Mary E. Townsend, *The Rise and Fall of Germany's Colonial Empire 1884–1918* (Macmillan, 1930). Russia: B.H. Sumner, *Tsardom and Imperialism in Far East and Middle East 1880–*

1914 (London: H. Milford, 1942); A. Malozemoff, *Russian Far Eastern Policy 1881–1904* (Berkeley: University of California Press, 1960). England: Walter P. Hall, *Empire to Commonwealth* (New York: Henry Holt, 1928); Robin Winks (ed.), *British Imperialism* (Holt, Rinehart & Winston, European Problems Studies). In relation to world politics, the painstaking work of a great American scholar, *The Diplomacy of Imperialism*, by W.L. Langer (2d ed.; New York: Alfred A. Knopf, 1951), deals with the period 1890–1902. See also E.M. Earle, *Turkey, the Great Powers, and the Bagdad Railroad* (Macmillan, 1943), for a significant chapter in the diplomacy of empire. Herbert Feis has written *Europe, the World's Banker 1870–1914* (W.W. Norton).

Finally, for an insight into some individual imperialists, a few good biographies of representative figures may be mentioned: A. Maurois, *Cecil Rhodes* (London: Collins, 1953); Geo. Seaver, *David Livingstone, His Life and Letters* (New York: Harper & Row, 1957); Olga Hall-Quest, *With Stanley in Africa* (New York: E.P. Dutton, 1961); Charles Beatty, *De Lesseps of Suez* (London: Eyre & Spottiswoode, 1956); Margery Perham, *Lugard: The Years of Authority 1898–1945* (Collins, 1960), the second volume of a two-volume work.

Sources. Joseph Chamberlain, *A Political Memoir 1880–1892*, edited by C.H.C. Howard (London: Batchsworth, 1953), sheds light on the thinking of a leading imperialist statesman. Margery Perham has edited the *Diaries of Lord Lugard*, a major work of scholarship (3 vols.; Evanston, Ill.: Northwestern University Press, 1959), and, in addition, *African Discovery: An Anthology of Exploration* (London: Faber & Faber, 1957). Louis Snyder has edited *The Imperialism Reader* (Princeton, N.J.: D. Van Nostrand, 1962), and George Bennett *The Concept of Empire, Burke to Attlee*, in the British Political Traditions series (London: A. & C. Black, 1953). From an earlier epoch, Philip D. Curtin, *Africa Remembered: Narratives by West Africans from the Era of the Slave Trade* (University of Wisconsin Press, 1968) collects valuable personal accounts from 1730 to 1830.

24

Democracy, socialism, and progress: 1870-1914

London at the turn of the century

chronology

1861
Emancipation of Russian serfs. 1864, Zemstvo law, reform of judiciary.
1868–74
First Gladstone ministry, Great Britain: Irish Land Act, 1870, Education Act, 1870, Trade Union Act, 1871.
1872–78
So-called *Kulturkampf*, Bismarck's struggle with Catholic church. May Laws, 1873.
1875
Constitution of Third French Republic (series of laws) passed.
Gotha Conference: organization of German Social Democrats.
1876
Narodnik (To the People) movement in Russia.
1878
Leo XIII, Pope. Liberal trend in papacy. Settlement of *Kulturkampf*.
Antisocialist laws passed in Germany.
1879
Germany adopts protective tariff.
Terrorist movement in Russia.
1880–85
Second Gladstone ministry. Employers' Liability Act, 1880; extension of suffrage, 1884.
1881
Assassination of Tsar Alexander II. Reactionary regime of Alexander III begins.
1883–89
Bismarck's welfare laws: sickness insurance, 1883; accident insurance, 1884; old age, 1889.
1884
Trade unions legalized in France.
1886
Irish Home Rule Bill introduced by Gladstone.
1888
William II becomes Emperor of Germany.
1889
Threat of coup by General Boulanger, popular French leader. Flight and suicide of Boulanger.
Great London dock strike.
1890
Resignation of Bismarck. End of antisocialist laws in Germany.
1891
Rerum Novarum, papal encyclical on social question.
1892
Home Rule chief issue in 1892 elections in Britain; fourth Gladstone ministry, 1892–94; Home Rule bill defeated by Lords.
1893
Founding of socialist Independent Labour Party in Britain.
Panama scandals, France. Corruption scandals in Italy.
1894
Beginning of Dreyfus Affair in France. Arrest of Capt. Dreyfus, charged with treason.
Nicholas II becomes Tsar of Russia.
1895
Kiel Canal opened.
1898
Trial and acquittal of Major Esterhazy; Zola's *J'accuse;* peak of Dreyfus case excitement.
Russian Social Democratic party founded.
1899–1903
Extension of social insurance laws in Germany.
1900
Assassination of King of Italy by anarchist; wave of anarchist assassinations.
1903
Dispute over army between Hungary and Austria in Dual Monarchy.
1904
General strike in Italy; wave of strikes.
1905
Separation of church and state in France.
Russian Revolution. Granting of Constitution.
1906
Stolypin reforms in Russia. Failure of Duma to function effectively.
Influence of *Action Française* group in France.
Liberal ministry in England: Trade Disputes Bill, 1906; Old-Age Pension Law, 1909.
1907
Universal suffrage in election of Austrian parliament. Government by parliamentary majority impossible.
1909
Wave of strikes in France. General strike, 1910, fought by Radical government.
1910–11
General election on issue of House of Lords, Great Britain; Parliament Act of 1911 reduces power of Lords.
Strikes in Britain. National Insurance Act passed.
Assassination of Stolypin, 1911.
1912
Reichstag elections in Germany make Socialists strongest party.
Extension of suffrage in Italy.
1913
Dispute over military service term in France. Cabinet instability.
1914
Home Rule bill enacted, not put into effect; civil war threatened in Ireland, with possibility of mutiny of British forces stationed in Ulster.
Antimilitary riots in Italy.

The march of scientific and technological progress

Practical inventions

After midcentury a series of discoveries in science, and in related areas of technology, gave to European man a sense of wonder and amazement. He thought, quite understandably, that he was living in the greatest of ages, one which had brought more changes than all the preceding centuries together. It would be difficult to enumerate them all. On the level of the practical, of new objects and processes used in everyday life, there were such miracles as telephone and telegraph, the Atlantic cable (finished in 1866), mass production of steel (made commercially feasible by the Bessemer, Siemens, and Gilchrist-Thomas processes, 1856–70), electrical power (developing gradually out of Michael Faraday's discovery of 1831 that electric current can be produced by the motion of a conductor in a magnetic field; the electric light was beginning to come into homes in the 1880's), synthetic dyes, photography, and many other things. Equally dramatic and practical was the work of Pasteur, Lister, and Koch—a Frenchman, an Englishman, and a German—between 1857 and 1880 in determining the role played by microorganisms in decay and disease. While preventive and curative medicine contended against grim sickness and death as never before, railroads and the new steam-driven ships made possible the transfer of foodstuffs across great distances, and helped confute the gloomy theories of the Rev. Thomas Malthus. The first practical automobile was probably that of Daimler in 1887, and by the end of the century it was possible to predict an age of internal combustion transport in the air as well as on the land. The first airplanes were to come in the 1900's.

Even atomic power was then almost predictable: in theoretical physics the threshold of the modern age appears to be James Clerk Maxwell's electromagnetic laws in 1864, and by 1897 the world of subatomic particles had opened up. There were X-rays by 1895 and knowledge of radioactivity by 1900. Chemistry made sensational gains, especially after the working out of the periodic table of atoms by a Russian, Mendeleyeff, in 1869. All this, and much more which may be read in the history of the various sciences, made almost every year a miracle year to the late Victorians, and made science the new god. In 1884 a prominent British yearbook reported that hardly any sphere of intellectual activity except the sciences was attracting much serious attention.

Optimism

The march of science sometimes brought less comforting things, such as religious skepticism and various dismaying revelations about the nature of the universe. The more meditative worried not only about the implications of Darwinism but about the second law of thermodynamics, which suggested that the universe was running down. But the average man scarcely allowed such doubts to intrude. Science seemed to be grinding out not only a myriad of practical advantages but solid knowledge about the ultimate constitution of reality. Popular philosophers such as Herbert Spencer or Ernst Haeckel conveyed the impression that all merely metaphysical or religious concepts

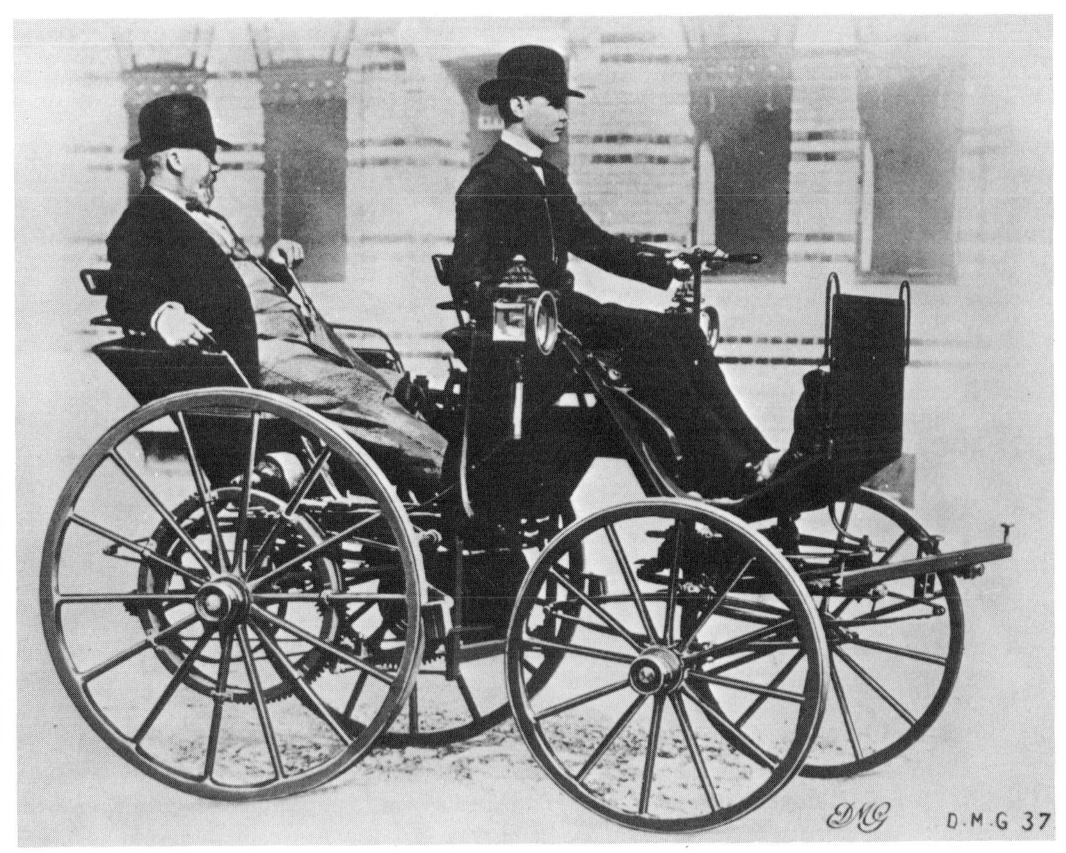

Gottlieb Daimler and his son in Daimler's first "horseless carriage"

of the world were obsolete, and that the only possible kind of knowledge is the scientific.

Most Europeans in the last decades of the century accepted the gospel of progress and evolutionary improvement without question. Industrial development was bringing a new vision of well-being to the masses of people. "There is not a poor man in England," wrote the American E.L. Godkin, "who is not conscious that he is vastly better off . . . than his grandfather was." "The history of the human race is the history of a growth," the Comtean historian, Frederic Harrison, told his audience. And a few years later the philosopher-statesman, Lord Balfour, refuting some who had found decadence in the modern world, stated flatly to the applause of his countrymen that "There are no symptoms either of pause or regression in the onward movement which for more than a thousand years has been characteristic of Western civilization."

Economic progress

This optimism seemed justified despite some serious problems that arose. The industrial nations of western Europe continued to increase their wealth, the largest strides being made by Germany while the others also grew. The

Growth of iron and coal production, 1870–1910

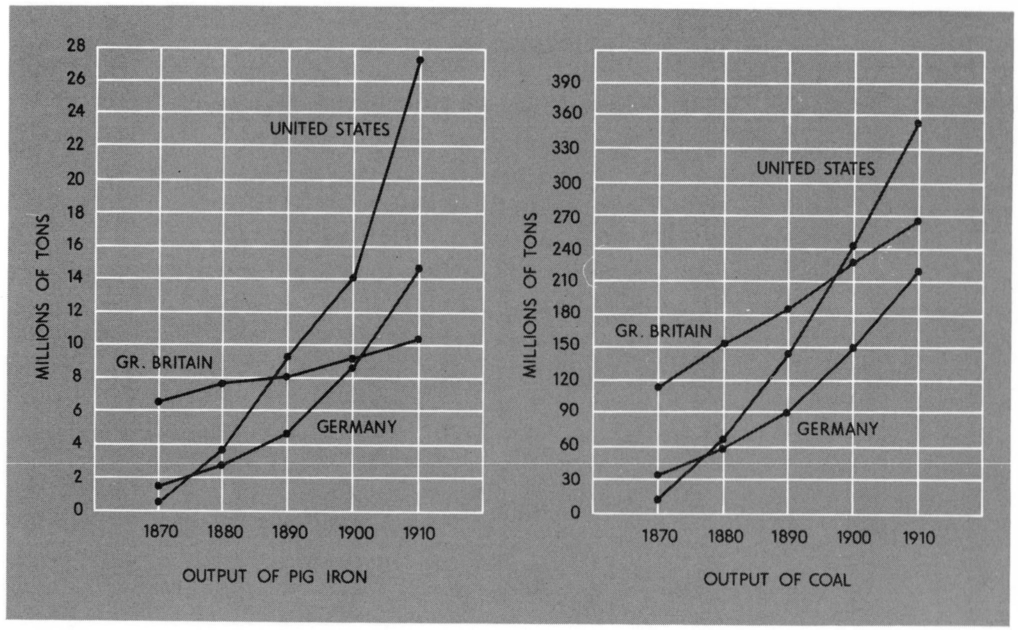

United States joined a world economy which exchanged goods and services as never before. With the victory of the North in her great Civil War, the United States advanced rapidly into an era of unparalleled industrial growth, in its initial stages drawing heavily on European capital, absorbing many millions of laborers from the European poorer classes, and in turn exporting cheap wheat from it fabulous western grain fields. There was to be sure some backsliding from free trade, but an international gold standard assisted a global interchange of goods which moderate tariff walls could not seriously discourage. The new imperialism, discussed in the previous chapter, acted as an economic stimulus.

As capitalism grew, it developed disturbing tendencies toward periodic breakdown, in major "depressions" such as marred each decade, especially the 1870's and 1890's. It also created giant monopolies or cartels which were popularly felt to be sinister. Socialism and other anticapitalist movements vehemently attacked this system of private enterprise as both unjust and inefficient; and, on the Marxist view, it was scientifically certain to destroy itself to be replaced by social ownership. These clashing ideologies were extremely important in this epoch. Still, neither capitalist nor socialist doubted the rosy colors of the future; they merely disagreed about the proper form of industrial organization. Nor was it impossible for them to compromise, as the example of England showed. The rise of real wages belied Marxist predictions of the increasing misery of the workers under capitalism. Economic historian John Clapham estimates the rise in real wages between 1850 and

1900 at no less than 75 percent. But between 1885 and 1913 the total capital wealth of Great Britain increased by a whopping 500 percent.

Political development

Politically, the epoch was in some ways a turbulent one: there were fierce party struggles in all countries. France was nearly torn apart by the Dreyfus affair; Bismarck attacked both the German Catholics and Social Democrats; and the question of Ireland, among others, disturbed British politics. Eastern Europe was far more conflict-ridden. Still, this strife stopped short of extensive armed violence; parliamentary systems with political parties functioned more or less successfully in all the major countries except Russia. Even in backward Russia, the reforms of Alexander II brought in agencies of local self-government, while the revolution of 1905 forced the establishment of a national parliament. That the steady extension of the suffrage, and the entrance of the masses into active political participation, had not caused any more commotion than it did was a matter of congratulation. There were serious problems, but believers in progress did not doubt that further education would remove them.

Most encouraging of all was the absence in international war. The longest of all periods of sustained peace among the major powers followed 1871. This despite serious clashes of national interest and ambition, described in the next chapters, and a rise in nationalistic feeling.

The truth is that major European intellectual figures of this generation turned toward pessimism—at least a deep sense of tragic possibilities, of things wrong with society at its very roots. But popular thought was never more optimistic. "Democratization" is a word that provides the key to this period, and democracy meant not only political forms but much more fundamentally a major alteration in society. In most of western Europe, at least, class barriers were going down, the "masses" were becoming literate, and a new kind of society was taking shape. In the elevation of formerly virtually outcast portions of the lower orders to membership in society, in their education and their acquisition of political importance, many found cause for profound satisfaction.

Democracy

Great Britain

The most striking development of the day was that toward political democracy. Felt to be remorsely advancing early in the century, it had been set back by the 1848 debacle, which had led to a generation of skepticism about it, marked by authoritarian regimes in most countries. Great Britain, not much affected by 1848, led the way toward extension of power to the masses. The advance was steady after 1867, if typically Anglo-Saxon in its piecemeal and gradual nature. After the second Reform Act of 1867 had increased the electorate, another in 1884 brought the vote to a large majority of adult males, and in the 1900's the women "suffragettes" were energetically campaigning for it. In 1888 a new local government act, called by one M.P. "the most significant measure ever submitted to Parliament," made county and city government truly democratic. Gladstone's so-called Midlothian campaign of 1881 was a landmark in popular electioneering, something previously considered both unseemly and dangerous; by the 1910 election, things had progressed so far in the direction of wooing the voter with all the devices of ballyhoo and propaganda that many traditionalists lamented the loss of English dignity. By 1910 members of parliament were being paid salaries, something the Chartists had demanded in vain more than a half century earlier. In 1892, the first socialist workingman ever to invade that gentleman's club, the House of Commons—the Scottish labor leader Keir Hardie—created a sensation with his cloth cap and tweed suit. (Someone said he woud have been no more conspicuous had he arrived stark naked!) Within the next few years a number of representatives of the new Labour Party joined him, though this group remained a small minority prior to 1914.

The Ballot Act and Corrupt Practices Act helped insure electoral honesty and protect against intimidation of voters. In 1909–10 a famous struggle in Parliament during which the House of Lords once again sought to block an important measure—the controversial budget of that year—resulted in the 1911 Parliamentary Act which clipped the peers' wings: the upper house could no longer defeat measures if these were passed three times by Commons. These were all changes in the direction of political democracy. Perhaps even more basic were reforms in the army and in education which sought to end the system of aristocratic privilege and make opportunity genuinely equal. While illiteracy had almost ceased to exist by 1900 and the universities were now open to non-Anglicans, British society remained class-conscious and, as Fabian Society socialists pointed out, poverty, inequality, and social injustice were terribly prevalent. Even here, something was done to bring government to the aid of the laboring poor (see next section). By 1910 the "welfare state" had made a respectable beginning, though far from completed.

Two-party system

Democratic politics worked in Great Britain because of a stable two-party system and a delicate balance of constitutional powers worked out over many decades. The power of the throne, save as a symbol of national unity, waned in favor of government by a cabinet, headed by the Prime Minister, drawn from the majority party in Commons. Between 1870 and 1914 the Liberals and Conservatives shared just about equally in control of the government, alternating with a decent deliberation; the longest domination by one party was 10 years (Conservative, 1895–1905), the shortest 2. It became firmly established that dissolution of Commons and a new election must follow any major defeat on a parliamentary vote; but such defeats were rare enough to insure political stability to go with the freedom of choice provided by alternate parties. The British parliamentary-cabinet system was the admiration of the world.

France: The Third Republic

In this respect France provided a contrast. The Third Republic emerged slowly from the collapse of the Second Empire in the disastrous war of 1870–

English suffragette being removed from a 1913 meeting addressed by David Lloyd George

71 and the civil strife that followed it. It began as a provisional government, with the expectation that there would probably be a return to monarchy, since France had once again shown herself to be too divided and mercurial to afford a democracy. But the monarchists could not agree on a candidate and it became apparent that "the Republic divides us least." Despised at first by both left and right, the Republic gradually won acceptance. The only major European state in this era that did not have a crowned head, France remained notoriously unstable in that cabinets rose and fell with alarming rapidity, the average life being less than a year. There was no stable two-party system, but many small parties which tended to change. Several monarchist plots threatened to overthrow the Republic, most notably one led by the popular general Boulanger in 1889. But the Republic survived, and took on strength.

Émile Zola, famous French novelist and embattled crusader for justice in the Dreyfus affair

"Dropping the Pilot." Bismarck is dismissed by Emperor Wilhelm II

The Dreyfus case

In the 1890's it survived a series of scandals and affrays, including a Panama Canal scandal and the celebrated Dreyfus affair. Capt. Alfred Dreyfus, a Jewish officer attached to the French general staff, was arrested in 1894 and charged with treason for the crime of passing military secrets to the Germans. He was convicted in secret court-martial, but subsequently there were demands to reopen the case on the grounds that evidence indicated that Dreyfus had been framed and the real culprit was another officer. The famous writer Émile Zola published a sensational indictment of the general staff and received a prison term for this. By 1898 public opinion was in a frenzy with all France lining up on one side or the other. A virulent anti-Semitism arose before the case against Dreyfus crumbled and he was at length vindicated. The affair finally discredited the right, and united socialists and liberals in defense of basic liberties. In its aftermath came legislation to separate church and state (1901, 1905). The years just prior to 1914 witnessed further conflicts between a socialist left and a monarchist right, but the nation prospered despite these political storms, and there was no real threat to the democratic Republic from either direction. Thus, despite the fact that French politics became a byword for turbulence, the once scorned Third Republic was to endure the great war of 1914–18 and last until 1940, when its life was ended by shattering defeat in another war. Socially, France was probably the most democratic country in Europe.

Germany: The Bismarck era

Germany was much less so. A democratically elected Reichstag or national parliament existed, but it lacked the power to control the government. It suffered under the domination of the great Bismarck, who held the office of Chancellor, created especially for him, and was responsible to the Emperor alone, not the Reichstag. Bismarck was able to manipulate the several political parties in such a way as to make the Reichstag a tool of the government and prevent it from developing any great power. Presiding over the diplomacy of Europe with a masterful hand, the gruff old Chancellor was less enlightened in his internal policies; he engaged in struggles with the Catholic church (1871–79) and the Socialists (1878–90), whom he outlawed. The prosperity which Germany experienced after unification, and the preeminent role in world affairs she held, prevented any great amount of discontent.

In 1890 the new Kaiser, Wilhelm II, dismissed Bismarck and ceased to persecute the Socialists. Wilhelm adopted more of the social legislation begun under Bismarck: factory laws; industrial courts for settling wage disputes; sickness, old age, and accident insurance administered by the state. In these respects Germany was the most advanced among the major states of the world. She also had a world-famous and widely imitated educational system, from the kindergarten to the universities; one which was more closely integrated with industrial technology than was true in France or Britain.

Approaching constitutional crisis

The Second Reich was in many ways an enlightened state, but Germany was too much dominated by aristocracy and bureaucracy for some tastes;

too lacking in individualism, too class-stratified, too regimented. It was a fairly free society, in the sense of basic liberties and judicial processes, but it was not a democratic one, either in the political or the social sense. German society included a class-conscious aristocracy of birth. The spectacular growth of German industry made the land increasingly urban, and after 1890 the Socialist party made rapid gains. On the eve of 1914, many people wondered whether Germany would not soon face a showdown on the constitution and whether the house Bismarck had built might not prove to have weak foundations. Reform of the constitution was blocked by the upper house, or Landtag, where the various regional states were represented, for there Prussia held sufficient power to veto basic change. And Prussia was the least democratic of German lands; its famous three-class voting system had not been altered since 1850.

Rising political discontent in the 1900's was associated partly with a lack of confidence in the Kaiser's leadership. An autocratic political system did not have an able autocrat, it seemed. No chancellor after Bismarck succeeded in winning the confidence of the German people. The Kaiser and his Chancellor constituted an essentially irresponsible government. But the great economic success of the nation operated to stifle protest and indeed to fill German hearts with an overweening pride. Nevertheless the elections of

Wilhelm II, Kaiser of Imperial Germany, 1888–1918

1912 made the Socialists (Social Democrats), who were pledged to a democratic constitution, the largest single part in Germany, with more than a third of the Reichstag members. Here as in France there were several political parties, not just two.

Much of the criticism of German society at the time came, however, from a small number of the more sensitive. The great majority thought it a supremely successful society, and indeed Germany excited the envy of much of the world as a supremely "go-ahead" nation. The Emperor Wilhelm II was made into an ogre (and called "the Kaiser") only after the war began. In the years from 1890 to 1914 he commanded widespread attention, if not always admiration, as a glamorous figure; mustached, resplendent in uniforms and medals, and astonishingly energetic, he was a kind of Teutonic Teddy Roosevelt (who was indeed one of his best friends), with interests ranging from the physical to the intellectual. He seemed a commanding and masterful figure, the foremost political personage of Europe by far. Only later did his reputation decline. The same might be said for his whole era.

Socialism and social welfare

Marxism

The democratization of the forms of politics had its counterpart in a trend toward social democracy. European socialism, born in the pre-1848 generation which produced the pioneer theorists Saint-Simon, Fourier, and Owen, had been all but crushed to earth in 1848; reviving in the 1860's, it suffered another severe blow with the suppression of the Paris Commune of 1871, widely if in part wrongly blamed on the socialists. But meanwhile it had continued to stimulate an important literature. While socialists theoreticians and leaders such as Pierre-Joseph Proudhon in France and Ferdinand Lassalle in Germany were notable, the chief formulator of socialist doctrine proved to be the team of Karl Marx and Friedrich Engels, Germans living in England after 1848. They forged a vast structure of theory that came to dominate the socialist movement and exert a remarkable influence on modern times. Employing the Hegelian dialectic but marrying it to a materialist or economic interpretation of history, Marx claimed to have created an exact social science which revealed that in the evolution of society capitalism remorselessly destroys itself to make way for the era of the classless society. His ambitious book *Capital* was never finished, but the first volume, published in 1867, was destined to a large influence. At the same time Marx and Engels tried to organize the Workers International; the so-called First International of 1864 broke up in quarrels between Marxists and Proudhonists. At Marx's funeral in 1883, his collaborator and patron Engels said that Marx had done for social science what Darwin did for biology. Some in Europe accepted this claim at face value and, impressed by the vigor of Marx's thought as well as his polemical denunciations of "capitalism," used him as the bible of the socialist movement that reemerged to become a great force in Europe in the years between 1890 and 1914.

Detailed exposition of Marx is impossible here. One point only: Marx's analysis in *Das Kapital* claimed to have demonstrated that capitalism is forced to exploit the working class ever more mercilessly and to destroy itself in the process. The capitalist derives his profit from the exploitation of human labor power; as machinery is introduced, he faces a declining rate of profit which requires him both to exploit his workers and to compete with his fellow capitalists more fiercely. The number of capitalists steadily diminishes, the misery of the working class rises, because of remorselessly operating laws; in the end, the transformation to a socialist order becomes almost automatic, since capitalism has so well if unintentionally prepared the ground. This Marxist prophecy did not come true. The condition of the working class, bad in the earlier stages of industrialism, was definitely improving by the end of the century. Private enterprises were not diminishing but increasing. Marx's was a beautiful theory slain by ugly facts. In Great Britain, the Fabian Socialists discarded his doctrine while continuing to work for a socialist society that would remedy injustice and inequality.[1] In Germany there were "revisionists" who wished to correct Marx drastically. But the dramatic power and sweep of his ideas continued to captivate many, including a majority of the strong German Social Democratic party.

Social Democrats

However, these Social Democrats were not revolutionaries. With the blessing of Engels (after Marx's death), they accepted political democracy as a legal path to attainment of socialism. Marx had taught them that the laws of social development inevitably and steadily operate to hasten the coming of socialism; not by revolutionary adventures but by steady progress would it be achieved. One might well wait patiently for the ripe fruit of socialism to drop from the capitalist tree, certain that it would one day do so. Meanwhile one should make sure that democratic political institutions were available, so that the great transformation could be brought about by the ballot.

Non-Marxian socialists

Organized after 1889 in the Second International, most West European socialists accepted the parliamentary system and the possibility of achieving socialism by democratic processes. In Great Britain, the movement which crystallized in the Independent Labour party, founded 1893, reflected a socialism which "did not rest on Marxian foundations" but was the heir of Owenism, Christian Socialism, Chartism, and a number of other literary and intellectual currents in Victorian England. The British mind was not agreeable to the dogmatic and heavily theoretical approach of Marx. French socialism, also, vigorous but not very unified, while much influenced by Marx was not in any monolithic sense "Marxist." Generally speaking, socialism in the West was a democratic, ethical protest against capitalism's various evils. It was inclined to drift close to what strict Marxists regarded as compromise with capitalism. It was not outlawed but given a place in capitalist society. The

---

[1] Founded in 1884, the society was named after the Roman general Fabius, whose tactics were those of delay; it included among its members such brilliant figures as George Bernard Shaw, Annie Besant, Sidney and Beatrice Webb, and for a time H.G. Wells.

Karl Marx (1818–83). His writings formed the theoretical foundation of growing socialist power, both evolutionary and revolutionary.

German Social Democrats were outlawed and persecuted by Bismarck, but after 1890 they regained a legal status and grew rapidly to become the largest single political party in Germany by 1912. If Great Britain developed no comparable socialist party, this was because the two major parties, and especially the Liberals, proved flexible enough to take over a good deal of the program of socialism.

Social legislation

Only a minority of Marxists thought differently than the "legalistic" Social Democrats. One of them, in the very different conditions of Russia, was the man known as Lenin. But in this optimistic period before 1914 even Marxian socialism was for the most part democratic and evolutionary. Meanwhile the Fabian idea, which saw socialism coming not only peacefully but gradually, piece by piece in the English manner, was the more prevalent one. The Fabians supplied an armory of facts in the form of studies of social questions and stirred enlightened middle-class opinion to work toward piecemeal social legislation. A movement of welfare-state opposition to the Victorian orthodoxy of laissez-faire emanated from a group around T.H. Green at Oxford, who taught a British version of Hegelian social philosophy stressing the definition of freedom as positive rather than negative, something to be provided by social planning rather than merely abstention from any interference with individual freedom. British economists such as Stanley Jevons revised the principles of David Ricardo and John Stuart Mill, and even Mill receded from laissez-faire in his later years. "We are all socialists now," a Liberal peer remarked in 1889, at which time such measures as workmen's compensation for injuries, municipal ownership of utilities, and recognition of trade unions were being enacted. Spreading from Germany, where Bismarck was responsible for the major initial example in Europe of such legislation (1883–89) was "social insurance"—sickness, accident, and old-age protection for workers, with government and the employers bearing part of the cost. The British National Insurance Act of 1911 added unemployment insurance.

Growth of unions

The growth of workingmen's unions was related to this move in the direction of the welfare state. Such working-class organizations, sporadically arising ever since the 1830's or even earlier, had heretofore been regarded as dangerously revolutionary and as illegal. England legalized them in 1870; the great dock strike of 1889 was a landmark in winning public sympathy for the goals of workingmen. In 1901 the Taff Vale decision of the House of Lords held unions liable for damages resulting from picketing, a decision which threatened to destroy the strike as a weapon and ruin the unions. But a Trades Disputes act a few years later relieved the unions from this threat. There was a similar pattern of trade union growth in other countries. In Germany the powerful unions and the Social Democratic (Marxist) party entered into a particularly close alliance. France, Italy, and Great Britain witnessed great strikes in the 1900's, and some of these led to raging conflict, violence, and bloodshed.

The violent instability of the new industrial order, with its periods of "panic" and depression when hundreds of thousands of workers might be thrown out of work, together with the gross extremes of wealth and poverty, helped advance this movement away from laissez-faire capitalism. The condition of the poor certainly made mockery of the complacent claims about progress. In his monumental survey of the London poor undertaken in the 1890's, Charles Booth wrote of the lowest orders that, "Their ultimate standard of life is almost savage"; he estimated that about one third of the population lived in "poverty," existing at the bare margin of subsistence. A good many more could lay little or nothing by as protection against sickness, accident, or old age. Little in the way of welfare provisions existed for the aged, the ill, the widowed or the orphaned. The state now began to throw a shield of protection over the workers against the worst disasters that might befall them.

Anarchists

This was only a beginning; severe hardships and inequities remained, as the sometimes bloody strikes testified. Socialists believed in the panacea of public ownership. Marxists held that "capitalism" would soon destroy itself. On the extreme left, revolutionary anarchists preached the purging power of class struggle and revolution; others dreamed of a great general strike of all the workers that would bring the power of capital to its knees. In the 1880's, 1890's, and 1900's, the anarchists threw bombs in Chicago and London, assassinated a Tsar of Russia, an Empress of Austria, a President of the United States (1901), and a King of Italy. Yet outside the "backward" areas of Europe they were more a nuisance than a threat. Optimists felt that, like political society, economic society was steadily if slowly progressing.

The other Europe

All the preceding generalizations about the relative success of democracy and social welfare hold true only of the wealthier, more favored parts of Europe. They were not true only of the large states, France, Great Britain, and Germany. Perhaps the only truly democratic country, in the sense of direct or pure democracy, was Switzerland, while other small lands such as Sweden, Denmark, and the Low Countries did better than the big ones. These peoples were often able to resolve truly major questions without violence. In 1905 the Norwegians decided to secede from their union with Sweden; this was accomplished peacefully, without war and even without much lasting bitterness. Scandinavian cooperatives and social welfare legislation became a model for the rest of the world.

Conditions unfavorable for democracy

But democracy encountered grave difficulties where (*a*) illiteracy and ignorance were prevalent; (*b*) there were pronounced cultural differences, such as more than one nationality or a deep gulf between the social classes; and (*c*) there were great extremes of wealth and poverty, with the poor dependent on the rich. Where all these conditions were unfavorable, democracy, if tried, became a farce. In Spain, from 1873 on there was supposed to be parliamentary government under a limited monarchy, with universal suffrage introduced in 1890; but political bosses in collusion with landlords herded ignorant peasants to the polls, as did political bosses in American cities teeming with recent immigrants. Hungary was another country where cultural and racial divisions along with extremes of wealth and poverty provided democracy with a barren soil. In Bulgaria, King Ferdinand, who ruled in the last part of the century, became notorious for managing parliament by applying government pressure and rigging elections.

Failures of Italian democracy

Equally adept at this were the political bosses of Italy, and elections in the landlord-ridden South were a farce. The political life of the new Italian nation, born with such high hopes in the *risorgimento* or national renewal of the Garibaldi epoch, proved disappointing. Between 1899 and 1914 the evil of ministerial instability was overcome at the price of a system of election "management" which many Italians felt to be a national disgrace. The "boss" and perennial premier, Giovanni Giolitti, reduced the parliament to impotence by controlling elections in the South of Italy through methods that combined corruption and governmental pressure—rather like the 18th-century British system—with outright intimidation. Giolitti was a personally enlightened and honest statesmen but the methods he used to maintain his government in power aroused bitter criticism. Of another Italian politician of this era, the famous sociologist Vilfredo Pareto said that he was "the leader of a syndicate of speculators" who ruled the country and robbed the state.

Italy worked hard to reduce illiteracy but it remained appallingly high. Beneath the veneer of unification old regional differences persisted. "We have made Italy, now we must make Italians," the remark attributed to Cavour, was all too true. The popes' refusal to accept the new Italian state added to difficulties, for millions of Italians faced an uncomfortable clash of loyalties between their country and their church. There was a huge gulf between the poverty-stricken South and the relatively prosperous north. In general, little success came Italy's way in this period, either economic or military, and men looking at the gap between the golden promises of the 1860's and the sordid realities of the 1890's and 1900's were inclined to blame the failure on the political order of democracy. This background is important in explaining the emergence of Fascism during and after World War I. Italy provided an example of the apparent failure of democracy in this period. Universal Suffrage[2] had proved to be no panacea.

Countries like Spain, Italy, Hungary, Bulgaria were examples of places where elections were held, sometimes even by universal manhood suffrage, yet "democracy" did not exist because the elections were "managed," the vote was meaningless, economic pressures or intimidation prevented a true and honest ballot. In Austria-Hungary a national parliament, elected by universal suffrage after 1907, had no power to control the government and was usually a scene of utter confusion because of the many national minorities. In one major European political state no national assembly or parliament existed at all until 1905. That was Russia.

Russia

Liberation of the serfs

A promising era of reform had opened with the advent of Tsar Alexander II just after the Crimean War. Defeat in that war had convinced everyone that if Russia wished to survive in the modern world she would have to reorganize her whole social order. The abolition of serfdom (for which read slavery) was the fundamental reform. Alexander courageously undertook it, and in 1861, just as the American Civil War began to destroy slavery in a

[2] After the Reform Act of 1882, when a restrictive tax-paying requirement was abolished, the Italian electorate was fairly democratic, but not fully so until 1912 because of a literacy requirement, which disenfranchised substantial numbers of Italy's impoverished masses. Though illiteracy fell steadily after 1870, it was still 38 percent in 1910. After the broadening of the suffrage in 1912, the elections of 1913 proved a fresh disillusionment to those who had expected marked improvement.

faraway land, its abolition was proclaimed—a decree which affected at least two thirds of the people of Russia. This enormous change in the social structure without violent revolution made a deep impression on world opinion. 1861, the year of Garibaldi, Lincoln, and Alexander, seemed at the time to liberals something like a year of miracles. And the Russian performance was the most impressive because it alone came about without war, or violent revolution.

Unfortunately the emancipation of the serfs did not prove the key that unlocked the door to a new Russia. It did not even end the "peasant problem," for the ex-serfs were burdened with debt: land was given to them only at a price, and having no money they were required to make annual payments over a period of many years. They had to live in the peasant villages under the communal organization until they paid off the debt, and thus remained a class apart, still poverty-stricken and not able to rise to the position of independent farmers.

The reforms of 1861–64 included some significant improvements in judiciary and local government, but stopped short of a national elected legislative assembly. That, Russia never had until 1905. There was no great demand for it. The Tsar considered himself an absolute autocrat, and was so considered by his subjects; the conception of limitations on the sovereign was alien to Russia. The peasant masses, unfree serfs until 1861, and long after that still a despised and illiterate caste, could not have known what self-government meant. The landlord nobility was jealous of its local right to rule over the peasants, but not much interested in traveling the enormous distances (via poor transportation) to sit in St. Petersburg. Many of the Russian "intelligentsia"—the small educated class—belonged to the bureaucracy employed by the Tsar's government to supply what national administration there was in Russia. A few of them dreamed of reform and progress; but of these the so-called Slavophiles considered the tsardom a precious Slavic institution, and only the Westerners asked for an adoption of such European practices as representative government and freedom of expression.

The radical movement

Alexander was soon frightened into calling off any further changes. In 1863 the Poles rose up in revolt, while the relaxing of the censorship brought forth a flood of pamphlets and articles in Russia, some of them quite radical. All this persuaded the Tsar that it was time to call a halt. He tightened the censorship and arrested people who demanded additional reforms, such as a national parliament. This in turn caused a minority of dedicated reformers to become embittered and eventually to resort to violence. The 1860's and 1870's created the radical movement in Russia, of which such men as Lenin and Trotsky were later offshoots. It was a remarkable movement, made up of idealists (many of them students) who burned with shame for Russian backwardness, were filled with European ideas of liberalism and socialism, and dedicated their lives to reform or revolution.

In the 1860's they organized "go to the people" campaigns in which they

Barricades in Moscow during the Revolution of 1905

tried to make contact with the peasants by living with them and instructing them; this met with little success. Frustrated in every direction, they turned to revolutionary conspiracy, which of course only intensified the government's persecution of them. In Russia, where "administrative arrest" by the dreaded Third Section and shipment to Siberian prison camps was the usual reward of political activism, it seemed impossible to act politically other than by violent revolution. Unable to persuade the sodden masses to rise up, the revolutionary intelligentsia began a campaign of assassination. In 1881 they succeeded in killing the Tsar, by hurling dynamite bombs at his carriage.

The wave of terrorism accomplished nothing except to cause the government to redouble its arrests and executions of revolutionaries or suspected ones, and to turn the autocracy even more toward repression.

Problems of nationalities

The reactionary advisers of Alexander III made the Siberian camps a byword for evil all over the world, unleashed a virulent anti-Semitism (the Jews being identified with subversion), and tried forcibly to "Russify" the various minority peoples. This latter aspect of the Russian scene should not be overlooked: to her other troubles, including the huge gulf between classes, social and economic backwardness, and communications problems, was added that of cultural disunity. By the end of the century, the Great Russians were less than 50 percent of the total population. Poles, Balts, Ukrainians, Finns, White Russians, some Germans, Jews, in the east Tatars and other Turkish peoples, to the south Georgians and Armenians—all these in varying degrees resented Russian cultural domination. Some of them, in the nationalistic 19th century, were becoming more and not less culturally conscious. The Ukrainians, for instance, though St. Petersburg insisted they were Russians, developed the view that they were historically and linguistically different, and culturally superior, to the Great Russians—in which there was some truth. The Poles were always desperately unhappy under Russian rule.

Revolution of 1905

In 1905, following her defeat in the war with Japan, a revolution shook Russia. The Revolution of 1905 was in reality a series of violent but unco-ordinated explosions, somewhat resembling the European revolutions of 1848 in that respect. Peasants rioted and seized lands; middle-class groups called for a constitution and a national legislature, some wanting it elected by universal suffrage; and the small but explosive industrial working class in several cities formed trade unions and went on strike. At the same time the national minorities expressed their discontent in various ways, demanding autonomy or cultural equality. But there was little unity of purpose. Bourgeois circles were uninterested in or hostile to what the factory workers wanted, for example. When the Tsar agreed to a Duma or elected legislature (The October Manifesto) with limited powers and a system of indirect election based on the propertied classes, the most conservative reformers were willing to accept this while others were not, thus further splitting the ranks of the revolutionists. The army remained loyal, and as soon as it could be rallied from its defeats in Manchuria it was used to restore order.

The Russian 1905, like the European 1848, had a great deal of enduring significance even if apparently a failure. Many forms of organization later to be used appeared for the first time here—notably, the "Soviets" or working-class committees or councils. It had been a great experiment in revolution, to be studied and learned from. Thousands of people had heroically defied the government, had suffered for it and left behind a tradition. A national legislature existed now, even if a most inadequate one. Russia, above all, had had a brief taste of freedom during these "days of liberty" and could not forget it. She remained, however, well behind the west of Europe in the development of democratic social and political forms, and only the most optimistic could believe that he would soon catch up. Progress in industrialization, especially after 1900, did not do much more than complicate her problems by introducing a dissatisfied urban working-class element.

A darker note

It is a notable fact that during these years in which industrial, political, and social progress seemed to bless Western civilization as never before, serious literature and thought became pessimistic as almost never before. It was a rich but disturbed era intellectually. The signs of this may be found in the novel, the drama, philosophy, religion, even science. While the vast majority of people were uncritically convinced of the gospel of unending progress, a small minority, increasingly "alienated" from society, indulged in almost hysterical denunciations of a shoddy civilization, or talked about the death of God, or found no hope in a world ruled by blind chance. Represented in this last group were the most brilliant and creative minds of a talented generation, including Dostoyevsky, Tolstoy, Zola, Hardy, Ibsen, Nietzsche.

Naturalism

Perhaps the central themes emerged from the post-Darwinian crisis of religion and philosophy. The world as a blind, cruel struggle, ruled by accident and not purpose, godless and without regard for moral values, permeated the profound pessimism implicit in the novels of Thomas Hardy and Émile Zola and in many other writings of the 1880–1914 period. Scientific naturalism had evidently destroyed not only traditional Christianity but any religious conception of the cosmos. Nietzsche and Dostoyevsky spoke of God's death. For a time men toyed with the thought that there might be a "religion of science" or a scientific religion, i.e., some valid revelation of purpose and order in the universe coming from the scientific laboratory; then, however, came a widespread realization that science, the realm of observable fact, does not provide such values.

Irrationalism

Will and instinct are evidently superior to "reason" according to Darwinian evolutionary naturalism; for the intellect itself is a product of the struggle for existence, forged by natural selection through the eons of evolution. Almost all the serious thinkers of the period 1880–1914 exhibited the impact of this shattering conclusion. They broke sharply with the older traditions of thought, and announced an "irrationalism" which recognized the basic role of some life force deeper than reason. The brilliant German philosopher Friedrich Nietzsche called it "will-to-power," while the French master Henri Bergson spoke of *élan vital* (vital force) and the great Viennese Jew Sigmund Freud postulated a *libido*. In political thought, Georges Sorel proclaimed the greater value of an apocalyptic religion of revolution over the pseudo-scientific rationalizations of the Marxists. All these representative men of ideas explored the interior dimensions of the nonrational human psyche, where myth and symbol reign and powers both terrible and potentially creative dwell. This generation discovered the unconscious irrational in the human mind.

Friedrich Nietzsche

Nietzsche, who himself spoke of Christianity as a "slave morality" invented by the weak and cowardly masses in revenge against the heroic elite—the reverse of Marx's view that it was invented by the ruling classes to keep the masses in subjection—nevertheless predicted a terrible "nihilism" that would

Count Leo Tolstoy (1828–1910), Russian master of the realistic novel.

Sigmund Freud (1856–1939) studied the nature of the mind, its lustful id, *and its repressive* superego, *and* created *the therapeutic techniques of psychoanalysis.*

result from the "death of God," or the loss of faith in Christian values. The elite who could respond creatively to nihilism might eventually, after a cycle of war and Caesarism, shape a new civilization; a race of supermen might even arise to transcend the present limitations of the species. But for the Europe of his own day, tame, bourgeois, and pallid, Nietzsche had only scorn and looked forward to its destruction with a fierce joy. If a kind of nihilistic optimism exists in Nietzsche, he predicted immediate chaos. "There will be wars such as there have never been on earth before." And after that, dictators. The course of events after 1914 proved him right. His writings of the 1880's, much discussed in the 1890's and 1900's, deeply moved a younger generation of restless youth.

Biblical criticism

From about 1870 on the so-called "higher criticism" of the Bible by philological and historical scholars undermined the old belief in the literal truth of the Jewish and Christian historical writings more effectively than Nietzsche's jeremiads. The higher criticism represented a continuation of Biblical studies which may be traced as far back as the Renaissance, but there was a startling breakthrough at this time. It was alleged that a good portion of the early books of the Bible were not written, as they stand, at the time of the events they relate, but many centuries later; that the four Gospels which narrate the life of Christ were not written until 50 to 100 years after his death and may contain mythical elements; and that the Bible contains much that may be found in other religious mythologies, undermining its claim to uniqueness. The new criticism caused a crisis in Christian circles, as some "Modernists" accepted the critical approach while others refused to believe what the critics and historians said.

The alienation of the artist

The other great scandal that cast some slight pall over Victorian optimism was the estrangement of the artist. In France as early as midcentury there appeared the phenomenon of the alienated, embittered writer or artist who cursed society and lived in "bohemia," a subculture of artists and intellectuals. In the aftermath of the disillusioning revolutions of 1848 sensitive spirits turned to a religion of art. Great Britain did not really know this phenomenon until the 1890's, when Oscar Wilde led a revolt of the esthetes which culminated in the scandal of his arrest for homosexuality. The French *poetes maudits*—accursed or damned poetic souls, as Verlaine dubbed them—had begun with Charles Baudelaire and especially Arthur Rimbaud in the 1860's. The Symbolist and Decadent writers of the 1880's and 1890's rejected the tasteless culture in which they lived and used a new kind of literature as the last solace of a dying civilization. If we concede that throughout all history the creative writer has been in some measure "different," and if we also agree that there have been some maladjusted and unhappy individuals in virtually every society, it still remains true that the profound alienation of the greater writers which began in the later 19th century is a significant and disturbing feature of modern times. The typical gesture was one of rejection, withdrawal, and refusal to engage in public communication. As the hero of Joris Huysmans' influential tract *Against the Grain* (*À Rebors*) isolates himself completely to live in a world of exquisite artistic sensibility, and the lovers of Villiers de l'Isle-Adams *Axel's Castle* prefer to commit suicide rather than soil their love with reality, so did the *fin de siècle* writers cease to be interested in the public, preferring to write highly esoteric verse to be read and understood by a few kindred spirits. Or, like Wilde, they deliberately insulted the bourgeois public and turned all its favorite values inside out.

To them this society which congratulated itself on its "progress" seemed engulfed by ugliness and greed, lacking in heroism, without a place for art and beauty. They might variously identify the enemy as democracy, capitalism, or the bourgeoisie. They might be Nietzschean atheists or they might seek for the foundations of some new religious faith. They might or might not be socialists, anarchists, revolutionaries. What they shared was a hatred of their civilization, and this hatred marked a serious crisis of modern culture. Probably the deepest question these alienated artists and intellectuals raised was whether modern technological society, rationalized and organized around the machine, held any place for art or the individual creative consciousness.

Revolution in the arts

The years between 1880 and 1914 brought to birth most of the modern styles in all the arts—a profoundly revolutionary generation, breaking sharply with tradition. Much of modern poetry lies under the influence of the brilliant French symbolists, Charles Baudelaire, Arthur Rimbaud, Stéphane Mallarmé, Paul Verlaine, Jules Laforgue. Such composers as Richard Strauss, Igor Stravinsky, and Claude Debussy produced a music no less revolutionary than the paintings of the post-impressionists, cubists, and futurists. A new architecture was being born in the 1900's, too. These exciting and disturbing paintings, poems, and musical compositions did certainly bespeak an atmosphere of revolt and novelty. (Stravinsky's "Rite of Spring" described a pagan bacchanalian orgy climaxed by a ritual murder.) They were created largely by "bohemian" artists, Picasso and his friends being denizens of the Paris slums, while the lives of Rimbaud, Wilde, and other poetic "decadents" were highly scandalous. There were violent protests against a "bourgeois" cultural pattern that seemed dull and spiritually dead.

Doubtless the man in the street remained oblivious of the fact that a painter named Picasso worked in poverty in Paris, or that James Joyce was writing in equal obscurity in Trieste. If he knew about the new art he was likely to be hostile to something violently strange, vaguely disturbing. When the modern artists were introduced to the American public in 1913, in Chicago the exhibition "had to be protected from verbal and physical attack by a large part of the population, enraged art students and the Law and Order League." The Parisian reception of Stravinsky in the same year may be compared. The average man was only slightly aware of Freud and Einstein,

"Head of a Woman," drawn by Pablo Picasso about 1909

Nietzsche and Bergson, unless he was unusually perceptive. He probably had the idea that men of letters, music, and paintings had suddenly become unaccountably queer, were doing incomprehensible things, and had lost contact with "normal" society.

The art and literature which shaped the 20th-century mind was made in garrets and slums by men who despised the society into which they had been born. Some of this art and literature was a conscious nose-thumbing at society. In one way or another, too, writers near the end of the century expressed the conviction that man had been corrupted, devitalized, dehumanized by this society. As Nietzsche suggested, the springs of creativity had dried up, and perhaps a "new barbarism" would be needed to restore them. It was in this mood of restless discontent and deep spiritual malaise that many artists and intellectuals welcomed the coming of war in 1914. It was at least a relief from the stodginess of "a world grown old and cold and weary," and might offer (as Nietzsche had predicted) the possibility of spiritual renewal through the purgative power of violence—a "holy madness."

Albert Einstein (1879–1955), author of the relativity theories, and of a revolution in man's conception of his universe.

Bibliography

Marx, Marxism, and international socialism: Isaiah Berlin, *Karl Marx: His Life and Environment* (Oxford University Press); H.B. Mayo, *Introduction to Marxist Theory* (Oxford University Press); R.C. Tucker, *Philosophy and Myth in Karl Marx* (Cambridge University Press); Julius Braunthal, *History of the International 1864–1943* (2 vols.; London: Thomas Nelson & Sons, 1967); Aaron Noland, *The Founding of the French Socialist Party 1893–1905* (Cambridge, Mass.: Harvard University Press, 1956); Richard Hostetter, *The Italian Socialist Movement 1870–1882* (Princeton, N.J.: D. Van Nostrand, 1958); H.M. Pelling, *Origins of the Labour Party 1880–1900* (Oxford University Press); G.D.H. Cole's *History of Socialist Thought: The Second International 1889–1914* (2 vols.; New York: St. Martin's Press, 1956); James Joll, *The Second International* (New York: Frederick A. Praeger, 1956); A.M. MacBriar, *Fabian Socialism and English Politics 1884–1914* (New York: Cambridge University Press, 1962). Carl Schorske, *German Social Democracy 1905–1917* (John Wiley & Sons), is interesting from a left-wing bias; see also Peter Gay, *The Dilemma of Democratic Socialism: Bernstein's Challenge to Marx* (Macmillan, Collier). There are far too many good recent books on this subject to list. But the anarchists should not be overlooked; see James Joll, *The Anarchists* (Boston: Little, Brown, 1964), and Paul Avrich, *The Russian Anarchists* (Princeton, N.J.: Princeton University Press, 1967).

There are also numberless books on the politics of the various countries of Europe in this eventful period. France is well covered in D.W. Brogan's general survey, *France under the Republic 1870–1939* (New York: Harper & Bros., 1959); while the outstanding episode of the period is the subject of Guy Chapman's *The Dreyfus Case* (London: R. Hart-Davis, 1955), which is also treated in a recent book by Douglas Johnson, *France and the Dreyfus Affair* (London: Blanford, 1966). Chapman also has written a general account of *The Third Republic of France* (New York: Macmillan, 1962). Harvey Goldberg's excellent *Life of Jean Jaurès* (Madison: University of Wisconsin Press, 1962) tells the story of France's leading socialist; the right wing figures prominently in two books on the *Action Francaise* movement, one by Edward R. Tannenbaum (New York: John Wiley & Sons, 1962), and one by Eugen Weber (Stanford, Calif: Stanford University Press, 1962). See also David Thomson, *Democracy in France since 1870* (Oxford University Press). Germany: John A. Nichols, *Germany after Bismarck: The Caprivi Era, 1890–1894* (Harvard University Press, 1958); Harry F. Young, *Maximilian Harden* (The Hague: Nijhoff, 1959), excellent biography of a leading German editor and journalist; J.C.G. Röhl, *Germany without Bismarck* (Berkeley: University of California Press, 1968). Italy: A.W. Salomone, *Italian Democracy in the Making, 1900–1914* (rev. ed.; Philadelphia: University of Pennsylvania Press, 1960); John A. Thayer, *Italy and the Great War: Politics and Culture 1870–1915* (University of Wisconsin Press, 1965); Benedetto Croce, *A History of Italy 1871–1915* (reprinted; New York: Russell & Russell, 1963), a classic by one of Italy's greatest philosophers. Spain: Raymond Carr, *Spain 1808–1939* (New York: Oxford University Press, 1966), has received high praise; more detailed, and revealing the weakness of Spanish democracy, C.A.M. Hennessey, *The Federal Republic in Spain* (Oxford University Press, 1962).

On Russia, W.E. Mosse, *Alexander II and the Modernization of Russia* (Macmillan, Collier); Hugh Seton-Watson, *The Decline of Imperial Russia 1855–1914* (Frederick A. Praeger); Franco Venturi, *Roots of Revolution* (Grosset & Dunlap), the latter a brilliant study of Russian populism in the 1870's. Seton-Watson is also the author of *The Russian Empire 1801–1917*, like Carr's *Spain* a volume in the Oxford University History of Modern Europe series (1967). Theodore H. Von Laue, *Sergei Witte and the Industrialization of Russia* (New York: Columbia University Press, 1963), contributes an important part of the pre-1914 Russian pattern. An unusual glimpse into the mind of a revolutionary terrorist was provided by David Footman, *Red Prelude: Life of the Russian Terrorist Zhelyabov* (reprinted; London: Barrie & Rockcliff, 1966). Solomon M. Schwarz, a one-time Menshevik, has recently published a book on *The Russian Revolution of 1905* (Chicago: University of Chicago Press, 1967).

Philip Magnus, *Gladstone* (New York: E.P. Dutton, 1954), is a modern biography of the leading British statesman of the 1870–95 period. The *Oxford History of England* for this period (1870–1914) is by R.C.K. Ensor and is very good on domestic matters. F.S.L. Lyons, *The Fall of Parnell* (London: Routledge & Kegan Paul, 1962), and A.P. Ryan, *Mutiny at the Curragh* (St. Martin's Press, 1956), recount two sensational political episodes, both connected with the crisis over Irish home rule. Daniel Roberts, *Victorian Origins of the Welfare State* (New Haven, Conn.: Yale University Press, 1960), tackles an important process; cf. Maurice Bruce, *The Coming of the Welfare State* (London: Batsford, 1961). A superb work of the life of the 1908–16 prime minister, though a little thin on Great Britain especially in the Edwardian period, is Roy Jenkins' *Asquith: Portrait of a Man and an Era* (New York: Chilmark, 1965).

On intellectual developments, Charles Gillispie has written a history of 19th-century science, *Lavoisier to Einstein*, in the series on the History of Scientific Thought edited by G. di Santillana and published in paperback by New American Library, Mentor. H. Stuart Hughes, *Consciousness and Society: European Social Thought 1890–1930* (Random House, Vintage), chiefly concerned with the sociologists, and Gerhard Masur, *Prophets of Yesterday* (Harper), more literary and philosophical, make a good team for the study of European thought during the prewar period. Roger Shattuck, *The Banquet Years: The Arts in France 1858–1918* (Doubleday, Anchor), is a valuable synthesis. Selected individual thinkers: Walter Kaufmann, *Nietzsche* (World Publishing, Meridian); J.A.C. Brown, *Freud and the Post-Freudians* (Penguin); E.H. Carr, *Dostoyevsky* (London: George Allen & Unwin, 1962).

Sources. Agatha Ramm (ed.), *The Political Correspondence of Mr. Gladstone and Lord Granville* (4 vols.; London: Royal Historical Society, 1952, and Oxford University Press, 1962); Albert Fried and Ronald Sanders (eds.), *Socialist Thought: A Documentary History* (Doubleday, Anchor). Useful sourcebooks for intellectual history include Eugen Weber (ed.), *Paths to the Present* (Dodd, Mead) and Eugene Black (ed.), *The Posture of Europe, 1814–1940* (Dorsey Press). Another convenient anthology is Walter Kaufmann (ed.), *Religion from Tolstoy to Camus* (Harper & Row). For Russia, Marc Raeff (ed.), *Russian Intellectual History* (Harcourt, Brace & World).

"Germania on the Sea." Germany was one of many countries experiencing the fever of nationalism. Painting by Lorenz Clasen.

25

Origins of the World War

chronology

1878
Eastern crisis; Treaty of Berlin attempts to compose Balkan region.
1879
Austro-German alliance.
1881
Three Emperors' League (Austria-Hungary, Russia, Germany).
1882
Triple Alliance (Germany, Austria, Italy).
1885–86
Bulgarian atrocities; another crisis in eastern Europe.
Austro-Russian tension.
1887
Reinsurance Treaty, Germany and Russia, for three years.
Revival of revenge feeling in France; Franco-German tension.
1891
Franco-Russian agreement, developed by 1894 into full military alliance.
1894–95
Sino-Japanese war.
Armenian massacres.
1896
Kruger Telegram; friction between Germany and England over South Africa.
1898
First German Navy bill, development of big-navy policy.
Fashoda crisis, Britain and France.
1899
Hague Peace Conference.
1902
Anglo-Japanese alliance.
1904–5
Russo-Japanese War; ended by Treaty of Portsmouth. Russian return to interest in Balkans as a result.
Anglo-Russian hostility; Dogger Bank episode.
Anglo-French Entente.
1905–6
First Moroccan crisis. Algeciras Conference, 1906, Anglo-French solidarity.
1907
Anglo-Russian entente (Persia).
Dreadnought battleships; naval race between Germany and Britain.
Second Hague Peace Conference, failure of disarmament.
1908
Young Turk Revolution.
Bosnian Crisis, following Austrian annexation of Bosnia and Herzegovina.
1909
London Naval Conference.
German-French agreement on Morocco.
1911
Second Moroccan Crisis.
Tripolitan War, Italy attacks Ottoman Empire.
1912
First Balkan War, Bulgaria, Serbia, and Greece versus Turkey.
London Peace Conference.
Haldane mission to Germany; failure to settle naval race between Great Britain and Germany; agreement reached on colonial affairs.
Anglo-French naval cooperation.
1913
Second Balkan War; Bulgaria against Greece, Serbia, Rumania, Turkey.
Austrian ultimatum to Serbia to get out of Albania, to which Serbs yielded.
Treaty of Bucharest closing Second Balkan War.
Crisis between Russia and Germany over German influence in Turkey.
1914
Assassination of Archduke Francis Ferdinand, June 28.
Backing to Austria given by Germany, July 5.
Austrian decision to crush Serbia. Ultimatum, July 23.
French and Russian decision to defend Serbia, July 25.
Austrian declaration of war on Serbia, July 28.
Russian order for general mobilization, July 29–30.
German ultimatum to Russia demanding cessation of military preparations on German border; German inquiry to Paris, July 31.
French, German mobilization; German declaration of war on Russia, August 1.
German declaration of war on France and invasion of Belgium, August 3.
British declaration of war on Germany, August 4.

The upsurge of nationalism

Despite the uneasiness of a few intellectuals, pre-1914 Europe felt a sense of security it would not know again, and entertained a belief in slow but steady progress as a virtual certainty. Most Europeans, looking back on the long interval of peace since 1870 (and that had been a short war), did not think a major war possible; any doubts they might have felt were banished by reassuring books proving that war had become obsolete in an age of economic internationalism. When war came to Europe at the beginning of August, 1914, few expected it; fewer still suspected it would last more than four agonizing years and drain the Old World of most of her energies, slaughtering a high percentage of her young men; or that it would break up three existing empires, bring a communist revolution to one, and set in train a whole sequence of troubles. It was one of history's great moments of decision. After avoiding war for more than 40 years, and having had no large-scale, protracted war among all the major powers for a century, Europe succumbed to Mars and embarked upon the biggest armed struggle the world had ever known. In so doing she nullified a century of progress and reversed the direction of her movement from up to down. Western civilization turned its highly developed guns on itself and came close to committing suicide.

It is difficult to exaggerate the blow to a whole civilization felt by representative European bearers of that tradition as a result of this war. "The lights went out"—whether they would ever come back on again became a serious question. The search for an explanation of how this could have happened, the search for the causes of the World War, the responsibility, the guilt, began immediately and was carried on at great length for years afterward. The specific events in the story of international politics, the motives of statesmen, the interests of great powers, the alliances and crises, especially but not exclusively during the last fateful month of peace between June 28 and July 31, 1914, received detailed attention. And occasionally somebody probed deeper, to ask whether there was not something fundamentally wrong with European civilization at its most confident hour, whether there was not a worm of spiritual derangement in the apple of material success.

Varieties of nationalism

One general judgment at least could confidently be made: from Ireland to Russia and the Balkans, nationalism had taken possession of Europe. It would be hard to think of any important state or region where it did not make itself felt. While Irish patriots clamored for independence for the Emerald Isle, French nationalists demanded the return of Alsace and Lorraine, Italians dreamed of another *risorgimento* to "redeem" a few Italians still living under Austrian or Turkish rule, and Germans meditated upon a union of the Germanic peoples in control of all central Europe. Catalonian nationalists found that their part of Spain really was different from the Castilians and ought to be independent; Ukrainians made a similar discovery in Russia. The Jewish Zionist movement, looking toward a restoration of the Jews to Palestine where they should have their own national state, made its debut.

Of all the forces present in pre-1914 Europe, a superheated variety of nationalism was undoubtedly the most disturbing to international peace. In most western countries there was an extremist group, like the Pan-German League (*Alldeutscher Verband*) in Germany, which hardly determined policy but exercised an influence on public opinion with its exuberant nationalist propaganda. The Pan-German League demanded vigorous policies looking toward the absorption into a single Reich of all Germans everywhere—and of course there were islands of Germans in Russia, toward whose ample plains the German expansionists looked with the cry of "Lebensraum" for the expanding population of Germany proper. Even the Scandinavians and Hollanders, who after all were Germanic, might become part of this great empire! If this viewpoint in Germany took on sinister aspects in the light of what happened later, we should not forget that it had its counterpart, roughly, in those Englishmen who vaunted their country's imperial mission to spread English institutions all over the world, in French conservative nationalist movements such as the *Action Française* group, and in Russian Pan-Slavism.

Irish nationalism

The Irish question churned up the normally placid surface of British politics just before 1914. An explosive issue in the 1880's and 1890's, it returned after 1910. The Irish, or at least the Catholic south of Ireland, demanded "home rule" and wanted complete independence from English rule. The Protestant minority in north Ireland (Ulster) bitterly fought this and many in England backed them. A home rule bill was passed; was delayed in the House of Lords the maximum two years, and became law just as World War I began, but did not go into effect, being suspended because of the war. At that point home rule seemed about to be met by an armed mutiny of the British forces in Ireland—an ugly situation indeed, which was to be continued during the war when Catholic Ireland rebelled against enlistments in the British army and sympathized with the enemy.

Pan-Slavism

The Russian government at Petrograd attempted to "Russify" all its subjects, including the proud Poles and Finns, bearers of a different cultural tradition, by methods of the most barbarous nature, even forcibly suppressing these peoples' native language and literature. Meanwhile doctrines of "Pan-Slavism" arose to preach, in varying accents, the mission of Russia to unite all the Slavic peoples under Russian leadership. This Russian counterpart of Pan-Germanism was equally fraught with explosive consequences, for there were numerous Slavic peoples in eastern and central Europe outside Russia. A half-dozen kinds of Slavs—Czechs, Poles, Slovaks, Ruthenians, Croats, Slovenes—lived within the Austrian Empire. These other Slavs developed their own versions of Pan-Slavism, in which they would not be swallowed by Russia but would form a league or confederation. Rising nationalism, especially among the South Slavs—the Serbs, Croats, and Slovenes—threatened to break the Hapsburg monarchy apart.

Troubles of Austria-Hungary

The minorities grew violently nationalistic and troublesome in the last years of the Dual Monarchy. The Czechs cherished an old and proud national tradition, and gave trouble first, after the Hungarians were appeased in 1867; later, the Slovenes and Croats were stirred by the exploits of their fellow Slavs in independent Serbia, who aspired to liberate them from the Austrian yoke. Men wondered how this polyglot state could hold together. A certain personal loyalty to the old emperor, Franz Joseph, seemed the only cement, and it was a feeble one. On the other hand, there was economic unity in this largely Danubian monarchy, and any disintegration of the area into petty states would perhaps be a worse solution. The oldest monarchy in Europe lived from day to day, hoping for the best amid growing chaos. The best idea seemed a further devolution of powers to give the Slavs, or some of them, autonomy within the framework of a federal state. But nothing was done for fear that the slightest movement would cause the ramshackle structure to fall in a heap. Perhaps the most talented and popular royal figure in Europe, the genuinely liberal Rudolf, heir to the Hapsburg throne, committed suicide in 1889 in a tragedy that shook Europe to its depths. His cousin, the heir to the

Emperor Franz Josef at a grand ball in Vienna, 1900

throne assassinated in 1914, was much less able and popular. The tragedy of Mayerling seemed like an omen of Hapsburg misfortune. Could Rudolf have solved the complex and difficult problems of the Empire? It is one of history's many unanswered questions; but one must doubt that he could have.

Seeds of conflict

It is difficult to harmonize this picture of a state living with its days numbered, destined to blow up in 1914 and blow Europe up with it, with the gayety and ease of life in Vienna in the later 19th century: Vienna the city of Johann Strauss, dance-mad, theater-mad, and music-mad, a city whose culture was in all likelihood the crowning achievement of the 19th-century bourgeoisie. Here by the beautiful blue Danube the Germanic ruling classes built a way of life renowned throughout the world for its popular love of the arts; as musical as Germany, it incorporated the lighter and gayer breezes from the south. But behind this glamour there remained the unsolvable problems of politics. In all the eastern states—Austria-Hungary, Russia, Ottoman Empire—political sovereignties did not correspond to nationalities, peoples being mixed together under dynastic states. Movements for national "liberation" could only mean the complete dissolution of the old states in revolutionary turmoil, and the creation of some entirely new system of smaller national states. Nor was it even easy to see how each national group could be given a territory both viable and free from minorities, for nature had not been so obliging as to sort the peoples out this neatly. One had Slavs, Hungarians, and Rumanians (for example) all living together in the area of Hungary, and one had Serbs, Greeks and Bulgars hopelessly intermingled in Macedonia. The "eastern question" which plagued Europe and finally exploded in 1914 was in good part the result of this factor. The emergent national consciousness of formerly downtrodden peoples was undeniably in many ways a sign of progress. But it also brought frightful conflict to much of Europe.

Cultural nationalism and the sovereign state as absolute values could mean serious trouble wherever they did not coincide, that is, wherever, as in Russia or Austria-Hungary, there were significant cultural groups under the rule of another people, groups which yearned for their own national state but did not have it, and could only get it by breaking up existing political units. These were to be the trouble spots of Europe. But there were also conflicts between the stabler, more contented national states of western Europe—France, Germany, and Britain—which reflected nationalistic pride. The border provinces of Alsace and Lorraine were one such: seized by Germany in 1870, they had been a rankling grievance to Frenchmen ever since, who made the claim that they were culturally French and ought not to suffer under the rule of the Teuton. As between Germany and England, the precipitant of jealousy and pride was sea power: England would tolerate no equal in her traditional domain of power, and the Germans aspired to build a fleet to rival hers.

Supremacy of the national state

It almost goes without saying that the great states of Europe recognized no outside limitations on their sovereign powers. Efforts made at the Hague Conferences of 1899 and 1907 to get them to accept a measure of compulsory arbitration of their disputes had failed except for some polite gestures made in the direction of internationalism; so also had efforts to secure disarmament. They were all old and proud, and their peoples looked to them as the defenders of national interest, not some putative international one. Bismarck had not been far wrong when he once said that "Europe" no longer existed, only the nations. This was true insofar as it was widely accepted that the national cultures of France, Germany, England, and so on, were unique, different, not to be understood in terms of a common civilization but only in terms of themselves. In the words of the French writer Maurice Barrès, "The German truth and the English truth are not at all the French truth and can only poison us."

This cultural and political nationalism consorted very strangely with the economic *inter*nationalism that was such a pronounced feature of the world. A global economy made peoples interdependent. But everywhere people not only looked gratefully to the national state, or dreamed of one, but they de-

Bulgarians hanged in the streets of Philippopolis in Eastern Rumelia in 1876

veloped a kind of religion of nationalism. At a time when traditional Christianity was declining, as many thought, substitute secular religions grew up, and of these the most potent popular one unquestionably was nationalism. It was surrounded with all the attributes of religion. Men adored the flag, pledged allegiance to it, sang national anthems. The French made a cult of Joan of Arc at this time—saint, martyr, national heroine—while the Germans built statues to "Germania" and Englishmen to "Brittania." The writing of history, in which there was a renaissance at this time, dwelt chiefly on the theme of the rise of the nation from its dim origins in the past to its present glories. Hegelian philosophy taught that the great purposes of world history are realized in and through the states, which embody the collective will of cultural peoples.

And when the moment came in 1914, everyone was more than ready to prove devotion to the nation by marching off to fight and die for it. At its beginning the war was immensely popular in all circles; wildly cheering crowds saw the deliriously happy soldiers off in London, Paris, Berlin, Petrograd.

Southeastern Europe

The Balkans were, of all places, the most dangerous repository of nationalism. It is necessary to understand carefully the status of the region which had been troublesome to Europe for many a decade and now started a fire destined to spread over the whole world. This largely mountainous area of southeastern Europe was mainly poor; and it was politically backward, largely because of its unhappy subjugation by the Turks long ago. The sultan's government had gone from bad to worse, until it was the scandal of Europe. In 1876, massacres of Bulgarians incensed European opinion; Russia intervened, and a great European conference at Berlin, in which Bismarck and Disraeli played major roles, sought to tranquilize the Balkans (1878).

Balkan crisis of 1878

The demand of Britain's Gladstone, that the Turks "one and all, bag and baggage, clear out from the provinces they have desolated and profaned," was regarded as far from an ideal solution because it might open up avenues to Russian expansion, or turn loose peoples who had not yet developed habits

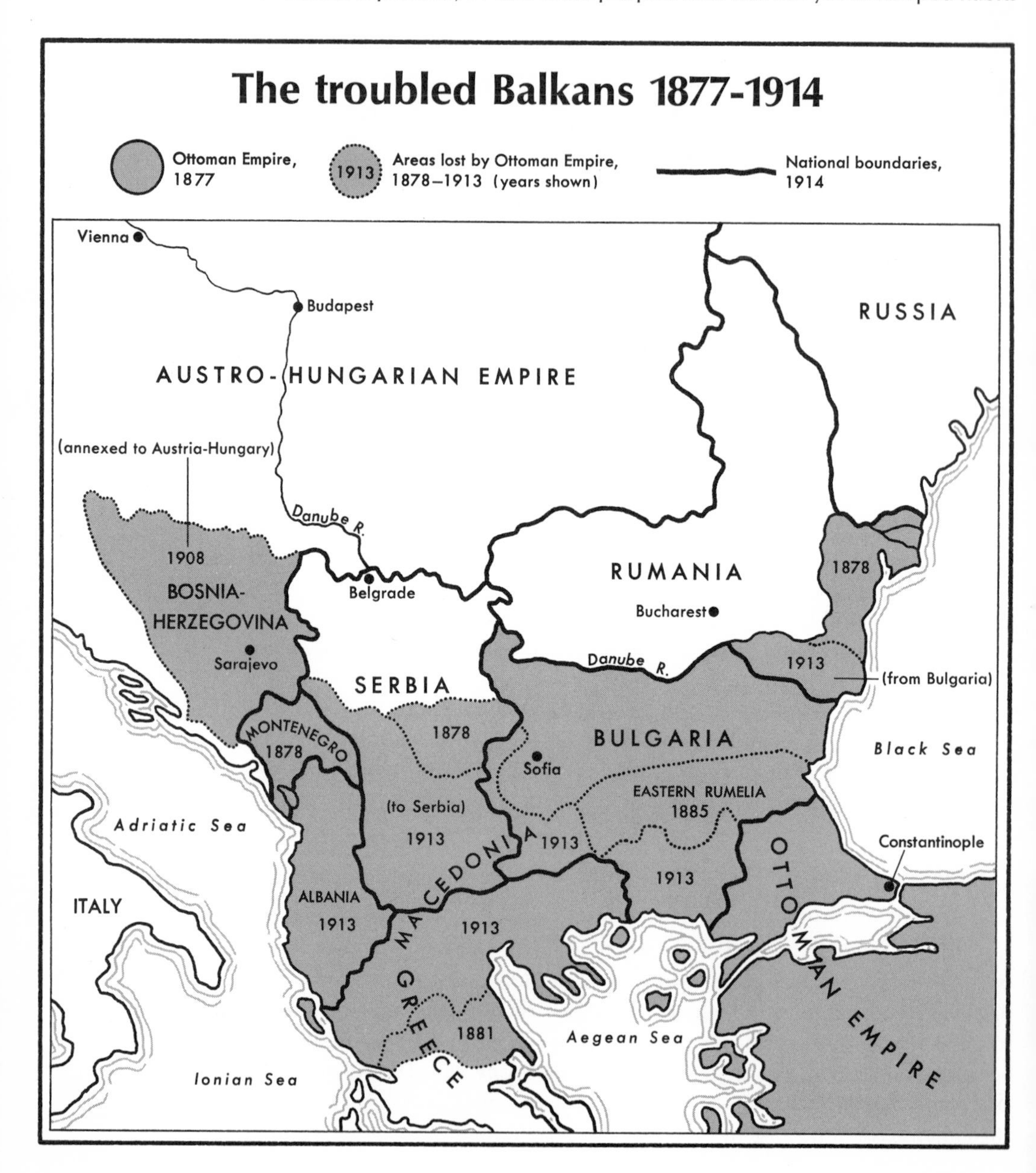

of orderly government. At Berlin in 1878, the powers destroyed the integrity of the Ottoman Empire in Europe but refused to throw the Turk out altogether, and supplied a solution which turned out to be productive of further trouble. The complex results of this major diplomatic settlement, in which Bismarck played the part of "honest broker" between the jealous rivals Russia, Great Britain, and Austria-Hungary, included a three-way division of Bulgaria, an Austrian *protectorate* over the important areas of Bosnia and Herzegovina (still technically under Turkish sovereignty), and outright independence for Serbia, Rumania, and the tiny state of Montenegro.

The arrangement did not provide stability. Though the Turk promised to reform, he did not, and a new rebellion occurred in 1885 in Eastern Rumelia, the portion of Bulgaria which had been left in the hands of the Turks. This then became a part of Bulgaria. But enlargement of the Balkan states usually served only to whet their ambitions. Serbia coveted Bosnia, Bulgaria Macedonia, in order to get valuable seaports, but the Austrian Empire had an eye on the same places. (See map.)

The chief difficulties of the 1900's stemmed from the rise of this little independent Balkan state of Serbia (together with its even smaller colleague Montenegro). The Serbs were proud and ambitious if few and poor. Serbian nationalism increased apace with the discontent of the South Slavs (Croats, Slovenes) in the Austrian Empire, who looked to their close relatives the Serbs for liberation from the Magyar yoke. Thus the fires of nationalism kept the Balkan pot boiling.

But the interests and rivalries of the great powers helped make this boiling pot a threat to set the world aflame. The vital interests of Austria-Hungary and of Russia were involved. While South Slav nationalism menaced the very existence of the Dual Monarchy, Russia felt a natural sympathy for the "little brothers" of the Balkans; and of course to both powers the strategic significance of this crossroads region was apparent. The stake was Constantinople itself, long believed to be a key to world power. Both states looked in this direction and saw much at stake in their rivalry for domination of the unstable Balkans.

Bosnian crisis of 1908

Russia, after defeat by Japan in 1905 caused her to lose interest in the Far East, turned with renewed interest to Balkan intrigue. After the murder of a king in 1903, Serbia fell under a dynasty (the Karageorgevich) hostile to Austria and friendly to Russia. To complicate matters came a revolution in Turkey in 1908, the Young Turk revolt, which encouraged people to believe that the time had come to move toward a final showdown in the Balkans. In 1908 Austria rather abruptly annexed outright the provinces of Bosnia and Herzegovina, which since 1878 had been under her administration. Russia had in fact begun the sequence of events that led to this move, by proposing to Austria that the time had come for a general sharing out of the Ottoman Empire; but Great Britain would not agree to the Russians' getting Constantinople, and while Austria took hers the Russians were left out.

Their howls of protest caused the Bosnian crisis, which ended in a Russian humiliation, France refusing to fight for her ally Russia in a Balkan quarrel. Germany was in fact angry with her ally, Austria, for having precipitated so dangerous a crisis; and many regarded the Austrian action as illegal. The Serbs were outraged. The Bosnian crisis left Serbia and Russia both dangerously angry.

Interests of the powers

The position of all the parties in this complicated area should be grasped, for the World War started here. Austria-Hungary was fearful of the revolt of her numerous Slavic minorities and had to control the source of nationalist agitation; hence her determination to keep down Serbia. Serbia was aflame with nationalistic righteousness, and aspired to free the other South Slavs who groaned under the Austrian or Hungarian yoke. Russia felt a natural sympathy for the "little brother" Slavs, and was ambitious to recoup her badly shaken prestige by defending them, a course which might achieve old and important Russian ambitions to gain Constantinople. And throughout the region, unstable political conditions provided an abundance of opportunity for intrigue. Through it all the most important fact making for change was the rise of national consciousness among the Balkan peoples themselves —not only Serbs, but also Bulgarians, Rumanians, Greeks, Macedonians, and others, in some places hopelessly intermixed. Macedonia was the best example of this, being a target for at least four brands of nationalism.

The Balkan Wars of 1912–13

Encouraged by Russia, the states of Serbia, Bulgaria, and Greece formed themselves into a Balkan League in 1912 and soon attacked Turkey, which was then engaged in a war with Italy, also descending upon the "sick man" in search of Tripoli. Perhaps the great European war began in 1911, not 1914, though at the time few people in western Europe paid much attention to such remote quarrels. The First Balkan War saw the three small Balkan powers successfully defeat the temporarily demoralized Turk. They drove him out "bag and baggage," taking generous slices of his territory, the Serbs particularly making substantial gains. Austria, alarmed, stepped in and vetoed the Serbs' bid for an Adriatic port in Albania. A diplomatic conference at London decided to put an independent Albania under guardianship of the great powers, which displeased the Serbs. But the powers could not prevent the Balkan states from quarreling over the spoils of the war with Turkey, Macedonia being the chief source of trouble. Bulgaria felt aggrieved at getting less than she thought her share in the war entitled her to. Greece and Serbia, joined by Rumania, fought against Bulgaria in the Second Balkan War of 1913. While Turkey took advantage of the situation to regain Adrianople, the Bulgars were beaten and deprived of territory. Serbia was again victorious, and Austria again was alarmed.

Dangers of War

What emerged from the complexities of Balkan affairs in these two wars of 1912–13 was that the Balkan countries were out of control, not listening

Bulgarian troops besieging the Turks in Adrianople in 1913 during the First Balkan War

to the great powers; that Serbia was ambitious, and Austria-Hungary extremely fearful and suspicious of her; that Russia would back Serbia at a pinch, while Germany would probably back Austria. It was a dangerous situation, and it exploded in 1914. Had the great powers shown a genuine will to cooperate, they could doubtless have solved it. The blindness of both Austria and Russia impresses one, for neither was in a position to endure a great war. But the uncertainty of the tsar's throne, and the precarious situation within Austria-Hungary, rendered both governments desperate for prestige and apprehensive about suffering any loss of face. In high circles of the Hapsburg state, the opinion grew that one way out of the frightful internal mess was to smash Serbia, thus removing the principal external irritant. In Russia, the "Pan-Slavs" worked themselves up into a veritable religious passion for the Balkan mission of their country.

European alliances

Franco-Russian alliance

It is a fact that while the World War started with an event in Bosnia and a quarrel between Serbia and Austria, it became a terrible war in the West between Germany and France–Great Britain. These countries were to be drawn in partly as a result of their alliances with the primary foes. France, since one memorable day in 1894, had an alliance with Russia—unpopular, at first, in republican circles there, but a source of security against Germany. The agreement between Russia and France provided that either would go to the other's help in the event of an attack by Germany, or by Austria supported by Germany. It did not commit France to support Russia in a war with Austria alone, nor commit either state to support the other in a war with anyone else, nor in an aggressive war. It had not meant much in 1904 or 1908, when Russia's quarrels in eastern places seemed of little interest to France. But France clung to it as her bulwark against isolation and in 1914 decided that she could not afford to desert Russia again. French capital poured into Russia to modernize her industries and improve her military efficiency in these years.

The central powers

Germany, for her part, was tied to Austria. She was not always happy about this, for it drew her into Balkan quarrels that offered dangers without

Kaiser Wilhelm II—*powerful German warships such as this stirred Britain to build the* Dreadnought

rewards. Bismarck had once made the memorable remark that the whole of the Balkan peninsula was not worth the bones of a single Pomeranian grenadier. However, in the 1900's Germany seemed always to back her sister Germanic monarchy, for she too had no other friend and felt that the *Mitteleuropa* bloc must not be sundered. And though some in Austria had nourished "revenge for Sadowa" feelings, the precarious Dual Monarchy now leaned heavily on her German friend.

Bismarck had regarded it as vital for Germany to keep on good terms with Russia and England, thus avoiding a situation in which Germany would have to support Austria as her only ally; but Bismarck's successors succeeded in alienating not only Russia but Britain. The previous record of amiable Anglo-German and also Anglo-Austrian relations should be stressed: as late as 1901 there was a significant move toward an outright pact between Germany and Britain, which testified to a strong feeling of solidarity. After all, Britain regarded Russia and, after her, France as the natural and historic enemies, and the Central Powers could help against both. The Franco-Russian pact was unpopular in England; Queen Victoria was always pro-German and intensely anti-Russian. If this picture changed startlingly in the 1900's the fault lay in good part with the aggressive naval program of the Kaiser which alarmed and angered the British.

The "Entente Cordiale"

France drew closer to Great Britain in the most significant diplomatic revolution of the 1900's. Prior to 1904, England had quarreled with France in Africa and had seemed to be on better terms with Germany. Of crucial importance in pushing England away from Germany was her fear of German sea power. Kaiser Wilhelm II and his advisers were naval-minded. The British were genuinely alarmed though their navy was larger than that of the Germans, and a naval race stirred the 1900's, with all efforts at limitation by agreement breaking down. Moreover, in the Moroccan crisis of 1905, Germany challenged France's supremacy in Morocco; and the British felt that Germany was bidding for an Atlantic base, which would thrust them right into the middle of world naval power.

First Moroccan crisis

The British and French had agreed to let France have a protectorate over Morocco, but unfortunately without consulting the Germans (naturally they did not consult the Moroccans, though the secret parts of this agreement provided for eventual partition of the country between France and Spain). The German government challenged this, the more boldly because France's ally Russia was for the time being wholly removed from the picture by the Russo-Japanese war then going on. The Germans had a strong grievance because of being ignored in Morocco, and chose to make the episode an occasion for a test of the strength of the new Anglo-French entente. Would the British back France? They did, and began secret military and naval discussions with France at this time. The Algeciras Conference of 1906, which terminated the crisis, largely went against Germany, though some concessions were made to her in Morocco, with a treaty being signed between France and Germany in 1909.

Certain circles in Germany were in favor of war at this time on the grounds that Germany's foes would never be weaker. However, the Kaiser did not favor such policies. In the aftermath of Algeciras, though, he appeased the German nationalists and militarists by enlarging upon the naval program. Arms limitation was discussed at the second Hague Peace Conference of 1907, but made no headway. A naval race between Germany and Britain, building the new British-invented "dreadnought" type of battleship, was soon in high gear.

A series of truculent speeches (and a newspaper interview) by the ebullient Kaiser William II also went far to persuade Englishmen that Imperial Germany was their foe. King Edward, unlike his mother Queen Victoria, was fond of the French (not least French ladies, it would appear). An undercurrent of hostility could be felt in Anglo-German exchanges of the 1900's, and from 1906 on, the British and French engaged in secret naval collaboration based on the assumption that in the next war they would be fighting together against Germany. This *Entente Cordiale* fell short of a formal alliance, and in 1914 no one quite knew what England would do. But the French were reasonably sure they could count on her at a pinch, while British opinion was prepared to believe the worst of Germany.

Russia and Britain

The French-British *rapprochement* facilitated a reconciliation between those old foes, Russia and Great Britain. Old foes they were: the Russian advance into Central Asia after mid-19th century confirmed British suspicions that the Russian bear was an animal not to be trusted. India, it was feared, was the prey she stalked; lively intrigue between Russians and British occurred in such places as Afghanistan and Persia. In 1902 the British made an alliance with Japan clearly aimed at Russia, whom she considered the most aggressive power in the Far East. Russia's "resignation" in Asia after 1905 took some of the pressure off, and France was eager to get her two new friends together.

A 1907 agreement concerning spheres of influence in Persia was the chief sign of this reconciliation. The Bear and the Lion, it was said, had sliced up the Persian pussy. They did not, however, get along well after that in Persia, and the average Englishman's opinion of Russia continued to be no very favorable one. Liberal circles in Britain and the United States denounced the tsarist persecution of minorities, of whom great numbers migrated to the United States in this era. So there was far from any close Russo-British understanding on the eve of the war.

France and Germany

France, of course, had never forgotten the humiliation of 1871 and the loss of the provinces of Alsace and Lorraine. There had been fears of a French war of revenge in 1875 and 1887. But few Frenchmen believed that France could win a war against Germany without help. The alliance with

Russia was a victory which overturned Bismarck's long success in keeping France isolated, but which created in turn a German fear of encirclement, making them trigger-happy in 1914. But with the Triple Alliance of Germany, Austria-Hungary, and Italy to offset Russia, France never felt that there was enough chance of victory to justify a war. As a French leader remarked in 1911 at the time of the Second Moroccan Crisis, France would probably go to war against Germany if the chances of success were as high as 70 percent. But she would hardly initiate such a war under any ordinary circumstances. In 1914 Germany felt that the Franco-Russian combination was increasing in strength as the French helped modernize the Russian army and industry, and apparently lived in terror of a two-front war. "Every nation in Europe has its bayonets pointed at Germany," the German Emperor told Colonel E.M. House, the American diplomatist, on the eve of the war. Thus in 1914 the two rival blocs looked at each other anxiously and were prey to fears of having the balance of power tip against them. It was a significant part of the pattern of war causation.

The road to war

We may need to repeat in summary the basic position of each of the powers. France desired revenge, recovery of the mastery of Europe, and recovery of the "lost provinces" of Alsace and Lorraine, but was hardly prepared to initiate a war against her powerful neighbor. She did break out of isolation to form an alliance with Russia, an alliance which encircled Germany and made her uneasy. Germany held on to Austria-Hungary as an ally and an approximate balance of power existed, but an uneasy one. The Balkan quarrels of Russia and Austria-Hungary might draw in their respective partners —this was the great danger. As for Great Britain, which had customarily stood apart from the alliances of the Continent, she drifted into a close understanding with France, primarily through fear of Germany's naval power.

A decade of crises

Some of the "crises" that preceded 1914 have been referred to. War came in 1914 partly because for a number of years Europe had managed to avoid war, at the price of exhausting both patience and room for compromise. There had been almost a decade of tension, beginning with the Russo-Japanese war, then the First Moroccan Crisis (1905–6). There followed, shortly, the Anglo-Russian entente and the Bosnian crisis, which made 1908 a particularly tense year. And no sooner had the Bosnian affair died away, leaving a sore Russia nursing her bruises, than the Second Moroccan Crisis loomed up. The agreement reached between France and Germany in 1909 concerning their interests in Morocco broke up in a controversy wherein Germany charged France with violating the agreement and the Algeciras Act. The French were indeed guilty of this, but again Germany overplayed her hand by sending a warship to Morocco (Agadir) and appearing to threaten war. Nevertheless neither side really wanted war and a settlement was reached, in which Germany yielded a free hand to France in Morocco in return for some territory out of the French Congo. The episode considerably stirred public opinion on both sides in 1910–11, the French talking of German blackmail, the Germans of French greed.

Immediately thereafter Italy attacked Turkey, and the Balkan League followed suit, leading on to the two Balkan Wars as described earlier. The Anglo-German naval race went on, and in 1912 a significant bid to end it (the Haldane mission) failed. The German price for cessation of her naval program was a promise of British neutrality in a European war; the British would not go this far. Thereupon Germany again announced a naval increase.

Germany and England nevertheless reached colonial agreements and tension did not seem to have increased. But when the murder of the Archduke of Austria at Sarajevo on June 28, 1914, launched Europe on the last crisis, all governments and all peoples had a tendency to feel that the lid had to blow off, and perhaps a war would relieve Europe from her intolerable tensions. Both sides felt they had backed down too many times and now had to stand firm. Russia, in particular, would not submit to another such humiliation as that of 1908, nor would Austria-Hungary tolerate any more provocation from Serbia. Their allies were ready to back them up this time.

To sum up: the decade between 1904 and 1914 saw a serious clash between Germany and France over Morocco, an apparently trivial matter which involved a testing of the Anglo-French entente, and a possible naval base on the Atlantic for Germany; it cemented the Anglo-French entente, caused a feeling that Germany was too inclined to employ the methods of gunboat diplomacy and international blackmail, and underscored the Anglo-German naval race. While France and Germany were not prepared to go to war over Morocco, these crises inflamed public opinion on both sides. The other major area of tension was of course the Balkans, where the chief clash was between Serbia, backed by Russia, and Austria-Hungary, backed by Germany. The 1907 revolution in Turkey, followed by the Italian war on Turkey and then the two Balkan wars of 1913, not only set a dangerous example of violence but rendered a tense situation even more explosive.

The Sarajevo assassination

The fateful assassination of Archduke Franz Ferdinand at Sarajevo, in Bosnia, by a Serbian nationalist, took place on June 28, 1914. It jolted Austria into carrying out its policy of war against Serbia, in order to extinguish Serbian independence. This was the decision that set off the chain reaction to war. The assassin[1] was associated with a secret terrorist society with headquarters in Serbia, founded in 1911 in order to carry on political warfare against Austrian rule in Bosnia. The Austrians blamed the act on the Serbian government, probably wrongly, but perhaps understandably. To the Austrians, this last brutal act was only the culmination of a long record of Serb provo-

[1] Gavrilo Princip was a restless, idealistic youth with literary interests and left-wing views, who had flunked out of school and had been rejected by the Serbian army during the Balkan Wars as physically unfit.

Powers of Europe and the Balkans, a 1912 view

The Archduke Franz Ferdinand moments before his assassination, June 28, 1914.

Gavrilo Princip is hustled into custody after shooting the Austrian prince.

cations, and a plan they had long meditated was now put into effect. They believed all Europe was shocked enough to deny Serbia any sympathy, and this at first seemed to be true.

The Austrian ultimatum

A severe ultimatum went from Vienna to Belgrade on July 23. Serbia's conciliatory reply was construed as a rejection, and on July 28 Austria declared war. Real military operations did not begin until August 12, though a few bombs were dropped on Belgrade July 29. Austria willed war against Serbia, using the assassination as an excuse; the real reason was the view of Austrian statesmen that their problems would get steadily worse unless Serbia were destroyed now.

Outbreak of general war

Austria wanted to be left free to deal with Serbia, and hoped the other powers would stand by. However, Russia decided she must fight to defend Serbia (July 24) and France decided she would have to stand by Russia (July 25, or July 22? What French President Poincaré said to the Tsar on the latter date has never been revealed.) Germany had been committed to Austria since July 5, on which occasion she gave a "blank check" of unqualified support to her ally, a grave decision about which she had some subsequent doubts but could not take back. When Russia on July 29–30 decreed a general mobilization of troops, despite German warnings, the Germans sent both an ultimatum to Russia and an inquiry to Paris, asking France what she intended to do. They did not get satisfactory replies. The Russians wished to fight only Austria, as the Austrians wished to fight only Serbia; but in mobilizing they caused the Germans to react in fear of a general war. On August 1 Germany declared war on Russia and on August 3 against France, immediately launching an invasion of France through neutral Belgium in accordance with war plans. England on August 4 declared war on Germany because of the violation of Belgian neutrality.

War guilt?

Europe had come to zero hour. Later, historians and statesmen filled hundreds of volumes in an effort to clarify such questions as war "guilt," war "responsibility," might-have-beens, causes, causes behind causes. Much was said in defense of and against everybody. In the course of the long investigation the cruder version of the Central Powers' "war guilt" theory (firmly believed by the Allied peoples during the war) went by the boards. None of the participants willed war in any evil or criminal sense; they all felt they had to act as they did. Each people believed passionately that it was fighting a war of defense. It was a cycle of fear rather than aggression. Austria, which willed the extinction of Serbia, felt that the Serbs had attacked her in her sorest place by propaganda, assassination, terrorism. It is easy to accuse the Austrian leaders (especially the chief of staff of the army, Conrad von Hötzendorf, who had for years urged preventive war on Serbia, and Count Berchtold, the foreign minister—not the old Emperor, who was duped) of criminal irresponsibility; but on the other hand few governments have endured as much at the hands of a smaller neighbor, and the situation of the Dual Monarchy was indeed a desperate one. One wonders what state would have acted otherwise under similar circumstances. Germany, which started the war in the west, claimed that she had to do so to forestall a Franco-Russian squeeze which would crush her. There are so many other examples in history of the powerful impulses toward preventive war in such circumstances (consider Israel in 1967) that Germany must probably be acquitted of having behaved abnormally here. The overt aggressors were apparently the Central Powers, Germany and Austria-Hungary, whatever provocation or extenuation they had. But some historians have blamed Russia for being the first to mobilize as well as for encouraging the provocative course of Serbian nationalism. The fact is that Russia could not allow Austria to crush Serbia, and Germany could not allow Russia to defeat Austria, while France could not allow Germany to smash Russia. These seem the salient points.

Mistakes that led to war

Their fears dominated the powers. Austria feared internal revolution; Russia feared loss of prestige, leading possibly to revolution; France feared isolation; Germany feared encirclement. No war is "inevitable." As usual there were many "might have beens" in this story. Germany should have held back Austria, instead of giving her a "blank check" of unconditional support, as she did on July 5. Austria should never have resorted to the desperate gamble of unilateral armed action against Serbia, great as was her provocation. The Serbian government should have controlled its unruly nationalistic fanatics. Russia should not have encouraged Serbian nationalism as a weapon against Austria. The great powers should not all have been armed to the teeth. Russia should not have decreed general mobilization, leading Germany to think that Russia might strike at her as well as defend Serbia. (But the Tsar's military experts told him partial mobilization was technically impossible.) France might have restrained Russia instead of promising her support. Great Britain might have bestirred herself more energetically to restrain both sides and mediate in the quarrel. Germany should not have been so trigger-happy. These were the chief errors—easier, of course, to detect with the advantage of hindsight than to see at the time. It does not seem as if there were any great statesmen in 1914—none like Disraeli and Bismarck, who had saved the peace in 1878 under similar circumstances.

No one felt really strongly about avoiding war; everyone went to war with a certain complacence. The Darwinian, realist mood permeated the statesmen; Conrad von Hötzendorff wrote that ". . . men and nations alike are dominated by the struggle for existence. Force is the law of life, and the statesman must shape his course accordingly." The great majority of military experts expected a fierce but short war, like that of 1870–71 or 1904–5. Nothing like the horror of what lay ahead was expected. War was regarded as a more or less normal method of settling otherwise unresolvable disputes, as even the peace planners at the Hague Conferences implied by the attention given to the rules of war.

The fact remains that during and after the war an earnest search for the "war guilt" quite naturally took place. It is a complex question, in the last analysis probably an unanswerable one. One popular opinion has been this: that the Germans, listening too much to purely military advice, made a monumental blunder—whether or not it was a crime—when they chose to attack first in the west and strike through neutral Belgium. In the quarrel between Serbia-Russia and Austria-Hungary over the Balkans, neither France nor England really cared very much to take the former's side in any major war. Is it possible that the war could have been localized had the Germans stayed on the defensive in the west? By their drastic action they brought Britain into the war, sacrificed much of world opinion, and inspired the French to an effort that was to be, this time, no equivalent of 1870.

Against this, however, it must be repeated that obviously for Germany the situation was fraught with the gravest dangers, and she could hardly count on France remaining passive. The French could not stand aside and watch the Central Powers crush her ally, Russia—the result would have been pure disaster for her, clearly.

In this chain of fear it is not easy to figure out the solution that might have saved western civilization its gravest blow perhaps in all history, and one may well conclude with many an historical analyst that this was a tragedy in the

Londoners cheer their king on the announcement of war, August 4, 1914.

deepest sense—not a simple case of right versus wrong but "right versus right." Meanwhile so far as most Europeans were concerned, they were far from apprehending the tragedy. The war was anything but unpopular at the beginning. As the soldiers marched off to the sound of cheering throngs, even the socialists, who had vowed never to go to war against their fellow workers in other countries, rallied to the defense of the fatherlands. The full horror of modern war had not yet made itself known to the world. It would soon do so.

Bibliography

Shelves have been filled with the fruits of more or less scholarly inquiry into the causes of World War I. Almost the last word in this long debate seems to have been said by the Italian historian Luigi Albertini, whose *Origins of the War of 1914* (3 vols.; New York: Oxford University Press, 1952–57) is both meticulous and fair. Another recent summary is A.J.P. Taylor's *Struggle for the Mastery of Europe 1848–1914* (Oxford University Press, 1955). A sampling of the controversy may be obtained in Dwight E. Lee (ed.), *Outbreak of the First World War* (Raytheon Education, Heath Problems in European History series). Vol. II of the *Journal of Contemporary History*, entitled *1914: Origins of World War I*, edited by Walter Laqueur and George L. Mosse (Harper Torchbook), contains a series of essays by leading American and European historians on the origins of the war. Among the abler monographs are E.L. Woodward, *Great Britain and the German Navy* (Oxford: Clarendon Press, 1935); W.L. Langer, *European Alliances and Alignments* (Random House, Vintage); A.P. Pribram, *England and the International Policy of the European Great Powers 1871–1914* (Oxford University Press, 1931); E.C. Helmreich, *The Diplomacy of the Balkan Wars 1912–1913* (Cambridge Mass.: Harvard University Press, 1938); J. Remak, *Sarajevo* (New York: Criterion Books, 1959). The earlier tangled history of Balkan diplomacy has been investigated by W.N. Medlicott, *The Congress of Berlin and After* (London: Methuen Publications, 1938); Medlicott is also the author of *Bismarck, Gladstone, and the Concert of Europe* (London: Athlone Press, 1956). For a closer look at the peoples of this area, see Charles and Barbara Jelavich, *The Balkans* (Englewood Cliffs, N.J.: Prentice-Hall, 1965). The recent book by V. Dedijer, *The Road to Sarajevo* (New York: Simon & Schuster, 1966), is probably the last word on the background of the assassination. George Monger, *The End of Isolation: British Foreign Policy 1900–1907* (London: Thomas Nelson & Sons, 1963), is a careful and fairly objective account, based on all the sources, of how Britain swung to the side of France. A sound older textbook is Raymond Sontag's *European Diplomatic History 1871–1932* (New York: Appleton-Century-Crofts, 1933); recently a semipopular account has been offered by Laurence Lafore, *The Long Fuse* (Lippincott). The affairs of the Dual Monarchy, essential to any understanding of how the war began, can be grasped via A.J.P. Taylor, *The Hapsburg Monarchy 1809–1918* (Harper & Row); Oscar Jaszi, *The Dissolution of the Hapsburg Monarchy* (University of Chicago, Phoenix); or A.J. May, *The Hapsburg Monarchy 1867–1914* (Harvard University Press, 1951).

Important nationalist movements are the subject of Mildred Wertheimer, *The Pan-German League* (New York: Columbia University Press, 1924); Eugen Weber, *The Nationalist Revival in France 1905–1914* (Berkeley: University of California Press, 1959), and Frank Fadner, *Seventy Years of Pan-Slavism in Russia* (Washington: Georgetown University Press, 1962). On the general subject of nationalism, see standard treatments by Hans Kohn, *The Idea of Nationalism* (New York: Macmillan, 1944), and Carlton J.H. Hayes, *The Historical Evolution of Modern Nationalism* (New York: R.R. Smith, 1931). Stress on the play of diplomacy is found in the engaging books by G.P. Gooch,

Studies in Diplomacy and Statecraft and *Before the War* (London: Longmans, Green, 1942, 1936–38), while individual statesmen of prominence have been studied by Keith Eubank, *Paul Cambon, Master Diplomatist* (Norman: University of Oklahoma Press, 1960), and Harold Nicolson, *Portrait of a Diplomatist* (Boston: Houghton Mifflin, 1930), this being his father, a leading architect of British policy in 1914.

The sources are particularly important on this topic, and many have been printed. *The British Documents on the Origins of the War*, edited by G.P. Gooch and H.V. Temperley, in 11 volumes, were published 1926–38; the *Documents diplomatiques français 1871–1914* were completed in 20 volumes in 1959; largest of all was the German set, *Die Grosse Politik der Europaischen Kabinette, 1871–1914*, 40 volumes (Berlin, 1922–26), of which a 4-volume selection was printed in English translation, *German Diplomatic Documents 1871–1914* (London: Methuen, 1928–31). For the less ambitious student, there is fascinating reading in G.P. Gooch's *Recent Revelations of European Diplomacy* (4th ed.; Longmans, Green, 1940), which summarizes and comments on the many volumes of personal memoirs by leading statesmen which appeared in the years after the war. Among the more important of these memoirs were those by Grey, Poincaré, Bethmann-Hollweg, Conrad von Hötzendorff, and Sazonoff.

26

The World War: 1914-18

chronology

1914

Vast German invasion of Belgium and France, beginning August 4. Battle of the Marne, September 5–12. Stabilization of western front across northeastern France by December.

Russian offensive against both Austria and Germany, forcing Germans to withdraw troops from western front. Defeat of Russians, battles of Tannenberg (August 26–30) and Masurian Lakes (September 6–15).

1915

Dardanelles campaign, February–December, finally abandoned in failure by British. Great Austro-German offensive against Russia on eastern front, inflicting huge losses and capturing Poland, Baltic region.

Tsar Nicholas assumes personal command of Russian armies, September.

Entrance of Italy into war on Allied side.

Sinking of *Lusitania* by German submarine; American protests.

1916

Renewal of major action on western front. Battle of Verdun, February–July, enormous loss of life on both sides, no decisive result. Allied offensive on Somme, July–November, small gains of territory at great expense.

Naval battle of Jutland, May 31–June 1.

Brusilov offensive by Russians, summer and fall, with initial successes but eventual collapse with loss of a million men as Germans strengthened Austrian armies. Rumania defeated and invaded by Austro-German forces.

Efforts at mediation by American government, also by Pope.

Lloyd George replaces Asquith as head of British government.

1917

Unrestricted submarine warfare announced by Germany. U.S. declaration of war against Germany April 6. Heavy toll of Allied shipping taken by subs, but convoying, more shipbuilding, and other countermeasures effective by summer.

Mutiny in French army, May–June, brought under control by General Petain. Collapse of Nivelle offensive.

March Revolution in Russia, abdication of Tsar, liberal government installed. Further military defeats, leading to Bolshevik Revolution in November.

British offensive at Ypres (Passchendaele), July–November, another failure with large losses.

Shattering Italian defeat at Caporetto, October–December.

Trench warfare in France—British infantry charge "over the top"

Clemenceau becomes head of French government. War-weariness in all countries. German Reichstag passes resolution for peace without annexations.
Greece finally enters war on Allied side.

1918

Treaty of Brest-Litovsk, March 3, humiliating peace made by Russian revolutionary government. Loss of Poland, Baltic provinces, Finland, Ukraine. Rumania also forced to make peace. Civil war begins in Russia.
Allied war aims stated, January 5, 8, by Lloyd George and President Wilson of United States; Wilson's "Fourteen Points."
Great German offensive in West, March–July; initial successes, but American troops help cause ultimate collapse of offensive.
British successes under General Allenby in Palestine area; Turks seek armistice.
Collapse of Bulgaria. Disintegration of Austria-Hungary with secession of minorities.
Allied offensive on western front, August–November. General Ludendorff seeks armistice terms. Collapse of German morale; mutiny at Kiel, November 3, revolution in German cities, November 4–9. Abdication of Kaiser Wilhelm II, November 9.
Armistice signed 11 a.m., November 11.

Armageddon: The first act

Apart from a few bombs dropped on Belgrade, the first noise of the greatest of wars in history (prior to 1914) was the mighty thunder of the German assault through neutral Belgium aimed at France. The Germans put into effect a plan long prepared for such an eventuality. They must crush France before slow-moving Russia could bring her vast manpower to bear on Germany from the east—so the German general staff had assumed. This could be done by violating Belgian neutrality, pledged by treaty since 1831; this "scrap of paper" would have to yield to the higher interests of national security. Moving five powerful armies on the right wing in a thrust to encircle and trap the French armies, the Germans expected to defeat France in a few weeks. They had done so in 1870, and they would do so again in 1940. They did not quite pull it off in 1914.

German attack through Belgium

The Germans gambled that their invasion of Belgium could win the war in one great thrust. Neutral opinion all over the world formed the impression that Germany had begun the war in a particularly brutal manner, and it was this which swung Great Britain to come in immediately on the side of France: it is unlikely that Britain would have entered the war at this time but for this violation of Belgian neutrality, though it is doubtful that she could have stayed out for long. The British position fundamentally was that of preserving the balance of power, and she could not allow Germany to smash France. If the gamble on initial victory did not pay off, the Central Powers might find themselves in a bad situation.

The Schlieffen plan

Memories of 1870 encouraged the Germans to feel that they could dispose of France soon, and the military plans had long been studied. But the Schlieffen plan, famed document which formed the basis of the Belgian invasion, was an alteration of the older Moltke's strategic ideas. It reflected the greater confidence, or cockiness, of the younger generation of officers after about 1890. It was a gigantic gamble which would leave the eastern front virtually denuded against Russia and would use almost all available troops in a giant enveloping movement to sweep through Belgium, send troops pouring into northern France and surround and capture Paris, on a time schedule of some six weeks. It was an imaginative and daring strategy, but it carried with it grave risks.

The bold offensive, which risked world opprobrium for the sake of quick victory, failed to win a quick victory due in part to lack of boldness. Troops were diverted from the great offensive sweep through Belgium, some to Lorraine, some to the eastern front where the Russians marched quickly on Germany. Moving into action with a speed they were not thought capable of, the Russians forced some diversion of troops from the western front: on August 25 Moltke, the German commander-in-chief, ordered six corps to East Prussia. The British Expeditionary Force came quickly to the aid of France and Belgium, but it was relatively a small force, for the British alone of the great powers had no conscript, mass army; they were accustomed to putting most of their money into the Royal Navy. The little Belgian army escaped destruction by retiring to Antwerp, where it pinned down some Greman troops. But during the hot weeks of August it looked as if the well-prepared Germans would succeed in their bold objective. The French army seemed unready for modern warfare, much as in 1940, or 1870.

Battle of the Marne

However, the steel-nerved Marshal Joffre withdrew his armies in good order and the Germans captured relatively few prisoners or guns. The attackers eventually grew exhausted from the rapidity of their advance. They did not have tanks as they did in 1940; despite some primitive automobiles, the foot soldier still bore the brunt of battle, while guns and supplies were mostly horse-drawn. Both armies suffered from fatigue; but the Germans were vulnerable to the counterattack Joffre launched across the Marne River in the last days of August. Joffre's alleged remark became a French legend:

Marshall Joseph Joffre, 1914 hero of the Marne

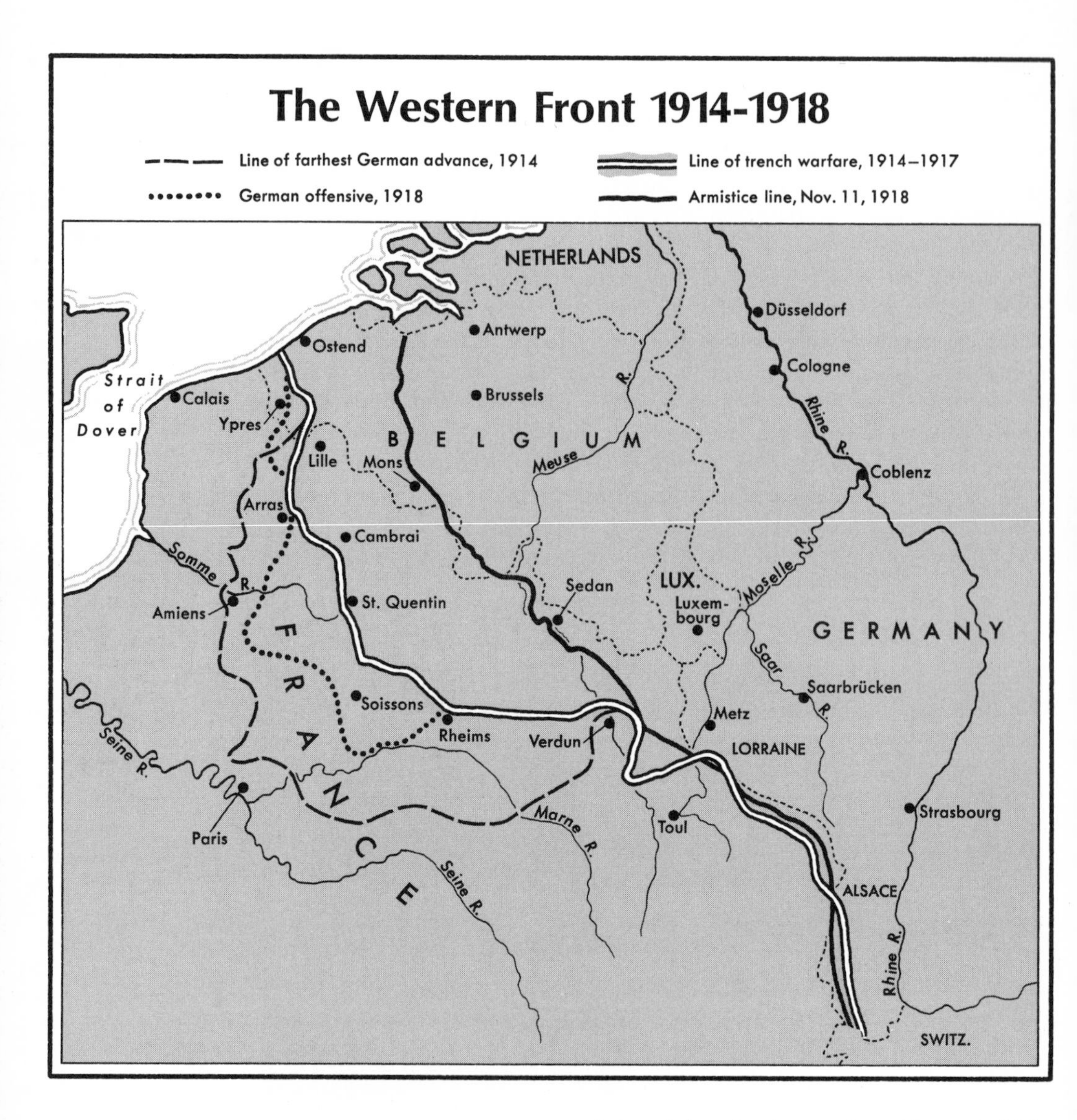

"my right wing is defeated, my left is falling back; good, I will attack." The Germans had gotten within 30 miles of Paris, where the guns were heard. They were deep in French territory. But they had not destroyed the French armies and they were forced to withdraw from their deepest penetration, never thereafter to secure a breakthrough. The Germans sought to go around the Allied end near the sea, but were checked here also. From this time on (October, 1914), both sides dug in behind trenches and barbed wire and the long stalemate began.

The first act of the great war thus ended in deadlock—a stalemate that continued on the western front for the next four deadly years. From the North Sea to Switzerland, each side dug in with trenches, barbed wire, and concrete "pill boxes," and defied the other to attack. Moved by desire to win the war, each side did occasionally launch an offensive, only to sustain incredible losses against the enfiladed fire of machine guns.

Once the initial German gamble had failed and the war became a long one, the odds were evidently all against the Central Powers. France, Russia, Great Britain, Belgium, and Serbia were at war with Germany and Austria-Hungary. Of the numerous powers that joined the war within a year or so, the Allies gained Italy, Japan, and Rumania as major additions, while the Central Powers added Turkey and Bulgaria. The population of the Allied or Entente states was double that of the Central Powers, and their resources greater—this counting only Europe, in addition to which the enormous colonial empires of Britain, France, and Belgium would be of value. (The smaller German overseas empire would be largely useless because of Allied command of the seas.) It was exactly these calculations which had persuaded Germany to risk everything for an immediate victory.

Stalemate on the western front

However, the war actually worked out to a stalemate—grimly and dramatically revealed in that long western front from the North Sea to the Alps which did not move more than a few miles for the next three and a half years. "No man's land" marked the stationary battle line, across which guns roared and, periodically, men charged, to be mowed down in the worst slaughter war had even seen. The two armies were about of equal strength. Interior lines enabled the Germans to use a few less troops. Until Great Britain could raise a mass army, the Central Powers had more divisions than France, Britain, and Belgium. A good part of the Allied total superiority in numbers was accounted for by Russia, but except in the initial phase, Russia was never able to make this strength count for her western allies. Her inadequately equipped and transported troops were smashed so badly by the Germans that they never quite recovered. In 1916 Allied supplies sent via Murmansk helped Russia to launch an offensive against the Austrians which was successful for a time; but by that time the Russians were running out of officers, and again the Germans defeated them. But the Germans could not win the war by mauling the Russians, and they could not crack through in the west either.

The western stalemate involved not merely an approximate equality of forces, but the nature of warfare at this moment. The defensive had the upper hand. The greatly increased firepower of modern weapons, plus the ability to construct barbed-wire fortifications and concrete "pill boxes" in vast quantities, gave the defense its ascendancy. Machine guns and barbed wire seem fairly humble commodities, but they controlled this war. It was not possible for unprotected infantry to charge against the enfiladed fire of machine guns; nor could any amount of cannonading get rid of the enemy trenches and pillboxes. Literally days of continuous firing, by cannon placed wheel to wheel, prepared the way for offensives, but still the gains would be measured only in yards, if at all, and the casualties would be counted in the tens of thousands.

Total war

The spectacular beginning of the war saw troops deployed in unprecedented numbers. At least three million soldiers were striving to kill each other in Belgium and France alone. Now they grimly held on, encouraged by propaganda and atrocity stories, determined to destroy the enemy. Moltke, the thoughtful German commander (soon, crushed by the terrible ordeal, to retire from the scene), had written just prior to the war a remarkably accurate prophecy of what lay ahead:

> It will become a war between peoples which will not be concluded with a single battle but which will be a long, weary struggle with a country that will not acknowledge defeat until the whole strength of its people is broken; a war that even if we should be the victors will push our own people, too, to the limits of exhaustion.

None of the powers except Austria was sure of its war aims when the fighting started. Fear and blundering had pulled them in; now they feared to get out. How could you let go without inviting defeat? And how could you afford not to win some tangible tokens of victory after having shed so much blood?

Military plans and failures

This uncomfortable and bloody war, which caused men to crouch in filthy trenches over which shells burst until, after months of boredom, they would be sent out to be slaughtered, was a supreme test of courage and morale. For a long time these remained surprisingly high. Plied as it was with an unprecedented campaign of propaganda, in which all the resources of the modern state were mobilized, the public was patriotic; it bought war bonds, denounced the savagery of the enemy against whom all kinds of atrocities were alleged, mobbed pacifists who protested against the war. The men in the trenches were quickly embittered, but they stuck it out. There seemed no alternative. The two sides were locked in a deadly embrace and neither could let go. Ghastly, fantastic as it was, there seemed no way to escape from the dance of death.

From the beginning, both sides accused the enemy of monstrous outrages against the "laws of war." The Allied peoples read stories of Belgian children bayoneted by brutal Germans; the Germans read similar stories with the roles reversed (chivalrous German soldiers barbarously tortured by black French African troops, for example). Fired by hate, public opinion demanded prosecution of the war to complete victory.

Failure of the generals

There were many efforts to break out of the deadlock. To many people then and later, the generals seemed stupid. David Lloyd George himself, who became Prime Minister of Great Britain halfway through the war, quarreled with his generals and declared that "the incredible heroism of the common man" was "squandered to repair the incompetence of the generals." This verdict has seemed unjust to some students; it is at least true that all kinds of ideas were tried out. Unfortunately they ended, with dismal regularity, in lethal failure, which usually caused the fall of some high commander. Over a hundred French generals were removed by Commander-in-Chief

Men suffered from dirt and boredom in the trenches while waiting to be sent out to be slaughtered.

Joffre in the first few months. Every chief commander at the beginning of the war was removed long before its end, including Joffre himself, the hero of the Marne. German Generals Falkenhayn and the younger Moltke vanished along with their British foes John French and Douglas Haig. On both sides, the ghastly failures were more notable than the successes.

On the decisive western front, the chief reliance was on big guns, fired at a speed and in numbers heretofore unapproached. Ammunition was used at a rate calculated to have equaled in one week the entire output of the Napoleonic Wars. Heavy bombardment was counted on to cut the barbed-wire entanglements and knock out the trenches, but several lines of interlaced trenches, dugouts, and pillboxes could not all be immobilized. With enough effort an initial advance might be made, but a well-timed counterattack usually wiped out the gain before it could be consolidated. Each side

Battery fire of eight-inch howitzers at the battle of the Somme

had to undergo the frightful experience of losing hundreds of thousands of men in order to learn that no assault could get far. The war became one of attrition.

Gallipoli

Tanks and airplanes received their baptism in this war, but were not yet well enough developed to have a decisive effect. The Germans introduced gas warfare, but it proved of limited value. The submarine was another weapon developed by the Germans, while the Allies tried an offensive aimed at Turkey, designed to open lines to Russia and eventually break through the back door of the Central Powers. It foundered at Gallipoli in 1915. First Lord of the Admiralty Winston Churchill was the chief architect of this plan to capture the Dardanelles, which Prime Minister Asquith backed; but others within the British high command, notably Naval Lord Sir John Fisher, objected to taking away strength from the home waters, and the whole enterprise fell afoul of considerable misplanning when it was launched. It was realized too late that an expeditionary army corps would be needed to complete the work of the fleet by landing and occupying the Turkish forts, and when it was realized, objections were raised against taking men away from the western front. Amid this wrangling and miscalculation the element of surprise was lost, and Turkish defenses organized with the aid of German technicians finally proved too strong to crack. A cabinet crisis and at length the resignation of Churchill accompanied the painful termination of the Dardanelles offensive in frustration and failure. It had gained initial successes but finally failed at the cost of some 100,000 lives and much suffering leaving behind a long controversy about exactly why and how it had failed

"Dogfight"—planes were lightly armed, fragile, and unreliable

Battle of Jutland

This was one of the few major engagements of the war involving navies. One other was the great Battle of Jutland. In another desperate effort to break the stalemate by breaking the blockade, the German fleet ventured forth to meet the British in the spring of 1916. Since the beginning of the war the British had been content to keep watch in the North Sea to see that the Germans did not get out with the main body of their fleet to challenge Allied control of the Atlantic sea lanes. In addition to the submarines, a few German cruisers slipped through to do some raiding of the English coast, but the battleships had remained in the Baltic. Jutland is the northern province of Denmark, between which and the southern coast of Norway flows the passage from Baltic to North Sea known as the Skagerrak. There the great naval engagement would naturally take place. The Germans did not expect to be able to defeat the much larger British fleet altogether, but they hoped to lure a part of it into a trap and destroy it. The ruse did not work, and the ensuing engagement involved both main fleets; the Germans soon disengaged themselves. In the battle of the afternoon and evening of May 31, they inflicted substantially heavier damages on the British than they suffered, from which feat they could extract much glory; but the fact remains that the German navy did not again dare risk such an encounter. The well-trained and well-equipped German navy, pride of the Kaiser's heart, had to sit idle in port, and ultimately exploded into revolution—evidence, perhaps, that critics of the Wilhelmine naval policy had been right. The British, for their part, gained a wholesome respect for the German navy at Jutland, and were not of a mind to track it to its lair. The Royal Navy contented itself with blockading the Central Powers in the hope of sooner or later starving them out. Both sides accepted the war of attrition in this area of battle, too. It should be noted that by remaining in existence the German fleet forced the British to remain on guard in the North Sea, unavailable for activities elsewhere.

The widening war

Italy's entrance into the war

In 1914 Germany and Austria-Hungary, the Central Powers, faced Serbia, Russia, France, and Great Britain. By 1915, with the war lengthening, other states in both Europe and Asia began to come in. Their motives varied. But they all might be said without much hesitation to fall, alas, in the category of what the president of the Italian cabinet called "sacred egoism." Italy bargained with both sides. At the cost of considerable future embarrassment, the Allied powers promised Italy territory to be taken from Austria and from the Ottoman Empire, as well as African colonies. This was the most celebrated of the war's "secret treaties," this 1915 Treaty of London. Italian public opinion flamed up against the traditional foe, Austria; Italy declared war only on her, not on Germany. The Italians were not to prove very effective warriors even against Austria-Hungary, and their entrance discouraged the Serbs, along with the dissatisfied Slavs within the Dual Monarchy. The cessions promised in the Treaty of London caused difficulty later at the peace conference, conflicting as they did with the principle of "self-determination" of peoples announced by the Allies. The Allies sought Italian support out of desperation, eager for even a diplomatic victory.

Other states enter

They had also gained Japan in 1915; not a very useful addition, since the Japanese had not the least intention of fighting anywhere near Europe but only wanted to seize the German leasehold area in China along with German island possessions in the Pacific. In 1915 Turkey and Bulgaria entered the war on the side of the Central Powers. Bulgaria held a grudge against Serbia stemming from the Second Balkan War, and watched the tide of battle in the east favoring Germany rather than Russia. Turkey had a treaty with Germany, motivated chiefly by her fear of Russia, and only awaited a favorable moment to intervene. (By secret treaty among the Allies, Russia was to be rewarded with Constantinople in the event of victory—reason enough for the Turkish position.) Turkey strengthened the German side considerably, because with German help the Turks successfully held the Straits of the Dardanelles and closed a line of communication between Russia and the western Allies.

The war in the desert

Though frustrated at Gallipoli, the British won successes in turning the Arab subjects of the Ottoman Empire against their rulers. Few Muslims responded to the call that went out from Constantinople to wage a "holy war" of religion against the Allies (it seemed obvious that Christian "infidels" were also allies of the Turks!). Arab nationalism was rising. The British were later to pay for the promises they made to the Arabs in 1916, but, at the time, anything to help win the war was naturally the sole consideration. They also promised Palestine to the Jewish Zionists as an eventual "national home" for the Jewish people. Solidly entrenched in Egypt, the British launched an offensive in 1917 from there against Palestine, defeated the Turks, and gained ascendancy over the Arab world. This signal achievement by the army of General Allenby in the colorful "war in the desert" gained some measure of revenge for Gallipoli. Still, it was of marginal significance for the much vaster struggle in Europe.

Serbia

Where else could one turn for relief from the grim deadlock in France? Serbia, the original cause of the war, could not be defended by her Allies once Bulgaria decided to join her foes. In 1915 German, Austro-Hungarian, and Bulgarian forces launched a combined offensive from three directions which overran Serbia despite her little army's valiant resistance, as the Allies stood helplessly by. They did succeed in rescuing the remains of the Serbian army, which escaped through the mountains of Albania and was carried by ships to the island of Corfu. The English and French had a small army at Salonika, which they managed to maintain there. This was on Greek soil, though the Greeks were technically neutral. To use this as the base for a Balkan campaign that would hit at the vulnerable Austro-Hungarian Empire with its discontented Slavic minorities became a dream of some Allied commanders. But two years passed before this dream could be realized. Eventually, that small force at Salonika would prove valuable. Meanwhile the Central Powers seemed firmly established throughout southeastern Europe.

Russian campaign

Russia was already showing signs of grave weakness. She began bravely, but the German corps withdrawn from the west checked her sharply in East Prussia early in 1915. Able to hold in the west with fewer men than the Allies because of their interior lines, the Germans decided to turn on Russia in 1915. They needed victories to restore public morale, and thought they might deal Russia a knockout blow. Generals Hindenburg and Ludendorff, ablest German commanders of the war, directed a highly successful campaign which drove the Russians from Poland and Lithuania and inflicted huge losses. But the Russians were able to withdraw the bulk of their forces. Unlike Hitler in 1941, the German high command decided against being drawn deeply into Russia. They remembered Napoleon, and they also could not forget the western front, from which it was dangerous to take too many troops. In 1941 Hitler had won his war in France, and could concentrate virtually all his strength against Russia; even so, he ultimately failed, a victim of the vast spaces into which the Russians could retreat. So, despite the weakness of Russia in 1915–17, it may have been wise of the Germans not to pursue this strategy. Hindenburg wanted to invade Russia, but was overruled by Falkenhayn at central headquarters.

The Russians had been badly mauled, and their backward economic society could not keep up with the demands of modern war for material, transportation, officers. All countries suffered from a shortage of lower-grade

General Paul von Hindenburg on the Eastern front in 1914

officers, needed to direct the huge armies at the front line, under the demanding conditions of modern warfare with its use of many technical devices. Casualties were always high in this category. Russia lacked an educated class from which such officer material could be drawn, most of the Russian population being illiterate peasants. Yet the Central Powers could not determine the outcome of the war on this front. Reluctantly they concluded that a decision could be reached only in the west.

Slaughter on the western front

After the disappointments in 1915, both sides reached the nadir of frustration in 1916. It was the year of Verdun and the Somme; of the naval battle of Jutland, the beginning of the end for Russia, and the death of Emperor Franz Josef. At Verdun, the Germans launched a giant offensive based on calculations that the losses on the side of the defenders of that great fortress would be heavier than those of the attackers. The result was horrible losses on both sides. In return, Joffre planned a vast offensive on the Somme, the brunt of which was borne by the British—and here fell the flower of young British manhood of this generation. The net result of these bloodbaths was negligible ground gained, and losses so great on both sides that the question seriously arose of which side would run wholly out of manpower first.

The Germans were less able to stand the losses. But 1917 brought the Allies to the brink of defeat. The so-called "Nivelle offensive" failed so badly that a mutiny swept the French armies. General Nivelle, who had replaced Joffre, was relieved in turn after this. The Russians, staggering under the demands of this war, were knocked back after the Brusilov offensive of 1916 had begun promisingly; they had a revolution in March, another in November. Rumania, which had entered the war on the Allied side in 1916, had to yield in 1917. On the Austro-Italian front the battle of Caporetto came close to knocking Italy out of the war. The Italians broke under pressure and before the line could again be stabilized, with French and British aid, lost perhaps 700,000 troops and the morale of the whole army. Germany inaugurated unrestricted submarine warfare, an act which caused the United States to declare war against her but threatened to knock out Britain. The British failed in another attack in Flanders in the autumn. All in all, it was a bad year for the Allies.

U.S. entry into the war

Looked on in this light, the decision to use submarines without restriction was a monumental German blunder. The chance the U-boats offered to win the war in a hurry proved irresistible, but by bringing the United States into the war Germany sealed her doom, for the Americans could put fresh men and money into the Allied camp and eventually break the stalemate. On April 6, 1917, after a long period of indecision, the United States declared war on the Central Powers, alleging that submarine warfare was not only hostile to American interests but a crime against humanity. Within a year she was shipping hundreds of thousands of troops to France.

Actually the Allies had found the United States an indispensable source of supplies long before this, a fact which strongly affected Germany's decision to risk American displeasure by renewing all-out submarine warfare. The United States had not wished in the beginning to be anything but strictly neutral. But she insisted on selling goods to whoever would buy. Since the Allies controlled the Atlantic, they were able to ship goods from the United States while their control of the Atlantic prevented the Germans from doing so. They also obtained large loans or credits in the United States to enable them to finance a large trade. Without these supplies they might have succumbed to Germany. The Germans were understandably upset and protested to the United States that she should either cut off trade with Britain and France or else make them grant Germany access to the sea lanes. The American government could not agree to either of these alternatives, and believed her course, one-sided as it was, had the sanction of international law.

Early in the war German submarines or U-boats had angered American opinion by sinking the British passenger ship *Lusitania* with considerable loss of American lives. In response to American demands Germany greatly restricted her use of the submarines (which sank ships without warning or provision for passenger safety) in 1915 and 1916. But early in 1917 she decided, as a desperate win-the-war measure, to use this weapon for all it was worth and take the risk of American hostility. There seemed a good chance that the British Isles could be starved out if the now numerous U-boat fleet blockaded them. So the German government announced that all ships of whatever type or nationality within a certain zone around Britain would be sunk without warning. The fateful decision was forced by the military against the advice of Chancellor Bethman-Hollweg. The American government, which had previously tried earnestly but vainly to interest the fighting nations in making a compromise peace, now broke relations with imperial Germany and her allies and soon (April 6) declared war. It was some time before American troops arrived in any numbers, but the assurance that they would do so sustained the weary Allied soldiers, and meanwhile American aid was important in helping Britain beat down the German threat from underneath the sea.

The crisis of morale

In his great poem "Dulce et decorum est," the young English poet Wilfrid Owen, himself killed in 1918, wrote of a comrade killed by gas:

If in some smothering dreams, you too could pace
Behind the wagon that we flung him in,
And watch the white eyes wilting in his face,

. . . .

If you could hear, at every jolt, the blood
Come gargling from the froth-corrupted lungs

. . . .

My friend, you would not tell with such high zest
To children ardent for some desperate glory,
The old lie: Dulce et decorum est
Pro patria mori.[1]

And young Siegfried Sassoon, living with the common soldiers "in foul dugouts, gnawed by rats," hearing "with sweat of horror in his hair" the boom of shells, lashed out bitterly at the higher-ups:

If I were fierce and bald and short of breath,
I'd live with scarlet Majors at the Base,
And speed glum heroes up the line to death.
You'd see me with my puffy petulant face,
Guzzling and gulping in the best hotel,
Reading the Roll of Honor. "Poor young chap,"
I'd say—"I used to know his father well.
Yes, we've lost heavily in this last scrap."
And when the war is done and youth stone dead,
I'd toddle safely home and die—in bed.

---

[1] "Sweet and fitting it is to die for one's country."

In February 1915, Germany declared a submarine blockade around the British Isles. After the sinking of British passenger liner Lusitania *on May 7, with large loss of life including 139 Americans, they called it off until 1917.*

Comment unfair, no doubt, but natural. "War is hell, and those who institute it are criminals," Sassoon declared. This is how most of the men in the trenches saw it, in this miserable and degrading war.

Such horrified revulsion against war and bitterness against its leaders appeared in many a novel, poem, or play published after the war. At the time, there seemed no choice but to stick it out. Patriotic fervor for the war ran high at the start of it; there were scenes of ecstatic joy as the troops marched off or departed from the railroad station. Most of the various nation's intellectual and spiritual leaders blessed the war as a sacred cause. Few

Wartime propaganda. In this typical American cartoon, the Allies shield civilization against a German monster preying on helpless peoples.

indeed dared to oppose it, and these invited grave unpopularity or worse. Bertrand Russell, a British dissenter, has described how he was set upon by a mob and saved only because he was identified as the brother of an earl—his status as distinguished philosopher and mathematician not being sufficient. He was subsequently imprisoned. In France, a distinguished public figure was sentenced to three years in prison for seeking a compromise peace. The German Marxist, Rosa Luxemburg, spent most of the war in prison. While the enemy was painted as bestial (Germans became widely known as "Huns") and also as a threat to civilization ("Prussian militarism" invoked images of the world forced to march the goose step if the Germans won), the other side of the propaganda coin exhibited the fair face of a noble postwar world once victory was attained. It would be (writer H.G. Wells was the first to say it in England) a "war to end war." British Prime Minister Asquith announced that Britain fought for no selfish interest but for "the enthronement of public right." Subsequently American President Woodrow Wilson proclaimed it a war "to save the world for democracy."

War losses

But morale gradually eroded under the pressure of defeat and slaughter. For the Germans, Verdun was the shocker. For the Allies, the mowing down of the flower of their youth, with little to show for it, came on the Somme. These epic struggles cost literally millions of casualties without achieving any significant change in the line of battle. Their horror and heroism will always be remembered, as long as there are literate men, as the greatest of historic battles, and the most futile. It may be best to pass over these bloody scenes, so often described, and simply indicate the magnitude of total losses sustained in this war—the vast bulk of them, of course, on the western front. For France, these were as follows: around five million killed, wounded, or captured. Nearly eight million Frenchmen were conscripted, a figure representing one fifth of the entire population and nearly every able-bodied man between 16 and 45. Thus about two of every three Frenchmen in the prime of life was a casualty. To say that an entire generation was wiped out would be only a slight exaggeration. The figures for Germany were no lower, for Great Britain only slightly so; for Russia they were apparently even greater, if one counts the cost of the revolution and civil war that grew out of the war. The total number in Europe of all those who suffered death or permanent injury as a result of the war has been estimated at 20 million.

Crises of 1917

This was destruction of life on a scale unmatched in Europe since the medieval Black Death. If one wonders how the peoples stood it, the answer is in part that they didn't, despite the unceasing din of public propaganda. In the awful year 1917, leaders both military and civil fell in France and Great Britain, a great mutiny swept the French army, and revolution came to Russia, as it subsequently would to Germany and Austria-Hungary. 1916 had been the year of Verdun, leading to the dismissal of General Falkenhayn from the German top command post; it had been the year also of an ill-fated last desperate offensive by Russia, the Brusilov offensive, which began bravely but ended in disaster and left Russia exhausted, bleeding, and ripe for revolution. In March the first Russian revolution of 1917 took place, at this stage under moderate leadership. It was the year of Caporetto, the nearly disastrous Italian rout. In France the great Joffre fell, replaced by General Nivelle, who promised victory and launched a great offensive only to see it fail with staggering losses. It was this defeat that brought on the French mutiny. How close this brought France to disaster only became fully known in later years. General Petain replaced Nivelle and restored order, but the hero of Verdun—a defensive battle—wanted no more attacks.

New Allied leaders

Yet at the same time, to counteract this defeatism, the old "Tiger," Georges Clemenceau, assumed the premiership. Disliked by most politicians for his sharp tongue and intractable temperament, Clemenceau was fierce and tough, breathing defiance at the foe, refusing to consider talk of compromise. "My war aims?" he replied to a questioner. "My war aim is to be the victor." "*Je fais la guerre*"—I make war. So in her hour of sorest distress

France found a fiery leader in the aged politicial rogue, Clemenceau. At the same time, in Great Britain Asquith yielded to David Lloyd George as Prime Minister. The "Welsh wizard" was a far more effective orator and popular figure than the reserved and aristocratic Asquith. Thus by sacrificing old leaders and substituting new ones the democracies managed to keep up morale, to some extent.[2] They held on until American help arrived to turn the tide.

The Russian Revolution

Their gallant but hopelessly under-equipped ally, Russia, was not so lucky. It was her fate to succumb to revolution and Communism, a development which was in all probability the most important single result of this fateful war.

Most European socialists had closed ranks behind their governments in the first few days of the war, ignoring slogans to the effect that the workers of the world would not fight each other in wars probably cooked up by wicked capitalists. They assumed their country was in danger and argued that the other side was the aggressor. (The German Socialists rationalized their position by pointing out that Russia was the most reactionary state.) They received places in the "patriotic front" governments. While the renowned socialist Jean Jaurès was assassinated in France as the war began, Jules Guesde led the French socialists into a government of national unity. In Germany the Social Democrats voted 92 to 14 to support the war; the first signs of opposition appeared in 1915, led by Karl Liebknecht. In Great Britain, the future Labour party leader Ramsay MacDonald refused to enter the government, but he was thrown out of the party and an overwhelming majority of the small band of Labour members of Parliament supported the government. In Russia, the Mensheviks, largest faction of the Russian Social Democratic party, were loyal. Only a small group of the more radical Bolshevik faction, directed from abroad by Lenin, carried on an illegal opposition to the war. Lenin was one of the few socialists in Europe who denounced the war from the very beginning. Between 1914 and 1917 he was in Switzerland.

Russia reeled under the shock of defeat in the war; her inadequate industrial, transportation, and administrative machinery broke down and the government forfeited all respect, as hunger came to the cities and the army could not even secure ammunition. "By the spring of 1915 it had become obvious that Russian industry was incapable of coping with the tremendous military problems imposed by the war." The heroic Russian soldier kept going under frightful conditions longer than any other soldier in Europe would have, but was reduced literally to fighting with his bare hands. The

---

[2] Not in Ireland, where resentment at the drafting of Irishmen, added to prewar discontents, touched off the uprising of Easter week, 1916, and led on to sporadic underground war between Irish patriots of the National Revolutionary Army and the British government.

Allies were unable to give much help to the tottering tsarist government. There were those at Petrograd who wished to make a separate peace with the Central Powers. Especially was this true after the discouraging failure of the 1916 offensive which began well, only to fall back under German pressure. But most Russians wanted to carry on the war while exchanging the old government for a new one that would be based on broader popular support and could organize the war efficiently.

The February Revolution

The revolution which began on March 8, 1917 (February 25 by the old-style Russian calendar then in use) was a spontaneous national movement against a regime that had lost the ability to govern. The occasion was a food shortage in the capital, leading to protests and strikes in which the soldiers made common cause with the strikers and mutinied rather than fire on them. The Tsar abdicated, seeking vainly to turn the crown over to his brother; Russia was a republic (March 16–17). The provisional government set up in March was a moderate one, headed by a prince and a professor (Lvov, Miliukov), and was expected to inaugurate constitutional, parliamentary government on the model of western Europe. But conditions were far too abnormal for that. At best, observers of Russia wondered whether this country with its illiterate peasant masses could yet sustain anything like a liberal, democratic system. As as was, the war went on and the misery of both soldier, peasant, and urban worker increased. And as the March Revolution swept away all restraints on free speech and political activity, the political prisoners were released, leaving Lenin, Trotsky, Stalin, and other leaders of the Bolsheviks free to plot revolution. Lenin arrived on April 16 to take charge of the Bolshevik faction, having been given safe passage on a sealed train by the Germans from his Swiss exile to Petrograd. He also received German money.

Failure of Kerensky

Lenin and Trotsky's Bolshevik faction was as yet an insignificant minority. The largest party in Russia was the Social Revolutionary party, based mostly on the peasants and advocating confiscation of the land from the landlords and its redistribution among the peasants. The mood of the Russian people was increasingly for an end to the dismal war and a beginning of sweeping social reform, as all the old discontents came to the surface—most particularly, the demand of the peasant for land. In May, a Bolshevik-inspired insurrection failed, but Miliukov had to resign as foreign minister and a new government including Mensheviks and Social Revolutionaries took office, its leading personality being the moderate socialist Alexander Kerensky, who assumed the War Ministry and subsequently, in July, became the Prime Minister. Kerensky believed that the war might be continued *if* the government repudiated imperialistic goals and proclaimed a peace without reparations or indemnities. He tried to reform the army by democratizing it, and to boost its low morale by personal visits and speeches at the front. For the time being Kerensky was more popular than Lenin, his fellow townsman (by a coincidence, both came from the same small city of the middle Volga). But the chief result of this was soon to discredit the Mensheviks and Social Revolutionaries, for they did continue the war, and only the Bolsheviks were wise enough, or brash enough, to call for immediate peace and the beginning of social reform. The cry for peace became the strongest Bolshevik slogan. The Bolsheviks promised not only an end of the war but a program of immediate socialism, nationalization of the land, and freedom for the national minorities.

Lenin

Lenin, the great Bolshevik, appears in the light of history as a magnificent, unscrupulous opportunist. Though a leading Marxist theoretician, he was always ready to adjust theories to realities and move toward power with a sure instinct. He was a dedicated revolutionist who believed simply that any means were justified in order to seize power, exterminate the "ruling class," and set up a socialist state. He was quite thoroughly authoritarian. Against other Marxists he held that the revolution would have to come by the ener-

Lenin in Moscow, 1919

getic action of a small revolutionary elite, not by the votes of the masses. And this revolutionary elite Lenin shaped as the instrument of his own will. Though Leon Trotsky believed that Stalin perverted the original Russian Communist system, most historians feel that the Stalinist dictatorship of the later period was a logical outgrowth of Lenin's authoritarianism and elitism—his creation of the Communist party as a fanatically disciplined political army accustomed to carry out the commands of its leaders.

Leninism

Lenin's Bolshevist version of Marxism showed considerable imagination in his adaptation to suit the Russian scene, while retaining recognizable links with traditional Marxist doctrine. In general, it may be recalled, Marx's followers in western Europe were the Social Democrats who not unreasonably interpreted the master to mean that the plant of revolution ripened naturally on history's soil, and therefore could be awaited with some passivity, for the fruit of socialism would fall into their laps as they sat beneath the tree. Parliamentary institutions in western Europe seemed to guarantee that if Marx were right in his social analysis, passage of political power to the proletarians was inevitable in time. Of course such institutions did not exist in Russia, and any democrat had to be a revolutionary—a dilemma which affected the middle-of-the-road "bourgeois" liberals and kept them weak. Revolutionary conspiracy was not new in Russia, as we know. Lenin's task was to square it with Marxist historical determinism. He did so by suggesting that because Russia was a backward society with a distorted development, the socialist revolution might *begin* there and then spread to the other parts of world capitalism. Lenin was, and remained, faithful to internationalism, holding that the more advanced industrial nations of Europe would have to play the major role in the socialist victory over capitalism. But Russia, precisely because she was the "weakest link," might crack first. Lenin differed sharply from the more orthodox, and usually more numerous, Mensheviks of the small Russian Social Democratic party, who had resigned themselves to waiting a long time for socialism in Russia, and were prepared for the time being to cooperate with liberal parties for the furtherance of capitalism, a stage which they believed had to come first. Lenin declared that a trained revolutionary nucleus should be ready to seize power and hold it until the proletarians of Europe joined in a world revolution.

The Bolshevik seizure of power

At any rate the genius of the Bolshevik Revolution guided his party with a sure hand in the summer and fall of 1917. The Bolsheviks captured control of the soviets, or committees of workers and soldiers, especially in the large cities, Moscow and Petrograd. They took advantage of continuing failures in the war, the wholesale collapse of the army, and a right-wing insurrection led by General Kornilov which further weakened Kerensky in September. At the first all-Russian Soviet Congress in June the Bolsheviks had only a sixth of the delegates, trailing Social Revolutionaries and Mensheviks considerably; in July they attempted an uprising and failed. But events played into their

Muscovites await news from Petrograd of the July, 1917 Bolshevik uprising.

hands. A tiny minority in March, not taken seriously by anyone, Lenin and Trotsky's faction miraculously came into possession of Russia on November 6 when the Bolsheviks seized power virtually without opposition in Moscow and Petrograd. They had captured control of the troops garrisoned in these cities, and no one appeared willing to fight for the discredited Kerensky government. They quickly established a complete dictatorship, dismissing the assembly by force and suppressing the other parties.

Russia in collapse

The whole country was in chaos, and it seemed to most observers that the Bolsheviks would not be able to hold it. Russia, in fact, appeared to be dissolving into small pieces, as the Austrian Empire did a few months later. The nationalities were seceding and setting up governments. They did so in Finland, the Ukraine, the Baltic States, and Poland; elsewhere local governments of various kinds took power. Soon, in order to carry out their promise of peace, the Bolsheviks had to make the peace with Germany (Brest-Litovsk) which cost them huge chunks of territory. The war had destroyed the Romanov empire and with it the somewhat misshapen unity that Russia had been. Ruin and anarchy were the essential features of Russian society as it appeared at the time to most observers. Lenin and Trotsky seemed like horrible clowns who had arisen but for a moment in this catastrophe. Only some time later did it become clear that Bolshevism had the strength to reunite and reorganize Russia.

The Armistice

Treaty of Brest-Litovsk

Brest-Litovsk came too late to save a weakening Germany. There, early in 1918, the newly established Soviet government of Russia under the dominance of Lenin and the Bolsheviks, carrying out its promise of peace at any price, gave up not only Finland, the Baltic region, Russian Poland, but also the Ukraine, while Rumania soon formally capitulated. But the Germans were never able to remove great numbers of troops from this disturbed region, nor was Bolshevik propaganda without its effects on them. At home, unity was broken as the socialists felt Brest to be a betrayal of the allegedly nonimperialistic war aims of the government. The hollowness of their triumph in the east apparently underscored the strategic lesson that only the western front was vital; and yet in the end it was collapse in the east which marked the beginning of the end for the Central Powers.

Collapse of Austrian Empire

Germany's ally, Austria-Hungary, had never shown any sustained ability to carry on the war and was now falling apart, the Allied army based on Salonika supplying a push. In the spring of 1918 the Germans tried another desperate offensive, but it failed, and with Americans pouring into the western front while the rear caved in, a Germany rapidly running out of soldiers, supplies, and morale was in desperate condition from the summer on. However, no one ever made a real breakthrough on the western front. Even in the last few months, when the Allies, using numerous tanks, steadily pushed the Germans

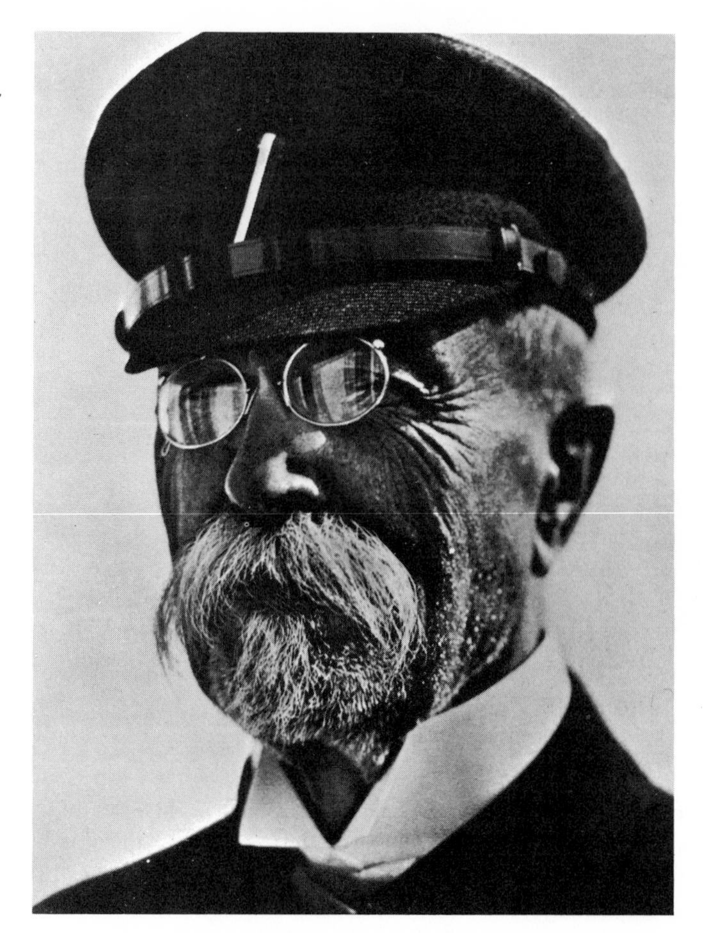

Thomas G. Masaryk (1850–1937), World War I Czech leader, then president of the new state of Czechoslovakia, 1918.

back, there was no rout, and ground was yielded grudgingly. Down to the end the defensive maintained its ascendancy in this war, and victory really came only when the Central Powers literally ran out of everything—including hope.

Allied propaganda concentrated on Austria-Hungary, where from the start of the war morale was weak. The imperial armies were filled with Czechs and Croats of doubtful loyalty. (The Poles, who hated Russia more, were more reliable.) Thomas Masaryk, the Czech leader, fled to London and set up a Czech liberation government. While the Austrian armies could occasionally beat the Russians and Italians, they required stiffening from the Germans to be an effective force. Desertion, especially among the Czechs, became an increasing problem. The death of the old Emperor in 1916 removed the last link holding the Empire together, and finally, in 1918, the Dual Monarchy simply dissolved. The various minorities—Czechs, Poles, South Slavs, Rumanians—proclaimed themselves independent, as the army melted away and revolutions broke out in Budapest and Vienna. What was left of Austria-Hungary had no choice but to give up and accept Allied terms on November 3.

Signing the Armistice

The collapse of Austria, opening the whole back door to Allied troops, was the last straw for Germany, which since midsummer had all but given up hope for victory anyway. The Germans only hoped for favorable terms. In the west their troops still held, and as long as morale held up there seemed no reason to surrender. The German war leaders, Generals Ludendorff and Hindenburg, were ready to negotiate for an armistice in September but did not contemplate total defeat. In October a change of government in Berlin brought in as Chancellor Prince Max of Baden, who had long favored a compromise peace. At the beginning of November, coinciding with the collapse of Austria, Germany suddenly caved in. A naval mutiny at Kiel on November 3 began a series of revolutions all over Germany. Hastily the German leaders sought an armistice, only to learn that the Allies insisted upon the abdication of Kaiser William II. On November 9 he did abdicate, and socialist leaders proclaimed a republic. Germany was in near anarchy. On November 11 in the woods of Compiègne, the German armistice team decided to accept severe terms dictated by Marshall Foch, the Allied commander-in-chief (since late 1917 there had been a unified Western command). Representatives of the new German Republic were faced with demands that the Germans withdraw their armies behind the Rhine; surrender all heavy artillery, submarines and major fighting ships; allow Allied garrisons at Mainz, Coblenz, and Cologne, the major German Rhineland cities. They saw nothing to do but sign. Quite unjustly, Adolf Hitler and his Nazis later blamed these men for betraying Germany from within. In fact, the Kaiser's regime had lost the war and brought on revolution against itself; now the painful task of surrender was left to the revolutionary government. It seems an incredible blunder that the Allies wanted it this way.

Bibliography

General histories of World War I have been attempted recently by Cyril Falls, *The Great War 1914–1918* (G.P. Putnam's Sons), and Hanson Baldwin, *World War I* (Grove Press). For its brilliance and style, Winston Churchill's *The World Crisis* (4 vols.; New York: Charles Scribner's Sons, 1923–29, or one-volume condensed version, 1931) will always find readers; another well-written account was that of John Buchan, *History of the Great War* (4 vols.; Boston: Houghton Mifflin, 1922). Gerhart Ritter has shed new light on *The Schlieffen Plan* (New York: Frederick A. Praeger, 1958). Recently there have been some excellent accounts of particular campaigns, such as Alan Moorehead's *Gallipoli* (London: Hamish Hamilton, 1956); Brian Gardner's *The Big Push* (London: Cassell, 1961); and Leon Wolff's *In Flanders Field: The 1917 Campaign* (Ballantine Books). Others include John Williams, *Mutiny 1917* (London: William Heinemann, 1962); John Terraine, *The Western Front 1914–1918* (London: Hutchinson, 1964); and Barrie Pitt, *The Last Act* (Cassell, 1962). Barbara Tuchman, *The Guns of August* (Dell) is popular. Corelli Barnett, *The Swordbearers* (New American Library, Signet), is an excellent study of strategy. Jere C. King's *Generals and Politicians* (Berkeley: University of California Press, 1951), discusses clashes within the French government; compare Paul Guinn, *British Strategy and Politics 1914–1918* (New York: Oxford University Press, 1965). Geoffrey Bruun has a biography of the French war leader *Clemenceau* (Cambridge, Mass.: Harvard University Press, 1963).

Among other interesting biographies of war leaders civil and military are Thomas Jones, *Lloyd George* (Harvard University Press, 1951), and J.W. Wheeler-Bennett, *Wooden Titan: Hindenburg* (New York: William Morrow, 1936). James M. Read, *Atrocity Propaganda* (New Haven, Conn.: Yale University Press, 1941), exhibits that unpleasant side of the war. The war's end is the object of a careful investigation by Henry Rudin, *Armistice, 1918* (Yale University Press, 1944); while Z.A.B. Zeman has examined *The Breakup of the Hapsburg Empire* (Oxford University Press, 1961), which accompanied the war's end. Perhaps the best authority on the war at sea is Arthur J. Marder, whose *Jutland and After* is the third volume of a series on the British navy (Oxford University Press, 1966).

Needless to say the war left in its ebb a rich deposit of memoirs. In Britain these include Lord Beaverbrook's *Men and Power* (Hutchinson, 1956), giving insights into high cabinet matters, while Duff Cooper's *Haig* (New York: Doubleday, 1936) contains much personal material of the British commander, and Lord Hankey has supplied a valuable memoir on *The Supreme Command 1914–1918* (2 vols.; New York: Macmillan, 1961). Sir Philip Magnus, *Kitchener* (New York: E.P. Dutton, 1959), ably handles an important war figure. Out of the war came such famous pieces as T.E. Lawrence's account of the Arabian war, *Revolt in the Desert* (New York: Doran, 1927), and a great deal from the men in the trenches, such as Siegfried Sassoon, *Memoirs of an Infantry Officer* (New York: Coward-McCann, 1930). The War Diaries of *Albert I, King of the Belgians* have been published in English (London: W. Kimber, 1954). Clemenceau's *Grandeur and Misery of Victory* (New York: Harcourt, Brace & World, 1930) is brief compared to the lively but allegedly sometimes unreliable *War Memoirs of David Lloyd George* (6 vols.; Houghton Mifflin 1933–37). On the German side Erich von Ludendorff, *The General Staff and its Problems* (2 vols.; Hutchinson, 1920), is from the ablest military figure Germany produced during the war. Brian Gardner (ed.), *Up the Line to Death* (London: Methuen Publications, 1964), is a poignant collection of war poetry. B. Bergonzi, *Heroes' Twilight* (London: Constable, 1965), deals with wartime literature. John Terraine has a pictorial history (Macmillan, 1965). Arthur Marwick's *The Deluge: British Society and the First World War* (Oxford: Bodley Head, 1965), is a survey of the impact of the war on all phases of society.

A satisfactory, though popular, account of *The Russian Revolution* is that of Alan Moorehead, in a Bantam paperback. The more intensive study by E.H. Carr, *The Bolshevik Revolution*, comprises several volumes of his projected History of Soviet Russia (Macmillan, 1951–53). Bertram Wolfe, *Three Who made a Revolution* (Beacon Press), is a popular older account; a major work of scholarship is Isaac Deutscher's multivolume biography of Trotsky, *The Prophet Armed, The Prophet Unarmed,* and *The Prophet Betrayed* (Random House, Vintage). Other major studies include George F. Kennan's close analysis, *Russia Leaves the War*, studying the Bolshevik road to Brest-Litovsk (from the American point of view), an analysis which he carries on in the sequel, *The Decision to Intervene*, i.e., the Allied intervention in Russia 1919–20 (Princeton, N.J.: Princeton University Press, 1956, 1958); and L.B. Schapiro, *Origins of the Communist Autocracy 1917–1922* (Harvard University Press, 1955). An outstanding account is M.T. Florinsky, *The End of the Russian Empire* (Macmillan, Collier); T.H. Von Laue, *Why Lenin? Why Stalin?* (Lippincott), is a searching commentary on historical continuity. The best biography of Lenin is by Louis Fischer, *The Life of Lenin* (New York: Harper & Row, 1964). Paul Miliukov, *Russia and its Crisis* (Macmillan, Collier), is by a participant. Other participants in this drama have told their own story: Leon Trotsky's *The Russian Revolution* is almost a classic work of literature (Doubleday, Anchor), while Alexander Kerensky has published *The Catastrophe* (New York:

Appleton-Century-Crofts, 1927) and recently (1967) his *Memoirs*. A good eyewitness account comes from N.N. Sukhanov, *The Russian Revolution* (Harper & Row, 2 vols.). Other sources include J. Bunyan and H.H. Fisher (eds.), *The Bolshevik Revolution 1917–1918: Documents and Materials* (Stanford, Calif.: Stanford University Press, 1961); R.P. Browder and Alexander Kerensky (eds.), *The Russian Provisional Government 1917: Documents* (3 vols.; Stanford University Press, 1961); and Z.A.B. Zeman (ed.), *Germany and the Revolution in Russia: Documents from the Archives of the German Foreign Ministry* (Oxford University Press, 1965).

27

The peace settlement of 1919-23

chronology

1919

Peace Conference opened at Paris, January 18. Germans excluded.

Council of Four (Wilson, Clemenceau, Lloyd George, Orlando) assumes control, March 25, after experiment with Council of Ten.

Covenant of League of Nations completed, April 28.

Controversy over terms of peace with Germany; Wilson threatens to return to the United States, April 7.

Departure of Italians from conference, April 23–May 6, after controversy over Italian territorial claims.

Treaty of Versailles with Germany, including League of Nations covenant, submitted to Germans on May 7. After vain protests Germans sign treaty, June 28.

Treaty of St. Germain with Austria, signed September 10.

Treaty of Neuilly with Bulgaria, signed on November 27.

United States Senate rejects League of Nations and Treaty of Versailles, November.

1920

U.S. Senate again rejects Treaty of Versailles.

Serious disturbances in India, Ireland, Middle East, Korea.

Treaty of Trianon with Hungary, June 4.

Treaty of Sèvres with Turkey, August 20.

Treaty of Riga between U.S.S.R. and Poland. Other treaties with Finland, Latvia, and Rumania establish Russia's western boundaries, 1920–21.

Clash between Poland and Czechoslovakia over Teschen; agreement reached.

1921

Treaty of Rapallo between Italy and Yugoslavia establishes boundary.

Irish Free State established.

Washington Conference convened; treaties relating to Far East and naval ratios signed, 1922, between U.S., Great Britain, France, Japan, and other powers.

Struggle between Poland and Lithuania over Vilna.

1922

Renewal of war between Greece and Turkey.

1923

Treaty of Lausanne sets new boundary between Greece and Turkey, more favorable to latter.

Problems of peacemaking

Secret treaties

Throughout the war, the question of "war aims" and the shape of the future peace arose, in various ways. One way in which the future settlement was influenced was by a series of promises given during the war, usually for the purpose of winning allies. Italy, when the Allies got her to enter the war on their side in 1915, received pledges of territory to be taken from Austria-Hungary and Turkey (secret treaty of London). Another secret treaty, which became known after the Russian Revolution, promised Constantinople to the Tsar. Japan also wrested from the Allies their consent to her taking over much of the German Empire in the Pacific and concessions in China. These "secret treaties" embarrassed the Allies at the peace conference in 1919. Russia's, and also Rumania's, treaties were nullified by the later withdrawal from the war of those countries, but Italy and Japan remained. In addition, to gain Jewish support Britain had given the Balfour Declaration pledge of a Jewish national home in Palestine. Great Britain and France had evidently shared out the whole of the former Turkish possessions in the Near East between themselves, too, by the Sykes-Picot agreement of 1916.

The "Big Four" at the Paris peace conference: Orlando, Lloyd George, Clemenceau, Wilson

These secret treaties and agreements, which wore the air of old-fashioned diplomacy at its most sinister, clashed with the slogan of "self-determination" that appeared in wartime propaganda utterances. Everyone, on this view, should be free to choose what government he wanted to have; and boundaries should follow lines of nationality as closely as possible. But by the secret treaties Germans and Slavs had been promised to Italy, Chinese to Japan, and Palestine to almost everybody.

Allied war aims

"Reorganization of Europe on the basis of nationalities"—the Allies named this the basis of the peace when in 1916 they replied to the American President Woodrow Wilson's request to both sides to state their terms. Specifically, they called for freeing of the national minorities in the Austrian and Turkish Empires (nothing was said about the minorities under Russian rule). When Russia went Bolshevik and left the war, the way was clear for the Allies to step up this war aim, which not only sounded most exalted but would have the practical effect of encouraging revolt in the enemy countries, Austria-Hungary and Turkey. President Wilson featured it in his famous "Fourteen Points," which in 1918 became the leading statement of Allied war aims and peace foundations. Somewhat similar words had earlier come from Kerensky and the short-lived Russian Republic, as well as other Allied leaders.

Also mentioned in the Fourteen Points were disarmament, reduction of tariffs, freedom of the seas, establishment of a League of Nations, and other rather general objectives. The war brought forth voluminous discussion of such ideals; it seemed that the liberal mind of Europe sought compensation for the awful descent into murderous war by spinning dreams of a beautiful postwar paradise. No other war ever produced such a proliferation of peace plans. Widely approved were statements to the effect that the old order in diplomacy and international relations was bankrupt, and a completely new one must be devised. While statesmen made secret treaties, publicists denounced secrecy and called for "open covenants openly arrived at." Pope Benedict's proposals for peace in 1917 included the theme of clemency and fair play which Wilson also stressed in his Points. So did a resolution passed by the German Reichstag in 1917. There should be no punitive indemnities, no seizure of territory for the sake of vengeance, no settlement except on the basis of a fair and impartial examination of claims. Whether the victorious Allies could apply such a generous spirit after so hateful a war remained to be seen.

The League of Nations idea

In liberal circles the idea of a League of Nations took hold and was endlessly discussed during the war. There were several different versions, none very precise, but the most influential groups arrived at a plan which would have member states agree to go to war together against any state which resorted to war without first submitting the dispute to mediation or arbitration. It was not clear how far they were to be required or only requested to do so. Critics pointed out among other things that sovereign states could hardly be compelled to go to war, and that going to war to prevent war was a paradox. Nevertheless the idea caught on with the public, and the words "League of Nations" became a formula of hope. Public opinion demanded a "new deal" in international relations. The concept of "collective security," as it would later be called, meant to many that somehow the old system of national self-interest and balances of power would give way to a new one based on international cooperation.

The Big Four

All these factors and considerations pressed on the leaders of the victors as they gathered at Paris early in 1919 to hold a peace conference. The world waited to see what they produced. The defeated power, Germany, was in the throes of revolutionary disorder; as was Russia, where the Bolsheviks were now fighting various anti-Bolshevik movements in a civil war; and portions of the old Austrian state. Numerous peoples all over the globe looked to the men at Paris to right their wrongs: to Georges Clemenceau, the old "tiger," who had assumed the premiership of France late in 1917 in time to receive credit for victory; David Lloyd George, the Welshman, who also rose during the war to be the chief of the British government; and President Woodrow Wilson, sailing from the United States to be the first American President ever to come to Europe while in office. Premier Vittorio Orlando of Italy rounded out the original "Big Four."

Though many countries sent representatives to the peace conference, the victorious great powers kept the reins firmly in their own hands, just as in 1815. Wilson, Lloyd George, and Clemenceau were the architects of a peace which, cynics were soon to say, was worse than the war. Meeting in close secrecy, the Big Three or Big Four seemed to be repudiating the first of the Fourteen Points, "open covenants openly arrived at." (An initial experiment with a larger body broke down.)

"Paris was a nightmare, and everyone there was morbid." A "sense of impending catastrophe" brooded over the scene, John Maynard Keynes added, in one of the most famous of commentaries on the Paris Peace Conference of 1919. "The Treaty," U.S. Senator William Borah declared in evaluating the results of the conference, "is a crime born of blind revenge and insatiable greed." More moderately, President Woodrow Wilson's chief adviser, Colonel E.M. House, one of its chief framers, confided to his diary at the conclusion of the Treaty of Versailles in June, 1919, that

> To those who are saying that the Treaty is bad and should never have been made and that it will involve Europe in infinite difficulties in its enforcement, I feel like admitting it. But I would also say in reply that empires cannot be shattered and new states raised upon their ruins without disturbance. To create new boundaries is always to create new troubles.

The Paris peace settlement of 1919 (of which the Treaty of Versailles with Germany, which also included the covenant of the League of Nations, was the chief but not the only instrument) has received more than its share of obloquy. Men soon spoke of "the peace that passeth understanding."

It was wrong to expect a miracle of the fallible mortals who came together at the peace conference. Too much damage had been done, and too many decisions were beyond their reach. They could not have been expected, for example, to put back together the Austrian Empire, even had they been so minded, for the peoples of southeastern Europe had taken matters into their own hands.

The end of the Hapsburg monarchy, and of imperial Russia, were facts accomplished before the peace conference met, largely by hands other than theirs. Thus one sin with which they have been reproached, the "Balkanization" of Europe into smaller pieces, was scarcely theirs. The statesmen who met at Paris had not made the secret treaties, either. Circumstances held them in rein everywhere.

Public opinion and the peace

They were the victims, not least among the many circumstances, of public opinion in their own countries. Whatever may have been said about clemency, the people who had fought and suffered through the long war wanted things which were not consistent with a mild peace. For one thing, they wanted the enemy to pay for it. Lloyd George in the famous "khaki elections" of 1918, on the eve of the conference, had promised (against his better judgment) to make the "Huns" pay for the war. And people demanded security for the future, a pledge against any renewal of the war. To the French this meant the destruction of German power forever, by the dismemberment and economic crippling of that country. The terrible Clemenceau was less terrible toward the Germans than was French opinion as a whole.

Holding the conference so soon after the war, and in the French capital where public opinion against Germany was hottest and nearest, came in for criticism. So did the personal participation of President Woodrow Wilson, who, some felt, could have exerted a moderating influence more effectively had he stayed aloof from the day-to-day proceedings and intervened only at crucial moments. These and other controversies made the events in Paris between January 18 and June 28, 1919, long a subject for the sharpest debate. On the latter date, the Treaty of Versailles with Germany, including the League of Nations "Covenant," was signed, and Wilson went home. Other work was done after that for many months, including treaties with Austria, Hungary, Bulgaria, and Turkey. But the dramatic moments were from January to June.

Wilson's role

World opinion to a remarkable degree had focused on the American president as its hope for a better world. Cheering millions greeted him in Europe, Italian mothers burnt candles to him as to a saint, eminent writers told him he was the modern Solon. After June 28, 1919, there was some tendency to write him off as a failure. He had turned out to be no more than an empty orator, as Keynes wrote, quite unable to "clothe with the flesh of life the commandments which he had thundered from the White House." Some

German minister signs the treaty in the Hall of Mirrors at Versailles, June 28, 1919.

Americans believed the wily Europeans had pulled the wool over his eyes; others said his mental powers were failing. In actuality, Wilson was far from a superman and knew relatively little about the complexities of world politics (few Americans did); but at Paris he came out about even in his clashes with the other Allied leaders. He had to withstand terrific pressure for a peace of vengeance. France was determined to destroy Germany as a nation and impose a "Carthaginian" peace, while Great Britain, though she did not believe in the partition of Germany, did insist upon massive reparations to rescue the staggering British treasury.

The settlement with Germany was criticized firstly because the Germans were not consulted. The terms as agreed upon by the Allies, working as the Council of Four, were handed over to the German delegation after they were completed. The Germans protested, but the Allies refused all changes of substance and Germany was confronted with a choice between signing and having the war renewed. (The punishing blockade had not been lifted with the armistice, and would continue until the peace was signed.) Under humiliating circumstances the Germans marched in and signed on June 28. There were no precedents in modern European history for a major peace settlement made without the participation of the defeated. Perhaps such participation might have made a difference in the terms of the treaty, or rendered it more acceptable to the Germans.

Terms of the peace

But the terms of the treaty were probably more important than the way it was drawn. Certainly Germany was not handled so drastically as the French

British boarding party and a German destroyer sinking at Scapa Flow, June, 1919. The Germans scuttled their ship rather than surrender it.

military and French public opinion wished. The most acute clash of wills at Paris occurred when the British and Americans joined in refusing the French demand for a territorial dismemberment of Germany, the western Rhineland portion to be made into a separate state. While Wilson stood by his principle of self-determination, the British had in mind the balance of power, for despite popular hatred of Germany the Foreign Office view was against any drastic weakening of Germany for fear of the consequences—one of which might be the extension of Bolshevism. So Germany was not "partitioned." She did lose territory. While she restored Alsace and Lorraine to France, and a small portion of territory to Belgium, her most galling losses were to the new Polish state in the east. This territory was mixed Polish and German; but the German cities of Danzig and Memel were given to the Poles and an unpleasant conflict bequeathed to the future. The "Polish Corridor" now once again separated part of Prussia from the rest of Germany.

Reparations

More punishing yet was the vast bill for "reparations" handed to the Germans. In return for denying the French their project of a Rhineland state, Wilson and Lloyd George gave in on the issue of reparations or indemnities. Indeed, Lloyd George was bound by his promises to get German money for his country and gave Wilson no help here. The sum of damages levied against Germany was controversial for several reasons: because it exceeded the bounds of war damage by including indirect or civilian damages; because it violated one of the Fourteen Points; and especially because it added up to a sum so vast that experts doubted whether it could be paid without deranging the entire German economy. In later years the bill was scaled down considerably (1924, 1929), but not before it had done damage to Germany and to

Europe. Reparations claims rested legally on Article 231 of the treaty, which declared that Germany must bear responsibility for the war—widely construed as her "war guilt."

Two other penalties were inflicted upon Germany: she was deprived of all her colonies (a rather clear violation of one of the Fourteen Points), and she was drastically disarmed (a small army and navy was left to her, but no major armaments or fortifications). The Allies were to occupy the Rhine bridgeheads for at least 15 years, and Germany was not to have troops in a demilitarized zone which extended to 30 miles east of the Rhine. Military experts believed that the key to control of Germany was the Rhine, and the bridges crossing it. That was why France wanted this region detached from Germany. She now had somewhat more doubtful security. The French thought that if after 15 years of occupation Germany was still a danger, they might find pretext to prolong the occupation. As a matter of fact, it ended in 1930.

A victors' peace

This settlement with Germany, some critics said later, was either too harsh or too lenient: it left Germany sore, but it did not destroy her. On the other hand, it was a logical outcome of the balance of forces at Paris. Lloyd George and Wilson were sure they were right in resisting the extreme French plan which sought to destroy the historic German state. They did not much like the reparations bill but could not stand out against it; they hoped that in a few years when passions had abated the terms might be moderated, as in fact they were. All in all, the Treaty of Versailles can be defended, or at least extenuated. But when all is said and done it was a treaty which Germany could not honorably accept, which she had not had any hand in drawing, and which therefore it became her object to revise or terminate. This great fact dominated the postwar era. And the treaty was vulnerable above all in having failed to live up to its own ideals, vulnerable to the charge of hypocrisy. The Fourteen Points, on the basis of which Germany had substantially been granted the armistice, had been honored more in the breach than in the observance. This peace was much more a victors' peace than the brave new world of unselfish internationalism which had been proclaimed from the housetops as the Allied war aim.

Features of the new Europe

Nine new nations

At Paris in 1919 and 1920 other treaties made peace between the western nations and Austria (Treaty of St. Germain), Hungary (Treaty of Trianon), Bulgaria (Treaty of Neuilly), and Turkey (Treaty of Sèvres). In other ways other boundaries were settled within the next few years: notably by the Treaty of Riga between Poland and Soviet Russia, ending the fighting in that area in 1920, and a treaty between Italy and Yugoslavia in the same year. Out of the vast convulsion of the war and the revolutions which it engendered, and out of the efforts of postwar conferences to clarify the confusion, emerged a Europe politically much changed. No fewer than nine new states appeared on the map, carved from the now extinct Austro-Hungarian monarchy or

Europe before World War I 1914
The Central Powers:
Germany
Austria-Hungary
North Sea
NORWAY
SWEDEN
St. Petersburg
Baltic
Sea
DENMARK
RUSSIAN EMPIRE
GREAT
BRITAIN
NETH.
Berlin
Warsaw
BELG.
GERMANY
LUX.
Prague
Paris
FRANCE
Vienna
SWITZ.
Budapest
AUSTRIA-HUNGARY
Trieste
RUMANIA
Sarajevo
Belgrade
Bucharest
MONTENEGRO
Black Sea
SERBIA
ITALY
BULGARIA
Sofia
Adriatic
Sea
ALBANIA
TURKEY
Mediterranean
Sea
GREECE

Europe after the war 1919-1923
Areas lost by Germany
Areas lost by Austria
Areas lost by Russia
Areas lost by Bulgaria
FINLAND
1917
NORWAY
SWEDEN
Leningrad
ESTONIA
1918
Baltic
Sea
North Sea
LATVIA
1918
LITHUANIA
1918
UNION
OF
SOVIET
SOCIALIST
REPUBLICS
DENMARK
GREAT
BRITAIN
Danzig
EAST
PRUSSIA
(Ger.)
NETH.
Berlin
Warsaw
GERMANY
POLAND
1918
BELG.
Malmedy
(to Belgium)
Paris
LUX.
Prague
Versailles
CZECHOSLOVAKIA
1918
ALSACE-LORRAINE
(to France)
Vienna
BESSARABIA
FRANCE
SWITZ.
AUSTRIA
Budapest
HUNGARY
RUMANIA
Trieste
YUGOSLAVIA
1918
Belgrade
Bucharest
Black Sea
ITALY
BULGARIA
Sofia
Adriatic
Sea
ALBANIA
(to
Yugo.)
(to
Greece)
TURKEY
Mediterranean
Sea
GREECE

from the former Russian and German states. Several of these had never before in history existed as independent states; others were reviving after centuries of extinction. Specifically, there were Poland, brought back to life after a century under the yoke of Russia, Germany, and Austria (of which, it may be noted, the latter had been the mildest); Czechoslovakia, which bore some resemblance to the ancient kingdom of Bohemia; Yugoslavia, a greatly enlarged Serbia; and the countries which had declared and maintained their independence from Russia, namely Finland, Latvia, Estonia, Lithuania.

New minorities for old

It was the "victory of the nationalities"—or was it? "To create new boundaries is always to create new problems." Unfortunately, there remained some serious minority problems. It had not proved possible to divide Europe up giving to each linguistic or cultural unit its own independent government. Czechoslovakia was an amalgamation of Czechs and Slovaks, with some Germans, the latter two groups giving signs of being more or less unhappy under Czech domination. The Croats, Slovenes, and Serbs who were now to try living together might or might not succeed, while Hungarians now lived under Rumanian rule, some Russians and Germans under their former subjects the Poles, and Turks under Greeks—the last situation producing a new war for Europe in 1922. Quarrels soon arose between Yugoslavia and Italy, and between Poland and Czechoslovakia, over areas where population was hopelessly mixed. This same situation prevailed in those portions of the new Poland which had formerly been in Prussia.

These areas of stress and strain, along with the substitution of small, new, and therefore less stable states for the old empires, caused people to talk of the "Balkanization of Europe" and did indeed make the future security of the Continent uncertain. Was there a stable balance of power? Would these new countries prove able to make the grade, economically and politically? Would new "irredentas" plague Europe, leading to wars of revenge and redemption? What would happen when and if Germany regained something like her former strength? Or Russia? Would the newly founded League of Nations be able to fulfill the hopes placed in it?

Trouble spots in the new Europe

A few sources of potential trouble may be singled out for comment. The new states of Poland and Czechoslovakia both were left with substantial German minorities, which Germany would probably try to reclaim if she ever recovered her strength. The awkward Polish Corridor running through Germany, separating East Prussia from the rest of Germany and including the German city of Danzig, would be a palpable irritant. Russia, too, would aspire to regain the Baltic states, as well as Bessarabia from Rumania and a slice from Poland, if she again became a great power. Austria and Hungary, formerly the rulers of an empire, were now left high and dry, hardly viable as countries—especially was this true of Austria, which might therefore try to attach herself to Germany, a move which the French would certainly veto.

Disunity of the victors

The outlook was the more dismaying because the Allies of the late war had lost their unity. Russia, of course, had defected altogether, and her Bolshevik rulers denounced all the "capitalist" powers, the western democracies even more than the defeated Germans. In 1921 Lenin's government signed a treaty of friendship with the German Republic, a case of two outcasts coming together for solace. The United States inclined to a withdrawal from interest in European political affairs, disillusioned with it all; Great Britain, and especially her overseas Dominions which had contributed so much during the war (Australia, New Zealand, Canada, South Africa), reacted similarly if less pronouncedly.

Italy had left Paris deeply aggrieved, as the result of a dispute concerning her claims to former Austro-Hungarian territory which President Wilson balked at delivering to her. In 1915 the Allies promised these rewards to Italy as the price of her entering the war, it will be recalled; but the United States did not feel bound by this secret treaty, which conflicted with Wilson's ideal of self-determination. Areas along the Dalmatian coast, in question here, were largely Slavic in population though with Italian communities intermixed; and the new and friendly state of Yugoslavia laid claim to them. The city of Fiume became a hot issue; the Italians at one point stormed out of the peace conference, and the eventual compromise did not altogether assuage wounded feelings. In 1920 by the Treaty of Rapallo Italy compelled Yugoslavia to grant some additional areas. The Italians got the impression that

"The Mask Falls," German expectations to the peace treaty contrasted with their reactions. German cartoon, 1919.

their allies had deserted them, a feeling which contributed something to the triumph of Fascism in Italy a short time later, and to Italy's becoming on the whole a "revisionist" power in the 1920's and 1930's.

Shantung issue

To which, as a footnote, it might be added that the Arabs, who had fought with the British against their Turkish overlords, now bitterly reproached the Allies for not giving them their liberty; and in the Far East both China and Japan, for different reasons, lacked confidence in their wartime partners. Japan had entered the war with a promise that she would receive the former German island possessions in the Pacific and the German leasehold in the Chinese province of Shantung. China entered the war in its later stages chiefly to have a voice at the peace conference to make an appeal against imperialism. At Paris Japan got her rewards, imperialism received no rebuke, and the Chinese were bitter. In the United States especially, a strong reaction against this seemingly cynical "deal" caused angry denunciations of both Japan and the Paris peace. Shantung as much as anything was in the minds of those Americans who decided to repudiate the Treaty of Versailles, refuse to enter the League of Nations, and write off the European world as morally lost. Thus did the war leave behind a devil's brew of hatreds and misunderstandings, of new conflicts born of the old, destined within another 20 years to cause another and even greater war.

The League of Nations

Could Europe and the world find security in the new and exciting idea of a general League of Nations under whose roof all nations might find shelter against attack? At Paris, President Wilson devoted a great deal of his personal attention to the drafting of the "Covenant" of the League—his own word, one intending to convey the solemnity of a Biblical rite. The League was indeed the object of an almost religious faith. It was widely believed that the "old regime" in foreign affairs was now as obsolete as the pre-1789 internal political order, to be swept aside by a revolution in the conduct of international relations. This discredited old way employed such dubious means as secret treaties, alliances, and diplomacy; it represented national selfishness dependent on armed might, and tried to keep the peace only through the balance of power. Had it not failed so badly in 1914 that an entirely new way must be found? One must replace power blocs and national militarism with international cooperation.

Plans for a League of Nations

In a general way, almost everybody approved the popular idea of a League of Nations during the war. And a number of groups had attempted to work out the specific plans of such a league. When one got down to details, though, agreement often broke down in the face of practical difficulties. Would the greater nations really relinquish control of their armed forces to an international institution—which would then be a world government or superstate? Would they agree in advance to abide by the decision of such an international body in any dispute? If not, could the League be anything more than a place to exchange views? On the one hand, utopian expectations surrounded the notion of a League of Nations—it was expected somehow to abolish war and usher in the international millenium. On the other hand, when the moment of truth arrived nations were simply not prepared to hand over to it any real power, for this would mean surrendering the jealously guarded sovereign power to choose war or peace, to defend the nation, to provide for national security.

Wrestling with such contradictions at Paris, Wilson and the other Allied statesmen hammered out the Covenant and wrote it into the Treaty of Versailles. Some people thought it a mistake to tie it so closely to the peace settlement. Some thought it too weak; others feared it might be too strong. It was attacked as a "Holy Alliance" of the big powers rather than true international democracy, because it gave somewhat more power to the larger nations who held permanent seats on the Council or upper chamber. Briefly, the member nations who joined the League (initially it excluded Germany and the other Central Powers, a feature often criticized) agreed to submit their disputes to conciliation or adjudication before going to war; that is, they had first to try to settle conflicts by peaceful means through the machinery of international organization. If after trying this procedure they still could not agree, presumably they might go to war with the League's blessing —another point criticized, by those who hoped to do away with war. If they went to war before going through this procedure, they were liable to punishment such as the breaking off of normal relations, economic boycotts, or even war.

Another article of the Covenant, one put in at the insistence of President Wilson, declared that each member state had its political independence and territorial integrity guaranteed by all the other members; however, in case of a violation the League might only recommend action, it could not demand it. The meaning of this Article 10 was somewhat obscure, probably not by accident, since it represented an ambiguous compromise between those who (like the French) wanted a strong League and others who wished to avoid ironclad commitments. Article 10 was destined to cause the most controversy when the United States Senate debated the League and finally refused to approve it, after proposing a number of "reservations" which Wilson refused to accept. Its foes claimed Article 10 violated the U.S. Constitution and endangered the nation by constituting an obligation to go to war automatically at the behest of a foreign body. In fact it obviously did not mean that; yet its lack of clarity helped discredit the League.

While all members sat in the Assembly, only 12 held seats on the Council, and the latter body would make the important decisions, such as deciding when a violation of the Covenant had occurred. The major powers held permanent seats on the Council, and the unanimous vote of this body was required on important matters. But the parties to a dispute could not vote when it came up for decision.

Awaiting delegates to the first meeting of the League of Nations, November 15, 1920.

There were other important features of the League. To deal with the thorny issue of imperialism, the League provided for a mandate system; countries holding colonies held them as trustees of the League and were supposed to report to the League on their progress. Also established were various agencies for international cooperation in such fields as health, conditions of labor, collection of information. A permanent Secretariat was to administer the League's activities from headquarters in Geneva, Switzerland. An affiliated World Court was expected to develop into a real instrument of international law.

Powers of the League

What did all this mean? Those who had dreamed of a world state obviously were disappointed, for the League had no real power except as the separate member nations chose to grant it on any particular occasion. The League did not possess its own armed force, for example, but would have to request forces from the various member states in case of an emergency. That the Covenant ventured as far as it did, in Article 10, was sufficient to frighten off the United States, which in refusing to join dealt the young institution a serious blow. Americans, already a little regretful about their crusade in Europe, had a mortal fear of being drawn in to police the endless quarrels of the Old World, or forced to fight in wars they did not want to fight in. As it turned out, there was nothing to be afraid of in the Covenant on this score; it became quite evident within a few years that no nation was going to accept an obligation in advance to uphold any frontier. In effect, they all held a veto power and refused binding commitments. This only reflected the fact that nationalism and the system of sovereign national states were far from dead. Governments felt a responsibility to their own people that they did not feel toward others. Regrettable no doubt, this was a fact of life. The war itself strengthened nationalism almost everywhere.

What the League might amount to only time would tell. With the refusal of the United States to take part, the French felt that a blow was dealt to their hope for security in Europe backed by American and British power. Her allies, as France saw it, had politely declined to take any appreciable part in guaranteeing and upholding the peace settlement they had helped write.[1] France would have to rely on her own might, plus whatever allies she might find of value from among the numerous smaller states. *Or* she would have to perform the difficult task of repairing her friendship with the hated foe, Germany. In the 1920's French diplomacy explored both paths, while continuing to hope that the United States and Great Britain could be drawn back into more active European roles.

The world beyond Europe

Imperialism and the peace

Though the great war of 1914–18 was waged almost entirely in Europe, its effects extended throughout the world and left little of it unchanged. The war had spread into the Middle East and resulted in the liquidation of the Turkish Empire; it had affected Africa and the Far East by means of the German colonies and Russia's Far Eastern possessions; Japan and China had entered the war and come to the Paris peace conference. Indeed, all kinds of "suitors and suppliants" flocked to Paris hoping for redress of wrongs: Arabs, Koreans, Indians, Irishmen, and others. (One young Indo-Chinese who came there to ask for independence for his people was named Ho Chi-minh. He left, disappointed, to begin an association with Communism; 50 years later, the chickens of Versailles were still coming home to roost in Vietnam.) Somewhat naively, these representatives of the colonial world expected or hoped that the fine phrases in the Fourteen Points meant that imperialism was to be ended and all subject peoples liberated. They were to be disappointed. At Paris the Japanese requested, and were refused, a statement affirming the equality of races; also rejected was the Chinese demand for an end of the "unequal treaties." Men later said that a great opportunity had

---

[1] In addition to the ambiguous pledges of the League, the French had obtained from Wilson and Lloyd George promises of a guaranty treaty pledging Great Britain and the United States to defend the Versailles Treaty frontiers. This too the United States refused to ratify; in fact, it was never even brought to a Senate vote.

been missed at Paris to repudiate imperialism—doomed in any case—and thus win the peoples of Asia and Africa. But the victor powers had not come there to liquidate their empires, or destroy the colonial system.

The Middle East

The Arabs pleaded for their freedom, but the Allies were trapped in a morass of wartime promises. A wit remarked that Palestine had become the much-promised land. For joining the Allied side and rebelling against their Turkish rulers, King Hussein and other Arab leaders had been promised that they should have independence; but in 1916 the Sykes-Picot agreement appeared to divide up many of the Arab lands between France and Britain. Then there was the famous Balfour Declaration, issued in 1917 by the British government in support of the Jewish Zionists who wished to reestablish the Jewish people in their ancient home in Palestine. These various inconsistent commitments, extracted during the war by the harsh duress of circumstances,[2] stored up trouble for the future; for the time being, the Allies chose to keep control of the situation by maintaining their position as "mandate" powers over the Middle East. The French, or at any rate many influential Frenchmen, enthusiastically embraced visions of French influence in this former theater of the Crusaders and Bonaparte. The British, well ensconced in Egypt, were concerned about the "lifeline of empire," while the threat of Communism lurked vaguely in the background. Britain and France would have welcomed American participation in the protectorate system but the Americans shied off from such "imperialistic" commitments.

If the Arab world seethed with discontent as a result of the peace conference, so did Iran, where the Persians were pro-German because hostile to Both Russia and Britain, the powers that had dominated them. In 1921 Iran turned toward the Bolsheviks, though within a few years she grew disillusioned with the new Russia too. All over the colonial world, the war deflated the white man's image and encouraged demands for liberation from western domination. It scarcely lay within the province of the peace conference to tell the British to grant independence to India, or Japan to Korea, or France to Indo-China. Nevertheless the war had led to demands from these peoples and others for their freedom. Never again would the European powers dominate the globe as they had done before the suicidal strife of 1914–18. The ensuing years brought severe difficulties for them as they struggled to maintain this domination.

The Turks were the only one of the defeated peoples to fight back against the harsh decrees of the victorious powers. They did not object to being deprived of their subjects, including Armenians as well as Arabs; but, in a resurgence of patriotic unity, they rallied around a great new leader, Mustapha Kemal Ataturk, and fought a war in 1922–23 to regain a portion of their Anatolian homeland which had been awarded to Greece. They succeeded

---

[2] One motive for the Balfour Declaration, though assuredly not the only one, was a desire to gain Jewish support for the war, not least in the United States, where for a long time Jewish opinion was pro-German chiefly because the greatest persecutor of the Jews was Russia, one of the Allied states.

The Balfour Declaration

Foreign Office,
November 2nd, 1917.

Dear Lord Rothschild,

I have much pleasure in conveying to you, on behalf of His Majesty's Government, the following declaration of sympathy with Jewish Zionist aspirations which has been submitted to, and approved by, the Cabinet

"His Majesty's Government view with favour the establishment in Palestine of a national home for the Jewish people, and will use their best endeavours to facilitate the achievement of this object, it being clearly understood that nothing shall be done which may prejudice the civil and religious rights of existing non-Jewish communities in Palestine, or the rights and political status enjoyed by Jews in any other country"

I should be grateful if you would bring this declaration to the knowledge of the Zionist Federation.

Yours,
Arthur James Balfour

in defeating the Greeks, as the Allies showed no willingness to get involved, and securing a revision of the original treaty. Turkey was a rare example of a country on which the war turned out to have worked beneficially. Purged of a useless empire, she turned in new directions and experienced something of a spiritual renewal.

The Far East

The withdrawal of Western strength in East Asia during the war and after caused the Japanese to feel that destiny had smiled on their dreams of power and influence in this theater. Seizing the German islands and the German sphere in China, Japan went further and confronted a disorganized China with the Twenty-One Demands. In 1911 the Chinese had a major revolution, which deposed the old Manchu dynasty and proclaimed a Republic, but the immediate effect was to dissolve any central authority and lead to local warlord rule. Japan, admittedly the most westernized and progressive of the Asiatic peoples, believed in her mission to lead the eastern Asiatics, and towards her huge but perennially ill-governed neighbor, China, she looked with a mixture of desire and irritation. Japan's ambition was to govern China and throw out the Europeans who had traded on China's weakness. At the peace conference, it will be recalled, she refused to give up any of the German possessions she had seized, especially the German Shantung leasehold; it was with difficulty that Wilson got her not to annex it outright. There was even talk of war between the United States and Japan, a prospect which Great Britain looked upon with alarm since she was an ally of both (the old 1902 Anglo-Japanese Treaty expired in 1920, subject to renewal).

The Washington Conference

The delicate Far Eastern situation led to an important conference soon after the war, at Washington in 1921–22. By this time the United States Senate had rejected the Treaty of Versailles with its provision for American membership in the League of Nations, and the party of President Woodrow Wilson had gone down to overwhelming defeat in the election of 1920. The American people were experiencing a profound reaction against the war and the conception of an enduring American involvement in the politics of Europe. However, they seemingly felt less hostility toward Asian affairs, and the Washington Conference addressed itself to these as well as to the partly connected question of naval disarmament. In addition to her acquisition of Shantung and the important strategic islands of the Caroline and Marianas groups, which greatly strengthened her naval position, Japan had taken advantage of the confusion and civil war in Russia to intervene in the Vladivostok region. The result of the Washington Conference was to get Japan to withdraw from this Siberian intervention, remove her troops from Shantung, withdraw the threatening demands on China, and agree to respect the status quo in China; in return, a naval ratio on capital warships of 5:5:3 between the United States, Great Britain and Japan was agreed upon, actually favorable to Japan in Pacific waters, the more so as the United States agreed not to fortify her Philippine Island bases. The three powers, together with France, established machinery to deal with any future disputes. Soviet Russia was as notably absent from this conference as from Paris; China, too, though the object of much of this, played little part. The Anglo-Japanese treaty was allowed to lapse. The significance of the Washington Conference lay largely in the restoration of good relations between Japan and the western Allies, on the basis of a compromise which worked reasonably well for a few years, only to break down in 1931.

Thus did statesmanship attempt to restore order to a world shattered and disarranged by the great war and its manifold consequences. Most impartial observers found little reason for comfort. "No one believes that the inequalities temporarily established by the Treaty of Versailles can be made the basis of a real peace," wrote Swiss professor William Rappard. Lord James Bryce, one of the leading architects of the League of Nations, saw "lunacy everywhere in Europe now [1920]. We all say to one another the war was bad, but this sort of peace is worse." Bad as the situation looked in Europe, it looked even worse in other parts of the globe. The months following the "peace" of 1919 saw violence in Ireland, India, Egypt, Korea, Greece, and Turkey, among other places; they gave evidence that in the Far East and Near East as well as in Europe the status quo was not likely to last.

The civil war in Russia

Of all the areas of international policy, the one that looked worst was probably that adopted toward the Russian Revolution. The Allies wasted an immense amount of time and effort trying to decide what to do about Russia. Perhaps there was nothing that could have been done. Yet the policy, if it may be called that, of half-hearted intervention against Lenin's regime, which failed to overthrow that regime yet convinced it of the West's implacable hostility, has seemed peculiarly inept to most historians.

After the peace of Brest, shorn of the Ukraine, Russia plunged toward actual famine and a crumbling economy. Thirty thousand Czech prisoners of war got loose and fought the Bolsheviks, as did other opponents who emerged. The Allies adopted a policy of limited intervention, chiefly to protect military supplies in such places as Archangel, the Crimea, and the Baltic states. The Japanese entered Vladivostok and Siberia, followed by

American, British, and Czech forces greet Japanese troops arriving in Vladivostok in 1918.

some Americans. At one time various "White" regimes held a good part of Russia, receiving some aid from the Allies and capitalizing on peasant disillusionment with the Bolsheviks, who seized grain from them to feed the cities. But the White groups could not cooperate with each other and some of them were viciously reactionary. For example, the Finns, Poles, and Balts could not cooperate with Great Russian chauvinists, such as the White leaders Wrangel and Denikin. To enable the Bolsheviks to regain control, Leon Trotsky created the Red Army, a notable triumph of energy and organizational skill. After the war ended, the Allies lost their enthusiasm for supporting most of the Whites and by early 1920 the last of them had surrendered or been evacuated. The French took General Wrangel and some 135,000 of his followers from the Crimea. At the Washington Conference the western statesmen persuaded Japan to abandon her intervention in Siberia. The Russian Reds failed to win back Finland, the Baltic states, and Poland; the Poles, strengthened by French help, finally defeated the Russians in a see-saw war and made favorable terms at the Treaty of Riga, 1921. The vigorous Finn, Baron Mannerheim, led a White force to victory in his country. Nevertheless, by 1921 the Bolsheviks had the rest of the former Russian Empire under control, though they seemed to have inherited a ruined country. The civil war was waged with weapons of terror and torture on both sides.

Doutbless it would have been difficult to formulate an effective policy for dealing with all this. The Allies badly underestimated the Bolsheviks at first, then badly overrated some of their White rivals. Divided among themselves, they could decide definitely neither to intervene nor not to intervene. The halfway measures they pursued probably guaranteed them the worst of both worlds: they earned the hatred of the Bolsheviks (though this already existed, it was intensified) without securing their defeat. Invited neither to the Paris nor the Washington conferences, an utter outcast in the world of international relations, the government of Soviet Russia, one of the world's greatest nations, could not be counted on to play a constructive role in world reconstruction. They would try, instead, insofar as they were able, to foment revolution and destroy the "capitalist" societies of the West.

Bibliography

One excellent study of wartime discussion of peace plans is Henry R. Winkler's *The League of Nations Movement in Great Britain 1914–1919* (New Brunswick, N.J.: Rutgers University Press, 1952). It can be supplemented by the exhaustive study of *Woodrow Wilson* by Arthus S. Link, of which several volumes have thus far appeared (Princeton University Press) which delve deeply into the mind of the American president. Hans W. Gatzke has contributed to the history of war aims and diplomacy with his book *Germany's Drive to the West: A Study of Germany's War Aims during World War I* (Baltimore, Md.: Johns Hopkins University Press, 1950). Arno W. Mayer, *Political Origins of the New Diplomacy* (New Haven, Conn.: Yale University Press, 1959), has some unusual insights, continued in his *Politics and Diplomacy of Peacemaking* (New York: Alfred A. Knopf, 1967). Cf. some chapters in R.N. Stromberg, *Collective Security and American Foreign Policy* (New York: Frederick A. Praeger, 1963). For an interesting study of Wilson in relation to European ideas, see Laurence W. Martin, *Peace without Victory: Wilson and the British Liberals* (Yale University Press, 1958).

H.M.V. Temperley edited a six-volume *History of the Peace Conference of Paris* (London: Froude/Hodder & Stoughton, 1920–24), which along with the 13 volumes of the official U.S. State Department documents, *Foreign Relations of the United States: The Peace Conference, 1919* (Washington: U.S. Government Printing Office, 1942–47), are the fullest record of the proceedings. Of the high participants Lloyd George, *The Truth about the Peace Treaties* (2 vols.; Boston: Houghton Mifflin, 1938), and Wilson's aide Col. E.M. House, *The Intimate Papers of Col. House*, edited by Charles Seymour (4 vols.; Houghton Mifflin, 1926–28), reveal the most. Harold Nicolson's *Peacemaking 1919* (G.P. Putnam's Sons, Capricorn), and Stephen Bonsal's *Unfinished Business* (New York: Doubleday, 1944) and *Suitors and Suppliants* (Englewood Cliffs, N.J.: Prentice-Hall, 1946), written by eyewitnesses with a flair for style and an eye for the historically significant, are the best treatments for the general reader. Among worthwhile secondary accounts are R. Albrecht-Carrié, *Italy at the Peace Conference* (New York: Columbia University Press, 1938); Jere C. King, *Foch versus Clemenceau* (Cambridge, Mass.: Harvard University Press, 1960), an account of the struggle within the French delegation; T.A. Bailey, *Woodrow Wilson and the Lost Peace* (W.W. Norton); Seth P. Tillman, *Anglo-American Relations at the Paris Peace Conference of 1919* (Princeton, N.J.: Princeton University Press, 1961); Ivo Lederer, *Yugoslavia at the Paris Peace Conference* (Yale University Press, 1963); John M. Thompson, *Russia, Bolshevism and the Versailles Peace* (Princeton University Press, 1966).

On the Russian civil war and Allied intervention, in addition to Kennan and other works cited in the previous chapter, see Richard H. Ullman, *Anglo-Soviet Relations 1917–1921*, of which two volumes have been published so far (Princeton University Press, 1961, 1968). In his second volume, covering the years 1918–20, Ullman traces the debate over policy within the British government. Other contributions to this subject include John A. White, *The Siberian Intervention* (Princeton University Press, 1950), and George A. Brinkley, *The Volunteer Army and the Allied Intervention 1917–1921* (Notre Dame, Ind.: University of Notre Dame Press, 1966). Elie Kedourie, *Britain and the Middle East 1914–1921* (London: Bowes & Bowes, 1956), is among the books that deal reliably with the tangled diplomacy of this area; see also Zeine N. Zeine, *The Struggle for Arab Independence 1914–1956* (Beirut: Khuyat, 1960); and, in connection with the Jewish Zionist issue, Leonard Stein, *The Balfour Declaration* (New York: Simon & Schuster, 1961), as well as the important testimony of Chaim Weizmann in *Trial and Error* (Schocken Books). H.C. Armstrong, *Gray Wolf: Life of Kemal Ataturk* (G.P. Putnam's Sons, Capricorn); and Arnold J. Toynbee, *The Western Question in Greece and Turkey* (reprinted; New York: Howard Fertig, 1968)—an early work of one of the most famous of living historians—deal with the wars of 1922–23. Among other troubles of the post-1919 years, those of Ireland have been chronicled in such books as E. Holt, *Protest in Arms: The Irish Troubles 1916–1923* (New York: Coward-McCann, 1961), and Desmond Williams (ed.), *The Irish Struggle 1916–1926* (London: Routledge & Kegan Paul, 1963). Perhaps the best book on China and Japan in relation to the Paris peace conference is Russell H. Fifield, *Woodrow Wilson and the Far East* (Hamden, Conn.: Shoe String Press, Archon, 1965); on the Washington Conference of 1922–23, John Chalmers Vinson, *The Parchment Peace* (Athens: University of Georgia, 1955).

28

Postwar Europe; Communism and the rise of Fascism

chronology

1920

Postwar economic difficulties in Europe.

Defeat of Clemenceau for French presidency.

End of civil war in Russia. Economic ruin of Russia, famine. Dictatorship of Communist Party under Lenin.

Attempted Kapp Putsch against Weimar Republic in Germany fails. Attempted Communist uprising in Ruhr. *Freikorps* disorders in Germany.

1921

Great coal strike, Great Britain.

Communist-Fascist clashes in Italy. Widespread disorders.

Little Entente of Czechoslovakia, Yugoslavia, and Rumania formed.

New Economic Policy, Russia, "temporary retreat" from Communism. Revolt at Kronstadt put down.

1922

Fall of Lloyd George ministry, Britain.

Rapid increase of Fascism in Italy; March on Rome; Mussolini granted dictatorial powers.

Treaty of Rapallo between Germany and U.S.S.R.

James Joyce, *Ulysses* (widely banned). Completion of Spengler's *Decline of the West.*

1923

French and Belgians invade the Ruhr, break with Britain over this action. Passive resistance in Ruhr. Great German inflation.

French efforts to set up separate Rhineland state.

Dictatorship of General Primo de Rivera in Spain.

Attempted seizure of Bavarian government by General Ludendorff and Adolf Hitler, National Socialist Workers' party leaders, in Munich. Hitler sentenced to prison.

1924

First Labour government, Britain, lasts eight months. Baldwin (Conservative) ministry, 1924–29.

French failure in Rhineland; Dawes Plan; resignation of Poincaré after elections. Easing of reparations crisis.

Murder of Socialist Deputy Matteotti by Fascists. Tightening of Mussolini's dictatorship.

Death of Lenin; struggle for power in U.S.S.R. among high Bolsheviks.

1925

Locarno treaties. Stresemann-Briand era of Franco-German cooperation, 1925–29.

General Hindenburg elected President of German Republic.

Surrealist movement in art.

1926

Germany admitted to League of Nations.

General strike in Great Britain.

Ottawa Declaration on equality of dominions with Britain within Empire.

1927

Lindbergh's transatlantic flight.

Consolidation of Chinese Revolution under Chiang Kai-shek's Nationalists.

Victory of Stalin in U.S.S.R.; banishment of Trotsky.

1928

Kellogg-Briand multilateral peace pact signed, Paris.

First Soviet five-year plan proclaimed. War on "kulaks" begins.

D.H. Lawrence, *Lady Chatterley's Lover.*

1929

Young Plan, scaling down reparations.

Second Labour government, Ramsay MacDonald Prime Minister, 1929–31.

Lateran Treaties, settling disputes between Italy and papacy.

King Alexander dictatorial ruler of Yugoslavia.

Stock market crash in United States, October; beginning of great world depression.

Lenin and Stalin in 1923

Soviet Communism: From Lenin to Stalin

The Communist structure of power

After they had finally defeated the "Whites" in the civil war which followed their seizure of power, the Communists who ruled Russia faced a serious crisis. In addition to the moral and physical desolation of a country which had endured disastrous war, two revolutions, terrible civil war, followed by a racking famine in 1921, there was the almost total destruction and flight of the old educated class. There was also uncertainty among the Bolsheviks. They had come through the civil war under Lenin and Trotsky's leadership with the aid of toughness as well as ability; they had Russia firmly in their grip of iron, and unblushingly butchered their opponents even when these were workers, soldiers, and peasants sick of the new tyranny of the Bolsheviks. They destroyed all opposition including the other socialist parties. They had built a centralized power structure. In theory power belonged to the soviets, or people's councils, but the All-Russian Congress of Soviets delegated its power to an executive committee, which in turn delegated it to a council of commissars made up solely of Communists. The Communist party, which was the real organ of power—no other parties being tolerated—also had a hierarchy culminating in the central committee and its various "bureaus," especially the Politburo. A small group of men, sitting on both the Politburo and the Sovnarkom, ruled Russia. They directed a dread secret police system (the GPU) which made the tsar's "Third Section" look like an amateur operation, and they also controlled the new Red Army in addition to the fanatically devoted party, the most formidable apparatus of power yet invented by man. But the party leaders at first were not quite sure what to do with this power.

Stalin's secret of success

Lenin died in 1924. In the struggle for control of the party as his successor, which first seemed to range the brilliant and popular Leon Trotsky against the field, Joseph Stalin, Communist party secretary, finally turned out to be the strong man. This outcome was a lesson in the power of organization against individual brilliance. Trotsky and the other high Communists, Kamenev, Bukharin, and Zinoviev, woke up too late to find that while they had been making the speeches, Stalin had worked quietly behind the scenes to put his men in key party positions. The wily Georgian used his seemingly unobtrusive post as General Secretary of the Central Committee of the party to influence selection of members to the powerful Politburo, to the "purge" apparatus, and indeed to administrative and executive positions at all levels of the political system. Lenin before his death had warned against Stalin's ruthlessness and power hunger (he had also criticized Trotsky as too mercurial). There is evidence of a personal feud between Trotsky and Stalin reaching back into the civil war of 1918–21. Stalin exploited jealousies between Trotsky, Kamenev, and Zinoviev. Eventually he became strong enough to maneuver them all out of the picture.

Issues in the Soviet debate

One of the issues debated by the top Communists during this rather confused struggle for power was the question of relative stress on world revolution and the possibility of building socialism in Russia alone. Should the Soviet Union continue to work toward world revolution, or should it accept that it was going to have to go it alone for the time being? Other difficult decisions had to be made about domestic policy. Marx had said remarkably little about how to organize socialism. Should the peasants be conciliated by allowing them to hold small farms and sell produce to the cities, or should they be forced into collective farms? Should industrialization be pushed forward rapidly, or slowly? On these issues there were, broadly speaking, a right wing and a left wing group among the Communist bigwigs. Stalin's strategy was usually to stand in the center as far as possible, and avoid committing himself to any position.[1] In this he displayed the instincts of a practical politician.

Trotsky's exile

By 1926 Stalin was strong enough to take the offensive and get Zinoviev, Kamenev, and Trotsky removed from the Politburo and other high posts, accusing them of disloyalty to the party. In 1927 Trotsky's group was expelled from the Party Congress and Trotsky himself shipped out of the capital. As

---

[1] A Russian joke of the time, related by Arthur Koestler, took the form of a questionnaire.

Q: What does it mean when there is food in the town but no food in the country? *A:* A Trotskyite deviation.

Q: When there is food in the country but no food in the town? *A:* A Bukharinite deviation.

Q: When there is no food in the country and no food in the town? *A:* The correct (Stalinist) line.

Q: And what does it mean when there is food both in the country and in the town? *A:* The horrors of capitalism!

the former hero continued to try to oppose Stalin, he was finally forced to leave the country. Trotsky subsequently lived in Turkey, Norway, and Mexico, always hounded by Stalin's secret agents and finally murdered in Mexico. Then, having used the right against Trotsky's left-wing group, Stalin adopted a good part of what the latter had been proposing and proceeded to maneuver the right-wing group out of the picture. Some years later, in the sensational "purge" of 1936–38, Zinoviev, Kamenev, and Bukharin, along with thousands of lesser officials, were tried, convicted, and executed or imprisoned. Stalin wanted no rivals, no equals. He intended to be the absolute boss of the Communist country, and he had achieved that goal by a most skillful campaign of utterly unscrupulous politics.

His victory meant the end of whatever democracy there had been in the Soviet Communist party, or for that matter the international Communist party, and the beginning of an iron dictatorship. In 1929 the practice of intraparty democracy, by which major issues were settled by a majority vote of the entire Communist party, came to an end. Stalin intended to make Russia over completely, using the powers of the state and the party, centralized in his hands. He wished to build socialism in Russia and believed it was possible

Trotsky in 1920

to do so; this would then prepare the way for Communist expansion throughout the world at a later date. But it would require the use of enormous power and great ruthlessness. Tough as nails, Stalin was just the man for this job. It is difficult to imagine Trotsky or any of the others being as good at the job of Communist dictator as Stalin was. But the strain of crudeness and power hunger that Lenin had sensed in him cost both Russia and the world dearly until his death in 1953, after 25 years of power, during which he led the Soviet Union through the huge socialization and industrialism plans and through the ordeal of World War II.

New economic policy

In order to secure a breathing space, the "new economic policy," a qualified return to capitalism and the free market, had been introduced after the war. But Stalin, beginning in 1928, launched the "great socialist offensive" designed to industrialize Russia within the framework of socialism, and catch Russia up with the capitalist societies. Rural Russia was to be collectivized and the dispossessed peasants driven to the cities to work in state-owned factories. Emphasis on farm mechanization and heavy industry meant that the consumer was left out; and the misery of the working classes who were supposedly laboring for a "worker's paradise" can seldom have been equaled in history. But the party drove ahead with a grim determination to modernize backward Russia by sheer will power. The results were sometimes awful. The leading "offensive" of the first five-year plan was a brutal war against the "kulaks" or allegedly rich peasants, waged in the name of the "class struggle" against capitalism. Between 1929 and 1931 these peasants unfortunate enough to own their own land were driven from their homes, sometimes deported and forced into labor gangs, while the land was put into "collective farms."

As well as they could the peasants fought collectivization with passive resistance, killing their animals rather than surrender them to the collective farms, and in 1931 famine struck Russia again. The Communists then slowed down the pace of collectivization, but they did not abandon it.

In the Urals, where new cities were created, to quote an American engineer who took part in their building, "Men froze, hungered, and suffered, but the construction work went on with a disregard for individuals and a mass heroism seldom paralleled in history." In the swelling cities housing was miserable, workers unable to leave their jobs without permission. It was something like economic slavery, but it presented itself as the opposite: freedom from "capitalism."

Five-year plans

The gigantic offensive, with its dynamism and courage as well as suffering and cruelty, caught the world's imagination. It happened that at this time the great depression ran its devastating course in the capitalist countries. Beginning in 1929 with the American stock market crash, depression slowly seeped through Europe and by 1932 reached a stage which made it the worst of all international economic collapses. It left in its wake unemployment, economic stagnation, and the ruin of farmers and small businessmen as well as industrial workers. This fact helps explain why the Soviet Russian system with all its repulsive features attracted favorable notice in the western countries. There was no unemployment in Russia! The Stalinist state saw to that. There was stir rather than stagnation; planning rather than drift. Soviet Communism produced the five-year plans in which national goals were set and then the nation strained every nerve to reach them, with all the excitement of a race.

The goals were not exclusively economic. Proclaiming their determination to do nothing less than create a wholly new civilization, a "proletarian" one to replace the tired old bourgeoisie, the Communists waged relentless war on such various things as illiteracy, Christianity, the bourgeois family. They sought a new art and a new literature, even a new science. The crudities and fallacies of dogmatic Marxism made some of this absurd, but in the cultural area too there was a vitality and exuberance which contrasted, many thought, with the decadence of the West. The Bolshevists had roughly awakened the slumbering giant, Russia, and like a veritable army of Peter the Greats they whipped her toward the goal not merely of equaling western Europe but surpassing it. It was an ideal which captured something of the spirit of the Slavophiles as well as the historic westernizers.

Elsewhere than in Russia, Communism fared badly in the 1920's. Lenin had confidently expected the Russian Revolution to trigger world revolution; indeed, his actions make no sense except on this hypothesis. (He could cheerfully sacrifice half of Russia in the peace of surrender with the Central Powers because he was sure he would get it back, with interest, in the revolution soon to come in Germany and all over the capitalist world.) But revolution did not come. Communists briefly held Hungary in 1919, briefly held scattered areas of Germany, but were crushed and failed to profit by the chaotic conditions that prevailed in Germany down to 1923. The reasons included the very fact of Russian control. As a recent historian of "the Stillborn Revolution" in Germany (Angress) observes, "As long as the Communists insisted on being bound by Moscow's directives rather than pursuing an independent policy, they could not hope to win the confidence, much less the support, of German labor." The Stalinized KPD (German Communist party) was led by mediocrities, the only sort who would meekly take orders from a foreign headquarters. Their tactics as well as their programs were wildly unrealistic. They abused the moderate socialists and trade unionists whom conciliatory policies might have won over. In France as well as Germany their influence was slight in the 1920's; it remained for the great depression of the 1930's to cause a sharp rise in their numbers. The most dynamic political movement and ideology of postwar Europe was led by an apostate leftist whose ideology featured anti-Communism. Communists did no better in the colonial world, where Lenin had theorized that their chances of striking at capitalism's weakest point were good. In 1927 the right wing of the Chinese Nationalist party turned against and very nearly destroyed the Communist left wing; many years passed before the Chinese Reds were able to put down their roots in rural areas. This resounding defeat marked the collapse of the Communist hopes for a world revolution and determined Bolshevik Russia to begin her Stalinist "socialism in one country" program.

The Fascist dictatorship in Italy

For once, both France and England found themselves in the shade politically. A world accustomed to look to the French for new political ideas and England for practices looked mainly in the 1920's to two other countries: Italy and Russia. Certainly the Fascism of the former and the Communism of the latter were the most exciting and controversial political developments; and Benito Mussolini and Nikolai Lenin were the outstanding political personalities.

Benito Mussolini

Of humble birth, Mussolini commenced his political career as a left-wing socialist, but turned away from the pacifism and internationalism of the socialists during the war, when he became an advocate of Italian entrance into the war. But for this, Mussolini might have followed Lenin's path; as it was, he became bitterly estranged from his former socialist comrades, who accused him of betraying the cause while he charged them with cowardice. An inquisitive and intellectual turn of mind brought Mussolini into contact with the more advanced ideas of the pre-1914 generation: Nietzsche, Sorel, Bergson. From them he got the concept of a revolution of values, the need to rescue civilization from decadence, the superiority of intuition over intellect. These philosophers were not, however, nationalistic, and Sorel repudiated Mussolini decisively when the latter turned in that direction.

Mussolini was at some pains to elaborate the philosophy of Fascism, which he declared to be a rejection of liberal utopianism, individualism, materialism, and pacifism. Life is a flux and a struggle, Fascists held. Man is a social being, living for and through the state. He is capable of heroism, and in war he finds his greatest nobility. As against Marxism, Fascism denied the materialism, the class-struggle idea, the tendency to make happiness consist in mere physical well-being. Fascism assailed the "lie of universal suffrage," asserted the inequality of man, and held that parliamentary institutions were corrupt and inefficient. Respecting the religious spirit, this dynamic creed tended to offer a religion of power and national glory in place of historic Christianity. Eloquently proclaimed by Mussolini, Fascism was a not unattractive doctrine, somewhat vague, but full of the fashionable Nietzschean concepts of spiritual heroism making over a corrupt world, with valiant "supermen" teaching the masses how once again to be virile and strong. In practice, however, Fascism all too readily became mere hooliganism, the cult of violence for its own sake, appealing most to immature and unadjusted people. The *Fasci di Combattimento* with their Black Shirt uniforms, their levies and their parades, usually ended by going out to beat somebody up, as did the Nazi brown shirts in Germany.

Roots of Fascism

Why did Italy give birth to Fascism and fall under its sway? One answer lies in the frustrations from which she had suffered over since the rebirth of the nation in 1861. The *Risorgimento* had aroused dreams of recovering ancient Roman glory, or at least a place in the sun somewhat befitting the descendants of the Caesars. Instead, the new nation encountered a series of humiliations. Apart from sore difficulties in "making Italians" out of various deep-rooted local loyalties, a parliamentary system that worked only with the aid of corruption, and economic difficulties, there was the shameful defeat by Africans in Ethiopia, and the growth of socialism and anarchism among the distressed workers—to mention only the most prominent of Italy's troubles. Millions of Italians migrated from the country, many to the United States—the sons of the Romans might be found in the ghettoes of New York, laughed at as fruit peddlers or deplored as a "criminal class." Unlimited immigration into the United States was closed off, however, after 1914, thus stopping up a safety valve for surplus Italian population. All this naturally galled Italians. Then came the war, and an opportunity to prove Italy's right to be a major power. But Caporetto stunned her anew, and at the Peace Conference the Italians thought they had been treated with contempt. From an outside point of view, it was their own greed that had brought this on them, but national pride is seldom rational. People in Italy talked of "the mutilated peace."

Italy after the war

Meanwhile Italy, less able to bear the costs of war, had suffered and was suffering from inflation and other symptoms of the economic dislocations caused by the war. All countries encountered difficulties in demobilizing literally millions of soldiers, and changing abruptly from war production to peace. For Italy the problem was made worse by the chronic weakness of government. The parliamentary system commanded little respect, produced no able leaders—or at any rate no popular and glamorous ones. Conditions after the war became chaotic. While unemployed ex-soldiers sometimes took to lawlessness, as in Germany, the strong Italian socialist movement pondered whether it should imitate the example of Lenin and make a revolution. It decided not to, but at the same time it would not take part in the government, and it called strikes which did no good and, by frightening the propertied classes, much harm. The socialist course was a foolish and disastrous one, in retrospect. Actually it was a perfect reflection of the confusion in the socialist position developed prior to the war: not sure whether to be revolutionary or democratic, it ended by being neither.

D'Annunzio in Fiume

The Socialists were the largest single party in 1919, but they would not help form a government. The Communists split off from them and declared their intention of inciting violent revolution. At about this time the swashbuckling novelist, Gabriele D'Annunzio, put himself at the head of some ex-soldiers and marched into the city of Fiume, which was in dispute between Italy and Yugoslavia. He accompanied his seizure of the city, where he remained for almost a year, with flamboyant gestures of the sort later copied

Benito Mussolini after the March on Rome, October 1922

by Mussolini—the uniformed private army, the parades and mass meetings, the leader addressing crowds of followers from the balcony as they roared slogans back at him. ("Whose is Fiume? OURS! Whose is the future? OURS!") D'Annunzio at least offered something exciting.

Reasons for the rise of Fascism

The government became paralyzed by the inability to form any cabinet that could long command the support of a majority in the legislature. Here, just as in Germany and France, parliamentary, cabinet government did not work very well owing to the number and variety of political parties. Coalition governments and juggling politicians were the rule. While inflation, strikes, riots, and revolutionary socialism disturbed Italy, the government seemed impotent. Meanwhile, the movement known as Fascism grew with phenomenal rapidity. Even the Pope, Pius XI, fell under Mussolini's spell, calling him "a man sent by God." Between May, 1921, when the Fascists won only a negligible number of seats in the elections, and the "March on Rome" in October, 1922, Fascism rapidly gained converts. As nearly as can be judged, this was because (*a*) many people were weary of ineffective government and wished for strong leadership; (*b*) property owners feared socialist revolution, from which the Fascists promised to save them; (*c*) the paralysis and disunity of the socialists prevented them from taking any action except ineffective striking, rioting, and boycotting of the government, which only made things worse; (*d*) the Fascists managed to project an image of dynamic leadership, aimed at restoring order to Italy and making her again a respected world power. Fascism was a mixture of many things, and received support from various quarters. Some industrialists and rich landowners supported it because they thought it would protect them from the socialists and Communists. Indeed, *squadristi* or local gangs hired by the upper classes to fight the socialists, break strikes, and protect property, were the power centers of the movement. On the other hand, some radicals joined it, too.

Perhaps the best analysis of Fascism is in terms of the error of Marx, who had predicted the extinction of the "bourgeoisie" and the proletarianization of practically everybody. This did not happen; on the contrary, the middle classes increased with the advance of capitalism—quite often a lower middle class of small merchants and manufacturers, who felt insecure both in relation to the bigger bourgeoisie (finance capital, big business) but also in relation to the propertyless working classes. Bolshevism captured Russia where there was little capitalism and a weak middle class; it could not win in any of the advanced capitalist societies because, quite contrary to Marx, the middle classes remained strong in these societies. They were severely frightened by the threat of Communism, though also susceptible to propaganda against big capital.

Triumph of Fascism

The Fascist program was vague in the extreme. All it talked about was action; it promised just to be dynamic. It denounced liberalism, parliamentary democracy ("the lie of universal suffrage"), socialism, and communism—all, alike, were products of modern decadence and materialism. One had to be heroic, and believe in something, and fight for it. One should follow Nietzsche's command to "live dangerously"; one should "believe, obey, fight." And evidently one ought to join a Fascist squadron, put on a black shirt, and go out to beat up some socialists. There was something of the Ku Klux Klan in Fascism.

Fifty years before Mussolini, Thomas Carlyle, famed English writer, had said that in the worship of great men we express our religious feeling, and had advocated this as a remedy for modern skepticism and money worship. Fascism offered this same advice. The Great Man turned out to be this Mussolini, son of a blacksmith; in his younger days rather handsome, with a pugnacious jaw and flashing eyes, a flair for colorful speech, and at least a superficial acquaintance with philosophy. Benito in reality was far from a superman, but he was bold enough to act the part, and ignorant enough to believe he could solve all Italy's problems. Ignorant people believed him.

Unfortunately one of his converts was the King of Italy. Mussolini could hardly have gained power without his aid. But Vittorio Emanuele (Victor Emmanuel) may have felt simply that Fascism had become so popular it should be given a chance. The Fascists organized a march on Rome, and

Mussolini was invited to head the government as Prime Minister. In actuality this was the end for the parliament; Mussolini then secured a law changing the electoral rules to penalize the splinter groups and maximize the Fascist parliamentary strength (the party with the largest number of votes would get two thirds of the seats). The ensuing election was not free from strong-arm methods by the Fascist *squadristi*. Most Italians shed few tears for a system that had fallen into disrepute because it could not produce stable and responsible government. This system broke down under the extraordinary demands of the postwar crisis, and under the weight of a bitter class struggle. Many respectable people, including some distinguished intellectuals (Benedetto Croce, Italy's leading philosopher, is the best example), supported Mussolini at the time; not because they agreed with him, but because they were somewhat mesmerized by Fascism's energy and, the situation being desperate, approved of giving it a chance.

Emergence of Fascist dictatorship

Given a grant of emergency powers, Mussolini soon had done away with parliamentary control over his government. The party militia or *squadristi* became employees of the state, thus providing a Fascist military force. At first Mussolini moved cautiously; only in January, 1925, did he fully reveal the mailed fist that lay underneath his kid gloves. Opposition to his regime arose then, following the brutal murder of the respected Socialist deputy, G. Matteotti, by Fascist thugs, after he had criticized Mussolini. The opposition was crushed, free speech was abolished, the Chamber of Deputies (parliament) purged of critics of Fascism. Great newspapers, whether of the socialist left or the bourgeois right, were badgered or coerced into appointing Fascist editors. From this time on whatever attractive features Fascism had possessed vanished, to reveal just the age-old face of tyranny.

While there were courageous men and women who suffered imprisonment or death fighting this system, it must be conceded that most Italians supported it. At least, they did not dislike it strongly enough, or see any attractive enough alternative, to persuade them actively to oppose it. In power, Mussolini's regime proved corrupt and incompetent, as well as tyrannical, but it carefully curried favor with many powerful forces in society; thus proving, rather depressingly, that freedom and intelligence can be dispensed with if a regime is politically astute, and controls the press. There were Fascist labor unions, replacing the older socialist or Catholic ones. Strikes were now forbidden, but some concessions made to the workers. A great many people, of course, got jobs as party functionaries or members of the government bureaucracy—greatly enlarged under Fascism, despite Mussolini's initial claims that he stood for the individual against the state. Big business, needless to say, did not find a world without strikes displeasing; Fascism restored order and, according to a famous saying, made the trains run on time. Like other dictatorships, Fascism went in for a public building program. Farmers were doubtless delighted at Mussolini's acting the role of dirt farmer and praising the simple virtues of the agriculturalist.

Mussolini arranges a concordat with the Pope, 1929.

In 1929 Mussolini negotiated a concordat with the Vatican which regularized relations between church and state for the first time since the feud had begun in 1870. Mussolini aped Napoleon in other matters as well as this one. For example, he conferred titles of nobility, creating a new Fascist nobility; he put members of his family in key positions, and he tried to take part in the formulation of a new code of laws. It does not seem that Fascism really did much to solve the economic problems of Italy, but it got credit for the restoration of more normal and orderly conditions as the postwar crisis waned. In the 1920's, people all over the world praised Mussolini as the strong man who had saved Italy.

Fascism borrowed something from Russian Communism in that it moved toward state planning and announced economic crusades such as the "battle for grain." The "corporate state" replaced individualistic capitalism, a planned economy replaced laissez-faire—at least on paper. All this was more sound than fury. More sinister, and perhaps more effective, was the use of education and youth societies to impregnate young minds with Fascist propaganda. Here they learned that Mussolini could do no wrong and that 1922 was the key date in all history; they were taught that Il Duce's eyes followed them everywhere and they must obey the leader blindly. And they were taught that war is good.

Fascism and war

One of Benito's pronouncements, hammered into the minds of Italian children and citizens, was as follows: "War alone brings all human energies to their highest state of tension, and stamps with the seal of nobility the nations that dare to face it." Not at first warlike in his foreign policy, Mussolini may have been indulging only in romantic rhetoric. But a good part of Fascism's ballyhoo always concerned the grandeur of the nation. Maps were exhibited everywhere showing the ancient Roman Empire, to remind Italians of their former world role. Italy was actually not a strong power. Mussolini tried to cut a wide swath in European affairs, but his talk was mostly bluff. In 1934, when Hitler's Germany began to be menacing, he joined with Britain and France, the allies of World War I, to try to check Germany. In 1935, the Italian dictator became involved in a war with Ethiopia, which caused him to clash with Britain. By 1936 he had moved closer to his fellow totalitarian dictator, Adolf Hitler, in a reversal of alliances. Never entirely happy in this relationship, Mussolini put his bets on Germany as a winner and went into World War II as her lackey. He would lose that war, and at the end of it an infuriated people would destroy him; long before that he had become an abject and pitiful figure. The war showed how woefully unprepared Italy was after 15 years of Fascist rule.

So in the end Fascism was one of history's great failures, and Mussolini, the man of destiny, the would-be superman, a joke. Italy has returned to parliamentary democracy, and seems likely to live with it despite its occasional difficulties. For the Italians found out that there is something worse than the inefficiency of democracy.

Other postwar dictatorships

There were other dictatorships in postwar Europe, as the palpable "victory of the democracies" in World War I slipped away in a swamp of disillusionment. Most dictatorships were not as novel as those of Communism and Fascism. In Rumania, Yugoslavia, and Bulgaria, unsatisfactory experiences with parliamentary government gave place to old-fashioned personal monarchies, of a rather traditional sort, usually bound closely to a landed aristocracy. In

Kemal Ataturk, a beneficent dictator, led the national renewal of the Turkish Republic after its defeat in World War I.

Poland, which had no king, the upshot was a military junta, a "government of colonels," after the popular military leader Marshal Pilsudksi had for a time exercised power. In Spain, a figure emerged from behind the throne in the form of Primo de Rivera, another general who became dictator (1923–30); a picturesque personality in whom there was perhaps something of Mussolini, but who lacked an ideology ("His model was not Mussolini but Haroun al Raschid," remarks Gerald Brenan in *The Spanish Labyrinth*). In Turkey there emerged possibly the most appealing of all the postwar strong men, Mustafa Kemal Ataturk, a courageous former soldier and genuine leader of his backward people toward a western orientation.

Reasons for failures of democracy

So it went nearly everywhere. The reasons included a lack of experience or unsuitable national temperament for the difficult, often exasperating procedures of parliamentary democracy. That system requires a spirit of compromise, which must rest on a deep-seated unity. A democracy of dogs and cats is not likely; and in some of these countries national and class animosities were not far from being of the dog-cat quality. Yugoslav democracy came to an end after a Croat leader was assassinated on the floor of the parliament—a procedure hardly calculated to encourage respect for parliamentary procedures. Primo's dictatorship in Spain emerged on the ruins of a parliamentary regime, and Spain's experiment in self-government from 1931 to 1936, after his fall, revealed how little that country was prepared to make such a government work; it culminated in open civil war after failing to achieve anything like a national consensus. Racial or national hatreds, such as those between Croats and Serbs, or Poles and Jews, were one sort of corrosive, while class conflict was another: in Spain, it was mainly a case of the poor hating the rich. Hatreds of this sort prevented the compromise and consensus upon which successful parliamentary democracy must rest. In analysis Fascism and dictatorship were the bitter fruits of hatred and bigotry.

Germany: The Weimar Republic and the rise of Nazism

Postwar disorders

In postwar Germany the Republic proclaimed in Berlin by the socialists, following the abdication of Kaiser William, struggled for several years against violent enemies on both left and right. The extreme socialists (Spartacists, as they were called in Germany) who wanted to follow Lenin's lead all but captured Germany early in 1919, their revolt being crushed only with the aid of the army and right-wing groups. The Weimar Republic was born amid defeat, as well as revolution, its first assembly having the unpleasant job of approving the Versailles Treaty, and was to be unfairly accused by some embittered nationalists of having betrayed Germany. The Weimar constitution provided for a most democratic system of government, but it never won the confidence of all Germany.

The great inflation

For the first few years, there were wild internal disorders. Bands of ex-soldiers roamed the country under freebooting leaders, terrorizing citizens and assassinating republican leaders. In 1920 one of them attempted to seize the government. Spartacist uprisings were renewed, especially in the Ruhr industrial region. In 1923 the French marched into the Ruhr, alleging failure to meet reparations payments, and it appeared that the French government wished to exploit the opportunity for another effort at its pet scheme of creating a separate Rhineland state. Rendered desperate by the desertion of her allies and her mordant fear of a potential German revival, France undertook an action one historian has characterized as the cause of Hitler and thence of World War II. It proved a complete miscalculation. The German workers went on strike, the government supported them, and during six months of "passive resistance" Germany's economy deteriorated amid the most spectacular inflation in modern history. The mark ceased to be worth anything at all; a wagon load would buy a loaf of bread. Before this disgraceful orgy ended anyone who had saved money had lost it, and the stabler classes of society were ruined and disillusioned. A few of the biggest industrial tycoons, however, took advantage of the chaos to increase their wealth and power, squeezing out smaller businesses.

Recovery of stability

It was during 1923, while inflation raged and the French tried to set up a Rhineland republic, that military hero Marshal von Ludendorff and an ex-corporal named Adolf Hitler tried to seize the Bavarian government. This "beer hall putsch" failed ignominiously, and for the next five years Hitler's extremist National Socialist Workers' party was all but forgotten, only to reemerge later. The nightmare experiences of the first four postwar years gave way to a much more stable period in Germany between 1924 and 1930, as they did in Europe generally. Almost miracuolusly, the mark was stabilized, following settlement of the Ruhr crisis with a new French government; after which loans from abroad and a revision of reparations payments cleared the way for a remarkable economic recovery. Separatist movements whether in Rhineland or Bavaria faded away, and the troublesome "free corps" bandits were brought under control. Responsible conservatives gave support to the Republic, and though its life was never easy, it seemed to be making progress in these years. The election of old Marshal Hindenburg as President strengthened the Republic. The government of the Republic always had to be based on a coalition of parties, which made for weakness and potential instability, but during the years of economic prosperity this defect was less noticeable than later.

In these years also Germany began to regain her position among the nations of Europe and even draw closer to France. The failure of armed intervention in the Ruhr in 1923 caused the fall of Poincaré's rightist government and the victory of a left bloc. Prime Minister Edouard Herriot, and after him Aristide Briand, who remained as foreign minister through a typical series of French governments, 1925–29, were willing to forget wartime hatreds and move cautiously toward reconciliation with Germany, perhaps within the framework of a federated Europe. On the German side the impressive Gustav

German cartoon on inflation, 1921. "I now have a million. Three quarters of it goes for rent and heating, and I may be able to get some bread and cheese with the remainder."

Stresemann had a long tenure as foreign minister, and he and Briand worked together well. These two men, Briand and Stresemann, both colorful and able, caught the imagination of the world as a symbol of Franco-German reconciliation and a new era of peace.

The Stresemann era

Stresemann was an extraordinary personality who impressed many, in Germany and throughout the world as being the ablest German statesman since Bismarck—indeed the only able one since Bismarck. It was he who steered Germany out of the collapse of 1923, by using his emergency powers to establish a new currency, and who secured Anglo-American financial cooperation while accepting the Dawes Plan for scaled-down reparations payments. While extremists of both left and right denounced him for surrendering to the Allied capitalists, Stresemann preached reconciliation and cooperation with her former foes as Germany's only possible path back to national strength. He found a response in the Allied countries, and Germany under his skillful leadership moved toward fairly good relations with France and Great Britain—a western orientation which ended the flirtation with Soviet Russia evident in the 1922 Treaty of Rapallo.

In 1926 Germany entered the League of Nations, from which she had previously been excluded, and received a great-power position on the League Council. A year before, the Locarno treaties had seemed to signal a new era. In these agreements Germany, France, and Britain joined in guaranteeing the existing frontier between Germany and France-Belgium. This meant that Germany accepted the cession of Alsace and Lorraine and Malmedy. How-

Final session of the Locarno conference of 1925. Mussolini, Stresemann, Briand, and Beneš were there.

ever, she did not promise to accept her eastern borders as final and doubtless expected some revision of the Treaty of Versailles there. Occupation by Allied forces along the Rhine ended before schedule, in 1930, while the Young Plan of 1929 further scaled down reparations and the thorny problem of disarmament was tackled. The "spirit of Locarno" was making headway between men of good will when the ugly rise of Hitler's party in Germany spoiled it. Unfortunately, Stresemann and Briand both passed from the scene, Stresemann dying in 1929 and Briand in 1932 after being rebuffed politically in 1931.

The German situation looked hopeful for a time. Bitterness left over from the war remained very much alive, but seemed gradually melting on both sides. Germans of all political complexions still rejected the Treaty of Versailles with its "war guilt" clause, and wanted extensive revision of it, but much opinion on the Allied side in these years was against the Versailles treaty, too. The historians searched for the causes of the world war and, with archives published to an unprecedented extent, sorted out the evidence and tended to acquit Germany of any criminal war guilt. The unilateral disarmament of Germany did not seem just to British and American opinion or to much neutral opinion in Europe. Even the French were willing to discuss the question in the great Disarmament Conference which held preparatory meetings from 1926 on, finally convening formally at Geneva in 1932. Sadly enough, under the impact of depression and the weakness of its government, Germany was to fall into the hands of the radical, hate-filled nationalist demagogue, Adolf Hitler, in 1933. The rise of his party from 1930 on frightened off the French from further concessions.

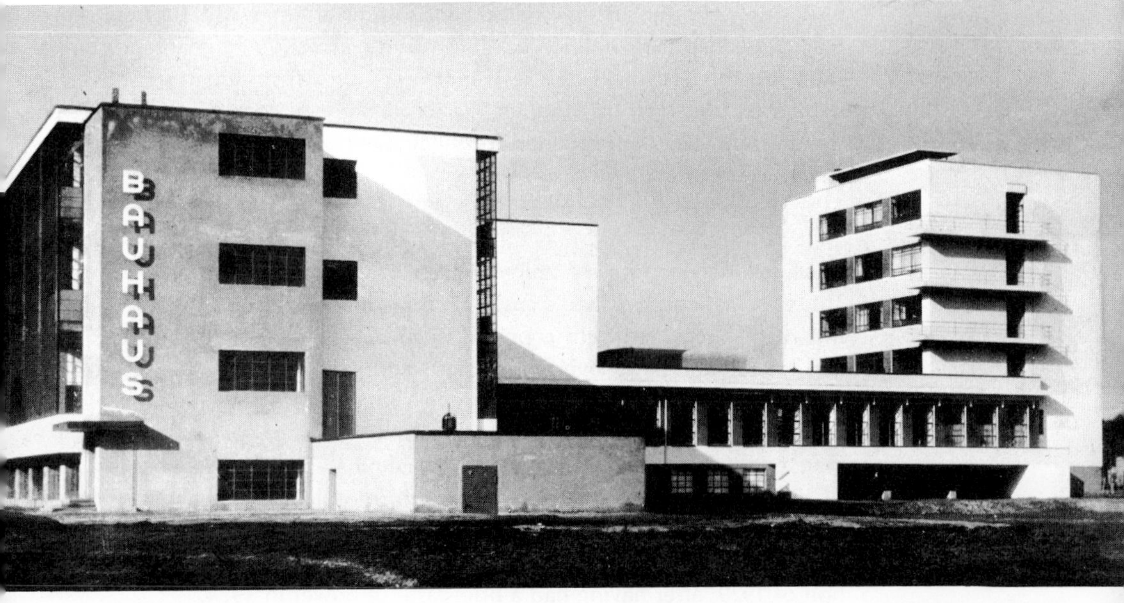

Walter Gropius founded the famous design school and in 1925 designed its building in Dessau. Among the faculty were Breuer, Kandinsky, Klee, and later, Mies van der Rohe.

Despite the Versailles treaty, a certain amount of clandestine German rearmament took place, winked at by the Allies, in the late 1920's. Especially significant were mutually advantageous arrangements with Russia. More significant was the work of General Hans von Seekt in building a quality army out of the small number (100,000) permitted Germany. Making a virtue of necessity, the Germans turned to intensive development of new modes of warfare based on a high degree of skill and mechanization. It was a singular achievement, one which Hitler subsequently took advantage of, though it was not a Nazi feat.

The Weimar renaissance

In the 1920's people spoke of a "Weimar renaissance" in the arts, for Germany became an exciting center of the new architecture and painting—for example, the Bauhaus school in Weimar, then Dessau, as a scene of modernistic painting. German scientists continued to excel, never more so than in the age of Planck, Einstein, and Heisenberg. But underneath the surface, German morale was not healthy in the 1920's. Humiliating defeat in war was not the only cause of this. The great inflation had left the middle classes impoverished and mistrustful. Communism on the left and antidemocratic extremism on the right both were potentially strong enough to bring down the Republic. People had become accustomed to violence in politics. And the moral damages of the war left the younger generation—the "fatherless generation," Germans called it—restless, rootless, cynical, vaguely idealistic but prepared to break with all past values. It was a mood not confined to Germany; one found it everywhere. Nowhere, however, was it stronger than in Germany. The postwar generation renewed contact with the rebellion in philosophy and the arts that dated back to prewar times. More ominous even than this collapse of traditional values was the attitude of a generation brutalized and made cynical by the war. Hitler's brown-shirted Nazi movement named its units "storm troopers," a word derived from World War I—the shock troops who were trained to toughness, hatred, and brutality.

The victorious democracies

England's crisis

It can hardly be said that the victorious states, France and Great Britain, much less Italy and Russia, enjoyed many of the fruits of victory in the 1920's. There was talk of "England's crisis." Foreign markets lost during the war were not readily regained with a pound pegged at its prewar rate of exchange, and for Britain loss of overseas markets and capital returns was disastrous—it meant unemployment. When employers sought to lower wages in order to improve British export prices, the result was a series of strikes. Strikes plagued the whole postwar period, and culminated in the great general strike of 1926, which seemed to some like a British proletarian revolution. It finally collapsed in a resounding defeat for the unions. But the Labour party, which moved up rapidly at the expense of the Liberals in these years, won the election of 1929, after having had a brief taste of power in 1924.

The decline of the Liberal party

"The strange death of Liberal England," as one historian has called it, was a notable political phenomenon. The Liberal party, with roots deep in English history, reaching back to the Whigs who had virtually made the 18th-century constitution, dominated British politics through much of the later 19th century and was in power from 1906 through the world war, though its margin had been a narrow one then, dependent on Irish votes and on a deal with Labour. In embracing a program of social legislation in 1909, the Liberals alienated some of their old-line supporters to whom liberalism meant exactly the opposite of such state interference in the free economy. Liberalism was thus caught between two opposing conceptions, the positive and the negative definitions of liberty. Moreover, the Boer War left a legacy of bitterness which pointed to another dilemma, that of the Liberal party's traditional antiimperialism versus the national interest in an age of power. When the Liberal party took Great Britain into the war in 1914, there were a few angry resignations. More important, when Lloyd George maneuvered Asquith out of control of the government in 1916 he and his followers may well have acted in the national interest (for Lloyd George was a more dynamic war leader), but they left behind another feud, which weakened the party for a number of years.

Rise of the Labour party

Meanwhile Labour was gaining in strength. Unlike other countries, Britain clung to the two-party system, her whole political structure being premised on it; there was not room for a third major party, and the Liberals fell as the socialist Labourites rose. The latter profited by a disillusionment with the war, which their leader Ramsay MacDonald had had the courage to oppose; but even more by the economic hardships of the post-war decade, turning the

The 1926 general strike in England—troops escorting food from the docks in London

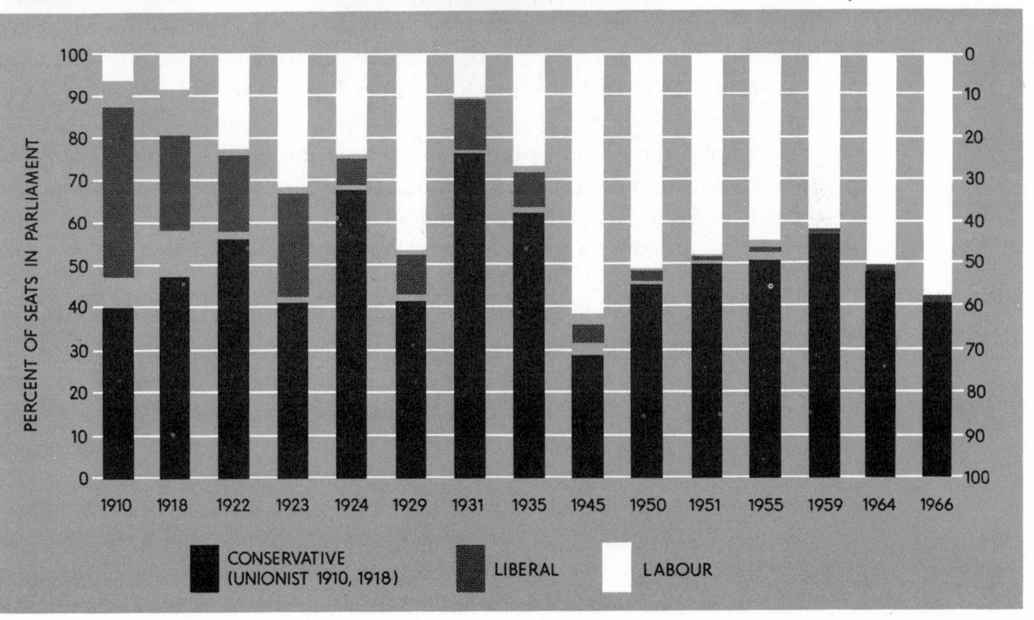

The changing pattern of British politics, 1910–66

depressed British workingman toward the socialist program. Labour found solid strength in two camps: the trades unions, and an important group of middle-class intellectuals who carried on the tradition of Fabian socialism. The war itself had done much to foster socialism; for had not the government taken over and directed the entire economy in the interest of winning the war? If such emergency powers could be used against the Germans, why not also use them in the "war against poverty"? "Homes fit for heroes" had been a wartime promise, assuring such servicemen as returned that the state would see to it they had the best. In such ways the socialist cause advanced in the 1920's. There was a short-lived first Labour government in 1924 and another in 1929. But most of the time the Conservatives, profiting from the Liberal collapse, were in power. (See chart.)

Problems of Empire

In addition to economic troubles at home, Great Britain faced crisis in her overseas Empire. The war had greatly stimulated nationalism among colonial peoples. Rebellion broke out in Ireland during the war and again after the war; fighting between the Irish independence party (Sinn Fein) and the British "black and tans," or constabulary police, became furious. World opinion was somewhat shocked at the methods the British government employed in this civil strife, which was savagely fought by both sides. Soon the British granted dominion status within the Empire to the southern part of Ireland, a solution accepted by a narrow majority of the Sinn Feiners but rejected by the rest, who continued the insurrection. The Irish problem did not entirely quiet down until about 1927, when an assassination caused a reaction against the extremist Republicans.

There was a similar pattern in other parts of the Empire. A serious insurrection in Egypt led by the Nationalist (Wafd) party required the attentions of a British army in 1919 and flared up on several other occasions. In 1922 the British declared their protectorate over Egypt at an end, but since British forces remained in Egypt to protect the canal the Egyptians were not satisfied. Elsewhere in the Arab world there were also outbreaks based on a sense of grievance from the war. The British had difficulties in Palestine and Iraq, the French in Syria as they faced Arabs angered by their failure to gain independence and self-government. In Palestine the entry of some Jews under the Balfour agreement was another Arab grievance.

Most serious of all for Britain was India. Near the close of the war the British announced that India would be granted an additional mete of self-government, but to the impatient Indian nationalists the offer was not enough. Though the national leader Mahatma Gandhi believed in nonviolent methods, incidents occurred. The British tried repressive tactics, and an ugly massacre at Amritsar in April, 1919, stirred India to renewed resistance. There was intense rioting in 1921 and 1922, and thereafter strikes, and campaigns of "civil disobedience" under the leadership of Gandhi, kept India in excitement all through the decade. The second campaign of civil disobedience began in 1930, quickly became anything but civil, and led to the arrest of Gandhi for

Mohandas K. Gandhi, preacher of revolution by peaceful means, hero of the Indian nationalist movement

the second time in the decade. The man whose "nonviolent" methods always seemed to lead to violence was, to Winston Churchill, a "naked fakir" bent on stirring up trouble. He was a kind of revolutionary saint to millions of Indians. But Gandhi only crystallized around his remarkable personality the stirrings of the entire world of nonwhite Asiatics in a movement aimed at independence. As the leading imperialist nation, Great Britain caught the brunt of this movement.

France in political crisis

France had less trouble regaining her economic balance than Britain, but her notorious political instability continued, and the French were obsessed with insecurity against a possible German revival. In regard to the first, a factor may have been that the French franc, unlike the British pound, was finally officially devalued by a resounding 80 percent, thus helping French exports; while the iron industry of Lorraine now came back to France, and, in addition, reconstruction of the devastated areas was a stimulus to investment. The demands of the veterans and widows of the war created a financial burden, and one cause of the 1923 invasion of the Ruhr was the popular slogan "Germany will pay," reflecting the belief that somehow the cost of the war could be extracted from the hated *Boche*. When the effort to collect proved an economic disaster for all concerned, France got hurt along with Germany, but the international entente of 1924, including evacuation of the Ruhr, the Dawes Plan, and the Locarno pacts, worked miracles for Europe, and prosperity settled on France for a few happy years. (The depression of 1929–31 missed France in its first onslaught, though she was eventually hit.)

The rise and fall of French cabinets continued to be a notable phenomenon occasionally disturbing the European scene. After the war an electoral system designed to minimize the smaller parties was introduced; the elections of 1919 resulted in victory for a conservative "bloc national" largely swept in on the coattails of the great wartime leader, Clemenceau. But such are the vicissitudes of French politics that only a few months later the old Tiger received a striking rebuff when he was refused the presidency, an honor he coveted. The man who had held France together in war was almost deserted in peace; the right thought he had yielded too much at the peace conference, while both the socialists and the Catholics had felt the cruel shafts of his terrible wit: disabused, skeptical, ironic, the old man entertained no illusions and believed in no fairies. The "bloc national" had little unity, and after Poincaré failed in the "battle of the Ruhr," the elections of 1924 brought in a "cartel of the left," a coalition of Socialists and Radicals which represented a reaction against Poincaré's aggressive nationalism and sought security in internationalism.

French security efforts

During the "years of hope" from 1924 to 1929, M. Briand remained steadily at the foreign office to carry on his policy of cautious reconciliation with Germany along with subtle efforts to bolster French security. But a series of French governments tried out all sorts of coalitions, Briand being about the only fixture. Poincaré returned to "save the franc," his grim determination being needed in this task of devaluation and financial retrenchment; then there was a cabinet shuffle under Poincaré, a Briand ministry, a Tardieu ministry keeping Briand on in his foreign ministry post. Save for the Communists on the far left, and the Socialists (diminishing in number), parties tended to deteriorate into factions, and the game of cabinet-building encouraged a popular cynicism about the whole process of parliamentary government. M. Tardieu himself eventually retired from the game to write some pages of disillusionment about the democratic system.

One should not exaggerate the ill effects of this cabinet instability, for the "government" went on regardless—that is, the administrative bureaucracy stayed and only the top men changed, generally speaking. But it undeniably made for paralysis at times when quick and courageous decisions were required, as the French found out in the 1930's. Meanwhile the rather uneasy détente of 1924 masked an international situation that was still dangerous for France. At Paris in 1919 France got promises of a guaranty treaty in which the United States and Great Britain would join in defending her frontiers, but both reneged. The League of Nations was supposed to guarantee them; it turned out to lack the power and the will to be a "league of force." The United States turned it down altogether, and British rejection of measures designed to put teeth in the covenant in 1924 left France with no choice except to grab at Locarno and a reconciliation with the Weimar Republic.

The left, and some of the right, followed Briand in his experiments in Franco-German friendship, but with qualms and uncertainties.

The French continued to feel misunderstood and badly used by their former allies, the British and Americans, who rebuffed every French effort to get them into a general security system and who put pressure on France to disarm. French diplomacy sought to make the most of what states remained. Soviet Russia being hostile, these were only the rather weak and precarious states of Poland, Yugoslavia, Czechoslovakia, and Rumania, with Italy an outside possibility. These powers were themselves at odds, and the best France could do was an alliance with Poland (which turned out to lack substance) and with the "Little Entente" of Yugoslavia, Czechoslovakia, and Rumania. It was little enough, should Germany regain her strength and seek to overturn the Versailles system. Briand gambled on the friendship of an appeased Germany, but had to consider French public opinion, which hated to give up the superiority in arms and position granted by the Versailles treaty—Germany disarmament, Allied occupation of the Rhine, a ban on German military forces in the Rhineland zone.

French Fascism

We have described the triumph of Communism in Russia, Fascism in Italy, and the emergence of National Socialism in Germany, which resembled Italian Fascism in basic ways. These dynamic ideologies of left and right appeared also in the democratic countries, though in France and Great Britain they were never more than ineffectual minorities. A great many intellectuals affected a sympathy for Soviet Communism; this became a major trend in the 1930's. A few adopted Fascism. The Communists won a significant if numerically small number of supporters among trade unionists and elected a handful of members to the national parliament (there were a dozen out of some 600 members in the French Chamber of Deputies in 1930). The extreme right in France exhibited a spirit akin to Fascism. The prewar *Action Française* movement, which had organized political activities in groups known as the *Camelots du Roi*, has been seen as an important predecessor of Mussolini's and Hitler's crusades; and from 1924 there were "Fascist leagues" in France which were in debt to the old *Action* but partly inspired by Mussolini's Fascism. In 1934 the fascist leagues seemed for a moment to be a serious threat. The great depression everywhere caused an increase in extremist factions, weakened the moderates, and threatened the overthrow of existing regimes. Democracy, the apparent victor of World War I, looked like it might be on the way out in Europe in the gloomy aftermath of that war.

Thought and culture in the twenties

By and large the postwar decade was marked intellectually by political disillusionment, a weary skepticism about values, and a turn toward art and literature as consolation—a reaction much like that which followed 1848. Pessimism about the future of the West was natural in the aftermath of the terrible war and the unsatisfactory peace. It could be found in Oswald

Caricature of T.S. Eliot

Lindbergh with U.S. Ambassador Herrick in Paris after his 1927 solo flight

Spengler's *Decline of the West*, a work which brilliantly posited the thesis that civilizations have life cycles and reach their peak of creativity only once —an hour long past for the West; or in the technically dazzling poems of T.S. Eliot, transplanted American who reigned as the literary mogul of the English-speaking world, poems immersed in the mood of desolation, death, paralysis of will:

> *Think.*
> *Neither fear nor courage saves us. Unnatural vices*
> *Are fathered by our heroism. Virtues*
> *Are forced upon us by our impudent crimes.*
> *These tears are shaken from the wrath-bearing tree.*
> . . . .
> *Thoughts of a dry brain in a dry season.*

Art and literature

Art and literature were never more brilliant than in these years, which saw the publication of James Joyce's *Ulysses*, the novels of D.H. Lawrence and Ernest Hemingway, the mature poetry of W.B. Yeats, the maturing of the modernist schools in painting and architecture. Joyce, Picasso, and Le Corbusier were at work creating the contemporary esthetic. The Freudian influence added to the excitement of the artistic revolution, opening up realms of the unconscious mind hitherto unexplored. Literature, so often controversial in this decade of *Ulysses* and *Lady Chatterly's Lover*, showed more interest in sex, the unconscious, the symbolical, the experimental, than in handling themes of social realism, despite the presence of many war novels. Esthetically and intellectually memorable, the 1920's displayed a marked disdain for the merely political. In reaction against ideas of progress, there was a notable "return to religion" in the neoorthodoxy of such theologians as Emil Brunner, Karl Barth, and Jacques Maritain. This marvelously creative "lost generation" saw life and history as tragic—in marked contrast to the flippant silliness of much "popular" culture, from which they were profoundly estranged.

Popular culture

This postwar decade was also the "Jazz Age," the "Long Weekend," the time of flappers and gangsters. In 1927 the American flyer Charles Lindbergh flew the Atlantic and, landing in Paris, was acclaimed by multitudes and became an international idol, though his was not really the first transatlantic flight. "Records" were broken every month or so, it seemed: first woman to fly the Atlantic, fastest flight over Atlantic, fastest automobile speed, first person to swim the English channel, first woman to swim the English channel, and so on. Plenty of other diversions existed: the movies, especially. Popular culture tended to be international: American movies went everywhere, and the popular actor Rudolph Valentino caused as much female hysteria in England as in the United States. Animated cartoons, "Westerns," and slapstick comedies spoke a cosmopolitan language; so did Charlie Chaplin and Mary Pickford. It was a time of crazes, such as crossword puzzles, mah jong, midget golf. The automobile had come to stay, and so had the painting of women's faces, formerly a sign of moral turpitude.

These and similar signs of change in popular culture have been abundantly reported upon. The zany side of life in the 1920's has been overstressed, but it existed. The paradox was that crazes, the throwing off of restraints (as for example in the newspapers and theaters, where a glorious good-bye was said to Victorian prudery), speed races, and other forms of hilarity and wildness went along with a tendency toward flatness and conformity. There was no character to most of the building, and the mass-circulation newspapers and magazines tended to standardize thought; everybody saw the same movies, too. Modern technology combined with democracy and numbers to make what some regarded as a cultural desert.

All the same, there was constant improvement in the common man's standard of comfort, whether in housing, clothing, eating, or cultural activity. Appalling degradation of taste as measured by a former, aristocratic standard might be a decided elevation if the comparison was made with the Victorian lower class, which had dwelt in foul slums without manners or morals. The war had destroyed the old order and ushered in the age of the common man. A large gulf existed between the men of letters, art, and science on the one hand, and on the other the shopgirl or tabloid-newspaper mentality; but the shopgirl of the 1920's probably had more cultural awareness than her mother. She had probably at least heard of Freud and T.S. Eliot and the modern artists, if only as a scandal (there were numbers of scandals of this sort, as for example Jacob Epstein's statue of W.H. Hudson in 1925). She almost certainly knew of an ancient Egyptian, King Tutankhamen, who oddly enough became a craze after the discovery of his tomb at Luxor in 1923. In the newspapers she read about the antics of the Bright Young People, or the arty inhabitants of Mayfair, in London. And in this era when all standards were turned topsy-turvy, she might even marry a peer. In the giddy 1920's lords were known to wed chorus girls, at any rate.

The war had accelerated many of these cultural phenomena, if it had not directly caused them. Automobiles and radios would probably have made their way into the world in any event, but wartime demands for them had certainly enormously stimulated their production, and after the battlefields no longer needed them a domestic market had to be found. Feminism, and a revolt against Victorian straightlacedness, had been in evidence just before the war, but again the war functioned as a powerful catalyst. Women got the vote they had vainly agitated for in the 1900's, as a reward for the shouldering of men's work when the boys were all away at the front. The tabloid culture, the culture of the "common man," had been emerging rapidly ever since about 1880, an inevitable consequence of modern democracy. But the war contributed greatly to a sort of social democratization. It was the democracy of the trenches, the democracy of death; class lines dissolved in the common struggle. Labor leaders entered into governments, politicians promised that every soldier on his return should have the best regardless of his pedigree. Withal, the horrible ordeal encouraged a kind of desperate gayety which the disillusioning aftermath seemed to perpetuate.

James Joyce and his publisher, Sylvia Beach

A revolution in manners and morals

It is well known that a "revolution in manners and morals" went on at this time, precipitated by the war, by a general feeling of insecurity, a vague awareness of the intellectual revolution, and some rather more concrete phenomena such as the automobile, the radio, and the movies. Manners and morals were freer. These were signs of the cultural crisis that afflicted Europe in the aftermath of the war, and which elsewhere helped cause the Fascist and Communist revolutions. In the western democracies the crisis took the form of restlessness and forced gayety, as if people were trying to avoid reality by a mad search for amusement. "The long weekend" ended between Munich and Dunkerque, when reality at last jarred the democracies out of their hysteria.

Alienation of the intellectuals

The estrangement of the intellectual and the artist from a mass-technological civilization was revealed in the genius of virtually all the most creative spirits of the era. It was apparent in their techniques which, designed to express a private world and not to communicate public truths, were as difficult, demanding, to the plain man well-nigh incomprehensible, as the poetry of Eliot or Yeats (which demanded a vast knowledge of mythologies and literature of all ages, worked into the complex tapestry of its allusions), the novels of Joyce (eventuating, in *Finnegan's Wake*, in the invention of a new language, incredibly demanding too of historical and literary knowledge), or the nonrealistic paintings of Picasso, Kandinsky, and other abstractionists. The alienation of Joyce may be taken as typical. "I will not serve that in which I do not believe, whether it call itself my home, my fatherland, or my church," says Stephan Dedalus in one of Joyce's early works. *Ulysses* justifies itself as a work of art, not a message of its time. If it has any message, it is the futility of human existence. D.H. Lawrence, less esoteric in his style than the Irish giant, migrated to the Indians of Mexico, or the Etruscans, because he was convinced that Western civilization was played out and done for. "All warmth is gone entirely, the hearth is cold. . . ." The other great novelist of the era, the French master Marcel Proust, wrote a vast chronicle of the total decay of French upper-class society.

Of the new spirit in the arts, perhaps the least alienated was the modernist architecture of Le Corbusier, Gropius, and others of this school; but it was as much resented and rejected by the majority at this time as was Picasso or Joyce. Corbusier entered a modernist design for the League of Nations building to be erected in Geneva, in his native Switzerland. It engendered a controversy; the winning design was that of the stately neoclassical edifice which stands in Geneva today. The episode symbolized the refusal of the public to embrace the leading art of the era. Yet Corbusier, along with Picasso, Joyce, and Eliot, was at work creating the modern modes of expression in all the arts.

Bibliography

On Soviet Russia in the 1920's, D. Footman, *The Civil War in Russia* (London: Faber & Faber, 1961), does not cover the whole of that confused struggle but does have much interesting material. O.H. Radkey, *Agrarian Foes of Bolshevism* (New York: Columbia University Press, 1958) and *The Sickle Under the Hammer* (Columbia University Press, 1963), are vigorous studies of the Bolsheviks and peasants during the Civil War and after. Richard Pipes, *The Formation of the Soviet Union* (Cambridge, Mass.: Harvard University Press, 1954), is a work of impressive scholarship. Deutscher has also written *Stalin: A Political Biography* (Random House, Vintage) E.H. Carr continues his *History of Soviet Russia* (New York: Macmillan) with four volumes on the 1920's. Alexander Erlich, *The Soviet Industrialization Debate 1924–1928* (Harvard University Press, 1961), covers a vital issue. For the ensuing convulsive effort to launch industrialization at the expense of the peasantry, perhaps the older works of Maurice Hindus best convey its terrible impact: *Humanity Uprooted* (New York: Cape & Smith, 1929) and *The Great Offensive* (London: Gollancz, 1933). Trotsky's own indictment of *Stalin* may be obtained in a Grosset & Dunlap Universal paperback. His *Papers* are being edited by Jan M. Meijer and published by Mouton at The Hague, Netherlands.

In English there seems less on Fascism. Laura Fermi has essayed a biography of Mussolini which is hardly definitive but may do as an interim report (Chicago: University of Chicago Press, 1961). Ernst Nolte, *Three Faces of Fascism* (Holt, Rinehart & Winston), is especially stimulating on Mussolini. Roy MacGregor-Hastie, *The Day of the Lion* (Dayton, Ohio: E.F. MacDonald, 1964), is more popular; Christopher Seton-Watson, *Italy from Liberalism to Fascism* (London: Methuen Publications, 1968), and Denis Mack Smith, *Italy: A Modern History* (Ann Arbor: University of Michigan Press, 1959), provide excellent background. Federico Chabod, *A History of Italian Fascism* (London: Weidenfeld & Nicolson, 1963), has been translated from the Italian. In paperback, S.W. Halperin, *Mussolini and Italian Fascism* (D. Van Nostrand, Anvil), and Herman Finer, *Mussolini's Italy* (Grosset & Dunlap), are both older works.

Among a rich harvest of notable books on the Weimar Republic are R.G.L. Waite, *Vanguard of Nazism: The Free Corps Movement 1918–1923* (Harvard University Press, 1952); H.W. Gatzke, *Stresesmann and the Rearmament of Germany* (Baltimore: Johns Hopkins University, 1954); Henry A. Turner, *Stresesmann and the Weimar Republic* (Princeton University Press); H.J. Gordon, *The Reichswehr and the German Republic 1919–1926* (Princeton, N.J.: Princeton University Press, 1956); K. von Klemperer, *Germany's New Conservatism* (Princeton University Press, 1957), a study in political ideology; Klaus Epstein, *Mathias Erzberger and the Dilemma of German Democracy* (Princeton University Press, 1959). On social and political aspects, see R.N. Hunt, *German Social Democracy 1918–1933* (New Haven, Conn.: Yale University Press, 1964); W.T. Angress, *Stillborn Revolution: The Communist Bid for Power in Germany 1921–1923* (Princeton University Press, 1963); Eric Waldman, *The Spartacist Movement of 1919 and the Crisis of the German Socialist Movement* (Milwaukee: Marquette University Press, 1958); Andreas Dorpalen, *Hindenburg and the Weimar Republic* (Princeton University Press, 1964). For a general survey, the book by S.W. Halperin, *Germany Tried Democracy* (W.W. Norton) is adequate; a fuller account is Erich Eyck, *History of the Weimar Republic* (2 vols.; Harvard University Press, 1962–63).

Charles L. Mowat has surveyed the scene of *Britain between the Wars 1918–1940* (University of Chicago Press, 1955), as also does A.P. Havighurst, *Twentieth-Century Britain* (Harper & Row). Another excellent study is A.J.P. Taylor, *British History 1914–1945* (New York: Oxford University Press, 1965), which is in the Oxford History of England. More detailed is Richard W. Lyman, *The First Labour Government* (London: Chapman & Hall, 1958). G.M. Young's interesting biography of *Stanley Baldwin* (London: R. Hart-Davis, 1952) treats a central political figure of the period. James Joll (ed.), *The Decline of the Third Republic* (New York: Frederick A. Praeger, 1959), is one of the St. Anthony's Papers from Oxford University. D. Brogan's and D. Thomson's works on the Third Republic, previously cited (see Chapter 24) are relevant here also. A notable document is the memoir of Joseph Paul-Boncour, translated into English as *Recollections of the Third Republic* (New York: Robert Speller & Sons, 1957).

Elizabeth Wiskemann, *Europe of the Dictators 1919–1945* (Harper & Row), is a broad survey. The final volume of the New Cambridge Modern History, edited by David Thomson, is appropriately titled *The Era of Violence 1898–1945* (New York: Cambridge University Press, 1960). Those interested in a lighter touch might enjoy Asa Briggs (ed.), *They Saw It Happen: An Anthology of Eye-Witness Accounts of Events in British History 1897–1940* (Oxford: Blackwell, 1960).

Hitler youth parading on "Party Day" in Nürnberg, 1933

29

The troubled thirties: Depression, Nazism, and war

chronology

1931
Depression deepens. Britain leaves gold standard. Moratorium on war debts.
Fall of British Labour government, split in Labour party; national coalition government under Ramsay MacDonald.
Manchurian incident.
Rise of National Socialists in Germany.
Spanish Republic born.
1932
League report on Manchuria.
Geneva Disarmament Conference.
Famine in Soviet Union, result in part of Communist war on peasants.
Nazis become largest party in Germany, with about 40 percent of the Reichstag.
1933
Japan censured by League, resigns.
Hitler becomes Chancellor. Reichstag fire, new elections, 44 percent Nazi. Outlawing of other parties by Reichstag.
Geneva Disarmament Conference breaks up; Germany leaves it and League of Nations.
World Economic Conference fails.
Four-Power Pact, England, France, Germany, Italy, on Mussolini's initiative.
Stavisky scandal in France. Rise of French Fascist Leagues.
1934
Russia joins League of Nations.
Assassination of King Alexander of Yugoslavia and French Foreign Minister Barthou at Marsailles.
Hitler purges party, murders opponents on night of June 30. Assumes presidency.
Attempted Nazi coup in Austria, assassination of Prime Minister Dollfuss.
German-Polish nonaggression pact.
1935
Germany repudiates disarmament clauses of Versailles treaty.
Stresa Conference, England, France, Italy.
Ethiopian crisis. Sanctions declared against Italy by League of Nations.
Stanley Baldwin, Conservative Prime Minister of Great Britain.
Saar votes for reattachment to Germany.
1936
Hoare-Laval proposals for Ethiopian settlement, withdrawn after public reaction. Resignation of Hoare, fall of Laval government.
End of Ethiopian war with Italian victory.
Beginning of Civil War in Spain.
German reoccupation of Rhineland, not opposed by Versailles powers, though denounced.
Death of George V, abdication crisis in England; abdication of Edward VIII. George VI comes to throne.
Popular front government in France.
Anti-Comintern pact; between Italy, Germany, and Japan.
Purge trials begin in Russia with execution of many old Bolsheviks. New Soviet Constitution goes into effect.
1937
War between Japan and China.
Neville Chamberlain becomes British Prime Minister.
Purge trials continue in Soviet Union.
1938
Austria annexed by Germany.
Anglo-Italian Pact. Hitler visits Rome.
1938
Czech crisis; Germans demand Sudetenland. Munich Pact following conferences at Godesberg and Berchtesgaden, giving Sudetenland to Germany.
Breakup of Popular Front in France. Daladier government.
Severe persecution of Jews in Nazi Germany. Hitler purges army.
1939
Hitler occupies Prague, Memel.
Anglo-French guarantee to Poland, Rumania, Greece.
Italian invasion of Albania, April.
Victory of Nationalists in Spanish Civil War.
Anglo-Russian conversations fail to achieve agreement.
Nazi-Soviet Pact.
Polish crisis over Danzig; German attack on Poland September 1, beginning World War II. Russians occupy part of Poland.

"Annus terribilis"

Thus historian Arnold J. Toynbee dubbed 1931—a "terrible year" for Europe. The world depression raged to its devastating climax in this year, as Europe felt the full impact of the slump which the roaring, boom-and-bust American economy experienced beginning late in 1929. Perhaps the depression may be best accounted for in terms of the profound dislocations in the world economic pattern which World War I caused. The United States had soared to world economic leadership as Europe faltered, spent her savings, lost markets during the fearful military struggle. After the war, currencies fluctuated and trade balances showed grave disequilibria as Europe struggled to right herself. The great German inflation, followed by pouring of foreign capital (chiefly American) into Germany in order to repair the damage, and the whole question of reparations and of the war debts owed to the United States, added to the disturbance. Tariff walls went up, as many countries sought self-sufficiency or "autarchy"; and a serious world overproduction of primary products developed during the 1920's, the result of these policies of autarchy, of new technology, and of large areas coming into production for the first time. Among many disturbing consequences of World War I, the effect on colonial areas ought not to be overlooked. These became considerably less profitable because of those movements of protest we previously noted.

The capitalist economy had always been subject to the ups and downs of the "business cycle." It is the price paid for a free economic system, in which individuals are left free to make their own economic decisions with the hope that the outcome will be beneficial to all. Free capitalism did provide incentives to wealth, both "the carrot and the stick"—the lure of profits, the fear of want. But it was prone to instability. According to economic theory accepted ever since the age of Ricardo and Say, these periods of disequilibrium were strictly temporary or local; the economic order as a whole supposedly tended naturally to full employment and the maximum use of resources. The business cycle was like the needle on a sensitive meter which might swing violently for a moment in one direction or the other but always came back toward its natural center. In the light of later and more sophisticated analysis—based on sad experience—this theory, while not without its element of truth, came to seem naive. It assumed all kinds of "normal" conditions which in the real world might go awry: for example, substantial free trade among nations, which did not exist at this time. It assumed perfect competition, obviously lacking in an era prone to both corporate monopoly and trade union influence; likewise political stability, with protection for property and no great amount of government intervention. It made no allowances for wars, reparations, the dismemberment of countries, and all kinds of political factors.

Whatever their causes, the economic earthquakes that shook Europe in 1931 were obviously not merely normal tremors. Banks failed, countries were forced to leave the gold standard for the first time in modern history.

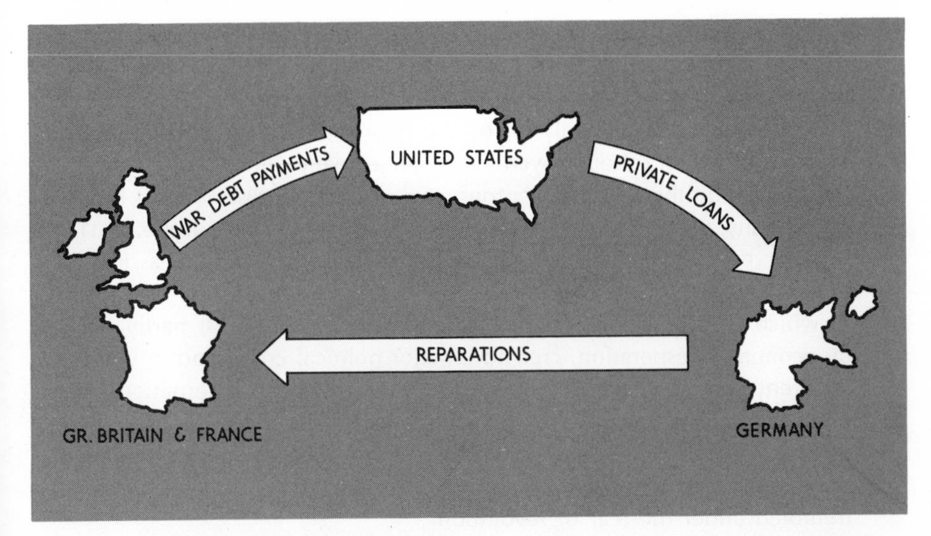

The cycle of war debts and reparation payments in the 1920's

In 1931, after the World Court refused to allow Austria to enter a customs union with Germany, this economically distressed country collapsed. The failure of Austria's central bank touched off a panic which led to the withdrawal of American funds from Europe; and from this event, and the already serious state of the American depression, panic spread through Europe, for she had not yet become able to live without American credit. President Hoover of the United States proposed a moratorium on all war debts and reparations, but French opposition delayed its acceptance; in any case reparations and war debts were at an end, because Germany simply could not pay to the Allies and they could not pay to the United States. In September, the Bank of England left the gold standard, and a symbol of economic stability passed away—the free interchangeability of currencies in terms of gold. For generations London had been the central clearing house for the moneys of the world. Now the pound itself was no longer backed by gold, and depreciated substantially.

This British decision caused country after country to take a similar step, which they felt necessary in order to stop the flight of gold under conditions of an adverse balance of trade. The flight from gold was followed by all kinds of nationalist economic policies—exchange controls, import quotas, tariffs. International trade fell seriously, since in the absence of an international money and the free movement of goods, nations were reduced to the primitive device of barter in the exchange of goods.

Most governments of Europe pursued "orthodox" economic policies. That meant keeping the government budget in balance, in order to lower costs so that markets might be recovered and the depression might quickly run its course. The idea of having the government borrow and spend to counterbalance deflation in time of depression ran counter to orthodox economic theory, though it was to be advocated by Swedish economists and the Englishman John Maynard Keynes—and practiced by Sweden during the great depression. The orthodox tactics seemed to have no effect, or at any rate it took them too long this time, and mass unemployment demoralized society.

Fascist Italy was as badly hit by the depression as the liberal countries; in Great Britain, a Labour government had as many difficulties as any "capitalist" one. But the most momentous results of the depression were to be felt in Germany, where the depression was the most severe in Europe. 1931, the terrible year, saw the rise of the National Socialist party as well as the Communist party in a Germany ravaged by unemployment. It was also the year in which Japan's absorption of Manchuria, a move at least partly inspired by economic desperation, created a major political crisis; and in which the apparent success of the first Soviet five-year plan made international Communism a distinct world factor. Political factors interacted with economic ones to bring about a mood of panic, which only deepened the depression as those with capital to invest hoarded it, as governments fell and societies trembled under the fear of revolution.

The triumph of national socialism in Germany

The collapse of German democracy took place under the hammer blows of this great depression. That democracy had never been very strong. Only since 1919, it will be recalled, had Germany had a true parliamentary system, and the Weimar Republic suffered from having been born of defeat and nourished on humiliation. Those who did not accept its underlying principles included a strong minority of extremists on both left and right—Communists and Nationalists. The cabinets of the 1920's had to rest upon a coalition of various parties, normally the Social Democrats, the Center Party (Catholic), and the middle-class Liberal and Democratic parties. These parties were not very congenial, and when the depression struck they were less so. After all, the Social Democrats represented the trade unions while the bourgeois parties spoke for industrial ownership and management.

When the depression hit Germany, the extremist parties increased their following. This meant the Communists on the left and, on the right, Adolf Hitler's National Socialist party, which suddenly burst forth as a major party in the election of September, 1930, the Communists increasing their representation in the Reichstag at the same time. Previously obscure, and rendered ridiculous by his failure in the Bavarian putsch of 1923, Hitler had emerged from prison, where he wrote his long, rather turgid book *Mein Kampf*, to hold his little group together. But it was a distinctly disreputable group of failures and malcontents, and its sudden rise to power belongs among history's most surprising, and tragic, stories.

Breakdown of parliamentary government

The sudden success of the Nazis in 1930, along with that of the Communists on the other extreme, may be interpreted as simply a protest vote—against rather than for something. Suffering from unemployment and all the other disasters of the great depression, Germans voted against the government in power, which seemed to be doing nothing much about their troubles, as naturally as Americans voted against the Republican party in 1932. They could hardly vote *against* the coalition government without voting *for* one of the extremist parties not identified with that government. A protest vote in the United States, under a two-party system, could go to the other major party, the Democrats. But a protest vote in Germany had to go to the Communists or the Nazis.

With nearly a half of the members of the Reichstag Communists or Nazis, each prepared to vote against any government, and with the Socialists unable to agree with the other parliamentary parties, it became impossible to find a majority in the Reichstag for any government. The parliamentary system, quite simply, failed to work. Under that system, a cabinet has to have the support of a majority of the parliament. No such majority could be found. In this situation the President resorted to government by decree, which was provided for by the constitution as an emergency solution, but which became the regular thing in Germany in 1931 and 1932. Brüning and von Papen headed governments which bypassed the Reichstag, since there seemed no alternative. They gambled on finding a cure for the depression which would cause the extremist votes to dwindle. But economic conditions grew worse, not better.

Rise of National Socialists

Elections held in July, 1932, sent the Nazi vote up to 230 in the Reichstag, making them the largest single party. Uniformed Nazi "storm troopers" paraded the streets and used violence on political opponents in a campaign of intimidation which seemed to meet little resistance from the forces of law and order in Germany. By this time, too, some financial support from big business flowed toward the Nazis, but they were by no means a party of the

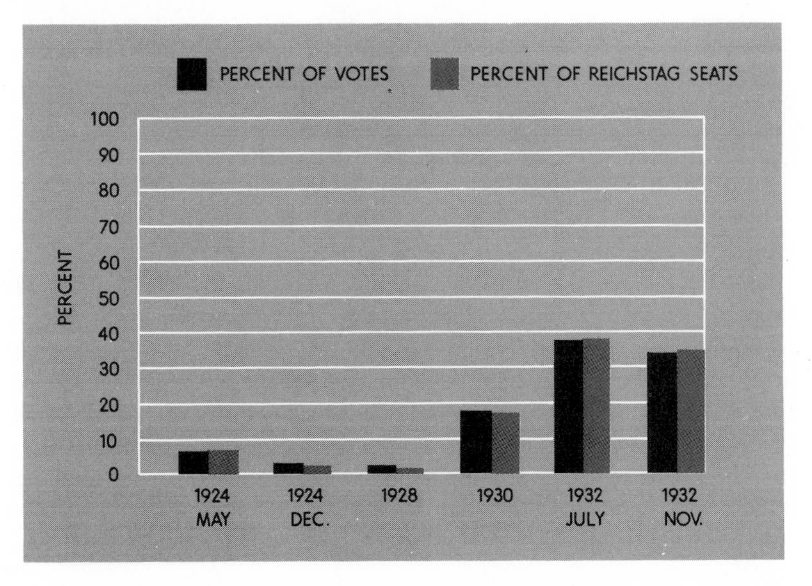

Strength of National Socialist (Nazi) party in Germany, 1924–32

Adolf Hitler

business class, and most respectable burghers despised them. Hitler got some financial aid from Mussolini, whom he regarded as the spiritual father of his movement. His votes came chiefly from ruined lower bourgeoisie, farmers, and to a lesser degree the working class.

The Austrian-born demagogue, Hitler, was a dynamic and almost hypnotic individual with little education but much insight into human nature and a large supply of superficial political ideas. He inveighed against the Jews, liberal intellectuals, pacifists, Marxists, and international capitalists. He appeared to believe in a doctrine of racism, according to which the biologically superior Nordic race had a right and duty to dominate or even exterminate inferior types, represented principally by Jews and Slavs. Those who argued that Hitler did not really believe such nonsense but only used it as propaganda were to be grimly confuted by the genocide programs of World War II.

Nazi ideology

The movement was fervidly nationalist, denouncing the shameful peace treaty and demanding a national resurgence under strong leadership to "throw off the shackles of Versailles." However, there were other nationalist parties, more respectable than the Nazis; Hitler had no monopoly on patriotism. Nazism added a vicious anti-Semitism, attacking the Jew as the enemy not only of German unity but of civilization itself, and paraded wildly inaccurate thories of history and of a Jewish conspiracy.[1] What really marked off the Nazis from other political groups was their rabble-rousing activism. They organized gangs of toughs, recruited from among the restless ex-soldiers or fatherless youth of the land. They called for revolution. This was a revolutionary rightism, something relatively new. It borrowed, of course, from Mussolini's Fascism. One ought not to categorize Nazism as something peculiarly German. If it drew in different ways on Richard Wagner and Friedrich Nietzsche, it also resembled the French *Action Française*. Anti-Semitism had made its modern debut in France during the Dreyfus Affair, and raised its ugly head all over Europe, usually being much more virulent in Russia, Poland, and Rumania than in western Europe. Hitler found it in his native Austria. Nazi racism owed much to an Englishman, Houston Stewart Chamberlain, who in turn derived it not only from Wagner but from the Frenchman, Comte de Gobineau. The corpus of ideas on which the Nazis drew was European, not exclusively German. They derived revolutionary nihilism from Nietzsche; but Nietzsche had been no German nationalist. The concept of an integral, organic, *völkisch* culture was found in France as well as Germany, though perhaps more widespread in the latter.

The National Socialist ideology picked up crumbs of doctrine from many sources and baked, or half-baked, these into a loaf that offered a little something for all appetites. It appealed to the anticapitalist feelings of the little man, but avoided the divisive class-struggle doctrine by claiming that only Jewish international capitalism was bad. The Nazis told the German people they had not really been defeated in the war but had been betrayed from within—"stabbed in the back"—by Jews and Marxists. To the intellectuals and the idealistic young, they offered scraps of Nietzsche and other fashionable creeds stressing heroism, rebirth, sacrifice, purgation of decadent elements, leadership, supermen. They offered to replace a stagnant parliamentarianism with the leadership principle. German farmers responded to an element in the Nazi ideology which deplored the uprootedness of modern man and preached a return to the soil with its eternal verities. The Nazis touched responsive strings in philistine hearts when they denounced modern art and literature as decadent, blaming the decay of classical standards and traditional morality on Jewish corruption of sound Germanic culture.

Nazi showmanship

The Nazis were good showmen, too. Like the Fascists, they clad their followers in a distinctive uniform, gave them insignia and a salute, organized

[1] The famous forgery, *Protocols of the Elders of Zion*, purporting to reveal the secret Jewish conspiracy against Western civilization, first gained currency in tsarist Russia, where prior to 1914 anti-Semitism was the most vicious in Europe. It seems to have originated as a satire or hoax in mid–19th-century France. Among others in addition to the Nazis who took it seriously was the American industrialist Henry Ford, who published an anti-Semitic paper in the 1920's.

them into military-like formations; they paraded, sang songs, held huge and colorful meetings, and made martyrs out of some of their hoodlums killed in street fights with the Communists. Better than their more staid opponents, they understood something about mass psychology. Hitler remarked that World War I had shown how easy it is to dupe the masses with propaganda, and also expressed his indebtedness to the American advertising industry, whose horrible but effective methods of mass hypnosis were becoming well known at this time. The Nazis S.S. corps owed something to the Jesuits, the Communists, and Nietzsche's idea of a superior elite—a small body of dedicated spirits trained in fanatical obedience and service to the cause. The notion of giving idealistic youth a cause to serve has been perpetuated elsewhere in Boy Scouts and Peace Corps; clearly it is psychologically sound. The National Socialists succeeded notably in capturing Germany's restless revolutionary youth, much as these young people might later regret their captivation. The Nazis also pandered to an element of brutality in youth, the gang spirit, for they encouraged street brawling and beating up political opponents.

In power, Hitler began to crush with brutal violence all that was finest in Germany, including its respect for law and its intellectual freedom, and quickly proceeded along the road to war. But one must not overlook the sense of terrible crisis in the world in 1931 to 1933. Even in the United States, millions of the unemployed sought breadlines while farmers rioted and banks closed; in this atmosphere Congress turned over virtually dictatorial powers to the new President, Franklin D. Roosevelt. In the Soviet Union, Stalinism began to silence all opposition and suppress the last remnants of freedom. Terrified by economic collapse, men were ready to sell their freedom for bread and jobs.

Hitler gains power

In 1933 the failure to take the ex-corporal and his band of freebooters seriously was perhaps a factor working in his favor. When his time came, Hitler proved as shrewd and ruthless a politician as Europe had seen. Circumstances worked in his favor in 1933. With the Nazis controlling around 35 percent of the electorate, enough to make them the largest single party, there seemed no choice but to allow them into the government, or else use the army to smash them and alter the democratic basis of the government. General Kurt von Schleicher entertained the latter idea but the army refused, believing itself too small and the risks too great. Old President Hindenburg, who had earlier disliked Hitler, then gave his consent to Franz von Papen to organize a coalition of Nazis with some other conservatives, hoping to tame the Nazis. But Hitler held out for the chancellorship for himself, and the ministries of defense and interior (army and police) for his lieutenants. Once this far in, Hitler used his power to establish a Nazi dictatorship. Early in 1933, the Nazis took advantage of a fire at the Reichstag,[2] denouncing the act as a Communist

[2] It was widely believed that the Nazis deliberately set the fire themselves, but careful students of the episode have concluded that though the Nazis were quick to take advantage of the act they did not initiate it.

President Hindenburg was in his 80's when Hitler came to power.

plot, and obtained emergency decrees suspending free speech and press. An election subject to Nazi tactics of intimidation produced a vote of only 44 percent for them. But with the aid of votes from other parties, laws were passed granting extreme emergency powers to the government. One by one, Hitler then outlawed the other parties, fastened the control of his highly disciplined party on all organs of government, dissolved trade unions, took over press and radio, and in all possible ways proceeded toward the erection of the most extreme dictatorship western Europe had ever known.

The Hitler regime: Toward world war

Hitler's success

The world was dismayed at the ease with which Hitler subverted and destroyed German democracy. On the long remembered night of June 30, 1934, he simply seized and murdered a number of enemies both within his own party (where he had tough and ruthless rivals) and outside it. In possession of the organs of opinion, he seemed able to control and mold the German mind. But Hitler was able to cement his grip on Germany largely because of his achievements, which made him seem like a savior, whatever his methods may have lacked in delicacy.

These were partly in solution of the internal economic crisis, where there was recovery, owing perhaps chiefly to the stimulus provided by rearmament. Hitler profited by the services of economic experts, especially the non-Nazi Hjalmar Schacht, who guided economic policy until 1935, resigning when Hitler turned to a war economy. Schacht was a genius at the new game of manipulating the rate of exchange and making favorable trade agreements on that basis. In other significant internal policies, National Socialism destroyed the trade unions and abolished the right to strike; and it set up work projects similar to the CCC and WPA in President Roosevelt's American New Deal. As in the New Deal, too, agriculture received some relief through the artificial raising of prices. Between 1932 and 1937, German economic recovery was greater than that of the United States under the New Deal. The similar recovery of the United Kingdom under conservative policies suggests that natural tendencies toward an upswing of the cycle might have brought about recovery regardless of the government's measures. But it was natural that the government in power should get credit. By 1936, Hitler had begun to spend money on large-scale rearmament, stimulating the economy.

As of about 1936, many people who later regarded Hitler as an evil maniac were granting him grudging praise. Winston Churchill praised him for having restored to his people their self-respect. (Old David Lloyd George was an enthusiastic British convert.) Undeniably dynamic, National Socialism early shocked much of world opinion by its crudities and especially by its persecution of the Jews. However, the systematic terrorization of the Jews, seizure of their property, and arrest by the dread Gestapo secret police became a world scandal only after November, 1938, following assassination of a Nazi official by a Jew. Until about that date, Nazification of German life was far from

After Germany's March 1935 declaration of its intent to rearm, France, Italy, and Britain joined temporarily in the so called "Stresa Front," but Italy soon broke with the democracies over Ethiopia. Laval, Mussolini, MacDonald, and Flandin at Stresa in April, 1935.

complete despite Nazi oratory, and optimists might still have hoped that Hitler and his movement would eventually be tamed by the responsibilities of power. This was considerably to underestimate the ideological fanaticism of the little Austrian, and also the grandeur of his plans for the rebuilding of Germany. For these included immense territorial expansion.

German rearmament

Immediately upon assuming power in 1933 Hitler took Germany out of the Geneva Disarmament Conference, where already it had been agreed in principle that Germany should have arms equality, erasing the stigma of the 1919 treaty, but where practical agreement on the meaning of this equality had foundered on French resistance. He went ahead to rearm Germany in defiance of the Versailles treaty, and in 1935 he openly denounced that treaty. Having gotten away with this, in 1936 he sent German troops into the demilitarized zone of the Rhineland, in defiance of the Locarno pact as well as the Versailles treaty. It was a bold move, for it was upon this that the French had relied for their security. But Hitler had calculated his chances correctly. Britain and France permitted this move to pass without resistance. Needless to say this added enormously to Hitler's popularity in Germany. In 1935, also, a plebescite held in the Saar, coal-rich region between France and Germany, returned this area to Germany after it had been administered by France ever since 1920.

Hitler's aims in Europe

Thus far Hitler had done no more than rectify manifest injustices stemming from the Versailles treaty, and asserted no more than a right to arm and occupy territory indisputably German. But he had no intention of stopping here. What were his goals? For one thing, he shared much of the old Pan-German aim of bringing all Germanic peoples in Europe under one roof. For another, his Nazi racist ideology convinced him that Slavs as well as Jews were "sub-men" who should rightly be ruled by the superior "Aryans." Most important of all, Hitler believed that even the restoration of her 1914 borders would not suffice for Germany's security. Had she not been beaten in that war? The Reich must be expanded and strengthened so as to render a recurrence impossible. A combination of these views led Hitler to look especially toward the east, toward Russia. He was always prepared to let France and England be junior partners in his "new order" provided they meekly accepted his domination. Toward Russia, controlled by the hated Bolsheviks, he looked with an eye to conquest and annexation.

Annexation of Austria

Meanwhile, the disarray of Europe and the weakness of his foes presented him with magnificent opportunities. While Britain and France struggled with depression and internal political crises, Soviet Russia was going through the great purge of all Stalin's real or imagined foes which almost shattered the Communist state in the 1936–39 years. Some of the smaller countries of Europe had trouble surviving. An Austrian born, Hitler was not likely to overlook the prospects of annexing that small country, left stranded by the dissolution of the Hapsburg Empire in 1918. He had explored this prospect as early as 1934, only to be checked by Italy. In 1938, much stronger and having made a friend of Mussolini, he conducted a ruthless *coup d'état* that attached Austria to the Reich, partly by internal Nazi subversion and partly by threats. There is much evidence that a majority of Austrians did not wish the *Anschluss* with Germany though many did. In this case, there was the justification that Austrians were Germans and that the little country could not survive separately. Again the Allied powers, though they had vetoed this annexation in 1931,[3] allowed Hitler to have his way, at the cost of Austrian independence.

Pact of Munich: Dismemberment of Czechoslovakia

Afterwards, it was widely agreed that someone should have checked Hitler's ambitions early. This was not quite so obvious at the time. But in 1938 the opinion grew that Germany's territorial ambitions were dangerously great. Each time he took something, the Nazi dictator effusively assured the world that this was his last demand; yet there was always another. In the summer of 1938, having swallowed Austria, he turned immediately to Czechoslovakia, fulminating against alleged mistreatment of the German minority in that country and demanding the cession of the Sudetenland region to Germany.[4] This time there was genuine alarm in London, Paris, and even in Moscow and Washington. To allow this dismemberment of Czechoslovakia, while it might again be defended on grounds of nationality and "self-determination," would be to render the Czechs defenseless and unlock all of southeastern Europe to German dominance. It would be sure to stimulate the Germans to fresh demands. Yet Britain and France had no boundaries with Czecholslovakia and, much more significant, no national will to fight a war in central Europe. After a long, tense crisis and threats of war, a series of conferences held in Germany between the leaders of France, Britain, Italy, and Germany resulted in a full victory for Hitler at Munich in late September, 1938, and the consequent dismemberment of the Czech state.

"Munich" marked the peak of the Nazi dictator's successful aggrandizement of Germany by diplomatic blackmail, wresting concessions from the beleaguered British and French with a combination of appeals to fair play and threats of war. They had bought peace at the price of another country's freedom—a democratic country—but the victory for "peace in our time" left so bitter a taste that public opinion in France and Britain, heretofore on the side of "appeasement," hardened against any further concessions to Hitler. The sadistic persecution of the Jews that began in Germany in November, 1938, did not lessen this reaction.

---

[3] The World Court had decided against it by a narrow margin; German opinion assumed this was a politically motivated decision.

[4] As in the case of Bismarck, there is an erroneous tendency to attribute to Hitler a master plan. He was undoubtedly guided by the turn of events. The Germans in Czechoslovakia, full of real or imagined grievances against the government at Prague and incited by Nazi propaganda, began this imbroglio, and Hitler responded. In terms of real priorities, Hitler and the Germans in general placed Poland higher than Czechoslovakia.

Hitler at his zenith

But Hitler had not finished with his demands. He intended to play what in terms of German opinion was his trump card: the return of the territory ceded to Poland in 1919, and especially the German city of Danzig. Tension rose in Danzig in 1939, and Hitler shrilly denounced the Poles for their crimes against Germans. This crisis was to bring on World War II. As the coming of that terrible war involved the attitudes and policies of other powers, including Soviet Russia as well as the western democracies, we may postpone a final verdict on it until after a glance at these other countries in the 1930's. Indisputable is the fact that Hitler had given Germany the initiative. He had won for her the ascendancy of Europe by 1939 and perhaps, had he had the sense to stop, she might have maintained it. But he was swept on by arrogance and by inordinate ambitions. He talked of "living space" in the east, of "settling the Baltic problem" (i.e., annexing the Baltic states), and of building a Reich so strong that it would last a thousand years. By this time he had completely mastered Germany. In 1938 the proud German army yielded up to him its honor and independence in the Fritsch affair, allowing Hitler to frame and depose its leader and appoint one of his Nazi stooges as its commander. At the time of the Czech crisis, plotters against Hitler hoped to depose him, but the stunning victory he won at Munich destroyed their

Chamberlain with Hitler at Munich, September, 1938. Britain and France bought a year's peace at the expense of Czechoslovakia.

chances. His opponents either fled or were killed or imprisoned. Many brave Germans paid the price of opposition to him, but the vast majority—what else could be expected?—hailed his triumphs.

France and Great Britain

While Hitler and Stalin were imposing a total conformity on their peoples, divisive ideological and political quarrels afflicted Britain and France. When the depression struck Britain a Labour government was in power, though dependent on votes from the diminishing Liberal party to sustain a narrow majority over the Conservatives. Split by the question of whether to cut the "dole" (unemployment relief payments) in order to balance the budget, the Labour government of Prime Minister Ramsay MacDonald resigned, MacDonald and a few other Labourites joining a coalition government with Conservatives and Liberals while the majority of Labour read him out of the party. With Labour badly disorganized by this split, the National Coalition government had things its own way for some years; in 1935 Stanley Baldwin became the cabinet chief in what was now hardly more than a straight Conservative government. The Baldwin government, succeeded by that of Neville Chamberlain in 1937, held to relatively orthodox, budget-balancing economic policies, at the cost of much bitterness among unemployed workers seeking state aid, but with the reward of some degree of economic recovery by 1937. There were nevertheless some extensions of government economic activity, notably in the field of public housing. The bitterness of those who suffered from the depression had much to do with British lack of morale in facing Hitler's challenge.

French Fascism and Communism

France was even more bitterly rent by ideological and social conflict. The extreme positions, Fascism and Communism, were stronger here than in Britain though not so strong as in Germany. In 1934, a year after the Nazi victory, the so-called Fascist Leagues, led by Col. François de la Rocque's *Croix de Feu* (Fiery Cross) organization, rioted in Paris and thereafter for some time greatly increased their membership. But they never really threatened a putsch or revolutionary seizure of the government and eventually subsided. On the far left, French Communists responded to instructions from Moscow and began to advocate a "popular front" of all antifascist groups.[5] They supported Leon Blum's popular-front government of 1936–38. Under this distinguished socialist intellectual a French "new deal" of fairly extensive proportions came into effect, including the nationalization of a few industries and prolabor union legislation. It encountered bitter resistance from businessmen.

Confronted with the critically deteriorating international situation and a fiscal crisis, Blum's government had anything but easy sailing; and the "popular front" of Communists, Socialists, and Liberals broke down altogether at the time of the Munich Pact, which the Communists denounced and the Socialists refused to support. A coalition headed by Radical Socialist (liberal) Edouard Daladier then found support on the right rather than on the left to the disgust of the latter and to the accompaniment of a wave of strikes. France on the eve of World War II presented, even more than Britain, a picture of internal disunity, of turbulent conflict between social classes and

[5] During the Nazi victory of 1933 the Communists' role was among the most inglorious of all inglorious roles in that bungled event. They helped the Nazis bring down the German Republic in the mistaken view that Communism would profit from this in the end. Their rigid ideology holding no place for Hitlerism, they believed it to be of no consequence, a kind of last gasp of decadent capitalism before the socialist revolution. After 1934 they were forced to readjust their thinking and changed to a "popular front" strategy. Prior to that they scorned liberal and moderate socialist parties as tools of the bourgeoisie.

political factions, despite the Daladier government's use of emergency powers to prepare for the impending conflict. Her diplomatic weakness before 1939 and the shattering defeat she was to receive in 1940 unquestionably bore some relation to this lack of civic morale.

This ideological warfare between left and right was a hallmark of the 1930's, in the democratic countries and elsewhere. The extremes of left and right were Communism versus Fascism or Nazism; they made Spain, and sometimes the streets of Paris, a battleground. Hitler and Mussolini shrilly denounced all degrees of liberalism and socialism as but preparation for Communism; while Communists and their often gullible "fellow travelers" called everyone who was conservative a fascist. Somewhere in between, the Roosevelt New Deal, or the Keynesian economics, or the Swedish welfare state, offered a "middle way" through the shoals of the great depression. Literature and thought reflected these "ideologies" of left and right. A part of the tragedy of the 1930's, with its drift toward devastating war, lay in the failure of the western democracies—Great Britain and France chiefly—to find any clear definition of a common will and purpose to pit against the all-too-united entities of Communist Russia and of Nazi Germany.

The role of the intellectuals

The depression mood of the 1930's caused a pronounced swing toward social and political consciousness among the intellectuals, a mood sharply different from that of the politically disenchanted 1920's. It is true that an infatuation with the Soviet Union on the part of intellectuals had been somewhat in evidence ever since the Revolution. Disillusioned with their own society, they felt an attraction for the Russian experiment. "In this muddy age its ten years shine," wrote the American liberal magazine *The Nation* on the 10th birthday of the Communist state in 1927. After this came the great drive to industrialize, contrasting with economic depression in the West, and the enthusiasm of some European and American writers for Russia grew almost immoderate. In some cases they adopted Communism and entered the party. Repudiating their preoccupation with art for art's sake in the 1920's, they now imagined they were participating in the class struggle and adopted a simple style appropriate to proletarian soldiers:

Singing I was at peace,
Above the clouds, outside the ring. . . .

None such shall be left alive:
The innocent wing is soon shot down,
And private stars fade in the blood-red dawn
Where two worlds strive.

The red advance of life
Contracts pride, calls out the common blood,
Beats song into a single blade,
Makes a depth-charge of grief.

(The poet who wrote these lines lived long enough to become Poet Laureate!)

Sidney Webb, veteran British Fabian socialist, who announced his approval of Communism in 1935.

The intellectuals and Communism

In 1935 Sidney and Beatrice Webb, the patriarchs of British Fabian socialism, published an admiring book on Soviet civilization, praising it for "its abandonment of the incentive of profit making, its extinction of unemployment, its planned production for community consumption, and the consequent liquidation of the landlord and the capitalist." This movement of the intellectuals towards Communism, as Marxist "fellow travelers" if not members of the party, became extremely significant in the early 1930's.

A few intellectuals were attracted toward Fascism for a time, too. But these were a small minority. This was to be the Pink Decade. The love affair of the writers with the Reds in most cases lasted but a few years. Even as they gravitated toward the Communist party, Stalin was tightening his iron grip on the whole apparatus, making any independence of thought impossible for party members; they had to follow the line from Moscow, which might require them to change directions from one day to the next. In 1939 it required them to do an abrupt about-face on Nazism, following the Nazi-Soviet pact of that year. The purge trials of the midthirties confronted them with a painful example of Soviet intolerance. Western intellectuals were of all people the least likely to abdicate their independent judgment. They sometimes found a halting place in Trotskyism, but for the most part the retreat from communism had begun by 1936 and there was a mass exodus in 1939. Many writers subsequently recounted their leftist adventures with amazement and mystification at their own actions. But in the 1930's the attraction of Communism was not surprising. There was, first of all, the fact that economic blight afflicted the democracies; Nazism was on the prowl; their own governments seemed impotent and their society decadent; in Russia, the great five-year plans were going forward with energy and drive, man was being transformed. It should be noted that Stalinism did not put all thought and literature in the Soviet Union into a propaganda straitjacket until about 1936. There was considerable freedom in the arts before that, and Russian music, drama, and cinema were making brilliant contributions. Prokofieff, Shostakovitch, Eisenstein, and Gorky helped make friends for Russia in their respective arts: music, the cinema, the novel.

Issues of the 1930's

Whether they admired or were disillusioned with the cause of Communism and the Soviet Union, writers found much to enlist their interest in the social sciene. There were hunger marches, strikes, riots of the unemployed. Politics became exciting under the influence of the grim battle against economic collapse. From the United States came news of the personality and program of President Franklin D. Roosevelt's "New Deal," featuring a variety of *ad hoc* innovations for alleviating the depression by government activity, presided over by a colorful political figure. Attacks on the old theory of economics came from economists such as the brilliant John Maynard Keynes, British proponent of government spending and an unbalanced budget, which horrified the orthodox school. The decade throbbed with social issues and social action. Few could stand aside from politics.

Pacifism

Above all, memories of the last war and the resolve not to fight again filled the social consciousness of the embattled political activists. Revulsion from the horror of 1914–18 filled bookstores, theaters, and movies with the theme of "no more war." Vociferous proponents of unilateral disarmament occupied leading posts in the British Labour party and similar groups. The Marxism fashionable in intellectual circles insisted that wars were always fought in the interest of capitalist profiteers and not the toiling masses, implying that there could not be such a thing as a war in the national interest. Students taking the famous "Oxford oath" swore they would bear arms under no circumstances.

Antifascism

The pages of the burgeoning left-wing periodicals and books radiated this hatred of war as much as they talked about another cause: antifascism. "Fascism" was a word loosely used to cover all manner of enemies of the human race, including not only Mussolini's Black Shirts and Hitler's hoodlums but any conservative, businessman, or opponent of Stalinism. (To the Communists, at least, Trotskyists were disguised fascists and Social Democrats were "social fascists" until 1936). The left intellectuals were sure that all the enemies were on the right.

They joined with many others in seeing Hitler's swastika emblem as the gravest danger civilization faced, but their pacifiism involved them in contradictions. Pacifism left the democracies open to the blackmail of Hitler. This hatred of war extended beyond the intellectuals to embrace wide segments of the population. Another war, surely, would totally destroy Western civilization. Feeling this way, men could not bring themselves to face the prospect of war and the Nazi dictator exploited this fear. In 1935 Stanley Baldwin, the genial, easy-going Conservative Prime Minister of Britain, did not dare tell the electorate the truth about German rearmament, as he later confessed, or ask the British people to accept substantial rearmament. This was part of the reason why the Western democracies were so tardy in responding to the aggressive German challenge.

The Spanish Civil War

Failure of the republic

One of the principal events which focused and dramatized this ideological conflict was the Civil War in Spain, 1936–39. The rest of Europe had not been accustomed to paying much attention to a country that seemed romantic but out of touch with the modern world, dreaming of her glorious past, politically and economically hopeless. In 1931, following a period of dictatorial rule, Spain began an experiment with a democratic republic which proved to be as turbulent as the famous Spanish temperament. In a country racked by depression, the leftist parties which were dominant in the Republic compounded political trouble by waging an aggressive campaign against the church, the army, and the big landlords, forces which represented traditional conservatism. Catalonian separatism again arose to complicate matters. By 1934, the socialists and the bourgeois parties had fractured their alliance and begun to quarrel. The revolutionary anarchists increased in strength and began to organize strikes. Amid this confusion and strife, in 1936 occurred a rightist, army-led rebellion to overthrow the Republic and restore authoritarian, upper-class control. It foundered on the heroism of Spanish workers and resulted in a protracted, bloody civil war, fought with all the ferocity of a class and social war by a people never known for their restraint. The Nationalists, as the followers of General Francisco Franco called themselves, and the forces of the Republic (Loyalists) fought indecisively in a conflict marked by acts of terrorism and atrocity.

Foreign intervention

The war involved all the great powers and became an international issue. The Republican Loyalists received some French aid early in the war; the Nationalist rebels turned to Mussolini who saw a chance for Italian glory and sent in troops, eventually to the number of some 60,000. Hitler, too, responded, but sent only a few thousand Germans; he evidently saw it as a chance chiefly to detach Italy from her ties to France and Britain (somewhat in evidence since 1934, though now threatened by the Ethiopian affair described further below). The Soviet Union supported the Republicans. Volunteers to the Republican cause flowed in from all over the world as idealistic young leftists pictured Spain as the great battleground of the apocalyptic

General Franco during the Spanish Civil War

Italian cycle troops in Franco's victory parade in Madrid, May 19, 1939

struggle between democracy and fascism. The Republican forces contained all shades of socialist, anarchist, and liberal opinion, but the Communists, profiting from the Soviet aid, finally attained a dominant position in the latter stages of the war and sometimes used their power to purge other factions.

The major powers tried to organize a nonintervention pact. Germany and the U.S.S.R. as well as France and Great Britain signed such a pact, but the first two continued to send aid to the rival Spanish factions anyway. Friends of the Republic complained bitterly that the democracies should have aided the Republic but instead adhered to the nonintervention principle while the totalitarian powers did not. General Franco's Nationalists finally won the war, largely, it seems, on their own, for the Italians did not distinguish themselves in battle, German aid was not great, and despite nonintervention the Republic probably got almost as much help from the Soviet Union and the international volunteers. Like so many glorious crusades, the Spanish Civil War ended in confusion and a blurring of the outlines; yet it had an enduring symbolic significance for this ideology-tormented decade.

Significance of the Spanish Civil War

The war produced a large literature and Picasso's famous mural depicting its horror, violence, and heroism—"Guernica." The war became a kind of symbol of the era. "It had quality, that war," the veteran journalist Herbert Matthews later recalled. "Something in it reached deeply into our hearts as well as our minds." The brooding ferocity and tragic dignity of the Spanish character were imprinted on it, but also the world's battle of ideals and ideologies. In the end, many of the idealistic liberals who had gone to do battle for righteousness against fascism in Spain became disillusioned, for the Communists gained control of the Republican cause and were as little interested in liberty as the fascists.

Most liberals in Britain, France, and America sympathized with the Republic and believed that its defeat at the hands of the fascists represented not only a victory for fascism but a chapter in the mournful story of "appeasement" of the dictators. The story was not quite that simple. General Franco's regime was not "fascist" except by the broadest extension of that term, though the movement known as Falangism, often close to the Spanish leader, contained elements resembling Italian Fascism and German Nazism. Franco showed in World War II that he had no intention of leading Spain into war on the side of Hitler and Mussolini. Catholic and traditionalist, the Franco regime was conservative but hardly fascist, any more than was the personal rule of Salazar in neighboring Portugal. Yet it had accepted aid from the Fascists and exacted a terrible vengeance on the Republicans whatever their shade of leftism. The war cost the lives of some 300,000 soldiers and 150,000 civilians. From its moral and physical shock Spain only began to recover 20 years later.

The Spanish Civil War went on simultaneously with the series of international crises, chiefly instigated by the Nazis, which set nerves on edge all over the world: Rhineland reoccupation, Austrian *Anschluss*, Sudetenland annexation, Polish crisis. From 1935 on Europe was rarely without its monthly war threat. The Spanish melodrama took its place along with the Italo-Ethiopian war of 1935–37, and the Japanese-Chinese conflict in the Far East, as major preliminaries to the global holocaust that broke out in 1939. Posterity would see it as rather a sideshow to the main event, yet at the time it looked like the very center.

Other diplomatic crises; The reaction to the Nazi challenge

Essential features of diplomacy

Historian E.H. Carr called the entire period between 1919 and 1939 a "twenty-year crisis" and there is a very real sense in which it was only a "long armistice." For Germany never really accepted the Paris peace, and the architects of that peace never really had the strength to enforce it. The victorious alliance of 1917–18 was shattered by the triumph of Communism in Russia and by the return to noninvolvement of the United States of America, as well as Italy's defection to Fascism. In the 1920's Germany and Russia were still recovering from their wounds, but as soon as they regained their strength they would be sure to make demands for the revision of the 1919 settlement. The main hope of the 1920's was that Franco-German reconciliation, perhaps within the framework of a European federation (Briand dreamed of a United States of Europe), might pave the way to a peaceful and gradual satisfaction of German claims. As we know, the Briand–Stresemann era lasted all too short a time and with the rise of Hitler in Germany the chances of peace rapidly dimmed. In the 1930's the German dictator violently overturned the Versailles treaty and then was emboldened to bid for the dominion of Europe. Britain and France, too weak to resist, burdened by domestic problems and economic crisis, failed to respond to the Nazi challenge until too late. This is the main theme of the tragic story of the coming of history's greatest war; the details, and the controversies, are numerous.

Italy and Ethiopia

The year 1935 brought not only Hitler's defiance of the Versailles treaty's disarmament provisions but also an outbreak of actual violence, in Ethiopia, which had the effect of alienating Italy from the Anglo-French side. In her desperate search for an ally against Germany, France looked frequently in the direction of Italy, whose martial spirit Benito Mussolini seemingly had revived and which in spite of Fascism did not appear to be necessarily a friend of Germany. In 1933 and 1934 the Italian *duce* showed no signs of friendship with his German disciple, and in fact appeared ready to join an alliance against him. In 1934 Mussolini prevented a German *coup* in Austria. But in 1935 he waged war on Ethiopia, and Great Britain led an action in the League of Nations which condemned this action and imposed economic penalties against Italy. Mussolini may have thought that French foreign minister Pierre Laval had promised him Ethiopia as a reward for a pact against Germany. The Italians had never forgotten their humiliation of 1896 at the

The Ethiopian army was limited in modern arms and some fought on the side of the Italians.

hands of the Ethiopians, nor their failure to get a due share of colonial territory. They regarded the Ethiopians as primitive and backward, and felt that Great Britain, who disciplined her own colonial subjects from time to time, was being hypocritical in opposing Italian domination of Ethiopia. For their part the British were undeniably concerned about the threat to Suez as well as to international morality.

League of Nations

But the apparently flagrant nature of the assault on a small and weak state aroused public opinion, especially in Britain, to rally behind the League of Nations and "collective security." The idea that the League might keep peace by banding together against any case of aggression had been present in the thinking of its founders, but had lain dormant heretofore. The League did attempt to impose economic "sanctions" on Italy, but apart from enraging the Italians it did not turn out to be successful. Oil was never included in the sanctions; nor did the United States cooperate with the League. French diplomacy was reluctant to lose Italian support against Germany, which was then much more threatening to the French. The British, who began the disciplinary action against Italy, had second thoughts about it in midstream. The affair ended in fiasco as Mussolini subdued the Ethiopians anyway while the League looked on helplessly. From this time on Mussolini drew closer to Hitler. The civil war in Spain helped cement their friendship.

Mussolini did not wish to play second fiddle to Hitler, whom he privately

The two dictators found more common ground after the Ethiopian war and exchanged visits. In this 1936 photo Hitler is wearing the fascist emblem.

regarded as a barbarian and a bore. The Italians were not exactly pleased when the Nazis took over Austria in 1938, though Hitler promised his Italian friend gratefully that he would "never forget" Mussolini's giving his consent. The once virile *duce* was now old, fat, and a bit weary. He found himself led in Hitler's wake into war in 1940, playing a jackal-like role in the attack on France. The "Axis" of Berlin-Rome-Tokyo came into existence as a formal alliance in the Tripartite Pact of 1940. Italy thus reversed her role between World Wars I and II, with consequences which were to be disastrous for her. The ideological linkage between Fascism and Nazism was in part responsible for this change. More so, perhaps, was the Ethiopian affair, in which the aggressive course of Italy and the reaction against it in the democracies caused the bitterest of feelings on both sides.

Reasons for policy of appeasement of Germany

We have recounted Hitler's increasingly audacious moves, as he tested the *status quo* powers and found them weak. An answer was promised to the highly important question, why the British and French allowed the German *Führer* to rearm, militarize the Rhineland, absorb Austria, dismember Czechoslovakia, and threaten Poland before they decided to make a stand. They also seemingly missed chances to make an ally first of Italy, as just noted, and then Russia, a more decisive failure. When, in the spring of 1939, having watched Hitler complete the destruction of the Czech state, the Allies finally decided that appeasement would never work, gave guarantees to Poland and undertook negotiations with Russia for an alliance. They failed; Stalin preferred to deal with Hitler, who offered him for the time being a share in the spoils of eastern Europe. Thus the British and French found that they had missed all the trains. Soon they were to enter into war against Germany on the worst possible terms. Innumerable postmortems asked the reasons for this sorry record and usually drew up a long list of indictments. Still, hindsight is always an inestimable advantage and one can offer a partial defense of Anglo-French diplomacy.

In the beginning, public opinion, especially in Britain, believed that Germany had been unfairly treated after World War I and had a just right to claim arms equality and occupation of her own territory. They could not see that intervention in German affairs would improve matters; it seldom does. As we have noted, public opinion was profoundly opposed to war. While the left was antifascist but pacifist, a significant current of opinion on the right believed that a strong anti-Communist Germany was a bulwark against Bolshevism, and adopted the alleged motto of French and British conservatives, Better Hitler than Stalin! In the long run, France had to live with Germany; she could not keep her down forever without an alliance with Russia, which was now unthinkable. So reasoned Pierre Laval, the able French foreign minister in 1934–36, destined to be led down this path to collaboration with Germany in World War II and finally execution at the hands of the returning Free French after the war.

Such much-maligned statesmen as Neville Chamberlain and Edouard Daladier, who gave in to Hitler at Munich, were motivated by a laudable desire to save Europe from what would certainly be a disastrous war, and resolved to make every conceivable effort to avert that catastrophe. Doubtless they misread the character of Hitler and failed to understand that fear of war is no basis for national policy in a world that contains Hitlers. But their economically troubled countries had failed to keep up their armaments and adequate rearmament began late. There is a controversy concerning whether the year of time bought at the price of the Munich Pact profited Britain and France more than Germany; certainly the former used it well, in that the British built up their air force and air defenses so that these were adequate to the test they had to meet in 1940–41. At this time, there was simply no national will in England or her Dominions—must less in her future invaluable ally, the United States—to go to war in central Europe. The leaders of the democracies had to follow the popular will. They were not, it must be admitted, a very inspiring set of personalities.

It should be added that the Allies, following what seemed the lessons of the first World War, put their military preparations into the defensive. The

French built a vast wall of concrete and steel, the so-called Maginot Line, along their border with Germany. (In 1940 the Germans went around it through Belgium.) They had no plans for an offensive against Germany. But such a strategy was useless against Hitler's expansionist drive; you could not protect Czechoslovakia and Poland by crouching behind the Maginot Line.

Failure of negotiations with Russia, 1939

If an earnest desire for peace dictated the attempt to appease Germany, honorable motives also seem to to have handicapped the Anglo-French in their negotiations with the Russians. Certainly the Soviets were justifiably angry at being excluded from the Munich settlement, which they interpreted as a conspiracy to turn Hitler eastward against Russia.[6] But in 1939, when approached by both Germany and the Allies, they preferred the former because Hitler offered them a generous share of eastern Europe: recovery of the Baltic states, Finland, and part of Poland. By contrast, the Western powers had to reckon with the hostility of Poland and Rumania to Russia; these countries would not agree in advance to allow Soviet troops entrance into their territory in the event of war with Germany. They feared Stalin as much as or more than Hitler. This was an obstacle at the time of Munich as well as in 1939. In view of misrepresentations often made, it should be stated as strongly as possible that the Western powers lost Russia to the Nazis in 1939 because they would not betray the smaller countries of eastern Europe to Stalin—a course of action honorable in the highest degree. But Hitler had no such scruples; he was prepared to offer Stalin another partition of Poland, reminiscent of 1773.

The role of the Soviet Union

The Communist state was the key to the riddle. It was itself a riddle to the rest of the world in many ways. For many years after 1918 relations between it and the other major states were always strained and sometimes nonexistent. The U.S.S.R. was not officially recognized by the United States until 1933, not admitted to the League of Nations until 1934. It had declared a kind of war against every other state by proclaiming itself the center of world revolution, with the objective of bringing about the overthrow of other governments in favor of Communist regimes. Not until the 1930's did it systematically seek to normalize relations with other sovereign states, and even then it insisted on maintaining the headquarters of the Communist International (Comintern) in Moscow.

Great socialist offensive

Vast changes were going on in Russia, and Stalin's goal of "building socialism in Russia alone," not waiting for the anticipated world revolution, implied a demand for peace and even aid from the "capitalist" countries.

[6] Though the Russians claimed that they stood ready to stand by Czechoslovakia if France and Britain did, this appears doubtful. They were no more ready for war than the democracies, and probably paraded their virtue because they were quite sure the bluff would not be called. This is controversial.

One of the many underground forts of the Maginot Line as they were in January, 1939

Though temporarily derailed in 1931 by peasant resistance, the drive to force the peasants into large "collective farms" went ahead. Millions of people went to the cities, where a rapid growth of heavy industry was taking place in coal, steel, oil, electrical power, heavy machinery, agricultural machinery. Whole new cities sprang up, such as Magnitogorsk in the Urals. It was difficult to accept all the extravagant Soviet claims of industrial miracles, and indeed by their own occasional admission this overrapid industrialization was accomplished at a vast human cost, accompanied by incredible foul-ups. Emphasis on investment in capital goods, while likely to pay off in the long run, meant a lowered standard of living in the present; consumer goods were scarce and poor by the standards of any western country. The attempt to plan an entire economy from the center proved top-heavy and grossly inefficient. Still, gains were made, and a wholly new economic system was gradually hammered into some kind of shape. Astonishing gains in literacy, too, were recorded, as Communist dynamism pushed backward Russia forward toward an industrial society.

Five-year plans

The first five-year plan, ending in 1932, had made progress in modernizing agricultural methods, but at the cost of a terrible conflict with the peasantry, described in the previous chapter, which so set back Russian agriculture that Soviet experts believe it never did reach 1916 levels in per capita production during the interwar years. But heavy industry showed large if uneven gains. The second five-year plan, 1932–37, promised to increase the production of consumer goods and thus raise living standards, but the stress in fact continued to be on heavy industry, transport, power plants. It should be noted that this progress of "socialism" was coercive and unfree in the highest degree. Workers were moved about by command; there was no right to strike against the state; the paradise of the workers had become, for the time being at least, the most rigorous system of industrial slavery ever invented. It was a "command economy" in which decisions were made by the state, and everything was "planned." During the 1930's, also, Stalin waged war on "egalitarianism," introducing unequal wages and a system of incentives for longer hours and increased production by the workers.

Those who were fascinated by the spectacle of a planned economy admired this system, as did those who believed as an article of faith that the Communist party could do no wrong. Much of the rest of the world was appalled at the cruelty of Stalin's totalitarian state, the increasing lack of freedom as well as the actual starvation and the imprisonment of millions in forced-labor camps. It is believed that Stalin's wife herself committed suicide in acute distress over the sufferings involved. But amid all this suffering Russia did drive ahead. Plants were built, great engineering projects such as the Dnieper dam were conceived and carried out. Critics noted a tendency toward "giganticism," the publicizing of certain huge projects at the cost of general progress. But progress in basic industrialization undoubtedly went on, and many Russians took pride in it. Stalin was another Peter the Great: terrible, cruel, but dominated by a vision of forcing backward Russia into the modern technological age.

The great purge

The most spectacular and publicized events in Russia in the years 1934–38 were the trials of the political enemies of Stalin, who, it seemed, included almost everybody. The "purge" swept virtually all the old Bolsheviks into the discard, caused literally hundreds of thousands to be arrested, and extended deeply into the high military command. Trial after trial, obviously "staged" in a manner peculiar to Soviet justice, brought confessions galore of treason, sabotage, and deviations from the correct Marxist-Leninist-Stalinist party "line." If these confessions were taken at their face value, then the Communist state seemed to be shot full of disaffection. If not, then Stalin was a tyrant who framed his rivals and wrung confessions from them by sinister methods. In later years, after the fall of Stalin, Russians wrote about their experiences in these mad years. Perfectly loyal officials were arrested, probably because someone under torture had signed a false confession incriminating them, and were taken down to be themselves forced to sign such statements naming still others as traitors. Thus the circle of arrests spread like a chain letter. The great majority of people seem, understandably, to have much preferred signing to withstanding torture. The demoralization resulting from this hysteria was only just being remedied at the time of the German invasion. Unquestionably the army was still in poor condition when Hitler struck.

Popular front strategy

Stalin, therefore, was as anxious to avoid war as Chamberlain and Daladier. He attempted to guide Soviet foreign policy closer to the Western democracies between 1935 and 1938, a move which coincided with the pursuit of "popular front" alliances by the Communist parties abroad. This was an abrupt change from previous Soviet policy. Seeing Nazi Germany as the greatest threat, Soviet strategy was to form a temporary alliance with the lesser danger from the capitalist world. The Communists had not previously distinguished in this way between capitalist states, regarding them all as absolutely hostile to Communism. Though Stalin in his way did honestly wish to cooperate with the democracies against Hitlerism, old hostilities proved hard to break down. The conservative British government entertained the deepest suspicions of Russia. Neville Chamberlain commented in 1939 that there seemed to be an impenetrable curtain between the two worlds. The Spanish Civil War helped keep them apart, and when at Munich the British and French yielded to Hitler while excluding the Soviets from the talks, Stalin evidently wrote off the Anglo-French governments as hopelessly craven as well as hostile to Russia. When Britain and France changed course in 1939 and attempted to repair the line to Moscow, Hitler beat them by offering Stalin a share in the spoils of conquest.

Nazi-Soviet pact

The greed of the Soviet chiefs was aroused, and they seem to have figured that they could buy time in this way for their defense against Hitler, whose eventual hostility they must have reckoned upon. And they no longer trusted the Western powers at all, or believed in their capacity to resist. They may also have reasoned that if Hitler did attack them later, Britain and France would already be in the war on their side. The alternative was to risk war with Germany at a time when they were not ready for it, and when they could expect little or no help from the democracies.

German Foreign Minister Von Ribbentrop and Stalin watch as Molotov signs the Nazi-Soviet pact.

The last days of peace

The Nazi-Soviet pact of August 23, 1939, which contained secret articles arranging for the partition of Poland, was, then, from the Soviet point of view, a way to buy time. There was much subsequent controversy over whether the British-French effort to woo Stalin might have succeeded if pressed with more determination; what really doomed it was the military weakness of the western powers, plus their commitment to defend Poland. They had given a pledge to defend that country and were determined to honor it.

Hitler threatens Poland

Public opinion in the democracies had abruptly changed since Munich and wanted no more "appeasement" of the arrogant Nazi dictator, no more "deals" with him. But Hitler was determined to destroy the Polish state and incorporate most of it into the German Reich. The immediate and ostensible issue was the city of Danzig. Danzig had been set up in 1919 as a free city under League of Nations supervision. Nazis had won control of the local administration, and were prepared to demand annexation to the Reich. It was a German city, and the Western powers in principle would probably not have opposed a solution giving it to Germany. But the Poles would not and could not yield. Though the war was to shatter their country and destroy their independence, the Poles were a proud people who aspired to be a great power and had no intention of being browbeaten into submission as the Austrians and Czechs had been.

Poland refuses to be intimidated

Hitler undoubtedly thought that they would yield, under pressure from France and Great Britain as well as Russia. He fulminated and threatened war, as he had done before, but many scholars do not think he really wanted or expected war in 1939. Germany was not militarily prepared for it. Hitler expected to win another war of nerves, and was sure the Allies would finally back down as they had done at Munich. Why should they fight for Poland, far less accessible and defensible, when they had abandoned Czechoslovakia? A part of the story of the coming of World War II in Europe was Polish pride and Polish stubbornness. Threatened from two directions, a small power lying between two greedy giants, both of whom had reason for conspiring against her independence, Poland never for a moment seems to have contemplated surrender or even compromise. It seems likely that Chamberlain and the French would have again been willing to avoid war by agreeing to the retrocession of some of Poland to Germany, but this was prevented by Poland's refusal to consider this, as well as by public opinion in their own countries. For his part Hitler, fortified by his pact with Russia, was supremely confident, as well he might be. He knew that Britain and France could do nothing to save Poland.

The war begins

On September 1 German troops marched on Poland. When they failed to heed British and French ultimata to withdraw, these powers declared war on September 3. Mussolini had proposed another conference at the last minute, but it came too late and could have achieved nothing. The Soviet Union, not declaring war, soon moved in to occupy portions of eastern Poland. There was no cheering this time, but war had come again for the second time within 25 years.

Causes of the war

Not many historians have ever doubted that the demonic will of Adolf Hitler and the insatiable dynamism of the National Socialists were the war's primary causes. On the other hand, the unfortunate vacillations of the other powers not only made Hitler's ambitions grow but probably even deceived him about their intentions in 1939. A strong and firm Allied front, concerned both to remove Germany's just grievances and to make it unmistakably clear that force would be met with force, might have contained the Nazis. The reasons why such a front was not formed lead one to consider chiefly popular opinion, leadership in the democracies, and the relations between Soviet Russia and the West.

Analysis of the causes of World War II would prove as endlessly attractive for the historian as those of World War I; the difference was that this time there was not much controversy about "war guilt." That lay with Germany. The main realm of controversy concerned whether in September, 1939, Hitler thought the Allies would yield Poland to him as they had yielded Czechoslovakia at Munich, or whether he was aware that he was plunging Europe into a general war. There is a good deal of evidence that Hitler did indeed think Britain and France were bluffing and that he did not anticipate a major war at this time. But there still remains the probability that in the long run his policies would have precipitated general war. He had said many times both publicly and privately, ever since his earliest speeches, that Germany must conquer the east of Europe and "Germanize it ruthlessly." His philosophy and his actions reflected his profound conviction that a Teutonic "elite" must enslave the allegedly weaker and inferior races. His goals, then, were nothing less than Nazi domination over all Europe, and sooner or later that meant war. Hitler glorified and apparently yearned for war. The German people, on the other hand, did not, to judge by their lack of enthusiasm for the war. Yet they followed the leadership of the Nazis, partly hynotized by it and partly intimidated. Hitler had succeeded in persuading them that he fought for the interests of the historic German state against a combination of Bolshevists and plutocrats, who wished to strangle it.

Bibliography

The two leading themes covered in this chapter are the Nazi regime in Germany and the coming of World War II. Both have given rise to huge quantities of scholarship. One might begin the former topic with Alan Bullock's popular biography, *Hitler: A Study in Tyranny* (Harper & Row). William A. Jenks, *Vienna and the Young Hitler* (New York: Columbia University Press, 1960), is among books which contribute additional perspectives on the Nazi leader. George L. Mosse, in *The Crisis of German Ideology: Intellectual Origins of the Third Reich* (New York: Grosset & Dunlap, 1964) and also in *Nazi Culture (ibid.*, 1967), a collection of writings from the Nazi era, illuminates the phenomenon of National Socialism. See also Walther Hofer (ed.), *The Nazis* (World Publishing, Meridian). William L. Shirer, *The Rise and Fall of the Third Reich* (Fawcett Publications), a popular treatment, should be read critically. From among recent specialized studies, Jacques Delarue, *The Gestapo: A History of Horror* (New York: William Morrow, 1964); Oron J. Hale, *The Captive Press in the Third Reich* (Princeton, N.J.: Princeton University Press, 1964); Arthur Schweitzer, *Big Business in the Third Reich* (Bloomington: Indiana University Press, 1964), showing that big business retained a degree of independence under the Nazis; Z.A.B. Zeman, *Nazi Propaganda* (New York: Oxford University Press, 1964); Charles H. Bewley, *Hermann Goering and the Third Reich* (New York: Devin-Adair, 1962). Hitler's *Mein Kampf* (Houghton Mifflin) and *Hitler's Secret Book* (Grove Press, Evergreen) throw some light on the Fuehrer's mind. E.M. Robertson, *Hitler's Pre-War Policy and Military Plans 1931–1939* (2d ed.; London: Longmans, Green, 1968), is authoritative on this important question.

Reginald Bassett's examination of the Sino-Japanese issue, *Democracy and Foreign Policy* (Longmans, Green, 1952), is a brilliant analysis of the episode that opened a stormy decade in international relations. Gordon Craig and Felix H. Gilbert (eds.), *The Diplomats* (Atheneum, 2 vols.); Elizabeth Wiskemann, *The Rome-Berlin Axis* (Oxford University Press, 1949); Keith Eubank, *Munich* (Norman: University of Oklahoma, 1963), are other outstanding contributions to an understanding of the developing tragedy. On *The Origins of the Second World War* (Fawcett Publications), A.J.P. Taylor is penetrating, but his construal of events has been vigorously challenged; compare Walther Hofer, *War Premeditated* (London: Thames & Hudson, 1955). A.J. and V. Toynbee (eds.), *The Eve of War, 1939* (Oxford University Press, 1958), and other volumes in the Royal Institute of International Affairs series for 1938–39 provide extensive documentation. The *Documents on British Foreign Policy 1918–1939*, third series, and *Documents on German Foreign Policy 1918–1945*, series C and D, devote numerous volumes to the diplomatic records, while as always the memoirs of statesmen are illuminating if used with due caution: see among others those of Lord Templewood, *Nine Troubled Years* (London: Collins, 1954); A. François-Poncet, *The Fateful Years* (New York: Harcourt, Brace & World, 1949); Anthony Eden, *Facing the Dictators* (Boston: Houghton Mifflin, 1962); and Galeazzo Ciano, *The Ciano Diaries* (New York: Doubleday, 1946). *Nazi Conspiracy and Aggression*, published by the U.S. chief of counsel at the Nuremberg Trials (Washington: U.S. Government Printing Office, 1947), is not exactly objective but prints valuable data. Francis L. Loewenheim (ed.), *Peace or Appeasement? Hitler, Chamberlain and the Munich Crisis* (Houghton Mifflin), includes a selection of documents and also the commentaries of various historians. Among many other recent studies, G. Brook-Shepherd, *The Anschluss* (New York: J.B. Lippincott, 1963); Roman Debicki, *The Foreign Policy of Poland 1919–1939* (New York: Frederick A. Praeger, 1962); Gerhard L. Weinberg, *Germany and the Soviet Union 1939–1941* (Leiden: Brill, 1954).

The Spanish Civil War has been competently handled by Gerald Brenan, *The Spanish Labyrinth* (Cambridge University Press), and Hugh Thomas, *The Spanish Civil War* (Harper & Row); and also Gabriel Jackson, *The Spanish Republic and The Civil War 1931–1939* (Princeton University Press, 1965). On the ideological strife of the decade, see Julian Symons, *The Thirties* (London: Cresset Press, 1960); G.D.H. Cole, *Socialism and Fascism 1931–1939*, Vol. V of A History of Socialist Thought (New York: St. Martin's Press, 1960); Neal Wood, *Communism and the British Intellectuals* (Columbia University Press, 1959); David Caute, *Communism and the French Intellectuals* (New York: Macmillan, 1964). The interesting symposium edited by R.H.S. Crossman, *The God That Failed* (Harper & Row) records the disillusionment of western intellectuals with Communism.

The U.S.S.R and its startling progress can be viewed in such works as N. Jasny,

Soviet Industrialization 1928–1952 (Chicago: University of Chicago Press, 1961), an expert analysis; L.P. Schapiro, *The Communist Party of the Soviet Union* (New York: Random House, 1960); Robert V. Daniels (ed.), *The Stalin Revolution* (Raytheon Education, D.C. Heath Problems series); Francis B. Randall, *Stalin's Russia: An Historical Reconsideration* (New York: Free Press, 1965); Kermit E. McKenzie, *Comintern and World Revolution 1928–43* (New York: Columbia University Press, 1964). Among the personal accounts of the Stalinist repression, A. Weissberg, *Conspiracy of Silence* (London: Hamish Hamilton, 1952), is an absorbing and perceptive account; F. Beck and W. Godin, *Russian Purge and the Extraction of Confession* (New York: Viking Press, 1951), seeks to piece together this whole picture from the numerous accounts of survivors. H. Kostiuk, *Stalinist Rule in the Ukraine: A Decade of Mass Terror 1929–1939* (Frederick A. Praeger, 1960), is a painstaking piece of research on a repelling subject.

Reginald Bassett, *1931: Political Crisis* (St. Martin's Press, 1958), is an exceptionally penetrating study of British politics at a decisive moment. Ian MacLeod's biography of *Neville Chamberlain* (London: Fred. Muller, 1961) is a sympathetic portrait of a controversial statesman. A good study of French political opinion is Charles Micaud, *The French Right and Nazi Germany, 1933–1939* (Durham, N.C.: Duke University Press, 1943). Paul Reynaud, *In the Thick of the Fight 1930–1945* (New York: Simon & Schuster, 1955), is an illuminating French memoir translated into English. Joel Colton, *Leon Blum: Humanist in Politics* (New York: Alfred A. Knopf, 1966), a splendid portrayal of one of the outstanding French political personalities of the 1930's, and John T. Marcus, *French Socialism in the Crisis Years 1933–1936* (St. Martin's Press, 1963) combine to give a good picture of the French left in this decade.

30
The Second World War

chronology

1939
German conquest of Poland; division of Poland between Germany and Soviet Union.
Soviets attack Finland, November, 1939–March, 1940.

1940
Annexation of Baltic states by U.S.S.R.
Denmark, Norway occupied by German forces after British and French mining of Norwegian territorial waters, April.
German invasion of Low Countries and France, May–June; fall of France, British evacuation at Dunkerque. Vichy regime in unoccupied part of France.
Winston Churchill becomes the British Prime Minister.
Air offensive against Britain, August, 1940–June, 1941.
Italian attack of Greece. German demands on Rumania. Nazi-Soviet tension over Axis push into Balkans.
Treaty of alliance between Germany, Italy, and Japan, September.
Japanese occupation of French Indo-China.

1941
British defeat Italians in North Africa; capture of Tobruk, January.
Lend-Lease Act passed by U.S. Congress, providing aid to foes of Axis, March.
German invasion of Yugoslavia and Greece. Evacuation of the British expeditionary force from Crete.
Vast German invasion of Russia, June 22. Advance to outskirts of Moscow, December 6.
American lend-lease aid extended to Russia.
Atlantic Charter, meeting of Roosevelt and Churchill, August. Warning to Japan.
Japanese surprise attack on Pearl Harbor, December 7, bringing United States into War.

1942
Advance of Japanese, capturing Philippines, Malaya, Dutch East Indies.
Japanese checked in naval battles of Midway, Coral Sea.
Renewal of German offensive in Russia; capture of Sebastopol, siege of Leningrad, penetration as far as Volga. Great battle of Stalingrad begins in September.
General Rommel drives British back in North Africa; finally stopped at El Alamein. British counteroffensive under General Montgomery.
India demands independence.
U.S. troops invade North Africa, November.

1943
American-Australian counteroffensive in Pacific, capturing islands from Japanese.
German army lost at Stalingrad. Russian counteroffensive pushes Germans back on broad front in Russia.
Casablanca Conference, Roosevelt and Churchill. "Unconditional surrender" of Axis demanded.
Final victory of Allies in Africa. Allied invasion of Italy, July–October.
Arrest of Mussolini, surrender of Italian government under Badoglio; Germans occupy Italy.
Teheran Conference between Stalin, Roosevelt, and Churchill, December.

1944
Invasion of Normandy, opening second front, by Allied forces, June.
Liberation of Paris, August; German frontier reached by September.
Red Army completes recovery of Russia, pursues Germans into Poland, Rumania. Warsaw uprising (crushed by Germans), August 1.
Advance of Americans in Pacific war, seizing islands near Japan for bombing attacks; Second Battle of Philippine Sea; reconquest of Philippines.
Dumbarton Oaks Conference to plan United Nations.

1945
Yalta Conference, February.
Russians drive through Poland, invade Germany. Allies cross Rhine, March 8.
Death of President Roosevelt, April 12.
Mussolini killed by Italian partisans, April 29.
Battle of Berlin; suicide of Hitler, May 1. Germans surrender, May 7.
San Francisco Conference completes Charter of United Nations.
Potsdam Conference, July.
Atomic bomb dropped on Hiroshima, August 6. Entrance of Soviet Russia into war against Japan, August 8. Surrender of Japan, August 10.
Formal signing of Japanese surrender terms, end of World War II, September 2.

Allied bombers over Germany in 1943

The German victories

The phony war

At the beginning of World War II a massive German attack smashed the Polish armies in a matter of days, and the world first heard the word *Blitzkrieg*. Within a month of September 1, 1939, there was a new partition of Poland, between Germany and the U.S.S.R. (with tiny morsels to Lithuania and to Slovakia, the rump of the former Czechoslovakia). Though France and Great Britain had declared war on Germany, there was no military action between them in the winter of 1939–40, and people began to talk of a "phony war." The Western powers had been unable to get troops to Poland before the Germans overran her, and they seemed reluctant to undertake any other kind of offensive. The Germans found it surprising that 110 French and British divisions did not move against only 23 German divisions in the west at the time of the invasion of Poland; but this inactivity reflected the defensive strategy that was a heritage of World War I in the French army. (This helps explain also why France did not react in 1936 or 1938.) Hitler too waited.

But this winter was not without its wars. The chief one was between the U.S.S.R. and Finland. Given a free hand in this area by the Nazi-Soviet pact, Stalin hastened to cash his chips; he forced the Baltic states to give him military bases, and made similar demands on the Finns, who refused. Thereupon at the end of November Russia attacked Finland, in a particularly bald specimen of aggression for which the Soviets were expelled from the dying League of Nations. They crushed Finnish resistance, though it took until March, and formed an unfavorable comparison with German efficiency in Poland.

Action in Norway

In April, action flared up in Norway. The British and French had mined Norwegian waters, and in retaliation the Germans invaded Norway, using parachute troops as well as naval forces. The British navy and an Anglo-French expeditionary force tried to help the Norwegians, but despite some losses the Germans were able to complete the conquest of Norway and Denmark by May. The legitimate government of Norway followed that of Poland to exile in London, while the Germans enforced dictatorial rule over the conquered peoples. In 1942, the world gained another new word, "quisling," taken from the name of the Norwegian who served as the head of a government subservient to Germany.

While startling, these events were small compared to the eruption of war in the west in the spring of 1940. Would the "phony war" end in some sort of negotiated peace? People sometimes hoped so, but the speeches of Winston Churchill on the one side, and of Adolf Hitler on the other, gave no reason for such a view. Churchill, who was not yet Prime Minister and did not become so until the Germans attacked in May, had been First Lord of the Admiralty since the beginning of the war. He had been an early critic of "appeasement" of Germany. He now gained fame by not only eloquently denouncing Hitler's system but predicting its early collapse. "When we look behind the brazen fronts of Nazidom . . . we see many remarkable signs of psychological and physical disintegration." "Let the great cities of Warsaw, of Prague, of Vienna banish despair even in the midst of their agony. Their liberation is sure." He explained the passivity of British strategy by the need to repair deficiencies in military supplies, too long neglected. The British, at least, gave no indication of backing out on the war. The French, who felt secure behind their vaunted Maginot Line of defenses, also had the feeling that time was on their side. The democracies rebuffed peace feelers from Hitler during the winter; they were now fully determined to crush him. Once the combined strength of the two democracies was mobilized, they could surely deal with Hitler's cumbersome, corrupt, and perhaps unpopular dictatorship. Certainly the German public had not seemed to welcome the war with any enthusiasm. But for his part, Hitler periodically spewed forth hatred and contempt of the democracies, with predictions that they would be swept from the earth. Those who talked about a "phony war" cannot have paid much attention to the true situation. The war only waited a chance to erupt into the most ferocious struggle of all times.

The fall of France

It did so in May. Bypassing the powerful Maginot defenses, the Germans again struck through Belgium, this time through the forested Ardennes section of southern Belgium which was considered impossible terrain for mechanized forces. The advance of war techniques since 1918 had brought the tank and the airplane to the fore and the Germans proved to have studied these new developments more assiduously than the French. Swiftly moving German panzer divisions knifed through behind the French lines and spread confusion. This was no repetition of 1914. There was no stopping the Germans. The fortress of Verdun, which they could never pass in World War I, fell to them within five weeks. The whole British expeditionary army, cut off from the French, had to be evacuated from the channel port of Dunkerque where it was penned up. This was accomplished, with great loss of equipment, and the British got some lift out of the almost miraculous salvation of a seemingly doomed army. Churchill pledged "We shall go on to the end . . . We shall never surrender."

But for France, Belgium, and the Netherlands—attacked this time by the Germans, with a devastating aerial bombardment of Rotterdam—there was no solace. On June 17, six weeks after the start of the invasion, France asked for an armistice, and signed it on June 22. More than half of France, including Paris, was surrendered to German control, while the remainder set up its capital at Vichy with old Marshall Pétain heading a dictatorial, semipuppet government. The French military leader Charles de Gaulle set up a government-in-exile in London and hoped to carry on the war from the French Empire, but this seemed a forlorn hope. The Third Republic was at an end, France had fallen, and Britain stood alone. Apparently she too was destined for early defeat. The world gasped at these events and a shiver of alarm went through even the United States, thus far neutral and "isolationist."

The Battle of Britain

The Germans opened a fierce air attack on England, which subjected British morale to the sternest test between July and November and was renewed in the spring of 1941. Apparently the Germans believed that terror from the air could break the will of a people and lead to surrender. But despite severe damages and suffering the British did not think of quitting. They were beginning to get aid from the United States. Their excellent fighter planes and antiaircraft defenses took such a heavy toll of the *Luftwaffe* that the German air force never again was quite the same. A prime factor in the RAF's victory in the skies in this Battle of Britain was radar, a scientific discovery made almost by accident but ably developed by the British under the direction of Sir Henry Tizard just before the war.

Accompanying the air assault were attacks on British shipping by air and submarine designed to cut off the island's food supplies. But American aid sustained the British. When Britain ran out of money late in 1940, the American Congress passed a Lend-Lease Act authorizing unlimited credits. The Americans had virtually joined the war on the side of Great Britain by March, 1941, and the British were confident they would soon come in all the way.

The U.S.-to-Britain supply line took the form of large convoys of cargo ships.

Here was another difference, destined to be fatal to Germany: this time the United States did not wait three years before entering the war. Profoundly dissatisfied with its World War I experiences, the United States had vowed neutrality in the next European war and in 1935–37 enacted legislation designed to insure a complete detachment from such a war. But after the fall of France American opinion shifted dramatically toward a policy of "all aid short of war" to the British; it had suddenly been made clear to the Americans how much their security could be threatened by the fall of Britain to a hostile power. Much "isolationist" sentiment in the United States, including disillusionment with World War I and some pro-German sympathy, was swept aside chiefly by revulsion against the character of Hitler, the kind of government he headed, and its ruthless military efficiency as a grave threat to the entire world balance of power.

The invasion of Russia

Hitler toyed with the idea of a cross-channel invasion of the British Isles and undertook some preparations for it, but decided it was impractical. Frustrated in his assault on England, but roused now to the full peak of a megalomaniac ambition, Hitler considered what to do next. He astonished the world by deciding on an invasion of Russia, launched June 22, 1941. The ideological foundations of Nazism had always included the concept of expansion at the expense of "inferior" Slavs with their degraded Communist philosophy. More concretely, Hitler and Stalin had not made congenial allies, but on the contrary had quarreled over spheres of influence in southeastern Europe, in a controversy somewhat reminiscent of 1914. Certainly Hitler found the Soviets surprisingly unafraid of him, unwilling to surrender eastern Europe to his control even when he tempted them with vague promises of rewards in Asia. Stalin ignored a number of warnings, including some from Churchill and Roosevelt, that the Nazis were planning an attack, and was still apparently taken by surprise on June 22. It is not clear why he misjudged the Germans so badly. Probably he was still misled by Marxist ideology about the character of the Nazi regime.

Yugoslav revolt

Hitler believed that war with Russia was inevitable sooner or later—better soon than later. The attack would have come a month sooner had not the preliminary campaign in the Balkans got off schedule because of a desperate revolt in Yugoslavia. Hungary, Rumania, and Bulgaria succumbed to Nazi pressure without a struggle, but when a pro-Axis government was installed by a *coup d'état* in Yugoslavia, popular revolution overthrew it and tried to resist the Germans. A war against Yugoslavia quickly succeeded in overcoming organized resistance, though guerrilla forces operating in the mountains were to plague the Germans all through World War II. But the timetable had been thrown off. Hitler himself thought this delay cost him victory in Russia, though this is problematical. In addition, Germany had to go to the help of Italy when Mussolini's legions bogged down in an attack on little Greece. The British hesitantly sent an army to the aid of Greece, but they and the Greeks were beaten by the Germans.

German strategy in Russia

The invasion of Russia turned out to be as disastrous in the long run for Hitler as it had been for Napoleon. Hitler did not doubt the ability of his panzer divisions to win an easy victory. The great plain of Russia seemed an admirable place for the tank warfare in which they excelled, and the Russian army was not thought to be up to the German in equipment or morale. But the Germans were not adequately prepared for the conditions of Russia. Poor roads and swampy plains turned out to be not so good for mechanized warfare. The Russians were thrown back, losing large numbers of men and vast quantities of equipment, but they retreated skillfully and drew the Germans in ever deeper while keeping their armies in existence, much as in 1812. And the Red Army was no contemptible fighting force. It showed a capacity to learn fast, after initial defeats, and its equipment was good. Soon it was receiving American equipment. Most of the outer world was sure Hitler would beat Russia by winter, but he failed by a narrow margin to take Moscow. Hitler, who was personally directing grand strategy, split the offensive into three parts. German armies swung far to the south to trap great numbers of Russians in the area of Kiev, and continued on in the direction of the Don river and the Maikop oil fields. But the northern attacks directed at Moscow and Leningrad were thereby weakened and halted short of their objectives in early December, amid a Russian winter. One of many postwar arguments, second-guessing on strategy, was about the wisdom of this strategy. As in 1914, the Germans had not quite dared to put all their strength in one punch, and had failed to land the knockout blow.

Thereafter the Germans never quite regained their feet in the Russian campaign. Hitler and his generals argued bitterly about the proper strategy, with Hitler gradually removing all the former *Wehrmacht* commanders, taking supreme command personally and allowing generals in the field little freedom. Military strategists and historians also still debate whether Hitler's inept strategy was to blame for the subsequent disasters. He does seem to have failed in judging the strength of the Russians, and refused to retreat when a strategic withdrawal might have yielded better results. A huge German force found itself trapped and forced to surrender in the great battle at Stalingrad in the early winter of 1942–43. In 1943 Hitler still insisted on undertaking a great offensive when his forces were no longer capable of it. Like Napoleon, he refused to retreat and refused to compromise, and eventually lost contact with reality. In the vast spaces of Russia, all military leaders seemed to lose their bearings, were drawn ever deeper into the country without achieving any real strategic success.[1]

The war in North Africa

Pundits have speculated that Germany would have done better to pursue a wholly different strategy. She should have followed up victory in Africa, they urge, by a Mediterranean strategy designed to cut off Britain's lifeline. When Italy entered the war in June, 1940, striking France after Germany had already disabled her, Italian forces also opened a campaign in Africa, invading Egypt from Libya. In December, 1940, the British counterattacked and drove them rapidly back across the Libyan desert. But in April, 1941, came General Erwin Rommel, "the desert fox," with trained German troops to reinforce the Italians and turn the tide again. Rommel advanced to the border of Egypt but was weakened by the withdrawal of men for the Russian front. He received reinforcements in May, 1942, after he had been driven back, and once again raced across to El Alamein near Alexandria where he was held in a crucial battle that marked the high tide of Axis success in the whirling North African war.

Clearly Germany and Italy could have won the war in Africa had Hitler not preferred to expend his major effort against Russia. Some strategists have felt that this would have offered them better possibilities. But such second-guessing is a little futile. Hitler did not want Africa; had he not wanted eastern Europe, he probably would not have plunged into war in the first place. He always considered Russia the major enemy and toward England held a kind of ambivalent attitude: sometimes he visualized a world in which Germany dominated the whole of Europe while Great Britain held the colonial world in partnership with her. He approached the British with an offer of

---

[1] It should be pointed out that not all military experts on World War II disparage Hitler's grasp of warfare; some would blame the German defeat primarily on other factors.

The war in Europe 1939-1945
Axis powers, Aug. 1939
Axis occupation and conquests to Nov. 1942
Allied offensives, Nov. 1942–May 1945
ICELAND
Murmansk
Atlantic Ocean
FINLAND
SWEDEN
NORWAY
SOVIET
UNION
ESTONIA
Moscow
Baltic
Sea
North Sea
LATVIA
LITHUANIA
GREAT BRITAIN
GER.
Stalingrad, Nov. 1942
London
NETH.
Berlin
Elbe R.
Warsaw
POLAND
NORMANDY June 6, 1944
BELG.
GERMANY
Prague
Paris
HUNGARY
RUMANIA
SWITZ.
VICHY FRANCE
Black Sea
YUGOSLAVIA
ITALY
BULGARIA
SPAIN
ALBANIA
Rome
Salerno
Aug. 1944
Anzio, Jan. 1944
TURKEY
GREECE
Sept. 1943
SICILY
Oran
Algiers
Tunis
July 1943
Mediterranean Sea
ALGERIA
TUNISIA
Tripoli
El Alamein, Nov. 1942
(Controlled by Vichy France)
Cairo
EGYPT
LIBYA
(Italian)

El Alamein. The Scots Guards advance under protection of their tanks and a smoke screen.

peace on such terms and was genuinely surprised when they spurned it. He did not think in terms of a naval or Mediterranean strategy, not being naval- or colonial-minded. (He hated the sea, and always got seasick!) That much indeed he seems to have learned from Bismarck, or, more likely, from his Austrian background and pan-German ideology. Hitler also had studied and believed in the "geopolitics" of such writers as the German Haushofer and the British Mackinder. General Haushofer's writings mingled political science with German nationalism and suggested that the key to world domination lay in control of the Eurasian continent. In regard to England, also, Hitler reasoned with some show of logic that if he destroyed Russia the British would have to accept whatever terms he chose to offer them.

The war in the Pacific

Japan's role in the 1930's

Japan, which had a long record of good relations with Great Britain and the United States, and had fought on their side in World War I, had embarked in 1931 upon a course which brought her into conflict with those powers and into a loose alliance with Germany and Italy in World War II. In 1931–33 she converted Manchuria into a Japanese-protected puppet state, was rebuked for it by the League of Nations, and resigned from the League. The United

States, in particular, strongly objected to the Japanese action, revealing more interest in the Far Eastern balance of power than she then showed in Europe. Japan was not on particularly good terms with Germany, but after 1937 her relations with Great Britain and the United States grew so bad that she turned in that direction for support. In the summer of 1937 Japan and China began a war which was a consequence of the seizure of Manchuria and which found Japan seeking to conquer and control the northern provinces of China proper. This attack on the territorial integrity of China seemed a clear violation of the Nine-Power Treaty of 1922, as well as international morality, and the United States objected with especial force.

Efforts to negotiate a settlement of this "China incident" never succeeded. China still suffered from weak and divided government, but her rising nationalist sentiment deeply resented the Japanese actions. In 1927 the Nationalist party headed by Chiang Kai-shek had finally attained control over China, ending a period of acute anarchy and warlordism. At this time Chiang also purged the party of its Communist elements. But conditions remained so bad that outside observers were not sure Chiang's government could last. Communism revived in some provinces and defied all efforts to crush it.

Japanese war aims

Japan, which feared Soviet Russia more than perhaps any other state, was shocked by the pact between Germany and Russia in August, 1939. However, she joined the Tripartite Pact with Germany and Italy (1940) and fought on their side in World War II. It cannot be said that Berlin and Tokyo cooperated closely or even much trusted each other. They were fighting separate wars. Japan took advantage of the fall of France to acquire a position of dominance in French Indo-China. Her objectives were the economic resources of southeast Asia, especially oil; she developed grandiose schemes of presiding over a great eastern Asia economic union that would provide her with markets for her industries. This brought her increasingly into conflict with Great Britain and especially with the United States. The British feared for Malaya and even India; the United States was by this time committed to the British side against Germany as well as entertaining strong prejudices against the Japanese imperialists.

Attack on Pearl Harbor

The United States gradually put more pressure on Japan to abandon her conquests of China and Indo-China. Meeting in mid-Atlantic in July, Prime Minister Churchill and President Roosevelt agreed that the time had come to warn Japan. An American embargo against Japan soon followed. Japan faced a choice between making peace on Anglo-American terms or waging war on them, as she saw it. Believing that Hitler was winning in Europe, Japan daringly embarked upon war and mounted the famous air attack of December 7 on the American naval base at Pearl Harbor, Hawaii.

The result was to arouse the United States to full entry into the war. Previously, the United States had been content to send supplies to Britain and China, later to Russia, without going on a war basis. While American military advisers counseled full entry into the war against Germany, President Roosevelt had not believed the American people would approve such a step unless the United States were directly attacked. Subsequently, he was accused of deliberately provoking Japan into the attack in order to solve this problem. Roosevelt was surely not that Machiavellian, but the Japanese action did bring the United States with its vast resources into the war, and thereby doomed the Axis. Japan's gamble was a reckless one, destined to rebound not only against her but against Japan's ally, Hitlerite Germany.

Japanese victories

The first six months of the war in the Pacific brought Japan spectacular successes. Her conquest of Hongkong and Singapore constituted, Winston Churchill later wrote, the greatest disaster to British arms in all history. The debacle at Pearl Harbor, where the U.S. fleet was taken entirely by surprise and heavily damaged, followed by the surrender at Corregidor of the Philippines in early May certainly constituted the greatest disaster to American arms. Java fell within three months, Burma followed, India appeared in danger; the British navy was mauled in the Bay of Bengal. Japan had seemingly won her Pacific empire. At her high tide in June, 1942, she occupied Attu in the Aleutian Islands near Alaska, close to the North American mainland. Within a few months Japan had control of all East Asia from Guam to Burma.

Japanese attack Pearl Harbor. The crew of the U.S.S. California *is rescued as the battleship sinks.*

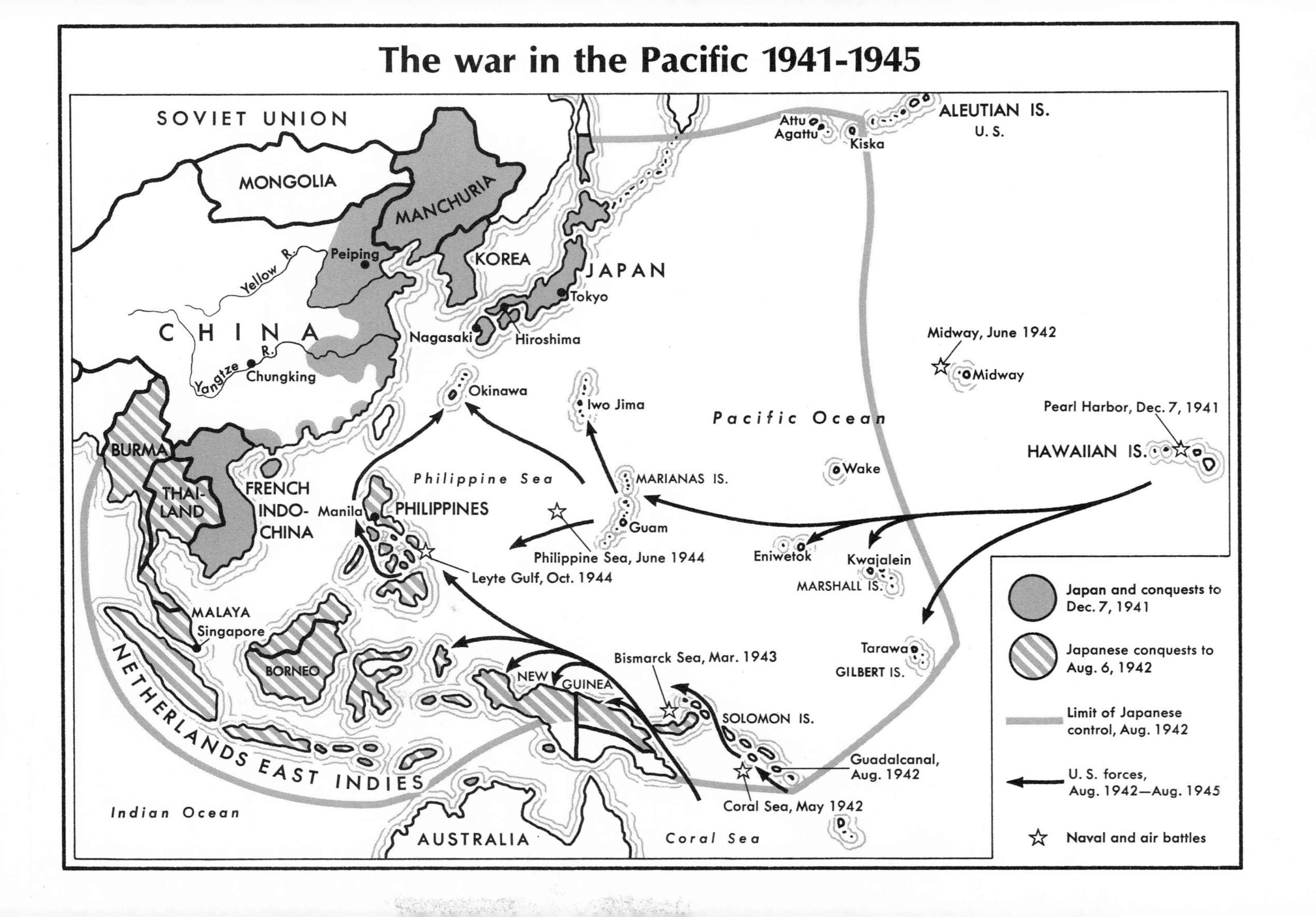
The war in the Pacific 1941-1945
SOVIET UNION
MONGOLIA
MANCHURIA
KOREA
JAPAN
Tokyo
Hiroshima
Nagasaki
Peiping
Yellow R.
CHINA
Yangtze R.
Chungking
Okinawa
Iwo Jima
ALEUTIAN IS.
U. S.
Attu
Agattu
Kiska
Midway, June 1942
Midway
Pearl Harbor, Dec. 7, 1941
HAWAIIAN IS.
Pacific Ocean
Wake
MARIANAS IS.
Guam
Philippine Sea
Philippine Sea, June 1944
BURMA
THAI-LAND
FRENCH INDO-CHINA
Manila
PHILIPPINES
Leyte Gulf, Oct. 1944
Eniwetok
Kwajalein
MARSHALL IS.
MALAYA
Singapore
BORNEO
Tarawa
GILBERT IS.
Bismarck Sea, Mar. 1943
NEW GUINEA
SOLOMON IS.
Guadalcanal, Aug. 1942
Coral Sea, May 1942
NETHERLANDS EAST INDIES
Indian Ocean
AUSTRALIA
Coral Sea
Japan and conquests to Dec. 7, 1941
Japanese conquests to Aug. 6, 1942
Limit of Japanese control, Aug. 1942
U. S. forces, Aug. 1942—Aug. 1945
Naval and air battles

The United States turns the tide

The tide began to turn with the naval battles of the Coral Sea and of Midway in May and June, 1942. Once in high gear for war, American industry was able to turn out ships, planes, weapons, and everything else in far greater quantities than Japan. It could sustain the demands of the European war and have enough left over to take care of Japan. Carrier-based aircraft became a devastating American arm of war. The Japanese found that defending a long string of islands could have its problems. The Americans, who bore the chief brunt of the war against Japan, though Australia also contributed along with British units and of course the Chinese, developed great proficiency in "island hopping" and worked their way close enough to the Japanese mainland to bomb the highly concentrated Japanese cities from land bases. Gradually the buildup of American strength in the islands adjacent to Japan became overwhelming. By early 1943 the Americans showed ability to capture island bases with consistency, working their way slowly but surely toward the heart of Japan, beginning in the New Guinea-Solomon Islands area and proceeding through the Gilberts. Guadalcanal in the Solomons, Kwajalein in the Marshalls, and Tarawa in the Gilberts were among the first important islands captured by the American counteroffensive. The inner line of defense in the Marianas and Philippines was not breached until 1944. Two naval battles in the Philippine Sea paved the way for the recapture of the Philippines in 1944.

The Japanese, like the Germans, failed *politically* in that they failed to reconcile conquered people to their rule or knit together their conquests in a lasting structure. Applying the Nazi conception of racial superiority and treating non-Germans as inferiors, the Germans made the peoples of eastern Europe hate them. The Japanese proclaimed themselves the liberators of Asia from the white man's rule, but in fact their goal was to reenslave these peoples to a Japanese imperialism. At least that is what the great majority of Chinese, Burmese, Malays, Thailanders, Vietnamese, Filipinos, etc., thought. Japan never solved the political problem of knitting together her far-flung empire.

Turning of the tide in Europe

Stalingrad

The decisive engagement in the Russo-German war was the titanic battle of Stalingrad, where Hitler lost an army early in 1943 after a long struggle, followed shortly afterward by another disaster at Kursk. German generals thought they could have staved off disaster even after that with a more conservative policy, but Hitler mounted another offensive in the spring of 1943 which achieved temporary success at the cost of being thrown back later by a Russian counteroffensive. By late 1943 the pattern had become clear and there was little hope for the Germans, who were being chased back toward the Russian borders. American military equipment poured into Russia, too, in large quantities. After winning the "Battle of the Atlantic" against German submarines, American power could be concentrated in Great Britain, whence air attacks might prepare the way for an invasion of Europe; also ships could

MacArthur wades ashore at Leyte in the Philippines on his "return" in October 1944.

carry much-needed supplies to Russia from there via the far northern, Murmansk route. (The other main route to Russia lay through the Persian Gulf and Iran.)

Operation Torch

By 1943 the western Allies, Britain and the United States, were not only bombing Germany in incessant, terribly damaging air raids, but they had launched an invasion of North Africa, in which they were joined by Free French forces. The Allied push into North Africa (November, 1942) at length carried them to conquest of the whole North African coast and then across the Mediterranean to the invasion of Sicily (July, 1943) and Italy proper (September). Anxious to launch an invasion from England across the English Channel as soon as possible, the Americans engaged in often acrimonious disputes with the British about the timing of this invasion, the British being more cautious and perhaps more realistic. The cross-channel invasion was postponed, to Stalin's disgust as well as that of some Americans. The African offensive was a substitute. It could secure firm control of the Mediterranean, thus keeping Britain's lifeline open as well as the Persian route to Russia; put pressure on vulnerable Italy and perhaps knock her out of the war; prevent neutral Turkey and Spain from deciding to join the Axis; and open up southern France as a possible invasion route. Torch, the North African invasion, coincided with British General Bernard Mongomery's El Alamein offensive against the formidable General Rommel and was designed to crush the German forces between the pincers.

That was what happened. The Americans entered North Africa without much opposition, though not without the political discord resulting from a deal with the Vichyite French in that area, and soon received their baptism of fire in an encounter with crack German troops in Tunisia. Though not disgraced, Rommel was outnumbered and had to flee, leaving behind a substantial number of soldiers to be captured by the Allies. North Africa and the Mediterranean, where the British island base of Malta held out under heavy attack, were in the hands of the Allies.

Italian campaign

In the summer of 1943 they struck at Sicily from Africa, and early in September invaded the mainland of Italy. Italy, which had never had much stomach for the war, was ready to quit, and anti-Mussolini forces working through the King were able to force out the now weary dictator. A new Italian government surrendered to the Allies soon after the Sicilian landing. Unfortunately for them, the Germans moved in to make Italy virtually an occupied country, restore Mussolini to power, and put up a stout resistance in the rough country and narrow defiles of the Italian peninsula. An attempt to outflank the German line by a landing from the sea at Anzio, near Rome, early in 1944 failed with heavy losses. Thereafter the Italian front lost in importance as the Allies prepared to make their major effort in the cross-channel invasion. It was said in its defense that it tied down numerous German troops and constituted good practice for the more important invasion. In actuality it seems to have served little purpose.

The Normandy invasion

The often delayed cross-channel invasion, Operation Overlord, finally was launched on June 6, 1944. It was a tremendous achievement, overcoming enormous difficulties and involving immense preparations. More than 100,000 men and 20,000 vehicles, transported across the English Channel by thousands of craft, took part in the first wave alone. The landings succeeded after heavy initial losses, and overcame stubborn German resistance to break out from the beaches and begin the sweep through France. The Germans no longer had the strength to hold off such splendidly equipped forces. They were retreating on both fronts through most of 1944, though still capable of brief counterassaults such as that in the Ardennes ("the Battle of the Bulge") in December.

The same was true of Japan, where fearful bombing had to be endured after June, 1944, the Americans having breached the inner line of island outposts—Saipan in the Marianas and Iwo Jima, taken after a bitter battle, being important bases. In the Burma theater the British moved forward, using Chinese troops; in naval engagements, the autumn brought the end for the Japanese fleet in the Second Battle of the Philippine Sea. By the close of 1944 no rational man could doubt that the war had been decided. It did not end,

Winston Churchill with General Bernard Montgomery in North Africa

General Eisenhower with U.S. paratroopers before the Normandy invasion

The horror of war: Wesel, Germany, after tactical bombing attacks to clear the way for Allied crossing of the Rhine

however, until far into 1945. The reasons for this lead one toward the realm of politics and diplomacy, which were of the first importance in this war.

Total victory and total inhumanity

These battles we have been describing so summarily were not less bloody than those of World War I for being of a rather different kind. This war was far harder on civilians, far more damaging to property. It left gaping ruins in most of the cities of Europe. While the atomic bomb, with its ability to wipe out most of the entire city of Hiroshima and kill upwards of 100,000 people at one explosion, did not make its grisly appearance until the last days of the war, fleets of superbombers, carrying tons of high explosives and bombing around the clock, inflicted damage that was cumulatively just as great. The war was unparalleled in its inhumanity, its disregard for the rules of war or for any sentiment except blind hate.

The candid historian must admit that the Allied side was almost as bad as the Axis. While the Germans began the rain of hell from the skies with the pulverizing of Rotterdam and the terror assaults on England (especially the raid which virtually wiped out the city of Coventry), the British and Americans later far outdid them—the official figures were that they were repaid 315 to 1, surely a generous rate. (For every ton of bombs dumped on England the United States and Britain eventually put down 315 tons on Germany.) The Allied bombing was officially "strategic," aimed at factories, depots, and rail centers, but often seemed terroristic.

The war on civilians

The theory, widely entertained, that precision bombing aimed at strategic industrial targets could quickly bring the enemy to his knees, proved to be one of the war's biggest fallacies. The Allied bombing attacks ran into prohibitive casualties and failed to shatter or even decrease German war production; by 1942, the decision had been reached to abandon precision bombing for "area bombing," which really was terror bombing, aimed at breaking the national morale. It did not succeed either, despite the unprecedented tons of horror dumped from the skies on residential areas. Though its advocates (especially British strategic bombing chief Sir Arthur Harris) continued to believe that it would make invasion of the Continent unnecessary, and even disapproved of Overlord when it came, in fact German arms production was not impaired; and bomber losses continued to be heavy. Sober students of the subject have frequently concluded that the strategic air offensive was a total failure, in a military sense: the men and money might have been more effectively applied in other kinds of military activity. To the end, however, the air chiefs maintained a strong ascendancy over strategy and the raids with their sickening toll of civilian life went on to the last. The old city of Nürnberg, a priceless medieval heritage but also scene of the Nazi rallies, was destroyed. Late in the war, when the Germans were already evidently beaten, a great air raid on refugee-crowded Dresden killed some 30,000 people. Few parts of any cities in Germany escaped severe damage.

Further testimony to the Allied inhumanity may be found in the fact that "within seven hours" after the attack on Pearl Harbor, American orders went out to "execute unrestricted submarine and air warfare against Japan," regardless of international law. During the war American submarines took the lives of over 100,000 Japanese civilians. (Shades of 1917, when the United States went to war accusing Germany of extreme inhumanity after the loss of 200 American lives!) The use of the atomic bomb, of course, constituted a final example of war at its cruelest.

The final solution

On the other hand, the inhumanity of the Nazi regime defied description. Their concentration camps, where all who criticized the regime were taken, surpassed anything ever seen in the systematic extermination of human beings, as well as in sadistic cruelty.[2] During the war there was conceived the

[2] See Morton Grodzins, *Americans Betrayed* (University of Chicago Press, 1949), for the story of amazing mistreatment of the Japanese minority in the United States during the war, which, however, stopped far short of Hitler's and Himmler's murderous methods.

German army photo of the forced evacuation of the Warsaw ghetto, used as evidence in the Nürnberg Trials.

Concentration camp victims of the Nazis were found in this mass grave at Belsen, April 1945.

infamous scheme of destroying the entire Jewish race. The imagination can scarcely conceive the motivations for such a scheme, save sheer insanity; but it was pushed through with frightful efficiency. The Jewish population of Germany was not large and some of them were able to escape. It was the unfortunate inhabitants of the ghettoes of Poland and Rumania who were marked for extermination in the gas chambers. According to careful estimates made later, the number of Jews put to death by or because of the Nazis was in excess of 4 million—perhaps as many as 4.5 million. The vast majority of these were eastern European, mostly Polish. For this ghastly business there was no rational reason, such as military necessity; indeed, the resources employed in carrying it out often actually impeded the war effort. Mass murder became a mechanized industry at such places as Auschwitz and Belsen. This vast crime overshadowed all committed by the SS, elite corps of the Nazi party, but there were others. In 1914–18, the world had been too gullible and believed all kinds of fabricated atrocity stories; this time, the truth was more horrible than most people were willing to believe until they saw the mass graves, the gas chambers, the concentration camps, and the walking skeletons who came out of them at the war's end.

Unconditional surrender

The war's inhumanity was one reason for its being waged to the bitter end without thought of terms. The Allied terms were announced officially as "unconditional surrender." Hitler for his part preferred to go down in ruins with Germany before surrending. Japan as well as Germany was asked to abandon herself completely to the will of the Allies. These terms were later criticized, not on the grounds that Hitler deserved any better, but on the grounds that, first, it might have been possible to encourage anti-Nazi elements in Germany, whereas the official policy refused to distinguish between regime and people; and, second, that the consequences of unconditional surrender included destruction of the European balance of power and necessarily entailed bringing Russia into the middle of Europe. The whole of eastern Europe, extending as far as the middle of Germany, would fall into Soviet Russia's hands if German power were to be totally destroyed. Similarly in Asia, the destruction of Japan's Empire would mean that much of it would probably pass to Russia as the only strong power on the spot there. Huge "vacuums of power" would be created which somebody would have to fill; and that somebody could only be the Soviet Union, almost in the nature of the case. No other strong power existed in Europe or Asia; the Americans entertained hopes for China, but the British regarded these as illusory. So, afterwards, there were to be bitter reproaches for the war that was lost in winning it—won from the Nazis and the Japanese warlords, the gains turned over to Communists who were equally hostile to the West, equally dangerous to world peace, equally greedy for power.

At the time, however, the Allies permitted themselves to hope that collaboration with the Soviet Union would be possible. Wartime friendship blossomed. "Uncle Joe" Stalin became an almost revered, avuncular figure.

Russian courage was admired and their suffering at the hands of the Nazis sympathized with. Dream took shape of a wonderful postwar world presided over by the United Nations, resting on the firm friendship of the three great powers, joined in due course by China and possibly France. In a series of wartime conferences, especially those at Casablanca, Teheran, and Yalta, the leaders of the Allies, Roosevelt, Churchill, Stalin, paraded their personal amity and laid plans for the peace. At Dumbarton Oaks in Washington a conference prepared a charter for the United Nations organization. While renewing the pledge to accept nothing less than total victory and total

Churchill, Roosevelt, and Stalin at the Yalta Conference, where early in 1945 the Allied leaders tried to agree on postwar zones and peace plans

annihilation of the enemy, the Allied leaders believed they could remake the world in a peaceful image by their postwar cooperation. It was a picture which overlooked many of the terrible problems of a war-shattered world, as well as fundamental differences between the Soviets and the West, but it functioned as almost the messianic hope of the Allied peoples.

The end of the war

Winston Churchill, writing of the last months of the war in his famous historical volumes some years later, titled this volume *Triumph and Tragedy*. The tragedy was not immediately evident to the soldiers and to the civilians at home who went literally mad with joy upon the announcement of the war's end. German resistance collapsed in March–April on all fronts, and Allied soldiers poured across the Rhine, up through Italy, and into Prussia, Austria, and Czechoslovakia from the east. On April 28 Mussolini was caught and murdered by Italian partisans. Three days later Adolf Hitler committed suicide in Berlin. There was really no German government, but some generals signed surrender terms at Reims on May 7 and the war in Europe was declared over the next day. American soldiers received orders not to speak to or trust any German. The entire German Empire was in chaos, but the Allies had agreed on occupational zones and their armies governed. The Russians liberated Prague, Vienna, Budapest, and Berlin. There were four zones of occupation in Germany, the French receiving one along with the Big Three, and a central control committee.

Russian control of eastern Europe

The Russians were in sole control of all of eastern Europe, their armies having occupied these countries en route to Germany (Poland, Bulgaria, Hungary, Czechoslovakia, Rumania). Only in Yugoslavia was there an armed force in existence, the partisan forces led by the fabulous guerrilla chieftain Tito. The Poles accused the Russians of having deliberately betrayed their partisan forces to the Germans, while murdering others. The Hungarians and the Czechs had not been given aid in setting up partisan forces, though they had asked the Western powers for it. The east of Europe had been, in effect, conceded to Russia. In the aftermath of the Teheran Conference late in 1943, when Churchill and Roosevelt first found out how tough Stalin could be, Churchill arrived at an agreement with Stalin in which the U.S.S.R. was to have "90 percent" influence in Rumania, 75 percent in Bulgaria, and presumably 100 percent in Poland and Czechoslovakia, while the Western powers were to have 90 percent of Greece, and Yugoslavia and Hungary were somehow to be shared equally.

At the Yalta (Crimea) Conference in February, 1945, when so many momentous and controversial decisions were made, Roosevelt and Churchill got pledges from Stalin to hold free elections in Poland but they had to sacrifice the Polish government-in-exile to a Communist government set up by the Soviets, and the promises of elections turned out to be worthless. In after years some were to recall with regret that Churchill had wanted to use the Balkans as an area for British-American offense but had been overruled by Roosevelt. Churchill saw the pattern of Soviet domination emerging as the war ended and was, as he writes, sick at heart. But few ordinary folk felt anything but joy that the war was over and the Nazis were crushed.

The end of the war in the Far East

Japan held out for three more months. She was invited to surrender from the Potsdam Conference in July by Stalin, the new American President Harry Truman (Roosevelt died on April 12), and Churchill—along with Labour leader Clement Attlee who was soon to be England's Prime Minister. The evidence indicates that the Japanese might well have surrendered before the fateful atomic bomb was dropped, had the Allies clarified their position in regard to the Emperor, who was finally permitted to keep his throne, and if the Russians had been candid about approaches which the Japanese had tried to make through them. On August 8 the Russians declared war on Japan, as they had agreed to do at Yalta in return for a number of territorial rewards, and marched into Manchuria. Two days before this, the first atomic bomb had been dropped on Hiroshima, and one day after this a second one fell on Nagasaki. Lengthy and arduous would be the controversy about this decision to use the "absolute weapon." It amazed and shocked the world, and was a dreadful precedent to set. Japan was already beaten without it, though as far as could then be seen she might have prolonged the war for some time. But it, together with Russia's declaration of war, did bring the war to an immediate end, as the Japanese offered to surrender if they could keep their Emperor, which condition the Allies now accepted.

Hiroshima, Japan, after the atomic bomb

In the Far East the situation also was to the advantage of the Communists, as universal disorder attended the collapse of Japan's sprawling Empire. Where the Japanese had thrown out European rulers, as in the Dutch Indies or French Indo-China or British Malaya, the people were not ready to return to their former masters. China had been seriously weakened by the long struggle; her Communist guerrillas were to be strengthened by contact with the Russians in Manchuria. The Soviet Union, in one of Yalta's more controversial clauses, had been promised a dominant position in the Manchurian port cities of Dairen and Port Arthur, keys to the control of Manchuria by China, and they were the occupying power in Manchuria and northern Korea.

One of the more dismaying features of the end-of-the-war situation was the haste with which the Americans prepared to disband their armed forces and come home. The war was over. The Americans were not accustomed to keeping large numbers of soldiers under arms except in wartime. War oratory had led them to believe all would be well once the Axis powers were crushed; thus they were not psychologically prepared for the continuing struggle. They had performed astonishing feats during this war, accomplishing miracles of production and raising huge armies. They honestly believed that they might now settle back and enjoy the fruits of victory.

Results of the war

The cost of the war

Only Spain, Sweden, and Switzerland escaped some involvement in this war. General Francisco Franco's regime in Spain, clerical and authoritarian, was widely regarded as "fascist" in the democracies but actually had no love for Nazism and no desire to be involved in Germany's war; by dint of careful maneuvering the Spanish kept out. Spain was politically boycotted for six years after the war by the Allies because of her alleged pro-German neutrality. Othewise, few places escaped a devastating experience. The statistics of death and destruction overwhelm one. Writing after the war, British author Sisley Huddleston spoke of the estimated 75 million persons who lost their lives (hardly much of an exaggeration) and the 150 million their homes, and pointed out that

> The sum spent on that war would have given every family in America, Russia, England, France, Germany, and many other countries, a fully furnished house and a substantial capital. Moreover, every city of 200,000 inhabitants could have been provided with new schools, sports grounds, hospitals and libraries.

Estimates of losses inevitably vary widely. Figures of such magnitude can have little meaning after a certain point. Apart from the millions upon millions killed, it is calculated that in Europe alone (counting the Soviet Union) between 1940 and 1945 over 30 million people were transplanted from their homes; immediately after the war, another 25 million were forcibly removed. Russia, Germany, Japan, and China suffered the most, but Italy and France had also been battlefields of this war which revealed the frightening powers of modern destructiveness, and Britain had been pounded from the air.

Nürnberg Trials

The defeated powers, occupied by the Allied troops, faced total reconstruction; their conquerors and occupiers came bearing plans for "reeducation" along with political constitutions framed in their own image; but what the future might hold was uncertain. For the moment, life in Germany and Japan was reduced to its lowest denominator; just to stay alive became the only possible objective. The conquerors and occupiers might talk generously of reeducation, but they also bore hatred for the late enemy and they were greedy for reparations. The Nürnberg (Nuremberg) Trials prosecuted the Nazi leaders for their crimes against humanity, against the rules of warfare, and for the crime of beginning a war of aggression; these trials were hailed as breaking new ground in international law, but were to be criticized on the grounds that they represented simply "victor's justice," or revenge under the disguise of law. The trial and execution of high Nazi leaders (such of them as had survived) by the Allied tribunals, followed by trials of lesser Nazis, gratified much of world opinion, which was hardly in doubt as to the guilt of these men; but it was all too evident that inhumanity on the Allied side had also existed, though lesser in magnitude, and would not be admitted to the Nürnberg record.[3] But through the trials, and in other ways the Allies hoped to "denazify" Germany.

---

[3] One of these acts was the Katyn Massacre, the shooting of several thousand Polish officers by the Russians in the spring of 1940. When the graves were found during the war the Russians blamed it on the Nazis and denounced the Polish government-in-exile as "fascist" for suggesting that Russia might be guilty. Evidently the Western Allies accepted the Soviet view, but much subsequent investigation has clearly demonstrated Soviet guilt.

Other Allied plans for Germany were not entirely clear, but there had been discussion of partitioning her into several small states, of entirely destroying and shipping away the factories of the Ruhr (the Morgenthau plan, once approved and then withdrawn), of giving Russia 10 or 20 billions of dollars in reparations (mentioned in the Yalta agreement), of keeping the Germans on a minimum calorie diet until everyone else was satisfied. Meanwhile the four powers each had a zone. While the Russians and French proceeded to strip theirs ruthlessly, the British and Americans turned before long to tasks of reconstruction, but without clear objectives or machinery for some time.

For Germany and Italy, in any case, the war was a traumatic experience which left them stunned and devoid of national purpose. There had been some resistance to the Nazi and Fascist rulers: Italian partisans had appeared late in the war, valiant German conspirators in the army had plotted against Hitler and narrowly missed killing him when a bomb misfired on July 20, 1944. But the great majority had not participated.

Liberated France

France had gone through the experience of national defeat, rule by the Vichy regime in unoccupied France, and the creation of a Resistance movement which fought the Germans and the "collaborators." She also suffered heavy war damage during the last year of the war. The return of the Allies to liberate Paris, in company with General Charles de Gaulle's Free French forces, was a glorious moment. But the war had left deep divisions in French life, which in some ways carried on the old political cleavage between left and right. General Pétain and Pierre Laval, his chief minister, leaders of the Vichyite "collaborationist" regime, had only been doing the best they could for their country, on one view; but they were tried, condemned, and treated as traitors by the restored Free French–Resistance elements. Many Pétainists drew a distinction between the old General who, a true patriot, had tried to stand between France and Hitler as best as he could, and the more frankly pro-Nazi Pierre Laval. Yet both were treated as equally guilty. Laval was executed, Pétain spared only because of his advanced age. Meanwhile a new government had to be started, and France debated the terms of the Fourth Republic's new constitution. With the further cleavage of Vichyites and Gaullists added to her historic factional disputes, could France manage to build a stable democratic government? Because of their participation in the Resistance, the Communists were a strong force in the new France; more hopeful was the emergence of a Christian Democratic party.

The Soviet Union, victorious, had suffered hugely from the German armies which had ranged far into the industrial and agricultural heart of the land for two years, leaving behind destroyed villages and shattered cities. Soviet authorities later estimated that 20 million persons died in the war. But victory left the Stalinist regime firmly entrenched, with Russian power and influence greatly enhanced. As already noted, Russia in many ways was the chief gainer from this war, or seemed likely to be. But for the moment she was deeply wounded by the long war waged with such disregard for life and on such a monstrous scale. It must not be forgotten that Russia absorbed the chief blows of the German armies and was chiefly responsible for their defeat. It was the Red Army which tore the entrails out of the *Wehrmacht;* when the Western allies invaded Europe in 1944, they met only its hollow shell.

Soviet gains

During the war, despite the wishful thinking in the West about post-war harmony between Russia and the West, there had been signs that the Communists continued to believe in their mission to overthrow all the "capitalist" countries and win the world victory of Communism. They had not ceased to subscribe to the Marxist-Leninist faith just because of an alliance with some of the capitalist powers dictated by necessity. They did not propose to forget the gulf that existed between the worlds of socialism and capitalism, and they took advantage of the situation to impose Communist domination on the countries which they occupied, i.e., Poland, Rumania, Bulgaria, Czechoslovakia, Hungary, and their portion of Germany. They had directly annexed the Baltic countries and a portion of eastern Poland, as well as Bessarabia from Rumania, thus recouping World War I losses.

At Potsdam the Western leaders agreed to the staggering inhumanity of uprooting millions of Germans from the region of east Prussia, including Danzig, and replacing them by Poles. Germany thus lost much territory to the Poles—though this has never been officially recognized in a treaty by the Western powers—and was forced to absorb some 10 million refugees in the postwar years, including also many expelled from the Sudetenland by the Czechs. One must add that in the view of the people as well as the government of the Soviet Union, such measures were absolutely necessary in order to insure that never again could the Germans unleash terror against their homeland. The Western powers were moved by similar feelings against the Germans, and approved these transfers of population as one way to end the problems created by German minorities in Poland and Czechoslovakia.

The victors exhausted

The nominal victors were not much better off than the vanquished. Great Britain had further impoverished herself to pay for the war, and stood to lose colonial territory. India and Burma were clamoring for independence, and got it soon after the war. There were to be additional difficulties for Britain as the harassed mandate power in Palestine; and she found herself saddled with many of the burdens of sustaining the balance of power in Europe as the Americans gaily prepared to go home. There was a serious problem of civil war in Greece which involved the British. This role of buoying up the defenses of the free world against Communist movements was to prove more than Britain could now afford. She negotiated a loan from the United States on terms that some thought onerous, and there were to be some bad times for Britain before the United States returned to shoulder her share of the burdens in 1947. She almost went under in the severe winter of 1946. Economic conditions were dreadful throughout the Continent in the postwar year; such a massive derangement of the world economy was bound to afflict all.

No peace conference

Machinery for bringing the world back to a semblance of normality was paralyzed by the emerging chasm between Soviet Russia and the West. After all previous great wars in modern history there had been a peace conference. This time there was to be no equivalent of the great settlements of Westphalia (1648), Utrecht (1713), Vienna (1815), and Paris (1919). That fact registered how much order and unity the European world had lost. There gradually came about a number of separate peace treaties in the next few years, but there never has been a formal German settlement, and nothing like a single great European settlement such as those mentioned above, when a European conference dealt with the problems of all Europe at the end of major wars.

The United Nations

One result of the war, widely heralded, was the establishment of the United Nations organization. The League of Nations, created in 1919, was allowed to die. The United States had never joined it, and the Soviet Union had been thrown out of it in 1940. Though it had organized a sizable amount of international cooperation in various minor ways, it had seemed to fail in the major concern of preserving peace. There were those who pointed out that one could hardly blame the League for this failure, since it was not and could not be more than the sum of its parts, meaning principally the great powers. No nation had surrendered any sovereign powers to the League; it had been essentially a permanent congress of sovereign nations, with the big powers reserving for themselves special privileges in it. The United Nations organization was not really any different. Apparently some people expected that the nations would disarm, and turn over military power to the new world organization, which would thus be a superstate. But such hopes proved far too optimistic. While the U.N. Charter granted broader powers than the League Covenant to the Security Council to investigate and act on "breaches of the peace," it also gave the big powers a rock-ribbed veto power on that Council. Some thought that only Russia had insisted upon this veto, but this view was mistaken, for all the great powers wanted a veto on any substantive matter affecting vital decisions.

In other words, none of the great powers could be bound against its will, and any significant decision of the Council required the unanimous approval of the United States, Great Britain, the Soviet Union, France, and China. So long as the great powers were in agreement, they could keep the peace. But disagreements between them would paralyze the United Nations as the agent of "collective security" to preserve peace throughout the world. And of course these disagreements were forthcoming, especially between Russia and the West. For all that, the United Nations grew quickly into a symbol of the will to peace after its birth at the San Francisco Conference of May–June, 1945.

Vacuums of power

Objectively looked at, the chief political ailment from which the war-shocked world suffered was the existence of enormous vacuums of power in Europe and Asia left by the total collapse of Germany and Japan. In Asia this region of the former Japanese Empire ranged from Indonesia through Malaya and Indo-China up to China itself; indeed, little if any of the Far East was unaffected. In Europe too the entire Continent, but especially the eastern half, was in question. If the Western democracies could not fill this vacuum—and, with the Americans leaving and the British and French exhausted, it seemed they could not—then it would pass by default to Soviet Communism. This was the grim situation which led Sir Winston Churchill to write of "triumph and tragedy," and others to speak of "defeat in victory," at the end of the costliest war in human history.

Bibliography

Jacques Benoist-Mechin, *Sixty Days That Shook the West: The Fall of France 1940* (New York: G.P. Putnam's Sons, 1963), translated from the French, memorably evokes the campaign that began World War II. Walter Ansel, *Hitler Confronts England* (Durham, N.C.: Duke University Press, 1961), deals with the crucial days of 1940–41. No other war has been anything like so much written about. The official histories—American and British, especially—have operated on a scale which may be indicated by the 91 volumes of the War Department's *History of the U.S. Army in World War II*, while individual accounts, memoirs, and so on, are almost countless. Sir Winston Churchill's celebrated work itself runs to six volumes (*The Second World War*; Boston: Houghton Mifflin, 1948–53); there is an abridged one-volume edition (1959). The reader seeking somewhat shorter accounts has such excellent ones as Chester Wilmot's *Struggle for Europe* (Harper & Row), the story of the Anglo-American invasion of the Continent in 1944–45, and Arthur M. Byrant, *The Turn of the Tide* and *Triumph in the West*, based on the diaries of Field Marshal Lord Alanbrooke (London: Collins, 1957, 1959). John F. Turner, *Invasion '44* (London: George C. Harrap, 1959), is yet another of the many fine battle accounts. So is Martin Blumenson, *Anzio: The Gamble that Failed* (New York: J.B. Lippincott, 1963). P.K. Kemp, *Victory at Sea 1939–1945* (London: Muller, 1958), covers the naval campaigns.

One of the more significant of the U.S. official series is *Command Decisions*, edited by Kent R. Greenfield (New York: Harcourt, Brace & World, 1959); in the British series, several volumes on *Grand Strategy* by J.R.M. Butler and John Ehrman (London: Her Majesty's Stationery Office, 1956–57) also focus on the high-level decisions about which there was so much acrimonious debate. Sir Charles Webster and N. Frankland have produced a notable work in the British official series, *The Strategic Air Offensive against Germany 1939–1945* (4 vols., H.M.S.O.). For the Far Eastern picture, F.C. Jones, *Japan's New Order in East Asia 1937–1945* (New York: Oxford University Press, 1954), is a useful and scholarly synthesis. The Soviet Union is publishing a six-volume official history of the Russian war; more useful for most readers will be Alexander Werth, *Russia at War* (Avon). Alan Clark, *Barbarossa: The Russian-German Conflict 1941–1945* (New York: William Morrow, 1965), is also learned and interesting; it tends to defend Hitler against the German generals. Trumbull Higgins, *Hitler and Russia: The Third Reich in a Two-Front War*, also scholarly and readable, concentrates on the period 1939–43 (New York: Macmillan, 1966). Arthur L. Funk, *Charles de Gaulle: The Crucial Years 1943–1944* (Norman: University of Oklahoma, 1959), and Robert Aron, *De Gaulle Triumphant: The Liberation of Paris 1944–1945* (G.P. Putnam's Sons, 1964) tell the Free French story. The end of the war is treated in R. Dabrowski, *Mussolini's Twilight and Fall* (New York: Roy Publishers, 1956), and H.R. Trevor-Roper, *The Last Days of Hitler* (3d ed.; Macmillan, 1956). F.W. Deakin, *The Brutal Friendship: Mussolini and Hitler* (New York: Harper & Row, 1962) contains rich materials on the Italian scene in the last part of the war.

Among the more interesting primary sources on military affairs are Felix Gilbert (ed.), *Hitler Directs His War* (Oxford University Press, 1956); B.H. Liddell Hart, *The German Generals Talk* (Berkley Publishing), and (ed.) *The Rommel Papers* (Harcourt, Brace & World, 1953); Field Marshal Bernard Montgomery, *El Alamein to the River Sangro* (Hutchinson, Grey Arrow); and *The Alexander Memoirs 1940–1945*, of Field Marshal Earl Alexander of Tunis (London: Cassell, 1962). A respected German account, very critical of Hitler, is Field Marshal Erich von Manstein, *Lost Victories* (London: Methuen, 1958). See also Heinz Guderian, *Panzer Leader* (Ballantine Books). The five volumes of General Charles de Gaulle's *War Memoirs* have been published in English by the Viking Press (New York, 1955–60).

On the various nonmilitary aspects of the war: Gerald Reitlinger, *The Final Solution* (A.S. Barnes, Perpetua), and Raul Hilberg, *The Destruction of the European Jews* (Quadrangle Books), document the horrible attempt to exterminate a race. Eugen Kogon, *Theory and Practice of Hell* (Berkley Publishing), gives the flavor of Nazi concentration camp life, for those with strong stomachs; also Primo Levi, *If This is a Man* (London: G. Allen & Unwin, 1960), one of the most perceptive of the numerous books which seek to describe the awful experience of life in these places. *The German Resistance to Hitler* has been covered by Gerhard Ritter, in a major work in German of which this is a somewhat abridged translation (New York: Frederick A. Praeger, 1959); see also Hans Rothfels, *The German Opposition to Hitler* (Chicago: Henry Regnery, 1948). Charles F. Delzell, *Mussolini's Enemies: The Italian Anti-Fascist Resistance* (Princeton, N.J.: Princeton University Press, 1961), is a work of careful scholarship. Robert Aron is the chief historian of *The Vichy Regime 1940–1944* (Macmillan, 1958). Two books on the atomic bomb may also be mentioned: Robert Jungk's brilliant *Brighter Than a Thousand Suns* (Grove Press), and Ronald W. Clark, *The Birth of the Bomb* (London: Phoenix House, 1961). The important matter of wartime diplomacy can be approached via Herbert Feis, *Churchill-Roosevelt-Stalin; Between War and Peace: The Potsdam Conference;* and *Japan Subdued* (Princeton University Press); or the more critical E.J. Rozek, *Allied Wartime Diplomacy: A Pattern in Poland* (New York: John Wiley & Sons, 1958). Useful also is John L. Snell's *Wartime Origins of the East-West Dilemma in Germany* (New Orleans: Hauser Press, 1959); while a fascinating and indispensable source is the *Foreign Relations of the United States* series, which has published volumes of official records on the *Conferences at Cairo and Teheran, Conferences at Yalta and Malta,* and *Potsdam Conference* (Washington: U.S. Government Printing Office, 1955, 1960, 1961).

31

Europe since 1945

chronology

1946

Constitution of Fourth French Republic approved.

Foreign Ministers, Conferences of Allies fail to agree on peace terms.

Economic difficulties in Europe.

1947

U.S. military and economic aid to Greece and Turkey.

Marshall Plan for European economic recovery. European Economic Organization set up.

Purge of non-Communists in Soviet satellite countries of eastern Europe.

India granted independence, remains within British Commonwealth.

Revolt against French rule in Indo-China, led by Communists.

1948

Seizure of Czechoslovakia by Communist coup, February.

Brussels Treaty (West European allies).

Yugoslavia breaks with U.S.S.R.

British withdraw from Palestine mandate; war between Jews and Arabs begins.

Separate governments set up in North Korea (Communist) and South Korea.

Currency reform, West Germany; beginnings of economic recovery.

1949

Victory of Communists in China; withdrawal of Nationalists to Formosa.

North Atlantic Treaty.

Berlin crisis; airlift. German Federal Republic (West Germany) established.

Expulsion of Arabs from Palestine by Jews; foundation of state of Israel.

Russia explodes atomic bomb.

Indonesia granted independence.

1950

Korean War begins. United Nations declares North Korea the aggressor.

Intervention of Chinese in Korea after advance of United Nations forces to frontier.

Europe Coal and Steel Community established.

1951

Stabilization of Korean front. Truce negotiations begin.

Peace Treaty with Japan signed, also U.S.–Japanese security pact.

Victory of Conservatives in British elections.

Antiwestern movement in Iran, attempts to nationalize oil properties.

1952

Egyptian revolution, fall of King Farouk; regime of Colonel Nasser.

Mau-Mau revolution in Kenya.

1953

Death of Stalin. Execution of Beria. Malenkov, Soviet Prime Minister, Khrushchev First Secretary of Communist party.

Uprising against Communist rule in east Berlin.

Completion of Korean truce negotiations.

1954

European Defense Community rejected by France; agreement reached on limited German rearmament within West European structure.

Beginning of Algerian revolution.

British agree to evacuate Suez Canal zone.

Indo-China crisis; Geneva Conference, partition arranged.

H-bomb developed.

1955

France recognizes Morocco's sovereignty.

Mild thaw in cold war: Austrian peace treaty, reconciliation between Tito and Kremlin, Russian recognition of West German state. Failure to agree on German unification at Geneva conference.

1956

Nationalization of Suez Canal by Egypt.

Israeli attack on Egypt, October 29; Anglo-French ultimatum followed by air attacks on Egypt and (November 5) landing of troops at Port Said.

United Nations condemns British-French-Israeli action, calls for ceasefire and withdrawal. Threats from United States, U.S.S.R.

Riots in Poland, June; Hungarian revolution against Soviet domination, November; crushed by intervention of Soviet troops.

1957

First Soviet earth satellite.

Rome treaties, beginning of European Common Market, economic integration.

Republic of Ghana (former British Gold Coast and Togoland colonies) becomes independent; beginning of series of new African nations.

1958

Khrushchev assumes premiership of U.S.S.R.

Berlin crisis.

Formosa Straits crisis (offshore islands between Taiwan and Red China).

Middle Eastern crisis; U.S. troops sent to Lebanon.

Fifth French Republic established under presidency of General de Gaulle.

Guinea, new African state.

John XXIII becomes Pope.

1959

Khrushchev visits United States.

1960

Cameroun, Togo, Malagasy Republic, Somalia, Dahomey, Niger, Upper Volta, Ivory Coast, Chad, Central Africa Republic, Congo Republics, Gabon, Mali, Senegal, Nigeria, Mauritania—new African states.

Conflict in Belgian Congo, Portuguese Angola.

Chinese-Russian breach.
Algerian War ends with Algerian independence.
1961
Renewal of Berlin crisis.
Tanganyika, Sierra Leone become independent.
United Nations intervention in Congo.
Russia launches first astronaut.
Meeting of uncommitted nations at Belgrade.
1962
Cuba crisis.
Chinese-Indian hostilities.
1963
Franco-German treaty of friendship.
Konrad Adenauer retires as German Chancellor.
British membership in Common Market rejected.
Escalation of Vietnam War.
1964
Labour government in Britain, first time in 13 years.
China explodes H-bomb.
Greek-Turkish conflict over Cyprus.
1965
President de Gaulle reelected in France.
Khrushchev replaced as Soviet Russian leader.
1966
Disturbances in Red China.
Kiesinger replaces Erhard as German Chancellor.
EEC achieves basic agreement on common agricultural policy.
1967
Israeli-Arab war.
Civil war in Nigeria.
1968
Student riots in Berlin and Paris.
Crisis in French government.
Russian occupation of Czechoslovakia.
Vietnam peace talks begin.

Baja California and the Pacific from space

The cold war

Between World War I and World War II there had been at least a "twenty years' truce"; for a while after World War II it seemed there would be no pause at all, but a direct passage into the next round. Not, this time, another round with Germany and her allies, which lay utterly crushed, but a struggle over the spoils of victory between the allies of the war, which in fact held to hostile ideologies and could not cooperate to meet all the distressing problems of a shattered and unstable world.

The vacuum of power

General George C. Marshall, chief American high commander of World War II, explained to his countrymen some two years after the war's end that the war had "created a political vacuum" in the whole of Europe, which the Soviet Union and its organization of international Communism was seeking to fill. At that moment Marshall was not sure whether "a healthy European community" could be recreated; he *was* sure that unless it was, there was no chance of a "lasting peace." From the utter destruction of Germany and Japan, American policy soon swung to their reconstruction. In area after area, from Korea and Japan to Germany and Greece, "cooperation" with Russia broke down. A few still insisted that the Russians were ready to cooperate but had not been given a fair chance. Far more in the West turned from idealization of the Soviet Union to bitter disenchantment, and talked of its methods of "international gangsterism." More objective persons were inclined to put their finger on this vast vacuum of power as the main cause of the "cold war" between the Soviet Union and the Western powers.

The Marshall Plan

Economic demoralization of great areas to the point of actual hunger or starvation was not confined to the defeated powers. The postwar years revealed that the European economy would have to recover as a whole: you could not make Germany a pasture and expect France and Britain to prosper. The latter countries, nominal victors, suffered as severely as the defeated. The winter of 1946–47 was a particularly terrible one for Britain. Such expedients as UNRRA (the United Nations Relief and Rehabilitation Agency), an American loan to Britain, and allowing the French to plunder Germany were clearly not solutions to the problem. On June 5, 1947, Secretary of State Marshall—as he now was—observed that "the rehabilitation of the economic structure of Europe quite evidently will require a much longer time and greater effort than had been foreseen." Marshall then proposed a bold approach through cooperative action and long-range American aid given in great quantities. Much as the United States had provided lend-lease aid to her allies in World War II without counting the cost, "Marshall Plan" aid would now be sent. It was offered to all, but the Communist countries indignantly rejected it as virtually a declaration of "cold war"—a plot by American capitalists to ensnare other nations.

In 1946 and 1947 Western diplomats had sought in vain to get the tough Soviet foreign minister, Molotov, to agree to peace treaties in a series of

U.S. Secretary of State Marshall in 1948 urging Senate passage of his foreign aid proposal

frustrating conferences. They assumed that such treaties would be made in the traditional manner, but the Russians were aware that it suited their interests to avoid final settlements, since it seemed that time was on their side. With the United States disarming and Europe a prey to disorder and collapse, why should the Soviets not wait to see if all did not fall into their hands? Germany remained occupied by the four powers; soon the Western zones were to be merged, but in Germany as in Korea the Russians refused to agree with the Western powers on a formula for reunification. What was intended to be a short-term military expediency thus became a permanent arrangement. Little Austria, too, was occupied by the four powers, "four elephants in a canoe," as the Austrian premier Renner once happily phrased it, until finally in 1955 as a sign of the mild thaw in the cold war which took place in that year, a peace treaty was signed.

Russian enslavement of eastern Europe

Continued occupation of Germany and Austria provided the Russians with a good excuse to maintain troops in the countries of eastern Europe which lay in between the Soviet Union and Germany-Austria. The Russians had shown determination to hold on to these countries which they "liberated" en route to the invasion of Germany. The Western allies felt strongly about these peoples not merely because of a general belief in free political processes but because they had gone to war in the beginning for the sake of Poland and Czechoslovakia, the victims of Hitler. These unhappy peoples had fallen out of Hitler's frying pan into Stalin's fire. The Russians obviously intended to stay, regardless of what they may have promised. They established puppet governments with increasing audacity. Some non-Communist politicians were at first tolerated in the governments of Poland, Hungary,

Czechoslovakia, Rumania, and Bulgaria. But in 1947 and 1948 these leaders were killed or forced to flee whenever they sought to play an independent role. The sad story of these victims of Communist intolerance soon appeared in books written by them in the free world. In 1948 the West was shocked by the apparent suicide, perhaps the murder, of the famous Czech leader, Jan Masaryk, amid a *coup d'état* which ended all independence in that symbol of the war against Hitler. Stalin had coolly picked up all the chips, at the cost of liberty in half of Europe.

This zone of states in eastern Europe the Russians thought of as a security cordon, or their just reward for fighting the Germans. In other areas they let go when opposition was firm enough. Energetic protests caused them to withdraw from Iran after they had overstayed their treaty rights. They put pressure on Greece and Turkey, but when these states received extensive American aid under the so-called "Truman Doctrine" of 1947, the Russians did no more than protest. They were defied in 1948 by the able independent Communist leader of Yugoslavia, the partisan hero Marshal Tito, who resented being dictated to from Moscow and was a strong enough national figure to risk talking back to the Kremlin. Though launching threats and boycotts, the U.S.S.R. did not make war on the spunky Yugoslavs. They also showed respect for Finland's independence when party influence flagged.

But in the nominally independent states of Poland, Czechoslovakia, Rumania, Bulgaria, and Hungary the Russians set about doing what the West construed as cynically imposing Communism by force, against the will of the peoples, and thus converting them into puppet states, agents of Soviet imperialism. The Soviet leaders certainly did not see it this way. They naturally thought that extending their way of life was conferring a great benefit on these peoples, liberating them from "capitalism"; and they also believed that control of this zone was necessary to their future security, in order to see to it that never again would a murderous war be launched from Europe against Russia. Finally, they thought it reasonable that the Western powers not intervene in the natural Russian sphere of influence, since Russia did not intervene in theirs. It is true that Communist parties in the democracies did not try to foment revolution right after the war.

In fact, the Western powers did no more than protest about the situation in East Europe. The Hungarian uprising of 1956, crushed by the Russians, revealed dramatically that the West would not intervene forcibly to free the Soviet satellites. But Soviet tactics here deeply alarmed and alienated the West, while Western protests, recriminations and welcoming of refugees angered the Soviets. Thus did the cold war grow.

First Berlin crisis

Germany, the divided and occupied enemy, was a more serious bone of contention, because here the confrontation was direct. Most especially was this true in the city of Berlin. The German capital city had been placed under the joint administration of all four of the occupying powers. It lay surrounded by the Russian zone of occupation. The Russians were therefore in a position to put pressure on it by cutting off supply routes. As cooperation between the occupying powers in Germany broke down, Stalin attempted to force the other powers out of the German city in 1948. Using an airlift to bring supplies into Berlin and showing a determination to fight rather than surrender their position, the Western powers held on and the Russians finally dropped their harassments. Berlin then became divided into two hostile halves like the rest of Germany. By this time, Britain, France, and the United States were proceeding with plans to merge their own zones and set up a German government in the western half of the country. Soon there were two Germanies, one bound to the West and one to the East. It was the symbolic and most dangerous point of cold war conflict, and long remained so.

Containment

Western policy-makers gained the impression in 1947 and 1948 that the Communists would take all that they could get, regardless of promises; that they looked toward the communizing of the world and had no intention of sharing it with any "decadent democracies" or "capitalistic imperialists," words which embraced the world of western Europe and the United States; but that they would usually retreat if confronted with determination backed by force. They were tough, resourceful, and unscrupulous foes, eaten by a fierce hatred of the democracies. But their Marxist ideology assured them that time was on their side. Marxists worshipped the god of historical inevitability, and fervently believed in the final triumph of Communism as a kind of apocalytical ending to the long saga of the human race. Their international manners were the worst possible, but they did not think in terms of launching major wars. The logical policy for the West was to "contain" them with armed strength and with policies designed to prevent the economic and political breakdown on which Communism thrived and which it confidently predicted.

NATO

The Truman Doctrine and the Marshall Plan brought American aid back to Europe on a massive scale, and in general the Americans, gradually awakening to their inevitable responsibilities as leader of the free world, began to break ancient traditions and move toward a world political role. In 1949 they proposed the North Atlantic Treaty, an alliance between the United States and much of non-Communist Europe. In 1948 Belgium, Britain, France, the Netherlands and Luxembourg had signed the Treaty of Brussels, forming a military alliance; this, along with the 16 nations of Europe associated with the United States under the Marshall Plan in an organization for economic cooperation (OEEC), proved to be the nucleus of NATO, the North Atlantic Treaty Organization. Initially the NATO countries were Great Britain, Belgium, France, Netherlands, Italy, Luxembourg, Iceland, Denmark, Norway, Portugal, Canada, and the United States. It was later extended to include Greece, Turkey, and West Germany (Federal Republic of Germany). Thus it included all the non-Communist countries of Europe except Austria, Sweden, and Switzerland, along with Spain, which in time became a sort of *de facto* member. NATO was a military alliance pledging its members to mutual defense ("an armed attack against one or more . . . shall be considered an armed attack against them all"); it also became in many ways an integrated military force, with its own organization and staff. The United States returned to Europe with tens of thousands of troops and a vast military establishment. Thus was the United States at long last knit closely to the affairs of Europe. For their part the Soviets declared NATO to be an offensive alliance aimed at the destruction of the U.S.S.R. by the warmongers of Washington. In the next few years NATO moved forward to develop its own organization (at Paris) and the beginnings of an effective military establishment, under the hastening impact of the Korean War. General Dwight D. Eisenhower became its supreme commander in the crucial year of 1951, with Field Marshal Bernard Montgomery as his deputy; thus did the highest Allied military leaders of World War II again join forces to organize the defenses of free Europe against the threat of Soviet Communism. Within a few years a German general was to be one of NATO's principal commanders!

Revival of European morale

"Containment" worked in Europe, not only because of American aid but because, their morale restored by it, the peoples of Europe rallied in defense

of their freedom. Economic health was restored, confidence returned, and tension gradually eased in Europe. A momentarily ominous minority of Communist votes in France and Italy diminished with the restoration of prosperity. The common danger from the East united Europeans as nothing had done before; even the Franco-German feud thawed as Germans were admitted to NATO and became an integral part of the community of western Europe. There could be no chance of Soviet Communism subverting western Europe, nor conquering it except in a major war drawing in the United States. In this sense the Russian threat, if such it was, proved a tonic for western Europe.

The cold war in Asia

In the Far East events took a more discouraging trend from the Western democratic point of view. The West had nourished hopes of a strong and democratic China taking its place in the United Nations as one of the global policemen. Instead, a violently antiwestern Communist regime swept to power after the war. The West was inclined to see Communism as a single entity, a great global conspiracy against peace and freedom. Subsequent events were to reveal that the Chinese Communists and the Russians, though they carried the same label and paid obeisance to the same modern religion, were far from operating as a monolithic bloc. History might have suggested this; but in the atmosphere of the cold war it was not clear, and on any showing the rival and hostile world of Communism was growing much too strong for comfort.

The Chinese Communists, aided by the Russian presence in Manchuria to some extent but much more so by the corruption and unpopularity of the Nationalist regime of General Chiang Kai-shek, defeated the latter and gained power in China in 1949, as the United States shrank from the forbidding task of sustaining a free China along with a free Europe. In its official apologia the United States government declared that nothing could have been done to save the Nationalist regime. The triumph of the Chinese Reds was a direct result of World War II, which had brought grievous damage to China while consoling her with few of the sweets of victory, since the United States had clearly defeated Japan with little apparent aid from the Chinese. Then, all over East Asia, the sudden withdrawal of Japanese power in 1945 created conditions of anarchy—another "vacuum of power" resulting from the total defeat of the Axis enemy. This vacuum was far less successfully filled by Western strength.

The Korean War

The Communist challenge for Asia next appeared in Korea. In June of 1950 troops of the Russian Communist–dominated government of North Korea, in that unhappy country also, like Germany, left divided in two by the quarreling victors of World War II, crossed the boundary line of the 38th parallel in what the Western world construed as an act of military aggression. It had done little to secure the defenses of South Korea prior to this time. In the absence of the Soviet deputy on the United Nations Security Council, that body condemned the action and invited participation in collective resistance to it by all the members of the United Nations. The United States bore the chief burden, while Great Britain sent significant numbers of troops and more than a dozen others sent token forces. The Korean War alarmed Europe both at the possibility of general war and at the diversion of American strength to the Far East, away from Europe. Thus most Europeans rejoiced to see resistance to Communism but worried lest that resistance leave Europe open to attack, and they were not displeased with the eventual outcome, substantially a restoration of the *status quo*, after more than a year of terribly destructive war. During the Korean War, Red China intervened on the side of the North Koreans while the United States with its fleet protected the island of Formosa, whence Chiang Kai-shek had fled to set up his Nationalist government, still claiming to be the rightful government of China. So the outcome was further to envenom relations between China and the Western powers.

Indo-China

Events of the next few years were to cause doubts about the security of other parts of the Far East. As the Japanese withdrew, France attempted to reassert her control over Indo-China, rich in so many economic resources; Communists assumed leadership of the movement of nationalist liberation from French rule. The French took the region in 1873 with 180 men, and held it in 1885 with 500. Between 1946 and 1954 she could not hold it with 200,000 troops, and finally had to abandon a hopeless task—one which the United States was later to take up with similar results. Elsewhere, too, antiimperialist nationalism fell into the hands of Communists, or threatened to do so: Malaya, Burma, Indonesia. But this struggle was really an aspect, not of the cold war between Soviet Russia and the United States, each with its allies or satellites, but of the struggle for independence of peoples who wanted no part of adherence to any European system. It is best left for later treatment.

The easing of tensions and the progress of Europe

End of the Stalinist era

In March, 1953, Joseph Stalin died. The world paid tribute to a man who had swayed the affairs of the human race more perhaps than any individual in modern history; then it breathed a sigh of relief. The master of the Kremlin had become for most of Europe a symbol of tyranny and slavery. The next reaction was to wonder what the shape of post-Stalinist Russia would be like, and post-Stalinist world Communism. Would the passing of the patriarch-

Stalin's funeral in 1953. The pallbearers (from right to left), are Beria, Malenkov, Stalin's son Vasily, Molotov, Bulganin, Kaganovich, and Shvernik.

tyrant open an era of liberalizing trends, or would it precipitate a bloody struggle for power out of which might emerge either violent disintegration of the Soviet empire or a new tyrant? A June 17 revolt in East Germany indicated that there might be revolutionary possibilities at least in the satellite countries.

New Soviet leadership

It is not easy to relax a dictatorship. The successors of Stalin in the high circles of the Soviet Union may have had such ideas—in particular G. Malenkov, who at first seemed the man destined to supplant Stalin. A complicated struggle for power within the party ensued, involving the execution of longtime Stalinist secret-police aide, Beria, and the demotion of other Stalinist wheelhorses such as foreign minister Molotov; the subsequent elimination of Malenkov; and the emergence of N. Khrushchev as the ultimate Communist leader, not, however as another Stalin. Khrushchev sensationally denounced Stalin within three years of his death, calling him an inhuman tyrant. By this he seemed to mean not so much that Stalinism repressed popular freedom as that Stalin, personally, had made his lieutenants in the Soviet power hierarchy "dance the gopak." "Back to Lenin" was a motto which scarcely meant Western-style democracy, and the Soviet Communists needless to say did not propose to renounce Communism, with its hatreds and its drive to world revolutionary conquest. They only denounced Stalin's personal dictatorship. But the new Soviet leadership introduced some striking changes in the tactics if not the strategy of Soviet foreign policy. In particular there was a new approach to the "neutralist" nations of Asia and Africa, together with some effort to relax the iron hold on the European satellites. At home, the new Russian leadership moved slowly to thaw the glacier of Stalinist despotism, introducing small measures of freedom. It seemed to wish to divert funds from military to consumer-goods production, something demanded by a growingly articulate Russian public.

Within a few years observers were agreeing that Soviet Russia was successfully moving into a new phase, marked by less revolutionary fanaticism, somewhat more personal liberty, more economic and social stability, a cautious retreat from the more dogmatic features of Marxist ideology, more stress on internal economic progress toward a consumer economy, and a collective rather than personal political leadership. It had had to surmount more than one crisis. In 1956 the Hungarians rose up in revolt. They were mowed down by Russian tanks in the streets of Budapest as the West looked on impotently; but the episode was a jarring one to the Soviets, costing them immense international prestige and almost destroying what was left of the Communist party outside the Soviet world. Thereafter for some years the trend was toward greater autonomy for the satellites, within the framework of Communist rule but with a *de facto* liberalization. The bloc was still knit together economically and politically. It had its counterpart of the NATO pact and the Marshall Plan. But culturally the successors of Stalin insisted on less conformity in the satellites, where in the name of "national Communism"

A portion of the wall the Russians built in 1962 to divide Berlin

some criticism of the reigning party bigwigs occasionally appeared. In the Soviet zone as well as in the West, economic conditions improved and brought a softening of the political dictatorship.

Renewal of Berlin crisis

Fear of Russia gradually waned in Europe. The cold war did not altogether end. In 1958 and 1961 the Berlin situation flared up in new crises. Khrushchev saw this enclave of Western influence in the middle of East Germany as a "bone in his throat" which he exerted every diplomatic effort to remove. While the Federal Republic of Germany, the western two thirds of Germany, successfully rebuilt its economy and became a flourishing community, the Democratic Republic, or East Germany, the Soviet-dominated part, did much less well, and hundreds of thousands fled each year to the freer and wealthier West. This embarrassing flight of population occurred chiefly via the western half of the city of Berlin, and made urgent in Russian eyes its elimination. For a Europe divided uneasily into the two worlds of Soviet Communism and the Western democracies, Berlin was the sorest point of friction where the two worlds rubbed abrasively against each other. The men in the Kremlin saw it as a threat to their entire position in eastern Europe; the West would not yield its 2.5 million citizens to a Communism they abhorred, and believed them to be a vital part of the West German economy, which in turn was now a vital part of the economy of the free world. A long crisis in 1961 and 1962, which frightened the world with the specter of nuclear war between the United States and the Soviet Union, finally subsided when the Russians walled off the western part of Berlin from the east, checking the mass exodus from east zone to west. The serious crisis of October, 1962, connected with Russian delivery of missiles with nuclear warheads to the anti-American regime in Cuba on the American doorstep, which also threatened World War

Nuclear test explosion in 1946 before development of the more powerful hydrogen "device"

III, was perhaps a by-product of Berlin, in that Khrushchev hoped to use that as a bargaining point in getting rid of the Western presence in Berlin.

After 1962 the cold war thawed and relations between the two worlds improved, without eliminating rivalry and some serious issues. The German question remains unresolved, but competition between Communism and the West tended to shift to the non-European world and to involve less threat of war. "Peaceful coexistence," in the phrase of the colorful Khrushchev —by which he certainly meant something less than close friendship—has prevailed. The two blocs became less monolithic. Corresponding to the progress of "depolarization" in the Communist bloc, which included the sensational rift between Red China and the U.S.S.R. from 1961 on, was a loosening of NATO ties. The European members of NATO had been tightly bound to the United States through their weakness and their fear of Russia. As fear waned and strength returned, some of them began to be slightly less uncritical of their powerful transatlantic protector. France especially adopted an independent position and began to develop its own nuclear weapons. This situation was changed, and a renewal of cold war threatened when in the summer of 1968 Russian troops suddenly occupied Czechoslovakia to halt the liberalizing trend in that country.

Nuclear weapons and the balance of terror

The superpowers, the United States and the Soviet Union, possess the ability to destroy each other and perhaps the entire human race, a "balance of terror" which has induced caution in each. The United States developed the atomic bomb during World War II, successfully testing it on July 16, 1945, and using it to compel the surrender of Japan a few weeks later.[1] When a committee of distinguished atomic scientists petitioned the American government not to use the dread weapon, they pointed out that it could not possibly long remain an American monopoly. In 1949 the Russians exploded their first atomic device. By 1954 far more destructive nuclear explosives had been developed, and the two superpowers began a race to build long-range missiles capable of carrying their multimegaton loads of death halfway around the world and into each other's population centers. In any all-out war, neither side could possibly escape virtually total destruction from the air. Even to contemplate war on such terms was to will the suicide of the human race. The "balance of terror" virtually forced some sort of détente between the United States and the U.S.S.R. They had to agree at least on the obsolescence of total war.

---

1 The scientific knowledge on the basis of which it was built came largely from Europe. From British scientist Ernest Rutherford's experiment of 1919, in which he achieved atomic disintegration, to Austrian physicist Lise Meitner's theory of uranium fission in 1939, and so to the role played by refugee European scientists working, during World War II, in the United States, fundamental theoretical atomic science was largely European. In August, 1939, the famed scientist Albert Einstein, who had fled from German anti-Semitism to the United States, wrote a letter to President Roosevelt urging that work be begun on the superweapon. Other exiles from Nazi or Fascist Europe, among them the Italian Enrico Fermi and the Hungarian-born Leo Szilard, made basic contributions; the United States contributed some scientists and the advanced technological know-how needed to convert idea into reality.

Meanwhile much had been done to eliminate that "vacuum of power" that had existed in an exhausted and weakened Europe. The economic and political recovery of Europe seemed almost miraculous to those who had written her off as finished in 1946. After receiving massive injections of American aid in the late 1940's, western Europe made spectacular economic gains in the 1950's, experiencing a boom of impressive proportions. West Germany, a heap of smoking ruins in 1945, had once again become a thriving economy, perhaps the most bustling in the world; and another remarkable case of recovery was Italy. All of free Europe shared in the boom, and by comparison the "people's democracies" of Communist East Europe, supposedly proletarian paradises, seemed dingy and depressed, though there too there was spectacular reconstruction out of wartime ruins.

The European Economic Community

A milestone on the road to European recovery was the 1957 Treaty of Rome which created the European Common Market, an economic union of the six continental countries of France, West Germany, Italy, Belgium, the Netherlands, and Luxembourg. The shattering blows of World War II were enough to persuade even a hate-torn Continent that it must unite or perish. Europe was not only outpaced economically by the Soviet bloc and the United States, she was in danger of losing her independence. Just as the proud Greek cities of antiquity had perished at the hands of cruder but bigger Macedon and Rome, so the nation-states of Europe, once so large and powerful, were now dwarfed by the giants on the fringes of the Continent. Western Europe could indeed shelter behind the American shield against Communist Russia, and was glad to do so, but it was a humiliating experience and in the long run probably unworkable. The Americans urged union on them so that the United States might be relieved of some of the burden. The European states found that they were too poor to afford atomic power unless they joined forces. They had, in brief, no choice this time.

There were many landmarks on the road to integration, beginning in 1950 with the plan of French Minister Robert Schuman for a Coal and Steel Community, from which the next step was the establishment in 1955 of goals for the removal of all tariffs, quotas, and other obstacles to trade: a customs union, or "common market." In 1954, the cause received a setback when the idea of a European Defense Community foundered on the hostility of France to any sort of German rearmament and to the loss of complete French military sovereignty. But conditions changed; the Suez crisis of 1956 (discussed below) helped persuade France to seek a more European orientation. Euratom (joint atomic energy development) and the Common Market, or European Economic Community, came into being at the same time with the signing of the treaties in Rome March 25, 1957. It is a date that might some day become memorable in European history. Almost miraculous was the approval of the Common Market treaty by the French Assembly in July, followed quickly by Germany, Italy, and the BENELUX states (Belgium, Netherlands, and Luxembourg, which had earlier formed a customs union).

The Common Market treaty did not immediately abolish all duties on goods between the member countries, but set up a timetable of 12 years, or three 4-year periods; the Common Market would thus not be a full reality until 1970, but the knowledge that it would certainly come made everyone begin preparing for it. In 1962 and 1965 the Common Market passed crucial milestones with the achievement of agreements on agricultural policy, while Great Britain had made overtures toward joining. Britain had initially held aloof, pleading Commonwealth ties. But within four years of the Rome treaty, the success of the Six in their joint venture was so notable that she too began to move toward them. Unfortunately there were to be serious obstacles in the way of thus expanding the original Six.

Future of European union

Grave questions remained about the scope, extent, and nature of the European integration process. French President Charles de Gaulle, while vetoing British entrance into the Six for the time being, held firmly to a conviction that complete political unification should not follow economic cooperation, as many of the Europeanists believed—not at least for the time being. The French insisted that the sovereign national states were too solidly based to yield to any superstate and postulated a "Europe of the Fatherlands," a Europe of states bound together closely by agreements of many sorts, but basically a federation and not a European superstate. This involved de Gaulle in acrimonious quarrels with the "functionalists" who wanted to begin early handing over powers to a truly sovereign European superstate. Did France wish to dominate the others? Was nationalism indeed still too strong and deeply rooted in the ancient communities of Europe? What about other European countries, loosely grouped in a Free Trade Association but apparently willing to follow Great Britain into the Common Market? (Switzerland; the Scandinavian countries of Denmark, Norway, and Sweden; Austria, Portugal, Spain.) Was the Six an exclusive club, or could it be enlarged? And, assuming the Gaullist position, would it be possible in the long run to maintain economic integration while denying political integration? Despite these doubts the movement had great momentum and enlisted the idealism of Europe as well as serving its practical advantage. The Common Market was popular in all the member countries and other countries were clamoring to join it.

In this respect the terrible war had included some blessings in disguise. No one could have expected that within 15 years after Hitler's death France and Germany would have buried their ancient animosities and clasped hands in cordial friendship. (They did so in a treaty in 1963.) Technologically, destruction made possible renewal and modernization; European railroads, for example, having had to be rebuilt, became the best in the world. A technological revolution came to somnolent France, and Italy began to dig itself out of its perennial poverty. American capital, and American tourists, became interested in Europe as never before, and European exports to the United States zoomed. The whole miracle was expressed succinctly by the French

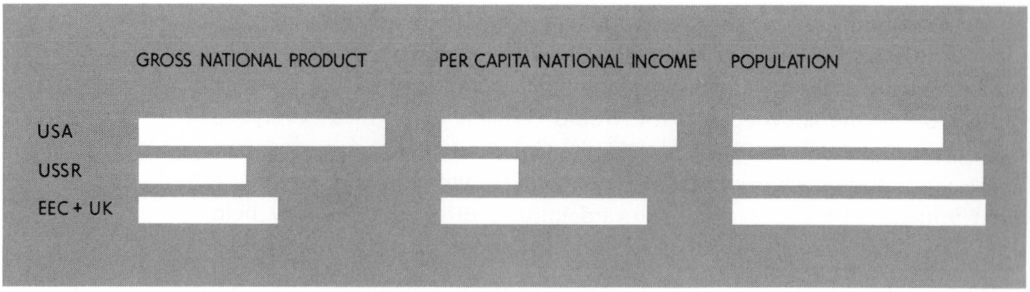

GROSS NATIONAL PRODUCT | PER CAPITA NATIONAL INCOME | POPULATION

USA

USSR

EEC + UK

Comparison of wealth and population of the United States, Russia, and the European Economic Community and United Kingdom, 1966

STEPS ON THE ROAD TO EUROPEAN UNITY, 1947–67

1947: Marshall plan proposed: American aid to Europe on condition that European countries cooperate economically.
Belgium, Netherlands, and Luxembourg form economic union (BENELUX).

1948: Organization for European Economic Cooperation (16 nations) established.
Treaty of Brussels: military alliance between Britain, France, and Benelux.

1949: North Atlantic Treaty signed; North Atlantic Treaty Organization (NATO) set up.

1951: European Coal and Steel Community treaty signed. Begins to operate, 1952. North Atlantic military headquarters (SHAPE) set up in Paris.

1954: European Defense Community treaties, drawn up in 1952 to create a joint European military force into which German units would be integrated, rejected by French Assembly. Western European Union treaties then approved. West Germany becomes member of NATO.

1957: France, West Germany, Italy, and BENELUX sign Treaty of Rome creating the European Economic Community (EEC); also treaty creating European Atomic Energy Community (EURATOM). Treaties go into effect January 1, 1958.

1960: EEC accelerates timetable for establishing the Common Market.

1962: First phase of common agricultural policy takes effect. Several nations including Great Britain seek membership or association with EEC.

1963: Negotiations for British membership in EEC break down on French objections.
Treaty of alliance and friendship between France and Germany.

1965: Crisis in EEC over agricultural policy and powers of European Parliament. France boycotts EEC meetings for seven months.

1966: EEC resumes full functioning. EEC council agrees to complete removal of all tariffs between EEC nations, and common farm policy, by July 1, 1968.

1967: British approach to EEC again rebuffed by France.
France withdraws from unified military aspects of NATO.

commentator Raymond Aron, writing in 1963: "In 1945, western Europe was a mass of ruins; today it is one of the most prosperous regions of the world." There was hope that western Europe might prove economically and politically, if not militarily, as strong as the superpowers, Russia and the United States, and function as a friendly buffer between them, virtually a "third force."

At the end of the 1960's there were some doubts. Commentators in France and Britain pointed to increasing dependence on the United States technologically, and an alarming invasion by American capital, a trend which if not halted would soon vest majority control of much of European industry in American hands. The pace of economic advance had apparently slowed, and the international monetary crisis of 1967–68, which forced Great Britain to devaluate her currency in the fall of 1967, produced a feeling of impending crisis in the world economy. These were complex questions involving the American economy and balance of payments as well as the need to devise some permanently effective medium of international exchange. It could scarcely be doubted that the economy of the western European countries was part of a highly complicated global structure and could be affected by everything from the Vietnam war to the American political situation. But in this world economy Europe's role was now a major one.

Political trends in European countries

The internal politics of the various European nations since 1945 showed a trend toward conservatism. Immediately after the war, it was leftward: the Labour party beat Mr. Churchill's party in 1945, the Communists had gained adherents during the war especially in France and Italy (where they stood forth as among the most dedicated foes of fascism), and the Christian Democrats or Christian Socialists had emerged as a strong force of the moderate left on the Continent. This war, like the last one, had encouraged a kind of apocalyptic fervor for some expected utopia of social justice, a mood which favored the left. And once again the war experience had brought a degree of statism which made socialist principles seem quite acceptable. "Full Employment" and "Fair Shares" were the mottoes of the day in Great Britain, where the Labour government's nationalization of basic industries (coal, railways, utilities, Bank of England) hardly surprised a people accustomed to government direction by the war.

British postwar politics

The Labour government in Britain proceeded to try to carry out an ambitious "welfare state" program, including socialized medicine, expanded educational opportunities, and increased welfare payments, under conditions of basic economic difficulty for Britain, reflected in a balance of payments deficit in her foreign trade. Most of these measures were not undone by the Conservative government which entered in 1951 upon a long season of power. Labour declined in the 1950's, torn by a struggle between left wing and right which reflected a crisis in its position. Its cure-all of nationalization was bankrupt and obsolete. When the Labour party returned to office in 1964, it was under the moderate, realistic leadership of Prime Minister Harold Wilson, pursuing policies very little different from those of the rival Tories. The latter had fully accepted the need for the state to guide the economy, not by ending private capitalism and assuming ownership by the state, but by a variety of indirect controls designed to channel the free enterprise order in the right direction and keep it from stagnating. Thus the distance between the parties had narrowed and the fierce ideological quarrels of the 1930's had somewhat receded.

Frustrations of the Fourth Republic

In France, as in England, the immediate postwar trend was leftward: a coalition of Communists, Socialists, and Christian Socialists (the MRP, or Popular Republican Movement), over which for a time General de Gaulle presided, experienced a brief honeymoon during which banks, utilities, insurance companies, and an automobile concern were nationalized, in accordance with state socialist dogma. This combination soon broke up, however, and the left declined, the Socialists and Christian Socialists very much so. The Communists maintained their strength but were isolated from other parties by the cold war. With five million Frenchmen voting Communist, a right-wing coalition emerged and won the premiership in 1952. Incessant government changes aided the growth of de Gaulle's position, which demanded drastic strengthening of the executive power. As so often before in French politics, governments rested on fleeting and uncertain coalitions. The dwindling Socialist party, MRP Christian Socialist (itself prone to internal feuds), the old Radical Socialists, and smaller splinter groups experimented in various cabinet combinations without ever finding a strong one. Whenever there was need for a major national decision, such weak governments, forced to propitiate every sort of minority interest in order to survive, could not make it. Brilliant leaders such as the glamorous Pierre Mendès-France found that a commanding presence and a will to act were sure recipes for parliamentary disaster.

After liquidating France's ruinous involvement in Indo-China, Mendès-France fell early in 1955 on the issue of North Africa, that is, the question of the relationship between France and Algeria and Tunisia. Rising Arab nationalism demanded an end to colonialism, but several million Frenchmen lived here, and the region possessed the highest strategic military importance in French thinking. Algeria had become a French Ireland, and was destined to cause immense anguish before the terms of its independence were finally arranged in 1962 amid the violent resistance of the embittered French settlers.

Charles de Gaulle and the Fifth Republic

The great decisions that faced France at the end of the 1950's included Algeria and the Common Market. There was the further thought that unless France found strong leadership she would be eclipsed within NATO and Europe by the Germans. Charles de Gaulle was the one personality who could provide such leadership, and for many years he had been building a

Charles de Gaulle, president of France's Fifth Republic

movement of this sort. In 1958, the Fourth French Republic, established right after the war, gave way to the Fifth, representing a transfer of power from the elected legislature to the President, General Charles de Gaulle, who had persuaded a majority of the French people that only his authoritarian leadership could save the nation he so ardently loved and had so well served. It had appeared to more and more Frenchmen that the old political system of democratic parliamentary government was unable to deal with all the problems France faced.

"Gaullism" rested on the gloomy view that democratic parliamentary government could not work in France, because of the deep divisions within it; but also on the hopeful opinion that underneath these divisions there existed a national will which would rally to the symbol of a strong executive. No dictatorship, de Gaulle's republic was distinctly authoritarian, depositing most power in the President rather than the assembly: a reversion almost to the regime of Louis Napoleon, in many ways. The president appoints the prime minister, whereas in parliamentary systems the prime minister and cabinet must have the approval of the parliament or assembly. The president may also legally assume dictatorial powers in time of national emergency (Article 34). Resting heavily on the personal prestige of the distinguished symbol of the French national will to fight in World War II, the Fifth Republic might not survive de Gaulle, many observers felt. But it served the purpose of strengthening the government to deal vigorously with grave national emergencies such as the Algerian war and France's role in the new Europe.

France flourished under de Gaulle. The General began by effectively and courageously liquidating the Algerian problem, giving Algeria independence.

His foreign policy of opposing the American dominance of Europe, equally as much as the Russian, might not be realistic but it was popular. He spoke up in mighty accents for France and for historic Europe, though he may have sometimes confused the two; and within France there was rapid economic growth. A flexible and nondogmatic realism might be said to mark most of the Gaullist policies. Gaullism claimed to stand above the parties and the ideologies. In 1965 President de Gaulle was reelected for a second 7-year presidential term, by popular vote, with a reduced margin; then in the 1967 elections to the National Assembly the various foes of Gaullism managed a marriage of convenience and their electoral union almost won a majority. In the spring of 1968 serious riots and strikes shook France, but elections held after this sensational event resulted in a victory for the Gaullists. After 10 controversial years of vigorous rule, de Gaulle had certainly lost ground, but his foes remained very much divided at bottom and no alternative government seemed conceivable. What would happen when the aging hero left remained an open question. But it appeared likely that Gaullism was a watershed beyond which France would never return to the old parties and ideologies.

Germany under Adenauer

In the Federal Republic of Germany—West Germany, with its capital at Bonn on the Rhine—the grand old man of Europe ruled for many years after the war at the head of a coalition chiefly dominated by the Christian Democrats, and steered Germany to her spectacular recovery with the aid of economic policies stressing classical free competition and private enterprise.

John F. Kennedy and Konrad Adenauer—the American President and the German Chancellor meet at the White House, April, 1961.

Konrad Adenaur, *Der Alte*, emerged as Germany's chief political personality soon after the establishment of the Bonn regime in 1949, and remained as Chancellor thereafter for the next 14 years. The opposition to Adenauer's party came from the Socialists, or Social Democrats as they had long been known in Germany; but this strong party, while dominating some of the local states or *Länder* (including West Berlin since 1953) produced no personality or program able to defeat Adenauer nationally, until finally in 1961 he suffered a considerable decline in his electoral majority. Like British Labour, the S.P.D. recanted and abandoned its "socialism" to become not significantly different on basic principles from its rivals. (See its 1959 Godesberg platform.) The situation in West Germany, living along side the Communist tyranny which enslaved the eastern part of the divided country, enhanced the role of foreign policy, as well as telling against any ideology smacking of Communism. Adenauer's Germany by no means did without welfare-state measures, but under the able guidance of economic minister Ludwig Erhard it administered large doses of old-fashioned capitalism to the German economy —and got rich doing so. At the same time, in the realm of foreign policy, Germany advanced from pariah nation to a trusted member of the NATO alliance under Adenauer.

Erhard replaced Adenauer as Chancellor in 1963, to be replaced in turn in 1966 by a grand coalition embracing Social Democrats as well as Christian Democrats and Free Democrats, the rightist party. The death of Adenauer in 1967 brought statesmen from all over the world to the funeral of the remarkable man who at the age of 70 began his leadership of postwar Germany and led it back from the ashes of defeat and disgrace. He had dedicated himself to democracy and to the Western alliance, but had hoped for eventual reunification of his partitioned country. He had clasped hands with France and led Germany into the European community. He had not seen the hoped-for reunification of his country, but had watched the Federal Republic become economically prosperous, politically stable, at peace with the world and gaining back the respect forfeited during the Nazi years.

The end of ideology

The politics of Western Europe in the postwar generation showed a tendency to depart from the old ideologies and move toward what might be called a realistic conservatism. This was quite often sophisticated and effective. There was no reversal, on the whole, of that "mighty invasion of government into economic life" which, it has often been noted, forms "one of the most fundamental contrasts between the 20th century and the 19th." The *dirigiste* state, directing and supervising the private sector (consisting, for the most part, of great corporations themselves heavily bureaucratized), assumed great power; within the state apparatus, the administrative bureaucracy of the government absorbed power at the expense of the legislative body. This was almost as true of Britain, where Parliament remained formally supreme, as of Gaullist France, where a powerful executive cut the parliament down to a lesser role. At the same time voters grew more sophisticated in that they less often followed a basic philosophical commitment to one party—whether ideological socialism or conservatism—and more often judged a government and its candidates by how practically effective it was. Some British Tories backed Labourite Wilson because he was a good administrator and skilled politician in dealing with specific issues; German socialists supported conservative (one-time Nazi) Kiesinger (Erhard's successor); Frenchmen of all hues voted for de Gaulle. (The General even appealed to some leftists by his policy of friendship with the Soviet Union.)

Economic "planning" was widely assumed necessary, even in Germany and the United States. It was less centralized in Britain than in France, for historic reasons. Its "style" varied from country to country; nowhere was it as dogmatic and omnipotent as in the Communist countries; but neither did anyone any longer suppose that economic systems regulate themselves by the automatic operation of natural law.

If this entailed an "end of ideology," and sometimes a consequent loss of interest in politics, it also meant the exploration of fresh horizons, and a greater degree of expertise in economic and social policy. In solving their economic problems many European countries showed intelligence and ingenuity. In terms of traditional schools, perhaps this was closest to Saint-Simon's dream of a socialist society run by an elite of experts and "technocrats." The world had grown too complex to be run in the old negative way.

Decline of Communism

With economic prosperity and political stability the appeal of Communism in free Europe went down. In Italy, possessor of the largest Communist party of free Europe, the decline was slight; in France it was considerable. In no other countries outside the Soviet zone except neighboring Finland and tiny Iceland was the percentage of legal Communist voters more than a tiny one (4.5 percent in Sweden being the largest); in countries where the party was illegal, only Greece had a significant movement. The denunciation and exposure of Stalin by his successors in the Kremlin, along with the brutal crushing of Hungarian independence in 1956, took its toll. One could hardly say that Communism had ceased to be a problem to the free nations of Europe but it seemed to be diminishing. It remained true that in France and Italy the Communists had dug deep roots in the working class and had a degree of respectability among the intellectuals not found elsewhere; yet by and large it seemed that, in Raymond Aron's words, "the end of the socialist myth" might be at hand.

Student riots in 1967 and 1968 suggested that the technocratic state and the end of ideology left a vacuum in the restless souls of young people which might be filled by all sorts of apocalyptic and revolutionary urges. The pluralist and affluent society produced its own discontents; pragmatism left no room for heroic ideals. Muddled as they seemed to be, the New Left's destructive cadres protested against materialism and bureaucracy, political quietude and careerism. They usually repudiated Soviet Russian Communism as strenuously, and for the same reasons, as they rejected their own technocratic society. They too accepted the "end of ideology" and strove for a political movement that would be utterly spontaneous and, apparently, without formal creed.

Parliamentary democracy

Had parliamentary democracy on the 19th-century model also outlived its day? We have already referred to Gaullism in France and to a general tendency for the administrative bureaucracy—an appointive elite of experts—to take over more power. Needless to say, parliamentary government had not revived in Franco's Spain, and it did not exist in the Soviet orbit; in 1967 a military *coup d'état* dismissed parliament and established dictatorial government in Greece. In the world of newly independent African and Asian states (see further below), the effort to install Western-style political institutions failed more often than it succeeded and parliamentary government seldom survived. Parliamentary institutions were uniquely strong in Great Britain and her offshoots, but even in Britain many complained that Parliament counted for less than it once did. Representative government was nonetheless taken for granted in most of western Europe. Even de Gaulle did not dream of doing without a legislature or defying constitutional rules. Civil liberties, the rule of law, constitutional government were safe enough in the major nations of western Europe. Was a recurrence of Nazism possible in Germany? Few careful observers thought so. Fascism was as much a casualty of history in the West as Communism or old-fashioned liberalism and socialism.

The quality of civilization

The democracies of western Europe found many tasks awaiting them as they sought to improve the quality of life for their people. Higher education was just beginning to move toward a mass phase, wherein the many and not just a few might have the advantage of studying at one of the traditionally excellent, but highly restricted, European universities. To keep up with the United States and Russia in industrial technology was a constant and difficult challenge. Highway construction had not kept apace with the swelling automobile population. The major countries had not yet succeeded in adequately housing everyone. Critics of General de Gaulle's nuclear armaments and space probe programs asked whether France could afford all this and social welfare too, implicitly endorsing a policy of giving up all attempts to compete with the superpowers in military power while concentrating on building a *quality* civilization in which all might live with dignity, culture, and beauty. Perhaps this would indeed be western Europe's future role in the world.

Soviet Russia

The success or failure of the above hopes might rest on the future of Russia. President de Gaulle, making overtures toward Moscow which sometimes drew frowns from Washington, invoked the vision of cultural Europe extending as far east as the Urals. If this were true, Europe's grand future would be assured. But ever since 1918 the men in the Kremlin had not seen it this way. They had declared war in the name of the "proletariat" on all the historic governments of Europe, and believed that the good society would never exist until Communist revolution had overthrown and completely destroyed them. The alliance of World War II against Germany had proved to be highly temporary, for the postwar era indicated that the two worlds could never mix and seldom agree. For its part the West tended to see Soviet Communism as a sinister conspiracy against the freedom of man, and its leaders as power-hungry and unscrupulous tyrants. In 1949, at the peak of cold war hysteria, American Ambassador to the United Nations Warren Austin listed the following:

> The depredation of Manchuria, the forced partition of Korea, guerrilla warfare waged against Greece, the threats to Turkey, the obliteration of freedom in Czechoslovakia, the ruthless destruction of all democratic opposition in Bulgaria, Hungary, and Rumania . . . the subjugation of Poland . . . all these are power-grabbing actions by the Soviet Union that peaceful words cannot hide.

The iron curtain

It was Winston Churchill who spoke of an "iron curtain" that had descended across Europe. In return, the U.S.S.R. denounced the NATO alliance as "by no means required for self-defense, but for the realization of the policy of aggression, for effecting the policy of unleashing a new war . . . to establish by force Anglo-American dominion over the world." There seems no reason to doubt the sincerity of either side. Each was inclined to irritate the other by self-righteous assumptions of having all virtue on its side. And they expressed the utmost abhorrence of each other's ideologies and systems, the Communists believing with a fervent faith that Western "capitalism" was depraved, decadent, and degenerate, impoverishing its exploited masses while it plotted wars of aggression to hide its shame.

The progress of Russian society and policy toward something more relaxed and normal doubtless owed something to the death of Stalin, but it was helped by a process of recovery that removed some of the grimness from Russian life. The Soviet leaders had undoubtedly feared the West, as much as it feared them, for it possessed atomic weapons and surrounded the U.S.S.R. with a powerful network of NATO and American bomber and missile strength. Soviet confidence, coming with their development of nuclear missile power, made for less nervousness. At the same time an inevitable second-generation effect cooled the fanatical ideological ardor of the revolution. Russian citizens yearned, as the French had done after their great revolution, for the fruits of the revolution without the strain of it.

Changes in Russian society

Brutal repression of the 1956 revolt in Hungary convinced many in the West that the Soviet regime had lost none of its repressive features. But in most of the satellites the next few years brought some slight liberalization. Meanwhile Russia-watchers believe that Soviet society is in progress toward something more "normal." "Bourgeois" materialism seems to be in evidence, in a society that is very definitely *not* "classless," with people asking for more comforts and less propaganda. Legal institutions and procedures afford more adequate safeguards and are less prone to interruption by "political" pressures; some relaxation of the iron censorship on thought and literature has occurred; contact with the outer world has increased. A middle class has grown up, reluctant though dogmatic Marxists would be to admit such a horror; and a technological elite, in the opinion of some experts on Soviet society, is gaining power at the expense of the old revolutionists. Stalin's slave labor camps were liquidated, and political arrest became less common.

In 1958 the Russians decided to decentralize their economic planning in a way that suggested possible evolution toward a more capitalistic type of economy. There remained serious problems of administering the cumbersome apparatus of the totally planned economy. A part of the Soviet riddle is that Russia can take the lead in space exploration yet cannot supply good automobiles to its citizens, can build intercontinental missiles yet possesses hospital equipment or gadgets of everyday life still much inferior to any country of western Europe or the United States. Pride in sending the first man beyond the earth's atmosphere, as the U.S.S.R. did in 1961, following the first "Sputnik" orbit of 1958, may be less comforting to the average Russian citizen than adequate transportation, lighting, refrigeration, and other home comforts. It is likely that the Soviet bosses will be under increasing pressure to deliver these consumer products.

The "thaw" in the world of Russian Communism made it possible for the first time in many years to publish literature and thought in Russia critical of the Soviet system. The theme of Dudinstev's popular *Not by Bread Alone* (1956) was roughly that "once a man has learnt to think nobody can stop him," that the overorganized and repressive machine can be beaten by courageous defenders of human values. Such unprecedentedly bold criticism was occasionally still censored but appeared to be the trend. Meanwhile non-Marxist Western philosophers and scholars were permitted to lecture in Russia and the country was opened to foreign visitors; the iron curtain had developed at least a crack or two. Among the leading factors working for liberalization of the Soviet totalitarian order was the awakening of a significant public opinion, a genuine power to which the rulers were forced at least in some degree to bow. The new leaders, such as Kosygin and Brezhnev who replaced the ebullient Khrushchev in the top echelons of Soviet power in the 1960's, seemed more like bureaucrats or business managers, more interested in the efficiency of Soviet production than in revolutionary adventures.

On the 20th anniversary of the murder of Jan Masaryk and the enslavement of Czechoslovakia to Communism, the Czechs forced the resignation of their pro-Russian President and proclaimed such heresies as democratic elections and the existence of an opposition party. The monolithic unity of world Communism, organized by the Comintern, was threatened. The Russians marched troops into Czechoslovakia disillusioning many who had thought Stalin's days gone forever. Yet in fact the Communist world lacked unity; most Communist parties in the West quickly denounced Moscow's action in strong terms.

Occupation of Prague by the Soviet Army, August 22, 1968

The Sino-Soviet quarrel

Proof of this disunity could be found in the acrimonious dispute which broke out in 1960 between Red China and the Soviet Union. To the former, the Soviet chiefs were guilty of the most heinous of crimes, betraying the world Communist revolution, because they had lost their zeal and grown complacently cautious. What infuriated Mao Tse-tung and his Chinese Communists most was the Russian willingness to embrace "peaceful coexistence" with the United States. The Chinese were disappointed in 1958 when Khrushchev failed to back them up in their challenge to the U.S.-supported Chinese Nationalist regime on Taiwan (the Formosa Straits crisis), furious when he visited the United States in 1959 to hobnob with President Eisenhower, and disgusted with his doctrines that war and violence are obsolete as methods of attaining Communist goals. They accused Khrushchev of cowardice when he backed away from the Cuban crisis. They declared that the Soviet Union under his leadership had become nothing more than a bourgeois capitalist state! When Khrushchev's successors in the Kremlin showed no signs of reversing his policies, the Soviet-Chinese estrangement became extreme and the world looked—on the whole delightedly—at the spectacle of the two great Communist centers feuding with each other more venomously than with the capitalistic enemy. Clearly there was this much truth in the charges of the Mao circle: Russia indeed preferred not to risk war, because she was becoming a "have" rather than a "have-not" nation, because she knew quite well that nuclear war with the United States would destroy her massive industries built at such great cost, and because she felt on the verge of a new era in which the fruits of industrialism would finally become available to the common man.

Communist polycentrism

The unseemly squabble between Moscow and Peking aided the process of depolarization in the Communist world. The European satellites seized the opportunity to assert a degree of independence. While little Albania sided with China, and Tito's Yugoslavia denounced the Chinese, Rumania attempted to arbitrate and others rejoiced in the chance to play a role other than that of helpless puppet of Moscow's will.

Communist parties in the West began to do strange things: the strong Italian party entered into a dialogue with the Catholic church. Disturbed adolescents on college campuses no longer rallied to Moscow's side but sought confusedly to dissociate their rebellious instincts from it, perhaps glorifying Cuba's Castro or China's Mao (themselves involved in a quarrel, though both disliked Russia), but more often turning to a kind of desperate nihilism of the left.

Some people, however, were *too* prepared to certify the ex-Bolsheviks as respectable bourgeoisie or even democratic believers in all the liberties. "Peaceful coexistence" no more means capitulation to Western values than "collective leadership" in the party means parliamentary democracy. Ruling out direct confrontations with the United States as too dangerous, Soviet policy has concentrated all the more on the weapons of propaganda and diplomacy. Communist dogma may be weakening but it is not dead in the U.S.S.R. There is no indication that the masters of the Kremlin have resigned their worldwide ambitions, or that they regard the Western "capitalist" states as anything other than their irreconcilable rivals in a struggle for world power. Within the U.S.S.R., only one political party is tolerated and nothing like real freedom of expression exists; that would be in flat contradiction to the Marxist-Leninist credo which teaches that politics is class war wherein the bourgeois enemy must never be given an advantage. In the later 1960's the party evidently took fright at an excess of freedom and began to prosecute writers for "revisionism." It destroyed Czechoslovakian autonomy.

Khrushchev, Mao Tse-tung, and Ho Chi-minh in Peiping, celebrating the 10th anniversary of the Communist government in China, October 1959

In its war for the world with the class enemy, Soviet policy has turned increasingly toward the Asian and African countries, proclaiming Communism as the friend of national independence and the enemy of imperialism, hoping and expecting that these new nations, so frequently poverty-stricken and revolutionary, would join the Communist side. Communist rebels, with aid from China, succeeded in destroying French control of northern Indo-China in 1954, as her allies gave France little help. In the 1950's Communists held posts of high influence in the Indonesian government, they waged guerrilla war in Malaya, and they seemed to have good opportunities in India, Burma, and other Asian countries. In Africa and the Middle East, the Egyptian revolution of 1952 brought to power a radically socialist and anti-Western regime, and indeed the whole colonial world swarmed with seemingly good Communist prospects. Orthodox Marxist-Leninist theory taught that the route to the destruction of the major capitalist states ran through their colonies, whose blood they sucked like vampires to keep themselves alive: take away this nourishment and the European bourgeoisie would die. So the Russians looked with high interest and expectation of vast rewards at the great process of liquidating imperialism which went on so rapidly in the 1950's. They were destined to much disappointment. In their dealings with the "Third World" the Soviet leaders could soon count a ghastly catalog of errors; they lavished billions of dollars on leaders who fell, leaving the Russians holding the bag, or who proved to be expensive encumbrances, or who turned ungratefully against their benefactor. For the *jeunes états*, as the French call them, were not of a mind to be towed in anyone's wake.

Europe and the outer world: The dissolution of colonialism

The neutralist nations

In 1961 at Belgrade, Yugoslavia, the heads of state of 24 of the neutral or "uncommitted" nations of the world held a meeting. Apart from Yugoslavia, whose famed President Tito had the distinction of being a Communist who had defied the Kremlin and remained independent of it, most of these leaders represented Asian and African nations. The most distinguished of them in addition to Tito included India's patriarch, Jawaharlal Nehru, unquestioned spokesman for that vast, potentially powerful state; Egypt's Abdul Nasser, who aspired to the moral leadership of the Arab world; and "Kwame" Nkrumah of Ghana, one of the new black Africa's chief symbols. Large differences separated these varied peoples, but they felt unity both in wishing to extricate themselves from the vendetta of the nuclear-armed great powers and in seeing the world's great issue as something other than Communism versus capitalism or democracy. To the "imperialists" both Soviet and Western they cried "a plague on both your houses," as they announced the arrival of a new force in the world, the erstwhile exploited colonial colored peoples, to whom the most important issue was their own freedom, self-determination, and struggle to find a place in the sun while becoming mature national peoples. For Communism as such they cared little, though some of them were attracted by the Marxist ideology and all

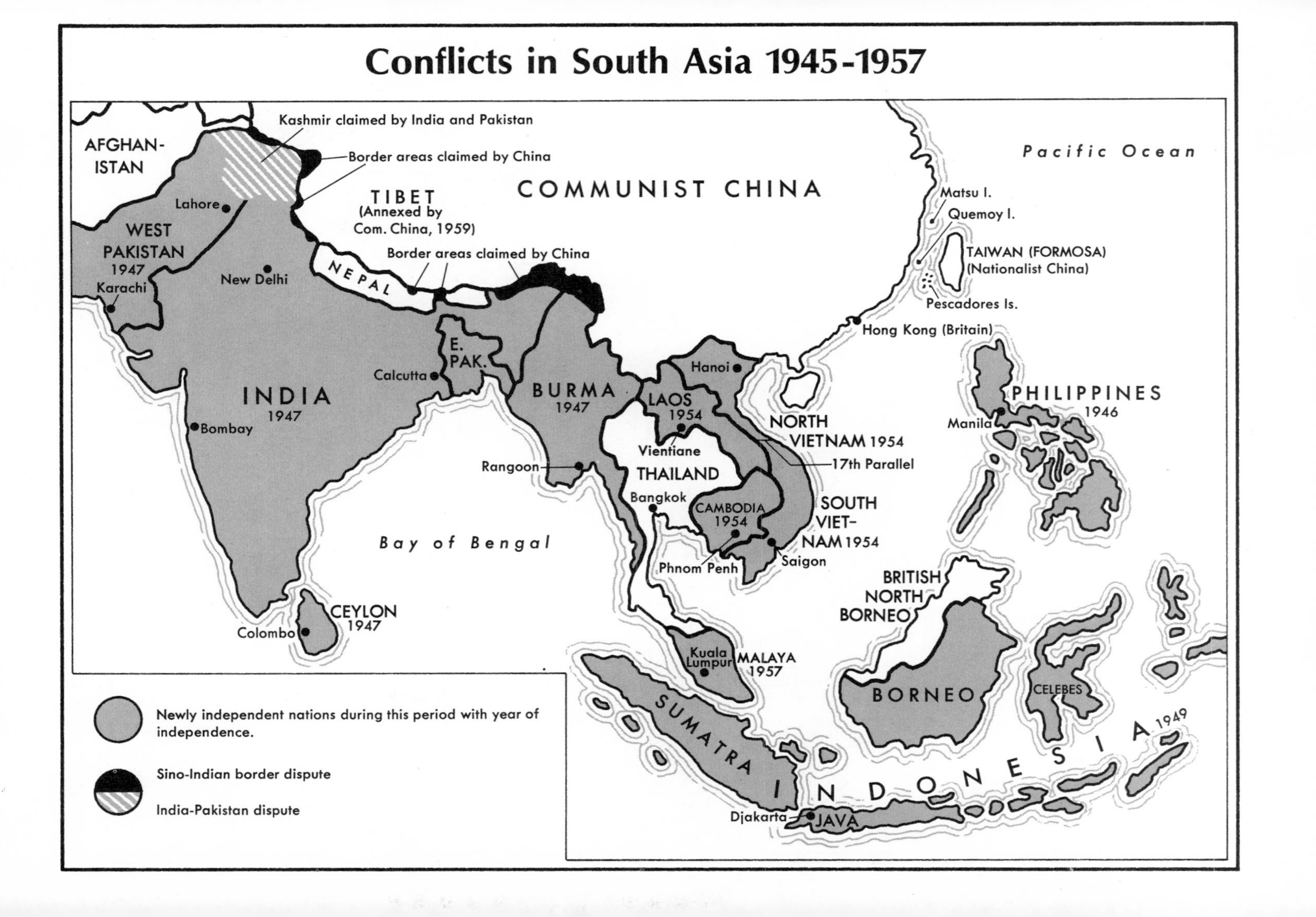
Conflicts in South Asia 1945-1957
AFGHAN-
ISTAN
Kashmir claimed by India and Pakistan
Border areas claimed by China
TIBET
(Annexed by
Com. China, 1959)
COMMUNIST CHINA
Pacific Ocean
Lahore
WEST
PAKISTAN
1947
Karachi
New Delhi
NEPAL
Border areas claimed by China
Matsu I.
Quemoy I.
TAIWAN (FORMOSA)
(Nationalist China)
Pescadores Is.
Hong Kong (Britain)
E.
PAK.
Calcutta
INDIA
1947
Bombay
BURMA
1947
Hanoi
LAOS
1954
Vientiane
NORTH
VIETNAM 1954
17th Parallel
PHILIPPINES
1946
Manila
Rangoon
THAILAND
Bangkok
CAMBODIA
1954
Phnom Penh
SOUTH
VIET-
NAM 1954
Saigon
Bay of Bengal
CEYLON
1947
Colombo
BRITISH
NORTH
BORNEO
Kuala
Lumpur
MALAYA
1957
BORNEO
CELEBES
SUMATRA
INDONESIA
1949
Djakarta
JAVA
Newly independent nations during this period with year of independence.
Sino-Indian border dispute
India-Pakistan dispute

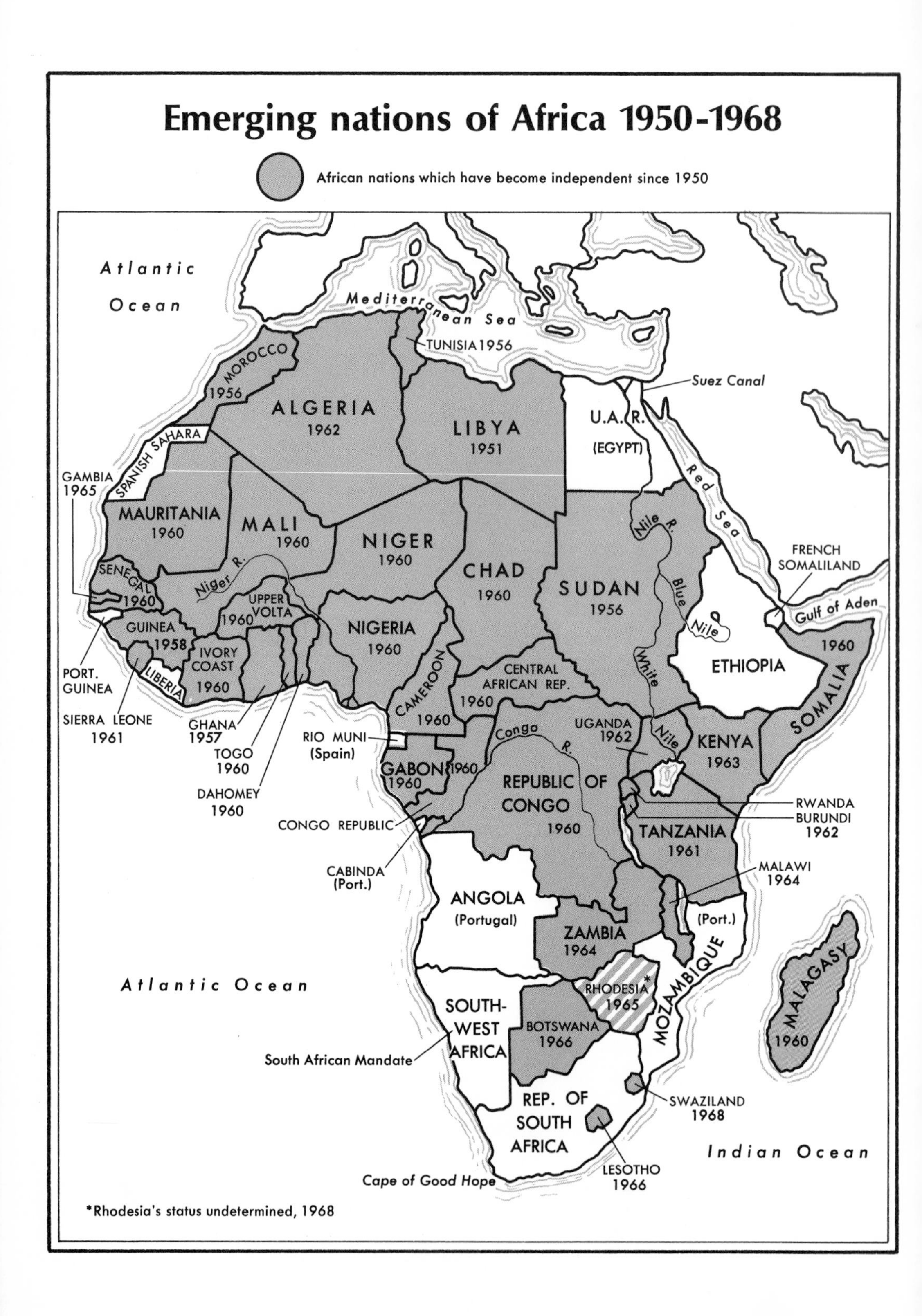
Emerging nations of Africa 1950-1968
African nations which have become independent since 1950
Atlantic Ocean
Mediterranean Sea
TUNISIA 1956
MOROCCO 1956
ALGERIA 1962
LIBYA 1951
U.A.R. (EGYPT)
Suez Canal
SPANISH SAHARA
GAMBIA 1965
MAURITANIA 1960
MALI 1960
NIGER 1960
CHAD 1960
SUDAN 1956
Red Sea
Nile R.
Blue Nile
White Nile
FRENCH SOMALILAND
Gulf of Aden
SENEGAL 1960
Niger R.
UPPER VOLTA 1960
GUINEA 1958
PORT. GUINEA
IVORY COAST 1960
LIBERIA
NIGERIA 1960
CAMEROON 1960
CENTRAL AFRICAN REP. 1960
ETHIOPIA
SOMALIA 1960
SIERRA LEONE 1961
GHANA 1957
TOGO 1960
DAHOMEY 1960
RIO MUNI (Spain)
GABON 1960
1960
Congo R.
UGANDA 1962
KENYA 1963
REPUBLIC OF CONGO 1960
RWANDA
BURUNDI 1962
CONGO REPUBLIC
TANZANIA 1961
CABINDA (Port.)
MALAWI 1964
ANGOLA (Portugal)
ZAMBIA 1964
(Port.)
MOZAMBIQUE
MALAGASY 1960
Atlantic Ocean
RHODESIA* 1965
SOUTH-WEST AFRICA
South African Mandate
BOTSWANA 1966
SWAZILAND 1968
REP. OF SOUTH AFRICA
Indian Ocean
LESOTHO 1966
Cape of Good Hope
*Rhodesia's status undetermined, 1968

Tito, Nehru, and Nasser at the meeting of neutralist nations in Belgrade, 1961

echoed its denunciations of "capitalistic imperialism." But for Western-style democracy they also showed meager enthusiasm, much as they talked about freedom and democracy: parliamentary institutions of the European variety usually did not work well as yet in these countries still struggling to achieve political stability and well-defined national unity. In any case they mistrusted the European states as their former or present imperialist "enslavers."

The retreat from empire

Six years later, Nehru was dead, Nasser was discredited, Nkrumah had been deposed, and others who had attended the 1961 congress, such as Algeria's Ben Bella, had also passed from the scene. This fact illustrates the instability of the Afro-Asian world. This was only to be expected. The vast process of "decolonization" has been one of the greatest of contemporary revolutions, and one necessarily marked by turbulence. In one year, 1960, no fewer than 17 African states were admitted to the United Nations; between 1955 and 1965, the total was twice that number. Except for Portugal, the European nations relinquished their African possessions and these became independent states. In Asia, the British had released India and Burma, the Dutch had somewhat reluctantly retired from the Indies, which now became Indonesia; the French attempted to hold Indo-China only to be defeated in 1954. Such was the story of the great retreat from empire. One of its final chapters contributed to the accession of the de Gaulle regime: the agony of Algeria forced France to turn to a government strong enough to take painful decisions and cut through the knot that bound France to a colony where several million Frenchmen lived.

The Commonwealth (British?)

The European powers did not give up their empires altogether willingly. It is true that the British showed more flexibility than did the French or Dutch, but this was because they entertained the illusion that the crown colonies were going to turn into members of the British Commonwealth, thus keeping at least some connection with the home country. The British cherished the noble ideal of a worldwide, multiracial Commonwealth, truly cooperative, where the white dominions of Australia, Canada, New Zealand, and South Africa would be joined by India and by the new African republics—a sort of little United Nations bound together by ties of sentiment and common political institutions. India, which got her independence in a momentous decision made by the postwar Labour government headed by Prime Minister Clement Attlee, joined the Commonwealth of Nations, but it has not meant much. The membership in the Commonwealth of Britain's former African possessions likewise in no way qualified their independence. Unlike the white dominions, these peoples felt little in the way of a sentimental attachment to the former governing power. Almost all of them chose not to honor the monarch of England as head of state but became separate republics, though members of what now ceased to be the British Commonwealth and became just The Commonwealth. The organization allowed some contact between the peoples but had trouble preserving its unity in the face of various conflicts; South Africa and Rhodesia quit entirely. In the 1960's the dream of any empire at all melted away, as Kipling, the poet of imperialism, had long ago foreseen:

> *Far called, our navies melt away,*
> *On dune and headland sinks the fire.*
> *Lo, all our pomp of yesterday*
> *Is one with Nineveh and Tyre!*

Some other dream than the imperial one would have to possess the soul of the British.

The British fought the "Mau-Mau" rebellion in Kenya and there was sporadic rioting elsewhere in her African possessions before they secured independence. The French, who also tempted their colonies with the idea of a "Community" between them and France, only to see most of them spurn the offer for outright independence, faced their greatest African ordeal in the bloody and protracted Algerian struggle, already referred to. Since about 1959 both France and Britain have accepted with good grace the independence of their African colonies and have given them economic aid and technical assistance, competing with Russia, the United States, and sometimes China in this bidding for favor. On the whole the vast process of decolonization went remarkably smoothly.

Postindependence headaches

Independence was sometimes the beginning of trouble. In Africa, the worst of the postindependence conflicts occurred in the erstwhile Belgian Congo—a bloody civil war which elicited the intervention of a United Nations peace force. Such troubles were due to a lack of political experience, to an economic situation that often worsened with the withdrawal of European control, and sometimes to boundaries that were improperly drawn. The meteoric rise and abrupt fall of Nkrumah in Ghana, leaving a country almost ruined by excessively ambitious and utterly unrealistic economic programs; the collapse of parliamentary government in country after country in favor of military dictatorship; tribal feuding in Nigeria leading to secession of part of the country and then civil war (1967); a general tendency to political demagoguery and exaggerated expectations from independence—such dismaying difficulties were counterbalanced by encouraging trends here and there. Awakening the morning after the celebration of independence, African peoples faced the sober realities of poverty, backwardness, and an absence of well-tried social and political institutions. They were receiving considerable aid from Europe, Russia and the United States, but in the last analysis they would have to build nations by their own efforts and this would necessarily be a work of time.

Europe's cultural influence

What interests the historian of Western civilization is the relationship, in a widening world, between these new peoples and the civilization of the West. That the world of power and civilization has broadened to include the peoples of Asia and Africa is obvious; they have entered into the consciousness of Europe, too, as never before. They changed the United Nations from a society dominated by Europe and North America to one filled mostly with the issues raised by the "new nations." Would they live on friendly terms with the European nations, and receive the influence of Western civilization as well as give something in return? Despite old grievances about colonialism, there were signs that Europe's cultural influence would indeed mean much to these peoples. If they rejected much they also borrowed much, sometimes unconsciously. The borrowings range from industrial technology through radio, movies, and television, to intellectual and cultural things. Africans moving rapidly from tribalism to an urban culture are creating that culture in the general image of the West's urban culture. Their education, press, and popular culture, as well as their buses, motor cycles, and phonographs, bear a Western imprint. Determined to be free from the West's political control, they wish to be included in its culture. Europe's influence on world civilization remains, even if the power of the European nations has declined. In the ex-colonial world of Asia and Africa today one often finds fierce denunciation of the wrongs and evils of "imperialism"—and at the same time a strong attachment to European intellectual and cultural influences. Indeed, the very language with which Asian or African leaders attack the West is derived from Western sources: the ideas of these men, who typically have received a Western education, come largely from liberal, socialist, and nationalist European ideologies. In Cambodia, Indo-China, and French Africa the war of liberation against France did not end French intellectual domination in the native universities and cultural influence among the ruling classes, any more than Indian independence has meant a discarding of British political institutions, language, and thought habits. For better or for worse, in liberty or dependence, these peoples have received the stamp of Europe and will not again be without it.

The mixture of old and new in these countries is often startling. The head of one of the African states, according to report, sacrificed a bull before he boarded an airplane, in order to insure his safety; some of the Arab countries display modern skyscrapers alongside of Bedouin tents. We are reminded of the mingling of the peoples, barbarian and otherwise, in the Roman Empire.

The mingling of peoples

Another feature of contemporary Europe is the extensive borrowing from the United States, in part a product of the occupation and American participation in Europe's defenses through NATO (several hundred thousand American troops have long lived in Europe from Scotland to Turkey), but more fundamentally, one suspects, the result of a long cultural process. Having long since learned to watch American movies and listen to American jazz music, Europeans of all cultural levels find themselves affected too by such innovations as supermarkets and suburbs. Technologically and economically, western Europe and America have interpenetrated each other as never before. The pattern of a kind of cosmic modern democratic culture, a present-day Hellenistic phenomenon, extends beyond Europe and America to embrace Japan and in some measure other Asiatic and African countries. Europe and America have not been immune to oriental influences such as Zen Buddhism, Japanese plays and movies, Indian philosophy, Chinese literature.

Europe and world conflict

The world had moved unsteadily through a series of international crises that shook it repeatedly during the two decades after the close of World War II, like a succession of secondary tremors touched off by the main earthquake. To name them is to recite much of the history of these disturbed years: the Korean War, the Berlin crises, the war in Indo-China (Vietnam), the Suez crisis, the series of wars between Arabs and Jews in the Middle East, the 1962 confrontation between the United States and the U.S.S.R. over Cuba, the Formosa Straits crises, and so on. Few if any years escaped having at least one. Each time, the world trembled at the thought of nuclear extinction. The causes of this cycle of trouble include the coincidence of several great upheavals and revolutions: the Asiatic-colonial rebellion against Western dominance, the vacuums of power left behind by the great war, the huge accretions of power to the two superstates, the United States and the Soviet Union, and their ideological and power conflict. So far as concerns Europe, an important factor was the ending of its power throughout wide areas of the globe and the shifting of this power into other hands.

Vietnam

Sometimes Europeans watched in chagrined frustration as power slipped from their weakened grasp into the stronger but inexperienced hands of the Americans. At the end of the war in 1945 American agents gave aid to the Vietnamese rebels against French rule, acting on the naive American theory that nothing but good could come of giving independence to the victims

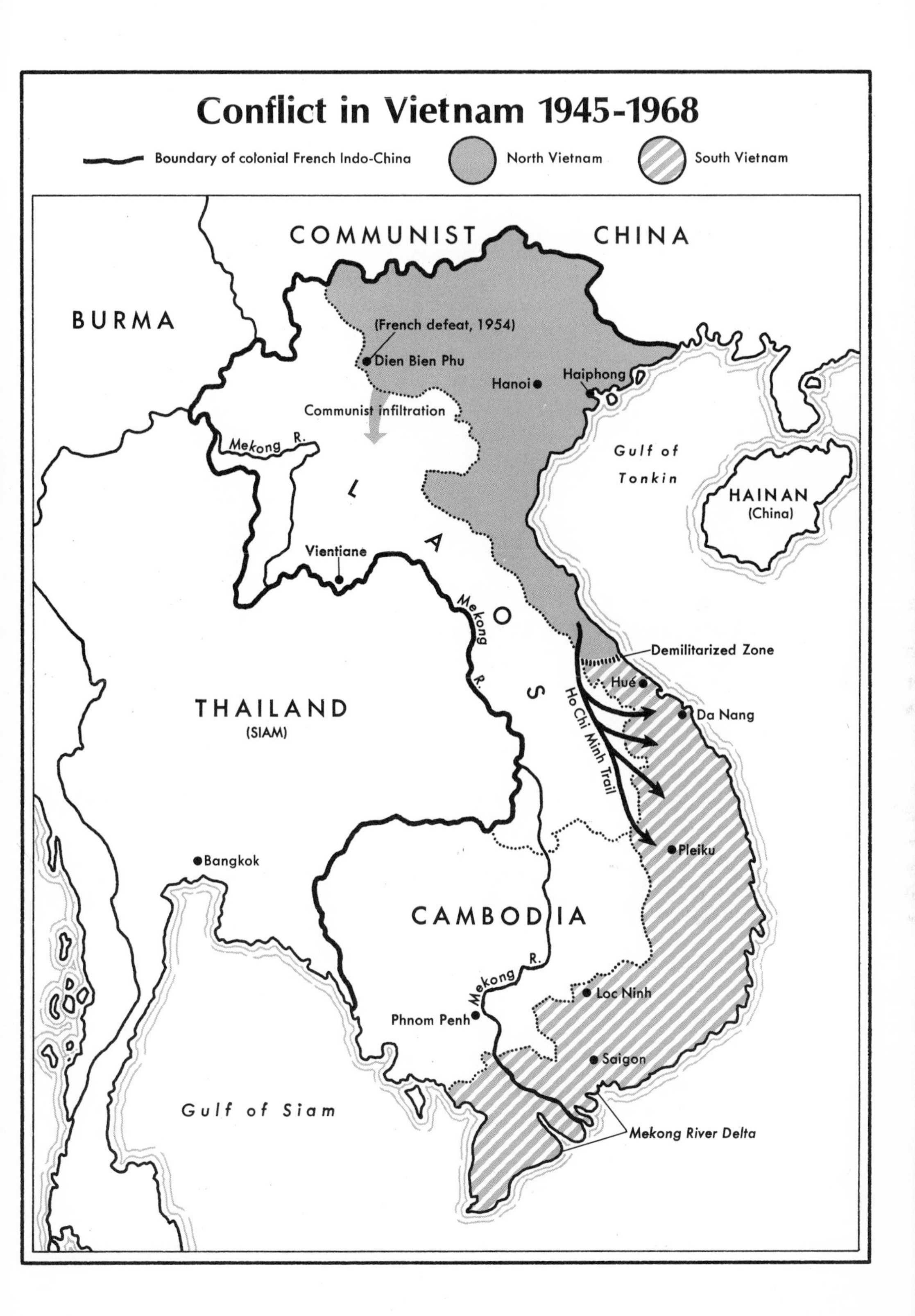
Conflict in Vietnam 1945-1968
Boundary of colonial French Indo-China
North Vietnam
South Vietnam
COMMUNIST CHINA
BURMA
(French defeat, 1954)
Dien Bien Phu
Hanoi
Haiphong
Communist infiltration
Mekong R.
Gulf of Tonkin
HAINAN (China)
LAOS
Vientiane
Mekong R.
Demilitarized Zone
Hué
Da Nang
Ho Chi Minh Trail
THAILAND (SIAM)
Pleiku
Bangkok
CAMBODIA
Mekong R.
Loc Ninh
Phnom Penh
Saigon
Gulf of Siam
Mekong River Delta

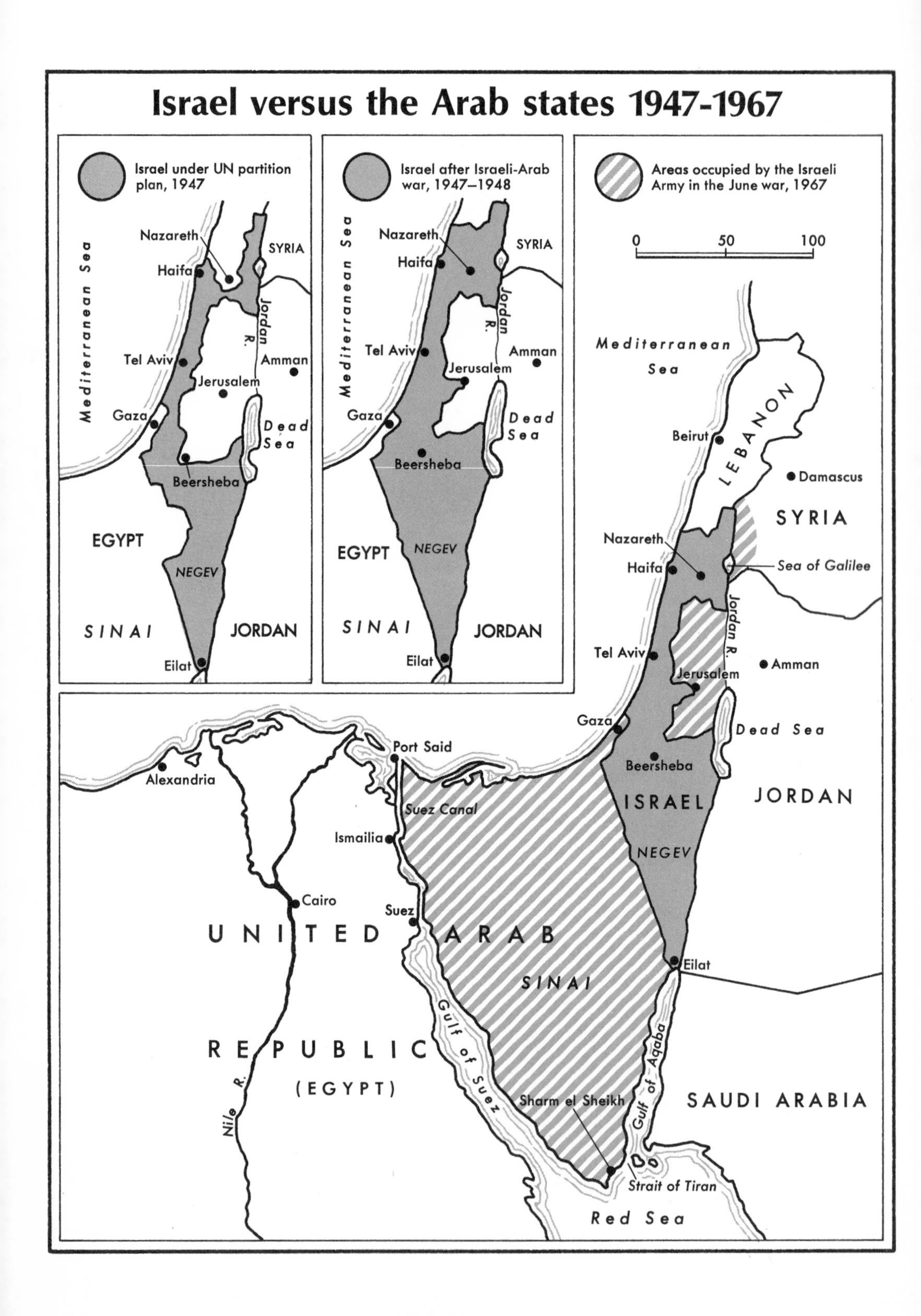
Israel versus the Arab states 1947-1967
Israel under UN partition plan, 1947
Nazareth
SYRIA
Haifa
Mediterranean Sea
Jordan R.
Tel Aviv
Amman
Jerusalem
Gaza
Dead Sea
Beersheba
EGYPT
NEGEV
SINAI
JORDAN
Eilat
Israel after Israeli-Arab war, 1947–1948
Nazareth
SYRIA
Haifa
Mediterranean Sea
Jordan R.
Tel Aviv
Amman
Jerusalem
Gaza
Dead Sea
Beersheba
EGYPT
NEGEV
SINAI
JORDAN
Eilat
Areas occupied by the Israeli Army in the June war, 1967
0
50
100
Mediterranean Sea
LEBANON
Beirut
Damascus
SYRIA
Nazareth
Haifa
Sea of Galilee
Jordan R.
Tel Aviv
Amman
Jerusalem
Gaza
Dead Sea
Port Said
Alexandria
Beersheba
ISRAEL
JORDAN
Suez Canal
Ismailia
NEGEV
Cairo
Suez
UNITED ARAB REPUBLIC
(EGYPT)
Eilat
SINAI
Gulf of Suez
Gulf of Aqaba
Nile R.
Sharm el Sheikh
SAUDI ARABIA
Strait of Tiran
Red Sea

of European imperialism. Then the Americans watched with some indifference, though giving small amounts of aid to the French, as the latter were defeated and thrown out of Indo-China. A few years later, the United States, spurning advice from the ex-rulers, embarked upon a war to hold Vietnam against the Communist-dominated nationalists which soon brought hundreds of thousands of American troops to Vietnam to wage a war of extermination.

Europe watched the United States first passively accept Communist rule in China and then turn bitterly on this regime, refusing all intercourse with it. Most European countries have granted diplomatic recognition to Red China and entered into trade with it, only to earn stinging rebukes from American politicians to whom such "dealing with the enemy" is little short of treason to the cause of Western democracy. Europeans have felt that American policy is erratic, emotional, and at times dangerously belligerent, at other times incredibly innocent. In 1956, perhaps the highwater mark of Euro-American misunderstanding occurred in the famous Suez crisis of that year, when France, Great Britain, and Israel attacked Egypt in a campaign aimed at teaching the brash Arab leader Nasser a lesson for having nationalized the Suez Canal, declared his hatred of the French and British "imperialists," accepted arms from the Russians, and tried to organize a war of revenge against the Jewish state of Israel which had been installed in the Middle East in 1948. Remaining aloof from such violent and conspiratorial measures, the U.S. government denounced the "aggression" and joined with the U.S.S.R. in forcing a halt on the French, British, and Jews. Eleven years later, however, the United States strongly supported the state of Israel when she again attacked Egypt and other Arab states. (This time France's President de Gaulle sympathized with the Arabs!)

The Suez crisis

The Suez crisis, coinciding almost exactly in time (apparently quite by coincidence) with the Hungarian uprising against the Russians, constituted a kind of watershed for the postwar years. In one way it led back to Hitler's war, and his persecution of the Jews, for the Jewish state of Israel—established after the war to the intense indignation of the Arabs, many of whom were displaced to make room for it—was in good measure a product of worldwide sympathy for the Jews. With the perversity typical of human history, this gesture only led to new violence and new persecutions. The Suez crisis related also to antiimperialism in the colonial world; the Egyptian revolution of 1952 was directed against colonialism. It was related to Vietnam, for the French, humiliated there in 1954 and compelled to accept the end of their rule at the Geneva Conference of 1955, did not feel like accepting another defeat in Algeria, with whose rebellion they connected Nasser. It was mixed up with the cold war because both the United States and the Soviet Union were wooing the Arabs in hopes of obtaining them as friends or allies. It was also related to memories of the coming of World War II; both British Premier Anthony Eden and French minister Guy Mollet thought they saw another Adolf Hitler in Colonel Nasser, and suffered from what has been called the "Munich reflex" (never appease anyone, especially a dictator). Finally, Suez brought to a head differences between the United States and her European allies, who felt that the Americans often did not aid them where they needed it most. The Americans were appalled by "imperialism" and refused to contemplate using force against Arabs in the interests of French and British domination. The results of the Suez fiasco included the French turn toward a European program, expressed in the Common Market union and a reconciliation with Germany, and also the nuclear program (which antedated de Gaulle, as did most of the attitudes and policies for which the General is frequently blamed).

Attention has already been drawn to the depolarization of the power blocs, which meant, to the evident dismay of the Americans, a loosening of the bonds uniting the NATO powers. The desire of much of Europe to become less bound to the Americans, to pursue a partly independent course in foreign policy, to avert the hegemony of *either* the Soviets or Americans, irritated Americans—who pointed out, correctly, that they had rescued Europe's democracies first from Hitler and then from economic collapse and Communism after the war. But many Europeans in the 1960's were appalled at the American commitment to far-off Vietnam in a dubious cause. No longer as fearful of Russia, they were far from willing to continue indefinitely as satellites of the United States, often treated with disdain. Americans who expressed extreme annoyance at General de Gaulle's anti-Americanism might have forgotten the numerous times, dating back to World War II, that he had been pushed aside as an Anglo-American team made decisions affecting the fate of France. In a notable snub, de Gaulle was refused an equal place in the NATO councils with Great Britain and the United States soon after his assumption of the presidency in 1958. France was also turned down on access to nuclear knowledge, causing her to go ahead on her own, at much greater expense, to develop her own atomic capacity.

By 1967 France had withdrawn from the unified military aspects of NATO, though not yet from the treaty itself—which might happen in 1969, when the treaty is up for review—and was busy pursuing a diplomacy of reconciliation both with the Soviet Union and the smaller Communist states of eastern Europe, who were themselves eager to lessen their dependence on the U.S.S.R. by developing contacts with the West. But the United States was also pursuing a détente with the U.S.S.R., which West Germany suspected might be at its expense. For its part the Federal Republic turned rather sharply away from the old policy of demanding unification and expecting NATO strength to bring this about; it now seemed willing to relax tensions with the countries of eastern Europe and hope for a friendly reconciliation with the east German state (German Democratic Republic). Meanwhile the heavy American involvement in Asian wars caused it to ignore Europe; as the European countries reduced their military commitment to NATO, so did the United States, the better to fight the war in Vietnam.

These misunderstandings are not surprising in view of the problems involved. Countries such as France and Great Britain have found it difficult to adjust to their new role as second-rate powers compared to the two giants who possess a virtual monopoly of military might; while the United States is new at the game and undeniably shows it at times. Contemplating their future role in the world from the vantage point of their considerable recovery of wealth and confidence in the 1950's, European nations think they may still have a major role to play in the world's affairs. They believe, for one thing, that they understand the former colonial world of Afro-Asia better than the Americans and can offer aid to the new peoples. They believe that European culture and European knowledge is still the world's finest. They think they may possibly function as a bridge between Russia and the United States.

Quite obviously Europe will have to cement its own solidarity more firmly than it has done if it wishes to exert any large influence on the world. Even if a few steps have been taken toward it, a United States of Europe is still a long way off and only such a union can enable Europe even to hope to speak on equal terms with the Soviet Republic and the American nation. But power is not everything. One revealing development of the 1960's, indeed, might be dubbed the impotence of power: the two major powers with their awesome armories of earth-destroying weapons could not control some very small peoples. The United States was frustrated by a handful of Vietnamese guerrillas; Russia could not prevent tiny Albania from thumbing a nose at her within her own bloc; and petty African potentates made Russian and American agents line up for the privilege of providing free aid. Small wars in "backward" countries cannot be handled by the launching of intercontinental rockets with multimegaton explosives. The kind of war the superpowers are equipped to wage is the kind that cannot be waged. Inability to solve elementary problems within their own lands has cost the superpowers prestige, too. Neither the American city nor the Russian countryside will evidently stand too close an inspection. The two superpowers also suffer from certain moral restraints just because they are so powerful. The United States could crush Cuba easily if it unleashed its mighty forces, but few things are more certain than that Castro will be allowed to continue his anti-American tirades unchecked.

In a world filled with conflict, poised precariously on the "balance of terror" between nuclear powers, marred by bitter hatreds, containing great extremes of wealth and poverty with the poor impatient of their poverty, there seems room for all the knowledge and wisdom and material aid that can be mustered. In the fruitful cooperation of Europe with America, with the Communist world, and with the Afro-Asian peoples, lies the hope of the future. Europe has much to give. With due respect for the histories of other civilizations, which no longer can be overlooked, it is still true that no other civilization has yet matched Europe's record of achievement in the realms of material welfare and political development.

Bibliography

It is difficult to compile a bibliography on recent history which leaves out the merely topical and therefore ephemeral books, useful for the hour but destined to be superseded in time by works based on fuller research and a better perspective. The following are, however, worthwhile interim reports at least: G.F. Hudson, *The Hard and Bitter Peace: World Politics since 1945* (New York: Frederick A. Praeger, 1967), and D.W. Brogan, *Worlds in Conflict* (London: Hamish Hamilton, 1967), are both incisive and stylish examinations of the course of world politics in the cold war and afterwards. For more detailed study of various portions of this canvas, F. Roy Willis, *France, Germany, and the New Europe 1945–1967* (Oxford University Press); Richard Lowenthal, *World Communism: The Disintegration of a Secular Faith* (Oxford University Press); Tang Tsou, *America's Failure in China* (Chicago: University of Chicago Press, 1963); W. Phillips Davidson, *The Berlin Blockade* (Princeton, N.J.: Princeton University Press, 1958); David Rees, *Korea: The Limited War* (New York: St. Martin's Press, 1964); Edgar O'Ballance, *The Algerian Insurrection 1954–1962* (Hamden, Conn.: Shoe String Press, Archon, 1967), and *The Arab–Israeli War, 1948* (London: Faber & Faber, 1956). On the Suez crisis, Hugh Thomas' *Suez* (New York: Harper & Row, 1967) may be supplemented by Peter Calvocoressi *et al.*, *Suez Ten Years After* (London: British Broadcasting Company, 1967), and the memoir of Anthony Nutting, *No End of a Lesson* (New York: C.N. Potter, 1967). Among many books on the Hungarian revolt of 1956, Paul E. Zinner, *Revolution in Hungary* (New York: Columbia University Press, 1962), and Ferenc A. Vali, *Rift and Revolt in Hungary* (Cambridge, Mass.: Harvard University Press, 1962).

On the various European countries: France: Edward Tannenbaum, *The New France* (University of Chicago Press, 1961); Stanley Hoffman *et al.*, *In Search of France* (Harper & Row); D. MacRae, *Parliament, Parties and Society in France 1946–1958* (St. Martin's Press, 1967); Edward Ashcroft, *De Gaulle* (New York: Odhams Press, 1962), one of the best studies of France's leading modern political personality, to which may be added W.W. Kulski, *De Gaulle and the World: The Foreign Policy of the Fifth Republic* (Syracuse, N.Y.: Syracuse University Press, 1966), a fair and searching appraisal. West Germany: Alfred Grosser, *The Federal Republic of Germany: A Concise History* (Frederick A. Praeger, 1964), is a useful survey, as also is Rudolf W. Leonhardt, *This Germany: The Story since the Third Reich* (Penguin). Peter H. Merkl, *The Origin of the West German Republic* (New York: Oxford University Press, 1963), is a careful monograph.

Other countries of western Europe: G. Mammarella, *Italy after Fascism: A Political History 1943–1963* (Montreal: M. Casalini, 1964); Brian Crozier, *Franco* (London: Eyre & Spottiswoode, 1968); and Stanley G. Payne, *Franco's Spain* (Thomas Y. Crowell). Integration: Ernest Haas, *The Uniting of Europe* (Stanford, Calif.: Stanford University Press, 1960); Uwe Kitzinger, *The European Common Market and Community* (New York: Barnes & Noble, 1967). In *Modern Capitalism: The Changing Balance of Public and Private Power* (Oxford University Press), Andrew Shonfield attempts a comprehensive analysis of contemporary economic society with stress on varieties of public planning. Great Britain: One of the best approaches to the British scene is through the series of studies of parliamentary elections, beginning with R.B. McCallum and Alison Readman's *The British General Election of 1945* (1947), and continuing with D.E. Butler and his collaborators on *The British General Election of 1951* (1952); *of 1955* (1955); *of 1959* (1960); *of 1964* (1965); *of 1966* (1966); all published by Macmillan in London and St. Martin's Press in New York. See also John D. Hoffman, *The Conservative Party in Opposition 1946–1951* (London: MacGibbon & Kee, 1964), and Kenneth Younger, *Changing Perspectives in British Foreign Policy* (Oxford University Press, 1964). There are numerous memoirs, e.g., Herbert Morrison and Hugh Dalton on the Labour side, Harold Macmillan and Anthony Eden on the Conservative. Eastern Europe: H. Ripka, *Eastern Europe in the Postwar World* (Frederick A. Praeger); Kurt London (ed.), *Eastern*

Europe in Tansition (Baltimore: Johns Hopkins University, 1966); Joseph Korbel, *The Communist Subversion of Czechoslovakia* (Princeton University Press); the memoirs of statesmen who were forced to flee their countries, such as Ferenc Nagy of Hungary and S. Mikolajczyk of Poland. Z.K. Bryzezinski, *The Soviet Bloc: Unity and Conflict* (Harvard University Press, 1967), is a reliable guide to a complex and shifting subject. The Soviet Union: Hugh Seton-Watson, *From Lenin to Khrushchev* (Frederick A. Praeger); Robert Conquest, *Power and Policy in the USSR* (Harper & Row); Leonard B. Schapiro, *Government and Politics of the Soviet Union* (London: Hutchinson, 1967); W. Leonhard, *The Kremlin since Stalin* (Frederick A. Praeger); Carl A. Linden, *Khrushchev and the Soviet Leadership 1957–1964* (Johns Hopkins University Press)—these but a selection from the large number of excellent studies on Soviet Russia.

For anything recent, the student would do well to consult the better periodicals dedicated to world affairs, such as *Foreign Affairs* or *Orbis*. The memoirs of important statesmen in the realm of international affairs are numerous and important; Sir Anthony Eden and Anthony Nutting have already been mentioned (Eden: *Full Circle* and *The Reckoning* [Boston: Houghton Mifflin, 1960, 1965]). George F. Kennan, *Memoirs 1925–1950* (Boston: Little, Brown, 1967), is a fascinating American record. Arthur M. Schlesinger, Jr., *A Thousand Days* (Houghton Mifflin, 1965), deals with the Kennedy administration, 1961–63, including the Cuban confrontation and other major decisions.

The world outside Europe presents a vast surface and our bibliography will not attempt to do it justice. C.E. Carrington, *The Liquidation of the British Empire* (London: George C. Harrap, 1961), offers a brief summary of the huge process of decolonization; so also Margery Perham, *The Colonial Reckoning* (New York: Alfred A. Knopf, 1962). Three Penguin paperbacks are good basic treatments of the Far East: C.P. Fitzgerald, *The Birth of Communist China;* Bruce Grant, *Indonesia;* and Richard Storry, *A History of Modern Japan*. Benjamin Schwartz, *Chinese Communism and the Rise of Mao*, and Bernard Lewis, *The Middle East and the West*, come from the fine Harper paperback series while Oxford University Press has Percival Spear, *India, Pakistan and the West*. V.C. Ferkiss, *Africa's Search for Identity* (New York: George Braziller, 1966), may be singled out from a crowd of recent studies of emergent Africa; another brief but thought-provoking commentary is Margery Perham's *African Outline* (Oxford University Press, 1966). In view of its enormous impact on the 1960's, a few books on the Vietnam war may be cited: Ellen Hammer, *The Struggle for Indo-China 1940–1955* (Stanford University Press, 1966), and D. Lancaster, *The Emancipation of French Indo-China* (Oxford University Press, 1961), deal with the French phase, while the late Bernard Fall, in *The Two Vietnams* (Frederick A. Praeger, 1966) and *Street without Joy* (Harrisburg, Pa.: Stackpole Books, 1966), stands out among the many authors who have written about the more recent conflict. See also Victor Bator, *Vietnam: A Diplomatic Tragedy* (Oceana Publications).

Epilogue

The future of man in Europe and the world

The great human communities

Among the questions confronting Europe at the end of the 1960's were some relating specifically to its own future and destiny, which lay at a crossroads. Would the Common Market community of the Six lead on to political union? Would it expand to embrace the rest of Europe? Would the division of Europe into a Russian-dominated Communist bloc in the east and an American-backed (or dominated?) bloc in the west prove permanent, or temporary? "I am convinced that the future belongs to the great human communities," said Belgium's Paul Spaak, first president of the United Nations General Assembly, one-time secretary-general of NATO, but more famed as the father of European Union. "Europe is one of those communities." If "Europe" (extending how far east and west? including Russia? Great Britain?) was indeed to become a single "community," it might conceivably lead the way to an age of larger groupings, built around natural human communities: Arab world, East Asia, western Hemisphere. Or it might bring about a resurgence of European world dominance. What would be Europe's relationship to the United States? Satellite, a true partnership, or a renewal of the bickering that has so often marred the mother-and-daughter cultures?

The continuing strength of nationalism

Perhaps the future lies with the larger human communities, if not with the often dreamed-of "one world" of a universal state and single human race. If we look at Africa's new nations, and some of Asia's, or even at older nations like France, Russia, and the United States, we shall hardly be able to say that nationalism is a spent force. Despite economic cooperation in Europe, only a rash prophet would flatly predict the merging of those historic entities, France, Germany, Britain, into a superstate; they are still alive and looking not a whole lot weaker. In Africa and Asia "Pan-African" or "Pan-Asian" movements vaguely seeking continental union make very little headway, and there is really no unity to these continents. The two superpowers, the United States and the U.S.S.R., though given to oratory about world unification, the one alleging it will come through international communism and the other through international democracy, display not the slightest desire to surrender control of their affairs to any international body. The United Nations is little more than the meeting place of sovereign states. To the dismay of its dedicated followers, it has made small progress in establishing new principles and practices of international behavior. An end to war between sovereign states seems as far away as ever; the years since the termination of the most destructive war in history in 1945 have seen the Chinese and Vietnamese civil wars, the Korean War, three Arab-Israeli wars, strife in the Congo and Nigeria, threatened war between India and Pakistan, India and China, China and Russia, Russia and the United States, etc., etc.

A European city today shows an amalgamation of old and new. This view of Brussels, capital of Belgium and of the European Economic Community, reveals a Gothic cathedral and Renaissance buildings side by side with modern office buildings.

These patterns of conflict are not just of one or two varieties. The cold war rivalry between the United States and the Soviet Union has been and remains a potent source of conflict, and so has the alignment of the former colonial areas as against their former imperialist rulers. But, as these animosities have in some cases cooled, so that Russia and the United States can flirt with a détente and African leaders cooperate with Europeans, one has the spectacle of Semitic Arabs and Jews implacably at odds over their corner of the earth, which all logic says they should cultivate together; of India squabbling with Pakistan, Indonesia with Malaya, and so on. Amid signs of cultural internationalism, political nationalism was never stronger.

The gap between rich and poor

Enormous economic and welfare gaps between the affluent American and West European worlds on the one hand, and squalid Asia and Africa, add

A symbol of modern belief—Le Corbusier's church in Ronchamp, France, in the Vosges Mountains

to the difficulties of visualizing anything like world unity. There seems general agreement on the rather dismaying point that despite all efforts to bridge this gulf, the tendency has been for it to widen rather than narrow; the rich are getting richer and the poor poorer, relatively speaking. A "revolution of rising expectations" has not been accompanied by realization of these dreams, and so from the ghettoes of Detroit and Newark to the villages of Borneo and Syria, revolutionary violence is engendered.

The title of the volume in the New Cambridge Modern History for our own era is "the age of violence." Mournfully, we would have to agree that it is an apt one. The 20th century, ushered in under the sign of the idea of progress, has had to witness the blasting of its dreams of eternal peace, of orderly evolution toward better and better social and political conditions, the breaking down of barriers between peoples. Its outstanding events have been the two devastating world wars, with ominous threats of a third. The violence has not yet ceased and it encompasses all parts of the globe.

Mingling of peoples

On the other hand it is clear that the world is knit more closely together today than ever before. This is revealed in all sort of ways, in war as much as in peace. Civil strife in Vietnam, which at one time would not even have been heard of in the United States, now involves hundreds of thousands of her soldiers. People travel more easily from Tokyo to New York or London to Melbourne than they used to from one town to the next. Television and other modern modes of communication teach formerly alien peoples all about each other. More Americans visit Europe in one summer than used to hear about it in a decade. These are all familiar clichés of modern life. Rapidity of travel, tourism, television would seem bound in the long run to wear away national provincialism, just as village and regional provincialism once surrendered to national unity. There are intellectual reflections of this in all sorts of amalgamations of ideas: while Zen Buddhism is stylish in the West, the Christian sects strive for "ecumenicalism" (today there are Japanese, Chinese, Syrian, African, and Indian cardinals of the Roman Catholic Church), and American Negroes adopt Islam. The present phase, as more than one historian has noted, resembles the Hellenistic era of ancient times, which preceded the Roman Empire.

Innumerable questions, then, to which only the future can provide answers, spring to mind concerning this particular moment in history and the directions that may next be taken. Deeper wonderings arise. Does history, in its huge entirety, have any meaning? It is clearly a story of struggles, defeats, occasional triumphs, amid much suffering and tragedy; of the rise and fall of empires and peoples, the writing of literature and the study of man and nature, of, in brief, a great deal of human activity in which the indomitable will of man to build civilization is evident. Sparta and Prussia erected civilizations on hardihood and discipline, Athens and England on commerce and representative government; the Venetians wrested a marvelous city from the sea, the Egyptians from the desert. All of them struggled to the heights of greatness—and fell. Men believed passionately in Marduk, in Jesus of Nazareth, in Mohammed, in Socialism and Democracy—only to have new generations arise who "saw through" the "myth" and did not believe as their fathers. The story is not ended, and therefore we cannot say what it means. Is it proceeding toward some culmination, desirable or undesirable, or is it simply a tale told by an idiot, full of sound and fury, signifying nothing? Does it perhaps go around in endless circles, as some have thought, or is there a direction?

If there is a goal, we are entitled to say that it will have been attained at a staggering cost. But for all we know it might well be worth it. To the mystery of life and why it exists at all the historian can give no answer. He can only display what has happened, and let wiser men mull it over. Experience itself is no guide to certainty. But without experience there is nothing; history offers us the record of human experience in all its inexplicable vitality and variety.

> *So many a million of ages have gone to the making of man;*
> *He now is first, but is he the last? is he not too base?*

Astronomers now are inclined to believe that life has come into existence at many millions of other places in the universe. If so, and if we might look forward to interstellar communication, we would be able to make some interesting comparisons between world histories. Perhaps ours is only one of an enormous number of experiments being conducted in Life. Many billions of ages may have gone into the making of all kinds of men, some of whom may well be less base and less limited than ourselves. But we do not know; perhaps ours is the highest form yet developed.

In regard to this particular experiment of man on earth, so far as we can judge it, we can hardly say that it has proved itself a success. It has produced some extraordinary things, but the possibility of its destroying itself clearly cannot be ruled out. A creature of contradictions, torn by conflicting impulses, only partly guided by reason, man has yet to learn to avoid war, live at peace with himself, abolish crime, remove poverty and racial prejudice; he has not yet created a civilization without ugliness, disease, vulgarity. On some of these tasks he has made a good start, but sometimes only at the cost of worsening other problems. For example, having found the cure for many once deadly diseases, he faces the problems of overpopulation and of the aged. Overpopulation raises the question of the possible extinction of wild life all over the world, with unpleasant consequences both esthetically and biologically. Are we to have no more wild animals except in zoos, and if so what becomes of the balance of nature? Will all rivers and even all the air be polluted by industrial products? Will there soon be no more open spaces at all, no more "nature"? What will be the effect on humanity of this loss? Will humanity finally choke and die of its very wealth?

The grimly ironic fact that physical science's most brilliant achievement, the discovery of atomic energy, has been used chiefly to make and threaten war on a new scale of destructiveness might suggest an even gloomier prospect from the biological sciences. Probably the most exciting and astonishing scientific discovery of recent years has been in the area of molecular biology, where since the 1953 breakthrough on the structure of the acid (DNA) which is the essential constituent of chromosomes and genes, much has been learned about the mechanism of heredity. Can this amazing knowledge be used to improve the human race, or will it be used in forms of biological warfare too terrible (so was the atomic bomb) to contemplate? Will it be used to liberate man from diseases and deformities while enriching his intellectual endowment, or does it open up dreadful visions of an ant-like "utopia" presided over by engineer-tyrants, such as haunted the imagination of Aldous Huxley (*Brave New World*) and George Orwell (*1984*)?

If the wealth of the "affluent societies" only seems to increase the gap

Human crowds on a street in Cologne, Germany.

Elephants huddled together in South Africa suggest the danger of extinguishing wild life on a planet ever more crowded.

"The Tribe," by Fred Berger, seems to depict an existential awareness of man's struggle for spiritual freedom in a mass society.

Modern man looks like this to sculptor Henry Moore, whose "Family Group" is in the Museum of Modern Art.

between them and the less fortunate parts of the world, are the affluent really happy in their world of endless gadgets? The records of crime, delinquency, drug addiction, alcoholism, divorce, do not suggest it. A literature of black pessimism or cynical absurdity is the highest expression of the West's spirit these days. It seems at times to be choked by too much knowledge as well as too many goods. The brilliant literature and philosophical thought of 20th-century Europe has been marked by a profound alienation of the artist from his civilization, by a desperate effort to find new values to live by in the teeth of the erosion of all the old values, by a disturbed awareness of man's forlorn condition in a world whose meaning he cannot find. Technological success, bigness, wealth, all have undeniable value, but they overwhelm the spirit and the mind of man; they have all but destroyed art and religion, in any meaningful sense, as a part of life. There is abundant evidence that man cannot live happily without these things. Perhaps the end will come for man not when he exhausts the planet's physical resources, or incinerates it in nuclear war, but when he uses up all his myths and can find nothing further to believe in—no further reason for joy and work, loyalty and courage, love and steadfastness.

Existentialism

The most interesting and significant recent intellectual and literary manifestations in the Western world relate to this loss of faith and the attempt to find new faith. While academic philosophy, especially in Sweden, Great Britain, and the United States, has been dominated by neopositivists and analytical schools who severely refuse to speculate on anything beyond the empirically verifiable, and while traditional religion has continued in decline, moralists, theologians and popular philosophers going under the general rubric of existentialism have spoken of the anguished crisis of values that arises in modern man. He feels the absurdity of a world without God or any clear standard of values, as well as of a complex and overorganized society which works to depersonalize the individual, reducing him to a faceless cipher. He has seen through the fallacy of revolution or any merely external social change as a means to utopia. He experiences a frightful loneliness and despair; but finds solace in the sheer fact of his human awareness, his individual existence as a radical reality capable of choosing and acting on values. What these values are is far from clear. But they must be created from within in absolute sincerity.

The various kinds of existentialism may be an expression of the defiant energy and will of the West, but they also testify to a fairly desperate searching for values amid the ruin of all values. This anarchic spirit portends the destruction of ancient social institutions. While Protestant clergymen shed their clerical colors and churchly ceremonies in an attempt to make their religion relevant to the modern world, so do Roman Catholics often rebel against the old church, papacy, rituals and all, in the name of Vatican II and their own radically revisionist theologians. These frankly secularizing forces may prove the undoing of the churches as a distinctive and separate element

Students riot in Paris, May 1968

in society. They are part of a mood that appears to endorse action for action's sake, startlingly like the Fascist program in this respect, though ostensibly dedicated to a liberal or radical goal.

Literature, art and music have spun futilely in experimental grooves, becoming ever more grotesque in their quest for novelty. So far as serious drama flourished in the 1950's and 1960's, it was the Theater of the Absurd. Interesting, often existential and expressive of a profound metaphysical inquiry (see such plays as Samuel Beckett's *Waiting for Godot,* Jean-Paul Sartre's *No Exit,* and Archibald MacLeish's *JB*), drama included under this category also embraced a variety of gestures of loathing and disgust, simply nihilistic in content; frankly intended to be an enormity, a scandal, a shock effect. It is always difficult to evaluate the art of an era when one is in the middle of it, to know what will survive and what will prove to be ephemeral. Of the creative spirit in the second half of the 20th century, so far as one could judge it in the 1960's, the verdict would have to be that its frenetic revolutionary qualities might as well portend the death of all art as the birth of a new one.

Meaningless riots by students in Germany, France, England, and the United States mirrored this dead-end of thought and expression. The cultural condition of Western man could give no one cause for complacency. Yet a glance at the Communist world suggests what happens when the freedom to experiment, accepted in the West, is blocked. Writers and artists in Russia are attempting to escape the straitjacket of intellectual and artistic conformity enforced by bureaucratic power. While the young radicals of the West sometimes demand Communism, the young radicals of the Communist world demand freedom.

Yet to anyone prepared to look upon all the manifold manifestations of the human spirit as interesting—its follies, insanities, delusions, contradictions as well as its triumphant achievements—no age has been as exciting as the contemporary. Whatever the future may bring, in the end we come to the quotation from David Hume with which we began this book. What spectacle is so fascinating as the march of the human race?

Bibliography

Speculations on the present and future state of Europe may be found in Stephen R. Graubard (ed.), *A New Europe?* (Beacon Press); George Lichtheim, *The New Europe: Today and Tomorrow* (New York: Frederick A. Praeger, 1963); David Calleo, *Europe's Future* (New York: Horizon Press, 1965). C. Northcote Parkinson, *East and West* (New American Library, Mentor), is among those who have commented on the interesting theme of cultural interaction; cf. Arthur Koestler, *The Lotus and the Robot* (New York: Macmillan, 1961). Raymond Williams, *The Long Revolution* (Harper & Row), and Charles Frankel, *The Democratic Prospect* (Harper & Row), are interesting commentaries on the modern cultural situation. Adrienne Koch (ed.), *Philosophy for a Time of Crisis* (E.P. Dutton), is a selection from leading modern philosophers on the situation of modern man. F. Copleston, *Contemporary Philosophy* (Newman Press), and Paul Roubiczek, *Existentialism: For and Against* (Cambridge University Press), are among a battery of books dealing with the leading theme of modern philosophy.

Illustrations

Index

B

C

D

G

H

I

J

M

N

O

P

T

This book has been set in 9 point Optima, leaded 3 points, and 8 point Optima, leaded 2 points. Chapter numbers and titles are 24 point Optima Semibold. The size of the type page is 33½ by 46.

Kiølen Mts.
North Sea
Baltic
Thames
Atlantic Ocean
Rhine R.
Elbe
Seine
E U
Loire R.
Danube Rive
Alps Mts.
Po R.
Pyrenees
Rhone
Ebro R.
Tagus R.
Adriatic Sea
Apennine Mts.
Mediterranean
Atlas Mountains
AFRICA